Windows
Server® 2008
Bible

Windows Server® 2008 Bible

Jeffrey R. Shapiro

WILEY

Wiley Publishing, Inc.

Windows Server® 2008 Bible

Published by
Wiley Publishing, Inc.
10475 Crosspoint Boulevard
Indianapolis, IN 46256
www.wiley.com

Copyright © 2008 by Wiley Publishing, Inc., Indianapolis, Indiana

Published simultaneously in Canada

ISBN: 978-0-470-17069-4

Manufactured in the United States of America

10 9 8 7 6 5 4 3 2 1

About the Author

Jeffrey R. Shapiro (Orlando and Miami, Florida) has worked in Information Technology for nearly 20 years. He has published more than 18 books on IT, network administration, and software development, and has written for numerous publications over the years. He also regularly speaks at events, and frequently participates in training courses on Microsoft systems. In 2003, he was selected to lead Broward County's NetWare to Windows Server 2003 migration project. Over the course of many years, Jeffrey authored several newsletters, which included the *Java Developers* newsletter for Network News magazine, *Online Business Today* (Home Page Press), and was a contributor to *Server Pipeline* newsletter. He was also a contributor to *Computer Telephony Magazine* for several years.

Jeffrey has specialized in Microsoft technologies since 1989. From 1992 to 1998 he was CTO for a leading software development company specializing in telephony solutions for business and was credited with developing one of the first Windows LAN-based computer telephony platforms.

In early 2003 he was selected to lead Broward County's (Florida) NetWare to Windows Server 2003 migration project. The mandate was to replace NDS with Active Directory to support more than 80 agencies and to architect three mission-critical high-performance data centers supporting about 6,000 users serving one of the largest population centers in the USA. One of his key missions for Broward County was to consolidate from hundreds of NetWare Servers to about 50 high-performance Windows Server 2003 Servers. He was also tasked to architect the county's SQL Server 2003 data tier comprising multiple data centers.

He is a highly effective engineer with a distinguished career leading all facets of software development, systems implementation, migration, analysis, network administration, systems architecture and design, deployment, and support. He has consulted for a large number of corporations of various sizes from small insurance agencies and motels to the likes of IBM, Disney, Gartner, ProSource, AmeriServe, Sun International, Microsoft, Old Mutual, Universal Property, KLM Airlines, Philips, State of Idaho, and more.

Besides various ongoing consulting projects, Jeffrey has his hands full authoring a number of highly specific deployment, operations and maintenance manuals, reports, and training material covering Microsoft infrastructure and software engineering technologies. He can be contacted at his company, Jacaranda Communications, Inc. at www.misiq.com.

Credits

Acquisitions Editor
Katie Mohr

Senior Development Editor
Tom Dinse

Technical Editors
Doug Holland, Andrew Edney

Production Editor
Angela Smith

Copy Editor
Kim Cofer

Editorial Manager
Mary Beth Wakefield

Production Manager
Tim Tate

Vice President and Executive Group Publisher
Richard Swadley

Vice President and Executive Publisher
Joseph B. Wikert

Project Coordinator, Cover
Lynsey Stanford

Proofreader
Publication Services, Inc.

Indexer
Jack Lewis

Acknowledgments

God knows how hard writing a book is ... and then to get it published. I am thankful for the team that has helped me bring this baby into the world.

I would first like to thank my agent, Carole McClendon, for her effort over the past few years in bringing me together with the team at Wiley Publishing. Special honors also go to the Wiley Publishing editorial team. In particular, I would like to "flag" my development editor, Tom Dinse, who did an outstanding job of bringing together the pieces of the puzzle.

The technical editor "Oscar" goes to Doug Holland and Andrew Edney, not only for reading my lines, but for reading in between them as well. In addition, I would no doubt have gotten no farther than this acknowledgments page without the expert cyber-pencil of copy editor Kim Cofer.

For every hour spent writing these words, at least ten were spent testing and toying with Windows Server 2008. How do you get this far? Simple — you gather around you a team of dedicated professionals who help you build a killer lab and then help you test everything from the logon screen to the shutdown command.

The "home" team always gets the last mention, but without their support, input, and love, the soul in this work would not have taken flight. Special thanks to Kim and Kevin Shapiro.

Contents at a Glance

Contents

Contents

Contents

Contents

Contents

Contents

Contents

Contents

Contents

Contents

Introduction

Welcome to Windows Server 2008, the long awaited OS once known only as "Longhorne."

Gone are the days when the Windows Server operating systems could be covered in a single book or a week's crash course at a training center. If I told you that this is the only book that you need about Windows Server 2008, I would be lying. Many of the features that I cover warrant advanced treatment under separate cover. In fact many features and roles of Windows Server 2008 need to be presented in specialized publications, hands-on seminars, and highly detailed, narrow focus, technical manuals.

But I have attempted to build as complete a hands-on reference as possible, while still providing a broad scope of coverage of the most important aspects and implications of the Windows Server 2008 platform.

This version builds on the solid foundation of an already released and widely used and tested operating system; namely Windows Vista. In this regard the server and client code share a common code base. In fact, Windows Server 2008 is the first release to manufacturing (RTM) of an operating system that already incorporates fixes and changes that would in the past need to be applied incrementally over time after shipping, or in one wallop as a giant service pack. Service Pack 1, which was applied to Vista, was "folded" into Windows Server 2008. The title of the book could actually have been "Windows Server 2008 SP1" but there is now no such thing as SP1. That might be a great marketing trick by Microsoft, but it also means deciding whether to adopt Windows Server 2008 now or later is no longer a matter of waiting for the first service pack.

If you are still supporting Windows 2000 (or, Heaven forbid, Windows NT), Windows Server 2008 offers many new and improved features that present you with both exciting and daunting challenges. This book is the culmination of thousands of hours spent testing, evaluating, and experimenting with just about everything that Windows Server 2008 can throw at you.

One of the most pervasive changes in Windows 2000 was the Active Directory, and Windows Server 2008 expanded on and improved implementation of the Active Directory. In Windows Server 2003 R2, Active Directory came with the so-called *Active Directory Federation Services* (ADFS), light-weight directory services, and branch office services built-in. This technology makes it easier than ever, and much more reliable, to extend AD to remote locations and branch offices or integrate them with a variety of different services, operating systems, rights management systems, and authentication services. These services are now further enhanced and built into the operating system and are now entrenched in the core code of the OS.

AD affects most aspects of Windows Server 2008, including the areas of security and user and group administration, network and domain topology, replication, DHCP and DNS, and more. Other important changes include changes to the Distributed File System (DFS), which enable you to build a homogenous file-system structure from shares located on various servers across the network. The concept of presenting shared folders to users as a grouping called a *namespace* has been further extended and enhanced. The enhanced DFS Namespaces (DFS-N) provides for easier management of file system roots within a DFS network infrastructure. DFS-N gives you far greater flexibility in deploying DFS; you now have a much more sophisticated tool to create multiple DFS roots and manage them. The tools allow you to manage and maintain DFS, as well as managing a dovetail into the Network File System (NFS) to interoperate with Unix or other "X"- based operating systems.

The changes in DNS and DHCP enable DHCP clients to dynamically request updates of their host records hosted by Windows Server 2003 DNS servers, enabling you to maintain up-to-date host records for all systems in the enterprise, even when they are assigned an IP address dynamically, or their host or domain names change. However, many services are now available against IPv6 of TCP/IP.

If you have been creating and managing Windows Server 2003 networks, you should find many features in Windows Server 2008 welcome improvements. A good example is Group Policy. A lot of the tools, such as the Group Policy Management Console (GPC), were late add-on tools for Windows Server 2003. These tools are now part and parcel of Windows Server 2008. You know from all the previous versions of the OS that you cannot implement a Windows Server 2008 network without Group Policy, but Group Policy is difficult to master without supporting tools. Windows Server 2008 greatly improves Group Policy technology with increased functionality, such as Resultant Set of Policy (RSoP) built into the GPMC and the capability to more easily report on Group Policy application with Resultant Set of Policy and so on.

There are also a number of revolutionary features of Windows Server 2008. The most dramatic feature of the OS is the Server Core concept. For the first time Microsoft has created an OS that lets you install a "core" operating system kernel without any additional roles and features added and without the overhead of the Windows Server 2008 user interface. This means you can install a headless server and provision it as a highly streamlined, light, and dedicated file server, or DNS server, or DHCP server, or domain controller, and so on.

You can also install the OS as usual with the standard GUI but now the basic installation comes with no roles or features added. Once you have a base OS running with the user interface, you can incrementally add roles (such as DNS, DHCP, or IIS) and only maintain the surface area you are actually exposing to the network. This provides a level of security for Windows Server that can be highly sophisticated and advanced at the same time that it is easy to manage and maintain. In the rapidly changing security landscape this is a very welcome feature of the OS and a worthwhile reason to upgrade your servers ... and if upgrading all your servers is not currently practical, then your public facing or most vulnerable servers would be excellent candidates to upgrade.

A number of services are no longer available in Windows Server 2008. These include add-ons like Netware Services, Service for Macintosh, and even Services for UNIX (although the word is still out on the latter service). Thus it is critical that you understand everything that Windows Server 2008 offers and does not offer, lest your upgrade plans succumb to a gotcha you never expected.

Who Should Read This Book

Windows Server 2008 Bible is for anyone involved in network administration, server management, MIS, and so on. This book is for you if the questions you have are along the lines of "How do we handle this?"

Windows Server 2008 makes waves in all IS infrastructures. The audience covers a wide spectrum … as broad as the number of services that the product offers. Not only does this book cater to network or server administrators, but many chapters are aimed at people tasked with certain responsibilities, such as security, user-account administration, service level, customer-relationship management, and so on.

Although I assume that you are familiar with the Windows environment (from Windows 9x through Windows XP and Vista), much of what I offer here is of value to administrators working in heterogeneous environments — even midrange and mainframe facilities. I have also focused on issues of concern to managers and information offices. This is very much an integration book, so you find conversion tips aplenty, culled from an eagle eye cast on every process that may create problems for business systems and processes that are still in place.

Whether you're just trying to get a handle on what's new in Windows Server 2008 and the effect that it's sure to have, looking at installing new Windows Server 2008 systems, considering an upgrade from Windows Server 2003 Server, or are tasked with converting from the ancient Windows NT Server to Windows Server 2008, you will find a wealth of information between the covers of this book that can help you meet your goals.

Everything that I discuss in these pages has been tested and deployed in several early adoptions, in one form or another, so step into my shoes and get a heads-up on the road ahead. You will no doubt go on to learn a lot more about Windows Server 2008, as will I. If you would like to comment on anything or add to what I've written, I value your contributions. You can write to me at jshapiro@misiq.com.

I have also made a number of white papers and reports available to readers of this book. If you visit my Web site at www.misiq.com you'll find a wide range of free documents covering various aspects of Windows Server 2008, from architectural plans to deployment plans to implementation. Information on late additions to the operating system, such as Hyper-V, is also available at the Web site.

How This Book Is Organized

The *Windows Server 2008 Bible* is divided into several parts. The following section summarizes the parts, their topics, and how they are structured.

Part I: Windows Server 2008, Core, Configuration, Networking, and Communication Services

Part I explores installation and several key networking and communications services in Windows Server 2008. Chapters 1 and 2 cover basic installation, Server Core installation, Server Manager, and the Microsoft Management Console. I also describe the various roles you can install to the basic or Server Core operating system, the many additional features (such as Telnet Server, WINS, clustering, and so on) that you can add, the various applets in Control Panel, and the Computer Management console.

The chapters in Part I also explore in detail several key networking and communications services. Chapter 3 lays the groundwork by covering the ubiquitous TCP/IP protocol, along with routing, troubleshooting, Network Address Translation (NAT), SNMP, and legacy protocols. DNS and client resolution management is covered in Chapter 4. Chapter 5 provides help configuring and deploying DHCP for automatic IP-address assignment and administration. Chapter 5 also covers WINS, while Routing and Remote Access and the Network Policy Server are covered in detail in Chapter 6.

Chapters 7 through 11 cover core services such as the registry, auditing, the .NET Framework backup and restore, and so on. Chapter 11 helps you develop and implement a backup and recovery strategy and explores the new Windows Server 2008 Windows Backup utility, configuring removable storage, and media pools.

Part II: File, Print, and Storage Services

Chapters 12 through 15 explore file, print, and storage services. Chapter 12 covers high-end print topics such as Internet printing, printer management, and troubleshooting. Chapter 13 deals with storage features. Windows Server 2008 adds extensive fault tolerance, storage management, recovery, and other availability features. Storage management in Chapter 13 includes removable storage, fault tolerance, RAID, general file-system management, and related topics.

File systems are covered in Chapter 14. This chapter details the various advanced file system features, such as DFS and NFS, available. Chapter 15 explains how to configure and optimize file sharing and security, and manage file sharing effectively. It also provides thorough coverage of file and folder encryption.

Part III: Security and Active Directory

Active Directory represents one of the most important parts of Windows Server 2008. Part III provides a complete look at AD, starting with Chapter 16, which covers security in general and Active Directory Certificate Services in particular. Chapter 16 takes a broad look at security in Windows Server 2008, including Kerberos, certificates, encryption, and many other security-related topics. A section on installing certificate authorities facilitates the establishment of smart card systems, IPSec, encryption services, secure sockets, and so on.

Chapter 17 provides a concise introduction to AD for newcomers, and Chapter 18 goes into planning for AD implementation. Chapter 19 looks at AD's logical structure and what it really represents, and examines the issues involved in developing a logical domain structure. Chapter 20 explores the physical structure of AD to explain it in the context of domains, sites, servers, and security. Chapter 21 covers AD planning, installation, and deployment, and Chapter 22 explores AD management.

Part IV: Change Control and Workplace Management

Managing users and groups is covered in detail in Chapter 23, and Chapter 24 adds to this section with coverage of change management and how Group Policy facilitates change control over users, computers, security, and the work space.

Chapter 25 takes a detailed look at Windows Server 2008's service-level tools, such as the new Reliability and Performance Monitor (which incorporates and enhances the legacy Performance Logs and Alerts).

Part I

Windows Server 2008, Core, Configuration, Networking, and Communication Services

Chapter 1

Installing Windows Server 2008

This chapter reviews the installation of Windows Server 2008. It discusses a number of hardware configurations and setup options and reviews potential obstacles. Several recipes are discussed in this chapter, and most of them use minimum hardware requirements; keep that in mind when ordering your server. We also explain how to achieve a fresh install or upgrade with different server configurations, installation of the Server Core image, and installation of the base OS with Windows Server 2008 GUI. We will have a look at Server Manager and the variety of server roles and features it allows you to install. Several other topics, including SQL Server, ASP, IIS, and Exchange, are also covered to help you understand how they are incorporated into Windows Server 2008.

It's All About the Core

Before we begin, let's review Microsoft's so-called Core Server installation paradigm, a new type of barebones OS that can also be headless, keyless, and mouseless . . . and Windowless. During the years of Windows NT, Windows 2000, and Windows Server 2003 (pre-R2) installing the operating system was a nail-biting event. We would always stand and gawk at the screen and hold our breath as certain stages in the installation were completed. Once we got through to the restart procedure it was high-fives all round.

By Windows 2000, installing on various hardware platforms was a lot easier. Gone, for the most part, were blue screens during installation or mysterious restarts that had everyone scratching their heads. But another problem arose. The Internet exploded in popularity and along with it the scourge of viruses and hostile cyberspace junk.

The problem was compounded by the need to connect a server to the Internet and patch it with all manner of fixes and updates that Microsoft issued after release to manufacturing (RTM). The result was that unless you sealed the server on a secure network and applied all the patches from a local update server, the chances that the server would be infected and compromised were almost 100 percent.

One of the problems of updating a new server is that the process would usually include patches, fixes, and configuration for just about every service running or not running on a server. It was a tedious and time-consuming task. But that has now been changed with Windows Server 2008.

You no longer need to install the OS and worry about all the services and functionality on it that you will not be using. Now you can install Server Core (a special build of the OS) or base OS with GUI, and incrementally install and apply only the services and bits needed for specific server functions. Server Core is like the birth of a baby, all naked and uncorrupted but not exposed, while the base OS installation with Windows user interface is like a 3-year-old, ready for "intelligence" to be added but with some exposure required.

What Is Server Core?

The Server Core installation lets you install a minimal OS for running just the chosen server roles that would not even need a GUI. This means that you don't have the huge "attack" surface that will ensue from all the service requirements. One more thing: Once you install just Server Core you can stand your server up in a secure environment, both physical and online, and worry only about securing the services you are actually running. Once Server Core has been installed you can then open Server Manager (remotely or via scripting) and install, among many others, the following server roles:

- Active Directory Domain Services (AD DS)
- Application Server
- DHCP Server
- DNS Server
- File Services
- Print Services

Here are some more benefits of the Server Core installation alternative:

- **Lower maintenance.** You only need to maintain on the server what is actually installed on the server. Why worry about maintaining File Services on a server that is nothing more than a simple domain controller?
- **You need less disk space.** The Server Core requires only about 1 gigabyte (GB) of disk space to install and approximately 2GB for operations after the installation.
- **Less management.** Management costs in realms like security, availability, and service level are far less than previous installation scenarios. You would not have to worry about supporting a bunch of services and code that you are not using.

More details of the server roles are presented throughout this chapter and in Chapter 2. We will return to actual installation of the Server Core OS later in this chapter.

Installation and Configuration Strategy

If you have done your homework and have an installation plan and architecture document ready, you are now ready to begin installing Windows Server 2008 in your lab. For help creating an installation plan and an architecture document (including an architecture template) visit www.misiq.com/whitepapers. You may be tempted (or you may have an urgent need) to go directly to a working or production system in a production environment. Perhaps your DHCP server died or a new DNS server is needed urgently. Resist — or stick with what you know. If you have a Windows Server 2003 network and need to raise a new service to fill an urgent need, stick with Windows Server 2003 until you have fully implemented a test lab and are familiar with the way things work under Windows Server 2008. In many respects it is a very different operating system. Microsoft Server 2008 has the same core kernel and presentation functionality as Windows Vista, but with server bits added in. So in many respects it is new code from the ground up compared to Windows Server 2003.

Conversely, if you are a seasoned administrator and you know what you're doing, you probably have issues such as a hardware checklist, remote or unattended installation, hot standby, and so on well taken care of. Proceed directly to a production system only if you know what you are doing and the production system is part of a conversion and rollout project.

Generally, you should always raise servers in a lab. Then you should burn them in (run them continually) for about a week; hit them with work for at least another week. After that, and if all test items check off, ship or go live. No two environments are the same. The following sections look at various installation and configuration scenarios.

NOTE A lot of people want to know how to burn in a server that is standing idle and has no users connected to it. One simple way is to set up Windows Server Backup to run continually. Running Backup is great physical therapy for a server. It works the hard disks, memory, system buses, access control, permissions and the NTFS, removable storage functions, transactional file system, and more. You can also configure Backup (or any other backup utility, for that matter) to perform both pre- and post-backup routines, such as sending alerts and moving files around the house. Depending on your stress test, you may need to write a backup script to automatically overwrite media and so on. In addition, if you want to test disk I/O and other routines, you may need to write some custom software for the job.

Getting psyched up about installing

This chapter takes you through the basic install routines and then to rollout a sophisticated deployment strategy. We are going to help you cook up a variety of server meals. Microsoft has spent many millions on the installation and configuration process, so Windows Server 2008 generally installs easily and performs well considering the power that it wields. It is certainly a lot smoother and friendlier to install than any other server operating system in existence (other than the machine you receive pre-installed from the factory).

We have installed the operating system numerous times and on at least ten different platforms with a variety of hardware, from scrap piles to brand names. We have also deliberately sabotaged our systems (such as taking away drives, drivers, memory, and certain system files) and tried a variety of recovery techniques. Our final verdict? If you experience any difficulty installing Windows Server 2008, you must be using very unconventional methods, thrift store hardware, or you're not paying attention to details and recommended strategy.

Take a moment to sit back, close your eyes, and imagine that you are in a class going through installation training.

Server recipes

In evaluating the various needs in the enterprise, we classify our installation options into various recipes of server installation, which are discussed in the following sections.

Server Core or bare-bones system recipe

This option consists of using minimum hardware requirements as recommended by Microsoft and some testing. All servers require at least 1GHz for x86-based computers except Datacenter Server, which requires 1.4GHz for x86-based computers. These are bare minimums for production servers, but you could get away with less in lab or testing environments. For production servers you'll likely deploy Windows Server 2008 in the 2GHz and higher range, especially for x64. We suggest a bare-bones minimum of 512MB of RAM for all servers except Datacenter Edition, which requires a bare-bones minimum of 1GB of RAM. You also want a DVD-ROM (the OS no longer fits on CDs), a 1.4MB floppy disk drive, a standard network card, and a mouse, keyboard, and monitor.

We have raised servers (Standard Server, Enterprise Server, and Web Server Edition) on CPUs ranging from old Pentium 866s, 1.2s, 1.4s, and so on. You can raise the mentioned servers on less, but we don't recommend it for anything more than the smallest test server, described in the section "Overview of Hardware," later in this chapter. On the other hand, an old horse with a lot of RAM might serve many of your needs. You can usually pick these servers up on the Internet for a song; and if they are good brands, they do well for many years, especially for servers only running Server Core.

Small file and print server recipe

The IT department needs the capability to efficiently utilize file and print resources and keep them available and secure for users. Networks tend to expand, with greater numbers of users located onsite, in remote locations, or even in partner companies, and IT administrators face an increasingly heavier burden. Windows Server 2008 now provides many enhancements to the file and print infrastructure to help solve the never-ending administrators' burden.

You should still use the bare-bones components but add a second large IDE hard-disk drive for file and print services, the usual peripherals, and so on. The amount of RAM that you need depends on the number of connections and users. Printing services require a lot more RAM than file services.

Your hard-disk demands are higher, and you should now consider adding a second drive. You can stick to a cheap IDE disk (even the cheap IDE or EIDE drives are good disks) or begin thinking about SATA and SCSI. Hold the thought about hard disks for the section "Overview of Hardware," later in this chapter.

NOTE   You may have read information elsewhere calling for more firepower in Windows Server 2008. My assessment is based on various experiments, projects, pilot systems, and deployments. Every situation is different, and the only way to really know what you need to throw at a situation is to test.

Application-server installation recipe

The Windows Server 2008 application environment builds on the solid enterprise capabilities of Windows Server 2003 Server security, availability, reliability, scalability, and manageability. The application development seems to be more dependable because the environment can be managed by fewer people, and it delivers lower TCO with better performance. Developers are one of the most highly leveraged resources in IT. By integrating .NET Framework into the Windows Server 2008 application-server development environment, developers are now freed from writing "plumbing" code and can instead focus their efforts on delivering business solutions.

You may want to install applications on servers for users who load them into local memory at their workstations. The application is thus loaded across the network, but the "footprint" and ensuing resource consumption is local to the user's hardware.

You may also have applications that are server-based or server-oriented. These may include database front ends, communications software, processing-oriented software, and network-management applications. Hundreds of applications may be suited to server-side execution and need no user interaction, such as process-control applications and data processing.

You could use the recipe for file and print servers that we give in the preceding section; raising the ideal configuration for your purpose takes some testing. Depending on the availability requirements, you may need to add RAID, hot-swap drive-bays, and so on, which are discussed in the section "Partitioning Hard-Disk Drives," later in this chapter.

Terminal Services installation recipe

A Terminal Services application server is a whole new ball game. The WinFrame licensing arrangement between Citrix Systems, Inc., and Microsoft was the origin of Terminal Services. Terminal Server, under the Hydra project name, first made its debut in Windows NT 4.0 in late 1997. It was then launched as a separate NT 4.0 operating system called Windows NT 4.0 Terminal Server Edition (TSE). It was even further enhanced in Windows Server 2003. Terminal Server in Windows Server 2008 is still called Terminal Services but it is now installed as role. However, you can still connect to a server using Remote Desktop Connection (RDC) in administrative mode. RDC provides substantial improvements over previous releases. RDC provides administrators and users with a simplified user interface that still connects to previous versions of Terminal Services (Windows NT 4–Terminal Server Edition and Windows 2000). See Chapter 2 for more information about the Terminal Services and RDC.

Windows Server 2008 Terminal Server supports more users on each high-end server than previous editions. Windows Server 2008, Enterprise Edition, provides a superior load-balancing support than previous editions. Session Directory maintains a list of indexed sessions by user-name, enabling users to reconnect to the Terminal Server and resume working in that session. It also provides unsurpassed remote manageability by taking advantage of technologies such as Group Policy and Windows Management Instrumentation (WMI), which provides management with complete remote capabilities through a comprehensive read/write system.

With Windows Server 2008 acting as a Terminal Services application server, all your users run all their applications on the server. No such thing as a local Terminal Services client even exists. The client can be a browser, a fat client running a Terminal Services terminal application (such as a TN3270 character-based terminal running on Windows and accessing a DB2 database on the mainframe), a dumb terminal (known as a Windows-based terminal), or terminals running on the Windows CE or Pocket PC platforms. Your users' terminals can also be installed on any non-Windows platform, such as Macintosh, DOS, and Unix, but these require extras from Citrix, which uses the ICA protocol.

Terminal Servers can be raised with any of the recipes discussed so far. What matters is not what you start up with but what the terminal users do after they are attached to the server. We have tested these services and deployed them in vigorous real-life situations with every version of the OS, and the following configuration pointers, which apply to a different configuration recipe that we discuss shortly, are key:

- Restrict your users from having more than four applications open at one time. Make sure, for example, that they can comfortably open and run a database application, a word-processing application, e-mail, and a Web browser.
- Configure the applications to run without fancy splash screens, animations, or any resource-intensive software.
- Assign and enforce hard-disk quotas. This is important to do for all users but is especially useful if you are dealing with terminal users.

A server hosting no more than RDC users should be running on a CPU of no less than 1.4GHz. Each user (depending on the applications and the type of processing) should be assigned no less than 32MB of RAM. 128MB and higher should be your goal to cope with the high demand of memory from many of today's memory hungry applications, especially applications from suites like Office 2007. You should also install fast SATA or SCSI drives and support them in hardware RAID configurations on fast controller cards. In short, no bare-bones situation is possible for Terminal Services and application hosting. After all, if you were deploying to standard clients, they would likely each have more than 1.6GHz with 1 or 2 GB of RAM.

At 128MB each, the recipe thus calls for the following total server RAM:

- Operating system = 1GB
- Five users at 128MB each = 640MB
- Total RAM needed = 2GB

You're likely to have a hard time adding a small amount of RAM into a modern motherboard. Your configuration would thus be at least 2GB for a modern application server hosting one to five RDC users.

Line-of-business role-server installation recipe

Role servers are servers running services such as DHCP, WINS, DNS, and Active Directory. Your application and needs may vary widely, depending on the service and how many subscribers it has. A small company may get away with a lightweight configuration, such as the small file- and print-server recipe offered in the section of that name, earlier in this chapter. In other cases, you may require much more firepower, especially on medium to large intranets. You can easily run DHCP, WINS, and DNS on Windows Server 2008 on 1GHz machines with 1GB of RAM in each, servicing several thousand users across a nationwide WAN, but you have a lot more replication and dynamic configuration overhead with Windows Server 2008, so you may need to shell out for more powerful machines.

High-road, or mission-critical recipe

Mission-critical servers should have no less than 1.6GHz in CPU capability. For the most part, and especially if you have more than a handful of users, your CPU should be more than 1GHz. You may consider equipment running two-CPU configurations or possibly deploy quad systems.

Hard-disk needs may vary, but you need to configure a second drive letter running at RAID-5 under hardware control. (In case you're wondering, these are SCSI devices, which we discuss in the section "Partitioning Hard-Disk Drives," later in this chapter.)

Redundant or standby system recipe

Any of the server recipes mentioned in the preceding sections can be cloned to provide an offline or hot spare. These are obviously not clustered or automatic failover machines. If the primary server goes down, you could pull dynamic volumes out of the primary arrays and install them into the hot spares. A better solution, if you can afford it, is to install Enterprise Server and run cluster services and network load balancing.

Large systems, clusters, and Datacenter Server installations

Advanced clustering (high availability) and Datacenter Server solutions are beyond the scope of this book, although most of the configuration information in this book applies to the high-end operating systems. Any large system calls for an external SCSI-based storage silo under hardware RAID-5.

The various recipes that we've discussed so far are summarized in Table 1-1.

TABLE 1-1

Hardware Guide for Server Recipes

Recipe	CPU/GHz	RAM/GB	HDD
Bare-bones	1.6	1-2	SATA, eSATA or SCSI
Small File and Print	1.6	1-2	SATA, eSATA or SCSI
App server	2	1-2	SATA, eSATA/SCSI
Terminal Services	2	2+	SCSI-RAID
Role server	2	1+	SCSI-RAID
LOB	2	1+	SCSI-RAID
Standby	1	1+	SATA, eSATA/SCSI
Large	2X2 or 2X4	4+	SCSI, eSATA – RAID

Overview of Hardware

Choosing hardware is not a difficult exercise at all for Windows Server 2008. You really don't put a lot into your system. The list of hardware that we discuss in the following sections is as follows:

- Motherboards
- CPU
- Memory
- Hard-disk drives
- HDD controllers
- Network interface cards (NICs)

Hardware compatibility

Before you go buy parts, review the Windows Server Catalog for hardware compatibility at http://www.windowsservercatalog.com/. The "Designed for … " or "Ready for … " Windows logo identifies software and hardware products that have been designed for and work well with Microsoft products. Software and hardware products displaying the logo must pass rigorous testing to ensure that they provide ease of use and stability and that they take advantage of the new features in Windows products. Software is tested by an independent testing lab. All PCs and peripheral hardware must be tested by Microsoft approved labs.

Businesses that use products meeting Windows logo criteria stand to gain the following benefits:

- Lower support costs
- Support for mixed Windows environments
- Correct use of the operating system
- Compliance with the Americans with Disabilities Act and other equal-rights legislation

According to Microsoft policy, Microsoft does not support you if the item is not on the so-called "HCL," or hardware compatibility list, but not many items may be on the HCL yet. If you offer to spend $195 with Microsoft to figure out whether hardware is the reason a server does not start, do they refuse to take your money? They never have to date. Microsoft's paid support team is very responsive and helps you determine whether hardware is your problem. If they tell you that you have a hardware-compatibility problem, that's probably all the advice that you need.

The compatibility issues aside, you should heed the following advice: Most large companies buy brands from the likes of IBM, Dell, HP, and so on; and if the budget is there, a small company looking for one business server should go this route as well. The servers are burned in and tested, and the manufacturer stands behind the compliance of its product running Windows Server 2008, logo-compliant or not. The servers also come with warranties and various levels of support.

If, however, you plan to build your own server, or if you need to upgrade a machine down the road, by all means, buy your own parts and knock together your own server. For best mother-board results, however, try to stick to made-in-America components or well-known and popular foreign imports. For RAM, only a handful of factories are left, but you're okay buying products from the likes of NEC, HP, IBM, TI, and others. For hard disks, IBM, Quantum, Western Digital, Maxtor, and Seagate are the leaders now, and really the only players. For CPUs, you have Intel and AMD. If you are thinking other marginal CPUs, you need to talk to the likes of IBM or Motorola. The other peripherals do not interfere with your server.

Installing Windows Server 2008

We have found, after dozens of installations, that the best practice for installing Windows Server 2008 is to follow this specific checklist of events:

- Check system requirements — visit Microsoft's site and review the System Requirements for Windows Server 2008.
- Read the setup instructions and release notes included with the Windows Server 2008 Installation DVDs.
- Determine whether to upgrade or install.

- Determine what licensing schema to use: per server or per seat.

- Determine whether you want the capability to choose between different operating systems each time that you start the computer.

- Determine whether you need an NTFS or FAT32 file system.

- Determine whether a special partition is necessary for this installation.

- Choose the correct components to install. Determine the server's purpose.

- Determine how to handle networking, IP, TCP/IP, and name resolution.

- Determine whether you want workgroups or domains.

- Disconnect any UPS devices. The setup process tries to detect devices connected to serial ports or USB ports; therefore, UPS equipment can cause problems with the detection process.

Start setup after you have considered each of the events in the following sections and prepared a checklist that is right for your installation.

Partitioning hard-disk drives

Give Windows Server 2008 a hand, and it takes an arm . . . or at least another drive. Installation assesses all the hard-drive resources in the system, and if you have two drives (or partitions), the OS attempts to use both. The first active partition gets snagged for the system files . . . the minimum required to raise the system to a point where you can run recovery tools or the Recovery Console. Windows Server 2008 calls this volume — you guessed it — the system volume.

Windows Server 2008 then snags a second drive or partition and uses it for the boot files, the files needed to boot the rest of the operating system all the way to the desktop on which you can log in. Windows Server 2008 calls this volume the boot volume. (This is a reversal of the old naming convention for boot and system partitions.)

Two reasons exist for the dual-disk consumption. First, Windows Server 2008 is optimized to use more than one hard-disk drive. Second, a minimum boot disk can be configured to hold just the boot files and can be formatted as FAT or FAT32 instead of NTFS. The theory is that if you lose the base operating system — that is, if you cannot boot to the desktop — you can at least boot to a DOS diskette and then, from DOS, copy new base files over the corrupt ones (or replace a defective drive). Many NT and NetWare systems have been configured this way. However, a well-designed and managed system need not retain a FAT boot disk, which, because of its poor security, is a risk to the entire system because it does not support file-level security.

Windows Server 2008, however, enables you to boot to the Boot Options console (whenever it detects a disaster). Here you have several options, such as Safe Mode with Networking, and from there you can attempt to boot without certain services and debug the problem after you have the OS up and running. You can also boot the Recovery Mode Console, which takes you to a command line that you can use to access NTFS partitions and the boot disks. The practice of leaving boot or system files on FAT volumes is old-fashioned — the result of bad memories from Windows NT days. We recommend the partition arrangement options described in the following sections.

Option 1: One HDD

This arrangement uses one hard-disk drive, which forces Windows Server 2008 to put both boot files and system files onto the same drive and partition. To use this option, follow these steps:

1. Configure the system with one hard-disk drive of about 12GB in size. (Microsoft's official recommendation is to supply at least a 10GB partition, but with roles and features to be added, as well as patches and fixes and new features coming down the road, you need to leave room for expansion.)

2. Format the partition during the install as NTFS.

3. Have Windows Server 2008 choose the default partition name.

The pros of this partitioning option are as follows: First, you save on hard-disk drives. Second, you can mirror this disk for fault tolerance. (Unfortunately, you can mirror the disk only under hardware disk mirroring because Windows Server 2008 does not enable you to mirror a disk that was installed as a basic partition ... even if you make the disk a dynamic disk.)

The negatives of this partitioning option are that, if you must format the system or boot volumes as FAT, you end up with a disk consisting of numerous partitions. This is not necessary on a server and can later lead to problems, such as no capability to mirror or diminishing hard-disk space and the advanced features of dynamic disks. You may also have trouble providing dual-boot capability, but dual boot is not recommended, and besides, you have no need to provide dual boot on a production server.

Option 2: Two HDDs

This arrangement uses two hard-disk drives: Windows Server 2008 puts boot files on one disk and system files on the second disk. To use this option, follow these steps:

1. Configure the system with two hard-disk drives of about 2GB each in size.

2. Format the drives as NTFS during the install.

3. Have Windows Server 2008 choose the partition names and the default and put the files where it needs to.

The positive aspect of this partitioning option, as far as we can tell, is that you have the option of leaving the boot volume formatted as FAT (or FAT32) and formatting the rest of the partitions and drives as NTFS.

The negatives of this partitioning option are that you use up a second drive for a small amount of hard-disk space, but if you are bent on dual or multi-boots, the second drive can hold the additional OS.

Although you have a performance incentive to use a second hard disk, the increased performance is not worth the effort and the second drive, considering the speed and response of modern hard disks. We are also talking about Server Core here and not Active Directory, LOB servers, SQL Server, or Exchange, which are built to take advantage of additional drives. You would be better off using a second drive as a mirror of the first to gain a fault-tolerance feature.

Performing a Server Core install

To create a server running on Server Core installation you need to have the following handy:

- The Windows Server 2008 installation media
- The product key
- A computer with the recommended configuration for a Server Core installation

Before you begin, make sure you have clean or newly formatted hard disks or volume that you can allow installation to format for you. You cannot upgrade from a previous version of Windows Server to a Server Core installation. You also cannot upgrade from a full installation of Windows Server 2008 to a Server Core installation. Only a clean installation is supported.

Be sure of your needs and configuration before you start. Once you start a Server Core installation you cannot go back later and try upgrading it to a full installation of Windows Server 2008 with the Windows UI. Microsoft does not support that route and you would have to blow away the Server Core installation and start all over again.

To install a Server Core installation, perform the following:

1. Insert the Server Core Windows Server 2008 installation media into the DVD drive.
2. The auto-run dialog box will now appear. Click the Install Now option.
3. The installation wizard takes you through the instructions to complete Setup.
4. After the installation, press Ctrl+Alt+Delete and click Other User. At the login enter Administrator with a blank password, and then press Enter. You will now be able to log in and you will have the chance to set a password for the Administrator account.

Performing an unattended Server Core install

As with previous versions of the OS, you use an "unattend" file for a Server Core installation or a regular Windows Server 2008 image. The unattended server install enables you to perform most of the initial configuration tasks during Setup. The following section describes an unattended installation of the Server Core image. If you have a number of servers to install, the unattended installation of Server Core can provide a host of benefits.

There is no need to perform initial configuration using command-line tools because you can include options in the unattend file that will enable remote administration. Once Setup completes you will be able to connect with various tools and applications and continue to fine-tune and configure.

To install a Server Core installation by using an unattend file, do the following:

1. First create an .xml file titled `unattend.xml`. You can use any text editor or the Windows System Image Manager.

2. Next copy the `unattend.xml` file to a local drive or place it on a shared network resource.

3. Place the Windows Preinstallation Environment (Windows PE), Windows Server 2003, or Windows XP media in the machine's CD drive and start your computer.

4. Next place the CD of the Server Core installation image of Windows Server 2008 into your disk drive. As soon as the auto-run Setup window appears, click Cancel. This will bring you to the command prompt.

5. Next, change to the drive that contains the installation media, enter the following command, and press Enter:

```
setup /unattend:<path>\unattend.xml
```

The `<path>` is the path to your `unattend.xml` file described in step 2. Setup will run to completion with whatever you have in the `unattend.xml` file.

Performing a basic install

The CD install consists of several stages, prompting you for information, copying files, and restarting. Setup concludes with the Installation Server Wizard, which guides you through the server configuration.

Initial setup: Using the DVD

To use the DVD for initial setup, follow these steps:

1. Insert the media into your DVD drive and then reboot your machine. Alternatively, you can run Setup from the DOS command line by typing `D:\setup.exe`. Executing Setup from the command line or from reboot loads a minimal footprint of Windows Server 2008 into memory. The code in memory contains the functions that start the setup program. The machine is rebooted, and the text-based version of Setup starts.

2. Next you can check online if any new bits need to be downloaded for the installation or you can continue with the bits you have on your DVD. Click Next to continue.

3. You are now required to add in your product key. Click Next and you will see the option to install Server Core or the regular Server 2008 image (this is shown in Figure 1-1). Click Next.

4. The next screen gives you the license terms and you have to agree to them to continue. Check the agreement checkbox and click Next.

   If you are installing on a server that already has a Windows Server installed you will be prompted to upgrade or install a fresh image. You should install a fresh copy of Windows Server 2008 on a newly formatted partition.

FIGURE 1-1

Choose standard installation image or Server Core.

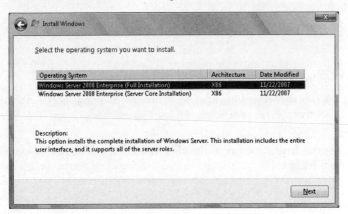

5. Setup next asks you to choose the partition on which to install the operating system. You can select existing partitions or choose to create a new partition. (You also have the option to load disk drivers at this point.) After choosing the partition, click Next. Once you have confirmed the file system you are on your way to installation.

6. Setup immediately begins installing files to the partition. If you have more than one disk in the system and want to install to one disk, do not format or partition any other media at this time.

7. Setup then saves the initial configuration and restarts the machine.

On boot up, the first screen that you see is the Windows Server 2008 Setup Wizard. The Windows Server 2008 operating system files are installed in the C:\Windows folder.

Running the Setup Wizard: Information to have handy

When you install Windows Server 2008 you will be asked for information about yourself, the organization or company licensing the software, and the computer.

Windows Server 2008 takes this information and begins installation in which it copies software to support machine configuration, installed devices, and so on. After this phase, Windows Server 2008 prompts you for the following information:

■ **Language options.** You are asked to customize language, locale, and keyboard settings. If you are installing in the United States, you can, for the most part, leave these at the default settings. You can also configure the server to use multiple languages and regional settings. Choosing multiple languages forces Windows to install the character sets from multiple languages.

■ **Name and organization.** Provide the name of the person responsible for the software and the name of the organization that owns the license.

■ **Licensing mode.** You can choose to select licensing on a per-server, per-seat, or per-device basis. If you choose to license per seat, you must enter the number of client access licenses (CALs) purchased. If you are going to provide application services by using the Terminal Services in Application mode, choose the CAL option.

■ **Computer name.** This is where you get to add the NetBIOS name. Windows Server 2008 chooses a default name for you, which you should change because it doesn't make very much sense. Coming up with a convenient naming convention that your users recognize is far better.

Windows pretty much leaves you to your own devices in naming your computers. The best rule to follow is to name the machine according to any convention you dream up that works for your situation . . . just be consistent. Resist cute names for several reasons: The names may be hard for your users to relate to, and some may find them annoying. (Not everyone loves Disney.) Server names are also the prefixes for the new Dynamic DNS names assigned to the server. A simple machine name for the genesis.mcity.us domain name would be MDENTS02.MCITY.US, which is far better than BULLWINKLE.MCITY.US. Be careful, too, about using names that attract security problems. We once used the name Checkpointcharlie, which was subsequently hacked the following week.

■ **Password for the Administrator account.** This account is installed into the local domain's Administrator account except for domain controllers.

■ **Windows Server 2008 components.** The next step is to add the optional components and services. Ignore most of these services in trial installations and go directly to Networking Options. Here, you must provide DHCP information, the DNS server address, and other information.

■ **Terminal Services.** You can also choose the operating mode of Terminal Services. For now leave it as is, in Administration mode. There's no point in installing Application Server mode until you are ready, and the mode can be changed at any time.

■ **Display settings.** These settings enable you to configure the screen resolution, number of display colors, and video-related information such as refresh rate. You can leave many of these settings at the default. Change your screen resolution, however, to at least 800 × 600. Many Windows Server 2008 folders and menus are jam-packed with icons and information, and 640 × 480 just does not work. In many cases, you should go with 1,024 × 768 resolution.

■ **Time and date.** These settings enable you to set time zones and daylight saving information and to adjust the current date and time. After this information is applied, Windows Server 2008 starts Phase 3 of the installation process: the network install.

Windows network install

This phase installs the networking components. Windows Server 2008 attempts to detect the network interface cards (NICs). If you use standard well-known brands such as Intel, you'll have no problems getting through the installation. The following list describes the steps, both automatic and interactive:

- **Network card detection.** After detecting and installing the drivers for the NICs, Windows Server 2008 attempts to locate a DHCP server on the network. It does this by broadcasting on DHCP Port 75 and then listening for a response from a DHCP server. If Windows Server 2008 cannot obtain an IP address, it uses the auto-configuration protocol and assigns itself an IP address. You can then continue with the installation, installing to a new workgroup, and make the necessary network connections later.

- **Networking components.** Next, you are asked to choose the networking components. The basic options to choose are the client for Microsoft Networks, File and Print Sharing for Microsoft Networks, and TCP/IP. You can install other services and components at any time after installation. If you are installing into an existing NT domain that does not have DNS or WINS servers in place, install NetBIOS as well.

- **Workgroup or domain.** If you are installing into a domain, you need the name of the account and password that has the authority to create new accounts in the domain. If you have problems installing into the domain, install into a workgroup. If you do not have a workgroup, create any workgroup name on the fly, such as awshucks, because you can always change it after installation or change to a domain whenever you are ready, post installation.

Final installation setup

This is the fourth phase of the installation, which involves final file copy, configuration, and removal of temporary files. The Setup program copies all remaining files to the hard disk. These include bitmap files, accessories, and services or component files that are either installed into service or left dormant until activated. Setup then applies configuration settings specified during earlier interactions.

The new configuration is saved in the registry databases and on disk to be used for the configuration after the computer starts anew. At this time, all temporary files are removed from the computer. After this activity, the machine is rebooted.

Installing from the network

You can also install servers from network sharepoints, which are called distribution drives or servers. Network installs should obviously be limited to local area network installation because anything less than the standard 100-Mbit/sec network speed makes installation an excruciatingly slow experience.

If you have not created a distribution share, simply copy the I386, I486, or ia64 (for Itanium-based systems) folder on the Windows Server 2008 DVD to a drive and share it. Apply the necessary access control to prevent unauthorized users from accessing the distribution files. The process, after you have a distribution point in place, is as follows:

1. Create a FAT partition on the target machine. This partition should be within the earlier recommended parameters. You can use the old faithful DOS FDISK command to create the partition, but if you are using a very large disk (more than 2GB), only Windows 98's FDISK for FAT32 enables you to configure all the space as one huge drive.

2. Boot to a network client. You can use Windows 95/98 boot disks (if you can still find them), but a simple DOS may be all that you need. Your DOS client contains the following software:

   ■ TCP/IP protocol files

   ■ DOS operating system files for minimum machine life

   ■ Network interface card drivers (another reason to use good cards that require no configuration)

3. You also need to create configuration files that log the target machine onto the network and enable it to use the source distribution sharepoint.

4. After you have connected to the network sharepoint, you start the installation by executing setup from the distribution server.

As Windows Server 2008 performs an upgrade, it first gathers information relating to installed hardware and software and reports this to you before installation begins. If some components preclude Windows Server 2008 from installing, you are given an option to remove those components or circumvent attempts by the installation process to support them in the new environment. After you have removed or dealt with the offending components, Windows Server 2008 enables the installation to proceed.

Roles, Features, and Applications

After you install the operating system and log in for the first time as an administrator, Windows Server 2008 automatically presents you with the Server Manager console. This tool enables you to configure role services such as Active Directory, DHCP, DNS, IIS, and more. If you do not need to use the tool immediately, you can close it. It can be accessed again from the menu items in Administrative Tools, from the Control Panel, and the command line. The OS, however, presents this tool to anyone who logs on to a server interactively in the capacity of an administrator.

Once you have completed a basic or Server Core installation, you have a variety of services and applications that can be installed on the server. These are grouped by roles, features, and applications. We will go into these in more detail shortly.

Standalone servers

Standalone servers do not connect to any domain but rather to a workgroup. You can create a workgroup from one standalone server or join the server to another workgroup, Windows for Workgroups–style. Standalone servers can share resources with other computers on the network, but they do not receive any of the benefits provided by Active Directory.

For a standalone server, you need the following items:

- Workgroup name
- An administrator's password
- Network protocols
- IP address
- DNS IP addresses and host names
- NetBIOS name of host

Member servers

Member servers are members of domains. A member server is running Windows Server 2008, a member of a domain, and not a domain controller. Because it is not a domain controller, a member server does not handle the account logon process, does not participate in Active Directory replication, and does not store domain security-policy information.

Member servers typically function as the following types of servers:

- File servers
- Application servers
- Database servers
- Web servers
- Certificate servers
- Firewalls
- Remote-access servers
- Print servers

Member servers also have a common set of security-related features, as follows:

- Member servers adhere to Group Policy settings that are defined for the site, domain, or organizational unit.
- Resources that are available on a member server are configured for access control.
- Member server users have user rights assigned to them.
- Member servers contain a local security-account database, the Security Account Manager (SAM).

To install a member server into a domain, you need to add the following items to your checklist:

- Domain name
- Network protocols

- IP address
- NetBIOS name of host

Role servers

A server on a network — standalone or member — can function in a number of roles.

As the needs of your computing environment change, you may want to change the role of a server. By using the Server Manager and the Add Roles Wizard, you can install Active Directory Domain Servers to promote a member server to a domain controller, or you can install individual roles or combinations of various roles, such as DHCP, WINS, and DNS. It is also relatively straightforward to demote a domain controller to a simple role server or remove any number of roles and features from a server.

Server Manager is the key configuration console you will use for installing server roles and features on your server. It can be configured to open automatically as soon as you log in to the Windows console or desktop. Figure 1-2 shows Server Manager opened to the File Services role details page.

FIGURE 1-2

The Server Manager console.

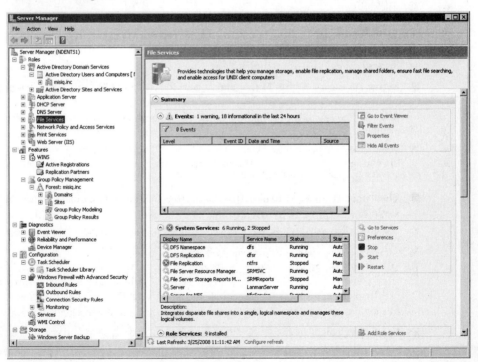

Types of roles

Let's look at the various roles and features you can install on Windows Server 2008.

- **Active Directory Certificate Services (AD CS).** AD CS role services install on a number of operating systems, including Windows Server 2008, Windows Server 2003, and Windows 2000 Server. Naturally the fullest implementation of AD CS is only possible on Windows Server 2008. You can deploy AD CS as a single standalone certification authority (CA), or you can deploy multiple servers and configure them as root, policy, and certificate issuing authorities. You also have a variety of Online Responder configuration possibilities. AD CS is discussed in depth in Chapter 16.

- **Active Directory Domain Services (AD DS).** This is the role in the Windows Server 2008 operating system that stores information about users, computers, and other resources on a network. AD DS is also used for directory-enabled applications such as Microsoft Exchange Server. AD also stores all information required for Group Policy. See Chapters 17–24.

- **Active Directory Federation Services (AD FS).** AD FS employs technology that allows users over the life of a single online session to securely share digital identity and entitlement rights, or "claims," across security and enterprise boundaries. This role — introduced and supported on all operating systems since Microsoft Windows Server 2003 R2 — provides Web Single Sign-On (SSO) services to allow a user to access multiple, related Web applications.

- **Active Directory Lightweight Directory Services (AD LDS).** This service is ideal if you are required to support directory-enabled applications. AD LDS is a Lightweight Directory Access Protocol (LDAP) compliant directory service.

- **Active Directory Rights Management Services (AD RMS).** This service augments an organization's security strategy by protecting information through persistent usage policies. The key to the service is that the right management policies are bound to the information no matter where it resides or to where it is moved. AD RMS is used to lock down documents, spreadsheets, e-mail, and so on from being infiltrated or ending up in the wrong hands. AD RMS, for example, prevents e-mails from being accidentally forwarded to the wrong people.

- **The Application Server role.** This role supports the deployment and operation of custom business applications that are built with Microsoft .NET Framework. The Application Server role lets you choose services for applications that require COM+, Message Queuing, Web services, and Distributed Coordinated Transactions.

- **DHCP and DNS.** These two roles install these two critical network service services required for every network. They support Active Directory integration and support IPv6. See Chapters 3 and 4 for DNS and DHCP, respectively. WINS is not classified as a key role for Windows Server 2008, and you install it as a feature, discussed later.

- **Fax Server role.** The fax server lets you set up a service to send and receive faxes over your network. The role creates a fax server and installs the Fax Service Manager and the Fax service on the server.

- **File Server role.** This role lets you set up all the bits, bells, and whistles that come with a Windows file server. This role also lets you install Share and Storage Management, the Distributed File System (DFS), the File Server Resource Manager application for managing file servers, Services for Network File System (NFS), Windows File Services, which include stuff like the File Replication Service (FRS), and so on. The File Server role is discussed in Chapters 13 through 15.

- **Network Policy and Access Services.** This provides the following network connectivity solutions: Network Access Protection (NAP), the client health policy creation, enforcement, and remediation technology; secure wireless and wired access (802.1X), wireless access points, remote access solutions, virtual private network (VPN) services, Radius, and more. The Network Policy and Access Service is discussed in Chapter 6.

- **Print Management role.** The print services provide a single interface that you use to manage multiple printers and print servers on your network. Printer management is discussed in Chapter 12.

- **Terminal Services role.** This service provides technologies that enable users to access Windows-based programs that are installed on a terminal server. Users can execute applications remotely (they still run on the remote server) or they can access the full Windows desktop on the target server.

- **Universal Description, Discovery, and Integration (UDDI).** UDDI Services provide capabilities for sharing information about Web services. UDDI is used on the intranet, between entities participating on an extranet, or on the Internet.

- **Web Server role.** This role provides IIS 7.0, the Web server, ASP.NET, and the Windows Communication Foundation (WCF).

- **Windows Deployment Services.** These services are used for deployment of new computers in medium to large organizations.

Features

Server Manager also lets you install dozens of "features" on Windows Server 2008. These so-called features are actually programs or supporting layers that support or augment the functionality of one or more roles, or simply add to the functionality of the server.

A good example of a feature is the clustering service. Now called Failover Clustering, this feature can be used to support mission-critical roles such as File Services, Printer Services, and DHCP Server, on server clusters. This provides for higher availability and performance.

Other features you will likely install include SMTP Server, Telnet Client and Server, Group Policy Management (for use with Active Directory), Remote Assistance, and more.

Net's now look at some specific scenarios.

Windows Server 2008 as a domain controller

Member Servers or just standalone servers can be promoted to domain controller. The Active Directory Wizard can help you install and configure components and enables you to provide directory service to network computers and users. Before installing or even considering a domain controller, however, review the following checklist:

- Review the Active Directory topic "Introduction to Active Directory" in your Windows Server 2008 Help guide.
- Make sure that you review the role of a domain controller.
- Review concepts about security.
- Review concepts about Domain Name Service (DNS) namespace planning and integration with DNS.
- Verify that the server has an NTFS partition.
- Verify that DNS is correctly configured.

Promoting member servers to domain controllers either creates new domains or adds additional domain controllers to existing domains. In creating the first domain, you must have already created one domain controller in that domain. The act of creating the domain controller also creates the domain.

If your organization needs additional domains, you must create one domain controller for each additional domain. New domains in a forest must be either a new child domain or the root of a new domain tree. If you decide to create a child domain, the name of the new domain must contain the full name of the parent. To hierarchically organize domains within your organization, make sure that you use the domain tree structure. If you would rather create the root of a new domain tree, make sure that its name is not related to the other domains in the forest.

To improve the availability and reliability of network services, add additional domains to a single domain. You can create new domain controllers across the network or from backup media.

Windows Server 2008, Windows Enterprise Server 2008, and Windows Datacenter Server 2008 all support Active Directory. AD uses a structured datastore for logical, hierarchical organization of directory information. The datastore is also known as the directory, and it contains information about Active Directory objects. Active Directory objects include shared resources such as servers, volumes, printers, and the network users and accounts.

Active Directory is tightly integrated with security through logon authentication and access control to objects. This makes managing directory data and organization throughout the network easy for an administrator. Schemas also help administrators with daily tasks by setting constraints and limits on instances of objects. Schemas consist of classes of objects and attributes contained in the directory. Global catalogs consist of the information about each and every object in a directory; therefore, a global catalog provides easy access to directory information regardless of which domain of the directory actually contains the data.

The following list summarizes the Active Directory features that are enabled by default on any domain controller running Windows Server 2008:

■ The selection of multiple user objects and the capability to modify common attributes of multiple user objects at one time.

■ The capability to drag and drop Active Directory objects from container to container or to a desired location in the domain hierarchy. You also have the capability to drag objects to group membership lists.

■ Enhanced search functionality is object-oriented and provides an efficient search that minimizes network traffic associated with browsing objects.

■ The capability to save queries, enabling you to save commonly used search parameters for reuse in Active Directory Users and Computers.

■ Active Directory command-line tools, which give you the capability to run directory-service commands for administration scenarios.

■ You can now create instances of specified classes in the base schema of a forest and instances of several common classes, including country or region, person, organizationalPerson, groupOfNames, device, and certificationAuthority.

■ The inetOrgPerson class is added to the base schema and can be used in the same manner as the user class.

■ You can configure replication scope for application-specific data among domain controllers running Windows Server 2008.

■ The capability to add additional domain controllers to existing domains by using backup media, thus reducing the time necessary for an administrator to create additional domain controllers.

■ Universal group membership caching to help prevent the need to locate a global catalog across a WAN.

Active Directory can provide a companywide network solution with one domain, reduced sign-on capabilities, and one single point of management. Active Directory helps eliminate unnecessary domains and reduces server hardware and maintenance costs.

CROSS-REF Please refer to Chapters 17–22 for a more in-depth view of Active Directory.

Two approaches to installing a domain controller are possible. First, you can raise the machine as a member server and promote it post-installation — and even post-burn-in. Alternatively, you can promote it to domain controller status during an automated installation. The latter option naturally requires a script.

We don't recommend the latter option unless you are really confident about your machines and their configuration or you have a huge rollout. If you are an Original Equipment Manufacturer (OEM), you would not need to be concerned about domain controllers and Active Directory because the domain specifics, such as creating a new tree or forest or joining existing trees and forests, is done on the customer's network. Conversely, if you, as a consultant or network engineer, have created an extensive unattended or remote installation regimen that automatically raises the machine as a domain controller, you know what you are doing.

For now, you have several reasons to not promote during or just after initial installation. First, promoting a domain controller is a time-intensive operation. (Active Directory goes through extensive self-configuration before the installation completes.) Second, if you experience a problem with the machine, you must demote the domain controller, which can be a complicated process. Third, after you have installed and raised a domain controller, you do not want to demote it because of a hardware problem or risk trashing your domain controller.

If Active Directory is demoted, it tears down everything that it created and restores the machine to the control of the registry and the local SAM. In fact, it is like watching a movie in reverse. Active Directory asks you for a new administrator account name and password for the rollback. All configuration changes made to the machine, such as desktop settings, are restored to the default, newly created settings. After you reboot the machine, you are back to where you started. You do not even get earlier changes that you made to the registry because the registry is essentially reinstalled after Active Directory comes down (because it is wiped out if you promote the server).

A good reason lies behind this. Everything configured on a domain controller is stored in the directory databases, and after the registry is restored, you can re-promote it from scratch. Promoting a domain controller is dealt with in Chapter 21.

To promote a role server into a domain controller, you need to add the following items to your checklist:

- Domain name
- An administrator's password
- Network protocols
- IP address
- DNS IP addresses and host names
- NetBIOS name of host
- Role service information

The checklist for a domain controller is as follows:

- Domain name. If you are creating a new domain, you need the name of the parent domain that you are installing under or the existing tree name (or the forest name if you are installing a new domain tree). If you are adding a domain controller to an existing domain, you need to have that name handy as well.
- An administrator's password
- Network protocols

- IP address
- NetBIOS name of host
- DNS IP addresses and host names

Windows Server 2008 as a Communications Server and Microsoft Exchange

Microsoft Exchange Server unites users with knowledge anytime, anywhere. Exchange is designed to meet the messaging and collaboration needs of small organizations, large distributed enterprises, and everything in between. Microsoft Exchange integrates with Windows Server 2008, although there have been a few hairy incompatibility problems with Exchange 2007 on the RTM build of Windows Server 2008. We list a few of the Exchange Server main services in the following sections.

Internet Information Services integration

Exchange is also integrated with IIS to provide for high-performance mail protocols, SMTP protocols, and POP protocols. Exchange also provides a browser interface to access the Microsoft Outlook Web Access client.

Active Directory integration

Active Directory, which is covered in more detail in the final chapters of this book, is an enterprise directory service that is highly scalable and fully integrated with Exchange at the system level. Exchange takes full advantage of the Windows Server 2008 Active Directory; with but a single point of administration, it enables users to control all messaging services seamlessly. All directory information, including users, mailboxes, servers, sites, and recipients, is stored in Active Directory. Administrators benefit from the unified administration, experience no user-interface changes, and require no retraining after switching to Active Directory. Integration features of Exchange Server and Active Directory include the following:

- Unified administration of Exchange Server and Windows Server 2008 enables an administrator to manage all user data in one place using one set of tools.

- Security groups in Windows Server 2008 can be automatically used as Exchange distribution lists, removing the need to create a parallel set of distribution lists for each department or group.

- Active Directory's schema extensibility enables the management of distributed information and easily configurable Exchange user and server information.

- Lightweight Directory Access Protocol (LDAP) is a native access protocol for directory information.

Distributed services

Distributed services enable subsystems to use storage, protocol, and directories on different computers, providing for scalability for millions of users. This system is extremely configurable, providing extensibility and flexibility for system architecture.

Security

Exchange Server offers you the only messaging system that is fully integrated with the Windows Server 2008 security model. Administrators use the Windows Server 2008 security model to define the permissions for all messaging and collaboration services, including public folders. This means that administrators can learn a single permissions model for managing both Windows Server 2008 and Exchange and can create a single set of security groups to apply to either Windows Server 2008 resources or Microsoft Exchange objects. This helps simplify your domain administration, and Exchange Server enables permissions to be set at the item or document level. Security descriptors can be set for messages and components. These features provide for new levels of security.

Single-seat and policy-based administration

Microsoft Exchange uses a graphic administration and monitoring system that integrates with Windows Server 2008's Microsoft Management Console (MMC) to provide single-seat administration. The MMC does not provide you with management capabilities, but with a common interface that enables you to manage all your needs. The Microsoft Exchange System Manager, Microsoft Active Directory, and Internet Services Manager are snap-ins that provide the management for Server 2008. Policy-based management provides the administrator with the capability to perform single operations made up of hundreds of objects. Policies are a set of objects defined by the administrator. The administrator can also define recipient policies that could potentially affect hundreds of thousands of users, groups, and contacts in Active Directory.

SMTP message routing

Exchange Server supports SMTP, POP, LDAP, IMAP, HTTP, NNTP, S/MIME, and X.509 version 3. This versatility enables Exchange Server to act as an organization's gateway to the Internet. Providing high-performance routing of e-mail services, SMTP is, by default, the transport protocol for routing all message traffic between servers, within an Exchange site and between sites. Your organization's use of SMTP results in increased performance and new opportunities for integration with the Internet. Exchange Server's message algorithms have been enhanced to provide fault-tolerant message delivery and to eliminate messages that bounce, even when multiple servers or network links are down. This provides for increased message bandwidth and performance. SMTP routing provides customers with considerable flexibility in designing a reliable, high-performance messaging backbone by using Exchange Server.

Internet mail content

Exchange Server can significantly increase performance of e-mail, because you use e-mail clients to store and retrieve Multipurpose Internet Mail Extensions (MIME) content directly from the base, without any form of content conversion. Client software such as Outlook enables you to stream data in and out of the database. This process helps performance immensely.

All the features discussed in the preceding sections provide low cost-of-ownership, which makes Microsoft Exchange Server a valuable asset to every organization.

System Monitoring Using Windows Management Instrumentation

Windows Management Instrumentation (WMI) helps simplify the instrumentation of computer software and hardware. It provides you with a means of monitoring and controlling system components, both locally and remotely. The sole purpose of the WMI is to define a set of environment-independent specifications, thus helping you share management information that works with existing enterprise-management standards, such as Desktop Management Interface and the Simple Network Management Protocol (SNMP). The WMI provides a uniform model that complements these standards.

WMI is fully integrated with Windows Server 2008 to provide a simplified approach to management. Such tools as Microsoft Management Console help simplify the task of developing well-integrated management applications, therefore enabling vendors to provide Windows Server 2008 customers with enterprise-scalable management solutions. Combining local and remote events and the WMI query language provides you with the tools that you need to create complex management solutions.

The WMI also provides you with the Windows Driver Model (WDM), a kernel-level instrumentation technology. This technology provides you with consistent, open access to management data. WMI extensions are available for the following WDM capabilities:

- Publishing kernel instrumentation
- Configuring device settings
- Providing kernel-side event notification
- Publishing custom data
- Enabling administrators to set data security
- Accessing instrumentation by way of WMI

You can run the WMI console from the command line in interactive mode or non-interactive mode. Interactive mode is used for entering commands at the computer, and noninteractive mode is useful for processing batch procedures.

The console installs the first time that you run it. If a change is introduced to the managed object format (MOF) files, the console automatically compiles the alias. To start the WMI console from a command prompt, type **wmic**. The prompt now should look as follows: `wmic:root\cli>`. The WMI console enables you to enter aliases, commands, and global switches, or you can enter /? for Help.

You can also run WMI console in noninteractive mode, whereby the command prompt returns to you after executing the command. An example is as follows:

```
<PROMPT>wmic os get /format:hform>OperatingSystem.html
```

The output from the command is redirected to an HTML file.

Windows Server 2008 for Database Services with SQL Server

If you have a modest understanding of database connectivity, you should find SQL Server's command syntax uncomplicated and easy to use. If you are an experienced developer, you are sure to appreciate the scalable, high-performance access that SQL Server provides.

If you are concerned about backward compatibility, we suggest connecting using ODBC.

You want to avoid any security issues so we are going to go through the steps to create an account for SQL Server to access data on a remote computer. Start by opening Management Studio; then, in the console tree, select Microsoft SQL Server ➢ SQL Server Group ➢ SQLComputerName. Select Databases and then double-click your database; proceed by right-clicking Users ➢ New Database User. The login name should be domain\username, and the Public checkbox should be selected for all the following items:

- db_owner
- db_accessadmin
- db_securityadmin
- db_ddladmin
- db_datareader
- db_datawriter
- db_backupoperator

Do not select db_denydatareader or db_denydatawriter. These options, if selected, deny members read and write permissions to the database.

You can choose between the TCP/IP Sockets and Named Pipes connection methods for accessing a remote SQL Server database. Named Pipes database clients must be authenticated by Windows Server 2008 prior to establishing a connection. Alternatively, connections using TCP/IP Sockets connect directly to the database server without connecting through an intermediary computer. Because connections made with TCP/IP Sockets connect directly to the database server, users can gain access through SQL Server authentication, rather than Windows Server 2008 authentication.

One of the main challenges of designing a sophisticated Web database application seems to involve managing database connections. After you open and maintain a database connection, it can severely strain a database server's resources and result in stability issues. Database servers experiencing a sudden increase in activity can become backlogged, greatly increasing the time necessary to establish a database connection.

Windows Server 2008 for IIS and ASP.NET

Windows Server 2008 offers integration between Visual Studio 2008 and IIS. This tight integration provides developers with very high levels of functionality. Now that the request-processing architecture is integrated with IIS 7.0, it should provide an improved experience for those of you using ASP.NET and the Microsoft .NET Framework. The new Windows Server 2008 Web Edition delivers a single-purpose solution for Internet Service providers, application developers, and others wanting to use only the specific Web functionality.

Windows Server 2008 for Application Services

Windows Server 2008 builds on the core strengths of the Windows family, providing security, manageability, reliability, availability, and scalability across the board. Many advancements were made in Windows Server 2008 that provide benefits for application development, resulting in lower total cost-of-ownership and better performance. The following list describes a few of these benefits:

- Simplified integration and interoperability
- Improved developer productivity
- Increased enterprise efficiency
- Improved scalability and reliability

- End-to-end security
- Efficient deployment and management
- Simplified integration and interoperability

Windows Server 2008 delivers a revolutionary application environment to build, deploy, and run XML Web services. Microsoft has provided integrated support for XML Web services, which enables applications to take advantage of the loosely coupled principles of Internet computing. The Windows Server 2008 application environment improves the productivity of developers by providing integrated application services and industry-leading tool support. The following feature set helps increase the productivity of developers:

- **ASP.NET.** Besides standard Web-based applications ASP.NET XML Web services allows developers to write their business logic in Web services, and the ASP.NET infrastructure is responsible for delivering that service via SOAP and other public protocols.

- **Automatic memory management.** The .NET Framework runs in the common-language runtime, which is a garbage-collected environment. Garbage collection frees applications that are using .NET Framework objects from the need to explicitly destroy those objects, reducing common programming errors dramatically.

- **Industry-leading tools.** Visual Studio 2008 provides an integrated, multilanguage tool for building Web applications.

- **Microsoft .NET Framework.** By integrating the .NET Framework into the Windows Server 2008 application-development environment, developers are freed from writing the day-in, day-out code and can instead focus their efforts on delivering real business value.

- **Reusable code.** Visual Studio 2008 provides an architecture that is easy to learn and that enables improved code reuse.

- **Separation of code from content.** This enables developers and content creators to work in parallel by keeping content separate from application code.

- **Server-side Web controls.** Visual Studio 2008 Web controls are compiled and run on the server for maximum performance, and can be inherited and extended for even more functionality.

Applications that are developed using Windows Server 2008 tend to be more responsive and available because Windows Server 2008 can be managed by so few people. This helps lower the total cost of ownership and provides better performance. Microsoft has also made many programming-model enhancements, providing component aliases, public and private components, process initialization, and services without components. Component aliasing enables you to configure the same physical implementation of a component as many times as you want. This provides component reuse at the binary level. The public and private components enable you to individually mark components as public for use in other applications, or private if the component can be seen and activated only by other components in that same application. Process initialization provides the developer with the capability to execute code as the hosting process starts and finishes. This helps your component take the opportunity to take any action, such as initializing connections, files, caches, and so on. Services without components enable you to programmatically enter and leave a service domain. This enables you to build components that use transactions without needing to inherit from ServicedComponent.

Building and deploying your application on Windows Server 2008 gives you better performance and more options for the design and architecture of your system.

Windows Server 2008 for Resolutions Services

The following sections describe what you need to create a plan to prepare and configure your server by using DNS, WINS, and DHCP. These sections focus on decisions that you must make for a complete Windows Server 2008 installation.

DNS

Before you begin using DNS on your network, decide on a plan for your DNS domain namespace. Coming up with a namespace plan involves making some decisions about how you intend to use DNS naming and what goals you are trying to accomplish by using DNS. Some questions that you may have at this stage include the following:

- Have you previously chosen and registered a DNS domain name for use on the Internet?
- Are you going to set up DNS servers on a private network or the Internet?
- What naming requirements do you need to follow in choosing DNS domain names for computers?

Choosing your first DNS domain name

In setting up DNS servers, you should first choose and register a unique parent DNS domain name that can be used for hosting your organization on the Internet. Before you decide on a parent DNS domain name for your organization to use on the Internet, search to determine whether the domain name is already registered to another organization.

 DNS, as it relates to Active Directory, is covered in more detail in Chapter 17.

DNS namespace planning for Active Directory

Before a DNS domain namespace can be correctly implemented, the Active Directory structure needs to be available, so you must begin with the Active Directory design and support it with the appropriate DNS namespace.

Active Directory domains are named by using DNS names. In choosing DNS names to use for your Active Directory domains, start with the registered DNS domain-name suffix that your organization has reserved for use on the Internet and combine this name with something significant in your organization to form full names for your Active Directory domains.

> **TIP** In planning your DNS and Active Directory namespace, we recommend that you use a different set of distinguished names that do not overlap as the basis for your internal and external DNS use.

Only use characters in your names that are part of the Internet standard character set permitted for use in DNS host naming. Permitted characters are all letters (a–z), numbers (0–9), and the hyphen (-).

DHCP

If you are still in the decision-making process as you are deciding how many servers your organization needs, consider the locations of the routers on the network and whether you want a DHCP server in each subnet. If you are planning on extending the use of a DHCP server across more than one network, you may need to configure additional DHCP relay agents and use superscopes as well. If DHCP service is provided between segments, transmission speeds may also be a factor. If your WAN links or dial-up links are slower, you may need a DHCP server on both sides of these links to service clients locally. Currently, the only limit that a DHCP server can serve is determined by the number of available IP addresses.

Following are some Windows Server 2008 factors that could enhance DHCP server performance:

- The primary contributing factor to improving DHCP server performance is the amount of random access memory (RAM) and the speed of the server disk drives installed.
- You should carefully evaluate disk-access times and average times for disk read/write operations in sizing and planning for your DHCP-server hardware specifications. You should also try to increase RAM to the point where server performance is maximized.

> **TIP** For the best possible DHCP server design in most networks, we recommend that you have, at most, 10,000 clients per server.

Most networks need one primary online DHCP server and one other DHCP server acting as a secondary, or backup, server. If you choose not to implement two DHCP servers, using the 80/20 rule for balancing scopes, but want to continue to provide a measure of potential fault tolerance, you may consider implementing a backup or hot standby DHCP server as an alternative.

WINS

The first decision that you need to make is how many WINS servers your organization needs. A single WINS server can handle NetBIOS name-resolution requests for a large number of computers, but you must also consider the location of the routers on your network and the distribution of clients in each subnet as you decide how many WINS servers are actually required.

Determine whether you want to configure WINS servers as pull or push partners, and set partner preferences for each server. WINS servers are designed to help reduce broadcast traffic between local subnets; WINS creates some traffic between servers and clients. This can be particularly important if you use WINS on routed TCP/IP networks. Consider the effects of slower speed links on both replication traffic between WINS servers and NetBIOS registration and renewal traffic required for WINS clients. In addition, consider how temporarily shutting down a WINS server can affect your network. Use additional WINS servers for failure recovery, backup, and redundancy.

The following two factors can enhance WINS server performance:

- Installing dual processors on the computer running WINS. This can help increase performance by almost 25 percent.

- Installing a dedicated disk drive, separate from the system drive, for the WINS database

TIP After you establish a WINS server on your intranet, adjusting the renew interval, which is the time between a WINS client-name registration and name renewal, can help you trim server-response times.

You can also sometimes estimate WINS client traffic based on the behavior of the WINS clients. In estimating WINS client traffic, however, you also need to consider the network topology and the design or configuration of the network routers. In some cases, predicting the traffic load on a specific network router is not possible because the routers are configured to autonomously route traffic based on factors other than traffic load. By testing the performance of your network installation of WINS, you can better identify potential problems before they occur. Use WINS server performance counters, which are available through the use of System Monitor. One last point about WINS: it is not installed as a server role, but rather as an add-on feature.

Summary

This chapter took you through the Windows Server 2008 basic install procedure. We recommend that you install only what you need to get the system up and running. Later, you can begin adding advanced components to the server and establish its role on the network or promote it to an Active Directory domain controller.

We also took you through an exhaustive discussion of hardware. Unless you plan to install complex adapter or interface cards for specialized purposes, such as modems, telephony cards, sound cards, and so on, you won't have problems as long as you stick to tried-and-tested components.

The next chapter provides the information that you now need to configure and deploy your running server.

Chapter 2

Configuring Windows Server 2008

This chapter explores the many tools for configuring and managing the system, managing users, and controlling other aspects of Windows Server 2008.

Using the Microsoft Management Console

One of the many changes in Windows 2000 from Windows NT that is expanded in the Windows 2003 and 2008 interfaces and administrative structure is the switch to a more homogenous approach to administrative utilities. Although many system and operating properties still are controlled through the Control Panel, most administrative functions have moved to the Microsoft Management Console (MMC), host for a variety of so-called "snap-ins" used to manage the myriad roles, features, and applications of the server. The MMC runs under Windows Server 2008, Windows 2000– Windows Server 2003, Windows 9x, and Windows XP and Vista. This section of the chapter examines the MMC and its component tools for Windows Server 2008.

Understanding the function of the MMC

The MMC itself serves as a framework. Within that framework are various administrative tools called consoles. In particular, the MMC provides a unified interface for administrative tools. This means that after you learn the structure of one tool, you will be able to apply that knowledge to the rest, which are going to follow suit (within limitations imposed by the differences in the function of the various tools). Figure 2-1 shows the MMC with the Computer Management snap-in loaded (more on snap-ins shortly). As you'll learn later in this chapter, you use the Computer Management snap-in for most aspects of a system's hardware and software configuration.

FIGURE 2-1

The MMC serves as a framework for a wide variety of administrative tools.

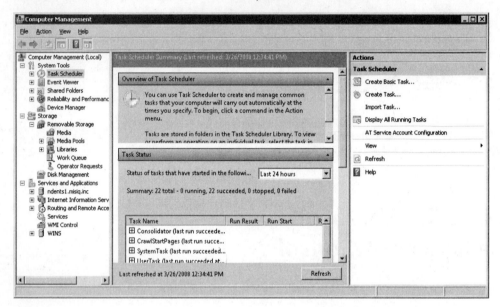

Perhaps more important than a unified interface is the fact that the MMC lets you combine administrative tools to build your own console configuration, which you can store by name on disk. The next time you need to work with it, you run the MMC console from the Start menu or double-click its icon or shortcut. For example, let's say that you want to put together a custom console for managing a Windows Server 2008 Internet server. You can integrate the tools for managing DNS, DHCP, Application Server, and IIS all under one interface. This custom console gives you quick access to most of the settings you need to configure on a regular basis for the server.

The MMC window usually consists of two panes, although many consoles in MMC on Windows Server 2008 comprise a single console divided into three panes. The left pane typically contains the Tree tab. The Tree tab generally shows a hierarchical structure for the object(s) being managed. When you use the Active Directory Users and Computers console, for example, the tree shows the containers in the Active Directory (AD) that pertain to users, groups, and computers.

The right pane is the details pane. The details pane varies depending on the item you select in the tree. When you select Services in the tree, for example, the details pane shows the list of installed services. The details pane typically offers two views: single details pane and extended Actions pane, which usually shows various tasks. The extended view adds an additional area that typically shows instructions or additional information about a selected item.

MMC provides two different modes: user mode and author mode. In user mode, you work with existing consoles and several variations of the user mode from full access to limited access. Author mode enables you create new consoles or modify existing ones. Figure 2-2 shows the Services console opened in user mode. Figure 2-3 shows the console opened in author mode. As indicated in the figures, author mode offers access to commands and functions not available in user mode.

FIGURE 2-2

Author mode, shown here, enables you to create new consoles while user mode restricts the actions that a user can perform within a console.

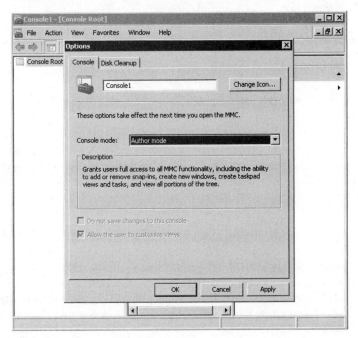

User mode actually offers three different options: full access, limited access with multiple windows, and limited access with a single window. With full access, an MMC user can access all the window management commands in MMC but can't add or remove snap-ins or change console properties. The limited access options limit changes to the window configuration of the console and use either a single window or multiple windows depending on the mode. A console's mode is stored in the console and applies when you open the console. Console modes can be changed via the Options property sheet (click File ➤ Options). Setting console options is discussed later in the chapter.

FIGURE 2-3

Author mode provides the capability to change console options and add new snap-ins.

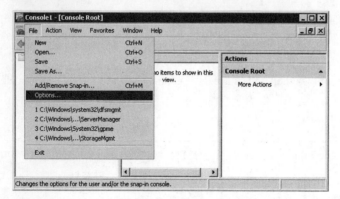

 The default mode in Windows Server 2008 is user mode — limited access, single window.

As mentioned earlier, you use author mode to author new consoles or modify existing ones. In author mode, you can add and remove snap-ins, change window options, and set options for the console.

Opening the MMC

You can open MMC consoles by selecting them from the Administrative Tools folder in the Start menu or by double-clicking their icons in Explorer. You also can start consoles using a command prompt. The format of the MMC command is as follows:

```
MMC path\file.msc /a
```

The following list explains the options for MMC:

- Path\file.msc. Replace path with the path to the console file specified by file.msc. You can use an absolute path or use the %systemroot% variable to reference the local computer's path to the Windows Server 2008 folder. Using %systemroot% is useful when you're creating shortcuts to consoles for use on different systems (where the system root folder might be different).

- /a. Use the /a switch to enter author mode and enable changes to the console. Opening an existing console with the /a switch overrides its stored mode for the current session.

- /32. This starts the 32-bit version of MMC. This is only needed when you want to run the 32-bit version on a 64-bit Windows version.

- /64. This starts the 64-bit version of MMC. This option works only on a 64-bit version of Windows.

For example, let's say that you want to open the DNS console in author mode to add the DHCP snap-in to it. Use this command to open the DNS console in author mode:

```
MMC %systemroot%\System32\dnsmgmt.msc /a
```

> **TIP** You can right-click an `.msc` file and choose Author from the context menu to open the file in author mode.

After opening the DNS console, you add the DHCP console using the Add or Remove Snap-In command in the Console menu. Snap-ins are covered in the next section.

> **TIP** If you prefer, you can open the MMC in author mode and then add both snap-ins using the Add or Remove Snap-In command in the Console menu.

Windows 2008 Server provides several preconfigured consoles for performing various administrative tasks. Most of these console files are stored in `\systemroot\System32` and have `.msc` file extensions (for Microsoft Console). Windows 2008 Server places several of these consoles in the Administrative Tools folder, which you access by clicking Start ➤ All Programs ➤ Administrative Tools. In essence, each of the preconfigured consoles contains one or more snap-ins geared toward a specific administrative task.

In an apparent effort to simplify the Start menu, Microsoft includes only some of these consoles in the Administrative Tools folder. However, you can open any console by double-clicking its file. When you do so, the MMC loads first and then opens the console. You also can open the MMC and add snap-ins to your own consoles. This gives you the ability to create a custom console containing whichever group(s) of snap-ins you use most often or that are targeted for specific administrative tasks.

Using snap-ins

Although the MMC forms the framework for integrated administrative tools in Windows Server 2008, the tools themselves are called snap-ins. Each MMC snap-in enables you to perform a specific administrative function or group of functions. For example, you use the DHCP snap-in to administer DHCP servers and scopes. The various MMC snap-ins serve the same function as individual administrative tools did in Windows NT. For example, the Event Viewer snap-in takes the place of the standalone Event Viewer tool (see Figure 2-4). The Disk Management branch of the Computer Management snap-in replaces Disk Administrator. The Active Directory Users and Computers snap-in takes the place of User Manager for Domains, and so on.

Snap-ins come in two flavors: standalone and extension. Standalone snap-ins usually are called simply snap-ins. Extension snap-ins usually are called extensions. Snap-ins function by themselves and can be added individually to a console. Extensions are associated with a snap-in and are added to a standalone snap-in or other extension on the console tree. Extensions function within the framework of the standalone snap-in and operate on the objects targeted by the snap-in. For example, the Services snap-in incorporates four extensions: Extended View, Send Console Message, Service Dependencies, and SNMP Snapin Extension.

FIGURE 2-4

Snap-ins perform specific administrative functions and replace standalone tools such as Event Viewer.

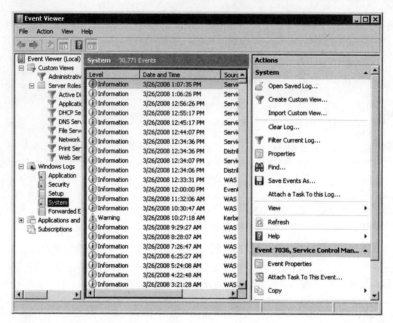

You can add snap-ins and extensions when you open a console in author mode. By default, all extensions associated with a snap-in are added when you add the snap-in, but you can disable extensions selectively for a snap-in.

To add a snap-in, open the MMC in author mode and choose File ➤ Add/Remove Snap-In. The Standalone page of the Add/Remove Snap-In property sheet shows the snap-ins currently loaded. The Extensions tab lists extensions for the currently selected snap-in and allows you to add all extensions or selectively enable/disable specific extensions.

In the Standalone page, click Add to add a new snap-in. The Add Standalone Snap-In dialog box lists the available snap-ins. Click the snap-in you want to add and click Add. Depending on the snap-in, you might be prompted to select the focus for the snap-in. For example, when you add the Device Manager snap-in, you can select between managing the local computer or managing another computer on the network. Adding the IP Security Policy Management snap-in enables you to choose between the local computer, the domain policy for the computer's domain, the domain policy for another domain, or another computer.

After you configure snap-ins and extensions the way you want them, save the console so that you can quickly open the same configuration later. To do so, choose File ➤ Save, or Save As, and specify a name for the console. By default, Windows Server 2008 will place the new console in the Administrative Tools folder, which appears on the Start menu under Programs, but you can specify a different location if desired.

Getting to know taskpads

A taskpad is a page on which you can add views of the details pane and shortcuts to various functions inside and outside of a console. These shortcuts can run commands, open folders, open a Web page, execute menu commands, and so on. In essence, taskpads enable you to create a page of organized tasks to help you perform tasks quickly, rather than use the existing menu provided by the snap-in. You can create multiple taskpads in a console, but the console must contain at least one snap-in. Figure 2-5 shows a taskpad for performing a variety of tasks in the DNS snap-in.

FIGURE 2-5

Use taskpads to create tasks for performing specific actions, such as these DNS-related tasks.

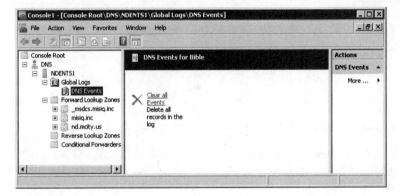

 You must open a console in author mode to create taskpads.

A taskpad can contain a list from the details pane in horizontal or vertical format. Horizontal works well for multiple-column lists (many fields per item), whereas vertical works well for long lists (few fields per item). You also can configure a taskpad to show no lists. In addition to the list, the taskpad includes an icon for each task with either a pop-up description or a text description of the task. You click a task's icon to execute the task.

Creating a taskpad

To create a taskpad, right-click the object in the tree that you want to be the focus of the taskpad and then choose New Taskpad View. MMC starts a wizard to help you create the taskpad. In the second page of the wizard right after the introduction screen (see Figure 2-6), you define the appearance of the taskpad. As you make selections, the wizard shows the results to help you determine the effect of your choices.

FIGURE 2-6

This wizard page helps you configure the way the taskpad appears.

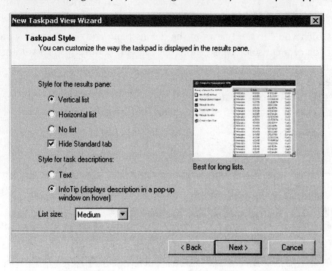

In the next page of the wizard, you specify the items to which the taskpad applies. The following list summarizes the options:

- **Selected Tree Item.** This option applies the taskpad to only the selected item in the tree. Using the DNS snap-in as an example, creating a taskpad for Forward Lookup Zones and using this option will cause the taskpad to appear only when you click Forward Lookup Zones. It will not appear if you click Reverse Lookup Zones.

- **All Tree Items That Are the Same Type as the Selected Tree Item.** This option applies the taskpad to all objects in the tree that are the same type as the selected object. In the previous DNS example, choosing this option would cause the taskpad to display when you click either Forward Lookup Zones or Reverse Lookup Zones.

- **Change Default Display to This Taskpad View for These Tree Items.** Select this option to have the MMC automatically switch to taskpad view when the user clicks the object in the tree associated with the taskpad. Deselect the option to have the MMC default to the normal view instead.

The next page of the wizard prompts you for a taskpad view name and description. The name appears at the top of the taskpad and on the tab at the bottom of the taskpad. The description appears at the top of the taskpad under the taskpad name.

On the final page of the wizard, you can click Finish to create the taskpad. The Start New Task Wizard option, if selected, causes the Start New Task Wizard to execute when you click Finish. This wizard, described in the next section, helps you create tasks for the taskpad.

Creating tasks

After you create a taskpad, you'll naturally want to create tasks to go on it. Select the Start New Task Wizard option if you are in the process of creating the taskpad. Alternatively, right-click the node in the tree that is associated with the taskpad, choose Edit Taskpad View, click the Tasks tab, and then click New.

The first functional page of the wizard prompts you to select the type of task to add. These prompts include the following:

- **Menu Command.** Choose this option to execute a menu command. In the subsequent wizard page, you specify the source for the command and the command itself. The available commands fall within the context of the selected source. Select an object and then select the desired command.

- **Shell Command.** Choose this option to start a program, execute a script, open a Web object, execute a shortcut, or perform any other task you can execute from a command line. The wizard prompts you for the command, optional command-line parameters or switches, the startup folder, and window state (minimized, normal, maximized).

- **Navigation.** Choose this option to add an icon for an existing item listed in Favorites.

The wizard also prompts you for a task name, description, and icon to associate with each task and gives you the option at completion of running the wizard again to create another task.

Modifying a taskpad

You can modify an existing taskpad to add or remove tasks or change taskpad view options. Right-click (in the tree) the object associated with the taskpad and then choose Edit Taskpad View. MMC displays a property sheet for the taskpad. The General page shows the same properties you specified when you created the taskpad, such as list type, list size, and so on. Change options as desired.

The Tasks tab, shown in Figure 2-7, lists existing tasks and lets you create new ones. New starts the New Task Wizard. Remove deletes the selected task. Modify lets you change the task name, description, and icon for the task but not modify the task itself. To modify the task, remove the task and re-create it. You also can use the up and down arrows to change the order of tasks in the list, which changes their order of appearance on the taskpad.

Other add-in tools

Snap-ins are just one of the objects you can add to an MMC console. Other objects include ActiveX controls, links to Web pages, folders, taskpad views, and tasks. The previous section explained taskpad views and tasks. The following list summarizes the additional items:

- **ActiveX controls.** You can add ActiveX controls to a console as the details/results view (right pane) for the selected node of the tree. The System Monitor Control that displays system performance status in Performance Monitor is an example of an ActiveX control. Choose Console ➤ Add or Remove Snap-In, select ActiveX Control from the list, and then click Add. The MMC provides a wizard to help you embed ActiveX controls, prompting you for additional information when necessary.

- **Links to Web pages.** You can add links to URLs in a console, which can be any URL viewable within a browser (Web site, ftp site, and so on).

- **Folders.** Insert folders as containers in the console to contain other objects. You can use folders as a means of organizing tools in a console.

 Would you like to add a local or network folder to a console? Just use the Link to Web page object and point it to the folder instead of an Internet URL.

FIGURE 2-7

Use the Tasks tab to add, remove, and modify tasks.

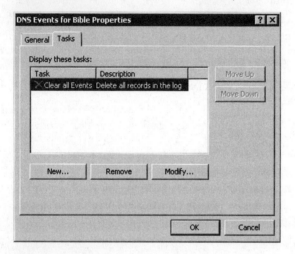

Customizing MMC to suit your needs

Like most applications, you can customize the MMC to suit your needs or preferences. First, you can configure the settings for a console when you author it to determine the way it is displayed in subsequent sessions. For example, you might want to configure a console for user mode — limited access, single window — to limit the actions the users can perform with the console. To configure a console, first open the console in author mode. Choose File ➤ Options to open the Options dialog box for the console (see Figure 2-8). Specify settings and then save the console. The changes will take effect the next time the console is opened.

The following list explains the available options:

- **Change Icon.** Click to change the icon associated with the .msc file. You'll find several icons in systemroot\system32\Shell32.dll.

- **Console Mode.** Choose the mode in which you want the console to open for the next session. Choose between author mode and one of the three user modes discussed previously.

- **Do Not Save Changes to This Console.** Select this option to prevent the user from saving changes to the console — in effect, write-protecting it.

- **Allow the User to Customize Views.** Select this option to allow users to add windows focused on items in the console. Deselect to prevent users from adding windows.

FIGURE 2-8

Use the Options dialog box to configure the console for future sessions.

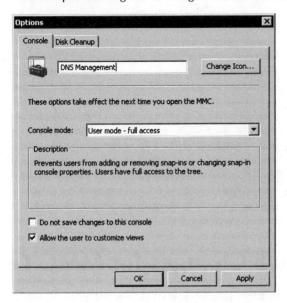

You also can control view options within the MMC. To do so, choose View ➤ Customize to access the Customize View dialog box, shown in Figure 2-9. The options in the Customize View dialog box are self-explanatory.

Control Panel versus MMC

Even though the MMC now serves as the focal point for many of the administrative tasks you'll perform on a regular basis, the Control Panel hasn't gone away. The Control Panel is alive and well and contains several objects for the system's hardware and operating configuration. The tools provided for the MMC do not take the place of the Control Panel objects or vice versa. However, you will find some of the MMC tools in the Administrative Tools folder in the Control Panel.

The Control Panel in Windows Server 2008 works much like the Control Panels in Windows Server 2003 and earlier Windows platforms. In fact, many of the objects are the same or similar. Later sections of this chapter explore the Control Panel objects. The following section examines the core set of MMC tools for managing a Windows Server 2008 system.

FIGURE 2-9

FIGURE 2-9

Use the Customize View dialog box to set view properties in the MMC.

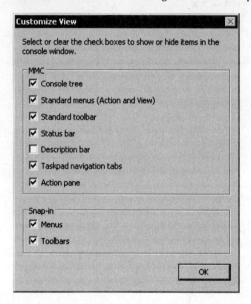

Windows Firewall Changes for MMC Tools

Before you learn about specific MMC tools included with Windows Server 2008, you should understand some limitations imposed by the Windows Firewall changes in Windows Server 2008. These changes affect the capability to remotely manage a Windows Server 2008 computer with many of the MMC tools. Here's why.

Windows Firewall by default blocks incoming traffic on port 445. This port is used by many of the administrative tools for remote management. If you receive one of the following error messages when attempting remote management, this firewall policy could be the culprit:

- Unable to access the computer Computer_Name
- Failed to open Group Policy object on Computer_Name. You might not have appropriate rights.
- Details. The network path was not found.
- An object (Computer) with the following name cannot be found. "Computer_Name." Check the selected object types and location for accuracy and ensure that you have typed the object name correctly, or remove this object from the selection.

- Computer Computer_Name cannot be managed. The network path was not found. To manage a different computer, on the Action menu, click Connect to Another Computer.

- System error 53 has occurred. The network path was not found.

To remediate this problem, configure Windows Firewall on the remote server to allow port 445. You can do so through the Windows Firewall GUI interface on the server, through a command line, or through Group Policy (see Chapter 24 for details on configuring Windows Firewall through Group Policy).

Getting to Know the MMC Tools

As explained previously, Windows Server 2008 contains several predefined consoles for managing a variety of tasks both on local computers and across the network. The following sections provide an overview of these tools. If you look for some of these "snap-ins" and can't find them, the reason could be that roles or features are not installed on the server.

Certification Authority

The Certification Authority console appears in the Administrative Tools folder but is installed only if you configure the server as a Certification Authority (CA). You can set up a CA once Active Directory Certificate Services is installed. Certificate Services enables the server to create certificates for itself and for other servers, workstations, and users on the network, either locally or across the Internet. For example, if you need to configure your Web server to require SSL for authoring, you need to install a certificate for that purpose on the server (Certificate Services are not required on the Web server itself to support SSL, only the certificate). A Windows Server CA can generate the certificate, eliminating the need for you to purchase one from a commercial CA, such as Thawte or VeriSign. However, unless the people viewing your site add your CA to their list of trusted sources, they'll receive certificate warnings when they view the site.

You use the Certification Authority console to manage Certificate Services on the local server or a remote server. You can configure certificate policy settings, view pending and failed certificate requests, and view issued and revoked certificates. You also use the console to manage general CA properties such as the capability to publish certificates to the Active Directory, configure how the server responds to certificate request, control CA security, and other options.

CROSS-REF Several sections in Chapter 16, including "Understanding Active Directory Certificate Services," explain Certificate Services in detail and how to manage them with the Certification Authority console.

Failover Cluster Management

The Failover Cluster Management console is available with Windows Server 2008 Enterprise Server and is the primary means by which you configure clustering. Clustering allows a group (cluster) of servers to function as a single logical unit for failover capability.

 The Standard Server and Web Server platforms do not include clustering.

You can use the Failover Cluster Management console to create and configure a cluster and for performing common tasks such as adding cluster nodes, configuring node and cluster properties, pausing the cluster service, and so on.

Component Services

The primary function of the Component Services console (see Figure 2-10) is to provide management tools for COM+ applications. COM+ provides a structure for developing distributed applications (client/server applications). The Component Services console enables you to configure a system for Component Services, configure initial service settings, install and configure COM+ applications, and monitor and tune components.

FIGURE 2-10

Use Component Services to configure COM+ applications as well as general Windows Server 2008 services.

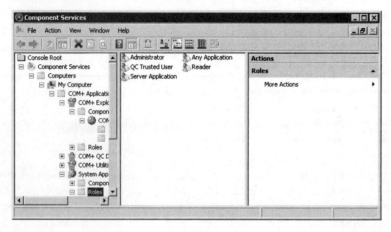

 Configuring COM+ applications goes hand-in-hand with COM+ application development. For that reason, this book doesn't provide detailed coverage of COM+ configuration.

The primary branches of the Component Services node under each computer are as follows:

- **COM+ Applications.** Use this branch to configure Component and Role properties and settings for COM+ components.

- **DCOM Config.** Use this branch to configure Distributed COM (DCOM) components, including setting security for them.

- **Distributed Transaction Coordinator.** Use this branch to view the DTC transaction list and monitor transaction statistics.

■ **Running Processes.** Use this branch to monitor and debug running processes. Right-click an application and choose Dump to dump the application state to a file for debugging and analysis.

> **NOTE** You'll notice that the Component Services console provided with Windows Server 2008 includes nodes for Event Viewer, Active Directory Users and Computers, and Services. These are also available as separate consoles. See the sections "Event Viewer," "Services," and "Using Event Viewer" later in this chapter, for more details. See Chapters 17–23 for a discussion of Active Directory.

Computer Management

The Computer Management console (see Figure 2-11) provides tools for managing several aspects of a system. Right-click My Computer and choose Manage or click Start ➤ All Programs ➤ Administrative Tools ➤ Computer Management to open the Computer Management console. Computer Management is composed of three primary branches: System Tools, Storage, and Services and Applications. System Tools provides extensions for viewing information about the system, configuring devices, viewing event logs, and so on. Storage provides tools for managing physical and logical drives and removable storage. Services and Applications enables you to configure telephony, Windows Management Instrumentation (WMI), services, the Indexing Service, and IIS. Other applications can appear under this branch as well, depending on the system's configuration.

FIGURE 2-11

Computer Management integrates several snap-ins to help you manage a system, its storage devices, and services.

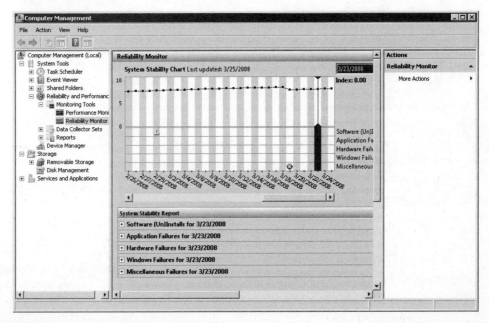

You can use Computer Management to manage either the local computer or a remote computer. Right-click the Computer Management node and choose Connect to Another Computer to manage a remote system. The tasks you can perform are usually the same whether local or remote, but some tasks can be performed within the context of the local system only. This chapter assumes that you're using Computer Management to manage the local system.

> **TIP** This section covers the snap-in extensions provided in the Computer Management console. However, many of these extensions can be used individually within their own consoles. For example, you can open `Services.msc` to configure services, rather than use the Services node in Computer Management. Look in `systemroot\System32` for available snap-ins (`.msc` file extension).

Event Viewer

Use Event Viewer to view events in the Application, Security, and System logs, as well as to configure log behavior (size, rollover, and so on). See the section "Using Event Viewer" later in this chapter for more information.

Reliability and Performance

The Reliability and Performance branch of the Computer Management snap-in provides tools for setting up performance monitoring. You can configure counter logs, trace logs, and alerts. This branch is useful only for viewing or modifying settings — it doesn't enable you to actually execute any performance monitoring. Instead, you need to use the Reliability and Performance MMC snap-in. See Chapter 25 for detailed information on configuring performance logs and alerts and monitoring system performance.

Shared Folders

The Shared Folders branch of the Computer Management snap-in enables you to view and manage shared folders, connections, and open files. The Shares node enables you to view shares on the selected computer. In addition, you can double-click a share to view and modify its properties and share permissions. See Chapter 15 for information on publishing folders in Active Directory.

> **TIP** You can create and manage shared folders through the Explorer interface. The advantage to using the Shared Folders console instead is that you can see all shares on the system at a glance.

You'll notice that a system includes a handful of shares by default, most of which are hidden shares (suffixed with a $ sign). These shares include the following:

- `drive$`. Windows Server 2008 shares the root of each drive as a hidden share for administrative purposes. You can connect to the share using the UNC path `\\server\drive$`, where `server` is the computer name and `drive` is the drive letter, such as `\\appsrv\d$`. Members of the Administrators and Backup Operators groups can connect to administrative shares on Windows 2000 Professional, Windows

XP, and Vista systems. Members of the Server Operators group can connect to administrative shares on Windows Server 2008 systems, as well as Administrators and Backup Operators.

- `ADMIN$`. This administrative share points to the systemroot folder on the system (typically, `\Windows` or `\WINNT`) and is used by the system during remote administration.

- `IPC$`. The `IPC$` share is used to share named pipes and is used during remote administration and when viewing a computer's shares.

- `PRINT$`. This share enables remote printer administration and points by default to `systemroot\System32\spool\drivers`.

- `NETLOGON`. This share is used to support user logon, typically for storing user logon scripts and profiles. In Windows Server 2008 and Server 2003 domains, the `NETLOGON` share points to `sysvol\domain\Scripts` on the domain controller(s).

CROSS-REF   For a complete discussion of sharing and security, offline folder access, and related topics, see Chapter 15.

The Sessions node enables you to view a list of users currently connected to the system. You can disconnect a user by right-clicking the user and choosing Close Session. Disconnecting a user could result in lost data for the user, so you might want to broadcast a console message to the user first. To do so, right-click the Shares or Shared Folders branch and choose All Tasks ➤ Send Console Message.

TIP   When you are viewing sessions for a remote computer, your connection appears as an open-named pipe and can't be closed.

The Open Files branch enables you to view files opened by remote users. Right-click an individual file and choose Close Open File to close the file. Alternatively, right-click the Open Files node and choose Disconnect All Open Files to close all files. As when disconnecting users, closing files could result in a loss of data, so try to broadcast a console message to the user first.

Device Manager

Device Manager provides a unified interface for viewing and managing devices and their resources (DMA, memory, IRQ, and so on). Device Manager displays devices using a branch structure. Expand a device branch to view the devices in the branch. No icon beside a device indicates that the device is functioning properly. A yellow exclamation icon indicates a potential problem with the device, such as a resource conflict. A red X indicates that the device is disconnected, disabled, or not in use in the current hardware profile.

Device Manager is the primary tool you use for configuring a system's hardware. To view or manage a device, locate it in the details pane and double-click the device (or right-click and choose Properties) to display the device's property sheet. The contents of the property vary according to the device type. Figure 2-12 shows a typical property sheet for a network adapter.

The General tab, shown in Figure 2-12, provides general information about a device, such as device type, manufacturer, and so on.

FIGURE 2-12

Use a device's property sheet to view and configure settings such as resource usage.

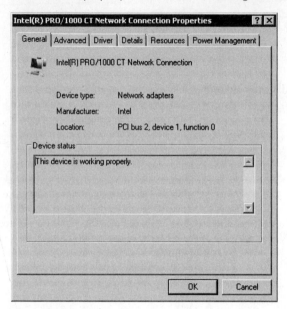

It isn't practical to cover every possible setting for every possible type of device in this chapter. The following sections explain tasks common to most devices: changing drivers and modifying resource assignments.

Driver changes

The Driver property page enables you to view details about, uninstall, and update a device's driver. Click Driver Details to view a list of the files that comprise the device's driver. This list is useful for checking the file or driver version to make sure that you're using a specific version. Use Uninstall if you want to remove the selected device's driver.

The Update Driver button opens the Upgrade Device Driver Wizard. Use the wizard to install an updated driver for the device. The wizard gives you the option of searching your system's floppy and CD-ROM drives, other specific location (local or remote share), or the Microsoft Windows Update Web site. Just follow the prompts to complete the update. In some cases, changing drivers requires a system restart.

Resource assignment

Because it supports plug and play (PnP), Windows Server 2008 can assign device resources such as DMA, IRQ, I/O base address, and UMA memory allocation automatically. In some cases, particularly with legacy devices (those not supporting PnP), you'll have to configure resource allocation manually. To do so, open a device's property sheet and click the Resources tab. If the Resources page doesn't provide any resources to change, click Set Configuration Manually to switch the page to manual property configuration (see Figure 2-13).

FIGURE 2-13

Set a device's resource utilization through its Resources property page.

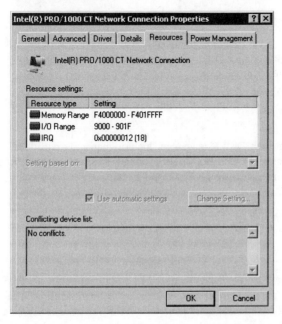

In most cases, Windows Server 2008 provides multiple, predefined configurations for devices, such as a combination of a specific IRQ and I/O range. Deselect the Use Automatic Settings option and then select a different configuration set from the drop-down list. To modify individual settings, first click in the Resource Settings list the resource you want to change and then click Change Setting. Specify the desired setting in the resulting dialog box and click OK.

Local Users and Groups

The Local Users and Groups branch of the Computer Management snap-in enables you to create and manage local user accounts and groups on Windows Server 2008 standalone and member servers. This branch is absent on a domain controller because you use the Active Directory Users and Computers snap-in to create user accounts and groups in the Active Directory.

CROSS-REF Users and groups are covered in detail in Chapter 23.

If you're familiar with creating user accounts and groups under previous versions of Windows Server, you'll have no problem using Local Users and Groups to create accounts. If not, see Chapter 23 for a detailed description of how to create accounts and groups. The primary difference between creating local accounts and groups and the same objects in the Active Directory is that the Active Directory provides for additional account and group properties. In addition, creating accounts and groups requires an understanding of permissions, rights, group policy, and user profiles, all of which are explained in Chapter 23.

Disk Management

The Disk Management node is the place to go to manage physical disks and volumes. Disk Management takes the place of the Windows NT Disk Administrator. Unlike the Disk Administrator, Disk Management performs most tasks immediately. In Disk Administrator, you must commit changes for most tasks (such as creating or deleting a partition). If you're an experienced Windows NT administrator, keep this important point in mind when making storage changes with Disk Management.

Some of the tasks you can perform with Disk Management include managing partitions, converting basic disks to dynamic disks, creating volumes (basic, spanned, striped, mirrored, RAID-5), creating and deleting physical volumes, formatting disks, and so on.

CROSS-REF For a complete discussion of storage devices and management (including Disk Management node), see Chapter 13.

Disk Defragmenter

As a disk is used over time, the data on the disk is scattered into noncontiguous clusters, becoming fragmented. Disk performance is greatest when data is not fragmented, as it takes less time to read the data (because the drive heads don't have to move as much to reassemble the data). The Disk Defragmenter node in Computer Management enables you to analyze a disk for fragmentation and then defragment the disk.

CROSS-REF See Chapter 13 for a discussion of Disk Defragmenter and other options for improving disk performance.

Removable Storage

The Removable Storage node provides a tool for configuring and managing removable storage devices and media. You use Removable Storage to track media such as tapes and optical disks and their hardware devices (jukeboxes, tape changers, and so on). Removable Storage is a technology subset of Hierarchical Storage Management (HSM). These new technologies provide a means for automatic data archival and retrieval of archived data.

The Removable Storage node enables you to create and manage media pools, insert and eject media, mount and dismount media, view media and library status, inventory libraries, and assign permissions for security on media and libraries.

Telephony

The Telephony node provides a centralized tool for managing telephony properties for the selected computer, including configuring telephony providers and assigning user permissions for various providers.

WMI Control

The WMI Control node in Computer Management provides tools for configuring and managing Windows Management Instrumentation (WMI) on a computer. WMI works in conjunction with the Web-Based Enterprise Management initiative to provide a means of collecting data about computers and their component devices both locally and remotely. WMI functions at the device-driver level, providing event notification from drivers and enabling WMI to collect data for analysis and management purposes. WMI is a key component in enterprise management. The WMI Control node provides a means for configuring general settings, logging, backing up and restoring the WMI repository, and security to control WMI access.

Services

In Windows Server 2008, services are applications that perform specific functions such as networking, logon, print spooling, remote access, and so on within the operating system. You can think of services as operating-system-oriented applications that function by themselves or in concert with other services or user applications to perform specific tasks or provide certain features within the OS. Device drivers, for example, function as services. Windows Server 2008 includes several standard services by default, and many third-party applications function as or include their own services. A background virus scrubber is a good example of a possible third-party service.

In Windows Server 2008, the Services node in the Computer Management snap-in (and by itself as the `Services.msc` console) takes over that function (see Figure 2-14). Services lists the installed services on the target system, and when Detail view is selected, displays description, status, startup type, and the account the service uses to log on.

Starting and stopping services

A running service processes requests and generally performs the task it was designed to accomplish. Stopping a service terminates the service and removes it from memory. Starting a service initializes and activates the service so that it can perform its task or function. For example, the DNS client functions as a DNS resolver, processing requests for names to address mapping in the DNS namespace. If you stop the DNS Client service, it is no longer available to process DNS queries.

Windows Server 2008 supports three startup modes for services:

- ■ **Automatic.** The service starts automatically at system startup.
- ■ **Manual.** The service can be started by a user or a dependent service. The service does not start automatically at system startup unless a dependent service is set for automatic startup (therefore causing the service to start).
- ■ **Disabled.** The service cannot be started by the system, a user, or a dependent service.

FIGURE 2-14

Use Services to configure, start, stop, and pause services, as well as view service dependencies.

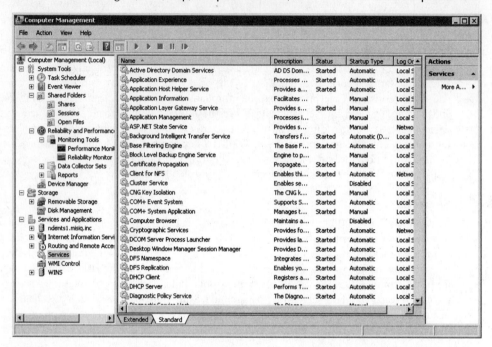

You set a service's startup mode through the General page of the service's properties. Open the Services node in the Computer Management MMC snap-in (or open the Services.msc console in systemroot\System32) and double-click the service. Figure 2-15 shows the General property page for a typical service. From the Startup Type drop-down list, choose the desired startup mode and click Apply or OK.

The General tab also enables you to start, stop, pause, or resume a service. Starting and stopping were explained previously. Pausing a service causes it to suspend operation but doesn't remove the service from memory. Resume a paused service to have it continue functioning. Open a service's General property page and then click Start, Stop, Pause, or Resume, as appropriate.

You also can start and stop services from a console prompt using the NET START and NET STOP commands along with the service's name, which you'll find on its General property page in the Service Name field. For example, use the command NET START ALERTER to start the Alerter service. Use NET STOP ALERTER to stop it.

> **TIP**   NET START and NET STOP are very useful for controlling services remotely. If the telnet service is running on the remote computer, you can telnet to the computer and use NET START and NET STOP to start and stop services on the remote system.

Setting General service properties

Other settings on a service's General property page control how the service is listed in the details pane and how the service starts up. Use the Display Name field to specify the name that will appear under the Name field for the service in the details pane. Specify the service's description in the Description field. Use the Start Parameters field to specify optional switches or parameters to determine how the service starts. These are just like command-line switches for a console command.

FIGURE 2-15

Use the General tab to configure service startup, control the service (start/stop), and set general properties.

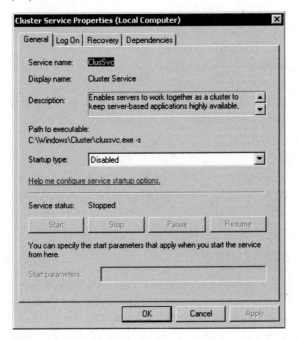

Configuring service logon

The Log On property page for a service specifies how the service logs on and the hardware profiles in which the service is used. Most services log on using the System account, although in some cases, you'll want to specify a different account for a service to use. Some types of administrative services often use their own accounts because they require administrative privileges. Therefore, you would create an account specifically for the service and make it a member of the Administrators group or give it the equivalent permissions, subject to its specific needs.

TIP   Avoid using the Administrator account itself. When you change the Administrator password, which you should do often if you use this account, you also have to reconfigure each service that used the Administrator account to change the password in the service's properties. Using a special account for those services instead enables you to change the

Administrator account password without affecting any services. See Chapter 16 for a discussion of how to protect the Administrator account and discontinue its use.

The Log On property page contains the following controls:

- **Local System Account.** Select to have the service log on using the local System account.

- **Allow Service to Interact with Desktop.** Select to allow the service to provide a UI for the currently logged-on user to interact with the service. This setting has no effect if the service isn't designed to provide a UI.

- **This Account.** Select and specify an account in the associated text box (or browse through the account list) to have the service log on with an account other than the local System account.

- **Password/Confirm Password.** Enter and confirm the password for the account specified in this account.

- **Enable/Disable.** Select a hardware profile from the list of profiles and click Enable to enable the service in that profile, or Disable to disable the service in the profile.

Configuring service recovery

Another behavior you can configure for services is what happens when the service fails. You can configure the service to restart, execute a file, or reboot the computer. In addition, you can configure a fail counter to track how many times the service has failed. You set a service's recover options through its Recovery property page (see Figure 2-16).

The Recovery page contains the following options:

- **First Failure/Second Failure/Subsequent Failures.** With these three drop-down lists, select the action (or no action) to take on the specified failure. You can choose to take no action, restart the service, execute a file, or reboot the computer.

- **Reset Fail Count After.** Specify the number of days after which the fail counter is reset to zero.

- **Restart Service After.** Specify the number of minutes that will pass between service failure and restart. Increase from the default of one minute if the system needs more time to stabilize after the service fails.

- **Run Program.** Use this group of commands to identify a program or script that will execute when the service fails. For example, you might create a script that broadcasts a message with the fail count and other information to the Administrators group. Use the Append Fail Count option to append the current fail count to the end of the command line (passing the fail count to the command for internal processing).

- **Restart Computer Options.** Click this button to specify the number of minutes to wait before restarting the computer and an optional message to broadcast on the network prior to restart (such as a reboot warning to users).

FIGURE 2-16

Configure service recovery options to specify what actions the service should take when it fails.

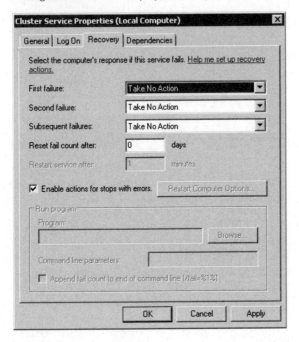

Viewing dependencies

You can use the Dependencies page to view other services on which the selected service depends as well as services that are dependent on the selected service. This property page displays information only and doesn't allow you to configure or modify dependencies. The page is self-explanatory.

Indexing Service

The Indexing Service is still available for backward compatibility in Windows Server 2008. It uses document filters to read and create a catalog of documents on a system and enables a quick text-based search through the catalog for documents that meet the search criteria. You should rather use the new Windows Search Service if you are starting search and indexing for the first time on Windows Server 2008. The service is discussed in Chapter 15. You cannot install both the new Search Service and the Indexing Service at the same time (as part of the File Services role). When installing the File Services role, you have the option of choosing one or the other, but not both.

The document filter extracts information from the document and passes that information to the Indexing Service for inclusion in the catalog. You can search using the Search command in the Start menu, the Query the Catalog node of Indexing Service in Computer Management, or a Web page. You can search based on a variety of criteria, including document name, author, contents, and so on. You might, for example, use the Indexing Service to build a catalog of internal documents or to catalog your organization's Web site(s). The Indexing Service will index the following document types:

- HTML
- Text
- Microsoft Office
- Internet Mail and News
- Other documents supported by an appropriate document filter (such as a third-party filter)

> **TIP**   Indexing Service is useful even on a workstation to index user documents and to speed up searching for specific documents or groups of documents.

Use the Indexing Service branch of the Computer Management console to configure the Indexing Service and query the index for a list of documents matching your query criteria. The Indexing Service branch appears in Computer Management, even if the Indexing Service is not yet installed. To install the Indexing Service, open the Control Panel and run Add or Remove Programs. Click Add or Remove Windows Components in the left toolbar, select Indexing Service in the Components list, and then click Next and follow the prompts to install the service.

Planning for the Indexing Service

When planning for the Indexing Service, understand that the system configuration determines the service's performance. Indexing Service has the same minimum hardware requirements as Windows Server 2008, but increasing the number of documents to be indexed increases the memory requirements. See the Help file for Indexing Service (press F1 with Indexing Service selected in Computer Management) for specific recommendations.

You also need to plan the file system to accommodate Indexing Service. Placing the catalog on a FAT volume will enable users to see the catalog even if they have no permission to view individual documents in the catalog. Placing the catalog on an NTFS volume offers the best security because Indexing Service maintains all NTFS security ACLs (Access Control Lists). Users will not see documents in the results list of a query if they don't have the permissions necessary to view the documents. In addition, the Indexing Service uses the System account to log on. If you deny the System account access to a given folder or file, Indexing Service will not be able to access the folder or file and won't index it. Encrypted documents are never indexed.

Where you store the index catalog(s) is also important. You should not store catalogs within a Web site (in the Web site's folder), because Internet Information Services (IIS) can lock the catalog and prevent it from being updated. Also avoid running antivirus or backup software that locks the catalog files, which would cause Indexing Service to time out while attempting to update the catalogs. The best practice is to create a folder on an NTFS volume specifically for your catalog files and place each catalog in its own subfolder of that primary folder.

> **TIP** You can change the location of the default System catalog created automatically when you install Indexing Service. First, create the folder to contain the catalog. Then right-click Indexing Service and choose Stop to stop the service. Open the Registry Editor and modify the value of `HKEY_LOCAL_MACHINE\SYSTEM\CurrentControlSet\Control\ ContentIndex\Catalogs\System\Location` to point to the desired location. Close the Registry Editor and restart the Indexing Service.

Creating and configuring a catalog

You can create multiple index catalogs to suit your needs. To create a new catalog, open the Computer Management snap-in and right-click the Indexing Service branch. Choose New ➤ Catalog. Specify a name for the catalog and its location and then click OK. The catalog remains offline until you restart the Indexing Service.

Next, expand the newly created catalog in the Indexing Service branch in Computer Management. Right-click Directories under the catalog's branch and choose New ➤ Directory to display the Add Directory dialog box, shown in Figure 2-17. Specify options according to the following list:

FIGURE 2-17

Add directories to a catalog to include their contents in the index.

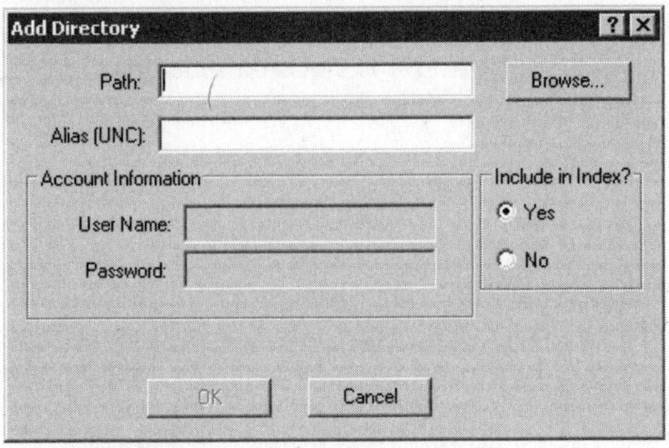

- **Path.** Specify the path to the folder you want to add in the catalog or click Browse to access the folder.
- **Alias (UNC).** If you're specifying a folder on a nonlocal computer, type the UNC path to the share in the form \\computer\share, where computer is the remote computer's name and share is the share where the folder is located.
- **Account Information.** For a directory on a remote computer, specify the domain\account and the password to be used to access the computer.

- **Include in Index?.** Select Yes to include the folder or No to exclude it from the catalog. This option enables you to exclude a subfolder of a folder that is included in the catalog. Add the parent folder and set it to Yes and then add the subfolder separately and set it to No to exclude it.

After you define the directories for the catalog, stop and restart the Indexing Service to populate the catalog. The Properties branch will be empty until you stop and restart the service.

Querying the catalog

As mentioned previously, you can query a catalog through a computer's Search command in the Start menu, a Web page, or the Computer Management snap-in. To perform a query using the snap-in, open the Indexing Service branch and click Query the Catalog under the desired catalog entry. Windows Server 2008 provides a query form in which you can specify the query criteria and options and view the results of the query.

Tuning performance

On a system with a large number of documents, you might want to fine-tune Indexing Service for best performance. Right-click Indexing Service in the Computer Management snap-in and choose Stop to stop the service. Right-click Indexing Service again and choose Tune Performance to display the Indexing Service Usage dialog box (see Figure 2-18). The options on the dialog box enable you to specify how often Indexing Service is used on the computer, and Windows Server 2008 automatically configures the service based on your selection. Choose the Customize option and then click the Customize button to specify custom settings for indexing and querying. For indexing, you can set a slider control between Lazy and Instant. Lazy causes indexing to function more as a background task, and Instant grants it maximum system resources, which takes resources from other running tasks. For querying, you can set a slider between low load and high load, depending on how many queries the computer receives. Be sure to restart the service after you finish configuring it.

Using Event Viewer

Microsoft defines an event in Windows Server 2008 as any significant occurrence in the operating system or an application that requires users (particularly administrators) to be notified. Events are recorded in event logs. Events and the event log are important administrative tools because they're indispensable for identifying and troubleshooting problems, tracking security access (logon, logoff, resource auditing, and so on), and tracking the status of the system and its applications.

> **NOTE** Some features are not available if you use the Event Viewer console within the Computer Management console. This section assumes that you are opening the Event Viewer console directly from the Administrative Tools folder.

FIGURE 2-18

Use the Indexing Service Usage dialog box to optimize Indexing Service's performance.

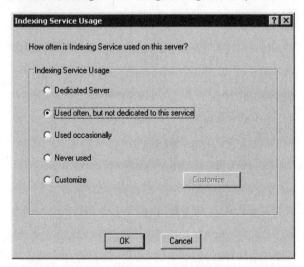

Events fall into these general categories:

- **System.** These include system-related events such as service startup and shutdown, driver initialization, system-wide warning messages, network events, and other events that apply to the system in general.

- **Security.** These include events related to security, such as logon/logoff and resource access (auditing).

- **Application.** These events are associated with specific applications. For example, a virus scrubber might log events related to a virus scan, cleaning operation, and so on, to the application log.

- **Setup.** These events are associated with setup processes such as adding roles and features.

- **Forwarded Events.** The Forwarded Events log contains log entries from another computer system. Here you create a subscription to an event log on another system, and then filter the event log that you have subscribed to so that only the desired events are retrieved. The retrieved events are placed into the Forwarded Events log.

NOTE In addition to the three default event logs, other Windows Server 2008 services create their own logs. The Directory Service, DNS Service, and File Replication Service are some examples of services that create their own event logs. You view these logs with the Event Viewer, just as you do the three standard logs.

Events range in severity from informational messages to serious events such as service or application failures. The primary event categories include informational, warning, error, success audit, and failure audit. The severity of an event is identified by an icon beside the event in the log. For example, warnings use an exclamation icon and errors use an X in a red circle. Each event has common properties associated with it:

- **Date and Time.** This is the date and time the event occurred.

- **Source.** This identifies the source of the event, such as a service, device driver, application, resource, and so on. The source property is useful for determining what caused the event (cause and event source are not synonymous).

- **Category.** The source determines the category for an event. For example, security categories include logon, logoff, policy change, and object access, among others.

- **Event.** Each event includes an event ID, an integer generated by the source to identify the event uniquely.

- **User.** This property identifies the user who caused the event to be generated (if applicable).

- **Computer.** This property identifies the computer that caused the event to be generated (if applicable).

The Event Viewer MMC snap-in is the tool you use to view and manage the event logs. The Event Viewer presents the logs in the tree pane as individual branches. When you click a log, its events appear in the pane on the right (see Figure 2-19).

Viewing and filtering events

Viewing an event is easy — just open Event Viewer, locate the event, and double-click it (or select it and press Enter). Event Viewer opens a dialog box showing the event's properties (see Figure 2-20). The top of the dialog box includes general information about the event such as time and date, type, and so on. The description text provides a detailed description of the event, which usually (but not always) offers a decipherable explanation of the event. The bottom portion of the dialog box displays additional data included with the event, if any. You can choose between viewing the data in byte (hexadecimal) or DWORD format. In most cases, it takes a software engineer to interpret the data because doing so requires an understanding of the code generating the data.

Use the up and down arrows in the right side of the dialog box to view previous and subsequent events, respectively. Click the Copy button to copy the selected event to the Clipboard.

By default, the Event Viewer shows all events for a selected log. In many cases, it is helpful to be able to filter the view so that Event Viewer shows only events that meet specific criteria. To apply a filter, click a log and choose View ➤ Filter to access the Filter property sheet for the log (see Figure 2-21).

FIGURE 2-19

The new greatly enhanced Event Viewer.

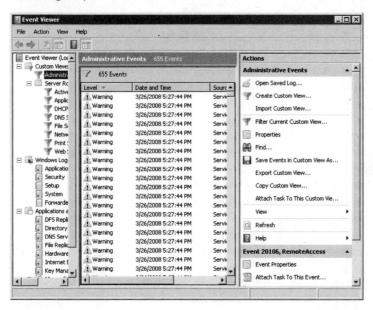

FIGURE 2-20

An event's property sheet provides detailed information about the event.

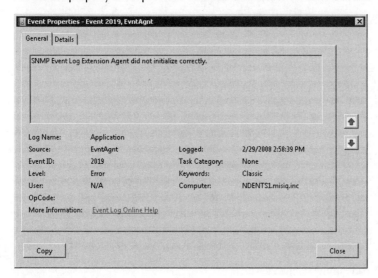

FIGURE 2-21

Use the Filter page to determine which events are displayed for the selected log in the Event Viewer.

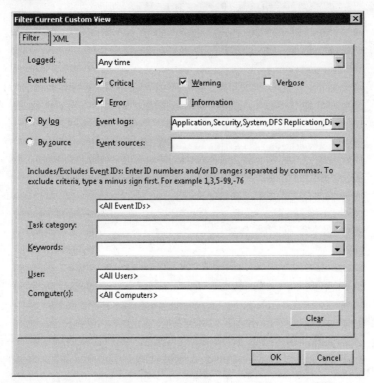

You can choose to view events based on their type, source, category, ID, user, computer, or date range. For example, you might want to filter based on source if you're trying to troubleshoot a problem with a specific application, service, or driver. To create the filter, select your criteria in the dialog box and click OK. Choose View ➤ All Records to remove the filter and view all events in the log.

Setting log properties

Each log includes general properties that define the way the log appears in Event Viewer, the size of the log, how it reacts when the maximum size is reached, and so on. Select a log and right-click to choose Properties to display its General property page (see Figure 2-22).

Some of the information displayed in the General page is read-only, such as the location of the log file. You can change the Display Name property to change the name by which the log is listed in the tree pane in the Event Viewer.

FIGURE 2-22

Configure a log's appearance and size through its General property page.

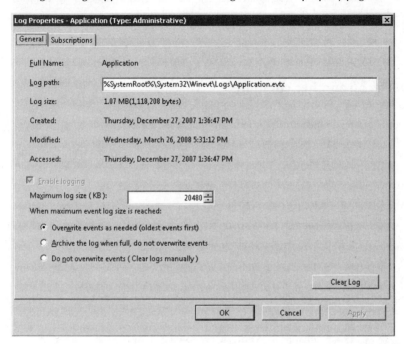

The Log Size group of controls specifies the maximum log size and the action Windows Server 2008 takes when the maximum size is reached. The options are generally self-explanatory. Keep in mind, however, that if you select Do Not Overwrite Events, Windows Server 2008 will stop logging events to the log when it fills up. Although Windows Server 2008 will notify you when the log is full, you'll need to monitor the event log and clear it periodically to ensure that you don't lose events.

TIP   Using a low-speed connection prevents Event Viewer from downloading all of the event data before you specifically request it and is useful when the logs are located on another computer, which is accessible through a slow network connection (such as dial-up).

Saving and clearing logs

Occasionally, you'll want to save an event log and/or clear the log. Saving a log copies it to another event file of a name you specify. Clearing a log removes all the events in the log. You might want to create a benchmark, for example, prior to troubleshooting a problem, or you might want to periodically archive your event logs. In any case, you save the log and then clear it.

To save a log, select the log and choose Action ➤ Save Log File As or right-click the log and choose Save Log File As. Specify a name and location for the log file and click OK. After you save a log file, you can open the log again in Event Viewer to view its contents. Keep in mind that a saved log is static and doesn't gather additional events.

When it's time to clear a log, open the log's General property page and click Clear Log. Windows Server 2008 will prompt you to confirm the action.

Viewing logs on another computer

You can use Event Viewer to view the log file of other computers in your network (or across the Internet via a VPN connection). To open another computer's event logs, open Event Viewer, right-click the Event Viewer branch, and choose Connect to Another Computer. Specify the computer's name or browse the network for the computer and then click OK. Select the Local Computer option to reconnect to the local computer's event logs.

Arranging the log view

You can arrange the Event Viewer results pane to specify which columns appear and their display order. If you seldom need to see the User or Computer columns, for example, you can turn them off.

To control column display, click any node in the Event Viewer and choose View ➤ Add/Remove Columns to open the Modify Columns dialog box. Add and remove columns as desired and use Move Up and Move Down to change the display order. Click OK to apply the changes.

> **TIP**   You can drag columns in Event Viewer to change their display order.

Server extensions

In addition to the MMC snap-ins described in previous sections, Windows Server 2008 incorporates several other snap-ins for managing specific services. For example, the DNS, DHCP, and IIS services all have their own snap-ins. Because these snap-ins are the primary means by which you control these services, they are best discussed in the context of the service. You'll find these snap-ins discussed throughout this book where appropriate.

Using the Security Configuration Wizard

Windows Server 2008 improves on the Security Configuration Wizard introduced in Windows Server 2003 to help administrators fine-tune security on a server. The wizard configures security settings based on server roles. The wizard prompts for information about the server and its roles, and then stops all services not required to perform those roles, locks down ports as needed, modifies registry settings, and configures settings for IIS and other components to apply the desired level of security.

NOTE Rather than cover the wizard step by step, this section explains the purpose of the wizard and its general function. You should have no trouble following through in the wizard once you understand this background information.

The Security Configuration Wizard is now installed by default. You no longer have to add it like you did with Windows Server 2003.

The first step in the wizard is to specify the policy action you want to take:

- **Create a New Security Policy.** Create a new policy based on the server's roles.
- **Edit an Existing Security Policy.** Modify a policy created previously on the server or another server.
- **Apply an Existing Security Policy.** Apply a previously created policy to the server.
- **Rollback the Last Applied Security Policy.** Roll the server back to its previous state prior to the last security policy application.

After you select the policy action and specify a server to use as the baseline for the policy set (you can choose the local server or a remote server), the Security Configuration Wizard steps you through several key areas:

- **Selecting server roles.** In this phase of the wizard, you specify the roles that the target server will perform. As explained earlier in this section, the wizard does not add or remove server roles.
- **Selecting client roles.** Each server performs several client roles, such as automatic update, DNS client, domain member, and others. Choose the client roles the server will fill.
- **Selecting administration and other options.** Specify options the server will include, such as backup methods, specific services, optional applications, and specific tasks (see Figure 2-23). The wizard uses the selections you make to determine which ports should be opened and which services enabled. When you click Next, the wizard displays a list of any additional third-party services it found installed on the server to enable you to include or exclude those services from the security configuration.

TIP To view additional information about any item in the wizard, click the arrow button to the left of the item name (refer to Figure 2-23).

- **Determine handling of unspecified services.** Choose how services not specified by the policy are handled. You can choose to have a service's startup modes set to Disabled or direct the wizard to ignore the services (not make a change to the startup mode).
- **Confirming service changes.** The Confirm Service Changes page of the wizard (see Figure 2-24) simply displays the changes that will be made to individual services. If you need to modify the actions the wizard will take for a particular service, note the contents of the Used By column for that service. Then, click Back to reach the appropriate page where you can configure the role(s) identified in the Used By column. Make changes as needed, move forward through the wizard to reach the confirmation page, and verify that your change was applied.

FIGURE 2-23

Select the options, services, and tasks required for the server.

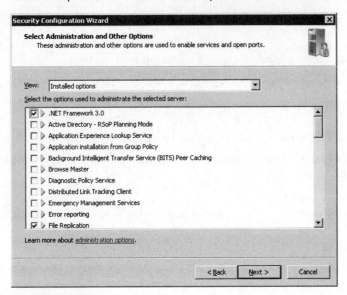

FIGURE 2-24

Confirm service changes before moving on and then adjust roles as needed.

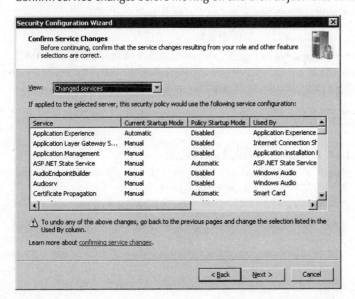

■ **Configuring network security settings.** In this stage of the wizard, you specify which ports will be opened in the firewall and which ports will be blocked (see Figure 2-25). The wizard offers several view options to help you identify specific ports. You can also click Add to add additional open ports or allowed applications. The wizard displays a confirmation page to help you validate your choices before continuing.

FIGURE 2-25

Specify ports to be opened on the server.

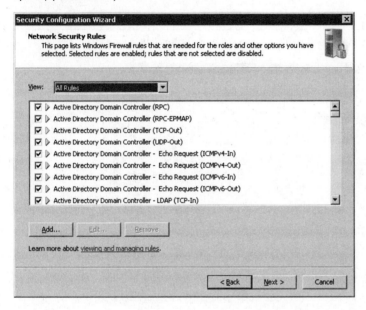

■ **Configure registry settings.** The wizard offers a handful of pages to obtain information about protocols used to communicate with other computers, authentication methods used, and minimum operating system requirements for other computers. The wizard uses the information gathered to modify selected registry settings to improve security and prevent specific exploits. It displays a confirmation page you can use to verify the target changes.

■ **Configure system audit policy.** This section of the wizard helps you specify an audit policy for the security policy set.

- **Configure Internet Information Services.** If the Application Server role is selected, the wizard displays a set of pages to prompt for options for Web service extensions, virtual directories, and anonymous authentication for IIS. Use these pages to specify IIS configuration for the security policy.

At the completion of the wizard, you are prompted to specify a security policy filename under which the wizard will store the policy configuration (see Figure 2-26). The wizard stores the settings as an XML file. You can then use the file to apply the configuration to other servers.

FIGURE 2-26

Specify the name of an XML file in which to store the policy settings.

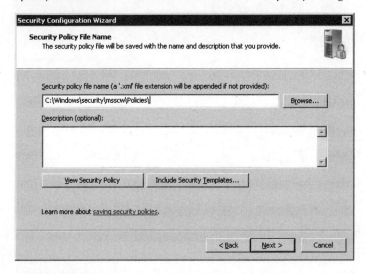

The Security Policy File Name page also provides two additional tasks you can perform. If you click View Security Policy, the wizard opens the SCW Viewer application (see Figure 2-27), which you use to view the settings specified in the policy.

You can also add security templates to the policy. These templates are located by default in `%systemroot%\securit\templates` as a set of INF files. You can view and modify these security templates (as well as create additional templates) with the Security Templates MMC snap-in. To add a template to a security policy in the Security Configuration Wizard, click Include Security Templates on the Security Policy File Name page to open the Include Security Templates dialog box. Here you can add and remove templates from the policy as needed.

FIGURE 2-27

The SCW Viewer page shows you policy settings.

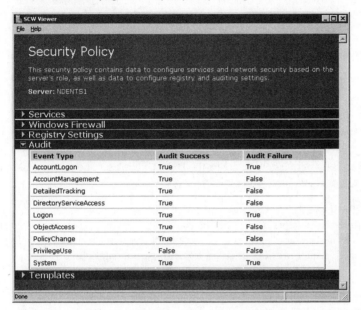

Working with Data Sources (ODBC)

ODBC, which stands for Open Database Connectivity, provides a framework for database engines to communicate with client applications. ODBC drivers serve as a middleman between a database and a client application, coordinating transactions and translating between the client and the database. In some cases, they can take the place of the database engine. For example, a server doesn't need Microsoft Access installed to enable clients to query an Access database file stored on the server, which is a typical practice of report engines such as Seagate Crystal Reports.

In order for client applications to communicate with a data source stored on a computer, you must configure the appropriate ODBC driver and connection on the target server. For example, if the client application needs to access an Access database, then you need to first configure the Access ODBC driver on the computer where the database is located. The Data Sources administrative tool enables you to configure and manage ODBC drivers and their associated data sources. This section of the chapter explains how to configure ODBC drivers.

 **NOTE** The Data Sources tool is one of the few administrative tools that functions as a standalone utility, rather than an MMC snap-in.

Defining DSNs

You make data sources available to clients by creating a Data Source Name (DSN). Three types of DSNs exist:

- **User.** A user DSN is visible only to the user who is logged on when the DSN is created.
- **System.** A system DSN is visible to all local services on a computer and all users who log on locally to the computer.
- **File.** A file DSN can be shared by all users who have the same drivers installed and who have the necessary permissions to access the DSN. Unlike user and system DSNs, file DSNs are stored in text files, rather than the registry.

The DSN identifies the data source, the driver associated with a data source, and other properties that define the interaction between the client and the data source, such as timeout, read-only mode, and so on. You use the same process to create a DSN for most database types. The exception is SQL Server, which provides a wizard for setting up a data source.

Defining a data source

To create a data source, you first open the ODBC Data Source Administrator. To do so, click Start ➢ All Programs ➢ Administrative Tools ➢ Data Sources (ODBC). In the ODBC Data Source Administrator, click the tab for the DSN type you want to create and then click Add. Select the desired data source type and click Finish. Except in the case of the SQL Server driver, ODBC prompts you for information, which varies according to the driver selected. Define settings as desired and click OK to create the DSN.

Setting up an SQL Server data source

The Microsoft SQL Server ODBC driver provides a wizard to configure an SQL data source. This section explains the options you find when setting up an SQL Server ODBC driver. The first wizard page contains the following options:

- **Name.** This name appears in the Data Sources list on the DSN page for the data source.
- **Description.** This optional description appears with the DSN name on the DSN page for the data source.
- **Server.** Here, you specify the IP address or host name of the SQL server computer.

The second page of the wizard, shown in Figure 2-28, prompts for connection and authentication options for the data source. The following list summarizes the options:

FIGURE 2-28

Specify connection and authentication options.

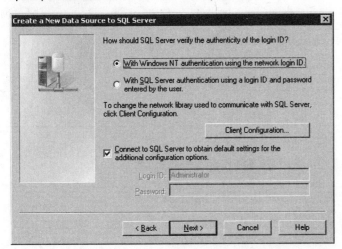

- **With Windows NT Authentication Using the Network Login ID.** Select this option to have the SQL Server ODBC driver request a trusted connection to the server. The driver uses the current client logon username and password to authenticate the request on the server. In the case of a service or Web server, the credentials are assigned to the service or specified in the code that makes the query. The specified username and password must have an association to an SQL Server login ID on the SQL Server computer.

- **With SQL Server Authentication Using a Login ID and Password Entered by the User.** Select this option to require the user to specify an SQL Server login ID and password for all connection requests.

- **Connect to SQL Server to Obtain Default Settings for the Additional Configuration Options.** Select this option to have the SQL Server ODBC driver connect to the SQL Server identified on the first page of the wizard to obtain the correct settings for options in remaining Configuration Wizard pages. When you click Next with this option selected, the driver connects to the SQL Server and obtains the data. Deselect this option to use default settings rather than connect to the SQL Server to obtain the information.

- **Login ID.** Specify the username to connect to the specified SQL Server to retrieve the settings for subsequent wizard pages (see the preceding bullet). This username and the associated Password field are not used for actual data connections after the data source is created, but are used only to retrieve information from the SQL Server for the remaining configuration pages.

- **Password.** Specify the password to use with the username specified in the Login ID field.

■ **Client Configuration.** Click to use the Network Library Configuration dialog box. Although you usually don't have to configure the network client configuration for the data source, sometimes you might need to specify the network connection mechanism and other options that define how the client connects to the data source. The options in Connection Parameters are specific to the network connection type you select from the Network Libraries list of options.

In the next page of the wizard, shown in Figure 2-29, you specify the database name and other options for the data source. The following list describes its options:

FIGURE 2-29

Specify the database name and other database options.

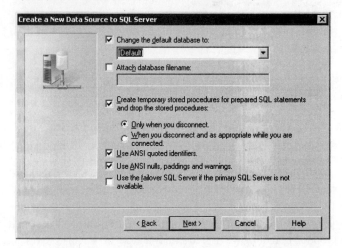

■ **Change the Default Database To.** Choose a database from the drop-down list to define the default database for the data source, overriding the default database for the specified login ID. Deselect this option to use the default database defined for the login ID on the server.

■ **Attach Database Filename.** Specify the full name and path of the primary file for an attachable database. The specified database is used as the default database for the data source.

■ **Create Temporary Stored Procedures for Prepared SQL Statements and Drop the Stored Procedures.** Select this option to have the driver create temporary stored procedures to support the SQLPrepare ODBC function and then choose one of the associated options (see the following bullets). Deselect this if you don't want the driver to store these procedures.

■ **Only When You Disconnect.** Have the stored procedures created for the SQLPrepare function dropped only when the SQLDisconnect function is called. This improves performance by reducing the overhead involved in dropping the stored procedures while the application is running, but it can lead to a buildup of temporary stored procedures. This particularly applies to applications that issue numerous `SQLPrepare` calls or that run for a long time without disconnecting.

■ **When You Disconnect and as Appropriate While You Are Connected.** Have the stored procedures dropped when `SQLDisconnect` is called, when `SQLFreeHandle` is called for the statement handle, when `SQLPrepare` or `SQLExecDirect` are called to process a new SQL statement on the same handle, or when a catalog function is called. Using this option entails more overhead while the application is running, but it helps prevent a build-up of temporarily stored procedures.

■ **Use ANSI Quoted Identifiers.** Enforce ANSI rules for quote marks so that they can only be used for identifiers such as table and column names. Character strings must be enclosed in single quotes.

■ **Use ANSI Nulls, Paddings and Warnings.** Specify that the `ANSI_NULLS`, `ANSI_WARNINGS`, and `ANSI_PADDINGS` options are set to on when the driver connects to the data source.

■ **Use the Failover SQL Server if the Primary SQL Server Is Not Available.** Have the connection attempt to use the failover server if supported by the primary SQL Server. When a connection is lost, the driver cleans up the current transaction and attempts to reconnect to the primary SQL Server. The driver attempts to connect to the failover server if the driver determines that the primary server is unavailable.

The final page of the wizard, shown in Figure 2-30, prompts for miscellaneous options as described in the following list:

FIGURE 2-30

Specify miscellaneous database options from the final page of the wizard.

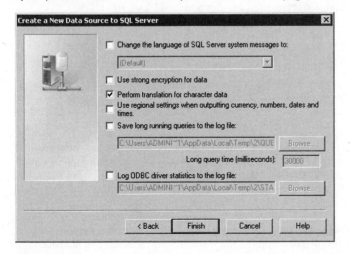

- **Change the Language of SQL Server System Messages To.** Specify the language used to generate SQL Server system messages. The server can contain multiple sets of system messages, each in a different language. This option is grayed out if the server has only one language installed.

- **Use Strong Encryption for Data.** Encrypt data using strong encryption.

- **Perform Translation for Character Data.** Select this option to convert ANSI strings using Unicode. Deselect the option to disable translation of extended ANSI codes.

- **Use Regional Settings When Outputting Currency, Numbers, Dates and Times.** Select this option to have the regional settings of the client computer used to display currency, numbers, dates, and other region-specific elements.

- **Save Long Running Queries to the Log File.** Log any query that takes longer than the time specified in the Long Query Time field.

- **Long Query Time (Milliseconds).** This specifies the maximum threshold value for logging long-running queries.

- **Log ODBC Driver Statistics to the Log File.** Log driver statistics to a tab-delimited log file.

ODBC Component Checker

A nonhomogenous set of ODBC components can lead to all sorts of strange and difficult-to-trace problems. For example, a Web application that queries an ODBC connection might receive a nonspecific server error when it attempts the connection if the ODBC component versions do not match one another. Keeping the components synchronized is therefore very important.

Microsoft offers a tool called the Component Checker to help you scan the system and determine whether the Microsoft Data Access Components (MDAC) are synchronized. You'll find the Component Checker at www.microsoft.com/data. You'll also find the latest version of MDAC at the site, along with additional technical information on MDAC and ODBC.

Viewing driver information

The Drivers page of the ODBC Data Sources Administrator enables you to view information about installed ODBC drivers. The Drivers page is useful for verifying driver version but doesn't provide any options you can change.

Tracing

Use the Tracing page of the ODBC Data Sources Administrator to configure tracing options to help you troubleshoot problems with a client connection. With tracing turned on, ODBC actions are logged to the specified file. You can view the log using any text editor.

Connection Pooling

Use the Connection Pooling page to specify whether or not ODBC drivers can reuse open connection handles to the database server. You can improve performance by eliminating the need for applications to establish new connections to a server, because the time and overhead involved in establishing the connection is reduced. Oracle and SQL connections are pooled by default, but others are not.

Understanding Control Panel Applets

As in other Windows platforms, the Windows Server 2008 Control Panel serves as a control center for configuring hardware and operating system settings. Some Control Panel applets control fairly simple sets of options, while others are relatively complex. The following sections explain the more complex Control Panel applets and their functions. Applets that require no explanation (such as configuring the mouse, game controllers, and so on) are not included. In addition, note that not all applets appear in the Control Panel by default. The Wireless Link applet, for example, only appears on systems with infrared ports or similar wireless hardware.

TIP You can configure the Start menu to display the Control Panel applets in the menu, enabling you to access individual Control Panel applets through the Start menu without having to open the Control Panel folder. To display the Control Panel applets on the Start menu, right-click the taskbar and choose Properties. Click the Advanced tab, select Expand Control Panel in the Start Menu Settings group, and click OK.

To open the Control Panel, click Start ➤ Control Panel. If you've configured the Start menu to expand the Control Panel and want to open the Control Panel folder, click Start, then right-click Control Panel and click Open. You also can open the Control Panel from My Computer.

Ease of Access applet

This applet enables you to configure interface and input/output functions designed to assist users with various physical challenges, such as limited vision. You can configure a variety of settings and features for the display, keyboard, mouse, and sound.

Add Hardware applet

The Add Hardware applet, when selected, runs the Add Hardware Wizard, which helps you add new hardware, remove hardware, unplug a device, and troubleshoot problems with devices. The wizard scans the system for changes and helps automate the process of installing drivers to support new devices.

If you choose to add or troubleshoot a device, Windows Server 2008 automatically performs a search for plug and play (PnP) hardware. If it finds and recognizes a new device, it takes you step-by-step through the process of installing support for the device. If it finds but can't recognize the device, the wizard prompts you to select the device from a list and manually specify the device's driver(s).

To troubleshoot a device, allow Windows Server 2008 to perform the hardware detection and then locate the device in the Choose a Hardware Device list and click Next. The wizard will help you perform steps to troubleshoot the device. To add a new device, choose Add a New Device from the list and then click Next. Follow the prompts to insert the Windows Server 2008 CD or provide a path to the appropriate driver files when prompted.

If you choose to uninstall a device, Windows Server 2008 presents a list of all devices. Select the device you want to remove, click Next, and follow the prompts to complete the process. If you're unplugging a device, Windows Server 2008 presents a list of devices that can be unplugged. Select the device, click Next, and follow the prompts (if any) to complete the process.

Default Programs applet

The Add or Remove Programs applet is no more. Much of the old functionality in the old applet in Windows Server 2003 has been integrated into Server Manager (role and features). Instead you now have the Default Programs applet. Windows Components are in Server Manager, split between roles and features (and no longer known as Windows Components).

The Default Programs applet is essentially a custom or third-party software installation and management interface. As you can see in Figure 2-31, the only application that I have installed on the example server is Skype. You do not have to do anything special when you install applications to ensure they end up being managed by the Default Programs applet.

Like the old application, the applet serves three main functions. It enables you to change the installation of or remove existing programs, install new programs, and turn Windows features on or off. The first two options are geared typically toward user-oriented applications. You use the latter option to add or remove features such as Indexing Service, Certificate Services, IIS, additional tools, and so on, to or from Windows Server 2008. The big difference between Windows Server 2008 and Windows Server 2003 is that on the latter you actually removed the application from the server, whereas now you can turn off the application without actually having to remove its bits and pieces from the server. At any time you want to add the application back, simply toggle the option "Turn Windows features on or off." However, you should know that only applications that support this API or that are Windows Server 2008 or Vista logo compliant support this feature.

FIGURE 2-31

Use Program and Features to add or remove or reconfigure and update programs.

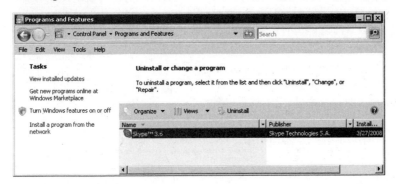

TIP   The list of installed applications does not, by default, include updates and patches. To view these installed items, click the View Installed Updates option in the applet as shown in Figure 2-31.

Administrative Tools applet

The Administrative Tools applet in the Control Panel serves as a container for various administrative tools, including the Computer Management MMC snap-in, the Services snap-in, Event Viewer, and others. Each of these tools is covered where appropriate in this chapter or in other chapters.

Windows Update

This applet (see Figure 2-32) enables you to specify how or if the server uses the Automatic Updates feature. In most situations, you will likely not use automatic updates for a server because of the need to test and validate updates prior to rollout. You can use Windows Server Update Services (WSUS) in conjunction with Group Policy to carefully control how and when automatic updates are deployed to servers and client systems. See www.microsoft.com/technet/prodtechnol/windowsserver2008/technologies /featured/wsus/default.mspx for details on WSUS.

Date and Time applet

This applet is the same one that appears if you double-click the clock on the system tray. The resulting dialog box enables you to set the server's date, time, and time zone, all of which are self-explanatory.

FIGURE 2-32

You can configure Automatic Updates behavior for the server.

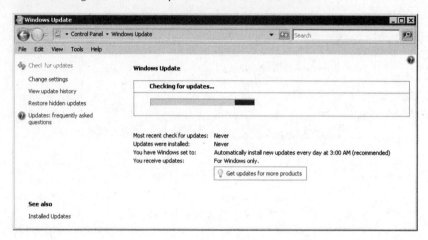

Having an accurate time on a server is extremely important for authentication purposes but is also important for error and event tracking, as well as security. For example, if you receive a denial-of-service attack from a particular dynamic IP address, knowing the time the attack occurred will enable you to track down the user of that IP at the specified time. Accurate timestamps are also important for reliable backup and restore operations.

Computers in a domain perform their own synchronization. Workstations and member servers automatically synchronize with the domain controller serving as the operations master in the domain. This DC should be checked and adjusted periodically for the accurate time, but a better option is to configure it to take its time from an Internet time source such as time.nist.gov. Domain members will then receive an accurate time when they synchronize with the DC.

> **NOTE** The Windows Time service is the component responsible for time synchronization. This service is set for automatic startup by default.

You can configure time synchronization settings through Group Policy. You'll find the policies in the \Computer Configuration\Administrative Templates\System\Windows Time Service Group Policy branch. Use the Global Configuration Settings policy to enable and configure a wide variety of properties that determine the way the server handles the time samples it receives from time providers.

The policies in the Time Providers sub-branch control time synchronization from both a client and server standpoint:

- **Enable Windows NTP Client.** Enabling this policy allows the server to synchronize its time with the server specified in the Configure Windows NTP Client policy. Disable this policy if you don't want the server to synchronize its time.

- **Configure Windows NTP Client.** Enable this policy if you want the server to synchronize its time with a remote time server. When you enable the policy, you gain access to several properties that specify the time server, update frequency, server type, and other time synchronization aspects.

- **Enable Windows NTP Server.** Enable this policy if you want the server to act as a time server, enabling it to service NTP requests from other computers on the network.

 You don't need Windows Server 2008 to host your own time server. Windows Server 200X, Windows XP, and Vista also offer the capability to act as a time server.

Display object . . . Personalization

The Display applet in no longer available on its own. It has been moved into the Personalization applet. It still, however, enables you to configure desktop settings such as wallpaper, background, color scheme, color depth, and desktop size (resolution). You also can configure a screen saver, enable and configure Web effects, and set general desktop effects and settings. If the system contains multiple display adapters, you can configure settings for each as well as configure how each adapter fits into the desktop.

Folder Options applet

The Folder Options applet in the Control Panel enables you to configure how Explorer folder windows appear and function. You can use it to enable/disable the active desktop, specify the type of window used for displaying folders (Web content or classic), and specify whether new folders open in the same window or in a new window, and so on. You also can configure other options such as file associations and offline files.

Internet Options applet

The Internet Options applet offers several property pages that enable you to configure settings for Internet Explorer and related programs such as Outlook Express and NetMeeting:

- **General.** Set the default home page, delete cached files, clear the URL history, and set general properties such as fonts, colors, languages, and accessibility features.

- **Security.** Use the Security page to configure security level for various zones. A zone is a group of Web sites that share a common security level. Click one of the predefined zones and click Sites to add or remove Web sites from the zone. Then use the slider on the Security page to set the security level for the zone or click Custom Level to specify individual settings for the way Internet Explorer handles cookies, ActiveX controls and plug-ins, scripts, file downloads, and so on.

- **Privacy.** Use the Privacy page to change the way Internet Explorer handles cookies, both globally and for individual Web sites.

■ **Content.** Use the Content page to enable and configure Content Advisor, which helps guard against access to restricted sites (such as sites with adult content). You also use the Content page to configure certificates for use on secure Web sites and for e-mail. Use the Personal Information group on the Content page to create a profile with your name, address, phone number, and other information. Bear in mind that this information is visible to Web sites you visit unless you configure the security zones to prevent it.

■ **Connections.** Use the Connections page to configure your Internet connection(s) and to specify how and when Internet Explorer uses auto-connect to connect to the Internet. Click Setup to run the Internet Connection Wizard to create a new Internet connection. Click LAN Settings to configure proxy server settings.

■ **Programs.** This page enables you to associate specific programs with tasks such as e-mail, newsgroups, and so on.

■ **Advanced.** This page contains several individual options that determine how Internet Explorer handles HTTP versions, multimedia, printing, security, and a variety of other properties.

Network and Sharing Center applet

The Network and Sharing Center applet in the Control Panel opens the Network and Sharing Center applet. This applet contains icons for each of your network connections, including LAN and dial-up connections. Click the "Manage network connections" link to configure the connection's protocols, bindings, clients, services, sharing, and other properties.

CROSS-REF For more in-depth coverage of network configuration, refer to Chapter 3.

Power Options applet

The Power Options applet in the Control Panel controls power-saving features on the computer, such as turning off system peripherals after a specified idle time and setting up hibernation (suspend to disk). You can configure power settings and save the configuration as a power scheme, making it easy to switch between different groups of settings.

The UPS page of the Power Options property sheet controls the UPS service. If a UPS is connected to the computer via one of the computer's ports, the UPS page shows UPS status such as estimated runtime and battery condition. You can configure the UPS through the UPS page or select a different UPS.

Printers Control Panel applet

The Printers Control Panel applet opens the Printers folder, which contains an icon for each installed printer, as well as a wizard for adding local or remote printers.

CROSS-REF For detailed information on the Printers folder and printing services, see Chapter 12.

System applet

The System applet provides access to general system properties. You also can open the System applet by right-clicking Computer and choosing Properties. The first page of the System property applet provides basic information about your system, including OS version, installed memory, CPU type, and registration information.

Clicking Advanced Systems Settings loads the Systems Properties dialog box. The first tab is the Computer Name page.

Computer Name

The Computer Name tab is the place to go to change the workgroup or domain to which the computer is assigned, as well as to change its computer name. You also can change the primary DNS suffix for the computer, as well as its NetBIOS name.

Hardware page

The Hardware page offers a handful of features for controlling the system's hardware and resource settings (see Figure 2-33). The Hardware Wizard was covered earlier in this chapter in the section "Add Hardware Applet." The Device Manager was covered earlier in the section "Device Manager."

FIGURE 2-33

Use the Hardware page to add, remove, and configure hardware and hardware profiles.

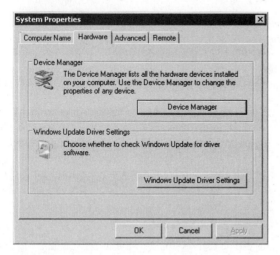

In Windows Server 2008, drivers can be signed digitally by Microsoft to certify that the driver has been tested and meets certain compatibility criteria defined by Microsoft. Clicking Windows

Update Driver Settings opens a dialog box you can use to configure driver installation. You can choose between the following:

- Check for Drivers Automatically (Recommended).
- Ask Me Each Time I Connect a New Device Before Checking for Drivers.
- Never Check for Drivers When I Connect a Device.

> **TIP**   You can configure driver signing behavior through Group Policy.

Advanced page

You can use the Advanced page of the System properties applet in the Control Panel to configure performance options for the computer, to view and set environment variables, and to configure system startup and recovery options.

User Profiles

User profiles store a given working environment, including desktop configuration, mapped drives and printers, and other properties. When a user logs on, the user profile applies the desktop configuration and other properties. User profiles are most useful for providing a consistent user interface for each user even when other users share the same computer. They're also useful for providing a consistent UI for users who log in from a variety of computers (roaming users).

> **TIP**   You access user profiles through the Settings button in the User Profiles group of the Advanced tab in the System property sheet.

A user profile comprises a registry file and a set of folders. The registry file applies settings to the UI such as mapped drives, restrictions, desktop contents, screen colors and fonts, and so on, and is a cached copy of the HKEY_CURRENT_USER portion of the registry. The folders include the user's My Documents, My Pictures, and other folders stored under the Documents and Settings folder for the user.

The three types of profiles are personal, mandatory, and default. Personal profiles enable users to modify their working environments and retain those changes from one logon session to the next. Mandatory profiles enable certain configuration changes (subject to restrictions in the profile itself), but those changes are not saved for future logon sessions. The only difference between a personal profile and a mandatory profile is the profile's file extension. Personal profiles use a .dat extension for the registry file portion of the profile, and mandatory profiles use a .man extension.

A default profile is preconfigured by Windows Server 2008 and is applied for new users that log on with no pre-existing profile. The profile then is stored as the user's profile for later logon sessions.

You specify a user's profile through the user's account properties when you create or modify the account. You use the Local Users and Groups MMC console to create and modify local accounts and use the Active Directory Users and Computers console to create and modify domain accounts in the Active Directory. The Profile tab of the user's account properties (see Figure 2-34) specifies the path to the user's profile, the logon script, and other properties. When the user logs on, Windows Server 2008 applies the profile located on the specified path.

FIGURE 2-34

The Profile page defines the path to the user's profile.

CROSS-REF Chapter 24 has more information about Group Policy objects and how they're integrated with Active Directory.

Creating a profile

Windows Server 2008 provides no specific utility for creating user profiles. Instead, you first log on as the target user to a system with similar video hardware as the user's target workstation (because video settings are stored in the profile and you need to ensure compatibility). You configure the working environment as needed, mapping drives and printers, setting desktop schemes, and so on. When you log off, the profile is stored locally along with the user's folder structure.

Copying profiles

In order to copy a user profile from one location to another, you use the User Profiles page of the System object in the Control Panel. Open the User Profiles page on the system from which you're copying the profile. Select the profile from the list of profiles stored on the computer and click Copy To. Select the local folder or network share where you want the profile copied and click OK.

Supporting roaming users

A roaming profile is the same as a local personal profile except that the profile is stored on a network share accessible to the user at logon. You specify the UNC path to the user's profile in his or her account properties so that when the user logs on, the profile can be applied regardless of that user's logon location. If a profile exists on the specified path, Windows Server 2008 applies that profile at logon. If no profile exists on the specified path, Windows Server 2008 creates a new profile automatically, stores it on that path, and uses the profile for future logon sessions.

Creating a mandatory profile

You create a mandatory profile in the same way you create a personal profile, but with one additional step. After you create the profile and copy it to the target location (such as the user's local computer or a network share for a roaming profile), change the name of the profile's registry file from `Ntuser.dat` to `Ntuser.man`.

Performance options

Click Settings under the Performance group on the Advanced page to display the Performance Options dialog box. The Visual Effects tab enables you to configure a variety of interface options that can affect overall system performance. In the default configuration, 2008 disables all visual effects except visual styles on windows and buttons. Essentially all of the visual effects are eye candy and have no significant administrative benefit, so you should leave them turned off.

You can select options on the Advanced tab to optimize the system for applications or background services. In most cases, you'll select Applications for a Windows Server 2008 Workstation or Background Services for a Server.

The Performance Options dialog box also enables you to change the system's virtual memory allocation (size of the system's swap file) and space allocated to the registry files. Why change swap file size or location? The swap file is used to emulate memory (thus the term virtual memory), making the system appear as if it has more physical memory than it really does. As memory fills up, Windows Server 2008 moves memory pages to the swap file to create space in physical memory for new pages, or it swaps pages between physical and virtual memory when an existing page stored in the swap file is needed. Windows Server 2008 automatically selects a swap file size based on physical memory size, but in some cases, you might want to increase the swap file size to improve performance. You also might want to move the swap file from the default location to a different disk with greater capacity or better performance (such as moving from an IDE drive to a SCSI drive).

Click Change on the Advanced tab of the Performance Options dialog box to access the Virtual Memory dialog box, shown in Figure 2-35. Select a drive for the swap file, specify the initial and maximum sizes (Windows Server 2008 will resize as needed within the range), and click Set. Specify the maximum registry size in the field provided and click OK to apply the changes.

FIGURE 2-35

Use the Virtual Memory dialog box to control swap file size and registry size.

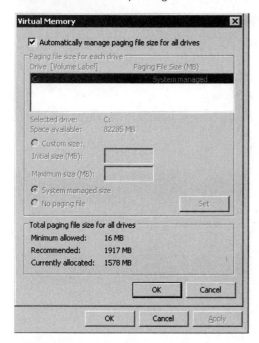

TIP   **Changing the maximum registry size doesn't change the size of the registry. It imposes a maximum size that when reached, causes Windows Server 2008 to generate a warning message that the maximum registry size has been reached.**

Environment Variables

Click Environment Variables on the Advanced tab to open the Environment Variables dialog box, which you can use to view, delete, and add environment variables. The variables you define in the upper half of the page apply to the user who currently is logged on. Variables defined in the bottom half apply to all users.

Startup/Shutdown options

The Startup and Recovery page (see Figure 2-36) enables you to configure boot options, how the system handles a system failure, and how debugging information is handled. The options in the System Startup group enable you to specify which boot option is selected by default and how long the boot menu is displayed. These settings are stored in the Boot.ini file, located in the root folder of the drive on which the boot loader is located. You can edit the file manually with a text editor to change values if you prefer.

FIGURE 2-36

Configure startup, recovery, and debugging options in the Startup and Recovery dialog box.

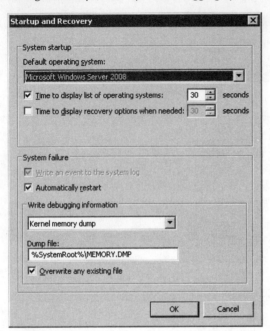

TIP   Click Settings in the Startup and Recovery group on the Advanced tab to display the Startup and Recovery dialog box.

The System Failure group of controls determines how Windows Server 2008 reacts when a system failure occurs. The system always attempts to write an event to the system log, if possible. If you need to see the blue screen of death after a system failure to gather information for troubleshooting, deselect Automatically Restart.

Use the Write Debugging Information group of controls to specify the action Windows Server 2008 takes to create a memory dump file when a system failure occurs. Microsoft support engineers can use the debugging information to determine the cause of the failure and recommend or develop a fix for the problem.

Remote tab

The Remote tab, shown in Figure 2-37, controls Remote Desktop/Terminal Services access to the server, as well as Remote Assistance.

The Remote Assistance group enables you to allow remote users to connect to the server through the Remote Assistance feature. If you click Advanced, you can enable or disable the option

Allow This Computer to Be Controlled Remotely. When this option is enabled, a remote user is allowed remote control over the server; disabling the option allows the user to view the server but not control it. You can also set the period of time during which a Remote Assistance invitation can remain open.

 **TIP**   You can send Remote Assistance requests with MSN Messenger or by e-mail.

FIGURE 2-37

Use the Remote tab to configure remote control features.

Remote Desktop is, essentially, a stripped-down version of Terminal Services. Enabling the Allow option in the Remote Desktop group allows remote users to initiate a Remote Desktop or Terminal Services connection to the server. Click Select Remote Users to specify the users that can log in through this service.

Windows XP and Vista include a built-in Remote Desktop client that you can use to connect to Windows Server 2008. In addition, users can employ a Terminal Services client to connect to the server through Remote Desktop. The Remote Desktop Web Connection ActiveX component enables Internet Explorer users to access a computer hosting Remote Desktop connections through their Web browser. Remote Desktop Web Connection is included with Windows XP and Vista and is available for download from Microsoft's Web site.

As handy as it is for remote control and management, Remote Desktop has security implications. You should read through Chapter 16 to ensure that you understand these security implications before enabling Remote Desktop on a server.

> **TIP** If you're having problems getting Terminal Services clients to connect to Windows Server 2008 running Terminal Services, be sure to enable the Allow Users to Connect Remotely to This Computer option on the Remote tab of the System Properties sheet. Disabling this option prevents Terminal Services clients from connecting, even if you've enabled access through Group Policy.

Windows PowerShell

A new addition to the server administration tools on Windows Server 2008 is the Windows PowerShell. Released before the server RTM, it is a new command-line shell and scripting language that lets you automate or organize repetitive administrative tasks on the server.

Windows PowerShell is great for server administrators because you don't need to be a code guru to use it like you would have to on Windows Server 2003 with VB and JavaScript, or complex C# applications. The Windows PowerShell is built to sit atop the .NET common language runtime (CLR) and the .NET Framework, accepting and returning .NET objects that you can interact with.

Windows PowerShell works with the so-called cmdlet. This "let" is a simple, single-function command-line tool built into the shell. More than 130 standard cmdlets ship with the system, and you can open them and manipulate them for your own use. You can also easily write your own cmdlets. The cmdlets can be used on their own or they can be combined and dovetailed with each other to perform tasks on a server that would be very difficult through the regular command line or via Control Panel applets and features.

You can use Windows PowerShell to manage Windows Server 2008 roles, such as IIS 7.0, DNS, DHCO, Terminal Server, and so on. You can also create cmdlets for line of business servers like Exchange Server 2007, SQL Server, and Microsoft Operations Manager.

To use PowerShell take the following action: Click Start ➤ All Programs ➤ Windows PowerShell 1.0 ➤ Documents, and then drill down to the folder that holds the GettingStarted manual. This is a WordPad file that will get you running cmdlets in short order. There is also a user guide in the same folder, release notes, and more.

Summary

Windows Server 2008 provides several tools for administering system hardware, operating environment properties, users, and other objects. Although most of the administrative functions are incorporated into Microsoft Management Console (MMC) snap-ins or extensions, a few — such as the ODBC Data Source Administrator — still exist as standalone utilities. The Control Panel serves as a control center for configuring hardware and OS settings and properties.

Understanding the administrative tools available to you is an important step in configuring and monitoring a system. This chapter examined the majority of the administrative tools you'll work with on a regular basis. Other chapters cover additional administrative tools or cover in more detail some of the tools mentioned here.

Chapter 3

Networking Windows Server 2008

This chapter provides a detailed discussion of Windows Server 2008 networking, including an explanation of Transmission Control Protocol/Internet Protocol (TCP/IP), versions 4 and 6, routing, network address translation (NAT), legacy protocols, and other topics related to Windows Server 2008 network configuration.

TCP/IP on Windows Server 2008

A little more than a decade ago, TCP/IP was used by a relatively small number of computers connected to the Internet. As the number of networks connected to the Internet grew explosively, and as companies expanded to include more and more networks within the enterprise, TCP/IP has come to be the protocol of choice for most organizations. The reasons are many, but they commonly include the organization's need for standardization, the capability to route, and of course, Internet connectivity.

Windows Server 2008 offers strong support for TCP/IP. TCP/IP is the primary protocol for, and the foundation of, Active Directory (AD), which is the keystone of Windows Server 2008 networks. On the client side, the TCP/IP protocol enables full support for connecting to both peer and server computers running TCP/IP, the Internet, and TCP/IP-based services such as networked printers.

> **NOTE** The stack has been completely rebuilt. It is called Next Generation TCP/IP Stack. This new stack is also included in Vista.

On the server side, Windows Server 2008 offers the configuration and management tools you would expect, including support for dynamic address allocation through Dynamic Host Configuration Protocol (DHCP), name resolution through Domain Name System (DNS), Network Basic Input Output System (NetBIOS) name resolution through Windows Internet Name Service (WINS), and a full range of configuration and troubleshooting tools.

Windows Server 2008 builds on features introduced in previous versions of Windows Server to support additional capabilities for TCP/IP clients. Windows 2000, 2003, XP, and Vista DHCP clients, for example, can request updates for their host records with a Windows Server 2008 DNS server, enabling DHCP clients to have up-to-date host entries in their domains. Windows Server 2008 DHCP servers can also initiate updates on behalf of TCP/IP clients, including those that are not designed to support dynamic DNS. Windows Server 2008 DHCP servers can request an update of the client's pointer record in DNS as well.

> **TIP**   Windows Server 2008 includes other features related to TCP/IP, such as the capability to bridge network connections; Internet Connection Sharing (ICS), which enables a single Internet connection to be shared by other users on the local network; and Windows Firewall, a rudimentary firewall. For more information on ICS and other remote-access-related topics, see Chapter 6.

On both the client and server side, Windows Server 2008 provides easy TCP/IP configuration. As with other Windows applications, you configure TCP/IP through various dialog boxes, but Windows Server 2008 also includes command-line utilities such as `ipconfig` to help you view and manage a system's TCP/IP configuration. A very useful feature is the capability to change IP addresses and other settings without requiring the system to reboot.

Before you begin configuring and using TCP/IP in Windows Server 2008, you need to understand the basics of how TCP/IP works, which are covered in the following section. If you're already familiar with TCP/IP and are ready to configure it in Windows Server 2008, turn to the section "Configuring TCP/IP" later in this chapter.

> **NOTE**   The following section explains IP version 4, generally referred to as IPv4. The next generation IP protocol, IPv6, is also included in Windows Server 2008. See the section "Understanding and Using IPv6" later in this chapter for a detailed explanation of IPv6 and its use.

TCP/IP Basics (IPv4)

TCP/IP is actually a suite of protocols. The IP portion of TCP/IP provides the transport protocol. TCP provides the mechanism through which IP packets are received and recombined, ensuring that IP traffic arrives in a usable state. TCP/IP arose from the ARPANET, which was the precursor to today's Internet. TCP/IP is standards-based and supported by nearly every operating system, including all Microsoft operating systems, Unix, Linux, Macintosh, NetWare, OS/2, Open VMS, and others. This wide compatibility and the capability to interconnect dissimilar systems are the primary reasons why TCP/IP has become so popular.

Although TCP/IP is most often used to provide wide-area networking (such as on the Internet), it is an excellent choice as a local network transport protocol, particularly where organizations want to serve network resources to local clients through an intranet. You can use TCP/IP as your only network protocol, or you can use it in conjunction with other protocols, such as NetBIOS.

IP addressing

Any device that uses TCP/IP to communicate is called a *host*, including a computer, a printer, and a router. As smart devices begin to pervade our daily existence, it's conceivable that even your washing machine or microwave oven will become a host, if not on the Internet, then at least on your home intranet. This will enable the device to notify the manufacturer (or you) when it needs service.

Each host must have a unique *IP address* that identifies it on the network so that IP data packets can be routed to and from it. *IP data packets* are simply data encapsulated in IP format for transmission using TCP. Each address must be unique; identical addresses on two or more hosts will conflict and prevent those computers from communicating properly. In fact, Windows Server 2008 shuts down the TCP/IP protocol on a computer if it detects an address conflict at TCP/IP initialization.

IPv4 addresses are 32-bit values usually expressed in dotted decimal notation, with four octets separated by decimals, as in 192.168.0.221. Each IP address contains two separate pieces of information: the network address and the host address. How these two items of information are defined in the IP address depends on its class.

There are five classes of IP addresses, class A to class E, but only three classes are relevant to you in relation to Windows Server 2008 networking: A, B, and C. Class A networks yield the highest number of host addresses, and class C networks yield the lowest number. Table 3-1 provides information about each class. The designation w.x.y.z indicates the portion of the IP address that defines network and host ID portions of the address.

TABLE 3-1

IP Address Classes

Class	Network ID	Network Host ID	Number of Available Networks	Number of Hosts per Network
A 1–126	W	x.y.z	126	16,777,214
B 128–191	w.x	y.z	16,384	65,534
C 192–223	w.x.y	Z	2,097,151	254

As Table 3-1 indicates, the address range 127.x.y.z is missing. 127.x.y.z is reserved on the local computer for loopback testing and can't be used as a valid network address. Addresses 224 and higher are reserved for special protocols such as IP multicast and are not available as host addresses. In addition, host addresses 0 and 255 are used as broadcast addresses and can't be used as valid host addresses. For example, 192.168.120.0 and 192.168.120.255 are both broadcast addresses that are not available for use as host addresses.

The number of addresses in a given address class is fixed. Class A networks are quite large, with more than 16 million hosts, and class C networks are relatively small, with just 254 hosts. The class you choose depends on how many hosts you need to accommodate; most important, it depends on whether you are using a public address range or a private one. The address ranges listed here are reserved by convention for private networks:

- 10.0.0.0, subnet mask 255.0.0.0
- 169.254.0.0, subnet mask 255.255.0.0
- 172.16.0.0, subnet mask 255.240.0.0
- 192.168.0.0, subnet mask 255.255.0.0

However, if you are not connecting your systems to the Internet, you can use any IP address class except the loopback addresses. For example, a class A addressing scheme can provide a large number of host addresses for your enterprise; but if you're connecting the network to the Internet, at least some of the addresses need to be valid, public addresses that fall in the range described in Table 3-1 (excluding the private ranges mentioned previously).

If all your systems connect to the Internet directly, rather than through a proxy server or other device that performs NAT, each host must have a unique, valid, public IP address. If you use NAT, only those hosts on the public side of the Internet connection need valid, public addresses. Those hosts on the private side can use one of the private address ranges described previously, but only NAT and proxy services will allow the public addresses to translate to the private ones. This means you can accommodate a large class A network internally, if needed. Figure 3-1 illustrates a network that uses a private IP range but connects to the Internet through a proxy server and router with public addresses.

FIGURE 3-1

This network uses private IP addresses internally and a proxy server to connect to the Internet.

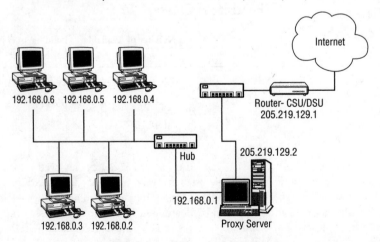

Subnetting

Each host, in addition to an IP address, needs a subnet mask. The *subnet mask*, like an IP address, is a 32-bit value typically expressed as four octets separated by periods. The subnet mask serves to mask the IP address into its two components, network ID and host ID, which enables traffic to be routed to the appropriate network and then to the destination host. Table 3-2 shows the subnet masks for the three standard network classes.

TABLE 3-2

Standard Subnet Masks

Class	Binary Value	Subnet Mask
A	11111111 00000000 00000000 00000000	255.0.0.0
B	11111111 11111111 00000000 00000000	255.255.0.0
C	11111111 11111111 11111111 00000000	255.255.255.0

In addition to masking the host ID from the network ID, a subnet mask also can serve to segment a single network into multiple logical networks. For example, assume that your small company obtains Internet access from a local ISP. The ISP uses a class C address space to accommodate a group of small business clients, of which your company is one. The ISP uses a subnet mask of 255.255.255.224 to divide the network into eight subnets with 30 hosts each. Table 3-3 lists the host ranges for each subnet.

TABLE 3-3

Sample Subnet

Subnet	Host Range
0	205.219.128.1–205.219.128.30
1	205.219.128.33–205.219.128.62
2	205.219.128.65–205.219.128.94
3	205.219.128.97–205.219.128.126
4	205.219.128.129–205.219.128.158
5	205.219.128.161–205.219.128.190
6	205.219.128.193–205.219.128.222
7	205.219.128.225–205.219.128.254

In this example, the ISP uses the first address range (subnet 0) for a *routing cloud* (a network subnet that functions solely for the purpose of routing), and the remaining seven subnets to accommodate the customers. You are the first customer and you get subnet 1, with addresses from 33 through 62. Figure 3-2 illustrates the network.

FIGURE 3-2

This ISP serves seven customers with a class C address space and a subnet mask of 255.255.255.224.

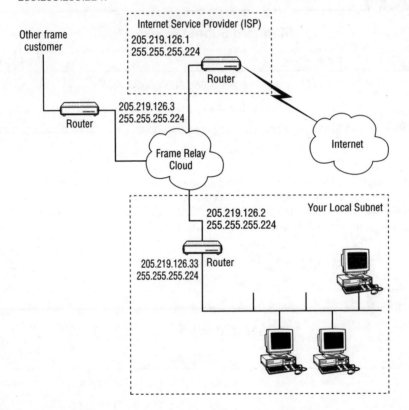

TIP You can calculate subnet masks manually, but it's a real chore. Instead, download a copy of Net3 Group's IP Subnet Calculator from www.wildpackets.com /products/free_utilities/ipsubnetcalc/overview. Alternatively, search your favorite shareware/freeware site, such as www.tucows.com, for additional tools such as Advanced Subnet Calculator, also available at www.solarwinds.net/download-tools.htm.

As you're designing your network and assigning IP addresses and subnet masks, keep in mind that all nodes on the same logical segment need to have the same subnet mask. This places them in the same logical network for routing purposes.

NOTE A full understanding of subnetting is essential for deploying Active Directory across multiple sites in an enterprise or the Internet. For more information, see Chapters 22 through 25.

Classless Interdomain Routing notation

Given the length of a subnet mask, it isn't always efficient to specify an address using the address and subnet mask. Classless Interdomain Routing (CIDR) simplifies addressing notation by enabling you to specify the network ID using the number of bits that define the network ID. Table 3-4 illustrates the concept.

TABLE 3-4

Classless Interdomain Routing Notation

Class	Binary Value	Network Prefix
A	11111111 00000000 00000000 00000000	/8
B	11111111 11111111 00000000 00000000	/16
C	11111111 11111111 11111111 00000000	/24

For example, the class C address space 192.168.0.0/255.255.255.0 can be expressed using CIDR as 192.168.0.0/24.

TIP CIDR is also known as *network prefix notation.*

CIDR is not limited to specifying these three network IDs. You can also use CIDR to identify the network ID for networks with different subnets. To determine the network prefix, simply add the number of subnet bits. For example, assume you create a subnet using the mask 255.255.255.224, or three additional subnet bits. The notation for the address range 192.168.0.*n* with this subnet mask would be 192.168.0.0/27. Table 3-5 shows the network prefixes for subnets of a class C network ID.

TABLE 3-5

CIDR Subnets of a Class C Network ID

Number of Subnets	Subnet Bits	Subnet Mask/CIDR Notation	Number of Hosts per Network
1–2	1	255.255.255.128 or /25	126
3–4	2	255.255.255.192 or /26	62
5–8	3	255.255.255.224 or /27	30
9–16	4	255.255.255.240 or /28	14
17–32	5	255.255.255.248 or /29	6
33–64	6	255.255.255.252 or /30	2

Obtaining IP addresses

How you assign IP addresses depends on whether your systems are connected to the public Internet. Systems connected to the Internet directly, rather than through a proxy server or other device doing NAT, must have unique, valid IP addresses, often termed "legal" addresses. This means you can't arbitrarily choose an address range for these systems. Instead, you need to obtain an address range from your ISP to ensure that you are using unique addresses (and that proper routing takes place). The number of addresses you need to obtain depends on how many hosts you will have on the public side of your proxy server or other NAT device, if any. For example, assume you configure your network so that a proxy server sits between the router and all other hosts. You would need only three public addresses: one for each side of the router and one for the public side of the proxy server. The hosts on the private side of the proxy server can use private addresses.

If your network is not connected to the Internet, you could theoretically choose any network address range, including a public range in use by someone else, but you will not be able to connect your network to the Internet. You should, however, follow the convention of using one of the reserved address ranges for your private network (discussed previously in this chapter), because it will make life easier for you if you install NAT services. You won't have to re-address all of your hosts later if you decide to connect the network to the Internet — you simply provide some means of NAT through a router (such as Routing and Remote Access Service, RRAS, discussed later) or a proxy server.

Gateways and routing

TCP/IP subnets use gateways to route data between networks. Usually, a *gateway* is a dedicated router or firewall, but it could be any device running routing services, such as a Windows Server 2008 server running RRAS. The router maintains IP address information about remote networks so it can route traffic accordingly. Traffic coming from the local network with a public address is routed through the appropriate port on the router. Figure 3-3 shows a simple network with two connections to the Internet. The second connection provides redundancy in the event that the primary connection fails.

FIGURE 3-3

A simple network with two gateways to the Internet.

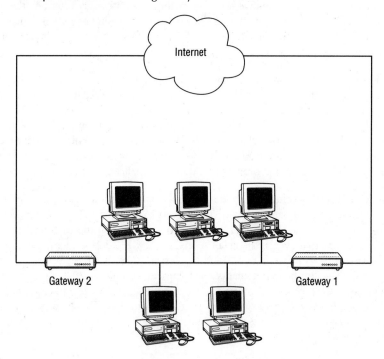

On the host, IP inserts the originating and destination addresses into each packet. The host then checks (using its subnet mask) the destination address to determine whether the packet is destined for another host on the same local network or for a host on another network. If the packet is for a local host, it is sent directly to the local host on the same subnet. If the destination host is on a remote network, IP sends the packet to the local host's *default gateway*, which routes the traffic to the remote network. You can configure multiple gateways if more than one is present on the network, and the local host attempts to connect through them in turn. If the default gateway is down, the host attempts to reach the next gateway in the list. The packet then travels through (possibly) several other routers until it reaches its destination.

Standalone subnets do not require gateways because there is nowhere for the traffic to go — all traffic is local. Subnets connected to other subnets or to the Internet require at least one gateway.

Dynamic Host Configuration Protocol (DHCP)

Because every host must have a unique IP address, how you allocate and manage addresses is an important consideration when setting up an IP network. You can allocate addresses in one of two ways: static addressing or dynamic addressing. With *static addressing*, you simply assign a specific IP address to each host. The address doesn't change unless you manually reconfigure the host's TCP/IP properties (thus the term *static*). Static addressing is fine for small networks for which you don't need to add or remove nodes or change addresses very often. As the number of nodes increases, however, static addressing can become an administrative nightmare. It's easy to accidentally assign conflicting IP addresses, and when subnet properties change (such as a default gateway address), you have to manually reconfigure those properties.

Dynamic addressing through DHCP is a much better solution than static addressing, particularly for large networks or dynamic networks in which IP properties change. DHCP enables a server to automatically allocate IP addresses and related properties (gateway, DNS servers, and so on) to clients as they boot. A dynamically assigned address and associated properties is called a *lease*. Depending on the configuration at the DHCP server, a lease can have an infinite duration or expire after a certain period. If a lease expires, the client can renew the lease to obtain a new IP address (which could be the same one provided by the previous lease).

DHCP in Windows Server 2008 offers some additional benefits in its interaction with Windows Server 2008 and Windows 2000 Server–based DNS servers. A Windows 2000 or Windows XP DHCP client can request that the DNS server update its host address in the DNS namespace for its domain. This means that even if the client receives a new IP address each time it boots, its host record in DNS will remain accurate. Windows Server 2008 DHCP servers can also request host record updates on behalf of clients, including non-Windows 2000/XP clients that don't support dynamic DNS updates. Remember, however, that the DNS records are updated locally. Servers that are hosting secondary records for the domain(s) will have to perform a zone transfer to retrieve the up-to-date records. Local clients that have DNS entries cached will obtain up-to-date queries when their caches expire.

 See Chapter 4 for detailed information on DHCP and how to configure Windows Server 2008 DHCP clients and servers.

Domains and name resolution

IP hosts communicate using IP addresses, but humans would have trouble remembering more than a few IP addresses. How would you like to try to remember the addresses of all the Web sites you visit in a week's time? *Domain names*, *host names*, and *name resolution* help simplify internetworking for the user.

Domain names identify networks using a dotted format similar to IP addresses, except that domain names use letters (usually words), rather than numbers. For example, the domain mcity.us identifies a specific network in the .us domain. Each host in the mcity.us domain has a host name that identifies the host uniquely on the network. The host name and domain name combine to create a Fully Qualified Domain Name, or FQDN, that uniquely identifies the host. For example, a host in the `mcity.us` domain might have the host name `server1`. The FQDN for the host would be `server1.mcity.us`. If the domain contains delegated subnets, those figure into the FQDN as well. For example, assume `mcity.us` includes a subdomain called `support`. The host named `fred` in `support.mcity.us` would have the FQDN `fred.support.mcity.us`.

NOTE There is not necessarily a correlation between a computer's FQDN and e-mail address. Although the user in the previous example might have the e-mail address `fred@support.mcity.us`, there is no correlation with his computer's FQDN. The host name and e-mail account have nothing in common.

There isn't any direct connection between FQDNs or IP addresses, so some method is required to map host names to IP addresses. When you type `http://www.mcity.us` in your Web browser, for example, some translation needs to occur to map `www.mcity.us` to its IP address so your browser can connect to the site. That's where DNS comes in.

DNS

Domain Name System (DNS) provides a distributed database to enable host names to be mapped to their corresponding IP addresses. DNS name servers maintain records for domains they host, and they respond to queries for a given host name with the IP address stored in the DNS database for that host. For example, when you attempt to connect to `www.mcity.us`, your computer submits a DNS request to the DNS server configured in your computer's TCP/IP properties to resolve the host name `www.mcity.us` into an IP address. The DNS server looks up the data and passes the address back to your computer, which connects to the site using the IP address. The only interaction you provide in the process is to enter `http://www.mcity.us` in your browser. Everything else happens behind the scenes.

NOTE The name resolution process described here is simplified for the purpose of this discussion. See Chapter 5 for a detailed explanation of how DNS works.

WINS

Another name resolution service provided by Windows Server 2008 is WINS. WINS provides much the same service for NetBIOS names that DNS provides for TCP/IP host names. NetBIOS is an application programming interface (API) that programs can use to perform basic network operations such as sending data to specific computers on the network. NetBIOS is used by earlier Microsoft operating systems to identify and locate computers on the network. Just as DNS provides a means for mapping host names to IP addresses, WINS provides a means for mapping NetBIOS names to IP addresses for systems running NetBIOS over TCP/IP.

NOTE NetBIOS is not required in Windows Server 2008, because Windows Server 2008 uses host names and DNS to locate hosts on the local network. See Chapter 5 for a complete discussion on how to configure WINS.

Unless you are using applications that use NetBIOS over TCP/IP, you don't need to configure WINS on your computer.

Obtaining a domain name

You should obtain a domain name if your network will be connected to the Internet, and to protect a root Active Directory domain name (discussed in Chapters 18 through 22). The domain will identify your computers on the Internet. Some years ago, domain management was managed by a single organization, Network Solutions. Now, you can register a domain through any authorized domain registration organization, like GoDaddy. See Chapter 5 for additional information on domain names and domain registration.

Preparing for installation

You now have enough information to begin configuring TCP/IP. Before you jump in with both feet, however, do a little planning. Make sure that you have the following information:

- **Network address and domain.** Obtain valid public addresses from your ISP for computers connected directly to the Internet. Decide which private, reserved address space you'll use for computers on private network segments. Register your domain with a domain registration authority. This step is required only if you intend to use DNS to enable users on the Internet to connect to your network and its resources.

- **Identify an IP address for the computer.** Obtain the IP address(es) you will be assigning to the computer if you are allocating them statically. If you're using DHCP, you don't need to obtain a specific IP, nor do you need the IP address of a DHCP server on your network. Windows Server 2008 TCP/IP locates the DHCP server automatically at startup.

- **Subnet mask.** Determine the subnet mask you'll need for the computer based on the way your network is configured.

- **Default gateway(s).** Determine the IP addresses of the router(s) that will function as the computer's gateway(s).

- **DNS servers.** Determine the IP addresses of the computers that will serve as the client's DNS servers.

- **WINS servers.** Determine the IP addresses of the computers that will serve as the client's WINS servers (if any).

Setting Up TCP/IP

Windows Server 2008 installs TCP/IP by default unless you override the installation during setup. However, you can add the protocol later if it was not installed by Setup or was deleted after installation.

> **TIP**   Setup installs TCP/IP by default when you install Windows Server 2008. In fact, you can't uninstall TCP/IP, although you can disable it for a particular interface.

Although you can't uninstall TCP/IP, there might be occasions when you would like to have that capability. For example, the registry settings for TCP/IP might have become so corrupted that you need to reset the protocol back to its initial post-Setup state. You can use the `netsh` command from a console to reset the protocol. The following example shows the syntax for the command:

```
netsh int ip reset c:\ResetIP.txt
```

The last parameter specifies the name of a log file in which `netsh` logs the results of the reset operation. When `netsh` completes, the TCP/IP registry keys and values will be reset to the just-installed configuration.

The following sections explain how to configure TCP/IP.

Configuring TCP/IP

Open the Network Connections folder from the Control Panel to configure TCP/IP. Right-click the network interface whose TCP/IP properties you want to change and click Properties to open its property sheet. Double-click TCP/IP or select TCP/IP and click Properties to display the General property page (see Figure 3-4).

FIGURE 3-4

Use the General tab to set a static IP address or configure the server for DHCP.

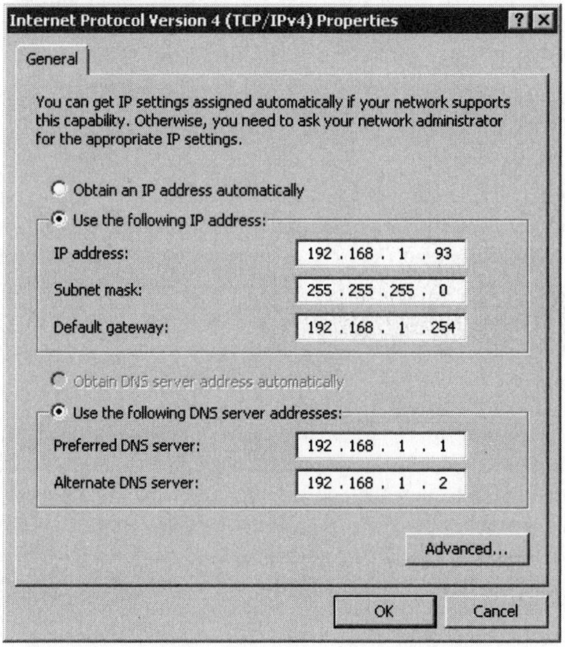

Use the following list as a guide to configure options:

- **Obtain an IP Address Automatically.** Select this option to use DHCP to automatically obtain an IP address and other configuration properties.
- **Use the Following IP Address.** Select this option if you need to assign a static IP address.
- **IP Address.** Specify a static IP address in dotted octet format.
- **Subnet Mask.** Specify the subnet mask for the interface in dotted octet format.
- **Default Gateway.** Specify the default gateway your computer should use to route nonlocal IP traffic.
- **Obtain DNS Server Address Automatically.** Select this option to automatically retrieve the list of DNS servers from a DHCP server. This option is available only if you obtain the IP address automatically.
- **Use the Following DNS Server Addresses.** Select this option to statically assign DNS server IP addresses.
- **Preferred DNS Server.** Specify the IP address of the DNS server you want to use by default for resolving host names to IP addresses.
- **Alternate DNS Server.** Specify the IP address of the DNS server you want to use for resolving host names if the preferred DNS server is unavailable.

These properties are sufficient for computers connected in a small private network, but in most cases, you'll need to configure additional properties. Click Advanced on the General tab to access the Advanced TCP/IP Settings property sheet. The following sections explain the options on each property page.

IP settings

Use the IP Settings tab (see Figure 3-5) to configure additional IP addresses for the computer and additional gateways. The Add, Edit, and Remove buttons in the IP Addresses section enables you to add, modify, and remove IP addresses and associated subnet masks on the computer. You might add multiple IP addresses to a server to host multiple Web sites, for example, with each site at its own IP address. Click Add to display a simple dialog box in which you type the new IP address and subnet mask to add. Select an existing address and click Edit or Remove to modify or remove the address, respectively.

Use the Add, Edit, and Remove buttons in the Default Gateways section to add, modify, or remove gateways. In small networks, there is often only one gateway, but in larger networks, multiple gateways are used to provide fault tolerance and redundancy, enabling users to connect outside their local network should one gateway become unavailable. Click Add to specify the IP address of another gateway, or select an existing address and click Edit or Remove to respectively modify or remove the selected gateway. The metric value of a gateway specifies the relative cost of connecting through the selected gateway. When routing is possible through more than one gateway, the one with the lowest metric is used by default.

FIGURE 3-5

Use the IP Settings tab to configure additional addresses.

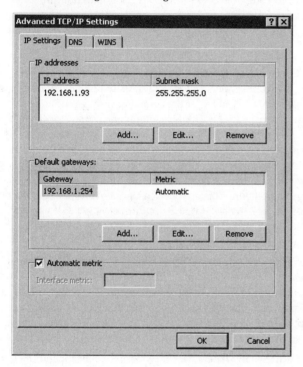

TIP   Here's an example of when the metric value comes into play: Assume your network has two connections to the Internet. Connection A is the one you want to use most because you pay a flat, monthly fee for it. Connection B is charged by bandwidth usage, and you only want to use B when A is unavailable. Therefore, you'd assign a metric of 1 to A and a higher value to B to ensure that traffic always goes through A if it's available.

The interface metric value on the IP Settings page specifies the relative cost of using the selected network interface. The default value is 1. This setting performs the same function for multi-homed systems (those with multiple network interfaces) as the metric value assigned to the default gateway(s). However, this value determines which interface is used to route traffic when multiple interfaces can be used to route the traffic. The interface with the lowest metric is used by default.

DNS

Use the DNS tab (see Figure 3-6) to configure DNS settings for the connection. In addition to specifying DNS servers, you can configure other options that control the way the client performs name resolution and enable dynamic DNS updates. The following list explains the available options:

- **Append Primary and Connection Specific DNS Suffixes.** Select this option to append the primary DNS suffix and connection-specific DNS suffix to unqualified host names for resolution. Define the primary DNS suffix for the computer through the computer's Network Identification property page (right-click My Computer, choose Properties, and click Network Identification). The primary DNS suffix applies globally to the system unless overridden by the connection-specific DNS suffix, which you set in the property "DNS suffix for this connection" (described later). For example, assume your primary suffix is `mcity.us` and your connection-specific DNS suffix is `support.mcity.us`. You query for the unqualified host name `fred`. This option then causes Windows Server 2008 to attempt to resolve `fred.mcity.us` and `fred.support.mcity.us`. If you have no connection-specific DNS suffix specified, Windows Server 2008 will attempt to resolve only `fred.mcity.us`.

- **Append Parent Suffixes of the Primary DNS Suffix.** This option determines whether or not the resolver attempts resolution of unqualified names up to the parent-level domain for your computer. For example, assume your computer's primary DNS suffix is `support.mcity.us` and you attempt to resolve the unqualified host name `jane`. The resolver would attempt to resolve `jane.support.mcity.us` and `jane.mcity.us` (attempting to resolve at the parent level as well as the computer's domain level).

- **Append These DNS Suffixes (In Order).** Use this option to only append the specified DNS suffixes for resolving unqualified names.

- **DNS Suffix for This Connection.** Use this option to specify a DNS suffix that is different from the primary DNS suffix defined in the computer's Network Identification property page.

- **Register This Connection's Addresses in DNS.** Select this option to have the client submit a request to the DNS server to update its host (A) record when its host name changes or its IP address changes. The client submits the full computer name specified in the Network Identification tab of the System Properties sheet along with its IP address to the DNS server. You can view the System properties through the System object in the Control Panel, or right-click My Computer and choose Properties.

- **Use This Connection's DNS Suffix in DNS Registration.** Select this option to have the client submit a request to the DNS server to update its host record when the host name changes or the IP address changes. The difference between this and the previous option is that this option registers the client using the first part of the computer name specified in the System properties along with the DNS suffix specified by the option "DNS suffix for this connection" on the DNS page. You can use this option along with the previous option to register two different FQDNs for the host.

FIGURE 3-6

The DNS tab controls how the client interacts with DNS servers.

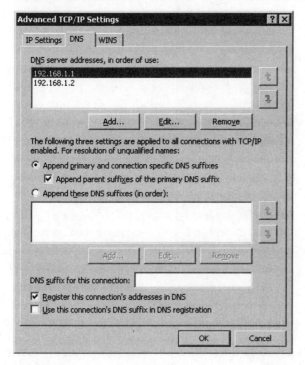

 Use the DNS tab when you need to add more than two DNS servers.

WINS

Use the WINS tab (see Figure 3-7) of the connection's TCP/IP properties to configure WINS services. You can use the Add, Edit, and Remove buttons in the WINS Addresses group to add, modify, and remove WINS servers by IP address.

FIGURE 3-7

The WINS tab specifies Windows Internet Name Service properties for the interface.

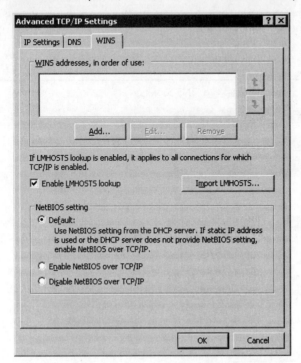

The following list explains the other options on the page:

- **Enable LMHOSTS Lookup.** Select this option to enable the computer to use a local LMHOSTS file to resolve NetBIOS names to IP addresses. LMHOSTS provides a way to supplement or even replace the use of WINS servers to resolve NetBIOS names. See Chapter 5 for more information on using LMHOSTS.

- **Import LMHOSTS.** Click to import an LMHOSTS file into your local LMHOSTS file.

- **Default.** Use this option to have the DHCP server automatically assign WINS settings.

- **Enable NetBIOS Over TCP/IP.** Select this option to use NetBIOS over TCP/IP (NetBT) and WINS. This option is required if the computer communicates by name with other computers running NETBIOS. NetBT is not required in a homogeneous Windows Server 2008 environment or when connecting to computers on the Internet through DNS.

- **Disable NetBIOS Over TCP/IP.** Select this option to disable NetBT in situations where it is not needed (see previous item).

Understanding and Using IPv6

With the proliferation of IP-based devices, the pool of available IPv4 IP addresses will eventually run dry. The lack of more addresses won't stop you from wanting that new integrated cell phone/PDA with wireless Internet connectivity, so something needs to be done about the dwindling pool of addresses. IPv6 is that something.

IPv6 is intended to be the eventual replacement for IPv4. The goals of IPv6 naturally include expanding the available address space, but they also target routing performance improvements, Quality of Service (QoS) for low-latency applications, increased security, and other improvements.

IPv6 terms and concepts

As with IPv4, a *node* in IPv6 is any device that implements IPv6, and it is either a router or host. The connection to a transmission medium through which packets are sent is called an *interface*. The medium used to transmit IPv6 is called a *link*, and can be loosely associated with an IPv4 subnet. *Neighbors* are nodes connected to the same link. Each link supports a specific *maximum transmission unit* (MTU) size, which is the maximum packet size that the link supports. The IPv6-capable portion of the Internet is called the *6bone*.

IPv4 supports both unicast routing and multicast routing; IPv6 supports these as well as anycast routing. Unicast traffic is directed at a particular interface. Multicast traffic is directed at a set of interfaces. Anycast addresses reference multiple interfaces, but anycast traffic is directed only to the closest interface to the sender, rather than to all interfaces.

IPv6 addresses are also different from IPv4 addresses: Whereas IPv4 uses 32-bit dotted decimal values, IPv6 uses 128-bit hexadecimal values comprising eight 16-bit sections. Here's a typical IPv6 address:

```
ABCD:EF12:0000:7890:0000:3412:0006:A327
```

Fields that contain leading zeros can omit the leading zeros, so the preceding example can be simplified as follows:

```
ABCD:EF12:0:7890:0:3412:6:A327
```

In addition, any fields that contain all zeros can be represented by a blank set (::), although a blank set can be used only once in an address. The following is an example:

- **Full address.** `ABCD:0:0:1234:0:0:0:5678`
- **Simplified address.** `ABCD:0:0:1234::5678`
- **Not acceptable.** `ABCD::1234::5678`

In addition, in mixed-mode environments that support IPv4 and IPv6 nodes, the six leftmost fields use hexadecimal values, but the remaining bits are entered as dotted decimal values, as in the following examples:

- `0:0:0:0:0:0:206.10.22.150`, or `::206.10.22.150` compressed
- `1234:FFFF:0:0:0:0:206.12.15.108`, or `1234:FFFF::206.12.15.108` compressed
- `::ACF5:0:206.142.68.11`

In an IPv6 address, a variable-length field of bits identifies the address type. This variable-length field is called the Format Prefix (FP). The following sections discuss the various IPv6 address types and their corresponding FPs.

Unicast addresses

The FP value 11111111, or FF, identifies an IPv6 address as a multicast address, so any address with an FP value other than FF is a unicast address. As with IPv4, unicast addresses identify a single node on the link. There are several types of unicast IPv6 addresses.

> **TIP** You can assign a single unicast address to multiple interfaces on a single node as long as the interfaces are recognized by the upper layers of the protocol as a single logical entity.

There are two reserved IPv6 unicast addresses. The first, `0:0:0:0:0:0:0:0`, or `::` in compressed format, is called the *unspecified address*. This address is used during IPv6 initialization before a node has obtained its own address. You can't assign `::` to a node, and it can't be used as the source address in an IPv6 packet or routing header.

The second reserved address is the loopback address. It corresponds to the 127.0.0.1 loopback address in IPv4. The IPv6 loopback address is `0:0:0:0:0:0:0:1`, or `::1` in compressed format. The loopback address enables the node to send a packet to itself, which is useful for testing proper function of the protocol stack.

Local-use unicast addresses support communication over a single link where no routing is required. They are also used for automatic configuration of addresses and neighbor discovery, which is the process used to discover neighboring nodes on the link. Table 3-6 shows the structure of a local-use unicast address.

TABLE 3-6

IPv6 Local-Use Unicast Addresses

10 Bits	54 Bits	64 Bits
1111111010	0	Interface ID

Site-local unicast addresses provide connectivity within a single private network and are similar to reserved private addresses used in IPv4. Just as these private IPv4 addresses are not routed, IPv6 routers do not route traffic for site-local unicast addresses. Table 3-7 shows the structure of a site-local unicast address.

TABLE 3-7

IPv6 Site-Local Unicast Addresses

10 Bits	38 Bits	16 Bits	64 Bits
1111111010	0	Subnet ID	Interface ID

The third type of unicast address is an IPv6 address with embedded IPv4 addresses. This type of address is used for tunneling IPv6 packets over IPv4 networks, and serves as a transitional mechanism to move from IPv4 to IPv6. There are two primary address types. In the first, only the 32 lower-order bits contain address data; the upper-order bits contain zeros. The second form is called an IPv4-mapped IPv6 address, and precedes the 32-bit IPv4 address with FFFF. Table 3-8 illustrates the structure of IPv6 addresses with embedded IPv4 addresses.

TABLE 3-8

IPv6 Addresses with Embedded IPv4 Addresses

80 Bits	16 Bits	32 Bits
0000 ... 0000	0000 or FFFF	IPv4 Address

Aggregatable global unicast addresses are used to allocate public address pools and are used primarily by ISPs to carve up the public address space on the 6bone (the IPv6 backbone network). Table 3-9 illustrates the structure of aggregatable global unicast addresses.

TABLE 3-9

Aggregatable Global Unicast Addresses

	Public Topology			Site Topology	Interface
FP	TLA ID	RES	NLA ID	SLA ID	Interface ID
001	13 bits	8 bits	24 bits	16 bits	64 bits

The Public Topology portion of the address hierarchy is managed by the large ISPs that maintain the structure of the 6bone and enable them to allocate address pools (aggregates) to smaller organizations, including individual companies and smaller ISPs. The Site Topology portion of the address hierarchy represents the internal routing information needed to route the packets internally. The interface ID provides the information needed to route to individual nodes. Table 3-10 defines the individual components.

TABLE 3-10

Aggregatable Address Components

Item	Field	Bit Length	Description
FP	Format Prefix	3	The value 001 identifies the address as an aggregatable global unicast address.
TLA ID	Top-Level Aggregation	13	Identifies the top-level authority for the routing hierarchy.
RES	Reserved	8	Reserved for future expansion of TLA and NLA fields, when needed.
NLA ID	Next-Level Aggregation ID	24	Used by top-level authorities to define and identify the routing hierarchy for the sites that they service.
SLA ID	Site-Level Aggregation ID	16	Used by organizations to create the internal routing structure to support their networks.
Interface ID	Interface	64	Identifies the interfaces on a link.

Multicast addresses

IPv6 multicast addresses serve much the same purpose as multicast IPv4 addresses, replacing broadcast addresses used in the IPv4 design. A multicast address is assigned to multiple nodes, and all nodes with the same multicast address receive the packets sent to that address. Table 3-11 shows the structure of a multicast address.

TABLE 3-11

IPv6 Multicast Addresses

8 Bits	4 Bits	4 Bits	112 Bits
11111111	Flags	Scope	Group ID

The Format Prefix of 11111111 identifies the address as a multicast address. The Flags field identifies the address type, and the first three bits of the Flags field are reserved as zero. A fourth bit of zero indicates a permanent multicast address assigned by the IANA. A fourth bit of 1 indicates a dynamically assigned address not under the authority of the IANA.

The Scope field defines the scope of the address, as shown in Table 3-12.

TABLE 3-12

Scope Field Values

Value	Scope
0	Reserved
F	Reserved
1	Node-local scope
2	Link-local scope
5	Site-local scope
8	Organization-local scope
E	Global scope
All others	Unassigned

The Group ID field identifies a particular group.

Anycast addresses

Anycast addresses use the same physical structure as unicast addresses. Unlike unicast addresses, however, anycast addresses are assigned to multiple nodes. Currently, only routers can use anycast addresses. A router that needs to send a packet to an anycast address uses a neighbor discovery mechanism to locate the nearest node that owns the specified address. The router then sends the packet to that node.

 See the following section to learn how you can assign IPv6 addresses in Windows Server 2008.

Using IPv6 in Windows Server 2008

Windows Server 2008 includes support for the IPv6 protocol, so you can assign IPv6 addresses to Windows Server 2008 computers. In addition, the RRAS in Windows Server 2008 supports IPv6 packet forwarding and route announcements. This section of the chapter explains how to install and configure the IPv6 protocol in Windows Server 2008.

Installing and configuring IPv6

Installing support for IPv6 in Windows Server 2008 is easy. Open the Network Connections folder from the Control Panel, right-click the interface on which you want to install IPv6, and choose Properties. On the General tab, click Install. Select Protocol and click Add. In the Select Network Protocol dialog box, select Microsoft TCP/IP version 6 and click OK. Then, click Close to close the interface's property sheet. To configure IPv6, click the Properties button. The dialog box in Figure 3-8 appears.

FIGURE 3-8

The IPv6 protocol appears in the interface's properties.

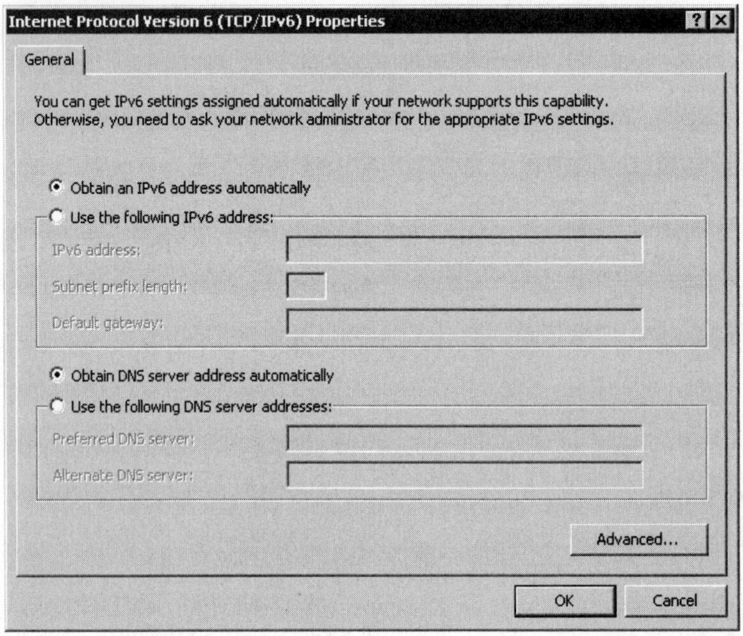

IPv6 address assignment

As with IPv4, you can assign IPv6 addresses either statically or dynamically, but the implications and implementation of automatic address assignment are very different from IPv4. Let's take a look at automatic address assignment first.

IPv6 address autoconfiguration

IPv6 doesn't require the use of a configuration protocol such as DHCP to assign addresses automatically, although IPv6 supports automatic assignment through DHCPv6 servers. Automatic configuration without a DHCPv6 server is called *stateless autoconfiguration*. With this method, the host configures its address using router advertisement messages received from the routers on its link. The result is similar to IPv4 address assignment with APIPA (Automatic Private IP Addressing), which enables Windows platforms to derive a valid IP address from the private 169.254.x.x/16 address space (class B with subnet mask 255.255.0.0). Windows Server 2008 supports stateless autoconfiguration.

IPv6 also provides for *stateful autoconfiguration*, which relies on a DHCPv6 server to allocate the address. However, Windows Server 2008 does not at this point support stateful autoconfiguration, nor does the DHCP service included with Windows Server 2008 support DHCPv6 address allocation. Therefore, you need to either rely on stateless autoconfiguration or configure the address and other properties manually.

Static IPv6 address configuration

Unfortunately, Windows Server 2008 doesn't provide a graphical means to configure IPv6. Instead, you must use the `netsh` command from a console to configure IPv6. Open a command console and issue the following commands to initiate a `Netsh` session to configure IPv6:

```
NETSH
INTERFACE IPV6
```

Next, add the interface and address using the following command:

```
ADD ADDRESS INTERFACE=string ADDRESS=address
```

Replace `string` with the string that identifies the IPv6 interface; `address` specifies the IPv6 address.

Generally, even if you assign the address statically in this way, the computer will determine the default router from router advertisements; however, you can assign the default router statically if need be. Still in the `netsh` IPv6 interface, execute the following command:

```
ADD ROUTE PREFIX=IPv6Address/Integer INTERFACE=string
```

Replace `IPv6Address` with the valid IPv6 address, and `Integer` with the prefix length. Replace `string` with the interface name on which to add the route. If you need to remove a route, use the following commands:

```
SHOW ROUTES
DELETE ROUTE PREFIX=IPv6Address/Integer INTERFACE=string
```

Use the results of the `SHOW ROUTES` command to determine the route prefix and interface index for the route to be deleted. Then replace the `IPv6Address`, `Integer`, and `string` values accordingly.

 See Chapter 5 for a discussion of the implications of IPv6 for DNS. See Chapter 6 for a complete discussion of using Windows Server 2008 for routing and remote access.

Troubleshooting TCP/IP

When TCP/IP works well, life is good. Occasionally, however, TCP/IP connections will fail and you will need to determine the cause of the problem. Windows Server 2008 includes a handful of TCP/IP utilities you can use to test connectivity and troubleshoot connections. This section of the chapter examines TCP/IP troubleshooting in general and the tools included with Windows Server 2008 for that purpose.

Common troubleshooting concepts

As is the case when troubleshooting any problem, the first thing to consider when troubleshooting TCP/IP connections is whether anything has changed in the system's configuration. Problems with a newly installed computer typically point to an invalid IP address, a wrong subnet mask, or an incorrect default gateway. If TCP/IP has never worked on the system, open the TCP/IP properties for the connection and verify that they are correct.

For systems that have been working but have stopped, you need to more narrowly define the problem. For example, if you've been able to connect to a specific Web site but can't anymore, see if you can connect to other sites. If the problem lies with one site, it's almost surely a problem on the server side and not something you can correct on your end. However, if a range of Web sites work but others do not, you probably have a DNS or routing problem. The same holds true for FTP sites and local resources such as other computers on your local segment.

A methodical, logical approach will help you identify the point of failure, if not the cause. Though you could work from the problem backwards, we prefer to troubleshoot from the local computer outward until we find the point of failure, using Packet InterNet Groper (ping). For example, you should first ping the loopback address (type ping 127.0.0.1 or ping localhost from a command prompt) to verify that TCP/IP is functioning on your computer. You can then begin moving farther out into the network and Internet until you find the point at which communication breaks down. Ping a computer on the local segment, and if successful, ping the internal side of the router. If that works, ping the external side of the router, and then a system past the router. If the ping fails at any point, it typically indicates that the packets generated by the ping command are not being returned, either because the remote node is configured to discard ping traffic or a problem with the routing table is preventing the packets from being returned. If ping localhost fails, you probably have a problem with your network interface card or a corrupt TCP/IP protocol stack.

NOTE If you have problems pinging a particular host and know that the host does not discard ping traffic, verify that the host has a properly configured default gateway. If not, the ping traffic will not be properly routed back to you.

The following list describes common problems and potential solutions:

- **TCP/IP won't initialize on the host or a service fails to start.** These problems typically point to a configuration error. Open the properties for the interface and check the settings for TCP/IP closely to make sure they are correct, particularly that you haven't specified a conflicting static IP address. For multi-homed systems, check the priority order of the interfaces. To do so, open the Network Up Connections folder and choose Advanced ➤ Advanced Settings. On the Adapters and Bindings tab, use the Up and Down arrows for the Connections list to move the primary adapter to the top of the list. In addition, verify in the same property page that TCP/IP is bound to the selected adapter.

■ **Communication to other hosts fails, or other hosts don't respond.** This often results from an IP address conflict, network hardware failure, or possibly an incorrect DHCP lease. Use the `ipconfig /all` command to check your IP address, subnet mask, and default gateway settings.

■ **Pinging localhost works but you can't communicate with local or remote hosts.** Verify that you have the correct subnet specified. The ability to ping local hosts but not remote hosts can be caused by incorrect default gateway setting or router problems.

■ **You can ping the local computer by name, but you cannot ping remote computers by name.** You're having a problem with DNS. Verify that you are specifying valid DNS servers in the system's TCP/IP configuration and that those servers are available.

■ **You can ping a non-Windows 2000/XP workstation but can't connect to it using a Windows Server 2008 console command.** You might be experiencing a problem with NetBIOS name resolution. Check WINS settings and verify that you haven't disabled NetBIOS over TCP/IP on the WINS page of the computer's TCP/IP settings. You might also have a problem with the workstation service on the local computer or the computer to which you are trying to connect. This is not a TCP/IP problem, but you would not be alone thinking it is. If the workstation service is stopped, try restarting it. If you can restart it and still have the problem, then name-to-IP address resolving is the likely cause. If you cannot restart the workstation service, you will likely have to reboot the culprit machine. A dead workstation service points to an installation that went bad.

■ **You can connect to a host or Web site by IP address but not by host name.** This is clearly a DNS issue. Verify that your system is configured for valid DNS servers and that the servers are available. (See Chapter 5 for troubleshooting DNS entries.)

Windows Server 2008 includes several utilities for troubleshooting TCP/IP connectivity. The following sections explain these tools, starting with the most basic and sometimes most useful tool: the `ping` command.

ping

In its most basic use, `ping` works like a submarine's sonar: It bounces a packet off a remote host and listens for the return packet. If the packet comes back, you have basic TCP/IP connectivity between the two hosts. Lack of a response can indicate routing problems, a configuration problem with TCP/IP on the local host, unavailability of the remote host, or increasingly, that the remote host is configured to ignore ping traffic.

The `ping` command generates Internet Control Message Protocol (ICMP) packets and transmits them to the designated host, and then waits for a response. The version of `ping` included with Windows Server 2008 sends four packets by default and waits for a period of one second for the response from each. You can specify the number of packets to transmit and the timeout period to override the defaults, if desired. For example, you might send a larger number of packets to test response time over a more realistic sample period. Following is sample output from `ping`:

```
C:\>ping 192.168.0.6

Pinging 192.168.0.6 with 32 bytes of data:

Reply from 192.168.0.6: bytes=32 time=16ms TTL=128
Reply from 192.168.0.6: bytes=32 time<10ms TTL=128
Reply from 192.168.0.6: bytes=32 time=16ms TTL=128
Reply from 192.168.0.6: bytes=32 time<10ms TTL=128

Ping statistics for 192.168.0.6:
    Packets: Sent = 4, Received = 4, Lost = 0 (0% loss),
Approximate round trip times in milli-seconds:
    Minimum = 0ms, Maximum =  16ms, Average =  8ms
```

`ping` is also useful in identifying name resolution problems. If you can ping a host by IP address but not by host name, one of the following could be the cause:

- There is no valid host record in the remote host's domain. Add an entry to the DNS zone or add an entry in your local Hosts file for the remote host.

- You have an incorrect entry in your local Hosts file for the host. Remove or correct the entry in the Hosts file. See Chapter 5 for a discussion of the Hosts and LMHOSTS files.

- Your DNS configuration is incorrect (pointed to wrong or unavailable DNS servers). Correct the configuration and try again.

Before you begin testing any connectivity problem, verify that you can ping your own workstation. Use `ping` to perform an internal loopback test that verifies whether or not TCP/IP is functioning on your computer. Use one of the following commands to ping your own computer:

```
ping 127.0.0.1
ping localhost
ping YourIPAddress
Following is the syntax for the ping command:
ping [-t] [-a] [-n count] [-l size] [-f] [-i ttl] [-v tos]
[-r count][-s count] [[-j HostList] | [-k HostList]]
[-w timeout] [-R] [-S srcaddr] [-4] [-6] target_name
```

Table 3-13 describes the switches you can use with `ping`.

TABLE 3-13

ping Command Switches

Switch	Function	Use
-t	Pings continuously until terminated by Ctrl+C. Press Ctrl+Break to view statistics.	Perform extended testing or check for intermittent problems.
-a	Resolves address to host name	Test name resolution and troubleshoot Hosts file.
-n count	Specifies number of packets to send	Perform extended testing.
-l size	Specifies packet size in bytes; the default is 64, the maximum is 8,192	Check for packet fragmentation and response time.
-f	Sets Don't Fragment flag in packet	Prevent routers from fragmenting packet.
-i ttl	Sets packet time-to-live	Increase timeout on slow connections.
-v tos	Sets Type of Service field	Specify type of action remote router should perform on the packet.
-r count	Records packet route; specify from 1 to 9	Determine route of outgoing and incoming packets.
-s count	Sets timestamp for number of hops specified by count	Set current hop count for the packet.
-j HostList	Routes packets using host list; specify maximum of 9 hosts	Direct traffic through specific route; hosts can be separated by intermediate gateways (loose source route).
-k HostList	Routes packets using host list	Similar to -j but hosts can't be separated by intermediate gateways (strict source route).
-w timeout	Sets packet timeout in milliseconds	Increase timeout value to overcome timeout on slow connections.
-R	Traces a round-trip path	Trace back to client; used on IPv6 only.
-S srcaddr	Source address to use	Specify source address to ping from; used on IPv6 only.
-4	Forces IPv4	Force ping to use IPv4; not necessary if specifying IPv4 address.
-6	Forces IPv6	Force ping to use IPv6.
target_name	Specifies remote host(s) to ping	Specify destination to ping.

ping and IPv6

You can use the ping command to test connectivity to systems that use IPv6. To test the function of the stack, ping the local interface using the following command:

```
ping ::1
```

If that works, try pinging the local computer using its IPv6 address, rather than the localhost address. Use the following command to ping a link-local node:

```
ping address
```

Replace address with the link-local address of the other node. Next, try pinging a different host using the same format, replacing address with the IPv6 address of the remote node and optionally using -s to specify the source interface. See Table 3-13 for a list of additional command switches you can use with ping to test IPv6 connectivity.

ipconfig

Use the ipconfig command to display configured TCP/IP properties for all adapters, set certain properties, renew or release address leases, and update host records through dynamic DNS. The ipconfig command is useful for determining TCP/IP settings on any system, but is most helpful for determining settings on systems that obtain settings through DHCP. Knowing your address and related settings is the first step in troubleshooting any connectivity problem. In addition, you can use ipconfig to release and renew a lease, set a class ID, manage the DNS cache, and request an update of the host record in DNS.

 The equivalent tool for ipconfig in Windows 9x is WINIPCFG.EXE.

The following shows the syntax for ipconfig:

```
Ipconfig [/all | /renew [adapter] | /release [adapter] | /flushdns |
/displadns | /registerdns /showclassid [adapter] | /setclassid
adapter [classid]
```

Table 3-14 lists the switches and their uses.

netstat

The netstat command provides three primary functions: monitoring connections to remote hosts, viewing protocol statistics for a connection, and extracting the IP address of a host to which you've connected using domain names (or determining domain name if connected by address). The syntax for netstat is as follows:

```
netstat [-a] [-enos] [-p protocol] [-r] [interval]
```

Table 3-15 describes the options you can use with netstat.

TABLE 3-14

ipconfig Command Switches

Switch	Function	Use
/all	Shows all TCP/IP properties, including MAC address	Obtain complete information; omit to view only address, subnet mask, and gateway.
/renew [adapter]	Renews DHCP properties on adapter	Omit adapter to renew DHCP properties on all adapters.
/release [adapter]	Releases current DHCP lease on adapter	Release address, disabling TCP/IP for adapter; omit adapter to release all leases.
/flushdns	Purges local DNS resolver cache	Overcome problems with bad cache entries.
/registerdns	Refreshes all leases and register host name with DNS	Ensure up-to-date host records in DNS; dynamic updates require a Windows Server 2003 DNS server.
/displaydns	Displays contents of local resolver cache	Check cache for potential bad entries.
/showclassid	Displays all class IDs allowed for adapter	Class IDs enable DHCP to assign properties on a client-by-client basis, using the class ID as the client identifier.
/setclassid	Sets the current class ID for *adapter*	See above.

TABLE 3-15

netstat Command Switches

Switch	Function	Use
-a	Displays all connections	Show all connections, including server connections.
-b	Displays executable that created connection	Identify programs that open specific connections.
-e	Shows Ethernet statistics	Use with -s.

continued

Switch	Function	Use
`-n`	Shows addresses and port numbers in numerical format	Use numerical rather than `host.domain` format.
`-o`	Displays owning process ID	Show the ID of the process that owns each connection.
`-s`	Shows statistics on per-protocol basis	`netstat` by default shows TCP, UDP, ICMP, and IP.
`-p protocol`	Shows connections for `protocol`	View connections for a specific protocol.
`-r`	Shows contents of routing table	Troubleshoot routing problems.
`-v`	Shows components that created connection	Use with `-b` to identify programs that open specific connections.
`interval`	Specifies interval for update; terminate with Ctrl+C	Omit `interval` to display information a single time.

TABLE 3-15   (continued)

As mentioned earlier in this chapter, you can use `netstat` to determine the IP address of a remote host. To do so, issue the command `netstat -n`. The following examples first issue `netstat` with no parameters, and then use `-n` to derive IP addresses:

```
C:\>netstat

Active Connections

    Proto  Local Address          Foreign Address          State
    TCP    bart:netbios-ssn       NOTE2KSRV:1117           ESTABLISHED
    TCP    bart:3454              ftp.BayNetworks.COM:ftp  ESTABLISHED

C:\>netstat -n

Active Connections

    Proto  Local Address          Foreign Address          State
    TCP    192.168.0.1:139        192.168.0.2:1117         ESTABLISHED
    TCP    209.105.38.181:3454    134.177.3.22:21          ESTABLISHED
```

This example shows two connections: a local connection to a server named NOTE2KSRV and another to `ftp.baynetworks.com`. Note that the second example displays the IP address, rather than the host name.

hostname

Use the `hostname` command to derive the host name of the local computer. If no host name is set through the DNS properties for the computer, the computer name set in the

Network Identification tab of the computer's properties is used as the host name. Using the `hostname` command is often easier than opening the properties for the connection to hunt for the host name. There are no options for the `hostname` command.

tracert

Being able to determine the route used to connect to a given host is extremely useful in troubleshooting routing problems. Use `tracert` to trace the route used to connect to another host and determine where, if at all, a connection is failing. For example, if you're having problems reaching sites on the Internet, you can use `tracert` to locate the problem and identify the router where the traffic is dying.

Like `ping`, `tracert` generates ICMP packets, but the `tracert` command sends a series of ICMP packets to the destination host using steadily incrementing time-to-live (TTL) values. Each gateway decrements the TTL value by one. The first packet has a TTL of 1, so it is decremented to 0 by the first gateway, which then sends an ICMP Time Exceeded packet back to the originating host (your computer) along with the transit time in milliseconds. The local host then transmits the next packet with a TTL of 2. The first gateway decrements it to 1, and the second gateway decrements it to 0. The second gateway then sends back the ICMP Time Exceeded packet. Subsequent packets make it one gateway, or *hop*, further than the previous one before being expired. The result is a table showing the data for each packet. When the packets stop coming back, you've potentially identified the problem router.

The following is a sample output from `tracert` (text in bold is the typed command):

```
C:\>tracert ftp.happypuppy.com

Tracing route to ftp.happypuppy.com [199.105.102.130]
over a maximum of 30 hops:

  1   110 ms   109 ms    125 ms   USR1RRT-TS1.DialUp.rrt.net
[209.105.38.198]
  2   109 ms    94 ms    125 ms   CISCO1RRTGW-TS.DialUp.rrt.net
[209.105.38.50]
  3   281 ms   110 ms     94 ms   border1-h4-0.ply.mr.net
[207.229.192.1]
  4   109 ms    94 ms    110 ms   core1-A0-0-0-722.PLY.MR.Net
[137.192.7.141]
  5   125 ms   109 ms    109 ms   Serial5-1-0.GW2.MSP1.ALTER.NET
[157.130.98.189]
  6   109 ms   109 ms    125 ms   152.ATM3-0.XR2.CHI4.ALTER.NET
[146.188.209.134]
  7   141 ms   125 ms    125 ms   194.ATM3-0.TR2.CHI4.ALTER.NET
[146.188.208.230]
  8   140 ms   141 ms    125 ms   106.ATM7-0.TR2.EWR1.ALTER.NET
[146.188.136.126]
  9   141 ms   125 ms    140 ms   196.ATM6-0.XR2.EWR1.ALTER.NET
```

```
[146.188.176.81]
 10   172 ms   141 ms    140 ms   192.ATM9-0-0.GW3.EWR1.ALTER.NET
[146.188.177.169]
 11   907 ms   953 ms    891 ms   ftp.happypuppy.com [199.105.102.130]

Trace complete.
```

The following is the syntax for `tracert`:

```
Tracert [-d] [-h max_hops] [-j hostlist] [-w timeout] [-R]
[-S srcaddr] [-4] [-6] target_name
```

Table 3-16 describes the switches for `tracert`.

TABLE 3-16

tracert Command Switches

Switch	Function	Use
-d	Does not resolve names of interim systems	Simplify output.
-h max_hops	Specifies maximum hops to trace	Limit testing to specified number of hops.
-w timeout	Sets time in milliseconds to wait for reply	Overcome slow connections.
-j hostlist	Specifies a loose-source route along hostlist	Perform a trace along the specified route.
-R	Traces round-trip path	Use on IPv6 only to trace back to the source.
-S srcaddr	Specifies the source address	Use on IPv6 only to specify the source IP address.
-4	Forces IPv4	Force tracert to use IPv4; not necessary when specifying IPv4 address.
-6	Forces IPv6	Force tracert to use IPv6; not necessary when specifying IPv6 address.
target_name	Returns the FQDN or IP address of destination host	Specify the destination.

arp

The `arp` command, which stands for Address Resolution Protocol, enables you to view the arp table on your local computer, which associates physical MAC addresses of other computers on the local network with their IP addresses. The arp table speeds up connections by eliminating the need to look up MAC addresses for subsequent connections. Viewing the contents of the arp table can be useful for troubleshooting connections to specific computers on the network.

The following are the syntaxes for the `arp` command:

```
arp -s inet_addr eth_addr [if_addr]
arp -d inet_addr [if_addr]
arp -a [inet_addr] [-N if_addr]
```

Table 3-17 describes the options for `arp`.

TABLE 3-17

arp Command Switches

Switch	Function	Use
-a or -g	Shows arp table data for all hosts	Provide a detailed view.
-d inet_addr	Removes entry for inet_addr from arp cache	Clear up a connection problem due to a bad arp cache entry.
-s Inet_addr eth_addr	Adds new arp cache entry for Inet_addr pointing to eth_address	Add an entry for specified host.
-N IfAddr	Displays arp entries for interface specified by IfAddr	Display arp entries.

route

You can use the `route` command to view or modify entries in the local computer's static routing table. Static routes are used in place of implicit routes determined by the default gateway for the computer. For example, you can add a static route to direct traffic destined for a specific host through a gateway other than the default to improve response time, reduce costs, and so on. The `route` command is also useful for troubleshooting, either for identifying incorrect static routes or for adding temporary routes to bypass a problem gateway.

The syntax for `route` is as follows:

```
route [-f] [-p] [print|add|delete|change] [destination] [MASK
netmask] [gateway] [METRIC metric]
```

Table 3-18 explains the options for `route`.

TABLE 3-18

route Command Switches

Switch	Function	Use
-f	Clears all gateway entries from table	
-p	Use with add to create a persistent route	Nonpersistent routes are lost at each boot.
Print	Prints a route	
Add	Adds a route to the table	Use -p to make the route persistent for subsequent sessions.
Delete	Deletes a route from the table	
Change	Modifies an existing route	
Destination	Specifies the host address	
MASK netmask	Uses subnet mask specified by netmask	If MASK isn't used, defaults to 255.255.255.255.
Gateway	Specifies the address of gateway for route	
METRIC metric	Specifies the metric, or cost, for the route using the value metric	
IF interface	Specifies the interface for routing table to modify	

You can use the wildcards * and ? with the print and delete switches. As with filenames, a * matches any number of characters, and a ? matches one character.

nbtstat

Use the nbtstat command to display statistics for NetBIOS-over-TCP/IP (NetBT) connections. You also can use nbtstat to purge the name cache and reload the Hosts file, which offers the benefit of reloading the LMHOSTS file without rebooting.

The following is the syntax for nbtstat:

```
nbtstat [-a RemoteName] [-A RemoteAddress] [-c] [-n]
[-R] [-RR] [-r] [-S] [-s] interval
```

Table 3-19 describes the switches for nbtstat.

TABLE 3-19

nbtstat Command Switches

Switch	Function
`-a RemoteName`	Shows the NetBIOS name table for computer `RemoteName`
`-A RemoteAddress`	Shows the NetBIOS name table for computer at the IP address `RemoteAddress`
`-c`	Shows contents of the NetBIOS name cache
`-n`	Shows NetBIOS names for the local computer
`-R`	Purges the NetBIOS name cache and reloads `LMHOSTS`
`-RR`	Submits Name Release packets to WINS, then refreshes
`-r`	Shows NetBIOS name resolution statistics
`-S`	Shows current NetBIOS workstation and server sessions by IP address
`-s`	Shows current NetBIOS workstation and server sessions by name
`Interval`	Returns number of seconds between subsequent display of protocol statistics

Legacy protocols

Microsoft has continued to support a number of legacy protocols in Windows Server. Windows Server 2008, however, clearly puts these protocols behind the network administrator, and you should begin to phase these out like an old OS such as Windows NT. I have left this section in for network administrators who have legacy protocols to support. These will need to be supported on your Windows Server 2003 machines. The following sections explain these protocols and their properties, but I do not provide a detailed explanation of how these protocols are structured or how they function.

NetBEUI

NetBEUI is one of two protocols that support NetBIOS, the name resolution method used by previous Microsoft operating systems, including DOS, Windows 3.x, Windows for Workgroups, Windows 9x, and Windows NT.

NetBEUI is useful on small networks because it is easy to install and configure. As the number of nodes on the network increases, however, NetBEUI becomes less practical due to the amount of network traffic it generates. In addition, NetBEUI is not routable, which limits it to local segments only.

> **TIP** NetBEUI can be routed if encapsulated in PPTP or L2TP for a VPN connection. This enables you to use NetBEUI for accessing resources on remote networks, but it also requires a TCP/IP link between the two networks.

There are no configurable properties for NetBEUI. Simply install the NetBEUI protocol on the selected interface and ensure that all nodes using NetBEUI on the network have unique names.

IPX/SPX

Like TCP/IP, IPX/SPX is actually two protocols: Internetwork Packet eXchange and Sequenced Packet eXchange. IPX/SPX provides connectivity for Novell NetWare servers and clients, but it can also serve as a primary network protocol when no NetWare servers are present.

With IPX/SPX, two types of numbers are used to route traffic: the external network number and the internal network number. The *external network number* is associated with the physical network adapter and network. All nodes on the network that use the same frame type (explained shortly) must use the same external network number. You can specify an external network number manually or allow Windows Server 2008 to detect it automatically. The external network number is a hexadecimal value between one and eight digits.

The *internal network number* identifies a virtual network in the computer, and programs identify themselves as being located on this virtual network, rather than the physical network identified by the external network number. Each virtual network appears as a separate network to the user. By default, Windows Server 2008 assigns the value 00000000 as the internal network number. The internal network number helps improve routing in multi-homed systems or in a system where more than one frame type is used on a single adapter.

The following are the configuration properties for the IPX/SPX protocol:

- **Internal Network Number.** This property defines the internal network number associated with the interface.

- **Auto Frame Type Detection.** Select this option to allow Windows Server 2008 to automatically detect the frame type. If multiple frame types are detected in addition to 802.2, NWLink defaults to 802.2.

- **Manual Frame Type Detection.** Select this option to manually configure the frame type or to configure multiple frame types. Specify the internal network number for each: Choose 802.2 for NetWare 3.3 or later on Ethernet; choose 802.3 for other Ethernet configurations; choose 802.5 for Token Ring adapters.

DLC

DLC stands for Data Link Control. All network adapters have a DLC address or DLC identifier (called a DLCI, pronounced *del-see*). Some protocols, including Ethernet and Token Ring, use DLC exclusively to identify nodes on the network. Other protocols use logical addresses to identify nodes. TCP/IP, for example, uses the IP address to identify a node. However, at the lower layers of the network, some translation still needs to take place to convert the logical address to the DLC address. Address Resolution Protocol (ARP) performs this translation for TCP/IP.

DLC is required as a protocol only for those situations where DLC is used rather than a logical address. For example, DLC enables Windows Server 2008 computers to connect to IBM mainframe systems and use DLC-enabled network printers.

There are no user-configurable properties for DLC.

SNMP

Simple Network Management Protocol (SNMP) provides a standardized means for managing hosts on TCP/IP (and IPX) networks. SNMP enables hosts to communicate with one another and is commonly used for remote monitoring and configuration. For example, you might use an SNMP management tool to manage routers or other devices in your network, gather information about workstations on the network, detect unauthorized attempts to reconfigure certain network devices, and so on.

Understanding how SNMP works

SNMP functions through SNMP management systems and SNMP agents. A *management system* is an application that requests information from SNMP *agents* and directs agents to perform certain tasks, such as setting options on the remote device or returning configuration data. For example, you might have a non-Windows Server 2008 router on the network that contains firmware to enable it to function as an SNMP agent. You use a management system (SNMP-aware application) on your local workstation to manage the router, by viewing and changing the router's configuration and monitoring its status.

SNMP management systems send SNMP *messages* to agents, which respond to those messages. In most cases, the management system requests information from a *management information base*, or MIB, managed by the agent. The MIB is a set of objects that function as a database of information about the managed host. The only message an SNMP agent generates on its own is a *trap*, which is an alarm-triggered event on the agent host. A system reboot on the agent host is an example of a trap.

SNMP uses *communities* to provide a limited amount of security for SNMP and a means of grouping SNMP management systems with agents. Agents respond only to management systems in the list of communities to which they belong. The community name serves as a password for access by the management system to the agent. Agents can belong to multiple communities.

The SNMP service included with Windows Server 2008 enables a Windows Server 2008 computer to function as an SNMP agent to allow remote administration of the following:

- Windows 2000/2003, Windows Server 2008
- Windows 2000/XP/Vista
- Windows Server 2008–based DHCP

- Windows Server 2008–based WINS
- Internet Information Services (IIS)
- LAN Manager
- Exchange 2000/2003, 2007 and later
- SQL Server 2000, 2005, 2008 or later

Windows Server 2008 core does not include any management system software, and the SNMP service functions only as an SNMP agent. However, there are third-party SNMP management tools for Windows Server 2008 and related services.

Installing and configuring SNMP

You add the SNMP service through the Add Features wizard.

TIP Also install the WMI SNMP Provider if you want to be able to manage the server through the Windows Management Interface.

The following sections explain how to configure the SNMP service (set community names and other tasks). You manage the SNMP service through the properties for the SNMP service. You can access the service through the Services console in the Administrative Tools folder or through the Services snap-in in the Computer Management console.

Configuring agent properties

After installing the SNMP service, you need to configure agent properties, which includes general information such as who is responsible for managing the agent host and the types of services with which the agent will interact on the computer.

Right-click the SNMP service in the Services console and choose Properties to open the properties for the SNMP Service, or select the service and choose Action ➢ Properties to display the service's property sheet. The General, Log On, Recovery, and Dependencies pages are the same as for other services. Click the Agent tab to configure the following agent properties:

- **Contact.** Specify the name of the person responsible for managing the host computer.
- **Location.** Specify the physical location of the computer or the contact's location or other information (phone number, extension, and so on).
- **Physical.** Select this option if the agent host manages physical hardware such as hard disk partitions.
- **Applications.** Select this option if the agent uses any applications that transmit data using the TCP/IP protocol.
- **Datalink and Subnetwork.** Select this option if the agent host manages a bridge.
- **Internet.** Select this option if the agent host is an Internet gateway.
- **End-to-End.** Select this option if the host uses IP. This option should always be selected.

Configuring traps

Use the Traps tab of the SNMP service to configure computers to which the SNMP service sends traps. From the Community Name drop-down list, select the community for which you want to assign a trap destination. If you have no communities set yet, type the community name in the combo box and click Add to List. Then, click Add to display a simple dialog box in which you specify the host name, IP address, or IPX address of the remote computer to receive the trap notification. Repeat the process to add other trap destinations as needed.

Configuring security

Use the Security tab of the SNMP Service's properties to configure the communities in which the agent participates and optionally a list of hosts from which the agent accepts SNMP packets. By default, the agent accepts packets from all hosts. This presents a security risk, however, so take care to configure security settings to allow SNMP traffic only from authorized hosts. The Security page contains the following options:

- **Send Authentication Trap.** Select this option to have the agent send a message to all trap destinations if the agent receives an SNMP request from a host or community not listed in the "Accepted community names" list or the "Accept SNMP packets from these hosts" list. The message is sent to all hosts in the trap destination list on the Traps property page to indicate that a remote management system failed authentication (potentially indicating an unauthorized access attempt).

- **Accepted Community Names.** Use this list and the associated buttons to modify the list of communities in which the agent participates and the community rights for each. You can select from the following rights:

    - **None.** This option prevents the agent host from processing any SNMP requests from the specified community. For example, you might configure None for the Public community for enhanced security.

    - **Notify.** Select this option to allow the agent host to send traps only to the selected community.

    - **Read Only.** Use this option to allow remote consoles to view data in the local MIB but not change it. This option prevents the agent from processing SNMP SET requests.

    - **Read Write.** Use this option to allow remote consoles to make changes on the managed system. This option allows the agent to process SNMP SET requests.

    - **Read Create.** Use this option to allow the agent to create new entries in the SNMP tables.

- **Accept SNMP Packets from Any Host.** Select this option to allow the agent to process requests from all hosts in the "Accepted community names" list.

- **Accept SNMP PACKETS from These Hosts.** Select this option to define a specific list of hosts from which the agent will process SNMP requests.

Translating events to traps

To trap events and enable the agent to transmit the traps to the management systems defined in its Traps properties, you need to first translate the event to an SNMP trap. For example, to trap a system shutdown, you need to convert the system event 513 to an SNMP trap.

Windows Server 2008 provides two utilities you can use to translate local events to SNMP traps. The first, `evntcmd.exe`, is a command-line utility you can integrate in batch files or use dynamically from a command console. For a description of command switches for `evntcmd`, issue the `evntcmd /?` command at a console prompt. The other tool, `evntwin.exe`, provides a graphical user interface for translating events to traps. Click Start ➤ Run and enter `evntwin` to run the Event to Trap Translator.

To translate a trap, select the Custom option and click Edit to expand the dialog box to include the Event Sources and Events lists (see Figure 3-9). Search through the Event Sources list to find the source of the event you want to trap (such as Security for system shutdown, startup, logon, and so on). In the Events list, locate and select the event you want to trap, and then click Add. Windows Server 2008 displays the Properties dialog box, which contains the following two options:

- **If Event Count Reaches.** Specify how many times the event can occur before a trap is generated.

- **Within the Time Interval.** Specify an optional time interval in which the number of events specified by the previous option must occur to generate a trap.

After you specify the properties for the trap, click OK to add it to the list. Repeat the process for any other events you need to trap.

Setting general properties

You can configure a handful of settings in the Event to Trap Translator to limit trap length and throttle the number of traps transmitted by the agent. With the Event to Trap Translator program open, click Settings to display the Settings dialog box. Configure the following options as needed:

- **Limit Trap Length.** Select this option to limit the length of data sent with the trap to the number of bytes specified by the following option.

- **Trap Length *n* Bytes.** Set the size in bytes for the trap. Any additional data is truncated if the trap exceeds the specified length.

- **Trim Insertion Strings First.** Trim insertion strings from the trap data before truncating the data when the trap exceeds the specified length.

- **Trim Formatted Message First.** Trim formatted message text from the trap data before truncating the data when the trap exceeds the specified length.

- **Apply Throttle.** Select this option to limit the number of traps that can be sent in a given period of time.

- **Don't Apply Throttle.** Setting this allows an unlimited number of traps to be transmitted.
- **Number of Traps.** Set the maximum number of traps allowed in the given time frame when throttling is turned on.
- **Interval of Time (Seconds).** Set the interval, in seconds, that the specified number of traps can be transmitted before throttling takes effect.

FIGURE 3-9

The Event to Trap Translator, expanded to show event sources.

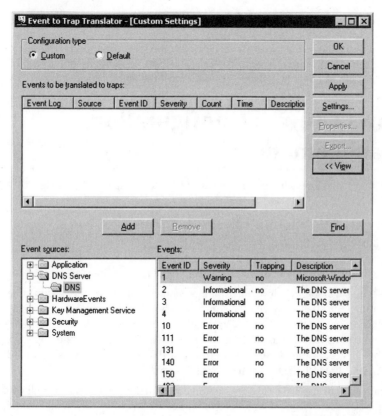

Exporting the trap list

After you've taken the time to weed through the Events list and create traps for a number of events, you probably will want to archive the data in case you experience a problem with the Event to Trap Translator or the system and need to reconfigure the traps. You might also want to configure the same traps on several other systems without having to reconfigure them manually. The solution in both situations is to export the trap list. After you have the traps configured as needed, click Export in the Event to Trap Translator. Windows Server 2008 prompts you for a filename. Save the file in an appropriate archive location or where you can access it from the other workstations. The file automatically receives a `.cnf` file extension.

Use the `evntcmd` command to load the Events list into the system. For example, the following command will load the file `events.cnf` from a network share into the local computer:

```
Evntcmd \\srv2\config\events.cnf
```

Use the following command to load the file from a local file named `netevents.cnf` to a remote system named work23:

```
Evntcmd -s work23 c:\snmp-stuff\netevents.cnf
```

When configuring traps on a remote computer, the SNMP service need not be running on the local computer. You will, however, have to copy the `evntcmd.exe` application to the local computer, because it is not installed by default (it installs with the SNMP service).

Windows Firewall Configuration and Management

This section explores Windows Firewall and explains how to configure and manage it.

Overview of Windows Firewall changes

Windows Firewall is secure, yet geared to deliver performance:

- ■ **On by default.** Windows Firewall is enabled for all network interfaces by default.
- ■ **Boot-time security.** Windows Firewall incorporates a selection of boot-time filters that restrict the traffic that can reach the computer while it is booting and until the system loads and initializes the network drivers and run-time firewall. Traffic is restricted to only those ports required to boot the system, such as DNS, DHCP, and application of Group Policy. Boot-time security is controlled with the run-time firewall; if you disable the run-time firewall, the boot-time firewall is also disabled.
- ■ **Global configuration.** To simplify firewall configuration, Windows Firewall by default uses the same configuration for all network interfaces. You can then modify settings for individual interfaces as needed.
- ■ **Local subnet restriction.** Windows Firewall includes the capability to restrict incoming traffic to one of three sources:
  - ▪ **My network (subnet) only.** Allow traffic from sources in the same subnet as the server.

◼ **Any computer (including those on the Internet).** Allow traffic from any source.

◼ **Custom list.** Allow traffic from a list of individual computers or subnets, or a range of IP addresses you specify.

◼ **On with No Exceptions Mode.** This mode ignores any preconfigured exceptions and drops all unsolicited traffic, making it easy to temporarily lock down the interface without reconfiguring ports or application exceptions.

◼ **Windows Firewall Exceptions Lists.** You can configure specific application exceptions to allow those applications to receive incoming traffic through ports that are blocked for all other applications. The benefit is that Windows, rather than the application, controls the port and can close it if the application hangs.

◼ **Multiple Profiles.** You can configure different firewall profiles for different situations. This feature is primarily targeted at client systems, but it can be useful for servers in troubleshooting situations.

◼ **RPC Support.** ICF did not support RPC traffic, which is required for several common services such as file and printer sharing and remote administration. With Windows Firewall in place, an application can request that Windows Firewall open the necessary ports as long as the application is running in the Local System, Network Service, or Local Service security contexts. You can also configure the RPC application on the exceptions list to enable it to accept incoming traffic on dynamic ports.

◼ **Restore Defaults and Unattended Setup.** You can easily restore the default firewall settings, as well as modify what Windows Firewall maintains as its default settings. In addition, you can specify a custom firewall configuration for unattended Windows Server setup.

◼ **Group policy support.** Windows Firewall can be fully configured and managed with Group Policy settings.

◼ **Multicast and broadcast traffic.** Windows Firewall will allow a unicast response for three seconds on the same port from which multicast or broadcast traffic came. This feature makes it possible for applications and services to alter firewall policy to accommodate client-server scenarios that use multicast and broadcast traffic, without unduly exposing ports.

◼ **IPv4 and IPv6 support.** Windows Firewall supports unified configuration for both IPv4 and IPv6 traffic, eliminating the need to configure firewall settings separately for each protocol.

Configuring Windows Firewall

To configure Windows Firewall on a server through a GUI, open the Windows Firewall applet in the Control Panel. If the Windows Firewall/Internet Connection Sharing (ICS) service is not running, the applet asks if you want to start the service. Figure 3-10 shows the Windows Firewall property sheet.

FIGURE 3-10

The Windows Firewall configuration interface.

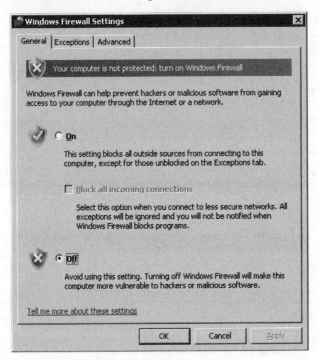

Turning on the firewall is as easy as clicking On and then clicking OK. However, you'll likely want to configure exceptions and set advanced settings. To configure exceptions to allow specific applications or ports, click the Exceptions tab, shown in Figure 3-11.

As Figure 3-11 indicates, Windows Firewall includes a small selection of exceptions by default. These include File and Printer Sharing, Remote Desktop, and UPnP Framework. However, none of these exceptions is enabled by default. To enable one, place a check beside its entry.

To add a program exception, click Add Program. Windows Firewall displays an Add a Program dialog box in which you select the application's executable. If adding a port, click the Add Port button instead, which displays the Add a Port dialog box, in which you specify a name and the port number (see Figure 3-12).

FIGURE 3-11

Add application or port exceptions on the Exceptions tab.

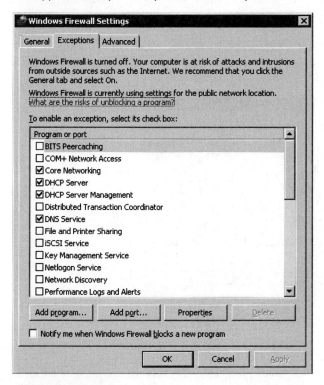

FIGURE 3-12

Use the Add a Port dialog box to open a port in the firewall.

When adding an application or port exception, you must specify the scope for the exception. The scope determines the source traffic to which the exception will be applied. To set the scope, click the Change Scope button on the Add an Application or Add a Port dialog box. Figure 3-13 shows the resulting Change Scope dialog box.

FIGURE 3-13

Specify rule scope with the Change Scope dialog box.

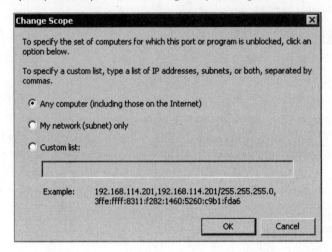

As mentioned previously in this chapter, you can specify that the rule apply to all sources, to only addresses on the local subnet, or to a custom list of addresses, hosts, or IP ranges.

> **TIP** The Exceptions tab includes an option labeled "Notify me when Windows Firewall blocks a new program." Enable this option if you want the firewall to notify you when an application attempts to access ports for which it has not be designated an exception.

You can also configure a selection of advanced options for the firewall. To do so, click the Advanced tab (see Figure 3-14). The network interfaces installed on the computer appear in the Network connection list. You can enable or disable Windows Firewall for a specific interface — just select or deselect the checkbox beside the interface name.

The final group on the Advanced tab, Default Settings, enables you to quickly restore Windows Firewall to its default settings. Just click Restore Defaults to do so.

FIGURE 3-14

Configure additional settings on the Advanced tab.

Managing Windows Firewall with Group Policy

In a well-managed network, it's likely that you will want to manage Windows Firewall settings using Group Policy. Windows Server 2008 adds several Group Policy settings to the Computer Configuration\Administrative Templates\Network\Network Connections\Windows Firewall Group Policy branch. This branch contains two sub-branches, Domain Profile and Standard Profile (see Chapter 24). The settings control Windows Firewall in domain and nondomain environments, respectively.

Managing Windows Firewall from a console

In many situations, you'll find it useful to be able to manage Windows Firewall settings from a console, whether for a local or remote server. The netsh console command also allows Windows Firewall configuration. The commands available in netsh for firewall management include the following:

- **Add.** Add programs or ports to the exceptions list and specify scope for the new rule.
- **Delete.** Remove programs or ports from the exceptions list.

- **Dump.** Dump the current configuration to a script.
- **Reset.** Reset Windows Firewall to its default settings.
- **Set.** Configure individual Windows Firewall settings (allow programs and ports, ICMP configuration, and so on).
- **Show.** Show the current firewall configuration.

To manage Windows Firewall with `netsh`, open a command console and execute the `netsh` command. Then, execute the firewall command in the `netsh` interface to enter firewall management mode. For help with specific commands, type a command followed by the ? character.

Windows Firewall with Advanced Security

Windows Server 2008 ships with an advanced security version of the firewall. Called Windows Firewall with Advanced Security, it resembles a traditional firewall configuration utility a la ISA Server. To open this console, double-click the option in Administrative Tools or Server Manager (under Configuration). The console that loads is shown in Figure 3-15.

FIGURE 3-15

Windows Firewall with Advanced Security console.

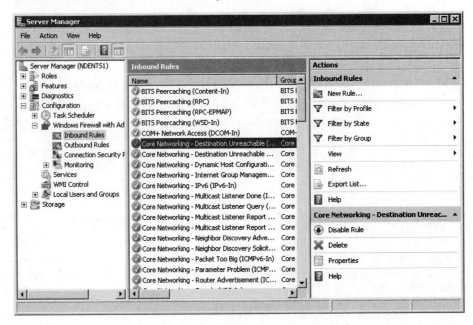

The console lets you set inbound and outbound filtering rules as well as connection security rules. Rules can be set for applications, ports, various predefined services, and custom settings.

The Ports option, for example, lets you filter according to the protocol (UDP or TCP) and the ports being targeted. Figure 3-16 demonstrates setting up a new Protocol/Port rule.

FIGURE 3-16

Creating a new Protocol and Ports rule.

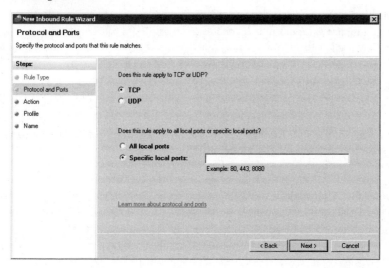

The ICMP and the Security Logging setting are now managed from the Windows Firewall with Advanced Security console. Security Logging enables you to configure logging options for Windows Firewall. Click the Customize button to open the Log Settings dialog box, where you can specify which events are logged, the location of the log file, and the maximum size of the file.

ICMP options are now enables by creating inbound and outbound rules using the ICMPv4 or ICMPv6 protocols.

Summary

The Transmission Control Protocol/Internet Protocol (TCP/IP) is the protocol of choice for many networks, partly because of the proliferation of the Internet, but also for the flexibility the protocol offers. TCP/IP is a complex protocol, however, so you need to address several issues when you configure a network for TCP/IP. Once you understand addressing and subnet issues, you need to decide how systems will receive their IP addresses (statically or dynamically) and assignments for name servers, gateways, and so on. You can use DHCP to automatically configure TCP/IP settings for clients on the network, which simplifies administration and helps protect against address conflicts from statically assigned addresses (see

Chapter 4). You can have local clients retrieve IP address leases from an external network through a DHCP relay agent. A Windows Server 2008 server running RRAS can function as a DHCP relay agent. RRAS is covered in Chapter 6.

Although its use is still currently rather limited, IPv6 will continue to gain popularity as development of the 6bone continues and companies realize the benefits offered by IPv6.

Several tools included with Windows Server 2008 will help you troubleshoot TCP/IP connections. The `ping` command, for example, is one of the most useful tools for checking basic TCP/IP connectivity. Other tools enable you to trace network routes, view IP configurations, view routing tables, and perform other troubleshooting tasks.

One final topic covered in this chapter is SNMP, or Simple Network Management Protocol. Windows Server 2008 includes an SNMP agent that enables the computer to respond to SNMP requests from local and remote management services. You can configure a Windows Server 2008 server to generate traps for specific events and have those traps transmitted to specific management services for monitoring and administration purposes.

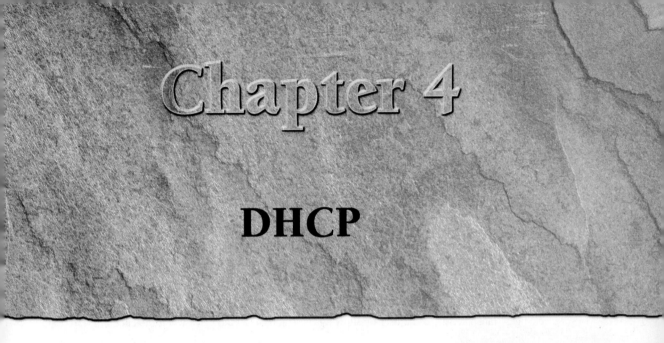

DHCP

This chapter covers configuring and managing a Windows Server–based Dynamic Host Configuration Protocol (DHCP) server and DHCP clients.

Overview of DHCP

The TCP/IP protocol, which is required for Internet connectivity and has become the protocol of choice for most intranets, requires that each node on the network have a unique IP address. This includes any individual network object, such as a server, workstation, printer, or router. You can assign IP addresses to network nodes either *statically* or *dynamically*. With a statically assigned address, you specify a fixed address for a given node, and that address never changes unless you manually change it. Static assignment is the option used when the network node must always have the same IP address. Web and FTP servers or devices such as printers that don't support anything other than static assignments are prime examples of devices with statically assigned addresses.

You also can assign IP addresses dynamically through the Dynamic Host Configuration Protocol (DHCP). DHCP enables network nodes to take IP address assignments from a DHCP server automatically at startup. Although dynamic assignment means that IP addresses for network nodes can (and do) sometimes change each time the node is restarted, that poses a problem only when a computer needs the same IP address for every session. In all other situations, including for most workstations and many servers, dynamic assignment enables you to manage a pool of

IP addresses more effectively to prevent address conflicts. DHCP also enables you to allocate a smaller number of IP addresses than the number of computers using them, provided the maximum number of live nodes at any given time doesn't exceed the number of available addresses. An example would be when you're using a server to provide dial-up access for multiple users. You might allocate 20 IP addresses to accommodate 50 dial-in users. Each user would receive a unique IP address assignment from the DHCP server at connection time, to a maximum of 20 concurrent connections.

Perhaps the most important benefit of DHCP is in the area of administration. DHCP makes it much easier to manage the IP address configuration of clients because you can effect all changes from a central server, rather than require changes on individual clients. The more computers on the network, the greater the advantage DHCP brings to address management. Rather than manually reconfigure network settings at several hundred (or more) workstations when a network change occurs, you can simply change the settings at the server, either pushing the changes transparently to the user or allowing the changes to take place when the clients restart.

The Windows Server DHCP Service

Windows Server 2008 includes a built-in DHCP service that offers excellent functionality for allocating and managing addresses. The DHCP Server service is built on industry standards (Request for Comments, or RFCs) defined by the Internet Engineering Task Force (IETF). This adherence to standards ensures that the DHCP service will accommodate not only Windows clients, but also other clients, including Unix, Macintosh, and so on.

As with other services, you manage DHCP on a Windows Server through the Microsoft Management Console (MMC). The DHCP service console snap-in enables you to create DHCP scopes (a range of addresses and corresponding properties), assign global properties, view current assignments, and perform all other DHCP administration tasks.

In addition to supporting the IETF standards, the Windows Server 2008 DHCP service extends the functionality of standard DHCP to include logging, monitoring, and other features that integrate DHCP with the Windows Server 2008 operating system. In addition to the many powerful features added to previous versions of the operating system that improve DHCP's usefulness, administration, and integration with other services, such as DNS, Windows Server 2008 includes Dynamic Host Configuration Protocol for IPv6 (DHCPv6) support. This and other features are discussed in the following sections.

Support for dynamic DNS

DHCP provides for dynamic address assignment and can therefore make it difficult to maintain accurate name-to-address mapping in DNS servers. As soon as a node changes its address, records in the DNS database become invalid. Windows Server 2008 DHCP integrates with

DNS by enabling the DHCP server and clients to request updates to the DNS database when addresses or host names change. This capability enables the DNS database to remain up-to-date even for clients with dynamically assigned IP addresses.

Dynamic DNS (DDNS) functions through a client-server mechanism. Windows Server and Windows XP/Vista DHCP clients support DDNS, and they can directly request that a Windows Server 2008 DNS server update their host resource records (also called A records) when the clients' IP addresses or host names change. Windows Server 2008 servers can also submit requests on behalf of clients, although a DHCP server can request an update to both the clients' host and pointer (PTR) records. Host records are used for host-to-address mapping, and pointer records are used for reverse lookup.

A Windows Server 2008 DHCP server also can act as a proxy for non-Windows 2000/XP/Vista DHCP clients to perform dynamic DNS updates. For example, a Windows Server 2008 DHCP server can perform updates for Windows 95/98 and Windows NT clients, which do not natively support dynamic DNS and are unable to submit requests to either the DHCP server or the DNS server to update their resource records. Figure 4-1 illustrates how DHCP and DNS interact.

FIGURE 4-1

DHCP supports automatic updates to DNS when host name or IP address changes occur.

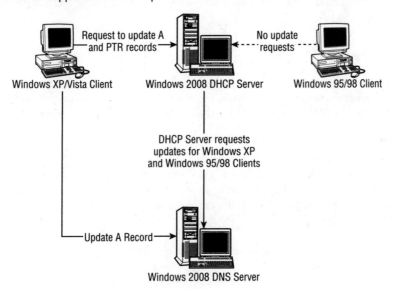

Windows XP/Vista Client   Windows 2008 DHCP Server   Windows 95/98 Client

Windows 2008 DNS Server

CROSS-REF See the section "Configuring Windows DHCP Clients," later in this chapter for an explanation of how to configure clients to use DDNS.

Vendor and user classes

Vendor classes enable you to define a set of DHCP settings for a specific equipment vendor and apply those settings to any node falling into that class. User classes enable you to do much the same thing, defining DHCP settings to apply to a specific group of nodes. Vendor and user classes offer enhanced flexibility in assigning custom settings to individual nodes or groups of nodes without affecting others on the same network. Through a vendor or user class, a node can request a custom set of DHCP settings to suit its configuration. For example, you might assign shorter lease durations to notebook PCs because they leave the network more frequently. You define a user class called Notebook and assign to it a shorter lease period; the client, which presents the user class to the server, receives the shorter lease based on that user class.

Multicast address allocation

Multicast addresses enable IP traffic to be broadcast to a group of nodes. They are most commonly used in audio or video conferencing. A standard IP address is also known as a *unicast* address because traffic is broadcast to a single address. A *multicast* address, however, enables you to send a group of computers the same data packets with a single broadcast, rather than using multiple broadcasts to a group of unicast addresses. The use of multicasting enables a group of computers to receive the same data without duplicating the packets, thereby reducing packet traffic.

Unauthorized DHCP server detection

Unauthorized DHCP servers can cause real problems in a network by allocating incorrect or conflicting configuration information to clients. For example, an administrator or power user might install and start a DHCP server, unaware that one or more DHCP servers already exist on the network.

The Active Directory (AD) stores a list of authorized DHCP servers. When a Windows Server 2008 DHCP server in a domain starts, it attempts to determine whether it is listed as an authorized server in the AD. If it is unable to connect to the AD or does not find itself listed in the AD as an authorized server, it assumes it is unauthorized and the service does not accept DHCP client requests. If the server does find itself in the AD, it begins processing client requests.

Workgroup DHCP servers (standalone servers not belonging to a domain) behave somewhat differently. When a workgroup DHCP server starts, it broadcasts a dhcpinform message. Any domain-based DHCP servers on the network respond with dhcpack and provide the name of the directory domain of which they are a part. If the workgroup DHCP server receives any dhcpack messages from domain DHCP servers, the workgroup server assumes it isn't authorized and does not service client requests. If a workgroup DHCP server detects no other servers or detects only other workgroup DHCP servers, it begins processing client requests. Therefore, workgroup DHCP servers will not operate on a network where domain-based DHCP servers are active, but they can coexist with other workgroup DHCP servers.

Automatic client configuration

Windows 200X, XP, and Vista DHCP clients attempt to locate a DHCP server at startup and renew any unexpired leases (a lease is an IP address and the associated data allocated from a DHCP server). If no DHCP server is found, the client pings the default gateway defined by the lease. If the ping succeeds, the client continues to use the lease and automatically attempts to renew the lease when half the lease time expires.

If the client is unable to locate a DHCP server and pinging the default gateway fails, the client assumes that it is on a network without DHCP services, automatically assigns itself an IP address, and continues checking for a DHCP server every five minutes. The client assigns itself an address in the subnet 169.254.0.0/16 (class B, subnet mask 255.255.0.0), but prior to assigning, the client tests to confirm that the address is valid and doesn't conflict with other nodes.

Automatic address assignment is a useful feature, particularly for small peer networks, such as a home network, without a DHCP server. It enables users to move between networks with relative ease, and eliminates the need to reconfigure their systems. For example, a user can move his or her notebook from the office to home and have a valid address within the current network without having to reconfigure TCP/IP each time.

Monitoring and reporting

The DHCP service performs its own monitoring, and logs events to the System log, which you can view with the Event Viewer console. DHCP also provides additional monitoring and statistical reporting. For example, you can configure DHCP to generate alerts when the percentage of available addresses in a given scope drops below a specified level.

Installing and Configuring the DHCP Server

The process of installing DHCP is relatively simple. Configuring a server and putting it into service is much more complex, however, particularly if you are new to DHCP. The following sections explain how to install the DHCP service and configure global and scope-specific settings.

Installing DHCP

As with other services, you add DHCP through the Add Roles wizard, which you can access though the Server Manager or the Initial Configuration Tasks application. Select Dynamic Host Configuration Protocol and click Next. Then follow the prompts to complete the software installation. After the software is installed, you can begin configuring and using DHCP without restarting the server. (See Chapter 2 for information about using Server Manager and the Add Roles wizard.) While installing DHCP Server you will be able to add DHCPv6 features as well.

 You should configure a DHCP server with a static IP address prior to adding the DHCP service.

Using the DHCP console

Windows Server 2008 provides an MMC console to enable you to manage DHCP servers both locally and on remote computers (see Figure 4-2). You can perform all DHCP administrative functions through the DHCP console. To open the DHCP console, choose Start ➢ All Programs ➢ Administrative Tools ➢ DHCP.

FIGURE 4-2

The DHCP console.

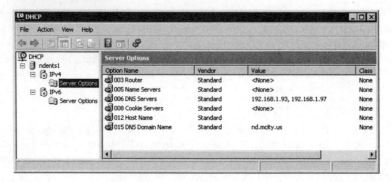

By default, the DHCP console connects to the local DHCP server, showing the server's IP address in the left pane. You can use the console to manage DHCP servers both locally and remotely. To connect to a different server, right-click the DHCP node (the topmost node) in the left pane and choose Add Server. Type the name or IP address of the server you want to manage and click OK. DHCP adds the server to the list.

Like most MMC consoles, DHCP functions as a two-pane console, with the tree pane on the left and the contents pane on the right.

Creating scopes

A DHCP *scope* is a set of properties that define a range of IP addresses and related settings, such as DNS servers, default gateways, and other information that the client needs to obtain from the DHCP server. Before you can begin using DHCP to assign addresses, you need to create at least one scope. Scopes can be active or inactive, so you also need to make the scope active before the server can allocate addresses from the scope to clients. This chapter assumes you are going to fully define the scope before activating it.

DHCP provides a New Scope wizard to take you through the process of creating a scope. To do so, right-click IPv4 or IPv6 nodes under the server in the tree and choose New Scope. Alternatively, select the server and choose Action ➤ New Scope. Click Next, and the wizard prompts you for the following information:

- **Name.** This is the friendly name that appears in the DHCP console for the scope. An example might be "Miami Office scope."

- **Description.** This optional description appears on the scope's General property page (right-click the scope and choose Properties to view). Assign a description to help you recognize the purpose of the scope. For example, you might use the address range in the description.

- **Start IP Address.** Specify the beginning address of the range of IP addresses you want to assign to the scope using dotted octet format.

- **End IP Address.** Specify the ending address of the range of IP addresses you want to assign to the scope using dotted octet format.

- **Length or Subnet Mask.** You can specify the subnet mask for the address range using either the address length or subnet mask in dotted octet format.

- **Exclusions, Start IP Address and End IP Address.** Use this page to specify one or more ranges of addresses to be excluded from the scope. Addresses in an excluded range are not used by DHCP or allocated to clients. If the addresses you want to exclude fall outside of the address range defined for the scope, you don't have to explicitly define an exclusion. For example, assume you create a scope with the included range 192.168.0.100 through 192.168.0.254. You do not have to create an exclusion for 192.168.0.1 through 192.168.0.99, which are implicitly excluded. Using this same example, however, you would need to create an exclusion if you wanted to prevent the address range 192.168.0.150 through 192.168.0.160 from being allocated to clients. If you choose an exclusion range, it must fall within the scope created on the previous page.

- **Lease Duration.** This property defines the length of time an IP address assignment is valid and is applicable to all clients unless modified by a user or vendor class assignment (in effect, it is the default lease period). When the lease duration expires, the client must request a renewal of the address. Failing that (because the address might already have been reassigned while the client was offline, for example), the client must request a new address lease. The default is eight days. See the section "Defining and Implementing User and Vendor Classes" later in this chapter for additional information.

- **Configure Other Options.** The wizard gives you the option of configuring the default gateway and DNS server properties to assign to the scope. See the section "Setting General Scope Options" later in this chapter for more information.

- **Activate the Scope.** Although you can activate the scope immediately after creating it, you should make sure you've fully defined all required scope properties prior to activation in order to ensure that clients receive all necessary DHCP properties. You can activate the scope later after fully defining it.

After you create a scope, it shows up in the DHCP console as a branch under the server's node in the tree pane, as shown in Figure 4-2. You'll see multiple scope branches when the server hosts more than one scope. Each scope branch includes the following objects:

■ **Address Pool.** This branch lists the included address pool for the scope along with any exclusion ranges. Each scope has only one inclusion range, but it can contain multiple exclusion ranges.

■ **Address Leases.** This branch lists current client address leases, including the IP address, name, and lease expiration.

■ **Reservations.** This branch lists address reservations, which reserve specific IP addresses for specific users based on the user's MAC address (physical network adapter address). See the section "Creating Reservations" later in this chapter for more information.

■ **Scope Options.** This branch lists additional properties passed to clients when they receive address leases from this scope. Typical properties include default router, DNS server assignments, time server, and time offset. The following section explains how to configure these settings.

Setting general scope options

You can specify a wide range of scope properties in addition to those discussed so far. These properties are given to clients when they receive a lease from the server. For example, the scope's properties can assign the default gateway and DNS servers the client should use, a time server for synchronizing the client's internal clock with the network or server, and many other properties. In most situations, you will need to configure only the default gateway and DNS servers, although some situations might warrant configuring other properties as well.

To configure general scope options, open the DHCP console and then open the scope whose properties you want to modify. Right-click Scope Options and choose Configure Options to display the Scope Options property sheet, shown in Figure 4-3.

The General tab enables you to configure properties that apply to all clients receiving address leases through the scope. You select an item by clicking it, and then you specify the value(s) for the item in the lower half of the property sheet. Enable or disable properties by selecting or deselecting their checkboxes in the list. Set the value for each one and then click OK.

The Advanced tab, shown in Figure 4-4, enables you to configure global properties for specific vendor and user classes. The default vendor classes are as follows:

■ **DHCP Standard Options.** These are the same options that appear on the General tab by default and apply to all client connections for which no vendor or user class is specified.

■ **Microsoft Options.** These options define Microsoft-specific DHCP properties for Microsoft clients.

- **Microsoft Windows 2000 Options.** These options define Microsoft Windows 2000/XP/Vista–specific properties for Windows 2000 and Windows XP/Vista clients.

- **Microsoft Windows 98 Options.** This selection can be used to define Windows 98–specific options, although by default none are defined.

FIGURE 4-3

The Scope Options property sheet.

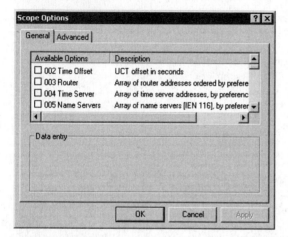

FIGURE 4-4

The Advanced tab.

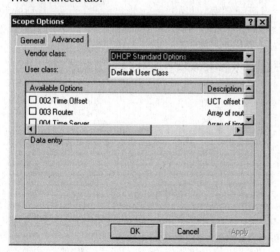

By default, three user classes are defined:

- **Default BOOTP Class.** These properties apply to clients that receive a lease via `bootp`. The command `bootp` enables clients to retrieve a valid address along with a boot image, which enables the computer to boot; it is typically used as a mechanism to boot diskless workstations.

- **Default Routing and Remote Access Class.** These properties apply to clients that receive a lease through RRAS connections.

- **Default User Class.** These properties apply to all clients not handled by a different user class.

> **NOTE** See the section "Defining and Implementing User and Vendor Classes" later in this chapter for detailed information on configuring and using vendor and user classes to customize lease properties for specific systems and users.

The following sections explain how to configure the most common DHCP properties.

Default gateway

The router lease property defines the default gateway assigned to the DHCP client. You can specify an array of addresses, giving the client multiple gateways to use. If the client's primary gateway fails for some reason, traffic will route through the next available gateway, providing fail-over insurance against a loss of connectivity. To assign a gateway to the array, enter the IP address in the IP Address text box in dotted octet format, and then click Add. You can enter a host name in the Server Name text box and click Resolve if you know the host name of the gateway but not its IP address. Clicking Resolve performs a DNS lookup and returns the IP address in the IP Address field if successful. You can specify multiple IP addresses, clicking Add to add each one to the array. Use the Up and Down buttons to change the order of the list. The client then tries the routers in sequence, starting with the top router.

Domain name and DNS servers

In addition to assigning one or more gateways, you will probably also want to assign at least one DNS server. Select 006 DNS Servers in the list and then add the IP addresses of the DNS servers to the list, just as you would when adding a router to the router list. The order of servers in the list defines the order in which the client will attempt to resolve names to addresses. Use the Up and Down buttons to change the order.

Domain name

Another property you should consider setting is the domain name. This property defines the client's domain and is used to create the user's fully qualified domain name (FQDN). The client prepends its host name to the domain name to create the FQDN. You can specify the domain name within the client's DNS properties, but setting it through DHCP instead enables the domain name to be changed dynamically when the client is granted a lease. If all the systems on the network use DHCP, you can change your entire organization's domain without changing any client settings — you simply change the domain name property in the DHCP server. Because of potential unseen pitfalls (clients with statically assigned domain names, for example), this isn't the recommended way of changing domain names.

Other scope properties

You can configure a wide range of other properties that are passed to the DHCP client when a lease is granted. Review the list of properties and configure those that apply to your network and client needs.

Configuring global DHCP options

Within each scope, you can configure properties such as domain name, gateway, and DNS servers, as explained earlier. These properties apply to all leases granted through the selected scope. You also can configure these properties to apply globally to all scopes defined on the server. These global options are used unless overridden by a scope-assigned property.

To configure global DHCP options, open the DHCP console, right-click the Server Options node, and choose Configure Options. The DHCP console displays the same property sheet you use to assign properties for a scope. Select and configure properties as needed.

Creating reservations

A *reservation* reserves a specific IP address for a specific Media Access Control (MAC) address. The MAC address is a unique hardware-based address that identifies a network adapter (Network Interface Card, or NIC) on the network. Reservations enable a specific adapter to receive the same IP address assignment from the DHCP server, and prevent the address from being leased to any other adapter. In effect, reservations let you enjoy the flexibility offered by DHCP while still enabling you to assign a static IP address. Through reservations, you ensure that the NIC always has the same IP address, but other configuration changes can be applied dynamically (such as domain name, router, DNS servers, and so on).

NOTE   Reservations do not assign the same IP address to a computer per se, because the reservation is associated with the NIC's MAC address, not the computer name. This is only a real distinction in multi-homed systems (those containing multiple NICs).

Before creating a reservation for a NIC, you need to know the NIC's MAC address. On Windows NT, Windows 2000, Windows XP/Vista, and Windows Server 2008 systems, you can use the ipconfig command at a console prompt to view MAC addresses for NICs in the computer. Open a console prompt on the system and issue the command ipconfig /all. The command lists network configuration data for each NIC, including the MAC address.

For Windows 9x and Me systems, use the WINIPCFG utility to determine the MAC address. WINIPCFG includes the adapter address in the information it displays, along with the IP address, the gateway, and other configuration information.

When you have the MAC address of the client's NIC, open the DHCP console and then open the scope where you want to create the reservation. Right-click the Reservations node and choose New Reservation to open the New Reservation dialog box (see Figure 4-5). Use the following list as a guide to configure the reservation:

- **Reservation Name.** This name appears in the DHCP console next to the reservation IP address (left pane). You can specify the computer's name, the username, or other information to help you identify the NIC for which the address is reserved.

- **IP Address.** Specify the IP address within the scope to reserve for the specified NIC.

- **MAC Address.** Enter the MAC address of the NIC for which the address is reserved.

- **Description.** This optional description appears in the contents pane of the DHCP console.

- **Supported Types.** You can designate the type of client (DHCP, BOOTP, or both) that can use the reservation.

FIGURE 4-5

Reservations assign an IP address to a specific network adapter.

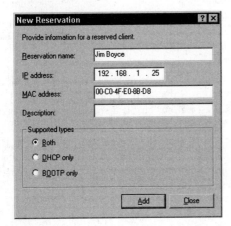

Setting global scope properties

Before you activate a scope and begin using it, you should configure a handful of properties that apply to the scope on a global basis. To set these, open the DHCP console, right-click the scope, and choose Properties to display the Scope Properties sheet. Use the General tab to modify the scope-friendly name, IP address range, lease period, and description. These options are self-explanatory.

The DNS tab determines how DHCP integrates with DNS. You'll learn how to configure DHCP clients to use DDNS in the section "Configuring Windows DHCP Clients" later in this chapter. For now, you can use the following list as a guide to configuring settings on the DNS page:

- **Enable DNS Dynamic Updates According to the Settings Below.** Select this option to direct the DHCP server to attempt to update client DNS information in the DNS server. The server will, by default, attempt to update the client's host and pointer records to associate the client's host name with its IP address.

- **Dynamically Update DNS A and PTR Records Only if Requested by DHCP Clients.** Select this option to have the server update the DNS records only if the client requests the update. Currently, only Windows 2000, Windows XP, and Windows Server 2003/2008 clients can request the update.

- **Always Dynamically Update DNS A and PTR Records.** Select this option to update the DNS records regardless of whether the client requests an update.

- **Discard A and PTR Records When Lease Is Deleted.** Select this option to have the DNS server discard the host record for a client when its lease expires and is deleted.

- **Dynamically Update DNS A and PTR Records for DHCP Clients That Do Not Request Updates.** Select this option to enable the DHCP server to update host and pointer records with DNS for clients that don't support dynamic update (such as versions of Windows prior to Windows 2000).

Use the Advanced property tab to configure the types of clients the DHCP server will handle with the selected scope. You can support DHCP only, bootp only, or both. If you select bootp only or both, you can configure the lease duration for bootp clients using the lease duration group, specifying a lease duration or configuring the scope to provide unlimited leases to bootp clients.

Activating and deactivating a scope

At this point, you should have enough data in the scope to activate it, although you might want to further configure your DHCP server by implementing vendor or user classes, using superscopes or multicast scopes, and so on (both are discussed later in this chapter). When you're ready to activate the scope, open the DHCP console. Right-click the scope in question and choose Activate. To deactivate a scope and prevent it from being used to assign leases, right-click the scope and choose Deactivate.

Authorizing the server

An additional step for domain-based DHCP servers is authorizing the server. *Authorizing* a server lists it in the Active Directory as an authorized DHCP server. As explained earlier, Windows Server 2008 DHCP servers attempt to determine whether they are authorized at startup and prior to processing client lease requests. Domain-based DHCP servers attempt to check the AD to determine whether they are listed as an authorized server. If the server is unable to contact the AD or doesn't find itself listed, it does not begin servicing client requests. A workgroup-based DHCP server queries the network for other DHCP servers; if it identifies any domain-based DHCP servers, it assumes it is not authorized and does not service client requests. If no domain-based DHCP servers respond, however, the server starts servicing client requests. This means that multiple workgroup-based DHCP servers can operate on the network concurrently.

When you install the DHCP service on a domain-based server, the server is unauthorized by default. You must authorize the server before it can begin servicing client requests. Authorizing a server simply lists the server in the AD. To authorize a domain-based DHCP server, open the DHCP console, right-click the server in the left pane, and choose Authorize.

Defining and Implementing User and Vendor Classes

Vendor and user classes are new features incorporated into the Windows Server 2008 DHCP service. Vendor classes enable you to create new, predefined scope options without having to go through the lengthy process of submitting RFCs and getting approval for adding new options. You can use vendor classes to create options specific to a particular device or operating platform, and then assign those options based on user classes.

User classes enable you to assign unique scope options to individual clients. For example, you may apply to all notebook users a specific DHCP configuration that, among other things, sets the lease expiration at eight hours rather than the default of eight days. You can incorporate other special properties to suit that group's requirements as well.

Vendor classes

In many respects, a vendor class is really just a container object that groups together custom DHCP options. You name the vendor class and assign to it new scope options not otherwise defined by the standard options. To create a vendor class, you specify a display name for the vendor class, a description, and an ID. The display name and description are primarily for convenience and identification within the DHCP console. The ID uniquely identifies the vendor class.

Creating a vendor class

To create, modify, or remove a vendor class, open the DHCP console. Right-click the server on which you want to work with vendor classes and choose Define Vendor Classes. DHCP displays a DHCP Vendor Classes dialog box that lists all currently defined vendor classes. Click Add to display the New Class dialog box, shown in Figure 4-6.

The display name is the friendly name for the vendor class within the DHCP console. You can include an optional description to further identify the vendor class. The ID is the data that clients use to request a specific set of DHCP options based on their vendor class. Click in the ID box under the Binary column if you want to enter the data in hexadecimal, or click under the

ASCII column to enter the ID in ASCII characters. Choose a string that uniquely identifies the vendor class but is also easy to remember (and perhaps easy to type). Bear in mind that this is an identifier string only and doesn't need to have any real relationship with the actual vendor name or other product information. However, using the vendor name in the ID will help you recognize the purpose for the vendor class.

FIGURE 4-6

The New Class dialog box.

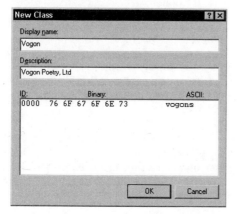

Configuring vendor class options

After you create a new vendor class, you need to specify the DHCP options that will be available to that vendor class. To do so, open the DHCP console, right-click the server on which you want to define vendor class options, and choose Set Predefined Options. DHCP displays the Predefined Options and Values dialog box. Select the option class for which you want to modify values and click Add. DHCP displays the Option Type dialog box, shown in Figure 4-7.

FIGURE 4-7

Use the Option Type dialog box to add vendor class options.

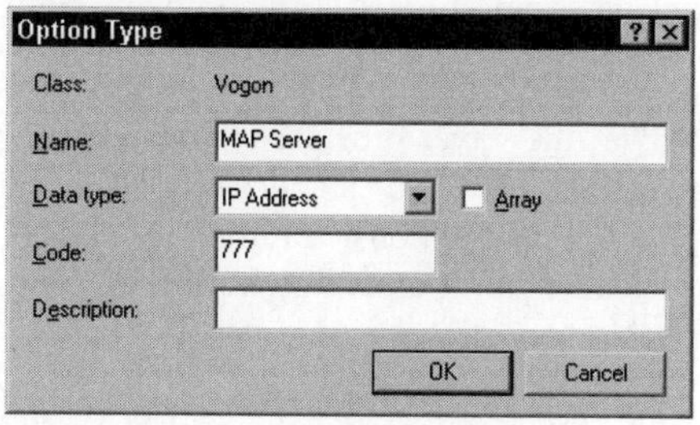

Provide information in the dialog box using the following list as a guide:

- **Name.** This is the name of the option as it appears in the Available Options list of the Scope Options property sheet. Specify a descriptive name such as Name Servers.

- **Data Type.** Select from this drop-down list the type of data represented by the class option (byte, word, long, IP address, and so on).

- **Array.** Select this option if you are creating an array, such as a DNS server list or gateway list.

- **Code.** Specify a unique numeric code for the option.

- **Description.** Specify an optional description to help identify the function of the option value.

You may have surmised that creating a vendor class and assigning class options to it can be a time-consuming task, particularly if you need to assign many options. Whenever possible, you should use standard DHCP options and override selected options with vendor class options only when needed.

> **NOTE** Windows Server 2008 incorporates three predefined vendor classes: Microsoft Options, Microsoft Windows 2000 Options, and Microsoft Windows 98 Options. The Microsoft Options and Microsoft Windows 2000 Options currently define three options: Disable NetBIOS, Release DHCP Lease on Shutdown, and Default Router Metric Base. You can use these options to implement the associated features for Windows 2000 clients. There are no predefined scope options for Windows 98 clients.

User classes

Although vendor classes enable you to define new DHCP scope options, user classes enable you to allocate DHCP scopes (whether standard or vendor class-defined) on a client-by-client basis. Each client can be configured with one or more user class IDs that the client submits to the DHCP server. The server responds with an appropriate lease based on the settings defined for that user class ID. For example, you might create a user class ID called notebook and configure its DHCP options to decrease the lease period, or you might have a group of computers that requires a different set of DNS servers or default gateway. You can use user class IDs in all of these cases to assign DHCP options on a selective basis.

> **NOTE** User classes must be supported at the client level. Currently, only Windows 200X, Windows XP, and Windows Vista clients support user classes. This capability is not included with Windows 98 or Windows NT clients.

When a client submits a class ID to a DHCP server, the server provides all the default options defined for the scope not otherwise defined by the class ID. You can allocate DHCP options using the default options for the scope and apply selective options with the user class. This means you do not have to duplicate the default settings for a user class; you need to configure only those settings that are unique to clients in that user class.

Creating a user class

You define a user class in much the same way that you define a vendor class. Open the DHCP console, right-click the server for which you want to define the user class, and then choose Define User Classes. Click Add in the DHCP User Classes dialog box. As you do with a vendor class, specify a display name to appear in the DHCP console, an optional description, and the class ID. The class ID is the data you will configure at the client level to enable it to request a lease based on the class ID. You can enter the class ID in either hexadecimal or ASCII format.

Configuring user class options

After you create a user class, assign to it the DHCP scope options that need to apply to each client having the specified class ID. To do so, open the DHCP console and expand the server in question. Right-click Scope Options, choose Configure Options, and click Advanced to display the Advanced tab (refer to Figure 4-4). You can select options from the DHCP Standard Options vendor class or use any other defined vendor class. Select the desired user class from the User Class drop-down list. The scope options predefined for the selected vendor class appear in the Available Options list. Browse through the list and configure scope options as you would the default options.

There is no need to configure options that will otherwise be assigned through the global options for the scope. Instead, configure only those options that are unique to the user class. For example, if all you are doing with the user class is reducing the lease period, then you need to configure only the lease value within the user class. All other settings can be assigned to the client through the global scope properties. When you have configured all necessary properties, click OK.

Configuring a client to use class IDs

You can assign multiple class IDs to Windows 200X and Windows XP/Vista clients, although only the last one assigned is actually used to retrieve DHCP data. Each client, by default, assumes the class ID "Default BOOTP Class," which enables Windows 200X/XP/Vista clients that require bootp to retrieve settings from the DHCP server. If you assign any other class IDs, however, the class ID assigned last takes precedence and the client takes on all global scope options plus the scope options assigned to that last class ID. The scope options are not cumulative — the client will not take on all options for all class IDs assigned to the adapter in question.

Use the ipconfig command to assign a class ID to a Windows 200X/XP/Vista client. You can assign class IDs manually through a command console or startup script. The syntax for assigning a class ID is as follows:

```
ipconfig /setclassid [adapter] [ClassIDString]
```

To configure a client with the class ID "portable" on the default network connection (Local Area Connection), use the following command:

```
ipconfig /setclassid "Local Area Connection" portable
```

> **TIP** You might want to rename your network connections using simpler names, if only to make it easier to perform `ipconfig` commands. To rename a network connection, open the Network and Dial-Up Connections folder, right-click the connection, and choose Rename. For example, you might rename "Local Area Connection" to simply "LAN."

Creating and Using Superscopes

As Windows 2000/2003 Server does, Windows Server 2008 also supports a DHCP feature called *superscopes*, an administrative feature that enables you to create and manage multiple scopes as a single entity. You can use superscopes to allocate IP addresses to clients on a *multinet*, which is a physical network segment containing multiple logical IP networks (a logical IP network is a cohesive range of IP addresses). For example, you might support three different class C logical IP networks on a physical network segment. Each of the three class C address ranges is defined as one of three individual child scopes under a superscope.

In many cases, you won't plan or set out to use a multinet because using a single logical IP network is much simpler from an administrative standpoint; however, you might need to use a multinet as an interim measure as your network size grows beyond the number of addresses available within the original scope. Or, you might need to migrate the network from one logical IP network to another, such as would be the case if you switched ISPs and therefore had to switch address assignments.

> **TIP** Superscopes are useful on high-speed wide area networks, especially when planning for and managing shallow Active Directory domain trees (trees with multiple Active Directory sites and few domains). This is discussed in Chapter 25.

You also can use superscopes to support remote DHCP clients located on the far side of a DHCP or `bootp` relay agent. This enables you to support multiple physical subnets with a single DHCP server. Figure 4-8 illustrates a single DHCP server supporting multiple logical IP networks on the local physical network, as well as logical IP networks on the far side of a relay agent.

Naturally, you will want to assign certain scope options, such as the default gateway within each scope, to place the option within the context of the scope. You can assign global options that apply to all scopes in a superscope at the server level. All scopes on the server, whether in a superscope or not, will use the global options when options are not specifically defined within the individual scopes. For example, all clients can probably use the same set of DNS servers, so you would define the DNS server array at the server level.

> **TIP** Keep in mind that superscopes are just an administrative feature that provide a container for managing scopes as groups on the same server. A superscope does not actually allocate options of its own. DHCP options come either from the server (global) or from the properties of the individual scopes within the superscope.

FIGURE 4-8

A single DHCP server can support multiple local IP networks and remote networks.

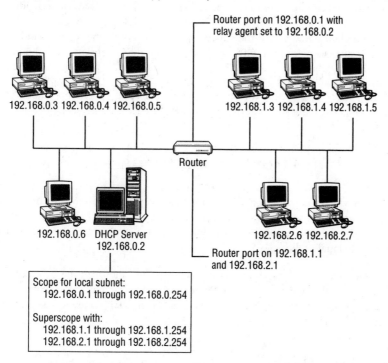

Router port on 192.168.0.1 with
relay agent set to 192.168.0.2

192.168.0.3 192.168.0.4 192.168.0.5

192.168.1.3 192.168.1.4 192.168.1.5

Router

192.168.0.6   DHCP Server
192.168.0.2

192.168.2.6 192.168.2.7

Router port on 192.168.1.1
and 192.168.2.1

Scope for local subnet:
 192.168.0.1 through 192.168.0.254

Superscope with:
 192.168.1.1 through 192.168.1.254
 192.168.2.1 through 192.168.2.254

Creating a superscope

You can create a superscope only after you define at least one scope on the server (this prevents you from creating an empty superscope). Windows Server 2008 enables you to select which existing scopes will be moved to the superscope. You can create additional scopes within the superscope afterwards. You can also create multiple superscopes and create scopes both inside and outside of a superscope. Therefore, a given server might have two superscopes with four scopes each, along with three scopes defined at the server level that are not part of either superscope.

To create a superscope, open the DHCP console. Right-click the server in which you want to create the superscope and choose New Superscope (the command is not available if no scopes exist on the server), and then click Next. Windows Server 2008 prompts you to choose a friendly name for the scope and to specify which existing scopes will be added to the superscope. Hold down the Shift key to select multiple scopes.

Activating and deactivating a superscope

Windows Server 2008 automatically activates the superscope if one or more scopes in the superscope are active when you create the superscope. If not, you can activate individual scopes in the superscope, and then activate the superscope itself. To activate individual scopes, right-click the scope and choose Activate. If the superscope contains only one scope, Windows Server 2008 activates the superscope as well. Otherwise, right-click the superscope and choose Activate.

You can deactivate an individual scope within a superscope, or you can deactivate the super-scope, which deactivates all scopes in the superscope. Deactivating a scope prevents it from servicing additional client requests for address leases. Right-click either a scope or superscope and choose Deactivate to deactivate it.

Removing scopes from a superscope

You can remove one or more scopes from a superscope if necessary to restructure the scopes on the server. Removing a scope from a superscope does not delete the scope or deactivate it. Instead, it simply makes it a scope directly under the server branch, rather than a child scope of the superscope. This enables you to add it to a different scope or eliminate the superscope without affecting its individual scopes.

To remove a scope from a superscope, open the DHCP console and open the superscope in question. Right-click the scope and choose Remove from Superscope. If the scope being removed is the only scope in the superscope, Windows Server 2008 removes the superscope because you can't have an empty superscope.

Deleting superscopes

Deleting a superscope removes the superscope and places its child scopes directly under the server branch of the DHCP server. The scopes are unaffected and continue to service client requests — they are simply no longer a member of a superscope. Open the DHCP console, right-click the superscope to be deleted, and choose Delete.

Creating Multicast Scopes

A *multicast scope*, as explained earlier, is used to broadcast IP traffic to a group of nodes using a single address, and is traditionally used in audio and video conferencing. Using multicast addresses simplifies administration and reduces network traffic because the data packets are sent once to the multicast address, rather than individually to each recipient's unicast address.

A Windows Server 2008 DHCP server can allocate multicast addresses to a group of computers much as it allocates unicast addresses to individual computers. The protocol for multicast address allocation is Multicast Address Dynamic Client Allocation Protocol (MADCAP). Windows Server 2008 can function independently as both a DHCP server and a MADCAP server.

For example, one server may use the DHCP service to allocate unicast addresses through the DHCP protocol, and another server may allocate multicast addresses through the MADCAP protocol. In addition, a client can use either or both. A DHCP client doesn't have to use MADCAP, and vice versa, but a client can use both if the situation requires it.

Because the use of multicasting is somewhat specialized, this chapter assumes you have a working knowledge of multicast addressing, routing, and so on, and focuses on explaining how to configure a Windows Server 2008 DHCP server to act as a MADCAP server.

TIP For additional information on using multicast scopes, open Help in the DHCP console and search for "multicast scope."

You can create multiple multicast scopes on a Windows Server 2008 DHCP server as long as the scope address ranges don't overlap. Multicast scopes exist directly under the server branch and cannot be assigned to superscopes, which are intended only to manage unicast address scopes. To create a multicast scope, open the DHCP console, right-click the server in which you want to create the multicast scope, and choose New Multicast Scope. Windows Server 2008 starts a wizard that prompts you for the following information:

- **Name.** This is the friendly name as it appears for the scope in the DHCP console.
- **Description.** Specify an optional description to identify the purpose of the multicast scope.
- **Address Range.** You can specify an address range between 224.0.0.0 and 239.255.255.255, inclusive, which gives you a large range of addresses to use.
- **Time to Live (TTL).** Specify the number of routers the traffic must pass through on your local network.
- **Exclusion Range.** You can define a range of multicast addresses to exclude from the scope, just as you can exclude unicast addresses from a DHCP scope.
- **Lease Duration.** Specify the duration for the lease. The default is 30 days.

You can choose to activate the scope through the wizard or activate the scope later. Right-click a multicast scope and choose Activate to activate the scope.

Configuring Global DHCP Server Properties

After configuring scopes and other DHCP options, turn your attention to a handful of global DHCP server properties that you can configure to fine-tune your DHCP server. To configure these settings, open the DHCP console, right-click the server, and choose Properties. Some of the server override settings you configure at the scope level. For example, the settings on the DNS tab correspond to the settings covered earlier in this chapter in "Setting Global Scope Properties."

FIGURE 4-9

Configure global settings with the General tab.

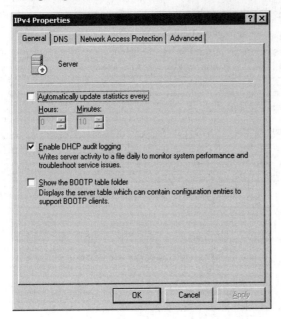

The General tab is shown in Figure 4-9.

It contains the following three settings:

- **Automatically Update Statistics Every.** Use this option to have the DHCP server refresh statistics in the DHCP console at the specified interval. The statistics update when you open the console; you can also refresh them manually by choosing Action ➤ Refresh. Use this option if you keep the console open for extended periods for monitoring.

- **Enable DHCP Audit Logging.** Enable this option (the default) to record DHCP server events to a log file. See the following material on the Advanced tab for more information.

- **Show the BOOTP Table Folder.** Enable this option to add a BOOTP Table branch to the DHCP console. You can then right-click the BOOTP Table branch and choose New Boot Image to display the Add BOOTP Entry dialog box (see Figure 4-10). Use this dialog to specify the boot image file, path, and TFPT server for the boot image.

The Advanced tab (see Figure 4-11) provides several settings for logging, backup, network configuration, and authentication.

FIGURE 4-10

Add BOOTP images through the BOOTP Table branch.

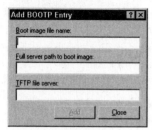

FIGURE 4-11

Configure a variety of settings with the Advanced tab.

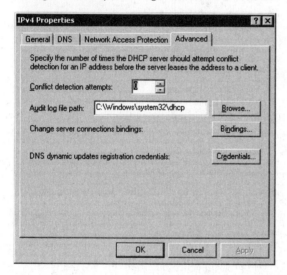

These settings include the following:

■ **Conflict Detection Attempts.** Specify the number of times the server should attempt to detect address conflicts before leasing an address to a client. Increase the value in situations where detection typically takes longer, such as in heavily saturated networks or when clients take longer to respond because they are operating in power-saving mode.

- **Audit Log File Path.** Specify where you want the DHCP server to place its audit log files. The default location is %systemroot%\System32\dhcp.

- **Bindings.** Click this button to open a dialog box in which you choose the network interfaces on which the DHCP server will respond to DHCP client requests. The list will be empty if the server has no static IP addresses.

- **Credentials.** Click this button to specify the account credentials, including domain, that the DHCP server will use when authenticating dynamic DNS requests to a Windows DNS server. You need to specify credentials only if the DNS server is configured to require secure updates.

> **NOTE** Windows Server 2008 also supports stateless and stateful DHCPv6 server functionality. DHCPv6 stateless mode clients use DHCPv6 to obtain network addresses and configuration in addition to the IPv6 address. The IPv6 parameters include DNS server addresses. See Chapter 3, which covers IPv6.

Managing the DHCP Database

Windows Server 2008 makes it easy to back up and restore the DHCP database, which provides recoverability from server failures and an easy means to move DHCP data to a different server. The DHCP data you can back up includes all defined scopes, reservations, and leases, as well as all options at the server, scope, reservation, and class levels. The default location for the backup is %systemroot%\System32\dhcp\backup. Consider copying the backup folder to another server frequently for improved recoverability in case the DHCP server fails and the backup folder is lost.

To specify the database and backup paths, right-click the topmost node representing the DHCP server and select Properties. The dialog box that appears provides the following two options.

- **Database Path.** Specify the location where the DHCP server will place its database files. The default location is %systemroot%\System32\dhcp.

- **Backup Path.** Specify the location where the DHCP server will back up its database. The default location is %systemroot%\System32\dhcp\backup. See the following section for information on backing up and restoring the DHCP database.

Backing up and restoring the DHCP database

The DHCP server provides three backup mechanisms. It backs up its database automatically to the backup folder every hour, which Microsoft terms a synchronous backup. You can also manually initiate a backup with the DHCP console, which Microsoft terms an asynchronous backup. The final method is to use the Windows Server 2008 Backup utility or third-party backup utility to perform scheduled or as-needed backups.

All of these methods back up the items mentioned previously, but do not back up authentication credentials, registry settings, or other global DHCP configuration information such as log settings and database location. Instead, you need to back up the registry key `HKEY_LOCAL_MACHINE\SYSTEM\CurrentControlSet\Services\DHCPServer\Parameters` to back up these additional items.

> **TIP** The easiest way to back up the DHCP registry key is to export the key from the Registry Editor. Open the Registry Editor, select the key, and export it to the same backup location as the other DHCP backup files.

To perform an asynchronous backup of the DHCP data, open the DHCP console, right-click the server, and choose Backup. In the resulting Browse for Folder dialog box, select the folder location where you want the data to be backed up. You can create a new folder through this dialog box, if needed.

To change the interval for synchronous backups from its default setting of 60 minutes, open the Registry Editor and open the key `HKEY_LOCAL_MACHINE\SYSTEM\CurrentControlSet\Services\DHCPServer\Parameters`. Modify the value BackupInterval as desired. (See Chapter 9 for information on how to edit the registry.)

> **TIP** With the Edit DWORD Value dialog box open, switch to decimal view and specify a value in minutes for the backup interval.

If the DHCP server suffers a failure, you can quickly restore the DHCP service by restoring the DHCP database. Bring the server back online and install the DHCP service. If you backed up the DHCP registry key, stop the DHCP service, import the key, and restart the service; then, open the DHCP console. Right-click the server in the console and choose Restore. Select the location to which you previously backed up the DHCP database and restore the data.

> **CAUTION** You can only restore a backup that you created manually with the DHCP console. Do not use the DHCP backup files created automatically by the DHCP service during a synchronous backup. This will cause the DHCP service to fail. The synchronous backups are used only by the DHCP service to automatically restore the database if the service detects that the DHCP database has become corrupted.

Moving the DHCP database to another server

Whether you are upgrading servers or simply migrating the DHCP service to another computer for performance reasons, moving the DHCP database is relatively easy. On the source server, open the DHCP console and back up the DHCP database to a location accessible by the target server. Stop the DHCP service on the source server and, if needed, export the DHCP registry key to a file, as explained in the preceding section.

> **TIP** Stopping the DHCP service prevents the DHCP server from responding to client requests and potentially conflicting with the new server when it comes online.

Next, install the DHCP service on the target server. Stop the DHCP service and import the registry file. Copy the contents of the DHCP database backup folder from the source server to the appropriate location on the target server (the default is `%systemroot%\System32\dhcp`). Then, start the DHCP service.

 Make sure you authorize the new DHCP server in the Active Directory.

Configuring Windows DHCP Clients

Configuring Windows 2000, Windows XP/Vista, and Windows 2003/2008 clients to use DHCP is a relatively simple process. At the client, right-click My Network Places and choose Properties, or choose Start ➢ Settings ➢ Network and Dial-Up Connections to open the Network Connections folder. Right-click the connection you want to configure for DHCP and choose Properties. Double-click the TCP/IP protocol in the list of installed components or select it and click Properties to display its property sheet.

NOTE On Windows 2000 systems, the Network Connections folder is named Network and Dial-Up Connections.

To configure a Windows 9x or Me client, right-click Network Neighborhood on the desktop or open the Network applet in the Control Panel. Locate and double-click the TCP/IP protocol in the list of installed network components.

You can configure the client to obtain its IP address from the DHCP server, obtain DNS server addresses through DHCP, or both. The controls on the General tab are self-explanatory.

Configuring DNS options for DHCP

You can configure a Windows 2000, Windows XP, Vista, or Windows Server 3003/2008 client to use Dynamic DNS (DDNS) to automatically update its host record when its host name changes or its IP address changes (including through DHCP lease renewal). Click Advanced on the General property page for the TCP/IP protocol for the connection in order to display the Advanced TCP/IP Settings dialog box; then, click the DNS tab to display the DNS page. This is illustrated in Figure 4-12.

Two settings on the DNS page control integration of DHCP and DDNS for the client:

- **Register This Connection's Addresses in DNS.** Select this option to have the client submit a request to the DNS server to update its host (A) record when its host name changes or IP address changes. The client submits the full computer name specified in the Network Identification tab of the System Properties sheet along with its IP address to the DNS server. You can view the System properties through the System object in the Control Panel, or right-click My Computer and choose Properties.

■ **Use This Connection's DNS Suffix in DNS Registration.** Select this option to have the client submit a request to the DNS server to update its host record when the host name changes or the IP address changes. The difference between this and the previous option is that this option registers the client using the first part of the computer name specified in the System properties along with the DNS suffix specified by the option "DNS suffix for this connection" on the DNS tab.

FIGURE 4-12

The DNS tab of the Advanced TCP/IP Settings dialog box.

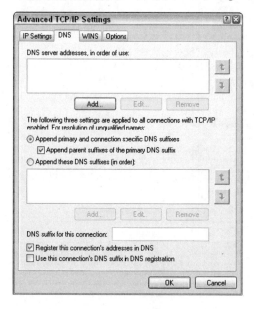

Network Access Protection

Network Access Protection on Windows Server 2008 makes use of DHCP enforcement features. In other words, a client computer must meet compliance levels in order to obtain an unlimited access IP address configuration from a DHCP server. For noncompliant computers, network access is limited by an IP address configuration that allows access only to the restricted network.

DHCP enforcement policy kicks in when a DHCP client requests a lease or asks to renew an IP address configuration from the server. The DHCP enforcement policy also actively monitors the NAP client, and if it falls into noncompliance the server will renew the IPv4 address configuration and limit the client to the restricted network until the client becomes compliant.

NAP compliance and DHCP can be set on the Network Access Protection tab of the IPv4 Properties dialog box. This tab is shown in Figure 4-13.

FIGURE 4-13

The Network Access Protection tab of the IPv4 Properties dialog box.

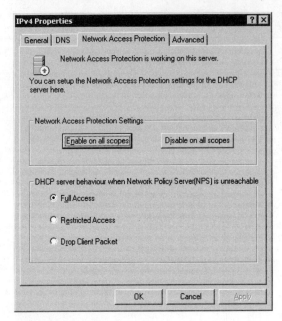

Summary

DHCP provides a means through which you can allocate IP addresses to clients automatically when the clients boot, making it much easier to manage IP leases and corresponding properties in a network. Rather than modify clients manually when a required change occurs (such as DNS server change, router change, and so on), you simply modify the properties of the scope on the DHCP server and allow the clients to retrieve the new data when they renew their leases. Through class IDs, you can allocate specific scope properties to clients to satisfy unique requirements of the client, such as gateways, DNS servers, lease duration, and so on.

The DHCP server service provided with Windows Server 2008 also enables a Windows Server to act as a multicast address provider, allocating multicast addresses to clients that require them. A server can function as a unicast scope server, multicast scope server, or both.

A new management feature provided with the DHCP server service is the capability to tie DHCP configuration issues to Network Access Protection policy. In addition, the DHCP server also supports IPv6 scopes.

Chapter 5

Windows Name Services

I n Part III of this book, you learn that Active Directory domains are
modeled on Internet domains. You learned in Chapters 2 and 3 that
Windows Server networks rely on TCP/IP as the network protocol of
choice. To resolve Windows Server domain controllers and many other
hosts running Windows services, you need to fully understand and know
how to configure Domain Name Service (DNS). This chapter explains the
services that you can use to create DNS. It also covers Windows Internet
Name Service (WINS) name servers, and includes coverage of Dynamic
DNS (DDNS), client configuration, and related topics.

Overview of the Domain Name Service

The Internet comprises many millions of devices, including computers,
routers, printers, and other devices, and each device is called a *node*.
Each node requires a unique IP address to differentiate it from others and
enable traffic to be routed to and from the node. Intranets also can employ
the TCP/IP protocol and require that each node have a unique address,
although in the case of an intranet, these IP addresses can come from
a nonpublic reserved address space such as 192.168.0.*x*. Nodes on the
Internet must have a unique, public IP address. IP addresses are difficult
for most people to remember, and their sheer number makes trying to do
so impractical. The Domain Name Service (DNS) overcomes this problem

by enabling users to work with names, rather than addresses. In effect, DNS provides a means of mapping names to addresses. Rather than type 146.57.248.13 to connect to Fox News' Web site, for example, you connect your browser to `www.foxnews.com`. DNS takes care of translating `www.foxnews.com` into the appropriate IP address. Mapping a name to an IP address is called *name resolution*.

The Internet arose from a network called the ARPANET, which comprised a relatively small number of computers in the 1970s (mostly defense and educational systems). With few nodes, it was fairly simple to provide name resolution. The Stanford Research Institute (SRI) maintained a single text file named `Hosts.txt` that contained the host-to-address translations for all the ARPANET's hosts. The operating systems (predominantly Unix) used the `Hosts.txt` file to resolve names to addresses. System administrators copied the `Hosts.txt` file from SRI to their local systems periodically to provide an updated list.

As the number of hosts grew, the continued use of a `Hosts.txt` file to provide name resolution soon became impractical. In the mid-1980s, the DNS system was developed to provide a dynamic name resolution system that no longer relied on a static name-to-address map. Before you learn about the DNS system, however, you need to understand domain names.

Understanding domain names

As mentioned in the preceding section, each device on an IP network is a node. Many nodes are also termed *hosts*. Generally, a host is a computer, router, or other "smart" device, but any device can be considered a host and have a host name associated with it. In Windows Server 2008, a computer's name as it appears on the LAN is typically its host name. Assume, for example, that your computer's name is "tia" and that your computer resides in the `mcity.us` domain. The host name is `tia`, the domain name is `mcity.us`, and the Fully Qualified Domain Name (FQDN) of your computer is `tia.mcity.us`. The FQDN identifies the host's absolute location in the DNS namespace.

Domain names are not limited to a single level, as in the preceding example. Assume that the `mcity.us` domain comprises several sites, each with its own subdomains. In addition, assume that each domain is divided into three subdomains: east, midwest, and west. The domain names would be `east.mcity.us`, `midwest.mcity.us`, and `west.mcity.us`. These domains could further be divided into subdomains, such as `sales.west.mcity.us`, `support.west.mcity.us`, and so on. Taking this example one step further, consider a host named "tia" in the `support.west.mcity.us` domain. This host's FQDN would be `tia.support.west.mcity.us`.

Table 5-1 lists the original top-level domains. Notice that the root of the domain namespace is a null, which is often represented by a dot (.). The dot is omitted from Table 5-1.

Table 5-2 lists new top-level domains.

TABLE 5-1

Original Top-Level Domains

Suffix	Purpose	Example
com	Commercial organizations such as businesses	microsoft.com
edu	Educational organizations such as colleges and universities	berkeley.edu
gov	Governmental organizations such as the IRS, SSA, NASA, and so on	nasa.gov
int	International organizations such as NATO	nato.int
mil	Military organizations such as the Army, Navy, and so on	army.mil
net	Networking organizations such as ISPs	mci.net
org	Noncommercial organizations such as the IEEE standards body	ieee.org

TABLE 5-2

New, Additional Top-Level Domains

Suffix	Purpose	Example
aero	Restricted to the air-transport industry	http://www.information.aero
biz	Businesses	latinaccents.biz
coop	Restricted to co-op organizations or those that serve co-ops	redriver.coop
info	Informational sites	windows.info
museum	Restricted to museums, museum associations, and museum professionals	smithsonian.museum
name	Personal names	boyce.name
pro	Restricted to credential-bearing accountants, lawyers, and doctors	shapiro.pro
us	Individual, businesses, and organizations with a presence in the United States	ford.us

TIP   See www.icann.org for information about the new domain namespaces.

Several other domain types exist in addition to the domain types specified in Tables 5-1 and 5-2. The .us domain, for example, is used by governmental, regional, and educational institutions in the United States. Other countries have their own domains, such as .uk for the United Kingdom, .jp for Japan, and so on.

> **TIP** NeuStar, based in Washington, D.C., has been assigned authority for the .us domain by the U.S. government. NeuStar's .us Web site provides links to enable you to research, register, and delegate within this domain. Point a Web browser to www.nic.us or www.neustar.us for more information on the .us domain or to request delegation for .us subdomains.

Until a few years ago, an organization called InterNIC was responsible for managing and allocating domain names within the top-level domains. InterNIC, however, became a for-profit business named Network Solutions, forfeiting its monopoly on the domain namespace. Network Solutions still can allocate domain names, however, as can a multitude of other companies on the Internet. To acquire a domain name for your organization, point your Web browser to www.icann.org to locate a domain registrar. Most domain registrars provide features on their Web sites to look up domain names — to determine whether the names are in use or are available, to register new domains, to modify domains, and so on.

Today's DNS system

Today's DNS system functions as a distributed database through a client-server relationship between DNS servers and clients requiring name resolution. The entire namespace of all domains comprises the DNS namespace. By using a distributed database architecture, DNS provides for local control of each domain while still enabling all clients to access the entire database whenever needed.

The DNS namespace comprises a hierarchical structure of domains, with each domain representing a branch on the tree and subdomains residing underneath. At the topmost level are the *root servers* that maintain the *root domains*, such as .com, .net, .org, .biz, and so on. The root of the domain namespace is a null, often represented by a dot (.). Figure 5-1 illustrates the DNS namespace.

The root servers maintain only a limited amount of information about a given domain. Typically, the information includes only the name servers identified as *authoritative* for the zone (that is, those having authority over the domain's records). Records that map names to addresses within individual domains reside on the name server(s) for the domains in question. These name servers are typically managed by ISPs for the ISPs' clients or by companies that manage their own domains. Certain other domains are delegated to other organizations (ISPs, state agencies, educational institutions, and so on) that manage the domains for the respective domain holders. Distributing the DNS namespace in this way enables users to control their own domains while still remaining a part of the overall namespace.

FIGURE 5-1

The DNS namespace is a hierarchical distributed database.

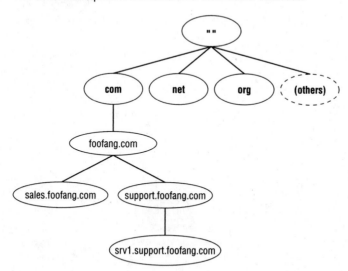

Resolvers, name servers, and forward lookup

DNS clients called *resolvers* submit queries to DNS servers to be resolved into IP addresses. Assuming, for example, that you want to connect to www.mcity.us, www is the host name (or an alias to a different host name), and mcity.us is the domain name. The resolver on your client computer prepares a DNS query for www.mcity.us and submits it to the DNS server identified in your client computer's TCP/IP settings, which in this case we assume is a DNS server on your LAN. The DNS server checks its *local cache* (which stores results of previous queries) and database and finds that it has no records for www.mcity.us. Therefore, the DNS server submits a query to the root server for the .us domain. The root server looks up the mcity.us domain and responds with the IP address(es) of the name servers for the domain. Your DNS server then submits a query to the specified DNS server for mcity.us, which responds with the IP address of the host www. Your DNS server in turn provides this information to your resolver, which passes the data to your client application (in this case, a Web browser), and suddenly the www.mcity.us site pops up on your browser. Mapping a host name or alias to its address in this way is called forward lookup. Figure 5-2 illustrates a forward-lookup request.

TIP Keep in mind that domains and IP address ranges have no direct relationship. A single domain can use any number of different subnets, and host records in a domain can point to hosts outside your local network and even outside your domain. You might outsource e-mail for your organization, for example, which would mean that your domain contains mail-related records that point to a server outside your subnet and LAN.

FIGURE 5-2

A forward-lookup query.

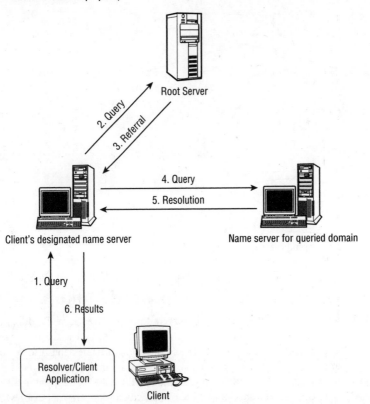

Name servers range from the root servers all the way down to the name servers at your department or organizational level. In most cases, a given name server manages all the records for some portion of the DNS namespace called a *zone*. The terms "zone" and "domain" are generally synonymous, but not always. A *zone* comprises all the data for a domain, with the exception of parts of the domain delegated to other name servers. (See the section "Configuring Subdomains and Delegation" later in this chapter for details.) A zone is the part of the domain hosted on a particular name server. The *domain* comprises the whole of the domain, wherever its components reside. Whenever the entire domain resides on a single name server, zone and domain are synonymous.

A name server that has full information about a given zone is said to be *authoritative* or has authority for the zone. A given name server can be authoritative for any number of zones and can be both authoritative for some and nonauthoritative for others. In addition, a name server can be either a primary master or a secondary master. A *primary master* maintains locally the records for those domains for which it is authoritative. The system administrator for a primary master can add new records, modify existing records, and so on, on the primary master. Figure 5-3 illustrates the relationship between zones and domains.

FIGURE 5-3

Portions of a domain can be delegated to name servers in subdomains.

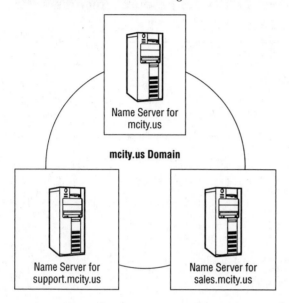

A *secondary master* for a zone pulls its records for the zone from a primary master through a process called a *zone transfer*. The secondary master maintains the zone records as a read-only copy and periodically performs zone transfers to refresh the data from the primary master. You control the frequency of the zone transfers according to the requirements of the domain in question, the desired amount of network traffic (reducing network traffic by reducing zone transfers if needed), and any other issues pertinent to your domain(s). A secondary master is essentially a backup DNS server. A server can function as a primary master for some zones and a secondary master for others. The difference lies in how the server handles the zones and not in the zones themselves.

Domain records and zone files

Each zone contains records that define hosts and other elements of the domain or a portion of the domain contained within the zone. These records are stored collectively in a zone file on the DNS server. A *zone file* is a text file that uses a special format to store DNS records. The default name for a zone file is `domain.dns`, where *domain* is the name of the domain hosted by the zone, such as `mcity.us.dns`. Windows Server 2008 stores zone files in `%systemroot%\System32\Dns` and provides an MMC console to enable you to manage the contents of the zone files with a graphical interface.

Each zone contains a certain number of *resource records* that define the hosts and other data for the zones. Several different types of records exist, with each serving a specific purpose. Each record has certain properties associated with it that vary from one record type to the next. Table 5-3 lists the record types and their purposes.

TABLE 5-3

Windows Server 2008 DNS Resource Records

Record	Purpose
A	Maps host name to an address
AAAA	Maps host name to Ipv6 address
AFSDB	Location of Andrew File System (AFS) cell's database server or Distributed Computing Environment (DCE) cell's authenticated server
ATMA	Maps domain name to Asynchronous Transfer Mode (ATM) address
CNAME	Creates an alias (synonymous) name for the specified host
HINFO	Identifies the host's hardware and operating system type
ISDN	Maps host name to Integrated Services Digital Network (ISDN) address (phone number)
KEY	Public key related to a DNS domain name
MB	Associates host with specified mailbox; experimental
MG	Associates host name with mail group; experimental
MINFO	Specifies mailbox name responsible for mail group; experimental
MR	Specifies mailbox name that is correct rename of other mailbox; experimental
MX	Mail exchange server for domain
NS	Specifies address of domain's name server(s)
NXT	Defines literal names in the zone; implicitly indicates nonexistence of a name if not defined
PTR	Maps address to a host name for reverse lookup
RP	Identifies responsible person for domain or host
RT	Specifies intermediate host that routes packets to destination host
SIG	Cryptographic signature record
SOA	Specifies authoritative server for the zone
SRV	Defines servers for specific purpose such as `http`, `ftp`, and so on
TXT	Associates textual information with item in the zone
WINS	Enables lookup of host portion of domain name through WINS server
WINS-R	Reverses lookup through WINS server
WKS	Describes services provided by specific protocol on specific port
X.25	Maps host name to X.121 address (X.25 networks); used in conjunction with RT records

The primary record is the *SOA*, or Start of Authority. The SOA record indicates that the server is authoritative for the domain. Whenever you create a new zone, Windows Server 2008 automatically creates the SOA record for the zone. *NS* records identify name servers, and a zone should contain NS records for each name server in the domain.

Address, or *A*, records map host names to IP addresses. *Multi-homed hosts* — those that have multiple IP addresses — can be represented by multiple A records, each mapping the same host name to the different addresses of the host. A DNS lookup retrieves all matching records when multiple A records reference the same name. To improve performance, the name server sorts the address list so that the closest address is at the top of the list when the resolver and name server are on the same network. Otherwise, addresses are rotated through subsequent queries to respond in round-robin fashion. One query responds with the address of the first address in the list, for example, and subsequent queries respond with the second and third, respectively.

CNAME (Canonical Name) records map an alias name to a Fully Qualified Domain Name (FQDN) and are, therefore, called *alias* records. Therefore, A and CNAME records typically work hand-in-hand. You create a host (A) record for a host and then use CNAME records to create aliases. You may create a host record for `server.mcity.us`, for example, and then use CNAME records to create aliases for www and ftp that point to that server.

Mail Exchanger, or *MX*, records are another common resource record type. MX records enable servers to route mail. The MX records in a zone determine how mail is routed for the domain hosted by the zone. An MX record includes the FQDN of the mail server and a preference number from 0 to 65535. The preference number determines the priority of the mail server specified by the MX record. If multiple mail servers exist for a domain, then the zone includes multiple MX records. Mail delivery is attempted based on the preference number, with the lowest numbered server(s) tried first. If the MX records all have the same preference number, the remote mail server has the option of sending to any of the domain's mail servers with the given preference number.

Service Locator (*SRV*) resource records offer the same flexibility for other services that MX records offer for mail routing. You create SRV records for specific services such as HTTP, FTP, LDAP, and so on. Resolvers that are designed to work with SRV records can use the preference number to connect to hosts offering the specified service. As with MX records, servers with lower preference numbers are attempted first.

The Pointer (*PTR*) record is another common record type. Pointers map addresses to names, the reverse of what host records do, in a process called *reverse lookup*. You learn more about reverse lookup in the following section. For now, be aware that whenever you create or modify resource records for forward lookup, the Windows Server 2008 DNS service can automatically create or modify the associated PTR record.

Each record has certain properties associated with it, and many properties are common to all records. Each record, for example, has a *time-to-live*, or *TTL*, property. The TTL value, a 32-bit integer, specifies the number of seconds for which the resolver should cache the results of a query before it is discarded. After the specified TTL period is reached, the resolver purges the entry from the cache, and the subsequent query for the item is sent to the name server, rather than pulled from the cache. Although the TTL value and caching can speed performance by caching frequently used queries, the dynamism of the Internet requires that records can change. Mail servers, Web servers, FTP servers, and other hosts can and do change addresses, and those changes need to be reflected in the DNS namespace. The TTL value enables caching, but also enables query results to grow stale and the resolver to query for fresh results. You need to adjust the TTL value for records to suit the type of record and how often you want the record updated across the intranet/Internet. If you're not sure what value to use initially, use the default value.

> **TIP**   The TTL value is optional for most resource records. The minimum default value specified with the SOA record is used if no TTL is specified for a record. In addition, the Windows Server 2008 DNS GUI presents some data differently from the way it is stored. The TTL is a 32-bit integer in the data file, for example, but the GUI represents it in the format *DD:HH:MM:SS* (days:hours:minutes:seconds) for readability.

Reverse lookup

Forward lookup maps names to addresses, enabling a resolver to query a name server with a host name and receive an address in response. A *reverse query*, also called *reverse lookup*, does just the opposite — it maps an IP address to a name. The client knows the IP address but needs to know the host name associated with that IP address. Reverse lookup is most commonly used to apply security based on the connecting host name, but it is also useful if you're working with a range of IP addresses and gathering information about them.

Address-to-name mapping through the regular forward lookup mechanism is simply not practical, because it requires an exhaustive search of the entire DNS namespace to locate the appropriate information. Imagine scanning through the New York City phone book trying to match a phone number with a name: Multiply that task by the number of computers on the Internet and you begin to understand that reverse lookup requires a special mechanism to make it practical.

The solution is to create a namespace of IP addresses — in other words, a domain in the namespace that uses IP addresses, rather than names. In the DNS namespace, the `in-addr.arpa` domain serves this purpose. The `in-addr.arpa` domain serves as the root for reverse lookup. To understand how the `in-addr.arpa` domain and reverse lookup work, you need to first examine IP addresses.

Each IP address is a dotted octet, or four sets of numbers ranging from 0 to 255, separated by periods. An example of a valid IP address is `206.210.128.90`. The `in-addr.arpa` domain delegates each octet as a subdomain. At the first level is `n.addr.arpa`, where n represents a number from 0 to 255 that corresponds to the left-most octet of an IP address. Each of these domains contains 256 subdomains, each representing the second octet. At the third level are subdomains that represent the third octet. Using the IP address given in this example, the reverse-lookup zone is `128.210.206.in-addr.arpa`. Figure 5-4 illustrates the reverse lookup domain `in-addr.arpa`.

FIGURE 5-4

The domain `in-addr.arpa` provides the capability to perform reverse lookup, mapping addresses to host names.

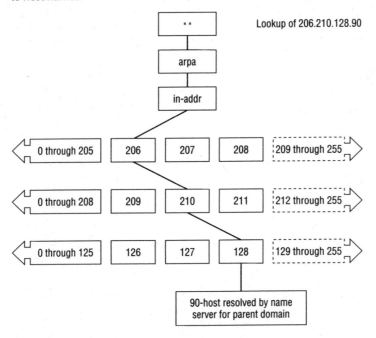

As the example in Figure 5-4 illustrates, reverse-lookup zones are structured in reverse notation from the IP address ranges that they represent. Take a forward lookup as an example, assuming that you're querying for the host `bob.support.midwest.mcity.us`. The lookup starts in the `.us` domain, moves to `mcity`, to `midwest`, to `support`, and then finally locates the `bob` host record. Reverse lookups happen in the same way, moving from least significant to most significant, right to left. Using the address from the preceding example, the reverse lookup starts in `in-addr.arpa`, moves to the `206` subdomain, to `210`, and then to `128`, where it finds the PTR record for the `.90` address and maps it to a host name. Using reverse notation to create the reverse lookup zones enables the query to start with the first octet of the address, which in this example is `206`.

The upper-level reverse lookup domains are hosted primarily by large ISPs such as AT&T, which delegate the subdomains to individual customers (or handle reverse lookup for them). Your primary concern is probably creating reverse-lookup zones for your subnets. Creating a reverse-lookup zone is a relatively simple task and is much like creating a forward-lookup zone. The only real difference is that instead of manually creating records in the reverse-lookup zone, you rely on the DNS service to do it for you automatically as you create records in forward-lookup zones. (You can find detailed steps for creating both forward and reverse lookup zones in the section "Microsoft Domain Name Services" later in this chapter.)

Delegation

Delegation is the primary mechanism that enables DNS to be a distributed namespace. Delegation enables a name server to delegate some or all of a domain to other name servers. The delegating server in effect becomes a "gateway" of sorts to the delegated domain, with individual domain records residing not on the delegating server but on those servers to which the subdomains are delegated. Figure 5-5 illustrates the process.

FIGURE 5-5

Delegation enables local control of subdomains where another organization has control and responsibility for the parent domain.

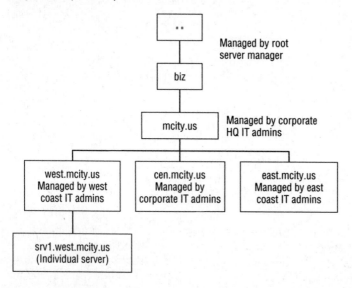

In the example of delegation shown in Figure 5-5, the root server for the .biz domain controls the mcity.us domain. The west.mcity.us domain is delegated to the West Coast IT staff, which hosts its own DNS servers and manages the DNS records for the subdomain. The subdomains for cen.mcity.us and east.mcity.us are managed by the corporate IT staff in Miami.

Delegation provides two primary benefits. One, it reduces the potential load on any given name server in the delegation chain. Suppose that all domains in the .com domain were hosted by one company. The company would need to host millions of domains, imposing an impossible load on their servers. More important, this situation would place a significant load on the poor administrators who would administer the zones. This load reduction leads to the second benefit: Delegation enables a decentralized administration, further enabling other organizations, such as subsidiaries of the company, to administer their own domains and have control over their resource records. (See the section "Configuring Subdomains and Delegation" later in this chapter for detailed steps on creating and delegating subdomains.)

Caching, forwarders, and slaves

The number of queries that could potentially hit an active and popular domain on the Internet could easily overwhelm a name server. Caching helps reduce that load and reduce network traffic. Each server caches successful and unsuccessful resolution queries for a period of time defined by the server's administrator. Whenever a resolver queries the server for an address, the server checks its cache first for the data, and, if the data exists in the cache, submits the cached data to the client, rather than look up the data again.

> **NOTE** Caching unsuccessful queries is called *negative caching*. Negative caching speeds response time, reduces server load, and reduces network traffic by eliminating repeated queries for names that can't be resolved (such as non-existent domains or hosts). As with positive caching, however, negative-cache results age and expire, enabling lookups to succeed when the domain or host record does become available.

Name servers can function as *caching-only servers*, which don't maintain any zone files and are not authoritative for any domain. A caching-only server receives queries from resolvers, performs the queries against other name servers, caches the results, and returns the results to the resolvers. Therefore, a caching-only server essentially acts as a lookup agent between the client and other name servers. At first glance, caching-only servers may seem to make little sense. They reduce network traffic, however, in two ways: Caching-only servers reduce zone transfers because the caching-only name server hosts no zones and, therefore, requires no zone transfers. Caching-only servers also reduce query traffic past the caching-only server as long as query results for a given query reside in the server's cache. Because the cache is cleared after the server restarts, the most effective caching-only server is one that remains up for extended periods.

A name server typically attempts to resolve queries against its own cache and zone files and, failing that, queries one or more other name servers for the information. In certain situations, you may not want all name servers for an organization to be communicating with the outside world — for network security, bandwidth, or cost reasons. Instead, you'd forward all traffic through a given name server that would act as a sort of agent for the other name servers in the organization. Assume, for example, that you have a few relatively slow or expensive Internet connections to your site and one with higher bandwidth or that is less costly. Servers A, B, and C connect through the former, and server D connects through the latter. Rather than have all servers generating traffic through their respective links, you might want to funnel all traffic through server D. In this case, server D would act as a *forwarder*, which forwards offsite name queries for other name servers on the network. Servers A, B, and C would handle queries against their local caches and zone files, and, failing those queries, would pass the query on to server D.

Name servers can interact with forwarders either exclusively or nonexclusively. If interacting nonexclusively, the server attempts to resolve queries against its cache and own zone files first. Failing that, the server forwards the request to the designated forwarder. If the forwarder fails the query, the server attempts to resolve the query on its own through other name servers. To prevent a server from doing this, you need to configure it as a *slave*, which makes it function in exclusive mode with the forwarder. When functioning as a slave, a name server first attempts to resolve a query against its cache and local zone files. Failing that, it forwards the query to the designated forwarder. If that fails, the forwarder responds with an unsuccessful query, and the local server fails the request to the client resolver without attempting any further resolution.

You also can configure a slave name server as a *caching-only slave*. In this configuration, the server hosts no zone files. It attempts to resolve queries against its local cache only and, failing that, forwards the query to the designated forwarder and takes no further action to resolve the query. It does not itself fail the request to the resolver.

Recursion, iteration, and referrals

Figure 5-6 illustrates a query for resolution of the host name `jane.west.mcity.us`. As the figure shows, the name server directly queried by the client must perform several queries to find a definitive answer. The other name servers do relatively little work, mostly responding with referrals, which simply point the originating server to a different name server farther down the namespace hierarchy. In effect, these other servers are saying, "I don't have the answer, but so-and-so does," referring to the name server contained in the referral.

FIGURE 5-6

Resolution of the host name jane.west.mcity.us shows recursion and referrals.

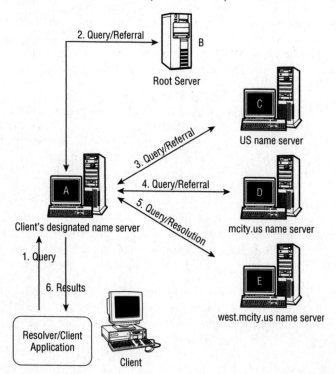

DNS uses two primary means to resolve queries: *recursion* and *iteration* (also referred to as *nonrecursive*). A recursive query is the method used by server A in Figure 5-6. In this example, the resolver sends a recursive query to server A, which starts the resolution process by querying the root server B. Server B responds with a referral to server C, which hosts the root of the .biz domain. Server C responds with a referral to server D, which hosts the *mcity.us* domain. Server D responds with a referral to server E, which hosts the delegated west.mcity.us subdomain. Server E contains the appropriate host record and returns the address for jane.west.mcity.us. In other words, in a recursive query, the queried server (in this case A) continues to query other servers until it finds a definitive answer; then it returns that answer to the resolver. A recursive query places the most load on the client's name server.

An iterative query places the majority of the load on the client. In the iterative query shown in Figure 5-7, the client resolver requests resolution of the same host, jane.west.mcity.us. In this example, however, name server A simply responds with the best information that it already has for the query. If the resolved query resides in Server A's cache, it responds with that data. Otherwise, it gives the client a referral to a name server that can help the resolver continue the query on its own. In the case of Figure 5-7, server A provides a referral to server B, which gives the client resolver a referral to C, and so on, until server E finally provides the answer to the resolver.

FIGURE 5-7

An iterative query of jane.west.mcity.us.

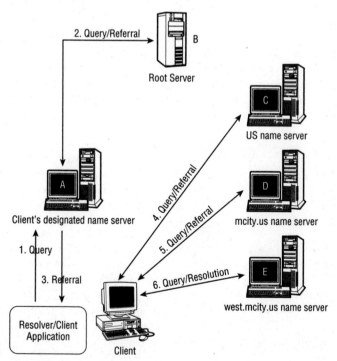

One main difference between recursive and iterative queries is the fact that recursive queries place the majority of the responsibility for resolving the query on the name server, whereas the iterative query places the responsibility with the client resolver. To adequately process iterative queries, therefore, a client resolver must be more complex and "smarter" than one that relies only on recursive queries. Recursive queries also tax the client's designated name server(s) much more than iterative queries. Name servers in general and Windows Server 2008 in particular enable you to disable the server's support for recursive queries, forcing the clients to use iterative queries. You might choose this option in situations where you need to limit the load on the server. Another reason to disable recursion is if you're setting up a name server that services only the LAN or WAN and you don't want it to attempt to resolve queries for domains outside that general area.

Microsoft Domain Name Services

Windows Server 2008 includes the Microsoft Domain Name Services (DNS) service, which you can use to set up and manage a Windows Server 2008 DNS server. As with other services, Windows Server 2008 provides a Microsoft Management Console (MMC) to enable you to manage DNS servers, zones, and resource records. The previous sections of the chapter explain the concepts behind the DNS service. The following sections focus on installing and configuring DNS and setting up zones and domains.

Installing DNS

You can install DNS through the Add or Remove Programs applet in the Control Panel. Open the Add or Remove Programs applet and in the Add or Remove Programs window that appears, click Add/Remove Windows Components. Double-click Networking Services or select the item and click Details. Select Domain Name System (DNS) and click OK. Follow the remaining prompts to complete installation of the software.

Overview of the DNS console

The *DNS console* included with the DNS service enables you to set up a DNS server, create and manage zones, create and manage resource records, and so on. In short, the DNS console is a single point of contact for all DNS management. Figure 5-8 shows the DNS console. Open the DNS console from the Administrative Tools folder.

By default, the DNS console shows the local server, but you can connect to any Windows Server 2008 DNS (or the DNS servers of previous versions of Windows Server) through the console. The console now provides you with the ability to set up conditional forwarding — this is not available with versions prior to Windows Server 2008. Conditional forwarding is a new feature that improves conventional forwarding by forwarding according to domain names provided in the queries. In other words, you can configure the DNS servers to forward queries to other forwarders by the provided domain names contained in the queries.

FIGURE 5-8

Use the DNS console to manage DNS servers locally and remotely.

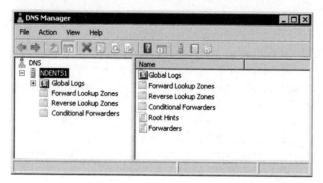

To connect to a server, right-click DNS in the left pane and choose Connect to DNS Server. Select The Following Computer radio button and then specify the computer's name or IP address in the corresponding text box. Click OK to connect.

After you connect to a server, you find three primary branches in the left pane: Forward Lookup Zones, Reverse Lookup Zones, and Conditional Forwarders. Expanding the Forward Lookup Zones, branch displays all forward-lookup zones, each under its own sub-branch. Expanding the Reverse Lookup Zones branch displays all reverse-lookup zones in their own sub-branches.

How the contents of a zone branch appear depends on whether the zone is for a Windows Server 2008 Active Directory domain or simply a DNS domain. If it's for a Windows Server 2008 domain, you find additional branches for domain-related services and objects, such as Kerberos, LDAP, sites, and more (see Chapters 20 and 21).

Creating forward-lookup zones

Each domain that you host for DNS requires a forward-lookup zone, a zone file, and associated records. You create the zone in the DNS console by using one of the following three options:

- **Active Directory Integrated.** This option creates the zone in the Active Directory, or AD, which provides for replication, integrated storage, security, and the other advantages inherent in the AD. The zone file is stored within the AD. You can create an AD-integrated zone only on a domain controller, giving the DNS service direct access to the database mechanisms of AD. You can't create AD-integrated zones on member servers that function as DNS servers.

- **Standard Primary.** This option creates a standard primary zone using a .dns file in %systemroot%\System32\Dns (default location). You can add and modify resource records in a primary zone.

■ **Standard Secondary.** This option creates a standard secondary zone using a `.dns` file in `%systemroot\System32\Dns`. This is a read-only copy of a zone on another server. You cannot create or modify resource records in a secondary zone.

Windows Server 2008 provides a wizard to help you create a zone. Right-click either the server name or on the Forward Lookup Zone branch and choose New Zone from the context menu to start the New Zone Wizard. In addition to prompting you for the type of zone (AD-integrated, primary, secondary, stub), the wizard prompts for the following information:

■ **Forward Lookup Zone/Reverse Lookup Zone.** Choose the type of zone that you want to create. In this case, choose Forward Lookup Zone.

■ **Zone Name.** Specify the full name of the zone, such as `mcity.us`, `west.mcity.us`, and so on. If you are specifying a second-level zone such as `west.mcity.us`, make sure that you first create the first-level zone for `mcity.us` on its designated name server. You then delegate `west.mcity.us` on that server to the current server.

■ **DNS Zone File.** Specify a zone-file name under which to store the zone's records if you're creating a standard primary or standard secondary zone. Specifying an existing file enables you to migrate existing resource records to the new zone. AD-integrated zones are stored in the AD and don't require an external file.

After you create a forward-lookup zone, you can begin populating it with resource records. Before doing so, however, first create any required reverse-lookup zones. Creating the reverse-lookup zone(s) before creating the resource records enables DNS to automatically create the PTR records in the reverse-lookup zones for resource records that you create in the forward-lookup zones.

Creating reverse-lookup zones

You create a reverse-lookup zone in much the same way that you create a forward-lookup zone. The primary difference is that you specify the subnet for the zone, and the DNS console converts that to the appropriate reverse zone name. Enter `208.141.230` after you're prompted, for example, and the DNS console creates the reverse lookup zone `230.141.208.in-addr.arpa`. You do not need to specify three octets unless you're creating a reverse-lookup zone for a domain that uses a class-C address space. Specify the appropriate number of octets to define your reverse lookup zone. In addition, you can choose to specify the DNS filename yourself, but remember to enter it in reverse notation.

Creating resource records

After you create a zone, you can populate it with resource records. As you create a zone, the Windows Server 2008 DNS service automatically creates the SOA record and NS record for you.

To create new records, right-click the zone in the left pane or right-click the right pane and choose New Host, New Alias, or New Mail Exchanger from the context menu to create A, CNAME, or MX records. Alternatively, choose Other New Records to create other types of resource records. The information that you provide will vary slightly depending on the type of record that you're creating.

Host records (A)

Host, or A, records map a host name to an IP address and are the primary means by which names are resolved. Each host in your network that you want visible through DNS needs to have a host record in its corresponding zone.

In creating a host record, you specify the host name (such as www, ftp, tia, server, and so on) and the IP address to map to that host. You can't add a host name containing periods, because anything after the period is considered part of the domain name. Select the Create Associated Pointer (PTR) Record option after creating the record in the DNS console to have DNS automatically create a pointer record in the reverse-lookup zone for the domain. DNS chooses the appropriate reverse-lookup zone based on the IP address that you specify for the host.

> **TIP** If you need to create a host name that contains a period, first create a parent-level zone for the second half of the name. If you're attempting to create joe.west in the mcity.us domain, for example, you first need to create a west zone as a subdomain of mcity.us. Then create the host record for joe in the west.mcity.us subdomain.

Alias (CNAME) records

Alias, or CNAME, records map an alias name to an existing FQDN. Assume, for example, that you're the administrator for mcity.us and you have a server in your network named srv1, with a corresponding A record for srv1 that points to the server's IP address. You want to use the server as a Web server, so you create an alias for www that points to srv1.mcity.us. Users connect to www.mcity.us, and DNS actually routes them transparently to srv1.mcity.us.

In creating an alias record, you specify the alias name and the Fully Qualified Domain Name of the host to which the alias points. As with a host record, you can't include a period in the host name for the alias. The FQDN for the alias can and does have periods in it, because by definition an FQDN contains the domain name in which the host resides.

Mail Exchanger records (MX)

Mail Exchanger, or MX, records enable mail to be routed through or to a domain. They specify *mail exchangers*, or servers that process mail for the domain. For MX records, specify the single-part name for the Mail Exchanger in the Host or Domain field. If you leave this field blank, the Mail-Exchanger name is the same as the parent domain name. In the Mail Server field, specify the FQDN of the server that acts as the Mail Exchanger. The FQDN that you specify here must resolve to a host (A) record in the zone, so make sure that you create the A record for the Mail Exchanger as well as the MX record. You can click Browse to browse the DNS namespace for the appropriate host name if you're not sure what it is. Finally, specify the preference number for the Mail Exchanger in the Mail Server Priority field.

Service Location records (SRV)

Service Location, or SRV, records are another common resource record type that offers excellent flexibility if a domain contains multiple servers for specific services, such as multiple HTTP servers. SRV records enable you to easily move a service from one host to another, and to designate certain hosts as primary for a given service and others as secondary for that same service. You might designate a server as the primary Web (HTTP) server, for example, and two others as secondary servers to handle HTTP requests whenever the primary server is heavily loaded or offline.

Resolvers that support SRV records submit a request to the DNS server for servers in the subject domain that provide a specific TCP/IP service (such as HTTP). The DNS server responds with a list of all servers in the domain that have a corresponding SRV record for the requested service type.

To create an SRV record, right-click the zone in the DNS console and choose Other New Records from the context menu. Select Service Location from the list and click Create Record to open the New Resource Record dialog box (it opens to the Service Location tab), as shown in Figure 5-9.

FIGURE 5-9

Use the Service Location (SRV) tab of the New Resource Record dialog box to create SRV records for specific services offered by specific servers.

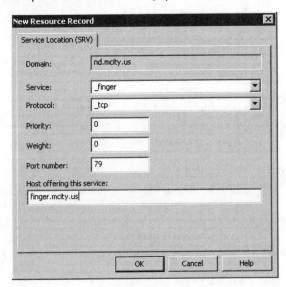

Fill in the fields for the SRV record, using the following list as a guide:

- **Service.** Select the predefined service type offered by the target server (FTP, HTTP, and so on).
- **Protocol.** Select either tcp or udp, depending on the requirements of the service.

- **Priority.** Specify an integer between 0 and 65535. This value specifies the preference order of the server, just as the preference number for an MX record identifies the priority of the target Mail Exchanger. A lower value places the server higher in the priority list (0 is highest priority); a higher value gives the server a lower priority. The client tries the server with the highest priority first. Failing that, it attempts connections to other servers in decreasing priority. Multiple servers can have the same priority value.

- **Weight.** Specify an integer between 0 and 65535 to allocate a weight to the target server for load-balancing purposes. If multiple servers have the same priority value, the weight value serves as a secondary priority indicator. Hosts with a higher weight value are returned first to the resolver client. Use a value of 0 to turn off weighting if you don't need load balancing. Using a value of 0 speeds up SRV queries and improves performance.

- **Port Number.** Specify an integer from 0 to 65535 to indicate the tcp or udp port number used by the target service.

- **Host Offering This Service.** Specify the FQDN of the target server offering the service. The FQDN must resolve to a valid name supported by a host record in the server's domain.

- **Allow Any Authenticated User to Update All DNS Records with the Same Name.** Apply an ACL to the record, enabling any authenticated user to update the record. This setting is available only for resource records of zones stored in the Active Directory.

Other record types

You can create other types of resource records by right-clicking the zone in the DNS console and choosing Other New Records from the context menu. The DNS console displays the Resource Record Type dialog box. Select from this dialog box the type of record that you need to create and then click Create Record. DNS displays the New Resource Record dialog box, which prompts for the required data, which varies from one record type to the next.

Configuring zone properties

A zone's properties determine how the zone performs zone transfers, ages resource records, and other behavior for the zone. The following sections explain the options available for a zone. To set these options, open the DNS console, right-click the zone, and choose Properties.

General zone properties

A zone's General property page enables you to configure the following options:

- **Status.** Click Pause to pause a zone and stop it from responding to queries. Click Start to start a paused zone. You might pause a zone while making extensive changes to the records in the zone or performing other administrative tasks on the zone.

- **Type.** You can change a zone's type on the General page to any of the three supported types (AD-integrated, standard primary, or standard secondary). If a server for a primary standard zone fails, for example, you can change its secondary zone on a different server to a primary zone.

- **Zone File Name.** Use this property to change the file in which the zone records are stored. By default, the zone filename is `zone.dns`, where `zone` is the name of the zone. The resource records for `west.mcity.us`, for example, would be stored by default in `west.mcity.us.dns`.

- **Dynamic Updates.** Use this option to enable/deny dynamic updates by Dynamic Host Configuration Protocol (DHCP) clients and servers to resource records in the zone and corresponding pointer records. See the section "Dynamic DNS" later in this chapter for detailed information.

- **Aging.** Select this to specify aging properties for records in the zone. See the section "Configuring Scavenging" later in this chapter for a detailed explanation.

Start of Authority properties

The Start of Authority (SOA) property page for a zone enables you to configure the zone's SOA record. This property page contains the following properties:

- **Serial Number.** DNS uses this value to determine when a zone transfer is required. The DNS service increments the value by 1 each time the zone changes to indicate that the zone is a new version. Other servers performing zone transfers with the server use this value to determine whether a zone transfer is needed. If the value is higher than the remote server's records for the zone, the server initiates a zone transfer to update the remote server's zone records. Use the Increment button to increment the serial number and force a zone transfer.

- **Primary Server.** This specifies the host name of the primary master for the selected zone. If you need to change the value, type the host name of the primary master or click Browse to browse the network for the primary master. Make sure that you include a period at the end of the host name.

- **Responsible Person.** This property specifies the e-mail address of the person responsible for managing the zone. The data takes the form of an FQDN. The address `administrator@mcity.us`, for example, should be entered as `administrator.mcity.us`, replacing the @ symbol with a period.

- **Refresh Interval.** This value specifies how often servers that host secondary copies of the zone should check the currency of their zone data against the primary zone data. The default is 15 minutes.

- **Retry Interval.** This value specifies the amount of time that must elapse before a server hosting a secondary copy of the zone retries a connection to the primary zone when a previous connection attempt failed. This value should usually be less than the refresh interval and defaults to 10 minutes.

- **Expires After.** This specifies the period of time that a server hosting a secondary copy of the zone can wait before discarding its secondary data if its zone data hasn't been refreshed. This prevents the secondary servers from serving potentially stale data to client requests. The default is 24 hours.

- **Minimum (Default) TTL.** This value specifies the amount of time that querying servers can cache results returned from this zone. After this period expires, the remote server removes the record from its cache. The default is one hour.

- **TTL for This Record.** This value specifies the time-to-live for the SOA record itself. The default is one hour.

Name servers properties

The Name Servers page enables you to modify the NS records for the zone. The advantage to using this method, rather than manually changing each record, is that you can view all NS records in the zone in a single dialog box. To modify a record, select the record and click Edit. Windows Server 2008 DNS displays a dialog box that you can use to modify the host name, IP address, or time-to-live value for the NS record. When modifying the host name, make sure that the name contains a period at the end. You can click Add to add a new NS record.

WINS properties

The WINS page determines whether the DNS service attempts to resolve through WINS any names that it can't resolve on its own. Use the following properties to configure WINS integration:

- **Use WINS Forward Lookup.** Select this option to enable the DNS service to query WINS for any names that it can't resolve on its own through DNS.

- **Do Not Replicate This Record.** Select this option to prevent the DNS server from replicating WINS-specific resource data to other DNS servers during zone transfers. You need to use this option if you are performing zone transfers to servers that don't support WINS (such as non-Microsoft DNS servers).

- **IP Address.** Specify the IP addresses of the WINS servers to query.

- **Advanced.** Click to set the cache timeout and lookup timeout periods. The cache timeout specifies the amount of time other servers can cache results returned through a WINS lookup. The lookup timeout specifies the amount of time that the DNS server can wait for a response from the WINS server(s) before generating a "Name not found" error.

Zone transfer properties

The Zone Transfers page of a zone's properties specifies the servers that can request and receive a copy of the zone's data through a zone transfer. You can configure the zone to enable all servers to request a transfer, only servers listed on the zone's Name Servers property page, or only servers included in a list of IP addresses that you define.

Click Notify to specify how other servers are notified of zone updates. You can configure the zone to automatically notify servers listed on the Name Servers property page for the zone, or servers included in a list of IP addresses that you define. Deselect the Automatically Notify option if you don't want the DNS server to notify the other servers whenever the zone data changes.

Managing DNS Server Options and Behavior

You can use the DNS console to configure various options that determine how the DNS service functions. The following sections explain the different properties and behavior that you can configure, including how to set up a forwarder and perform monitoring and logging.

Configuring multiple addresses on a DNS server

By default, the DNS service responds on all IP addresses bound to the server. You face no real performance penalty in enabling the DNS service to respond on all bound IP addresses, but in some situations, you may want to reduce the addresses to only those that you specifically want associated with the DNS service. You might allocate two addresses that are always used for DNS, but, in effect, "reserve" the other IP addresses on the server for other uses. Assume, for example, that you have the addresses 192.168.0.2 through .10 bound to the server. If you enable the DNS service to respond on all addresses, users may conceivably start using 192.168.0.10 for DNS if they know that it's there. A few months down the road, you remove .10 from the server because you want to use it elsewhere. Suddenly, those users who have been using .10 as a DNS server find themselves unable to resolve. If you start out limiting DNS to a specific set of addresses that is always used on the server for DNS, you can avoid the problem. In addition, you might want to restrict DNS to a subset of the available addresses for security, firewall configuration, or other infrastructure reasons.

You configure the addresses on which the server responds through the Interfaces tab of the server's property sheet. Open the DNS console, right-click the server, and choose Properties from the context menu to open the property sheet for the server. On the Interfaces page, choose All IP Addresses if you want the server to respond to DNS queries on all IP addresses bound to the server. Choose the Only the Following IP Addresses option if you want to limit the server to responding on only the IP addresses listed in the associated box. Use Add and Remove to change the contents of the list.

Using a forwarder

The section "Caching, Forwarders, and Slaves" earlier in this chapter discusses the use of forwarders and how they enable you to funnel DNS requests through specific servers for purposes of administration, access, or bandwidth control. You configure a Windows Server 2008 DNS server to use a forwarder through the Forwarders page of the server's property sheet. Open the DNS console, right-click the server, choose Properties to display the property sheet, and then click the Forwarders tab. Use the following controls to configure forwarding:

- **DNS Domain.** Click New to add the domain name to which queries will be forwarded.
- **Selected Domain's Forwarder IP Address List.** Specify the IP address of a server to which queries should be forwarded. You can specify multiple servers.

- **Number of Seconds Before Forward Queries Time Out.** Specify the time in seconds that the DNS server waits for a response from a listed forwarder. At the end of this timeout period, the local DNS server submits a query to the next server on the list until it receives a response or cycles through the list.

- **Do Not Use Recursion for This Domain.** Select this option to configure the server as a forwarding-only slave, preventing the server from attempting to resolve queries on its own if the forwarder cannot resolve the query. Leave this option deselected (the default) to enable the local server to attempt resolution if the forwarders cannot respond to the query.

Configuring advanced settings

The Advanced page of a DNS server's property sheet enables you to set several advanced options that control the way the server functions. To configure the following settings, open the DNS console, right-click the server, choose Properties, and click the Advanced tab:

- **Disable Recursion.** Select this option to prevent the server from performing recursive queries. With this option selected, the server replies with referrals instead of recursively querying until a resolution is reached.

- **BIND Secondaries.** To optimize zone transfer speed, Windows Server 2008 DNS servers (by default) use compression and submit multiple resource records in a single TCP message whenever performing zone transfers. This method is compatible with servers running BIND (Berkeley Internet Name Domain) version 4.9.4 and later, but is incompatible with earlier versions of BIND. To optimize performance, leave this option deselected if your server is not going to be performing zone transfers with these earlier systems. Select this option to have the Windows Server 2008 DNS server perform slower, uncompressed zone transfers to ensure compatibility with these older systems.

- **Fail on Load if Bad Zone Data.** The Windows Server 2008 DNS service, by default, continues to load a zone even when it detects errors in the zone data, logging the errors but not failing. Select this option if you want the DNS service to stop loading the zone when the zone data contains errors.

- **Enable Round Robin.** The Windows Server 2008 DNS service, by default, rotates and reorders a list of host records if a given host name is associated with multiple IP addresses. This round-robin behavior enables an administrator to perform load balancing, directing traffic to multiple computers with the same host name but different IP addresses (such as multiple servers hosting www.mcity.us). With this option selected, the server responds to queries with each address in turn. Deselect this option if you want to disable round robin and have the server return the first match in the zone.

- **Enable Netmask Ordering.** If a given zone contains multiple host records that map the same host name to multiple IP addresses, the Windows Server 2008 DNS service can order the response list according to the IP address of the client. Windows Server 2008 DNS checks the IP address of the client against the addresses of the host records and if a record falls in the client's subnet, the DNS service places that host record first in the list.

This directs the client to the requested host that is closest and typically fastest for the client to access, which is very important for Active Directory services. This option is selected by default. Deselect this option to prevent the DNS service from reordering responses based on subnet. Netmask ordering supersedes round-robin ordering, although round robin is used for secondary sorting if enabled, and it is useful where subnets are in different geographical locations.

■ **Secure Cache Against Pollution.** The Windows 2003 DNS service does not add unrelated resource records added in a referral from another DNS server to the Windows Server 2008 server's cache. It caches referrals that might not match the queried host name, however, such as caching a referral for `www.sillycity.com` if querying for `www.mcity.us`. Selecting this option prevents the DNS service from caching nonrelated referrals.

■ **Name Checking.** Internet host names were originally limited to alphanumeric characters and hyphens. Although this limitation was maintained after DNS was developed, it posed a problem in some situations, particularly for supporting international character sets. This option controls how the DNS service performs name checking. By default, Windows Server 2008 uses the UTF8 (Unicode Transformation Format) character set, which provides the broadest and least restrictive character set support. Select Strict if you need to limit names to the standard format. Use Non-RFC to permit names that do not follow the RFC 1123 specification. Use Multibyte to recognize characters other than ASCII, including Unicode.

■ **Load Zone Data on Startup.** By default, the Windows Server 2008 DNS service loads zone data from the Active Directory (for AD-integrated zones) and from the registry. You can configure the server to load only from the registry or from a BIND 4 boot file. This latter option enables you to essentially duplicate a BIND server under Windows Server 2008, importing all the zone data. Notice that the boot file — typically called `Named.boot` — must use the BIND 4 format, rather than the newer BIND 8 format.

■ **Enable Automatic Scavenging of Stale Records.** Stale records typically are those that point to hosts no longer on the network. Accumulation of stale records can lead to decreased storage space, degradation of server performance, incorrect name-to-address resolution, and no capability for a host to have the DNS service create its resource record (through Dynamic DNS). Scavenging, which is turned off by default, enables the DNS server to use timestamps and other properties to determine when a resource record is stale and automatically remove it from the zone. Records added automatically through DDNS are subject to scavenging, as is any record manually added with a timestamp that you have modified from its default of zero. Resource records with a timestamp of zero are not subject to scavenging. Select this option and configure the associated scavenging period. Notice that scavenging must be enabled for individual zones in their properties as well. For additional information on scavenging, see the section "Dynamic DNS" later in this chapter.

■ **Reset to Default.** Select this option to reconfigure all advanced settings to their defaults.

Setting root hints

Root hints direct a name server to the root servers for domains at a higher level or in different subtrees of the DNS namespace and, in effect, provide a road map for a DNS server to resolve queries for domains outside of its area of authority. For DNS servers connected to the Internet, the root hints should point to the Internet root name servers. For DNS servers that provide services only to a private network, the root hints should point to the root server(s) for your domain or organization. Servers that function as forwarders for local clients requesting resolution of Internet names should have their root hints point to the Internet root servers, while the other name servers in the organization should point to the local root server for the organization's private network.

By default, the Windows Server 2008 DNS service uses a `cache.dns` file that contains the list of Internet root servers. You find `cache.dns` located in `\%systemroot%\System32\Dns`. Browsing the file in Notepad or WordPad shows you that the file contains entries for NS and A records for the Internet root servers. If you're connecting a name server to the Internet, use the `cache.dns` file to ensure that you have the appropriate root hints. If you're creating a name server for your internal network, however, you should instead use a `cache.dns` file that contains the NS and A records of the name servers higher in your local namespace, rather than the root Internet servers.

You can edit the `cache.dns` file directly by using Notepad or WordPad if you need to modify its entries. If you prefer, you can use the interface provided by the DNS console to modify the `cache.dns` file. To do so, open the DNS console, right-click the server for which you want to modify the `cache.dns` file, and then choose Properties. Click the Root Hints tab to display the Root Hints page. Use Add, Edit, and Remove to add, modify, and remove entries from the `cache.dns` file, respectively.

NOTE Entries in the `cache.dns` file consist of an NS record and a corresponding A record for each name server, located on two separate lines. The first line specifies the NS record. This line begins with an @ symbol, followed by a tab, and then NS, another tab, and then the FQDN of the root server. On the next line, specify the FQDN of the server, a tab, and then A to indicate an A record, another tab, and finally the IP address of the server.

If you are running internal name servers that don't need root hints to servers higher in the local area, you should eliminate root hints altogether. The easiest way to do this is to rename or delete the `cache.dns` file and then stop and restart the DNS server.

TIP Although the root name servers change infrequently, the root servers can change for a variety of reasons. You can acquire a new list of root server records via FTP from Network Solutions by downloading the file `ftp.rs.internic.net/domain/named.root`. You can use the file directly as your `cache.dns` file without modifications. You can also click Copy from Server on the Root Hints page to copy the root hints from another server. (You specify the IP address of the other server.)

Configuring logging

By default, the DNS service does not perform extensive logging because the number of potential queries in a relatively small amount of time can be quite large, particularly for servers that serve a large portion of the namespace or a large number of clients. You can configure logging for reasons related to troubleshooting, security, and so on through the properties for the DNS server. The service provides two types of logging: event logging and debug logging, described in the following sections.

Configuring basic logging

Basic logging (or *event logging*) is useful for identifying potential problems and basic troubleshooting. You configure basic logging through the Event Logging page of the DNS server's properties. Open the DNS console, right-click the server, choose Properties, and click the Event Logging tab. Select the items to be logged and click OK. The DNS service stores log entries in `\%systemroot%\System32\Dns\Dns.log`. If yours is a busy server, however, understand that logging even a few items can consume a lot of server time and create a potentially very large log file.

Using debug logging

If basic logging fails to help you identify the cause of a DNS server problem, you can enable *debug logging*, which records packets sent and received by the DNS server. Debug logging generates a very significant amount of log traffic and corresponding server overhead, so you should use debug logging only if basic logging does not provide the information that you need to address the problem at hand.

To configure debug logging, open the DNS console, right-click the server, and choose Properties. Click the Debug Logging tab to display the Debug Logging page of the server's property sheet (see Figure 5-10). Use the Packet Direction group of controls to log incoming packets, outgoing packets, or both. Use the Transport Protocol options to choose which protocol(s) to log.

The Packet Contents and Packet Type groups of controls enable you to choose the types of packets that the DNS service logs. Enable the Details option if you want the entire contents of the packets logged, rather than a subset of the contents.

If you're having problems with certain servers or clients, you can enable the Filter Packets by IP Address option, which causes the DNS service to log the IP addresses of the source and destination servers. You can then click Filter to specify a list of servers (by IP address) that are logged.

Finally, use the File Path and Name field to specify the path and filename for the log file, and the Maximum Size field to specify the maximum log file size.

FIGURE 5-10

Configure extended logging on the Debug Logging page.

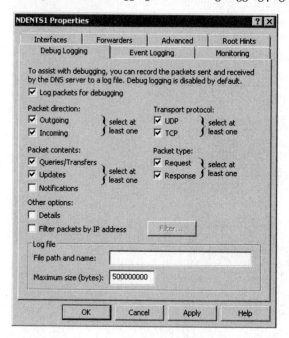

Monitoring and testing

The Monitoring property page for a DNS server enables you to issue test queries against the local server and recursive queries against other name servers. This helps you test the server and its capability to communicate successfully with other name servers. This is an extremely useful tool, because most other methods for this type of testing typically use a cumbersome command-line interface. To display the Monitoring page to perform testing, open the DNS console, right-click the server, choose Properties, and click the Monitoring tab, as shown in Figure 5-11.

The following list explains the options on the Monitoring page:

- **A Simple Query Against This DNS Server.** Choose this option to perform an iterative test against the local server.

- **A Recursive Query to Other DNS Servers.** Choose this option to perform a recursive query against other DNS servers (which start with the DNS servers defined in the local server's TCP/IP properties).

- **Perform Automatic Testing at the Following Interval.** Select this option to perform periodic, automatic testing by using the preceding two testing options.

- **Test Interval.** Specify the frequency of automatic tests.

- **Test Results.** This list shows the results of tests and includes the test date, time, and results.

FIGURE 5-11

Use the Monitoring page to issue test queries.

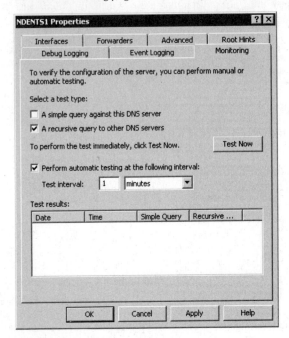

Applying security

Windows Server 2008 provides the capability to restrict access to a DNS server and/or selected zones, enabling you to control who can modify the server, add records, remove records, and so on. You can configure security for a server overall only if the server is a domain controller participating in the Active Directory. You can't configure security on member servers that host the DNS service or on standalone DNS servers. In addition, you can configure security on individual zones only when the zones are stored in the AD (set up as AD-integrated zones).

To apply security to a server overall, open the DNS console and connect to the server. Right-click the server and choose Properties to display its property sheet. In addition to the property pages discussed in the preceding sections is a Security tab. Click the Security tab to display the Security page, where you can define the permissions that groups or users have within the DNS server. Security at the server level acts as the first line of defense in protecting the server in general and the zones housed on the server.

You also can configure security for individual zones as a second layer of security, giving specific users or groups the capability to manage a given zone. Open the DNS console, right-click the zone in question, and choose Properties. Use the Security page in the zone's property sheet to configure security for the zone.

Managing the server and cache

You use the DNS console to manage the DNS server in addition to managing individual zones. The following list describes common administrative tasks and explains how to accomplish them using the DNS console:

- **Update data files.** The DNS service automatically stores changes to the data files at set intervals, and whenever the service shuts down, writes changes in memory to disk. A good practice is to update the data files manually whenever you add several records or make other changes to ensure that those changes are written to disk in the event of a problem with the server that would otherwise prevent the updates from occurring. To update the data files within the DNS console, right-click the server and choose Update Server Data Files.

- **Stop, start, pause, resume, or restart the DNS service.** You can control the DNS service on the local computer through the Services branch of the Computer Management console (which you access by right-clicking My Computer and choosing Manage). You might find using the DNS console easier, however, particularly in managing a remote DNS server. In the DNS console, right-click the server, choose All Tasks from the context menu, and choose the desired action (Start, Stop, and so on).

- **Clear the cache.** If a server's cache becomes polluted with bad records or you're having problems correctly resolving queries, clearing the cache can fix the problem if the problem is related to the cached queries. In the DNS console, right-click the server and choose Clear Cache to clear the contents of the cache. Note that this command does not affect the root hints defined by the `cache.dns` file.

Configuring Subdomains and Delegation

If yours is a small organization, you're likely to have only a single domain. Larger organizations, however, often segregate services and delegate responsibility and administration for different parts of the organization's namespace, or you may simply be hosting the DNS records for another organization. You accomplish these tasks through *subdomains* and *delegation*.

A *subdomain* is a child of an existing domain. The domain `west.mcity.us`, for example, is a subdomain of `mcity.us`. The domain `west.west.mcity.us` is a subdomain of `west.mcity.us`. The `mcity.us` domain serves as the primary domain for all of these. The `mcity.us` name server could host the resource records for all its subdomains, providing centralized management of the organization's namespace. Queries for hosts in the subdomains would be handled by the `mcity.us` name server(s). The `mcity.us` domain, however, could also *delegate* the subdomains to other name servers, such as name servers hosted at the sub-domain location. The domain `mcity.us` — located in Florida — may, for example, delegate `west.mcity.us` to the name servers for the support group located on the West coast. In this case, queries directed to the `mcity.us` name server would be referred to the `west.mcity.us` subdomain. The only real difference is that in the former example, all the zones and data reside on the `mcity.us` server, and in the latter, they are parceled out to other servers as required by the domain structure.

Setting up subdomains

Whether you're hosting a subdomain on the primary name server for the organization or dele-gating it, the first step is to create the subdomain. You accomplish this task through the DNS console. In the console, open the server on which you want to create the subdomain; then open the parent domain. To create the subdomain `west.mcity.us`, for example, open the `mcity.us` zone. Right-click the parent zone and choose New Domain. Windows Server 2008 prompts you for the subdomain name. Enter the single-part name (west in this example) and click OK. The subdomain appears as a sub-branch under the parent domain. After you create the subdomain, you can begin adding records to it. Just right-click the subdomain and choose the type of record that you want to create. As in creating records for a parent domain, you can specify only the single-part name for the host. If you're creating a host record for `jane.west.mcity.us`, for example, you would create a host record for jane in the `west.mcity.us` subdomain.

> **TIP**   Before creating resource records in a subdomain, verify that you have created the reverse-lookup zone for the subdomain. This enables the DNS service to automati-cally create pointer records for hosts that you define in the subdomain.

Delegating a subdomain

Rather than host a subdomain's records under the parent domain's name server, you may prefer to delegate the subdomain to another server. Assume, for example, that the Support group hosts its own DNS records on its own servers. In this case, you need to perform the following steps to delegate `support.mcity.us`:

1. On the Support group's name server, create the zone `support.mcity.us` and support reverse-lookup zone, as explained in the section "Reverse Lookup" earlier in this chapter; then populate the zone with the appropriate resource records for the hosts in `support.mcity.us`.

2. On the parent name server hosting `mcity.us`, open the DNS console and then open the `mcity.us` zone. Right-click the zone and choose New Delegation to start the New Delegation Wizard.

3. In the wizard, specify the delegated domain name (in this example, support). The wizard automatically assembles the FQDN for the delegated domain by using the parent domain as a postfix. Click Next.

4. On the Name Servers page, click Add to add the FQDN and IP address of the server(s) on which the subdomain's records are hosted. In this example, you'd specify the name and address of the server that hosts `support.mcity.us`.

5. Repeat Step 4 to add other name servers that host the subdomain's records, click OK, and then click Finish to complete the process.

DNS and Active Directory

The Windows Server 2008 DNS service provides integration with the AD to provide to the DNS service the advantages inherent in the AD's security, ease of management, replication, and so on. In fact, DNS integration with the AD is required for domain controllers (DCs) because the Windows Server 2008 Netlogon service uses DNS for locating DCs. A DC can run the DNS service itself or rely on other servers in the domain to provide DNS services, but a name server that supports dynamic updates and that is authoritative for the domain must be present. (See the section "Dynamic DNS" later in this chapter for more information on DDNS and dynamic updates.)

Integrating DNS in the AD provides a measure of fault tolerance for DNS. Because the DNS data for integrated zones is replicated throughout the DCs for the domain, any DC running the DNS service can handle client requests for resolution of names in the hosted domains. This means that you have no single point of failure for a given domain as long as it is hosted in an AD-integrated zone. One server can go offline, and others can continue to process requests for the domain. Changes to records in an AD-integrated zone are automatically replicated to other DCs running the DNS service, simplifying administration. If you bring a new DC online that is running the DNS service, the zone records are automatically replicated to the new DNS server. Synchronization of AD-integrated zones is also potentially more efficient than a standard zone transfer, because data is selectively transferred, rather than transferring an entire zone.

Security, discussed in the section "Applying Security" earlier in this chapter, is another important advantage to AD integration. You can apply access control lists (ACLs) to a server and to individual zones to define which users or groups can modify the server and records in the secured zones.

> **TIP** Only primary zones are supported for AD-integration. Secondary zones must be stored in standard zone files. By migrating all zones to the AD, however, you effectively eliminate the need for secondary zones, because the zones are replicated to other servers for redundancy and fault tolerance, the main purpose of secondary zones. If you maintain Windows NT-based DNS servers, however, you still need to rely on secondary zones.

Whenever you create a zone by using the DNS console, the wizard gives you the option of creating three types of zones: *AD-integrated*, *standard primary*, and *standard secondary*. Choose AD-integrated if you want to take advantage of the benefits offered by the AD for DNS.

CROSS-REF The AD is a complex topic that requires quite a bit of explanation in its own right. Refer to Part III for a detailed explanation of the AD's structure, function, replication, and administration.

Dynamic DNS

Dynamic DNS (DDNS) enables a Windows Server 2008 DNS server to automatically update resource records for clients if their host names or IP addresses change. Host name changes can occur when the remote computer changes computer name or becomes a member of another domain (which implicitly changes its FQDN). The use of DHCP is another argument for DDNS. As DHCP leases expire, a client computer's address can, and is likely to, change. This makes maintaining accurate DNS records for hosts on the network that use DHCP for address allocation difficult. DDNS resolves the problem.

DDNS functions through a client-server mechanism. Windows 2000, 2003, and XP DHCP clients support DDNS and can directly request that a Windows Server 2008 DNS server update their host resource (A) records whenever the clients' IP addresses or host names change. Windows Server 2008 DHCP servers can also submit requests on behalf of clients, although a DHCP server can request an update to both the clients' host and pointer (PTR) records.

A Windows Server 2008 DHCP server also can act as a proxy for non-DDNS-capable DHCP clients to perform dynamic DNS updates. A Windows Server 2008 DHCP server can, for example, perform updates for Windows 9x and Windows NT clients, which do not natively support Dynamic DNS and, therefore, cannot submit requests to either the DHCP server or DNS server to update their resource records. Figure 5-12 shows how DHCP and DNS interact.

CROSS-REF For a detailed discussion of configuring a Windows Server 2008 DHCP server to support DNS, see Chapter 4.

Configuring DDNS

Most of the configuration to support DDNS occurs on the client side. You do, however, have some configuration steps to take on the server side to implement DDNS. You enable dynamic updates on a zone-by-zone basis, and the types of updates permitted depend on whether the zone is stored in the AD. AD-integrated zones give you the additional option of permitting only secured updates, which use the ACL for the zone to determine who can perform an update. Standard zones not stored in the AD can be configured only for unsecured updates or no updates.

TIP Windows Server 2008 clients, by default, attempt to perform an unsecured update; failing that, they attempt a secured update. If you're having problems getting client records to update from servers or clients outside of a domain, make sure you haven't configured the zone for secured updates only. For optimum security, avoid using a DC as a DHCP server, because updates from the DHCP server always succeed, even if the zone is configured for secure updates only.

FIGURE 5-12

DHCP supports automatic updates to DNS if host name or IP address changes occur.

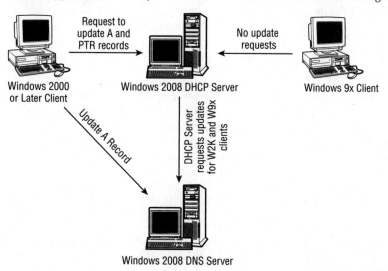

You configure a zone's DDNS behavior through the zone's properties. Open the DNS console, right-click the zone, and choose Properties. The Dynamic Updates option determines whether the server accepts dynamic updates for records in the zone. You can choose one of the following three options:

- **None.** Select this option to prevent DHCP clients or servers from updating resource records in the zone.

- **Nonsecure and Secure.** Select this option to enable DHCP clients and servers, including those outside the domain, to perform unsecured updates to the zone's resource records. DHCP servers can also update pointer records for dynamically updated host records.

- **Secure Only.** Select this option to require the DHCP client or server to authenticate in the domain in order to be capable of performing dynamic updates of host or pointer records.

CROSS-REF See Chapter 4 for information on how to configure a client for DDNS.

Configuring scavenging

As explained in the section "Domain Records and Zone Files" earlier in this chapter, records can become stale in a zone. A notebook user's computer, for example, may update its host record in its zone, but then the user disconnects from the network without shutting down. The computer remains off the network for an extended period, but the computer's host record still remains in the zone. As a result, the record becomes stale and potentially points to the wrong IP address (or the user might change her computer's host name). You can configure Windows Server 2008 DNS to *scavenge* records, removing those that are stale.

Windows Server 2008 uses a timestamp to determine whether a record is stale. The server scans the data at an administrator-defined interval, checking the resource records' timestamps to determine whether they have exceeded the refresh interval. If so, the server scavenges the record (removes it from the zone). Scavenging, by default, applies only to dynamically created records and has no effect on records that you create manually. The DNS server, however, applies a timestamp to resource records that you create manually, setting the timestamp to zero to indicate that the record is not subject to scavenging. You can modify the value to enable the DNS service to scavenge these records as well.

You configure scavenging in two places: at the server level and at the zone level. At the server level, you enable scavenging globally for the server and set the scavenging frequency, how often the server performs scavenging. The default value is seven days, and the minimum is one hour. To configure scavenging at the server level, open the DNS console, right-click the server, and choose Properties. Click the Advanced tab to display the Advanced property page. Select the Enable Automatic Scavenging of Stale Records option and then use the Scavenging Period control to specify how often the server should perform a scavenging operation. The more dynamic the network, the more frequently you should have the server perform scavenging. Choose a value that fits your network needs.

You also need to configure scavenging on a zone-by-zone basis. Scavenging can be applied only to primary zones. Open the DNS console, right-click the zone for which you want to configure scavenging, and choose Properties. On the zone's General property page, click Aging to open the Zone Aging/Scavenging Properties dialog box (see Figure 5-13).

FIGURE 5-13

Configure the zone's scavenging properties in the Zone Aging/Scavenging Properties dialog box.

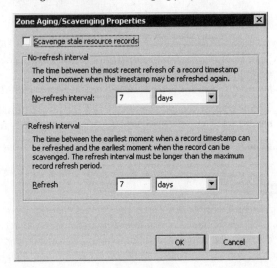

The dialog box contains the following two controls:

- **No-Refresh Interval.** This property essentially specifies the timestamp's time-to-live. Until this period expires, the record's timestamp can't be refreshed.
- **Refresh Interval.** This property defines the period of time that the timestamp can remain unrefreshed before the server scavenges the record.

Scavenging occurs automatically at the interval defined in the server's general scavenging properties. You can also manually initiate a scavenge. Open the DNS console, right-click the server, and choose Scavenge Stale Resource Records.

Windows Internet Name Service (WINS)

NetBIOS, described in Chapter 3, is a legacy API that has for many years served as the means by which you connect to file systems and network resources on corporate local area networks. Then along came TCP/IP and crashed the NetBIOS party, spiked the punch, and became the protocol of choice everywhere, not asking permission from authority higher up the OSI stack. As a result, many clients on a network cannot see the IP-flavored host names that map to IP addresses; instead, they can see only NetBIOS-flavored names. The solution' maps the NetBIOS names to IP addresses.

Windows Internet Name Service (WINS) was developed by Microsoft to provide a DNS-like Net-BIOS Name Service (NBNS) to map NetBIOS names to IP addresses. The "Internet" in WINS is a little misleading, because a NetBIOS name on the Internet is like a goldfish trying to breathe in olive oil. In essence, it also signifies taking a NetBIOS name and turning it into a neo-host name that can be mapped to an IP address, and as long as IP rules supreme and you take the input/output out of NetBIOS, it is nothing more than a label, even at the functional or application levels of the network.

WINS is more than just a name-IP address resolver, however. It enables centralized management of NetBIOS namespace data and eliminates the need to remotely manage multiple LMHOSTS files (which perform the same function for NetBIOS lookup that Hosts files perform for DNS lookup).

WINS also helps reduce NetBIOS broadcasts on the network to maximize bandwidth utilization, because clients can query the WINS server for a name-to-address mapping, enabling them to communicate directly with remote hosts, rather than generate broadcast traffic on the network.

WINS is needed on old Windows networks because the only way that the down-level operating systems flag their presence is via NetBIOS; and in many respects, it has been convenient even since the days that TCP/IP first showed up. Imagine a Windows network on which every server were listed under only its IP address.

WINS is also essential for getting those NetBIOS names resolved over TCP/IP subnets. NetBIOS is not routable, and it was never intended to be; nor are the primary protocols that carry Net-BIOS names, such as NetBEUI (although they can be encapsulated in TCP/IP communication packets that can be routed, a practice often used to route SNA traffic over TCP/IP). The only way, then, for NetBIOS to coexist in the routable world of IP addresses and IP internetworks is via WINS.

> **NOTE**   WINS communications take place in datagrams over the UDP port 137, which is reserved for NBNS.

Microsoft's strategy, in line with all the other Internet builders, is to abolish reliance on NetBIOS and to support TCP/IP and its successors as the only routable protocol on all networks. This strategy enables network administrators to gradually abolish NetBIOS from their networks as they replace down-level or NetBIOS-named computers and devices, and enables them to switch to native mode Windows Server 2008 deployment, which is more secure and rich.

However, for many companies, expect WINS and NetBIOS to be around for many years. In fact, we predict that the last vestiges of NetBIOS, and thus WINS, are not going to vanish for a few years yet. Change is not an overnight phenomenon in large corporate environments, where huge investments in corporate intranets are also underway. In fact, had it not been for Y2K, many companies would have kept Windows NT 3.51 around. The reasons to keep WINS around are patent if you consider the following two inescapable facts:

- **Investment in legacy systems.** NetBIOS has been the driving force on Windows networks since the advent of the networkable personal computer. In all those years, Windows has become the pervasive desktop operating system, and it is now poised to become the dominant server operating system.

- Our guess is that no one really knows how many copies of Windows are running in the world. Estimates range from tens of millions to hundreds of millions, so a huge investment in legacy, or so-called *down-level*, Windows operating systems still exists, from simple clients to mega-servers, and is likely to remain so for many years to come. Insofar as these systems, especially the servers, still use NetBIOS names, WINS is needed to resolve these names into IP addresses. In short, the best of both worlds — an entrenched namespace coexisting with an indispensable protocol.

- **Investment in legacy applications.** Many applications still use NetBIOS names in their code, so NetBIOS remains a fact on these networks until all applications no longer depend on NetBIOS or they can be removed from your network and information systems.

How WINS Works

All Windows 9x and later operating systems can request services of WINS. To request a name-IP address resolution, the client queries any WINS server designated to it on the network. It tries to contact WINS servers in the order assigned in the WINS address list in its TCP/IP configuration.

The client tries to connect to the WINS server three times before giving up and moving on to the next WINS server in the list.

After the client boots and authenticates on the network, it registers its name and IP address with the designated WINS server. If the client does not register automatically, the registration takes place whenever the client next makes a query or targets a folder on a remote server.

The process to connect to a NetBIOS name by using TCP/IP is as follows:

1. Computer MCSQL01 logs on to the network and makes a registration request with WINS. The NetBIOS name and IP address are thus recorded to the WINS database.

2. You come along and you need to connect workstation SQLCLIENT (at 10.5.4.132) to \\MCSQL01\SHARE1 (at 100.50.2.32), which you see in the browse list. SQLCLIENT needs to make a request of the WINS server for the IP address of MCSQL01 to effect a connection to the server via TCP/IP. In other words, the client needs to turn the target address \\MCSQL01\MYSHARE into \\100.50.2.32\MYSHARE because the only way to connect to the remote server, via several routers, is TCP/IP.

3. If the WINS server is unavailable, then SQLCLIENT tries two more times before trying the next WINS server in its list. Assuming that MCSQL01 happens to register with WINS and an IP address exists, the resolve is successful and the connection can be established.

4. Finally (and we are not being cheeky because we have needed to do this on many occasions with the old WINS), if you cannot see or connect to the share, you can phone the owner or admin of the server and ask for the IP address. For network *administrators* to do this to troubleshoot connections is okay. For *users* to do this every time that they need a file or a printer, however, is not okay.

WINS registration

The WINS architecture is very different from that of DNS. WINS maintains a database of name-IP address mappings. It is not hierarchical. After a client registers a mapping, the WINS server issues a successful registration message to the client. Encapsulated in that message is a time-to-live (TTL) value, which is like a "lease" on the name, held in trust by WINS for a certain period of time.

What if the name is already registered with WINS and the client makes a new registration attempt, or another client tries to register with the same NetBIOS name? WINS does not ignore the request; it sends out a verification request to the currently registered owner of the mapping. The request goes out three times at 500-millisecond intervals. If it has more than one IP address for the client, which is often the case on Windows NT, Windows 2000 Server, or Windows Server 2003/2008, WINS tries each address that it has for the registered owner. This verification regimen continues until all IP addresses are "called" or the owner responds.

If the owner responds, the client requesting the registration gets a polite decline. If the owner does not respond, however, the client requesting registration gets free passage.

Mapping renewal

WINS mappings are not persistent, and the WINS database is in a constant state of change. Leases on mappings are assigned on a temporary basis to enable other computers to claim the mapping later. The short-term lease method also enables clients with DHCP-assigned IP addresses to register their new addresses with WINS.

If the WINS client remains online, it needs to renew its lease before expiration on the WINS server. The client achieves this task by renewing automatically after one-eighth of the TTL has elapsed. If the client does not receive a renewal notification from the server, it continues to attempt renewal every two minutes, until half the TTL has elapsed. After that, the client moves on to the next WINS in its list and begins the renewal attempt with that server. WINS is a multimaster replication architecture, and which of the WINS servers honors the WINS registration request doesn't matter as far as the client and the networking-resolving process are concerned. If the next WINS in the list fails to honor the request, however, the client "hits" the leading server again.

On a successful registration renewal, the client attempts to renegotiate the next lease renewal after 50 percent of the TTL has elapsed.

If WINS clients are powered down normally — that is, by issuing the shutdown command — they send a message to WINS requesting release of the mapping. The message includes the entire mapping NetBIOS-IP address. The WINS server honors the request as long as the records check out. In other words, the mapping must exist or the values for IP address and name must be the same as in the message. If the request checks out, the record is *tombstoned* (marked for deletion); otherwise, it remains in the database.

WINS Forever

As important as WINS has been for many diverse Windows-based networks, the WINS service on NT 4.0 is not something that we look back on fondly, and for many with thousands of users spread over dozens of subnets, it has been more a case of WINS and "LOSSES."

Although WINS offered a measure of fault-tolerance on small intranets, it often let us down on large networks, losing connections, missing replication with its peers, and collecting garbage that needed to be manually deleted from the database. Often, intra-domain communications between sites would break down because records were not updated and the clients could not succeed with connections to critical services in other domains. Many network managers pleaded with Microsoft to rebuild the WINS service, and Microsoft did so with Windows 2000 Server. Thus WINS continues to be an integral and important "feature" of Windows Server 2008.

WINS features do not mean much to new administrators working with WINS, but they are welcome news for the old and the brave among you. Two important features are worthy of mention in this chapter: *persistent connections* and *manual tombstoning*, discussed in the following sections.

Persistent connections

WINS should never be implemented as a single-server solution unless a very small collection of users depends on the service and the business can afford the downtime and collapse of service level. For networks serving a lot of users or small offices that need to maintain critical connections across the intranet, WINS should be implemented in groups of two or more servers. Not all servers need to be on the same subnet, however, because should a local WINS fail, the client can hit a secondary on another subnet because it already knows the static address (via DHCP) of the secondary WINS server.

WINS servers thus coexist as loose clusters. (They interoperate but do not really function as a single logical unit.) After a client registers with WINS or whenever WINS tombstones a record, the information is replicated to WINS servers that are configured as replication partners. Often, replication on the old WINS on NT 4.0 would fail because requests to reestablish wouldn't occur. This would result in widely dispersed WINS databases being inconsistent and out of touch with each other.

Users on the intranet depend on the maintenance of connections between clients and servers placed at opposite ends of the intranet. If WINS servers cannot comply with requests, the user usually gets the "Network Path Not Found" error message, and the attempted connection fails. This message may seem to suggest that the host is down, but often it is WINS that is at fault, so first try to ping the host by name to rule out a WINS problem.

TIP Always keep a database of your static IP addresses handy. If you can ping the host that is not being resolved by WINS and you can manually map to a known share on the host, such as \\192.168.4.8\shares, you can be almost certain that WINS is in trouble.

Windows Server 2003 and 2008 WINS can be configured to request a permanent connection across the intranet with any or all replication partners. Persistent replication offers two major advantages.

Significant overhead associated with starting and stopping connections is reduced. Legacy WINS would need to reestablish connections with replication partners every time that it needed to replicate. A chance always exists on a very large intranet that a connection cannot be established automatically and requires human intervention.

The speed of replication has also been greatly increased, because updates can be sent directly to the replication partner, obviating the need to first establish connections.

Manual tombstoning

You can manually mark records for deletion by using the manual tombstoning feature in Windows Server 2008 WINS. This means that manual deletion requests get orderly and consistent propagation to replication partners. On Windows NT WINS, manual deletes on one server were problematic, because a chance existed that a replication partner could reestablish the previously deleted record.

If you manually tombstone a record, the information is propagated to all replication partners (which occurs quickly with the persistent connection option). Tombstoned records are deleted from all servers after the propagation and after all partners have received the tombstoned records.

WINS Installation and Configuration

WINS does not require a dedicated server or your most powerful CPU. The service can also be installed on a DNS, DHCP, or DC server — even on a Remote Access Service (RAS) server.

Installing WINS

To install WINS, the server needs a static IP address — preferably one dedicated to WINS traffic. You can either *multi-home* the machine (that is, install more than one NIC) or assign another IP address to a single interface.

If you did not install WINS with the operating system, follow these steps:

1. Open Server Manager; right-click the root node and select Add Features. The Add Features Wizard appears.

2. Click Start, and then click Server Manager. You will now see the left pane of Server Manager. Click the Features option, which brings up the Features Summary. Now click the Add Features label. The Add Features Wizard now opens.

3. Scroll down the Select Features list, select WINS Server, and click Next. Click Install.

4. Review your installation results, and click Close.

Configuring WINS

WINS, like DNS and many other services in Windows Server 2008, now uses the Microsoft Management Console (MMC) for configuration and management. To launch the WINS snap-in, go to Administrative Tools and select the WINS option or (easier) open the Run dialog box and run the `winsmgmt.msc` shortcut. The WINS snap-in is shown in Figure 5-14.

One of the perks of WINS is that clients register themselves with the service, and for the most part, you do not need to manually enter mappings. One exception is non-WINS clients and static entries.

Static entries

By entering static mappings, you ensure that WINS clients can resolve the IP addresses of non-WINS clients. Non-WINS clients include machines running under other operating systems, networks, network devices, domains, and so on. You can even insert a static IP address for another WINS server, if the connection to that WINS server is unreliable and you cannot afford to have the server lose a lease and not be capable of renewing it.

FIGURE 5-14

The WINS MMC snap-in.

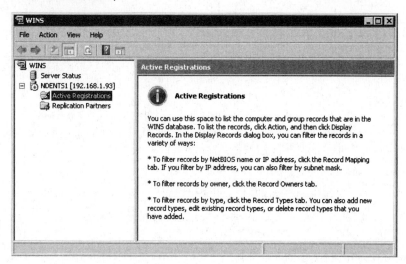

To create a static mapping, open the WINS console as explained in the preceding section and follow these steps:

1. Right-click the Active Registrations node on the WINS tree. Choose New Static Mapping from the context menu.

2. In the New Static Mapping dialog box, type the name of the target to be resolved in the Computer Name field.

3. Although you can add a scope name in the optional NetBIOS Scope field, this field should not be used because NetBIOS scopes are not recommended. The support is included for advanced NetBIOS solutions and applications.

4. From the Type drop-down list, select the type of name to be resolved. The following list explains the static entry types:

   ▪ **Unique.** This is a unique name that can be mapped to a single IP address. Use this type if you need to add a static mapping for a server — usually another WINS server.

   ▪ **Group.** Choose this type for a name that maps to a group. A group is a logical unit on the intranet. Group members, regardless of their nature, usually have their own IP addresses, but these do not need to be stored in WINS.

   ▪ **Domain Name.** Choose this type to map an IP address to a domain name.

■ **Internet Group.** Choose this type to group resources, such as routers, hubs, and printers. You can store up to 25 members in an Internet group.

■ **Multihomed.** Choose this type for the name of a host that has more than one IP address. (*Multi-homed* usually refers to a host with more than one network interface card, but Windows Server 2008 can assign multiple addresses to a single interface.)

5. In the IP Address field, enter the IP address of the client and click OK to store the entry.

The proxy agent

The WINS proxy agent extends the WINS services to non-WINS clients by listening for their name-registration requests and broadcast-resolution requests and then forwarding them to the WINS server. To set up this service, you need to tinker in the registry.

Open the Registry Editor and go to the following subkey:

```
HKEY_LOCAL_MACHINE\SYSTEM\CurrentControlSet\Services\NetBT\Parameters
```

Under the `Parameters` key, you find the entry for `EnableProxy`. Change this value to 1 (enabled). Unfortunately, you must then restart the server.

After it's enabled, the proxy agent forwards the non-WINS client's broadcasts, requesting name registration to the WINS server. The name does not get registered; the intention of the proxy is to verify that the name is not already registered.

Whenever the agent detects a name-resolution broadcast, it checks its NetBIOS name cache and attempts to resolve the name to an IP address. If the name is not cached, the agent forwards the broadcast as a resolve request to the WINS server. The WINS server responds to the agent, and the agent then responds to the non-WINS client.

Configuring Windows Clients for DNS and WINS

Configuring Windows clients to use DNS and WINS is a relatively simple task. It primarily means configuring the clients with the appropriate DNS and WINS server IP addresses. If you're using DHCP, you can configure the DHCP server to provide the DNS and WINS server data to the DHCP clients automatically.

CROSS-REF To learn more about DHCP and how to configure both DHCP servers and clients, see Chapter 4.

If you're not using DHCP or need to configure the DNS or WINS settings separately from the dynamically assigned IP address on the client, you can configure the client's DNS/WINS settings manually. To do so, log on to the client computer and open the properties for the client's TCP/IP connection. On the General page, locate the TCP/IP protocol in the list of installed components and choose Properties to display the TCP/IP property page, shown in Figure 5-15.

FIGURE 5-15

Configure DNS and WINS settings through the connection's property page.

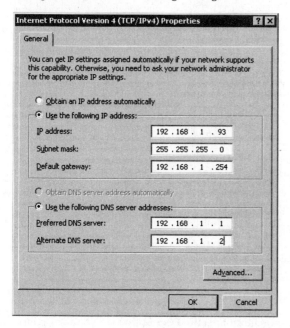

If you select the Obtain an IP Address Automatically option, you can select the Obtain DNS Server Addresses Automatically option to receive the DNS server address list from the DHCP server. If you prefer, you can specify the addresses explicitly by choosing the Use the Following DNS Server Addresses option and then filling in the IP addresses of the preferred and alternate server. The client resolver attempts to resolve through the preferred server first; and if the preferred server fails to respond, the client tries the alternate server.

To configure additional DNS properties, click Advanced and then click the DNS and WINS tabs to display the DNS and WINS property pages, shown in Figure 5-16. You can specify more than two DNS servers if you want and change the order of DNS servers in the list. The resolver tries the DNS servers in order from top to bottom.

FIGURE 5-16

Use the DNS page to configure additional DNS options.

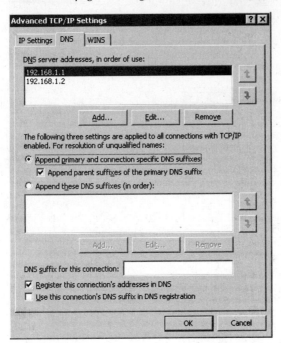

The following list explains the options on the DNS page:

- **Append Primary and Connection Specific DNS Suffixes.** Select this option to append the primary DNS suffix and connection-specific DNS suffix to unqualified host names for resolution. You define the primary DNS suffix for the computer through the computer's Network Identification property page (which you access by right-clicking My Computer, choosing Properties, and clicking Network Identification). The primary DNS suffix applies globally to the system unless overridden by the connection-specific DNS suffix, which you set in the field DNS Suffix for This Connection. Assume, for example, that your primary suffix is mcity.us and your connection-specific DNS suffix is west.mcity.us. You query for the unqualified host name tia. This option then causes Windows Server 2008 to attempt to resolve tia.mcity.us and tia.west.mcity.us. If you have no connection-specific DNS suffix specified, Windows Server 2008 attempts to resolve only tia.mcity.us.

- **Append Parent Suffixes of the Primary DNS Suffix.** This option determines whether the resolver attempts resolution of unqualified names up to the parent-level domain for your computer. Assume, for example, that your computer's primary DNS suffix is west.mcity.us and you attempt to resolve the unqualified host name jane.

The resolver would attempt to resolve `jane.west.mcity.us` and `jane.mcity.us` (attempting to resolve at the parent level as well as the computer's domain level).

- **Append These DNS Suffixes (in Order).** Use this option to append only the specified DNS suffixes for resolving unqualified names.

- **DNS Suffix for This Connection.** Use this option to specify a DNS suffix for the connection that is different from the primary DNS suffix defined in the computer's Network Identification property page.

- **Register This Connection's Addresses in DNS.** Select this option to have the client submit a request to the DNS server to update its host (A) record when its host name changes or IP address changes. The client submits the full computer name specified in the Network Identification tab of the System Properties sheet, along with its IP address, to the DNS server. You can view the System properties through the System object in the Control Panel, or you can right-click My Computer and choose Properties.

- **Use This Connection's DNS Suffix in DNS Registration.** Select this option to have the client submit a request to the DNS server to update its host record whenever the host name changes or IP address changes. This differs from the preceding option in that this option registers the client by using the first part of the computer name specified in the System properties, along with the DNS suffix specified by the DNS Suffix for This Connection option on the DNS page. You can use this option along with the preceding option to register two different FQDNs for the host.

TIP   Configuring Windows NT and Windows 9x clients for DNS is very similar to configuring Windows 2000/XP/Server 2003/2008 clients. Right-click Network Neighborhood and choose Properties, or open Network in the Control Panel. Locate and double-click TCP/IP and then click DNS to set the DNS properties.

Using Hosts and LMHOSTS Files for Name Resolution

DNS servers resolve host names to IP addresses, and WINS servers primarily resolve NetBIOS names to IP addresses. In some cases, however, the capability to resolve host names to addresses without contacting a DNS or WINS server is helpful. You may, for example, have several hosts on the local network with host names and addresses that don't change, so you have no real need to put a load on the local name server for resolution if you can avoid it. Or you may not have a name server available for some reason but still need to enable an application to resolve host names.

Windows Server 2008 offers two methods for resolving host names to addresses that you can use in conjunction with or in place of name servers to provide name resolution. These two methods rely on ASCII files to store a database of host-to-address entries, just as the original ARPANET relied on the Hosts file for name resolution. You can use a local Hosts file in conjunction with or in place of DNS and a local LMHOSTS file in conjunction with or in place of WINS.

Using a Hosts file for name resolution

A `Hosts` file maintains a host table that maps host names to IP addresses. Windows can look up entries in the `Hosts` file to resolve names without needing to query a DNS server for resolution. Windows Server 2008 creates a file named `Hosts` in the `\%systemroot%\system32\drivers\etc` folder. `Hosts` is an ASCII file that you can edit in Notepad or any other word processor. The file uses the same format as the `Hosts` file on 4.3 BSD Unix (stored in `/etc/hosts`) and by default includes an entry that maps `localhost` to `127.0.0.1` (which is used for loopback testing and troubleshooting).

> **TIP** Make a backup copy of the `Hosts` file before modifying it in case you experience any problems modifying the file. Do not change or remove the entry for `localhost`.

Entries in the `Hosts` file take the format `IP Address <tab> host name`. You can specify more than one host name for a given IP address, but you must use multiple entries for hosts in different domains, each entry on its own line. Entries in `Hosts` are case-sensitive, so in the following example, the first two entries enable a correct resolution if the user specifies the host name in either uppercase or lowercase:

```
192.160.0.124    joe.mcity.us
192.160.0.124    JOE.MCITY.US
192.168.0.203    jane.west.mcity.us
```

You can include a single host name for each entry or specify multiple host names for a single IP address if they fall in the same domain. The following, for example, are valid entries:

```
192.168.0.224    me     tarzan   jim.west.mcity.us
192.168.0.198    you    jane     jane.east.mcity.us
```

Each of the entries in this example specify three host names for each IP address.

Windows Server 2008 parses the entries in the `Hosts` file in sequential order until it finds a match. You can speed up lookup time by placing the most frequently used host-name entries at the top of the file.

Using the LMHOSTS file for name resolution

Windows Server 2008 automatically resolves NetBIOS names for computers running TCP/IP on a local network. You can use an `LMHOSTS` file to resolve IP addresses of computers on other networks to which yours is connected by a gateway when a WINS server isn't available.

`LMHOSTS` is an ASCII file, with the entry format similar to entries in a `Hosts` file. In addition, `LMHOSTS` supports special keywords, explained later in this section. Windows Server 2008 includes a sample `LMHOSTS` file in `\%systemroot%\system32\drivers\etc`. As with the `Hosts` file, you should make a backup copy of `LMHOSTS` before modifying it.

Windows Server 2008 parses each line in `LMHOSTS` sequentially at startup, so you should place frequently accessed names at the top of the file for best performance. Following are a few rules for structuring an `LMHOSTS` file:

- Each entry must include the IP address in the first column, with the NetBIOS name in the second column. Additional keywords, if any, appear in subsequent columns. Columns are separated by at least one space or tab character. Some LMHOSTS keywords follow entries, while others appear on their own lines (discussed later in this section).

- Each entry must reside on a separate line.

- Comments begin with the pound (#) character, and special LMHOSTS keywords also begin with the # character. Keep comments to a minimum to improve parsing performance. Place frequently accessed entries near the top of the file for best performance.

- The LMHOSTS file is static. As with the Hosts file, you must manually update the file to create new entries or modify existing ones.

Windows Server 2008 TCP/IP reads the LMHOSTS file at system startup, and entries designated as preloaded by the #PRE keyword are read into the name cache at that time. Other entries are read only after broadcast name-resolution queries fail. Remember to place frequently used names near the top of the file and to keep comments to a minimum to improve performance.

You can include the following special keywords in an LMHOSTS file:

- #PRE. Preloads the entry into the name cache at startup. If you want names stored in a remote LMHOSTS file to be added to the name cache at startup, use the #INCLUDE and #PRE statements in combination, as in the following example:

  ```
  #INCLUDE     \\srv1\public\lmhosts       #PRE
  ```

- #DOM:<domain>. Designates remote domain controllers located across one or more routers. Entries that use the #DOM keyword are added to a special Internet workgroup name cache that causes Windows Server 2008 TCP/IP to forward requests for domain controllers to remote domain controllers as well as local domain controllers. The following example identifies a domain controller named server1 in the domain west.mcity.us and preloads the entry into the name cache at startup:

  ```
  192.168.0.212  server1  #PRE  #DOM:west.mcity.us
  ```

- #INCLUDE<filename>. Includes entries from separate LMHOSTS files. Use #INCLUDE to include entries from a common, shared LMHOSTS file or your own set of entries stored on your own computer. If you reference a remote LMHOSTS file on a server outside of your network in an #INCLUDE statement, you must also include an entry for the IP address of the remote server in the LMHOSTS file before the #INCLUDE statement that references it. Do not use #INCLUDE to reference an LMHOSTS file on a redirected network drive unless your drive mappings remain the same from one session to another. Otherwise, use the UNC path for the file. The following example includes an LMHOSTS file from a network server:

  ```
  #INCLUDE  \\server1\public\Lmhosts     #Includes shared Lmhosts file
  ```

- #BEGIN_ALTERNATE. Signals the beginning of a block inclusion, a block of multiple #INCLUDE statements. The statements within the block designate primary and alternative locations for the included file; the alternative locations are checked if the primary file is unavailable. Successful loading of any entry in the block causes the block to succeed, and subsequent entries in the block are skipped. You can include multiple block inclusions within an LMHOSTS file. Following is an example of a block inclusion:

```
#BEGIN_ALTERNATE
#INCLUDE     \\server1\public\lmhosts           #Primary source
#INCLUDE     \\server2\public\lmhosts           #Alternate source
#INCLUDE     \\netserv\shared\lmhosts           #Alternate source
#END_ALTERNATE
```

 Addresses of servers specified in a block inclusion must be preloaded through entries earlier in the file. Entries not preloaded are ignored.

- #END_ALTERNATE. This signals the end of a block of multiple #INCLUDE statements.
- \0xnn. Use this keyword to specify nonprinting characters in NetBIOS names. Enclose the NetBIOS name in quotation marks and use the \0xnn keyword to specify the hexadecimal value of the nonprinting character. The hexadecimal notation applies to only one character in the name. The name must be padded to a total of 16 characters, with the hexadecimal notation as the sixteenth character. The following is an example:

```
192.168.0.89   'janetrs   \0x14'     #Uses special character
```

Summary

This chapter described how DNS provides the primary means through which Windows Server 2008 clients resolve host names to IP addresses. The client's computer uses a resolver to request resolution of a name from one or more DNS servers. The client can also use a Hosts file to statically map names to addresses and bypass the need to access a DNS server for name resolution.

DNS in Windows Server 2008 is dynamic, enabling clients and DNS servers alike to request that a DNS server that is authoritative for the client's zone update the client's host and pointer records. A client can directly request an update of its host record, and a DNS server can request an update of both the host and associated pointer record on behalf of the client. Zones that are stored in Active Directory can be secured through ACLs to require authentication before dynamic updates are permitted.

WINS provides the same capabilities for resolving NetBIOS names to addresses that DNS provides for host names. Windows Server 2008 includes a WINS server service that enables a Windows Server 2008 server to function as a WINS server and integrates DNS and WINS to provide additional capabilities. Although WINS is not always an optimum solution, it nevertheless offers several advantages for name resolution where NetBIOS names are still used.

Chapter 6

Routing and Remote Access

This chapter covers the remote access services provided with Windows Server 2008 that enable dial-up and IP access (client and server) for remote connectivity, including dial-up connections to the Internet. It also covers the many features in Routing and Remote Access Service (RRAS) that enable Windows Server 2008 to function as a router.

Windows Server 2008 RAS and Telephony Services

RAS stands for Remote Access Services. In Windows Server 2008, RAS enables Windows Server 2008 clients to dial or directly connect to other systems for access to remote networks, including the Internet, and enables Windows Server 2008 computers to act as network and dial-up access servers to route remote clients into a network. The Routing and Remote Access Service (RRAS) enables Windows Server 2008 to function as a router. RAS and RRAS are integrated into a single service in Windows Server 2008. This chapter examines the dial-up networking features in RRAS that enable a Windows Server 2008 computer to function as both a dial-up server and dial-up client.

The following sections provide an overview of these RRAS features. Later sections explain protocol, security, and configuration issues.

Overview of Windows Server 2008 RRAS

Remote access enables a client computer to connect to a remote computer or network and access the resources of the remote computer or network as if they were local. For example, users who are frequently on the road can access the company file server(s), printers, mail system, and other resources from remote locations. Clients also can use remote access services to connect to public networks such as the Internet. Figure 6-1 illustrates one implementation of remote access.

FIGURE 6-1

RRAS enables remote users to connect to the local computer or network and supports dial-out connections from Windows Server 2008 clients.

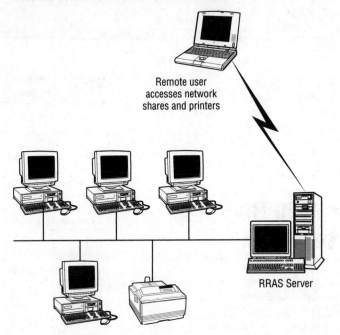

Remote user
accesses network
shares and printers

RRAS Server

The Routing and Remote Access Service in Windows Server 2008 provides three primary functions:

- **Dial-up client.** You can use RRAS to create and establish dial-up connections to remote networks, including the Internet, through a variety of media such as a modem, ISDN, infrared, parallel ports, serial connection, X.25, and ATM. Windows Server 2008 dial-up clients support a wide range of authentication protocols and other connectivity options, which are discussed in depth later in this chapter. Support for tunneling protocols enables clients to establish secure connections to remote networks through public networks such as the Internet.

■ **Dial-up server.** A Windows Server 2008 can function as a dial-up server, enabling remote clients to connect to the local server, and optionally to the local network, through the same types of media support for dial-out connections. You can also use RRAS to support Terminal Services client sessions because RRAS issues an IP address to the connecting clients and binds the necessary protocols to the RAS connection.

Windows Server 2008 supports several authentication protocols and can authenticate users against local or domain user accounts, or it can use Remote Authentication Dial In User Service (RADIUS), an industry standard authentication mechanism. Once connected, a remote user can browse, print, map drives, and perform essentially all other functions possible from either the local server or local area network.

■ **Routing services.** The routing components of RRAS enable Windows Server 2008 to function as a unicast and multicast router. Windows Server 2008 provides for routing, packet filtering, connection sharing, demand-dial routing, and several other features that make it a good choice for LAN and WAN routing. Windows Server 2008 also adds limited firewall capability.

Although Windows Server 2008 RRAS integrates dial-up networking and routing into a single service, they are treated as separate issues in this book because of the different focus for each.

One of the key benefits of Windows Server 2008 RRAS is its integration with the Windows Server 2008 operating system. On the client side, integration means that once a remote connection is established, the client can access resources on the server transparently as if they were local resources. The client can map remote shares to local drive letters, map and print to remote printers, and so on. Except in very rare circumstances, applications can use remote resources seamlessly without modification to make them RAS- or network-aware.

On the server side, integration means that Windows Server 2008 can use a single authentication mechanism to authenticate users both locally and from remote locations. RRAS can authenticate against the local computer's user accounts or accounts in the domain, or it can use an external authentication mechanism such as RADIUS. Through its support for RADIUS, Windows Server 2008 RRAS enables a Windows Server 2008 to function as a gateway of sorts to the network while offloading authentication to another server, which could be any RADIUS platform, including a Unix server.

NOTE Remote Authentication Dial-In User Service (RADIUS) is a standard, cross-platform protocol for authentication commonly used for dial-in authentication.

Windows Server 2008 RRAS also provides close integration with Active Directory (AD). This AD integration provides users with the replication of remote access settings, including access permissions, callback options, and security policies, among others. AD integration also means simplified administration with other AD-related services and properties.

As you learn later in the section "RAS Connection Types and Protocols," Windows Server 2008 RRAS supports a wide range of connection protocols, including Point-to-Point Protocol (PPP), Serial Line Internet Protocol (SLIP), and Microsoft RAS Protocol. Windows Server 2008

RRAS supports multiple authentication methods, including Microsoft Challenge Handshake Authentication Protocol (MS-CHAP), Extensible Authentication Protocol (EAP), Challenge Handshake Authentication Protocol (CHAP), Shiva Password Authentication Protocol (SPAP), and Password Authentication Protocol (PAP). Network protocols supported include TCP/IP, IPX/SPX, and AppleTalk to support Microsoft, Unix, NetWare, and Macintosh resources and clients.

New features of Windows Server 2008 RRAS

If you're familiar with RAS or RRAS in Windows NT or Windows 2000, you'll find all of those same features in Windows Server 2008 RRAS. You'll also find several enhancements to existing features, along with many new features, including those described in the following sections.

AD integration

As mentioned previously, Windows Server 2008 RRAS integrates with the Active Directory (AD). AD integration enables client settings to be replicated throughout the organization to provide expanded access by clients and easier administration. Integration with the AD also can simplify administration by enabling you to browse and manage multiple RRAS servers through the AD-aware RRAS management console snap-in, providing a single point of management for RRAS services in an organization.

Bandwidth Allocation Protocol and Bandwidth Allocation Control Protocol

The Bandwidth Allocation Protocol (BAP) and Bandwidth Allocation Control Protocol (BACP) enable Windows Server 2008 RAS to dynamically add or remove links in a multilink PPP connection as bandwidth requirements for the connection change. When bandwidth utilization becomes heavy, RAS can add links to accommodate the increased load and enhance performance. When bandwidth utilization decreases, RAS can remove links to make the connection more cost efficient. You configure BAP policies through a Network Policy Server (NPS) policy that you can apply to individual users, groups, or an entire organization.

MS-CHAP version 2

Previous versions of RAS supported Microsoft Challenge Handshake Authentication Protocol (MS-CHAP) to authenticate remote clients. MS-CHAP v2 provides stronger security and is designed specifically to support Virtual Private Network (VPN) connections, which enable remote clients to establish secure connections to a private network through a public network such as the Internet. MS-CHAP v2 provides several security enhancements:

- LAN Manager coding of responses, formerly supported for backward compatibility with older remote access clients, is no longer supported. This provides improved security. MS-CHAP v2 no longer supports LAN Manager encoding of password changes for the same reason.

- Mutual authentication, which provides bi-directional authentication between the remote client and the RAS server, is supported. Previously, MS-CHAP provided only one-way authentication and did not provide a mechanism for the remote client to determine whether the remote server actually had access to its authentication password for verification. Version 2 not only enables the server to authenticate the client's request, but also enables the client to verify the server's ability to authenticate its account.

- Stronger encryption is provided in MS-CHAP v2. The 40-bit encryption used in previous versions operated on the user's password and resulted in the same cryptographic key being generated for each session. Version 2 uses the remote client's password, along with an arbitrary challenge string, to create a unique cryptographic key for each session, even when the client password remains the same.

- Better security for data transmission is provided by using separate cryptographic keys for data sent in each direction.

Extensible Authentication Protocol

The Extensible Authentication Protocol (EAP) enables authentication methods to be added to RAS without redesigning the underlying RAS software base, much like new features in NTFS 5.0 enable new functionality to be added to the file system without redesigning the file system. EAP enables the client and server to negotiate the mechanism to be used to authenticate the client. Currently, EAP in Windows Server 2008 supports EAP-MD5 CHAP (Challenge Handshake Authentication Protocol), EAP-TLS (Transport Level Security), and redirection to a RADIUS server. Each of these topics is covered in more detail later in this chapter.

RADIUS support

Windows Server 2008 RRAS can function as a RADIUS client, funneling logon requests to a RADIUS server, which can include the Internet Authentication Service (also included with Windows Server 2008) running on the same or a different server. The RADIUS server doesn't have to be a Windows Server 2008 system, however, which enables RRAS to use Unix-based RADIUS servers or third-party RADIUS services you might already have in place. One of the advantages to using RADIUS is its capability for accounting, and several third-party utilities have been developed to provide integration with database backends such as SQL Server to track and control client access.

CROSS-REF See the section "Using RADIUS" later in this chapter for detailed information on configuring and using RADIUS.

Network access policies

Windows Server 2008 improves considerably on the flexibility you have as an administrator to control a user's remote access and dial-up settings. Earlier versions gave you control only over callback options, and settings were assigned on a user-by-user basis. Although Windows Server 2008 still lets you assign remote access permissions through a user's account, as with Windows Server 2008 RRAS, you also can use an NPS policy to define the remote access settings for one or several users. This is achieved using the Network Policy Server policy service (NPS). NPS access policies give you a fine degree of control over the users' settings, controlling options such as allowed access time, maximum session time, authentication, security, BAP policies, and more.

CROSS-REF See the section "Policy Server" later in this chapter for additional information on configuring and using NPS policies. See the Windows Server 2008 Security chapter (Chapter 16) for security aspects of NPS policy.

Account lockout

Windows Server 2008 RAS enhances security by supporting account lockout, which locks an RRAS account after a specified number of bad logon attempts. This feature helps guard against dictionary attacks in which a hacker attempts to gain remote access by repeatedly attempting to log on using a dictionary of passwords against a valid account. You can configure two settings that control lockout — the number of bad logon attempts before the account is locked out and how long the account remains locked before the lockout counter is reset.

The Routing and Remote Access management console

The Routing and Remote Access service is installed using Server Manager using the Network Policy and Access Services role. Please refer to Chapter 2.

Microsoft has integrated most administrative and management functions into Microsoft Management Console (MMC) snap-ins, and RRAS is no exception. The Routing and Remote Access console snap-in enables you to configure and manage an RRAS server. Figure 6-2 shows the Routing and Remote Access console.

FIGURE 6-2

The Routing and Remote Access console.

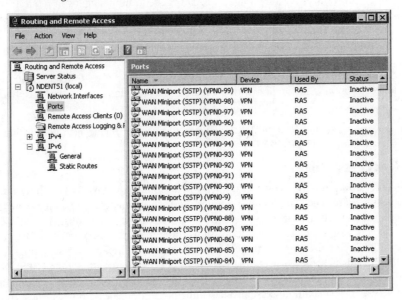

The RRAS console serves as a central control center for managing most RRAS properties. In addition to configuring ports and interfaces, you can configure protocols, global options and properties, and RRAS policies through the RRAS console. Later sections of this chapter explain how to use the RRAS console to perform specific configuration and administration tasks. Open the console by choosing Start ➤ All Programs ➤ Administrative Tools ➤ Routing and Remote Access.

RAS Connection Types and Protocols

Windows Server 2008 supports several connection types and network protocols for remote access. The following sections explore these connection types and network protocols.

> **NOTE** The NetBEUI, NetBIOS, NWLink, IPX/SPX, and NetBIOS protocols are not included with Windows Server 2008, so Windows Server 2008 does not support them for routing and remote access. Serial Line Internet Protocol is also removed and SLIP configuration automatically gets converted to the Point-to-Point protocol.

Point-to-Point Protocol

The Point-to-Point Protocol (PPP) was developed as a standardized alternative to SLIP that offered better performance and reliability. Unlike SLIP, PPP is designed around industry-designed standards and enables essentially any PPP-compliant client to connect to a PPP server. Windows Server 2008 supports PPP for both dial-in and dial-out connections. On a Windows Server 2008 RAS server, PPP enables remote clients to use TCP/IP. Windows-based clients, including Windows Server 2008, Windows NT, Windows 9x, and Windows 3.x, can use any TCP/IP client. Macintosh clients can use TCP/IP. PPP no longer supports authentication protocols CHAP and PAP.

Point-to-Point Multilink Protocol and BAP

The Point-to-Point Multilink Protocol (PPMP, or simply Multilink) enables multiple PPP lines to be combined to provide an aggregate bandwidth. For example, you might use Multilink to combine two analog 56 Kbps modems to give you an aggregate bandwidth roughly equivalent to 112 Kbps. Or, you might combine both B channels of an ISDN Basic Rate Interface (BRI) connection to provide double the bandwidth you would otherwise get from a single channel.

The Bandwidth Allocation Protocol (BAP) works in conjunction with Multilink to provide adaptive bandwidth. As bandwidth utilization increases, BAP enables the client to aggregate additional connections to increase bandwidth and improve performance. As bandwidth utilization decreases, BAP enables the client to drop connections from the aggregate link to reduce connection costs (where multiple connections incur their own charges).

CROSS-REF See the section "Using Multilink and BAP" later in this chapter for information on configuring and using multilink connections.

Point-to-Point Tunneling Protocol

The TCP/IP protocol suite by itself does not provide for encryption or data security, an obvious concern for users who need to transmit data securely across a public network such as the Internet. The Point-to-Point Tunneling Protocol (PPTP) provides a means for encapsulating and encrypting IP for secure transmission. PPTP is an extension of PPP that enables you to create a Virtual Private Network (VPN) connection between a client and server.

PPP frames in a PPTP session are encrypted using Microsoft Point-to-Point Encryption (MPPE), with the encryption keys generated using the CHAP authentication process. PPTP by itself does not provide encryption, but rather encapsulates the already encrypted PPP frames. In order to provide a secure connection, the client must use either CHAP or EAP authentication. Otherwise, the PPP frames are encapsulated unencrypted (plain text). Figure 6-3 illustrates how PPTP encapsulates data. PPTP is installed by default when you install Windows Server 2008 RRAS.

FIGURE 6-3

PPTP and L2TP use different methods for encapsulation and encryption.

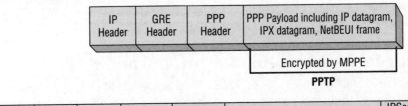

TIP PPTP is a good choice for creating secure connections to a private network through a public network, such as the Internet, when the remote network isn't configured to support IPSec.

Layer Two Tunneling Protocol

Layer Two Tunneling Protocol (L2TP) is a protocol that combines the features of PPTP with support for IP Security (IPSec) to provide enhanced security. Unlike PPTP, which relies on MPPE for encryption, L2TP relies on IPSec to provide encryption. Therefore, the source and destination routers must support both L2TP and IPSec. Figure 6-3 illustrates how L2TP encapsulates data. L2TP is installed by default when you install Windows Server 2008 RRAS.

TIP   L2TP provides better security than PPTP by supporting IPSec. L2TP is a better choice for creating VPN connections than PPTP when the remote network is configured to support IPSec.

Transport protocols

As mentioned previously in this chapter, RRAS basically supports TCP/IP. When you install RRAS, Windows Server 2008 enables all currently installed protocols for incoming and outgoing RAS connections. As you learn later in the section "Configuring RAS for Inbound Connections," you can configure the supported protocols to enable clients to access only the RAS server or the LAN. You configure access on a protocol-by-protocol basis.

TCP/IP

As a dial-out protocol, TCP/IP enables you to connect a Windows Server 2008 client to nearly any TCP/IP-based network, including the Internet. You can statically assign the IP address, subnet mask, default gateway, and other settings for the dial-out connection or allow the remote server to assign the connection properties. As a protocol for incoming connections, TCP/IP enables essentially any client that supports TCP/IP and PPP to connect to a Windows Server 2008 RAS server. As you learn later in the section "Configuring RAS for Inbound Connections," you can allocate addresses from a static pool or use DHCP to allocate addresses and other connection properties to remote clients. In addition, clients can request a predefined IP address (defined on the client side through the connection properties).

Enabling and Configuring RRAS

Although RRAS is installed by default when you install Windows Server 2008, you still need to enable the service in order to configure and use it. To do so, choose Start ➤ All Programs ➤ Administrative Tools ➤ Routing and Remote Access to open the RRAS console. Right-click the server in the left pane and choose Configure and Enable Routing and Remote Access to start the RRAS Setup Wizard. You can use the wizard to automatically configure RRAS for specific applications or configure the service manually.

TIP   If you enable RRAS and choose to configure it manually and then later decide you'd like to run the wizard, you can do so, but you will lose the current configuration settings. To reconfigure the service through the wizard, open the RRAS console, right-click the server, and choose Disable Routing and Remote Access. After the service stops, right-click the server again and choose Configuring and Enabling Routing and Remote Access.

The wizard provides five basic options for configuring RRAS:

- **Remote access (dial-up or VPN).** Sets up the server to accept incoming remote access connections, whether dial-up or VPN.

- **Network address translation (NAT).** Sets up the server to provide NAT services to clients on the private network that need to access the Internet.

- **Virtual private network (VPN) access and NAT.** Sets up the server to support incoming VPN connections from the Internet and NAT-protected client connections from the local network out to the Internet.

- **Secure connection between two private networks.** Establishes a demand-dial or persistent connection between networks, with the server acting as a router.

- **Custom configuration.** Enables you to choose individual services you want RRAS to offer, such as NAT, LAN routing, and VPN access.

NOTE If the Windows Firewall service is running, you cannot enable and configure RRAS. Open the Services console, stop the Windows Firewall service, and configure it to Disabled startup. Then, try running the RRAS wizard again.

The following sections explain how to use the wizard and the custom configuration option to set up RRAS to perform specific functions.

IP Routing

Except in self-contained private networks, routing plays an important role in TCP/IP. Routing enables packets destined for external subnets to reach their destinations, and for traffic from remote networks to be delivered to your network. Windows Server 2008 includes a service called Routing and Remote Access (RRAS) that enables a Windows Server 2008 to function as a dedicated or demand-dial router (establishing connections only as needed). This section of the chapter discusses IP routing in general and the routing elements of RRAS in particular.

IP routing overview

A *router* works in concert with other network hardware to direct network traffic to its intended destination. For example, when you open your Web browser at the office and connect to www.foxnews.com to check the current news, your network router directs the traffic out to the Internet. At that point, other routers take care of getting the traffic to the site and back again with the responses. Another example is when you dial into your ISP from home. The ISP's router(s) connects its network to the Internet and processes traffic going to and from your computer and to and from the computers of other connected customers.

A typical router essentially sits on the fence between two or more subnets. This fence is typically known as a *hop*, and each time a packet traverses a router, its *hop count* is incremented. The router exists on all subnets to which it is connected and therefore has connectivity to each subnet. When traffic comes into the router from a particular interface, the router directs the traffic to the appropriate interface. Figure 6-4 illustrates a typical routing scenario. If the number of hops a packet takes to reach a destination is determined to be excessive by a router, the packet will be terminated and a message will be sent back to the sender indicating that the packet expired in transit. This is a safeguard that prevents data that cannot be routed to an interface from eternally moving around the Internet. The typical hop limit is 30 for most routers.

FIGURE 6-4

Several networks connected to the Internet through a router.

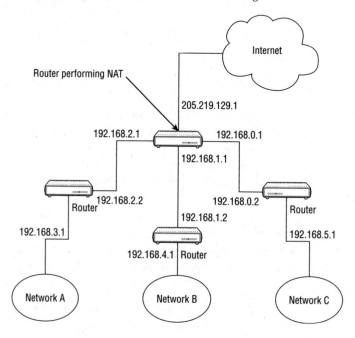

A router examines each packet that comes in to determine the destination network for the packet. It does this by examining the destination address stored in the packet's header. The router then decides which of its interfaces to use to route the traffic (based on its knowledge of adjacent routes) and sends it on its way. For example, assume that a router has four interfaces as shown in Figure 6-4: one for each of the local networks and one that connects to the Internet. A packet comes into the router from subnet A with the destination address 192.168.4.99. The router routes the packet out through the interface connected to subnet B, and the adjacent router at 192.168.1.2 routes the packet on to network (B). Another packet comes from network (A) with the destination address 205.135.201.130. The router sends that packet out through the interface connected to the Internet because it doesn't belong in any of the local subnets.

Routers use *routing tables* containing *routes* to determine where to send packets. Routes help the router know where different networks are located relative to its interfaces so that it can send packets out on the appropriate interface and have them delivered to the proper destination. Each route in the routing table falls into one of the following types:

- **Network route.** These provide a route to a specific network ID and therefore to all host addresses within that network.

- **Host route.** These provide a route to a specific host, defining not only the network but also the address of the host.

- **Default route.** The default route is used to route all traffic for which there is no specific network route or host route. For example, a router connecting a local network to the Internet would have a default route pointing all traffic to the Internet interface.

Each route in the routing table has certain general properties:

- **Network ID/host address/subnet mask.** These properties identify the destination network ID or host address and the destination subnet. The router checks the destination addresses in the packets against these entries to determine a match. If the packet address matches the criteria, the router uses the forwarding address and interface data associated with the route to process the packet.

- **Forwarding address.** The router forwards matching packets to this address. The address could be that of another router or the address of a network interface on the local router (directing the traffic out a specific port on the router).

- **Interface.** This is a port number or other logical identifier of the port through which the traffic is routed for the given route.

- **Metric.** The metric specifies the relative price of the route based on cost, available bandwidth, and so on. Where multiple routes exist to a given network or host, the route with the lowest metric is used.

When a packet comes in to the router, the router checks the destination address in the packet's header against the routing table to determine which route applies to the packet. If the router matches the destination address with a route, it forwards the packet using the forwarding address associated with the route. If the router finds no matching route, it forwards the packet using the default route (if one is configured on the router). The default route is used to handle any traffic for which a specific route is not indicated.

How do routers learn their routes? One method is to learn routes dynamically from other routers and propagate them to other routers. Routers communicate with one another using routing protocols, with the two most common protocols for IP routing being Routing Information Protocol (RIP) and Open Shortest Path First (OSPF). Windows Server 2008 supports both (and can support additional protocols). RIP and OSPF are explained shortly.

A second method is for routers to use static routes. When you configure the router, you create the static route, which creates the static route entry in the routing table. A router can use static routes to handle all its traffic, a common situation for small to mid-size organizations. For example, if you only connect a few local subnets to the Internet, you can use static routes to handle all traffic, with a default route handling traffic to the Internet. You can read more about static routes later in the section "Configuring Static Routes."

RIP

RIP for IP, one of the two routing protocols included with Windows Server 2008 for routing IP traffic, offers the advantage of being relatively easy to configure. RIP is appropriate mainly for small to mid-size businesses because it is limited to a maximum hop count of 15. RIP considers any address more than 15 hops away to be unreachable.

When a router using RIP first boots, its routing table contains only the routes for physically connected networks. RIP periodically broadcasts announcements with its routing table entries so that adjacent routers can configure their routes accordingly. After a router starts up, it uses RIP announcements from adjacent routers to rebuild its routing table.

RIP also uses triggered updates to update routing tables. Triggered updates occur when the router detects a network change, such as an interface coming up or going down. The triggered updates are broadcast immediately. Routers that receive the update modify their routing tables and propagate the changes to adjacent routers.

 Windows Server 2008 supports RIP v1 and v2. RIP v2 adds additional features such as peer security and route filtering.

OSPF

OSPF offers an efficient means of handling routing for very large networks such as the Internet. OSPF uses an algorithm to calculate the shortest path between the router and adjacent networks. OSPF routers maintain a *link state database* that maps the inter-network. The link state database changes as each network topology change occurs. Adjacent OSPF routers synchronize their link state databases and recalculate their routing tables accordingly.

Because of its scalability, OSPF is geared toward large networks. It's also more complex to configure. If yours is a very large network, OSPF may be a good choice for your routing needs. For smaller networks, consider using RIP. In situations where you're only connecting a few networks together, static routes could be the best and easiest solution of all.

Routing with RRAS

In addition to providing remote access services to enable a Windows Server 2008 to act as both a dial-up server and client, RRAS enables a Windows Server 2008 to function as a router for persistent connections and as a demand-dial router, connecting only when requested by a client to do so. For example, you might have two divisions of a company that need to transfer data between networks only occasionally. Maintaining a leased line or a direct Internet connection between the two isn't feasible because of the cost involved. Instead, you can set up a demand-dial router that will call the other router (over a dial-up connection, for example) when any traffic needs to be routed to the other network.

All of the functions supported by Windows Server 2008 RRAS require routing. When you use the wizard to configure a RRAS server, routing is enabled on the server. In this section of the chapter, we limit RRAS specifically to functioning as a router to explain how to configure routes, protocols, and other components. Later sections explain how to configure a RRAS server to function in other ways (such as a VPN server).

Configuring a basic router

As mentioned previously, RRAS can use static routes, dynamic routes, or a combination thereof to provide routing services. This section of the chapter explains how to set up a simple router that uses static routes, rather than dynamic routing. Most of the steps in this section also apply to a dynamic router, so even if you won't be using static routes, you should read this section before moving on to "Dynamic Routing," later in this chapter.

At this point, assume that you have yet to enable RRAS. To configure a LAN router, open the RRAS console by choosing Start ➤ All Programs ➤ Administrative Tools ➤ Routing and Remote Access. Right-click the server and choose Configure and Enable Routing and Remote Access to start the wizard. Then, choose Custom Configuration and click Next. Choose LAN routing, click Next, and click Finish. Click Yes when asked if you want to start the RRAS service.

Configuring the router address

By default, the router uses the first IP address bound to an interface to process routing tasks on that interface. An interface that has only one address assigned therefore doesn't require configuration of its address. You might, however, have multiple addresses assigned to each interface for other purposes. In such a case, you need to configure which address the router interface will use.

To do so, open the RRAS console, expand the IP Routing branch, and click General. In the right pane, right-click the interface you want to configure and choose Properties to display its property sheet. Set the IP address, subnet mask, and gateway (if required) for the interface on the Configuration page. Click Advanced if you need to specify a metric for the interface.

Configuring static routes

After you set up RRAS for routing, you need to either add static routes or configure the router to use RIP or OSPF. The exception is when you have only two networks connected by a router. In this situation, the router can route the traffic without a specific route.

To add a static route, open the RRAS console and expand the IP Routing branch. Click Static Routes, right-click the right pane (or Static Routes), and choose New Static Route to display the Static Route dialog box (see Figure 6-5).

FIGURE 6-5

Use the Static Route dialog box to add a static route.

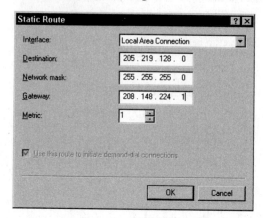

The following list explains the options in the Static Route dialog box:

■ **Interface.** Select the network interface to be used to forward packets that fit the criteria for the route. For example, to route traffic destined for the Internet, select the network interface on the server that is connected to the Internet.

■ **Destination.** Specify the address criteria for matching packets. RRAS will check the destination address in the packet header against this address to determine whether the route applies to the packet. You can specify a network address, a host address, or a default route of 0.0.0.0. For a network address, use the low broadcast address for the network. For example, for the class C network 205.219.128.x, use 205.219.128.0. For a host, specify the actual IP address of the host.

NOTE Creating a default route using 0.0.0.0 causes all traffic for which there is no other applicable route to be forwarded through the interface defined by the default route entry.

■ **Network Mask.** Specify the network mask for the destination network or host. For a default route, enter 0.0.0.0.

■ **Gateway.** Specify the address to which the packets will be forwarded for this route. It must be an address directly reachable on the router's external network segment (interface for the route). For example, you might specify the address of the router port on the same subnet for the next adjacent router.

■ **Metric.** Specify a value to define the relative cost for the route. A lower metric indicates a lower cost. In many cases, administrators use the number of hops to the destination as the metric. When multiple routes apply to a given packet, the route with the lowest metric is used unless it is unavailable.

- **Use This Route to Initiate Demand-Dial Connections.** Select this option to cause the router to initiate a demand-dial connection when it receives packets applicable for the selected route. This option is available only if at least one demand-dial interface is configured for the router.

Create static routes to accommodate each specific network segment in your network. Create a default route to handle all other traffic.

Adding and configuring a demand-dial interface

You need to add a demand-dial interface if you're installing RRAS to include the capability to function as a demand-dial router as well as a LAN router. A demand-dial router automatically dials a connection to a remote network when traffic from the local network needs to be routed to the remote network reachable through the demand-dial connection as defined by the route for that network.

To install a demand-dial interface, open the RRAS console and expand the server on which you want to install the interface. Right-click Network Interfaces in the left pane and choose New Demand-Dial Interface to start the Demand-Dial Interface Wizard. The wizard prompts for the following information:

- **Interface Name.** Specify a friendly name for the interface. By default, RRAS suggests the name Remote Router. Keep in mind that if you configure the demand-dial interface to allow remote users (routers) to connect to this interface, the interface name is automatically used as the local account name. Using the suggested name Remote Router, for example, causes Windows Server 2008 to create a user account named Remote Router.

- **Connection Type.** Select between physical devices such as modems, ISDN, network adapters, and so on, or specify that the connection will use a virtual private networking (VPN) connection. Selecting the VPN option will cause the wizard to prompt you for the tunneling protocol to use (PPTP or L2TP). You can also choose PPP over Ethernet (PPPoE).

- **Phone Number or Address/Alternates.** For a dial-up device, specify the phone number of the remote interface. Specify the IP address of the remote interface if connecting through a non-dial-up device (such as a physical network connection).

- **Route IP Packets on This Interface.** Select this option to enable IP routing on this demand-dial connection. TCP/IP must already be installed on the server.

- **Add a User Account So a Remote Router Can Dial In.** Select this option if you want to create a user account remote routers can use to dial in to this demand-dial connection. When the remote router receives a packet that needs to be forwarded to the local demand-dial interface, the remote router uses the account and password stored in its dial-out credentials to connect to the local router. The credentials at the remote router must match the account and password you create through the wizard. See "Dial-Out Credentials" at the end of this list to configure the local account and password that the local router will use when connecting to remote routers.

- **Send a Plain-Text Password if That Is the Only Way to Connect.** Select this option to allow RRAS to transmit its credentials using plain text rather than encryption if the remote router doesn't support encryption or doesn't support the types of encryption supported by the local router.

- **Use Scripting to Complete the Connection with the Remote Router.** Use this option to specify a script RRAS will use when connecting to the remote router. Scripts can be used to automate the logon process and other connection tasks. Scripts are most applicable to dial-up connections that require menu-based selections to authenticate and log on.

- **Dial-Out Credentials.** Specify the user name and password the local router will use to authenticate its access to the remote router. On a remote Windows Server 2008 router, you would use the option "Add a User Account So a Remote Router Can Dial In" discussed previously to configure the associated account on the remote router.

Setting demand-dial filters

By default, RRAS allows all IP traffic through the demand-dial interface. However, you can create filters to restrict the type of traffic allowed. For example, you might want to restrict TCP port 80 to block Web browser traffic through the interface. You can create filters to restrict traffic going to or from specific networks, or you can create a filter that blocks specific packets to or from all addresses. The demand-dial interface will establish a connection to the remote router only if the packet is not blocked by the configured filters.

To configure filters, open the RRAS console and open the server on which you want to configure filters. Drill down the IPv4 or IPv6 nodes and select the General node. In the right pane, right-click the interface where you want to configure filters and choose Properties. Then choose the Inbound or Outbound filter options. The dialog box shown in Figure 6-6 loads.

FIGURE 6-6

Use filters to restrict traffic through the interface.

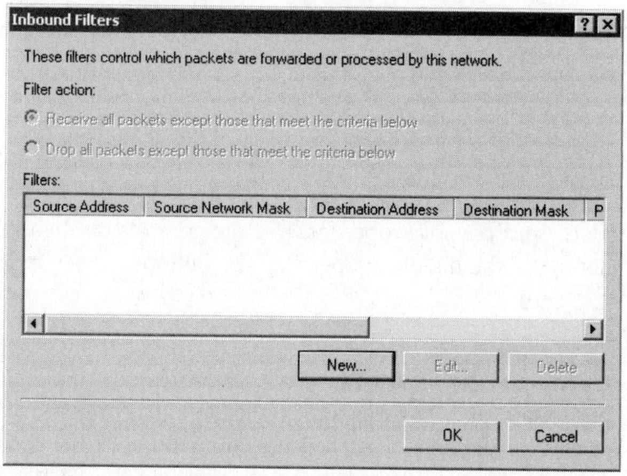

Click New . . . to set the new filters. Configure the filter using the following list as a guide, click OK, and repeat the process to add any other required filters:

- **Source Network.** Select this option to base the filter on the network from which the packet was sent. Specify an IP address and subnet mask to define the source network or host.

- **Destination Network.** Select this option to base the filter on the destination address in the packet's header (where the packet is going). Specify the address and subnet mask of the destination network or host.

- **Protocol.** Specify the protocol type to filter. Select Any to filter all the traffic or select a given protocol type and specify the accompanying information, such as the source and destination ports.

Setting permitted dial-out hours

You might want to restrict a demand-dial connection to specific hours to limit the times at which the router will forward traffic on the interface. For example, you might want to disable the demand-dial interface during the weekend. To configure dial-out hours, open the RRAS console and then open the server you want to configure. Click the Network Interfaces branch, right-click the demand-dial interface, and choose Dial-Out Hours. Use the Dial-Out Hours dialog box to specify the hours at which the interface can be used. The options in the dialog box are self-explanatory.

Changing dial-out credentials

You can modify the credentials the router uses to connect to the remote router when it initiates a demand-dial connection. You might have entered it incorrectly when you set up the router, the remote administrator may have changed the account at the other end, or you might need to change the account and password for other reasons. Open the RRAS console and the server you want to modify. In the RRAS console, right-click the demand-dial interface you want to change and click Set Credentials. Specify the new user name, domain, and password as needed.

Setting dialing properties

In some situations, such as when you're using a modem connection, you'll want to configure dialing properties such as redial attempts, redial interval, idle time before disconnect, and so on. To configure dialing properties, open the RRAS console, open the Network Interfaces branch, right-click the demand-dial interface, and choose Properties. Use the controls on the General and Options property pages to configure the dialing properties. The options are self-explanatory.

Configuring security methods

RRAS gives you the capability to configure the security/authentication methods that RRAS uses for authenticating with the remote router for a demand-dial connection. To configure authentication methods, open the properties for the demand-dial connection and click the Security tab. The settings you can configure here for the authentication methods are the same as those you can configure for incoming RAS connections. For a detailed description of authentication methods, see "Configuring RRAS for Inbound Connections," later in this chapter.

Modifying network settings

RRAS uses the protocols and other network properties configured for an interface when you add the interface. You might need to remove or add a protocol or make other network property changes for a routing interface. For example, you might want to add the capability to route IPX as well as IP, requiring that you install IPX on the interface. You can do so through the RRAS console. Open the property sheet for the routing interface, choose Properties and click the Networking tab. You can configure dial-up server settings, network protocols and bindings, and other network properties.

Enabling or disabling routing

On occasion, you might need to enable or disable a router, such as taking the router down for maintenance. You can stop or pause the RRAS service to stop routing on all interfaces, or you can take down a specific interface. To stop, pause, or restart RRAS, open the RRAS console, right-click the server you want to manage, and choose the task you want to perform (stop, start, and so on) from the All Tasks menu.

To take down a specific interface, open the RRAS console and then open the IP Routing branch. Click General to display the routing interfaces, right-click the interface to bring the menu down, and choose Properties. Deselect the option Enable IP Router Manager and click OK to take down the interface. Reselect the option and click OK to bring it back up.

Dynamic routing

If yours is a more complex network than the one described in this section, you might want to use a routing protocol such as RIP or OSPF to provide dynamic route table creation and management. The following sections explain how to add and configure RIP and OSPF. This section assumes that you have some knowledge of RIP or OSPF and primarily need to know where to go to add and configure routing protocols in Windows Server 2008 RRAS.

Adding and configuring RIP

Before you can configure RIP on an interface, you need to add it. In the RRAS console, open the server you want to manage and then expand the IP Routing branch. Right-click General and choose New Routing Protocol. Select RIP Version 2 for Internet Protocol from the list and choose OK. A new node labeled RIP appears under the IP Routing branch.

Next, you need to specify the interface on which RIP will run, because by default no interfaces are configured when you add RIP. Right-click RIP and choose New Interface. RRAS displays the available interfaces. Select the one on which you want to run RIP and click OK.

The next step is to configure RIP. RRAS presents a property sheet for RIP when you add the interface. You can also display the RIP properties by double-clicking the interface in the right pane with RIP selected in the left pane. The following sections describe the options you can configure for RIP.

General

Use the General page to configure how RIP handles updates, to enable or disable authentication, and for other general properties, as explained in the following list:

- **Operation Mode.** Choose the method RIP uses to update routes. You can choose the auto-static update mode or periodic update mode. With auto-static mode, RRAS sends out RIP announcements only when other routers request updates. Any routes learned through RIP when in auto-static mode are treated as static routes and remain in the routing table until manually deleted, even if RRAS is restarted or you disable RIP. This is the default mode for demand-dial interfaces. The periodic update mode generates RIP announcements automatically at the interval defined by "Periodic announcement interval" on the Advanced property page. Routes learned through RIP with this mode are treated as RIP routes and are discarded if the router is restarted. This is the default mode for LAN interfaces.

- **Outgoing Packet Protocol.** Select the protocol RIP should use for outgoing RIP announcements. Select RIP version 1 broadcast if no other adjacent routers support RIP version 2. Select RIP v2 broadcast in a mixed environment with adjacent routers using RIP v1 and RIP v2. Select RIP v2 multicast to send RIP announcements as multicasts, but only when all adjacent routers are configured to use RIP v2 (RIP v1 doesn't support RIP v2 multicast announcements). Select Silent RIP to prevent the router from sending RIP announcements and to function in listen-only mode, listening for announcements from other routers and updating its routing table accordingly, but not announcing its own routes.

- **Incoming Packet Protocol.** Specify how you want the router to handle incoming RIP announcements. Select Ignore Incoming Packets to have the router function in the announce-only mode and not listen to announcements from other routers. Otherwise, select the required mode depending on the mix of adjacent routers and their support for RIP v1 and/or v2.

- **Added Cost for Routes.** This number is added to the hop count for a route to increase the relative cost. Increase the number to help limit the traffic on the route if you have other, less costly routes that can be used if they are available. The default is 1, and the maximum number of hops for IP and RIP can't exceed 15.

- **Tag for Announced Routes.** You can use this value to assign a tag number to be included with all RIP v2 announcements.

- **Activate Authentication/Password.** Select this option to enable the inclusion of a plain-text password for incoming and outgoing RIP v2 announcements, and then specify a corresponding password in the Password field. If this option is enabled, all routers connected to this interface must be configured for the same password. This option serves only as a means of identifying routers and doesn't provide security or encryption of RIP traffic.

Security

The Security tab enables you to specify which routes to accept or reject that come in via RIP announcements from other routers. You can accept all routes, accept only routes that fall within a specified network range, or ignore all routes in a specified range. For outgoing RIP announcements, you can configure RRAS to announce all routes, announce only those routes that fit a specified network range, or exclude routes that fit a specified range.

Neighbors

The Neighbors tab enables you to define how the router interacts with neighboring routers. The options are as follows:

- **Use Broadcast or Multicast Only.** Select this option to issue RIP announcements only using the outgoing packet protocol specified on the interface's General property page.

- **Use Neighbors in Addition to Broadcast or Multicast.** Select this option to define specific routers to which RRAS sends unicast RIP announcements as well as to issue RIP announcements using the outgoing packet protocol specified on the General page.

- **Use Neighbors Instead of Broadcast or Multicast.** Select this option to define specific routers to which RRAS sends unicast RIP announcements and not issue RIP announcements through the broadcast or multicast protocol specified on the General page. Use this option in networks that don't support RIP broadcasts.

Advanced

You can use the Advanced tab to set several advanced options for RIP on the selected interface, including the interval between RIP announcements, the route expiration period, and other settings. The following list summarizes the settings:

- **Periodic Announcement Interval.** Specify the interval in seconds at which RIP announcements are issued from the local router. You can specify a value between 15 seconds and 24 hours (86,400 seconds), and this setting is only applicable if you've selected periodic update mode on the General tab.

- **Time Before Routes Expire.** This value defines the time-to-live of routes learned through RIP. Routes that do not update in the specified time are marked as invalid. You can specify a value between 15 seconds and 72 hours (259,200 seconds). This setting only applies if the interface uses periodic update mode.

- **Time Before Route Is Removed.** Specify the number of seconds a route learned through RIP remains in the routing table before it expires and is removed. Valid values range from 15 seconds to 72 hours. This setting applies only if the interface uses periodic update mode.

- **Enable Split-Horizon Processing.** Select this option to prevent routes learned on a network from being announced on the same network. Deselect the option to allow those routes to be announced.

■ **Enable Poison-Reverse Processing.** Select this option to assign a metric of 16 (marking them as unreachable) to those routes learned on a network that are announced on the same network.

■ **Enable Triggered Updates.** Select this option to allow the router to generate triggered updates when the routing table changes. Set the maximum time between triggered updates through the option Maximum Delay on the General page of the global RIP property sheet. To view this property sheet, right-click the RIP node in the IP Routing branch of the RRAS console and choose Properties.

■ **Send Clean-Up Updates When Stopping.** Select this option to have RIP announce all routes with a metric of 15 to adjacent routers when the local router is going down, indicating to the other routers that the routes are no longer available. When the router comes back up, RIP will announce the routes again with their appropriate metrics, making those routes available again.

■ **Process Host Routes in Received Announcements.** Host routes in RIP announcements are ignored by default. Select this option to include them in received announcements.

■ **Include Host Routes in Sent Announcements.** Host routes are not included by default in outgoing RIP announcements. Select this option to include host routes in outgoing announcements.

■ **Process Default Routes in Received Announcements.** Default routes received in RIP announcements are ignored by default. Select this option to add them to the local routing table. Note that this could have the consequence of disabling routing if the default route is not applicable to the local router.

■ **Include Default Routes in Sent Announcements.** Default routes are not included by default in outgoing RIP announcements. Select this option to include them. In most situations, you should not include default routes unless those default routes are applicable to all other networks on the selected interface.

■ **Disable Subnet Summarization.** Select this option to have subnet routes summarized by class-based network ID for outgoing announcements on networks that are not part of the class-based network. Subnet summarization is disabled by default and requires RIP v2 broadcast of RIP v2 multicast support on all applicable routers.

General RIP properties

You can set a handful of general properties for RIP in addition to those described in the previous sections. To set these properties, open the IP Routing branch in the RRAS console, right-click RIP, and choose Properties. Use the General tab to configure logging, and the Security tab to define the routers from which the local router will process RIP announcements.

DHCP relay agent

A DHCP relay agent (BOOTP relay agent) functions as a sort of DHCP proxy, enabling DHCP clients on a given IP subnet to acquire IP leases from DHCP servers on other subnets. The

DHCP relay agent relays messages between DHCP clients and DHCP servers. The DHCP relay agent component provided with Windows Server 2008 RRAS serves that function. Figure 6-7 illustrates a Windows Server 2008 functioning as a DHCP relay agent.

FIGURE 6-7

A Windows Server 2008 operating as a DHCP relay agent

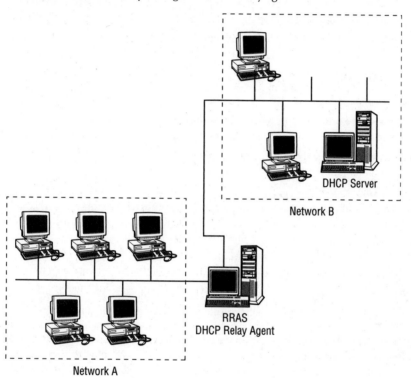

NOTE   The DHCP relay agent can't run on a Windows Server 2008 that also is running the DHCP Server service or network address translation (NAT) with automatic addressing enabled.

Setting up a DHCP relay agent is fairly simple. In the RRAS console, select the server you want to function as a DHCP relay agent. Open the IP Routing branch, right-click General, and choose New Routing Protocol. Select DHCP Relay Agent from the list and click OK to add it to the IP Routing branch.

Next, add the interface(s) on which the DHCP relay agent will function. Right-click in the right pane or on DHCP Relay Agent and choose New Interface. Select the appropriate network interface and click OK. RRAS displays a property sheet for DHCP Relay that includes the following options:

- **Relay DHCP Packets.** Select this option to enable DHCP relay or deselect it to disable DHCP relay.

- **Hop-Count Threshold.** Specify the maximum number of DHCP relay agents to handle DHCP relayed traffic. The default is 4; the maximum is 16.

- **Boot Threshold.** Specify the interval the server waits before forwarding the DHCP messages. Use this option to enable a local DHCP server to have a chance to respond to requests before forwarding the message to a remote DHCP server.

The final step is to define the list of DHCP servers to which the local relay agent relays messages. In the RRAS console, right-click DHCP Relay Agent under the IP Routing branch and choose Properties. RRAS displays a dialog box you can use to specify the IP addresses of the remote DHCP servers.

IGMP – multicast forwarding

Most IP traffic is *unicast*, or directed to a single destination. A Windows Server 2008 running RRAS can function as a *multicast* router, broadcasting Internet Group Management Protocol (IGMP) traffic to multiple hosts. Multicasting is most often used for audio or video conferencing to enable multiple hosts to receive the same data. Clients configured for multicast listen for the multicast traffic, and all others ignore it. Chapter 4 discusses how to configure multicast scopes for a DHCP server, enabling it to assign multicast addresses to clients that request them. This chapter explains how to configure RRAS to function as a multicast forwarder.

NOTE   Windows Server 2008 does not include any multicast routing protocols. Multicast routers exchange group membership information with one another to help determine how multicast traffic is routed. Windows Server 2008 only provides limited multicast routing, but does function as a multicast forwarder, forwarding multicast traffic to listening clients. Windows Server 2008 can be configured as a multicast router through the addition of third-party protocols.

Overview of multicast forwarding

A Windows Server 2008 multicast forwarder listens for multicast traffic on all attached networks and forwards the traffic (based on its multicast destination address) to attached networks where listening clients reside or to other routers for networks where participating clients reside. A Windows Server 2008 multicast forwarder also listens for IGMP Membership Report packets and updates its multicast forwarding table accordingly, enabling it to forward traffic to those destinations requesting it.

The IGMP routing protocol included with Windows Server 2008 is not an IGMP routing protocol per se, but enables a Windows Server 2008 to function as a forwarder. After you add the protocol to Windows Server 2008, you configure one or more interfaces to handle IGMP. You can configure the interface to function in either *IGMP router mode* or *IGMP proxy mode*, as explained in the following sections.

IGMP router mode

An IGMP interface running in router mode sets the network adapter for the interface in *multicast-promiscuous mode*, which passes all multicast packets received on the interface to the higher networking layers for processing.

> **NOTE** Not all network adapters support multicast-promiscuous mode. If you're setting up a multicast forwarder, verify with the NIC manufacturer that the adapter supports this mode.

The interface also tracks multicast group membership, querying periodically for IGMP Membership Report messages and updating its forwarding table accordingly. Each entry in the table specifies the network ID in which multicast clients are listening and the multicast address on which those clients are listening. The table does not reference individual hosts, but rather the interface forwards traffic to any networks where at least one client is listening for multicast traffic.

> **TIP** When multiple routers in a network function as IGMP routers, one is automatically elected to be the querier and performs all membership queries.

IGMP proxy mode

IGMP proxy mode enables a local intranet router to pass IGMP traffic to and from multicast-capable clients and routers on the Internet (referred to as *multicast backbone*, or MBone).

An interface running in IGMP proxy mode functions as a proxy for IGMP Membership Report packets. RRAS listens on the selected interface for IGMP Membership Report packets and retransmits them on all other interfaces running in IGMP router mode. This enables IGMP multicast groups connected to the proxy mode router to have upstream routers update their multicast tables.

The interface running IGMP proxy mode also serves as a gateway of sorts for IGMP traffic coming to the local network from the upstream multicast router, forwarding that traffic to the appropriate clients. Traffic from local clients to the Internet also passes through the interface. For both incoming and outgoing traffic, TCP/IP itself handles the forwarding.

Setting up a multicast forwarder

The first step in configuring a multicast forwarder is to add the IGMP protocol to the router. In the RRAS console, open the IP Routing branch of the designated server, right-click General, and choose New Routing Protocol. Select IGMP from the list and click OK to add it to the IP Routing branch.

Next, add at least one interface for IGMP. Right-click IGMP in the left pane and choose New Interface. Alternatively, select IGMP in the left pane and right-click anywhere in the right pane and choose New Interface. Select the interface on which you want to run IGMP and click OK. RRAS displays the IGMP Properties sheet. The General tab enables you to choose between router mode and proxy mode for the interface. Select the protocol version using the IGMP Protocol Version drop-down list if you select router mode.

The Router tab contains several options that control how IGMP functions on the interface:

- **Robustness Variable.** This variable indicates the relative robustness of the subnet to which the interface is attached.

- **Query Interval.** Specify the interval at which IGMP queries are broadcast on the interface.

- **Query Response Interval.** Specify the maximum amount of time the router should wait for a response for General Query messages.

- **Last Member Query Interval.** Specify the time, in milliseconds, the router waits for a response to a Group-Specific Query message, and the time between successive Group-Specific Query messages.

- **Startup Query Interval.** Specify the time, in seconds, between successive General Query messages sent by the router during startup. The default value is one-quarter of the query interval.

- **Startup Query Count.** Specify the number of General Query messages to send at startup.

- **Last Member Query Count.** Specify the number of Group-Specific Query messages sent with no response before the router assumes there are no more members of the host group on the interface being queried.

- **Automatically Recalculate Defaults.** Select this option to have RRAS automatically recalculate values for the Startup query interval, Startup query count, and Last member query count at startup. The default for the Startup query interval is one-quarter the query interval. The default for Startup query count and Last member query count is the same as the Robustness variable.

- **Group Membership Interval.** This read-only property displays the calculated group membership interval, which is the period of time that must pass before the router decides that there are no more members of a multicast group on a given subnet. The value is calculated as (Robustness variable) × (Query interval) + (Query response interval).

- **Other Querier Present Interval.** This read-only property displays the calculated querier present interval, which is the amount of time that must pass before the router decides that there are no other multicast routers that should be the querier. The value is calculated as (Robustness variable) × (Query interval) + (Query response interval) ÷ 2.

Network address translation

Windows Server 2008's RRAS provides full-featured network address translation (NAT) services. Network address translation is not new, and was born out of the high demand for IP addresses. With the Internet growing the way it is, it is virtually impossible to obtain a large range of IP addresses, especially for a small company. The most an ISP will assign to a small company is less than one-sixteenth of a class C subnet, and you have to be spending a lot of money on dedicated Internet services to get that many addresses.

Most small businesses are deploying asymmetric digital subscriber lines (ADSLs), which are cheaper and often faster than dedicated Internet access connections, such as Frame Relay or dedicated ISDN. However, an ISP will usually only assign you a small range of addresses (sometimes just a single IP address). If you plan to install several hosts on your internal network, such as DNS, mail, Active Directory, Web, and FTP services, and need to route Internet traffic to these hosts, you will need a NAT.

> **NOTE**   NAT services in Windows Server 2008 are typically aimed at small or home businesses. A larger company would most likely use a firewall, which has NAT built into its packet inspection technology. Most routers, even for small offices, now come with NAT support.

NAT alleviates the demand for a larger number of IP addresses by mapping externally assigned IP addresses to internally or privately assigned private addresses (translating from one IP address to another). This means that one IP address can typically be used to target a whole range of IP addresses on the concealed network.

Windows Server 2008 NAT and the RRAS service takes NAT further. NAT can inspect inbound packets to host names and query the internal IP address of the host from an internal DNS. It will then route the packets that have arrived at the public address to the internal hosts, and route the packets to the correct service via the ports it has been configured to use.

Configuring NAT

As described earlier, you might typically assign a private address range to an internal network in a small company and use NAT to connect your network to the Internet. Armed with the IP addresses of your internal hosts and the IP addresses assigned to you by your ISP, run the RRAS Setup Wizard to configure the server for NAT (right-click the server in the RRAS console and select Configure and Enable Routing and Remote Access). Select the option Network Address Translation, click Next, and provide the following information:

> **NOTE**   You can also manually add NAT, as explained a little later in this section.

- **Use This Public Interface to Connect to the Internet.** Select the network interface that is connected to the Internet. This might not actually be a public interface — a firewall or other private network segment might sit between the interface and a public presence on the Internet.

- **Create a New Demand-Dial Interface to the Internet.** Select this option if you want to create a new demand-dial interface for the Internet connection.

- **Enable Security on the Selected Interface by Setting Up a Basic Firewall.** Select this option to enable a firewall on the interface.

You can also manually add NAT if you have already enabled RRAS for another function. The following steps not only add NAT manually, but also take you through the configuration steps for NAT:

1. First add NAT as a routing protocol, which you do by right-clicking the General node and selecting New Routing Protocol. Select the server in the console tree and expand its node down to NAT. The interfaces (NICs) appear in the details pane on the right.

2. Add the interface to the protocol. Right-click NAT and select New Interface. You will have the option to configure the interface for the internal network or the external network (Internet). Select an interface and click OK to display the Network Address Translation Properties dialog box. Specify whether the interface is connected to the Internet or the private network and click OK.

3. Select the interface to configure and right-click. Then select Properties. The Local Area Connection Properties dialog box will appear.

4. On the Address Pool tab, enter the IP address assignment provided by your ISP. In many cases with ADSL, you will be given a dynamically assigned address, which should remain persistent, meaning the same IP address is renewed every time the DHCP lease expires. You can ask an ISP to reserve the number for you as well.

5. On the Services and Ports tab, place a check beside a service that you want translated. The Edit Service dialog box will load.

6. In the Private Address field, enter the IP address of the server hosting the specified service and click OK.

7. If you need to add a service not listed, click Add to open the Add Service dialog box. Enter a name for the service in the Description of Service field.

8. In the Incoming Port field, type the Well-Known port number typically assigned to the IP service in question: for example, port 21 for FTP or port 25 for SMTP.

9. In the Outgoing Port field, type the private port you wish to assign to the same service. It could be a Well-Known port of the outgoing IP service or any port used by your internal resources. (Using high port numbers, such as 5000, provides additional security; this makes it more difficult for hackers to focus on unknown ports.)

10. In the Private Address field, type the private address of the TCP/IP service (typically, the host).

11. Enter the public IP address to be translated (as opposed to the interface) in the field for this address pool entry.

That's all there is to configuring NAT; however, you should plan the deployment carefully. To point clients to the Internet for browsing and other services, you would configure the private outgoing IP address on the NAT as your gateway to the Internet. NAT will translate this address to the correct public address.

You can also configure services and ICMP behavior for the interface. The Services tab enables you to configure NAT translation to allow external requests coming from the Internet to be mapped to servers on the internal LAN. The ICMP tab contains settings that determine how the server reacts to ICMP messages it receives on the interface. You can configure these settings without enabling the firewall on the interface, but it's likely you'll do both.

Configuring Services and Ports

The next step in setting up NAT on an interface is to specify the services and port traffic that are allowed in or out. For example, if there is an FTP server on the internal network and you want external users to be able to access it, you need to enable FTP. In the RRAS console, click NAT and open the properties for the network interface in question. Click the Services and Ports tab (see Figure 6-8).

FIGURE 6-8

Use the Services and Ports tab to add or remove services allowed through the network.

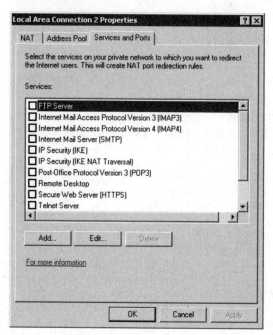

FIGURE 6-9

Configure the service settings on the Edit Service dialog box.

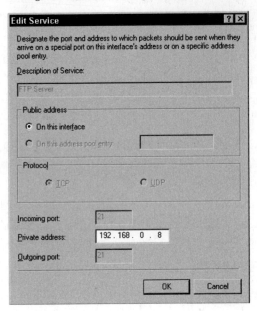

Adding a standard service is as simple as selecting the checkbox beside the service. Windows Server 2008 displays the Edit Service dialog box (see Figure 6-9), in which you can configure the settings for the service, such as the address of the server on the private network that provides the service. Using the FTP example, this would be the IP address of the internal FTP server.

You can only specify the IP address of the server for the standard services listed in the Services and Ports tab. You can configure additional properties by creating a custom service. To do so, click Add to open the Add Service dialog box (see Figure 6-10).

Enter a name for the service, and then select either TCP or UDP to specify the protocol for the service. In the Incoming Port field, type the port number to which the packets are targeted. For example, this would be port 80 for a Web server. In the Private Address field, enter the IP address of the server on the internal LAN. In the Outgoing Port field, enter the port on the server to which the packets will be directed. In most cases, the Incoming Port and Outgoing Port values will be the same. However, you can use different port numbers to remap the traffic. For example, you might map incoming port 80 traffic to port 8080 on the server if the server uses that port for HTTP traffic.

FIGURE 6-10

Define the settings for a custom service on the Add Service dialog box.

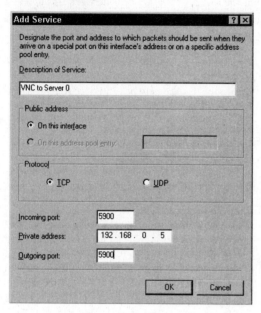

Configuring RAS for Inbound Connections

RRAS in Windows Server 2008 takes three distinct directions: routing, inbound connections (RAS server), and outbound connections (RAS client). This section explains how to configure a Windows Server 2008 as a RAS server. When you install Windows Server 2008, Setup by default installs RRAS, so you don't need to install it separately. You do, however, need to configure it. The following sections explain how to configure modems, ports, protocols, encryption, and other properties to set up and manage a RAS server.

Enabling RRAS

As explained earlier in this chapter, RRAS installs when you set up Windows Server 2003, but you need to enable and configure the service. The wizard offers a handful of options to help you automatically configure the service.

Remote access (dial-up or VPN)

Select this option to configure the RRAS server to enable remote access clients to connect through the server to access resources on the server or on the local network through a dial-up or VPN connection. You can choose either or both. The wizard prompts for the following:

- **Public interface.** For VPN connections, choose the public interface through which remote VPN clients connect to the RRAS server. You also have the option of enabling a basic firewall on the interface.

- **Network interface.** The wizard prompts for the network interface to assign to remote clients, which determines from where the addresses and other access properties come. In a multi-homed server, select the network interface where the DHCP server is located, if allocating addresses through DHCP.

- **IP address assignment.** You can choose to assign addresses through DHCP (see the previous option) or from a static address pool. If you choose to use a static pool, the wizard prompts you for the range of addresses to use. See the section "Configuring Protocols" later in this chapter for detailed information regarding address assignment.

CROSS-REF You can enable remote clients to request a preassigned IP address configured at the client side. See the section "Configuring Protocols" later in this chapter for a detailed explanation.

- **RADIUS.** You can configure the RRAS server to use RADIUS for authentication and accounting. Specify the IP address or host name for the primary and alternative RADIUS servers, along with the RADIUS shared secret, which essentially is a password the RRAS server uses to authenticate its right to access the RADIUS servers. Windows Server 2008 includes a RADIUS server called Internet Authentication Service (IAS) that you can use for RRAS and other applications requiring RADIUS authentication, or you can use any RADIUS server. See the section "Using RADIUS" later in this chapter for more information.

Network address translation

This option helps you set up a network address translation (NAT) server. Configuring NAT was covered earlier in this chapter.

Virtual Private Network access and NAT

Select this option to configure RRAS as a Virtual Private Network (VPN) server, enabling clients to use PPTP or L2TP to dial in from a public network such as the Internet (or direct dial-up) and to establish a secure connection to the local network. This option also sets up the server as an Internet gateway with NAT, enabling internal users to access the Internet through the server.

By default, RRAS configures 128 ports each for PPTP and L2TP, but you can add or remove ports as desired. The settings prompted by the wizard are the same as those settings explained previously in the section "Remote Access (Dial-Up or VPN)." The server also prompts for the network interface through which the RRAS server connects to the Internet. The VPN server must have a second network interface for the internal LAN.

Secure connection between two private networks

Select this option to configure the RRAS server to function as a router. The wizard prompts you to choose whether or not you want to use demand-dial connections to access remote networks. If you choose No, the wizard completes the configuration and terminates. If you answer Yes, the wizard asks whether you want to assign IP addresses through DHCP or a static address pool (if IP is installed on the server). Choosing Yes does not cause the wizard to configure any demand-dial connections; you configure those through the RRAS console after the wizard finishes. The wizard adds NAT/Basic Firewall to the configuration automatically.

Custom configuration

Select this option if you want to choose which functions the RRAS server will perform. You can run the wizard again if desired to automatically configure the server, although you'll lose the current configuration settings. See the previous section, "Enabling RRAS," to learn how to restart the wizard.

 The following sections assume you are configuring the server manually rather than using the wizard, or you are fine-tuning settings after running the wizard.

Configuring modems and ports

One of the first steps to take in setting up a Windows Server 2008 RAS server is to install and configure the hardware and ports that will handle the incoming calls. You configure a standard modem through the Control Panel. If the modem is not already installed, open the Control Panel and double-click the Phone and Modem Options icon. Click the Modems tab, and then click Add to start the Add/Remove Hardware wizard. You have the option of selecting the modem manually or letting Windows Server 2008 search for it. Repeat the process for any additional modems you are installing on the system.

Other types of dial-up equipment require different installation and configuration steps that vary from one item to the next. It isn't practical to cover every type in this chapter, so refer to the manufacturer's documentation to learn how to properly install the hardware. If you're setting up a server connected to the Internet to act as a VPN server for your local network, install the network hardware, connect the system to the Internet, and verify that the server has connectivity to both the LAN and the Internet.

You configure ports for incoming access through the RRAS console. When you click the Ports node, the console displays the installed RAS ports. Windows Server 2008 by default installs both the PPTP and L2TP protocols for VPN support and adds ports for each protocol (one incoming connection per port of each type). You can view the status of a given port by double-clicking the port in the list or right-clicking the port and choosing Status. Windows Server 2008 displays a Port Status dialog box for the port that shows line speed, errors, and protocol-specific data such as IP address.

To configure ports, right-click Ports in the right pane of the RRAS console and choose Properties. Windows Server 2008 displays a Ports Properties dialog box listing each of the port types. For example, all PPTP ports appear under a single item in the list, as do all L2TP ports and individual modems. Select the port type you want to configure and click Configure. Windows Server 2008 displays the Configure Device dialog box shown in Figure 6-11.

FIGURE 6-11

The Configure Device dialog box.

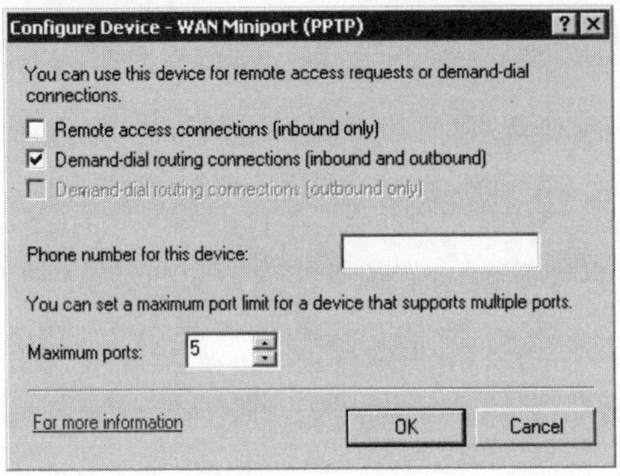

The following list explains the options in the Configure Device dialog box:

- **Remote Access Connections (Inbound Only).** Select this option to enable the selected port to handle incoming connections only and not function as a demand-dial router for outgoing connections.

- **Demand-Dial Routing Connections (Inbound and Outbound).** Select this option to enable the port to handle incoming calls and function as a demand-dial router to service local clients for outgoing calls.

- **Phone Number for This Device.** This option is used for Called-Station-ID and BAP-enabled connections and to identify the IP address for PPTP and L2TP ports. Some devices support the automatic recognition of the device's phone number for Called-Station-ID, so you need to add the number manually only if the device doesn't support automatic recognition. The number must match the number defined in the Called-Station-ID attribute of the NPS policy that is in effect, or the call is rejected. For BAP, this property is passed to the client when it requests an additional connection so it knows what number to dial for the new connection. For PPTP and L2TP ports, enter the IP address, in dotted decimal format, you are assigning to the VPN interface of the server.

- **Maximum Ports.** Use this control to specify the maximum number of ports enabled on a multiport device or protocol (such as PPTP or L2TP).

Configuring protocols

In addition to configuring the ports used by the RRAS server, you also need to configure the protocols to be used by remote access clients. Verify that you have the necessary protocols installed prior to attempting to configure the protocols for RRAS. The following sections explain the options you have for each of the supported RRAS protocols.

TCP/IP

You can assign IP addresses to remote access clients using one of three methods: DHCP, a static address pool, or by allowing the client to request a preassigned IP address.

Assigning addresses through DHCP

When the RRAS service starts, it checks for the availability of a DHCP server (if configured to use DHCP for address assignment) and obtains 10 leases from the DHCP server. The RRAS server uses the first lease for itself and assigns the remaining addresses to RAS clients as they connect, recovering and reusing addresses as clients disconnect. When the pool of 10 addresses is exhausted, the RRAS server obtains 10 more, and the process repeats as needed. When the RRAS service stops, it releases all the addresses, making them available for other DHCP clients on the network.

The RRAS service will use Automatic Private IP Addressing (APIPA) if it is unable to locate a DHCP server at startup. APIPA enables Windows Server 2008 to assign addresses in the class B address range 169.254.0.1 through 169.254.0.254 (subnet mask of 255.255.0.0). APIPA is designed to allow automatic IP configuration when no DHCP server is available. Because APIPA is intended for use in internal, single-segment networks, it does not allocate settings for default gateways, DNS servers, or WINS servers.

By default, RRAS selects a network interface at random from which to obtain the DHCP leases for RAS clients. You can, however, specify the interface to pull addresses from a specific network segment/server when the RRAS server is multi-homed (multiple network interfaces). You do so through the IP page of the server's properties. In the RRAS console, right-click the server and choose Properties, and then click the IP tab (see Figure 6-12). Use the Adapter drop-down list at the bottom of the property page to select the adapter, or choose Allow RAS to Select Adapter if you want RRAS to automatically select an adapter.

 The Adapter drop-down list appears only on multi-homed systems.

Using a static address pool

You can assign addresses to RAS clients from a static pool if you have no DHCP server on the network or simply prefer not to use DHCP for the RAS server. In previous versions of RRAS (Windows NT), you could configure included and excluded address ranges. In Windows Server 2008, however, you create included ranges only. You can achieve the same effect as an excluded range by creating multiple included ranges that don't include the address range you want to exclude.

You configure the static address pool through the IP property page for the server. In the RRAS console, right-click the server, choose Properties, and then click the IP tab. Select the option

Static Address Pool and click Add to display the New Address Range dialog box. You specify a starting address for the range, and then either the ending address or the number of addresses to include in the pool. Windows Server 2008 determines the ending address for you if you specify the number of addresses; it also determines the required subnet mask based on the selected address range. Click OK to add the range, and then repeat the process if you need to add other ranges.

FIGURE 6-12

The IP tab.

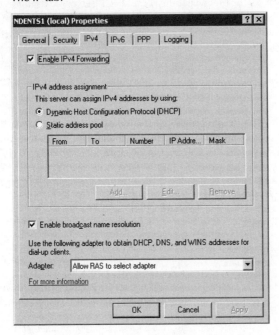

When defining static address pools for RRAS, make sure you don't use addresses already allocated to other systems or to DHCP servers on the network. If the static address pool is in a different subnet from the local network, you must either enable IP routing on the RRAS server (configured through the IP page of the server's global properties) or add static routes for the subnet.

Allowing clients to use preassigned IP addresses

In some situations, it's advantageous for clients to be able to use the same IP address for each remote session. For example, users might work with applications that expect remote users to be at specific IP addresses. Arbitrarily allowing clients to request preassigned IP addresses could lead to address havoc and potential routing problems, but Windows Server 2008 overcomes that problem by allocating the remote client's IP address through his or her account properties. Enabling a client to request a preassigned IP address requires two steps. First, you must configure the applicable NPS policy to allow the user to request a preassigned IP address. Second, you must specify the address in the user's account properties.

CROSS-REF You configure the NPS policy through the RRAS console. See the section titled "Policy Server" later in this section for detailed information on configuring and managing NPS policies.

Where you modify the user's account properties depends on the network configuration. On a standalone server (no domain), you modify the user's properties through the Local Users and Groups node of the Computer Management console. Open the account's properties and click the Dial-In tab. Select the option Assign a Static IP Address and specify the desired address in the associated text box. For information on other properties on the Dial-Up page, see the section "Policy Server" later in this chapter. You'll find the same properties for users in a domain in the Active Directory Users and Computers console. Configure properties as you would on a standalone server.

Enabling/disabling IP for RRAS

By default, Windows Server 2008 RRAS enables for RRAS all protocols installed on the server. You can selectively disable a protocol if you don't want to allow that protocol to be used for remote connections. To enable or disable IP for RAS, open the RRAS console, right-click the server, and choose Properties. On the IP property page, select or deselect the option "Allow IP-based remote access and demand-dial connections" to enable or disable IP for RAS, respectively.

IP routing and restricting access to the RAS server

By default, the RRAS server allows remote clients access not only to the local server, but also to the network (subject to permissions and policies applied to the remote client or local resources). As such, the RRAS server provides IP routing to the remote clients, routing traffic between the remote client and the LAN. You can prevent remote clients from accessing the LAN by disabling IP routing on the RRAS server. To do so, open the RRAS console, right-click the server, and choose Properties. On the IP page, deselect the option Enable IP Routing to prevent remote clients from accessing the LAN and to restrict their access only to resources on the RRAS server.

CROSS-REF IP routing must be enabled if you're using the RRAS server to provide LAN or demand-dial routing. See the section titled "IP Routing" earlier in this chapter for a detailed discussion of Windows Server 2008 routing through RRAS.

Configuring authentication

After you have configured protocols on the RRAS server, you need to turn your attention to authentication and encryption, configuring the server to suit your needs.

Configuring PPP

Windows Server 2008 offers a few options you can configure that control PPP connections to the server. In the RRAS console, right-click the server, choose Properties, and click the PPP tab. The PPP page offers the following options:

- **Multilink Connections.** Select this option to allow remote clients to request and use multilink connections. This option enables multilink connections but does not explicitly enable dynamic link management through BAP or BACP, which is controlled by the following option. See the section "Using Multilink and BAP" later in this chapter for additional information.

- **Dynamic Bandwidth Control Using BAP.** This option enables the server and client to use Bandwidth Allocation Protocol and Bandwidth Allocation Control Protocol to dynamically multilink connections, adding links when bandwidth utilization increases and removing links when bandwidth utilization decreases.

- **Link Control Protocol (LCP) Extensions.** LCP extensions enable LCP to send Time-Remaining and Identification packets, and to request callback during LCP negotiation. Deselect this option only if the remote clients don't support LCP extensions.

- **Software Compression.** Select this option to have the RRAS server use Microsoft Point-to-Point Compression protocol (MPPC) to compress data transmitted to remote clients. Deselect this option if the remote clients don't support MPPC.

Configuring authentication

As mentioned earlier in this chapter, Windows Server 2008 RRAS supports several authentication standards. You can configure RRAS to accept multiple authentication methods, and the server will attempt authentication using the selected protocols in order of decreasing security. For example, RRAS attempts EAP first if EAP is enabled, then MS-CHAP version 2, then MS-CHAP, and so on.

You configure the authentication methods for RRAS through the Security page of the RRAS server's properties (accessed from the RRAS console). Click Authentication Methods on the Security page to access the Authentication Methods dialog box, shown in Figure 6-13. Select the authentication methods you want to allow and click OK. The following sections provide an overview of each method and where applicable, and how to configure and enable them.

CROSS-REF You can require a specific authentication method for a client through a NPS policy. The following sections don't cover configuring authentication through a remote policy for each authentication protocol, but you will find coverage of that topic in the section "Policy Server" later in this chapter.

EAP

Extensible Authentication Protocol (EAP) enables the client and server (or IAS, if used for RAS authentication) to negotiate an authentication method from a pool of methods supported by the server. Windows Server 2008 EAP provides support for two EAP types: EAP-MD5 CHAP and EAP-TLS. Both the client and authentication server must support the same EAP type for authentication through EAP, and you can install additional EAP types from third parties on a Windows Server 2008.

FIGURE 6-13

You can configure multiple authentication methods through the Authentication Methods dialog box, and RRAS attempts them in decreasing order of security provided.

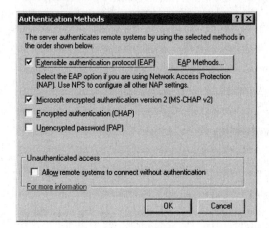

EAP-MD5 CHAP functions much the same as standard CHAP, but challenges and responses are sent as EAP messages. EAP-MD5 CHAP authenticates with user names and passwords. EAP-TLS, conversely, uses certificates to authenticate remote clients, using a secured private key exchange between client and server. EAP-TLS provides the most secure authentication of all the methods supported by Windows Server 2008.

 **Windows Server 2008 supports EAP-TLS only in domain environments (either mixed mode or native). RRAS on a standalone server does not support EAP-TLS.**

Enabling RRAS to support EAP requires three steps. First, enable EAP as an authentication method in the Authentication Methods dialog box through the RRAS server's properties. Then, if necessary, configure the remote client's NPS policy to allow EAP, as explained later in the section "Policy Server." Finally, configure the client to use the appropriate EAP type. See the section "Configuring Outgoing Dial-Up Networking Connections" for a detailed explanation.

Configuring EAP-RADIUS

In addition to supporting the two EAP types described previously, Windows Server 2008 also enables authentication messages for any EAP type to be relayed to RADIUS servers (such as Windows Server 2008 systems running IAS). EAP-RADIUS encapsulates and formats the messages going from the RRAS server to the RADIUS server as RADIUS messages. The RADIUS server encapsulates the EAP response as a RADIUS message and passes it to the RRAS server, which relays it to the client. In this way, the RRAS server functions as a relay and doesn't actually perform the authentication, nor does it require the EAP type used to be installed on the RRAS server. Instead, the EAP type must be installed on the RADIUS server.

In addition to configuring the client to use EAP and the appropriate EAP type, you must enable EAP authentication on the RRAS server, configure it to point to the appropriate RADIUS server, and install the required EAP type on the RADIUS server. You configure the RRAS server to accommodate EAP through the Authentication Methods dialog box for the server, as explained previously. To point the RRAS server to the RADIUS server, open the server's Security property page and select RADIUS Authentication from the Authentication Provider drop-down list. Click Configure ➢ Add to display the Add RADIUS Server dialog box, shown in Figure 6-14.

FIGURE 6-14

The Add RADIUS Server dialog box.

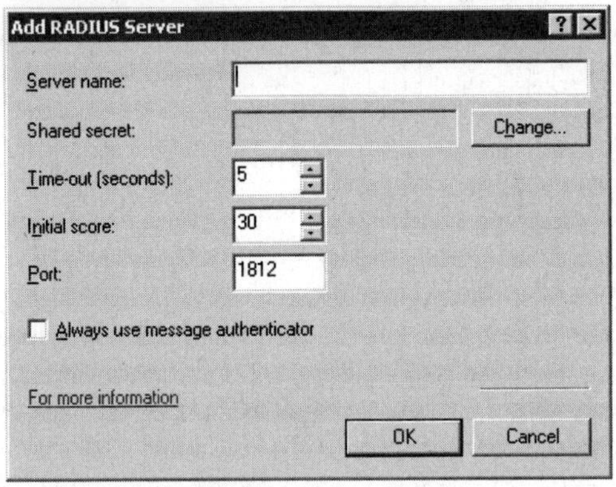

Use the following list as a guide to configure RADIUS server options:

- **Server Name.** Specify the FQDN or IP address of the RADIUS server.
- **Shared Secret.** Enter the secret string used by the RADIUS server to authenticate access to the RADIUS server. You can use any alphanumeric characters and special characters in the string, up to 255 characters. The shared secret is case-sensitive.
- **Time-Out (Seconds).** This is the period of time the RRAS server will wait for a response from the RADIUS server before timing out and failing the authentication.
- **Initial Score.** This value indicates the overall responsiveness of the RADIUS server. This number changes dynamically as the responsiveness of the RADIUS server changes. RRAS

queries the servers in order of highest to lowest score (the higher the score, the better the responsiveness). Use this option to specify an estimated initial score.

■ **Port.** Specify the UDP port used by the RADIUS server for incoming authentication requests. The default is 1812 for newer RADIUS servers and 1645 for older RADIUS servers.

■ **Always Use Message Authenticator.** Select this option to force the RRAS server to send a digital signature with each RADIUS message. The signature is based on the shared secret. Ensure that the RADIUS server supports and is configured for receipt of digital signatures before enabling this option. If you're using IAS and the client for this server is configured to require the RRAS server to always send a digital signature, you must select this option.

CROSS-REF See the section "RRAS Logging and Accounting" later in this chapter to configure the RRAS server for RADIUS authentication.

Repeat the process described previously to add other RADIUS servers as required.

NOTE Storing passwords with reversible encryption is similar to storing passwords in clear text and can therefore be a security risk. Only enable this policy if you have a specific need to do so.

You need to modify the default domain policy if you want to apply reversible encryption for all users in the domain. On a domain controller, choose Start ➢ All Programs ➢ Administrative Tools ➢ Domain Security Policy. Open the branch Security Settings/Account Policies/Password Policy and enable the option "Store password using reversible encryption." On a standalone server, choose Start ➢ All Programs ➢ Administrative Tools ➢ Local Security Policy to modify the password policy to enable reversible encryption.

Each user for which reversible encryption has been enabled needs to modify his or her password so that the new password will be stored with reversible encryption. Configuring the user's account or the domain or local policy for reversible encryption does not automatically change the way the passwords are stored. You can reset the users' passwords yourself or have the users change passwords during their next logon session. Because the users can't change passwords through CHAP authentication, they must either log on to the LAN to change their passwords or use MS-CHAP through the remote connection to change their passwords, and then switch to CHAP for future remote sessions. The alternative for those users who can't log on to the LAN or use MS-CHAP is for the administrator to reset the password.

CROSS-REF The final step is configuring the remote client to use CHAP. See the section "Configuring Outgoing Dial-Up Networking Connections" to learn how to configure remote access clients.

SPAP

SPAP stands for Shiva Password Authentication Protocol. Shiva is a corporation that develops and markets several remote access solutions, including the Shiva LAN Rover. Clients connecting to a Shiva LAN Rover use SPAP for authentication, as do Shiva clients connecting to a Windows Server 2008 RRAS server. SPAP is disabled by default for a Windows Server 2008 RRAS server. SPAP offers a lower degree of security than the methods described previously, so you should enable SPAP only if you need to support Shiva clients. You can enable SPAP through the Authentication Methods dialog box in the RRAS server's properties.

 SPAP is no longer supported for PPP connections.

PAP

Password Authentication Protocol (PAP) uses plain text to transmit passwords, making it susceptible to compromise. Therefore, only use PAP to support clients that don't support any of the other authentication methods, or when security is not an issue. Enable PAP for the RRAS server through the Authentication Methods dialog box in the RRAS server's properties.

Unauthenticated access

You can configure a Windows Server 2008 RRAS server to allow unauthenticated remote access, enabling any user to log on regardless of whether he or she provides a valid username and password. Though unauthenticated access can pose a security risk, it nevertheless has some uses. Because unauthenticated access is applicable in few situations, it is not covered in detail here. To learn more about unauthenticated access, open the RRAS console, select Help, and open the topic Remote Access/Concepts/Remote Access Security/Unauthenticated Access.

Disabling routing (Remote Access Server only)

If you're using RRAS only to provide dial-in remote access and don't require routing, you can disable routing and allow the server to function as a remote access server only. This reduces some of the overhead in the RRAS server and can improve performance somewhat. You also might want to disable routing for security reasons that might be applicable to your network.

To disable routing, open the RRAS console and then open the properties for the server on which you want to disable routing. On the General page, deselect the Router option and leave the Remote Access Server option selected. Click OK and allow Windows Server 2008 to restart RRAS for the change to take effect.

RRAS logging and accounting

Windows Server 2008 RRAS, like many other services, logs events to the Windows Server 2008 System log, which you can view and manage with the Event Viewer console. You configure logging options on the Event Logging page of the RRAS server's property sheet. Open the RRAS console, open the property sheet for the server, and click the Logging tab. The Logging page offers a handful of options that control the amount of information logged to the System event log; the options are self-explanatory. You also can enable logging of PPP events for troubleshooting purposes — just enable the option Log Additional Routing and Remote Access Information.

By default, a Windows Server 2008 RRAS server uses Windows Server 2008 accounting, which means that certain aspects of remote sessions are logged to the log file designated by the entry in the Remote Access Logging branch of the RRAS console. Windows accounting is applicable when you are using IAS to provide authentication. If you're using a RADIUS server, however, you'll probably want to configure RADIUS to perform the accounting for you. The following sections explain both options.

Using Windows accounting

By default, Windows Server 2008 RRAS does not log remote sessions, but you can enable logging for security and troubleshooting. To use Windows accounting, open the RRAS console, right-click the server, choose Properties, and click the Security tab. Select Windows Accounting from the Accounting Provider drop-down list, and then click OK to close the property sheet.

In the RRAS console, open the Remote Access Logging branch. You'll find an item in the right pane labeled Local File. Double-click Local File, or right-click it and choose Properties, to display the Local File Properties sheet. The Settings page contains the following options:

- **Accounting Requests.** Select this option to log accounting requests from the RRAS server to the accounting server to indicate that it is online and ready to accept connections or go offline, and to start and stop accounting for a user session.

- **Authentication Requests.** This option logs authentication requests sent by the RRAS server to IAS on behalf of the client, along with responses from IAS to the RRAS server indicating the acceptance or rejection of the remote client's authentication request.

- **Periodic Status.** This option enables you to log periodic status requests for a session sent by the RRAS server to IAS, although this option is generally not recommended because of the potentially large log file that usually results.

The Local File page of the Local File Properties sheet determines the format for the local log file as well as the log's location, filename, and how often a new log file is created. The options are self-explanatory.

Using RADIUS accounting

You configure RADIUS accounting through the Security tab of the RRAS server's properties. Open the RRAS console, right-click the server, choose Properties, and click the Security tab. Select RADIUS Accounting from the Accounting Provider drop-down list, and then click Configure. In the RADIUS Accounting dialog box, click Add to add a RADIUS accounting server and configure its properties. The following list explains the options:

- **Server Name.** Specify the FQDN or IP address of the RADIUS server.

- **Shared Secret.** Enter the secret string used by the RADIUS server to authenticate access. You can use any alphanumeric characters and special characters in the string, up to 255 characters. The shared secret is case-sensitive.

- **Time-Out (seconds).** This is the period of time the RRAS server will wait for a response from the RADIUS server before timing out and failing the accounting request.

- **Initial Score.** This value indicates the overall responsiveness of the RADIUS server. This number changes dynamically as the responsiveness of the RADIUS server changes. RRAS queries the servers in order of highest to lowest score (the higher the score, the better the responsiveness). Use this option to specify an estimated initial score.

- **Port.** Specify the UDP port used by the RADIUS server for incoming authentication requests. The default is 1813 for newer RADIUS servers and 1646 for older RADIUS servers.

- **Send RADIUS Accounting On and Accounting Off Messages.** Select this option to have the RRAS server send Accounting-On and Accounting-Off messages to the accounting server when the RRAS service starts and stops.

Configuring a VPN Server

A secure Virtual Private Network (VPN) connection enables remote access clients to establish secure connections to the RRAS server or to the local network to which the RRAS server is connected from a nonsecure network such as the Internet. Once connected by a VPN connection, the remote user has the same capabilities and security that he or she would have when connected locally to the network. A common use for VPN is to allow remote users to access files, printers, and other resources on the office LAN when they are on the road or working from other locations.

In a VPN connection, the data packets are encapsulated with additional header data that provides routing data to enable the packet to reach its destination. The segment of the connection in which the data is encapsulated is called a *tunnel*.

Data is encrypted before it is encapsulated to make the data secure as it travels through the public network. *Tunneling protocols* manage the traffic flow between the client and server. By default, Windows Server 2008 supports two tunneling protocols: Point-to-Point Tunneling Protocol (PPTP) and Layer 2 Tunneling Protocol (L2TP). These protocols are described earlier in this chapter in the section "RAS Connection Types and Protocols." All previous operating systems and Vista and Windows Server 2008 clients support PPTP; Windows Server 2008 clients in fact support both PPTP and L2TP. Non-Microsoft clients that support PPTP or L2TP can also connect to a Windows Server 2008 VPN server.

When you set up a Windows Server 2008 RRAS server manually as a remote access server, Windows Server 2008 automatically installs both PPTP and L2TP and configures five ports for each protocol, meaning you can connect five remote VPN clients with each protocol. If you use the wizard to configure the server as a VPN server, the wizard creates 128 ports each for PPTP and L2TP. In either case, you can change the number of virtual ports available for connections through the Ports branch in the RRAS console.

To easily configure a VPN server, run the configuration wizard and select the desired VPN option. See the section "Configuring RRAS for Inbound Connections" earlier in this chapter for a description of the options offered by the wizard. The following sections explain changes you can make after installation and how to configure the server for VPN manually.

> **TIP** Don't forget to enable the remote clients' accounts for remote access — either through the individual account properties or the NPS policy. This is required for VPN connections just as it is for standard RAS connections.

Configuring VPN ports

You use the RRAS console to make all changes to the VPN server's configuration. One of the changes you'll surely want to make at some point is the port configuration. Open the RRAS console, open the server to be changed, right-click the Ports branch, and choose Properties. The Ports Properties sheet shows the available ports, port type, and limited other information. Click a port type, and then click Configure to display the Configure Device dialog box, shown in Figure 6-15.

FIGURE 6-15

The Configure Device dialog box.

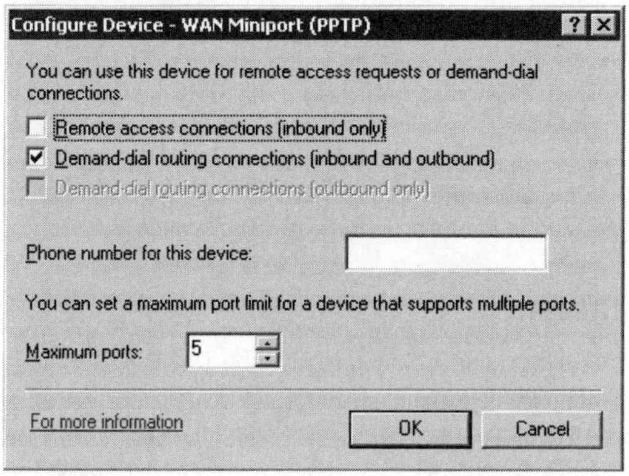

Use the Configure Device dialog box to configure port properties, which vary somewhat from one type to another.

Use the following list as a guide to configure port options:

■ **Remote Access Connections (Inbound Only).** Select this option to enable the port type for incoming remote access connections. Deselect the option to prevent incoming connections on the selected port type.

■ **Demand-Dial Routing Connections (Inbound and Outbound).** Select this option to enable incoming and outgoing demand-dial routing on the port type. Deselect to disable routing for the selected port type.

- **Demand-Dial Routing Connections (Outbound Only).** Select this option to allow only outbound demand-dial connections.

- **Phone Number for This Device.** For PPTP and L2TP ports, specify the IP address assigned to the VPN interface on the server through which the incoming connections arrive.

- **Maximum Ports.** Change the number of ports of the selected type with this control.

Enabling L2TP for VPN

By default, Windows Server 2008 configures five L2TP ports when you install RRAS for remote access and 128 ports when you install RRAS for VPN. You need to take some additional steps, other than configuring ports that you need, to ensure that L2TP provides a secure connection, as explained in the following sections.

Obtaining and installing a certificate

L2TP uses IPSec to provide encryption, which requires that you install a computer certificate on the RRAS server as well as the client to provide encryption/decryption capability for IPSec. You must have a Windows Server 2008 running Certificate Services on your network (or locally on the RRAS server) from which to obtain the certificate. This certificate server is called a Certificate Authority (CA). An enterprise root CA can be configured to allocate computer certificates automatically to computers in the domain, or you can use the Certificates console to request a certificate from an enterprise CA. You also can connect to http://server/cersrv, where server is the address or name of the CA, to request a certificate. Use this last option if your RRAS server is not a member of a domain or if you need to request the certificate from a standalone CA.

Configuring L2TP over IPSec filters

Unlike PPTP, which uses Microsoft Point-to-Point Encryption (MPPE), L2TP relies on IP Security (IPSec) to provide encryption to secure the VPN connection. You therefore need to configure IPSec filters accordingly on the RRAS server's public interface to restrict all but L2TP traffic. This will ensure that only secure L2TP traffic moves through the RRAS server. To configure the filters, first note the IP address of the RRAS server's public interface (the one connected to the Internet). Then, open the RRAS console, open the IP Routing branch, and click General. Right-click the interface on which you want to set the filters and choose Properties.

On the General page of the interface's property sheet, click Inbound Filters to display the Inbound Filters dialog box, as shown in Figure 6-6. Click Add to display the Add IP Filter dialog box. Select the option Destination Network. Then, in the IP Address field, specify the IP address of the server's Internet network interface. In the Subnet Mask field, enter **255.255.255.255.** Select UDP from the Protocol drop-down list, enter **500** in both the Source Port and Destination Port fields, and click OK.

Back on the Inbound Filters dialog box, click Add again and add another Destination Network entry for the same IP address and subnet mask as the first entry, but add UDP port entries of

1701 for both the Source Port and Destination Port fields. Click OK. Then, in the Inbound Filters dialog box, select the option "Drop all packets except those that meet the criteria below," and click OK.

Next, you need to add filters to restrict traffic for outgoing packets to the appropriate ports for L2TP. On the General page of the interface's property sheet, click Output Filters. Just as you did for the input filters, add two output filters for the server's public network interface IP address, subnet mask 255.255.255.255, with the first filter using UDP port 500 for Source Port and Destination Port, and a second filter using UDP port 1701 for Source Port and Destination Port.

Using Multilink and BAP

As mentioned earlier in this chapter, Windows Server 2008 supports the use of multilink connections, which enables a client to connect to the RRAS server using multiple, aggregated links. Bandwidth Allocation Protocol (BAP) provides a means for the bandwidth utilization to be dynamic. As bandwidth usage increases, the client can request another connection to improve performance. As bandwidth usage decreases, connections can be dropped to make them available to other clients or reduce connection costs. Enabling multilink and BAP requires a few steps: enable multilink, configure network access policies, configure the ports, and configure the clients.

First, open the RRAS console, expand the server node, then right-click and select Properties. On the PPP page, select Multilink Connections to allow clients to request multilink connections. Select "Dynamic bandwidth control using BAP or BACP" to enable clients to use BAP/BACP to dynamically manage aggregation. Click OK to close the property sheet.

The second step is to enable multilink in the appropriate network policy. The default policy allows all clients to use the settings defined globally for the RRAS server, so enabling multilink and BAP for the server enables it for all remote clients unless modified by a network policy. If you want to restrict the use of multilink and BAP to selected users, modify the policies accordingly. Apply one policy for those who require multilink support and a different policy for those who do not.

In the RRAS console, open the Servers branch and click Remote Access Logging & Policies. Double-click the policy you want to modify (or create a new one). Select the Settings tab for the Multilink policy (see Figure 6-16).

You can configure the settings based on the following list:

- **Server Settings Determine Multilink Usage.** Select this option to use the global settings defined by the RRAS server.
- **Do Not Allow Multilink Connections.** Select this option to disable multilink for remote clients covered by the policy and limit them to a single connection.

- **Allow Multilink Connections.** Select this option to allow remote clients covered by the policy to use multiple connections.

- **Percentage of Capacity/Period of Time.** Specify the utilization threshold value and duration the server uses to determine when to drop a link.

- **Require BAP for Dynamic Multilink Requests.** Select this option to require the client to use BAP to manage multiple links. If the client doesn't use BAP, multilink connections are refused and the client is limited to a single link.

FIGURE 6-16

The PPP page.

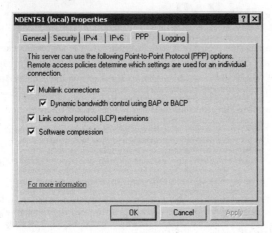

Next, specify the phone number for each port used for multilink connections to enable the server to pass that data to the client when the client requests another link. The client uses the link number to dial the next link. In the RRAS console, open the server, right-click the Ports branch, and choose Properties. Double-click the port for which you need to set the dial-in number, or select the port and click Configure. Specify the phone number in the field Phone Number for This Device and then close the dialog box and the Ports property sheet.

CROSS-REF See the section "Configuring Outgoing Dial-Up Networking Connections" later in this chapter to learn how to configure Windows Server 2008 clients to use multilink and BAP.

Policy Server

Although you can rely on global settings on the RRAS server to provide security and enable/disable access, you have much greater control over remote clients through the use of Network Policy Server (NPS). Like other group policies, NPS policies enable you to configure access on a user, group, or global basis. By default, Windows Server 2008 RRAS creates a single NPS policy. You can modify this policy and/or create additional policies to suit your needs.

You manage NPS policies through the NPS console. In the console, open the server to be managed and then open the Remote Access Logging & Policies branch. Right-click the node and choose Launch NPS. Then select the option to manage Network Access Policies.

Connections to RRAS and "other access servers" are actually configured to deny access to all dial-up users. Click the policy and note that the option Deny Remote Access Permission is selected. This setting applies unless overridden by per-user settings in each user's account, which effectively disables access for all users unless their accounts are configured to allow access. Selecting the option Grant Remote Access Permission for This Policy enables all users to gain remote access.

You can use the default NPS policies as-is, add other conditions to them, or create new policies to fit specific users, groups, or situations. For example, assume you want to grant remote access to a sales group but limit the group's members to one link (disable multilink). You want to also enable your Administrators group to gain access but allow them to use multilink. Therefore, you need to create two policies. We'll use this example to illustrate how to create and configure policies. First, create the policy for the Sales group.

Creating a new policy

In the RRAS console, open the server, and then open the Remote Access Logging & Policies branch. Right-click the right the Network Policy node and choose New to start the New Network Policy Wizard. You have two options in the wizard: create a typical policy for specific uses or create a custom policy. If you choose the former, Windows Server 2008 lets you choose from VPN, Dial-Up, Wireless, and Ethernet access methods (depending on configuration), which sets the policy condition NAS-Port-Type Matches *type*, where *type* specifies the appropriate connection type, such as Ethernet. You can open the policy and view the NAS-Port-Type setting for the policy. All policies that you create in this way are set to deny access based on the specified condition(s).

For each of the four typical policy options, you specify the policy name, which identifies the policy in the console. In addition to specifying the connection type, you must also specify the user or group to which the policy applies, as well as the authentication and encryption options.

If you choose the option to create a custom policy, the wizard prompts for the following information as you progress through the screens:

- **Policy Name.** This is the policy name as it appears in the RRAS console. Specify a name that identifies the purpose of the policy or affected users. In this example, use Sales as the friendly name.

- **Conditions.** Use the Specification Conditions page of the wizard to specify the criteria by which the policy grants or denies access. In this example, click Add, select Windows-Groups, and click Add. Select the Sales group ➤ OK ➤ Next. (This example assumes a Sales group in the Active Directory, used by your Sales department.)

- **Specify Access Permission.** Click Next, and then select which action is applied to the selected criteria. In this example, we want the Sales group granted access, so select Access Granted. If you wanted to explicitly prevent the Sales group from using remote access, you would instead select Access Denied.

- **Configure Authentication Methods.** Click Next and then select the authentication methods use on this access server. You can choose the more secure EAP authentication types or the less secure methods such as MS-CHAP or CHAP.

- **Configure Constraints.** Click Next and then select the constraints to configure. This screen gives you the option to set times of access, idle time out, and NAS port types.

- **Configure Settings.** Click Next and then select the RADIUS integration or general routing and remote access settings. The latter lets you set Multilink options, IP filters, encryption, and IP settings. Click Next to review all the options or go back to change settings. When you are happy with the policy, click Finish.

  If you double-click a policy, NPS displays your new policy Properties page to allow you to make changes or add stuff as needed. This is shown in Figure 6-17.

This sheet contains several tabs, which were described in the previous sections. After you configure the Sales group's policy to deny multilink, you run the wizard again to create another policy for the Administrator's group, this time granting multilink permission. Some of the options you have are further explained in the next section.

Dial-In Constraints

Dial-In Constraints determines when the user can connect, for how long, and other properties that define the user's connection in general. Use these options to specify which dial-in media types are available to users to whom the policy applies. For example, you might select Virtual Private Networking (VPN) to allow the remote users to connect through a VPN connection only.

IP

The options of the NPS policy's properties determines how the client IP address is assigned and which input/output filters, if any, apply to the connection. You can force the server to assign an IP, allow the client to request a specific IP, or let the global server settings define how the address is assigned (the default).

You can apply a filter to incoming packets to limit them to specific protocols or ports. See the section titled "Configuring L2TP over IPSec Filters" earlier in this chapter for more information on creating filters.

Multilink

The Multilink option determines whether or not the remote client can use multilink, the maximum number of ports, and criteria that determine when BAP drops a link if bandwidth usage drops. These options are generally self-explanatory. See the section titled "Using Multilink and BAP" earlier in this chapter for additional information.

The Policy Properties dialog box for a new policy.

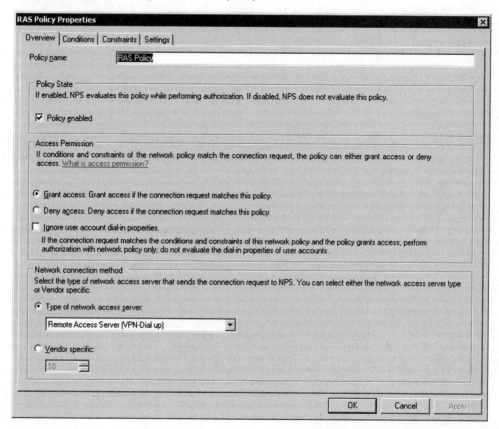

For our example, the Sales group needs to be denied the use of multilink. Select the option "Do not allow Multilink connections" to prevent anyone in the Sales group from using a multilink connection.

Authentication

The Authentication option determines the authentication method(s) allowed for remote clients covered by the policy. Through this page, you can enable EAP or other authentication methods allowed for the remote clients. You can select multiple methods or select a single method if you need to ensure that the selected group always uses the same authentication method.

The option "Allow clients to connect without negotiating any authentication protocol" enables remote clients to establish a connection without authenticating. Although this capability is useful in a limited number of situations, it presents a security risk because you have no control over who can gain remote access. Use this option sparingly.

CROSS-REF   For more information on authentication methods, see the section titled "RAS Connection Types and Protocols" earlier in this chapter.

Encryption

The Encryption option defines the levels of encryption that can be used by clients covered by the policy:

- **No Encryption.** Select this option to enable remote clients to connect without using encryption. If no other encryption options are selected, remote clients are prevented from using encryption.
- **Basic Encryption.** Select this option to enable remote clients to use IPSec 56-bit DES or MPPE 40-bit encryption.
- **Strong Encryption.** Select this option to enable remote clients to use 56-bit DES or MPPE 56-bit encryption.
- **Strongest Encryption.** Select this option to enable remote clients to use IPSec Triple DES (3DES) or MPPE 128-bit encryption.

RADIUS

The RADIUS option enables you to configure additional RADIUS connection properties for remote clients covered by the network policy access policy. Because there are so many, it isn't practical to cover all of them in this chapter. Click Add on the Advanced page and browse the list to determine which, if any, you require for the selection policy.

Prioritizing policies

As soon as you have configured a policy, you can manage the polices from the Network Policy Server console. As mentioned earlier the NPS console can be accessed from the RRAS console. The NPS console is shown in Figure 6-18. Each NPS policy has a unique order number, and policies are evaluated and applied in order of priority. You can change the order to define the way policies are applied, which determines the final applied result. To change the order, right-click a policy and choose either Move Up or Move Down to change its position and order number. You can also use the up and down arrows on the toolbar.

FIGURE 6-18

The Network Policy Server console.

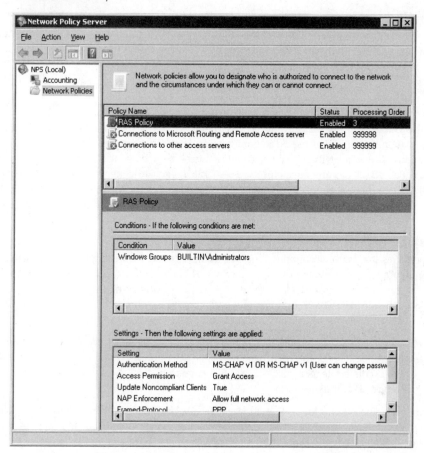

Using RADIUS

Windows Server 2008 uses the NPS to enable a Windows Server 2008 to function as a RADIUS (Remote Authentication Dial-In User Server) server. In addition to providing authentication services, RADIUS also performs accounting and keeps track of user logon, session duration, logoff, and so on. You can use NPS to provide authentication for RRAS, IIS, or other services, including providing authentication for non-Microsoft dial-up servers. Any dial-up modem pool that supports RADIUS, for example, can authenticate clients through a Windows Server 2008 running IAS.

> **NOTE**   The NPS service does not have to be installed on the same server as RRAS. In fact, the NPS server could be located not only on a different server, but also in a different subnet. You specify the IP address or FQDN of the NPS server when you configure the RRAS server to enable RRAS to locate it.

Configuring RADIUS

NPS uses certain security measures to restrict which services can connect to RADIUS for authentication. Services that use NPS to authenticate remote users are called *clients*. You need to configure RRAS and NPS to allow specific clients — such as your RRAS server — to connect to a RADIUS server to authenticate users. To enable a client to connect, open the NPS console and then open the policy. On the Properties dialog box click the Settings tab to manage RADIUS clients. You can choose Standard clients or Vendor Specific clients.

Configuring accounting

NPS performs logging of accounting requests, authentication requests, and periodic status. You can configure NPS to use one of two file formats: NPS-compatible or database-compatible. Both options create a delimited text file. The latter is useful for importing the log file into a database such as Access or SQL Server. You can also configure NPS to log to a SQL Server directly (covered next).

You configure logging through the NPS console. In the console, click the NPS node, and then click the Local File item in the right pane to display its properties. Use the Settings page to configure which events are logged. Use the Log File page to control the size of the log, how often the log is replaced, and its location.

You can configure NPS to log to SQL Server database. To enable SQL Server logging, click the SQL Server option in the right pane to open the SQL Server Properties dialog box. As with local file logging, you specify the types of events you want NPS to include in the log. Also specify the maximum number of concurrent client connections to the logging server, and then click Configure to open the Data Link Properties dialog box, where you specify the target SQL Server, database name, authentication credentials, connection permissions, and initialization variables for the database.

Configuring Outgoing Dial-Up Networking Connections

In addition to using RRAS to support dial-in users, you can also configure dial-out connections. For many users, this means creating a dial-up connection to the Internet, although with

Windows Server 2008, it's more likely that you'll be creating demand-dial router or client connections to another server or to a router. Network address translation (NAT) and routing are covered in detail earlier in this chapter. This section of the chapter assumes you need to configure Windows Server 2008 dial-up connections to a RAS server or the Internet.

Creating a connection

As with nearly every configuration issue, Windows Server 2008 provides a wizard to automate creation of dial-up connections. Click Start ➤ Network and open the Network console. Then right-click the Network node and click Properties. This will open the Network and Sharing Center. Under the Tasks option click "Set up a connection or network" option. You are now presented with several options to establish persistent connections to remote networks. If the OS detects a modem, you will be able to specify the connection method (modem, broadband, and so forth), authentication credentials, phone number, and other applicable information.

Configuring connection properties

After you create a connection, you can modify its properties. Most of the properties are self-explanatory, and you can configure such properties as the server's phone number or, in the case of a VPN server, the IP address, or FQDN. Other options configure such properties as redial attempts, idle time before hang-up, and so on. You should have no trouble configuring these settings. The following sections explain a handful of configuration issues that are perhaps not as intuitive as the others.

Security and authentication

The security option for a connection enables you to specify the authentication method used for the connection. By default, Windows Server 2008 sets up the connection to allow unsecured passwords, which means the client can send the password in plain text, making it susceptible to interception. This is shown in Figure 6-19.

After your connection is created, simply click the Connect to a Network option. This loads the Connect to a network panel, which contains a list of connections you have created. To edit the connection right-click the connection and select Properties. You can select Require Secured Password from the "Verify my identity as follows" drop-down list to force the connection to require encryption for the password. The method used for encryption depends on the authentication method negotiated with the remote server. The following two options work in conjunction with the Require Secured Password option:

- **Automatically Use My Windows Logon Name and Password (and Domain if Any).** Select this option to have the connection automatically use your current logon name, password, and domain for logon to the remote server.

- **Require Data Encryption (Disconnect if None).** Select this option to force data encryption for the connection and disconnect if the server doesn't offer a supported encryption method. You can prevent encryption through the Advanced properties (explained next).

FIGURE 6-19

Specify user credentials to connect to a network.

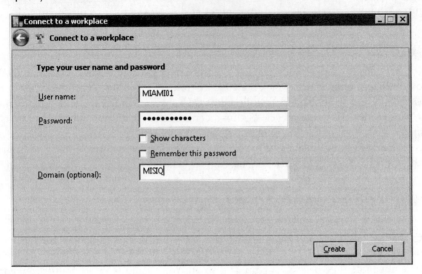

You also can use a smart card for authentication. Select the option Use Smart Card from the Validate drop-down list to use a smart card for authentication. This option must be supported by the remote server in order for the connection to succeed.

Select Advanced on the Security page and click Settings if you want a finer degree of control over authentication settings (such as configuring EAP or other protocols). Use the Data Encryption drop-down list to specify whether encryption can be used or is required for the connection. The options are self-explanatory.

If you choose any protocols other than EAP, you simply need to select which protocol(s) you want the connection to attempt. You can select multiple protocols. If dialing a Windows Server 2008 RRAS server, the server will attempt authentication based on the security offered by each method, choosing the most secure whenever possible.

Configuring EAP

Configuring a client to use EAP takes a little more effort. Select the option Use Extensible Authentication Protocol (EAP), and then select either MD5-Challenge or Smart Card or Other Certificate from the associated drop-down list. If you select Other Smart Card or Other Certificate, click Properties to display the Smart Card or Other Certificate dialog box. Select options using the following list as a guide:

- **Use My Smart Card.** Select this option if you have a smart card reader attached to your system and a smart card to use for authentication.

- **Use a Certificate on This Computer.** Select this option to use a certificate installed on your computer to provide authentication.

- **Validate Server Certificate.** Select this option to have your computer verify that the certificate provided by the server is still valid (not expired). Deselect the option to have the client accept the server's certificate without checking it.

- **Connect to These Servers.** Use this option to limit connections to servers that reside in a specified domain. For example, enter `mcity.us` if you only want to connect to servers in the `mcity.us` domain (`server1.mcity.us`, `ras.mcity.us`, and so on).

- **Trusted Root Certificate Authorities.** Select the trusted root certificate authorities for the server.

- **Use a Different User Name for the Connection.** Select this option if the username stored in the smart card or associated with the certificate you're using is not the same as the username you need to use to log on in the remote domain.

Configuring protocols

Just as you can with a LAN connection, you can configure a dial-up connection for more than one protocol, or perhaps you have more than one protocol enabled for a connection and want to turn off the protocol for dial-up but leave it enabled for the LAN. To change your protocol settings, click the Networking tab and click the Properties button. You can also remove a protocol, but keep in mind that removing it removes it from the computer altogether, and other connections won't be able to use it.

CROSS-REF For more information on configuring network protocols, see Chapter 3.

Multilink and BAP Revisited

As explained earlier in this chapter, some dial-up servers support multilink connections that enable you to connect to the RRAS server with multiple links (two or more modems, for example) to create an aggregate connection with a total bandwidth equal to the sum of all connected links. Windows Server 2008 dial-up networking supports multilink dial-out connections and can optionally use Bandwidth Allocation Protocol (BAP) to dynamically add and drop links as needed to accommodate changes in bandwidth usage. The remote server you connect to must support multilink and must also support BAP if you use BAP on the client side.

NOTE Most ISPs that support multilink also charge you for the capability to use multiple connections. Paying for multiple user accounts won't work for multilink, because Windows Server 2008 treats the individual connections as a single one and uses a single username/password pair for establishing all links. Moreover, the server needs to support multilink to enable bandwidth to be aggregated on the server side for your connections. Just dialing two separate accounts would give you two non-aggregated connections.

Before configuring multilink for a dial-up connection, you need to first install the multiple devices you'll be using to dial out. If you only have one device installed, the multilink options are not shown. If multiple devices are installed but only one is selected for the connection, the multilink options are dimmed.

After installing all connection devices, open the NPS console (from RRAS) and double-click the policy to edit. This action will open the Properties for the policy. You can then select the settings page, and click the Multilink option. If you need to configure different numbers for each one, or need to make sure that all devices call the same numbers, or if you need to hunt groups to distribute calls, and so on, you would do this in RRAS itself.

> **TIP** Windows Server 2008 does not automatically reinitialize dropped multilink links unless you're using BAP. Selecting the option Dial All Devices might get you an aggregate link, but there is nothing to prevent the connection from suffering attrition as links are dropped and not reestablished. You can force links to reinitialize by setting relatively low usage conditions. Select Dial Devices Only as Needed from the Options page of the connection's properties and then set automatic dialing to low values, such as 1 percent for five seconds.

Configuring dial-up networking to connect to the Internet

In most cases, you can re-run the Network and Sharing Center Wizard to create a new dial-up connection to the Internet and use it as-is without problems. However, you might want or need to fine-tune some of your settings for cost or performance reasons. The following sections examine common properties you might want to modify.

Controlling disconnects

Most ISPs implement an idle-disconnect period, causing a connection to be dropped when no activity is detected for a specified amount of time. In most cases, the idle-disconnect works well, but some ISPs don't implement it and others that are configured for idle-disconnect seem to work sporadically. If you're paying for your connection by the hour, idle-disconnect can save you a lot of money if you forget to disconnect or want the system to disconnect after a long, unattended download.

You'll find the option "Idle time before hanging up" on the Options property page for the connection. If your ISP doesn't use idle-disconnect or you want to ensure that your connection disconnects even when the ISP doesn't drop you, select the idle time that can occur before your system automatically ends the connection.

The other side of the disconnect issue is the fact that you might want your system to stay connected past the ISP's idle-disconnect period. For example, you might be performing a long, unattended download, but the remote server occasionally is idle for too long and the ISP drops your connection. In this situation, you can download and use one of the many connection utilities that maintains minimal traffic on your connection to ensure that it won't be dropped. You'll find several such utilities at www.tucows.com. Alternatively, simply open your e-mail client and configure it to check your e-mail every few minutes. The traffic going to the mail server will be sufficient to keep your connection alive.

Online security

Another potential problem is that in some cases, other users on the Internet can see your local folders and potentially gain access to your files. You can prevent that from occurring by disabling the File and Printer Sharing service from the dial-up connection. The default condition has this service disabled. Open the Network page of the connection's property sheet and deselect the File and Printer Sharing service. In addition, deselect any protocols other than TCP/IP if they are enabled and you don't need them for a specific reason.

You should also consider enabling ICF on the interface. You'll find ICF on the Advanced tab of the connection's properties.

Summary

Windows Server 2008 RRAS integrates routing with remote access into a single service. Remote users can connect to a Windows Server 2008 RRAS server to gain access to resources on the server or the network. Users can authenticate against the server's local accounts, against domain accounts, or against a RADIUS server. Windows Server 2008 includes the Network Policy Server Service, which you can use to configure a Windows Server 2008 computer as a RADIUS server, providing full authentication and accounting services. Windows Server 2008 supports several authentication methods offering varying degrees of security for both Windows and RADIUS authentication.

Virtual Private Networking support in RRAS enables remote clients to establish a secure connection to a Windows Server 2008 or its network through a public network such as the Internet. In addition to supporting PPTP, Windows Server 2008 RRAS also adds support for L2TP, which provides additional security over PPTP. Demand-dial router connections can also use PPTP and L2TP, making Windows Server 2008 RRAS a good solution for establishing secure network-to-network connections over the Internet.

Dial-up networking in Windows Server 2008 enables all versions of the operating system to function as a remote access client. Though RRAS dial-out is more prevalent on workstations, the same capabilities are available in Windows Server 2008. You can create dial-up connections to private networks, the Internet, or individual computers.

Chapter 7

Backup and Restore

E very MIS or network administrator has a horror story to tell about backing up and restoring systems or data. One organization for which we manage more than a dozen backup servers has data processing centers spread all across the United States, and all are interconnected via a large, private wide-area network. Not long ago, a valuable remote Microsoft SQL Server machine just dropped dead. The IT doctor said it had died of exhaustion ... five years of faithful service and never a day's vacation. After trying everything to revive it, we instructed the data center's staff to ship the server back to HQ for repairs.

The first thing we asked the IT people at the remote office was: "You've been doing your backups everyday right?" "Sure thing," they replied. "Every day for the past five years." They sounded so proud that we were overjoyed. "Good, we need to rebuild your server from those tapes, so send them all to us with the server." To cut a frustrating story short, the five years' worth of tapes had *nada* on them — not a bit nor a byte. Zilch. We spent two weeks trying to make sense of what was on that SQL Server computer and rebuild it. We refuse to even guess the cost of that loss.

We have another horror story to relate later, but this example should make clear to you that backup administration, a function of disaster recovery, which we discuss in more depth in the next chapter, is one of the most important IT functions you can have the fortune to be charged with. Backup administrators need to be trained, responsible, and cool people. They need to be constantly revising and refining their practice and strategy; their companies depend on them.

This chapter serves as an introduction to backup-restore procedures on Windows Server networks, the Backup-Restore utility that ships with the operating system, and the Windows Server 2008 Removable Storage Manager. Before we get into all of this, however, let's consider several angles on the backup/restore functions expected of administrators.

Why Back Up Data?

You back up data for the following two reasons, and even Windows Server 2008, with its fancy tools, rarely highlights the differences:

- Record-keeping (such as annual backups performed every month)
- Disaster recovery (DR) or system recovery

You should make an effort to determine whether a file is no longer valuable to the disaster-recovery period, and then it should be archived for record-keeping. Depending on your company's needs, this period may vary from a week to a couple of weeks or from a month to a couple of months — and even years. There is no point to buying media for annual backups for a site you know is due to close in six months.

What to Back Up

Often, administrators back up every file on a machine or network and dump the whole pile into a single backup strategy. Instead, they should be dividing files into two distinct groups:

- *System files* comprise files that do not change between versions of the applications and operating systems.
- *Data files* comprise all the files that change every day, such as word-processing files, database files, spreadsheets files, media files, graphics files, and configuration files (such as the registry, and the DHCP, WINS, DNS, and Active Directory databases). Depending on your business, data files can change from 2 percent per day on the low side to 80 percent per day on the high side. The average across many of the businesses for which we have consulted is around 20 percent of the files change every day. You must also consider the new files that arrive.

Understanding the requirements makes your life in the admin seat easier, because this is one of the most critical of all IT or network admin jobs. One person's slip-up can cause millions of dollars in data loss. How often have you backed up an entire system that was lost for some reason only to find out that in order to restore it, you needed to reinstall from scratch? "So why was I backing up the system," you may have asked yourself. And how often have you restored a file for a user who then complained that he or she lost five days' worth of work on the file because the restore was so outdated? It's happened to us on many occasions and is very disheartening when you are trying so hard to keep your people productive.

Nothing is worse than trying to recover lost data, knowing that all on Mahogany Row are sitting idle, with the IT director standing behind you in the server room, and discovering that you cannot recover. The thought of your employment record being pulled should be enough to make you realize how important it is to pay attention to this function.

We delve into these two subjects in depth in this chapter and explore how Windows Server 2008 can help you better manage your recovery and record-keeping processes. We start by focusing on the data side of the backup equation before leading this discussion into system backup/restore.

Understanding Backup

Before you can get started using the Windows Server 2008 backup program or any other backup program, you need to know how backing up works and have a basic backup strategy in mind.

Understanding archive bits

The *archive bit* is a *flag*, or a unit of data, indicating that the file has been modified. When we refer to the *setting* of the archive bit, we mean that we have turned it on or that we have set it to 1. Turning it off means that we set it to zero (0). If the archive bit is turned on since we last backed up the file, the file has been modified since it was last backed up.

Trusting the state of the archive bit, however, is not an exact science by any means, because it is not unusual for other applications (and developers) and processes to mess with the archive bit. This is the reason we recommend that a full backup be performed on all data at least once a week.

What is a backup?

A *backup* is an exact copy of a file (including documentation) that is kept on a storage medium (usually in a compressed state) in a safe place (usually at a remote location) for use in the event that the working copy is destroyed. Notice that we placed emphasis on "including documentation," because every media holding backups must include a history or documentation of the files on the media. This is usually in the form of labels and identification data on the media itself, on the outside casing, and in spreadsheets, hard catalogs, or data ledgers in some form or another. Without history data, restore media cannot locate your files, and the backup is useless. This is why you can prepare a tape for overwriting by merely formatting the label so that the magnetic head thinks the media is blank.

Various types of backups are possible, depending on what you back up and how often you back it up, as the following list describes:

■ **Archived backup.** A backup that documents (in header files, labels, and backup records) the state of the archive bit at the time of copy. The state (on-off) of the bit indicates to the backup software that the file has been changed since the last backup. When Windows Server 2008 Backup does an archived backup, it sets the archive bit accordingly.

- **Copy backup.** An ad hoc "raw" copy that ignores the archive bit state. It does not set the archive bit after the copy. A copy backup is useful for quick copies between DR processes and rotations or to pull an "annual" during the monthly rotation. (We discuss this in the section "Setting Up Schedules" later in this chapter.)

- **Daily backup.** This does not form part of any rotation scheme (in our book, anyway). It is just a backup of files that have been changed on the day of the backup. We question the usefulness of the daily backup in Backup, because mission-critical DR practice dictates the deployment of a manual or automated rotation scheme (described later in the "Performing a Backup" section). In addition, Backup does not offer a summary or history of the files that have changed during the day. If you were responsible for backing up a few million files a day . . . well, this just would not fly.

- **Normal backup.** A complete backup of all files (that can be backed up), period. The term *normal* is more a Windows Server 2008 term, because this backup is more commonly called a full backup in DR circles. The *full backup* copies all files and then sets the archive bit to indicate (to Backup) that the files have been backed up. You would do a full backup at the start of any backup scheme. You would also need to do a full backup after making changes to any scheme. A full backup, and documentation or history drawn from it, is the only means of performing later incremental backups. Otherwise, the system would not know what has or has not changed since the last backup.

- **Incremental backup.** A backup of all files that have changed since the last full or incremental backup. The backup software sets the archive bit, which thereby denotes that the files have been backed up. Under a rotation scheme, a full restore would require you to have all the incremental media used in the media pool, all the way back to the first media, which contains the full backup. You would then have the media containing all the files that have changed (and versions thereof) at the time of the last backup.

- **Differential backup.** This works exactly like the incremental, except that it does not do anything to the archive bit. In other words, it does not mark the files as having been backed up. When the system comes around to do a differential backup, it compares the files to be backed up with the original catalog. Differential backups are best done on a weekly basis, along with a full, or normal, backup, to keep differentials comparing against recently backed up files.

What is a restore?

A *restore* is the procedure you perform to replace a working copy of a file or collection of files to a computer's hard disks in the event that they are lost or destroyed. You often perform a restore for no reason other than to return files to a former state (such as when a file is mangled, truncated, corrupted, or infected with a virus).

Restore management is crucial in the DR process. If you lose a hard disk or the entire machine (for example, it is trashed, stolen, lost, or fried in a fire), you need to rebuild the machine and have it running in almost the same state (if not exactly) that its predecessor was in at the time of the loss. How you manage your DR process determines how much downtime you experience or the missing generation of information between the last backup and the disaster — a period we call *void recovery time*.

Understanding how a backup works

A collection of media, such as tapes or disks, is known as a *backup set*. (This is different from a *media pool*, which we discuss in the following section.) The backup set is the backup media containing all the files that were backed up during the backup operation. Backup uses the name and date of the backup set as the default set name. Backup enables you to either append to a backup set in future operations or replace or overwrite the files in the media set. It enables you to name your backup set according to your scheme or regimen.

Backup also completes a summary or histories catalog of the backed-up files, which is called a *backup set catalog*. If your backup set contains several media, the catalog is stored on the last medium in the set, at the end of the file backup. The backup catalog is loaded whenever you begin a restore operation. You can select the files and folders you need to restore from the backup catalog.

Removable Storage and Media Pools

Removable Storage (RS) was introduced in Windows 2000, so it's had nearly a decade to prove itself. It removes a lot of the complexity of managing backup systems. This service also brings network support to Windows for a wider range of backup and storage devices.

Microsoft took the responsibility of setting up backup devices and management of media away from the old Backup application and created a central authority for such tasks. This central authority, Removable Storage, is one of the largest and most sophisticated features of the operating system, worth the price of the OS license alone, and a welcome member on any network. If you are not ready to convert to a Windows Server 2008 network, you might consider raising a Windows Server 2008 Backup server just to obtain the reliable services of Removable Storage on a Windows Server 2008 platform.

Removable Storage is like an iceberg; in this chapter we can show you only the tip. Exposing the rest of this monster service and everything you can do with it is beyond the scope of this treatise, and a full treatment of the subject would run into several chapters. To fully appreciate this service — and if you need to get into some serious disaster-recovery strategies, possibly even custom backup and media handling algorithms — refer to the Microsoft documentation covering both the Removable Storage Service and its API and the Tape/Disk API. The following section provides an introduction to the service.

The Removable Storage Service

Removable Storage comprises several components, but the central nervous system of this technology is the Removable Storage Service and the Win32 Tape/Disk API. These two components, respectively, expose two application programming interfaces (APIs) that any third party can access to obtain removable storage functionality and gain access to removable storage media and devices. The Backup program that ships with the OS makes use of both APIs to provide a usable, but not too sophisticated, backup service.

By using the two services, applications do not need to concern themselves with the specifics of media management, such as identifying cartridges, changing them in backup devices, cataloging, numbering, and so on. This is all left to the Removable Storage Service. All the application requires is access to a media pool created and managed by Removable Storage. The backup application's responsibility is identifying what needs to be backed up or restored and the source and destination of data; Removable Storage handles where to store it, what to store it on, and how to retrieve it. Essentially, the marriage of backup-restore applications and Removable Storage has been consummated along client-server principles.

The interface to Removable Storage is the Removable Storage Snap-in. The interface runs in Microsoft Management Console, which can be configured as explained in Chapter 2. Before you can use the snap-in, the Removable Storage service first has to be installed. This can be done using the Add Features Wizard in Server Manager (see Chapter 2).

The Removable Storage Service can also be accessed directly by programming against the API. You can also work with it interactively (albeit not as completely as programming against the API) in the Removable Storage node found in the Computer Management snap-in (compmgmt.msc). Before we begin with any hard-core backup practice, we need to look at Removable Storage and how it relates to backup and disaster recovery.

CROSS-REF   Removable Storage is also briefly discussed in Chapter 13.

The service provides the following functionality to back up applications, also known as backup or data moving and fetching clients:

- Management of hardware, such as drive operations, drive health and status, and drive head cleaning.
- Mounting and dismounting of cartridges and disks (media).
- Media inventory.
- Library inventory.
- Access to media and their properties.

Access to the actual hardware is hidden from client applications, but the central component exposed to all clients is the media pool. To better understand the *media pool* concept in Removable Storage, you should first understand *media*.

Backup media ranges from traditional tape cartridges to magnetic disk, optical disk CD-ROM, DVD, and so on. More types of media are becoming available, such as "sticks" and "cards" that you can pop into cameras and pocket-sized PCs, but these are not traditional backup media formats, nor can they hold the amount of data you would want to store. DVD, a digital-video standard, however, is a good choice for backing up data, because so much can be stored on a single DVD disk.

Like the dynamic disk-management technology discussed in Chapter 13, Removable Storage hides the physical media from the clients. Instead, media is presented as a logical unit, which is assigned a logical identifier or ID. If a client needs to store or retrieve data from media, it does not deal with the physical media but with that media's logical ID. The logical ID can thus encapsulate any physical media, the format of which is of no concern to the client application.

> **NOTE** Although the client need not be concerned about the actual media, you (the backup administrator) have the power to dictate onto which format or media type your backups should be placed, by configuring media pools.

Media formats can be extremely complex. Some media enable you to write and read to both sides; others enable access to only one side. How media is written to and read from differs from format to format. Removable Storage handles all those peculiarities for you. Just as the Print Spooler Service can expose the various features of thousands of different print devices, so can Removable Storage identify many storage devices and expose their capabilities to you and the application.

Finally, and most important from a cost/benefit perspective, Removable Storage enables media to be shared by various applications. This ensures maximum use of your media asset.

The Removable Storage database

Removable Storage stores all the information it needs about the hardware, media pools, work lists, and more in its own database. This database is not accessible to clients and is not a catalog detailing which files are backed up and when they were backed up. Everything that Removable Storage is asked to do or does is automatically saved in this database.

Physical locations

Removable Storage also completely handles the burden of managing media location, a chore once shared between the client applications and the administrator, but the physical location service deals with more than knowing in which cupboard, shoebox, vault, or offsite dungeon you prefer your media stored; it is also responsible for the physical attributes of the hardware devices used for backing up and restoring data. Understanding the information in this section is worthwhile, because you need such knowledge to perform high-end backup services that protect a company's data.

Removable Storage splits the location services into two tiers: libraries and offline locations. When a storage medium is online, it is inside a tape device of some kind that can at any time be fired up to enable data to be accessed or backed up. When a medium is offline, you have taken it out of its drive or slot and sent it somewhere. As soon as you remove a medium from a device, Removable Storage makes a note in its database that the medium is offline.

Libraries can be single tape drives or highly sophisticated and very expensive robotic storage silos comprising hundreds of drive bays. A CD-R/W tower, with 12 drives, is also an example of a library. Media in these devices or so-called libraries are always considered online and are marked as such in the database. Removable Storage also understands the physical components that make up these devices.

Library components comprise the following:

- **Drives.** All backup devices are equipped with drives. The drive machinery consists of the recording heads, drums, motors, and other electronics. To qualify as a library, a device requires at least one drive.

- **Slots.** Slots are pigeonholes, pits, or holding pens in which online media are placed in an online state. If the medium is needed for a backup, a restore, or a read, the cartridge or disk is pulled out of the slot and inserted into the drive. After the medium is no longer needed, the cartridge is removed from the drive and returned to its slot. The average tape drive is not equipped with a slot, but all high-end, multidrive robotic systems are. The basic slot-equipped machine typically comes equipped with two drives and 15 slots. Slots are usually grouped into collections called *magazines*. Each magazine holds about five cartridges, and one magazine maintains a cleaning cartridge in one of the slots. You typically have access to magazines so that you can populate them with the cartridges you fetched from offline locations.

- **Transports.** These are the robotic machines in high-end libraries that move cartridges and disks from slots to drives and back again.

- **Bar code readers.** Bar coding is discussed in the section "Labeling Media" later in this chapter. It is a means by which the cartridges can be identified in their slots. You do not need a bar-code reader-equipped system to use a multidrive or multislot system, because media identifiers can also be written to the media, but bar code reading enables much faster access to the cartridges because the system does not need to read information off the actual media, which requires every cartridge to be pulled from a slot and inserted into a drive — a process that could take as long as five minutes for every cartridge.

- **Doors.** Doors differ from device to device and from library system to library system. In some cases, the door looks like the door to a safe, which is released by Removable Storage whenever you need access to slots or magazines. Many systems have doors that only authorized users can access. Some doors are built so strong that you would need a blowtorch to open them. On cheaper devices, especially single-drive/no-slot hardware, the door is a small lever that Removable Storage releases so that you can extract the cartridge. Other devices have no doors at all, but after Removable Storage sends an "open sesame" command to the "door," the cartridge is ejected from the drive bay.

- **Insert/eject ports.** IE ports are not supported on all devices. IE ports provide a high degree of controlled access to the unit in a multislot library system. In other words, you insert media into the port and the transport finds a free slot for it. By way of analogy, you can think of the IE port function as a valet service. You hand your car keys to the valet, who finds parking space for you.

If the hardware you attach supports any or all of these sophisticated features, Removable Storage can "discover it" and use it appropriately.

You have dozens, if not hundreds, of devices from which to choose for backing up and storing data. Removable Storage, as we discussed in the preceding sections, can handle not only traditional tape backup systems, but also CD silos, changers, and huge multidisk readers. If you want to determine whether Removable Storage supports a particular device, follow the steps to create a media pool discussed in the section "Performing a Backup" later in this chapter.

Media pools

A relatively new term in the Windows operating system is the *media pool*. If you are planning to do a lot of backing up or have been delegated the job of backup operator or administrator, you can expect to interact with media pools in your future backup-restore career.

A media pool, in the general sense of the term, is a collection of media organized as a logical unit. Conceptually speaking, the media pool contains media that belong to any defined storage or backup device, format, or technology assigned to your hardware, be it a server in the office or one located on the WAN somewhere, 15,000 miles away. Each media pool can only represent media of one type. You cannot have a media pool that combines DVD, DAT, and ZIP technology, but you can back up your data to multiple media pools of different types if the client application or function requires it.

Thinking of the media pool in terms of the hardware devices that are available to your system (such as a CD-R/W or a DLT tape drive) may be easier for you. Try not to work with media pools from dissimilar devices, especially in backing up zillions of files. For example, avoid creating media pools that consist of Zip drives, DLT tape drives, and a CDR-R/W changer. It would make managing your media, such as offsite storage, boxing, and labeling, very difficult, much like wearing a sandal on one foot and a hiking boot on the other and then justifying walking with both at the same time because they both represent "pools" of walking attire.

Removable Storage separates media pools into two classes: *system pools* and *application pools*. The Removable Storage Service creates system pools as it is first installed. By default, the Removable Storage Service is enabled and starts up after you boot your system. If you disable it or remove it from installation, any devices installed in your servers — or attached on external busses — are ignored by Windows Server 2008 as if they did not exist. After Removable Storage is activated, it detects your equipment; if compliant, they are used in media pools automatically created by the service or applications.

System pools

System pools hold the media that are not being used by any application. After you install new media into your system, the first action that Removable Storage takes is to place the media into a pool for unrecognized media. Then, after you have identified the media, you can make it available to applications by moving it to the free pools group. The system pools are built according to the following groups:

■ **Free pools.** Free pools enable any application to access the media pools in this group. In other words, these media pools can be made available to any application requiring free media. Applications can draw on these media pools if they need to back up data. After media pools are no longer required, they can be returned to this group.

■ **Unrecognized pools.** Media in these pools are not known to Removable Storage. If the service cannot read information on a cartridge, or if the cartridge is blank, the media pool supporting it is placed into this grouping.

■ **Import pools.** This group is for media pools that were used in other Removable Storage systems, on other servers, or by applications that are compatible with Removable Storage or that can be read by Removable Storage. Media written to by the Microsoft Tape Format (MTF) can thus be imported into the local Removable Storage system.

Application pools

If an application is given access to a free media pool, either it creates a special pool into which the media can be placed or you can create pools manually for the application by using the Removable Storage snap-in, shown in Figure 7-1.

FIGURE 7-1

The Removable Storage snap-in.

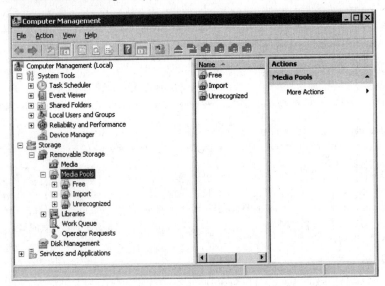

A very useful and highly sought-after feature of Windows Server 2008 media pools is the fact that permissions can be assigned to pools to enable other applications to use the pools or to protect the pools in their own sets.

Multilevel media pools

Media pools can be organized into hierarchies, or nests. In other words, you can create media pools that hold several other media pools. An application can then use the root media pool and gain access to the different data storage formats in the nested media pools. Expect to see sophisticated document storage, backup, and management applications using such media pools.

An example of using such a hierarchy of media pools can be drawn from a near disaster that was averted during the writing of this chapter. One of our 15-tape DLT changers went nuts and began reporting that our tapes were not really DLT tapes but alien devices that it could not identify. The only way to continue backing up our server farm was to enlist every SCSI tape and disk device on the network into one large pool. After the DLT library recovered, we could go back to business as usual.

Work Queue and Operator Requests

Note the nodes for both Work Queue and Operator Requests in the Removable Storage tree. These services provide a communications and information-exchange function between the operator (the backup operator or administrator or the backup operator group) and Removable Storage, respectively.

Work queue

Working backup applications and the RSS (Remote Storage Service) post their work requests to the Removable Storage Service. To manage the multitude of requests that result from applications and services, each request for work from the RSS is placed into the work queue. The work queue is very similar in concept to the print queue.

The work queue provides information on queue states on a continual basis, which is reported to the details pane in the Work Queue node. For example, if an application is busy backing up data, then an In Process state is posted to the details pane identifying the work request and its state. Table 7-1 describes the work queue states reported to the Work Queue details pane.

TABLE 7-1

Work Queue States

State	Explanation
Queued	The work item has been queued. It is waiting for the RS service to examine the request.
In Process	RS is working on the work item.
Waiting	The request is waiting for a resource, currently being used by another service, before work on the item can continue.
Completed	RS has handled the work item successfully. The request has been satisfied.
Failed	RS has failed to complete the work item. The request did not obtain the desired service.
Cancelled	The work item has been cancelled.

Operator requests

No matter how sophisticated Removable Storage is, it just does not do some things. These items are marked for the "human" work queue. For example, Removable Storage cannot fetch cartridges from the cabinet or the storeroom. This is something you must do. The details pane in the Operator Requests node is where Removable Storage posts its request states for you, the operator. Removable Storage can also send you a message via the messenger service or the system tray, just in case you have the habit of pretending the Operator Requests node does not exist. Table 7-2 lists the possible Operator Request states.

TABLE 7-2

Operator Request States

State	Explanation
Submitted	The described request has been submitted, and the system is waiting for the operator's input.
Refused	The operator has refused to perform the described request.
Completed	The operator has complied and has completed the described request.

Labeling media

Removable Storage can read data written to the labels on the actual tape or magnetic disk as well as external information supplied in bar code format. The identification service is robust and highly sophisticated and ensures that your media is not overwritten or modified by other applications.

You need to provide names for your media pools; and if you can afford a bar code reader, organize them according to serial numbers (represented as bar codes) for more accurate handling. If you are planning to install a library system, get one that can read the bar codes from the physical labels on the cartridge casing. This information is critical in locating a few files that need restoring from 5 million files stored on 120 30GB tapes. (The bigger the enterprise, the more complex is the backup and restore regimen and management.)

Another reason we prefer a numbering or bar code scheme for identifying media, as opposed to labeling it according to the day of the week, is that a cartridge can often be inadvertently written to on the wrong day. If that happens, you may have a cart named Wednesday but with Tuesday data on it, which can get confusing and create unnecessary concern. With a bar code or serial number, you can easily ensure that the Wednesday cart is returned to the Wednesday box without needing to scratch out or change the label.

Practicing scratch and save

Although Windows Server 2008 does not cater to the concept of *scratch and save* sets, such sets are worth a mention because you should understand the terms for more advanced backup procedures. Simply put, a *save* set is a set of media in the media pool that cannot be overwritten for a certain period of time. A *scratch* set is a set of media that is safe to overwrite. A backup set should be stored and cataloged in a save set for any period of time during which the media should not be used for backup. You can create your own spreadsheet or table of media rotating in and out of scratch and save sets.

The principle behind scratch and save is to protect data from being overwritten for predetermined periods.

A monthly save set is saved for a month, for example, while a yearly set is saved for a year. After a "safe" period of time has elapsed, you can move the save set to the scratch set. In other words, after a set is moved out of the save status into the scratch status, you are tacitly allowing the files on it to be destroyed. A save set becomes a scratch set if you are sure, through proper media pool management, that other media in the pool contain both full and modified and current and past files of your data and that destroying the data on the scratch media is safe.

Fully understanding the concept of save and scratch sets is important because they are the only way you can ensure that your media can be safely recycled. The alternative is to make every set a save set, which means that you never recycle the tapes ... making your DR project a very costly and risky venture because tapes that are being constantly used stretch and wear out sooner.

Establishing Quality of Support Baselines for Data Backup/Restore

Windows Server 2008 provides the administrator with backup and recovery tools previously seen only on midrange and mainframe technology (such as the capability to mark files for archiving). For the first time, Windows network administrators are in a much better position to commit to service level agreements and quality of service or support levels than before. Unfortunately, the new tools and technologies result in a higher and more critical administrative burden. (The service level shifts to the Windows administrator as opposed to being [typically] the domain of the midrange, Unix, or mainframe administrative team.) Let's consider some of the abstract issues related to backups before we get into procedures.

No matter how regularly you back up the data on your network, you can restore only up to the point of your last complete backup and then the subsequent incremental or differential backups. Unless you are backing up every second of the day, which is highly unlikely and impractical, you can never fully recover the latest OS data up to the point of meltdown (unless you had a crash immediately after you backed up) using standard backup software. Only advanced backup/restore systems that store data in specialized databases (such as the SQL Server transaction log) can do that. You need to decide how critical it would be for your business to lose even one hour of data. For many companies, any loss could mean serious setback and costly recovery, often lasting long after the disaster occurs.

Therefore, it's important to consider the numerous alternatives for backup procedures and various strategies. Decide on a baseline for backup/restores: What is the least acceptable recovery situation? You also need to take into account the quality of support promised to staff and the departments and divisions that depend on your systems, plus the service level agreements (SLAs) in place with customers.

NOTE Service level and quality of support are discussed fully in Chapter 25.

Before you consider other factors, decide what you would consider adequate in terms of the currency of backed-up data. Then, after you have established your tolerance level, you need to determine how to cater to it and at what cost. Starting with cost, consider the following list:

- Data restored is one month or more old.
- Data restored is between one and four weeks old.
- Data restored is between four and seven days old.
- Data restored is between one and three days old.
- Data restored is between six and twelve hours old.
- Data restored is between two and five hours old.
- Data restored is between one and 60 minutes old.

Depending on how the backups were done and the nature of your backup technology, just starting up the recovery process could take up to ten minutes (such as reading the catalog), depending on the technology. Therefore, level 7 wouldn't be an option for you as a tape backup solution. In cases where backup media is offsite, you would need to consider how long the media takes to arrive at the data center after you place a call to the backup bank. This could be anything from 30 minutes to six hours, and you may be charged for "rush" delivery.

Now refer to the preceding list and consider your options. How important (mission-critical) is it that data is restored, if not in real time, almost in real time? Many situations require immediate restoration of data. Many applications in banking, finance, business, science, engineering, medicine, and so on require real-time recovery of data in the event of a crash, corruption of data, deleted data, and so on.

You could and should be exploring or installing clustered systems, mirrors, replication sets, and RAID-5 level and higher storage arrays, as described in Chapter 13, but these so-called fault-tolerant and redundant systems typically share a common hard-disk array or a central storage facility. Loss of data is thus system wide and mirrored across the entire array. A mirror is a reflection — no more, no less.

This brings us to another factor to consider: the flawed backup. You consider this factor if your data is continuously changing. The question to ask is, "How soon after the update of data should I make a backup?" You may decide, based on the preceding list, that data even five minutes old is damaging to system integrity or the business objectives. A good example is online real-time order or delivery tracking. Backing up data with such narrow intervals between versions brings us to the subject of quality and integrity of backed-up data. (In the section "Establishing Quality of Capture" later in this chapter, we discuss versioning and how technology in Windows Server 2008 facilitates it.) What if the file that just got hit by a killer virus is quarantined and you go to the backup only to find that it is also infected or corrupt? What if all the previous files are infected, and now just opening the file renders it useless? It's something to think about.

Earlier this year, we rushed to the aid of our main SQL Server group, which had lost a valuable database on the customer ordering system (on our extranet). Every hour offline was costing the company six figures as customers went elsewhere to place their orders. Four-letter words were flying around the server room. We had to go back three days to find a clean backup of the database that showed no evidence of corrupt metadata.

Figure 7-2 illustrates data backed up on a daily basis; and in this case, bad data is backed up for three days in a row. You may consider some of the gray area as safe, where backup data is bound to have all the flaws of its source (corruption, viruses, lack of integrity, and so on), if you have other means of assuring quality or data integrity. Such assurances may be provided by means of highly sophisticated anti-virus software, quality of data routines and algorithms, versioning, and just making sure that people check their data themselves. Backing up bad data every ten minutes may be a futile exercise depending on the tools that you have to recover or rebuild the integrity of the data.

FIGURE 7-2

The narrower the interval between backups, the greater the chance that backed up data is also corrupted, infected, or lacks integrity.

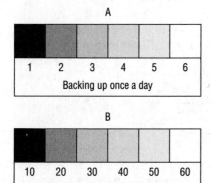

A

Backing up once a day

| 1 | 2 | 3 | 4 | 5 | 6 |

B

Backing up at 10-minute intervals daily

| 10 | 20 | 30 | 40 | 50 | 60 |

Most companies back up data to a tape drive. The initial cost is insignificant in relation to the benefit: the capability to back up and recover large amounts of data. A good tape drive can run anywhere from $500 for good Quarter-Inch Cartridge (QIC) systems to $3,000 to $4,000 for the high-speed, high-capacity Digital Linear Tape (DLT) systems, and a robotic library system can cost as much as $80,000. Now consider minimum restore levels, keeping the quality of backup factors described earlier in mind, as follows:

- Restore is required in real time (now) or close to it. Data must be no longer than a few seconds old and immediately accessible by users and systems even in the event that the primary source is offline. In the case of industrial or medical systems, the secondary source of data must be up-to-date, and latency can be measured in milliseconds, not seconds. Your SLAs may dictate that 24-7 customers can fine you if data is offline longer than x seconds or minutes. We call this the *critical restore* level.

- Restore is required within ten minutes of the primary source going offline. We call this *emergency restore*.

- Restore is required within one hour of the primary source going offline. We call this *urgent restore*.

- Restore is required within one to four hours of the primary source going offline. We call this *important restore*.

- All other restores that can occur later than the previous ones can be considered *casual restores*.

Figure 7-3 shows this in a visual hierarchy.

FIGURE 7-3

The data-restoration pyramid.

■ = data integrity

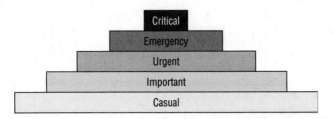

The pyramid in Figure 7-3 illustrates that the faster the response to a restore or recall of data request, the higher the chance of retrieving poor data. Each layer of the pyramid covers the critical level of the restore request. This does not mean that critical restores are always going to be a risk and that the restored data is flawed. It means that the data backed up closest to the point of failure is more likely to be at risk compared to data that was backed up hours or even days before the failure. If a hard disk crashes, the data on the backup tapes is probably sound, but if the crash is due to corrupt data or virus infection, then the likelihood of recent data being infected is high.

Another factor to consider is that the "cleanest" backup data is often the furthest away from the point of restoration or the most out-of-date.

If the level of restore you need is not as critical or the quality of the backup not too important, you could consider a tape drive system either to a backup server or local to the hosting machine. You could then set up a scheme of continuous or hourly backup routines. In the event that data is lost (usually because someone deletes a file or folder), you could restore the file. The worst-case scenario is that the data restored is one hour out of date and at such a wide interval that a replacement of a corrupt file with another corrupt file is unlikely. Consider the following anecdote: We recently lost a very important Exchange-based e-mail system. Many accounts on the server could be considered extremely mission critical. Thousands of dollars were lost every minute the server was down. (The fallout from downed systems compounds damages at an incredible rate. The longer a system is down, the worse it becomes.)

The last full backup of the server was performed on the weekend. The system went down on Wednesday. Because we were backing up only the files that changed on Monday and Tuesday, we could restore the e-mail server to the state that it was in the night before. This was good news to the MIS director but not very good news to people who felt that losing six to eight hours of e-mail was unacceptable. (For many, that would mean losing an entire day of work and a lot of wasted time rewriting and resending e-mail.)

The good news was short-lived, however, after we discovered that the transaction logs covering the Monday and Tuesday backups were corrupt on both the system and the tapes. The result was that we could restore the entire system to the state it was in on Friday, essentially losing everything between Friday night and Wednesday afternoon. For backup administrators, this was unacceptable. In the section "Backup Procedure" later in the chapter, we discuss how to prevent this from happening.

If you have several servers that need this level of protection, you must install some expensive backup equipment and advanced third-party software. Having a hot "clone" mirroring the entire system would be the way to go. Both disk and system mirroring, striping, and redundancy are discussed in Chapter 13. Full-blown redundant systems are required if applications need to continue, oblivious of the switch to alternative media and hardware. To summarize: Considering the checklists and matrices described previously, for a restore service level of five and up, you would be looking at regular tape backup systems. Anything more critical would require online libraries and a hierarchical storage management system — a service provided by Remote Storage Services (RSS), covered in Chapter 14.

Establishing Quality of Capture

In planning backup procedures and establishing quality of support levels for backups, it's vital to consider the quality of your backups before you begin designing rotation schedules and schemes and backup/restore procedures. Every business is different. Even businesses in like industries do things differently, so what you decide on may work for you but not for anyone else. What we suggest in the following sections are guidelines for establishing procedures. Before you get stuck in here, however, remember the following: Devise a plan, and if it works (after tests work under strict analysis), stick to it. If backup media get out of sync or lost or damaged, you may have a disaster on your hands when trying to restore critical data.

Best backup time of the day

Suppose that you decide to back up your data every night. One of the first items to consider is when to start your backups. If staff work late or your systems are accessed late into the night, you might wait until the early hours of the morning to begin backing up. In other words, the best time to start doing backups is whenever the files are least likely to be open and changing or whenever you are most likely to be getting the last possible version change before people go home for the night and systems become idle again.

You may run into problems backing up earlier in the evening or even late at night if, for example, a process or department swings around near midnight and updates 20 percent of the critical data you need to back up (such as night order processing). It can be especially tough to decide when to start backing up e-mail systems and database management systems because they typically are in use around the clock, especially if your organization is a national or global entity.

Some organizations restrict access to systems at certain times to ensure that the best backups are achieved at that time. This would naturally need to be coordinated with other departments and change control, because making a system unavailable could crash other processes that may be running at the same time, or they may need access to the data. We believe that systems should never be taken offline, even for backups. Moreover, in the age of the Internet, who would want to restrict access to systems? That's tantamount to closing shop in the middle of the day for international Web sites, which consider "after hours" to be an obsolete term.

Length of backup

You should also determine how long your backups take. Starting your backups at one minute to midnight may be prudent, but if morning swings around and your backups are still churning away, you have hardly performed a backup, and the file may become locked or substantially changed after systems and people log in and seize control again.

If your backup devices are backing up multiple servers, you may not get to the last machines until the next day. There's not much sense in a Thursday incremental backup that is part of a rotation scheme that takes place only on Saturday.

You have a number of options to consider in striving to ensure that the best quality backups take place in as little time as possible:

- **Files that do not change.** Repeatedly backing up system and application files is a waste of time. Many administrators, either from lack of time to plan their backups or ignorance, waste an incredible amount of time and resources backing up files that seldom change. System files are a good example, as are temp files and noncritical log files. Consider dividing your backups into the categories described in the next paragraph.

■ **Long-term system and system state files.** These files include program files and system state files that never change or change very seldom. As explained in the section "Rotation Schemes," later in this chapter, incremental and differential backup functions ignore these files after a full backup has occurred, but tying up time and media even on a weekly or monthly full routine that can often run into two or more days of continuous backup still makes no sense.

■ **Short-term state files.** These files include system or application state files that change often. Such files include configuration files, registry files, the Active Directory files, and so on. On servers, both registry and Active Directory files can change every day, whenever new users or resources are added or changed, so if short-term state files change daily on your servers, they need to be included in backups. Noncritical short-term state files, including .pagesys files, event log files, and temp files (.tmp), are not needed to restore downed systems, nor are they critical or useful to data.

■ **Data and resource files.** These files include word-processing files, graphics-related files, database files, transaction logs, e-mails and other communications files, spreadsheets, voice and audio recordings, and so on. These files (and they can often be listed or categorized by their extensions) change often, are almost always critical, and should always be backed up or included in all backup routines.

If you intelligently include or exclude certain groups of files, you can control and keep backup times to a minimum. You also save on media (at $30 to $50 a pop for DLTs and not much less for small packs of DAT cartridges); you can save a lot of money and wear and tear on systems, media, and backup devices.

NOTE Redundant systems that use replication services in products such as Active Directory, SQL Server, Exchange, and so on are more effective, in many cases, than fancy backup technology for high-availability initiatives.

Backup of servers and workstations

If you have not by now separated your backup procedures into backup of systems and backup of data, now is the time to do it. Often, system administrators repeatedly back up Windows servers and workstations in their entirety for absolutely no reason. We cannot count how many full versions or backups of our systems we have in storage. This has a lot to do with the lack of thought that goes into backup practice and little to do with the inflexible backup technology of earlier versions of the Windows server platform.

In some cases, we have several years of system backups for which the only files on the media that are different are the data files. From the get-go, you could probably recover 10 to 20 cartridges and put them back into the rotation without affecting your quality of service and backup integrity levels. (That could be worth a lot of money to you in media costs and time.)

How then do you deal with the backup of systems? If you have not already done so, consider taking an "image" of the system and saving it either on tape media, compact disk, DVD, or a remote storage volume. We don't recommend storing archival or version-based images on any remote storage volume or disk, which could fail or allow someone to delete the file, even if you secure it (although Windows Server 2008 security provides more protection than Windows NT 4.0, Windows 2000 and even Windows Server 2003).

Instead, burn the system image onto a CD or use a product that specializes in so-called bare metal capture of all data. Several popular products specialize in bare metal recovery. The Stac Replica system, for example, boasts the capability to back up a server and then restore it to any other machine with zero reinstallation required.

Workstations are viable candidates for image storage because they are usually never backed up. Most system administrators tell their users to put their data into server sharepoints where they are accessible to groups that have an interest in the files, and the data is backed up every day when the rotation sweeps around. Windows Server 2008 now offers such advanced control over the user's workspace that a policy dictating the storage of user's files on a server share is entirely enforceable. See Chapter 15 for information on how to redirect users' data folders to backup sharepoints.

Many users experience a considerable loss of computing time and inconvenience if they lose a workstation and no backup exists. Restoring such a system to its prior state before a hard disk crash, fire, or theft can take more than a day, and many critical processes take place from work-stations.

To restore a system from an image is relatively simple, and in many cases, recovery can take place in a morning. Images can also be kept in a safe place at work for quick access.

The upshot of this method is that when a system is blown away, you need only to set up identical or very similar hardware and restore from the image to get a machine that is in the same state it was in when the image was burned. You would then restore the data and any files that have changed since the image was burned.

Naturally, you need to ensure that you install the necessary service packs that were installed on the system from the time of the last image burning, or reburn the image after a new service pack, application software, or new system libraries are applied.

The best candidates for the image burning and bare metal backup techniques are servers on which the majority of files are static system files. A print server is a good example, and the Windows Server 2008 Resource Kit includes such a utility (`printmig`) to back up logical printer shares. It may not be much of a savings to burn an image of a server for which 89 percent of the storage space is dedicated to databases or e-mail files. Conversely, a Remote Access Server, one of a group of WINS servers, and volumes that have no changing data on them are ideal candidates for image burns.

The open files dilemma

Open files have always been the backup administrator's nightmare on Windows NT Server, and this is still very much the case on Windows 2000 and Windows Server 2008 volumes and

Windows Server volumes. What are these open files? Any resource file on a system needs to be opened for exclusive or shared use by a user or device that is exploiting or updating its contents. Backup software, backup schemes and rotations, and backup administrators hate open files for the following reasons:

- Open files cannot be backed up.
- Open files trash automated backup jobs.
- Open files cause the backup schedules to slow down and even grind to a halt.
- Forcing open files closed or shutting down services and systems causes headaches, inconveniences, missed deadlines, crashes and, worse, the Blue Screen of Death (although the latter is the least likely to occur).

Many relational database applications, for example, place "locks" on files while they are in use. The system also places locks on files. These files can range from simple configuration files, the registry and Active Directory files (their databases, for example), SQL servers, WINS servers, DHCP servers, and so on. E-mail applications are a good example of an open-files nightmare. These files are often huge and are almost always open and in use by the applications. Microsoft Exchange is a good case in point.

If a file is open or an exclusive lock is on the file, your backups are in trouble. On a mail server such as Exchange, the result of the open-files problem could be catastrophic for you. The information stores, the registry, the Exchange directory, the Active Directory, WINS, DNS, DHCP, and so on, are always open. If the backup fails because these huge files could not be backed up, you may be talking about hundreds if not thousands of users inconvenienced, at incredible cost.

Suppose that you face such a disaster: You do a full backup of Microsoft Exchange every weekend. Then, one day, your silent pager vibrates your hip joints with the message that the Exchange Server crashed. You try to revive the system but it doesn't respond, but that's okay because you have been diligently making full backups of Exchange every weekend. Unfortunately, after you do your backup, you find that the backup software was skipping exactly those files from which you need to do the backup. Career killer?

Database servers can cause even bigger headaches. Many, such as SQL Server, are self-contained domains of users and login mechanisms. From the outside world, you see only a huge database blob. In the case of SQL Server, it's the files with the `.mdf` extension, such as `hello.mdf`. In fact, any huge file that has a `.dat` or a `.?db` extension is likely to be a database.

NOTE   **Many high-end systems, such as SQL Server, now ship with their own built-in backup services.**

You have several ways to deal with this bugbear, from the cheapest to the most expensive solution.

First, you can shut down the open application's services prior to backup or force closure of the files by requesting users to close applications and even log off. (Incidentally, any restore of SQL Server requires the database to be placed into single-user mode so that the restore agent has unrestricted access to the databases.) This is by far the cheapest method (software cost), and you can force closure of services and files prior to backup with several batch files and scripts. If you have the budget, buy the backup agents for products like SQL Server and Exchange that enable you to back up open files while these systems are still running.

The second solution is to install an open-files utility that provides the backup software with a "window" to the data in the open files. The advantage of this solution is that your backup software has access to open files across the board. One such product is the Open File Manager (OFM) from St. Bernard software (www.stbernard.com). You can install this tool on your systems and never worry about open files not getting backed up. So important to backup and recovery is this utility that it is worth a special mention here. Thoroughly test it on your systems before going live. As important as it is, the product tinkers with files deep in the abyss of the file system, as does anti-virus software. OFM and NetShield from Network Associates have been known to collide, so test your implementation before going into production.

The third and most expensive solution is an agent or API that works with the backup software you are using. Products such as Backup Exec and ARCserve provide their own technologies that enable the Microsoft Server products to be backed up while they are online and in use.

Notice that, in this short list, we list the solutions in order of cheapest to most expensive, but that expense is only in terms of what buying the solution costs. In other words, if you think that you are saving money going for the option to shut down services, think again. This could be your most expensive solution. For example, just as you think you're being clever and shutting down services by using the nifty little batch files and scripts that we are about to create, the batch file breaks. For some reason, the service does not shut down, and the next day, your system crashes and you don't have a backup.

The open-files agents are not airtight technology. We run nightly backups of several huge SQL Server databases, Oracle, Lotus Notes, and more. Often, we notice that the open-files agent stopped for some reason, and the backup of critical data did not go through. You must watch the services like a cat sitting between a mouse and a hole in the wall.

The fact that Microsoft provides some limited open-file support for Exchange is worth mentioning here. Whenever you install Exchange, the installation updates the NT Backup utility to enable it to back up Exchange's directory and information store.

CAUTION   Never ever mix backup technologies on the same files. For starters, each backup job changes the state of the files to some degree, from changing the archive bit on one end to causing the applications to do housekeeping on the other end. Your restores may not work if a second backup application has altered the file system. In addition, if a restore job fails, you can forget about getting support from a vendor if another product has interfered.

Shadow Copy technology on Windows Server 2008, however, presents a whole new ball game with respect to open-file issues. See the section "Working with Shadow Copies" later in this chapter.

Backup Procedure

The path to Windows Server Backup's (WSB) door is Start ➤ All Programs ➤ Administrative Tools ➤ Server Manager ➤ Storage ➤ Windows Server Backup. Alternatively, just run the command-line shortcut `wbadminmsc` or `server` for Windows Server Backup in Search under All Programs.

For most uses of your computer, the WSB utility is sufficient to archive and store data, and to recover it in the event of a disaster, but that's as far as it goes. You certainly want to stick with the third-party products for enterprise-wide disaster recovery and data protection.

Before we get into the highs and lows of backup and restore, first we need to look at the limitations of the utility that ships with Windows Server 2008. It is a vast disappointment over the NTBackup that was bundled with earlier versions, but it still has some uses.

Basically, backup is not really useful for managing a mission-critical DR project from a single server devoted to DR. If you manage a server farm, performing backups on each machine is a huge waste of time and resources and a drain on the IT budget. The only advantage is better bandwidth, as described in the section "Backup Bandwidth" later in this chapter. You need to upgrade to a third-party suite if you want to devote to one server the job of backup system.

The most that WSB promises you is the capability to back up a server's volumes with limited source selection ability. You can't really do much with it. For example, many mail and groupware administrators want the capability to back up multiple Exchange Servers across the enterprise from a single DR location. If you use good equipment and sensibly manage an Exchange Server, you're unlikely ever to need to restore the machine and the databases in their entirety.

Any good Exchange administrator can confirm that 99 percent of all requests for restores to Exchange come from users who stand in your doorway drooping like basset-hound ears and say, "I can't find my Inbox folder. I think it got deleted somehow."

Pro-backup utilities enable you to expand and collapse a mailbox tree in the backup software like an unfolding deck of cards. Trust us. If you have more than a handful of users (we manage about 3,000 on just one of our 67 domains), your Exchange DR is mostly about restoring a folder. Backing up and restoring folders piecemeal is often referred to as a *brick-level* or *object-level* backup and recovery.

Database servers are also an example of specialist applications where machines are almost entirely devoted to the database. Backing up a SQL Server, such as Oracle or SQL Server, while it is in use is virtually impossible. The leading backup vendors have special agents that can attach to these servers as actual "users" (not domain accounts) created inside the database environment. If you have only a handful of users on a server or face no chance that anyone is using the server at certain times at night, you can probably get away with shutting down the database and all related services and backing up the closed files. In an enterprise-level DR project, this would be a practice unbecoming of the backup administrator, unless the entire domain were offline for maintenance.

Some advanced software suites come with "push" agents that send the files to the backup server. ARCserve, for example, provides backup agents that pump files to the server. The agents connect to the servers across IP or IPX, and any open files that cannot be pushed or that are in use are marked for later transmission after they are no longer being used.

So far we have really discussed only backups. Restoring files on running systems can be even trickier because you are attempting to replace a file, not make a copy of it. High-end software suites enable you to restore by session, media, objects in a tree, and so on.

As a rule of thumb, you need something a lot more robust than Windows Server Backup in a heterogeneous, mixed version, multivendor/OEM, chock-full-of-nuts environment. However, you always have a need to use Backup. We know of one sad case where the Exchange administrator of a Fortune 500 company got so tired of waiting for the backup operator to get around to doing a mailbox restore on her server that she went with Backup and "the heck with mailboxes." The next day, the CIO came over to whine about recovering his deleted mailbox, which he swore was more valuable than his 401(k). It was the Backup administrator who was relocated to an oil rig in the North Sea, not the Exchange administrator.

Performing a Backup

In this section, we show you how to actually perform a backup using the Windows Server Backup. The whole thing starts with creating a media pool. Throughout this example, we assume that you're using a simple media pool composed of 4 mm DAT cartridges.

 You also use Backup to create an emergency repair disk (ERD).

Creating a media pool

Attach your DAT drive or whatever removable storage device you have to the computer. If you have not already done so, go to Add Hardware in the Control Panel and install the device. If the device was installed at the time you installed Windows Server 2008, the Backup media pool is probably using it already. If not, you must manually create the pool and allocate it to Backup or nest the new pool in the Backup media pool.

In Computer Management or Remote Storage, expand the Removable Storage option and select Media Pools. Right-click Media Pools and choose Create Media Pool from the pop-up list that appears. The Properties page for the media pool is presented, enabling you to select from dozens of supported media formats and technologies, as shown in Figure 7-4.

Understanding rights and permissions

As with all Windows Server platforms, you need certain rights and privileges to work with files. Windows Server 2008 does not permit you to back up or restore files that you cannot claim rights to by virtue of your membership in a group, or *ownership*.

FIGURE 7-4

The Removable Storage media selection list.

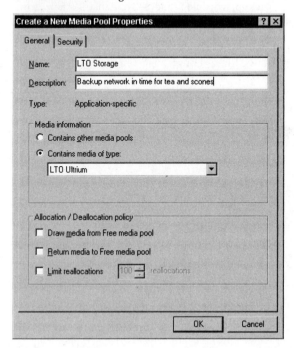

Here are the rules: If you are the owner of a file or folder, you can back up and restore the file on your domain or local computer, as long as you have logged on at the machine to restore to or have direct ownership. You must have access to the files in the form of one or more user permissions, such as read, write, or full access. You cannot back up files if they are not yours.

Backup software services must use the account of a backup operator to access and back up files, regardless of the rights associated with these files. If you are the administrator or a member of the Backup Operator's group in a local group, you can sign on and perform backup and restores to the local machine.

To perform backup and restores from and to any machine on the network, you must be either the administrator (signed on as) or a member of the domain's Backup Operator's group. As a domain Backup Operator, you can also do backups and restores in another domain if a trust exists between the domains.

Remember that you cannot back up the system state of another computer with NT Backup even if you are the Angel of Administration. The advanced evolution of the Windows Server 2008 subsystem must have a lot to do with such a restriction.

Understanding source and destination

We refer to sources and destinations when talking about backing up ... on any system. Open WSB and click the Backup Once or Backup Schedule Options. Note that if a tape drive is not installed, you can back up to a file. You can also back up to the media pool you created.

Now click the wizard to choose your options as illustrated in Figure 7-5.

FIGURE 7-5

Selecting a source and destination in Backup.

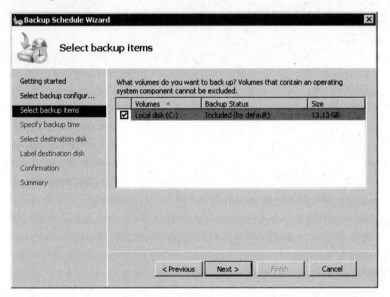

Verifying backups is not a bad idea, but it adds a lot of time to the length of a backup; in many cases, it can take almost as long to verify a backup as the backup itself. If you have a lot of files and servers to back up, by the time you get to verify a file (compare the original against the backup), the original may have changed. This is a problem in many data centers where about 30 percent of the files backed up (usually during a 15-hour process) are changed before the verification starts. Many professional packages offer various levels of verification. On several, for example, you can confirm that the label and catalog information is intact or reliable and then make the assumption that the rest of the tape is okay.

TIP If you have the time to verify your backups, by all means do it, but backup algorithms are so advanced today it is highly unlikely that a target file on the tape may not be the same as the source. Instead, set aside a day every so often (we do this once a month) to test restore the most critical data to a development server (even a special folder). You should also run disaster simulations, testing the restoration of the most valuable servers and their data.

Setting up schedules

Your next option is to start the backup now or schedule it to run later. Later may be whenever the computer is sure to be idle with no one logged on. On a Windows Server 2008 server, users can be logged on via terminals, shares, RAS, or via some network connection, such as FTP. Consider shutting down certain services or denying access for the time the backup is running,

The Backup Schedule option can be used to edit the job schedule.

Rotation Schemes

A *rotation scheme* is a plan or system by which you rotate the media that you use in your backup sets. At the most basic level, a rotation scheme may be a daily backup using one medium. You would not have much of a DR scheme because you would be writing over the medium every day, but this is a rotation scheme nonetheless. Another consideration in a rotation scheme is the dividing line between what you consider archiving: data backup, version control, system-state, and recovery.

Figure 7-6 shows one way to look at your data's value from a chronological point of view. The scale is a simple one, but it demonstrates the various stages of usefulness that backups go through, starting from the left. Data in the archival period need not be located onsite and is kept for record-keeping (annual backups), and data in the version control period is stored offsite and onsite for access to full weekly generations of the data. Data in the recovery period is stored both onsite and offsite and (depending on the critical nature of the data) is either online or within "arm's length" of recovery.

FIGURE 7-6

The stages of a backup's life.

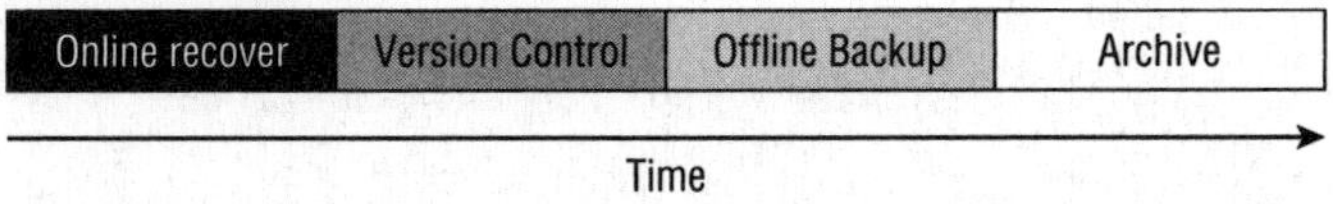

| Online recover | Version Control | Offline Backup | Archive |

Time

You can now expand your rotation scheme. The first option is to rotate the media every other day so that you could be backing up to one tape while the alternate is in safekeeping somewhere. If the worst were to happen — a tape is eaten by the device or something less common — you would still have a backup from the previous day. If the machine were stolen, you could restore it, but rotating every other day is useful only in terms of total data loss. You have a full backup of all your files every day, but what about wear and tear? A tape or a platter is a delicate device. Inserting it, removing it every other day, and writing to it repeatedly can put your data at risk. Tapes stretch and they get stuck in tape drives. Tapes should be saved according to the scratch-and-save discussion in the section "Practicing Scratch and Save" earlier in this chapter.

What about version control? Rotating with multiple media — say a week's worth — would ensure that you could roll back to previous states of a file. We could refer to such a concept of versioning as a *generation system* of rotation (not sufficient for critical restore, however). In fact, one such standard generation scheme is widely used by the most seasoned of backup administrators to achieve both these ideals: versioning, and protecting media from wear and tear and loss. It is known as the *GFS* system, or *Grandfather, Father, Son* system.

You now want to create a GFS scheme to run under Backup. Most high-end backup software can create and manage a rotation scheme for you, but for now and always with Backup, you need a legal pad. Put a label on one of your tapes or disks and call it Full, or First, Backup or Normal # 1 — whatever designates a complete backup of the system and collection of files and folders.

The first backup of any system is always a full backup, and the reason is simple. Back up and you need a catalog or history of all the files in the backup list so that you can access every file for a restore and so that Backup can perform incremental or differential analysis on the media. Do your backup according to the procedures discussed in the section "Performing a Backup" earlier in this chapter. You should have enough practice by now, and you are ready to go from a development or trial backup to a production rotation scheme.

As soon as you make a full backup set, label the members as discussed and then perform a second full backup (or copy the first). On the first backup set, add the following information to the label:

- **Full_First.** January Server 2008
- **Retention.** G (for Grandfather) or one year — for example, dd-January-2008
- **Serial number.** Your choosing, or automatically generated

On the second set, add the following information to your labels:

- **Full_First.** Week1-January Server 2008
- **Retention.** F (for Father) or one month, Weekly-February-Server 2008
- **Serial number.** Your choosing, or automatically generated

The next day, choose a second set of media, but this time only the files that have been changed are backed up by using differential or incremental options. Suppose that you are doing incrementals here for example's sake.

On the incremental set, add the following information to the label:

- **I_First (or a day of the week):** Monday, or First
- **Retention:** Seven days or every Monday
- **Serial number:** Your choosing, or automatically generated

The next day, put in a new backup set and perform the next day's incremental. This time, the label information is Tuesday or "Second"; retain these media in a seven-day save set and store them in a safe place. On Wednesday, perform the third incremental, and on Thursday, perform the fourth incremental. Now look at what you are achieving.

You have created a grandfather set that you store for a year. If you started this system in January 2006, you do not reuse these tapes until January 2008; the retention period is one year, the oldest saved data that you have.

The second copy set is the father set of the scheme, and this set is reused in four weeks' time. In other words, every four weeks, the set can be overwritten. This does not mean that you make a full backup only once a month. On the contrary: Notice that you made one full set and four incremental sets, so you are making a full backup once a week and four incremental backups Monday to Thursday. You retain the weekly set only for a month, meaning that at the end of each month, you have five full backup sets, one set for each week, retained for a month, and one set for each month, retained for a year.

What about the incremental sets? These sets are the grandchildren of your rotation scheme. You save them for seven days and return them for scratching on the same day the following week. What you back up on Monday is overwritten next Monday, Tuesday is overwritten next Tuesday, and so on. This also means that, at any given time, your people can access the previous day's data, the previous week's data, the previous month's data, and the previous year's data. What you have created is a traditional rotation scheme for performing safe and accessible backups of data.

Variations on this theme are possible, and you need more than just seven of whatever media you are using. For example, for the full GFS rotation, you would need the following for a single server that used one DLT tape drive:

- **Daily backups (incremental, rotated weekly):** 4+
- **Weekly Full (rotated monthly):** 4+
- **Monthly Full (rotated annually):** 12+
- **Total tapes:** 20+

The best days for such a rotation scheme are Monday through Thursday for incremental, and Friday for full. Even on big systems, you're unlikely to be doing an incremental into the following day; and on Friday, you have the whole day and the weekend to do the full backup, at a time when the system is most idle. You could start after the last person leaves on a Friday, and you would still have about 48 hours of backup time to play with.

Restoring Data

We left the subject of data restoring until now because it is usually the least time-intensive task to perform, and it is hoped that you are not asked to restore data too often. WSB has a restore option, Recover, that enables you to select the source.

You also have the option of restoring some or all of the files to their original location or an alternative. The following checklist thus applies to any restore that you are doing:

- Always make sure that restoring files to their original locations does not result in loss of data. This may seem illogical, but restoring files often results in further damage. For example, if a file is corrupt but up-to-date and you restore a file that is not corrupt but out of date, how much better off are you? It may be better to investigate saving the contents of the file that you want to replace or salvaging what you can before overwriting the file. You could restore to an alternative location or rename the corrupt file. Better to check whether a "corrupt" file is recoverable before you blow it away with all chances of ever recovering your data.

- Consider, too, the consequences of restoring. Windows Server 2008 stores all manner of information about a file: the folder that it's in, the volume, EFS, DFS, RFS, quota information, sharepoints, archive information, and so on. Restoring a file restores not only the contents, but also any attributes and information known about the file at the time it was backed up. Anything new applied to the file and its relationship with the rest of the universe is not recorded in the restore. A good example is restoring a folder that several new groups and users were given access to after the last backup. The restore now blocks these new users, and a critical process may bring things crashing down if you turn your back. Again, restore to an alternative location if you are unsure of the results.

- Block user access while performing a restore to original locations. Nothing causes more problems than having users trying to open files that have not been completely restored. Blocking access results in calls to the help desk, so make sure that customer service or help-desk representatives know about the process, and don't waste your time calling people to tell them about the block. If it is a big sharepoint, you always have someone messing things up. Conversely, if you are restoring a share that needs to be accessed by a critical process coming from another machine or software, let the owners of these processes know before their applications crash.

- Always check who is connected to the destination computer and what files they have open. If you restore to files that are open, you at least get access errors; at worst, you could corrupt the files you are restoring. You can check who is connected to the server by opening the File Management Console (or Computer Management) and expanding the Sessions node under the Shared Folders leaf. You can also see who is connected to what by running the NET SESSIONS and NET FILE commands at the Command Console. NET SESSIONS and NET FILE work for all versions of Windows Server.

One last item before we leave Restore. We spent a lot of time digging in the Remote Storage Manager looking for a place to erase, format, and catalog media. After all, RSM is where everything's supposed to happen for media. We guess Microsoft let this one slip by them, and we let them know. All is not lost. We discovered the missing erase and format utility in Backup. It is on the Restore tab, of all places. Just right-click the tape icon and format away your precious media.

Tape Location

Be sure to remove your valuable rotation sets from the premises as soon as the backup job is done, every day, and as long as online media are available. You can find many reliable media pick-up companies in all cities in the United States. If you don't have access to a media pick-up firm, find a safe place (such as a safe deposit box at a bank) and move your media to this remote location every day. You could also buy a small fireproof safe and keep that onsite.

Following are two chief reasons for moving the media offsite: First, if a disaster were to take out your building, it would take out your backups as well. Here in Hurricane Land, Florida, USA, we move backups to a secure location every day. Second, tapes and backup media grow legs and may walk out of your offices. Worse, someone may access your tapes and steal sensitive information without you knowing it.

We have a very secure computer room, and some time in the latter part of the last millennium, we removed a tape and then left the secure environment to fetch a new label. We were gone two minutes and returned to find the tape gone. We thought we had misplaced it and had to repeat a five-hour backup all over again. Later, we learned that in those two minutes, another administrator had asked the computer-room staff for a spare tape, who gave them our unlabeled tape, thinking it was blank. Lesson learned: Never leave your backup media unattended, even for two minutes.

Backup Bandwidth

Bandwidth is an important item in your Hardware/Media/Support Level equation. From the get-go, forget about doing any significant backup over a WAN or Internet connection unless you have upward of a 1.5-Mbit pipe to the source (and even that is a stretch given the size of data files these days). Anything less (unless it is a very small collection of files) does not provide a suitable facility for backing up. The only time you should try backing up over a low bandwidth connection (and for backup, low bandwidth could be considered anything under 10 Mbit) is when you need to grab a handful of important files. To back up a remote registry over a 64-Kbit pipe would take several hours.

On the other hand, we routinely back up thousands of server shares over a gigabit Ethernet network; if you have a 1-Gbit backbone (GigE) and have servers sitting directly on that, all the better. Remember, though, that even a 100-Mbit backbone is only as valuable as the speed of the server bus, network links, hard disk I/O, and the capabilities of the backup devices.

The minimum rate of backup you can expect over a 10-Mbit network is between 15MB and 45MB per minute, depending on the backup device. Local tape drives on fast computers using SCSI technology, and high-end hardware can even achieve levels of around 200MB per minute, and even higher on RAID systems and extremely high-speed disk arrays. However, placing a high-end backup device on every server can be very expensive.

Determine how much data needs to be backed up and then figure out how long backing up all that data is going to take you. If the data is mission critical, you may want to back it up more often. Remember that data changes every minute of the day. Database applications can see as much as 20 percent of the data changing on the low end and as much as 80 percent changing on the high end. E-mail systems change just about every second of the day in busy organizations.

Here is a very simple formula to determine how long it will take to back up your data. Say that you want to back up X amount of data to a certain device in Y time. Starting with the desired unknown Y, you would want to first figure out how much data you are going to try to back up on the local machine or over the network. After you have calculated this, your equation resembles the following:

$$Y = S/T$$

Here, Y = time, S = amount of data in megabytes, and T = transfer time, in minutes, of hardware (locally or across the network). The data transfer or backup rate of the DLT 7000 is around 300MB per minute (hauling data off the local hard drives). Thus, for a data store of 2GB, your equation would be $Y = 2000$, which would take just over six minutes to back up. Factor in another two minutes or more per 100MB for latency, cataloging, files in use, database updating, and so on. It would be safe to say that 2GB of data could be backed up in less than ten minutes. Across the local area network, you would be safe to divide the transfer rate by a factor of ten. The same 2GB over the network would take more than an hour to back up.

Working with Shadow Copies

In addition to the new design for backing up open files, the Shadow Copy function also goes a long way toward relieving the administrative burden on backup operators. How many times have you received a help-desk ticket or a call to retrieve a file that was mistakenly deleted or corrupted? If you're nodding your head, you're sure to be delighted with Shadow Copy's capability to restore previous copies of documents directly from the shadow copy maintained in the file system.

Shadow Copy backup/restore enables you to create shadow-copy backups of entire volumes, which makes exact copies of files, including all open files (that open-file magic again). Even databases, which are almost always held open exclusively, are backed up. If you are also the SQL Server administrator, you know how frustrating it is to need to close down database connections so that maintenance on the database can be conducted and backups taken.

Any files under Shadow Copy management that are opened by an operator or the system are automatically backed up during a volume shadow-copy backup. Thus, files that have changed during the backup process are copied correctly. This, of course, does not obviate the need to back up "real" files to tape or some other media, but it ensures that backing up the shadowed files means that you have not lost data because of the open-files dilemma. If this isn't reason enough for you to rush out and buy Windows Server 2008, you've been suffering too many long nights restoring data.

Shadow copy backups have terrific utility in that they ensure the following:

- Applications can continue to write data to the volume during a backup.
- Open files are no longer skipped during a backup.
- Backups can be performed at any time, without locking out users.

Because we do not live in a perfect IT world, some applications and backup systems may not believe that everything about Shadow Copy is cool. Check with the manufacturer of your software or hardware if you have some doubts that shadow copies on third-party products represent a reliable record of your data. Of course, you should always experiment with them in the lab before using them on your actual system.

To enable shadow copies, perform the following steps:

1. Open Computer Management (Local). In the console tree, right-click Shared Folders ➤ All Tasks ➤ Configure Shadow Copies. You can also right-click the volume in Explorer and select Properties ➤ Shadow Copies. Whichever route you choose, the dialog box tab shown in Figure 7-7 loads.

FIGURE 7-7

Selecting the volume for configuring shadow copies.

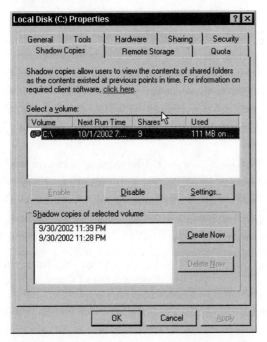

2. Select the volume in the list where you want to enable shadow copies and click the Settings button. This will open the Settings dialog box shown in Figure 7-8.

FIGURE 7-8

Configure your setting for shadow copies.

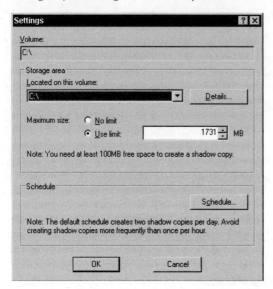

You can now configure Shadow Copy properties to suit your needs.

The Storage Volume option is for specifying where to store the shadow copies of the selected volume. The default is to use the same volume. Microsoft recommends that you use a separate volume on another disk because this approach provides better performance for heavily used file servers.

You can change the storage volume only if no shadow copies are present. If you need to change the storage volume for a volume that already is enabled, you must delete all the shadow copies on that volume before changing the storage volume.

Select the Details button to open a dialog box that lists the shadow copies currently stored. This dialog also provides information about the total space and available storage space on the disk.

The Storage Limits option enables you to configure the size of the part on the volume that holds the source files being shadow copied. The default size is 10 percent of the size of the actual volume. If the shadow copies are stored on a separate volume from the source files, change this default to reflect the amount of the storage volume you are willing to dedicate to shadow copies.

The storage limit must be at least 100 MB, which permits only a single shadow copy to be retained. If you set a restrictive storage limit, test to ensure that the number of shadow copies you scheduled can fit within those restraints. If shadow copies are deleted prematurely because of storage limits, you may be defeating the purpose of enabling shadow copies of shared folders.

The Schedule button launches the Task Scheduler with the information that you need to create a task schedule for taking shadow copies of shared folders on a regular basis. Before creating the schedule, look at your current users' work patterns and design a strategy that schedules shadow copies at a time of day that works best for your users. The default schedule is Monday through Friday at 7 A.M. and 12 P.M. Following are some rules to consider in enabling Shadow Copy:

- Do not enable shadow copies on volumes that use mount points. Any drive mounted into the volume that is enabled for Shadow Copy is not included as the copies are taken.

- Shadow copies should not be used as a replacement for regular backups. Keep backing up as you usually do, but spend less time restoring from backup tapes.

- Don't schedule Shadow Copy to copy too often. The default schedule is 7 A.M. and 12 noon, but we went nuts on this feature and shadowed every hour, running out of disk space very quickly. If you decide that you need copies more often, make sure you allot enough storage space and don't take copies so often that server performance degrades.

- Before deleting a shadowed volume, delete the scheduled task for creating shadow copies. If the volume is deleted without deleting the Shadow Copy task, the scheduled task fails and an Event ID: 7001 error is written to the event log. Delete the task before deleting the volume to avoid filling the event log with these errors.

- In considering Shadow Copy, think about file permissions: If you're restoring a file, the file permissions are not changed. Permissions remain the same as before the restore. If you're undeleting a file, permissions are set to the default permissions for the directory.

- As storage area limits are reached, the oldest shadow copy is deleted and cannot be retrieved.

- Shadow copies are read-only. You cannot edit the contents of a shadow copy. You can work with the copy only after it is restored.

- Shadow copies are enabled on a per-volume basis. You cannot enable shadow copies on specific shares.

Summary

This chapter deals more with backup practice and protocol than actual software or technology because quite frankly the backup software that comes with Windows Server 2008 is only useful for the most simple volume backup jobs. For peace of mind and ease of use choose a utility from a third-party software vendor. Most third-party applications perform backups and restores in the same way. The Microsoft tape and media APIs ensure that at the file backup level, the data state resulting (integrity) from all backup technology is no better or worse from vendor to vendor.

Some third-party vendors, however, do have software that better manages the backup process. Backup is a useful utility, but in many respects you are likely to use it for quick and dirty work or for recovery disks and ASR media. It is not a high-end utility for the application and data services that Windows Server 2008 is cut out to provide.

This chapter also touched on the Shadow Copy facilities now built into the file system that comes with Windows Server 2008.

Chapter 8

Disaster Recovery

ealing with a failed server is one of the most stressful parts of a
system administrator's job. You face the pressures of reinstalling
the operating system, recovering valuable data from the backup
media, and then reinstalling all the key services needed for the correct
operation of the server. Planning for disaster recovery involves a lot more
than simply knowing how to operate your restoration software. In this
chapter, we show you how to correctly use Automated System Recovery
(ASR) to recover a base operating system, as well as best practices for
creating and documenting a disaster recovery plan.

IN THIS CHAPTER

Creating documentation

Setting up a response plan

Recovery from backup

Recovery of key services

Disaster Recovery Planning

Disaster recovery is one of the most important things that you can learn in
system administration. Administering a server doesn't mean anything if you
can't bring it back to life should something happen to it, such as a catastrophic disk failure or an Active Directory database corruption.

The fine art of disaster recovery not only includes restoring files from a
backup device, but also locating potential problems that could lead to
a crashed server, restoring services after a reinstallation of the operating
system, and a multitude of other duties.

Policy and protocol

The first step in disaster recovery is to define a policy and protocol. The
policy should define what happens in what order to get things restored

to their normal working condition. The protocol should specify the conditions that must be met to perform certain actions. Under what circumstances, for example, should you reinstall the operating system, and what determines whether you should merely attempt to repair the server operating system? These are the issues that need to be resolved.

It doesn't make sense to lay out a generic policy for disaster recovery, which varies from company to company. You must take several things into account, such as whether your business performs 24 × 7 operations. If so, your guidelines to disaster recovery will be much stricter than a company that operates only eight hours a day. Define the response times for reacting to an emergency as well as estimates for how long systems should take to be back up and running.

Documentation

Documentation is the cornerstone of any disaster recovery plan. Without documentation, everyone involved in the disaster recovery plan must depend on memory. Considering the number of steps needed to bring a server back to life as well as to restore all data and ensure that all systems are functioning correctly, memory alone probably isn't of much use.

In considering a disaster recovery plan, you can take a clue from common household items. How many of you, for example, have a clock or appliance in your house that always flashes the ubiquitous 12:00? Many people fail to read an appliance's documentation — whether it's for setting a clock or recovering from a server crash — or don't understand it. In writing a disaster recovery plan, ensure that your documentation is read and that it makes sense.

In developing your plan, you need to anticipate budget overruns and time shortages. Typically, when a disaster recovery plan is running behind, time is taken from the documentation process to even things out. This obviously is a bad idea, but it is typically not a decision left up to the project leader in charge of the documentation process. You need to learn how to deal with a shortage of time and still develop usable documentation. Many technical writers and administrators suggest using a layered document as a practical approach. The document outline would contain five headings. Section 1 would be, for example, an overview of the disaster recovery plan. The sections of the document can be prioritized, which determines what is completed first. Sections containing nonessential information could be reserved until the end of the project in case time needs to be cut. Plan on prioritizing document sections according to the following guidelines (low to high priority):

- Nonessential informational
- Important information
- Necessary information
- Essential information

Using this approach, you are sure to complete all the essential items before time is taken from the project.

Before developing a usable plan, you must know how the document will be used. In many organizations, the sales team values the plan because it shows potential clients that your company is devoted to providing uninterrupted service. Managers may use the document to support budget requests for additional staff. Keeping all this in mind, ensure that you don't try to squeeze everything into the document. Its purpose is to function as the company's recovery tool in case of emergency — not as a marketing tool. The portions of the document that marketing and managers find useful are most likely the portions with a lower priority.

Equally important as being clear on the intent of the documentation is knowing who is likely to read the document. All companies have their own terms that are specific to their organizations. Using technical terms and phrases that your company doesn't typically use is pointless. If you are a consultant in an unfamiliar company, try to learn the language and read through other documentation that it may already have.

Another important aspect of the creation of the documentation is determining who has access to it. Quite often, these documents contain very sensitive information, such as the administrative password, firewall and router information, or user-account information. These documents, after they're developed, are usually stored on a network drive so that many other employees can proofread them, make corrections, and even add content. This location on a network drive must be accessible to authorized users only. You also need to determine who can access the documentation outside the directory. This directory is probably being backed up, for example. Find out who has access to the backup media and can extract the information. If the backups are performed across the network, consider that someone may be intercepting the packets. Extracting sensitive information this way would prove fairly easy. You may also want to consider that, at some point, this document may be shown to people who shouldn't have access to the sensitive information. Ensure that all the sensitive information is contained in a section that can be easily removed should the need arise — for example, in the appendix of the disaster recovery plan. Should a salesperson need access to the document, you can then provide it to that person, with the exception of the section containing the sensitive information.

Most important, keep the document simple. You need to convey very complex information in an easy-to-read manner. If you can do this, readers of all types should have no problem following along.

Disaster recovery training and action planning

Before you begin the training process, setting objectives is a must. Without objectives, how can you know whether you have accomplished what you set out to accomplish? Take these suggestions to heart before you begin training so that you can create a list of the objectives that you want to accomplish.

In creating a disaster recovery plan, use several layers for tasks and subtasks. Each one must have an objective, including procedures to follow to accomplish the objective. You can use Microsoft Word to generate a list like this because it is quite capable of numbering each item with the correct indentation for denoting levels. If you want a bit more control and the capability to set conditions on the items, sub-items, and even predecessors, consider using Microsoft Project. Using this type of layout can serve as a road map for the plan you are undertaking.

These plans are typically called use cases. A *use case* is actually a page (or pages) defining a typical scenario. For every possible scenario, you should have a use case.

Identifying Resources

As you are planning for disaster recovery, you need to identify several resources to make your job easier. If you have multiple people who manage servers, initiate an *On-Call* schedule — a schedule of who comes in and performs the necessary steps should a server go down. If you have fewer than a dozen servers, having just one person respond may work. The more servers you have, however, the more people you need to involve. Not only should you take administrators into account, but to effectively get things back up and running, you may also need a member of your network administration team on hand, as well as those of any other team that your servers may affect.

After you have created this On-Call schedule, keep a list of hardware vendors that you can call at a moment's notice should you need additional hardware. Server administrators aren't always the best at actually installing hardware, so you may require a consultant or a vendor's support representative to get the necessary hardware installed and configured before you can restore the server to its normal operating condition.

Although planning for disaster recovery in a company that has one location is pretty tedious, imagine the additional steps necessary should a remote server go down. Not only do you need to ensure that someone local to the machine can respond, you also must ensure that this person has intimate knowledge of the other servers on the WAN so that everything is correctly set up. A handy tool in this case is a Keyboard, Video, Mouse (KVM) switch that accepts TCP/IP connections. A KVM switch enables you to remotely connect to a server, reboot it, and configure it and anything else — all from the comfort of your sofa.

Keeping a diagram of your servers handy may help you identify resources. This diagram should look something like a tree diagram, showing each server and what services and applications each server hosts. If a server goes down, you can see at a glance which systems it affected. By using this information, you can make a well-informed decision about who needs to be contacted for additional support or who should be informed that systems are currently down.

Developing Response Plans

Developing a response plan isn't something you can do overnight. You need complete knowledge of the servers as well as all the applications they are hosting. To get this kind of information, you more than likely need to interview several dozen people in your organization. After obtaining a list of all the equipment and people you need to involve in the response plan, make a rough outline of the plan. Although you could easily spend a month writing it, you can never make your plan completely foolproof. Some portions are sure to be lacking. Unfortunately, you generally must use a bit of trial and error to get the plan to work correctly.

NOTE Several software packages enable you to inventory your systems, which is a first step in developing a response plan. These software packages provide an outline that you can use to begin your planning.

In developing your response plan, be generous with your allotment of response times. Assuming the worst and giving yourself ample time is better than taking 300 percent longer than the plan assumes to get all systems back up and running. After you have a response plan in place, the best way to determine whether it suits your needs is to test it.

Testing Response Plans

Disaster recovery planning is a bit like building a bridge with toothpicks. Just when you think you have the support beams in place, they float away. Disaster recovery planning can be an enormous task — and proportionally so with a larger network.

You have probably heard the adage "If you fail to plan, you plan to fail." This clearly applies to the disaster recovery process. You can develop a very robust plan, but if you never test it, how can you know how well it works? No matter what technique you choose to test a response plan, keep the following points in mind:

- **Failures don't exist.** No matter what you do during a test, any results that you receive are worth something. The only failure is not testing at all. All tests yield results, and these results help administrators gain a better knowledge of their system and the systems with which it interfaces.

- **Set objectives.** Because most administrators have very limited time, a thorough plan with objectives can drastically reduce the time necessary to test a system. This plan and its objectives can usually be performed in steps. Completing all the steps at once isn't necessary; you can complete a few steps one day and maybe a few more the next week. You can also quite possibly test the steps out of order, which might suit the schedule of the administrators. In testing a system, make sure that the objectives are well defined. Set time limits on the tests and compare those times to the actual results. This procedure ensures that the modifications you make to the test plan in the future accurately reflect the time that recovery takes for your particular system in its current environment.

- **Action items.** Every test should be timed and well documented, and all the steps and the final outcome should be well documented. This enables you to review all the steps and provide training material to other employees who may become responsible for portions of the system. Documenting a system, testing it, and then keeping all the results in your head doesn't do anyone any good. (If you should happen to, say, step in front of a bus, all progress is lost if you failed to document the test results.)

- **Frequency.** Test often! Creating a plan and testing it once is only good until certain aspects of your system change enough to make your plan obsolete. Not only should you schedule regular tests on your system, you should also ensure that you test it whenever anything major changes. If new routers or servers are added or the network topology changes, you should automatically begin a new test of your plan. If enough changes in your system and its surroundings, the plan is quite likely to need updating.

- **Consultants.** Some consultants specialize in testing systems. It may be helpful to pick their brains and gain some insight into the world of testing. Many software packages out there can also assist you in your testing. To be of any use, however, these software packages must be extremely configurable; some may even contain a scripting language. Look into these products and try to locate a consultant who specializes in them.

Response plans and their testing is a very large subject that can consume not only a single book but literally volumes. For many of the sophisticated technologies out there today, you can pick up a book that can help you narrow your testing and get very specific with it.

Mock Disaster Programs

The best way to ensure that your disaster recovery procedures are adequate is to put them to the test. Completely document several types of "disasters" and then play them out according to your disaster recovery plan. Some of these events, especially a particularly catastrophic one, take a bit more time because they may involve going to a remote location, installing servers, and performing restores of data to get things going. Not only are test procedures for recovering servers and data necessary, but you also need to take into consideration communication lines and so on. To simulate simpler problems such as hard-drive failures, you can simply have a co-worker remove a SCSI cable from your drive array. Table 8-1 shows what you could expect from a number of disaster situations.

Understanding fault tolerance

The idea of *fault tolerance* in a computer system revolves around the concept that the computer (or server, in this case) should have the capability to deal with a hardware or software failure. Probably the easiest failure to deal with is a power loss. To counter this type of failure, you can simply use an uninterrupted power supply (UPS), but would using a UPS actually constitute fault tolerance? A UPS doesn't have the capability to run forever, so you are actually merely postponing the inevitable. A better solution is to have two or more power supplies in the server that are both connected to uninterrupted power supplies. During a power outage, one UPS can supply power to the server, while the other one is charged offsite. Dual power supplies, however, brings up a topic all its own.

Having dual components is a must for any server that has to be extremely fault tolerant. To have a true fault-tolerant system, therefore, you need two network interface cards, two power supplies, multiprocessors, and two drives. All these items seem to be good ideas, but what good would two hard drives do? Assuming that all the data from Drive 1 is copied to Drive 2, a failure would result in you needing to power down the machine and move Drive 2 into the

Drive 1 position. That's why the use of a *Redundant Array of Independent Disks* (RAID) and hot-swappable drives is important.

TABLE 8-1

Expectations During a Sudden Disaster

Disaster	Expectation
Operating-system drive failure	Typically a simple recovery, given a recent backup of the partition. Restore the OS from backup with ASR and force replication.
Data-drive failure	Loss of the operating system can be dealt with, but a company works hard to build a large repository of data. This data could include orders, accounting records, client lists, and so on. With recent backups, you should still expect to lose some data.
Unknown hardware failure	An unknown hardware failure takes a fair amount of time to correct. Before you can check the validity of data or the OS, you must find the faulty hardware and fix it. This process can be very time-consuming and may require consultants or vendors to be onsite.
Fire	Ouch! A fire means that your server may have suffered smoke, heat, fire, or even water damage. Expect long hours of setting up new equipment before you retrieve offsite backups to restore your servers.
Catastrophic event (tornado, hurricane, and so on)	Such an event would probably require an offsite restore to get your system back up and available so that the company can continue with its day-to-day operations.
Security breach	Your first concern here is securing data. Hackers can destroy your OS if they want, but corrupting precious data could mean the death of your company. Secure the data and systematically shut down the systems to ensure your data's integrity.

You have several levels of RAID that you can use, but the most common is RAID Level 5. RAID 5 requires at least three drives and provides data-stripping and error-correction information. The drawback to RAID 5 is that it requires extremely complex hardware to function. A mid-level RAID 5 controller is now standard on all server motherboards, so cost is no longer a factor. Hot-swappable drives enable you to remove a failed drive from the server while the system is still running and replace it with a new drive without losing any data.

If you don't have a ton of cash to throw around — or maybe you just need a RAID setup for an individual user and not particularly for a server — you can purchase a motherboard with a built-in RAID.

Many boards contain the UDMA/ATA133 RAID controller functionality, and with most of these, you can expect the following:

■ RAID 0, 1,0+1 and Span

■ Hot-swapping a failed hard disk in a mirror array

■ Independent use of hard disks

■ Hot spare-disk support

■ Disk-error alarm

Although an IDE RAID configuration isn't as fast as a SCSI solution, it is very effective and can save you quite a bit of money.

Identifying the Weak Links

Most of you already know that your system is only as strong as its weakest link. Failing to identify the weakest link in your system almost always leads to a catastrophe. Keeping the weakest links in mind is also very helpful should you experience problems; knowing the weakest links helps you identify where to start in the troubleshooting process.

In examining your system for possible points of failure, you should start with the most obvious:

■ Hard-disk drives

■ Power supply

■ Network connection

■ HDD controller card

■ Processor

Ensuring that the preceding components don't fail is a fairly straightforward process — you double up on everything. Suppose you have a dual-processor system, with a RAID-5 hot-swappable hard-disk system running with dual power supplies and dual network cards. All this is neatly bundled and connected to a UPS or possibly a generator system. It almost sounds foolproof, right? What do you do if your RAMBus RAM dies? What if the video card fails? A memory problem is easily fixed by ensuring that your system contains more than one stick of memory. You can even go so far as to use a board that supports hot-swappable memory modules. Having more than one stick of memory ensures that if one dies, the system doesn't crash to its knees. It's likely to suffer some errors, but at least you should have the opportunity to shut down the system and fix the problem without losing data.

Normally, you would have a serious problem if your video card died. How could you safely shut down the system to fix the problem? Fortunately for you, Windows Server 2008 supports a *headless configuration*. You can install the OS, configure all your applications, and then remove the video card, keyboard, and mouse, and the machine still operates. You can do all the configuration by using a remote desktop or even via Web administration.

After you have considered all possible points of failure in your system and have taken the appropriate steps to fix weak links, take a step back and look again. Your system may be the very definition of redundancy, but what if a router goes out that connects your system to the WAN? This isn't a point of failure in the server, but it affects the system's operation. In planning your server configuration, keep the network configuration in mind. The more that you look at and consider, the better off you are when problems arise.

Recovery from Backup

Should the worst happen and a server goes down, one of the most important things that you must do is restore your system from a backup. Not only is this a time-consuming process, but you're probably under stress to get it done as quickly as possible. Without a computer system, most corporations are generally helpless. In this state, orders generally cannot be placed from vendors, nor can they be provided to customers. Time is money.

The restore process generally happens in two phases: restoration of the base operating system and restoration of configuration files such as Active Directory information.

Recovery of base operating systems

Restoration of the base operating system should be the second step that you take in the event that your server crashes. The first task, obviously, is the repair of the component that brought the system down in the first place — assuming, of course, that the reason for the crash was hardware related.

Restoring the operating system is just a four-step process:

1. Boot to the Windows Server 2008 CD and wait for the installation wizard.
2. Click "Repair your computer."
3. At the System Recovery Options page select "Windows Complete PC Restore." This will get you to the restore wizard.
4. Now if you have made a server backup, as described in the previous chapter, using Windows Server Backup or another application, choose a suitable backup (the latest available or another one of your choice). This page on the wizard provides several options you can choose for the recovery procedure.

These steps assume that you have created a backup set by using the Microsoft-provided Windows Server Backup application.

NOTE Intentionally downing a server just to practice the art of restoration with ASR is time-consuming and may not be justifiable for your network. A smart approach should you want the practice is to use VMWare to install Windows Server 2008. You can then set up the OS, perform a backup, delete the OS from the drive, and perform an ASR for training purposes.

Recovery of configuration

Configuration information for the server — such as screen resolution, folder views, share information, and so on — is all restored during an ASR. You're highly likely, however, to find that your Active Directory information is outdated. Backing up Active Directory information doesn't make a lot of sense if several servers reside on your network. If additional servers are in place, all the information is updated after replication takes place. If you have only one server, first and foremost, shame on you! Second, you can rest assured that all Active Directory information is backed up during a full backup using the Microsoft Backup application.

Mirrored Services, Data, and Hardware

Mirroring data — that is, copying it to another drive in the same form — can be accomplished by using RAID, as described in the section "Understanding Fault Tolerance" earlier in this chapter. To have a truly redundant system, you must mirror everything within your system — dual network cards, multiple processors, redundant power supplies, and so on. Without this type of hardware, your system is very prone to failure and down time.

Recovery of Key Services

Recovering key services can prove somewhat of a nightmare depending on the topology of your network. The following sections discuss some of the services that you may need to recover and what you should expect during the recovery process. Every possible scenario cannot be explained here, of course, because what you may face depends on how your network is set up. If we assume that you are running all services on one server, restoring a full backup to your server would fix everything. We doubt that this is the case, however, and expect that your services are spread across many machines.

Active Directory

A full backup of a server includes all Active Directory information. Whew! If your full backups are few and far between, make sure that you capture the system-state on the incremental backups. The system-state backup includes the Active Directory information. Without this information, you have a long road ahead in restoring the server to operating order.

If you happen to have more than one server in your forest, a full backup or system-state isn't necessary. After you have reinstalled the server OS and the system is somewhat operational, just add the server to the domain tree again and then kick back and wait for replication. If you can't wait around for this to happen, use the tools provided to forcefully start the replication process.

CROSS-REF You can find more information on manually starting the replication process in Chapter 22.

Because the amount of data in Active Directory can be very large, a full replication may seriously inhibit your network bandwidth. To make a good decision regarding what route to take, weigh the amount of time required to restore a backup of this data against that of a full replication of your server.

DNS

By default, all DNS files are stored in `C:\windows\system32\dns`. Incremental backups should catch any changes made to these files. If you have enabled dynamic updates to DNS, you quite often see this file change. After you have restored the operating system on your server, ensure that the DNS server is indeed installed. If it wasn't installed during your last backup, you can perform a reinstall by using the Configure Your Server Wizard. Accept all defaults on this wizard, which are of little consequence anyway because you overwrite the configuration files with backups.

After you have verified that the DNS server is installed and running, you need only restore all `*.dns` files from your backup media. After you have restored these files, shut down the DNS server and restart it to see the configuration changes.

Registry

The registry is probably one of the easiest things to restore after you have recovered from a server failure. A full backup of a server always includes registry information. Because incremental backups look at all changed files, the registry is backed up then, too. If your registry does not appear to have changed since the last backup, something is definitely wrong — the registry is constantly changing, regardless of anything actually happening on the server.

Crash Analysis

After a crash has occurred, the single most important thing you can do after you have restored the server and fixed all problems is to analyze the crash. If you don't fully understand what brought the system down in the first place, you cannot effectively prevent another crash from happening in the future.

Never take anything for granted in performing a crash analysis. Just because your RAID-5 array died doesn't actually mean that it was the root of the problem — it could be a defective cable or perhaps even the controller card. Put your CSI hat on for a few days and examine every inch of the system until you are 100 percent sure that you can explain the cause. After you have come up with a valid explanation, try to back it up. Assuming, for example, that a cable was to blame, use the same cable in a new machine and try to get the system to crash. If it does crash, try to determine whether everything happened in the same order that it did on the other machine. If so, you have your culprit.

Summary

A disaster recovery plan is like a smoke alarm in your house — you know that you need it, but you don't really appreciate it until disaster strikes. With the correct documentation and backups, as described in this chapter, you can quickly restore servers to operating condition and keep your business running — even after a major server failure. Not only is creating a disaster recovery plan very important, but practicing it and keeping the documentation up to date as the need arises is also vital to the health of your system.

Chapter 9

The Registry

The registry is the core repository of configuration information in Windows Server 2008, used for storing information about the operating system, applications, and user environment on standalone workstations and member servers (nondomain controllers).

The Purpose of the Registry

Early versions of the Windows operating system family (such as Windows 3.x) stored most of their configuration information in *initialization*, or .ini files. These files were text files containing various sections that stored settings for a variety of properties such as device drivers, application and document associations, user environment settings, and so on. Windows applications also used .ini files to store their configuration settings. Even today in Windows Server 2008 and applications, .ini files are still sometimes used for storing user, application, and operating system settings. A quick search of your hard drive for .ini files will illustrate that fact. I might add that XML-based configuration files have gone a long way to returning us to the days of text-based configuration files.

Although they provide a simple means of storing and retrieving settings, .ini files offer some disadvantages, particularly for storing important OS settings such as device drivers, configuration data, user environment settings, and so on. First, Windows Server 2008 needs a fault-tolerant system for maintaining its settings to avoid the problem of an unbootable system caused by a corrupt or missing .ini file. This information also needs to be secure, something .ini files can't really provide. Finally, managing all the settings needed to keep a Windows Server 2008 system up and running, plus applications and user-related settings, would be overwhelming if .ini files were the only solution. The registry comes to the rescue.

In Windows Server 2008, the registry stores configuration information about the system's hardware and software, both operating system- and application-related. The registry also stores information about users, including security settings and rights, working environment (desktop properties, folders, and so on), and much more. However, unlike Windows NT, it no longer stores domain user and computer accounts or information related to network objects. This job now belongs to the Active Directory, as explained in Chapter 22 and the chapters in Part III.

CAUTION When you promote a member server to a domain controller, all registry settings that also apply to a domain controller server (such as the desktop settings) are absorbed into Active Directory, but when you demote the server, the original registry settings are not restored, and you are returned to a clean registry. (The Demotion Wizard even asks you for a new Administrator password because the original account is lost.) Keep this in mind when you demote a domain controller, because Active Directory can easily outgrow the host machine on which it was originally installed.

The following list explains some of the ways certain components make use of the registry:

- **Setup.** When you install Windows Server 2008, Setup builds the registry based on your selections (or automated selections) during installation. Setup also modifies the registry when you add or remove hardware from the system.

- **Application setup.** The Setup program for an application typically will modify the registry to store the application's settings at installation. It also will typically read the registry to determine which components, if any, are already installed.

- **Applications.** Most applications that store their settings in the registry modify those settings during program startup, shutdown, or general operation to store changes made to application settings by the application or the user.

- **Device Manager.** The Device Manager console program detects hardware and attached peripherals, and it stores information in the registry about those items for use in subsequent boot steps to initialize device drivers for identified devices.

- **The kernel.** The Windows Server 2008 kernel reads the registry at startup to determine which device drivers to load and in which order, along with other driver initialization parameters.

- **Device drivers.** Most device drivers store their configuration and operating settings in the registry, reading the registry at initialization to determine how to load and function.

- **System.** The Windows Server 2008 operating system as a whole uses the registry to store information about services, installed applications, document and Object Linking and Embedding (OLE) associations, networking, user settings, and other properties.

- **Administrative tools.** One of the main functions of utilities such as the Control Panel, the various Microsoft Management Consoles (MMCs), and standalone administration utilities is typically to modify the registry. In this context, these utilities provide a user interface for registry modification.

- **The Registry Editor.** Windows Server 2008 provides one tool, `regedit.exe`, that enables you to view and modify the registry directly. Though you'll want to perform most modification tasks using other utilities, the Registry Editor makes possible tasks such as direct modification, selected registry backup, and more.

The registry is in many ways the "brain" of the Windows Server 2008 OS. Nearly everything the OS does is affected by or affects the registry. For that reason, it is important to not only understand the registry's function and how to modify it, but also how to protect it from catastrophe or unauthorized access. The following sections explain the structure of the registry and how to manage it.

The Registry Structure

The registry forms a hierarchical (tree) database with five primary branches called *subtrees*. A subtree can contain *keys*, which function as containers within the subtree for *subkeys* and *values*. Subkeys are sub-branches within a key. Values are the individual settings within a key or subkey. Perhaps the best way to understand the registry structure is to view it through the Registry Editor, as shown in Figure 9-1. (You'll find detailed information about the Registry Editor later in this chapter in the section "The Registry Editor.")

FIGURE 9-1

The Registry Editor shows the structure of the registry: a hierarchical tree, with each subtree serving as a primary branch.

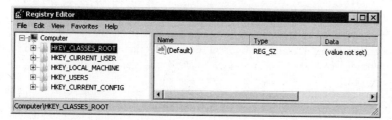

There are two physical subtrees in the Windows Server 2008 registry: `HKEY_LOCAL_MACHINE` and `HKEY_USERS`, the former containing system- and hardware-related settings and the latter containing user-related settings. These two physical subtrees are divided into the five logical sub-trees you see in the Registry Editor. Organizing the registry into five logical subtrees makes it easier to navigate and understand the logical structure of the registry. The five logical subtrees are as follows:

- HKEY_LOCAL_MACHINE. This subtree, often abbreviated as HKLM, stores settings that apply to the local machine, defining hardware and operating system settings that are the same regardless of which user is logged on. The settings in HKLM, for example, define device drivers, memory, installed hardware, and startup properties.

- HKEY_CLASSES_ROOT. Abbreviated HKCR, this subtree contains file association data, such as associating a document file type with its parent application and defining the actions taken on a given document type for various tasks (open, play, edit, and so on). This subtree is built from HKLM\SOFTWARE\Classes and HKEY_CURRENT_USER\SOFTWARE\Classes, with the value in HKCU taking precedence. HKCR provides user- and computer-specific class registration, providing different class registrations for each user. This per-user class registration is different from previous versions of Windows that provided the same registration data for all users.

- HKEY_CURRENT_USER. This subtree (HKCU) stores the user profile for the user currently logged on to the system locally. Settings include desktop configuration and folders, network and printer connections, environment variables, Start menu and applications, and other settings that define the user operating environment and UI. This subtree is actually an alias of HKEY_USERS*SID*, where *SID* is the security ID of the current user.

- HKEY_USERS. This subtree (HKU) stores user profile data for users who log on to the computer locally, as well as the default user profile for the local computer.

- HKEY_CURRENT_CONFIG. This subtree (HKCC) stores hardware configuration data about the local computer identified at startup, and includes settings relating to device assignments, device drivers, and so on. This subtree is an alias of HKLM\SYSTEM\CurrentControlSet\Hardware Profiles\Current.

Each of the subtrees listed previously represents a *hive*. Microsoft defines a hive as a body of keys, subkeys, and values rooted at the top of the registry hierarchy. An individual hive comprises two files:

- A registry file, in most cases stored in *systemroot*\System32\Config. This file contains the registry structure and settings for the given hive.

- A log file, stored in *systemroot*\System32\Config. This file serves as a transaction log for modifications to the hive registry file.

Table 9-1 lists the registry hives and their corresponding filenames.

TABLE 9-1

Registry Hive Files

Hive	Files
HKEY_LOCAL_MACHINE\SAM	Sam and Sam.log
HKEY_LOCAL_MACHINE\SECURITY	Security and Security.log
HKEY_LOCAL_MACHINE\SOFTWARE	Software and Software.log
HKEY_LOCAL_MACHINE\SYSTEM	System and System.alt
HKEY_CURRENT_CONFIG	System and System.log
HKEY_CURRENT_USER	Ntuser.dat and Ntuser.dat.log
HKEY_USERS\DEFAULT	Default and Default.log

Windows Server 2008 uses a process known as flushing to ensure a reliable, working copy of the registry at all times, guarding against attempted registry changes not being completed. Attempted changes to the registry, after a given number of seconds has passed or the modifying application explicitly requests it, are flushed or saved to disk. The following steps explain how flushing occurs for all but the SYSTEM hive (HKLM\SYSTEM):

1. Modified data is written to the hive log file so that the data can be reconstructed if the system halts or fails before the data is written to the registry file.

2. The log file is flushed upon completion of a successful update to the log file.

3. Windows Server 2008 marks the first sector of the registry file to indicate that it is in the process of being modified (dirty).

4. The changes are written to the registry file.

5. Upon successful completion of the write operation, the first sector is modified to indicate successful completion (clean).

When Windows Server 2008 reads the hive files to construct the registry, it checks the status of each file. If the system failed during a previous registry update operation, the registry file will still be marked as dirty. In that situation, Windows Server 2008 attempts to recover the registry file using the log file. The changes identified in the log file are applied to the registry file, and if successful, the file is marked as clean.

Having a backup of the registry is critical to being able to recover a failed system. Although Windows Server 2008 provides fault-tolerant management of the registry hive files, you should employ some additional procedures to ensure a valid, working copy of the registry. You'll find coverage of backup procedures in Chapter 7, and disaster recovery in Chapter 8.

Registry hive files

As mentioned earlier, the registry is divided into five logical hives. This section looks at each hive in a bit more detail.

HKEY_LOCAL_MACHINE

As explained earlier, the HKLM root key contains hardware and operating system settings for the local computer. HKLM contains the following subkeys:

- HARDWARE. This key stores the physical hardware configuration for the computer. Windows Server 2008 re-creates this key each time the system boots successfully, ensuring up-to-date hardware detection/configuration.

- SAM. The Security Account Manager (SAM) key contains security data for users and groups for the local machine.

- SECURITY. This key contains data that defines the local security policy.

- SOFTWARE. This key stores data about installed software.

- SYSTEM. This key stores data about startup parameters, device drivers, services, and other system-wide properties.

When corresponding settings are found in the HKCU key, those settings override settings in HKLM for the current user for certain data. If no corresponding settings exist, those in HKLM are used. For certain items such as device drivers, the data in HKLM is always used, regardless of whether the data also resides in HKCU.

HKEY_USERS

The HKU key stores user profile data for users who log on to the computer locally, as well as the default user profile for the local computer. It contains a subkey for each user whose profile is stored on the computer, in addition to a key for the default user (.DEFAULT). It's virtually impossible to identify a given user from the SID, but you wouldn't want to try to modify settings in this key anyway except through the administrative tools that modify the registry. If you do need to modify settings directly, use the HKCU key instead.

HKEY_CURRENT_USER

As explained earlier in this chapter, the HKCU key is an alias for the KHC*SID* key, where *SID* is the SID for the current local user. In other words, HKCU points to the registry key in HKU where the currently logged-on user's registry data is stored. It contains, among a few others, the following subkeys:

- AppEvents. This key contains data about application and event associations such as sounds associated with specific events. Select the Sounds and Multimedia icon in the Control Panel to modify settings in this key.

- Console. This key contains data that defines the appearance and behavior of the Windows Server 2008 command console (command prompt) and character-mode applications. Use the application or command console's Control menu to define settings in this key.

- Control Panel. This key contains data normally set through the Control Panel applets.

- Environment. This key contains environment variable assignments for the current user.

- Keyboard Layout. This key stores information about the user's keyboard layout and key mapping for international settings. Select the Regional Options icon in the Control Panel to modify these settings.

- Network. This key stores data about the user's network connections.

- Printers. This key stores data about the user's printer connections.

- Software. This key stores data about the user's installed applications.

- Volatile Environment. This key stores volatile operating environment data such as the user's application directory (usually \Documents and Settings\user \Application Data) and logon server.

 Your system might include additional keys depending on the server's configuration.

HKEY_CLASSES_ROOT

The HKCR key stores data about file associations and is built from HKLM\SOFTWARE\Classes and HKEY_CURRENT_USER\SOFTWARE\Classes, with the value in HKCU taking precedence. It contains numerous keys, one for each file/document type. Use the File Types tab of the Folder Options object in the Control Panel to modify file associations.

HKEY_CURRENT_CONFIG

The HKCC key is an alias of HKLM\SYSTEM\CurrentControlSet\Hardware Profiles \Current, and it stores hardware configuration data about the local computer relating to device assignments, device drivers, and so on. It contains two keys: Software and System. The Software key stores settings for system fonts and a handful of application settings. The System key stores a partial copy of the CurrentControlSet key in HKLM\SYSTEM\CurrentControlSet.

Keys and values

As you've read up to this point, *keys* serve as containers in the registry. Keys can contain other keys (subkeys). Keys can also contain *value entries*, or simply, *values*. These are the "substance" of the registry. Values comprise three parts: name, data type, and value. The name identifies the setting. The data type describes the item's data format. The value is the actual data. The following list summarizes data types currently defined and used by the system:

- `Binary Value`. This data type stores the data in raw binary format, one value per entry. The Registry Editor displays this data type using hexadecimal format.

- `DWORD value`. This data type stores data as a four-byte number (32-bit), one value per entry. The Registry Editor can display this data type in binary, hexadecimal, or decimal formats.

- `QWORD value`. This data type stores data as a 64-bit number, one value per entry. The Registry Editor can display this data type in binary, hexadecimal, or decimal formats.

- `Expandable string value`. This is a variable-length string that includes variables that are expanded when the data is read by a program, service, and so on. The variables are represented by % signs; an example is the use of the `%systemroot%` variable to identify the root location of the Windows Server 2008 folder, such as a path entry to a file stored in *systemroot*\System32. One value is allowed per entry.

- `Multi-String value`. This data type stores multiple string values in a single entry. String values within an item are separated by spaces, commas, or other such delimiters.

- `String value`. This data type stores a single, fixed-length string, and is the most common data type used in the registry.

The Registry Editor

Windows Server 2008 provides one Registry Editor (Regedit), `regedit.exe`, for viewing and modifying the registry. Windows 2000 and previous versions of Windows NT included an additional Registry Editor, `regedt32.exe`, which provided a few features that Regedit lacked. These features have been merged (finally!) into a single editor.

Regedit enables you to connect to, view, and modify a registry on a remote computer. Before you go tromping through the registry, however, keep two things in mind: You need a good backup copy of the registry, and you need to be careful with changes you make because you could introduce changes that might prevent the system from booting. That's why a backup copy is so important.

In addition, before you start playing with the Registry Editor, keep in mind that most changes, whether for the system, user, service, application, or other object, should be made with the administration tools for that object. Only use the Registry Editor to make changes not available through other administration tools. In addition, understand that Group Policy can modify the registry, and in many situations Group Policy is a better alternative for applying modifications where Active Directory is present.

Regedit.exe

Regedit displays the registry in a single, two-pane window. The registry tree appears in the left pane, and the results pane on the right shows the object currently selected in the tree. To view a particular key or setting, expand the tree and select the object you want to view.

 **NOTE** Click Start ➤ Run, type **regedit** in the Run dialog box, and click OK to start Regedit.

Modifying the registry

You can use Regedit to perform all registry browsing and modification tasks. You can even back up the registry by exporting it to a registry script; however, you should use Backup or a third-party backup utility that backs up other system data along with the registry. The following sections explain how to accomplish specific tasks in Regedit.

Creating and modifying values

You're most likely to modify the registry to change existing values rather than create new ones or modify keys. To change the value of a registry entry, locate the value in the editor and double-click the value. Regedit displays a dialog box (similar to the one shown in Figure 9-2) that varies according to the data type you're editing. Modify the data as needed, and then click OK.

FIGURE 9-2

Regedit provides a dialog box tailored to the type of data value selected.

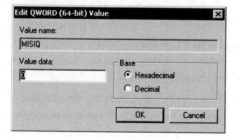

You can create a new value in an existing key. You might need to do this, for example, if a given application feature or property defaults to a hard-coded value in the absence of a registry value. Creating the value in the registry lets you control the application's behavior for that feature. To create a value, first locate and select the key in which you want to create the value. Click Edit ➤ New and select the type of value to create. Regedit creates a new value and names it New Value #*n*, but highlights the value name so you can type a new one to rename it. Double-click the newly created value to display a dialog box in which you set its data value.

Creating and deleting keys

Although you'll usually be creating and modifying values, you might need to create a new key. As you do when creating a value item, first locate the key in which you want the new key created. Select Edit ➤ New ➤ Key. Regedit creates the key and highlights the name (New Key by default) so you can quickly change it. Type the desired key name and press Enter.

Deleting a key is even easier than creating one, which may be dangerous. When you delete a key, all of its contents are deleted as well. There is no undo feature, so be very sure you've selected the right key and really want to delete it before proceeding. Then, choose Edit ➤ Delete. Click Yes to confirm the deletion or No to cancel it.

Importing and exporting keys

On occasion, you might find it useful or necessary to copy all or part of the registry to a file. For example, say you've gone through the trouble of installing an application that created its own registry section to store its settings. Now you want to move the application to a different computer, but don't want to go through the whole installation process. Instead, you'd rather just copy the files over to the other computer. In this case, you can export the application's portion of the registry to a text-based registry file. After you copy the application's files to the other system, you can import the registry file into the other computer's registry. A similar example would be installing an application on several systems remotely. You copy the files to the computer and then edit each computer's registry remotely to add the application settings.

NOTE   Migrating an application by copying registry values will only work if the application's setup process does not perform any other tasks other than copying files to a set of folders and modifying the registry. Changes such as registering DLLs cannot be duplicated with a simple registry copy. Therefore, running the installation process on the target servers is, in many cases, the only way to install an application. Even so, migrating the registry keys could enable you to duplicate the configuration of an application after installation.

With Regedit, you can save a key and its contents to a binary file that you can later load into a registry. To do so, select the key and choose File ➤ Export, and then specify a filename. From the Save as Type drop-down list, choose Registry Hive Files. Click Save to save the file.

You also can use Regedit to export a selected branch or export the entire registry to a registry script. There are other ways to back up the registry, so let's assume you want to export only a single branch (you use the same process either way). Locate and select the branch of the registry you want to export. Choose File ➤ Export. Regedit displays the Export Registry File dialog box shown in Figure 9-3. Specify a filename for the registry file and select either All or Selected Branch, depending on how much of the registry you want to export. Then click Save to create the file, which will have a .reg extension by default.

FIGURE 9-3

You can export a branch or the entire registry to a text file.

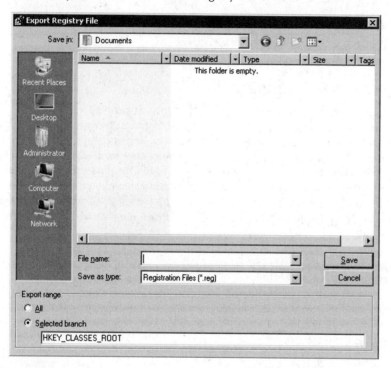

> **TIP** You can use any text editor to view and, if necessary, modify the exported registry file.

Importing a registry script adds the contents of the file to the registry, creating or replacing keys and values with the imported values. Using the application installation example described previously, you'd import the registry values for the application you want to add to the computer without running the application's Setup program.

> **NOTE** In most cases, simply copying registry settings does not fully install an application, so importing and exporting application registry keys is seldom a replacement for running the application's Setup program. Using the registry copy method works only when the application doesn't create user-specific settings or perform other, nonregistry modifications during installation.

You have two ways to import a registry file: import it in Regedit or simply double-click a registry script. To import a key in Regedit, choose File ➤ Import and select a registry file. Locate and select the text file and click Open. Regedit loads the registry file and applies its settings. Changes take effect immediately. In addition, double-clicking a registry script file causes Windows Server 2008 to incorporate into the registry the settings stored in the file (after prompting you to confirm).

> **NOTE**   You also can choose Start ➢ Run and enter the name of the registry file to import the file's settings into the registry.

Editing a remote registry

You can edit the registry of a remote computer, subject to your permissions and rights on the remote computer, as well as how the remote system is configured. To open the registry from another computer in Regedit, click File ➢ Connect Network Registry and specify the computer name or browse for it. The registry for the remote computer appears as a separate branch in the tree pane. You can view and modify settings just as you would for the local computer, although the tree includes only the HCLM and HKU keys for the remote computer; the others are not displayed. When you're finished, click File ➢ Disconnect Network Registry, and the computer's registry disappears from the tree. You can connect to multiple remote systems concurrently, if needed.

Loading and unloading hives

Regedit provides the capability to load and unload individual hives, which is useful for managing individual hives from another system or managing user registries. For example, you might use Regedit to edit the hive of a system that won't boot, repairing the damage so you can replace the hive on the target system and get it running again. You also can load a user's copy of Ntuser.dat to modify the user's registry settings.

Loading a hive affects only the HKLM or HKU keys, so you must first select one of those keys before loading the hive. The hive is loaded as a subkey of the selected hive, rather than replacing the existing key of the same name (you specify the name for the new hive). You can modify the settings in the key, unload the hive, and copy it to the target system, if necessary.

To load a hive, open Regedit and choose File ➢ Load Hive. Regedit prompts you for the location and name of the previously saved hive. Select the file and click Open. Specify a name for the key under which the hive will reside and click OK. To unload a hive, select File ➢ Unload Hive.

Securing the Registry

As you've probably surmised at this point, the registry is a critical part of the Windows Server 2008 operating system. It also can present a security risk because virtually every setting for the

OS and applications reside in the registry. For that reason, you might want to apply tighter security to certain keys in the registry to prevent unauthorized access that could potentially give a remote user or hacker the capability to change settings that would grant them access or cause damage. You also can prevent remote administration of a registry and protect the registry in other ways. This section of the chapter explains your options.

Preventing access to the registry

Perhaps the best way to protect the registry from unauthorized changes is to keep users out of it altogether. In the case of a server, keeping the server physically secure and granting only administrators the right to log on locally is the first step. For other systems, or where that isn't practical for a given server, you can secure the Registry Editor. Either remove the Registry Editor from the target system or configure the permissions on Regedit.exe to deny permission to execute for all except those who should have access. If you've removed the Registry Editor from a system and need to modify its registry, you can do so remotely from another computer that does contain a Registry Editor. See the section "Securing Remote Registry Access" later in this chapter if you want to prevent remote editing of the registry.

> **NOTE** Simply removing the Registry Editor from a server doesn't prevent registry changes. Someone could easily write a script to modify the registry from a command console or a telnet session.

Applying permissions to registry keys

Another way to protect the registry or portions thereof is to apply permissions on individual keys to restrict access to those keys. In this way, you can allow certain users or groups access to certain parts of the registry and deny access to others. However, use this capability sparingly. Changing the Access Control List (ACL) for a registry key incorrectly could prevent the system from booting. Either avoid configuring the ACL for preexisting keys and change only those keys you create yourself, or be very careful with the changes you make.

In Regedit, select the key or subkey on which you want to set permissions. Choose Edit ➤ Permissions to access the Permissions dialog box (see Figure 9-4). Add and remove users and groups as needed, and then set permissions for each. For more information about setting permissions, see Chapter 17.

Auditing registry access

If you do allow access to a system's registry, consider auditing registry access to track who is accessing the registry and what they're doing. Although you could audit all access to the registry, that would generate a potentially huge amount of load on the server, so consider auditing only success or failure in modifying a key or value.

FIGURE 9-4

Use the Permissions dialog box to configure access permissions on registry keys.

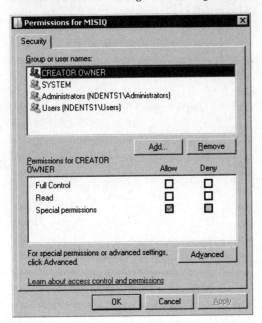

To enable auditing of the registry, first enable auditing on the target system. You can do this either through the local security policy or through Group Policy. Open the branch `Computer Configuration\Windows Settings\Security Settings\Local Policies\Audit Policy`. Double-click the policy Audit Object Access and select Success and/or Failure, depending on which events you want to track.

Enabling auditing of object access doesn't configure auditing for a particular object, but instead simply makes it possible (that is, turns on the capability to audit object access). You then need to configure auditing for each object you want to audit. In the case of the registry, this means you need to configure auditing for each key you want to track. To do so, open Regedit. Locate and select the key you want to configure and choose Edit ➢ Permissions. Click Advanced, click the Auditing tab, click Add to select the user or group whose access you want to audit for the selected key, and click OK. Regedit displays the Auditing Entry dialog box, shown in Figure 9-5. Select Successful/Failed as desired. Table 9-2 lists audit events you can configure for registry access.

TABLE 9-2

Registry Access Audit Events

Audit Event	Explanation
Query Value	Log attempts to view the key.
Set Value	Log attempts to set values.
Create Subkey	Log attempts to create subkeys.
Enumerate Subkeys	Log attempts to list subkeys.
Notify	Log attempts to open the key with Notify access.
Create Link	Log attempts to create links to the key.
Delete	Log attempts to delete a key.
Write DAC	Log attempts to determine who has access to a key.
Writer Owner	Log attempts to determine who owns a key.
Read Control	Log attempts to remotely access registry objects.

FIGURE 9-5

Use the Auditing Entry dialog box to configure auditing of the selected key.

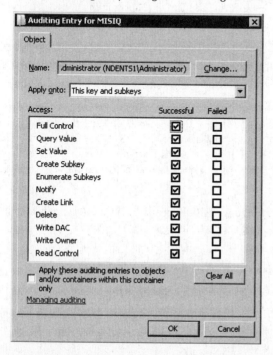

Securing remote registry access

A good security step to take to prevent hackers and others from making unauthorized changes to a system's registry is to prevent remote access to a system's registry. When a user attempts to connect to a registry remotely, Windows Server 2008 checks the ACL for the following registry key:

```
HKLM\System\ControlSet001\Control\SecurePipeServers\winreg
```

If this key is missing, all users can access the registry subject to the permissions assigned to individual keys. If the key exists, Windows Server 2008 checks the permissions on the key to determine whether or not the remote user can gain access to the registry (and levels of access). Individual keys then determine what these remote users can do with a given key. Therefore, winreg is the first line of defense, and individual key ACLs are the second line of defense. If you want to prevent all remote access to the registry, make sure you set the permissions on the winreg key accordingly.

Summary

Despite the towering authority of Active Directory at the domain level, the registry still forms the repository of essentially all data that determines the Windows Server 2008 configuration for hardware, the operating system, and applications. Although you can modify the registry directly, most changes can and should be accomplished through the Control Panel or other administration tools for OS- and hardware-related settings, and through applications for each application's registry settings.

When you do need to modify the registry, you can use the Registry Editor (Regedit) to do so. You can use Regedit to view and modify the registry, as well as perform additional tasks such as loading an individual hive from another computer.

Security on the registry is also important. Restricting registry access is vital to secure a system from local and remote viewing and modification of the registry. You can apply permissions on individual keys through Regedit and apply permissions to HKLM\System\CurrentControlSet \Control\SecurePipeServers\winreg to prevent unauthorized remote access to a system's registry. Auditing of registry access enables you to track who is accessing the registry and the tasks they're performing on it.

This chapter explored the concept of auditing registry access. Chapter 10 explores auditing in more detail, including security and object access auditing.

Chapter 10

Auditing Windows Server 2008

IN THIS CHAPTER

Discovering how auditing works and why to use it

Configuring policies for auditing

Examining the audit reports

Enabling auditing — effective strategies for specific scenarios

uditing provides a means of tracking all events in Windows Server 2008 to monitor system access and ensure system security. It is a critical tool for ensuring security, but it can overwhelm a server if not configured and used correctly. This chapter explains how and why you should implement auditing, and provides some specific tips on how to configure and use auditing for different situations. As you read through the chapter, keep in mind that auditing is just one weapon in your security arsenal. Locking down the server, using firewalls, and other security-management tools are even more important. This chapter also covers Active Directory auditing. If you are not familiar with security policy settings you can also use the Security Configuration Wizard (SCW), discussed in Chapter 16, to set up auditing. It provides a quick Wizard-based model for audit configuration. The SCW contains its audit settings in an audit policy.

Auditing Overview

In Windows Server 2008, *auditing* provides a means of tracking events. It is an important facet of security for individual computers as well as the enterprise. Microsoft defines an *event* as any significant occurrence in the operating system or an application that requires users (particularly administrators) to be notified. Events are recorded in *event logs* that you can manage by using the Event Viewer snap-in.

Auditing enables you to track specific events. More specifically, auditing enables you to track the *success* or *failure* of specific events. You may, for example, audit logon attempts, tracking who succeeds in logging on (and when) and who fails at logging on. You may audit object access on a given folder or file, tracking who uses it and the tasks that they perform on it. You can track an overwhelming variety of events in Windows Server 2008, as you learn in the section "Configuring Auditing," later in this chapter.

Windows Server 2008 provides several categories of events that you can audit, as described in the following list:

- **Account Logon Events.** Track user logon and logoff via a user account.
- **Account Management.** Track when a user account or group is created, changed, or deleted; a user account is renamed, enabled, or disabled; or a password is set or changed.
- **Directory Service Access.** Track access to Active Directory.
- **Logon Events.** Track nonlocal authentication events such as network use of a resource or a remote service that is logging on by using the local system account.
- **Object Access.** Track when objects are accessed and the type of access performed — for example, track use of a folder, file, or printer. Configure auditing of specific events through the object's properties (such as the Security tab for a folder or file).
- **Policy Change.** Track changes to user rights or audit policies.
- **Privilege Use.** Track when a user exercises a right other than those associated with logon and logoff.
- **Process Tracking.** Track events related to process execution, such as program execution.
- **System Events.** Track system events such as restart, startup, shutdown, or events that affect system security or the security log.

Within each category are several different types of events — some common and some specific to the objects or events being edited. If you audit registry access, for example, the events are very specific to the registry. Rather than cover every possible event that can be audited, this chapter explains how to enable and configure auditing, looks at specific cases, and explains how auditing improves security and monitoring in those cases.

Configuring Auditing

Configuring auditing can be either a one- or two-step process, depending on the type of events for which you're configuring auditing. For all but object access, enabling auditing simply requires that you define the audit policy for the given audit category. You have an additional step for object-access auditing, however — configuring auditing for specific objects. Enabling auditing for the policy *Audit Object Access*, for example, doesn't actually cause any folders or files to be audited. Instead, you must configure each folder or file individually for auditing.

Enabling audit policies

Before you begin auditing specific events, you need to enable auditing for that event's category. You configure auditing through the computer's local security policy, Group Policy, via the Security Configuration Wizard (SCW), or all three. If domain audit policies are defined, they override local audit policies. This chapter assumes that you're configuring auditing through the domain security policy. If you need to configure auditing through local policies, use the Local Security Policy console or the SCW to enable auditing. To configure auditing through the domain security policy you can open the Group Policy Management Console (GPMC) and edit the domain policy. To do this now, follow these steps:

1. Choose Start ➤ Administrative Tools ➤ Group Policy Management.

2. Expand the GPMC to the Default Domain Policy, right-click the node, and choose Edit. The Group Policy Management Editor will open. Drill down from the Policies node through Windows Settings to Security Settings, and open the Local Policies ➤ Audit Policy branch. As Figure 10-1 shows, each audit policy category appears with its effective setting.

 If you want to configure auditing on the Domain Controllers OU for the local domain, open the Domain Controller Security Policy console from the Administrative Tools folder.

FIGURE 10-1

Use either the local security policy or the domain policy to enable auditing.

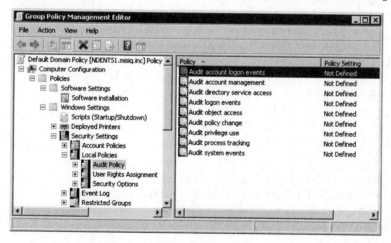

3. Double-click a policy in the right pane to display its settings in a dialog box (see Figure 10-2). You can enable the auditing of both Success and Failure of events in the selected category. You may, for example, audit successful logons to track who is using a given system and when. You may also track unsuccessful logons to track attempts at unauthorized use of a system.

4. Select Success, Failure, or both, as desired, and click OK.

FIGURE 10-2

Select the types of events (Success or Failure) for which you want to enable auditing.

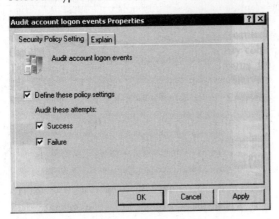

After you configure each category, close the security policy console. See the following section if you're configuring the auditing of object access. Otherwise, audit events begin appearing in the security log. Make sure that you configure the security log's size and overflow behavior to accommodate the audit events. You can configure the log and view it in the Event Viewer, which is located in the Administrative Tools folder.

Auditing object access

The second step in configuring object-access auditing is to enable auditing on the individual objects that you want to monitor (such as folders, files, registry keys, and so on). You typically configure the objects where you find them in the user interface, such as in Explorer for folders and files, in the Printers folder for printers, and in Regedit for the registry keys. The types of events that you can audit for a given object depend on the object itself. Events for file access, for example, are different from events for registry-key access. To configure auditing for a folder or file, follow these steps:

1. Open Windows Explorer and then locate the folder or file. Right-click the object, and choose Properties from the context menu to view its property sheet.

2. Click the Security tab and then click Advanced to open the Advanced Security Settings dialog box.

3. Click the Auditing tab of the Advanced Security Settings dialog box to open the Auditing page and then click Add. Select a user, computer, or group that you want to audit, and click OK. Windows Server 2008 displays an object dialog box that lists the events you can audit for the selected object (see Figure 10-3).

CROSS-REF   See Chapter 12 for more information on controlling and monitoring printer access.

FIGURE 10-3

Select the Successful or Failed checkbox as needed to configure auditing for each event type for the selected object.

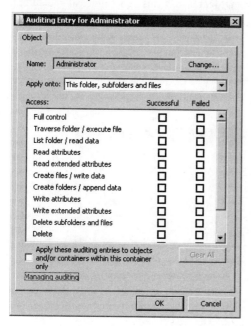

4. Select Successful for a given event if you want to record the successful completion of the event. Select Failed to monitor failed attempts. Selecting the Apply These Auditing Entries to Objects and/or Containers Within This Container Only checkbox applies auditing to only the contents of the selected container (such as the files in the selected folder). The contents of subfolders are audited unless this option is selected. After you're satisfied with the audit event selections, click OK.

CAUTION   As you're defining the audit policy for a selected object, keep in mind that you could potentially generate a huge number of events in the security log. Unless you have a specific reason to audit success on a given event, consider auditing only failure to reduce traffic to the log and load on the computer. Auditing failed access is typically most useful for tracking attempts at unauthorized access.

Repeat the preceding steps to add other users, groups, or computers to the list. In the Advanced Security Settings dialog box (see Figure 10-4) are the following two options that control how auditing entries are affected by the parent object and how they affect child objects:

■ **Include Inheritable Auditing Entries from This Object's Parent.** Include these with entries explicitly defined here. Select this option if you want auditing properties to be inherited by the current object from its parent object. Deselect this option to prevent audit properties from being inherited.

- **Replace All Existing Inheritable Auditing Entries on All Descendants with Inheritable Auditing Entries from This Object.** Select this option to clear and audit properties configured within child objects (such as subfolders) and to enable the audit properties for the current object to propagate to child objects.

FIGURE 10-4

Use the Auditing tab of the Advanced Security Settings dialog box to configure auditing for a selected object.

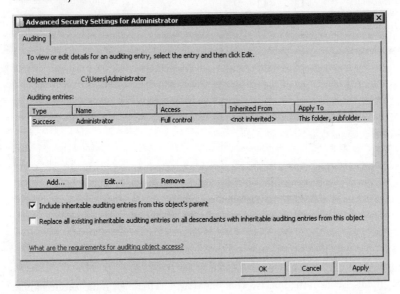

Close the object's property sheets after you finish defining the audit policy for the object. Auditing begins immediately.

Examining the Audit Reports

Windows Server 2008 records audited events to the Windows Server 2008 security log. You can use the Event Viewer snap-in to view the event logs, save logs as log files for future viewing, and save the logs in either tab- or comma-delimited formats.

Using the Event Viewer

You can use the Event Viewer to view and manage the event logs. In addition to the security log, you can manage the application and system logs, as well as any additional logs created by

Windows 2003 services or applications. By default, the Event Viewer displays the logs dynamically, meaning that new events are added to a log as you're viewing it. You also can save a log to disk to use as a benchmark or simply to archive a log before clearing it. Figure 10-5 shows the security log in the Event Viewer.

CROSS-REF For detailed information on the Event Viewer console snap-in, including how to save logs and configure log behavior, see Chapter 2.

FIGURE 10-5

You can browse the security log (and other logs) by using the Event Viewer.

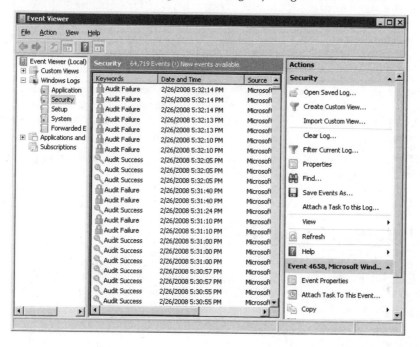

Using other tools

The Event Viewer provides the means through which you configure and view event logs. Because you can save a log to a text file, however, you can use other applications to view a log. You may save a log to a comma-delimited file, for example, so that you can import the file into Microsoft Access or another database application to create a database that you can easily organize by event ID, source, and so on. You may also export the data to a text file and import it into a word processor to create a report. Just make sure that you pick an application that can import tab- or comma-delimited files and export the log files in the appropriate format.

A handful of other third-party tools exist for viewing a system's log files. One in particular worth considering is RippleTech's LogCaster. Providing a mechanism to manage the event logs is just a small part of what LogCaster does. It not only provides a unified interface for viewing the event logs, it also serves as an excellent warning system for administrators. LogCaster provides real-time monitoring of the event logs, services, TCP/IP devices, performance counters, and ASCII logs. It provides automatic delivery of alerts through a variety of mechanisms, including paging, e-mail, ODBC, SNMP, and others. Whenever a given event occurs, you can have LogCaster automatically notify you regardless of where you are. Whether you're tracking system performance, want to be notified of audit events, or want to be warned of a possible system intrusion, you should find LogCaster an excellent resource. You can locate RippleTech on the Internet at www.rippletech.com.

You can also use several enterprise management tools to go beyond just managing event logs. Microsoft Operations Manager (MOM), for example, provides the capability to collect information across the enterprise from event logs, Unix syslog files, SNMP traps, and other sources to help you monitor availability and performance. MOM provides an excellent set of tools for monitoring systems and Microsoft applications such as Exchange Server, SQL Server, and others. For more information on MOM, check www.microsoft.com/mom.

Several other third-party enterprise-management tools are worth considering if you're looking for ways to improve data collection and monitoring. You should also consider CA Unicenter (at www.ca.com), HP OpenView (at www.hp.com), and the many tools from NetIQ (at www.netiq.com).

NOTE   Microsoft Operations Manager is derived from NetIQ Operations Manager. Microsoft licensed the technology and integrated additional features to target the product to Microsoft platforms and applications.

Strategies for Auditing

Although you could audit every event, doing so wouldn't be practical because you'd place an undue load on the system and either end up with an enormous log file or spend all your time worrying about archiving the logs. The following sections examine some specific scenarios and how you might employ auditing.

Leaving auditing off

One option is to leave auditing off altogether, which is not a bad option in some situations. If you're not concerned with security, you have no real reason to enable or perform auditing. Turning off auditing reduces system overhead and helps simplify log management; most organizations are (or should be) concerned with security at least to some degree, however, so this option is unlikely to fit your needs.

Turning all auditing on

At the other end of the auditing spectrum is complete auditing. If you're very concerned about security or shooting for C2 security certification, this may be an option. Bear in mind, however, that your system is likely to generate a huge number of events requiring very active management of the security log. As an alternative to full logging, consider logging only failure events and not success events.

Auditing problem users

Certain users, for one reason or another, can become an administrator's worst nightmare. In some cases, it's through no fault of the user, but instead results from problems with the user's profile, account, and so on. In other cases, the user can be at fault, frequently using the wrong password, incorrectly typing the account name, trying to log on during periods when they are not allowed, or even trying to access resources for which they have no permissions (or need). In these situations, you can monitor events associated with the given user. You may even need to retain the information for counseling or termination purposes.

Which types of events you audit for a given user or group depends on the problem area. Audit account logon events, for example, if the user has trouble logging on or attempts to log on during unauthorized hours. Track object access to determine when a user or group is attempting to access a given resource such as a folder or file. Tailor other auditing to specific tasks and events generated by the user or group.

Auditing administrators

Auditing administrators is a good idea, not only to keep track of what administrators are doing, but also to detect unauthorized use of administrative privileges. Keep in mind, however, that auditing affects system performance. In particular, consider auditing account logon events, account management, policy change, and privilege use of an administrator only if you suspect an individual. Instead, control administrators by delegating through the wise use of groups and organizational units.

Auditing critical files and folders

One very common use for auditing is to track access to important folders and files. In addition to tracking simple access, you probably want to track when users make or attempt to make specific types of changes to the object, such as Change Permissions and Take Ownership. This helps you monitor changes to a folder or file that could affect security.

Summary

Auditing enables you to monitor events associated with specific users, groups, and services. These events are recorded to the security log. The capability to monitor these events is not only useful for troubleshooting, but also is an important tool for monitoring and managing security. You learned how you can keep tabs on the actions of specific users or groups and monitor attempts at unauthorized access to the system or its resources.

As the chapter explained, configuring auditing for most types of events is a one-step process. You configure the policy for Success, Failure, or both in the local or group security policy. Configuring the auditing of object access, such as monitoring access to folders/files, printers, or the registry, requires the additional step of configuring auditing on each object to be monitored.

Auditing is a useful tool for tracking what is happening in the network and on given computers, and is one step toward providing a secure and reliable environment. Truly providing reliability and security requires an understanding of service level, which is covered in detail in Chapter 25.

Chapter 11

.NET Framework Services

The .NET Framework is included with Windows Server 2008 but like many other features, it needs to be specifically installed before it can be used. (See Chapter 2, "Configuring Windows Server 2008.") This framework for application developers enables your system to run very sophisticated programs that are extremely fast and extremely portable. The .NET Framework also enables many components to run on the server. A good example is Windows PowerShell, which is built on the .NET Framework. (Chapter 2 includes a discussion of Windows PowerShell.)

Along with this power also comes security concerns. Presumably, because the framework is integrated, applications that run on it can have a great deal of control over the server. To some degree that's true, but this is where security comes into focus.

In this chapter you learn about the components that make up the .NET Framework. You glimpse at its application programming interface as well as view how the garbage collection facility works and how you can monitor it.

The recent versions of the .NET Framework include versions 3.0 and 3.5. These bring many new features to the platform, for example: the .NET Framework now includes the XPS Viewer, which lets you view, sign, and protect XML documents; and Windows Communications Foundation (WCF) and HTTP Activation Components, which allow applications to start and stop dynamically in response to inbound requests from the network in general and from HTTP requests in particular, and so on. Another exciting addition is the Windows Workflow Foundation (WWF), which allows developers to build advanced workflow and queuing applications.

To run applications using the .NET Framework on Windows Server 2008, you need to add the Application Server role (see Chapter 2). Open Server Manager, select Server Roles, and choose Application Server. As soon as you check this role, the Add Roles Wizard pops up with a request to confirm what is about to be installed. This is shown in Figure 11-1.

Adding features required for the Application Server role.

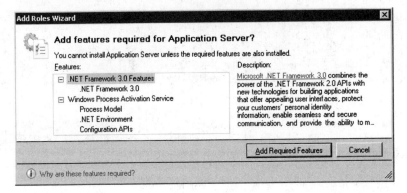

The wizard will now prompt you for more application server bits. These include IIS support (the Web server), Com+ Network Access, process activation, distributed transactions, and so on. Click Next and click the Add Required Role Services button. You will go through several additional screens for settings that are more granular or specific to the services you have chosen. If all you chose to do was install the Framework, the installation will be quick.

Introduction to the .NET Framework

The average Windows Server 2008 administrator may not have a lot of interest in the .NET Framework. The .NET Framework is, in a nutshell, an application programming interface that programmers can use when creating applications. This framework gives the programmer an extraordinary amount of control over the machine on which it runs, as well as over network operations as a whole. This may all seem a bit scary at first, but it comes with a very sophisticated toolset for configuring security within the framework and applications that utilize it. The job of the server administrator is to configure this security and deploy it across the network to protect network resources from rogue code.

On Windows Server 2008, the .NET Framework is a much more enhanced environment than its predecessors, versions 1.0 through 2.0. The following support is included.

64-bit platform support

The new generation of 64-bit computers is here, and its operating system is Windows Server 2008 all the way. This results in the capability to create applications that can run faster and take advantage of more memory than is available to 32-bit applications. We can now build 64-bit applications with managed code and write 64-bit unmanaged code on 64-bit computers, without the limitation of the 4GB memory barrier inherent in 32-bit systems.

Access control list

It is now possible to use an access control list (ACL) to grant or revoke permissions to access a resource on a computer. A host of new classes has been added to the .NET Framework, enabling managed code to create and modify an ACL; and new members that utilize an ACL have been added to the I/O, registry, and threading classes. See Chapter 16 for further discussion about ACLs.

ADO .NET and LINQ

ADO.NET includes a few new features that support user-defined types (UDT), asynchronous database operations, XML data types, large value types, snapshot isolation, and new attributes that enable applications to support Multiple Active Result Sets (MARS) with SQL Server 2005 and 2008.

Some database operations (generally command execution) can take considerable time to complete. Single-threaded applications must block and wait for the command to finish its work before continuing their own operations. The `SqlCommand` class and the `BeginExecuteNon-Query`, `BeginExecuteReader`, and `BeginExecuteXmlReader` methods, paired with the `EndExecuteNonQuery`, `EndExecuteReader`, and `EndExecuteXmlReader` methods, provide the asynchronous support.

As for LINQ — language integrated query — this is a new query language extension introduced with version 3.0 that provides support for data querying in a type-safe way.

Asynchronous processing

To further push the envelope on processing performance, the .NET Framework version 3.5 provides several standard asynchronous operations that enable you to have much more control over background threading. Such enhancements are ideal to free the user interface from bottlenecks, or to enable high-priority threads to complete other operations while some background task is executing.

When coupled with the technologies in ADO.NET, you can perform asynchronous database operations using an API that is modeled after the asynchronous model of the .NET Framework.

Other areas that have been enhanced include File I/O, Stream I/O, Socket I/O, HTTP, TCP, the remoting channels (HTTP, TCP), proxies, XML Web services created using ASP.NET, ASP.NET Web Forms, message queuing using the `MessageQueue` class, and finally, the asynchronous delegate class.

Understanding the .NET Initiative

A clear definition of what the .NET initiative is has been somewhat of a mystery. The .NET Framework is obviously a framework for application development, but what about Server 2008? It doesn't mean that Windows Server 2008 is meant for .NET development, but one distinct characteristic of the Windows Server 2008 operating system is that it comes with the .NET Framework already integrated into the operating system; you have no need to install it. Before we move on with a discussion of the .NET Framework, however, you first need to understand what brought it about and what Microsoft hopes to accomplish with it.

The .NET Framework is a set of libraries that enable programmers to build applications. The difference between the .NET Framework and, for example, MFC is that the .NET Framework enables extremely rapid development of applications that can be integrated very tightly with the operating system. The amount of time, for example, to build a Windows Service application that monitors remote Windows Services — or processes, for that matter — is reduced by an order of magnitude if you use the .NET Framework. This Framework also provides for Web services and remoting, which act as methods for invoking components on remote systems, over the Internet. This can obviously be a nightmare for network and/or server administrators who need to maintain the security of their systems. Fortunately for administrators, the .NET Framework has extensive security built into it.

The Common Language Runtime

The *Common Language Runtime* (CLR) is an environment that enables .NET application languages to run while providing each application with the same functionality set. The CLR also manages memory during program execution, as well as managing thread and other system services. The CLR also verifies that applications are permitted to run given the current set of security configurations.

The CLR can grant or deny security to items such as disk access, network access, memory, and peripherals such as printers. It also implements strict type and code verification by use of the *Common Type System* (CTS), which is discussed in the following section.

Unlike interpreted languages, the CLR uses *Just-in-Time* compilation so that all applications are compiled into native machine language for the system on which the applications are running. This offers dramatic performance gains over interpreted languages, ensures less of a strain on the OS, and limits the chance of memory leaks and the like.

Another definite benefit of the CLR is that it enables applications developed in separate languages to communicate with each other and maintain a high degree of integration. The benefit to Windows Server 2008 administrators is that they can write code in VB or C# that performs in exactly the same way and uses the exact same function calls, which means that one language doesn't have advantages over another. A benefit of writing scripts with a .NET Framework language (such as VB, C#, and so on) would be, for example, importing a list of users and automatically creating logins for them within Active Directory.

Common Type System

We briefly touched on the Common Type System (CTS) in the preceding section, and now you'll look at a few of the details of CTS from a server administrator's point of view. Figure 11-2 illustrates the CTS.

FIGURE 11-2

The collection of types that make up the Common Type System.

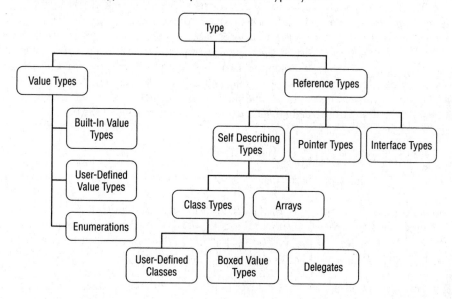

CTS ensures that all code within an application is *self-describing*, which means, for example, that the value of an integer type can be consumed by a long data type. Not a very thrilling concept for server administration perhaps, but CTS helps ensure that a programmer cannot insert bogus code within an application to intentionally cause an error. Why would someone do that, you ask? Well, suppose you hire a programmer to write a few backend components for your Web site running on IIS 7.0. This programmer inserts a few lines of code that, if correctly accessed, cause an error that perhaps drops the user into the system, providing him or her with complete access, or maybe — even worse — crashes your server.

Keep in mind that the .NET Framework and all its components are very security-centric. The actual security details and operation of the framework are beyond the scope of this book, but rest assured that any applications on your server that are written with a .NET Framework language can be configured for the utmost security conscious.

.NET security

.NET security can be configured in three different ways: at the enterprise level, the machine level, and the user level. This separation of security levels ensures not only that your enterprise can have a security policy in executing .NET applications, but also that, should your company hire contractors, a security policy can be applied to them as well so that they can't take advantage of your servers and the information they contain.

To drill down even further, each level of security (enterprise, machine, user) can also contain custom code groups. You could make a code group for enterprise applications that need Internet access as well as a code group that needs access to corporate print servers. After the .NET Framework determines security access, it essentially overlaps the three security zones and examines the privileges. If a privilege has been removed in any level, then the specific action isn't permitted. This ensures, for example, that a user security policy doesn't override an enterprise policy. (See Chapter 16 for information on security policies.) This kind of granular control is exactly what is needed for such a powerful programming framework.

Application domains

To better understand application domains, consider an example that many of us have been through. The corporate mail server has been in desperate need of a way to process automated help desk tickets. To achieve this, the IT department has created a COM object that watches the mail go through the mail server and routes the help desk ticket to the correct person for the job. Several weeks after this COM object is installed, the Microsoft Exchange Server mysteriously crashes; this hasn't happened to Exchange since it was installed.

This particular example may not be familiar to all of you, but the circumstances may be. So what happened to the Microsoft Exchange Server? The key to the mystery was that the COM object was an in-process object. The term *in-process* means that the COM object shared process space with Microsoft Exchange Server. Sharing process space allows the object (in this example, it is the COM object) to share memory with the host application (Microsoft Exchange Server). This allows for an incredible amount of integration because both application and COM object can share all sorts of information. Unfortunately, this also means that if the COM object dies, the application and all other objects in the process space die as well.

This type of incident is pretty typical on Windows Server 2008 because not all applications are perfect and quite often applications crash. On Windows 98 and ME, you could expect different behavior, however. These operating systems don't have protected memory segments, which means if one application crashes, it could quite possibly kill all running applications, including Windows! Since Windows 2000, we have been shielded from this because an application dying within its process space couldn't harm other applications, nor could it harm Windows.

Application domains solve this problem of multiple objects in the same process space threatening the lives of the other objects. Application domains involve a greater level of granularity, enabling multiple objects (or applications) to run within the same process space with isolation. This isolation means that even though multiple objects are executing, one of them can error and halt execution and not affect the others.

As a Windows Server 2008 administrator, this means that the pesky programmers can't bring your servers to their knees. Application domains are by no means foolproof, but they are a vast improvement over simple process space and a definite step in the right direction.

Garbage collection

The *Garbage Collection* (GC) facility within the .NET Framework is in charge of releasing memory as objects run out of scope and are no longer used within an application. The fact that programmers have almost always needed to specifically free resources is the number one cause of memory leaks within an application. Thanks to the .NET Framework, this is all handled behind the scenes.

If this sounds too good to be true, the truth is that it may be. Although GC does free up memory, it does so at an undefined interval. Function calls available to the programmer enable a manual invocation of garbage collection but don't guarantee when it occurs.

On a positive note, included with the .NET Framework are performance counters that enable you to monitor garbage collection — when it runs, how long it runs, and the amount of memory it frees up, just to name a few aspects.

.NET vs. the JVM

That Microsoft took a long hard look at the Java Virtual Machine (JVM) or the Java Runtime Engine (JRE) during the design phases of the .NET Framework is really no secret, so most of the useful features that you see in the JVM are also present within the .NET Framework. To avoid a war and lots of hate e-mail, we don't recommend one over the other here, but we do outline the two benefits to using the .NET Framework over the JVM:

- The .NET Framework has a great deal of support for graphical user interfaces (GUIs). Those who have ever tried to create a Windows-based application by using a text editor and the .NET Framework probably don't agree with us on this, but that's our story and we're sticking with it. Not only can you design Windows applications by using the .NET Framework, you can also design applications for the Web to be displayed in a browser, as well as applications for PDAs, cell phones, and many other Wireless Application Protocol (WAP) enabled devices. Java simply doesn't offer this luxury; a third-party package is needed for GUI creation within Java.

- The next obvious benefit of .NET over the JVM is performance gain. .NET simply beats the JVM in running almost any type of application, whether it is simply a GUI application with one screen or an n-Tier application accessing a database backend.

Configuring the Global Assembly Cache

Configuration of the Global Assembly Cache (GAC) should be done by a developer 99 percent of the time because developers are most familiar with what their applications do and do not need. We touch on the GAC briefly here so that you, as a server administrator, have an idea of what its configuration actually entails.

The .NET Framework is capable of side-by-side DLL execution. Therefore, you can have two DLLs with the same name on the same machine and in the same folder. This enables applications to use the DLL that fits their needs. Application A may need version 1.0 of a certain DLL, whereas a newer Application B may require version 3.0 of the same DLL.

Summary

The .NET Framework is a very powerful tool for application developers as well as server administrators. It enables you to create very powerful programs to ease server administration — such as importing large lists of users and adding them to your network or simply to monitor system conditions. The framework also allows for side-by-side execution of same-name DLLs, which typically leads to application crashes. Using the .NET Framework, you can also build components that can communicate across the Internet and through firewalls using open standards and common protocols to help propel your business.

The .NET Framework is merely just that — a framework. It contains many tools and utilities that enable specialized applications to run.

Part II

File, Print, and Storage Services

Chapter 12

Print Services

This chapter covers everything you need to know about the Windows Server 2008 printing service. Despite all of our efforts to create a paperless office, hardcopy and thus printers are not going away. For all intents and purposes, for good or for evil, printers are becoming more sophisticated, cheaper, and easier to use; and Windows Server 2008 isn't helping to conserve trees. In fact, the operating system now includes support for more than 4,000 printers, as well as support for industrial, high-performance, printing supporting devices that would cost a small island.

In addition, technologies such as e-mail and the World Wide Web have not done much to alleviate the need for printers. Instead, they have often succeeded in shifting the burden of hardcopy output from the sender to the receiver. Today, even attorneys e-mail contracts; and then ask you to print them out, sign them, and return them.

The network operating system lives and dies by its ability to host access to printers. The print service is the third leg of the "stool" that makes up a network operating system. Without it, a network OS simply falls over. Windows Server 2008 has inherited a rich and robust printing service, culled from years of research and development and the experiences of more than 100 million users. It is one of the reasons why Windows Server 2003 has done so well. In Windows Server 2008 the driver model has been extended to cater to the XML Paper Specification (XPS), which adds more efficiency and throughput to the print subsystem. We explore this a little later in the chapter.

For the most part, installing printers and printing is a no-brainer; that is, until the printer stops printing. In order to troubleshoot problems, a good understanding of the elements and components of Windows networking services is vitally important.

As an administrator, you need to understand the logical environment in order to troubleshoot printer problems effectively. Therefore, this discussion begins with an introduction to the components that make printing actually happen, and then moves on to installing printers. After the discussion, your properties and parameters setup will mean more to you. After you're equipped with the fundamentals, you can explore print-service troubleshooting.

The components described here are extremely complex objects and APIs that make up the Windows Server print service. This chapter should provide you with enough information to visualize the components and therefore be able to solve printing problems in Windows Server environments in an effective manner.

Before you can start setting up printers and printing you first need to set up your server with the Printer Services role. Do this using the Server Manager console as demonstrated in Chapters 1 and 2. Once the role is installed you will be able to access Print Management. This console provides a single interface with which you can administer multiple printers and print servers, including printers on legacy Windows 2000, Windows XP, Windows Server 2003, and Windows Vista.

Print Services

In Windows Server 2008, Microsoft has enabled the print administrator to set down policy and procedures for using printers. This is achieved with the Print Services subsystem. Print Services and its interface, the Print Management console, were given to us in Windows Server 2003, so it's a robust and well-oiled product of the last generation. It is now even better tuned to the management of printers over wide area networks, as well as printers that reside at branch offices and remote locations. (The Print Management console is shown later in the chapter in Figure 12-4.)

The Print Management console gives you a central portal that encapsulates all the printers connected to all the print servers on your network, no matter how remote. You can use the console to manage printer errors, and assist users in connecting to printers closest to them or at remote locations. The console also enables you to discover and install printers on local branch office subnets, and can even execute installation scripts you provide.

Understanding Windows Server Printer Services

To help you avoid getting hung up on terminology and concepts, look at the printer services from two different points of view: the logical environment and the physical environment. The logical environment is an abstraction of the physical device that the user sees. It includes the software required to interface to the physical environment. The physical environment represents the devices from which the final printed medium (usually paper) emerges.

Printer services: the logical environment

First of all, printers have no user interface other than a cryptic keypad and a small LCD screen. Their job is to receive data and to convert the data into information that a printer's electronics understands. The printer language or software lays out the page according to specifications in the data and goes about the task of sending this information to the physical parts that print the images onto a hard medium.

Therefore, if you're not able to print, and all the logical printer components check out, the only course of action you can take for a faulty printer is to ship it back to the factory or call a service technician (assuming you know little about corona wires, drums, and hoppers). For the most part, you need only know how to turn the printer or plotter on and off, change toner and paper, connect its interface cables, and clean it.

Windows Server, conversely, is both printer-aware and user-aware. Its task is to provide a logical printer interface that users can see and managers can manage and troubleshoot, as well as a holistic printer spooling and pooling environment. The logical printer, represented by the printer object, its icons, and properties, is representative of the hardware. The printer icon, or the printer share, is all the knowledge workers need to know about printing.

You can install logical printers on your client computers (local printers), but most of the time the logical printers are installed on servers dedicated to hosting logical printers (network printers).

The following list describes the basic user procedure to connect to and use a printer:

1. Install a logical local or remote printer to which you have access (the installation is persistent).

2. After you are connected, you can manage certain properties of the logical printer, such as paper size and layout, bins and trays, resolution and color, number of pages and copies, and so on.

3. You, or at least your users, then print documents and graphics to the logical printer. The action of printing is often called a job. The job encapsulates printing instructions for the printer service, telling the logical printer how the job should be printed to the physical printer. When a client application prints a document or image, the application calls the Windows graphic device interface (GDI), which loads the driver for the target printer. (The driver is downloaded from the server if it does not exist on the client machine. On Windows Server clients, the drivers are downloaded with every print job.)

   Using the driver for the target printer, the GDI renders the document in the printer language of the physical printer. After completion, the GDI then calls the local spooler, hands off the job, and closes. At this point, the GDI's work is done, and the client computer sends the job to the print server, via a routing service. The routing service transports the print job over the network using the remote procedure call service, the NetBIOS redirector.

4. After it has received the job from a print router or other interface, the logical printer, also called the printer service or client spooler, loads the necessary driver, which tells it how to interface to the physical printer and how to send it the document. This is done via the services of print providers and processors.

5. The print processor checks the job's data types and alters them or leaves them alone, depending on the requirements and the data types received. The print processor ensures that the job prints correctly.

6. If the data types call for separator page processing, the jobs are handed off to the separator page processor. The separator page is added to the front of the job.

7. Meanwhile, as printer administrator, you manage the logical printer's properties (the logical printer is an object), such as where it resides on the network, who has access to it, when they can use it, and so on.

The printer service, illustrated in Figure 12-1, includes several components and concepts, which are described in the following sections.

FIGURE 12-1

The Windows Server Print Service, represented as a stack of services.

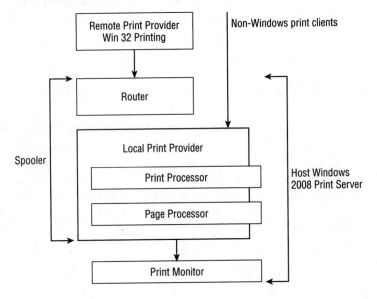

Print routers

Print routers sit between the client application and the print server (which can also be on the local machine, if printing to the parallel or serial port). The first job of the router is to route print jobs to the correct servers and print services. The second job of the router, once the target server is found, is to make sure the client has the correct driver for the job. The router checks the target server's driver with the client's, and if the client's driver is older or absent, the router updates the driver on the client machine.

> **NOTE** Routers are usually Win32 services. In other words, they cater to Windows printing. All other network clients, such as Unix, mid-range systems, and the Mac environment, get their jobs to the Windows Server print service via APIs that interface directly with the server service stack. As mentioned earlier, the XPS support in Windows Server 2008 extends the printing subsystem to allow XPS documents to print directly to XPS-compatible drives and devices.

Printer drivers

Printer drivers are the first variable components you provide when setting up logical printers. They are the software components sent to the user's software to enable it to create print jobs according to the capabilities of the target printers.

Printer drivers are built for specific printers or printer families. For example, you need one printer driver for jobs printed to the Hewlett Packard LaserJet 9000 printers and different drivers for jobs printed to LaserJet 3050 and LaserJet 21XX printers, respectively. However, LaserJet 4 and 5 drivers can print standard jobs printed to the old LaserJet III printers, but these older printers may not print a complex job generated by the LaserJet 4 or 5 driver (PCL and later).

Printer drivers are installed when you install and configure logical printing devices. You can also select alternative drivers after the logical printer has been installed.

Printer drivers are stored in the \system32\spool\drivers\ folder. Information about the drivers is stored in the registry of the hosting machine.

The drivers are grouped into raster printer drivers, which include the PCL standard and dot matrix printers and PostScript printer drivers, which are typically used for high-end graphics and publishing applications, the domain of the Apple/Mac computers and printers.

The spooler service stack

The spooler service is an engine — a collection of libraries — that controls each and every print job on a machine. It's best described as a stack, starting with a router service that can receive jobs handed off from client processes (refer to Figure 12-1). After arriving into the stack, the job is passed down to the print processor for rendering and then finally passed down to the Print Monitor for transmission to the I/O ports on the physical interfaces at either local or remote ports.

The spooler is also the service that controls client and server printer management, installation and administration of logical printers, and more. From the user's point of view, it's the functionality that exists behind the icons to which users send their print jobs. Each Windows Server machine has one spooler service.

The spooler is under the control of the service control manager. It can be stopped and started at any time. You need only shut down the spooler service (using the `net stop spooler` command) to stop all printing services on a machine. The spooler is part of the Win32 subsystem and is never deleted or relocated. It's owned by the local system account, and a number of child processes and services depend on it.

The spooler service is also responsible for client-side printer management. In fact, when you stop the service, the machine can't request or send print jobs to the logical shared printers on a server machine. In other words, the spooler service acts as either a client or server service, as needed.

The spooler service creates the files (spool jobs or files) in the directory where it resides. The service and files are installed by default in the `\windows\system32\spool\printers` folder, so if your server hosts a large number of print jobs, you should consider redirecting the print jobs to a volume dedicated to servicing printers. Changing the path value in the printer's registry key does this. The key in question is as follows:

```
HKEY_LOCAL_MACHINE\SYSTEM\ControlSet001\Control\Print\Printers
```

The XPS Document Writer keys are also located at the preceding registry hive. The value is a drive letter and subfolder path, not the UNC path. After the value has changed, stop and restart the print service. You can also set up separate folders for each printer's job, which is discussed next.

Spooler output files

These are the files that are generated by the spooler service (specifically, the print provider component) for each job it handles. After the job has been sent to the printer successfully, the spooler files are deleted. The spooler output files consist of two types of files — the spool file and the shadow file. They serve the following purpose:

- **Spool file.** This file has the `.spl` extension and is the print job — what gets sent to the printer.

- **Shadow file.** This file has the `.shd` extension. It contains the information needed for the print job, and is useful only to the print service components. It contains information related to the job's position in the queue, the job's owner, the printer's destination, and so on.

To redirect the spool files for each printer to a separate volume or folder, change the target printer's default spool directory key. The key in question is as follows:

```
HKEY_LOCAL_MACHINE\SYSTEM\ControlSet001\Control\Print\Printers
```

Drill down to the printer in question and then look for the SpoolDirectory data item. You can then change the value (the default is blank). Remember that the value must be a drive letter and folder, not the UNC. This is demonstrated in Figure 12-2. The reason for redirecting these spool files to custom directories is explained next.

FIGURE 12-2

Changing the spool directory for a printer.

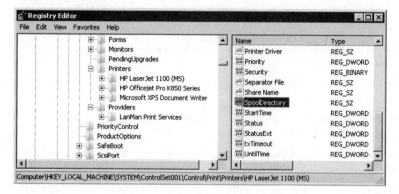

Print queues

Windows print queues are the previously mentioned print files (the collection of .spl files) waiting in the spool folder to be printed. Each spooled job prints in the order it is received. You can use the net print command at the command line to manage a job, or you can work with the document interactively via the respective printer's management interface (accessing the printer management interface for both local and remote computers is described later in this chapter).

If you manage a lot of printers, redirecting each printer's spool files to a separate folder can make it easier to manage the printer queue from the command line. If a print job hangs for some reason, you may begin your diagnostics with the print queue. If the queue receives the file from the user, the client spooler service process is not the problem. The next diagnostic step is to determine why the job is sitting in the queue but going nowhere.

The print processor

The print processor is the .dll file (such as Wntprint.dll) that resides in the \system32 \spool\prtprocs\w32x86 folder. This library of functions takes the print job data sent by the spooler and renders it into data the printer can understand (if the data is already understandable, it isn't rendered). Most print jobs don't require any intervention by the print processor, unless you have peculiar output requirements.

The default data type spooled to printers by the processor is NT EMF, which can be handled by most printers. EMF stands for Enhanced Metafile Format, and most printers can read it. You don't have to intervene and change the print processor libraries very often because the client applications determine the data type to be sent and because you can't choose or force a job to be handled by any particular print processor. This work is handled automatically.

Windows Server comes with built-in print processors. The one installed by default is known as WinPrint, and it handles the standard data types printed by Windows applications. You can find the libraries for the XPS Document Writer at \\system32\spool\tools. Another important print processor is SFMPSPRT — the Macintosh print processor — which handles jobs sent to PostScript printers. The Macintosh print processor is installed when you install Macintosh services on the host machine; however, you can only deploy Macintosh services on Windows Server 2003. WinPrint can handle the following data types:

- **NT EMF version 1.00x.** EMF stands for Enhanced Metafile Format. These files can be printed to most printers.

- **RAW.** This data type job indicates to the print processor that nothing further needs to be done to print the document.

- **RAW (FF appended).** This type forces the print processor to check whether a form feed has been added to the end of the job — to ensure that the last page exits the printer.

- **RAW (FF auto).** This type does not issue a form feed, and the print processor adds it to the end of the job automatically.

- **TEXT.** This data type is usually issued for printers that do not accept direct text. The print processor renders the text to meet the needs of the target printer.

NOTE The Macintosh print processor, SFMPSPRT, on Windows Server 2003 R2 SP1, renders jobs to non-PostScript printers for the benefit of Mac clients. However, the output is limited to the very basic "playout" (to use a Mac-DTP phrase for sending a job to the printer). The default data type is PSCRIPT1, which is a Windows bitmap format that prints to the non-PostScript printers. The best you can do for Mac clients is to install PostScript printers (or face the wrath of the Mac maniacs), which provides the high resolution and graphics capabilities DTP publishers require, regardless of whether the client is Mac or Windows or Linux.

Ports

The term *port* is loosely used to refer to the hardware connections that enable a data stream to flow from one device or medium to another. Print servers and printer interface equipment use ports to represent network and cable connections. Ports are assigned network addresses and reside between the printer and the spooler service.

Print monitors

Print monitors are important components to understand. They are soft devices that control the transmission process of the print job to the I/O ports on the devices that interface with the physical printer. Windows Server supports several standard print monitors. Print monitors perform the following tasks in the print service:

- They open a connection between the print processor and the port. The connection is then used to transfer the data to the I/O ports of the physical printer or remote printer interface. In essence, they touch the actual ports at the interfaces on the remote print servers or printer interface devices.

- They monitor the print job for error messages, progress, and completion.

The print monitor essentially monitors the entire print job and reports its status back to the spooler. If a print job times out for some reason, the monitor notifies the spooler, and the spooler sends a message to the client.

Several print monitors are built into Windows Server 2008. You can see the list when attempting to create a new port for the job data connection. Unfortunately, Windows Server 2008, like its predecessor, tends to create confusion between the monitor type and the actual I/O port, as illustrated in Figure 12-3.

FIGURE 12-3

The Ports tab in the Properties dialog box.

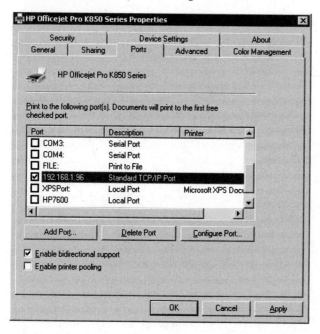

Why is it so important to understand the role of the monitor? It's usually the first component in the print service stack that alerts you to a print problem and its most common reason — inability to communicate with the local or remote port. If the print monitor reports that there's a problem connecting to a remote port, you have a network problem (IP, or lower on the network stack). Usually, a trip to the printer finds the network cable kicked out of the network drop or the interface unit.

Various monitors are bundled with Windows Server.

Local print monitor

The local print monitor (formerly `localmon.dll` and now built into `localspl.dll`) manages the following ports:

- **Parallel interface.** This interface caters to print jobs that are sent to the parallel port on the computer initiating the job. Most machines support parallel port printing. You choose this monitor when you set up a local printer connected directly to the host. The local printer can also be shared, which makes it a network printer.

- **Serial interface.** This interface provides the same service as the parallel interface. The data, however, is transmitted through the serial interface, a communications port (such as COM1 or COM2), instead of the parallel interface. Serial interfacing is not common on printers.

- **USB, infrared, and wireless (the likes of 802.1X and Bluetooth).** Windows Server 2008 supports USB printing, infrared, and various shades of wireless printing. The local print monitor and its user interface components provide the means to set up these printers in the same location as the legacy parallel and serial interfaces and the remote ports (such as LPR and IP).

- **File.** This interface enables you to spool the job to a filename. The job is identical to jobs that are spooled directly to print interfaces, local or network. The option of wrapping up the data into a file enables you to relocate the file to another system for printing. In other words, the physical printer does not have to be present or locatable on your network to be of service.

This option is convenient if you do not actually own or have access to the target physical printer. If you need to print to very expensive printers, such as the Linotronic typesetters and heavy-duty PostScript printers run by service bureaus and printing companies, you can print the job to a file and then send the file to the service via the Internet or on a disk. All you need to do is install the driver for the target printer. (By the way, PostScript print files are binary.) Print files are printed using various commands at the command prompts of the target machines from which they are printed.

LPR print monitor (TCP/IP printing)

As soon as you put some distance between the physical printers and the computers from which you are requesting the print service, you establish a network-printing environment. The protocol suite of choice for a heterogeneous computing/printing environment is TCP/IP, and you would be well advised to aim for a homogenous TCP/IP printer network. In particular, the Line Printer Remote (LPR) and Line Printer Daemon (LPD) service is used as a standard for TCP/IP printing. It was derived from the Berkeley Unix standards. LPR and LPD printing becomes available on Windows Server 2008 only after Services for Unix are installed on the server.

Windows Server 2008 supports LPR/LPD printing with the services of the LPR/LPD environment and the LPR print monitor. The LPR monitor is installed by default when you install Windows Server 2008. If you installed Services for Unix on Windows Server 2003, additional TCP/IP printing support were added to the printing system to support printers connected to Unix servers. Alas, Services for Unix are not supported on Windows Server 2008 as of RTM.

The LPR port can be used for all TCP/IP printing environments, especially for connecting to remote printer interface devices that do not support a custom TCP/IP daemon or service. You can also use the LPR service to connect to printers hanging off the local ports of Unix computers and to big iron, such as VAX, MVS, and AS/400.

The LPR/LPD facilities are provided by the TCP/IP Print Server service, which is installed when you install Windows Server 2008. Typing LPR at the command prompt returns several command-line commands for LPR printing.

Standard TCP/IP print monitor

By default, Windows Server 2008 also installs a standard TCP/IP print monitor that enables you to create a port to any network interface device or printer that supports IP.

Third-party print monitors

Third-party monitors may need to be loaded when you install printers that require custom or proprietary print monitors. All printer manufacturers create print monitors that can be installed into the printer service at any time, post-installation of Windows Server 2008. These include the following legacy print monitors:

- **Digital's print monitor.** Note the apostrophe after Digital. The possessive denotes that the monitor is technology belonging to Digital Equipment Corporation (or DEC, which is now part of Hewlett-Packard Company) and not "digital" as in binary, which is a common presumption.

   The Digital print monitor is not installed as a default monitor and ships with DEC products, such as the DEColorwriter. It requires the DECnet protocol from Digital, which runs atop TCP/IP, typical of the network protocol tomfoolery of the last century.

- **Hewlett Packard's print monitor.** The older Hewlett Packard monitor talks to HP's printers and plotters and JetDirect devices. This monitor requires that the DLC protocol be added to the network services. The old HP monitor is essentially useless because it does not support TCP/IP. In the event that you need to install it, possibly to enable the server to cater to printing from the mainframe and mid-range environments, remember that DLC is not a routable protocol. The server and printer must be on the same network segment.

   The JetDirect print monitor is a new technology that can use several protocols, including TCP/IP and IPX/SPX (no longer supported on Windows Server 2008). The JetDirect print monitor is installed during installation of the JetDirect printer drivers and management software. You can route IP print job packets to a JetDirect card anywhere on the planet.

- **Lexmark print monitor.** Another big printer manufacturer is Lexmark. Windows Server 2008 supports both Lexmark DLC and TCP/IP print monitors.

Printer services: the physical environment

To use Windows Server printer services, you need a computer that can act as a host for the services. If you support a large network, dedicate a server to the role of printer server.

All of the Windows Server operating systems support printer server services. The only difference is the degree of availability. The servers (Standard, Enterprise, and the 64-Bit Edition [Data Center]) are designed to host a large number of connections, whereas workstations are typically restricted to no more than ten concurrent connections (as was the predecessor to Vista). Windows Server 2008 enables you to cluster the printer service for maximum availability.

Experience has shown us over the years that the size of the company or group has little to do with how much hardware you need to throw at print services. For instance, we manage small insurance companies that print five times the number of documents that our larger clients do. Here are some "street" rules for determining the hardware resources needed for a print server:

- If you can determine that RAM holds 10 MB of print data at any given time, provide at least 30 MB for expansion.

- Provide three to five times more hard disk space for print spools and queues or enable the volumes to be easily extended (see Chapter 13). This might be hard for you to determine when first setting up the print service on a server, but you can easily predict your needs. If all your users are printing concurrently — or at least within a few minutes of each other — total the size of all their documents in the spool folders. These documents sit in the spooler on the hard disk until the service sends them to the printer, so provide at least three times more hard disk space than the total of all document sizes sent to the printer. You never know when someone will decide to send the entire tax rulebook of the Internal Revenue Service to the printer, over the weekend.

- Printing is a demanding service. At one of our clients, we have as many as 40 printers on one server alone, so it makes sense to ensure that the print server machine has a processor to be proud of.

- Color printing or printing complicated graphics requires a lot of processor bandwidth. A dedicated server should service these needs, especially in terminal environments.

Print servers

Several hardware components combine to complete the printing system. Unfortunately, the names of the components do not always mean the same thing to everyone. The print server, in our book, is a computer that "serves" printer interfaces to users on the network, as previously discussed. Printer interfaces (logical printers) are established on the server and act as representatives or portals to the printers, either on the network or attached directly to the parallel ports of the computer.

Print devices

A *print device* is what Microsoft calls the physical printer hardware. If you ask your user where his or her print device is, he or she will probably draw a blank, but the term seems to have become a Microsoft standard. To stay on the same page as your customers, stick with "printer" and avoid overcomplicating things with redundant phrases.

Local printers are connected directly to the parallel, serial, USB, and wireless ports of computers, whereas network printers can interface directly to the network with the help of network interface components (NICs). The components can be network interface devices or NICs built directly into the printer.

Network interface devices

The makers of these interface boxes say they have a claim to the term *print server*, and some even stamp "print server" on their product. We suggest referring to them by their brand names — such as Lantronix box or JetDirect card — it results in less explaining.

These guys are very useful and exist for the following reasons:

- They obviate the need to hook up a computer parallel port to every printer in the office. Instead, the printer cable is attached to a parallel port on the box, which attaches to the network via a network interface port.

- In large companies, the print servers (computers) are locked away in cooled server rooms, and the printers are located either near their users or in printing rooms. The interface device enables the printer and the print server computer to coexist some distance away from each other. At one of our clients, we support label printers in many distribution centers that are installed at loading docks and bays where food is packed and shipped. We would not want to locate an expensive Pentium or AS/400 at every dock just to print labels.

- They provide a network interface to the printer, enabling you to place a printer at any convenient location where you have a network drop.

- They support a variety of networks, such as Token Ring and Ethernet, and support all the most popular protocols, especially TCP/IP.

- They are packed with smart electronics and embedded software that enable you to manage their network protocols, such as assigning network addresses, printing capability, and communications with the printer. They are equipped with terminal access and daemons for remote management. You can telnet into them or even access their internals from a Web browser.

- They enable you to connect more than one printer to the network at a single network drop and address (many printers on one IPv4 or IPv6 address). The interface directs the inbound job to an IP port assigned to the printer. (Remember that standard IPv4 supports up to 65,536 ports.)

- They come with built-in memory to further queue documents sent by the server.

These interfaces are very useful, inexpensive, and compact. Keep them hidden out of harm's way, such as under the printer, in a printer cabinet, or behind the printer stand. We have a collection of dead Lantronix boxes — each no bigger than a pack of West Virginia's filtered finest — that have been tortured with cigarette butts, coffee spills, shoe prints, and electric shock. They also have a habit of going into indefinite seclusion, never to be seen or heard again.

Multi-function printers (MFPs) now come equipped with fax, scanning, and printing capability. The smaller models, and smaller single print-only devices, do not offer Ethernet ports and interface only to the USB ports of the host computer. To share these devices, you typically share them through the host workstation. You can share these devices without a host computer with a separate printer server device as described earlier, but it's best to share a printer specially built or configured for workgroup sharing, and one that has a built-in Ethernet port and print server functionality.

Print Services Strategy

Providing print services to the enterprise should be a well-planned exercise. Although it appears easy enough to install printers, it makes sense to create blueprints or policy governing printer installation, usage, access, naming, administration, and more.

Often, you arrive at a company only to find that your predecessor knew his or her printing environment like a palm tree knows where its coconuts fall. Troubleshooting such an environment is almost impossible, and it's best to scrap what you inherited and start all over again. Your best course of action would be to create a new logical printer environment and then move users to the new environment in phases.

As a starting point, the guidelines for setting up a strategic print service plan are discussed in the following sections.

Printer taxonomy

Printers that users print to are not the actual printer devices, but logical printers set up in Windows Server, and these printers can thus go by several aliases. As discussed later, one physical print device can be used by several groups that "map" to the printer as different shares, targeting different aliases. You must establish a consistent and practical naming scheme or convention to cater to a varied user environment.

Although it may not seem important if you already have hundreds of printers set up in many different places or if the printer administrator's job recently became your responsibility, create a naming scheme for your printers if you do not have any. A large company could have as many as 1,000 physical printers plugged in everywhere, and their logical printer namespace may contain as many as 1,500 names.

The naming scheme should be simple. Put "HP" in all Hewlett Packard printer names, "Xe" in all Xerox printer names, "Ne" in NEC printer names, and so on. For example: HP5LSI_MIS1 is the share name for the main MIS Hewlett Packard 5LSI printer, and the name HP5LSI_MIS2 may be the same printer shared for after-hour use.

You can also name printers by their location, which is especially useful if you have printers located all over. A naming convention could be two letters for region or continent, such as "NA" for North America; two letters for country, such as "US"; two or more letters for city, such as "BOCA," and then the number of the printer or device, such as "PRN01." The name of a printer could end up as NAUSBOCAPRN01.

If you are naming by location and type of device, populate the description and comment fields for each printer, described later in this chapter.

Keep the names simple and try not to leave blank spaces, such as HP MIS1b. Blank spaces make it difficult for advanced users or administrators to map to printers from the command line using the net use command, or from within scripts. Names with spaces need to be enclosed between quotes, which wastes time. Rather, use underscores to represent spaces in the name.

Keep the name as short as possible; it doesn't need to explain life itself. You can be as descriptive as necessary in the Description fields and in the Active Directory, as you'll soon discover. We have encountered printer names you need a cipher to read. If the admin can't shout the name across the room or over the telephone — "You need to map to HP_MIS1b" — then the name is too complex. Consider this e-mail recently received from an associate in a sister company: "You can send the reports to $_IKY14_T_MAT_MGT5." This "fifth" printer allegedly belonged to the materials management group on the fourteenth floor of the "Tier" building somewhere in Kentucky.

Easy share names also work well for users. In our accounting department, we named all our printers HP_ACT1 to HP_ACT12. The ACT is short for accounting, but it didn't take long before users associated the printers with Shakespeare.

Creating print groups

Here we go again reminding you not to give share access or permissions to individuals (in permissions and access control), but rather to work with groups. Even if the printer belongs to a group of one person, you never know when someone else may need to print to the same printer. A good example is an executive who has a personal printer in his or her office. If you create the logical printer in Windows Server and add only the name of the executive to the printer object's access control list, the executive's assistant can't print to that printer. If a group has access, then the assistant can be added to the group.

Using groups in access control and permissions enables effective printer management. Under our corporate policy of controlled access, groups are only given access to certain printers at certain times and for certain jobs. We believe it's best to limit group access to all network printers. Otherwise, a disaster awaits. We've seen a user send ten copies of a 1,500-page report to a small printer that could not handle the job, causing urgent smaller documents to wait indefinitely for a chance to print. If you plan well, you won't have to spend half your life deleting and purging failed jobs from print queues.

Not too long ago, we received a call from a CEO's assistant saying he sent a highly secret document to the wrong printer, which he couldn't find — anxiety was mounting. We found the document before it printed by tracing the queues and looking for his call sign (ownership). Now the CEO can only print to a printer that does not specifically deny him access.

Controlling access to printers is discussed later in this chapter.

Creating a print network

Creating a print network, used exclusively for printers, is a worthwhile exercise. It helps keep other devices and machines from invading the printer's address space and makes it easier to manage the printer requirement. Here are some points to consider:

■ **TCP/IP.** The protocol of choice for most printer networks is TCP/IP. If possible, stick to one network protocol. Managing a network of more than one protocol adds dollars to your total cost of ownership. Most models and makes support TCP/IP. Even modern PostScript printers can be assigned an IP address, even though AppleTalk drives them. Older printers and environments (such as VMS, MVS, NetWare, and so on) prefer to talk LAT, IPX, Pathworks, and so on, but for a Windows Server print network, you may as well introduce Klingon into the school syllabus.

■ **Subnet.** For organizations with several printers, it's best to create one or more subnets exclusively for printers. One class C subnet caters to 254 printers or more on printer inter-face devices, which would likely be more than enough addresses for a company of 3,000 paper monkeys. If you manage several interconnected offices or sites on a WAN, reserv-ing a block (10 or 20) of addresses out of the class C on the site should suffice. Don't add a second subnet to the site just for a bushel of printers; it adds stress to the routing and replication bandwidth on which DNS and Active Directory depend.

■ **DHCP.** Ensure that the printer IP address range doesn't get used by DHCP. This is easily handled by reserving the block of addresses in the DHCP service (see Chapter 4).

Keeping drivers current

The print routers receive the printer driver from the server every time they make a connection. Keep current and available the printer drivers for every make and model of printer you deploy. Windows Server 2008 ships with more drivers than FedEx and UPS combined, as opposed to the 2,500 (give or take a few) that shipped with Windows 2000, so the library on the disk is more than sufficient.

The following provides two good reasons for this important task:

■ **Staying current.** By regularly updating the drivers, you ensure that users always have access to the latest feature the drivers publish and that you have maintenance releases that fix earlier release defects. Printer drivers become out-of-date very quickly. You can keep drivers current using the Windows Update service.

■ **Availability.** Making sure servers hold and keep current printer drivers for every printer you deploy ensures that whenever a client connects to a printer (an old or new logical printer) the latest driver is available. This keeps printing delays to a minimum and reduces the volume of support calls.

Installing and Setting Up Printers

When you install printers on a server, they usually install as local printers printing to remote TCP/IP ports. Local printers, by definition, are printers that coexist with a server, which acts as its proxy. Local printers are shared as files and folders so that user groups may map to them and use their services.

Just because the physical printer is established out on the network somewhere does not mean it's a network printer; it must still be installed as a local printer (remember, you are installing a logical printer). Installing the network printer option does not make your server a proxy for the printer. It only gives you the capability to connect to and print from the remote network printer. Installing a network printer only makes you another client, which is not your objective.

Before you begin installing a new local printer, keep the following parameters and data handy:

- If you have a TCP/IP printer network, assign the new IP address for the remote port, be it on a printer interface device or on the printer itself. Ensure that the DHCP server reserves the IP address, and mark the IP address as assigned on an IP address allocation list or database you keep.

- If you are setting up a port on a remote printer interface device, make up a network name for the device. The name can be derived from the name of the device given by the manufacturer, a serial number, and even a MAC (hardware) address.

- Have all printer drivers handy. If you do not maintain an install directory on the server, you may need your Windows Server 2008 install CDs within arm's reach.

Installing the local printer

Follow these steps to install a local printer:

1. Log on to the Print Server computer as an administrator group member. You can do this from the console or log on over a terminal session.

2. From Administrative Tools, select Printers or the Print Management menu item. The Print Management console opens. This is illustrated in Figure 12-4.

3. Drill down to the Print Server node, right-click, and choose Add Printer. This launches the Network Printer Installation Wizard. The printer may be connected directly to your server, or your server may be in Little Rock, Arkansas, U.S.A., and the printer can be in Zululand, Natal, South Africa. As mentioned earlier in this chapter, choose Network Printer only when the printer you are installing is not going to be serviced by the local computer as its printer server, host, or proxy.

4. Next, choose the option "Search the network for printers." This is the fastest way to connect to a printer over the network. Print Management will find the printer on the network for you and present it for configuration. From here on you will be ask to supply a driver for the printer and search the list of supported printers to find a suitable library for the newly discovered printer. End of story.

FIGURE 12-4

The Print Management console.

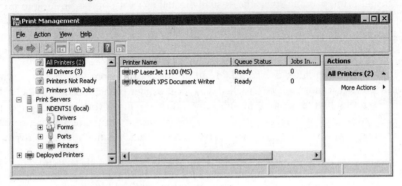

If the printer is indeed installed in Zululand, you need an IP address for the port on the printer or on the print device interface box to which your Zulu printer is connected. Note that you can also choose a parallel port (the LPT port) or a COM port if the printer actually is connected to the server computer with a data cable.

For demo purposes, let's assume the printer is a Zebra printer located 9,000 miles away in Zululand. In this case, you must create an LPR port and assign it the IP address you have handy. (If you don't have the IP address handy, stop everything and get it.) In this case you would choose the second option for TCP/IP printing and direct IP assignment by host name resolution. The remote IP address will be made available as a local port, or you can choose the option to add a new port.

5. Go ahead and choose the last option to add a port. After you click Next, you will be given the option to name the port. Next choose the option to install a new driver and click Next (this is demonstrated in Figure 12-5). If you are unable to find the correct driver on the server, simply choose the option to use a driver installation CD as the source.

6. Now, to use the LPD option for direct TCP/IP printer for Unix devices and the like you need to install the LPR Port Monitor. This can be done on the Add Features option in the Initial Configuration Tasks Wizard (see Chapter 2). On the Select a Printer Port screen of the Add Printer Wizard, check the Create a New Port option and then choose the LPR port option from the Type of Port drop-down menu. Click Next to load the Add LPR-compatible Printer dialog box. You are prompted to provide a name or IP address for the port. If possible, provide the IP address, because name resolution just slows things down (the IP address should be permanently assigned to this port in any event).

Now provide the name. The far-away printer is hanging off a Lantronix server, so the typical name we use identifies the port as being on a Lantronix printer "server."

Because we discussed the function of the print monitor earlier, note here that the LPR print monitor immediately tries to touch the remote IP address. The LPR Port Configuration Warning shown in Figure 12-6 pops up if the IP address or remote server does not respond to a test packet sent by the monitor. At this point, you can abandon the installation in order to test the IP address or the remote device or you can continue with the setup and return to troubleshooting later. Either option returns you to the same point. It's no big deal to return later to change the IP address or other settings, as shown later.

FIGURE 12-5

Choosing a printer.

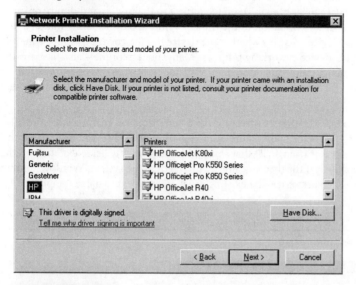

FIGURE 12-6

An LPR port error.

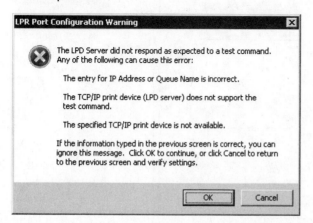

This message may occur for several reasons:

- The IP address could be bad or unreachable. Troubleshoot the address using ping, tracert, or other TCP/IP tools described in Chapter 3.

- If the address is valid, the interface device may not be working properly. Diagnose that problem with the tools that ship with the device.

- The device may not be connected to the network, or it may be connected but not have power. Whatever the reason, someone at the remote site must troubleshoot the device. Many interface devices enable you to connect to the printer and dump, or print setup and diagnostics information to the printer. Printing out the configuration and setting in the device tells you whether the device has the correct IP address installed and whether the device is working properly. Many modern printers also have the capability to print configuration and address information. If the device is set up with the wrong IP address, as is usually the case, then a simple change gets your device installed and working.

7. Click Next to load the printer driver for the printer from the manufacturer list, illustrated in Figure 12-5. If the printer you are installing is not in the list, you need to get the driver from the Internet or from a CD that ships with the printer. Click Next after you have selected the driver. If the driver is already installed on the system, Windows prompts you accordingly to replace or use the existing driver. Click Next to name the printer.

FIGURE 12-7

Location and comment information.

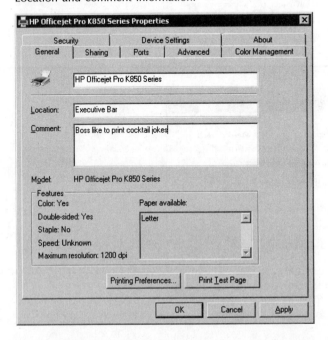

8. Click Next to share the printer. Then click Next to provide information about the location and use of the printer. You can also access the property pages of the printer once it is installed, as shown in Figure 12-7.

9. Finally, you can choose to print a test page. Do it. Click the test page but do not use the troubleshooter. In other words, respond Yes to the prompt asking whether the test page printed correctly, even if you have no idea what came out, halfway across the planet. It's not that we don't trust the troubleshooter. If we agreed that the test page did not print, we would not be wasting time hyperlinking our way around the help system. After you've troubleshot several printer problems, the troubleshooter becomes a waste of time. The test page is more useful as a means of sending a document to the printer without having to leave the printer configuration to send a page. You can then check the queue of the printer. If the test page has not printed after a few minutes, you need to troubleshoot. Meanwhile, your new printer service is installed. Before you have access to it, you must still do some fine-tuning.

Publishing Printers

Printers are a resource, but you can either make them available to users or hide them. When printers are made available — when they can be found on the network — users try to connect to them and print, oblivious to any permissions or policy you may have set. If you don't want certain printers used by various groups, you have to lock them down, even hide them away.

Conversely, if you are going to make a printer share available, you should make it easily locatable, not only to ease your workload, but also so that the user or the administrator installing the printer as a network printer can find it. This is what we call *publishing printers*.

Locating printers

Printers can easily be located by browsing the printer servers, as is the case with legacy Windows NT printer servers. The printer can then be installed on a client machine for printing — using the Add Printer Wizard or via the net use command.

Locating the printer in Active Directory

You can also publish printers in Active Directory. You can search an enterprise for a printer that serves your purpose. Let's say you are looking for a printer that can print on both sides of the page and that has stapling capability.

If the printer has been published in Active Directory, you can ask the directory to search for printers matching your specifications, as illustrated in Figure 12-8. You can then look up the printer's manager or contact person and request access to the printer. This is great for large or widely dispersed organizations, where machine count can run into the hundreds or thousands.

FIGURE 12-8

Searching for a printer in the directory.

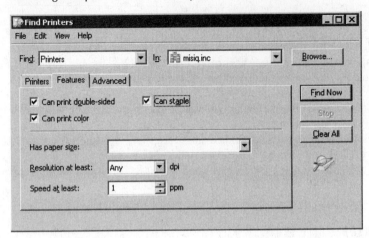

To publish or list the printer in Active Directory, you don't have to do anything other than ensure that the server is an active member of a domain. When a server is authenticated as a domain member, Windows Server 2008 enables the server to publish its shares in the directory. You can also expressly refuse to publish the shares by unchecking the List in the Directory checkbox found on the Shares tab or the printer properties.

The print server need not be a domain member to make its print shares available. You can map to the printer share of a standalone machine in the directory as follows:

1. Select the OU in AD in which to publish the share. Right-click the OU, select New, and choose Printer.

2. Enter a UNC name to the share name, as illustrated in Figure 12-9. Although the dialog box refers to pre-Windows Server 2008 print shares, this is how you list standalone Windows Server 2008 print server shares in the directory. You can also map to the IP address used by the server with \\192.168.10.57\HP1.

Locating printers over the Web

With Internet Information Services fully integrated into the Windows Server 2008 operating systems, clients can connect to the print server's printers via the HTTP protocol if IIS is installed and started. Upon connecting to a logical printer share on the server, the server automatically updates the client with the necessary printer driver.

This is a wonderful service for large intranets and service bureaus — a print manager with a flare for HTML can customize the pages for each printer, publishing its features, connection parameters, usage requests, and so on.

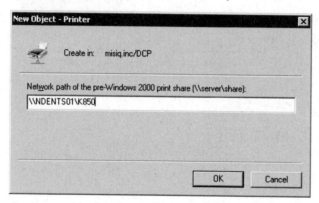

Manually listing a printer in Active Directory.

Clients connect to the printer using their Web browsers as follows:

- `HTTP//servername/printers`. This Web page lists all the logical printers hosted by the server identified in the URL. The information entered when the printer was first installed is listed on the page, as well as status information, and more.

- `HTTP//servername/logicalprinter_share`. This URL connects you directly to the logical printer.

Hiding printers

You can hide print shares the same way you hide folders — by appending the dollar sign ($) to the end of the share name, such as `HP_MIS8$`. You can still map to the share from the command line, using the `net use` command, but you must use the exact printer share name.

If you want to hide the share, remember not to list it in the directory when you first install it as a local printer.

Printer pools

Pooling is another means of publishing printers. Several printers can be grouped together to form a contiguous print resource. Note the checkbox on the Port tab that is checked, as illustrated in Figure 12-10.

Printer pooling is ideal for a shop that prints a high volume of documents. Print jobs don't have to wait for a job on one printer to finish. If another printer is free, the jobs automatically route to the first free printer.

FIGURE 12-10

Pooling logical printers.

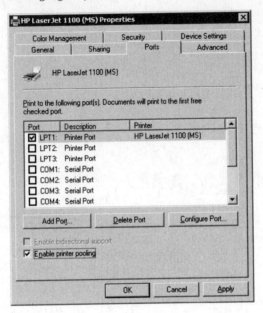

To create a pool of printers, do the following:

1. Install your group of identical printers as local printers. Create as many ports as printers to be added to the pool.

2. Check the Enable Printer Pooling checkbox.

3. Check all the ports on which a member of the pool is installed (see Figure 12-11 later in this chapter). It's important to ensure that each port has an identical printer connected to it.

Loading printer ports

Windows Server 2008 enables you to create multiple logical printers and assign them to the same port. We coined the phrase "loading the ports" to describe this technique, which can be considered a many-to-one setup: many logical printers to one physical printer or port. Each logical printer is a separate instance of the printer object. In other words, you can create several logical printers, all printing to the same physical device and the same physical port.

The following list describes the benefits of loading printer ports:

- **Printer configuration.** Each logical printer can be configured differently for various reasons. Availability, sharing, permissions, and device settings can be different for each logical printer. On one printer, you might provide access to group A to print certain jobs, while on another logical printer you might provide access to group B running other jobs. One printer might be available at night, while another is only available during the day (when the office is busier).

- **Job prioritizing.** Certain logical printers can be given priority over print jobs. Setting the `priority` property of the logical printer achieves this. One printer can be set up under a high priority to only enable access to users who can justify high-priority printing privileges.

- **Delegating Admin functions.** Each logical printer has its own print manager and queue. Document administrators can be assigned to manage the documents in the queues belonging to the logical printers installed in their OUs.

- **Sharing physical printers.** Several organizational units, or departments, can share a single printer. Instead of lumping all the users into one group, it makes more sense to create a logical printer for each group. Separator pages identify each group's job.

Prioritizing jobs can't be done automatically on the same logical printer. If one job requires priority over another job, you can pause the lower-priority job and enable the urgent job to "jump the queue." This becomes tricky and tiresome when several documents are queued. It's better to create another logical printer on the same port and then set a higher print priority for the latter logical printer

How can you do this? The logical printer has a `priority` property that can be set from the lowest value of one to the highest value of 99. Jobs that are sent to the printer with the higher priority setting print before the lower-priority jobs.

You can achieve this as follows:

1. Create a second logical printer on the same port (loading) as the regular printer.
2. Select the printer in Print Management and right-click its icon. Select Properties and zero in on the Advanced tab, shown in Figure 12-11. In the Priority text box, select the priority (you can make it the highest if this printer is the most important) and click OK.

Now when users need to print urgent jobs, they can print to the second printer. Create a special group for the latter printer, which can be used for people who have priority over others. When a user needs to print a job urgently, you can temporarily admit him or her to the group.

FIGURE 12-11

The Advanced tab in the Properties dialog box.

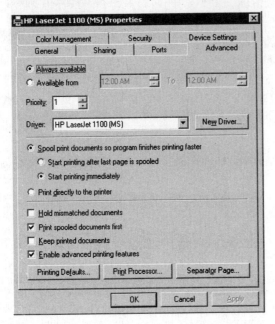

Printer Administration

Long gone are the days when the only printers we set up in the average office were simple laser printers and dot matrix printers. Today, it would be ridiculous to expect the OS to cater to all the features of the numerous printer brands and models. Instead, Microsoft publishes APIs that enable the printer manufacturer to hook into system management facilities to manage and configure the printer. Still, a number of common features are accessible from the printer configuration dialog boxes.

There are three tiers of Windows Server 2008 printer administration. First, we can control how and what printers print, and when they can print it. This is printer-centric management. Second, we can control which jobs print; we can delete them, pause them, redirect them, and cancel them. This is job-centric management. Finally, we can publish printer shares and control who has access to the printer, when they have that access, and what they can print. This is printer access control. Let's first deal with printer management functions.

Printer management

The job of the printer manager requires strong organizational skills. Using the techniques provided in this chapter, you can create logical printers, install network interface devices, install physical printers onto the network interface devices, provide access to the printers, delegate administration, and more. In essence, as a printer manager, you have to do everything this chapter covers, including the following chores.

Setting separator pages

Setting separator pages, or banners if you prefer NetWare terminology, can be tedious work, but in very busy printing environments producing substantial documents, they are essential.

Separator pages separate jobs. They also can be used to provide information about jobs and can print at the beginning of each print job, in front of the first page. They don't affect printing order of the jobs or pagination. Consider the following key reasons for using separator pages:

- **Tracking down job owners.** We had several high-end printers to which many people printed every day. At the end of each day, hundreds of documents were forgotten by their owners. At the end of the week, a huge pile of uncollected documents was getting thrown out (Web pages, white papers, press releases, e-mail, and so on). The situation got worse by the day, and it didn't take long to recognize the waste of time and materials. The situation called for separator pages, to enable a printer administrator to collect the jobs, identify the owners, and threaten them with disciplinary action if they did not collect their output. Habitual offenders were told they needed to clean up their act or they would lose their printing privileges.

- **Separating the print jobs in long runs.** If your printer is receiving large volumes of print runs, or continuous reports, the only way to pull complete jobs from the run or sort them easily is with separator pages. We have several printers that typically print reports on a round-the-clock basis, and all the jobs are separated by separator pages.

- **Organizing chaos at high-traffic printers.** After printing, many job owners dash off to the printer and wait for the paper to slide out of the hopper. If the printer is busy printing, eager beavers grab every freshly printed page, collecting pages and even whole jobs before other users can get to them. Meanwhile, uncollected jobs are stored in the pickup tray, and if separator pages don't exist, it doesn't take long to create job mayhem.

- **Job information.** Separator pages can be used with sophisticated printers to print job information, such as the owner, the language used (if the printer supports language changing on the fly), and so on.

Windows Server 2008 provides four types of separator page files, stored in the systemroot \System32 folder. Table 12-1 describes these pages.

The pages described in the Table 12-1 are not actually printed. They are script files that contain codes to instruct the print provider to print a separator page, and what to print on it. You can open and edit these files and customize them for your purposes. By default, the separator file instructs the printer to print the job owner's name, date, and job number.

TABLE 12-1

Separator Pages

Separator File	Purpose
PCL.SEP	Switches a dual-language HP printer to PCL mode printing
PSCRIPT.SEP	Switches a dual-language HP printer to PostScript mode printing
SYSPRINT.SEP	Used for PostScript printers
SYSPRTJ.SEP	Same as SYSPRINT.SEP but uses Japanese characters

To create your own separator file, copy the existing one (so you have an original) and modify the copy as needed. You can rename the file whatever you like, but give it the .sep extension. The contents of the Windows Server 2008 PCL file are as follows:

```
\
\H1B\L%-12345X@PJL ENTER LANGUAGE=PCL
\H1B\L&l1T\0
\M\B\S\N\U
\U\LJob : \I
\U\LDate: \D
\U\LTime: \T
\E
```

Note that the first character in each line of code is the backslash (\). This character denotes that the character following it is the escape code. You could use a character such as the @ sign as the escape code signifier (such as @E). The Windows Server 2008 escape codes are as follows:

- \B\M — Text is printed in double-width blocks until \U.
- \B\S — Text is printed in single-width blocks until \U.
- \E — Page eject.
- \Hn — Initiates a control sequence for which n is a hex code for the target printer (see the printer manual).
- \Fpath — Prints the contents of a file at path.
- \I — Job number.
- \Lxxx — Prints the characters in x following the escape code.
- \n — Skips n lines (zero moves to the next line).
- \N — Switches a dual-language HP printer to PCL mode printing.
- \T — Time the job was printed.
- \U — Turns off block character printing.
- \Wnn — Width of the separator page in characters.

Separator pages are set up on the print server computer as follows:

1. Select the printer from the Print Management dialog box. Right-click and select Properties. Then go to the Advanced tab, as illustrated in Figure 12-11.

2. Click Separator Page. You can type the name and path of the separator page, or you can browse for it. OK your way out of the Properties dialog box. The print provider now prints the separator page.

Some final advice about separator pages: They work well in high-print or high-job volume situations but are annoying for the small stuff. For every single sheet you print, out pops a separator page you have to throw away. To save the forests and your sanity, keep separator pages off the small jobs.

Mixing and matching forms and trays

Most printers today come with multiple trays for labels, envelopes, paper and form sizes, and more. Single-tray printers can be manually fed a form or you can enable the physical printer to automatically feed the form. You can also configure your printer to enable application users to select the paper or form size they need right from their applications.

To assign a form to a particular tray or form feeder, do the following:

1. Select the printer from the Print Management dialog box. Right-click, select Properties, and go to the Device Settings tab, shown in Figure 12-12.

2. Click the tray for which you want to assign paper sizes. A drop-down menu enables you to select from a list of standards-based paper sizes. Select a size and click OK.

FIGURE 12-12

Device settings.

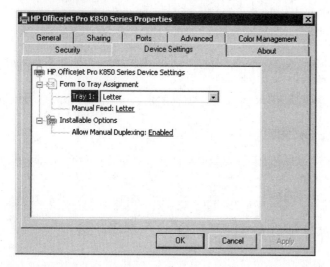

Job management

Server 2003 and printer administrators are frequently called to manage print jobs or documents. Windows Server 2008 enables you to delegate the job management function on an OU-to-OU basis. The following task list describes the job management functions that can be assigned to job management administrators. The job management options are accessible from the context menu (right-clicking), the Printer menu, and the Document menu in the respective print queues dialog box, as illustrated in Figure 12-13.

The Print queue dialog box for a printer.

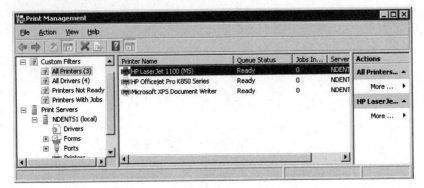

- **To pause a job.** Double-click the printer to open the queue or print job manager. Then select a printing document and right-click or click the Document menu. Select the Pause option. A checkmark appears next to the document to indicate that it's paused.

- **To pause all jobs.** Right-click the printer queue and select the option Use Printer Offline. All jobs are suspended.

- **To resume a job.** There are two ways to resume a job. You can pull down the Document menu again and select the Resume option, or you can right-click the job again and re-click the Pause option to clear the checkmark.

- **To cancel all jobs.** Right-click the queue window on any job and select the option to Cancel All Documents.

- **To delete a single job.** Select the document and press the Delete key.

You can redirect stalled jobs to another physical printer rather than delete them and resubmit them. The logical printer remains the same — just change the port and physical printer.

Open the properties of the logical printer, go to the Ports tab, and select a new port. As long as you know that the printer on the new port is working, is the same as the one you are redirecting from, and uses the same driver, your documents will print.

Advanced spool options

The default options on the Advanced tab work for the majority of printing environments, but the tab has several other options that are useful for troubleshooting and managing printers.

Available time

A logical printer is usually always available. However, it may be necessary to shut it down for some reason during the day. Some printers are so large and complex that refilling their trays can take up a lot of time, hoppers and bins may need to be cleaned, toner may need to be refilled, and so on.

In addition, you may shut down a logical printer to prevent certain groups from using it during specific hours. For example, a group might need exclusive access to the printer at a certain time, and they can't afford to have other users printing at that time (check printing is a good example).

To shut down the logical share at a certain time, toggle to the Time Available option to enable it and set the time range.

NOTE   Setting an available time for a logical printer does not shut down the physical printer at the time range you set. If other logical printers point to the same physical printer and availability is set to Always, other users can print. If you need to shut down the printer completely at a certain time, make sure all logical printers have the same available time range set.

To spool or not to spool

As mentioned earlier, you can opt to send print jobs directly to the printer. Simply toggle the options to use the spooler or to print directly to the printer. If you choose the latter, the print job bypasses the spooler and prints directly to the printer.

Choose the latter option only in rare situations, such as a broken spooler; otherwise, you lose the benefits of spooler-managed printing. For starters, print jobs complete much faster at the application level when they are sent to the spooler. A large document can tie up your application for hours as it prints directly to the printer, and you must wait for each printed page to emerge from the printer before the next page is sent.

Still, you might have a special reason to print directly to the printer, and you should explore the use of a sophisticated printer interface device that has sufficient memory to act as a buffer.

Most of the time, all logical printers make use of the spooler, but you can toggle between printing immediately when the spooler receives a page or waiting until it has received the entire document before it starts sending the job.

Choosing the latter delays printing, but it ensures that the entire job spools correctly before the printing process starts. You would do this if you had a large job to print and the application that produced the job was no longer available. An example would be a print service bureau, where customers bring in print files for processing.

Holding mismatched documents

Check this option for most of your logical printers, especially if they represent sophisticated devices with multiple feeders and hoppers. This option instructs the spooler to examine the codes in the print document and checks them against the setup of the physical printer. For example, suppose you print to a bulk cassette or special-size form feeder from the application, but that option has been disabled in the printer's device settings or it's offline for some reason. Instead of throwing an error, the printer holds the job until the problem has been corrected. This is illustrated in Figure 12-14.

FIGURE 12-14

Mismatched documents are held.

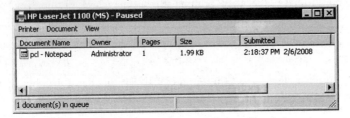

The spooler does not hold up valid jobs from printing. While your job is on hold, you can correct the problem at the actual printer or delete the job (Cancel) and reprint with new parameters.

Printing spooled documents first

When you tell the spooler to give jobs that have completed spooling priority over jobs that are still spooling, it overrides any priority a job has. In other words, if you are spooling a job consisting of 1,000 pages, why should all the one-page jobs have to wait in line?

If you turn this feature off in situations where all the jobs are roughly the same size, the spooler prints the jobs in the order it receives them.

Keeping printed documents

This is another feature that at first seems to make no sense — until you get a job to print that takes hours to set up. A good example of such a job is a sheet of labels for ZIP disks, or address labels, or CD labels, or high-resolution color jobs that don't change graphically but need to be reprinted from time to time.

If you have such a need, you can create a logical printer that keeps the documents after they have printed. When you need to reprint the job, right-click the job you need and select Restart from the context menu.

Creating a special printer that keeps the jobs makes more sense than toggling this property every time you want to keep the document and run the risk of every user's job having to be manually deleted from the hard disk. Use the techniques described earlier for creating a logical printer that redirects its jobs to a folder you created instead of the default queue folder, so that jobs that should be deleted are not co-mingled with your persistent jobs.

> **TIP** Another means of keeping the job is to print to a file and then later print it from the command line whenever you need it. This might be a better option for you if the environment in which you are working is not sufficiently secure and you run the risk that the queue gets "flushed" and your job is lost. The Copy command prints documents from the command line.

Access control

Providing access to printers is similar to providing access to files and folders. To give users access to the printers on the print server, you first have to share the printer. Sharing also enables users to browse the network to find the printers. Providing printer access is almost identical to providing access to sharepoints, with one difference: You can't decide who accesses the print share. Microsoft has hard-coded the share to be open to everyone. Sounds horrible? Fear not.

You can restrict access to printers via security permissions (access control). As with file shares, you may be tempted to just leave the Everyone group in the printer access control list. This may be a good idea if you have a huge printer or a collection of pooled printers set up as a free-for-all, only printing to blank white paper (and you are certain that no one can walk up to the printer and stick letterhead in the tray). In other situations, especially when it comes to smaller printers, or highly specialized printers (such as check and label printers) and plotters, it becomes essential to restrict the printers to only the groups specifically using the printers.

> **TIP** Consider creating groups along application needs and then admitting the application users to these groups. For example, we have a group of users who work with People-Soft applications all day long, and we installed a special Xerox system that prints payroll checks. To prevent people from printing to the checks in the tray, only members of the PeopleSoft-Check Printers group have access to this printer.

You can also provide access to — and information about — all printers in the organization by publishing the printers in the Active Directory (which is done automatically when you install printers on any server that is a domain member). You can delegate the administration task to printer administrators in any group established on an OU-per-OU basis.

Assigning permissions according to role

Windows Server 2008 separates access to printers into three roles or classes of users: people who print, people who manage the documents or jobs, and people who manage the printers. Incidentally, users can be assigned all the permissions. Table 12-2 summarizes the printer permissions.

TABLE 12-2

Printer Permission Types

Access	Print	Manage Documents	Manage Printers
Print	Yes	Yes	Yes
Manage Own Job	Yes	Yes	Yes
Manage Other's Job	No	Yes	Yes
Connect	Yes	Yes	Yes
Control Print Jobs	No	Yes	Yes
Delete All Jobs	No	No	Yes
Share Printers	No	No	Yes
Configure Printers	No	No	Yes
Delete Printers	No	No	Yes
Change Permissions	No	No	Yes

The Manage Own Job permission enables the user to pause jobs, resume jobs, restart jobs, and cancel any job he or she owns. Users have no access to documents in the queue over which they have no ownership. Administrators, however, may take ownership of documents.

The `printer` object is similar to the `file` object. You can assign the preceding permissions, and you can specifically deny any of them. Be careful, though — denying a permission may affect other weaker permissions. For example, denying Connect is as good as removing the group from the access control list. Deny is stronger than the allow permissions of any other group and overrides other permissions granted.

Permissions are fully described in Chapters 23 and 24, which offers techniques and suggestions.

Delegating printer and document administration

Delegating responsibility for the management of print jobs and printers is important, especially in large organizations. Instead of sending all the problems that users have with printers to one person, you should set up two printer groups per OU and assign people from the OU to deal with the OU's printer problems and needs, assuming you have the staff. The following list is a suggestion for the two groups:

- **Print Job Admins.** Members of this group can manage print jobs, including pause, restart, redirect, and cancel. This group cannot delete jobs or change printer properties.

- **Printer Admins.** Members of this group can perform print job management, install printers, configure printers, and delete printers. They can also change permissions, take ownership, and publish printers in the directory.

Creating groups and delegating administrative control is discussed in Chapters 23 and 24.

Taking ownership

You can take ownership of a logical printer in the same way you take ownership of a file or folder. Ownership rules for printers are no different from the ownership rules for files and folders. For example, the person who created the logical printer owns it; the user owns the created print job. Ownership is discussed in Chapter 16.

To take ownership of a printer, perform the following steps:

1. Open the logical printer's properties and select the Security tab. Click the Advanced button.
2. The Advanced Security Settings dialog box appears. Click the Owner tab. Your user account (your logon) and the Administrators group appear in the list of owners. Select the account and click Apply or OK. Click OK again to close the Properties dialog box.

Remember that you can't take ownership if you are not a member of an administrator's group that has been assigned the Manage Printers permission.

Troubleshooting

Now that you understand the Windows Server 2008 printing services, you're better equipped to troubleshoot printer problems when they occur, and they will occur. Out of all the services the mighty Windows Server 2008 networking environment has to offer, the printer services generate the most support calls, behind resource access issues.

It is important to limit the amount of third-party software that has a tendency to bog down a printer server when installing multiple printer models and makes. Manufacturers such as HP, Dell, Xerox, Ricoh, Kyocera, and Lexmark like to install their own drivers, utilities, print monitors, and so on. These can sometimes conflict with one another and cause problems, such as memory leaks. Some printer software regularly update themselves over the Internet, and this can also cause issues.

Best practice should be to drive all your printers using the standard Microsoft components, especially the monitors and drivers that are either present on the system or available through update services.

If you find that your high-volume printing (say, 30,000 pages a day) is leaking out all your memory, it will almost certainly be caused by third-party printer bits draining the server. You can clean this up by making sure all printers hook into the Microsoft parts that ship with the operating system, rather than something on a CD that came with the printer (don't be tempted to automatically install everything on the CD that came with the printer). If the driver that came with the OS does not expose the functionality available on the new printer, then check first with Microsoft to determine whether a new driver is available and use that one.

In addition, go through your registry on the server to ensure that orphaned keys are not causing problems. Delete the entries you don't need. Consult with Microsoft to do this if you are new to registry hacking or you could cripple operations on the server. Another reason to consult with Microsoft if you have determined that printing is leaking memory out of the server is to obtain guidance and software bits for any fixes and patches that you may need.

Be aware that not all third-party software is cluster-aware and new drivers from third-party vendors may not easily install to the cluster nodes (print server clustering is beyond the scope of this book).

The following troubleshooting suggestions and tips are a good place to start to resolve printing problems as quickly as possible.

Server-side print problems

We like to refer to jobs that do not print as being *blocked*. Blocked jobs arrive at the queues and just sit there, or they time-out with an error. Most calls to a support or help desk are complaints about jobs that have spooled to the logical printer but are not emerging from the physical printer.

If a job is sitting in the queue and not indicating an error, a mismatched document may be trapped by the printing service. Mismatch problems are easily corrected, as shown earlier.

Jobs that throw an error indicate they were unable to print to the physical printer. If the job can't print and an error is reported, take the following steps to correct the problem:

1. **Check the port assigned to the logical printer.** If the port is an IP address, ping it. If you get a reply from the port, you have connectivity to the network components involved in the printing process. In other words, jobs can get to the server and the server can see the port, or at least the print monitor can. (If you are some distance away from the print server, open a terminal session to the server and ping the port from the session.) If the IP address is correct and you get a reply from the port, you can check the IP port off your list. If the port is a parallel or serial cable connected directly to the server, you need to perform specific diagnostics there as well.

 Network addressing is seldom the problem, especially if you maintain your IP printing network as suggested earlier (and if your printer has been printing before and no IP address conflicts appear in the event logs).

2. **Check the hard disk space, memory, and event logs.** Resource starvation is a major cause of printer spooler service shutdown. (With Windows Server 2008, you can set and enforce disk quotas — described in Chapter 13 — to help prevent your print server from running out of hard disk space.) Freeing up space or shutting down memory hogs may be all it takes to get printing again. The event logs can tell you when the first jobs failed. These events may relate to other errors that could identify a reason for the sterile jobs.

You can also check the driver. Although this is an unlikely point of failure with a printer that has been printing with no problems to date, the driver may have been changed or deleted by another administrator.

If you can't get the print service printing to the physical printer within, say, five minutes of getting a call for help, go to Step 3.

3. **Attempt to redirect the jobs.** Redirect the jobs to another port and physical printing device as described earlier in this chapter under the "Publishing Printers" section. This is a quick fix that does not affect users and alleviates the pressure stemming from impatient users. They still print to the same logical printer.

   If the new target physical printer is located somewhere else in your offices, notify users where they can collect their jobs. Please don't redirect the jobs to another city in another state as one CNE once did; and make sure you are redirecting the jobs to another printer of the same type and using the same driver.

   If you can't redirect the jobs and the other port is printing — and the blocked jobs are not — you most likely have a problem with the spooler and spooler files. This could have been caused by the lack of resources. You need to act fast and proceed to Step 4.

4. **Stop and restart the spooler service on the print server computer.** If resources starvation is the problem or the spooler is down for some reason, the spool files can become corrupted. In fact, consider giving the spooler a sharp crack on the head when everything else seems to check out. Restart the spooler and then stop and restart it again. If the spooler starts up normally and responds quickly to the restart command, but the jobs are still not printing, it's likely that they are corrupt. Delete the jobs — kill the spool files and the shadow files. (You may have to take ownership to delete the files. If new jobs are still not printing, it's a drastic situation.) The files to delete are the SPL file and SHD files, previously discussed in this chapter.

5. **Take the logical printer offline.** The best way to do this is to prevent access to the logical printer completely. Selecting the option Use the Printer Offline does nothing but cause the queues to fill up with more sterile print jobs. Your users print and then rush to the printers to stare at empty hoppers like deer in headlights. It's better to tell them they have been denied access, and they will know why. We prefer to remove access from the printer completely. Go to the Security tab on the Properties dialog box and uncheck the permissions assigned to the groups using the printer. You may have to perform this exercise with several logical printers all using the port on which there is an error.

6. **Notify users that there is a problem, and notify your help or service desk.** When users discover they can't access a printer, they call for help. It's better to preempt the calls.

7. **If you can see the port, attempt to log in.** Some ports enable you to telnet into the interface box. If you can log in to the port, you can get diagnostics from the port. Many manufacturers now ship software that can query the printer for errors and diagnostics. If the printer reports errors, you may have to call in a service technician. If the printer is checking out, you may have a problem with the printer interface device — such as the Jet-Direct card or the Lantronix device. Often, we have found these to be problem children that were fixed when we downloaded new versions of their firmware.

8. **Check for problems on the client.** If clients are printing and you are not seeing the jobs in the queues, then check the client. Odds are good it's not a server-related problem. The spooler service on the client may be stopped.

Client-side print problems

Client-side printing problems are different from server-side problems, although they are certainly interrelated and may stem from the server. The following list represents the most common client-side print problems you may encounter:

1. **Pages print incorrectly or are garbled.** The cause of this problem is usually that the client has received the wrong printer driver. Check the server configuration and make sure the client is getting the correct driver. You may need drivers for all versions and types of operating systems running on your clients, possibly one for every version of Windows too.

   The clients may also generate error messages saying that they need to install a printer driver when connecting to a specific printer on a Windows Server 2008 printer server. This means that the correct drivers are installed on the Windows Server 2008 server, but they are not automatically sent to the legacy client every time the client prints.

   Finally, another cause of garbled text could be related to the physical printer. It may have special font requirements, it may be set to print only PostScript when the job you're sending is PCL (which could happen when you print to a file or restart a job from some time back), or the printer may be low on memory or faulty.

2. **Only some clients print.** This means the client has been misconfigured. Chances are good the client has printed — but to the wrong printer. You can minimize this problem by providing adequate information about the location of printers.

Enabling bi-directional printing

Enabling bi-directional printing enables smart printers equipped with the capability to transmit data to the printing service to talk to the server in real time. It also makes it easier to find out why a printer is not printing when all else checks out. The physical printer has the capability to report to the server that it requires paper, servicing, or toner, or reports its overall status, and more.

The default operation is bi-directional printing disabled. The option is found on the Ports tab of the printer properties. It's grayed out if the port selected does not support bi-directional printing. This does not mean you won't get sufficient status information from the printer because Windows polls the printer for information, but Windows only polls for standard information (out of paper, and so on), and the messages are not as detailed.

Auditing Printer Usage and Management

Windows Server 2008 enables you to track print job success and failure on a logical printer. Check out Chapter 10 on auditing Windows objects, if you have not already done so, and how to prepare the system for auditing.

You can audit access and usage to a logical printer as follows:

1. Select the printer you wish to audit for printing and management. Right-click and select Properties; then select the Security tab.

2. On the Security tab, click the Advanced button, which launches the Access Control Setting dialog box for the logical printer. Click the Auditing tab.

3. On the Auditing tab, click Add and select the group or groups you want to access. Choose the Success or Failure audits you want to trap and click Apply.

That's all there is to auditing printer usage. To check the audits, refer to the system log in Event Viewer.

Summary

This chapter was designed to get you up to speed on the elements of the Windows Server 2008 print services. We believe it's important to understand the service from the manager or administrator perspective — in order to correctly troubleshoot printing problems.

Chapter 13

Storage Management

This chapter introduces Windows Server 2008 storage. We start by presenting the "science" of disk management, and Hierarchical Storage Management (HSM). (Removable storage and remote storage are covered in depth in Chapter 14.) We also cover configuration and types of disks, partitions, and volumes (including a new partition style introduced in the 64-bit version of Windows Server 2008); software-based fault-tolerant disk configurations (using a Redundant Array of Inexpensive Disks, or RAID); and disk quotas. The chapter concludes with an overview of how to troubleshoot common storage management problems.

Before you can proceed with storage and file management you will need to install the File Services role. This role was demonstrated in Chapter 2.

Overview of Storage

Although there are few certainties in life, in storage management you can be fairly sure that no matter how much disk space you plan for, sooner or later, you will run out of it. You can also expect a disk crash to happen at the worst possible time.

At best, the failure of a storage device or even a shortage of disk space has a negative impact on running applications; more commonly, it leads to server downtime or data loss. This, in turn, translates into business losses, sometimes measured in millions of dollars. You can help prevent these losses by taking the following proactive approaches:

- Evaluate your storage needs.
- Design and implement highly available storage solutions.

- Restrict and monitor storage use.
- Provide disaster recovery and backup/restore mechanisms.

Storage Management

Storage management can be analyzed functionally by dividing it into three areas: *performance and capacity*, *high availability*, and *recoverability*. The following sections look at each of these areas.

Performance and capacity

Typically, a computer system requires local storage for system and boot files required by the operating systems (although Windows Server 2008 Server supports Storage Area Network [SAN] configurations whereby all disks are external). The boot partition (hosting the operating system) needs to be able to accommodate profiles of logged-on users, paging files, memory dumps, and installed programs. Make sure you set partitions large enough, especially because boot and system partitions, after being created, cannot be extended without third-party tools such as Partition Magic.

NOTE This chapter uses the terms *boot partition* and *system partition*, a counterintuitive naming convention used by Microsoft for partitions containing boot files (system partition) and system files (boot partition). Contrary to what you might expect, a Windows-based computer boots from the system partition and stores its operating system files on a boot partition. These terms can refer to the same partition or two separate ones (separate boot and system partitions are mandatory on Itanium-based Windows Server 2008 installations, covered later in this chapter, and optional on Intel 32-bit computers).

Conversely, ensure that your computer's BIOS supports Interrupt 13 Extensions if you plan to make your boot or system partition larger than 8GB.

NOTE One of the limitations of older versions of BIOS (Basic Input/Output System) was the way hard disk access was handled, by using the BIOS internal code invoked through Interrupt 13. The addressing implemented in the code allowed access to partitions no larger than 8.4GB, which at the time of its inception (early 1980s) was more than anyone expected to ever need. Earlier versions of Windows (up to Windows NT 4.0) relied on this feature to read the system files necessary to boot before the operating system was fully loaded. This is why the size of boot and system partitions was limited in those systems to about 8GB. The problem surfaced when one of the files needed during the boot ended up (typically through fragmentation, especially after service pack updates, on systems with high disk space utilization) beyond the boundary reachable through BIOS. In the late 1990s, computer manufacturers developed extensions to the BIOS code handling Interrupt 13 that allowed it to work with much larger partitions (up to 9TB). The newer operating systems, starting with Windows 98 and Windows 2000, can take advantage of the Interrupt 13 BIOS extensions, but you need to make sure that your computer's BIOS has this capability (you might be able to get updated BIOS from its manufacturer). Otherwise, ensure that your system and boot partitions are smaller than 8GB.

Do the disks storing boot and system volumes need to be particularly fast? Not necessarily, because access to boot files is needed only at startup, and more frequently used operating system files are cached in the server's memory. However, you should ensure that the paging file resides on a fast volume (you might need to move it from its default location) because this will significantly improve the server's responsiveness.

To accommodate these varying requirements, separate the operating system from the data. You can accomplish this by first grouping disks into arrays based on their purpose and then attaching each group to dedicated channels or disk controllers. Depending on your budget, you may be in a position to get faster disks, use striping volumes, or combine both by striping volumes on faster disks.

Collect information on applications to be installed, type of data, and number of users accessing the volumes. When dealing with extremely demanding applications such as busy commercial Web sites or On-Line Transaction Processing (OLTP) database management systems, take into consideration disk-related hardware parameters such as the following:

- **Access time.** This is the time it takes for a hard disk to register a request and prepare to scan its surface.

- **Seek time.** This is the time it takes for a hard disk to find and assemble all the parts of a file.

- **Transfer rate.** This is the time it takes for a hard disk to transfer data on and off the disk.

Closely observe the rate of disk consumption and plan accordingly. Leave a generous margin and ensure that your design allows for easy expansion. Keep your space utilization below the 70 percent threshold, which not only enables you to prevent sudden "Out of space" messages, but also helps keep disks defragmented (in order for the built-in Disk Defragmenter to work efficiently, the disk should have at least 15 percent of total disk space available). Implement monitoring tools that will notify you when disk space utilization approaches the threshold defined by you.

If you find that the capacity of a single volume does not satisfy your disk space needs, you have the following options:

- Volumes can be spanned or extended (providing they are unformatted or formatted with NTFS and they are not system or boot volumes). Spanning refers to the process of chaining together areas of unallocated space residing on separate physical disks. Extending involves adding extra unallocated space to an already existing volume. Extending is typically done when a volume runs out of free space and at least one unpartitioned area remains on the disk. This remaining area can be added on to extend the volume capacity. Dynamic volumes can be extended using any area from the same or different physical disks, but basic volumes are limited to contiguous areas on the same disk. You will explore this topic in more detail later in the chapter.

- If you want to increase the speed of I/O operations, you can create striped volumes (known also as RAID-0). Striped volumes, similar to spanned ones, are created using areas of unallocated space on multiple disks. What's different is the way data is written to the volume, which adds the requirement that striped areas be the same size. Another similarity between striped and spanned volumes is the lack of fault tolerance, meaning that the failure of any of the striped disks makes the entire volume inaccessible. If you want to add a level of fault tolerance (which is typically recommended), you can use striping with parity (RAID-5). This type of configuration provides redundancy by storing additional parity information as part of the volume. Another type of fault-tolerant volume, a mirror (RAID-1), creates an exact copy of the data, so it does not contribute in any way to increase available space (as a matter of fact, it wastes 50 percent of available space). Fault-tolerant solutions are discussed in the next section.

- You can enforce disk space quotas on a per-user basis. As shown later in the chapter, you can specify a maximum amount of space that can be used by each user, for each server volume.

- You can mount a volume onto an empty folder on another volume. This way, from the user's perspective, the available storage is increased by the free space on the mounted volume. This topic is covered in Chapter 14.

- You can redirect shared folders on one server to a shared volume or folder on other servers. This functionality is available with Distributed File System (DFS), presented in Chapter 14.

- You can compress data on volumes. Compression is also covered in Chapter 14.

- You can automatically move older files from a local volume to removable, locally attached media, such as tapes and portable disks. Refer to Chapter 14 for details.

The preceding options are frequently combined (for example, disk quotas can be applied to a DFS residing on a RAID-5 volume).

Windows Server 2008 and SANs

A SAN (Storage Area Network or System Area Network) is essentially a collection of disks and storage controllers. What makes it different from the much more common Directly Attached Storage (local disks attached to a local disk controller) is the fact that a SAN is physically separate and independently managed. A single SAN can (and typically does) provide storage to multiple servers. It is linked to them through one or more dedicated interconnecting devices, which can be as simple as external SCSI buses or as complex as a multilevel, fully redundant network of fiber switches.

NOTE SAN is sometimes confused with Network Attached Storage (NAS), which, similar to SAN, is an external, separately managed collection of storage devices, but is connected through a regular TCP/IP network, most often shared with client computers. NAS offers the convenience of SAN at lower prices. Its performance, however, does not match that of SAN because available bandwidth between server and storage is more limited due to lower media speed and, possibly, depending on design, contention with client traffic. Windows Server 2008 introduces a number of improvements in the area of NAS, such as support for multipath I/O and Volume Shadow Copy Service. Interestingly, recent developments in iSCSI (Internet-SCSI) technology are changing traditional SAN design by allowing the use of IP protocol for server-to-storage communication. Windows Server 2008 now supports iSCSI.

SANs, despite their high initial cost and increased complexity of management, are becoming a more popular choice for storage. Microsoft embraces this trend by extending the SAN support introduced in Windows Server 2003 geared toward SAN-based architecture, such as multipath I/O (the capability to simultaneously use several separate physical paths to storage devices), Winsock Direct (a protocol that bypasses networking layers and communicates directly with SAN hardware), support for SAN-based boot and system partitions, the capability to turn off volume automounting (with the MOUNTVOL.EXE utility), and Storage Explorer (a new tool for working with SANs).

High availability

Besides providing a sufficient amount of fast storage, you also need to ensure its availability. You can use one of the following technologies to reach this goal:

- **RAID-1 (mirrored) fault-tolerant volumes.**
- **RAID-5 fault-tolerant volumes.**
- **Clustered servers.** This refers to two or more servers sharing (typically) common storage and capable of automatic fail-over. Server clustering is available only in Windows Server 2008 Enterprise and Datacenter Server.
- **Hot standby server.** This is a server synchronized with the original data source via a replication mechanism. You can use the File Replication Service built into Windows Server 2008 when dealing with regular file shares (several third-party replication mechanisms are also available). Log shipping is one of the options for synchronizing replicas of Microsoft SQL Server.

Windows Server 2008's fault-tolerant dynamic volumes are given comprehensive coverage later in this chapter. You can also consider using DFS (described in Chapter 14) as another way of implementing high availability.

Recoverability

Recoverability features need to be able to secure your data against a number of threats, such as file corruption, theft, disasters, virus attacks, user-deleted files, or failed hard disks. The primary services that offer such support include the following:

- **Removable Storage Services (RSS).** This works with backup technology, media, and robotics to provide a comprehensive data protection media management system (you can find out more about it in Chapter 7).
- **The Backup/Restore Service** This is fully discussed in Chapter 7 and as part of the HSM concept in Chapter 14.
- **Volume Shadow Copy Service.** Introduced in Windows Server 2003, this offers a revolutionary approach to backup and restore operations. It works by creating an instant copy (snapshot) of the original disk volume. As new files are created or existing ones modified, the service keeps track of only the changes to the state of the volume captured in

the snapshot. This way, the volume can be backed up while the files are open and the applications are running (need for a backup window is eliminated) and a restore can return the volume to a specific point in time. The client portion of the service allows users to instantaneously restore previous versions of a modified file.

Issues with legacy systems

It is unlikely that you will run into issues relating to lack of support for Windows Server 2008 storage management features in previous versions of Windows. Older operating systems (other than Windows 2000 and XP Professional) are not capable of recognizing dynamic disks created by Windows Server 2008 Server unless the disks are local. The only scenarios in which this can happen occur when dual booting between Windows Server 2008 current and legacy systems and when transferring disks between such systems.

The introduction of a 64-bit version of Windows Server 2008 on Itanium-based computers added another degree of incompatibility. Its new partition style, called GUID (Globally Unique Identifier) Partition Table (GPT), is not supported on any other operating system (including 32-bit versions of Windows Server 2008).

Note that the restrictions described in this section apply only to local disk access. Volumes residing on dynamic disk and GUID partitions can be accessed via the network by any other operating system (providing proper permissions are granted).

Disk Management

In Windows Server 2008 Disk Management (DM) is found under the Storage node in the Server Manager console. The DM service handles two types of storage: basic and dynamic. Basic disks are practically identical to (and compatible with) those used in previous versions of Microsoft operating systems. Dynamic disks, conversely, are more technologically advanced, scalable, and robust; they were introduced in Windows 2000 and are supported only in Windows 200X, XP Professional/Vista, and Windows Server 2008 Server.

Management of dynamic disks and their volumes is handled by Logical Disk Manager (LDM). One of its features is replicating data describing dynamic disk structure across all of the local dynamic disks. This way, a corruption of such data on a single disk does not affect its accessibility. LDM is also the underlying component of DMS, which provides the following features:

- **Online Management.** This enables fault-tolerant RAID configurations and nonsystem or nonboot volumes to be created and rebuilt without rebooting the system (although your servers need to be hot-pluggable if you want to replace a failed disk or extend an existing volume by adding a new disk).
- **Mounted Volumes.** This is the feature that maps an entire volume into an empty folder on an NTFS-formatted basic or dynamic volume. Mounted volumes provide a convenient

and instantaneous way to add disk space to a volume, by using an empty folder on the volume as an access point to another volume on one of the local disks. If no local disks with free space are available, you can install another and use it for the mount. Removing a mounted volume is just as easy. Neither of these operations requires a reboot.

Mounted volumes can use practically any type of storage, including removable media. This gives you plenty of flexibility in handling disk space shortages. For example, you can mount a new volume onto the D: drive using one of its empty folders and then extend that volume if you start running out of space on the D: drive again.

Mounted volumes are available only when the volume where the mount point resides is formatted with NTFS, because reparse points (on which volume mounting is based) are not available in FAT or FAT32. However, the volume you mount can be formatted with any file system supported by Windows Server 2008, including FAT, FAT32, NTFS, CDFS, and UDF.

■ **Disk Defragmentation.** This is the process of rearranging data on a disk to make it contiguous. This reduces seek time and effectively speeds up access to data. Disk defragmentation, introduced in Windows 2000, has been improved in Windows Server 2008 through the addition of a command-line interface (defrag.exe), the Disk Defragmenter application, and scheduling capabilities. We cover it in depth in Chapter 14.

■ **Disk Management Tools.** These are part of Windows Server 2008 Server and include Disk Management console and several command-line utilities.

Disk Management is implemented as an MMC snap-in. It enables you to manage disks and volumes on local and remote systems. It is covered in more detail later in this chapter.

The diskpart.exe command-line utility provides a shell from which you can launch multiple, disk-management-related commands. It is typically used to automate disk management tasks. It can be run in either interactive mode or in batch mode, using a text file containing multiple commands as input.

The fsutil.exe command-line utility is used for the management of file systems and volumes. You can use it, for example, to determine volume characteristics (such as file system, volume name, and so on) or to query how much free disk space a volume contains. Run the following code to display total and free bytes on the C: volume:

```
FSUTIL VOLUME DISKFREE C:
```

You can also run the following code to list additional information about the C: volume:

```
FSUTIL NTFSINFO VOLUMEINFO C:

MOUNTVOL.EXE is a command-line tool used for volume mounting
```

> **NOTE** Managing GPT disks involves several Itanium-specific tools, in addition to the preceding ones.

Partition Styles

Partition style describes the arrangement of partitions and volumes on a disk. All x86-based systems store information about disk layout using the structure called Master Boot Record (MBR). Itanium-based computers running the 64-bit version of Windows Server 2008 Server can also use the GPT partition style, with disk and volume information stored in the GPT. Because the partition style is set on a per-disk basis, MBR and GPT disks also exist.

Despite significant differences between MBR and GPT disks, most of their features are identical. Both can be configured as basic or dynamic disks. Both can also contain the same types of volumes, with the exception of logical volumes residing on extended partitions, because extended partitions are supported only on MBR disks.

MBR disks

Operating systems based on Intel x86 processors communicate with hardware via BIOS, which recognizes disks configured using the MBR partition style. MBR consists of a set of predefined fields storing disk configuration information, initial bootstrap code, and the partition table.

GPT disks

Itanium-based operating systems communicate with hardware using the Extensible Firmware Interface (EFI). EFI specifications also include a definition of GPT partition style. GPT offers support for volume sizes of up to 18EB and up to 127 partitions on basic disks (compared to a practical limit of 2TB and 4 partitions with MBR partitions). It also includes performance and reliability improvements; for example, a GPT disk contains two copies of the partition table stored in a separate, hidden partition.

Itanium systems can use a mix of GPT and MBR disks, but they must boot from a GPT disk. (In other words, the system partition on Itanium systems has to be created on a GPT disk. This partition, called the EFI system partition, must be formatted using FAT and have a size between 100MB and 1GB.) System files must reside on a separate partition (called, as you probably recall, the boot partition) from the boot files stored on the system partition. Note that the files used during the boot process of Itanium-based computers are different from the ones on x86-based systems.

GPT has its limitations. As mentioned before, it is not backwardly compatible. Only 64-bit operating systems running on Itanium computers (64-bit versions of XP or Vista and Windows Server 2008 Servers) can access GPT-partitioned local disks. GPT partition style cannot be used for removable disks or for disks attached to shared storage devices on cluster servers in Windows Server 2008 Enterprise and Datacenter platforms. In addition, the EFI system partition cannot be mirrored.

Conversion between MBR and GPT disks requires deleting all volumes and partitions. After all of them are removed, you can use the Convert to GPT Disk or Convert to MBR Disk options in the Disk Management console or the Convert GPT and Convert MBR options of the diskpart utility.

Removable Storage

Removable storage includes any media that can (and is intended to) be easily swapped between multiple systems or relocated offsite for restore and disaster-recovery purposes. Most commonly, removable storage consists of tapes, recordable and rewritable CD and DVD disks, removable hard drives such as ZIP or JAZ disks, and optical drives.

Windows Server 2008 offers a uniform approach to removable storage management. It provides the same interface whether dealing with single tape drive units similar to Quarter Inch Cartridge or highly sophisticated automated archive systems such as optical drive libraries or multi-drive tape silos. Removable media, regardless of their physical type, are organized into collections called *media pools*. The media pools are organized based on common characteristics, typically related to their purpose. Tape devices and backup topics are discussed in Chapter 7.

Remote Storage and HSM

HSM is more of a concept than a practical implementation and consists of numerous interrelated components and services. Its purpose is to control the transfer of data throughout a computing environment. HSM not only provides data protection, but also takes care of space utilization by moving unused data off local storage. This can happen according to some arbitrarily chosen criteria, such as when the disks start getting full, or at preconfigured intervals.

The hierarchical system of data storage has several levels. The *data retrieval level* starts out at the top of the hierarchy. Data at that level is online and immediately available. It resides on local fast hard disks, in fast-access network storage silos and SANs, or arrays of hard disks servicing clusters. The bottom of the hierarchy, known as the *storage level*, represents data that is offline (stored on tape cartridges, compact disc libraries, or tape libraries). Intermediate levels correspond to slower hard disk arrays.

How does the data get from the immediate-availability state to the other end of the hierarchy? This is the task of Remote Storage. A file that does not satisfy certain conditions, such as "time since last accessed" being shorter than the interval you defined, is moved off the fast disks down the hierarchy to slower media. In a well-designed system, files that are not used at all end up eventually on library tapes. This file migration can be triggered when free disk space reaches dangerous limits.

Remote Storage replaces the moved file on the disk with a link pointing to its current location. From a user's perspective, the way of accessing the file does not change because the link emulates its presence (a user can tell whether a file has been archived, however; its icon is slightly modified and includes a tiny clock). At the first attempt to access it again, the file is checked out of the archive system and returned to its original location. The main drawback of this mechanism is the slower access time when opening such files, but this is a small price to pay in exchange for disk space savings.

When Remote Storage needs to move the data to a lower level of the storage hierarchy, it interfaces with the removable storage system — via the previously described media pools — to copy the data to an available media library. You can deploy low-cost storage as a means of continually offloading stale data from the local disks that need space for applications and current data. You can use this strategy as long as you have available secondary, online storage media, such as tape or recordable DVDs or CDs.

Remember that HSM is not a substitute for regular backups because only a single instance of the data exists. Make sure that you factor archived data into your backup strategy. Consider installing a system that makes regular, rotation-managed backups of the offline media.

The Disk Management Snap-in

The Disk Management MMC snap-in is automatically loaded into the Server Manager console, located in the Control Panel, under the Administrative Tools folder. You can also run it as a standalone snap-in by launching diskmgmt.msc or adding it to a custom console.

In the Server Manager console, the Disk Management snap-in is a leaf or node on the Storage folder. The snap-in is illustrated in Figure 13-1 outside of the Server Manager console.

FIGURE 13-1

The Disk Management snap-in.

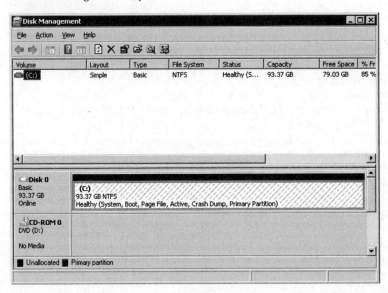

The Disk Management snap-in is the main application for managing disks and volumes in a Windows Server 2008 system via the graphical interface. You can use it to perform most operations on disks and volumes on both local and remote systems, as long as they are running Windows Server 200X Server, XP Professional and Vista, or Windows 2000. We describe how to use Disk Management for the most common disk and volume tasks later in this chapter.

Basic Storage

All disks start as basic disks with structures that make the disk recognizable to the operating system. Specifics depend on whether the disk is MBR or GPT type (as previously described). Besides presenting the disk to the operating system, these structures store a disk signature, which uniquely identifies the disk. The signature is written to the disk through the process called initialization, which typically takes place when a disk is added to the system. Before a basic disk can be used to store any files, it has to be divided into partitions and volumes. Partitions are areas of a physical disk that can host one or more volumes, depending on whether the partition is primary or extended.

Primary partitions

Primary partitions can exist on both MBR and GPT disks. MBR disks are limited to four primary partitions, whereas GPT disks can contain up to 127 of them (plus Microsoft Reserved Partition). From a practical point of view, a primary partition is equivalent to a volume. One of its unique features is its capability to store a boot sector, which is used when launching an operating system. As explained previously in this chapter, such a partition is called a system partition. In order for a primary partition to become bootable, you have to designate it as active and install appropriate operating system boot files on it. In pre-Windows 2000 operating systems, each primary partition was associated with the drive letter used to access it in Windows Explorer or via a command prompt, but this is no longer the case. In Windows Server 200X, you have the option of not assigning a drive letter to a partition (such a partition can be accessed, for example, by creating a mount point).

Extended partitions

Extended partitions are subject to several restrictions: They are supported only on MBR disks, only one such partition can exist per physical disk, and the operating system cannot boot from them. Their main benefit is the fact that they can contain multiple logical drives (volumes). You can use this feature if you want to work around the four-partition limit of MBR disks. Instead of creating four primary partitions, which translate into four volumes only, you can create three primary partitions and one extended partition. After the extended partition is created, you can divide it into any number of logical drives.

Basic volumes

Basic volumes are areas of the disk that can be independently formatted. The process of formatting assigns a specific file system to the volume (such as FAT, FAT32, or NTFS) and is required in order to store files on the disk. As mentioned previously, a basic volume can be located on a primary or extended partition. In the first case, a single volume occupies an entire partition; in the second case, one or more volumes can be created, with the portion of the partition unassigned to any volume left for later use.

When working with basic disks, you are limited to basic volumes only (which consist of a contiguous area of a single disk). To format any other type of volume (such as spanned, striped, mirrored, or RAID-5), you first need to convert two or more disks to dynamic disks (at least three for RAID-5 and two or more for the other types).

Basic volumes can be extended, which essentially involves adding more space to an existing volume. This, however, is not possible in any of the following scenarios:

- The volume is formatted using FAT or FAT32 (only NTFS or unformatted volumes can be extended).
- The volume is used as a system or boot partition.
- Unallocated space is not adjacent to (immediately following) the volume to be extended.
- The volume was created as a basic partition on a Windows NT 4.0 or Windows 2000/2003 installation that was subsequently upgraded to Windows Server 2008 Server.
- The simple volume has been modified using the `diskpart.exe` utility with the `retain` command (more about this later).

Note that you cannot extend a basic partition using the Disk Management utility; you must use `diskpart.exe` instead.

Extending a volume does not affect data residing on the volume and it does not require a reboot.

Dynamic Volumes and Fault Tolerance

Dynamic storage was introduced in Windows 2000. Its main advantage is support for multi-disk configurations, with additional performance and fault-tolerance benefits. The basic units of dynamic storage are dynamic disks.

Dynamic disks

All dynamic disks start as basic disks. The conversion is manual and performed using either the Disk Management console or the `diskpart.exe` utility. The conversion process creates a Logical Disk Management database containing the dynamic disk configuration for the entire system (shared with all other dynamic disks and updated for every disk configuration change).

GPT disks store it in a separate, hidden partition, whereas MBR disks need roughly 1 MB of free, unpartitioned space at the very end of the disk. The conversion fails if this space is not available. This will not happen if the MBR basic disk has been created in Windows 2000, XP, Vista, or Windows Server 200X (because these operating systems always reserve sufficient space at the end of the disk when the basic disk is initialized), but it might happen if the system has been upgraded from Windows NT 4.0 and partitions fill the entire disk. There is no workaround to this issue other than backing up the data and deleting and re-creating all the partitions.

> **NOTE** Storing disk information in multiple copies of the LDM database (one per disk) increases fault tolerance. This is a better approach than the one used for basic disks, whereby configuration information resides in the registry.

Conversion is a nondestructive operation, but to play it safe, make sure you have a solid backup before you start. When switching back from dynamic to basic disk, backup and restore is the only way to preserve the data because this operation requires deleting all of the disk volumes (along with their content).

Conversion of the disk from basic to dynamic typically does not require a reboot. The only exceptions to this involve conversion of basic disks containing system, boot, or paging files.

Dynamic disks are not supported on portable computers and removable disk drives. This is by design because laptop computers rarely use multiple disks and having a shared LDM database on a removable drive would require overwriting it every time the drive is transferred between computers. You also cannot use dynamic disks as shared storage devices for server clusters in Windows Server 2008 Enterprise and Datacenter servers.

You should not run the conversion for disks that contain other operating systems (on multi-boot computers) because this might prevent them from booting. This is because during conversion, references to all partitions (except for system and boot) are removed from the MBR.

Volumes created on dynamic disks are called, as you might have already guessed, dynamic volumes. If the basic disk contained any primary partitions or extended partitions with logical drives, they are converted automatically into dynamic volumes. This does not apply to original equipment manufacturer (OEM) partitions (vendor-specific configuration partitions), and system partitions on GPT disks. Even though the maximum number of supported dynamic volumes per dynamic disk is 2,000, more than 32 are not recommended. There are five dynamic volume types:

- **Simple volumes.** A simple volume is limited to a single disk only. Simple volumes on their own do not provide any advantages over basic volumes, but they can serve as a starting point for extending storage space on the local system or building fault tolerance into it. You need to start with simple volumes if your goal is to extend or span volumes. If you have additional dynamic disks, you can also add levels of fault tolerance by mirroring them. Simple volumes can also be mounted to NTFS folders. Simple dynamic volumes can occupy contiguous or non-contiguous areas of the dynamic disk (after it is extended).

- **Spanned volumes.** If you have multiple dynamic disks with unallocated space, you can extend a simple volume beyond a single disk. At that point, your simple volume becomes spanned. Spanned volumes can occupy multiple, non-contiguous areas on up to 32 dynamic disks on the same system. To span a existing simple volume, it must be formatted using NTFS. You also have the option of creating a spanned volume starting with multiple, unallocated areas of free space on several dynamic disks.

Windows Server 2008 writes data to spanned volumes sequentially, filling all the available space on the first disk before starting with the next one. This means that spanned volumes do not provide any performance benefits — data is accessed in the same way as if it were written to a simple volume. Nor is there any improvement in terms of fault tolerance, as no data redundancy is provided. As a matter of fact, data stored on a spanned volume becomes even more vulnerable, because a failure of any disk renders the entire volume unusable.

■ **Striped volumes**. On the surface, striping seems to be similar to spanning. In this case, you also combine areas of unallocated disk space from multiple disks into a single volume. The differences between them stem from the way the data on the resulting volume is written and read. Instead of the sequential approach used in a spanned volume, data is divided into 64 KB pieces and written across all disks participating in the volume. This means that each disk is utilized to the same degree and the size of each stripe is the same (unlike spanned volumes, where you could arbitrarily choose the size of each area).

Due to their structure, striped volumes provide significant performance benefits. If dynamic disks can be accessed simultaneously (depending on the type of disk controller), I/O operations on each disk can be executed in parallel. Data vulnerability, however, is increased (just as with a spanned volume). This is the main reason why striped volumes are typically used for read-only data that can be easily restored.

A striped volume can consist of up to 32 dynamic disks. Striped volume sets are also known as RAID-0 configuration.

■ **RAID-1 volumes (mirrors).** This is one of two software-based fault-tolerant disk configurations available in Windows Server 2008. A mirrored volume set consists of two identical copies of a simple volume residing on two separate dynamic disks. If one of them fails, the system can still remain operational using the other copy until the failed hardware is replaced and the mirror is re-created. Mirrored volumes are part of standard fault-tolerant solutions.

■ **RAID-5 volumes (fault-tolerant stripes).** This is the other type of software-based fault-tolerant disk configuration included in Windows Server 2008. As with striped volumes, data is written across all the drives in 64KB pieces. What is different is that for each of these pieces, the operating system adds parity information to one of the disks in the volume. The parity information is used to reconstruct the data if one of the disks fails. You need at least three dynamic disks to construct a RAID-5 volume. Fault tolerance and efficient use of disk space are two main advantages of RAID-5 volumes.

Simple and spanned dynamic volumes can be extended (just like the basic ones). They are subject to restrictions similar to those that apply when extending basic disks, except they do not require unallocated space to be adjacent; you can use free space on any dynamic disks. Essentially, it is possible to extend any non-system, non-boot, NTFS-formatted (or unformatted) dynamic volumes, as long as they have been created natively in Windows Server 2008. Note that it is not possible to extend striped, RAID-1, or RAID-5 volumes; if you are planning on using them, evaluate your space requirements ahead of time.

RAID-1: Disk mirroring

Windows Server 2008 allows the creation of a mirror using any dynamic volume, including those containing system or boot files, as long as the unallocated space on the other disk is sufficient. When you create a mirror, you can start with a simple volume and an unallocated area on another dynamic disk or two unallocated areas on two dynamic disks. In the first case, the data from the existing simple volume will be copied to the other disk during the initial resynchronization process. In the second case, parts of the volume will be populated equally starting with the first write operation.

The main drawback of mirroring is its degree of space utilization, which is always equal to 50 percent (for example, when using two 18GB disks, your usable space is 18GB). However, RAID-1 is the only disk configuration that can provide software-based fault tolerance for boot and system partitions (this limitation does not apply to hardware-based fault tolerance, discussed later in this chapter). With the costs of hard drives falling, configuring a server with a mirrored volume for system or boot files is a very cost-effective means of maintaining high availability.

Note that redundancy on the disk level does not prevent downtime if both dynamic disks participating in the mirror connect to the same disk controller. If availability of your system is critical, you might want to consider duplexing. Duplexing extends the concept of mirroring by using separate disk controllers, each connected to one of the mirrored disks.

RAID-5: Fault-tolerant striping with parity

RAID-5 is similar to a nonredundant stripe set, but additional parity information is calculated and written across the disks to provide fault tolerance.

To set up a RAID-5 configuration, first evaluate your storage requirements; then determine how many disks will be needed to satisfy your needs. Remember the following three rules:

- Each of the striped areas across all disks has to be the same size.
- The redundant data will occupy up to $(1/n)$th of the total space, where n is the number of striped disks.
- A RAID-5 configuration can contain between 3 and 32 dynamic disks.

For example, if you have one dynamic disk with 9GB of unallocated space and two others with 13GB, the biggest RAID-5 configuration you can create will have 18GB of available space. This is because you are limited by the smallest of the areas that will be used for the volume (9GB in this case). Three disks with 9GB each will give you 27GB. One-third of it is used for parity; therefore, you are left with only 18GB.

The amount of wasted space (space used for parity information) is exactly equal to the size of the RAID-5 volume on a single disk. In other words, if you havefive 36GB drives, and each in

TABLE 13-1

Feature Comparison between Basic and Dynamic Disks

Feature	Basic	Dynamic
Managing Legacy Volume Sets on Basic Disks	No[1]	N/A
Booting to Windows Server 2008 Server from a Volume	Yes	No[2]
Installing Windows Server 2008 Server to a Volume	Yes	Yes[2]
Creating/Managing Basic Volumes	Yes	No
Creating/Managing Spanned Volumes	No	Yes
Creating/Managing Striped Volumes	No	Yes
Creating/Managing Mirrored Volumes	No	Yes
Creating/Managing RAID-5 Volumes	No	Yes
Maximum Number of Volumes	4[3]	2000[4]
Creating/Managing Volume Mount Points	Yes	Yes
Extending Volumes	Yes[5]	Yes[5]
Support for FAT, FAT32, and NTFS	Yes	Yes
Support for Shared Storage on Server Clusters	Yes	No[6]
Support for Removable Drives (including USB and IEEE 1394)	Yes	No

[1]On Windows NT 4.0 and earlier, you could create mirrored sets, striped sets, spanned sets, and striped sets with parity on servers with basic disks (dynamic disks were introduced in Windows 2000). Support for these features was implemented by a driver, ftdisk.exe. For compatibility reasons, Windows 2000 continued support for these types of volumes on basic disks, but in limited capacity. After upgrading to Windows 2000, all fault-tolerant basic disk configurations were still accessible, but new ones could not be created. Windows 2003 Server and later eliminates completely legacy fault-tolerant disk components implemented by ftdisk.exe. Keep this in mind if you migrate from Windows NT 4.0 servers using a multi-disk configuration. You will have to back up data on the fault-tolerant volumes and restore it when Windows Server 2008 is installed.

[2]The capability to boot from a partition or a volume is strictly dependent on whether an entry for it appears in the partition table. This will happen if the dynamic disk has been converted from a basic disk that contained partitions created in earlier operating systems. It is also possible to use the retain command available in the diskpart.exe utility. This will force the simple volume entry to be retained in the partition table, even if the volume has been created in Windows Server 2008.

[3]Basic disks using the MBR partition style support a maximum of four partitions; if one of them is extended, you can create unlimited numbers of logical drives to it. Basic disks using the GPT partition style support up to 128 primary partitions (including Microsoft Reserved Partition), but do not allow you to create extended partitions.

[4]Even though it is possible to create up to 2,000 dynamic volumes on a dynamic disk, the recommended maximum is 32.

[5]A volume can be extended if it is formatted with NTFS (or if it is unformatted) and is not used to store operating system or boot files. You cannot extend a basic volume that has been created in Windows NT 4.0 or 2000 and upgraded to Windows Server 2008 Server. Basic volumes can be extended using the area on the same disk only. In addition, this area has to be contiguous (immediately following) the one used by the basic volume. Similarly, you can extend a logical drive in an extended volume, as long as there is free contiguous space available. Basic volumes must be extended using diskpart.exe (this feature is not available through Disk Management).

[6]Dynamic disks can be used only for local storage on cluster nodes.

its entirety is part of the RAID-5 volume, you will have 4 × 36GB worth of usable disk space. This is much more efficient than mirroring, because the percentage of overhead in this case is 20 percent as opposed to 50 percent. With 32 disks in a RAID-5 volume (the maximum number of disk supported), you waste only $1/32 \times 100$ percent, or 3.125 percent. Conversely, the more disks you have, the higher the probability that more than any two of them will fail.

RAID-5 is slower than other disk configurations because of the additional operations that need to take place to accommodate the calculation and writing of the parity information. Performance can be improved by using faster and more powerful hardware. Using drives of the same type and speed, as well as fast controllers with a large amount of battery-protected cache, will make a significant difference. Remember that within a RAID-5 configuration, the fastest and most expensive disk is only as good as the slowest and cheapest one.

Consider the type of data when determining the type of software-based fault-tolerant disk configuration. A mirror is the only type of volume that can be used for system and boot volumes; mirroring is also appropriate for storing data that is written sequentially (such as transaction logs). Conversely, if you require large, fault-tolerant volumes that will be accessed randomly, use RAID-5. For example, for large application servers such as SQL Server or Exchange 2008, place their databases on a RAID-5 volume and mirror the transaction logs.

Table 13-1 presents a comprehensive comparison of the features of basic and dynamic disks.

Hardware RAID

Our focus in this chapter has been on software-based RAID configurations available in Windows Server 2008. Although they can improve high availability or offer faster disk access, they are no match for equivalent hardware solutions, which range from relatively inexpensive internal RAID controllers to high-end, fiber-attached SANs containing hundreds of hot-pluggable drives, gigabytes of battery-backed cache memory, multiple, redundant, powerful, built-in storage controllers, and multi-channel I/O. They can also provide support for additional disk configurations such as RAID-1 + 0 (mirrored striped volumes) or RAID-0 + 1 (striped mirrors). This disparity is visible especially when dealing with RAID-5 configurations, where parity information needs to be calculated during data writes. Although software-based volumes use the local CPU, hardware solutions offload this task to dedicated processors on external RAID controllers.

Note that each of the hardware-based RAID configurations is presented to the operating system as a single disk. Therefore, if you have five physical disks and you set up two of them via controller as RAID-1 and the remaining three as RAID-5, once you boot to Windows Server 2008, you would only see two disks in the Disk Management console.

Dynamic Storage Management

Your introduction to practical dynamic disk management will start with the conversion from basic to dynamic disk. Then you will take a look at creating simple, spanned, striped, mirrored, and RAID-5 volumes.

Converting basic disks to dynamic

Upgrading a basic disk to dynamic takes only a few steps:

1. Start by backing up all data on any disks you intend to upgrade (even though the operation is nondestructive).

2. Launch the Microsoft Management console by typing MMC.EXE from the command prompt or select Start ➤ Run. Select Add/Remove Snap-in from the File menu, click the Add button from Add/Remove Snap-in, and choose the Disk Management option from the list. You will be prompted for the target computer, so pick the local one or type in the name of a remote one. Close all dialog boxes, and you will see the snap-in loaded in the tree pane. (Alternatively, you can use the Computer Management console, which contains the Disk Management node in the Storage tree. In all of the following sets of instructions, we will assume that this step has been taken.)

3. Make sure that either the top or bottom part of the details pane lists disks, not volumes. This is done by selecting View ➤ Top or View ➤ Bottom and then choosing either the Disk List or Graphical View option. Figure 13-2 shows the disk view in the top part of the pane and the graphical view at the bottom.

FIGURE 13-2

Selecting the option to convert a disk from basic to dynamic.

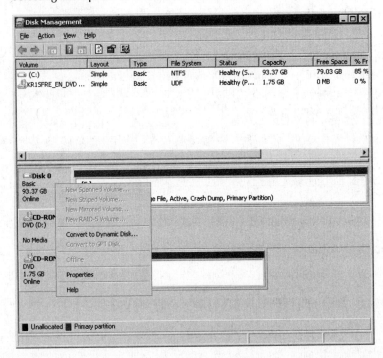

4. Right-click the basic disk you want to convert and select the option Convert to Dynamic Disk. The Convert to Dynamic Disk dialog box is displayed, prompting you for confirmation and giving you an option to choose another disk or convert multiple disks at once. If the disk contains any partitions, you will be presented with another window, listing your selection and volumes to be converted for each disk. You will be reminded that after conversion, other operating systems (other than Windows 2000, XP Professional and Vista, or Windows Server 200X) will not be able to access the volumes on the disk. Finally, another message box will notify you that all volumes on the disk will be dismounted (so you should not keep any files on these volumes open during the conversion). If you are converting the disk containing the Windows directory, the reboot will be required. (See Figure 13-3.)

FIGURE 13-3

Confirming the action to convert to dynamic disk.

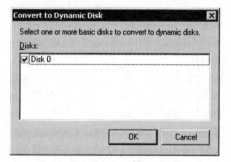

5. After you click the Yes button on the final message box, the conversion takes place. The process is almost instantaneous.

If you want to convert a dynamic disk back to basic, you need to first delete all the volumes it contains. Obviously, this will destroy any data stored on them, so back it up first. After both steps are completed, select the Convert to Basic Disk option that appears in the context menu for each of the dynamic disks displayed in the Disk Management console.

You can also use the diskpart.exe utility to perform both types of conversion with the following steps:

1. At the command prompt on the target server, type diskpart. This will launch the tool and display the diskpart > prompt.

2. At the diskpart > prompt, type SELECT DISK x, where x is the number of the disk to be converted to dynamic (you can obtain a listing of disks by typing LIST DISK at the diskpart > prompt). This will make the disk a target of any subsequent operations.

3. Type in CONVERT DYNAMIC. This completes the conversion process.

To convert back to the basic disk, start by deleting all of its volumes. To do so, select each of them with the `select volume` command (after selecting the disk), and then run the `delete volume` command for each. After this is done, execute `convert basic`. A quicker approach is using the `clean` command, which removes all disk configuration information from the disk. This command can also be used to convert the GPT disk to MBR. After running it, you will also need to re-initialize the disk.

Creating simple volumes

If a basic disk contains any partitions when it is upgraded, they all are automatically converted to simple volumes. You can also create them after the disk becomes dynamic. Simple volumes can exist only on dynamic disks.

Create a simple volume with the following steps:

1. In the Disk Management console window, select the Graphical View from the View ➤ Top or View ➤ Bottom menu. This will display a listing of the disks, with rectangles representing the layout of their volumes or partitions.

2. Bring up the context menu for the rectangle representing the disk layout of the dynamic disk on which the simple volume will be created.

3. Select the New Volume option to launch the New Volume Wizard. Depending on the number of dynamic disks and their layout, you will have an option to create Simple, Spanned, Striped, Mirrored, or RAID-5 volumes. Select Simple and then click Next.

4. The Select Disks page of the wizard will appear, listing Selected and Available disks that can contain the type of volume you chose. On this page, you can specify multiple simple volumes on multiple dynamic disks and provide the size individually for each of them. By default, the size of the simple volume is equal to the size of the remaining unallocated space on the disk (even if the areas of free disk space are not contiguous).

5. The next page of the wizard offers you three options: You can assign it to the volume drive letter, mount it in an empty folder on an existing NTFS partition, or leave it the way it is, not mounted and without a drive letter assignment.

6. The next page gives you an option to format the volume. The only option available from Disk Management console for volumes on dynamic disks is NTFS. You can, however, use FAT or FAT32 if you use `format.exe` from the command line. You can specify the allocation unit size and set the volume label. You can use quick format (if you are fairly confident that the disk does not contain bad sectors) and enable file and folder compression on the volume level.

7. The final page displays your choices. Click Finish to create the volume. If you formatted the volume without selecting the quick format option, the operation might take a while to complete (depending on several factors, such as volume size, system performance, disk speed, and so on). At any point, you can cancel formatting in progress and start the quick format by selecting the Format option from the Action ➤ All Tasks menu.

Extending simple volumes and spanned volumes

As explained previously in this chapter, simple volumes, once created, can be extended, provided that they are formatted using the NTFS file system (or are unformatted), they haven't been converted from basic volumes created in previous versions of Windows operating systems (other than Windows XP/Vista or Windows Server 2008), and they do not function as system or boot volumes.

A simple volume can be extended by adding unallocated space residing on the same disk or by adding unallocated space from another disk on the same system. In the second case, your simple volume will become a spanned volume. Spanned volumes can also be created by combining multiple areas of unallocated disk space on multiple dynamic disks with the New Volume Wizard (described in the previous section).

To extend a simple volume into a spanned volume, use the following procedure:

1. In the Disk Management console, switch to the Graphical View in the lower part of the pane by selecting View ➤ Bottom ➤ Graphical View.

2. Right-click the existing simple volume and select the Extend Volume option from the context menu (the same option appears in the Action ➤ All Tasks menu). This will start the Extend Volume Wizard.

3. A familiar Select Disk page appears. To convert a simple volume into a spanned volume, pick another dynamic disk with unallocated space from the Available list and add it to the Selected box. Decide how much space will be added to the existing volume. Because the existing volume is already formatted, the Format Volume page does not appear.

4. Click Finish. The volume will be extended, and your simple volume will become spanned.

Create a new spanned volume with the following steps:

1. In the Disk Management console, switch to Graphical View in the lower part of the pane by selecting View ➤ Bottom ➤ Graphical View.

2. Right-click the disk with unallocated space and select the New Volume option to launch the New Volume Wizard. The steps you go through are practically identical as before, although your selections will differ.

3. Select the Spanned option as the type of volume you want to create. Next, on the Select Disk page, all remaining dynamic disks with unallocated space will be listed in the Available box. Select the ones you want to include in the spanned volume and click Add. This will switch them to the list of Selected disks. For each disk, you can specify the amount of unallocated space you want to use for the spanned volume.

4. As with a simple volume, decide whether to assign a drive letter to the volume. You can also mount it using an empty folder on an NTFS partition.

5. Finally, specify the file system on the Format Volume page.

A spanned volume can be further extended by adding unallocated space from any of the local dynamic disks.

If you want to recover any of the space used by the spanned volume, delete the entire volume. Before you start, back up whatever data you want to preserve.

Delete a spanned volume with the following steps:

1. In the Disk Management console, switch to Graphical View by selecting View ➤ Bottom ➤ Graphical View.

2. Right-click any of the parts of the spanned volume. They will be displayed using the same color and will have the same label and drive letter (if assigned). Select the Delete Volume option.

After the delete operation is completed, space used by the volume returns to the unallocated state and can be used for any other type of disk configuration.

Creating and managing RAID-0 volumes (striping)

To create a striped volume, you need to have at least two dynamic disks with unallocated disk space. Each area from each of these disks used by the striped volume will have the same size. You do not need to be concerned about this when creating the striped volume because Disk Management will ensure that all pieces are equally large — it will simply allocate space on each disk using the size of the smallest unallocated space among all of them. However, keep this in mind when designing the layout of your volumes. Remember that boot or system volumes cannot be parts of a stripe. Evaluate your storage needs carefully, because striped volumes cannot be extended.

Create a striped volume with the following steps:

1. In the Disk Management console, switch to Graphical View by selecting View ➤ Bottom ➤ Graphical View.

2. Right-click the disk showing unallocated space and select the New Volume option. The New Volume Wizard launches and takes you through the previously described steps. Select the Striped option on the Select Volume Type page.

3. The remaining options are similar to the ones described in the previous section covering the creation of a spanned volume. The main difference is that once you decide which dynamic disks will be used for building the stripe, the amount of space allocated from each of them will be the same and based on the disk with the smallest amount of unallocated space. If you manually type in a smaller number, the size of the areas to be created on each disk will automatically change. Total volume size is the result of multiplying the number of disks in the stripe by this amount.

To delete a striped volume, simply select the Delete option after right-clicking the volume. Obviously, this destroys all data stored on it, so back it up first.

Creating and managing RAID-1 volumes

RAID-1 volumes are fault-tolerant mirrors. Creation of RAID-1 volumes always involves two dynamic disks. You can create mirrored volumes in one of the following ways:

- Create a simple volume and mirror it afterward using an unallocated area of the same or larger size on another dynamic disk.

- Create a mirror using two areas of unallocated space on two separate dynamic disks. As with striping, these areas do not have to be the same size. Choose the smaller one and decide which portion of it you want to use. When the mirror is created, an equally sized portion will be automatically allocated on the other disk.

Create a mirrored volume using the first method with the following steps:

1. In the Disk Management snap-in, switch to Graphical View by selecting View ➢ Bottom ➢ Graphical View.

2. Right-click the disk containing a dynamic volume you want to mirror and select the Add Mirror option.

3. You will be presented with the list of dynamic disks on your system with a sufficient amount of unallocated space to create the mirror. Select the one you want to use and click the Add Mirror button.

4. Right-click the disk containing a dynamic volume you want to mirror and select the Add Mirror option. This will start the process of synchronizing the content of the original simple volume with its replica. The length of time the process takes depends on the amount of data as well as your system's performance and utilization levels. After the synchronization is complete, your mirrored volume should display Healthy status.

Create a mirrored volume using the second method with the following steps:

1. In the Disk Management snap-in, switch to Graphical View by selecting View ➢ Bottom ➢ Graphical View.

2. Right-click one of the disks that will contain the mirrored volume and select the New Volume option. The New Volume Wizard will launch.

3. On the Select Volume Type page, select the Mirrored option.

4. On the Select Disk page, click the second dynamic disk listed in the Available box and click Add. The disk will appear in the Selected box. As with the striped volume, Disk Management will automatically adjust the size of the space used for the mirror to match the smaller area of unallocated space between two disks (as illustrated in Figure 13-4). You can make it smaller if you want.

5. The next two steps — selecting a drive letter or mounting the volume and formatting — are the same as the ones used for other types of volumes. After you click Finish, the mirror will be created instantaneously because no resynchronization needs to take place.

FIGURE 13-4

Selecting the disks used for a mirrored volume.

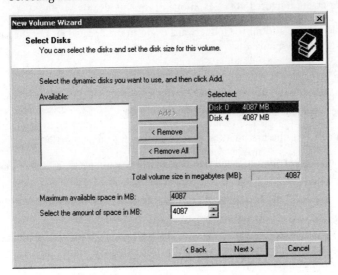

Creating and managing RAID-5 volumes

A RAID-5 volume is another type of fault-tolerant disk configuration available in Windows Server 2008 Server. In order to create a RAID-5 volume, you need to have at least three dynamic disks with unallocated space. As before, even though these areas might be of different sizes, Disk Management will ensure that only space equal to the smallest one will be used when creating the volume. It is not possible to extend a RAID-5 volume or create a RAID-5 volume using any existing volume.

To install RAID-5 volumes, complete the following steps:

1. In the Disk Management snap-in, switch to Graphical View by selecting View ➤ Bottom ➤ Graphical View.

2. Right-click the dynamic disk showing unallocated space and select the New Volume option. The New Volume Wizard will launch and take you through the previously described steps. In the Select Volume Type box, select the RAID-5 option. For this option to be available, you need to have at least three dynamic disks with unallocated space.

3. As with striped and mirrored volumes, on the Select Disks screen you will select disks that will be part of the volume. The size will be automatically adjusted by Disk Management (you can also make it smaller).

4. After selecting the drive letter assignment and formatting option, the wizard will display the final information page. Click the Finish button to instantly create a RAID-5 volume.

Importing disks

Typically, basic disks and dynamic disks containing simple volumes can be removed from one computer and installed into another Windows Server 2008 computer without any impact on the data stored on them. This is also possible when dealing with multi-disk volumes, as long as all the disks that the volume uses are moved together. The multi-disk volumes can be recognized on another system because information about their configuration is stored locally on each disk in the LDM database.

However, transferring dynamic disks between two systems requires an additional step called importing. This is necessary because all dynamic disks in a computer form a group, the name of which is computer-specific (derived from the computer name). In order for a dynamic disk to be imported into a new computer, its database information needs to be merged with the one existing on the new system and its computer group reference renamed.

Import foreign dynamic disks using the following steps:

1. Ensure that each disk is in a healthy state before removal.

2. After inserting the disks into the new host, open the Disk Management console. If the disk does not appear in the details pane, select Action ➤ Rescan Disks. You can also try launching Device Manager and select Action ➤ Hardware Changes.

3. Right-click the disk marked "Foreign" and then choose the Import Foreign Disks option.

4. The Foreign Disk Volumes dialog box will list all volumes detected on the disk to be imported. You can verify whether the list is complete. After you click OK, the disks will be imported into your system.

When the import process is completed, select the Rescan Disks option again to verify that the import worked.

Managing Storage with Disk Quotas

Disk quotas enable you to control space utilization of NTFS-formatted basic and dynamic volumes. In this section, we will take a closer look at the quota technology and the reasons for using it.

Why you need disk quotas

No matter how much hard disk space you think you need, it will never be enough. An insatiable appetite for space is common to users, applications, and operating systems. Just compare the current average size of a user's profile or home folder with those of a few years ago, or consider the space requirements of Microsoft Office 2008 and Windows XP.

Keeping track of available storage is an endless but essential effort. All computer functionality is affected by a lack of hard disk space. If your disk becomes full, services will stop, databases will crash, and backup jobs will fail.

Disk quotas provide a means of controlling and enforcing a user's ability to save data to a volume. It can be enforced at the user level and restricted on a per-volume basis. Typically, you set a user's quota and let Windows Server 2008 monitor the user's disk consumption. Then, when the amount of a user's data on the volume exceeds the first threshold defined by your quota limits, the OS will react with a warning. When the second threshold is reached, users can be prevented from saving any additional files until some disk space is freed. This can be accomplished by either deleting files that are no longer needed, moving them to a different volume, changing file ownership (more about this last option next), or asking the administrator to change the quota limits. Quotas, therefore, not only help you protect disk space, they also force your users to maintain their space utilization. Users can easily find out how much space they can use before reaching the second threshold by checking the volume properties. If the quota limits are enforced, volume properties will display only the amount of space left within their quota limits, rather than total amount of free space on the volume.

With disk quotas, you can set a limit on the hard disk space consumption for all your users. The quota system is not difficult to set up and manage, but you should understand how it works and know its limitations.

Ownership

Quota calculations are based on ownership. Every time a file or folder is created on an NTFS volume or partition, the operating system adds an ownership attribute to it. Permissions have no bearing on the quota system.

Using ownership seems like a good idea, because the person who created a file should be held accountable for usage of the disk space occupied by it. Conveniently, ownership is properly transferred when a copy of an existing file is made, because copying actually involves the creation of a new file. Unfortunately, there are also some drawbacks to using ownership for controlling quotas:

- In many cases, ownership of the file might unexpectedly change. The most common example is the restore scenario, whereby an administrator or backup operator uses a staging area instead of restoring files directly to their original location. In this case, the next step after the restore would involve manually copying restored files to their final destination, where the user requesting the restore can access them. If this copy is done by someone other than the user, that person becomes the owner of the copied files, and they no longer count toward the user's quota limits. One solution to this problem is using a staging area on the same volume and moving files instead of copying, because moving files between folders on the same volume retains ownership.

- Fixing ownership problems might be difficult and time-consuming. Windows does not provide a method for granting ownership to another user (you can only take ownership if you have sufficient rights, which are controlled by Take Ownership of Files and Other Objects user rights and granted automatically to members of local Administrators groups).

 **Several third-party products can be used to grant ownership. Refer to** www.pedestalsoftware.com **and** www.mks.com **for details.**

■ Migration of data between servers must be done using methods that preserve file and folder ownership. The best approach is using Windows Server 2008 backup and restore, or third-party backup programs that offer this feature. However, this might create a problem if local groups (rather than domain local groups) are used to grant permissions to data.

■ You need to pay special attention to services that are running in the context of a user account. Although typically such an account is a member of a local Administrators group, which is exempted from quotas, this might not be the case. In such situations, the service might suddenly stop running if an application using it exceeds disk space quota limits.

■ Disk quotas can be assigned only on a per-user basis, because (with the exception of local Administrators) a group cannot be listed as an owner of a file or a folder. This introduces administrative overhead, unless you apply the same limit to all users.

Caveats of quota systems

Besides the ownership-related issues listed in the preceding section, there are several other caveats for disk quotas in Windows. The quota system ignores compression, taking into account only the uncompressed size of a file when calculating space utilization. It uses the same rule with sparse files. Removing quota entries for individual users requires changing ownership for every single file owned by that person on the volume (or deleting or moving these files).

As expected, quota limits do not apply to any accounts that are members of the local Administrators group. You can change this, though, by creating a separate quota entry for each of them. The only account that cannot be restricted this way is the built-in Administrator account.

When configuring quotas, you can instruct the quota service to write entries into the event log. You can build a custom solution that would use these entries to trigger a notification or even some type of cleanup activities.

Establishing quotas does not automatically enforce them, but it enables you to collect the statistics about users' data. This, in turn, helps you make accurate estimates of disk space utilization and plan quota settings accordingly. Before you implement quotas, note that they impose a performance penalty. Their impact depends on the amount of data and overall system performance, so, just as with other solutions, you should test it properly first.

Remember that disk utilization statistics in the Quota Entries window are cached and might not reflect the actual values. You need to refresh the window by pressing the F5 key to update them.

Disk space/quota analysis

The quota service component, once enabled for a volume, gathers disk space usage information about all users who own files on it. This information is reported to the Quota Entries for New Volume as illustrated in Figure 13-5 (accessible from the Quota tab of the Volume Properties). This information provides a convenient way of determining ownership of file objects in a volume, without having to analyze the entire file system by checking the security properties of each file and folder.

FIGURE 13-5

The quota entries for a local disk.

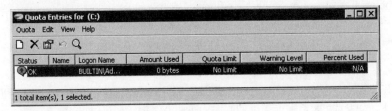

After collecting information utilization of the volume on a per-user basis, you can start setting disk quotas.

Setting disk quotas

To set up quotas on individual volumes, do the following:

1. Make sure you are logged on as a member of the local Administrators group on the server hosting the volume. This is required to set quotas. The volume must be formatted using NTFS. If not, run the `convert.exe` utility first if you want to preserve the data residing on it. Otherwise, format it with NTFS using the Disk Management console, Windows Explorer, or the command line.

2. Launch the Disk Management console.

3. Switch to Graphical View by selecting View ➤ Bottom ➤ Graphical View.

4. Right-click the volume for which you want to set the quotas and select the Properties option from the menu. This will display the Local Disk Properties dialog box. Click the Quota tab. This will display the options shown in Figure 13-6.

    If the volume has a drive letter assigned to it, you can also access it from the My Computer window by right-clicking that drive, selecting Properties from the context menu, and clicking the Quota tab. Both methods bring up the same dialog box, but the first one allows you to set up quotas on volumes (such as mounted volumes) without a corresponding drive letter.

5. Click the Enable Quota Management checkbox. This triggers the monitoring of user disk space consumption (the results can be viewed by clicking the Quota Entries button).

6. Click the Deny Disk Space to Users Exceeding Quota Limit checkbox. This option is required to enforce quota limits and send notification to users who exceed them. Checking this is not sufficient, though, to enforce quotas. You also need to set appropriate limits for everyone, or for individual users, through the Quota Entries for Local Disk window.

7. Leave the Do Not Limit Disk Usage option selected if you want to allow users to use as much hard disk space as they need; otherwise, check the Limit Disk Space To select box and specify the size limit. This value will apply to all users (with the exception of members of the local Administrators group).

8. Set the warning level to whatever amount you consider appropriate (but higher than the limit set in the previous step). This is the first threshold. After the warning has been issued, users can continue using hard disk space until they reach the second threshold.

9. The last two checkboxes on this tab control the logging of events for exceeding warning and quota limit thresholds in the Windows System Event Log. When searching for them, remember that they are listed as informational events.

FIGURE 13-6

The Quota tab of New Volume Properties.

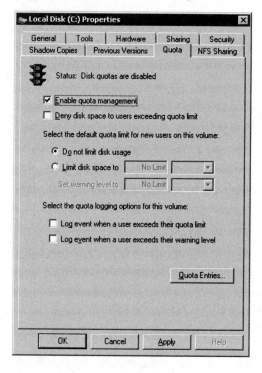

Adding disk quota entries

In the preceding section, we set the same quota thresholds for all users. If you want to be able to control disk space utilization in a more granular fashion, you can create separate limits for individual users. To add quota entries, click the Quota Entries button in the Local Disk Properties dialog box for the volume. Insert quota entries using the following steps:

1. From the Quota menu, select the New Quota Entry option. This brings up the Select Users dialog box.

2. From the Select Users dialog box, enter the username to which the limit will apply and then click OK.

Common-sense disk quota management

Disk quotas can help you manage disk space utilization, but they can also make common, otherwise straightforward, tasks more difficult. The following suggestions should help you make your quota management more efficient:

- When assigning quotas, leave some extra disk space unassigned. This will be useful if you need to customize quotas on a per-user basis. This extra space will also be used by NTFS metadata (taking roughly 64 KB per file) that is not counted toward a user's quota limits.

- Make users aware of the effects of disk quotas (without getting into details) and how to check the disk space available to them (all of them should be familiar with Windows Explorer). Most likely, enforcing quotas will bring them much closer to the space utilization limits than before. For example, let's say user JDoe owns 100 MB worth of files on a quota-enabled volume with total disk space of 36GB. The same volume is used by 50 other users with very similar space requirements. Assuming (for simplicity's sake) that all of them currently occupy the same amount of space, JDoe will see 31GB of free disk space when checking the volume properties. Suppose you set the quota threshold to 600 MB, which you get by subtracting the 6GB "cushion" from the total of 36GB and dividing it by the total number of users (obviously, your users' requirements will likely be completely different). As soon as you check the Deny Disk Space to Users Exceeding Quota Limits checkbox in the Quota tab of Volume Properties, and set the quota limit, free disk space properties for JDoe will show the value of 500 MB.

- Enable warning thresholds for all users and leave a sufficient buffer between the warning and hard disk limit. It makes no sense to warn users that they are about to run out of allocated space and then enforce a hard limit as soon as they try to save their files.

- Ensure that users will not be installing applications on the volume with the quota limits set. In rare cases when this happens, increase the quota limit to prevent application installations from failing, or install it using an administrative account.

- Monitor hard disk usage on a continuous basis. Take corrective actions (for example, increase allocated space for power users) if you encounter problems.

- Avoid sharing user accounts. Such a solution is insecure and makes proper quota management difficult.

- Account for the size of a user's roaming profile in your estimates of space requirements if they happen to be stored on a volume with disk quotas turned on.

- If the spool directory resides on a volume with disk quotas, account for the sizes of print jobs. Their ownership is set to the users who created them, so they also count toward the quota limits. If possible, move a spool directory to a separate volume.

- Try using Group Policies, Windows Management Instrumentation scripts, or the `fsutil.exe` command-line utility to manage disk quotas. To simplify management, you can also export and import quota entries between the servers (as long as they are located in the same domain).

- Remove quotas for users who no longer need access to the volume. This requires, though, that you first delete, move, or take ownership (as Administrator) of users' files. The easiest way to do this is from the Quota Entries dialog box. Attempting to delete an entry will invoke the Disk Quota dialog box shown in Figure 13-7. This dialog box lists all folders and files owned by the user. You can delete, take ownership of, or move individual files or multiple files. The only option available for folders is to take ownership.

FIGURE 13-7

Disk Quota dialog box.

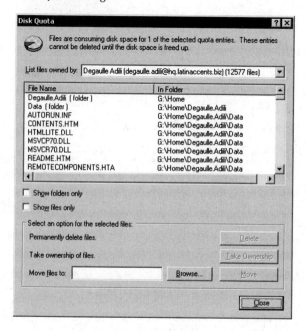

Troubleshooting

The following sections will help you troubleshoot disk- and volume-related issues.

Disk and volume states

During the lifetime of a disk or a volume, its integrity may change. The disk management utility indicates the status of each disk and volume through its state. The status of disks and volumes can be listed using the diskpart.exe utility with the list disk and list volumes commands. Table 13-2 lists possible volume states and the meaning of each one.

Table 13-3 lists possible hard disk states and the meaning of each one.

TABLE 13-2

Common Types of Volume Status

State	Description
Healthy	The volume operates in the normal fashion and no known problems have been detected. This status is displayed for both basic and dynamic volumes. Healthy status can contain additional sub-status information. Two examples are listed next.
Healthy (At Risk)	The volume is available, but Windows Server 2008 has detected read and write (I/O) errors on the disk. This state is only reported for dynamic volumes.
Healthy (Unknown Partition)	The volume is not recognized. It might have been created using a different operating system or it might be a non-recognizable OEM configuration partition. They can be deleted with both Disk Management and the `diskpart` tool (using the `delete partition` command with the `override` option).
Unknown	The boot sector is corrupted. This might be the result of disk corruption or a boot sector virus.
Resynching	This status applies to mirrored volumes. Resynching is the process of making both sets of data (one on each mirror) identical. The duration of the resynching process depends on the amount of data, and system performance and utilization. Try to limit access to the volume while resynching is in progress. When the resynching is complete, the disk status returns to healthy.
Formatting	The volume is being formatted. The percentage of the formatted volume is displayed to indicate the progress.
Regenerating	This status applies to RAID-5 volumes. It takes place after replacing a failed disk and involves writing missing information to a new member of the volume. Try to limit access to the volume while regeneration is in progress. When the regeneration is complete, the disk status returns to Healthy.
Failed Redundancy	This status applies to mirrored and RAID-5 volumes. It indicates that one of the disks failed and the volume is no longer fault tolerant. Even though the volume remains accessible, failure of another disk in the volume will cause loss of data. You should replace the disk as soon as possible and resynch or regenerate the volume.
Failed Redundancy (At Risk)	This status applies to RAID-5 or RAID-1 volumes. It means that the volume is no longer fault tolerant and that I/O errors have been detected on the media. This status appears for each part of the volume on each disk. The Failed Redundancy state can also appear with other sub-states, such as System or Boot, for a failing nonmirrored system or boot volume.
Failed	This status applies to both basic and dynamic volumes. It indicates that the volume cannot be started and will require intervention. This status also might be displayed after importing incomplete multi-disk dynamic volume.

TABLE 13-3

Common Types of Disk Status

State	Description
Online	The disk is fully operational and no known errors have been detected.
Online (Errors)	The disk is operational but I/O errors have been detected. You might be able to return the disk to the Online state by running the `Reactivate Disk` command from the context menu of the disk. This status is available only for dynamic disks.
Offline	The dynamic disk cannot be accessed. This is typically caused by physical disk or connector failures. Try using the Reactivate Disk option from the Action menu of the Disk Management console. If this fails, you must remove the physical disk from the computer and execute the Remove Disk option to remove references to the disk from the LDM database. This status is available only for dynamic disks.
Foreign	The disk has been moved from another computer. Import it using the Import Foreign Disks option from the disk's context menu.
Missing	The dynamic disk is damaged, corrupted, or disconnected. If the cause of the problem can be eliminated, you might be able to return the disk to Online status by selecting Reactivate Disk from the Action menu in the Disk Management console. Otherwise, use the Remove Disk option. This status is available only for dynamic disks.
Not Initialized	For MBR disks, a valid disk signature is missing from the Master Boot Record. For GPT disks, a valid GUID is missing from the GUID partition table. This typically happens when a new disk is installed in the computer. Initialization of the disk fixes the problem.
Initializing	This status is displayed when converting a disk from basic to dynamic. There is no need for intervention unless the system hangs and the status remains unchanged. Ordinarily, the status should return to Healthy.
Unreadable	The disk might be temporarily unavailable or corrupted. This status is available for both static and dynamic disks. Try rescanning the disk or rebooting the computer. If this does not change the status, replace the disk.

Fixing RAID redundancy failures

If the status of any volume reports Failed Redundancy, Failed Redundancy (At Risk), or just Failed, use one of the following procedures to fully recover it.

Procedure 1: To reactivate a volume in Failed Redundancy state, try the following:

1. In the Disk Management snap-in, switch to Graphical View by selecting View ➤ Bottom ➤ Graphical View.

2. If a disk hosting the volume is listed in Missing, Offline, or Online (Errors) state, right-click it and select Reactivate Disk. If the reactivation succeeds, the disk returns to Online and the volume to Healthy status.

Procedure 2: When a Failed Redundancy volume does not recover using the previous approach, try the following:

1. If the disk returned to the Online status, attempt to reactivate the volume manually. This is done using the Reactivate Volume option (although typically this should take place automatically after performing the steps in Procedure 1).

2. If the disk is still listed as Offline or Missing, then the problem is most likely related to a nonfunctioning disk or loose or failed connectors. To replace a failed mirror, right-click any of the disk areas participating in the mirror, select the Remove Mirror option, and follow the wizard. Replace the bad disk and follow the instructions for creating mirrors using existing dynamic volumes provided in the section "Creating and Managing RAID-1 Volumes," earlier in this chapter. To repair a RAID-5 volume, first eliminate the cause of the problem. If the disk needs to be replaced, do so, initialize it, and convert it to dynamic. Then, use the `Repair Volume` command from the context menu of the RAID-5 volume.

Procedure 3: To attempt the reactivation of a volume in a Failed Redundancy (At Risk) state, try the following:

1. Try to reactivate the disk hosting the volume (typically listed with Online [Errors] status) in the same fashion as in Procedure 1. If necessary, attempt to reactivate the volume manually using Procedure 2.

2. A change of status to Failed Redundancy (without At Risk) after the first step is usually a good sign, and repeating the steps in Procedures 1 and 2 (if needed) should return the disk to Healthy status. The likely problem is that the volume data is out of sync (for a mirror) or parity information needs to be regenerated (for RAID-5). Use the Reactivate or Resynchronize commands and then run `chkdsk` against the volume. If this fails, you may need to replace the hardware. You will need to have a valid backup.

Procedure 4: To replace disks, do the following:

1. If you have spare dynamic disks, import them using the Import Foreign Disk option. Otherwise, install the disks as basic and convert them to dynamic.

2. Using the methods described earlier in this chapter, return the volume to its original state.

Storage Explorer

Windows Server 2003 Release 2 storage management introduced SAN management resources for storage with the Storage Manager for SANS. In Windows Server 2008 this tool is now called Storage Explorer. Storage and SAN management software is very expensive, and although the new tool is not high-end, it will suffice for many small SAN storage implantations. SAN storage configuration is mostly used in clustering and high-availability environments, which are beyond the scope of this book; however, we touch on SAN storage again in the next chapter.

Summary

This chapter provided a thorough look at Windows Server 2008 storage services. In particular, we covered the Disk Management console and management of basic and dynamic disks and volumes, concepts and configuration of disk quotas, and troubleshooting disk and volume problems.

Chapter 14

Windows Server 2008 File Systems

This chapter explores the many aspects of the Windows Server 2008 file system, including file system structure, the Distributed File System (DFS), auditing, and system repair and recovery.

An Overview of Disk Structure

To understand the file system options in Windows Server 2008, you first need to understand some basic physical disk concepts and terms. This section covers concepts and terms that will help you understand file system structure in Windows Server 2008. This chapter does not cover basic hardware storage concepts such as heads and head gap in detail because these topics aren't germane to an understanding of file systems. This chapter focuses mainly on logical disk structure, rather than physical disk structure, but let's take a quick look at how physical and logical structure relate to each other.

The circular path a head traverses as it sits motionless over a disk platter is called a *track*. The tracks are magnetically encoded on the disk during formatting and define the physical structure of the disk's storage space. The tracks that reside in the same location on each platter form a *cylinder*. Each track is divided into a certain number of *sectors*, the number of which depends on the disk type and location of the track on the disk. Sectors are the smallest physical storage units on a disk, but they are grouped into *clusters*, which are the smallest *logical* storage units on the disk. Figure 14-1 illustrates basic disk structure.

FIGURE 14-1

Physical disk structure.

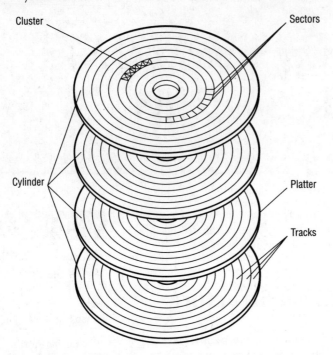

Each cluster comprises a certain number of sectors. The number of sectors in each cluster depends on the drive type, partition size, and file system (explained in the following sections). When the operating system stores a file, the storage space is allocated not by sector, but by cluster. The cluster size has a significant impact on the amount of free space on a disk, as you'll learn later in the section "Optimizing Storage Capacity."

Basic disks in Windows Server 2008 contain one or more *partitions* that consist of a series of clusters. A partition has a beginning and an ending sector, and the number of sectors in between determines the partition capacity. Each partition uses a particular file system type (FAT16, FAT32, NTFS, and so on). Each basic disk can contain up to four partitions, all *primary partitions*, or three primary partitions and one *extended partition*. Each primary partition represents a single drive with a single drive ID, while an extended partition can contain multiple logical drives. Each logical drive can be represented by a drive ID, although drive IDs are not required per se. For the sake of simplicity and consistency, the term *volume* refers to a logical drive entity, such as a drive defined by a primary partition or a single logical drive in an extended partition.

Dynamic disks are new in Windows Server 2008 and overcome the four-partition limitation of basic disks. Dynamic disks don't contain partitions. Instead, they contain *dynamic volumes*, which are a lot like a logical drive within an extended partition in the sense that the disk can contain multiple volumes and each appears as a unique object. However, you can create an unlimited number of volumes in a dynamic disk, subject to disk capacity. As with partitions in a basic disk, each dynamic volume has its own file system (FAT16, FAT32, or NTFS).

> **TIP** Although you can manage existing fault-tolerant volumes on a basic disk with Windows Server 2008, you can't create or extend these volumes on basic disks. Full support (creation and modification) for fault-tolerant volumes now requires a dynamic disk.

The Enterprise Server and Datacenter Server versions of Windows Server 2008 also support the GUID Partition Table, or GPT. Support for GPT volumes — introduced in Windows XP — requires the 64-bit versions of the server platforms, which run on the Intel Itanium processors.

GPT offers several advantages over the Master Boot Record (MBR) partitioning scheme. First, GPT supports 2^{64} logical blocks. Assuming a typical block size of 512 bytes means a theoretical size for a single GPT volume of 8ZB (zettabytes), although the practical size is limited to about 18 exabytes. GPT also supports a theoretically unlimited number of unique partitions per disk. This means that a single disk can be considerably larger than it could be with other partitioning schemes.

Windows Server 2008 systems with GPT disks can read and write to those disks, as well as to MBR-type disks. However, the 64-bit versions of Windows Server 2008 cannot boot from an MBR disk. The boot loader and boot partition must reside on a GPT disk. The GPT partition includes a structure called the Protective MBR, which starts at sector 0 and precedes the GPT partition on the disk. The Protective MBR exists for non-GPT-aware disk utilities, which would otherwise interpret the GPT partition as being unpartitioned space.

> **NOTE** You will find more information about GPT at www.microsoft.com/whdc/default.mspx.

Whether you choose to use basic disks with primary or extended partitions, or dynamic disks with dynamic volumes, each volume requires a file system. You can choose among three in Windows Server 2008: FAT16, FAT32, or NTFS. Each offers certain advantages and disadvantages. The following section explains the structure, advantages, and disadvantages of the FAT16 and FAT32 file systems.

FAT16 and FAT32

The FAT file system originated with DOS and is supported by DOS, all versions of Windows, Windows NT, Windows Server 2008, Unix, Linux, and OS/2. Because of that wide support, it is the most compatible between operating platforms (one of its advantages). FAT stands for File Allocation Table, which is the structure in a FAT volume that stores information about disk space allocation.

A disk formatted with the FAT file system contains five control areas. The first is the *reserve area*, which comprises one or more sectors depending on the disk type. The first sector in the reserve area is the *boot sector*, which contains the partition table and bootstrap program. The partition table stores information about the disk's partitions, including type, starting and ending sectors, and which partition is active. The bootstrap program executes at startup and boots the operating system or boot loader in the active partition. The boot sector is always located at cylinder 0, head 0, track 1 (the first sector on the disk).

The *File Allocation Table* (FAT) is the second control area and serves as a reference table of the clusters in the volume. Each cluster's entry contains a value defined by those listed in Table 14-1. The value defines the cluster's status, indicating whether the cluster is available, in use, bad, or reserved. A backup copy of the FAT makes up the third control area and can be used by utility applications to restore the file system when the primary FAT becomes corrupted.

TABLE 14-1

FAT Cluster Entries

Entry	Meaning
0	Cluster is available
BAD	Cluster contains a bad sector and is unusable
Reserved	Cluster is reserved for use by the operating system
EOF	End of File; marks the last cluster of a file
nnn	Number of the next cluster in the file

The fourth control area is the *root directory table*, which works in conjunction with the FAT to define files in the root directory, subdirectories (which are really just files in the root directory), and the starting cluster of each file. The fifth control area is the area in which file data is actually stored in the volume. When applications request a file read operation, the OS reads the FAT to locate the beginning cluster for the file. It then uses the FAT as a sort of road map to locate the other clusters for the file, using the FAT as a lookup table to determine which clusters to read and in which order to put a file back together.

Windows Server 2008 automatically determines the number of sectors per cluster for a volume based on the volume's size. Table 14-2 lists the default cluster size for FAT volumes. The sizes listed apply to disks consisting of a single partition and to logical drives in an extended partition. Floppy disks are not included. Cluster size is an important consideration when formatting a disk to optimize disk capacity.

The FAT file system originally used 12 bits to define the FAT entries. A 16-bit FAT, called FAT16, was introduced in DOS 4.0 to accommodate larger cluster values and therefore larger disks. FAT16 supports a maximum of 65,526 clusters, which limits FAT volumes to 4GB ($clustersize_{max} \times clusters_{max} = bytes$).

Windows 95 OSR2 introduced FAT32, which allocates 32 bits to the FAT, increasing the maximum number of clusters to 268,435,446. The maximum cluster size of 32,768 bytes means that FAT32 volumes can theoretically be up to 8TB (one terabyte equals 1,024 gigabytes), although the current hardware limitation of 512-byte sectors limits the actual size to 2TB. Windows Server 2008 limits the size of the FAT32 partition you can create within Windows Server 2008 to 32GB. However, it does support mounting any size FAT32 volume, including those larger than 32GB. This capability enables you to mount FAT32 volumes larger than 32GB created with another operating system or a third-party partitioning utility. Table 14-3 lists the default cluster sizes for FAT32 volumes of a given size.

TABLE 14-2

Default FAT Cluster Size

Volume Size	Cluster Size	Sectors per Cluster
Less than 32MB	512 bytes	1
33 to 64MB	1K	2
65 to 128MB	2K	4
129 to 255MB	4K	8
256 to 511MB	8K	16
512MB to 1GB	16K	32
1GB to 2GB	32K	64
2GB to 4GB	64K	128

TABLE 14-3

Default FAT32 Cluster Size

Volume Size	Cluster Size	Sectors per Cluster
Less than 512MB	Not supported	N/A
512MB to 8GB	4K	8
8GB to 16GB	8K	16
16GB to 32GB	16K	32
More than 32GB	32K	64

NOTE Microsoft reserves the top four bits of each cluster in a FAT32 volume, so there are only 28 bits for the cluster number, not 32; therefore, the maximum number of clusters totals 268,435,446. In addition, BIOS limitations can limit volume size on any given system. Finally, the 512-byte sector size is also a limiting factor.

NTFS

NTFS stands for NT File System, and NTFS is the third file system type supported by Windows Server 2008. It offers several advantages over the FAT16 and FAT32 file systems, although NTFS is not the optimum choice in all situations, as you'll learn shortly.

One primary difference from FAT16 is that NTFS is a recoverable file system. If a failure occurs that affects an NTFS volume, Windows Server 2008 reconstructs the volume automatically when the system restarts. Another important distinction is security. FAT16 and FAT32 allow you to apply limited share permissions to control access to resources shared from a FAT16 folder. The share permissions apply to all subfolders and files within the share. NTFS, however, allows you to apply not only share permissions, but *object permissions* as well. Object permissions provide a much more granular level of control over folder and file access, enabling access on a folder-by-folder and file-by-file basis. Object permissions apply not only to remote connections across the network, but also to local connections. NTFS, therefore, is the only Windows Server 2008 file system that provides adequate security for folders and files for users who log on locally. NTFS also allows object access auditing, something that is not supported for FAT16/FAT32 volumes.

In addition, the version of NTFS on Windows Server 2008 now has self-healing features built into it. In the past you would have used the Chkdsk.exe tool to fix problems with the NTFS file system volumes. This was always a tedious and time-consuming process that resulted in downtime.

With NTFS's self-healing features you do not need to take any action to fix the disk. When something goes wrong on the disk you get notified about the error and then offered several possible fixes and what actions to take. And you don't need to run Chkdsk.

CROSS-REF See Chapter 10 for a detailed description of auditing.

Similar to FAT32, NTFS supports larger volumes than FAT volumes, with a maximum of 2TB per NTFS volume. Also similar to FAT16 and FAT32, NTFS provides for a variable cluster size that adjusts automatically according to volume size. Table 14-4 lists the default NTFS cluster sizes for volumes of a given size.

As with FAT16 and FAT32, you can change the cluster size for an NTFS volume when you format the volume to optimize storage capacity. The cluster sizes identified in Table 14-4 are the default sizes Windows Server 2008 uses unless you specify otherwise. See the section "Optimizing Storage Capacity" later in this chapter for an explanation of why you would choose a cluster size different from the default values.

TABLE 14-4		

Default NTFS Cluster Size

Volume Size	Cluster Size	Sectors per Cluster
512MB or less	512 bytes	1
513MB to 1GB	1K	2
1GB to 2GB	2K	4
2GB to 4GB	4K	8
4GB to 8GB	8K	16
8GB to 16GB	16K	32
16GB to 32GB	32K	16
More than 32GB	64K	128

NTFS structure

The structure of an NTFS volume is considerably different from that of the FAT16 and FAT32 file systems. The boot sector, located at sector 0 in the volume, can be up to 16 sectors in size and comprises two structures: the BIOS Parameter Block (BPB) and the bootstrap program. The BPB stores information about the volume's layout. The bootstrap program loads the file NTLDR, which boots the system. NTFS stores a duplicate copy of the boot sector at the end of the volume for redundancy and fault tolerance.

How NTFS stores volume data also differs from FAT. NTFS uses a relational database called the *master file table* (MFT) to manage the contents of a volume. The MFT serves much the same purpose in the NTFS file system that the FAT serves in the FAT file systems. The MFT stores a record for each file and directory, including the MFT itself. Each entry includes the name, security descriptor, and other attributes. The MFT is an array of data with rows representing file records, and columns representing attribute fields for each record, as shown in Figure 14-2. The size of each MFT record is constant and determined when the volume is formatted. MFT record size can be 1K, 2K, or 4K, depending on disk size.

The Data field for each record stores the file's data. With very small files, the data is contained completely within the Data field of one MFT record. When all of a file's attributes — including its data — reside in a single MFT record, the attributes are called *resident attributes*.

FIGURE 14-2

The MFT is a relational database that maintains the data on an NTFS volume.

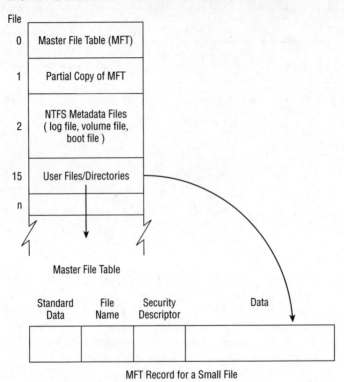

As a file increases in size or becomes fragmented, however, it requires multiple records to store its data. The primary record in the MFT for a file that spans multiple records is called the *base file record*. The base file record serves as the starting point in the file's data chain. NTFS creates additional areas called *runs* on the disk to store the additional file data. With volumes that have a cluster size of 2K or smaller, the runs are 2K in size. Volumes with 4K or larger clusters use 4K-sized runs. Attributes that don't reside in the MFT but instead reside in runs are called *non-resident attributes*. NTFS adds additional runs as needed when file size increases.

If you compare the way NTFS and FAT store information about data in the volume, you'll see that the MFT is similar to FAT. Windows Server 2008 uses the cluster entries in the FAT to locate the clusters in a file's data chain. Windows Server 2008 uses the records in the MFT to locate the data in a file's data chain. The clusters belonging to a file are referenced in the MFT using virtual cluster numbers (VCNs). Each file starts with VCN 0, and additional clusters are numbered sequentially up to the last cluster in the file. The Data attribute for the file contains information that maps the VCNs to the logical cluster numbers (LCNs) on the disk.

When there are too many VCN-to-LCN mappings to store in a single MFT record, NTFS adds additional records to store the additional mappings. Figure 14-3 illustrates VCN-to-LCN mapping in the MFT.

FIGURE 14-3

The MFT record for a file stores its VCN-to-LCN mapping, using multiple runs if necessary.

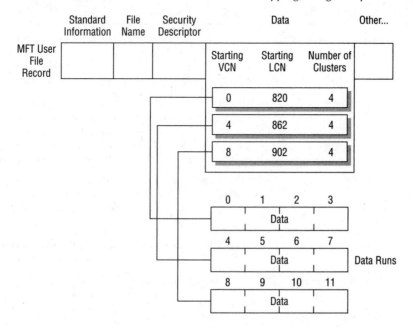

The first 16 records in the MFT are reserved by NTFS for *metadata*, which are the files NTFS uses to define the file system structure. Table 14-5 describes the metadata stored in the MFT.

Though the MFT performs a similar function to the FAT, the similarities between the two file systems stop there. NTFS provides considerably more features than FAT because of the differences in structure. As mentioned previously, NTFS provides much better security and recoverability than FAT. NTFS also provides built-in compression capability, enabling you to compress files on a file-by-file basis. The NTFS driver handles decompression on the fly, making compression transparent to the user.

NOTE For detailed information on using compression on NTFS volumes, see the section "Using Disk Compression in NTFS" later in this chapter.

NTFS's structure also makes it an extensible file system, so new features can be added without completely redesigning the file system. Several new features were added to NTFS version 5 in Windows 2000, and these improvements carry forward into Windows Server 2008. The following sections explain the most pertinent changes.

TABLE 14-5

NTFS Metadata

MFT Record	Description	Filename	Purpose
0	Master file table (MFT)	$Mft	Stores the base file record for each file and folder in the volume. Additional records are used when the number or size of files and folders exceeds the space available.
1	Master file table 2	$MftMirr	This duplicate MFT stores the first four records of the MFT to ensure access to the MFT in case of a failure. The boot sector stores the data segment locations for both $Mft and $MftMirr for recoverability.
2	Log file	$LogFile	Stores transaction history enabling NTFS to perform a recovery of the file system if an error occurs. The log can be up to 4MB in size.
3	Volume	$Volume	Stores volume data such as the volume version and volume label.
4	Attribute definitions	$AttrDef	Comprises a table of attribute names, numbers, and descriptions.
5	Root file name index	$	The volume's root directory.
6	Cluster bitmap	$Bitmap	Clusters-in-use table.
7	Partition boot sector	$Boot	Contains the bootstrap program on the bootable volume.
8	Bad cluster file	$BadClus	Bad cluster map.
9	Security file	$Secure	Stores unique security descriptors for all files in the volume.
10	Upcase table	$Upcase	Converts lowercase characters to uppercase Unicode characters.
11	NTFS extension file	$Extend	Enables file system extensions such as reparse points, quotas, and so on.
12–15			Reserved for future use.

Disk quotas

NTFS in Windows Server 2008 supports *disk quotas*, which enable you to restrict the amount of disk space a given account can use. Quotas enable you to more effectively manage storage space because you can parcel out the space on an as-needed basis. Quotas also force users to conserve their designated storage space, compelling them to delete files when no longer needed. You can configure how quotas are enforced when a given user's quota is reached, by either denying additional space to the user or simply displaying a warning message (see Chapter 13 and Chapter 15).

You assign quotas on a per-volume basis, which means that the entire volume shares the same quota properties. However, you can assign quota limits on a per-user basis, which enables each user to have a different quota limit, if necessary. You can also apply quotas on a per-group basis through the use of Group Policies. This flexibility enables you to tailor disk quotas to each user's or group's needs.

Although quotas apply to an entire volume, rather than a single folder, there is a way around the per-volume nature of quotas. For example, assume you want to apply quotas only to C:\Users but not to the rest of drive C. *Mounted volumes*, also supported in Windows Server 2008, enable you to mount a physical volume to an NTFS folder. The mounted volume appears to both local and remote users as the contents of the host folder. In this situation, you can apply quotas to the mounted volume but not to the volume where it is hosted (drive C in this case). The net effect is that to the user, quotas only apply in the folder C:\Users.

CROSS-REF For more information regarding quotas and quota assignment, see Chapters 13 and 15. See the section "Mounted Volumes" later in this chapter for a discussion of mounted volumes.

Reparse points

Reparse points enable Windows Server 2008 to implement a handful of other features (described in the following sections). Reparse points are NTFS objects that carry special attribute tags. They are used to trigger additional functionality in the file system, working in conjunction with file system filters to extend the capability of the NTFS file system. The combination of reparse points and these additional file system filters enables features and functions to be added to the file system by both Microsoft and third parties without the need to redesign or restructure the file system. The Encrypting File System, described in the next section, is an example of a feature that relies on reparse points.

In effect, reparse points are like red flags in the file system. When Windows Server 2008 encounters a reparse point during path name parsing, it passes the reparse attribute tag (which uniquely defines the purpose of the reparse point) back up the I/O stack. Each installable file system filter in the I/O stack examines the reparse tag. When a match occurs, the driver executes the feature associated with the reparse point, so this "red flag" tells Windows Server 2008 that a driver other than the standard NTFS file system driver needs to process the file I/O to accommodate the added functionality made possible by that other driver.

Encrypting File System

The Encrypting File System (EFS) is one feature made possible by reparse points in Windows Server 2008 that enhances security for local files on NTFS volumes. EFS is useful for securing files on any system, but it is most useful on systems that can easily be stolen or physically compromised, such as notebook and tablet PCs. EFS is integrated within NTFS and therefore is applicable only to files on NTFS volumes. FAT16 and FAT32 volumes do not support EFS. Only files can be encrypted; folders cannot, even on NTFS volumes. However, folders are marked to indicate that they contain encrypted data. EFS is designed to protect files locally, and therefore doesn't support sharing of encrypted files. You can store your own encrypted files on a remote server and access those files yourself. The data is not encrypted during transmission across the network, however, unless you use Internet Protocol Security (IPSec) to encrypt IP traffic (assuming you are using TCP/IP as the network protocol for transferring the file).

 For a detailed discussion of EFS and how to implement it, see the section "Securing Files by Using the Encrypting File System," in Chapter 15.

Hierarchical Storage Management

Hierarchical Storage Management (HSM) is another concept in Windows Server 2008 made possible by reparse points. HSM enables some or all of a file to be stored remotely, and reparse points mark these files accordingly. The reparse point data stores the location of the remote data and allows NTFS to retrieve the data when needed. HSM works in conjunction with remote and removable storage to enable files to be archived to tape or disk and automatically restored when requested by a user or process.

Directory junctions

Directory junctions are another feature of NTFS. Directory junctions mark NTFS directories with a surrogate name. When the reparse point causes the path name to be reparsed, the surrogate name is grafted onto the original name. Directory junctions enable local volumes to be mapped to local NTFS folders, and allow remote network shares to be mapped to local NTFS folders, thereby integrating these local and remote elements into a single local namespace. Directory junctions offer functions similar to the Distributed File System (DFS), explained later in the section "Managing the Distributed File System." Unlike DFS, directory junctions work solely within the file system and don't require a client-side driver.

The primary purpose of directory junctions is to enable you to create a single local namespace using local folders, other local volumes, and network shares. All of these appear within the local namespace and appear to the local user as part of the local volume. Figure 14-4 illustrates the use of directory junctions to map local volumes and network shares into a local namespace.

FIGURE 14-4

Directory junctions enable you to map local volumes and network shares into a single local namespace.

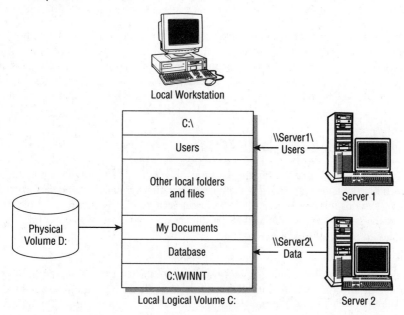

Mounted volumes

Another reparse point feature, volume mount points (mounted volumes), brings to Windows Server 2008 the same advantages for local file systems that the Unix operating system offers through its distributed file system. In effect, this capability enables you to mount a volume to an NTFS folder on a different volume, making the mounted volume appear as if it were physically contained on the host volume. You can mount multiple volumes within a file system namespace, creating a homogenous file system from disparate physical volumes on the local computer. A single volume can be mounted to multiple NTFS folders if needed.

> **NOTE** For a detailed discussion of mounted volumes, see the section "Working with Mounted Volumes" later in this chapter.

Transactional NTFS

The Transactional NTFS file system and the Transactional Registry, the kernel transactional technology in the Windows Server 2008 operating system, have been greatly improved and perform file handling and I/O via transactions. Transactions preserve data integrity and handle error conditions reliably, allowing developers of high-end, mission-critical applications to develop highly reliable applications for Windows Server 2008.

Although the server administrator will not do anything to the Transactional NTFS system, it is worthwhile to discuss how it operates. Basically all file operations on an NTFS file system are performed transactionally. This means that the full ACID properties common in database technology are employed on the file system. *ACID* stands for *atomic, consistent, isolated*, and *durable* transactions.

For example, an application will be able to execute file or registry operations on a large number of files or registry operations and either commit all of the transactions or roll them back if one in the collection fails (an all or nothing requirement). This allows a Server 2008 system to be very reliable and consistent and practically eliminates system or software crashes. This means that corruption of files and data due to inconsistent operations or system failures is avoided.

Choosing a File System

FAT offers a handful of advantages. First, it is compatible with nearly every PC operating system, which is useful for systems that must boot multiple operating systems and enable all (or multiple) operating systems to see a common FAT volume. Second, FAT is very recoverable because you can boot the system from a DOS diskette in the event of a failure and run a third-party FAT recovery utility to repair and recover a volume.

FAT also has some disadvantages. The fact that the boot sector is stored in a fixed location (the first track on the disk) makes it more susceptible to failure. If that track goes, the drive goes. In addition, the root directory structure in a FAT volume is limited by design to 512 entries, which limits the number of files in the root folder to 512, but more important, limits the number of folders under the root.

Another disadvantage of FAT16 is the 4GB limit it imposes on volume size, although in reality this isn't a true disadvantage because the overhead imposed by FAT16 on large volumes makes them undesirable. In addition, the relatively large default cluster size in a FAT16 volume makes FAT volumes less efficient in their use of storage.

FAT32 offers its own advantages. The 32-bit FAT increases the storage capacity to 2TB, considerably higher than the 4GB supported by FAT16. The smaller default cluster size for a FAT32 volume means that FAT32 volumes store data more efficiently than similarly sized FAT16 volumes.

Aside from different default cluster sizes and maximum capacities, there are a few key differences between FAT32 and FAT16. First, FAT32 offers better performance than FAT16. Second, FAT32 is more fault tolerant than FAT16 because Windows Server 2008 can automatically use the backup copy of the FAT32 if the primary becomes corrupted. Third, the boot record on a FAT32 volume contains backup data necessary to re-create the volume in the event that the boot record becomes damaged.

NTFS offers several advantages over the FAT file systems. In terms of speed, NTFS is not always the fastest of the three. With many mitigating factors on either side (structure, cluster size, fragmentation, number of files) and the fact that today's hardware allows for quick file system performance regardless of the file system type, speed is not a factor in most situations. Choosing the right underlying disk subsystem is often more important (SCSI or SATA versus other interfaces, for example).

One of the primary advantages offered by NTFS is security. Neither FAT16 nor FAT32 provides any local security for files. The security you can apply to FAT volumes is very limited for shared network access. Only NTFS enables you to assign permissions on a file-by-file basis with a high degree of granularity. Built-in support for compression is another advantage offered by NTFS that you won't find in FAT16 or FAT32 under Windows Server 2008.

Because you can control cluster size for FAT volumes under Windows Server 2008, as you can for NTFS, cluster size is not an advantage per se, but NTFS will always use a smaller default cluster size for a volume of a given size. Reducing cluster size improves storage efficiency by reducing sector slack (see the section "Optimizing Storage Capacity" later in this chapter), but it can also increase file fragmentation, which can reduce performance. Because of the difference in structure between FAT and NTFS, NTFS is more efficient at retrieving a fragmented file, which mitigates fragmentation as a factor in deciding on cluster size.

In short, the primary advantages offered by NTFS are those that pertain to functionality and security, rather than performance. Consider choosing NTFS for all new installations and converting existing FAT16 and FAT32 partitions to NTFS for upgrades. You'll not only gain the security advantages offered by NTFS's object permissions, you will also be able to take advantage of DFS, EFS, mounted volumes, disk quotas, and the other features discussed previously. The primary reason to retain a FAT file system is to enable other operating systems on a dual-boot system to see the volume. While the additional overhead imposed by NTFS could be considered a disadvantage, most systems are so fast today that the overhead is transparent or negligible.

Optimizing Storage Capacity

Although quotas can help you manage storage capacity on NTFS volumes, there are other issues to consider, including some that apply to FAT16 and FAT32 file systems. This section covers two topics that will help you optimize storage capacity: cluster size and compression.

Optimizing cluster size

As explained earlier in this chapter, a sector is the smallest unit of physical storage space on a disk. The smallest *allocation* unit, however, is the cluster. When Windows Server 2008 parcels out storage space, it does so by cluster. The significance of this is that cluster size has a direct impact on how efficiently the file system stores data. For example, assume a volume uses a cluster size of 64K. You store several files, each 32K in size. Although two files could possibly fit in one cluster, that's not how Windows Server 2008 allocates the space. Instead, each file resides completely in its own cluster. That means that each file takes up just half of its allocated space, with the rest being unused. This is often called *sector slack*. Take it to the extreme in this example and assume that all your files are like this, and you'll waste half of the space on the volume. A 32GB volume would hold only 16GB of data.

In reality, most files are much larger than 32K, so the amount of wasted space is reduced. Overall, however, sector slack can have a significant impact on storage capacity, leaving as much as 25 percent or more of a disk unusable. You can reduce cluster size to reduce sector slack and optimize your storage space. This has the net effect of increasing file fragmentation (see the next section), but a policy of frequently defragmenting the drive and the fact that NTFS efficiently retrieves even highly fragmented files can eliminate performance as an issue.

You can define the cluster size for a volume when you format it. To specify a nondefault cluster size for an NTFS volume, simply choose the desired cluster size from the Allocation Unit Size drop-down list on the Format dialog box (see Figure 14-5). There is no way to change the cluster size on an existing volume without reformatting the volume in Windows Server 2008.

The Format dialog box doesn't give you any options for using a nondefault cluster size for FAT16 and FAT32 volumes, however. You must format these volumes using the FORMAT command from a console prompt and specify the desired cluster size as a parameter of the FORMAT command. You can choose any of the cluster sizes defined in Tables 14-2, 14-3, and 14-4 for the respective file systems. In addition, FAT32 and NTFS support cluster sizes of 128K and 256K for volumes with a physical sector size greater than 512 bytes. For a description of the FORMAT command's syntax, open a command console and type format /?.

FIGURE 14-5

Use the Allocation Unit Size drop-down list to choose the cluster size when formatting a disk with NTFS.

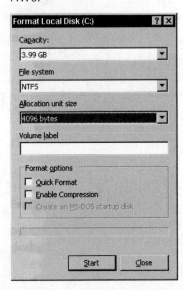

Defragmenting volumes

Windows Server 2008 allocates storage space in contiguous clusters whenever possible. This improves file system I/O performance because the disk heads don't have to move much to read or write a file. As files are added and modified, however, the amount of available space changes and files become *fragmented*, or stored in noncontiguous sectors. The more fragmented a volume, the poorer the performance because the drive heads have to move more to piece together the file. Even drives that use an efficient cluster size for the size of volume and size of files on the volume can suffer from fragmentation that reduces performance.

Windows Server 2008 includes a defragmentation utility called Disk Defragmenter that you can use to defragment a volume. Disk Defragmenter analyzes disk fragmentation and defragments drives that require it. It also provides a detailed fragmentation analysis report. See Chapter 13 for more information on Disk Defragmenter.

Using disk compression in NTFS

Another way to optimize storage capacity on NTFS volumes is to use compression. You can enable compression of an entire NTFS volume or configure individual folders and files for compression. Compression is not supported on volumes with a cluster size greater than 4K because the trade-off between storage capacity and performance degradation isn't worthwhile. The amount of storage increase achieved depends on the file types being compressed.

Enabling and disabling compression

You can enable compression when you format a volume or turn on compression at any time for an entire volume, a folder, or an individual file. To enable compression for a volume when you format the volume, select the option Enable Compression on the Format dialog box. Use the /C switch if formatting a volume with the FORMAT command from the command prompt. In either case, folders and files added to the volume will be compressed by default.

You also can enable or disable compression for a previously formatted volume. Right-click the volume and choose Properties. On the General page, select the option Compress Drive to Save Disk Space, and then click OK or Apply. Windows Server 2008 asks if you want to compress only the root folder or all folders and files. Select as desired and click OK. To turn off compression, deselect the option Compress Drive to Save Disk Space. Again, Windows Server 2008 asks if you want to apply the change to only the root folder or to subfolders and files.

To compress or decompress a single file, right-click the file and choose Properties. On the General property page, click Advanced to display the Advanced Attributes dialog box. Select or deselect the option Compress Contents to Save Disk Space, click OK, and then click OK or Apply.

> **TIP** You can use the COMPACT command to compress or decompress a folder or file from the command console. Issue the command compact /? to view the syntax and usage for the COMPACT command. Use COMPACT with no command-line parameters to view the compression attribute of a folder or file.

Moving and copying files affects their compression attributes:

- **Moving an uncompressed file to any folder.** The file remains uncompressed, regardless of the compression attribute of the destination folder.

- **Moving a compressed file to any folder.** The file remains compressed, regardless of the compression attribute of the destination folder.

- **Copying a file.** The file takes on the compression attribute of the destination folder. A compressed file copied to an uncompressed folder, for example, is uncompressed at the destination.

- **Replacing a file**. If you copy a file to a folder that already contains a file by that name (and you replace the original), the file takes on the compression attribute of the file it replaced.

- **Copying or moving from FAT16/FAT32 to NTFS.** The file assumes the compression attribute of the destination folder. Note that FAT16 and FAT32 do not support compression, so all files start out uncompressed and either remain that way if copied or moved to an uncompressed folder or are compressed if copied or moved to a compressed folder.

- **Copying or moving from NTFS to FAT16/FAT32 or to floppy.** Files are uncompressed, as neither FAT16/FAT32 nor floppy drives support compression.

Performance considerations

The degree to which compression affects performance depends on a handful of factors. As files are moved or copied, even on the same volume, the file has to be uncompressed and then recompressed. Files are uncompressed for transfer across the LAN, so you don't get any benefit from compression in reducing network bandwidth use.

Windows Server 2008 can experience significant performance degradation when compression is used, depending on the server's function and load. In general, lightly loaded servers or those that are primarily read-only or read-mostly do not suffer from compression degradation as much as heavily loaded servers or those with a lot of write traffic. In addition, compressing certain types of files (jpg, zip, and so on) is counterproductive and can actually result in larger file sizes, rather than smaller. The only real way to determine whether compression will affect a given system is to test it. If you find that you don't get the capacity savings you expected or if performance drops significantly, then simply uncompress the volume or folders.

Managing the Distributed File System

Windows Server 2008 includes an extremely useful feature called the *Distributed File System* (DFS) that enables you to simplify a user's view of the LAN and its resources. In essence, DFS enables you to bring local volumes, network shares, and entire multiple servers under a common file system namespace. Rather than require users to browse several different servers on the network for resources, those resources can all appear under the same namespace (such as a single drive letter). In other words, these distributed resources all appear to be located in the same place to the user, although they could actually be separated by continents.

DFS provides other benefits in addition to providing a unified view of a distributed file system and simplifying access to the file system by users. First, DFS uses link tracking to keep track of objects within the DFS namespace, which enables folders and their contents to move without breaking the logical link and structure within DFS. Because users see the logical location for a given folder, rather than the physical location, you can move a folder from one location to another, whether on the same server or to another server. Users can still access the folders from the same logical location even though they may have moved physically. In the case of a Web server, DFS enables you to move portions of a given Web site without affecting availability of the site or breaking any site links. In the case of an enterprise, DFS's link-tracking enables you to restructure storage as needs change without affecting users' access to the shared data or the way they access it.

Second, *availability* is another benefit to using DFS when integrated with Active Directory (AD). DFS publishes the DFS topology to the AD, making it visible to all users in the domain. You can replicate the DFS namespace through AD-integrated replication, making the folders in a given DFS namespace available even when a particular server is down or unavailable.

Load balancing is the third benefit offered by DFS. You can bring multiple replicas of a share under a common sharepoint, associating multiple identical shares with a single share name. While it may appear to a user that a folder or file is being accessed from a specific location each time, it can actually be pulled from a different server based on load.

DFS also lets you *replicate* content from server to server. The *DFS Replication* (DFS-R) component provides better efficiency and scalability over the old File Replication Service (FRS) in the first release of Windows Server. DFS-R supports multiple replication topologies, schedules, and throttles replication schemes, and utilizes *Remote Differential Compression* (RDC) to increase WAN efficiency (reducing bandwidth usage). RDC is a differential over-the-wire protocol that detects data changes in files and enables DFS Replication to replicate only those changes when files are updated.

In addition, Windows Server 2008 provides a new management interface for DFS called the *DFS Management console* (inherited from Windows Server 2003 R2). You use this console to create and manage DFS namespaces and replication groups. The DFS Management console provides a much richer management environment and the inclusion of features formerly available only through command-line tools.

DFS structure and terminology

Essentially, a DFS namespace is a shared group of network shares residing under a DFS root, which serves as a container for the namespace and performs much the same function for the distributed file system that a root folder serves for a physical volume. In other words, the DFS root serves as the sharepoint for the distributed file system. Rather than contain subfolders like a root directory does, the DFS root contains links to the shares (local and remote) that form the distributed file system. Each link appears as a subfolder of the root share.

A server that hosts a DFS root is called a *host server*. You can create root targets on other servers to replicate a DFS namespace and provide redundancy in the event that the host server becomes unavailable. A user can access the DFS root using a UNC pathname in the form \\host server\root name, where host server is the network name for the server hosting the DFS root and root name is the root's name. For example, if you created a root named Shares on a server named FileServer, users would access the DFS namespace from their computers using the UNC pathname \\FileServer\Shares. What they see when they get there is a function of the DFS itself, which might include shares local to that server, shares on other servers, or even shares on the clients' own computers. Users can also specify more highly defined paths, such as \\FileServer\Shares\George\Files\Somefile.doc.

NOTE   If you found yourself limited with Windows 2000 Server's DFS implementation, whereby a host server can host only one DFS root (whether domain or standalone), you'll find more flexibility in Windows Server 2008. DFS in Windows Server now supports multiple standalone and domain roots, giving you greater flexibility in creating and managing roots.

Figure 14-6 illustrates a sample DFS structure. The DFS root is called \\SRV1\root and contains data in shares from SRV2 and SRV3, program files in a share from APPSRV1, and data from a Windows Vista workstation computer.

FIGURE 14-6

The DFS structure (standalone DFS namespace).

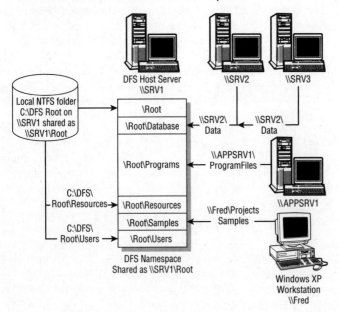

As illustrated in Figure 14-6, DFS links connect a name in the root to one or more shared folders called targets (called replicas in Windows 2000), or simply DFS shared folders. The links are essentially subcontainers within the root and serve much the same purpose as subdirectories in the root of a physical volume. Within the link object are one or more targets (pointers to shared folders) that define the share that a user sees when the link is opened. The ability to define multiple targets in a given link is what gives DFS its failover capability. DFS responds to a client request with the list of all targets in a requested link. The client then decides which one to use. If any particular target (share) referenced in a link is unavailable (the server sharing it is offline or times out, for example), the client can use a different one.

> **TIP** Although you might assume that each replica associated with a particular link will be a copy of the same folder, that isn't the case. DFS doesn't provide any replication of data between replicas by default. Nothing prevents you from defining multiple replicas in a DFS link, each pointing to completely different content. This presents interesting options for creating dynamic content on Web sites that use DFS in their underlying structure. Provide a means of replication and synchronization if you need to ensure that the content in the multiple replicas is identical. See the section "Replication with DFS" later in this chapter for more information.

Domain-based DFS namespace vs. standalone DFS namespaces

DFS supports two types of DFS namespaces: standalone and domain-based. Domain-based DFS namespaces integrate with the Active Directory and provide replication of the DFS topology across the domain (but not replication of folders unless you specifically configure them for replication). A domain-based DFS namespace must be hosted on a domain member server. The DFS's topology is automatically published to the AD to provide access to all users in the domain (and in trusted domains), subject to their access permissions.

Standalone DFS namespaces do not integrate with the AD and therefore do not provide the replication offered by domain-based DFS. Standalone namespaces are limited to a single namespace target, whereas domain-based namespaces support multiple namespace targets. You can create a maximum of 10,000 DFS links in a standalone namespace and 5,000 DFS links in a domain namespace.

> **NOTE** There is no explicit limitation on the number of levels that each target can have within its host share. The root only contains pointers to the shares, and those shares can contain essentially any number of subfolders. However, you are subject to the Windows Server 260-character limit for pathnames.

As mentioned previously, you can create namespace targets to replicate a DFS namespace from one computer to another. You can only do this within the framework of a domain-based DFS namespace. You cannot create namespace targets of standalone DFS namespaces. However, you can create a domain-based DFS namespace on any member server in a domain. The server need not be a domain controller.

As with replicas in a DFS link, there is no guarantee that a given namespace replica is an exact copy of another. Creating a root replica does not provide any means of folder replication or synchronization — it simply creates a logical relationship between namespaces on two or more servers that are referenced by the same name in the DFS namespace. You must configure that replication and synchronization separately to ensure that users see the same content regardless of the server to which they connect.

Client support

DFS provides full support for clients to access shared resources through a DFS namespace sharepoint, as long as those clients support the underlying network structure and protocol and are DFS-aware. These clients can browse both standalone and domain-based DFS namespaces on the network. Both Windows 98 and Windows NT 4.0 with Service Pack 4 include built-in support for browsing standalone and domain-based namespaces, as do Windows 2000, Windows XP, Vista, and Windows Server 200X platforms. Windows 95, Windows 98, Windows NT, Windows 2000, and Windows XP clients can host a replica (even Windows 95 clients without the DFS service installed) because at that level, DFS simply represents a share-redirection mechanism. As long as the folder is shared on the client computer, any DFS-aware client can be redirected to that share. In addition, the clients don't have to be in the same domain (or in a domain at all) to host a shared folder, even with a domain-based DFS root. While I mentioned many legacy operating systems earlier, I strongly suspect that if you are savvy enough to be thinking about DFS you probably would not be supporting anything earlier than 2000.

Replication with DFS

As mentioned briefly earlier in this chapter, DFS can provide a level of redundancy to ensure that shares within a given DFS namespace are available even when a server or share becomes unavailable for some reason. DFS does this through replication, which copies the root or link (and underlying data) to one or more other servers. Because DFS returns the complete list of root replicas or share replicas in response to a query, a client can try each one in the list to find one that functions when a particular server or share is offline.

Though DFS by default does not provide replication of a DFS root or any replicas associated with a given DFS link, you can configure DFS to replicate entire DFS namespaces or individual shared folders (DFS links). DFS relies on the File Replication Service (FRS) included with Windows Server 2008 to perform automatic replication. After you create a namespaces replica or a share replica, you can configure the replication policy for that object, which defines how the object is replicated. Automatic replication is only available for domain-based DFS namespaces and only data stored on NTFS volumes can be replicated. By default, FRS replicates the data every 15 minutes.

Automatic replication is not available for data stored on FAT volumes or for standalone DFS roots or replicas. In these situations, you need to use manual replication. Manual replication is just what its name implies. You replicate the data by copying the data periodically through drag-and-drop or a similar method as you would manually copy any file from one place to another. Although you could automate the manual replication through the use of

AT commands and batch files, that solution is somewhat awkward. Automatic replication through the use of domain-based DFS is by far the best method for sheer simplicity and low administration. Although you could configure a mix of automated and manual replication within a domain-based DFS namespaces, it's best to use one or the other to ensure that the copies remain synchronized.

You can configure your replication scheme such that one copy serves as a master and the other copies serve as read-only copies. To do so, first create the folder and share on the servers that will host the read-only copies. Set NTFS permissions on the main share folder to grant users read-only access but still allow FRS the control necessary to write changes to the share's child folders. Then set the replication policy for the root replica or folder replica to initiate the replication, specifying the dynamic source root or folder as the initial master.

 See Chapter 22 for detailed information on managing replication within Active Directory.

Replication with DFS-R

DFS Replication (DFS-R) takes the place of FRS for file replication. DFS-R shares many common points with legacy FRS:

- **Multimaster replication.** DFS-R is a multimaster replication engine, replicating changes that occur on all servers in a replication group to all other members in the group.

- **USN monitoring.** DFS-R detects file changes by monitoring the update sequence number (USN) journal, and replicates changes after the file is closed.

- **Staging.** DFS-R uses a staging folder to stage changes before sending and receiving the changes.

- **Conflict resolution.** DFS-R uses a conflict-resolution system to manage changes by multiple servers. For files, the last writer prevails. For folders, earliest creator wins. Files and folders that lose the conflict resolution are placed in a conflict folder for later resolution, if needed.

Although there are several similarities between FRS and DFS-R, many differences and improvements also exist. Here are some of the more important:

- **Limited replication.** DFS-R replicates only changed blocks, not the entire file. This feature alone provides a significant improvement in the performance of DFS, potentially reducing replication time by as much as 400:1 and having a corresponding positive impact on bandwidth usage.

- **Self-healing.** DFS-R is self-healing and can automatically recover from potential problems such as USN journal wraps, USN journal loss, or DFS replication database loss.

- **WMI integration.** DFS uses a Windows Management Instrumentation provider to obtain configuration and monitoring information from the DFS-R service.

Client-side caching

DFS provides for client-side caching of requests to improve performance and reduce network traffic. When a client issues a query to a DFS host server, the host returns the requested information along with a cache value. The client caches the returned results for the specified period of time. If the client makes another request for the same information within the cache period, the data comes from the client's cache, rather than the host. If the cache period has lapsed, the cached data is purged and the host server provides the data, which again is stored in the cache during the next cache period. Data writes are not cached.

You can configure cache values for an entire root or for individual folder replicas. You configure the cache value when you create the root or link. You can also modify the cache value at any time through the object's properties. Right-click a root or link and choose Properties to view its property sheet (shown in Figure 14-7), change the cache value on the Referrals page, and click Apply or OK.

FIGURE 14-7

You can specify cache time when you create the root or link.

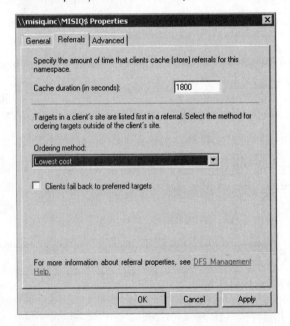

Working with the DFS Management console

As with most other administrative functions, Windows Server 2008 provides an MMC console for managing DFS. To open the DFS Management console, choose Start ⇨ All Programs ⇨ Administrative Tools ⇨ DFS Management, or execute the console file dfsmgmt.msc. Figure 14-8 shows the DFS Management console open at replication.

FIGURE 14-8

Use the DFS Management console to manage DFS replication.

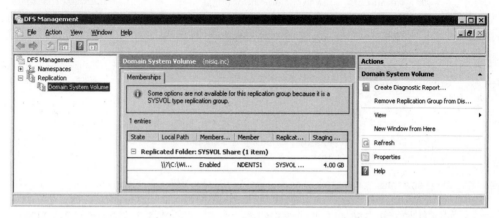

The DFS Management console enables you to manage multiple DFS namespaces across the network, thereby providing a single point of management for all DFS namespaces in your enterprise, subject to your access permissions within the enterprise. To view a DFS namespace not listed in the console, right-click Namespaces and choose Add Namespaces to Display. Specify the DFS namespace name or server host according to the three naming formats described on the resulting dialog box.

The following sections explain how to use the DFS Management console for specific tasks. See Chapter 2 to learn more about general MMC console operations.

You can create a standalone or domain-based namespace using the DFS console. You can create either type on a member server or domain controller. You are not restricted to creating domain-based DFS namespaces only on domain controllers. In addition, you can use the DFS console to create a DFS namespace on any appropriate target server in the network; you are not restricted to creating a DFS namespace only on the local computer. You can create multiple DFS namespaces on a server.

To create a DFS namespace, open the DFS console, right-click the Distributed File System node, and choose New Namespace to start the New DFS Namespace Wizard. The wizard prompts you for the following information throughout the process:

- **Namespace Type.** Select the type of DFS namespace you want to create. As explained previously, you can create either type of DFS namespace on a workgroup or domain member server or domain controller.

- **Domain Name.** Specify the domain name if you are creating a domain-based namespace.

- **Host Server.** The wizard prompts you for the name of the server on which the DFS namespace will be hosted. Specify the server's UNC name (such as \\someserver) or the fully qualified domain name (such as someserver.somedomain.com).

- **Namespace Name.** Specify the name of the sharepoint on the host server to which the DFS namespace will be anchored.

- **Comments.** You can include an optional comment for the namespace that identifies its function or provides other information about the namespace. This information appears when you view the namespace's properties (right-click the namespace and choose Properties).

- **Folder to Share.** Enter or select the folder that you want to serve as the namespace of the share.

To delete a DFS namespace, right-click the namespace and choose Delete Namespace. Windows Server 2008 will prompt you to verify the deletion. Note that deleting a DFS namespace prevents clients from accessing that namespace, although it does not delete the underlying folders or their contents.

You can replicate namespaces and shares in domain-based DFS namespaces. When you create a namespace target, you don't have the option of specifying a replication policy, but you can modify the properties after the namespace target is created. When you create a share target, you can specify that it participate in automatic replication. You can configure the replication policy only if there are at least two root targets. To modify the replication policy, right-click the root target in the DFS Management console and choose Properties.

Terminology and key features

With the introduction of new DFS features, Microsoft has changed terminology for certain DFS objects. These changes are reflected in Table 14-6.

TABLE 14-6

DFS Terminology Changes

Pre-Windows Server 2003 R2	R2 and Windows Server 2008	Definition
Link	Folder	Any folder under the namespace of the namespace, such as \\server\namespace\<folder>
Link target	Folder target	The UNC path of a shared folder or another namespace associated with a folder in a namespace
Root	Namespace	Virtual folder tree with a namespace at \\server\namespacename
Root server	Namespace server	Any server hosting a namespace

In addition to the new features described earlier, DFS with R2 exposes features that are difficult to configure with the previous release. These features are discussed in the following sections.

Client failback

When a DFS server fails or is removed from a namespace, clients attempt to fail over to another server in the namespace. In most situations, when the server is restored, you'll want clients to fail back to the original server because of affinity or other infrastructure reasons. Prior to Windows Server 2003 R2, you could not easily configure clients to fail back to their local servers. With the combination of the DFS Management console, Windows Server SP1, and a client failback hotfix for Windows XP and Windows Server 2003 clients, clients can be configured to fail back to their local servers in a Windows Server 2008 DFS environment.

Target priority

The new DFS Management console enables you to specify the order in which servers appear in a namespace referral, enabling you to prioritize namespace servers for clients. Windows Server 2008 (like Windows Server 2003 R2) obviates the cumbersome methods, such as configuring subnets and sites in Active Directory with high link costs to effectively force a priority.

Delegation

The DFS Management console assigns permissions as needed on namespace objects in the Active Directory (domain-based namespaces) or the registry (standalone namespaces) to eliminate the need for namespace managers to be a member of the local Administrators group on a given server.

Namespace restructuring

The DFS Management console makes it much easier to restructure a namespace. This capability is useful when you need to rename or move folders or restructure based on the addition of new folders or content, business reorganization, and so on.

Managing namespaces

The DFS Management console provides two branches: Namespaces and Replication. As you might expect, you create new namespaces with the Namespaces branch. To create a namespace, click the Namespaces branch and then click New Namespace in the Actions pane, which launches the New Namespace Wizard.

The wizard prompts for several items of information:

- **Namespace Server.** Enter the name of the server that will host the namespace and click Next. The wizard verifies that the DFS service is running on the target computer. If not, the wizard will ask if you want it to set the service startup mode to Automatic and start the service for you. You can accomplish these tasks manually if you prefer.

- **Namespace Name and Settings.** Specify the name to use as the namespace folder of the namespace. The wizard will create a folder for the namespace if needed. After you enter a folder name, you can click Edit Settings to open the Edit Settings dialog box, where you can specify the local path for the namespace folder and set access permissions.

- **Namespace Type.** On this page of the wizard, choose between a domain-based or a standalone namespace.

The final page of the wizard summarizes your selections and enables you to create the namespace. Click the Create button to create the namespace, and then click Close to close the wizard. The namespace then appears in the Management console.

To create folders, click the namespace in the left pane under the Namespaces branch. The central pane displays any existing folders under the Namespace tab.

To add a new folder, click the New Folder link in the right pane. DFS Management displays a New Folder dialog box in which you specify the name for the new folder (as it will appear in the namespace), and the physical folder(s) that will be targets of the folder in the namespace. As in the previous iteration of DFS, you can add multiple folder targets for a single folder name.

After you add a folder, it appears in the center pane. You can click the folder target in the left pane to add additional targets or configure replication for the folder.

Managing replication

You can use the DFS Management console to configure and manage replication for the namespace and folders. Bear in mind when planning your DFS infrastructure that replication requires a domain-based namespace and member servers or domain controllers as namespace servers.

When you add a second folder target to a namespace for a given folder, DFS Management asks if you want to set up replication for the folders. You can do so at that point or put it off until later. If you choose Yes, DFS Management launches the Replicate Folder Wizard. To launch the wizard later, click the folder in the left pane under its namespace. Then, in the center pane, click Replication. Click the Replicate Folder Wizard link in the center pane or the Replicate Folder link in the right pane to start the wizard.

The wizard prompts you to create a replication group for the folder and set properties for the group. These include the following:

- **Replication Group and Replicated Folder Name.** The replication group is used to identify the servers that host the folder, and the replicated folder name identifies the target folder.

- **Replication Eligibility.** The wizard evaluates the folders to determine whether they can participate in replication and indicates any problems so you can correct them before proceeding.

■ **Primary Folder Target.** Choose the server that is hosting the folder that will serve as the primary target. Other folders will initially replicate from this primary folder.

■ **Topology Selection.** Choose the replication topology you want to use for the group. You can choose hub and spoke (which requires at least three folder targets), or choose full mesh (for two or more folder targets). You can also choose the No Topology option at this point and create a custom topology after you finish with the wizard. However, no replication will take place until you create the custom topology.

■ **Replication Group Schedule and Bandwidth.** You have two options for specifying the replication schedule and amount of allowed bandwidth. The first option, Replicate Continuously Using the Specified Bandwidth, enables DFS to replicate the folders continuously, but throttles replication according to the bandwidth setting you choose. The default is Full, imposing no restrictions on replication. The alternate option, Replicate During the Specified Days and Times, enables you to set up a custom replication schedule to further manage bandwidth utilization.

If bandwidth is not really an issue, then the best option is to allow DFS to replicate the folders continuously using full bandwidth. However, available bandwidth and other issues can make continuous replication unattractive. For example, you might prefer to have all replication occur during down hours late in the evening or early morning, or you might need to exclude a certain time period from replication because of other events on the network that require as much bandwidth as possible. Perhaps you want to schedule replication to occur prior to backup events. Whatever the case, the Edit Schedule dialog box gives you full control over the schedule, as well as bandwidth used during any particular time slice.

Working with Mounted Volumes

The preceding section discussed the Distributed File System (DFS), which enables you to create a file system namespace using shares from multiple computers in the enterprise. Windows Server 2008 includes a feature called *mounted volumes* that does for the local file system what DFS does for the enterprise. Mounted volumes, which rely on NTFS's reparse points, provide a means for you to mount local volumes under NTFS folders on the local computer. This enables you to create a homogenous file system from multiple volumes so that, for example, volumes D:, E:, and F: can all show up as folders under volume C:. Figure 14-9 illustrates how mounted volumes work.

FIGURE 14-9

Mounted volumes enable you to create a homogenous file system namespace from multiple local volumes.

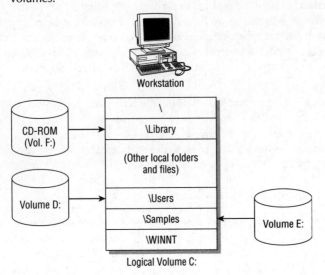

The primary benefit to mounted volumes is that they enable you to create a single file system namespace on the local computer that integrates multiple physical or logical volumes. This simplifies the user's view of disk resources and offers the following key advantages:

- **Selectively apply disk quotas.** As discussed in a previous section, you can apply quotas to a mounted volume to effectively apply quotas to a single folder within the logical namespace. This capability enables you to apply different quotas to different folders within a single logical volume. For example, you might apply different quotas to C:\Users\Documents and C:\Users\Programs to grant users different quota levels within each folder. (This example assumes that two different local volumes are mounted, one under each folder.) Because quotas apply to an entire physical volume, the only way to achieve different quota values is to mount separate physical volumes with different quota values to each folder.

- **Increase apparent volume size without hardware changes.** You'll probably find that in many situations, user storage-space requirements will surpass physical storage capacity over time, even when you apply quotas. Mounted volumes enable you to accommodate increasing storage requirements without replacing existing hardware. Instead, you add additional storage space locally and mount the new space to the existing volume. With servers that support the hot-swapping of drives and the ability to add new drives without taking down the system, the volume capacity increase can be accomplished without taking down the host server or affecting the services it provides.

- **Create a homogenous file system namespace from disparate volumes.** One of the chief benefits of mounted volumes is the ability they give you to create a single, homogenous file system namespace from various physical volumes.

- **Overcome the 14-letter drive ID limitation.** Mounted volumes do not require a drive ID, which overcomes the 14-volume limitation imposed by using letters for drive IDs. Rather than map local volumes to individual drive IDs, you can simply mount each one under its own NTFS folder on a host volume.

Although using a mounted volume can give you much the same effect as extending a volume, mounted volumes offer the advantages of selective quotas and can be used on basic disks. Extending a volume is supported only on dynamic disks.

Mounting a volume

You use the Disk Management console to mount volumes to NTFS folders. You can only mount a volume to an empty, local NTFS folder. The volume being mounted must also be local. To create a mounted volume, open the Server Management MMC console and open the Disk Management node. Right-click the volume you want to mount and choose Change Drive Letter and Paths from the context menu. Click Add to display the Add Drive Letter or Path dialog box, shown in Figure 14-10. Specify the path to the local NTFS folder in which you want to mount the volume and click OK.

FIGURE 14-10

Specify the local NTFS folder to which you want to mount the volume.

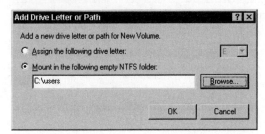

The way a mounted volume appears in Explorer depends on the volume type. Hard disk volumes appear as drive icons instead of folder icons. CD-ROM volumes appear with a CD icon.

NOTE You can browse only when creating a mounted volume on the local computer. You must specify the path in the text box if using Disk Management to manage a remote computer.

Unmounting a volume

Unmounting a volume is equally easy. Open the Disk Management node, right-click the volume you want to unmount, and choose Change Drive Letter and Path. Select the path you want to remove and click Remove. Click Yes to verify the operation or No to cancel it.

Services for Network File System

Windows Server 2008 integrates NFS components into Windows Server. These components are collectively called *Services for Network File System* (SNFS).

SNFS incorporates both the client and server components of NFS, along with related services and tools. Like Services for Unix, SNFS provides interoperability between Windows and Unix environments for file sharing. SNFS includes 64-bit support, better interoperability between Server Message Block (SMB) and NFS systems, enhanced reliability, and support for NFS Devices.

SNFS provides a management interface that is different from Services for Unix's (SFU) interface. Figure 14-11 shows the Microsoft Services for NFS Administration. The console provides management access to username mapping, NFS client, and NFS server components.

FIGURE 14-11

The SNFS management console.

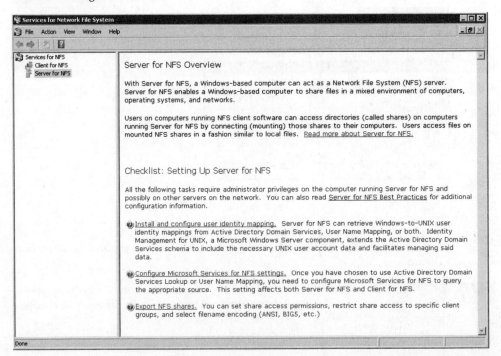

For the most part, the SNFS Administration console provides an interface that is similar to, but a somewhat simplified version of, the SFU management interfaces. Use the NFS Server branch to manage and configure the NFS service. To configure properties, right-click the NFS Server branch and choose Properties. The console displays the NFS Server Properties dialog box (see Figure 14-12), which you use to configure server settings, filename handling, locking, and logging.

FIGURE 14-12

The NFS Server Properties dialog box.

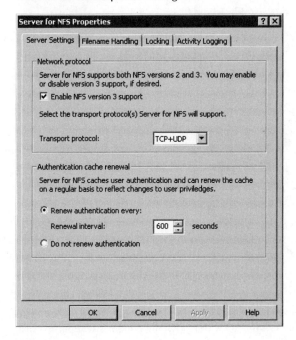

The NFS Client branch enables you to manage the NFS Client service and configure its settings. Right-click the branch and choose Properties to open the NFS Client Properties dialog box (see Figure 14-13), which you use to set transport protocol, mount type, buffer sizes, and file permissions.

Given that the management interface has been simplified, you should have no trouble configuring settings, particularly if you have used SFU in the past.

The Server for NFS component in SFU enables Windows Server 2008 to function as either a client or server in an NFS environment, offering folders and files to NFS clients or accessing a NFS network. This makes it possible for Unix hosts and other platforms running an NFS client to access folders and files on a Windows Server 2008 server and vice versa. Services for Network

File System is installed as a component of the file server role. Adding the role automatically adds the NFS bits supported on Windows Server 2008.

FIGURE 14-13

The NFS Client Properties dialog box.

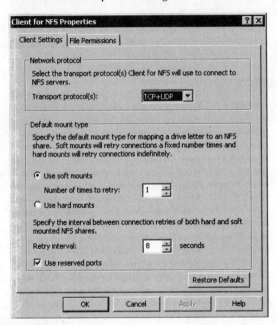

NFS overview

You have two options for authentication with NFS: use Server for NFS Authentication, or allow anonymous access to the shares. Using anonymous access is fine if you have no critical data or have no security concerns about allowing anonymous access to the NFS shares and their contents. However, it's more likely that you will want to control access, so we'll take that approach in this chapter. Authentication is explained in more detail in the next section.

Unix systems have different filename conventions than Windows systems, and because Unix clients will be placing files in the Windows file system, Server for NFS needs some mechanism to remap special characters that are not allowed in the Windows file systems. You accomplish this by creating a character-mapping file that tells Server for NFS how to handle the translation.

You also need to decide how you want Server for NFS to handle case sensitivity. Unix systems are case sensitive, but Windows Server 2008 is case preserving/case insensitive. Windows Server 2008 maintains the case of a file but does not consider case when locating files. In no situation can two files with the same name but with different case be stored in the same folder on a Server for NFS share because of the underlying reliance on the Windows Server 2008 file systems.

By default, Server for NFS considers case sensitivity when matching directory and filenames, but you can configure Server for NFS to ignore case. We'll cover how to do that shortly.

The type of underlying file system also has some bearing on how Server for NFS handles files. FAT and CDfs don't provide the ability to set individual ACLs, providing very little security. If you share a FAT or CDfs share through Server for NFS, the server returns the owner and group provided during authentication (the requester) as the owner and group for the file or folder in question. Essentially, this translates into "Everyone owns this file." Clients cannot change ownership of folders or files on FAT and CDfs shares.

The level of access a user has in a FAT or CDfs NFS share depends on the share permissions you apply to the share, just as for Windows clients who access a FAT/CDfs-based share. Users who are granted read access to the mountpoint receive read and execute permissions for owner, group, and other (-r-xr-xr-x). Users who are granted read/write or namespace access to the mountpoint receive read, write, and execute permissions (-rwxrwxrwx).

> **TIP** Share a FAT folder or volume as read-only if you want to prevent modifications to the files.

NTFS is a completely different animal in terms of file permissions. NTFS provides extensive access control, and those access permissions need to be mapped to their Unix equivalents. Unix is more restrictive in that it supports only three levels of permissions for owner, group, and other. NTFS allows you to set permissions for individuals or groups independent of other permission sets.

The Services for Unix Help documentation includes a more extensive discussion of how Server for NFS translates NTFS permissions to Unix file modes. In a nutshell, understand that SFU translates the NTFS permissions to maintain the level of access defined in NTFS for the Unix clients. You should avoid using chmod and similar Unix tools to change permissions on files or folders stored on an NTFS share because the access control list for everyone, owner, and primary group will be modified, leading to potentially unforeseen consequences. Instead, use NTFS permissions at the server to change permissions for folders and files when needed.

Configuring authentication

NFS clients can authenticate against domain accounts or accounts on the local Windows Server. If you're going to rely on domain accounts, you must install Server for NFS on each domain controller in the target domain. Server for NFS authenticates through the User Name Mapping server you've specified in SFU's configuration.

When an NFS client requests access, Server for NFS accepts the UID and GID from the client and passes them to the UNM server. The UNM server explores its database and returns the account based on the UID and group membership based on the GID. If there is no match, Server for NFS returns an error to the client.

NOTE If Server for NFS is configured to allow anonymous access and the client submits an anonymous request, Server for NFS passes the anonymous UID and GID instead.

Server for NFS passes the account and group information to Server for NFS Authentication, which logs on the user either locally or in the domain, depending on the credentials provided. Server for NFS Authentication responds with the user credentials, which Server for NFS then uses to request file access on the client's behalf. By default, SFU forces re-authentication if the client connection is inactive for ten minutes, but you can disable this behavior or change the interval, if needed, through the SFU console (explained later).

If you have not yet done so, you need to specify the UNM server that SFU will use for authentication. Open the SFU console, click the Services for Unix branch, and then click Settings in the right pane. This page provides only one option — Computer Name — where you specify the name of the UNM server. With that done, configure user and group mappings as described in the preceding section.

Configuring logging

Unless you have no security concerns for NFS (unlikely), one of your next steps should be to configure logging for Server for NFS. Enabling and configuring logging provides a trace path for identifying security problems and troubleshooting access problems.

To configure logging, open the SFU console, click the Server for NFS node, and then select Properties. Logging is configured on the Activity Logging tab. You can configure NFS to log to the event log.

CROSS-REF See the section "Working with Event Viewer" in Chapter 2 for detailed information on configuring the size of the Windows event logs, as well as the rollover behavior when the log fills up.

After you set the log location, you can choose which events to log. Simply place a check beside the events you want to log.

Configuring file locking

Use the Locking tab in the Server for NFS page to configure file locking for NFS. Server for NFS uses mandatory locks for all file requests, including those that come in through NFS, and Windows Server 2008 enforces those locks. You can configure the period that Server for NFS waits for clients to submit requests to reclaim a lock in the event that the connection is disrupted. To do so, open the Server for NFS node of the SFU console and click the Locking tab. Specify the waiting period in seconds in the field provided. You can also use this tab to view and release existing locks if needed.

Configuring filename translation

Earlier, you learned how Server for NFS must translate Unix-allowed filename characters to the Windows file systems. You control how characters are mapped by creating a translation file.

The translation file is a text file with each line in the file specifying a character-to-character mapping in the following form:

```
0xnn 0xnn : 0xnn 0xnn ; [comment]
```

The column to the left of the colon specifies the Unix character and the column to the right of the colon specifies the character to which it will map on Windows Server 2008. For example, you might want to change the colon (:) character, which is allowed in Unix filenames, to a dash (-) on Windows Server 2008 because a colon is an invalid filename character under Windows. The following would accomplish the mapping:

```
0x00 0x3a : 0x00 0x2d ; maps : to -
```

> **TIP** Everything to the right of the semicolon is treated as a comment and ignored for purposes of mapping the characters.

Setting up the map is a matter of deciding which characters need to be mapped, and to what they will be mapped, and then creating an entry in the file for each required translation. Take care not to create multiple mappings for the same client-side character, and don't remap periods, which are required by both Unix and Windows Server 2008.

After you create the translation text file, place it on the server and set permissions on the file or its parent folder to prevent unauthorized changes. Then, open the Server for NFS branch in the SFU console, and click the Server Settings tab in the right pane. Use the File Name Handling group of controls to enable translation and configure the location of the translation file.

> **TIP** To support Unix's convention of treating as hidden files those files whose names begin with a period, enable the option identified for that purpose in the File Name Handling group.

Setting authentication renewal and case sensitivity

The Server Settings tab also provides controls you can use to control authentication renewal and other behaviors. By default, Server for NFS requires a client to re-authenticate after 10 minutes. You can use the options in the Authentication Options group to change that interval, or, if desired, disable authentication renewal. For example, security might not be a major issue for you for the NFS shares, so you could turn off authentication renewal to reduce server overhead and improve client performance.

While you're working in the Server Settings tab, take a few seconds to configure how Server for NFS handles case sensitivity for each of the three supported file systems: CDfs, NTFS, and FAT. By default, Server for NFS preserves case for each of the three file systems, but you can configure it to return filenames as either uppercase or lowercase if desired.

Sharing a folder

After you've configured Server for NFS to behave in the way you need, you're ready to start making folders available through NFS. You configure sharing for NFS in much the same way you configure sharing for Windows. Open in Explorer the parent folder, right-click the folder or volume you want to share, and choose Sharing; then click the NFS Sharing tab (see Figure 14-14) and click the Manage NFS Sharing button. Then check the Share This Folder option.

Use the NFS Sharing tab to share a folder through NFS.

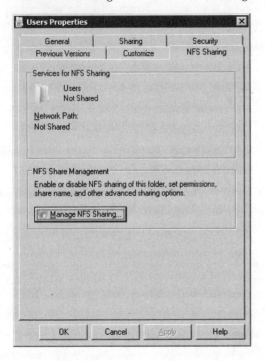

As you can for a Windows share, you can set the share name by which NFS will make the resource available. Use the Encoding drop-down list to specify the character encoding type to be used for the folder (the default is ANSI). If you want to allow anonymous access to the resource, select the option Allow Anonymous Access. You can change the anonymous UID and GID from their defaults of -2, if needed.

Next, configure permissions for the share to define the permissions that NFS clients will have in the share. Click Permissions to open the NFS Advanced Sharing dialog box (see Figure 14-15). By default, Windows Server 2008 grants all computers read-only access.

FIGURE 14-15

Configure permissions with the NFS Advanced Sharing dialog box.

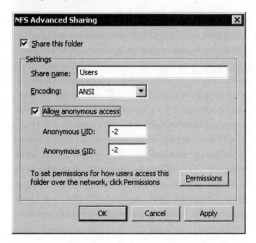

To add a new client or group, click Add to open the Add Clients and Client Groups dialog box. Select and add the name, select the desired access type from the drop-down list, set the encoding type, and if you want to grant namespace access, select that option. Then click OK. You can change these properties from the NFS Share Permissions dialog box if needed. When you're satisfied with the permission sets, click OK to close the NFS Share Permissions dialog box, and then click OK to close the properties for the folder or volume.

Summary

The topic of file systems in Windows Server 2008 covers a very broad range of technologies and features. Choosing the best file system depends on several factors, but in most cases, the best choice for providing the broadest range of features and the best security is NTFS.

NTFS not only provides enhanced security through NTFS object permissions, it can be extended through the use of file system filters from Microsoft and third parties, enabling certain capabilities not offered by FAT16 or FAT32. These additional capabilities include the Distributed File System (DFS), which enables you to create a single, homogenous file system namespace from shares on multiple computers across the enterprise. This homogenous file system simplifies administration, improves availability and failover capability, and most important, greatly simplifies user access to shared resources.

Another feature made possible by NTFS in Windows Server 2008 is mounted volumes, which bring the same concept to the local file system that DFS brings to the enterprise. You can use mounted volumes to create a homogenous file system namespace from multiple physical and logical volumes on the local computer, making those volumes appear as an integral part of a single logical volume.

Two mutually exclusive features made possible with NTFS are compression and encryption — you can use one or the other, but not both. NTFS can provide on-the-fly compression and decompression of files to increase storage capacity by as much as 80–90 percent, with the process remaining completely transparent to the user. The Encrypting File System (EFS), discussed in the next chapter, functions as an installable file system filter that performs encryption and decryption on the fly and transparently to the user. EFS provides a high degree of security for sensitive data that could be susceptible to theft, such as with notebook computers.

Chapter 15

Sharing and Securing Files and Folders

This chapter provides an understanding of access control to network file and folder resources. Chapter 14 provided an in-depth review of the Windows Server 2008 file system, especially NTFS and the DFS. In this chapter, you'll look at the file system from other viewpoints: users and applications, and, of course, administrators. You'll also learn how to configure the Encrypting File System (EFS) in this chapter.

Windows Server 2008 has enhanced the file-server role of the operating system with some cool new features, as the following list describes:

■ **Remote Document Sharing.** This feature enables access to files on Web servers through standard file-system calls through the new Web Distributed Authoring and Versioning protocol (WebDAV). This is very popular for use with document-sharing and document-control systems such as SharePoint.

■ **Enhanced Distributed File System.** Although this was the subject of Chapter 14, you learn about mapping to file services on the DFS in the section "Connecting to Shares," later in this chapter.

■ **GUID Partition Table.** The 64-bit support on Windows Server 2008 Enterprise Edition and Datacenter Edition includes the disk-partitioning technology that provides an alternate to the Master Boot Record (MBR) found on all 32-bit operating systems. Although the new technology is largely hidden from the user and the administrator, it greatly improves reliability and performance over that of the legacy MBR (see Chapter 13).

Most data is generated and stored on computer systems, using the file and folder metaphors inherited from our three-dimensional world. Since the advent of local and wide area networks, and particularly the Internet, however, your files and folders are accessible to anyone with a computer and a network connection unless you secure them. You need to secure the data within their files and the folders that contain those files while at the same time providing controlled access to authorized users. The NT File System (NTFS) enables you to do that on the following three security access levels:

- Shares
- Folder permissions and file permissions (called NTFS permissions)
- Encryption

> **NOTE** NTFS creates a hierarchy of folders in a volume, all starting from a root folder. Earlier versions of NTFS could store only a single folder hierarchy on a single hard drive or volume, maintained on a single computer. As described in Chapter 14, the folder hierarchy (or folder namespace) can traverse or span hard-disk volumes on any computer on the network. To keep things simple, this chapter discusses folders and files independently of where they may be located on the network.

Sharing and Securing Your Data

Windows Server 2008, as do all modern graphically managed or command-line managed operating systems, enables you to manage your files and folders in the same way you manage your hardcopy filing systems: in folders and filing cabinets. Consider the file room in a law firm or a newspaper morgue. It is unlikely you would be permitted to just walk into this room, which is usually locked or guarded, and you would need authority to enter, but you know that it's there. The company does not hide it away from you, because it is a shared resource, and the company usually wants you to know about it because you may need data in it to do your work.

Shares are the clubhouses of the network. A share is where users and groups of users go to share resources. You enable folder-sharing for your users and applications by creating a share, or in the lingo of mainframe, midrange, and legacy systems, a *sharepoint*. By owning the files and folders on your own machine (and we discuss ownership in the following section), you automatically have full access and control over your folders and their contents. Administrators own all the folders that they create anywhere on the network and can thus share them.

> **NOTE** Don't confuse the term *sharepoint* with Windows SharePoint Services, an add-on component to Windows Server.

Getting back to your brick and mahogany file room: By having access to the file room, you do not necessarily have access to every file or folder that it contains. Depending on your rank in the company, the department that you work for, and the work that you do, you may or may not have permission to open a file cabinet, read a file, check it out, change its contents, or add data to it. Similarly, by being a member of a group of users or by having individual authority, you may gain access to the NTFS share, but some files are not for your eyes. Others are accessible for reading only — you may not be permitted to change, delete, copy, or move them. The levels of access that you have to the folders and files are called *permissions*. Administrators, members of administrative groups (Administrator, Domain Administrators, or groups delegated administrative rights), and the owners of objects can assign permissions and control access to these objects, and they can also encrypt the files.

> **NOTE** Over the years, we have found that most calls to the support desk are related to a user or a group that cannot connect to shared resources, such as folders, files, and printers. When users can't connect and get the "Access denied" message, they assume that the world has ended. Usually, the culprit is a simple case of an incorrect permission. Permission misadventures cause much consternation and are a waste of time, so every administrator should become an expert in this subject.

Folder and file encryption is the third mechanism that you can now use for protecting your files and folders. It was added to the Windows 2000 file system and is naturally also supported on Windows Server 2008. If you add support for cryptography and distributed security services, such as Kerberos and digital certificates, to the file system, you have what is known as the *Encrypting File System*, or *EFS*. The EFS is fully discussed in the section "Securing Files by Using the Encrypting File System," later in this chapter.

Ownership

Another means of understanding shares or sharepoints is by understanding *ownership*. Ownership is not a configuration setting or a mere value in the registry or Active Directory; it derives from the security services of the Windows Server 2008 security system (which is discussed in more detail in Chapter 16).

If you've done some Windows programming, that usually helps you to understand ownership. The Win32 API has a function that creates objects such as folders and files. If the function that you are calling can take a security parameter, you can lock the object (pass a security descriptor) and keep other processes from accessing it. The lock is like a key that you, the owner, get to keep after you create the object. That is the essence of ownership. Of course, the whole process is managed by the OS and requires no user actions.

Whenever a process creates a file or a folder — objects — the file system assigns that process the rights of ownership and passes it a key. The process created it, so that process owns it . . . and it can do whatever it wants with that object. If *you* create a folder on the computer that you are logged onto or within a folder namespace to which you have access, *you* own the folder. Only you and the processes that operate within your security context (activated by the validation of your password) can access that folder.

Now, when other users or processes need access to the folder you just created, do you enable them to take ownership — hand them the key? No, not normally, because if you did, you would be losing your right to the object. By creating a share, you are essentially inviting others to access the folder (with restrictions, of course), but you don't give them the key. If someone else with bad intentions got hold of your keys, they may come back after dark and destroy your network. Remember the old adage: Possession is nine-tenths of the law. Moreover, remember what we say about safeguarding the Administrator account in Chapter 24. You can do tremendous damage with 50 lines of code and access to the Administrator account.

The owner of an object can actually enable a specified user or a group to take over the ownership of the object. (We describe that process in the section "Taking Ownership," later in this chapter.) Taking ownership is a one-way action. You can take ownership, but you cannot bestow it or return it. You can enable someone else to take ownership; you assign that person this permission. Ownership can be transferred only if the would-be benefactor is willing to take it. Because it lacks the capability to transfer ownership unilaterally, NTFS prevents users from hiding dirty work. In other words, you cannot lock up a folder and throw away the key and then make it look as though someone else did the damage.

Configuring the File Server Role

Before you can offer file services to your users, you need to configure the server to perform the role of a file server. As you learned in Chapters 1 and 2, installing a server from scratch makes this happen because the file server role is one of the most common roles for a server. The installation of the server roles is demonstrated in Chapter 2.

The flowchart shown in Figure 15-1 identifies the sequence of file-server chores that you are likely to perform in configuring your file server.

FIGURE 15-1

Steps you take to create, configure, and manage file servers.

Start

Configure the server role

Determine naming convention for folders

Build root share and folder hierarchy on data drive

Apply new rights and permissions to folders and shares

Build DFS and configure replication

Map users to home folders and share points

First you need to create the file-server role (see Chapters 14 and Chapter 2 for the specifics of installing roles). After you have a file server up and running, determine whether you need to set up additional file servers and configure a Distributed File System (DFS); if you do not need a DFS, you proceed directly to configuring a folder hierarchy and a collection of shares on one or more standalone file servers. After your file server is performing optimally, you need to turn your attention to the EFS.

When it's time to manage the file server, you have a handful of management tools at your disposal. The main file-server management tools on Windows Server 2008 are the File Server Resource Manager and the Share and Storage Manager. Both tools were in one console in Windows Server 2003. They have now been separated. The latter tool is shown in Figure 15-2; this console is a more dedicated management facility for file servers than is the Computer Management console introduced in Windows 2000. Although you can still perform many file-server chores from the Computer Management console, Windows Explorer, and even the command line, the File Server Management console provides a useful interface for the most common file-management responsibility: managing shares and sessions. For larger enterprises and for high availability solutions, Windows Storage Server 2008 takes file server resources and management even further.

FIGURE 15-2

The Share and Storage Management console.

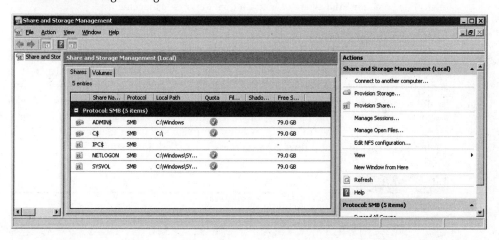

The easiest way to open the Share and Storage Management console is from the Administrative Tools menu. It is a Microsoft Management Console (MMC) tool in the system32 folder, and, thus, from there, you can create a desktop shortcut or link it to your custom menus.

You may notice that the console caters to two areas that dominated the old Computer Management console in Windows 2000 and Windows Server 2003: the creation and management of file shares and disk management. Disk management is discussed in Chapter 13.

File Server Resource Management console

Another addition with no new functionality in Windows Server 2008 is the File Server Resource Management console (see Figure 15-3). This console combines several file server–related management tools into a single interface and can generally replace the original File Server Management console included with earlier versions of Windows Server.

FIGURE 15-3

The File Server Resource Management console.

The tools integrated in the File Server Resource Management console include Quota Management, File Screening Management, and Storage Reports Management.

Quota Management

The Quota Management group enhances quota management capabilities over the interface built into Windows Explorer as demonstrated in Chapter 13. Use the Quotas node to create and manage quota entries through predefined quota templates or custom quota settings. Use Auto Quotas to apply a quota to a folder and have that quota template applied to all existing subfolders and any new folders created in the target folder. Use the Quota Templates node to manage existing quota templates and create new ones. A quota template specifies the quota limit, whether the quota can be exceeded, and how notifications are handled (see Figure 15-4).

FIGURE 15-4

Use quota templates to manage quota settings.

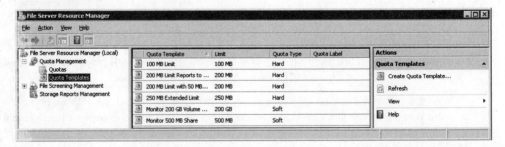

File Screening Management

The File Screening Management branch enables you to control the types of files that users can create in a given path. For example, you might use file screening to block MP3, AVI, and other types of time-wasting (and disk-wasting) files. You can also use file screening to block executables or other types of files that could pose a security risk.

To apply a screen, click the File Screens node in the left pane and then click the Create File Screen link in the right pane. The console displays the Create File Screen dialog box (see Figure 15-5).

FIGURE 15-5

You can apply screens to control file types that can be placed in a specified target folder.

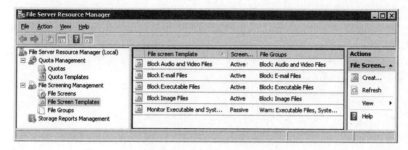

After you enter or browse to and select the path, you can choose from a predefined screen template or create a custom file screen. If you first create a new template, then select it in the list, right-click and select Edit Template Properties, the console displays the File Screen Template Properties dialog box shown in Figure 15-6.

Following are the options available to you:

- **Settings tab.** On the Settings tab, you specify the file groups to be screened. If the existing screen groups do not suit your needs, click Create to create a new, custom group. You can specify files by extension, filename, or both. You can also specify file types or names that should be excluded from the screen (and, therefore, allowed in the folder). The Settings tab also enables you to specify whether the screen is active or passive. If active, the file is blocked. If passive, the file is allowed, but a notification is sent to the user.

- **E-mail Message tab.** Use the E-mail Message tab to have Windows Server send an e-mail alert to one or more administrator (or manager) accounts. You can also direct Windows Server to send a notification to the user's e-mail address (which requires Active Directory integration to obtain the user's address). You can specify the message content and various message headers (From, Subject, Reply-To, and so on).

- **Event Log tab.** Use the Event Log tab to specify events that should be recorded to the event log when a violation occurs. You can customize the text that is used for the event.

- **Command tab.** On the Command tab, you can specify a script, executable, or other command to run when a violation occurs. Specify the command, optional parameters, working directory, and service under which the command will run.

- **Report tab.** Use the Report tab to determine the types of reports that will be generated for violations, when and how they are sent, or to view reports immediately.

FIGURE 15-6

Create a custom file screen and set screen options from the File Screen Template Properties dialog box.

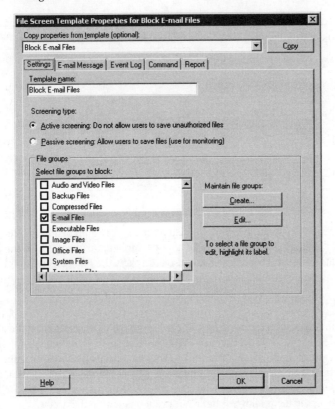

In most cases, you will probably prefer to create templates that define the actions for specific file types. The File Screen Templates node under File Screening Management lets you do just that. You can view and modify existing templates and create your own.

Finally, use the File Groups node to view existing file groups and create new ones. You can then use these file groups in templates or in custom settings.

Storage Reports Management

Keeping track of what is happening on a file server can be a critical task. The Storage Reports Management node of the Storage Resource Management branch enables you to define and generate a variety of reports related to the file system and file server.

To get started, click the Schedule a New Report Task link in the right pane. The resulting Storage Reports Task Properties dialog box (see Figure 15-7) enables you to choose which folders to include in the report, the types of reports to generate, and the report formats. Use the Delivery tab to specify e-mail addresses to which the reports are sent, and the Schedule tab to schedule when the reports are generated and sent out.

FIGURE 15-7

Create and schedule reports with the Storage Reports dialog box.

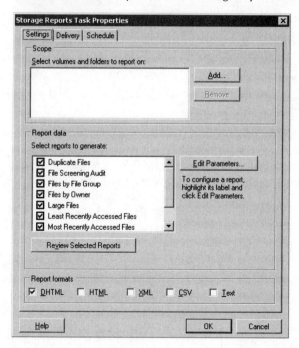

In addition to scheduled reports, you can also create reports immediately when needed. In the right pane, click the Generate Reports Now link. Doing so opens a dialog box similar to the one shown in Figure 15-7, minus the Schedule tab. You can also use the links in the right pane to cancel, modify, or delete a report task.

Publishing Shares in Active Directory

The idea of published shares is no longer new to the Windows networking environment, but it did begin with Active Directory. Windows Server 2008 users connect to shared resources on the domain by looking them up in Active Directory or mapping them out by using logon scripts.

Although connecting or mapping to sharepoints published in Active Directory is useful, the DFS provides the most utility and value for a company with extensive or widely distributed file serving needs. You explore the use of the DFS in the section "Connecting to Shares," a little later in this chapter.

Creating shares on Windows Server 2008 is really easy, and if you have Windows experience, you can read the following section only as a refresher and to pick up subtle yet important differences. Establishing shares on remote computers is another story, however, and the process is handled now by the File Server Management console. You can also create shares from Windows Explorer, the command line, and the Server Manager console as you set up your server in the file-server role. You can also create shares from the Active Directory Users and Computers console.

Creating a Share

As you first create a share, the file system automatically gives read access to the Everyone group, unless you have taken steps to prevent that (as described in the section "Share Attributes," later in this chapter). If the contents of the files are sensitive, remove the Everyone group and assign access only to authorized users or groups. Although read access stops unauthorized users from adding files to the folder or deleting files, it does not stop anyone from reading the files, and read access for Everyone means that all users can unnecessarily see the sharepoint, which is not a good idea, because shares should be shown on a need-to-know basis.

> **NOTE** In Chapter 13, we encourage you to use commonsense management practices and avoid assigning rights to individual users. The same advice applies to shares. Share folders with groups, not individuals, and don't share to the Everyone group unless you have a good reason to do so.

Sharing a local folder

If you are the owner of the folder or the folders within the local folder namespace or you have administrative access to the folders, sharing a folder involves little more than right-clicking the new or existing folder and then choosing Sharing and Security from the pop-up menu. Select the Share this Folder option in the folder's Properties dialog box that appears. (It is open to the Sharing tab.) The Share Name is enabled by default, as shown in Figure 15-8. (A Web Sharing tab also appears on this dialog box if you have Internet Information Services installed on the server.)

FIGURE 15-8

The Sharing tab on a folder's Properties dialog box.

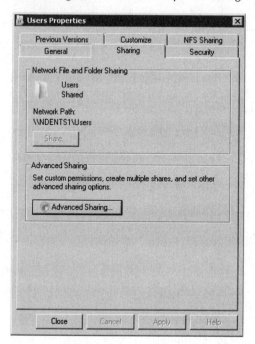

As soon as the fields on this dialog box are enabled, you can enter the following share data:

- **Share Name.** The actual folder name is used as the default share name, but you can change this to reflect any name that better suits the application for the share. Choose a descriptive share name for the share, one that clearly informs the user of the purpose of the share or that provides a hint of the share's contents. A folder may, for example, be already named SQLDATA. Rather than change that name, which would affect other applications, a better choice would be to make the share name SQL Server databases. Share names can be up to 80 characters in length, and they can contain spaces. If your users are attaching to the share from the command line or you have applications that may send share attach commands to the system console, however, stick to single names of between 8 and 12 characters (and stick to eight-character names with three-character extensions for those still using software built during the previous millennium). The best command-line-compliant substitute for the aforementioned share name is simply DATA.

- **Comments.** The Comments field takes more than 100 characters, so you can be creative here. Populate this field whenever possible because the data shows up in Explorer and Active Directory whenever users browse for a share. Although we've said that you can be creative, be conservative, too. A 100-character comment field forces most users to waste time scrolling to the right.

- **User Limit.** On server shares, you have no maximum connection limit, but you can restrict connections to shares for application-specific purposes or licensing by selecting the Allow This Number of Users radio button and then incrementing the number in the spin box to the right of the option. The Maximum Allowed radio button then toggles off. Client operating systems such as Windows 2000 Professional and Windows XP Professional prohibit more than ten concurrent connections and impose several other exclusions, which is why they do not make good file servers in a busy, yet small, office.

- **Permissions.** This button opens the Permissions dialog box. As soon as you enter the share name and description, you can click the Permissions button to admit users to the share and set the access types that you want. Permissions are discussed in depth in the section "Share Attributes," later in this chapter.

- **Caching.** This button was called Cache Settings in Windows 2000 and Windows Server 2003. Clicking it opens another dialog box that enables you to configure offline access to the shared folder. Offline folder and file access is touched on in the section "Offline Access (Caching)," later in this chapter, and explained in the context of Group Policy and change control in Chapter 24.

After you create a share, you have the option to create another share. Clicking the New Share button clears the fields in the dialog box but does not replace the old share; you can share a folder as many times as you want, each time with different access clients and permissions. Any time that you need to end a share, just select the share name from the drop-down list and click the Remove Share option, which becomes visible after the creation of a second share. If you need to stop sharing the folder completely, click the Do Not Share This Folder radio button and then click Apply. This option terminates all shares on the folder.

Establishing shares by using the Share and Storage Management console

You can connect to a remote computer and create a sharepoint on it in two ways. The first and hardest way is by using the NET SHARE command at the command prompt. The second, and by far the easiest, way is by opening the Share and Storage Management console. (You can also use the Computer Management console, as mentioned in the section "Configuring the File Server Role," earlier in this chapter.) If your Computer Management console shortcut is missing, simply create a new one by linking to the compmgmt.msc snap-in in the Windows Server 2008 installation folder — usually Windows.

After the Share and Storage Management console is open, select the first option, Shares (Local), in the folder tree in the left-hand pane. Right-click it and choose Connect to Another Computer from the pop-up menu, as shown in Figure 15-9. You can connect to a computer listed in Active Directory (the best way), or you can connect to a computer listed in the domain. After you have opened the remote computer in the snap-in, you can manage the remote computer's shared folders. From here on, the process of creating the sharepoint is no different from creating shares on the local machine.

To connect to another computer, simply enter the name of the file server to connect to in the edit box of the Select Computer dialog box, as shown in Figure 15-10, and click OK.

FIGURE 15-9

Right-click Shares (Local) in the File Server Management console to access its pop-up menu.

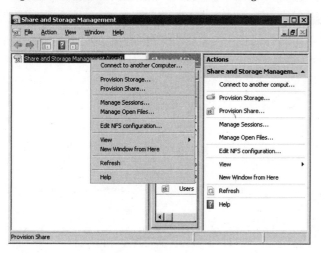

FIGURE 15-10

The Select Computer dialog box enables you to specify a file server to connect to or to browse for the server in Active Directory.

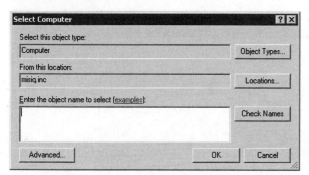

To create the share on the local or remote computer, run the Share and Storage Management console. Expand the nodes, select Shares, and right-click it. Then choose Provision Share from the pop-up menu. The Provision a Shared Folder Wizard opens, enabling you to provide shared-folder parameters, as shown in Figure 15-11.

Enter the path to the shared folder in the location field and then click Next. You will arrive at the NTFS Permissions screen of the wizard. This is shown in Figure 15-12.

FIGURE 15-11

The Provision a Shared Folder Wizard starts with Location settings.

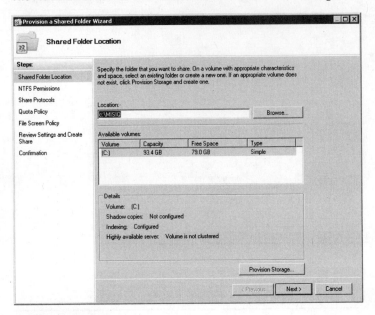

FIGURE 15-12

The NTFS Permissions screen.

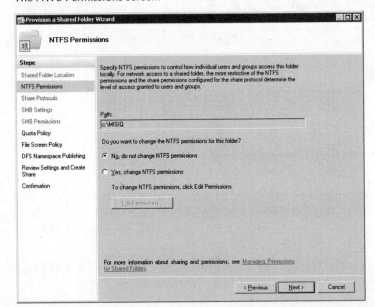

After setting your permissions, click the Next button or Finish to get to the Share Protocols options. You can share on SMB or NFS or both. This is shown in Figure 15-13.

FIGURE 15-13

The Share Protocols options.

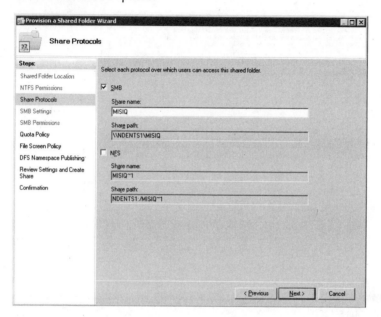

Each protocol option you choose will add an additional step in the wizard for configuration or the protocol. Figure 15-13 shows SMB. Click Next to configure the SMB options. The SMB Settings screen is shown in Figure 15-14.

Clicking the Advanced button will take you to the User Limits and Caching options. Once you are done with SMB or NFS or both, click Next to go to the screen for each protocol's permissions options. The SMB Permissions settings screen is shown in Figure 15-15.

Clicking Next takes you to the Quota Policy screen. This screen is shown in Figure 15-16. For more information on quota management see Chapter 13.

Click Next, and you are brought to the File Screen Policy screen as shown in Figure 15-17. File screen was discussed earlier in this chapter. Here you can apply file screening policy to the share. After provisioning for file screens, click Next.

Finally you will arrive at the DFS Namespace Publishing Screen after clicking Next. This screen is shown in Figure 15-18. You can elect to publish into the DFS according to the protocol, or simply ignore the DFS and click Next. You will then be able to review your settings, go back to make changes, or click Finish.

FIGURE 15-14

The SMB Settings screen.

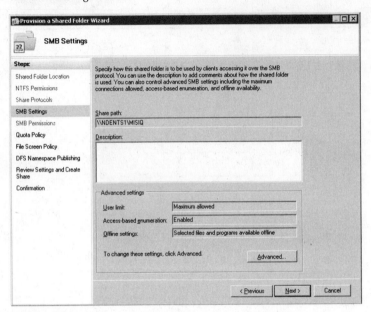

FIGURE 15-15

The SMB Permissions screen.

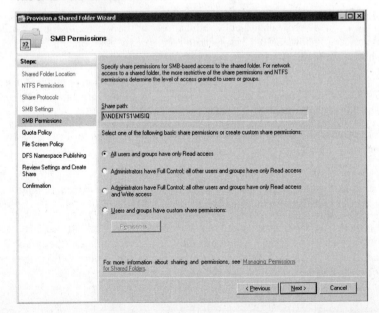

FIGURE 15-16

The Quota Policy screen.

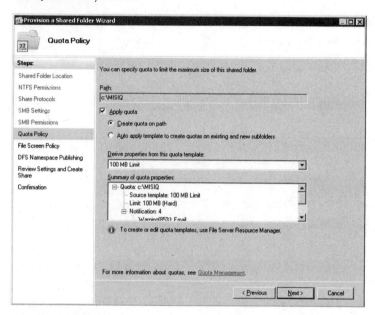

FIGURE 15-17

The File Screen Policy screen.

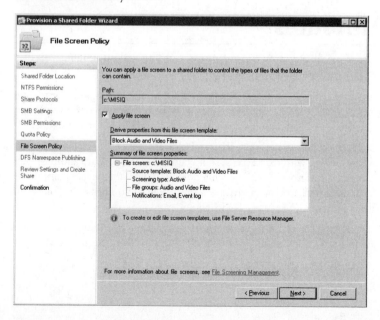

FIGURE 15-18

The DFS Namespace Publishing screen.

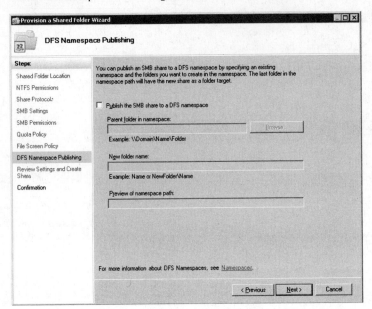

Once the share is created, it can be fully managed in the Share and Storage Manager.

Share Attributes

Share access can be given directly to users or processes or implicitly through group membership. Shared folders possess the following attributes:

- Folder shares work only on folder objects and not on the files that folders contain. You cannot select a file, x-file, and share it as x-file on the network, but you can share a folder called thexfiles and enable users to access the files in that folder.

- The default access permission on a share is Full Control. This permission is assigned to the Everyone group, with read access, so if you create such a share and have your Guest account enabled and not governed by any domain policy, then every computer user has access to it. Of course, you are a sensible administrator and are sure to follow our advice and make sure that your network is locked down.

- Shares can be established on most file systems, including FAT, but NTFS permissions, discussed in the section "Securing Files and Folders by Using Permissions," later in this chapter, are peculiar to the Windows NT, Windows 2000, Windows XP, Vista, and Windows Server 2003 and 2008 operating systems.

■ Shares are visible to you (if they are not hidden), even if you do not have permission to access the folder through share permission or security settings. This frustrates many NetWare file-server administrators, who can hide the share on that type of server from users who don't need to know that it exists.

■ A shared folder on your machine is represented as an icon of people sharing the folder; but across the network, the icon does not include the hand — the icon is either visible to the user as a folder sitting on the network or it is not seen at all because it is hidden. Hiding shares is a valuable security and administration tool that we discuss in the section "Connecting to Shares," later in this chapter.

NOTE Share permissions do not provide protection from local access to a folder or its contents. Therefore, use NTFS permissions to protect data from local access by unauthorized users.

Table 15-1 lists the folder permissions that apply to Windows Server 2008 shares. Remember that the access level is at the share only; NTFS permissions provide the "second line of defense" to locked-down resources at the object level. You set share permissions through the Share Permissions dialog box, which you can access by clicking the Permissions button on the Sharing page of the folder's Properties dialog box. If you click this button, the dialog box shown in Figure 15-19 opens.

TABLE 15-1

Shared Folder Permission Types

Permission	Privilege
Read	The user can see the entire shared folder tree (root shared folder and subfolders). The user can also see all the files in the folder tree (traversing) and open them for reading. The user can execute applications in the shared-folder hierarchy.
Change	This privilege inherits the read privileges and enables the user to change the folders and the data in the files within the shared folder's namespace. The user can also change file attributes and can copy, move, and delete files and folders. The user cannot change the actual share.
Full Control	This privilege enables the user to take ownership of the files and folders, within the shared folder's namespace. It inherits the privileges of the Read and Change permissions. Under NTFS, only Full Control enables a user to change permissions and take ownership of a file or folder.

FIGURE 15-19

Setting share permissions for a folder.

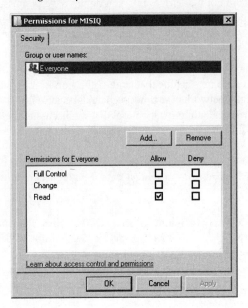

Deny

You can deny access to any of the permissions described in Table 15-1 by clicking the appropriate Deny checkbox on the Share Permissions tab in a folder's Permissions dialog box. If you deny Full Control, for example, you drop the privilege level down to Change. Deny is useful if you want to single out a user and deny that user permission. Deny is the strongest permission attribute; in other words, it takes precedence over every permission. If a user in a primary group has full access to a share, but you deny access directly or via a secondary group, for example, the individual user is denied access despite the access given in the primary group. Taking a user out of a group, however, is better than keeping her in the share and specifically denying her access individually.

Accumulation of share permissions

Share permissions accumulate. If a user is a member of one group that is given Read access but is also a member of another group that is given Change access (to the same share), the user's cumulative permissions in the share are Read and Change. The user's effective permission is Change, because it includes Read permission.

Moving or copying folders

If you move a folder, the shares assigned to it are deleted. The folder is not shared at the new location. If you copy a folder, the new copy is not shared, but the source folder remains shared.

Intradomain shares

Shares are not restricted to the users and groups of the domain in which they are created. If a trust relationship exists between two domains, a user or group in one domain can be given access to the share in another domain. The administrator of Domain A can provide access to a user or to a global or universal group from Domain B.

Who can share folders

Members of the predefined Administrators, Server Operators, and Power Users groups can share folders. In a domain on a member server, members of the Administrators or Server Operators groups can share folders that exist on any computer on the network. On a standalone computer, only the administrator and members of the Power Users and local Administrators groups can share a folder.

Workgroups do not enjoy such flexible sharing. Only members of the local Administrators group and the Power Users group can share folders. (Remember, however, that if you own the folder, you can share it, and an administrator can take ownership at any time.)

Hidden shares

The capability to hide shares is a useful feature of the Windows OS. It makes up for the problem of shares being visible to everyone on the network, even to users who do not have access to the shares. Relative hiding of shares is probably a very difficult and cumbersome technology to introduce into the OS, but exposing shares only to users who have access to them makes sense. To the other users, the shares should not be visible ... but available only on a need-to-know basis. Active Directory goes a long way in making selectively exposing shares to users possible by locating published shares in organizational units.

Hiding shares is possible simply by ending the share name with the dollar sign ($). You can still connect to the share if you have access to it, but it does not appear on the browse list (because nothing ending with the dollar sign appears in the browse list). You connect to the share by using the Run dialog box, as explained in the following section, or at the command line by using NET SHARE.

Here is a good example of a hidden share in action: A certain company in Florida transmits millions of dollars of direct-deposit information to the bank every afternoon. The application resides at the data center in Miami, but it logs in to a hidden share on the wide area network after an application in Los Angeles writes the direct-deposit information to a file in the same hidden share. Both applications or processes are members of the Banking group, and they have read and write access to the file in the share. No one else can see the share on the network, and the cloaking affords the share a measure of concealment. Of course, digging around on computers and looking for hidden shares is possible, but did you know that you can hide *servers* as well? Run the command NET CONFIG SERVER /HIDDEN:YES, and the server stops appearing on the browse list. You can still contact it if you know the IP address. To put the server name back on the browse list, change the /HIDDEN: option to NO in the command.

Connecting to shares

Ensuring that users have access to shares, typically through drive mappings, is one of the most frequently visited tasks that the network administrator has on his plate. You have several ways to connect to shares that are not visible in a browse list. You can connect by using interactive tools, such as Windows Explorer, or at the command line. You can also connect to published shares in Active Directory. DNS directs you to the domain controller hosting Active Directory, so connecting to a share is as simple as browsing for a Web page.

To connect to a Windows Server 2008 file server share using Windows XP or Windows Server 2003 by using the Map Network Drive Wizard (an option that assigns a drive letter), follow these steps:

1. Right-click the My Network Places icon on the desktop and then select Map Network Drive from the pop-up menu. The Map Network Drive dialog box appears.

2. Type the UNC path to the folder in the Folder field if you know it, or click Browse to search for the exact folder.

3. Enter a drive letter of your choice in the Drive field or use the default.

4. Select the Reconnect at Logon checkbox if you want the connection to remain persistent. Click OK to finish.

   You can also connect to the share under another username. All you need is the user's logon name and password. This option is useful if you need to connect to a resource on a domain for which you are not fully authenticated.

To connect to a share by using the Run dialog box, follow these steps:

1. Choose Start ➤ Run.

2. In the Run dialog box, type the UNC path to the folder if you know it or click Browse to search for the exact folder. Click OK.

To connect to a share from My Network Places, follow these steps:

1. Open My Network Places.

2. Find the computer that contains the share and locate the folder in the browse list.

3. After you find the share, double-click it to establish the connection.

To connect to a share in the Active Directory, follow these steps:

1. Open My Network Places.

2. Expand the Active Directory node until you locate the domain in which you want to locate a published share.

3. After you find the share, double-click it to establish the connection.

To connect to a Windows Server 2008 file server share from a Windows Vista machine or Windows Server using the Map Network Drive Wizard (an option that assigns a drive letter), follow these steps:

1. Click the Network icon on the Start menu and then right-click the Network folder and select Map Network Drive from the pop-up menu. The Map Network Drive dialog box appears. (Note: My Network Places is not on the default desktop in Windows Server 2008, but it is available in Windows Explorer and on the desktop of the alternate Windows 2000 [Classic] Start menu.)

2. Type the UNC path to the folder in the Folder field if you know it, or click Browse to search for the exact folder.

3. Enter a drive letter of your choice in the Drive field or use the default.

4. Select the Reconnect at Logon checkbox if you want the connection to remain persistent. Click OK to finish.

You can also connect to the share under another username. All you need is the user's logon name and password. This option is useful if you need to connect to a resource on a domain for which you are not fully authenticated.

Connecting users to published shares

You can connect users to shares published in Active Directory. This enables you to map users to shares according to their membership in organizational units (OUs). Say, for example, that you have an OU called US MIA, which belongs to NA OU; users who work in Miami should map drives to the file shares that they need in this OU. As long as a user is a member of the OU, that user can gain access to the share.

You can automate share connection via login scripts, demonstrated later in this section. Providing shares and mapping users' drives to them is performed according to the flowchart shown in Figure 15-20.

FIGURE 15-20

The procedures for setting up drive mappings for the members of various organizational units.

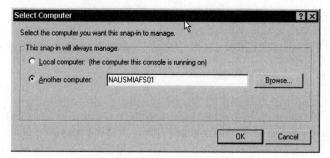

First you need to create some standards for the company. Table 15-2 lists the standard mapped drives assigned to the various hubs and sites in the `mcity` domain.

TABLE 15-2

Shared Folder Permission Types

Drive Letter	File Server Share
J (user folders)	\\ServerName\BusinessGroup\Users\UserName
K (common folders)	\\ServerName\BusinesGroup\Common
W (application data)	\\ServerName\BusinesGroup\Applications

This takes the share name off any browse lists. Next, you provide a login script for the user, as demonstrated in the following section.

You have several reasons for mapping to shared resources in this manner. First, it enables administrators to control what users have mapped access to. Forcing or simply enabling users to map to shared resources such as folders and printers tends to result in an administrative nightmare as well as a security risk.

Second, by not advertising the shares to browse lists, you add an extensive security layer on the shared resources. Security is further enhanced by locking the shares down so that users can access them only via login scripts or Group Policy, which are further protected with permissions and access control.

Third, script or policy-driven mapping keeps the mapping uniform and standard. In other words, users' home directories are mapped to J, all application data is mapped to W, and the common folders are mapped to K.

Mapping out the DFS namespace for users

As Chapter 14 demonstrates, one of the wonders of Windows Server 2008 is the Distributed File System (DFS) namespace. A DFS is a good idea for a company of any size, and living without one is hard after you apply it to a distributed company with file servers in many cities or even across multiple campuses.

The main hub for the `mcity.us` organization also supports a site in another town that has a busy file server, so we decided to build a DFS file system that spans both sites and provides a single file-system namespace to our users. After the DFS is built, as shown in Chapter 14, you can map your user's directory to folders in the namespace without needing to create hundreds of shares on the actual file servers. If you have recently escaped from a NetWare/NDS network, this section should pique your interest.

No matter where your user logs on, as long as you create a domain DFS, that user can map to a home folder and other folders as needed.

To set up the DFS and map users to a home folder in it, follow these steps:

1. Create a DFS root. This is done by opening the DFS Management console under Administrative Tools, as shown in Chapter 14, and right-clicking the root node to launch the New Namespace Wizard. Your DFS root is at the start, or root, of the folder branch containing all your users' home directories. The New Namespace Wizard takes you to the screen shown in Figure 15-21. Before you create the root name, add a dollar sign ($), as shown, to the end of the name to hide it on browse lists. After you have created the DFS root, you are done working on shares. All you need to do is map users to their folders on the namespace.

FIGURE 15-21

The new root name, with a trailing dollar sign ($) for hiding it, in the New Root Wizard.

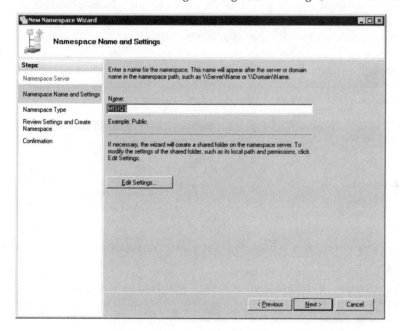

2. Create a simple batch file to be processed as a logon script. You can go to town with VBScript or JScript stuff, but for logon scripts, a simple batch (*.bat) file works (and you thought that DOS was dead). Figure 15-22 provides an example of a logon script to map users to home folders. (Note that you are not limited to batch language, and on Windows Server 2008, you can script this in more than 20 languages.)

FIGURE 15-22

Creating a logon script in Notepad to map users to home folders in the domain DFS.

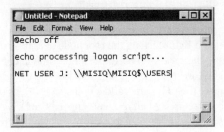

3. Place the script, or batch file, in a share that all client computers can access. SYSVOL or NETLOGON are usually the safest bets. Make sure that your client computers can see the volumes whenever they authenticate to the domain or the script is not processed. Run the NET USE command at a client workstation to see what the client workstations are using on the server. The Shares folder in the Share and Storage Management console, however, provides you with the server-side information, as shown in Figure 15-23.

FIGURE 15-23

Checking out the shares in the Share and Storage Management console.

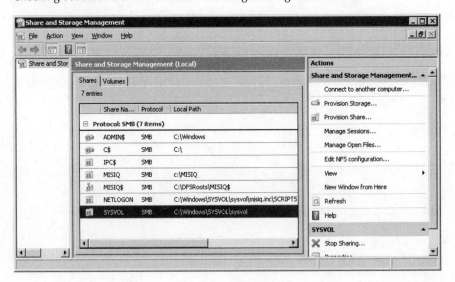

4. The next job is to enable Group Policy for the users. Create a Group Policy Object to affect the users in the organizational unit to control and then open the Group Policy Management Editor to edit the object, as shown in Figure 15-24. Expand the User Configuration node through Windows Settings and Scripts (Logon/Logoff). (This process is described in detail in Chapter 24.)

FIGURE 15-24

Configuring Group Policy to process logon scripts.

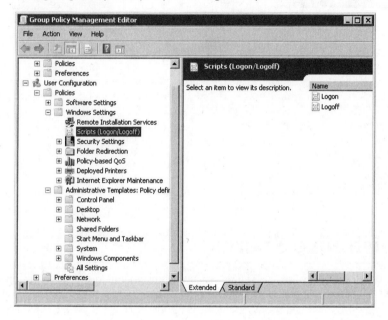

5. Double-click Logon in the right-hand pane and enter the path to the logon script on the server, as shown in Figure 15-25. Remember to use a UNC path or your clients may think that they need to process a script that's sitting on their own hard-disk drives.

6. Save the policy. Now, whenever users in the OU are under the influence of the policy logon, their J drives are automatically mapped to the folder on the remote share.

FIGURE 15-25

Providing the UNC path to the logon script for a Group Policy Object.

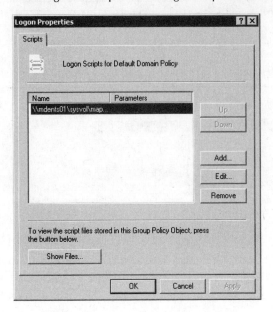

Administrative Shares

As you install Windows Server 2008, NTFS automatically creates administrative shares on your local volume. These shares are placed in strategic administrative folders, the most important being the one where you installed the Windows Server 2008 system files. These administrative shares are listed in Table 15-3.

Shutting off these shares is possible, but doing so may result in unpredictable results. You can, for example, shut down the NETLOGON share to prevent anyone from trying to obtain authentication at your machine — and you may have legitimate reasons for doing so — but the correct way is to stop the Net Logon service.

We have found that you can delete the share if you are an administrator or have ownership of the share. If you try to change permissions on the share, however, Windows Server 2008 denies access with a nasty message saying that built-in shares cannot be modified — absurd in light of the fact that you can delete the administrative shares at any time after you unseat the ownership.

Incidentally, if you delete an administrative share, it returns after you reboot the computer. The administrative shares are controlled by the server service. Anytime you restart this service, such as at reboot time, the shares are reestablished and reset to the factory default.

TABLE 15-3

Administrative Shares

Share	Purpose
Roots (C$, D$, E$, and so on)	The root of every volume on a Windows Server 2003 (and even on Windows 2000, NT 4.0, and earlier servers) is shared. If you can map to the share, you can access the entire volume.
ADMIN$	This share is the system root, the Windows Server 2003 system folder hierarchy. To map to this share, simply use \\SERVERNAME\ADMIN$.
PRINT$	This share is created as you install the first shared printer on the server. The share is established at \\SERVERNAME\SPOOL\DRIVERS, and its purpose is to enable clients to remotely pull printer drivers for installation on their machines. The Everyone group has Read access to this share, and administrators can install new drivers to the share as needed by using Full Control.
NETLOGON	This share is used for the Net Logon service, which is the mechanism to service logon requests to the server. It is also used for locating logon scripts. This share is not automatically created in Windows Server 2003. See Chapter 13 for related user management information.
IPC$	This is the share for the Named Pipes protocol, which provides intraprocess and interprocess communications between applications.

You may be concerned that the administrative shares pose a potential danger, and they do. In fact, all shares are dangerous if not managed with common sense. Mapping to the shared roots on each drive is feasible if you know how to use a server. If you can connect, you gain total access to the drive and the entire folder hierarchy within.

You would be right to say that these shares are the equivalent of leaving the hen-house door open for the fox to walk right in. Only administrators, however, have access to these shares. That limitation, however, is still not comforting, and the whole administrative-share quirk is another reason why we lock up the Administrator account. As long as the Administrator account's identity and password are locked away and security policy is in force, you won't experience any hacking of these shares.

Commonsense Strategies for Sharing Folders

Shares are not an easy facility to manage, and often they conflict with applications, restrict the wrong people, and expose the network to security risks. The following sections offer strategies for closing holes in your network with respect to shares.

Restricting shares

Many administrators prefer to keep shares wide open by leaving the Everyone group in the share with full access. Instead, they control access to subfolders via folder and file permissions. We understand this policy and the rationale to relieve some of the administrative burden (one less thing to worry about), but is this commonsense management? Not if it means that you are leaving doors unlocked on your network.

The problem is that the subfolders below the share become accessible to the users who are given access at the sharepoint, and if the Everyone group has access to the root, then it has access to all the subfolders. By not restricting the share, you are in effect giving yourself more work to do, because you must go to every subfolder and apply NTFS permissions. On a complex folder hierarchy, the task of locking up all the subfolders could prove next to impossible. If you want to keep shares (and your network) secure, your best course is to remove the Everyone group from the share and admit only the groups that require access to the folder namespace. Further security can be applied by using the file and folder permissions.

> **TIP**   Limiting use of the Everyone group makes troubleshooting user-related problems easier. The Everyone group forces you to be cognizant of every user account in your domain and every domain with which you share trusts.

Setting up application sharepoints

If users need to access a remote application, shortcuts are created on their systems (manually or via profiles, logon scripts, and Group Policy). The users run the applications from the network shares, and the applications run in the local memory space on the client computer. Most well-designed Win32 applications can be executed multiple times in this fashion, and you are often asked to install an application on the application's server and then share that folder. The following strategies are suggested for creating application shares:

- Create an application sharepoint. On our servers, we call this share the "Apps" sharepoint.

- Under the Apps sharepoint, you can create a share for each application that you are installing and then share each respective install folder. Creating more shares may not be necessary, however, because the subfolders are accessible to those given access to the sharepoint. If you need to restrict access to a subfolder, simply ensure that only the authorized group has access, through folder permissions, which are discussed throughout the latter part of this chapter.

- Provide access to an Administrators group (or whatever suits your purpose) for the root (Apps) share and make sure that the group has the Full Control privilege assigned. This enables only application administrators to manage the applications, such as patches and upgrades. You may also add a special *applications admins* group with Change control enabled to permit technicians or consultants to troubleshoot the applications.

- Remove the Everyone group from the share and provide access to either the Users group or a specific group that requires the access. Make sure these groups have only the Read privilege assigned.

Setting up data sharepoints

Data shares contain files that users or applications need to share. Users mostly share spreadsheet and document files, while applications (clients) need access to databases. Commonsense practice is to keep the data sharepoints separate from the application sharepoints, because data shares require more that just read access.

Data backup is another good reason for separate data sharepoints. Your backups should not be repetitively backing up application files, and the share is easy to identify and back up. The following points describe how to create a data sharepoint:

- Create a root data sharepoint for applications. Name the shares after the groups or projects that require them — for example, `Part 11 compliance docs` or `materials management`. Naming the shares after the application name is confusing, and you may have many shares that contain data generated by the same application. A share named Microsoft Access Files, for example, would be a bad idea. (We manage several hundred servers, and they all contain Microsoft Access files.)

- Give your users Change access so that their applications can update files and save the data. Administrative groups should be given Change or Full Control as needed.

Offline Access (Caching)

On Windows Server 2008, you can configure shared folders and their contents for offline access. The contents of these shares can therefore be seconded to the target computer. The remote or standalone computer disconnects from the network and maintains a mirror, or shadow copy, of the folder and files. You continue to work with the offline resource as if you were connected to it on the server. The following steps describe how to set up folders for offline access:

1. Open Windows Explorer, right-click a shared folder, and choose Sharing from the pop-up menu. The folder's Properties dialog box appears.

2. On the shared folder's Properties dialog box, select the Sharing tab and click the Caching button. The Offline Settings dialog box appears, as shown in Figure 15-26. All shares are cached for offline use by default, so you can select Only the Files or Programs That Users Specify Will Be Available Offline radio button if you do not need to cache the contents of the folder.

FIGURE 15-26

The Offline Settings dialog box.

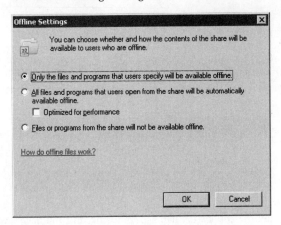

3. To keep caching for offline access, you can choose one of the options shown in Figure 15-21 and described in Table 15-4.

TABLE 15-4

Caching Settings

Caching Option	Purpose
Only the files and programs that users specify will be available offline.	This option enables users to select the files to be marked for offline access. This is the default setting for all shares, but only files marked for offline use are activated. Every file marked for offline is cached, regardless of whether or not the file was opened.
All files and programs that users open from the share will be automatically available offline.	This option enables every file in the folder that is opened to be automatically cached. This option saves on bandwidth because only files actually used are cached. You can further instruct the file server to optimize the offline setting activity to be optimized for performance. This is especially useful in low-bandwidth connections, such as a frame relay WAN, or for added file server scalability.
Files or programs from the share will not be available offline.	Selecting this option prevents users from obtaining offline access to files and programs.

Offline attributes

The following are attributes of the offline access features of Windows Server 2008:

- After a computer first connects to the share on the network, any files marked for caching on the server are copied to the client computer's hard disk.

- After a computer reconnects to the share on the network, any files that have been updated on the client computer are copied to the server.

- After the user logs off the network, the server and the client synchronize the files automatically.

Synchronizing cached resources

To manage the synchronization between offline files and folders and their sources on the server clients, you need to open Windows Explorer and choose Tools ➤ Open Sync Center ➤ Synchronize from the menu bar. In the Items to Synchronize dialog box, first select the items in the list to synchronize and then click the Synchronize button.

The synchronization management options, shown in Figure 15-27, can be used to determine when offline files are synchronized with the versions on the servers. You can do either a quick or a full synchronization. The latter takes longer but ensures that the current versions are saved to the network and copied to the client.

FIGURE 15-27

The Items to Synchronize dialog box.

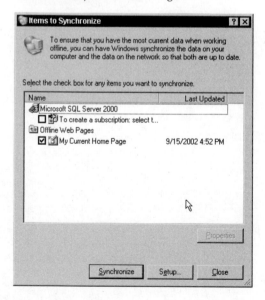

Securing Files and Folders by Using Permissions

As explained in Chapter 16, permissions are the means by which you control access to network objects. After shares, they are the second and third lines of defense in protecting data and network resources. File and folder permissions are controlled by NTFS. This section deals specifically with the permissions that control access to volumes, folders, and files, as opposed to permissions that control access to sharepoints.

Permissions kick in as soon as you format a volume to NTFS. Volumes are protected with NTFS permissions, just as are folders and files. As soon as you format a volume to NTFS 5.0, right-click the name of the volume in Windows Explorer and choose the Properties command on the pop-up menu. Click the Security tab of the Properties dialog box that appears. You'll notice a bunch of groups that have default access to the folder. The most suspicious group is Everyone.

These settings are still consistent with the Windows 2000 default, whereby the default behavior of the OS is to give Everyone access as well — that is, assign it rights to access the files in the folder. This access has now been locked down further in Windows Server 2008. Although the Everyone group is still added to the security settings, by default it gets no rights. We still advise that you change this default behavior, however, and remove the Everyone group from the default groups that are given access to every new folder that's created. To do so, see the flowchart in Figure 15-28.

FIGURE 15-28

The steps to removing access to new folders for the Everyone group.

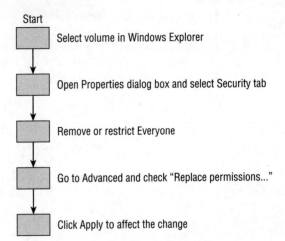

To remove the group, follow these steps (and please proceed with caution):

1. Select the disk volume in Windows Explorer and right-click it to select the Properties option, which loads the volume's Properties dialog box. Select the Security tab on the dialog box.

2. Click the Advanced button on the Properties dialog box. The Advanced Security Settings dialog box opens. If the Everyone group is included in the list of groups, remove the group or disable (deselect) any rights that it may have. Your best course is to remove the group because not having the group in the list in the first place is more secure than just denying it any rights. In addition, selecting Deny shuts down the whole share because it literally locks out *everyone*.

3. Select the Replace Permissions on All Child Objects radio button and click Apply. Do not deselect the Inheritable Permissions radio button. You are warned about the change; click OK in the warning dialog box to continue. The Everyone group is now removed from the list of groups that have access to all objects on the drive.

Now, only select administrators can create and manage new folders on the volume. The default thus prevents all and sundry from creating a folder on the volume; and each time that you create a folder, you automatically assign your administrators' group to the folder and nothing else. This setup is a good security practice and keeps the doors locked until the folder is ready for group access.

If you decide not to remove the Everyone group, remember that the group is automatically given carte blanche access to any share that you create (albeit with no rights).

Setting up security as just described can be performed on a drive that's in service for only a short time but is safest and most easily done on a new volume.

CAUTION We strongly recommend that you remove the Everyone group from the root of the volume. If you don't, you're creating a security risk, because giving Everyone permission at the root of the folder hierarchy and then forgetting about it is all too easy. If your volume has been in service for a while, however, removing the Everyone group this way may do some damage if you have been loose in dishing out rights to "Everyone." Many shares and access rights are given access to Everyone, so removing it this way is likely to prevent access to a user or an application that depended on it being there.

Permission Types

Table 15-5 lists the folder permissions that you can apply. Folder and file permissions are accessible from the Security tab of the folder's Properties dialog box. To access the folder's Properties dialog box, right-click the folder and choose Properties from the pop-up menu. Then select the Security tab, shown in Figure 15-29.

TABLE 15-5

Folder Permissions

Permission	Purpose
Full Control	This permission enables the user to take ownership and perform all the actions of the following permissions.
Modify	This permission enables you to authorize users to delete the folder under management and all earlier permissions.
Read & Execute	This permission enables you to authorize the user to traverse the folders from a root folder down. It also enables the user to read the files and execute applications in the folder under management and all subfolders.
Read	This permission is the first that provides access to the folder's contents. Without this permission, the user would get the dreaded Access Denied message. This permission enables the user to see ownership, permissions, and file attributes. All Write permissions are grayed out.
Write	Use this permission to authorize the user to create files and folders in the folder. It also gives the user the capability to change file attributes and view ownership and permissions.
List Folder Contents	This permission enables the user to see files and subfolders in the folder under management.
Special Permissions	This permission's checkbox is not selectable until special or advanced permissions are enabled. Advanced permissions are accessible only by clicking the Advanced button.

Table 15-6 lists the permissions that you can assign to files.

NTFS 5.0 also enables you to assign advanced versions of the permissions described in the preceding tables. These permissions are more specific versions of the general permissions. They enable you, through the extended selection lists accessible from the Advanced button, to pinpoint the level of access you want to provide to the user, such as *only* read a file or *only* execute an application ... as opposed to the Read and Execute options in the basic permissions.

To assign Advanced permissions, click the Advanced button on the Security page of the file or folder's Properties dialog box; then click the Edit button on the dialog box that appears. This launches the Advanced Security Settings dialog box, shown in Figure 15-30.

FIGURE 15-29

The Security tab of the folder's Properties dialog box.

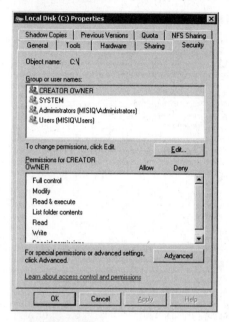

TABLE 15-6

File Permissions

Permission	Purpose
Full Control	This permission enables the user to take ownership and perform all the actions of the following permissions.
Modify	This permission allows the user to delete and perform all the actions permitted by the previous permissions.
Read & Execute	This permission allows the user to run applications, and applies the Read permission to the file.
Read	This permission allows the user to read the files and view their attributes, ownership, and permissions.
Write	This permission allows the user to change the files' contents and attributes and to view ownership and permissions.
Special Permissions	This permission's checkbox is not selectable until special or advanced permissions are enabled. Advanced permissions are accessible only by clicking the Advanced button.

FIGURE 15-30

The Advanced Security Settings dialog box for a folder.

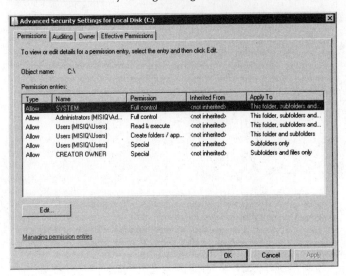

You can deny permissions at any time by selecting the Deny checkbox to the right of the permission. If you deny Full Control, you effectively deny all other permissions as well.

NOTE   The Permissions list on the Security tab and in the Advanced Security Settings dialog box is an abstraction of the Access Control List (ACL) maintained by the file system. The ACL can be accessed directly — but only programmatically.

Permissions Attributes

You can assign multiple permission types to users, groups, and computer accounts for tighter control of access to folders and files. As with shares, you need to understand the attributes of permissions to more effectively achieve your objectives. Permissions possess the following attributes:

- Permissions are cumulative. A user's total authority is the sum of all permissions granted over the use or access of an object. If, on a given collection of files, a user is granted Read permission by virtue of his or her membership in the Readers group, for example, and is a member of an Application Access group that bestows the Execute permission on the same set of files, the user's total access is Read and Execute.

- The Deny permission option overrides any and all permissions granted to a user for the specific object. If a user has Full Control of an object by virtue of membership in several groups, assigning him the Deny option in only one group locks that user out of the file or folder completely.

- File permissions are *not* stronger than folder permissions. Any file permission bestowed to a user does not override or supersede any permission granted at the folder level. In other words, if you give a user file access (even Full Control) but deny the user access at the folder level, the user cannot access the file. This mechanism prevents the user from connecting to the file from the command line by specifying a UNC path to the file.

Inheritance

The permissions that you assign to a given folder or file can, by default, propagate down to the child folders and files. In other words, if the Everyone group is given access to a folder and inheritance is turned on for all the subfolders in the hierarchy, the subfolders also enable the Everyone group to have access, as do the files. We recommend that you keep inheritance turned off by default or via domain policy so that you do not leave doors open by acts of omission or by failure to keep an eye on the propagation chain reaction.

Of course, the inheritance option is useful if you need to build a huge folder hierarchy and automatically provide one group with specific permission access to the entire folder and file namespace.

To prevent or enable permission inheritance, simply deselect or select the Allow Inheritable Permissions option on the Advanced Security Settings dialog box (accessed by clicking the Advanced button on the file or folder's Properties dialog box). You are prompted to Copy or Remove the inherited permissions every time that you deselect the checkbox. By turning inheritance off for a folder, you make the folder the new parent, and if subfolders have inheritance turned on, they become children.

In the section "Commonsense Strategies for Sharing Folders," earlier in this chapter, we advised you to remove the Everyone group from the volume's Group or User names list. You should keep the Reset Permissions on All Child Objects and Enable Propagation of Inheritable Permissions checkbox selected. The option can be selected from any level in the folder hierarchy. It brings back not-too-fond memories of the Replace Permissions on Subfolders and Files option on NT 4.0 and earlier versions of NTFS.

By running this option, you are replacing — not merging — the permissions on all child folders and files on the volume, so any permissions applied to subfolders and files are lost. If that is not your desired result, you could end up losing weeks of work restoring permissions so that users and applications can operate. Even worse, this action cannot be undone. You can only rebuild what you had from backups and documentation. Proceed with care here, because the wrong step could cost you dearly.

Taking Ownership

Administrators, owners, or users with Full Control of an object can set up a user or a group to take ownership of the object. This is done by first admitting the user or group to the *access control list* (ACL), via the Group or User names list, and selecting the Take Ownership checkbox on the Permission Entries list, as described in the section "Permission Types," earlier in this chapter, or by giving the potential owner Full Control (which is a security risk). Figure 15-31 shows the Owner tab of the Advanced Security Settings dialog box.

FIGURE 15-31

Use the Owner tab of the Advanced Security Settings dialog box to control object ownership.

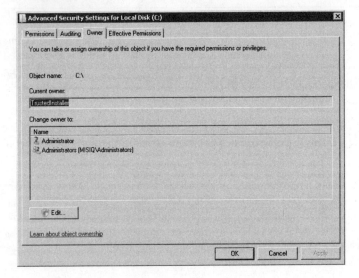

Administrators, as long as they inherit their power from an Administrator's group, can take ownership of objects regardless of the permissions in the object's ACL.

To take ownership of the object, follow these steps:

1. Open to the Security tab of the Properties dialog box for the object in question. (See the section "Permission Types," earlier in this chapter.) Click the Advanced button and then select the Owner tab from the Advanced Security Settings dialog box.

2. Select the Replace Owner on Subcontainers and Objects checkbox to take ownership of all child subfolders and files contained by the parent folder.

3. In the Change Owner To list box, select the User or Group account name that is taking ownership and click Apply.

Copying and Moving

Often, you may need to move or copy folders and their contents to other volumes or containers on the network. You can't do so, even as an administrator, if you don't have ownership or the permission to move or copy the folders, but you can take ownership and then assign yourself the necessary permissions.

Before you move a folder or a file, check and document the ownership and rights before the actual copy or move. After you have successfully completed the process, you can reapply any permissions along the way.

The following security behavior applies to copying, moving, and ownership of files and folders:

- Whenever you copy or move a file or a folder to a container within the same volume or on another volume, the permissions assigned to the object are dropped, and the object and its contents and children inherit the permissions assigned to the destination container.

- You cannot copy or move a folder or a file to the destination container if the destination container has not given you Write access, regardless of which volume you are moving or copying to.

- The user account that performs the actual copy or move becomes the owner of the objects after they reach their destination; usually that's the administrator.

- Permissions and ownership do not change at the source objects.

Strategies for Managing Permissions

Assigning permissions is not a complex art, but you need to be orderly and consistent about the process. It looks easy, but on a big network with a lot of resources, thousands of users, and mission-critical applications, you cannot afford to drop the ball.

Here's a good example: Every night at a certain company, a process on an AS/400 connects to a share on a Windows network, opens a file, and writes a million dollars' worth of business to the file. As soon as the file is closed and saved, another process connects to the same file and performs special functions on the data. What would happen if, by some mistake on the part of the administrator, the permission on that file were changed, and the file could not be opened? A million dollars' worth of business could potentially be lost. In our case, we had alerts on the AS/400 that raised an alarm if the process failed. The only damage done was that the administrator was beeped at 3:00 A.M. to fix the problem.

Consider the following guidelines for handling permissions:

- Create groups for access to folders and files and assign them only the permissions required to work on the files. If a group needs only the Read permission on a file, assign only Read permission to that group.

- Have team leaders or department heads formally request all permission levels for their teams or departments, and have them put the requests in writing. Then assign rights only according to the written request. That way, should a user accidentally delete a file, the damage is not on your head. All requests for permissions should be channeled through the help or support desk, where a case can be made specifically for the purpose.

- Document everything that you do on a permissions case. You always have something to refer back to if problems crop up later. It's common to get a request to restore a folder and permissions back to the way that they were previously because of some problem resulting from the change. Folders and files get deleted, and the backups do not always contain the latest permissions work performed on the object. Make sure that your documentation is clear and concise so that other administrators or support-desk staffers can handle the case.

- Use the Deny option only if implicitly denying access to a user or group is essential or urgent. Opt instead to remove a user from a group or remove the group from access control.

- Assign permissions on a folder-by-folder or file-by-file basis. Make sure that the permission requestor opens a separate support case for each permission required on a folder or a file.

- Avoid propagation if possible. In other words, don't simply set permissions for a root or parent folder and then leave all subfolders exposed to the inherited permissions. By the same token, don't just add a group to the parent folder if they specifically need access to only a single subfolder or file. (Prevention is better than a cure in dealing with deleted or damaged files.)

- In today's world of viruses and denial-of-service attacks, assigning only Read and Execute permissions to application folders or files makes sense (see Chapter 16). Doing so prevents any hostile attempt to delete or infect files in a folder or to replace the file with a Trojan horse.

- In working with public data folders, assign the Read and Execute permissions and the Write permission to the group requiring access to existing files. This practice enables the group to read or execute a file and to save changes whenever necessary. Adding the built-in Creator Owner principal to the folder and assigning it Full Control is a good and safe practice. Users who create their own files can thus safely perform all necessary functions on the file and even delete it if necessary.

- Assigning permissions to files at every corner can be tedious. Classify files according to their level of importance and application and then group them in folders only. Doing so enables you to assign permissions to the folders and not to each file.

For most enterprise work environments, share and folder and file permissions are sufficient security. If someone steals a server or a hard disk, however, and attempts to access its files from another operating system, that person may gain unfettered access to the data. If the data needs to be protected from such an attack, no NTFS permissions can keep the data safe. You need to encrypt your data, which can be done in Windows Server 2008 by using the Encrypting File System, as was the case with Windows 2000.

Securing Files by Using the Encrypting File System

Windows Server 2008 adds to the *Encrypting File System* (EFS), introduced in Windows 2000. The EFS enables users and administrators to encrypt and protect the file system in situations where the system is subject to unauthorized physical access. The additions, however, have more to do with managing file encryption and recovery than with the employment of stronger file encryption.

The EFS is an ideal agent for data protection in any situation, including that of a server in a small office that typically is not locked in a secure computer room or that of a public place that uses a server to support a transient workforce, such as a circuit court or polling station. EFS is invaluable on workstations where hard disks are accessible or on notebooks that are easy pickings for the criminally motivated. A *storage area network* (SAN) is also an ideal candidate for EFS, as in an intranet that enables many people to access secure corporate data, such as 401(k) or similar employee-related information that should not fall into unauthorized hands. EFS provides on-the-fly encryption and decryption, working transparently to the user, just as NTFS compression works behind the scenes without any interaction with the user. Although EFS does not protect the data from unauthorized access across the network, it does secure the data from a disgruntled employee who physically removes the storage device from the network.

NTFS provides a means of protecting data while it is safely tucked in a user's computer or on a server and that computer or server is not subject to a direct hacker attack, but little prevents someone from stealing a computer or a removable storage device and gaining access to the device by cracking the password or using one of the tools floating around the Internet — or available commercially — that enable access to NTFS volumes while bypassing NTFS security. The only viable solution, other than using only internal devices and wrapping hefty chains around your computers, is to use encryption.

Encryption on individual files is not always an answer either. Many applications create temporary files as you work with a document, and these temporary files are not encrypted unless you use an encryption system that automatically encrypts everything in the folder in which the temporary files are created. EFS addresses this potential problem.

EFS supports encryption of folders and files on NTFS volumes but does not support encryption on FAT volumes. (Because encryption is integrated with the NTFS, it relies on NTFS reparse points and an installable NTFS filter.) You can use encryption on folders and files stored locally as well as on remote servers. Encryption, however, doesn't protect file data as it moves from the remote server to your workstation across the network (or vice versa), because the network traffic is unencrypted. If you need to ensure security throughout the entire process, use IPSec to encrypt network traffic.

> **NOTE** Windows Server 2008 warns you that a file to be moved or copied from one encrypted file system to another is going to be decrypted. You had no such warning in Windows 2000, and as a result, many files were inadvertently left insecure.

How EFS works

EFS employs *public-key encryption* and the *CryptoAPI* architecture to encrypt and protect files. Windows Server 2008 encrypts each file with a unique, randomly generated file-encryption key. These keys are independent of the user's public/private-key pair. By using a different key for each file, Windows Server 2008 provides a very secure encryption method that is difficult to compromise at all, much less on a widespread basis (decrypting an entire volume of encrypted files, for example). The current implementation of EFS uses the *Data Encryption Standard X* (DESX), which provides 128-bit encryption, until recently available in Windows 2000 only in North America.

As an administrator, you need to do very little, if anything, to enable users to encrypt and decrypt files. EFS automatically creates a public-key pair and a file-encryption certificate for a user the first time the user attempts to encrypt a file. This eliminates the need for you to create a certificate or key pair for each user who needs to use EFS. The users' encryption certificates and keys are stored in their profiles, so they are available each time that a user logs on.

Whenever a user encrypts a file, EFS automatically generates a *bulk symmetric encryption key* and then encrypts the file by using the key. EFS then uses the user's public key to encrypt the bulk encryption key. (The user's key is called a *File Encryption Key*, or *FEK*.) EFS stores the FEK for an encrypted file within an attribute called the *Data Decryption Field* (DDF) in the file itself. In addition, EFS also encrypts the bulk encryption key by using the recovery agent's public key. This FEK is stored in the *Data Recovery Field* (DRF) of the file. The DRF can contain data for multiple recovery agents. Each time EFS saves the file, it generates a new DRF by using the current recovery-agent list, which is based on the recovery policy (explained in the following section). Figure 15-32 shows the encryption process.

Encryption and decryption happen transparently to the user as the file is read from and written to the disk, so a user can simply open an encrypted document by using the document's parent application without any special procedures. The application doesn't need to be EFS-aware because the encryption/decryption happens at the file-system level, independent of the application. EFS uses the private portion of the user's key pair to decrypt the FEK and enable the user to view the data. If the user doesn't supply the necessary private key required by the file (which happens automatically through the user's certificate store), the user receives an `Access Denied` message. Figure 15-33 shows the decryption process.

> **NOTE**   EFS does not require an entire file to be decrypted as it is being read. Instead, decryption occurs on a block-by-block basis, so only those portions of the file actually read are decrypted. As a result, EFS is extremely fast, and overhead is not noticeable in accessing encrypted files.

EFS under Windows 2000 was not designed to enable encrypted data to be easily shared among users; you could, however, enable multiple users to access and work with encrypted folders and files. The users simply need to share the same encryption keys. For more information, see the section "Sharing Encrypted Data," later in this chapter. Windows Server 2008 makes encrypted folder and file sharing a lot easier.

FIGURE 15-32

The encryption process used by EFS.

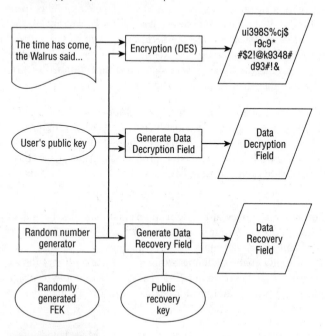

FIGURE 15-33

The decryption process used by EFS.

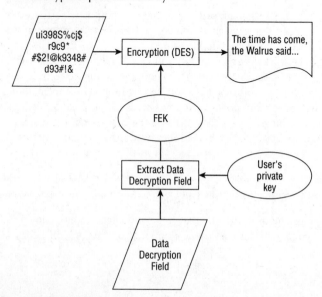

Recoverability and the encryption recovery policy

In most situations, you want the capability to recover encrypted data when a user leaves the organization or loses her encryption certificate and keys. EFS ensures recoverability of encrypted files by administrators by requiring that at least one data-recovery key be present on the system. These recovery keys enable a *recovery agent* who has the necessary public key to decrypt a file's FEK, thereby decrypting the file. The recovery key doesn't enable the recovery agent to retrieve any other information, such as the user's private key, ensuring continued security for an employed user while still enabling the agent to recover data.

On Windows 2000/Windows Server 2008 domains, the Domain Administrators account is configured automatically as the recovery agent in a domain. The local Administrator account is defined as the recovery agent on standalone computers and those participating in a workgroup. The recovery process is identical to the decryption process shown in Figure 15-33, except that the EFS uses the recovery agent's private key instead of the user's private key to decrypt the data.

You can define an encryption recovery policy at the domain level and enforce that policy on all computers in the domain through domain/group policies. Administrators can delegate recovery policies to specific security-administration accounts through the delegation features inherent in Active Directory (AD). This capability enables administrators to delegate authority for encrypted data recovery to one or more security administrators. EFS also enables multiple recovery-key configurations, which provides redundancy and greater flexibility in configuring and implementing the encryption policy.

If you have no domain (such as in a standalone, workgroup, or home-office environment), EFS automatically creates recovery keys and saves them as machine keys, enabling the local Administrator account to perform encryption recovery.

The EFS recovery policy is part of the domain security policy for computers participating in a domain and part of the local security policy for computers in a workgroup or for standalone computers. In each case, the security policy is applied through `Security Settings\Public Key Policies\Encrypted Data Recovery Agents`. You can use the Local Security Policy or Domain Security Policy MMC consoles, as appropriate, to add and configure recovery agents and their certificates. This includes importing and exporting certificates. By implementing the recovery policy in the system security policy, Windows Server 2008 provides centralized replication, enforcement, and caching of the policy. Because the user's security credentials are cached, the user can continue to work with encrypted files even if his system is not currently connected to the network.

 See the section "Configuring and Using a Recovery Policy," later in this chapter, for information on configuring the security policy and performing recovery operations.

Windows Server 2008 no longer requires that the recovery be in effect on the domain to decrypt files. Although the policy is configured for standalone computers as part of local policy, recovery on a Windows Server 2008 domain is configured as needed at the site, domain, and OU level; it can also be configured at the individual computer level. The policy applies to all Windows 2000, XP, and Windows Server 2008 computers that are within a defined scope of the policy. The recovery certificates are issued by a *Certificate Authority* (CA) using the Certificates console.

Using EFS

Because EFS is integrated with NTFS 5.0 and installed automatically, no installation or configuration is required for a user to begin encrypting folders and files. As long as a recovery agent is defined, the user can encrypt files. If no recovery agent is defined, EFS is disabled. Because Windows Server 2008 by default creates the recovery certificate and installs it in the domain or local security policy, as appropriate to the system, users can begin using encryption with Windows Server 2008 right out of the box.

Although you can encrypt individual files, applying encryption on a folder-by-folder basis is best (or in cases requiring extreme security, on a volume-by-volume basis). The main reason for not applying encryption to individual files is that many programs, such as Microsoft Word, create temporary files as you work, and EFS does not automatically encrypt these temporary files. To do so, the application would need to be EFS-aware and notify the operating system that the temporary file needs to be encrypted. By encrypting a folder, you effectively encrypt the contents of the folder. As you create new files in the folder (including automatically created temporary files), they are encrypted and enjoy the same security as the other files in the folder.

> **TIP** When you encrypt a folder, you aren't actually encrypting the NTFS field that defines the folder. Instead, you are setting the folder's encryption attribute. EFS uses this attribute to determine how to handle file creation and modification operations in the folder.

Recovery policy

The following three types of recovery policy can be defined in the domain by administrators:

- **Recovery-agent policy.** This is the default recovery policy. As soon as an administrator adds one or more recovery agents, the recovery-agent policy is in effect. These agents have the responsibility of recovering the encrypted data within the scope of their administration.

- **Empty-recovery policy.** This policy comes into effect when an administrator deletes all the recovery agents and their public-key certificates. Such a policy actually means that no policy exists. For Windows 2000 and Windows Server 2008 servers on the domain, this requires EFS to be disabled.

- **No-recovery policy.** If an administrator deletes all the private keys associated with a recovery policy, a no-recovery policy is in effect. Recovery of data, therefore, is not possible because you have no way to activate a recovery agent. Depending on the environment, this may be a desirable situation.

Encrypting and decrypting through Windows Explorer

Encrypting a folder or file is easy. Just right-click the object and choose Properties from the pop-up menu to display its property page. On the object's General property page, click Advanced to open the object's Advanced Attributes dialog box (see Figure 15-34). Select the Encrypt Contents to Secure Data checkbox, click OK, and then click OK again to close the object's property sheet.

FIGURE 15-34

The Advanced Attributes dialog box.

NOTE   NTFS compression and encryption are mutually exclusive, so encryption is not supported for compressed folders or files, or vice versa. If you enable encryption of a compressed folder or file, the file is decompressed. If you compress an encrypted folder or file, it is decrypted. This decryption doesn't happen automatically per se, but if you select the Compress Contents to Save Disk Space checkbox on the Advanced Attributes dialog box, the Encrypt Contents to Secure Data option is automatically deselected.

If you encrypt a folder, Windows Server 2008 displays the Confirm Attribute Changes dialog box, shown in Figure 15-35, when you click Apply. If you select Apply Changes to This Folder Only, EFS encrypts the folder but not any of its contents, including subfolders or files. Any new objects that you create in the folder, however, are encrypted. If instead you choose Apply Changes to This Folder, Subfolders and Files, EFS encrypts not only the folder, but also all its child objects.

FIGURE 15-35

The Confirm Attribute Changes dialog box.

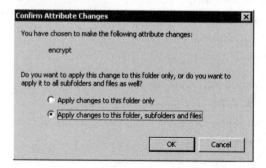

Encrypting and decrypting using the command prompt

If you work substantially in a command console or need to integrate encryption processes in batch files, you can use the CIPHER command to encrypt and decrypt folders and files. Following is the syntax for the command:

```
CIPHER [/E | /D] [/S:directory] [/A] [/I] [/F] [/Q] [/H]
[pathname [...]]
CIPHER /K
CIPHER /R:filename
CIPHER /U [/N]
CIPHER /W:directory
CIPHER /X[:efsfile] [filename]
```

The following list summarizes the command options for CIPHER:

- /E. Encrypts the specified folders. New files added are encrypted.

- /D. Decrypts the specified folders. New files are not encrypted; does not affect existing encrypted child objects.

- /S. Performs the specified operation on folders in the given directory and all subfolders.

- /A. Performs the specified operation for files as well as folders.

- /I. Continues the specified operation even when errors occur. By default, CIPHER stops whenever an error is encountered.

- /F. Forces the encryption operation on all specified objects, including those already encrypted. Objects already encrypted are skipped by default.

- /Q. Reports only essential information.

- ■ /H. Displays files with hidden or system attributes; these files are omitted by default.

- ■ /K. Creates a new file-encryption key for the user who is running CIPHER. All the other options are ignored when this option is used.

- ■ /N. Prevents keys from being updated. It works with the /U option.

- ■ /R. Generates an EFS recovery-agent key and associated certificate and then writes the files to a PFX file (which contains certificates and private key information) and CER files, which contain only certificate information. The administrator then adds the contents of the CER file to the EFS recovery policy to create a recovery agent for users. The PFX file is then imported to recover individual files.

- ■ /U. Used to affect all the encrypted files on a volume to update user file-encryption keys and recovery-agent keys when they are changed.

- ■ /W. Wipes data off volumes.

- ■ /X. Used for backing up EFS certificates.

- ■ pathname. Specifies a file or directory.

If used without parameters, CIPHER displays the encryption state of the current directory and any files contained in the folder. You can use multiple directory names and wildcards. Use spaces between multiple parameters.

Copying, moving, or renaming encrypted files

As with compression, a folder's encryption attribute also has an effect on the files that you copy or move between encrypted and non-encrypted folders or files and folders that you rename. The following list summarizes the effect of the encryption attribute in copying, moving, and renaming objects:

- ■ **Copying and moving encrypted folders or files to unencrypted folders (NTFS volumes).** The copies are encrypted regardless of the encryption attribute of the destination folder. If you are copying to another computer, the objects are encrypted only when the destination computer permits encryption. In a domain environment, the destination computer must be trusted for delegation — remote encryption is not enabled by default.

- ■ **Copying and moving unencrypted folders or files to encrypted folders (NTFS volumes).** The folders or files are encrypted when copied or moved through the Explorer interface. This applies to copies on the same computer and to a remote computer that supports encryption. The COPY console command causes the destination file to be encrypted, but the MOVE command does not because it simply renames the file.

- ■ **Copying and moving encrypted or unencrypted files to FAT volumes.** Windows displays a prompt indicating that the files cannot be encrypted and gives you the option to copy or move the files anyway, losing encryption. An exception to this is when you use the Backup utility to back up the files to a Backup file (BKF) on a FAT volume. In this case, the file remains encrypted in the backup set.

The COPY command used in a command console has been modified to support encryption. You can use the /D switch to copy an encrypted file to a non-EFS capable volume, but the file loses its encryption. Following is an example:

```
COPY /D sourcefile destinationfile
```

The XCOPY command also supports copying to non-EFS-capable volumes. XCOPY, however, uses the /G switch for this functionality. The syntax is similar to that for the COPY command.

If you rename a folder or file, the encryption attribute is unaffected. Therefore, you can rename an encrypted folder or file in place, and it remains encrypted. In addition, you can rename a folder or file to a different location (essentially a move operation), and the folder or file remains encrypted, even if it's renamed to an NTFS folder that is not encrypted.

Accessing encrypted data remotely

To access encrypted data, you must have the necessary security certificate and key. If you're logging on from the computer on which you encrypted the files, you have that certificate and associated private key in your local certificate store, provided you log on using the same account used when you encrypted the files. To access the encrypted data remotely from another computer, you must do one of two things: Use a roaming profile or import the certificate to the computer. If you use a roaming profile, your security certificates follow your logon, making them available regardless of your logon location.

If you're not using a roaming profile, you need to import the certificate that you used when the files were encrypted. You also can share a security certificate to enable multiple users to access the same set of encrypted folders and files. The following section explains how to share a security certificate.

Sharing encrypted data

To use files on a computer other than the one on which they were encrypted, you must have the required certificate and its associated private key on the computer at which you're logged on. This is true whether you're accessing data that you or someone else encrypted, so you need to install the certificate and its associated key on your computer. Use the Certificate Manager, which you can load as a snap-in for the MMC. First you export the certificate and its key on the computer on which the files were encrypted, and then you import the key to the computer(s) on which you want to access those files.

NOTE Using Certificate Services to share encrypted data requires you to install a *public key infrastructure* (PKI) and establish a Windows 2000, Windows Server 2003, or Windows Server 2008 network as a local or private Certificate Authority (CA). We introduce Windows PKI in Chapter 16.

To export the certificate and key, follow these steps:

1. Log on with the account that was used to encrypt the files and then open the Certificates MMC console snap-in focused on the user account (run `certmgr.msc` from the command prompt).

2. Select Personal ➤ Certificates, as shown in Figure 15-36, and locate the certificate issued for EFS. (Select the Intended Purposes column for Encrypting File System.)

FIGURE 15-36

The Certificates console.

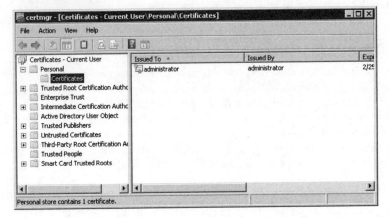

3. Right-click the certificate in the right-hand panel and choose All Tasks ➤ Export from the pop-up menu to start the Certificate Export Wizard.

4. In the wizard, choose the Export option to export the private key and click Next.

5. The default PKCS format option should be automatically selected on the next screen of the wizard; if not, select it (see Figure 15-37). Choose options from the wizard based on the following list and then click Next again:

   ■ **Include All Certificates in the Certification Path if Possible.** Select this option if you need to export multiple certificates from the selected store. In most cases, you do not need to select this option, because you probably have only one EFS certificate in your personal store.

   ■ **Enable Strong Protection (Requires IE 5.0, NT 4.0 SP4 or Above).** This option enables *iteration count*, which provides stronger security. This option is compatible with Internet Explorer 5.0 and later and NT 4.0 Service Pack 4 or later. If, in the unlikely event, you are exporting the key to systems that don't fit those criteria, deselect this option.

■ **Delete the Private Key if the Export Is Successful.** This option, if selected, deletes the private key associated with the certificate. In most cases, you probably do not want to delete the private key so you can continue to use the certificate on the originating system.

FIGURE 15-37

Use the Certificate Export Wizard to export the EFS certificate to other computers.

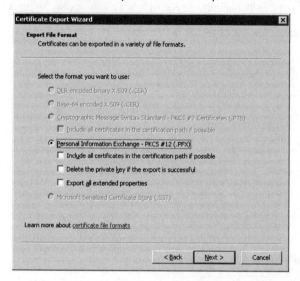

6. Specify and confirm a password in the wizard for the private key being exported. Doing so ensures that only those users who have the password can import and use the certificate. Notice that you can export the key with a blank password, but doing so reduces security for the key and enables anyone with access to the export file to import and use the certificate to decrypt the files.

7. Specify a filename for the file in the wizard and click Next; then click Finish to create the file.

After you have exported the certificate file, you need to import the file on the computer(s) and accounts from which you want to access the encrypted files. Follow these steps to import the certificate:

1. Log on at the computer where you want to use the certificate, or in the case of a roaming profile, simply log on at any computer in the domain, using the account through which you want to access the encrypted data.

2. Open the Certificate Manager MMC console; then open the Personal folder.

3. Right-click the Personal folder and choose All Tasks ➤ Import from the pop-up menu to start the Certificate Import Wizard.

4. Within the wizard, locate the file created in the preceding steps and click Next to display the File to Import screen of the wizard, shown in Figure 15-38.

FIGURE 15-38

Use the File to Import screen of the Certificate Import Wizard to specify or locate the file to import.

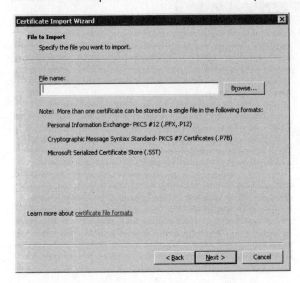

5. After you're prompted, specify the password for the private key in the certificate; then select options based on the following list:

   ■ **Enable Strong Private Key Protection.** Select this option if you want Windows Server 2008 to prompt you each time the private key is used by an application. This helps you track when the key is used.

   ■ **Mark This Key as Exportable.** Select this option if you want the capability to export the key in the future. If you don't select this option, you can't export the key.

6. Specify that you want to place the certificate in the Personal store and follow the prompts to complete the wizard and the import process.

You can provide the exported certificate to other users who need to access the encrypted data. You can also distribute the file as you would any other, such as by e-mail attachment or by placing the file in a network share. Because both methods make the file publicly available, make sure that you use a password when exporting the certificate and give the password only to those users who need to import and use the certificate.

Encrypting files for multiple users

After files are encrypted, you can share the files by using the file-sharing feature of Windows Server 2008. First, encrypt the files as described in the preceding section and then click the Details button on the Advanced Attributes dialog box, shown in Figure 15-34, to add users to the encrypted file. The user is added only if she has a valid EFS certificate.

You cannot share a file until it is encrypted, and the Details button is enabled only after you open the Advanced Attributes dialog box again.

You are now ready to add users:

1. Click Details. The User Access dialog box shown in Figure 15-39 opens. This dialog box shows existing users and the certificates cached in the Other People and Trusted People certificate stores on the local machine. The dialog box enables you to add users found in Active Directory as well.

FIGURE 15-39

The Encryption Details dialog box shows existing users.

2. To add new users, click the Add button. The dialog box, shown in Figure 15-40 opens, displaying the users who can be added from the local machine. To find a user in Active Directory, click the Find User button.

FIGURE 15-40

Use the dialog box to add more users to the encrypted file.

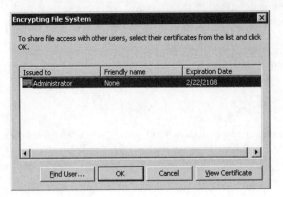

3. From the Select Users dialog box, you can choose to view a certificate. Click the View Certificate button and the certificate appears onscreen, as shown in Figure 15-41. Click the Details tab to view data concerning the key, as shown in the figure.

FIGURE 15-41

Viewing the user's certificate details.

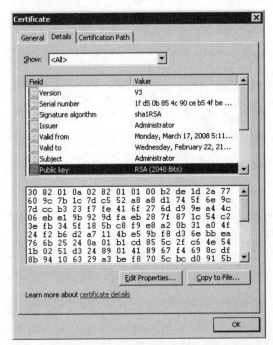

You cannot add groups of users to encrypted files, and the EFS header for a file has a limit of 256K for metadata. You can, however, add 800 users to the encrypted file.

Backing up and recovering encrypted data

The Windows Server 2008 Backup program can back up and restore files for which the backup operator (or account) doesn't have adequate permissions to actually view the data. The same is true for encrypted data. Backup can back up and restore encrypted data regardless of whether the backup account has the EFS certificate necessary to decrypt the data. The backup and restore operations also have no effect on the encryption state of the files — the files remain encrypted and secure.

You can also back up directly from the command line by using the /X parameter, or by clicking the Back Up Keys button in the Encryption Details dialog box (refer to Figure 15-39).

NOTE Even when encrypted files are backed up to media that doesn't support encryption (such as FAT volumes or floppies), Backup maintains the encryption on the files. If an unauthorized user gains access to the backup set and restores it — whether to FAT or NTFS volumes — the encrypted data is not restored. Backup creates the target files, but the files are empty.

In some situations you may need to recover encrypted data as a recovery agent. A user who has encrypted data on his computer may leave the organization, for example, or lose his certificate. In this situation, any recovery agent who has the appropriate recovery certificate, which Windows Server 2008 creates automatically, can recover the encrypted data.

Follow these steps to restore encrypted files:

1. Back up the encrypted files to a BKF file on a floppy disk or hard disk accessible from the recovery agent's computer.

2. Log on to the recovery agent's computer and restore the files from the backup set to a secure NTFS folder.

3. If you don't already have the required certificate, use the Certificates console to import the recovery key and certificate to the recovery agent's computer.

4. Open the property sheet for each file and deselect the encryption option to turn off the file's encryption attribute (decrypting the file). You can now send the decrypted files to any user who needs them. If the data needs to be re-encrypted, use a certificate shared by those users who need to access the data.

Configuring and using a recovery policy

EFS requires that a recovery agent be designated before encryption can occur. On a standalone computer or on those in a workgroup, the local Administrator account is designated as a recovery agent by default, and the appropriate recovery key is placed in the Administrator's personal certificate store. In a domain, the Domain Administrator account is designated as the default recovery agent. You can continue to use the default recovery agents if desired, or you can modify the recovery policy to accommodate specific security needs, such as redefining the role of recovery agents within the domain or disabling EFS on certain computers. The following sections examine administrative issues related to configuring and using a recovery policy.

Securing the default recovery key — workgroup/standalone computer

At the initial logon with the Administrator account on a standalone computer or a computer in a workgroup, Windows Server 2008 creates a default recovery policy on the computer that makes the local Administrator account the recovery agent for EFS. Windows Server 2008 does so by creating a recovery certificate for the administrator and placing it in the administrator's personal store.

In some situations, you may want to secure the local recovery key to prevent the local administrator account from being used to recover encrypted data. You may instead want to delegate this capability to a specific user. To secure the recovery key, export the key to a file and then remove the certificate from the local computer. Give the key to the designated recovery agent for import on the agent's computer or place the certificate file in a secure location for import whenever it is needed.

See the section "Sharing Encrypted Data," earlier in this chapter, if you're not sure how to export the recovery certificate. After you successfully export the certificate, remove the certificate from the local computer to prevent it from being used for EFS recovery.

Securing the default recovery key — domain

You may want to secure the default recovery key in a domain environment as well. You may, for example, want to create a group of administrators specifically for the purpose of EFS recovery, rather than enable any domain administrator to perform recovery. To secure the default recovery key in a domain, log on as Administrator on the first domain controller in the domain. Then use the procedure described in the preceding section to export the certificate to a file and delete the certificate from the Domain Administrator account's certificate store.

Obtaining a file-recovery certificate

If you are using the default recovery policy in a domain, requesting recovery certificates isn't necessary because the required certificates are already in place in the Domain Administrator's certificate store. If you are instead delegating recovery responsibility to a specific group of users or to individual accounts, you may want to use a Certificate Authority (CA) to generate recovery certificates when requested by recovery agents.

NOTE   You don't specifically need to use a CA to distribute recovery certificates. You can simply export the default domain-recovery certificate from the Domain Administrator's certificate store and then give the certificate to individual users designated as recovery agents for import on their computers. Using multiple certificates, however, can increase security by not putting all your recovery eggs in one basket. Instead, you can rely on the CA to issue a unique recovery certificate to each recovery agent.

Because this chapter focuses on file systems, it does not cover how to set up a CA. Instead, the following steps explain the general procedure for providing a means for recovery agents to request recovery certificates:

CROSS-REF See Chapter 16 for details on how to set up a CA.

1. If no CA is currently installed, log on to a domain controller and run the Add/Remove Programs object in the Control Panel. Install Certificate Services.

2. Create a group called Domain Recovery Agents in the domain and add the appropriate users to the group. Configure policies on the CA to enable the designated users or group to request recovery certificates from the CA. To do so, open the Certificate Authority console, right-click the server, and choose Properties. Click the Security tab, and grant Enroll and Read permission as needed.

3. Have each recovery agent request a recovery certificate from the CA. To start this process, the agents open the Certificates MMC console, right-click their Personal store, and choose All Tasks ➤ Request New Certificate from the pop-up menu to start the Certificate Request Wizard.

4. The wizard automatically locates a CA in the domain, but the agent can choose a specific CA if needed. Through the wizard, the agent specifies that she wants to obtain an EFS Recovery Agent certificate and follows the wizard's prompts to obtain it.

5. If the certificate is not automatically published to the AD, the agent needs to copy the certificate without the private key to a CER file. The domain administrator then uses this file to add the certificate to the domain recovery policy. Use the Certificates console to copy the certificate to the CER file (that is, to export the certificate to the file).

6. The agent exports the certificate to a secure PFX file by using the Certificates console and places the PFX in a secure archive. Then the agent deletes the certificate from the local computer, again through the Certificates console. This ensures that the certificate is applied through the domain policy, rather than through the local policy.

Defining a domainwide recovery policy

After you set up a CA, and the designated recovery agents have their certificates exported to CER files, set up the domainwide recovery policy. You do so by adding the recovery agents and their respective certificates to the default domain policy. The presence of the certificates in the `Security Settings\Public Key Policies\Encrypted Data Recovery Agents` container implicitly defines the domain recovery policy. Follow these steps to define the domain recovery policy:

1. Set up a CA and a Recovery Agents group and have the agents request certificates and then export them to CER files.

2. Collect the CER files into a common secure location on your local computer or on the domain controller.

3. Open the Default Domain Policy in the Group Policy Management Editor, shown in Figure 15-42.

FIGURE 15-42

The Default Domain Security Settings console.

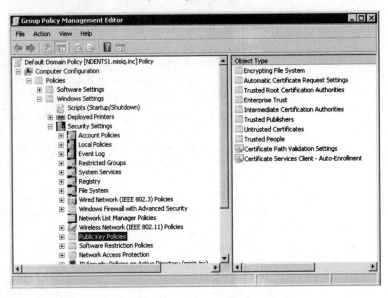

4. In the Security Settings node, open to Public Key Policies in the left-hand pane.

5. Right-click the Encrypting File System folder in the right-hand pane and choose Add Data Recovery Agent from the pop-up menu, to start the Add Recovery Agent Wizard.

6. Follow the wizard's prompts to complete the installation. Repeat the process to add any additional certificates. (If the certificates are already published in AD, they are listed in the wizard. You can also browse to the folder containing the CER files.)

CROSS-REF   See Chapter 16 for information about Certificate Authorities and how to set them up in Windows Server 2008.

Defining a recovery policy for an organizational unit

You define a recovery policy for an OU in essentially the same way that you define the domain-wide recovery policy. Rather than work at the domain level, however, you work at the level of the OU. Follow the same steps in the OU as those described in the preceding sections for the domain, adding recovery-agent certificates at the appropriate container in the OU.

Forcing EFS use

In some situations, particularly with notebook computers that contain sensitive data, you may want to force the use of EFS. Because encryption and decryption happen transparently to the user, forcing the use of EFS doesn't affect the user in any way and ensures that if a notebook is stolen, then the files on it are relatively safe from compromise.

To force EFS use, format the drives on the computer by using NTFS. Apply object permissions to folders to prevent the user from storing documents in any folder other than those you configure for encryption. You may restrict the user to only working within the My Documents folder, for example, setting permissions on all other folders to prevent the user from creating documents in them. Then configure My Documents for encryption. Secure the default recovery key if present on the computer by exporting it and then removing the certificate from the computer.

Disabling EFS

In some situations, you may want to disable EFS for specific standalone computers or certain computers in an OU. You can disable EFS by applying an empty recovery policy to the computer — one that contains no recovery certificates and, therefore, disables EFS. If the user tries to create an encrypted folder or file, she receives an Access Denied message.

An empty recovery policy is different from no recovery policy in a domain. With no recovery policy in place, the recovery policies defined at higher levels in the AD are inherited by the local computer. If no policy exists at a higher level, the local policy applies.

On a standalone computer or one in a workgroup, simply export the recovery certificate from the local Administrator's personal certificate store and then remove the certificate from the computer (along with any other recovery certificates, if installed). This defines an empty local policy, effectively disabling EFS. In a domain, define the empty policy at the OU level.

Summary

This chapter described how you share folders to enable users to access shared or network applications and to provide access to shared data. As we note, shares should not be left wide open by admitting the Everyone group to the share with Full Control. Users should be admitted to shares as members of groups and not individually.

Folder and file permissions are the domain of the NTFS. The permissions provide true network security and access control. Permissions can be complex and cumbersome to manage on a large network with many users, groups, and network resources. We stress strong documentation, change-control record keeping, and tracking as commonsense practices in providing access and security to network files and folders.

In situations where physical security of a server is critical, the Encrypting File System (EFS) provides an excellent means of securing files on the server, preventing unauthorized access through file copy to a disk or backup to offline storage. If you intend to implement EFS, keep in mind that encryption and compression are mutually exclusive, so if you're going to use EFS, it must be on an uncompressed volume.

Part III

Security and Active Directory

Chapter 16

Windows Server 2008 Security

This chapter starts you off with a discussion on the need for powerful distributed security before introducing you to the specifics of Windows Server 2008 distributed security. It also reviews the new Windows Server 2008 security protocols, and protection of services and data.

An Overview of Windows Server 2008 Security

While the new era of computing and Windows Server 2008 will bring forth many benefits, it will also herald dastardly attempts to rob you, beat you up, and shut you down. There are many forces out there that have only one thing on their evil minds, and that is to find any way to break into your network to plunder and pillage. And it's only going to get worse.

Before you start building your new corporate infrastructure around Windows Server 2008, it will pay for you to become thoroughly versed in the security mechanisms the operating system offers and how to go about locking down your assets. Without a doubt, it is probably the most secure operating system available today. Not only has it inherited the Windows 2000 and Windows Server 2003 C2 security compliance, but if there were showbiz awards for security, then Windows Server 2008 would clean up at the Oscars, the Golden Globes, the Grammies, and more.

But before we get into Windows Server 2008 security specifics, let's look at the problem holistically. You can then evaluate your current security status before devising a security plan.

You have probably heard the term "C2 security" everywhere, so what does it mean to you, the network, or server administrator? Absolutely nothing. C2 security is nothing more than a U.S. government sanction. The United States keeps a series of "books" that grade the security levels of operating systems. These specifications include object ownership, object protection, audit trail, memory protection, and user identification, all of which are discussed in various places in this book.

C2 is defined in the so-called "Orange Book," which is really titled the *Trusted System Evaluation Criteria*. C2 evaluation checks to see how secure a computer really is. However, C2 only applies to standalone computers. Microsoft is also testing to the specifications for network computers (Red Book and Blue Book). Microsoft has already gone above and beyond C2 with Windows Server 2008, so the term is really meaningless.

> **NOTE** The operating system is not C2 out of the box. A vendor or security service provider has to set up a machine and the OS to be C2-compliant. This means locking down objects, setting up audit trails, creating user accounts with secure password philosophy, and so on. Only when a machine has been fully locked down can it be rated as C2-compliant ... whether it's a washing machine or a file server. The first versions of Windows Server 2008 were more secure out of the box than Windows 2000 or Windows Server 2003; and now, with the threat of hostile software ready to pounce on a fledgling server, Microsoft has opted to lock the server down more fully until an administrator has fully configured it.

Windows Server 2008 can be as locked down as the space above your head, or it can be as tight as a hole on a pin head. You have the control to secure it or open it as you deem fit. The network is only as secure as you make it. If Windows Server 2008 is not properly configured, claiming awards like C2 will not get you out of a jam when a hacker pulls your pants down on the Internet. Blunt, yes, but security is part of the day-to-day life of a network administrator. If you don't take care of security problems, you will not have a network for very long.

The need for security

If you are new to network administration in general and Windows Server 2008 in particular, before you devise a security plan, you need to understand the risks to your network and yourself. Unless you plan to hire a security expert, you will probably have to come up with a plan yourself. Chances are good your company will ask this of you ... your superior will assume that you are well versed in the subject. If you are well versed about security threats, you can skip this part and go directly to the section titled "Rising to the Security Challenge."

A company's data is its lifeblood, and it needs to be vigorously protected. As the network administrator, you are charged with the responsibility to ensure that data is kept confidential and that it can be relied upon. Numerous mechanisms are in place to assist you with respect to data integrity and confidentiality, and they range from a sensible access control policy to encryption, backup, and availability.

Data input

Data is vulnerable to attack and capture from the moment a person types in a user ID and password. How often have you had to enter a password while someone was standing over your shoulder? You try to type as quickly as you can, but spies will watch you typing and pick up your passwords quicker than you think. Then, when you are not at your desk, they will get your user ID from the memo field at the sign-in screen and masquerade as you from any computer, anywhere.

With a smart card, a user is authenticated without the risk of being compromised because the thief needs the card to complete the hack. Smart card readers offer one of the most sophisticated domain authentication solutions available to Windows Server 2008.

Data transport

The PC's or input device's operating system must send the information down the network stack to the transport, all the way to the domain controller's (DC's) network interface and up the DC's respective stack. All along this route, the data is vulnerable to interception. If the data is not encrypted, or is encrypted very lightly, there is a risk that a person tapping the network will be able to pick up conversations between your input device and the domain controller, or any other partner for that matter.

To counter this, Windows Server 2008 employs extensive encryption technology both in data and network communications, and in file storage and protection.

Why the threat exists

There are many reasons why people threaten your security. Let's look at a short list of threats that you are most likely to encounter during your life as a Windows Server 2008 administrator:

■ **Espionage.** People attempt to break into your communications realm to learn company secrets, employee secrets, product plans, your financial situation, strategies, and so forth. This level of threat is the most virulent. The attackers have strong motives to get the attack under way and to ensure they succeed. They do not want to be discovered and will continue to hide in your environment as long as they need to. The damage is often irreparable if the attackers are undiscovered. This is the most difficult form of attack to counter because, for the most part, you do not know where they are hitting you or why.

Though bugging devices and spying are not usually the responsibility of the network or server administrator, espionage via the network is becoming more common every day because it is so easy and it is where all the jewels are located.

Over the network, hackers will read files and e-mail, and try to log in to databases wherever they can to steal credit card numbers, bank account numbers, and so forth. An attacker can, for example, find out the password of your voice mail system and then listen to your messages.

- **Denial of Service (DoS).** These attackers are intent on destroying you. They can attack your physical premises or locations, which is becoming harder to do all the time, or they can target your network, which is becoming easier to do because you are connected to the Internet or because you provide users with remote access. This is fast becoming the favorable means of attack for stopping your work — first, because of the dependency your company has on the network, and second, because the attacker does not need to be physically present for the attack.

  DoS attacks are made by flooding your network portal (targeting your gateway to the Internet) with massive floods of e-mail, or with *syn* attacks, which are the low-level communication barrages that suck up all the server's resources, finally causing it to crash. Sometimes the objective is to crash the server just to trigger backdoor code that spawns a process. There could be a million places on a network to hide a sliver of code that will be executed when certain files are loaded. Good examples are the boot files and startup files such as `AUTOEXEC.BAT`.

- **Hostile applications.** Hostile applications are placed on the Internet for unwary surfers to download. Upon execution of the code on your internal network, the application can begin its dirty work, which for a while might be to do nothing that can cause it to be detected, but rather to find information that would be valuable to the attacker. Such applications are also called Trojan horses.

- **Virus attacks.** By far, the most visible attack on the network comes in the form of viruses. Contrary to the claims that there are tens of thousands of viruses, only a handful of virus writers can actually claim to have invented one from start to finish. Most virus authors are not as brilliant as you may have been led to believe; they are just copycats. However, this information does not provide any relief.

  A lot of virus code is available on the Internet to be freely downloaded, manipulated, and enhanced or packed with a payload. This is why we see so many variations of viruses every month. Some can be detected by anti-virus software such as NetShield and cleaned up; others are more sinister, such as Backdoor-G, which can only be picked up by the anti-virus software after it has delivered its payload. Not only does it wreck your PC before it can be detected, but it also first attacks the anti-virus software.

Threats emanate from two locales: the external environment and the internal environment. A threat from the external environment is one that comes from people who have no contractual status with the enterprise. They are complete strangers, and the attack comes from the outside. A threat from the internal environment is one that comes from people who have a relationship with the company, from employees to contractors to customers. This attack usually comes from the inside. In some cases, it comes from the outside, with inside information. Other times, the threat does not stem from revenge or criminal intent, but from ignorance.

The external environment

Not too long ago, the only way to threaten or attack an organization, its people, or its business was through some sort of physical act. This is no longer the case. It costs far less money and is much safer for a hacker to stay in a safe haven and attempt to break into a network through a RAS portal or a connection to the Internet. For many attackers, it offers the possibility of financial reward; for others, the payoff is merely related to some demented feeling of achievement.

Now that many small companies can afford dedicated connections to the Internet, the pickings have become very attractive. Though we have not yet realized the paperless office, almost all data is placed on the network in sharepoints and databases. The network and server storage silos are thus loaded with valuable information.

Attackers also no longer need to proactively choose their targets. They create hostile code that is inadvertently downloaded from the Internet and executed by a number of mechanisms, from rebooting to the mere act of unzipping a file. The code then can gather intelligence and send it to its master. It is therefore essential that you establish a policy to ensure that code downloaded from the Internet is authenticated and signed with the digital signature (a public key) of a trusted software publisher.

E-mail is now very much tangible property, and it can be used in court cases as evidence and as a source of information that can be used to plan an attack on a person or an organization. We all communicate more by e-mail than we do by snail mail, yet e-mail is treated like a postcard. We do not enclose our messages in an envelope and seal it. We just put it in the mail for any-one to look at.

E-mail needs to be secured on two levels. One, we need to ensure that the people with whom we communicate are really who they say they are. Two, we need to ensure that our e-mail is not being read or changed as it traverses the Net. It is very easy to trace the route a message takes over the Internet and penetrate e-mail systems. Securing e-mail is becoming essential and falls under the auspices of public key encryption, which is discussed shortly.

Another tangible and visible property that has emerged in recent years (soon after the release of the Windows Server 2008) is Web services. Web services extend services of the company to the Internet, and thus assist customers and clients with interacting and transacting business easier over the Internet. However, Web services also expose potential targets to hackers, worms, and viruses. Windows Server 2008 thus further secures Web services with a host of security enhancements aimed at these business-critical technologies.

This is achieved in part with Active Directory Federation Services, which extends the value of Active Directory deployments to facilitate collaboration with partners, resulting in increased user productivity, greater IT efficiency, and better security. It also extends the value of Active Directory Rights Management Services in Internet-facing Web environments, enabling stronger authentication for extranet deployments, native delegated administration, and close integration with Microsoft technologies.

The internal environment

The internal environment threat includes employees who are either malicious or stupid, or who make honest mistakes. Threats come in the form of outright misuse of privileges to total ignorance or stupidity. For example, the perpetrator of outright misuse of privileges has administrative rights on the network and provides himself or herself with access to sensitive data.

The ignorance factor often involves users failing to keep anti-virus software current, or down-loading all forms of rubbish from the Internet, thereby introducing malicious content to the net-work from the external environment.

Outright stupidity and honest mistakes that often cause headaches for administrators are usually deleted files, corrupted databases, deleted mailbox folders, and so on. Deleted data can usually be recovered from backups, as long as the backup regimen is well practiced in your company. Most of the time, recovering deleted files is unnecessary administrative work. Often, the problems are not user-related issues at all, but just bad management on the part of a lazy network administrator or server administrator.

Rising to the Security Challenge

Over the years, there has been a lot of discussion about the security capabilities of Windows. Microsoft has often been criticized for not delivering a more secure operating system, but the charge isn't really fair, and the problem has not been all Microsoft's fault. For starters, the U.S. government has for years not allowed the export of 128K-bit encryption algorithms, although that did not deter many organizations from smuggling out the software.

Regarding comparisons with Unix, Unix systems are more at risk today than Windows Server 2008. Because the Unix source code is open for all to see, many hackers can read the code to look for weak points and plot their attacks. Server for server, there are still more Unix machines on the Internet than Window Server 200X machines. On Windows Server, hackers resort to scanning network communications to look for information with which to replay attacks. Data interception was and still is a common form of attack against a Windows Server network.

For Windows Server 2008 to compete and even excel over the competition in the risky and exposed world of e-commerce, it needed to be the most secure operating system. The following sections explore the standard Windows Server 2008 security mechanisms that are part of the web and woof of Windows Server 2008:

- Reducing the attack surface by server role
- Kerberos
- IPSec
- PKI
- NT LAN Manager (NTLM)

Before we get into a general discussion of security, let's investigate several roles and features that make Windows Server 2008 the most secure operating system from Microsoft.

Security Enhancements in Server Roles

In Chapter 1 and throughout this book we discuss the concept of the server role. Though this is not unique to Windows Server 2008 (roles were introduced in Windows Server 2003), roles installation using Server Manager is more geared to server security than it was in Windows Server 2003.

In Chapter 1 we started by discussing the Server Manager console snap-in and how it is used to install specific roles to a server. This model lets you reduce the attack surface because you now have the ability to configure just the functionality that you need for a particular server role. We also covered the Server Core feature of Windows Server 2008 in Chapter 1. This lets you reduce the attack surface of the server roles in your organization even further because at start up of Server Core you are running a server with no services or features or functionality that typically exposes the server to attack. Additionally, as each server role or feature is installed a default set of security settings are applied. Not only is the server incrementally upgraded, it is also incrementally secured as new bits are added to it.

To further lock down the server roles you can use the Security Configuration Wizard (SCW) to secure and enforce the security configuration implemented when you installed various roles and features. The SCW will help you create and deploy Group Policy Objects (GPOs) and further harden your servers. See Chapter 24 for coverage of Group Policy.

All the fancy encryption algorithms you use will be useless if your server stands in the middle of an open-plan office for anyone to plunder or sneak out. Unless a server or key systems and data storage are locked up behind secured barriers, you might as well forget the rest of this chapter. But what about the times when that is impossible to do? The following sections look at security enhancements aimed at several directory and configuration roles that are often the first targets of security attacks.

Active Directory Domain Controller role service

The Active Directory Domain Controller role includes the following security-related enhancements:

- **Attribute-change auditing.** The OS now logs both the old and new values of an AD attribute when a successful change is made to that attribute. In previous versions, AD logged only the name of the attribute that changed. With new subcategories for auditing AD DS, you can more scientifically evaluate or discover what security-related changes have taken place in the directory.

- **Fine-grained password policies.** You can now implement multiple password and account lockout policies within a single domain. In earlier versions of the OS, you could only create a single domain policy that extended the password policy to every OU. This has changed with Windows Server 2008. You can apply different password configuration and account lockout policies for different collections of user in the domain.

- **Read-only domain controller (RODC).** This is a new type of domain controller, which uses a read-only AD DS database and only supports inbound replication for all partitions and the SYSVOL.

- **No account passwords present on RODC.** No passwords, except for the RODC itself and the RODC specific Kerberos account, are stored on the RODC. This means you can deploy a DC in an environment that might not be safe, such as a factory floor or a remote location or branch office.

■ **Installation versus Deployment.** Active Directory Domain Services are now installed as one of the roles for a server. This act alone does not make the server a directory domain controller. You then need to promote the server to a DC. This further ensures that a DC is not compromised during the establishment or extension of a domain.

The DHCP Server Role

The DHCP Server Role and the DHCP Client service now include the following security-related improvements:

■ **DHCPv6.** Though IPv6 was introduced in Windows Server 2003, DHCPv6 functionality was not available until Windows Server 2008. The service can allow client computers to use the DHCPv6 stateless mode, which provides network configuration parameters excluding an IPv6 address. This means that you can configure client computers to receive an IPv6 address from local configuration or from other devices, such as IPv6 auto-configuration. DHCPv6 in stateful mode lets clients receive both IPv6 addresses as well as network configuration parameters.

■ **Network Access Protection (NAP).** The NAP service is part and parcel of DHCP. This service forces DHCP clients to obtain vetting on system and security health state before they can obtain an IP address from the server. Unfortunately, NAP is supported on DHCP only for IPv4 addresses at this time.

See Chapter 3, which covers IPv6, and Chapter 4, which covers DHCP.

The DNS Server Role

The DNS Server Role and DNS Client service now includes the following security-related improvements:

■ **Background zone loading.** Zone data is now loaded in the background as a server is rebooted. This means the DNS servers hosting large DNS zones stored in Active Directory can now respond more quickly to clients. Before, DNS query was delayed until zones were fully loaded, which widened the security breach window.

■ **Support for read-only domain controllers (RODCs).** The DNS Server role supports primary read-only zones found on RODCs. This means that RODCs can fully participate in DNS replication on border networks, remote locations and otherwise insecure premises.

For more on DNS see Chapter 5.

Before you tackle the protocols, services, roles, and features, you need to get up to speed on the cloak-and-dagger stuff.

Understanding Encryption Basics

This is a true story: A man walked into a diner one morning and ordered fried eggs. When the eggs were delivered, he changed his mind and advised the waitress that he had ordered scrambled eggs. The waitress, peeved at the cheek of the client, picked up a fork and with a quick whipping movement rendered the eggs into an unrecognizable heap. "There, now they are scrambled," she said, and stormed off.

The action of rendering eggs into an unintelligible mess is known as scrambling. Data is scrambled in similar fashion; we call it encryption. At first, the data is in whole recognizable form, often called *plain text*, like the fried eggs. The motion to scramble them is known as the *algorithm* . . . and the result is often termed *cipher text*. In the anecdote, the algorithm is the technique, style, or "recipe" by which the waitress used her wrist and fork to turn a perfect pair of sunny-side-ups into a mound of yolk and white. If she only took a few stabs at the eggs, the patron might be able to claim he still had fried eggs (not a strong encryption algorithm).

Knowing the key that reverses the process is vital to the recovery of the data, but that is the only difference between egg scrambling and data scrambling. If we knew how to unscramble eggs, Humpty Dumpty might still be alive, and our world would be very different.

In computer science, the standard that governs the techniques and recipes for encryption of data is known as the Data Encryption Standard (DES). DES data encryption algorithms (DEAs) specify how to encrypt data and how to decrypt that data. A number of important bodies, such as the American National Standards Institute (ANSI) and the National Institute of Standards and Technology (NIST), govern the specifications for DES. Each algorithm is rated according to the strength of its encryption capability (and resistance to duplication, attack of the encryption/decryption key).

DES, actually the DEAs, need to be continuously improved because the codes are often cracked by encryption experts (for science and crime). New standards are on the horizon, and the Advanced Encryption Standard (AES), has largely replaced DES. Other standards governed by these bodies include the Digital Signature Standard (DSS) and the Digital Signature Algorithm (DSA). Incidentally, the U.S. government does not regulate encryption.

 For more information on encryption standards, see the RSA Laboratories Web site at www.rsasecurity.com.

Getting to Know Cryptography

Cryptography dates back more than 4,000 years. Over the past millennia, it has protected many a culture's communications and has brought them through wars, treaties with neighbors, and more.

In recent years, electronic data communications have escalated to such volume and importance in our lives that without electronic or digital cryptography we would not be able to continue with business as usual.

In fact, we owe our computerized environment to cryptography. If you have time during the locking down of your networks, you should read the online biography of Alan Turing, who directed the British to build the first digital computers to break the Germans' Enigma code.

Pretty Good Privacy (PGP) is a software program written for no financial gain by Phil Zimmerman, who believed that the cryptography algorithms that were being protected by patents should be made public property ... worldwide. He created PGP in 1991, and over the years, it was disseminated around the world on the "undernet." Even though its export was expressly forbidden by the U.S. government's International Traffic in Arms Regulations, which classified his software as a munition, it became available everywhere on bulletin board systems and the first pioneer sites of the World Wide Web. In the past decade, PGP was pretty much the only means of securing data and communications on the Internet and corporate networks of the world.

However, encrypting data always required a user to make an effort to secure communications. Lethargy and a lack of knowledge have always left room for error and holes. Only with the incorporation of the encryption algorithms in the very core of the operating systems and standards-based network protocols would encryption become as pervasive and as transparent as air.

We have come a long way since Phil Zimmerman risked detention to make the slogan *encryption for everyone* a reality. Today, Windows Server 2008 incorporates it extensively. Only you, the administrator, need to ensure that it is configured correctly, through security policy, and everyone on the network will be able to use it, without even knowing it exists. Before we look at this native support for cryptography in Windows Server 2008 and how it is used, consider the following sections Cryptography 101.

Cryptography Next Generation

Windows Server 2008 now includes *Cryptography Next Generation* (CNG), which lets you create, update, and use custom cryptography algorithms in cryptography-related applications such as Active Directory Certificate Services, Secure Sockets Layer (SSL), and Internet Protocol security (IPSec). The CNG supports the U.S. government's Suite B cryptographic algorithms. These include algorithms for encryption, digital signatures, key exchange, and hashing.

The CNG is a set of APIs that provide the ability to carry out basic cryptographic operations, such as creating hashes and encrypting and decrypting data; creating, storing, and retrieving cryptographic keys; and installing and using various cryptographic providers. CNG also supports the current set of CryptoAPI 1.0 algorithms.

In addition CNG provides the following features:

- It lets customers choose their own cryptographic algorithms or use various implementations of the standard cryptographic algorithms. You can also add new algorithms as needed.

- It supports cryptography for kernel mode operations. The same API is used in both kernel mode and user mode to fully support cryptography features of the OS. SSL/TLS, IPSec, and various startup processes use CNG in kernel mode operations.

- CNG provides support for elliptic curve cryptography (ECC) algorithms. A number of ECC algorithms are required by the United States government's Suite B effort.

- CNG also applies to public key infrastructure (PKI) servers that require the use of Suite B algorithms. Servers running on Windows Server 2003 cannot be used in a CNG PKI.

To use the new cryptographic algorithms, both your CA and your applications should support ECC (or any other new algorithm you implement under CNG). Though the CA needs to issue and manage these new certificate types, applications must be able to handle certificate chain validation and use the keys generated with Suite B algorithms.

Keys

Cryptography is a lock, a means of securing information by rendering it undecipherable without a key. The key, or cryptographic key, is held closely by people sending and receiving the communication. The following is the simplest example of cryptography:

The communication: Package color baby burger

The Key:

Package = meet

color = same

baby = grand central station

burger = 14:00 hours

Deciphered: Meet me at the same place at Grand Central Station at 2 P.M.

Obviously, if you have the key, you can unlock the code and decipher the message.

Private keys

Private key encryption is also known as *symmetric key encryption* or just *conventional cryptography*. This encryption uses the same key to decrypt and encrypt the data. In other words, the key you use to lock the door is the same key you use to unlock the door. In the previous example, both the sender of the message and the receiver share a common codebook or key. The sender encodes the message with the key, and the receiver decodes the message with the same key. This form of encryption is not the most secure in the public domain, because for widespread communications, numerous parties must hold the key. As soon as the key falls into wrong hands, then all bets are off, but it can be used in network authentication where the compromising of a key is highly unlikely.

Public keys

Public key encryption uses two keys. One key is public, and the other is private. Both keys can encrypt data, but only the private key can decrypt the data. To be pervasive, the technology depends on a public key infrastructure (PKI), which Windows Server 2008 has greatly enhanced (more about PKI later in this chapter).

A mathematical process is used to generate the two keys, and the keys are related to each other by the product of that mathematical process. Therefore, the message encrypted with one key can be decrypted only with the other. This is how it works:

You want to send an encrypted message. The receiver has a public key, which he or she makes publicly available for encrypting messages. You encrypt the message using the public key and send it. When the receiver gets your message, he or she can decrypt it using the private key, which is mathematically related to the public key. No one, including you, can decrypt the message with the public key.

It goes without saying that the private key must be closely held or your messages will be compromised.

Session keys

The chief problem in making public keys widely available is that the encryption algorithms used to generate public keys are too slow for the majority of just-in-time communications (there are numerous algorithms used to create the keys, but the technology is beyond the scope of this book). For this reason, a simpler session key is generated, which in turn holds the "key" to the encrypted data. The following steps describe the process:

1. A session key is randomly generated for every communication that requires encryption. A *key distribution authority* (or the originator of the communication, or a vouchsafe process) creates the session key for the communication or message.

2. The data is encrypted with the session key.

3. The session key is then encrypted with the recipient's public key. The encryption of the data by the session key is a thousand times faster than the encryption of the data by the public key.

4. The encrypted data and the encrypted session key are then sent to the receiver, who can decrypt both by first decrypting the session key with the secret key and then decrypting the data with the session key.

Key certificates

Key certificates are containers for public keys. Key certificates usually contain the public key of the recipient, the identity of the public key's creator, the date the key was created, and a list of digital signatures.

Digital signatures

We add our written signature to most things we do in the material world, so why not in the digital world? Most of us spend our working lives in cyberspace. Our customers deal with us on the Net, they buy from us on the Net, and they expect that when they send us confidential communications, they are sending it to the right people. We also want some assurance that when someone sends us a message, hits our Web site, or connects to our computers, they are who they say they are. We also need to use digital signatures to prevent repudiation. In other words, if someone places an order with you over the World Wide Web or via e-mail, or enters into some form of contract with you, that person should sign the document so that they cannot later repudiate the transaction.

It is not always necessary to encrypt a message, which taxes computer resources. Sometimes, the message or data content or information is not sensitive. Sending someone a publicly available encrypted price list would be an absurd idea, but what if someone intercepted that message and changed the content? What if someone sent you a message saying, "I had to sack my assistant today," and a jokester intercepted the message and changed the content to read, "I had to smack my assistant today"? The effects of changing content could be devastating.

Digital signatures are thus used to authenticate the sender, to legally bind parties in digital transactions, to authenticate content, and to ensure that content has not been tampered with in any way.

Windows Server 2008 makes wide use of the encryption mechanics described previously. One of the most important implementations is in the use of the Kerberos protocol, which is now the most important means of authenticating and protecting data in not only Windows Server 2008, but all major operating systems.

Understanding Kerberos

What if we told you that every time you go to work, you have to go to a certain security officer who signs you in and issues you a clip-on tag that enables you to enter the building and go to your desk, but do nothing else? And that you had to check in with the officer every hour to renew your tag?

What if you then needed to go to this person for a new tag every time you needed to access a resource in the company, such as the file room or the copier? Suppose you had to present this tag to guards that protect each resource so that they can verify that you are legitimate?

You'd say, "Wow, this is overkill. Why is security so tight here?" It would probably be hard to work in such an environment. Imagine if several companies, or a whole city, adopted such stringent security practices. Life in such a city would be so secure that companies would be able to trust each other enough to share resources, but for all intents and purposes, it would still be hard to work in such an environment.

Yet, this is precisely how Kerberos works. The only difference is that the security check-ins and tag issues are handled transparently by the underlying protocols, and everything takes place in network transmissions. The user is oblivious to what is going on under the network hood.

Kerberos is based on a system of *tickets*, which are packets of encrypted data issued by a *Key Distribution Center* (KDC) — the security officer just mentioned. This ticket is your "passport," and carries with it a myriad of security information. Each KDC is responsible for a *realm*, and in Windows Server 2008 every domain is also a Kerberos realm. In addition, every Active Directory domain controller (DC) is a KDC.

When you log on to Windows, WinLogon and LSA kick in to first authenticate you to the KDC (see Chapter 17), which provides you with an initial ticket called the *Ticket Granting Ticket* (TGT), which is akin to a right-of-way coupon at the fairgrounds, or a passport. Then, when you need to access resources on the network, you present the TGT to the DC and request a ticket for a resource. This resource ticket is known as a *Service Ticket* (ST). When you need access to a resource, your processing environment presents the ST to the resource. You are then granted access in accordance with the ACL protecting the resource.

The implementation of Kerberos in Windows Server 2008 is fully compliant with the Internet Engineering Task Force's (IETF) Kerberos v5, which was originally developed by MIT. This specification is widely supported, which means that tickets issued in a Windows Server 2008 domain (now also known as a Kerberos realm) can be passed to other realms, such as networks running Mac OS, Novell NetWare, Unix, AIX, IRIX, and so forth.

Trusts can therefore be established between the Kerberos Domain Controllers (KDCs) in the respective realms. The KDC trusts, for all intents and purposes, work just like trusts for Windows NT systems, which are set up between the primary domain controller (PDC) in each domain. Moreover, because Windows Server 2008 still speaks NT LAN Manager (NTLM), trusts are maintained to legacy Windows domains.

Kerberos, however, does require more tweaking and administration than you may be used to on Windows NT domains using NTLM. That's because users have to check in with the KDC several times a day. For example, if you are logged on for 12 hours straight, you will probably have to check in with the KDC about 12 to 15 times in that period. If the domain supports 1,200 users, that will result in about 18,000 hits to the KDC.

In addition, trusts between heterogeneous networks are not as transparent as the trusts between Active Directory domains, in which the domain controllers can explicitly vouch for the users. Trusts between Windows Server 2008 forests, Windows Server 2008 and Windows NT, and Windows Server 2008 and other realms involve a manual setup between each domain's or realm's respective administrator. The process that takes place in the Unix or IRIX realm may be very different from the setup that takes place between Windows Server 2008 realms.

When planning the physical layout of the network, if you have multiple domains that communicate across a WAN, you will need to establish shortcuts or the best possible routes that ticket transmission can use to move from realm to realm. Shortcuts may be required so that authentication does not become bogged down in network traffic over a small pipe.

NOTE If authentication is slow due to slow links between networks, you may have a good reason to establish the site as a new domain. For more information on deciding when to create a new domain, check out Chapter 7.

Kerberos is a very fast protocol and an ideal environment for implementing the Single Sign-On paradigm in network authentication.

Kerberos and the Single Sign-On initiative

Single Sign-On is long overdue. From a security standpoint, it provides tremendous benefits. If a user has six or seven passwords, it means he or she has six or seven more opportunities to compromise security. Many people are so sick of the different passwords they have to deal with that they would rather not have a password. This is a problem in systems where password creation and application is in the hands of the user. A good example is a voice-mail system. Many systems ask the user not to enter 1234 or to leave the password blank, but a review of the password history on the system usually shows that many passwords are left blank or are simply 1234.

Other users go to the opposite extreme and type their passwords into a password database or a spreadsheet, or worse, a simple text file. An intruder will go to town on a document loaded with keys. Password databases are the mother lode; it takes a few seconds to crack the password that locks the file.

With Single Sign-On, the user authenticates once, and that authentication is respected by other network applications and services. Made possible by Kerberos and Active Directory, Single Sign-On is supported in SQL Server 2005 and Exchange 2007, and is supported by trusts set up between realms implemented by other operating systems and Windows Server 2008. It is the very reason why Windows Server 2008 trusts — between domains that share a common root or forest — are transitive.

Psst ... this is how Kerberos works

Kerberos is built around the idea of "shared secrets." In other words, if only two people know a secret, then either person can verify the identity of the other by confirming that the other person knows the secret. The shared secret in Kerberos is between Kerberos and the *security principal* (the human user or a device).

Here's an analogy: Two people send each other e-mail regularly and need to be sure that each e-mail cannot be repudiated by the other, or that someone else is not masquerading as the sender. To ensure that the sender or receiver is who they say they are, both agree offline that something in the messages between them will confirm that each one is "the one." However, if someone is analyzing e-mail and spotting word arrangements, it will not take them long to discover the hidden confirmation message. On a network authentication mechanism, this can be quite a problem because it would not take long to intercept a message and fool an authentication service into thinking the user is genuine.

Therefore, how do the two correspondents devise a plan to verify each other's identity? The answer is symmetric-key cryptography. The shared key must be kept secret, however, or anyone will be able to decode the message. As discussed earlier, a symmetric key is a single key that is capable of both encryption and decryption. In other words, as long as the two correspondents share the same key, they can encrypt their messages and be sure that the partner is able to decrypt it.

NOTE The terms *secret key* and *symmetric key* are often used interchangeably when discussing the use of a single key to encrypt and decrypt text. However, it is entirely possible for a secret key to fall into the wrong hands.

The practice of secret key cryptography is not new and goes back to before the Cold War days when insurgents perfected secret key techniques and cipher science. In the Kerberos implementation, however, authentication is a done deal as long as the information is decrypted, or as long as one party can prove they are the real thing by being in possession of the decrypting key in the first place. But what if someone on the network steals the key, or manages to copy previous authentication sessions? Kerberos then makes use of an unalterable factor that goes back to the Big Bang … time.

Time authentication

Kerberos authentication begins, literally, from the time a user tries to log on to the domain. When Kerberos receives an authentication request, it follows this series of steps:

1. Kerberos looks the user up and loads the key it shares with the user to decrypt the authentication message.

2. It then looks at the information in the message. The first item it checks is the time field, which is the time on the clock of the user's workstation or the machine from which the user requested logon authentication. If the time on the sender's clock is out of synch by five minutes, Kerberos will reject the message without further ado (Kerberos will compensate for the different time zones and daylight savings time). However, if the time is within the allowable offset of five minutes, Kerberos accepts the message pending one more item.

3. Kerberos determines whether the time is identical or older than previous authenticators received from the sender. If the timestamp is not later than and not the same as previous authenticators, Kerberos allows the user to authenticate to the domain.

However, it is also important to know that the authentication is *mutual*. Kerberos will send back a message demonstrating that it was able to decrypt the user's message. Kerberos returns only select information, the most important being the timestamp that it obtained from the original authentication from the client. If that timestamp matches the client's information, then the client is sure that Kerberos, and not an imposter, decrypted the message.

Key distribution

Authenticating to Kerberos works well for authentication to the domain, but what about accessing resources once the client has logged in? In that Kerberos is used for authenticating to domain resources, how does the client authenticate to other network resources?

Well, Kerberos is able to distribute keys. In other words, it acts as a broker. This, in fact, is where the name Kerberos comes from. In Greek mythology, you may recall that Kerberos was a three-headed dog that stood guard over the gates of Hades. Kerberos, the protocol, also has three heads: the client, the server, and a mediator, or proxy. The proxy is known as the Key Distribution Center ... it dishes out keys. In Windows Server 2008, the Key Distribution Center is installed on the Active Directory Domain Controller.

By now you are probably beginning to think one step ahead here, possibly muttering, "Cool, that whole rigmarole of decrypting the message and checking the timestamps just has to be repeated between clients and servers." You would be further correct if you assumed that the job of giving the network resources copies of every user's key would be that of the Key Distribution Center. However, you are correct in theory only, because so much key distribution would be a tremendous drain on resources. Every server would have to store keys from potentially thousands of users in memory. What is actually implemented is quite ingenious in its simplicity.

Session tickets

Instead of following the logical plan and sending the session key to the client and the server at the same time, the KDC in fact sends both copies of the key to the client and then gets out of the way. The client holds the server's copy of the key until it is ready to contact the server, usually within a few milliseconds. The illustration in Figure 16-1 may help you "decrypt" what is going on here.

FIGURE 16-1

Key distribution and mutual authentication.

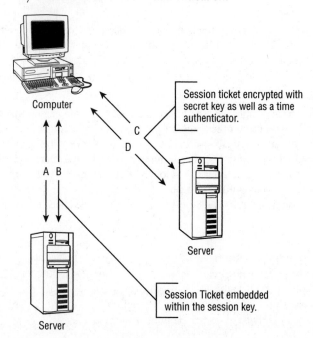

The KDC invents a session key whenever the client contacts it to access a resource (A). The server sends the session key to the client, and embedded in the session key is the session ticket (B). Embedded in the session ticket, which really belongs to the server, is the server's session key for the client. All that really happens here is that the KDC acts as a domain broker or proxy for secret key negotiations that take place between a client and the resource to which it requires access.

When the client receives the communication from the KDC, it extracts the ticket and its copy of the session key. It stores both items in secure volatile memory. Then, when the client contacts the server (C), it sends the server a message containing the ticket that is still encrypted with the server's secret key and a time authenticator that is encrypted with the session key. The ticket and the authenticator make up the client's credentials in the same fashion as the logon authentication process.

If everything checks out, the server grants access to the client (D) because the server knows that a trusted authority, the KDC, issued the credentials. As soon as the client is done using the server, the server can get rid of the session key that the client was using to communicate with the server. The client will instead hold the session key and re-present it to the server each time it needs to access it.

Session tickets can also be reused; and as a safeguard against ticket theft, the tickets come with expiration times. The time to live for a ticket is specified in the domain security policy. Typically, ticket life usually lasts about eight hours, the average logon time. When the user logs off, the ticket cache is flushed and all session tickets and keys are discarded.

Kerberos and trusts

Kerberos trusts are made possible by extending the concepts just discussed beyond domain boundaries. When a trust is established between two domains, which happens automatically between domains that are part of a contiguous namespace (an Active Directory tree), the two domains share an *inter-domain key*, and one KDC becomes the proxy for the other and vice versa.

After this inter-domain key has been established, the ticket granting service in each domain is registered as a security principal with the other domain's KDC, allowing it to issue ticket referrals. Clients in their home or native domains still contact their local KDCs for access to the foreign resource. The local KDC confirms that the resource needed by the client resides in another domain. It then sends the client a referral ticket for the resource in the other domain. The client then contacts the other domain's KDC and sends it the referral ticket. The remote KDC authenticates the user or begins a session ticket exchange to allow the client to connect to resources in the remote domain.

Locating KDCs

DNS is the locator service for Kerberos. The governing Request For Comment (RFC) 1510 specifies how DNS should resolve KDC hosts to IP addresses. Client computers need to send their messages to the IP address. If the IP address of the KDC cannot be resolved, it generates an error message to the client indicating that the domain cannot be located.

In a Windows Server 2008 domain, the KDC is usually installed on the Active Directory server. They are not connected in terms of application process space, and run as separate services. However, because the KDC is always installed on the DC, it is possible to resolve a KDC by looking up the host address of a domain controller.

It is also possible to install Windows Server 2008 servers in non-Windows Server 2008 domains, and they can still participate in Kerberos authentication. You will need to ensure that they resolve to the correct host addresses, which will not be to Active Directory domain controllers. The utility called ksetup.exe is used to configure clients and servers to participate in Kerberos realms that are not Windows Server 2008 domains.

Obviously, a lot more can be said about Kerberos than what is described here, but such a topic exceeds the scope of this book. You can find numerous books that deal exclusively with Kerberos. For now, understand that Kerberos security is the de facto pervasive security mechanism that protects Windows Server 200X domains. Kerberos is a good reason to move to native domains as soon as possible. As ugly as it may sound, the three-headed hound guarding your network is the de facto standard on Windows Server domains.

Getting to Know IPSec

IPSec, which is a contraction of IP and Security, is an Internet Protocol (IP) security mechanism employed in Windows Server 2008 for the maximum protection of network traffic. IPSec is mainly used for communication over an insecure IP network. One such network springs to mind — it's called the Internet.

The protection, encryption, is applied at the IP layer and takes place between two computers. The encrypted packets are not filtered in any way by firewalls or routers and simply pass through. Thus, it is also transparent to the users and applications deployed on either side of the correspondence.

IPSec operates on four levels: encryption and encapsulation, authentication and replay tolerance, key management, and digital signing and digital certificates.

The encryption is also known as *end-to-end*, which means that it remains encrypted en route to the other computer, and it can only be decrypted by the other computer. IPSec also uses public key encryption; however, the shared key is generated at both ends of the encryption, and it is not transmitted over the network.

The IP Encapsulated Security Protocol uses 40/56-bit DES or 112/168-bit DES to encrypt the IP address of the sender along with the datagram. This thwarts attempts to grab the packets in transit between hops and prevents attackers from learning the source or destination address, which would be required in order to mount an attack. The original packet is also encapsulated in a new packet, along with the contents of the packet and the header information. The packet is still transmitted to the destination IP address, but that is not apparent during transmission.

To guarantee data integrity, the secure data encryption algorithm (SHA-1 or MD-5 of RSA) ensures that the data cannot be tampered with en route. This is called IPSec anti-replay. Each datagram is tagged with a sequence number. When the datagram reaches its destination, its sequence number is checked to verify that it falls within the predetermined range. If it does not, the datagram is discarded.

The key management component is supported by the ISAKMP (Internet Security Association Key Management Protocol)/Oakley key management protocol v8 used to enable the use of a single architecture to secure transactions with different vendor products that are IPSec-compliant. The Digital Signature Standard (DSS) and RSA provide the proof of authorship for signatures on digital certificates.

IPSec also supports the capability to import your company's unique x.509 v.3 digital certificate into IPSec-compliant hardware and software. This means that you are essentially integrating IPSec into your Public Key Infrastructure (PKI), which is discussed later in this chapter. The integration between IPSec and PKI provides even stronger network security.

This is how IPSec works:

1. Computer A sends data to computer B across an insecure IP network. Before the transmission begins, an algorithm on computer A checks whether the data should be secured according to the security policy established on computer A. The security policy contains several rules that determine the sensitivity of the communication.

2. If the filter finds a match, computer A first begins a security-based negotiation with computer B via a protocol called *Internet Key Exchange* (IKE). The two computers then exchange credentials according to an authentication method specified in the security rule. The authentication methods can be Kerberos, public key certificates, or a predefined key value.

3. After the negotiations are underway, two types of negotiation agreements called *security associations* are set up between the two computers. The first type is called *Phase I IKE SA*, and it specifies how the two computers are going to trust each other. The second type is an agreement about how the two computers are going to protect an application communication. This is known as *Phase II IPSec Sec Sas*, and it specifies the security methods and keys for each direction of the communication. IKE automatically creates and refreshes a shared secret key for each SA. The secret key is created independently at both ends without being transmitted across the network.

4. Computer A signs the outbound packets for integrity and may or may not encrypt the packets according to the methods agreed upon in the earlier negotiation. The packets are then transmitted to computer B.

5. Computer B checks the packets for integrity and decrypts them if necessary. The data is then transferred up the IP stack to the application in the usual fashion.

Although IPSec was designed to protect data on insecure networks, it can also be deployed on an intranet, especially in light of the widespread implementation of TCP/IP in a Windows Server

2008 intranet. It has obvious application to protect against many of the threats discussed earlier in this chapter.

However, all encryption carries with it the burden of the actual encryption overhead on CPUs, so you need to test IPSec in various situations before you deploy it.

> **NOTE** Network Interface Card (NIC) vendors are supporting IPSec, and using a Windows Server 2008 IPSec driver may go a long way in reducing CPU usage. The idea is much like a hardware-based RAID controller that employs a CPU on the interface card to perform striping, as opposed to handing off that burden to the main system CPU.

Similar to Kerberos, IPSec is managed under Group Policy, which is discussed extensively in Chapter 24. You define it per site, per domain, or per organizational unit (OU). It can also be defined for computers that are not affected by domain or OU security policy. Specifically, IPSec can be configured to provide variations of the following services:

- You can specify the extent of authentication and confidentiality that will be negotiated between the communicating parties. For example, you can specify the minimum acceptable level of security allowed between clients, which is sending clear text over the network but hiding both sender and receiver information.

- You can set policy that communication over certain insecure networks takes place using IPSec, or not at all.

IPSec is discussed later in this chapter in "Security Planning," and in Chapter 24.

SSL/TLS

Secure Sockets Layer/Transport Layer Security (SSL/TLS) has been around in several Windows NT or BackOffice products for a while. It is a widely supported protocol both on corporate networks and on the Internet. SSL/TLS has been supported in IIS and Exchange.

Windows Server 2008 uses SSL/TLS and X.509 certificates (discussed next) to authenticate smart card users for network and data protection. SSL/TLS is used to secure a wide range of communications such as network traffic, IIS traffic (Web and FTP), e-mail, and client transactions created in browsers.

Understanding Active Directory Certificate Services

Two levels of public key cryptography are at work inside Windows Server 2008. One level is implicit and expressly built into the operating system. It is at work in Kerberos, IPSec, and the Encrypting File System (EFS), and does not require attention from you, other than some minor configuration management. The second level is explicit. It requires you to build a public key infrastructure to accommodate a pervasive use of public key cryptography throughout the enterprise.

CROSS-REF   See Chapter 15 for a detailed discussion of EFS.

Public Key Infrastructure

A *Public Key Infrastructure*, or PKI, is a collection of services and components that work together to a common end. It is used to build a protected environment that will enable you to secure e-mail communications both on the intranet and over the Internet, to secure your Web sites and your company's Web-based transactions, to enhance or further protect your Encrypting File System, to deploy smart cards, and more.

A PKI gives you the ability to support the following public key services:

- **Key management.** The PKI issues new keys, reviews or revokes existing keys, and manages the trust levels between other vendors' key issuers.

- **Key publishing.** The PKI provides a systematic means of publishing both valid and invalid keys. Keys can also be revoked if their security is compromised. PKI handles the revocation lists so that applications can determine whether a key can no longer be trusted (akin to the revoked and stolen credit card lists published by the banks for the benefit of merchants).

- **Key usage.** The PKI provides an easy mechanism for applications and users to use keys. Key usage is essential to providing the best possible security for the enterprise.

Digital certificates

As discussed earlier in this chapter, public keys are packaged in digital certificates. A good example of a digital certificate is the visa you are given by a foreign country permitting access. The visa number is the key; it is what enables you to get into a country and move around. The visa, issued by the country's consulate, and which is usually laminated or expertly printed so that it cannot be tampered with, is the digital certificate, an object of trust that proves that you received the visa or "key" from a trusted authority — in this case, the consular general — and that the number is authentic. Although visas can be forged and authorities are constantly working to come up with better certificates, passport control officers use verification equipment to check the authenticity of the visa. If a visa is forged, the immigration authority at the port of entry will be able to detect the forgery and deny access. Digital certificates, however, rely on certificate authorities for verification.

How do you verify a digital certificate? A certificate authority (CA), the issuer of your key, or the equivalent of the consular authority in the previous analogy, signs the certificate with its digital signature. You can verify the digital signature with the issuer's public key. Who vouches for the issuer? The answer lies in a *certificate hierarchy*, a system of vouchsafes that extends all the way up to a group of root certificate authorities that have formed an association of vouchsafes. You can obtain the public keys for the CA from Microsoft, but it is all transparently taken care of in Microsoft Certificate Services.

Creating the PKI with active directory certificate services

A PKI is based on many different services and components, all deployed in concert. For example, a Microsoft PKI depends on Active Directory for the publishing of information about issued keys. In addition, certificates, revocation lists, and policy information are all stored in the directory. Knowing your directory service thus brings you closer to realizing the reality of the ultimate secured enterprise.

Managing a Microsoft PKI is not difficult and is even less time-consuming than managing users, printers, or the network. Actually, many tasks you perform in your day-to-day activities already encompass management of the PKI. Chapters 21 and 24 will thus offer pointers and guidelines specific to the management of your PKI or Active Directory Certificate Services (ADCS) on Windows Server 2008.

Support for Legacy NTLM

The NT LAN Manager (NTLM) is a legacy protocol that Microsoft has included in Windows Server 2008 to support legacy Windows clients and servers. We will not be covering NTLM in detail here because our predecessors have published much information on it over the years. In addition, NTLM support is not configurable to the degree that Kerberos is, and it does not support transitive trusts and the Single Sign-On initiative.

In Windows Server 2008, the default authentication and security protocol between Windows Server 2008 machines is Kerberos. By continuing to support down-level or legacy Windows technology, you obviously leave room for infiltrators to maneuver; however, that does not mean NTLM is a weak protocol. After all, it has kept Windows NT networks together for many years and was key to the C2 award earned by the operating system at version 3.51.

NTLM is omnipresent; it only stops working when the last process that needs it signs off. NTLM will be invoked under the following circumstances:

- You have legacy clients and servers that need to log on to the network or locally.
- You have Unix clients that need to continue talking to NT servers.
- You have Unix clients that are using the server message block (SMB) daemon that authenticates to NTLM.

Consider the following strategy for phasing out NTLM:

1. Move your legacy Windows NT and 9x clients to Windows Server 2008. Servers can be upgraded or replaced; clients can also be upgraded to support Kerberos or moved to terminal services (so the clients do not actually log on to the domain from a remote operating system).

2. Configure your Unix services to authenticate to Windows Server 2008 domains using Kerberos. Phase out SMB usage.

3. Deploy Microsoft's services for Unix packages.

Smart Cards

A smart card is really dumb looking. It is no bigger than a credit card and is carried around like one. Smart cards work just like ATM cards; you slide the card into a slot, and then you are prompted for a personal identification number (PIN).

The smart card contains a smart chip that is wafer-thin and embedded in the card. The chip holds a digital certificate, the user's private key, and a load of other information that can be used for Single Sign-On, e-commerce, access control, and data protection and privacy, such as securing e-mail and Web access.

The more modern form of a smart card is not really a card at all; it's more like a plug or a dongle. Thanks to USB technology, the dongle plugs into the USB port of your workstation or server. The chip is installed inside the casing of the plug. These USB devices are easier to carry around, and typically allow for more data storage than the older credit-card-type smart cards.

To install smart card technology, you must have a public key infrastructure established. You must also install smart card readers, which can be a little expensive, but capitalized over many users, it will pay for itself in TCO and security.

NOTE   For further information on smart cards and Windows Server 2008, see "The Smart Card Deployment Cookbook" at www.microsoft.com. RSA Laboratories at www.rsasecurity.com is also a good starting point for smart card research. The "cookbook" is a little outdated. If you can't find the link, visit www.misiq.com — a link to a number of smart card white papers is maintained there.

Domains

Let's look at the basics. *Domains*, or network domains, are the logical containers of a network, which control access to all the resources placed in the custody of the domain. The domain does not exist in the physical sense, yet it is accessible from anywhere in the world if it maintains a portal to the Internet or a remote access service; all you need is a computer and a connection to a network or a modem.

A domain means different things to different technology vendors. The term *domain* is not exclusively used by Microsoft. It is used on the Internet and by technologies such as SNA (mainframe protocols and services still believed by many to be superior to the TCP/IP domain).

A domain is a loosely defined term, and it represents a collection of computer and data processing devices and resources collected together under one "roof" or security boundary. For the benefit of new administrators to both legacy Windows 200X and Windows Server 2008, let's look at some basic facts about domains. Undoubtedly, what makes a domain a domain is that it is held together by a security policy that dictates the protection of the resources within it.

You gain access to a domain at the application level of the OSI stack. Interactive software to let you manually present credentials to the domain is available on the computer or via a device into which you insert a token for your credentials, such as a smart card or magnetic card.

Domains are held together by *domain controllers*. These controllers are keepers of databases that can authenticate users by asking them to verify identity by confirming a password. This is known as *authentication*. The databases in question are the SAM in Windows NT and the Active Directory in Windows Server 2008.

Logon and Authentication

When you log on to a network, you do not have access to network resources. You simply land in a holding area (for a few milliseconds) before being further authenticated to the network's resources. Logon is much like using the international airport in a country after you've landed from abroad. You get rights of passage around the airport. Heck, you can even spend money on duty-free items, set up a home, get married, and pass out; but that's about all. If you want access to the city, you have to go through passport control and customs.

Windows Server 2008 logon

When a user or machine logs on to a domain, he, she, or it interacts with a collection of functions that make up the Windows Logon service, better known in development circles as Win-Logon. WinLogon is now fully integrated with Kerberos, which provides the initial Single Sign-On architecture now part of life on a Windows network. After the logon, the user continues to be attached to the security protocol its client software best understands, which could be Kerberos, NTLM, or Secure Sockets Layer/Transport Layer Security. These protocols transparently move the user's identity around the network.

The authentication model of Windows Server 2008 is the same as Windows NT and almost every computer system in the world. (Refer to Chapter 23 for a discussion on the Local Security Authority.) However, it is not so much the model that causes problems in network security, but rather the other missing or weak links in the chain.

Bi-factorial and mono-factorial authentication

Network login is a *bi-factorial* exercise, meaning that it requires the user or device to present two factors to the authentication mechanisms of the network: a user ID (also known as an account name or ID), and a password (or what is also known in the secret service as the cipher).

Every user ID must have a password. In order for the authentication system to validate the user, it asks for a password, and that is the only way it authenticates. However, the authentication is very weak. The authenticator cannot guarantee that the user is in fact the correct user; it could easily be an imposter pretending to be the user.

Besides the network login (user ID and password), other examples of bi-factorial authentication are ATM cards, smart cards, and the like. The user presents the card and either types in a user ID or a password. Two components have to match to unlock the door. However, it is still not 100 percent secure. ATM cards are stolen, passwords can be discovered, and so forth.

Mono-factorial identification is a far more secure and convenient form of authentication. There can be only one form, and it is more convenient for both the user and the authenticator.

The bottom line is that the user has to do less work to authenticate; he or she need not remember a password and does not have to type in a user ID. Examples of mono-factorial authentication include fingerprints, retinal scans, and voiceprints. These factors seldom require another factor of identification. A user has only one retinal pattern, voiceprint, and fingerprint in existence. In many cases, the password is not needed because the pattern itself is the cipher; and because it is attached to the user, there is no need to verify the user.

Trusts

For many reasons, it becomes necessary to create new domains. With Windows NT, big companies spawn domains like frogs' eggs because they are physically restricted by the technology (the SAM becomes unstable at more than 40MB). In Windows Server 2008, we create domains to compartmentalize or partition the directory, to represent distributed resources or corporate structure, for ease of management (delegation), security, and much more.

It often becomes necessary for resources in one domain, such as users, to access resources in another domain. In order for this to happen, the domains, if "genetically" different, have to set up trust relationships. Whereas domains that share a domain tree trust each other by default, domains on other trees in other forests, non-Windows Server 2008 domains, and realms from other environments do not, and you have to explicitly set up the trust. A domain that is trusted by another domain is known as a *trusted domain*. The domain that trusts the other domain is known as the *trusting domain*. This policy is the same in Windows NT as it is for Windows Server 2008.

If the trust is only one way, we call it a uni-directional, or one-way, trust. In other words, Domain A trusts Domain B, but Domain B does not trust Domain A. This is illustrated in Figure 16-2.

When the trust is mutual, the trust relationship becomes bi-directional, or two-way. Bi-directional trust enables the users or devices in each domain to access resources in the other's domains (see Figure 16-3).

Windows NT trusts are limited by the underlying database and security technology, which endows the operating system with a less than suitable "cognitive" ability. In other words, Windows NT domains are always mistrusting; and as such, whenever two domains need to interoperate, explicit trusts must first be set up between them.

FIGURE 16-2

Uni-directional trust relationship between two domains.

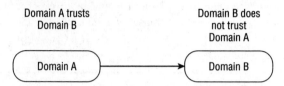

FIGURE 16-3

Bi-directional trust relationship between two domains.

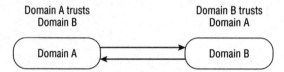

What's more, Windows NT trusts are not transitive, which means that just because Domain A trusts Domain B, and Domain B trusts Domain C, Domain C does not necessarily trust Domain A, or the other way around. This is illustrated in Figure 16-4.

FIGURE 16-4

Nontransitive trust relationships between three domains.

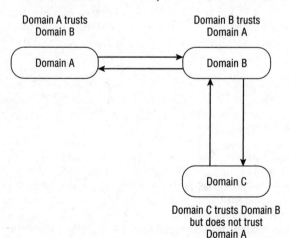

The domain container and security technology of Windows Server 2008 is very different. Enabled by a robust directory service, a hot security technology, such as the Kerberos v5 protocol, and a powerful policing capability, Windows Server 2008 domains that are part of the same namespace, or family, and even of the same tree in a forest, implicitly trust one another. Not only are the trusts already implied, but they are also transitive, as illustrated in Figure 16-5.

FIGURE 16-5

Transitive trust relationships between three domains in the same forest.

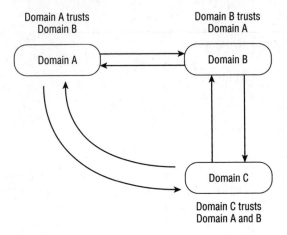

However, domains from one forest do not automatically trust domains from another forest. Let's take this a bit further. There are several domains in Sherwood Forest. All these domains fall under the auspices of Robin Hood (the root domain in Active Directory). This means that as long as you live in Sherwood Forest, you pledge allegiance to Robin Hood and can visit any domain (access control, however, still applies).

A domain that is part of another forest in the British countryside, however, is not automatically trusted by Robin Hood's realm, Sherwood Forest. The administrators of both root domains need to get together and formalize a treaty before the two forests and domains will be able to trust each other.

Windows NT does not have a treaty with Windows Server 2008, partly because it speaks the wrong security language — that is, NTLM. In order for Windows Server 2008 and Windows NT users to exchange vows, you have to set up a bilateral trust. Windows Server 2008 will talk to NT using NTLM.

Setting up trusts is awkward, and whenever mistrusting administrators from two domains try to set up trusts, it usually takes an assertive individual to lead the way. However, you have to know how to set up trusts between NT and Windows Server 2008; it is the only way for the two operating systems to coexist, and it is key to any conversion effort. The steps to creating trusts are explained in Chapter 17.

After authentication is successful, the user or application gains certain default rights to the network and its resources. The next level of protection steps in. It is called access control.

Access Control

After a user or device account is authenticated to the domain, it is given permission, through certain default privileges, to network objects. The objects represent files, devices (such as printers and computers), and the file system's structure. In Windows Server 2008, these objects are stored in the Active Directory and "point" to the actual network location (in Windows NT, they are stored in the SAM portion of the registry).

To gain access to an object, the object has an Access Control List (ACL) associated with it. This access control list is also stored in the directory. An analogy might be to think of your ACL as a bouncer standing at the door to a club. When someone tries to gain entry to the club, the bouncer checks his or her ACL. If the entry seeker is not on the list, then entry is denied. The items on the ACL are known as access control entries. You can view the ACL by opening the Security tab on an object's property sheet.

The property sheet lists the users and groups that have access to the object, and the level of access they have, such as Read, Write, or Execute. ACLs apply only to security principals — that is, user accounts, computer accounts, and security groups (as opposed to distribution groups). Security principals and ACLs are further discussed in Chapter 19.

Auditing

The word *auditing* strikes fear into the hearts of everyone. Even if you have nothing to fear, auditing is an ominous idea, a prying into your every move. But auditing is not only a practice defined within a security context; it is also an essential practice in troubleshooting and problem-solving. An audit trail, a requirement for C2 security compliance, can lead you not only to the wolf's den, but also to a solution to a problem that was affecting network resources or causing users grief.

Auditing leaves a trail that you can follow to see what was done or attempted by network objects. If the network object has a username attached to it, your audit trail will then be a history of what was attempted by whom.

A good example of an audit trail can be found on the RAS. When a user calls to say he or she cannot log on to the network remotely, you can check the audit logs and trace his or her attempts by searching for information related to his or her user ID. The audit trail will then tell you why the person was rejected and give you a possible remedy.

Auditing of objects is not enabled by default. It has to be enabled and applied to the object. Auditing is discussed in depth in Chapter 10.

Security Planning

Before you begin jumping up and down shouting, "Whoo, hoo, IPSec, PKI, SSL, way to go!", you should know that unless you are running a native Windows Server 2008 network, you will not realize the full potential many of these protocols have to offer.

Windows Server 2008 security is also so extensive that it is possible to get bamboozled in your efforts to provide the ultimate security. As you learn more about the capabilities of Windows Server 2008, you'll discover that the adage "less is more" applies to many Windows Server 2008 components in general and to Windows Server 2008 security in particular. The subject of security planning is therefore coupled to the subject of planning for Windows Server 2008 in general.

Firewalls

Firewalls are devices that protect your network and computers from malicious computer hackers. The Windows Server 2008 comes with what is known as the Windows Firewall. This firewall is fairly simplistic but provides some very necessary firewall services to the machine on which it resides, as well as any machine that may share its Internet connection.

Firewalls come in all shapes and sizes, and can be a PC running Windows or, perhaps, an embedded device. Embedded devices have a definite advantage over computers running firewall software in that they typically can be used a lot faster and can inspect packets at a very high rate. Computers, conversely, have many other tasks to perform as well as packet inspection, and therefore can lose performance. In any event, a well-equipped machine running Windows Server 2008 and routing services can be a very efficient firewall for your corporate network.

Active Directory Security Policy

Windows Server 2008 continues to implement the Key Distribution Center (KDC) as a domain service. It uses the Active Directory as its account database and the Global Catalog for directing referrals to KDCs in other domains.

As in other implementations of the Kerberos protocol, the KDC is a single process that provides two services:

- **Authentication Service (AS).** This service issues ticket-granting tickets (TGTs) for connection to the ticket-granting service in its own domain or in any trusted domain. Before a client can ask for a ticket to another computer, it must request a TGT from the authentication service in the client's account domain. The authentication service returns a TGT for the ticket-granting service in the target computer's domain. The TGT can be reused until it expires, but the first access to any domain's ticket-granting service always requires a trip to the authentication service in the client's account domain.

■ **Ticket-Granting Service (TGS).** This service issues tickets for connection to computers in its own domain. When clients want access to a computer, they contact the ticket-granting service in the target computer's domain, present a TGT, and ask for a ticket to the computer. The ticket can be reused until it expires, but the first access to any computer always requires a trip to the ticket-granting service in the target computer's account domain.

The KDC for a domain is located on a domain controller, as is the Active Directory for the domain. Both services are started automatically by the domain controller's Local Security Authority (LSA) and run as part of the LSA's process. Neither service can be stopped. If the KDC is unavailable to network clients, then the Active Directory is also unavailable — and the domain controller is no longer controlling the domain. Windows 2000/Windows XP ensures availability of these and other domain services by allowing each domain to have several domain controllers, all peers. Any domain controller can accept authentication requests and ticket-granting requests addressed to the domain's KDC.

The security principal name used by the KDC in any Windows Server 2008 domain is `krbtgt`, as specified by RFC 1510. An account for this security principal is created automatically when a new Windows Server 2008 domain is created. This account cannot be deleted, nor can its name be changed. A password is assigned to the account automatically and is changed on a regular schedule, as are the passwords assigned to the domain trust accounts. The password for the KDC's account is used to derive a cryptographic key for encrypting and decrypting the TGTs that it issues. The password for a domain trust account is used to derive an inter-realm key for encrypting referral tickets.

All instances of the KDC within a domain use the domain account for the security principal `krbtgt`. Clients can address messages to a domain's KDC by including both the service's principal name, `krbtgt`, and the name of the domain. Both items of information are also used in tickets to identify the issuing authority. For information on name forms and addressing conventions, see RFC 1510.

Secure Sockets

Secure Sockets is often referred to as the Secure Sockets Layer (SSL). SSL allows for a secure encrypted connection to a Web server. You will typically find SSL-enabled Web sites when you purchase goods online or perform other transactions that need to have a high degree of security so outside forces cannot intercept information.

SSL has changed a bit with Windows Server 2008, which incorporates a new Windows Service application, W3SSL, to handle secure communications to and from the Web server. SSL uses encryption on all data sent and received to prevent people from intercepting information, such as credit card numbers.

Dealing with W3SSL directly is almost impossible with the documentation provided, but if you wish to use it with an IIS application/Web site, this can be accomplished very easily by simply pointing and clicking.

Firewalls, Proxies, and Bastions

As we have discussed, firewalls keep people out of your network and away from all sensitive data that it may contain. Proxies are another way of maintaining security on a network. Proxies enable computers on a network to maintain a degree of anonymity while users surf the Web. All requests from client computers to the Internet are sent to a proxy server. The proxy server requests information from the Internet, and then transmits this information back to the client PC that wanted the information in the first place.

Typically, proxy servers also cache information, so if people on your network, for example, typically go to the same Web sites, the proxy server can retrieve the Web pages much faster from its cache than it could from the Internet connection. Policies can be set regarding how long to cache Web pages and the maximum amount of space to use when it does so.

Because proxy servers are capable of caching data from the Internet and returning that data to a client request, it can greatly reduce the amount of traffic over your Internet connection. If you have a large number of people that need to be on the Internet and you would like to conserve bandwidth, a proxy server may be the way to go. Aside from helping with the speed of the connection, a proxy server can almost always be set up to filter data as well. Setting up a proxy in a corporate environment would enable management to block Web sites that enable employees to search for jobs. Setting one up at your home on a broadband connection would enable you to ensure that your children aren't looking at Web sites you don't want them to visit. Even if you trust your Internet users to stick to sites where they belong, with the extreme amount of pop-up ads today, your users may be viewing other Web information whether they like it or not.

In today's risky world of open systems and widely distributed networks, protecting corporate data and information from compromise is a daily effort. One of the mandates of a Windows Server 2008 administrator is to deploy a solution that is simple and, by extension, not overly complex to administer. However, keeping deployment and administration simple often results in the compromise of security, even if unwittingly.

A good example is how the architectural elegance and sophistication of Active Directory makes it susceptible to compromise if its data streams are not secured. Though AD lowers the cost of administering complex networks dramatically through the use of easy-to-understand metaphors, easy-to-use interfaces, and a powerful delegation of the administration model, efforts to attack and compromise the network has risen by an order of magnitude recently. In addition, because AD is so widely used, it is thus the largest target in the crosshairs of most network attackers.

Introduction to the Public Key Infrastructure

Windows Server 2008 contains a very robust Public Key Infrastructure (PKI) that provides an integrated set of services and tools for deploying and managing Public Key applications. This enables application developers to take advantage of the shared-secret key mechanism and to provide the best security possible. The tools provided with Windows Server 2008 enable administrators to manage these keys from a central location for an entire enterprise.

Setting up and Configuring Active Directory Certificate Services

A key element in the PKI is Active Directory Certificate Services (ADCS), which enables you to deploy one or more enterprise CAs. These CAs support certificate issuance and revocation. They are integrated with Active Directory, which provides CA location information and CA policy, and allows certificates and revocation information to be published.

The PKI does not replace the existing Windows domain trust-and-authorization mechanisms based on the domain controller (DC) and Kerberos Key Distribution Center (KDC). Rather, the PKI works with these services and provides enhancements that enable applications to readily scale to address extranet and Internet requirements. In particular, PKI addresses the need for scalable and distributed identification and authentication, integrity, and confidentiality.

Support for creating, deploying, and managing PK-based applications is provided uniformly on workstations and servers running Windows Server 200X, Windows XP, Vista, Windows 2000 or Windows NT, as well as workstations running Windows 95 and Windows 98 operating systems. Microsoft CryptoAPI is the cornerstone for these services. It provides a standard interface to cryptographic functionality supplied by installable cryptographic service providers (CSPs). These CSPs may be software-based or take advantage of cryptographic hardware devices and can support a variety of algorithms and key strengths. Some CSPs that ship with Windows Server 2008 take advantage of the Microsoft PC/SC–compliant smart card infrastructure.

Layered on the cryptographic services is a set of certificate management services. These support X.509 version 3 standard certificates, providing persistent storage, enumeration services, and decoding support. Finally, there are services for dealing with industry-standard message formats. Primarily, these support the PKCS standards and evolving Internet Engineering Task Force (IETF) Public Key Infrastructure X.509 (PKIX) draft standards.

 **For more information on the Internet Engineering Task Force (IETF) or X.509, please visit their Web site at www.ietf.org.**

Other services take advantage of CryptoAPI to provide additional functionality for application developers. Secure Channel (schannel) supports network authentication and encryption using the industry standard TLS and SSL protocols. These may be accessed using the Microsoft WinInet interface for use with the HTTP protocol (HTTPS) and with other protocols through the SSPI interface. Authenticode supports object signing and verification. This is used principally for determining the origin and integrity of components downloaded over the Internet, though it may be used in other environments. Finally, general-purpose smart-card interfaces also are supported. These are used to integrate cryptographic smart cards in an application-independent manner and are the basis for the smart-card logon support that is integrated with Windows Server 2008.

Understanding Active Directory Certificate Services

Microsoft Certificate Services, included with Windows Server 2008, provides a means for an enterprise to easily establish CAs to support its business requirements. Certificate Services includes a default policy module that is suitable for issuing certificates to enterprise entities (users, computers, or services). This also includes the identification of the requesting entity and validation that the certificate requested is allowed under the domain PK security policy. This may be easily modified or enhanced to address other policy considerations or to extend CA support for various extranet or Internet scenarios. Because Certificate Services is standards-based, it provides broad support for PK-enabled applications in heterogeneous environments.

Within the PKI, you can easily support both enterprise CAs and external CAs, such as those associated with other organizations or commercial service providers. This enables an enterprise to tailor its environment in response to business requirements.

Setting Up and Configuring a Certificate Authority

Deploying Microsoft Certificate Services is a fairly straightforward operation. It is recommended that you establish the domain prior to creating a CA. You can then establish an enterprise root CA, or CAs. The Certificate Services installation process walks the administrator through this process. Key elements in this process include the following:

- **Selecting the host server.** The root CA can run on any Windows Server 200X/2008 Server platform, including a domain controller. Factors such as physical security requirements, expected loading, connectivity requirements, and so on, should be considered in making this decision.

- **Naming.** CA names are bound into their certificates and hence cannot change. You should consider factors such as organizational naming conventions and future requirements to distinguish among issuing CAs.

- **Key generation.** The CA's public-key pair is generated during the installation process and is unique to this CA.

- **CA certificate.** For a root CA, the installation process automatically generates a self-signed CA certificate, using the CA's public/private-key pair. For a child CA, a certificate request can be generated that may be submitted to an intermediate or root CA.

- **Active Directory integration.** Information concerning the CA is written into a CA object in the Active Directory during installation. This provides information to domain clients about available CAs and the types of certificates that they issue.

- **Issuing policy.** The enterprise CA setup automatically installs and configures the Microsoft-supplied Enterprise Policy Module for the CA. An authorized administrator can modify the policy, although in most cases this is not necessary.

After a root CA has been established, it is possible to install intermediate or issuing CAs subordinate to this root CA. The only significant difference in the installation policy is that the certificate request is generated for submission to a root or intermediate CA. This request may be routed automatically to online CAs located through the Active Directory, or routed manually in an offline scenario. In either case, the resultant certificate must be installed at the CA before it can begin operation.

There is an obvious relationship between the enterprise CAs and the Windows Server 2008 domain trust model, but this does not imply a direct mapping between CA trust relationships and domain trust relationships. Nothing prevents a single CA from servicing entities in multiple domains, or even entities outside the domain boundary. Similarly, a domain may have multiple enterprise CAs.

CAs are high-value resources, and it is often desirable to provide them with a high degree of protection, as previously discussed. Specific actions that should be considered include the following:

- **Physical protection.** Because CAs represent highly trusted entities within an enterprise, they must be protected from tampering. This requirement is dependent upon the inherent value of the certification made by the CA. Physical isolation of the CA server, in a facility accessible only to security administrators, can dramatically reduce the possibility of such attacks.

- **Key management.** The CA keys are its most valuable asset because the private key provides the basis for trust in the certification process. Cryptographic hardware modules (accessible to Certificate Services through a CryptoAPI CSP) can provide tamper-resistant key storage and isolate the cryptographic operations from other software that is running on the server. This significantly reduces the likelihood that a CA key will be compromised.

- **Restoration.** Loss of a CA, due to hardware failure, for example, can create a number of administrative and operational problems, as well as prevent the revocation of existing certificates. Certificate Services supports backup of a CA instance so that it can be restored at a later time. This is an important part of the overall CA management process.

Deploying a PKI

The architecture discussed here proposes a fully AD-integrated PKI to protect administrative data streams (as well as organization data and information) from compromise using asymmetrical (public key-private key) technology, backed by an industry-standard certification authority. The technology of choice (because of its ability to tightly integrate with AD and for purposes of support) is Microsoft's Certification Services (in particular, the services that ship with Windows Server 2008).

The following services are candidates for the PKI implemented herein:

- IP Security (IPSec)
- Smart card logon
- Web-based administration and secure Web communications (this is likely to become a critical need at MCITY)
- Secure e-mail (see also Microsoft Exchange 2007 architecture)
- Digital signatures
- File encryption
- Custom PKI-enabled applications
- IEEE 802.1x authentication

Note that by establishing a self-administered PKI, MCITY will be able to maintain complete control over the issuance of certificates used in the private environment, at the OS level. The additional benefit of the AD-integrated PKI is that the standard X.509v3 certificate is supported in all available Single Sign-On initiatives. It is also the technology of choice for eliminating password theft in the most sensitive departments of the organization.

A PKI is not only a workstation or server centric service. In fact all network devices can participate in the PKI for greater security. Network devices are able to use Active Directory Certificates Services on the Windows Server 2008 platform because Microsoft PKI now supports the Network Device Enrollment Service (NDES) directly.

NDES is the essentially the Microsoft implementation of the Simple Certificate Enrollment Protocol (SCEP), developed by Cisco Systems, Inc. It was implemented in Windows Server 2003 as an add-on. This communication protocol allows network devices such as appliances, switchers, routers, hubs, and ports to enroll and participate in X.509 services provided by the CA.

NDES uses the Internet Server Application Programming Interface (ISAPI) filter on IIS to generate and provide one-time enrollment passwords to administrators, receive and process SCEP enrollment requests on behalf of software running on network devices, and retrieve pending requests from the CA.

With NDES you can provide a much more flexible and scalable PKI

Trust model

Various trust models can be architected for a PKI. These models include the *hierarchical* (or deep) *model* comprising root certification authorities (RCA), intermediate certification authorities (ICA), and the subordinate (issuing) certification authorities (SDA, or just CA); the *flatter networked model*; the *hybrid model*; and the *cross-trust models*. The latter two enable you to include more than one root CA in the implementation.

The model that works best for a solution required typically for a network operating system is the hierarchical model. It is also known as the *rooted trust model*. This model is illustrated in Figure 16-6.

The hierarchical model.

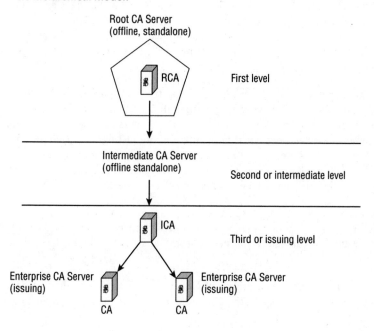

The hierarchical model to be implemented for this architecture consists of a tree of CAs (not unlike a tree in DNS, except that it does not represent a namespace). The root CA sits at the top of the hierarchy. It is the authorizing principal CA and the only component of the PKI authorized to sign its own certificate. The self-signed root certificate means that it is impossible for anyone to pretend to be the root CA unless he or she gains access to the root CA private key. In other words, only the root CA knows and possesses its key, and only the most trusted people in the organization should know where this key is kept and control access to it. Losing the key to the CA is like losing a key that opens every safety deposit box in a bank.

Root CAs certify their subordinate CAs to operate in the subordinate tier (which, as mentioned, are usually called intermediate CAs, or ICAs). These are also kept offline. The main difference between the ICA and the root CA is that the ICA's certificate is signed by the root. The ICAs can either issue certificates or authorize the next level of CAs, the issuing servers.

The root is taken offline after it is commissioned and issues the subordinate CA certificates. After its initial work, the CA's keys and credentials are stored on a smart card (or a token device) and placed in a vault with the hard disks that belong to the server.

The hierarchical model essentially provides delegation, which means that the CA can delegate all or part of its certificate-issuing responsibilities to a subordinated CA. The idea behind the hierarchy is to allow the intermediate CAs to be also taken offline and, thus, allow only issuing servers to remain contactable from the network. This installs a second layer of security.

To take the CA offline, you can simply turn it off or stop the CA service on the machine. As long as the computer is locked down and secured with a smart card for logon, its hard disks do not need to be locked in a vault like the root CA. If an issuing server or even an intermediary is compromised, it does not mean that the entire PKI has to be rebuilt. In the event of compromise, certificates will need to be revoked, the ICA or certificate issuer's keys will need to be regenerated (which implies a new certificate), and the root will need to be brought online (but not onto the network) to issue the new subordinate certificate.

Scalability is one of the most important aspects of the hierarchical model, enabling both growth and creative delegation. Certification issuance is a resource-intensive process, and even though a single CA can handle thousands of certificates, you may still need to load-balance the servers and scale them across sites.

You can also define different policies for different CAs in the hierarchy. In other words, a CA in the trust chain may issue certificates according to a different set of rules designated to another CA responsible for machine certificates.

The hierarchy can also provide an efficient certificate-validation scenario. In a large or widely distributed organization, every certificate issued by any CA in the hierarchy contains its certificate trust chain leading all the way to the secured root CA. To validate a certificate, it is thus sufficient to trust the root CA in the hierarchy. As long as the root CA is 100 percent secured and behind vault doors, a trust chain and its rock-solid trust anchor can be maintained.

The hierarchical model also obviates the need to maintain Certificate Trust Lists (CTLs), which represent an administrative burden. Figure 16-7 illustrates the architecture for the MCITY Active Directory implementation.

FIGURE 16-7

AD-PKI architecture.

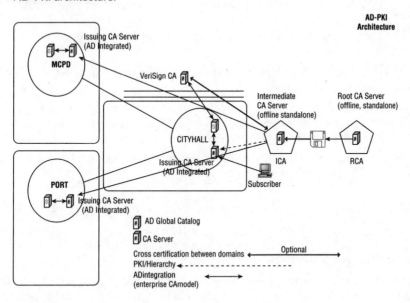

Certificate Policy

This book is not the ideal forum for a bit-by-bit discussion of the Certificate Policy (CP). However, for the purposes of this discussion, the following list serves as guidance:

- The provided policy module in Windows Server 2008 will not be changed.

- The exit model will allow for certificates to be issued to FTP, Web, File, and Active Directory locations on the BC network only.

- Any user — computer, application, or human — requesting a certificate shall state the purpose of the certificate. Valid uses of certificates provided by the PKI proposed in this architecture include the following: user and computer authentication, digital signing of software, encrypted e-mail, nonrepudiation, key encipherment, Encrypting File System, IPSec, SSL, secure e-mail, and data encryption.

- A user shall be entrusted with his or her private key. Should the private key become lost or compromised, the user must promptly notify the CA administrator so that the key can be replaced.

- All users (including end-users and operators of CAs) will be informed of the requirement to report unauthorized disclosure of their private key in an agreement, which they will sign prior to their being issued a certificate. Upon discovery of the unauthorized disclosure of the private key, users will be required to contact their CA, within one working day. The method of contacting the CA will be one of those listed in the CPS, to be defined in this CP.

- When not in use, users will be required to keep all copies of their private key either on their person or in a secure place.

- The CA and its administrators cannot be held liable for the compromise of private keys their CA servers have issued.

- Private keys shall be exportable from certificates only if a specific request is approved; otherwise, they will be issued as non-exportable. A complex alphanumeric password is required to allow the key to be exported from the certificate.

- The CP will cater to certificate enrollment and renewal, manual and automated.

- Issued certificate lifetime shall be one year, unless otherwise requested.

In line with these policy requirements, the policy module may need to be edited to reflect the policies required by the city.

Certificate Practice Statement

The Certificate Practice Statement (CPS) translates the CP into operational procedures at the CA level. This should be fully documented in your Active Directory Operations and Maintenance manuals. The embedded CPS provides for the following:

- Identification of CA
- Policies implemented
- Algorithms supported and key lengths available
- Lifetime of the CA
- Security of the CA (physical, network, and procedural)
- Certificate lifetime
- Certificate revocation practice (policies and practice)
- Certificate Revocation Lists (CRLs), CRL distribution, publishing intervals
- CA certificate renewal
- CA backup/restore
- CA administrators and delegated rights
- How certificates are issued at the OS level and to users

CA keys and certificate safety

By far, the safest way to store a CA's private key is to store it on a smart card or a token (usually on a USB-connected device, as mentioned earlier in the section "Smart Cards"), which gets locked away with the server's hard disks. By securing both server disks and cards belonging to the root CA, you achieve the ultimate security for the CA.

The smart card can also be used to log on to the server and authenticate without having to know the password and user identification to boot up and operate the server. The smart card and PIN number is all that is required. As mentioned earlier, it is much harder to steal a smart card and PIN than a user ID and password. (Once the CA's certificate is stored on the smart card, as opposed to the hard disk, the CA service cannot be started without the existence of the smart card.)

The ICA should also be set up with smart cards, and if the private key is installed on the card, it is not absolutely necessary to take the ICA offline. The ICA cannot be compromised if the private key is not stored on the server. The smart card for the ICAs can then be locked away in a vault until needed.

Certificate validation

The process of validating certificates entails having all users of certificates obtain access to the issuing server's certificate (which is essentially access to its public key). This is also true for intermediate and issuing CAs. This is done by issuing the certificate of the CA and publishing it to a contactable URL on the network. You can publish the certificate to a Web site, to a file share, and to Active Directory.

If the certificate of an issuing CA cannot be reached, then an application that relies on the certificate should follow protocol and reject further processing. However, some applications leave the onus to continue with the use of the certificate to the user. Under medium to high security conditions, the application will fail. Thus, it is critical that Windows can verify the issuance of the certificate by being able to "walk" the certificate chain from the issued certificate to the issuer's certificate.

Active Directory integration

To integrate a CA with AD, you specify at installation of the server that it should be an "enterprise" CA server (mode), rather than a standalone CA server. AD-integrated servers essentially install different CA policy modules. The standalone mode defaults to the issuance of only SSL and S/MIME certificates, but you can manually request certificates for any PKI-enabled application. The certificates on a root CA and on standalone CAs also require that the administrator manually approve the issuance of the certificate.

Installing the CA in enterprise mode provides the following benefits:

■ The CA uses Active Directory to store and publish certificates and certificate revocation lists (CRLs). In addition, the certificates are automatically mapped to the accounts of the requestors. Certificate requesting is a fully automated procedure in an AD-integrated PKI. However, it is also easy to manually map certificates to user accounts in AD and to use the CA for any PKI-enabled custom application.

■ AD contains the location of the CAs in the hierarchy, so anytime an application requests a certificate, it can query the GC to locate the certificate.

■ Applications can query AD to look up and retrieve the certificates from the AD repository.

■ Smart card logons are automatically mapped to the Windows Server 2000/2008 accounts during the smart card enrollment process. The process that makes this happen is elegant. When a user logs on to the network, the Kerberos KDC (see the section "Understanding Kerberos," earlier in this chapter) queries AD for a mapping between the user's certificate and an Active Directory account. The process validates the user's ID using the public credentials and thus does not need a password.

■ AD-integrated CAs can issue all of the different types of certificates required in the PKI. This is achieved with certificate templates, which are loaded in the CA's policy module.

AD also allows certificates to be issued to groups. By setting the ACLs on certificate templates, you can filter which objects can get certain types of certificates by group membership. This is useful for groups of computers for which you can control which computers' accounts can enroll for a certain certificate.

Certificate enrollment architecture

It is critical in a PKI that, before a CA can honor a request, the requestor must be identified according to established protocol. Once this requirement is satisfied, the process of linking the issued private key to the user's public key is straightforward.

The following methods might be catered to for a large enterprise PKI:

■ **At the OS level.** This is done via the Certificate Manager's MMC snap-in or transparently through the auto-enrollment process in the Kerberos architecture described earlier in this chapter. Because every computer user in the city will be using Windows XP, users have the potential to manually request a certificate from the CA in the domain.

■ **Via the intranet.** All authentication methods are available at the IIS level. A custom Web page can (and should) be developed for manual user-driven certificate requests of an issuing CA. The best way to do this is to create an ASP.NET application that is installed to one of the intranet's IIS servers. This technique will also require secure sockets and secure authentication to the Web server.

The restricted enrollment agent

The restricted enrollment agent is a new feature in the Windows Server 2008 Enterprise operating system. It limits the permissions that users designated as enrollment agents have for enrolling smart card certificates on behalf of other users.

An enrollment agent is an individual or a group in an organization that issues certificates for others, specifically for the issuing of smart card certificates. To perform the function the user must obtain an enrollment agent certificate, which enables the agent to enroll. In most companies the enrollment agent is usually the PKI administrator or members of the security team. However, in some organizations, such as an enterprise with many branches, the PKI or support teams might not be local to the users that need the service. The restricted agent thus can be used to designate a branch manager or other trusted employee to act as an enrollment agent without having to have a slew of security credentials.

Group Policy

Enterprise policy for certificates is kept in AD Group Policy Objects (GPOs). Policy can thus be defined and tailored to meet domain requirements (all users or computers, or both, affected by the same certificate policy) or at lower levels, such as at sites and OUs. The enterprise AD-integrated PKI provides the capability to force certificate usage for a specific purpose to a collection of computers organized in groups. The policies you can define include the following:

- **Automated certificate enrollment and renewal.** An example of this policy usage is enabling the computer accounts of administration workstations to automatically enroll in certificates to be used for IPSec communications with the domain controllers. This policy also allows the IPSec certificates to be automatically renewed.

- **Data recovery agents.** This policy will be defined to allow recovery of Encrypting File System (EFS) data. The EFS data recovery privilege can be delegated to the accounts listed in the Data Recovery Agent GPO.

Group Policy can also be used to cater to certificate trust lists (for incorporating external CAs into the enterprise PKI) and trusted root CAs, which lifts the burden of maintaining them at each workstation.

MCITY users are partitioned in AD according to a hierarchy of organization units. This will facilitate the mapping of user accounts to certificates as needed.

Certificate revocation architecture

CRLs are objects that list the certificates that have been revoked by a CA. They can be read by PKI-enabled applications (such as the certificate manager on Windows XP). CRLs are critical for maintaining security. If a PKI application has no way of verifying the validity of a certificate, then it either cannot operate or cannot continue with the processing of an application.

The CA has no way of knowing whether a certificate it has issued has been compromised. If a CA issues a certificate and its owner loses or compromises the key, then it is incumbent on the certificate owner to alert the CA of the compromise.

The CA can then revoke the certificate, and both legally (declaratively) and operationally force the certificate out of circulation. Of course, a PKI-enabled application (such as Internet Explorer) can continue to ignore the revocation, but custom PKI applications that work with highly sensitive or valuable data would typically suspend operations as soon as a certificate was revoked.

Windows Server 2008 PKI technology supports the concept of CRL distribution points (CRLDPs). The CRLDP is an extension to the X.509v3 standard and works as follows:

- The certificate generated by the CA includes one or more pointers to a CRLDP. These can be valid Internet or intranet URLs, an LDAP URL (Active Directory), or a file system share.

- When a PKI-enabled application starts up, or when it is about to engage in secure processing, it must check whether a new CRL has been published. If one has been published, then it is pulled from the CRLDP and cached to the client on whom the PKI-enabled application operates.

- CRLDP planning is critical because a CRLDP is more than just a place to fetch a CRL object. The certificate can also contain a variety of CRLDP locations so that if one URL is offline, the CRL can be located at the other locations published in the certificate. This architecture will publish CRLs to an intranet URL, a file share on the DFS, and in an AD container.

- The CRLDP architecture will be critical for the AD infrastructure proposed in this architecture document because AD will be an aggressive user of the PKI from the get-go. In fact, the root CA discussed herein will be created before the root AD domain controllers are commissioned.

- The PKI administrator will be responsible for the management of the CRLDPs and CRLs. The CAs for each hub site will publish to the CRLDPs closest to their PKI clients. CRLDPs can be changed at various intervals during the lifetime of a certificate. However, the old CRLDPs need to be maintained for certificates that are still in circulation.

Online Certificate Status Protocol support

An alternative to CRLs, the online responder, which is based on the Online Certificate Status Protocol (OCSP), can be used to manage and distribute revocation status information to client consumers of certificates.

Certificate revocation is a function certification authorities (CAs) and, as explained earlier, distributing certificate revocation lists has been the standard way clients find out the status of certificates. In situations where CRL use is impractical, an online responder can be used instead.

Online responders distribute OCSP responses about the validity of certificates. Unlike CRLs, which are distributed periodically and contain information about all certificates that have been revoked or suspended, an online responder can respond to requests about individual certificates. Online responders are more efficient than CRLs. Bandwidth, persistent services, or high-speed connections are no longer a criteria for receiving certificate status, which was often the case with downloading large CRLs.

The online responder services also better handle bottleneck periods, such as during morning logon when a large numbers of users come to work and authenticate during log on or reply to signed e-mails. And the protocol also allows an organization that needs an efficient means to distribute revocation data for certificates that are not issued from Active Directory Certificate Services.

Online responders are also more secure. Sending out CRLs of thousands of certificates exposes an organization to dangers because information on revoked or suspended certificates is open and insecure.

User certificates

User certificates can be issued in one of three processes, in no specific order:

- First, if allowed, a user can open the Certificate Manager's MMC console on the local XP workstation. Access to the console can be controlled via Group Policy. This process will be likely used by advanced users.

- Second, and controlled transparently, is auto-enrollment via the services of an enrollment agent (such as the agent for Exchange and the agent for IPSec). Most users will thus be using certificates and never know it.

- Third, administrators and advanced users will fill in requests from a Web-based interface and download the certificate to specific locations.

A final word on setting up a PKI is that it is critical that no single individual be in a position to compromise a PKI. Several roles are thus defined to meet this objective. Certificate Services on the Windows Server 2008 platform meet this objective by including several CA management roles.

 See Chapter 1 for installing the Active Directory Certificate Services role.

Summary

This chapter provided an overview of the key security protocols and mechanisms available in Windows Server 2008. Perhaps no other subject related to networking is as important as security. You can offer your users all manner of features and performance, integrate to perfection (almost), and maintain a server room that hums like a Rolls Royce engine, but even the tiniest security breach can decimate the best system.

The external environment of an enterprise is like an ocean of pressure, pushing and pushing until the rivets of your ship pop. Before you can plan your security strategy, you should first try to understand the technology that is at work in the Windows Server 2008 security subsystems.

In particular, this chapter covered security threats and risks, cryptography, the new authentication protocols, and the Microsoft Certificate Services, which are used to build a public key infrastructure to serve your enterprise.

Chapter 17

Windows 2008 and Active Directory

S ince the days of Windows 2000, Active Directory has become one of the hottest technologies on corporate networks. If you are familiar with the Windows 2000 implementation of Active Directory, then you are probably also familiar with its shortcomings. Understanding Active Directory is thus a prerequisite to any management or deployment of Windows Server 2008.

In the 1970s, all the computing resources you needed, or could use, resided on the same computer or terminal you were logged on to. In the 1980s, with the advent of the PC LAN, many files were located on remote machines and there were definite paths to these machines. LAN users shared the files and printers, and exchanged e-mail on the LAN. Before the end of the 1990s, we witnessed the beginning of the paradigm shift whereby all information and functionality could be accessed on any server on any network anywhere ... and the user did not need to know where the objects were physically located. Now it's 2008, and not only can you access any file on any server across a corporate network, but you can access it with PDAs, cell phones, and any number of wireless devices.

This is the ideal computing model, in which all network objects — servers, devices, functionality, information, authentication, and the transports — combine to provide a single continuous information system and computing environment. This environment enables users, whether human or machine, to attach — or remain attached — to systems from a consistent user interface at any point of entry on the network. No matter what users require — whether it's functions of a device, communication, processes, algorithms, or perhaps just information and knowledge — they must be able to access such an object regardless of its physical location.

IN THIS CHAPTER

Understanding the origins of Active Directory

Understanding the elements of Active Directory

Comparing flat account databases and Windows Server 2008 domains

The Active Directory was Microsoft's bold leap toward realizing the dream of a truly distributed environment and IT architecture. It has been talked about for many years. Headlines in the technical trades were always gloomy, so many network administrators and systems engineers forgot about the directory and worked hard to refine or improve what was already in place, at considerable investment. Now, however, the Active Directory is a proven technology, and the Windows Server 2008 iteration offers many enhancements. You probably have little idea what it is or how to use it. Don't feel ashamed. Not only are you not alone, if you are unfamiliar with the Windows Server operating systems, it is unlike anything you have ever used before.

This chapter describes the elements of Active Directory. We will kick off with a brief discussion of how and why we will use Active Directory, and where it came from. Then we break it down into its constituent components (its logical structure), and finally we discuss how the components work and interoperate with each other. You will notice that the subject of Windows domains and trusts is left until after a full discussion of Active Directory.

This chapter also features the appearance of Millennium City (MCITY), or `mcity.us`, which is the example Windows Server 2008 network infrastructure we use throughout the book (it was originally introduced in the *Windows 2000 Server Bible*). It's a network that runs the infrastructure of an entire city, and its Active Directory is what we used to test the limits of what Microsoft says it's capable of. MCITY is essentially one huge Active Directory laboratory.

You don't need to be in front of your monitor for this chapter. Just curl up with some snacks and postpone any appointments you might have.

The Omniscient Active Directory

The original Windows NT client-server architecture was a great improvement over other server and network offerings, both from Microsoft and other companies. However, it had a shortcoming that, had it not been resolved in Windows 2000, would have suffocated the advancement of this highly sophisticated operating system. Now, Windows Server 2008 has taken it a step further with increased performance and many enhancements that make configuration and management much easier. On any network — resources are not easily distributed. The interoperation and scalability of numerous servers, printers, shares, devices, files, knowledge resources, functionality, and the sustained availability thereof, collapse when the capability for all network components and objects to share information is absent. One of the most significant components of Microsoft's technology is the Active Directory. There is perhaps no other aspect of Windows Server 2008 that will have the impact the directory service will, because just about every new feature or capability of this product depends on a directory service.

Before we haul out the dissecting tools, know the following:

- The Active Directory service is critical to the deployment and management of Windows Server 2008 networks, the integration and interoperation of Windows Server 2008 networks and legacy NT networks, and the interoperation and unification of Windows

Server 2008 networks with the Internet. Its arrival is a result of the evolutionary process of Microsoft's server and network technology. One way or another, the directory service is in your future.

■ Active Directory is a powerful directory service, either as part of a Windows network or as a standalone service on the Internet. In the latter role, it is an apt contender as a directory service in the same way that Internet Information Services (IIS) is an apt contender for a Web server. In other words, no querying client on the Internet needs to know that the directory is Windows Server 2008 Active Directory. Active Directory is 100 percent LDAP-compliant and 100 percent IP-compliant.

Why do we need directories?

A directory provides information. At its most basic level, it is like a giant white pages that enables a user to query a name and get back a phone number ... and then possibly connects to the person by automatically dialing that number. However, a directory in the IT world is a lot more than a telephone book. Before getting into the specifics of Active Directory, let's look at some reasons why we need directories. We kick off by placing Active Directory at the center of all services provided by Windows 2008.

Single Sign-On and distributed security

Active Directory makes it easier to log in to and roam cyberspace. Imagine if you had to log in at every mall, highway, turnpike, newsstand, public facility, sports amenity, shop, fast-food outlet, movie house, and so on, in the brick-and-mortar world we live in. Why then should we have to do this in cyberspace?

In every company today, it is almost impossible to get anywhere on the network without going through at least three logins. Every day, we log in to Web sites, Windows domains, voice mail, e-mail, and FTP, to name just a few; we won't go into how many accounts and logins we have.

Not only do we have to log in dozens of times a day, and remember dozens of passwords and user or login IDs, but we also have to know exactly where information and resources are located on the network. The uniform resource locator (URL) on the World Wide Web has alleviated the resource location problem to some extent (it obviates having to know exactly where something lives on the Internet), but it is still not ideal and not very smooth. URLs are perishable, and for the most part unmanageable in large numbers, which means they often are not updated. They are not managed in any sensible, cohesive system.

The ideal is to have some sort of badge that enables us to log in once and then flash it wherever we go, much like a proximity badge that allows your presence to be sensed and your identity verified. For starters, every application and service on our LANs, from e-mail to voice mail to data access to printer access, should be made available to us through one universal login, at home or at work. The type or level of access we have will depend on the attributes or "clearance level" of our badges. The access token provided by Windows NT security comes close to this, but it is not accepted by other technologies as a valid means of authentication.

Figure 17-1 illustrates several systems that should be accessed and managed from a central login authority. In many cases, this is already possible with Active Directory–compliant applications such as SQL Server 2008 and Exchange 2007.

Active Directory is shown here in its rightful position as a central login authority.

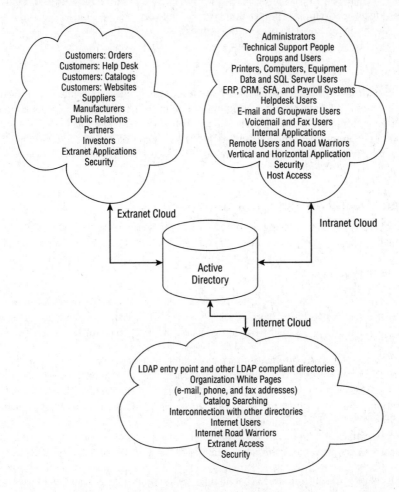

As you will learn in the chapters that remain, the single login dream is achieved by using the services of Active Directory and Windows Server 2008 support for MIT's Kerberos authentication. This service is known as *Single Sign-On* (SSO). SSO has become a quasi-standard among supporters of the Kerberos protocol, such as Microsoft, Apple, Sun, and, yes, in some cases, Novell.

Once a trusted user is authenticated via the Kerberos protocol, all other services that support the Kerberos protocol can accept and allow access to the principal. This is made possible by the Kerberos use of tickets — the badge idea previously discussed — which are issued by the directory service.

Change management

Active Directory makes it easy to manage the roamers and users of cyberspace and corporate networks and the computers they use to attach to the network. As administrators, we want to be able to manage our users and computing resources in one central omnipresent repository. We don't want to repeatedly manage users in the voice mail directory, on the NetWare servers' directory, in the Host systems database, in our e-mail directory, on our Windows domains, and so on.

As managers, we also need to be able to manage this information easier with changes. Mergers, acquisitions, new products, and services need to be continually managed on a cohesive and consistent basis. Group Policy, the change control and change management service of Windows Server 2008, stores all user and computer information in Active Directory.

Distributed administration

Active Directory enables you to delegate administrative function and responsibility and parcel out chunks of the network or domain for controlled administration. A distributed directory service makes it possible to delegate the administration of network resources and users throughout the enterprise. On legacy Windows NT systems, you can create users and groups with administrative rights, but it is impossible to hide other network resources from these administrators.

Because Active Directory can be partitioned as a mirror of the structure or organization of the enterprise, it is also possible to partition the administration of the compartments. In other words, it makes more sense to appoint a member of a department to perform repetitive management of that department's resources.

You will see later how administration of the directory can be delegated to individuals who are given only selective access or right of passage to delegated areas of the directory.

Application management

Active Directory makes it easy to develop and distribute applications. Application developers need consistent, open, and interoperable interfaces and APIs against which they can code functionality that stores and manages information relating to applications, processes, and services in a distributed information store. We want to be able to create applications and store application and persistent data to an "invisible" repository through an open interface. This information should be available from anywhere and everywhere on the network, including from an intranet or even the Internet (thanks to the .NET Framework).

Developers want to be able to create methods that install an application into a directory on the network for initial configuration and manipulation over the lifetime or use of the application.

We do not want to concern ourselves with the inner workings of the directory. We want to create our information or configuration object, initialize it, use it, and be done ... no matter where the user installs or invokes our product. Moreover, wherever the object we created is moved to, it should always be accessible to the application.

With all of the above, the cost of access and management has in the past been high. We are looking for solutions that will, in the long- to medium-term, reduce the cost of both management and operation of cyberspace and the information technology systems running our companies and our lives.

What Is Active Directory?

There are registries and databases that provide a directory-type facility for applications and users, but not one is interconnected, share-centric, or distributed in any way. Active Directory is a universal distributed information storehouse through which all network objects, such as application configurations, services, computers, users, and processes, can be accessed, in a consistent manner, over the full expanse of a network or inter-network. This is made possible by the logical structure of the directory. Before you start scratching your head, you should understand that without Active Directory, you cannot log in to a Windows Server 2008 domain, period.

CROSS-REF Chapter 19 discusses the Active Directory logical structure and illustrates the control you have over Active Directory's logical and physical structure.

We compare Active Directory to a database later in this chapter.

The grandfather of the modern directory: The X.500 specification

The directory service as we know it began with an interconnection model proposed by the International Organization for Standardization (ISO) a little more than 20 years ago. This model is popularly known as OSI, which stands for *open-systems interconnection*. In the late 1980s, OSI was given a huge boost by big business and government and quickly became the foundation for the information revolution we are experiencing today.

The OSI model and its seven layers lie at the root of modern information technology. Without a fundamental understanding of OSI, it is difficult to be an effective systems engineer, software developer, network administrator, CIO, or Webmaster. OSI is to IT what anatomy is to medicine. Although we assume that you are familiar with the OSI model, this brief discussion of X.500 serves to provide a common departure point for all systems engineers not familiar with a directory service.

The X.500 directory service can be found at the OSI application layer, where it sits as a group of protocols approved and governed by the International Telecommunications Union (ITU), formerly the CCITT. The objective of X.500 was to provide standards and interfaces to an open and interoperable global and distributed directory service.

X.500 is made up of many components (databases), all interoperating as a single continuous entity. Its backbone is the Directory Information Base (DIB). The entries in the DIB provide information about objects stored in the directory. Figure 17-2 represents the information contained in the DIB.

FIGURE 17-2

The X.500 hierarchy (a), and the DIB and the information it contains (b) are shown here.

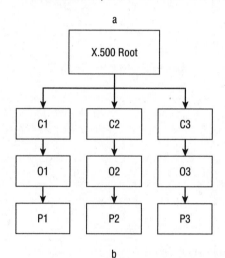

Entry Identifier	Classes	Attribute Values
P1	County Organization Person	US MCITY Jeffrey Shapiro

In order to access the information stored in the DIB, both users and computers needed a structure or model that would make it easier to understand where data could be located. The model proposed was an object-oriented, hierarchical structure that resembles an upside-down tree, as illustrated in Figure 17-3. The root of the tree is at the top, and the branches and leaves hang down, free to proliferate. This model ensured that any object in the tree is always unique as long as it is inherently part of the tree and can trace its "roots" to the single node at the top. Active Directory trees (and DNS) work the same way, as discussed later. The tree is read from the bottom to the top.

The objects in the X.500 tree represented containers for information representing people, places, and things. These objects would also be organized or grouped into classes (for example, groups of countries, companies, localities, and so on).

FIGURE 17-3

The X.500 tree structure illustrates the location of Active Directory domain information.

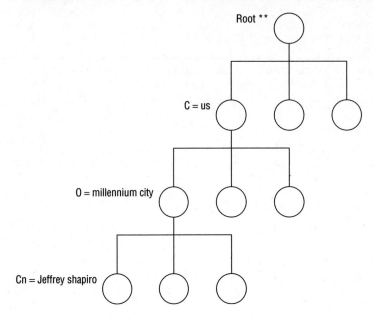

The X.500 standard included the following container objects:

- Country
- Location
- Organizational unit (OU)

Unfortunately, X.500 suffered from several limitations in its early days. It became bogged down under its own weight (the specification was exhaustive), and in many respects it was ahead of its time (especially with respect to its ties to OSI). It made its appearance in the late 1980s at a time when most innovators could not care less about managing information openly and globally, when we were all huddled in our garages inventing or writing code like crazy, and we were all competing for market share at every turn.

X.500 was also born before the advent of the World Wide Web and the mass utilization of the Internet by both the public and businesses. What really dragged it down was its ties to the OSI protocols (the datalink protocols — DLC — such as 802.2 and 802.3), which turned out to be its Achilles' heel, because the way of the Internet world was IP. Meanwhile, the Internet took off on the coattails of TCP/IP, leaving X.500 struggling in a protocol desert landscape.

Like so many innovations before it, X.500 provided nourishment for other inventions that followed, and much of the foundation for the modern directory service, especially Active Directory, can be directly attributed to the vision of X.500, as you will soon see.

The father of the modern directory: LDAP

The X.500 specifications defined a protocol whereby services would be able to access the information stored in X.500 databases. This protocol was known as the *Directory Access Protocol*, or DAP. It consisted of a comprehensive set of functions that would provide the capability for clients to add and modify or delete information in the X.500 directory.

DAP, however, was overkill and consisted of far more functionality than was required for the implementation of a directory service. Therefore, a simplified version of DAP was created, called the *lightweight directory access protocol* (LDAP). After several refinements, LDAP has begun to stand in its own right as a directory service. After adoption by the Internet Engineering Task Force (IETF), several important features of LDAP have garnered it widespread support:

- LDAP sits atop the TCP/IP stack, rather than the OSI stack. This means that every client with an IP address, able to send and receive packets over IP, can access and exploit LDAP-compliant directory services. The client needs only to know how to "talk" to LDAP (IP). TCP, the transport, takes care of the rest.

- LDAP performs hypersearching, which is the ability of a directory to refer to another directory for authoritative information. In other words, one LDAP directory can defer to another to chase information. An example is how Web-based search engines look to other search engines, via hyperlinking, for collateral information or information that does not exist in their own databases. Directory services on a worldwide Internet thus can become contiguous and distributed to form a transparent massive service, limited only by available servers and network resources.

- Early in its childhood, LDAP implemented a rich C-based API, making C the *de facto* programming language of the directory service. Using the most popular language of the day to call directory functionality ensured LDAP widespread support in the bustling developer community.

LDAP consists of the following components, which in some shape or form are the foundations of all modern directories, including Active Directory:

- **The data model.** This model represents how data is accessed in the directory. The data model is inherited directly from the data model of the X.500 specification. Objects are infused with information by way of assigning attributes to them. Each attribute is type-casted and contains one or more distinct values. The objects are classified into groups of classes, such as OUs or Companies.

- **The organization model.** This is the inverted tree paradigm described earlier, which is also inherited directly from the X.500 specification. It is the structure adopted by all modern directory services. Of particular note is how the Domain Name System (DNS) of the Internet is arranged around inverted trees. The DNS consists of several trees, the root or topmost levels, that sprout downward and contain millions of leaves (or nodes). Figure 17-4 illustrates the DNS forest and the seven roots. It also illustrates the .com tree and how it has fired the Internet into the commercial juggernaut it is today.

FIGURE 17-4

The organizational model revolves around the inverted tree, a hierarchical collection of objects.

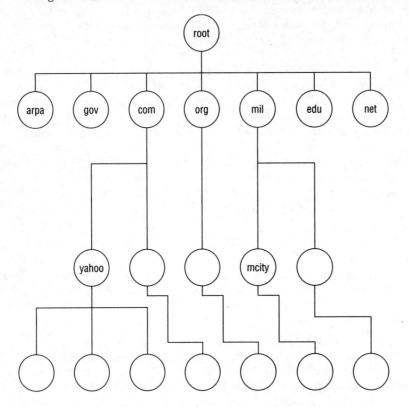

- **The security model.** This model specifies how information is securely and safely accessed. LDAP adopted Kerberos password authentication and has since added additional authentication layers with the inclusion of the Simple Authentication Security Layer (SASL). This SASL provides a tiered architecture for a multitude of service providers. Version 3.0 of LDAP also supports the secure socket layer (SSL) of TCP/IP, which was developed independently by the Internet community. Windows Server 2008 supports SSL in its browser; Internet Explorer also supports SSL in its Web server, IIS.

- **The functional model.** This model specifies the methods for querying and modifying the directory objects. It includes operations to add entries and to edit, to populate the attribute fields, to delete, and to query objects in the directory.

- **The topological model.** This model specifies how directory services integrate or interoperate with other compliant directories. The ability of LDAP directories to refer or defer to other directories is inherent in this model.

LDAP's popularity flourished with the Internet. Today, many popular applications and server technologies support the protocol. It can be accessed from most e-mail applications, Web-based applications, and even embedded systems such as routers and gateway devices.

After X.500

Several large technology companies are hard at work on directory services. The two of note that appear to have been at it longer than Microsoft are Banyan Systems and Novell. Others include Netscape and IBM (Lotus Notes).

Banyan perhaps has been at it the longest with its StreetTalk product, which has been part of the Vines OS for more than a decade. Novell entered the market midway through the 1990s with a directory service aimed at its installed NetWare base, called the Novell Directory Service (NDS), and it has been working on versions of NDS that will be independent of the NetWare OS, including a version for Windows NT.

NOTE Despite its immaturity, Active Directory has been built on proven technology. One technology on which it heavily depends is replication, which comes from Microsoft Exchange. The Exchange site integration and replication technology has been proven on millions of installations around the world.

From the ground up, Active Directory has been built on open, international standards. Note that Active Directory is not an X.500 directory, but it has borrowed heavily from the X.500 specifications. In particular, it uses LDAP as the access protocol, which opens it to everyone and everything. In short, Microsoft has taken everything that was great about X.500 and LDAP and combined it with proven technologies it has developed for other purposes over the years (such as Microsoft's Component Object Model, or COM). Active Directory can exchange information with any application or service that uses LDAP.

Active Directory also relies on DNS as its locator service, enabling clients to transparently locate domain controllers (Active Directory hosts) by merely connecting to a DNS server and looking up the IP addresses for the closest domain controller.

CROSS-REF We discuss the role of DNS in Active Directory in greater detail in Chapter 3.

The open Active Directory

Active Directory also provides a rich set of APIs to encourage the development of tools and applications. Active Directory will thus serve as a repository for application-specific information, particularly software that is group driven. For example, we have developed a Customer Relationship Management (CRM) system for several medical and dental clients. Our users typically log in to the application and become apparent as a community of active users to the rest of the practice or hospital, once authenticated in Active Directory.

The application is able to obtain enterprise-wide information about the state of the application at any given time, and we are able to group users according to service and access levels, governed by objects in Active Directory. In particular, the application publishes information about who is logged in and using the system, the files (data) they have checked out of the database management system (such as SQL Server or Oracle), and what they are currently doing.

We do not need to provide users with a second login just to use the application. Instead, when they run the CRM, it checks to see whether Active Directory has authenticated them, the machine from which they are accessing the system, and what they are allowed to access. Based on this information, we populate the Graphical User Interface (GUI) that drives the CRM with information the user is allowed to see or use.

How the registry fits in

Now that you can see why we need directory services and where they came from, where does the registry fit in? In the early days of Windows 95 and Windows NT, Microsoft improved the information repositories of applications running on the Windows platform with the creation of the registry. It was a great relief from the mess created by initialization and configuration files, insecure text files that anyone could access.

The registry, however, was more of a technology created to stabilize the OS, as a repository for managing information and the configuration of applications and computers. When users deleted their Windows 3.11 and earlier version .ini files in error, the application was, for better or worse, destroyed (if the .ini files were not backed up). The registry set out to change all that. Today, some of the largest software houses in the world still do not use it; many have opted for XML-based config files as well.

What's more, the registry also became the home for the so-called Security Account Manager (SAM). SAM is still used on Windows Server 2008 standalone servers today. This database stores and manages all the security and access control authority of network resources.

There are some similarities between the registry and Active Directory. Specifically, the registry is all of the following:

- A database, somewhat cryptic and complex, but still a database
- Open and accessible (except for the SAM part)
- Able to be programmed against
- A replicating structure (single master), providing some vestige of a distributed system
- A system of hierarchical structures, which contains records that hold configuration data

For the most part, the similarities end there. Comparing the registry to Active Directory is like comparing a JetSki to the USS Kitty Hawk: Active Directory is a completely different animal. Yes, you can still use the registry to store configuration data, and you would still use the registry on a standalone workstation or server, even a domain controller. Specifically, the difference is that Active Directory is also the following:

- A distributed multi-master database (peer directories update each other in real time, latency aside)
- Built on open, Internet-based standards

- Object-oriented

- Interoperable (almost coexistent) with DNS

- Able to service any network client using TCP/IP

- Able to grow to gargantuan proportions

Unfortunately, many applications today still store configuration information in unguarded flat text files, ignoring the registry for the most part. Ignoring both the registry and Active Directory will likely render your application incompatible with Windows Server 2008, from both a functional perspective and as a Microsoft logo requirement.

NOTE Active Directory is not meant to replace the registry. The registry still plays an important role in Windows Server 2008. In fact, even Active Directory uses the registry to store some configuration-related information. Microsoft began working on a directory or distributed information storage facility some time ago, possibly even at the same time it was developing the registry. We would one day like to see the registry based on an open standard such as XML.

From the outset, Microsoft believed it could only succeed with Active Directory by ensuring that it was based on open standards and interoperable with the Internet, period. In other words, any IP-based (LDAP) client will be able to access the Active Directory, and like IIS, FTP, and other services, this access is transparent (in terms of the OS on which it is sitting).

- Active Directory supports and coexists with both DNS and LDAP. Both are modeled on the X.500 standard, especially with respect to its structural and organizational model.

- Active Directory supports open and interoperable standards, especially with regard to the widespread naming conventions in use today.

- Active Directory is seamlessly integrated into the Internet by virtue of Microsoft's total adoption and commitment to TCP/IP. All other protocols that Microsoft supports essentially provide for backward compatibility with earlier versions of NT, other network operating systems, legacy transports such as SNA and the DLC protocols, and NetBEUI clients.

- Active Directory provides a rich set of C#, C/C++, J#, VB, .NET Framework, and scripting language interfaces, allowing it to be fully programmed against.

CAUTION If you need to program complex code against Active Directory, use a language that is based on the .NET Framework, such as Visual Basic .NET or C++. These languages offer a significant increase in speed compared to other languages.

- Active Directory is built into the operating system making it backwardly compatible with earlier versions.

- Active Directory is a fully distributed architecture, enabling administrators to write once and update everywhere from a single point of access, across any network.

- Active Directory is highly scalable and self-replicating. It can be implemented on one machine or the smallest network, and can scale to support the largest companies in the world. It has become the pervasive directory services technology within a short time.

■ Active Directory's structural model is extensible, enabling its schema to evolve almost without limits. In this regard, Active Directory has to comply with the X.500 specification that extending the schema requires you to register the new class with a X.500 governing body. This compliance is achieved by registering an Object Identifier (OID) with the authorities. In the United States, the authority is the American National Standards Institute (ANSI).

Active Directory has fully adopted the most popular namespace models in use today. It embraces the concept of an extendable namespace and marries this concept with the operating systems, networks, and applications. Companies deploying Active Directory are able to manage multiple namespaces that exist in their heterogeneous software and hardware.

The Elements of Active Directory

Active Directory is a highly complex product that will no doubt become more complex and more advanced in future versions. At the core of the product are several elements that are native to directory services in general and Active Directory in particular.

Namespaces and naming schemes

AD has adopted several naming schemes, which enables applications and users to access Active Directory using the formats in which they have most heavily invested. These name formats are described in the following sections.

RFC822 names

RFC822 is the naming convention most of us are familiar with, by virtue of our using e-mail and surfing the World Wide Web. These names are also known as user principal names (UPN) in the form of `somename@somedomain`; for example, `thepresident@thewhitehouse.gov`. Active Directory provides the RFC822 namespace for all users. If you need to find a person's extension number at a company (if they publish it), you need only query the directory and look up `someone@somedomain.com` (your software will translate that into the correct LDAP query, as shown later). The UPN is also the login name or user ID to a Windows Server 2008 domain. Windows users can now log in to a Windows Server 2008 network by simply entering their user ID and password, like this:

```
User: jeffrey.shapiro@mcity.us
Password: *************
```

TIP It is possible to assign any UPN to a domain for login. In other words, you might create a domain called MCITY but prefer users to log in as `someone@acmesales.com` so that they do not need to remember more than their e-mail addresses.

LDAP and X.500 names

The LDAP and X.500 naming conventions are known scientifically as *attributed naming*, which consists of the server name holding the directory (which we refer to as the *directory host*), username, OU, and so on, as shown in the following example:

```
LDAP://anldapserver.bigbrother.com/cn=jsmithers,ou=trucksales,
dc=bigbrother,dc=com
```

LDAP names are used to query the Active Directory.

Active Directory and the Internet

It is possible to locate Active Directory servers anywhere on the Internet or a private intranet. These Active Directory servers can be full-blown Windows Server 2008 domain controllers, or they can serve the single purpose of being LDAP directory servers. The information and access that users and clients enjoy from these servers is transparent.

The client needs only to resolve the closest Active Directory server to it to get information. The closest server might be on the same site as the client, in which case the DNS server will resolve to an Active Directory server on the same subnet as the client. Alternatively, it may be located on a site far away. This means that Active Directory can and will be used as an Internet directory server without ever being accessed for domain authentication. Multiple Active Directory servers will link together to provide a global directory service that spans the continent.

Active Directory everywhere

Microsoft also set out to ensure that Active Directory was highly scalable and would become pervasive as quickly as resources permitted. Active Directory is easy to install and set up on a simple server. It is also easy to set up and install Active Directory as a single-user repository, and it carries virtually no noticeable overhead on the simplest configuration (we discuss Active Directory configuration in the chapters that follow). In other words, when Active Directory needs to be small, it can be small, and when it needs to be big, it can grow at an astonishing rate.

This makes Active Directory ideal for even the simplest of application information storage requirements. Although it is no substitute for database management systems that provide advanced information management services such as information analysis and data mining (or the management of corporate data), it may not be uncommon to find a single-user application deploying Active Directory in the hope that later scaling up will be as easy as merely further populating the directory. Active Directory even installs on a standalone 133 MHz desktop machine with 64 MB of RAM, and is easily deployable as a domain controller supporting a small company (although this configuration is not what Microsoft officially recommends, and such a configuration should support little else but a directory with a small helping of user and computer accounts). As you will see in forthcoming chapters, you can install AD in read-only mode to support branch offices and remote locations that are insecure, like factories and warehouses.

Conversely, it is possible to deploy Active Directory in such a way that it scales to surprising levels. As a domain repository, Windows NT 4.0 or later repositories would max out at about 100,000 users, but Active Directory can scale to the millions — it can grow as large as the Internet. All the replicas of Active Directory are synchronized (which itself is quite an administration feat, as you will soon see). All copies of an organization's Active Directory system propagate changes to one another, similar to how DNS servers propagate domain records.

NOTE   In practice, account databases, like the old NT domain, become shaky at between 30,000 and 40,000 accounts, which is why many large companies created multiple resource and account domains. Because all versions of the OS from Windows 2000 and later use Active Directory, you will find no significant difference between them when it comes to scalability.

The key to the scalability of Active Directory is the domain tree — a data hierarchy that can expand, theoretically, indefinitely. Active Directory provides a simple and intuitive bottom-up method for building a large tree. In Active Directory, a single domain is a complete partition of the directory. Domains are then subdivided or partitioned into organizational units, enabling administrators to model the domain after their physical organization structure or relevant business models. A single domain can start very small and grow to contain tens of millions of objects; thus, objects can be defined at the smallest corporate atomic structure without the fear of overpopulation, as was the case with Windows NT 4.0, and NetWare 3.*x* and 4.*x*.

Inside Active Directory

The core of Active Directory is largely accessible only to geeks who see heaven in a line of C++ and Assembly code (the author included). It does not ship with special viewer tools, such as MS Access, that give you a feel for what exists in its structures or what these structures look like (a few Resource Kit tools provide some access). The following, however, describes the key components, with the objective of providing an insight into the innards of this directory service.

If it walks like a duck . . .

One area seriously lacking in administrator education is database knowledge. Database 101 should be in every engineering course. All too often, we see administrators "reinitializing" databases to free up space, only to discover that they wiped out valuable corporate data in the process. Later in this chapter, you will examine the anatomy of the directory from a very high level. To fully understand how the Active Directory engine works, the following is a mini-course on Active Directory, the database.

On the physical level, Active Directory is two things: a database and a database management system (DBMS) . . . pure and simple. The data it keeps can be viewed hierarchically. A *database* is a repository for data. It is a software structure in which data is stored, manipulated, and retrieved by any process seeking to gain access to and exploit the information it contains. If you are not sure this is a valid definition of Active Directory, then let's apply the definition of a database (the rules) to Active Directory.

A database is a database if the following are true:

- It contains functional layers — which include a schema — that define the structure of the database: how data is stored, retrieved, reviewed, and manipulated. Other functional layers include an "engine" that comprises I/O functions, maintenance routines, query routines, and an interface to a storehouse for the data. This is often known as a storage engine.

- The data, properties, and attributes of a thing are stored in containers, which comprise collections of records, known as tables (such as in a relational database) or some other cubby (such as in an object database).

The simplest definition of a DBMS is that it is a software application on top of which sits a user interface, used to manage the data in the database and the database itself. A DBMS can be used to extract data (query), format it, present it to users, and print or transfer it into a comprehensible form. Modern DBMS systems, such as SQL Server, provide users with the technology to interpret or analyze data, as opposed to simple quantification.

Users of databases and DBMS include both humans and machines. Software used by machines and computers saves and accesses data because it is a means by which a process can gain access to persistent information. Persistent data can and should be shared by multiple users, both human and machine. For example, an engineer puts data into a database so that a robot can perform repetitive work based on the data.

Active Directory is all of the above and more, but you would not use it to, for example, extract records of a group of individuals who pose a credit risk to your company, because such support is beyond the purpose of a directory service. Whether Active Directory is a relational database or an object database brings us to debatable levels in our discussion, so we won't go there. Our analysis of Active Directory will help you to make that determination on your own.

A relational database is made up of tables; it has columns (collections) that represent things, such as a column or collection of first names. Information about each individual entry is stored chronologically (for example, the fifth *first name* or *fn* in the collection is David). Figure 17-5 represents a column of first names.

You can have multiple tables in a relational database. You can also have "things" in one table that relate to things in another table, not only by chance, but also by design and purpose. In relational tables, you access the properties of a thing, and the information that it represents, by referencing its place in the collection, as shown in Figure 17-6.

An object database is a little harder to define, mostly because many forms of object databases evolved from relational databases. An object-model–compliant database might be more about how the information it contains is exposed to the users and how the underlying schema can be accessed than about the underlying makeup and technology or how it was created.

However, an object database might also be best described as a database that conforms to the object model as opposed to the relational model. We do not know enough about how Active Directory works because at the very core it is a proprietary technology. What we do know is that data is stored in Active Directory in a structure that resembles tables with columns and rows. In fact, Microsoft has used the very same database engine (Jet) it deployed in Exchange Server in Active Directory. It is thus a blood relative of Microsoft Access.

FIGURE 17-5

The column in a relational database contains records, which are members of collections or groups.

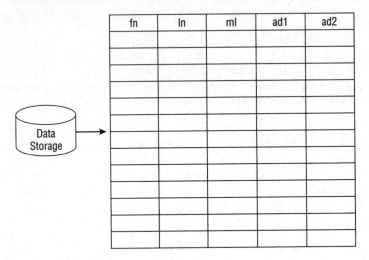

FIGURE 17-6

Two columns in a relational database contain records that are related to each other.

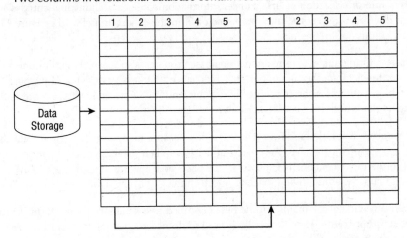

The Active Directory database structure

Active Directory has been implemented as a layered system comprising the Core Directory Service Agent (DSA), the Database Layer (DB), and the Extensible Storage Engine (ESE). Above these layers lie the interfaces that comprise the replication service, the Security Account Manager, or SAM (as with the NT 4.0 SAM), the LDAP interface, and the API (ADSI). The LDAP interface, as you will see later, provides the interface or access to LDAP clients. LDAP is supported in all 317-bit desktop and workstation environments. LDAP is also built into Outlook. SAM provides the security interfaces to Active Directory and hooks into the access control technology (see Figure 17-7).

FIGURE 17-7

Active Directory consists of three functional layers, on top of which lie the access and replication layers and the Security Account Manager (SAM).

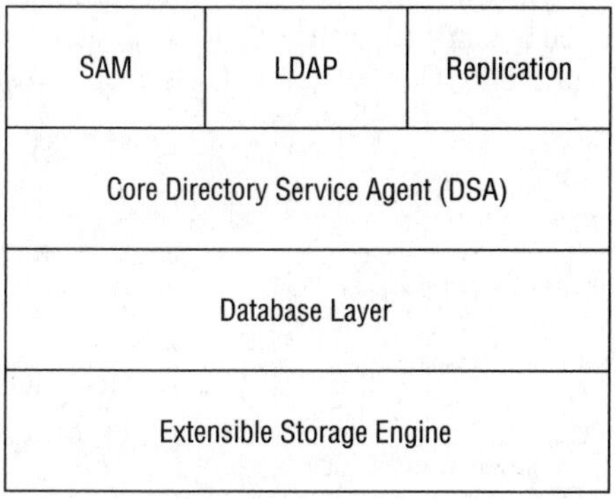

SAM	LDAP	Replication
Core Directory Service Agent (DSA)		
Database Layer		
Extensible Storage Engine		

NOTE It's time to dispense with the acronym SAM. The problem is that SAM stands for Security Account Manager, Security Accounts Manager, and Security Access Manager; Surface to Air Missile fits as well. If Microsoft would simplify this to SM for Security Manager, we could all agree on what the acronym stands for.

The ESE comprises two tables: a data table and a link table. The ESE database is used to maintain data on the structure of the directory, and is not apparent to clients. The Active Directory database, NTDS.DIT, conversely, contains the following collection of database tables that users will relate to, either transparently, via some cognitive processing, or directly:

■ **Schema table.** The *schema* dictates the type of objects that can be created in Active Directory, how the objects relate to each other, and the optional and compulsory attributes applied to each object. Note that the schema is extensible, and it can thus be expanded to contain custom objects that are created by third-party applications and services.

■ **Link table.** The link table contains the link information and how the objects relate to each other in the database.

■ **Data table.** The data table is the most important structure in the Active Directory database system because it stores all the information or attributes about the objects created. It contains all the compulsory and optional information that makes up the objects, such as usernames, login names, passwords, groups, and application-specific data.

Active Directory objects

If Active Directory is a casserole, then the objects are its ingredients. Without objects, the directory is a meaningless, lifeless shell. When you first install Active Directory, the system installs a host of user objects you can begin accessing immediately. Some of these objects represent user accounts, such as Administrator, without which you would not be able to log in and obtain authentication from the directory.

Objects contain attributes or properties — they hold information about resources they represent. For example, the user object of a Windows Network contains information (the attributes) of the user pertaining to his or her First Name, Last Name, and Logon ID. Figure 17-8 illustrates an object-oriented representation of a user object in the Active Directory. (The actual data structure is a table of columns or fields.)

FIGURE 17-8

An Active Directory user object and three attributes or properties.

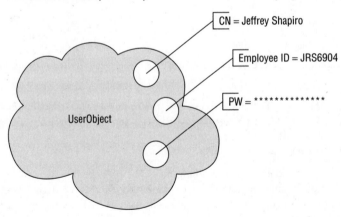

CN = Jeffrey Shapiro

Employee ID = JRS6904

PW = **************

UserObject

There can be many different objects in Active Directory. Some hold exploitable information, and some are merely containers for other objects. You might conclude that the entire Active Directory is one big object, inside of which are container objects, which contain other objects, and which in turn contain other objects, as illustrated in Figure 17-9, which depicts a *container object*, technically represented by a triangle, a popular storage symbol, which holds other container objects. This nesting can continue until the last object is a *leaf object*, which cannot be a container.

FIGURE 17-9

The container object contains other objects, which in turn may contain objects.

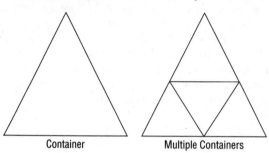

Container   Multiple Containers

Objects that are not container objects, such as user objects, are known as leaf objects, or end node objects, as illustrated in Figure 17-10. When a leaf object is added to the container, the nesting ends there.

FIGURE 17-10

The leaf object, or end node object, does not contain other objects.

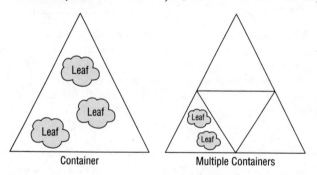

Container   Multiple Containers

Active Directory is like those Russian nesting dolls. Figure 17-10 provides a popular two-dimensional view of the container philosophy. However, the metaphor we are more familiar with in IT and Windows network administration is the object tree, which we discuss shortly.

We also talk in terms of *object classes* when working with Active Directory. The object class is less a class in the object-oriented technology sense and is more a collective noun for the type and purpose of objects organized as groups. Object classes can be user accounts, computers, networks, and more; actually, they can be any of the objects that Active Directory currently supports.

Another way to look at the object class, or simply class, is that it is a definition of an object that can be created and managed by the directory. *Content rules* govern how an object can be attributed. Classes are also endowed with certain rules that dictate which classes of objects can be parents, which can be children, and which can be both.

We mentioned earlier that the Active Directory schema is extensible. This means that programmers can code against the API and create and manage their own objects (refer to the discussion on ADSI later in this chapter, in the "My Active Directory" section). This enables application developers to use Active Directory and save configuration and state information about applications. Of course, the registry is still a valid place to store information, especially for hardware settings, but Active Directory offers features such as replication, propagation, and a wider "gene pool" of objects, such as users, with which to interact and coexist.

Active Directory schema

The *schema* is the Magna Carta of Active Directory. When you create an object in Active Directory, you have to also comply with the rules of the schema. In other words, you have to supply all the compulsory attributes required by the objects, or the object cannot be created. The schema governs data types, syntax rules, naming conventions, and more.

As just mentioned, the schema, which is stored in the schema table, can be extended dynamically. That is, a program can extend it with new custom classes and then provide the rules by which the schema can manage the classes. Once this has been accomplished, the application can begin using the schema immediately.

Extending or changing the schema requires conforming to programmatic and administration rules and is typically a one-way process, unless you restore from a backup. That the schema is itself part of the directory means that it is an enterprise-wide service in Active Directory. As such, a master schema has to be properly accessed before any peer schema receives propagated schema changes. We will not delve too far into this because it is a subject that belongs in a book devoted to programming Active Directory.

Object attributes

Objects contain *attributes*. Some are essential to the object's existence, such as a password for a user object. Some are not essential, such as a middle initial.

Walking the Active Directory

The route to an object in Active Directory is achieved by traversing a hierarchical path that resolves the object's name. This path includes all the container objects through which you can drill down to the end node. What might be a little difficult to grasp is that on the one hand, we talk about containership, while on the other, we talk about how you have to walk a long and winding road to discover the name of the leaf or end node object. The best way to understand this is by examining the diagram in Figure 17-11, which shows a system of boxes that contain smaller boxes, and so on. If you join all the left top corners of the boxes, you see the emergence of the hierarchical path described here.

FIGURE 17-11

If you join all the dots representing the ID of each box, a systematic, hierarchical collection of boxes begins to emerge.

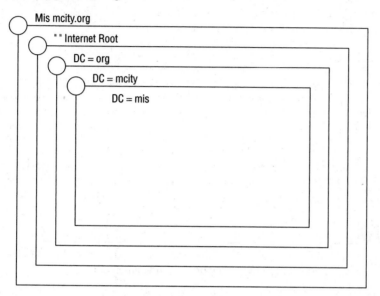

In Active Directory, this full path name (the names of all the dots joined together) is known as the *distinguished name* (DN) of the object. The name of the final object itself, apart from the path, is known as the *relative distinguished name*, in this case "mis."

We say the full path to the object and the object name itself is *distinguished* because it is unique in Active Directory. No other object contains the identical object DN. In other words, the object itself is unique. The purpose of this naming and tracing mechanism is to allow an LDAP client to track down an object and retrieve its information as quickly as possible.

The relative distinguished name (RDN) of the object is the object name itself. The RDN is an attribute of the object. The RDN is not necessarily unique, although it is unique in its container in Active Directory, because such a name can exist at the end of another DN somewhere else in Active Directory, down some other path. Figure 17-11 illustrates how two objects can have the same RDN but somewhere up the chain the similarity will end, at the root or the parent.

When we make a query to Active Directory, we naturally start at the root of the DN of an object and follow the path to the node. In LDAP, however, we start at the RDN and trace the name parts to the root. In this fashion, the entire DN is constructed during such a query, such as the following:

```
cn=box1,root=,container5=,container6=,container7=,container8=..
```

It might help to clear things up for you at this point if you construct a DN on a scrap piece of paper. For the exercise, let's say that you need to construct a query to the user named "jchang." To get to jchang, you need to start with the cn, which is jchang, then go up to office=232, floor=3, building=maotsetung, city=peking. LDAP works from the bottom up. Try not to think about an entry point into Active Directory, but to merely start at the object and parse your way up the path until a match is found when you hit the root object.

Naming conventions

Each section of the DN is an attribute of an object expressed as `attribute_type=value`. When we talk about the object name itself or the RDN, we refer to the *canonical* or *common* name of the object, expressed in LDAP lingo as `cn=`. If we are talking about a user, the common name takes the format `cn=jchang`.

Conversely, each object's RDN is stored in Active Directory, and each reference contains a reference to its parents. As we follow the references up the chain, we can also construct the DN. This is how LDAP performs a directory query. This naming scheme is very similar to the mechanism of DNS, as illustrated in Figure 17-12.

FIGURE 17-12

The domain hierarchy on the left represents a DNS domain namespace on the Internet. The domain hierarchy on the right represents an Active Directory domain namespace.

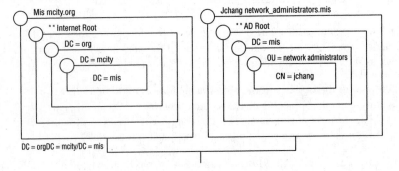

Now that we have discussed the naming mechanisms of Active Directory, you should know that Windows does not require everyday users to go through this exercise every time they access an object. The UI does all the work for you and hides this syntax. However, such attributes are required when you code directly to the Active Directory API (ADSI) or LDAP, or are using scripting languages or tools to query and work with Active Directory in a more advanced fashion than the standard tools allow.

Active Directory supports both LDAP v2 and LDAP v3 naming styles, which comply with the Internet's RFC 1779 and 2247 naming styles. This style takes the following form:

```
cn=common name
ou=organizational unit
```

```
o=organization
c=country
```

However, Active Directory drops the `c=country` and replaces `o=organization` with the `dc=domain` component, as shown in the following example:

```
cn=jchang,ou=marketing,dc=mcity,dc=org
```

> **NOTE** The use of commas in the DN is a separation or delimiter mechanism. LDAP functions parse the DN and go by the delimiters to break the DN into its relative parts.

In *dot notation*, this would read `jchang.marketing.mcity.us`. An LDAP algorithm translates LDAP names to DNS format and vice versa.

By complying with the LDAP naming convention, any LDAP client can query Active Directory via an LDAP Uniform Resource Locator (URL) as follows:

```
LDAP://ldapserver.mcity.us/cn=jchang,ou=marketing,dc=mcity,dc=org
```

Objects in Active Directory are stored and tracked according to an attribute consisting of the object's globally unique identifier, or GUID (pronounced *gwid* by some and *gooeyID* or *gooID* by others). The attribute is called the *objectGUID*. The object can thus be moved around and changed, even renamed, but its identity will always remain the same. The GUID is the 128-bit number that is assigned to the object upon its creation. An object cannot exist in Active Directory without a GUID; it is one of the compulsory attributes that are automatically assigned when the object is created. The GUID is available for external process reference and programmatic function; in other words, you can reference the object in Active Directory from an external program by its GUID. This mechanism ensures that the object will always be accessible as long as it exists. Ergo, wherever it is moved, it is still accessible.

Objects are protected in Active Directory via the SAM access control mechanisms, and security is achieved through the functionality of access control lists (ACLs). In other words, you need to be able to prove ownership and rights over an object if you want to edit or delete it.

Domain objects

When you set up Active Directory for an enterprise, your first exercise will be to create your root domain, or, in Active Directory terms, the root domain object. If this root domain will also be your Internet root domain, you should register it with an Internet domain administration authority (such as `GoDaddy.com`, Inc) as soon as possible. If you already registered a root domain, you will be able to create an object that represents it in Active Directory and link it to the DNS server hosting or resolving that name. If you have not registered your domain, you might not be able to match it to your company name, because domain names are being claimed every second of the day. This root domain in fact becomes the first container object you create in your chain of objects that represent the "expanse" of your local network logon domain in Active Directory. Under this domain, you create more container objects that represent the organizational units (discussed next) within your enterprise. For example, you might create a domain called `mcity.us` and register it with a registrar. There are also security considerations we address later.

For now, know that the domains you are creating here are full-blown security and administration entities of your network, in the same fashion that legacy NT 4.0 and earlier domains were. How they work will just confuse you for now, so we have left this discussion for the chapters to follow. Note, however, that we do not discuss integration and migration of legacy domains until Chapters 18 and 19.

Figure 17-13 represents a path (from the bottom up) of a user all the way up to the domain root. As you now know, you can have only a single domain parent in Active Directory. It is entirely feasible, and good practice, to create subdomains under the domain root that reflect the subdivision of resources, departments, politically and geographically diverse divisions of an enterprise, acquisitions, resource entities, and more.

FIGURE 17-13

A user object (account) on an Active Directory local domain. There is a direct connection between the Active Directory domain and the DNS domain.

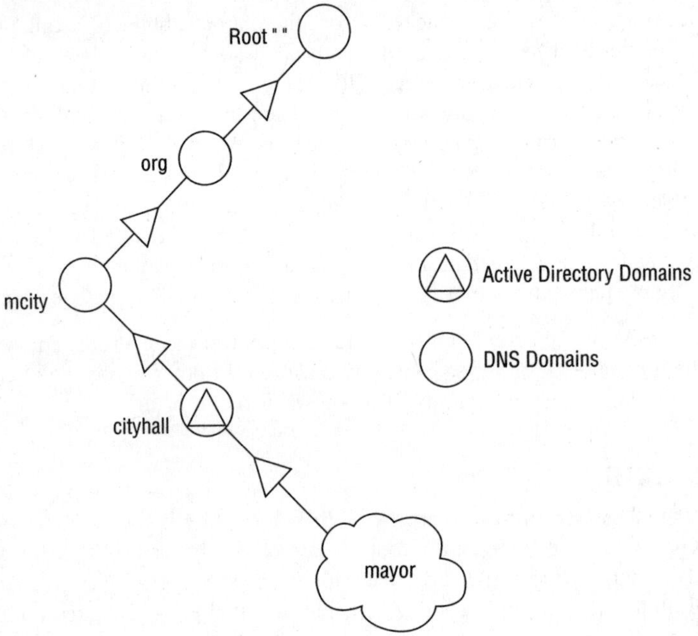

CROSS-REF Chapter 20 presents some reasons you would or would not partition Active Directory into several domains.

For example, a root domain of ABC Company might be `abc.com`. You could then easily create a subdomain of `abc.com` called `marketing.abc.com`. Note that the `.com` should not be your domain root, because the Internet authorities own that domain root. Keep in mind that we are still creating objects only from an Active Directory point of view. These domain objects are container objects, with name attributes for easy lookup and management (and GUIDs for internal tracking and identity). What we are actually asking Active Directory to do is to maintain the first domain as a root container object, which in turn contains subordinate domain objects.

Organizational units

OUs are key container objects in which you can group classes of objects. OUs can, for example, contain objects such as user accounts, printers, computers, files, shares, and even other OUs. Figure 17-14 illustrates the "containerization" of a group of user accounts into an OU.

FIGURE 17-14

User accounts grouped in an OU container.

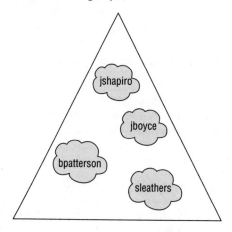

The OU is a welcome addition to the network. In Active Directory, you can create these containers to reflect your enterprise or organization. To illustrate, we re-created the organizational chart of a major U.S. city and merged it into the domain of a cyberspace city called Millennium City. This will become the sample enterprise we will return to during later discussions of Active Directory.

The organization chart on the left in Figure 17-15 shows the hierarchy of departments and divisions in Millennium City at the time a directory for this organization was being contemplated. You can see that the chart shows a diverse collection of departments, both local and geographically dispersed, and various sites and services. On the right in Figure 17-15, the same organizational chart is represented with OU objects in Active Directory.

In any domain on the domain path, you can create organizational units, and inside these organizational units you can create group, user, and computer objects. You can also add custom objects to the domains and OUs. Active Directory also enables you to create any end point or leaf object outside the OU.

FIGURE 17-15

The left side of the figure represents an organizational chart. The right side represents the same organizational chart as an object hierarchy in Active Directory.

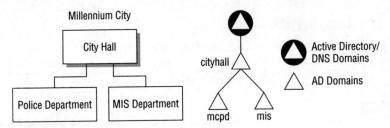

Trees

Active Directory refers to the domain structure just described as *domain trees*. Everything from the bottom of the object path is considered part of the domain tree — leading from the bottom up, all the way to the single domain parent at the top. The domain tree is unique in Active Directory because no two parent domains can be the same. The schema does not allow it.

As demonstrated earlier, the domain tree is a systematic collection of Active Directory domain objects that belong to a contiguous namespace. Remember that in Active Directory, the root domain can be extended or partitioned into multiple subdomains that share a common parent. Subdomain names must also be unique; however, they all share a common directory schema, which is the formal definition of all objects in the domain tree.

Active Directory deploys the DNS naming conventions for hierarchical naming of Active Directory domains and domain devices. In this regard, the Active Directory domains and the devices therein are both identified in DNS and Active Directory. Don't worry — Windows Server 2008 takes full advantage of Dynamic DNS, so DDNS names, such as WINS, do not have to be created in Active Directory and then manually entered into DNS. Although the two domain hierarchies have identical names, they still reflect separate namespaces. DNS manages your Internet namespace, while Active Directory manages your enterprise namespace. The enterprise namespace is, however, resolved via the services of DNS, which provides a directory to the servers that hold your Active Directory directories.

Forests

It is possible to create another parent domain in Active Directory and create objects under it that may appear identical to objects in adjacent domain trees. These collections of domain trees are called *forests*. Active Directory refers to a single domain tree as a forest of one tree. You can also set up trust relationships between these trees, and allow users of one tree in the forest to access the resources in another tree. You would find yourself adding trees to your forest, for example, when you acquire another IT department in a corporate takeover or merger, or when migrating objects from one domain to another, or integrating with legacy NT domains.

Trusts

Finally, we get to the issue of trusts. Like all Windows domains Windows Server 2008 domains interrelate or interoperate according to trust relationships. In other words, the security principals of one domain are trusted by the security services of another domain according to the trust relationship between the two domains. This is illustrated in Figure 17-16.

FIGURE 17-16

Domain A trusts domain B, and domain B trusts domain A . . . a two-way trust.

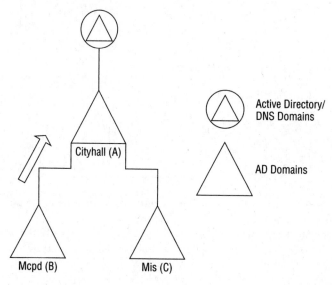

Cityhall (A)

Active Directory/
DNS Domains

AD Domains

Mcpd (B)   Mis (C)

Figure 17-17 illustrates the three domains that are linked by transitive trust relationships. This new trait, *transitive*, essentially means that if domain A trusts domain B and domain B trusts domain C, then A also trusts C. Another way to look at it is by stating that a friend of my friend is also my friend. Figure 17-17 illustrates the transitive trusts.

You might be wondering why, then, Windows Server 2008 domains are automatically transitive, whereas legacy NT domains are not. There is no magic in this, no nifty trick performed by Microsoft other than the adoption of an established security standard long overdue: Kerberos. The ticket-granting service that Kerberos and Active Directory bring to Windows Server 2008 creates a distributed security network. Like the Single Sign-On initiative discussed earlier, Kerberos tickets issued by one domain can be used as good currency in another domain. The Kerberos ticket is like a multinational visa or passport that allows the bearer to gain access to any territory that accepts it.

FIGURE 17-17

Transitive trusts: If domain A trusts domain B and domain B trusts domain C, then domain A trusts domain C.

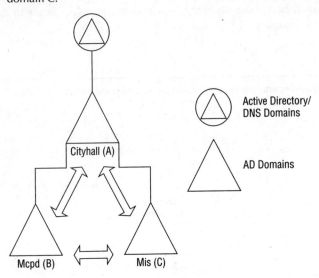

> **NOTE**   Transitive here really means that something is able to get from point A to point B by going via point *n*. Transitive can refer to the transient activity of other systems besides security. Replication is a good example.

The global catalog

As discussed earlier, in LDAP, the mechanism for searching or parsing a domain tree is to start from the bottom and travel all the way up to the domain root. LDAP also works on a system of referrals in which a search that ends in a dead end can be referred to other domain trees in the forest. However, LDAP searches only work when you know what you are looking for — in other words, you already have the DN or object name and all you are hoping for are the attributes you will be allowed to see. What if you want to find, for example, all the printers in the OU named Town Planning or all the users that have access to a certain folder? Enter the global catalog (GC).

Active Directory supports directory deep queries by means of a GC that is created as soon as the first domain root is created. It contains the attributes of all objects in Active Directory that are, by their nature, searchable. Last or first names are a good example; organization names, computers, printers, and users can be searched by supplying certain attributes as keywords. Applications and users are thus able to query the GC by using a known, or assumed, attribute as a keyword to find possible matches.

The GC also enables you to find an object without knowing in which domain it resides, because the GC holds a subset of all the objects of all domains in a forest. For example, a domain member tells you that he or she is unable to log on to the domain. When you search the domain, you find no object that represents this user's name or logon attributes. You can then search the GC to determine whether the user has perhaps been assigned to another domain, an account has not yet been created, or it is disabled.

My active directory

Of extreme importance to domain administrators is the ability to program against Active Directory. Custom access to account information has always been a limitation in Windows NT 4.0. Microsoft provided no easy way to access the SAM for customized administrative functions. Every organization has a particular need that cannot be satisfied by the base functionality alone: A good example is the need to find out which Windows NT accounts have dial-in access enabled, and who has used this privilege in the past three months. Building a tool to query this against the NT SAM and generate a report for management is like trying to add another face to Mount Rushmore.

Active Directory, however, provides several APIs you can use to access its data for such custom needs:

- **ADSI.** The most important API Microsoft has released is the *Active Directory Service Interfaces* (ADSI). ADSI is a collection of Component Object Model (COM) objects that can be used to manipulate and access the directory. Since its release, Microsoft has added Java support (JADSI), which enables any Java tool to program against the ADSI interfaces; but given the litigious atmosphere around Java, you would be better off programming Active Directory from the LDAP API using Java, as described in a moment.

- **MAPI.** This is the Windows Open Services Architecture (WOSA) Messaging API. One of Microsoft's oldest APIs, Active Directory supports MAPI to allow mail-enabled directory applications to gain access to the MAPI address book provider.

- **LDAP API.** This is a C API, which is the *de facto* standard for programming against anything LDAP-compliant. The LDAP API can be programmed from .NET, C, C++, Java, and so on (essentially any programming language capable of calling C functions).

However, through ADSI, you can access any LDAP-compliant directory (Active Directory, LDAP repositories, and third-party directories such as NDS). This means that ADSI can be used by anyone who wants to create applications that access any LDAP-compliant directory. In other words, write once to ADSI and support any directory (with Microsoft Windows, naturally).

ADSI provides an abstract layer above the capabilities of the directory (it wraps the LDAP API). In this fashion, it provides a single set of directory service interfaces for managing or accessing LDAP resources.

Developers and administrators will use ADSI to access LDAP directories in general, and Active Directory in particular. This opens Active Directory and LDAP to a host of possible applications.

Consider this: Under NT 4.0 and earlier, it was cumbersome to work with APIs to duplicate the functionality of User Manager for Domains and Server Manager. Administrators were pretty much saddled with these applications, no matter how creative they believed they could be in managing network resources through code or scripting.

ADSI will see both ISVs and corporate developers developing tools to make their administrative tasks easier and cheaper. Using traditional languages and scripting tools, a developer might create functionality that automatically sets up groups of users, applications, network resources, tools, devices, and more. These "applets" can also be targeted to the Microsoft Management Console (MMC), which makes their installation and deployment a cinch. In addition, developers will be able to easily "directory enable" their applications.

ADSI has been designed to meet the needs of traditional C and C++ programmers, systems administrators, and sophisticated users, but it is as easily accessed with Visual Basic, making it the most comprehensively accessible LDAP product on the market. ADSI presents the services of the directory as a set of COM objects. For example, an application can use the ADSI PrintQueue object to retrieve data and to pause or purge the print queue, leading to applications that coexist with the underlying technology (as opposed to applications that just run on the platform).

Active Directory is also MAPI-compliant in that it supports the MAPI-RPC address book provider. This support enables a MAPI-based application to look up the contact information of a user, such as an e-mail address or telephone number.

Bridging the Divide: Legacy Windows and Windows Server 2008

One of Active Directory's primary features is its accommodation of earlier versions of Windows domains. Most companies will not switch their entire operations to Windows Server 2008 overnight, but will instead run Windows Server 2008 alongside every shade of Windows Server from NT through Server 2003 for some time.

Many companies will adopt the Active Directory domain controller or several controllers as the new "PDC" of legacy Windows NT domains. NT servers, workstations, and clients view Active Directory servers as PDCs in mixed-mode (Windows Server 2008, NT, and 2000 mixed) environments. To users, applications, and services, the authentication by Active Directory is transparent, thus allowing NT domains to continue services oblivious to the fact that the PDC is in fact the proverbial disguised wolf, as Microsoft cunningly did with the File and Print services for NetWare, which made clients think the NT server was a NetWare server. Active Directory achieves this magic by totally emulating Windows NT 3.51 and NT 4.0 domain controllers. In a mixed-mode environment, the Windows Server 2008 domain controller acts and behaves like a Windows NT 4.0 domain controller. Even applications and services (including the ISV and third-party products) that are written to the Win32 API will continue to work without modification in an Active Directory environment.

A term you will encounter in subsequent chapters is *down-level compliance*. This down-level compliance enables many IT and LAN administrators to plan gradual and safe transitions to Windows Server 2008 domains in which Active Directory is the master logon authority. Thus, the transition in most cases will be evolutionary rather than revolutionary, while still guaranteeing that Active Directory is deployed right at the very beginning. Transition by phased implementation is the route we primarily advocate in the chapters to follow, and we discuss routes to Windows Server 2008-Windows NT integration that do not require Active Directory.

NOTE The routes to Windows Server 2008 are less of an issue because Windows 2008 is fully backwardly compatible with Active Directory in earlier Windows Server operating systems.

Active Directory provides or denies logon authority and access privileges to the network resources of a Windows domain. Before we proceed further with Active Directory, it's necessary to get certain information straight about Microsoft domains: we define "domains" in the Windows network sense (as opposed to what you have read about earlier in this chapter) so we all know what we are talking about. Not only should we try to clear up the confusion about domain generations or versions, you will almost certainly have to integrate or migrate legacy NT domains into Windows Server 2008 domains, and unless you understand the differences, you are likely to really foul things up. Philosophically, these are very different.

There are two types of Windows domains: the NT domain (now the legacy domain of the last millennium) and the Windows Server 2008 domain — a container object in Active Directory, a speck on the Internet, and conceptually the extent of your network. Both can be analyzed in terms of a logon "stack," and both share common traits.

Figure 17-18 represents the Windows NT and Windows Server 2008 local logon stack on the local machine and the logical order (from the top down) of the process to authenticate access to the local services. At the top of the domain stack are client processes; these reside on local machines or on other client machines, workstations, and network devices. When the client process requires access to a service, the local Security Account Manager, using data stored in the local SAM, controls the access (this works the same for Windows NT and Windows Server 2008).

FIGURE 17-18

The Windows NT and Windows Server 2008 logon and authentication stacks.

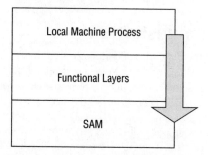

Figure 17-19 represents the Windows domain logon and authentication stack, which encompasses the Windows NT networking environment. The domain logon stack works in the same fashion, but the clients do not log on locally to a machine or network resource. Instead, the OS passes the access request to Active Directory, in Windows Server 2008, or the domain (PDC or BDC) registry (where an accessible copy of the SAM resides), on NT domain controllers.

FIGURE 17-19

The Windows NT and Windows Server 2008 domain logon and authentication stacks.

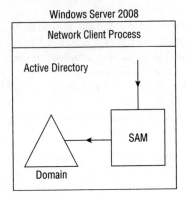
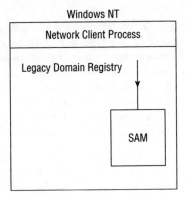

The Windows Server 2008 domain is a single collective, albeit extendable, unit that comprises all the network objects considered to be members. In many respects, the domain structure is one huge distributed container that embraces all your company's networking and IT assets. You can view a domain as a "collective," much as a fleet of ships comprises a flotilla or a navy, or a group of marines comprise a brigade or a corps.

Before we discuss Windows Server 2008 domains, let's discuss some quick similarities, which for many will provide familiar turf. The NT domain begot the Windows Server 2008 domain, and that's probably the best way to compare them (even if the kid somehow came out very different).

Single point of access and administration

NT domains enable an administrator to log on to the network and gain access to the administration tools at a server or workstation (even via scaled-down tools on older versions of the client OS). Users, groups, network devices such as printers and drives, and resources such as folders and sharepoints are accessible to administrators who have been assigned the necessary rights.

Windows Server 2008 domains provide the same single point of access and administration, but with a lot more flexibility to manage resources and users. The OU, for example, is a new entity in the Windows domain that enables you to group users in administrative structures, compart-ments, or diverse organization divisions or management entities. This means it is possible to create units and assign administrative functions to departments. For example, the materials management department is managed under the Mat-Mgt OU, and a user in this OU is assigned administrative rights to manage the contents of this OU and only this OU. This obviates the need to assign everything to a single administrator, or having an admin group with dozens of users gaining access to blanket administration authority on the domain.

Domains and more domains

The Windows network domain represents a logical grouping of computers and devices that are accessible to a group, or groups, of users and computers, regardless of their logon place or posi-tion. The domain provides a means of containing and controlling users on the network and pro-vides a defined boundary and a security shield behind which computers, users, and operators function in a secured environment. Windows Server 2008 domains perform an identical func-tion, as described in later chapters.

If you are new to Windows networking, here's a quick explanation of the Windows network domain: Compare it to a workgroup. When Microsoft launched Windows 3.11 and Windows for Workgroups back in the early 1990s, it provided a means for computers to connect to each other as peers so that each computer could share its resources. You would have to specifically permit access to the resources on a computer before anyone or anything could use it. This is already a pain to do at each computer in a small office of people, because each computer acts as a standalone server and has to be managed as such. Once your network begins to expand, it becomes impractical and well nigh impossible to manage.

The domain, conversely, was born of the capability to locate a central security, login, and access permissions authority on a master server, called the primary domain controller, or PDC. The SAM database, which lives inside the registry, provided a global access to the users in the central security database, to the resources on all the computers, and to devices attached to the network, such as printers, backup drives, and CD-Rs.

Intra-domain trust relationships

The only time you should have had to administer more than one domain in a company (70+ in one company is the record for me) is due to aggressive acquisitions, in which you might inherit domains from the various takeovers. Windows Server 2008 domains are modeled on Internet domains, have depth and perspective, and can be partitioned almost infinitely. They inherently trust each other, in much the same way that family members trust each other under the same roof, even though each person goes about his or her business in his or her own section of the house.

It makes sense to create multiple domains (actually domain extensions or partitions) on a Win-dows Server 2008 network for very different reasons — the most important being devolution of power and delegation of management. As you will see later, you can create domains that encom-pass subnets, sites, departments, locations, and the like. Moreover, as long as your domains are attached to a common ancestor, the domain root, trusts between them are full-blown two-way. Although the term *transitive* relates to two-way trusts that exist between many domains, not only on the same tree, but also across trees in the forest, this naturally does not mean that two domain groups (the forests) can be somehow grafted onto each other like you would two living plants. Still, it's a darn sight easier to migrate, move, and eventually eliminate orphan domains in a forest.

In short, Windows Server 2008 domains are modeled after Internet domains, have dimension, and can be partitioned. The old NT domains, if you remember, were flat.

Access control lists and access tokens

When a user (human or service) logs in to a domain, NT authentication and security management grants the user access to the network and resources it is permitted to use. This is done in the form of ACLs and access tokens. Seasoned or astute NT administrators will recall how it is possible to access and edit the ACL on a local machine. If you do not know how, you will learn later. Windows provides the user (login) with an access token, which the user wears as it browses the network. The access token works like the security badge you wear to work. As you approach doors or devices, they either open for you or deny access. Windows Server 2008 domains both control access using ACLs. In Active Directory, the SAM ACLs (in the directory) control who has access to objects and the scope of that access.

All Windows Server 2008 services are referred to as objects. These objects are either stored in the local Security Account Manager (SAM), which is a registry tree, or Active Directory is controlled by the ACLs. Each ACL contains permissions information, detailing which user can access the object and the type of access allowed (such as read-only or read/write). ACLs are domain-object-bound; they are not transient entities.

Summary

This chapter introduced Active Directory as one of the most impressive components of Windows networking. As applications developers, we need consistent, open, and interoperable interfaces and APIs against which we can store and manage information relating to applications, processes, and services. Many companies have risen to the challenge of providing directories. Directories and directory services will and must be free, open, accessible, and part of the network operating systems and technology we use. Active Directory is all this and then some.

Chapter 18

Planning for Active Directory

This chapter analyzes numerous models in planning for Active Directory and defines potential obstacles that may interrupt your planning process. Planning an Active Directory requires a methodology with a focus on your enterprise or organization's operational needs. You also want to take into consideration the big picture and how it evolves as you integrate new applications with Windows Server 2008. This is a constant battle in the ever-changing technical world. This chapter can help network managers, systems integrators, and consultants prepare for the required tasks and decisions to plan an Active Directory.

Active Directory Overview

Gaining a good understanding of Active Directory is critical before you start your planning. Directory services are nothing more than orderly ways of classifying and managing resources on a network, whether users, printers, servers, or security parameters. Directories become the points of reference for user services and applications. They help find a printer in a field office, locate a user and direct an e-mail, or verify that a user has access rights to a particular file. They also provide Single Sign-On (SSO), which gives a user access to the whole network from a single logon. Directories are becoming increasingly important as business networks expand to include connections with business partners and customers.

Four basic topological components make up the Active Directory structure: *forest topology*, *domain* or *domain tree topology*, *site topology*, and *organizational unit topology*. This chapter will help you create an architecture document that incorporates planning guidelines for each topology, discussing the important decisions throughout the process. This document will then serve as your Active Directory architecture document for both migration and ongoing operations and support.

Basic Design Principles

As you prepare your plan for Active Directory, you should follow a few basic principles to help you through the decision-making process. One of the main principles is to keep it simple. Simple structures are easier to maintain, debug, and explain. You do realize some value in adding complexity, although you must ensure that you weigh the added value derived against the potential maintenance costs.

Certain costs are associated with everything that you create. If you create a structure without a well-defined plan or reason, it could cost you in the long run; you must, therefore, try to justify everything in your structure.

Another main principle is to plan for changes in your organization. Normal changes occur in every organization, from enterprise reorganization or acquisitions to employees moving though the organization. These changes affect your Active Directory structure. You need to plan for these changes and analyze the effects that such changes impose on your structure. Again, try to keep the design simple and general so it can be flexible enough to handle significant changes.

Planning for the ideal structure, even if it does not currently reflect your domain or directory infrastructure, is important. Understanding what the ideal is, in the context of your organization, is useful, even if it is not actually in reach. Most designs require more than one attempt. You can compare multiple designs to devise the best design for your organization.

Active Directory Structure

Windows Server 2008 Standard Server, Enterprise Server, and Datacenter Server provide a directory service called *Active Directory*. Active Directory stores information about objects and enables administrators or users to easily access information. This information is stored in a *datastore* (also known as a *directory*) that provides a logical and hierarchical organization of information. The following plans help you model your Active Directory structure.

A domain plan

You need to consider several characteristics of a domain before attempting to create your domain plan. We discuss each characteristic in more detail in this section, providing you with a better understanding of the planning life cycle.

A *forest* consists of a database, whereby the database partitions are defined by the domains. This database is made up of many small databases spread across computers. Placing the individual databases where the data is most relevant enables a large database to be distributed efficiently. Each of these databases contains *security principal objects*, such as computers, users, and groups. These objects can grant or deny access to resources in your structure and must be authenticated by the domain controller for the particular domain in which the object resides. Objects are thus authenticated before they are eligible to access the resource.

Domain administrators control every object in the domain structure; Group Policy is associated with that domain and does not automatically propagate to other domains in the forest. For the domains and the Group Policy to be associated, they must be explicitly linked, so security policy for a domain user account must be set on a per-domain basis.

> **NOTE** Linking Group Policy across domains is complex, resource intensive, and not very practical. If you are entertaining the idea, then be certain that your domain architecture has gone awry somewhere.

A *domain* is identified by its *DNS name*, which provides a method for you to locate the domain controller for the given domain. This name indicates the domain's position within the forest hierarchy. The following list provides a step-by-step checklist for creating a domain plan for a single forest:

1. Determine the number of domains needed in each forest. Small to medium-size organizations (10 to 500 users) should not need more than one domain. Larger organizations of up to 10,000 users should not require more than a root and single child (resource) domain.

2. Determine the forest root domain.

3. Create a DNS name for each domain.

4. Create a DNS deployment plan.

5. Determine shortcut trust relationships.

6. Plan for changes in the domain and understand the effect of the changes.

7. Create teams to manage the network.

In determining the number of domains for the forest, consider a single-domain model, even if your existing structure has more than one domain. Several factors dictate that you create more than one domain, such as preserving the existing domain structure, administrative partitioning, and physical partitioning. Try to keep the plan simple if at all possible. If you can justify more than one domain, you need to detail this justification for administration purposes. Remember that adding additional domains has additional costs associated with it, in the form of additional management and administrative burden.

If, by chance, you still have NT domains in place, you may prefer to keep them as they are instead of consolidating them into Active Directory. If you decide to keep the NT domains, you should weigh the cost of maintaining more domains against the cost of migrating to Active Directory.

After you determine the number of domains that you need in your new forest, you need to determine the *forest root domain*. The *root domain* is the first domain created in the forest.

Forestwide groups, enterprise administrators, and schema administrators are placed in this domain. If your plan calls for only one domain, that domain will be your forest root. Consider the following possibilities in selecting the root domain:

- **Selecting an existing domain.** Usually, this domain is a critical part of your operation, and your organization cannot afford to lose this domain.

- **Selecting a dedicated domain.** This type of root domain serves solely as the root. It is an additional domain created for this purpose only.

After determining your root domain, you need to determine the *DNS naming structure* for your domains. DNS is globally recognized and can be easily registered. These DNS names are used by clients requesting access to the network to locate domain controllers. In creating your DNS hierarchy, you can divide your domains into trees, because a *tree* is a set of one or more contiguous named domains. (The names are contiguous because the names are different by only one label.)

Shortcut trusts are two-way transitive trusts that enable you to shorten the path in a complex forest. You explicitly create shortcut trusts between domains in the same forest. A shortcut trust is a performance optimization that shortens the trust path Windows security takes for authentication purposes. The most effective use of shortcut trusts is between two domain trees in a forest.

Shortcut trusts create performance optimizations that shorten the trust path for security. Consider the following: If a user requests access to a network resource, then the user's domain controller must communicate with the resource's controller. Considering that, you need to understand that the two domains must be related in a parent-child relationship; otherwise, the user's domain controller cannot communicate efficiently with the resource's domain controller. Depending on the network location of the controllers for that domain, the authentication hop between the two domains can potentially increase the chance of a failure. To reduce the chances of this happening, you can create a shortcut trust between the two domains, enabling them to communicate.

If you must change the domain plan after deployment, this is not a task to determine overnight. Domain hierarchies are not easily restructured after creation. Try to plan for such a contingency so that you don't end up creating only a short-lived domain structure. Put a lot of thought into your domain design, and it will pay off in the long run.

Site topology

The *site topology* is layered on top of the physical network that reflects the underlying network topology. The domain structure sits above the site topology, but below the network layer. Making a clear distinction between the domain structure and site topology plans is important. Domains contain objects, whereas sites reflect user groups. The domain is mapped to the site by placing a replica of the domain in the site, so the site contains the entire domain.

The site topology routes query and replication traffic efficiently and helps you determine where to place domain controllers within your structure. The site is known as a set of IP subnets; these subnets usually have LAN speed or better. Site links are used in the plan to model the available bandwidth between the sites. These links are usually slower than LAN speed. The following four parameters make up a site link:

- **Transport.** Used for replication.
- **Cost.** Determines the paths of replication.
- **Replication schedule.** Helps indicate when the link is available for replication traffic.
- **Replication interval.** Polls the domain controllers at the opposite end of the site link for replication changes.

After the user starts his or her computer, the computer communicates with the domain controller of the user's member domain. The user's site is then determined by the domain controller, based on the computer's IP address, which returns the name of the site to the user's computer. This information is cached and used for future queries. *Replication* uses the site topology to generate replication connections. A built-in process known as the *Knowledge Consistency Checker* (KCC) creates and maintains replication connections between domain controllers. The site topology is used to guide creation of the connections. *Intrasite replication* tunes the replication, while *intersite communication* minimizes bandwidth usage. Table 18-1 displays the differences in the site replication patterns.

TABLE 18-1

Differences between Intersite Replication and Intrasite Replication

Intersite Replication	Intrasite Replication
Bridgehead servers maintain replication connections.	Connections are made between two domain controllers located in the same site.
No compression is used to save processor time.	Compression is used to save bandwidth.
Partners notify one another if changes need to be replicated.	Partners do not notify one another.
Replication uses the remote procedure call transport.	Replication uses the SMTP or TCP/IP transport.

You need to consider a few processes before starting your plan. Make sure that you define sites and site links by using your network's physical topology as the beginning point. You may also consult the team manager for your TCP/IP and forest planning group. These managers should be involved in this process. In creating the topology for your forest, again use the physical topology of your network for reference. Keep this plan as simple as possible, based on your current bandwidth. Refer to the following section before you commit to creating your plan.

A forest plan

The *forest* is one of the main components of the Active Directory. It provides a collection of Active Directory domains. Forests serve two main purposes: simplifying user management within the directory and simplifying user interaction within the directory.

A few main characteristics also apply to the Active Directory: the *single configuration container*, the *schema*, *trusts*, and *global catalogs*. The *configuration container* supplies replication to all domain controllers in a forest. This container holds information about directory-aware applications that pertain to a forest, while the *schema* defines object classes and attributes of the object. These classes define types of objects that are created in a directory. The schema is then replicated to every domain controller. A *trust* automatically creates a two-way, transitive relationship between the forest and the domain and can be seen by any other group or user in all the domains in the trust. The *global catalog* (GC) contains every object in all domains in the forest, although it can see only a select set of object attributes, enabling fast, efficient full-forest searches. The GC also provides a seamless presentation to end users.

We suggest starting with a single-forest scenario, which is sufficient in most situations. Remember to keep the structure simple unless you can justify the creation of additional forests. If you create a single forest, all users can see a single directory in the GC; they are, therefore, oblivious to the structure of the forest. The trust is automatically created for you, and configuration changes need to be applied only once. They flow through all forests.

If your design requires administration across divisions within your organization, you may be required to create multiple forests. Remember that for each additional forest, you face an additional cost. Figure 18-1 represents a multiple forest configuration.

FIGURE 18-1

A multiple forest configuration.

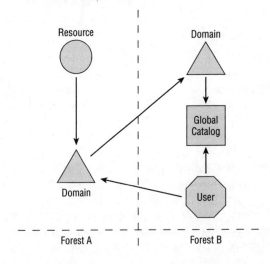

 Additional forests must contain at least one domain, thereby causing additional costs. This is why we stress keeping the plan simple.

The user who searches the GC in Forest B for a resource in Forest A can locate the requested resources and obtain direct access to the resource because of a one-way trust.

As you are determining how many forests are required, keep the users' needs in mind and not those of the administrators. Do not create multiple forests to solve administrative problems because this setup could possibly distort the users' view of the forests. In certain cases, however, such as where having a consistent view is not important for the users, this type of setup is tolerable.

Each forest that you create should have an associated *forest change control policy* as part of your forest-plan document. You use this policy to guide changes that have forestwide effects. You do not need to determine the individual processes before continuing, but understanding their ownership is important. The policy should include information about each of the shared elements in a forest.

Monitoring or setting up a schema change policy is also important. This policy would include the team names that control the schema administration, the total number of members of the group, and the guidelines for schema changes. You should also devise a configuration change policy that consists of the same policies as the schema policy, adding guidelines for creating or changing domains for the forest and modifying the topology.

A trust plan

The first step in creating a *trust plan* is to determine when you need to create a *trust* for your forest. If you create a forest trust between two forests, Windows Server 2008 by default creates a transitive relationship between every domain residing in the forest. Trusts are created only between the forest root in one directory and the forest root of another directory.

Before creating a forest trust, you need to ensure that all your domain controllers are running Windows Server 2008. The functional level must be set to Windows Server 2008, and you should verify that you have the correct DNS structure in place. The DNS structure must be authoritative for both forest DNS servers in which you want to create your trust, or you can create a DNS forwarder on both servers. (Refer to Chapter 3 for more information on DNS forwarding.) The following checklist can help you ensure that you follow the correct procedure in planning for a trust:

- Make sure that you have a good understanding of the various trust types.
- Make sure that your DNS structure is set up correctly for the trust.
- Make sure that your functional level is set to Windows Server 2008.

To create a trust, you must have enterprise administrator's rights on both forests. The new trusts each have their own password, which the administrators of both forests must know.

> **NOTE** To determine the forest root, you can use the ADSI edit tool to connect to the configuration container. The domain that contains the configuration container is the root. This tool is installed when you create an AD domain.

An organizational unit plan

An *organizational unit* (OU) is the container in which you create structure within a domain. Consider the following characteristics in planning an OU.

The OU can be *nested*, enabling you to create a hierarchical tree structure inside the domain. OUs are also used to delegate administration and control access to directory objects, thus enabling you to delegate the administration of objects in the directory in a very granular manner. Remember that OUs are not security principals, so you cannot make the OU a member of a security group.

You can associate OUs with Group Policy, enabling you to define desktop configurations such as users and computers. You can also associate Group Policy with domains, sites, and OUs, enabling you to use different policies in the same domain.

In defining your plan, you do not need to consider the end users. An end user can navigate through resources in an organizational-unit structure, but is not likely to do so because of the availability of the GC.

Planning for the Active Directory Enterprise

You need to have a good understanding of forests and trees before you can start planning for the naming conventions in your organization. Consider organizational growth in doing such planning. A good convention using meaningful names propagates down through all levels of your Active Directory.

Naming strategy plan

The organizational naming structure that you choose can reflect your company's organizational chart. Figure 18-2 shows a typical organizational naming structure of this type.

The naming structure shown in Figure 18-2 allows for growth, but also has some disadvantages. What if your company rewrites the organizational chart frequently? If this is the case in your organization, you can expect to reconstruct your network frequently. If the thought of such frequent restructuring scares you, this plan is not for you.

A *geographical naming structure* may be new to you. Depending on the size of your organization, this type of plan may or may not fit your needs. This plan separates your organization by location into manageable units. Figure 18-3 shows a simple geographical model.

FIGURE 18-2

An organizational naming structure.

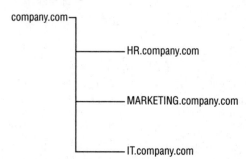

company.com
├──── HR.company.com
├──── MARKETING.company.com
└──── IT.company.com

FIGURE 18-3

A geographical naming structure.

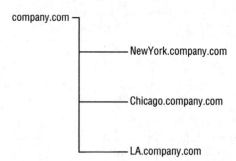

company.com
├──── NewYork.company.com
├──── Chicago.company.com
└──── LA.company.com

The geographical model tends to be consistent. After all, the names of the cities used in Figure 18-3 are not going to change anytime soon. This model tends to be more flexible compared to the organizational model. The major disadvantage is that geographical naming doesn't represent your company's true structure.

Another possibility is a mixture of the preceding two models. Because both models have some advantages and disadvantages, using the mixed-model approach may prove a benefit to your company. Figure 18-4 displays a simple mixed model. (The size and diversity of your organization greatly affects your naming schema.)

Generally, in the mixed model, the first domain is assigned a DNS name; then, for every child of the existing domain, you use *x.dnsname.com*. Make sure that you use only the Internet standard characters, defined in the Request for Comments (RFC) 1123 as A-Z, a-z, 0-9, and the hyphen. Doing so ensures that your Active Directory complies with standard software. Using the preceding models as guides, you should have sufficient information to create your own plan for a naming schema.

FIGURE 18-4

A mixture of the organizational and geographical naming models.

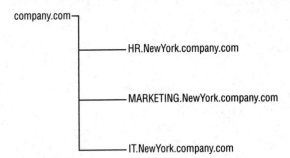

company.com

     HR.NewYork.company.com

     MARKETING.NewYork.company.com

     IT.NewYork.company.com

Domain and organizational units plan

In planning your OUs, first examine your company's organizational structure and administrative requirements so that you can form your company's OU structure. This examination helps you determine when creating an OU is appropriate. The following list shows a few different reasons for creating OUs:

- **Simplify resource administration.** OUs are essentially container objects that store printers, file shares, users, groups, and other OUs. By assigning permissions at the container level, you are essentially assigning the permission to each of the OU's stored objects.

- **Delegation of administrative tasks.** Grouping objects such as users, computers, and groups into an OU helps you define a distinct area of administration for delegation.

- **Helps divide users with policy requirements.** OUs help keep objects with identical security requirements together.

You must always create your first-level OUs unique to a domain. Doing so provides consistency throughout your structure. You have no limit to the number of OUs that you can put in a hierarchy, but the shallower your OU hierarchy, the better your administrators can understand it. Whenever you create an OU, make sure that it is meaningful, keeping in mind who is going to administer and view the OU.

Your organizational needs drive the OU hierarchy. We discuss in this section several common models that may help you determine your OU hierarchy. Remember that you may need to combine several of these models to complete your hierarchy.

The first model that we discuss is the geographic model. This model organizes your resources by location. Figure 18-5 shows North America, Europe, and Asia as examples of OUs. In using location as the factor for placing your OUs, you are laying the foundation for the OU organizational tree.

FIGURE 18-5

A geographic organizational model.

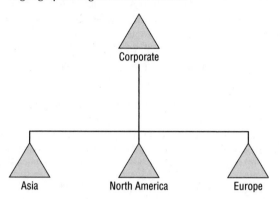

Geographic boundaries remain stable, helping administrators easily identify where resources are located. This model may not exactly mirror your business practices, but you may still want to use this model, making minor modifications to the design as necessary for your organization.

The *organizational model* divides OUs by department. This model looks similar to the geographic model, except that you are using your organization's structure to build your model. Because this model is based on your company's organizational structure, it is easily understandable by administrators, making the task of delegating administration easy. Departments can change, but that is not a problem because the OUs are easily reorganized.

The *object-based model* is divided by object classes. Generally, these divisions would include your users, computers, groups, printers, and shares. This model helps make resource administration easier because OUs are designed by object types. Using this model may produce potentially larger numbers of OUs.

Remember that OUs are the smallest scope or unit to which you can assign Group Policy or delegate administration, thereby enabling you to manage resources based on your organizational model and to give administrators the capability to delegate administration on all OUs or a single OU.

Branch office plan

A *branch office plan* consists of numerous branch offices, with links to a corporate hub. It can be deployed in both large and small corporate environments. This plan covers only the branch office plan's basics; for corporate branch environments, you need to spend additional time planning, configuring, and monitoring for a smooth transition to branch offices.

Structural planning

Domain and forest partitions make up the two main pieces of the structural planning process. The two main reasons why most administrators partition their Active Directory structure are to accommodate political organizational legal restrictions and to keep objects organized. If your organization does not agree on resource management and a common schema, you need to deploy multiple forests. In deploying multiple forests, you are greatly increasing your administrative requirements. Your organization would likely have two options if separate security boundaries exist.

If the business units can acknowledge that no security isolation between domains is necessary and can agree on common operations and security guidelines, then create a single forest. If your organization has a requirement for isolated domains, however, then you need to create multiple domains. You are unlikely to exceed the number of possible objects for one forest. You can support many forests, assuming that your hardware supports such a need.

Domain partitioning is the second piece of the structural-planning element. There are several advantages and disadvantages to creating both a single and multiple domain directory. You can reduce the amount of data that is replicated during DomainNamingContext replication, thereby increasing the amount of global-catalog data that is replicated. The general amount of network traffic is reduced if you're using the multiple-domain structure. We suggest that you keep your plan to a single domain if your WAN can carry the load. Remember to keep the plan simple if possible.

Replication planning

Active Directory replication and SYSVOL replication represent the two major components of domainwide and forestwide replication. These two components use the same replication topology, but are run independently from one another. File replication system (FRS) SYSVOL replication starts as soon as a replication window is opened, whereas Active Directory randomly starts within the first 15 minutes of a replication window opening. Active Directory replication with multiple partners, therefore, starts at different times within that 15-minute interval, whereas the FRS SYSVOL starts at the same time for all partners.

Active Directory uses serialized inbound replication, whereby inbound replication is incoming data transferred from a replication partner to a domain controller. Because the data is serialized, the hub domain controller can handle inbound replication with one branch domain controller. This plays a big part in determining the number of bridgehead servers that your organization needs. A bridgehead server should not have more than 50 simultaneous active replication connections at any given time. Try to keep the number lower than 50, which provides a significant effect on CPU utilization, network throughput, and I/O throughput. Data transfer from a domain controller to the replication partner is considered to be outbound replication. Outbound replication is not serialized, but it is multithreaded, thus causing the branch controller to pull changes from the hub domain controller.

The *file replication system* (FRS) is used by system policies and logon scripts stored in SYSVOL, causing domain controllers to keep SYSVOL for network clients to access. The FRS is a multithreaded, multimaster replication engine, meaning that changes to the SYSVOL can be made on any controller, with the controller then replicating the changes. FRS SYSVOL uses the timestamps on a file to determine the latest version of that file to distribute.

In determining your choice of bridgehead servers, you must first understand which servers should be bridgeheads. You also must understand the different load implications placed on a server depending on the replication type. Inbound bridgehead servers in a hub site travel through the list of replication partners one by one after the replication window opens. If the connection is slow and the window closes before the controller has finished replicating, it continues replicating until it is finished, potentially causing problems with the inbound sequences. Outbound replication is performed in parallel. The only limiting factors, therefore, are the performance of the bridgehead servers, CPU load, and disk I/O. In deciding how many bridgehead servers are needed, use inbound and outbound connections as the basis for the determination.

Hub site planning

Building the data center is the first step in the planning process, which includes configuration of DNS, root domain controllers, and bridgehead servers. Branch offices are usually connected through slow links to the hub, so setup of the domain controller first would mean replicating the whole directory. We don't think that you want to wait for that to occur. In many cases, no operations staff is located at the branches, so no one is willing to install and configure the domain controller. You have the option of using Terminal Services, but you still may need to be onsite to perform some configuration.

Administrators can install domain controllers in a central location, enabling quick creation of the domain controllers, and then ship them out to the branch offices. This location where the domain controllers are installed and configured can be a data center but usually is a staging site. You must consider the differences between the sites — for example, their TCP/IP and link speeds. If hundreds of computers are to be set up, then it's preferable to do this in one location (staging site), where the process has been proven and tools and experienced personnel are on hand. The setup process can cause increases in traffic for initial setup, so the staging site must have fast links for the replication process.

In building the root domain, make sure that the forest root domain controller is the first domain controller installed. Then the GC server must be installed; at least one domain controller in the forest domain must be the GC. The first domain controller that we installed was the GC server. We therefore installed GC on the domain controllers in the root domain. The GC role should be left on this computer. Additional domain controllers in the root domain should be only domain controllers. The forest root domain is special; it is the root of the Active Directory namespace. DNS configuration for the forest root domain controller is slightly different from all other domain controllers. DNS servers in the forest root domain (as long as they are domain controllers) hold a master copy of the _msdcs, which is used to store the CNAME records for replication. (The CNAME record is an entry in your DNS table that specifies another domain to which the user would be redirected.) You want to avoid isolation of a forest root domain controller after a configuration change; these DNS servers need to be configured to use another DNS server as the primary DNS server. You need at least two forest root domain controllers in the hub site, pointing to each other as primary DNS servers.

Five operation master roles exist in the root domain: the schema master, the domain naming master, the primary domain controller (PDC) emulator, the infrastructure master, and the relative ID (RID) master. The schema-master domain controller controls all updates to the schema. For you to update the schema of the forest, you must have access to the schema master. Only one schema master exists in the entire forest. The domain-naming master controls the addition or removal of the domains in the forest. The infrastructure master is responsible for updating references from objects in its domain to objects in other domains. The RID master processes all pool requests for the domain controllers of a particular domain. The PDC advertises itself as the primary domain controller to workstations, member servers, and domain controllers that are running earlier versions of Windows.

The root domain is usually a small domain, keeping the load to a minimum. On a small domain, you should try to keep all roles on one server so that whenever you take the server down, transferring the roles to a different domain is easy. On a larger network comprising several hub sites that service large centers of the employee population, such as our example Millennium City, you will need to install root domain controllers in each of the central hub sites.

You need to plan for recovery because the root domain is a crucial part in the Active Directory forest. It maintains the schema and the configuration information. If the root domain is lost, operations requiring the root domain do not operate correctly. Securing at least one domain controller of the root domain is of utmost importance. (Refer to Chapter 8 for more information on disaster recovery.)

Site staging planning

Your staging site can either be a separate site in your data center that helps you in preparing new domain controllers, or it can possibly be contracted out to a third-party company for staging. If you have hundreds of computers to be manufactured, the best practice is to do all staging in one location. Your tools are then in one location for easy access, debugging, and configuration. This also helps your replication traffic, as branch offices generally have slower links that can cost you valuable time.

A staging site has a set of requirements that must be adhered to for successful staging. You must have at least one permanent domain controller in the staging site for replication of the new domain controllers. You also must have a permanent network connection between the staging site and the hub. Finally, this site must be large enough to handle all the new domain controllers. By providing a domain controller in the staging site, you can use it to replicate the existing directory while the installation wizard is running. The network connection provides the server configuration to the new domain controllers. It's a good idea to keep domain controllers online for a while before they are shipped so that the RID pool is delivered, replication has sufficient time to complete, file-replication service replication succeeds, SYSVOL is shared, and the domain controller can advertise itself. You need a staging site that enables you to have sufficient time to complete the preceding processes and provide enough physical space for all your needs.

Domain controller planning

Building a domain controller and then shipping it to the final destination can cause many problems. Many things can be done wrong if the domain controllers are built in a location that is different from the destination location. Risks are involved in even the most thought-out plans. Consider the following pre-staging steps.

You need to install the correct operating system with the correct service packs, all troubleshooting tools, and monitoring tools. You may also have some in-house products that may need installation, depending on your organization. You need to verify that the preceding step was successful, as well as promote the server to a domain controller. You also need to verify that the promotion was successful and leave the computer online in the staging site. You then need to prepare your computer for transportation to its final destination.

In a perfect world, your new servers and domain controllers would be installed from a new image. This process is fast and less error prone. You should also document the software releases that were installed. Perform configuration and prepare a checklist. Make sure that you verify that the computer name, DNS configuration, and IP configuration are all correct. Whenever the server is ready to be promoted to a domain controller, run the Active Directory Installation Wizard to promote the server. Specify the domain controller that is to be used to provide initial replication. As you install the domain controller into the staging site, it is automatically configured. Verifying that the new domain controller is replicating correctly with the rest of the domain controllers is crucial.

Before you prepare to pack and ship your server to its destination, verify that each domain controller is correctly configured.

Administration Planning

Administration planning provides you with an understanding of your server administration needs. This section covers topics from delegating administration to building an administration hierarchy. This section should provide you with the information that you need to build your total administration plan. The point is to make administration as easy to manage as possible by preparing an administration plan.

Delegating administration

The main capability of Active Directory in Windows Server 2008 is the delegation of administration. Through this process, you can design a directory infrastructure to span multiple organizations that require unique management requirements. This helps your organization meet specific requirements for operational and structural independence. Administrators can delegate service management and data management to achieve isolation between organizations.

Many reasons exist to delegate administration, and you should understand why organizations may want to delegate administration. Table 18-2 describes several such reasons.

TABLE 18-2

Reasons to Delegate Administration

Reason	Description
Organizational structure	Provide the capability to operate independently from the organization
Legal requirements	Provide the capability to restrict access to sensitive information
Operational requirements	Provide the capability to place unique constraints on configuration, availability, and security

The administrative responsibilities that are delegated can be separated into two main categories, *service management* and *data management*. Service management generates responsibility for delivery of the directory service, and data management provides responsibility for the content stored in the directory service. The service administrator is responsible for administering service management, and the data administrator is responsible for the data management.

Delegating forests, trees, and organizational units

Three structures are used to delegate administration in forests, trees, and OUs. You need to know when selecting a structure based on the delegation requirements is appropriate. You should fully understand the preceding section before continuing.

The forest administrator is a member of a Domain Admins group and has control over the Enterprise Admins and the Schema Admins groups. This, by default, gives the forest administrator total control over the forestwide configuration settings. The forest owner, therefore, controls the domain controllers, which gives the forest owner the service administrator title. Domain Admins have control over domain controllers, giving them by default the title of service administrator. The OU object is controlled by the Access Control List; users and groups that have control over objects in the OU, therefore, are data administrators.

Implementing object security

Active Directory objects (such as files and registry entries) have security identifiers associated with each object. This association creates a security-identifier presence, indicating that the resources in the directory can be secured in the same manner that files can be secured. By assigning a security identifier to each of the objects, you are essentially granting read and write privileges to the object, to a grouping of properties, or to individual properties of that object. You therefore give administrators a granular-type control over the updating procedures of these objects and the users who can maintain and update the objects.

Simple and multilevel inheritance

Active Directory object permissions are automatically inherited, causing objects in one container to inherit the permissions of that container or parent container. This form of inheritance is enabled by default to help minimize object administration.

This design of permission inheritance flows downward in the hierarchy to the object's child objects, if they exist. If you create an OU named *marketing*, for example, and you permit the Marketing Admin group to have Full Control rights to the marketing OU, after the child units are created they inherit the same permission settings, and the group administrator has Full Control permissions to the objects as well.

> **NOTE** The domain and enterprise administrators have full reign in the following situation: They can enable or deny permissions for every object in the Active Directory, as can any other owners of the objects.

You can prevent this type of inheritance if you want to set a different level of security access to the child container than that of the parent container.

Defining object visibility in Active Directory

Object visibility is determined by the group scope that also determines what type of objects can be contained within a group. Three group scopes can essentially determine an object's visibility: *universal*, *global*, and *domain local*. Members of universal groups can include other accounts and groups from any domain in the tree or forest; security groups cannot be created if using this type of scope when in native mode. They can, therefore, grant permissions in any of the domains that belong to that tree or forest. Global groups could contain other accounts or groups from the domain in which the group is defined; they also have the capability to grant permissions to any domain in the forest. The domain local group incorporates groups and accounts from Windows Server 2008, Windows 2000, or NT. These groups can be granted permissions only within their respective domains.

Administrative roles

The administration team manages and maintains requirements as the system grows to meet your organization's needs. Depending on the size of your organization, the team may consist of one or two individuals or a series of interdependent groups. You need to identify who is going to perform administrative tasks such as account management and daily operations.

Efficient enterprisewide group nesting

OUs can be nested to create a hierarchy in a domain structure. This structure is independent of the domain structure, enabling each domain to create its own hierarchy. OUs don't seem to affect performance. Group Policy can be applied to these OUs to give administrators granularity in their administration of security.

Building the administrative hierarchy

Active Directory administration increases in complexity and difficulty with each administration level. The goal is to minimize the cost of administration while providing a high level of service. Table 18-3 describes each tier of the administration model.

TABLE 18-3

Three-Tier Administration Model

Administration Tier	Description
First-tier	Provides day-to-day administrative tasks such as creating users, help-desk support, and working with end users.
Second-tier	Provides in-depth knowledge of the organization's network and server apps. Administrators at this level are experts at problem-solving and are required to use monitoring and troubleshooting tools.
Third-tier	Handles critical or cross-application problems that may be escalated to this level from the first or second tiers. Evaluates and rolls new server applications.

System administration may not always be clearly defined, as shown in Table 18-3. You usually find a hierarchy of administration based on the skills and experience of the administrator.

Migration Planning

During the migration planning stage, you make several important choices. These choices determine the functionality of certain features. We hope to help you make your migration choices much easier by covering the two main concepts of migration: *upgrades* and *restructuring*. Depending on your organization, you may need to upgrade first and then restructure, or restructure first and then upgrade. This section should help you make these choices and help you complete your migration plan while identifying some areas of risk.

Upgrade plan

Upgrading from Windows 2000 or Windows Server 2003 to Windows Server 2008 enables you to take full advantage of the new features without restructuring your network configuration. Your existing directory service remains intact and provides you with improved group replication, application directory partitions, forest trust relationships, group caching, and an improved intersite replication-topology generator.

The three main tasks that you need to document in preparing your upgrade plan to Windows Server 2008 are *pre-upgrading*, *upgrading*, and *post-upgrading*. The pre-upgrading task takes you through all the necessary precautions that occur with a Windows Server 2008 upgrade. The pre-upgrade task's main points are securing all domain data and preparing your infrastructure.

The first task in pre-upgrading requires you to secure your domain data. This task may vary depending on the operations and procedures in your organization. You should at least allow for successful replication between two domain controllers in each domain, perform a full backup of all the domain controllers, and then successfully test all backups to make sure that they are not corrupt.

The second task in pre-upgrading requires you to prepare your infrastructure for the upgrade. The first step to completing this task is to successfully use the Active Directory preparation tool (ADPrep.exe) on the schema master to prepare the forest, and then once on the infrastructure master in each domain. Make sure this program successfully executes or Windows Server 2008 setup fails.

Use the following list to serve as a checklist for the pre-upgrading plan:

- Back up all domain data and verify its validity.
- Use the ADPrep tool to prepare your forest and check for successful completion.
- Use the ADPrep tool to prepare your domain and check for successful completion.

The next step in planning your upgrade consists of the upgrade itself. This task involves installing Active Directory, upgrading the first domain, and upgrading the remaining domains. You can plan to upgrade your Active Directory installation by using the Active Directory Installation Wizard. The wizard enables you to create an additional domain controller and join it to existing domains, to configure the local server, to create directory partitions, or to install and configure DNS. By completing this task, you have a domain controller.

 **After installing Active Directory, allow sufficient time for replication to take place and for all member servers to synchronize with the new member server.**

After you have allowed time for the replication to synchronize with the other domain controllers, you should upgrade your first domain controller. Then follow that by upgrading the remaining controllers.

As a checklist for the upgrading plan, make sure that you install Active Directory, upgrade your first domain, and follow that first upgrade by upgrading the remaining domains. You now need to follow up all the upgrading steps with your post-upgrade task. If you completed the preceding upgrade task successfully, you are now ready to raise the forest and domain functional levels. By default, the forest automatically functions at the Windows 2000 native functional level. If all your domains in the forest are in Windows 2000 native mode, raising the functional level of your forest to Windows Server 2008 automatically raises the domains' functional level.

As a checklist for the upgrading plan, make sure that you raise domain functional levels to Windows Server 2008 and also raise forest functional levels to Windows Server 2008.

Restructuring plan

Determining when to restructure is an important part of this plan. You need to restructure if your existing NT or Windows Server 200X structure does not fit your target structure. You may also want to migrate gradually, maintaining your backward compatibility. Before you make your decision, consider the following questions. Are you currently unhappy with your structure and believe that you could carry out a two-phase migration: upgrade to Windows Server 2008 and then restructure to fix any problems? Do you feel that you can't maintain a production environment while migrating to a new environment?

If your response to either of the preceding questions is yes, you should seriously consider restructuring. The main reason for restructuring is to maintain a network design in an ever-changing organization. Suppose you have department A and department B, each of which has its own individual domains, but then the departments decide to merge. In NT, you could create a trust between the two servers, but the two servers can never truly merge without re-creating all the users in one of the domains. Windows 2000 and Windows Server 2008 provide a much easier interface for restructuring Active Directory to match the changing organization. Combining can still be a lot of work, but with Windows Server 2008, you never need to resort to reformatting the server.

As is the case with most types of network restructuring, you can't just sit down and revamp the entire network. You must plan your changes and determine how the changes may affect the network. You need to familiarize yourself with the tools used for restructuring Active Directory.

Migration tools

The `ADPrep.exe` tool is essential in preparing Active Directory for Windows Server 2008. It prepares the forest and domain for an Active Directory upgrade by performing a collection of operations before the first domain controller is installed. This tool is located on the Windows Server 2008 CD (in the sources folder).

Current and old schema merge, preserving the previous schema modifications in your environment. You can run `ADPrep /forestprep` in a forest to accomplish the necessary forest preparation and `ADPrep /domainprep` to prepare a domain. To prepare the schema operations master, run `ADPrep /forestprep`.

 The `ADPrep` program creates a log file each time that it executes. This log file helps you troubleshoot errors that may occur and documents each step of the preparation process.

Test-lab plan

The test-lab plan is designed to help you prepare your testing strategy, basing it on a realistic scenario. In a test environment, you definitely need a realistic scenario that simulates your production environment. By preparing this scenario, you can verify your assumptions and uncover problems while optimizing the design. In doing so, you are verifying your plan and reducing your risk of errors and downtime.

Depending on your environment, you may even spread your test environments across numerous physical or even geographical locations. Several elements influence the type of lab that you choose, such as physical space or environmental limitations, budget, time and staff available for building the lab, existing labs, corporate culture, and the project's or corporation's goals. Based on the previous elements, you have two types of labs to choose from — an *Ad Hoc lab* and a *Change Management lab*. The Ad Hoc lab provides specific project testing. After the project ends, the equipment can be redeployed, used for a production environment, or returned to the vendor. The total cost of ownership (TCO) for an Ad Hoc lab varies, depending on the number of projects that you need it for, but the equipment can be redeployed, essentially keeping the TCO low. The Change Management lab presents a permanent environment. At first glance, you may think that the TCO for a permanent lab would be greater than that for the Ad Hoc lab, but if you view it across projects, the cost of a permanent lab is likely to be more reasonable. Ad Hoc labs are hard to track, and financial accountability is diluted. Change Management labs can be used in the following test environments:

- Network upgrades
- Service packs and software patches
- Business application compatibility
- Desktop configurations
- New hardware platforms
- Administrative and support processes
- Client computer management tools

In determining what model fits your goals, if circumstances (such as your budget) seem to dictate an approach other than the one that you consider the best, try to come up with creative ways to support your solution.

After you make the decision for the correct lab model for your environment, make sure that your lab simulates the full environment. You need to prepare a list of information about your environment that helps you design the lab. This list can include your current or new logical and physical network design, features that you want to explore and evaluate, administrative tools to explore or evaluate, and service packs, server drivers, and server bios that you need to configure and test.

This list needs to be able to grow, depending on your own test-lab needs. After you compile your list and determine your test-lab design, focus on documentation. We know that this is hard to do, but it can prove essential and helps keep lab users current regarding design changes. Testers can use lab descriptions and diagrams whenever they design test-case scenarios to ensure completeness in the testing plan.

Backup and recovery plan

Backing up your Active Directory on a regular basis is critical. The Backup tool provides several features that keep this process simple. You should integrate your Active Directory backup routine into your regular server backup procedures without causing interruption to the network.

The Backup tool enables you to back up the domain controller while it is still online, causing no user interruption. The backup should consist of Active Directory, along with old system files and data files. The Backup tool provides methods for backing up the data that are supported for a normal backup. The normal backup marks each file as having been backed up and truncates the log files of database applications.

Before you attempt to make a backup, document the existing structure, including the resource registry keys that map to resources. We also suggest that you catalog your backups and create a repair disk for each node that you can use for restoring that node, if necessary. You should use the Backup tool to create emergency repair disks in case the system files become corrupted or damaged.

The Backup tool should back up all the system components and all distributed services on which Active Directory depends. This data is known as the *dependent data*, which is collectively known as the *system state data*. This data encompasses the system startup files, the system registry, the class registration database, file replication, the certificate database, the domain name system, and Active Directory. Therefore, whenever you use the Backup tool, you cannot back up Active Directory alone; all the system state data must be backed up. We recommend that you schedule regular backups and keep them well documented.

You have two basic plans for restoring Active Directory. The first plan involves reinstalling Windows Server 2008 as a domain controller and then enabling the other domain controllers to populate Active Directory through replication. This plan keeps Active Directory in its current state.

The second plan is to restore the directory from the backup location. This automatically restores Active Directory to its last backed-up state. You have three options in restoring from backup: primary, normal, and authoritative restore.

The *primary restore* option is used for restoring servers of a replicated data set (SYSVOL and FRS). This should be used only if you are restoring the first replica set to the network. You should never use primary restore if you have already restored one or more of the replica sets; this restore should be your first replica restore. Primary restore is typically used if all domain controllers in the domain are lost.

The *normal restore* option is used in a nonauthoritative state. This restore keeps all original update sequence numbers intact, enabling replication to use this number to detect and propagate in the servers. If newer data is available from other servers, the newer data replicates to the server.

To use the *authoritative restore* option, you need to run the `Ntdsutil` utility after you restore the system state data, but before you restart the server. This utility enables you to mark objects for authoritative restore and automatically updates the sequence number so that the data is new. You are, therefore, replicating through the server, thus ensuring that you replace the data with restored data.

> **CAUTION** If you decide to restore your system state data but you forget to designate a different location for the data, the backup erases the data and restores the system state data from backup. You therefore lose any data that was not on the backup.

Deploying the Plan

After creating the appropriate plan for your Active Directory scenario, you need to organize your deployment team, based on their skill sets, and assign specific roles to the team members. The team should now be able to make projections on deploying the plan for your organization and on the final rollout. You then need to prepare a schedule and budget to meet the needs of your plan. If your plan requires additional resources, those issues need to be addressed and dealt with.

Summary

This chapter takes you through the basic planning process of Active Directory and the pieces that make up the directory. Depending on your organization, you may need to build your own scenario. Several planning steps and stages are discussed in this chapter, which we summarized into a basic plan that you can use for your own organization. We mention many times that you should try to keep your plan simple and consider alternative measures if needed, although doing so is not always possible.

The next chapter provides the information that you need to build your logical domain structure.

Chapter 19

Organizing a Logical Domain Structure

I f you've read Chapter 18, you are probably pretty psyched about Active Directory, and you probably thought that we were nuts in the opening chapters of this book, where we urged you not to install Active Directory and to deploy standalone servers until you are at home with the new operating system. In this chapter, we are going to go overboard. We are going to tell you *not* to build your new domain until you have read this chapter, done a psychoanalysis of your company, and designed your domain on a whiteboard or a math pad and come up with a blueprint.

While Windows Server 2008 provides a way for you to rename your current domains by using the Active Directory domain-rename tools, we still believe that documenting your domain structure before creating the physical structure is very important.

Before you start, know that if you delete from the server either the root domain or the last domain on a domain tree (a process known as *demotion*), then you uninstall the namespace. If you screw up the namespace and decide, after many hours of hard work, that you started wrong, you could end up losing all those hours that you spent creating user and computer accounts and configuring domain controllers. In addition, if you go into production, you also take down several colleagues. We thus offer you a mini-guide to enterprise analysis in this chapter in the hope that, as you get ready to break ground, you don't slice your toes off in the process.

IN THIS CHAPTER

Planning the logical domain structure

Partitioning the domain

Using organizational units to create domain structure

Creating the design blueprint

Keepers of the New Order

As a new Windows Server 2008 administrator, you now find yourself at the center of a paradigm shift. You are also a pivotal component in the change that is underway on the planet in all forms of enterprise and institutional management.

Windows Server 2008 is a great facilitator in that paradigm shift. Companies are changing; a new order is emerging. The way that businesses communicate with their customers is changing. Very little is currently regarded from a flat or unidimensional perspective. Today, corporate workers, owners, and administrators need a multifaceted view of their environment. Managers and executives need to look at everything from a 360-degree panorama of the business — its external environment and its internal environment.

You, the network administrator — specifically, the Windows Server 2008 network administrator — now have a lot more on your shoulders. Everyone is looking at you — what you're worth, what you know, how you conduct yourself — from the boardroom to the mailroom. You are the person to take the company beyond the perimeter of the old order.

The tools to facilitate the shift can be found, for one reason or another, in Microsoft Windows Server 2008. You learned a lot about the Windows Server 2008 architecture in the previous chapters, so we don't repeat it here, except to say that Windows Server 2008's Directory, Security, Availability, Networking, and Application services are in your hands and those of your peer server administrators. The tools that you use to manage all the information pertaining to these services and objects are the Active Directory and the Windows Server 2008 network.

As mentioned in earlier chapters, Windows Server 2008 domains are very different from legacy Windows domains. They are also very different from the network management philosophies of other operating systems such as Unix, Apple, and the mid-range platforms such as the AS/400.

Before you begin to design your enterprise's *Logical Domain Structure* (LDS), you have a number of important preparations to make. Besides items such as meditating, education, a lot of exercise, and a good diet, you also have some network administration specifics to consider. You'll examine these items in the following sections.

Active Directory Infrastructure Planning

Active Directory planning is a critical part of your Server 2008 deployment. The design of your Active Directory defines the success or failure of your organization's Windows Server 2008 implementation. A great deal of planning goes into an Active Directory infrastructure, such as creating a forest plan and a domain plan for the forests, planning the organizational units, and developing the site topology. These topics are all covered in more detail in Chapters 17 and 18, so if you study those chapters, you should have a good understanding of how to plan your Active Directory.

Planning for the Logical Domain Structure

If your task is the installation of, or conversion to, Windows Server 2008, the first item on your list should be to understand the steps to achieving the LDS and then implementing it. Unless you can create an LDS blueprint, the myriad of other management functions (such as creating and managing user accounts, groups, policies, shares, and more) are difficult to implement and cost you a lot in time and material. The following list represents the steps that you must take in this chapter to arrive at the point where you can begin the conversion process, or even install in a clean or new environment:

1. Prepare yourself mentally for the task.

2. Assemble an LDS team.

3. Survey the enterprise.

4. Design the LDS.

5. Produce the blueprint.

Preparing yourself mentally

Long gone are the days when installing a Windows-based network could be handled with a sprinkling of administrative experience gleaned from a few books or an education based on crammed MCSE courses.

Running a successful Windows Server 2008 domain (no matter what the size) is going to require more than a magazine education in networking, telecommunications, security, and administration. If you have been managing or working with Windows NT Server, you have a head start on the new administrators and administrators from the other technologies who have chosen to defect. Nevertheless, the conversion and installation process is arduous and mentally taxing, and how much time you spend on fixing problems in the future depends on how well you lay your foundations now. The following sections offer some advice that can help stem the migraine tide from the get-go.

Forget about conversion

Trying to think about retrofitting, upgrading, or converting your legacy Windows domains and even your NetWare or Unix environments only gets you into trouble. Forget about what everyone, including Microsoft, says about this, at least until you have the new domain structure in place and are fully versed in the techniques described in this chapter and others described in this book. Only after you fully understand the possibilities and the limitations of Windows Server 2008 domains should you begin to plan your conversion process.

If you try to convert before the Windows Server 2008 LDS is in place, you risk of an IT disaster and also risk losing money and opportunity in many respects. Set up a lab. We can't tell you everything that you need to know or be aware of in this book, nor can Microsoft. Only you can discover how Windows Server 2008 accommodates your needs and how you accommodate its needs. No two organizations are alike.

Stay out of Active Directory

Before you break out into a cold sweat, this advice applies only to this chapter. The Windows Server 2008 LDS is just that — logical. Until you have your blueprint in place, your plans approved, and the budget in the bank, you don't need to do a thing in Active Directory.

Yes, Active Directory is the technology that makes the new LDS a reality, and yes, we would not be discussing the LDS in such direct terms as we do here if Active Directory were not a reality, but trying to design an LDS while tinkering around in Active Directory is counter-productive. Don't assume that you can stumble your way to a design or blueprint.

We're not saying you shouldn't try to learn about Active Directory in a hands-on manner. Learn as much about it as you can; play around in the lab. If you know nothing about Active Directory, you should not be in this chapter just yet, because you should have an understanding of Directory service terms and concepts.

If you are not yet up to speed with Active Directory, study Chapter 17, read the wealth of information in the Help system, download as much information as you can from Microsoft, and check out books about Active Directory and LDAP. Chapter 17 is where you can test examples and concepts in Active Directory. In this chapter, you should be working with design tools and a whiteboard — a very large one.

> **NOTE** For information on LDAP, you can download RFCs 2254, 2255, and 2307 from the Internet. These can usually be located at the Internet Engineering Task Force Web site (at www.ietf.org), but you can find these and many other LDAP references at any main search engine.

Assembling the team

Before you begin, assembling a design team is vital. Whether you are a consultant or an administrator for a small company, whether you are attacking this single-handedly or as a leader or part of a team working in a mega-enterprise, designing the domain requires the input of several people. In small companies that are adopting Windows Server 2008, the team may consist only of you and the owner or CEO.

The domain planning committee

Your domain planning committee should include a number of people (especially if the task is huge) who can assist you in the enterprise analysis that you need to undertake. Your team may be made up of the following members:

- **Assistant analysts and consultants.** These are people to help you quickly survey a large enterprise. The Millennium City example in this book, which is an Active Directory domain structure that spans an entire city, replete with departments and divisions, may need to employ about a hundred analysts to get the survey job done as quickly as possible. How many such members you need depends on how quickly you need or want to move. If you plan to use your IT department as a test case (going from development to production), you could probably get away with one or two analysts.

- **Documentation experts.** These are people to assist you in getting information documented in an accessible form as soon as possible. These people should, as far as possible, be trained in desktop publishing and documentation software, illustration and chart-making software, groupware, and so on. The documents should be stored in a network sharepoint (using a product such as Windows Sharepoint Services, or WSS).

- **Administrators.** These people are to be involved in preparing the installation and conversion process. These may include technicians and engineers currently involved in the day-to-day administration of domains, technical support, special projects, and so on.

Domain management

As the LDS plan progresses from enterprise analysis to approval and then to implementation and conversion, you need to appoint people who initially are involved in the day-to-day administration and management of the new domains.

If you have the resources at your disposal, appointing newly trained staff or hiring and training administrators from the legacy pool makes sense. These people can help you build the new Windows Server 2008 domain and need to communicate with the administrators of the old domains, and so on. If you are doing everything yourself, you have your work cut out for you.

Change control management

To provide your users with a higher level of reliability and a more managed infrastructure, you need to appoint a person responsible for change management. After the development domain is ready to be rolled to production, the teams need to communicate to assess the effect of the domain and to prepare for it. As projects become more complex in the computing environment, collaborating on complex projects becomes even more important.

Users need consistent, reliable experience, including a well-configured operating system, up-to-date applications, and data that is always available. The IT department must meet a variety of needs on a network. For this to succeed, IT must respond to the various changes that occur in the computing environment. The following list describes a few of the factors that require change management:

- New operating system and applications
- Updates to operating systems and applications
- Hardware updates
- Configuration changes
- New users and business requirements
- Security requirements

The change-control manager helps provide a lower total cost of ownership (TCO) by ensuring reduced downtime, reduced disaster-recovery costs, and reduced data loss because of hardware failure.

Domain security

Domain security is a serious issue, so you need to appoint at least one person to manage all aspects of it. That person's role is to test security in the development domain and to apply the appropriate security mechanisms in the production domains. In addition, such a manager can help you to determine domain policy, Group Policy, delegation, workspace management, and so on.

CROSS-REF See Chapter 16 for information on Windows Server 2008 security and security policies in general.

Intradomain communication

An important component is intradomain communication, or the communication between Windows Server 2008 domain users and legacy domain users. Depending on your environment, different levels of domain functionality are available. If all your domain servers are Windows Server 2008 servers, the functional level is set to Windows Server 2008, providing all the Active Directory domains and forest features to you. If you still maintain NT 4.0 or Windows 2000 domain servers, your features are limited.

In Windows 2000 Server, both native and mixed modes existed. If the domain was set to mixed mode, it supported NT 4.0 backup domain controllers (BDCs), but not the use of universal security groups, group nesting, and security identifier capabilities. If the server was set to native mode, it supported all capabilities. Controllers running Windows 2000 Server are probably not aware of forest and domain capabilities. Now, with Windows Server 2008 (as was the case with Windows Server 2003), you have three domain functionalities. These functional levels are listed in Table 19-1.

NOTE Use caution in raising the domain functionality. After it's raised, the domain no longer supports legacy domains. A domain that is set to Windows Server 2008 for a domain functional level cannot add domains that are running Windows 2000 Server.

TABLE 19-1

Domain Functional Levels

Functional Level	Support
Windows 2000–2008 mixed	NT 4.0, Windows 2000, and Windows Server 2003–2008
Windows 2000/3/8 native	Windows 2000, Windows Server 2003, 2008
Windows Server 2003–2008	Windows Server 2003 to Windows Server 2008

You also need to appoint an Exchange administrator if you plan on integrating Exchange — or Lotus Notes administrators, Send Mail people, and so on.

A vital component of the LDS is that information can flow freely through the enterprise's information network and between the operational environments in which the company finds itself after a Windows Server 2008 domain greets the world.

Education and information

You need to generate information to keep management abreast of the development with respect to the conversion process and the emergence of the LDS. After a plan is approved, this information needs to be extended to educate people throughout the enterprise.

Surveying the enterprise

Before you can begin to plan the LDS, survey your enterprise. Consider the job of the land surveyor. A surveyor sets up the theodolite — the instrument that measures horizontal and vertical angles — and charts the hills and valleys, the lay of the land, the contours, and more. These scientists and engineers determine where it is safe to build a house or skyscraper, where to bring in a new road or a bridge, or where to place a town or a city. You need to do the same — not to determine where the company is going (which is what enterprise analysts do), but how to plan an LDS with what is already in place and what may be around the corner.

In surveying the corporate structure, you are not going to take on the role of offering management advice about its business, nor do you suggest that new departments or units should be added, moved, or removed to suit the new domain structure. Not only would that be impossible, but it also would likely get you fired or promoted out of networking.

On the other hand, the Windows Server 2008 LDS needs to be filtered up to the highest levels of management. In fact, the LDS blueprint is what the CIO or CTO is going to drop on the boardroom table, and the IT department is expected to implement the changes desired by management to affect the DNA, e-commerce, paradigm shift, and more. The Windows Server 2008 LDS, because of what it may expose, may indeed result in enterprise or organizational change; just don't say it too loudly.

Windows Server 2008 domains reflect the enterprise structure more than any other technology, and the domain structure is representative of the layout and the landscape of your company, from an administrative and functional point of view.

Windows NT domain administrators, network administrators, and IT/IS managers have never before contemplated that their careers would take them into enterprise analysis. Large organizations are no doubt going to hire expensive enterprise analysts, but for the most part, that's an unnecessary expense unless some serious first aid is needed before a conversion to Windows Server 2008 can be considered.

In many cases, you'll already have the resources at hand. They exist in you and in your peers. You do not need to go overboard studying enterprise analysis, enterprise resource planning (ERP), and customer relationship management (CRM). Of course, having that knowledge helps and may even get you the job that you're after. This chapter serves as a guide if you are not sure where to start. The following sections discuss the key concepts of enterprise analysis.

Enterprise analysis

Enterprise analysis is where enterprise land surveying and enterprise engineering come together for the future and good of the company. Enterprise analysts examine where the company is today, what business it is in (many don't know), where it wants to go (or where the board or shareholders want it to go), and then make suggestions about how the company should go about achieving its objectives. Enterprise analysts help suggest changes at all levels of the enterprise — in particular, in information systems and technology. They provide management with critical, actionable information — blueprints that start the wheels of change turning.

Without technology, very few of the desires of the corporation can become a reality. You do not need to look far to see how misguided efforts in IT/IS have wrecked some companies, making others more competitive and profitable. In your new role as enterprise analyst, you are surveying the corporate landscape to best determine how to implement a new Windows Server 2008–based logical domain structure.

You have two responsibilities. You must study the enterprise with the objective of implementing the new LDS as quickly and painlessly as possible. You may have a lot of money to work with, or you may not have much of a budget. In either case, you are going to need facts fast.

You also need to study the enterprise and forecast, or project, where it may be heading. Is the business getting ready for an IPO, to merge, to file Chapter 11, or to be acquired? Is it changing focus? All these items and more affect not only the LDS of a company, but also the LDS of a city, a hospital, a school, or a government.

You may consider that you are doing the enterprise analysis for the good of the company, but you are doing it for your own good. You are expected to cater to any change that may happen between sunrise and sunset, and not having the wherewithal to implement or accommodate the sudden business direction that management may throw at you is not good IT administration.

Where do you start? As mentioned earlier in the section "Planning for the Logical Domain Structure," you can't plan the LDS by just looking up all the groups that you created in Windows NT and assuming that just importing them all does the trick. That would be the worst place to start and the worst advice that anyone can take. Microsoft, we believe, makes too much noise about upgrading Windows NT; we believe that countermands strategic LDS planning.

> **NOTE**   Group Policy technology is so sophisticated that it makes upgrading an NT domain and inheriting its groups and user accounts a tricky business. Make sure that you fully understand Group Policy before you upgrade an NT domain. It is discussed in detail in Chapter 24.

Here is a short list of starting points. The following items may be better in another order for you, and you may add to the list as you deem fit:

- **Get management on your side.** This may not be difficult if you are the CIO or if the LDS directives come from the CIO or CTO, but to do the job well, you need access to more than would be expected of network or domain administrators. Management and

HR, therefore, need to trust you with sensitive information. We would add to this point: Get the CEO on board. You are going to need to set up appointments with the most senior staff in the enterprise. They need to know that your research is sanctioned at the very top. You are likely to encounter resistance at the departmental head level, where change may be deemed a threat. Advise department heads in writing that if you do not get cooperation, then their departments must be left out of the domain conversion or "new order." People tend to go crazy when their e-mail is cut off, so you can use this as a foot in the door.

- **Get hold of organizational charts.** Most enterprises and organizations have these. If you're fortunate, they are up to date. If they are not or they do not exist, you need to invest in a software tool that can make organizational charts.

- **Tell people what you are doing.** Be frank and open about the process, without exposing the team to security risks.

Enterprise environments

Before you begin an exhaustive enterprise analysis project, take some time to understand the environments in which the enterprise or organization operates. Enterprise analysts often refer to these environments as *operational environments*. We have been teaching companies about their respective operational environments for several years, long before the advent of Windows Server 2008. The elements in these environments feature heavily on both the LDS and physical domain structure (PDS).

Years ago, an enterprise operated in only two environments: *external* and *internal*. The advent of the Internet and wide area networks have resulted in a third environment: the *extra* environment, or the environment "in between." An analysis of these environments is essential in the formulation of both the LDS and the PDS.

To fully investigate the environments, you need to build lists of items to look for; otherwise, you do not know where to start and when to finish.

The external environment

The *external environment* is made up of several components: customers, suppliers, distributors, cleaning staff, and so on. At the physical level, the corporation or enterprise must deal with the elements of the external environment directly. Examples include providing access to cleaning staff, dealing with customers, delivery pick up, and more.

The most important technological factor in the external environment is the Internet. Like all enterprises and organizations, the Internet provides resources for dealing with the elements in the external environment electronically and offers a means of interconnecting partitions of the internal environment. Any modern company is as present in cyberspace as it is in the physical realm.

Today, the neural network in the external environment also is the Internet. The telephone system still plays an important and indispensable part, but it is becoming less pervasive as people find the Internet more convenient in many respects.

The enterprise depends on several components on the Internet that are vital to its existence in general. These include DNS, the locator service for the entity on the Internet, and the Internet registration authorities that provide the entity the right (for a fee) to participate in a global Internet infrastructure. These rights include the registration of your domain names and the assignment of IP addresses, without which you are unreachable.

Pay attention to the following short list of items as you examine the external environment:

- How is the company connected to the Internet?
- How does the company use the Internet's DNS system?
- What are the public domains used by the enterprise?
- Who keeps the domains and makes sure that the fees are paid on time?
- Are the domains that you need to register available?

The internal environment

The *internal environment* comprises all the departments, divisions, OUs, and Key Management Entities (KMEs) that work together for the benefit of the enterprise. This environment includes employees, contractors, executives and management, subsidiaries, divisions, acquisitions, equipment, intelligence, information, data, and more.

The internal environment's neural network is the private intranet and its relative KMEs and administrative functions. The intranet is a private network, which is the medium for the Internet protocols TCP/IP. The local area network (LAN) is fast becoming a passé term, associated with outmoded and confining protocols such as NetBEUI, IPX, and more. Windows Server 2008 is, for all intents and purposes, an intranet operating system that still knows how to function on a LAN for backward compatibility.

 NetBEUI, once the web and woof of the Microsoft network, is no more.

Very important to consider in the internal environment are all the legacy systems and mid-range systems that are going to need facilities in the new realm.

Consider carefully the following short list of items as you examine the internal environment:

- How many employees work for the company?
- How many remote divisions or branches does the company have?
- What functions do the remote divisions perform?
- How are the sites interconnected?
- Who is responsible for the management of the network that connects each of the sites?
- What is the bandwidth of the links between the sites?
- How is the company prepared for disaster recovery?

The extra environment

The *extra environment* is the interface — and the environment in the immediate vicinity of the interface — between the external environment and the internal environment. In some cases, the division may be obvious and thus easy to manage (such as a computer terminal in the public library or a voice-mail system). In other cases, the interface is harder to encapsulate or define, and thus more difficult to manage (such as how people hear about your product).

Examples in the extra environment are e-mail; communications between the internal and external environments that may need to be monitored, controlled, and rerouted; corporate Web sites that enable customers to access portions of the internal environment; and so on.

The network environment supporting this environment and its technology is known as an *extranet*. A good example of such an extranet is FedEx, which enables customers to tap into their tracking databases to monitor their shipments.

Pay attention to the following list of items as you examine the extra environment:

- What Web sites does the company use? Who manages them? Where are they located?
- What call center or help-desk functions are in place?
- How do contractors and consultants gain access to the enterprise to perform their work without risking exposure to sensitive data?

Working with organizational charts

With the organizational chart in hand, you can zero in on the *logical* units of the enterprise and begin enterprise analysis in a "logical" fashion. Figure 19-1 represents a portion of the organizational chart of Millennium City. (The entire chart is on the CD, in the Millennium City Domain Structure Blueprint PDF.) The chart has been adopted from the organizational chart of a major U.S. city, and we use it throughout the book to demonstrate examples of both LDS and PDS.

The full chart for Figure 19-1 is huge (more than 80 divisions and hundreds of boards and councils), but you must realize that the LDS that you are going to create may need to accommodate such an environment. Obviously, fully converting such an organization is going to take many years, and you're likely to be working with Windows 2006 before achieving 100 percent penetration with an organization of this size.

In fact, in organizations of this size, you're likely never to achieve a 100-percent pure Windows Server 2008 domain structure, and you wouldn't want to. Just a cursory glance at such a chart tells you that you are going to be up to your neck in integration with legacy and mid-range systems, Unix and Mac platforms, and more.

You need to start somewhere, however. You need to start conversion and installation with select departments, starting perhaps with your own department, where you can learn a lot about the conversion process, the fabric of Windows Server 2008, and the place to set up the labs and development environments.

FIGURE 19-1

Abridged organizational chart of Millennium City.

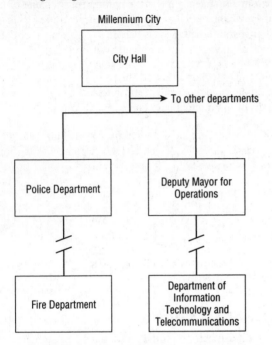

We have selected three entities out of the chart to use as examples. We are going to convert the Mayor's office (City Hall), the Department of Information Technology and Telecommunications (DITT), and the Police Department (MCPD).

Identifying the Key Management Entities

Key Management Entities (KMEs) are the management, administrative, or service components of a business or organization that, taken as a whole, describe what the entity does. These KMEs are not on the organizational chart and often span multiple departments. Payroll processing, for example, is a KME that spans the enterprise. Although the KME for payroll is concentrated in the Office of Payroll Administration, the KME spans Millennium City because it requires the participation of more than one logical unit or OU. Every department processes its payroll by processing time sheets, data input (time/entry databases), sick leave, raises, check issues, check printing, bank reconciliation, direct deposits, and so on. The KMEs need not be physical groups; they can be logically dispersed between several departments and across several domain boundaries, remote sites, and so on.

All KMEs, after they're identified, are best represented on a matrix of the enterprise. Each KME represents an area of responsibility that must be measured and evaluated. After you have identified the KMEs, you can learn about the IT/IS systems and technologies that have been implemented to assist them and ultimately how both LDS and PDS can emerge to accommodate them. Figure 19-2 shows the KME matrix for DITT.

FIGURE 19-2

KME matrix spreadsheets prepared in Microsoft Excel.

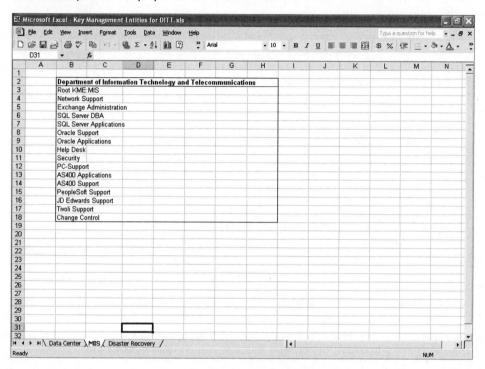

MIS people seldom research KMEs or even update previous reports and plans. An important benefit or payoff of such research is that MIS learns how it can improve efficiency in the KME.

Breaking the KMEs down further and extracting the components that require the services of IT/IS is also important. You need this information later as you identify where to delegate administration and control in various OUs and domains.

Strategic drivers

In the movie *Wall Street*, Michael Douglas's character identifies greed as the *strategic driver* in his effort to raid companies and make huge profits. Greed certainly is a strategic driver in many companies and organizations, but many others exist, and you could argue that they are subordinate to greed and profit. The Internet is a strategic driver; the ambitions of the CEO and major shareholders are strategic drivers; mergers and takeovers are others, as are investment in new technology and more.

Strategic drivers are also new laws, new discoveries, new technology, lawsuits, labor disputes, and so on. Knowing what makes the company work and what can keep it working is critical in domain planning and structure. You need to have as much information as you can about the enterprise and where it is headed so that you can give 100 percent where and whenever needed.

If you know the strategic drivers of the organization for which you work, then you can be in a position to cater to any IT/IS demands placed on you. More important and germane to the task at hand, you can implement a domain structure to cater to the drivers that influence the future of the enterprise.

Use your sixth sense, common sense, and logic in determining strategic drivers. Remember that with the new domain comes new threats, denial of service attacks, viruses, information and intellectual property theft, data loss, loss of service level, and more. Consider the following good example: In the weeks prior to New Year's Eve, Y2K, we anticipated heightened security concerns from the CEO of the large distributor that we support. Therefore, we preempted the request and investigated how best to lock down the company's RAS and still provide access to key support staff that might be required to dial in during the night. We effectively locked down all access and created a secure zone on the RAS machine, which authenticated users locally before providing access to the domain. Being a good system administrator means going beyond the theories that you learn at MCSE school or computer science class. Windows Server 2008 is the wake-up call for stodgy sysadmins.

Identifying the logical units

Looking at the organizational chart of Millennium City in Figure 19-1, the *logical units* jump out at you. Every department or OU within each department affects the LDS in some form or another.

The Mayor's office looks simple enough. It includes the mayor and the people who work for the mayor, such as public relations people, advisors, and administrative staff. The Mayor's office is probably one of the simplest logical units to represent or quantify in the LDS plan. For all intents and purposes, it can be represented as a single OU on the LDS.

In corporations, the offices of the CEO and executive staff can range from extremely complex to very simple, but the DITT is very different. What are the logical units within this department? We identify some of them in the following list (although we cannot deal with every OU within this department because the list would run into too many pages):

- **Operations.** This unit is responsible for disaster recovery and maintenance of critical systems. The people in this unit make sure that systems are online; they watch systems and applications for failures; they monitor production; they print reports; and so on.

  If Operations detects errors or problems, its members try to fix them within certain guidelines or parameters. They may be required to restore servers in the middle of the night or call the on-call staff as needed. Operations staff members are trusted employees with heavy responsibilities. They probably need high levels of access to certain systems. They may need to have authority to shut down servers, reboot machines, perform backup, and so on.

- **Help desk.** This unit may be part of Operations or a separate unit. The Help desk is responsible for getting staff members out of jams with technology, teaching them how to use new applications, and more. Help desk members also need special access to systems, and they often need to troubleshoot applications and systems in the context or stead of the users that its members need to help. They may need to log in to mailboxes, for example, troubleshoot print queues, and escalate calls to second- and third-level support.

■ **PC Support.** PC Support is a separate organizational or logical unit within the DITT. The people who work in this unit troubleshoot desktop PCs, including upgrade and maintenance, and ensure that all employees within the entire company — often across physical organizational divides — have the resources that they need to do their work.

■ **Security.** Security staff members are responsible for catering to requests for user and machine accounts, changing passwords, access to resources, and more. The security staff works closely with network support in determining group memberships, rights and permissions, access to shares and files, and so on.

■ **Network support.** That's where you (and we) come in. Network support deals with the upkeep of the intranet, servers, and WAN resources, as well as dealing with network providers, routers, circuits, and more. You also deal with the location of domain controllers and are responsible for upgrading servers; interconnecting protocols; establishing services; providing storage, backup and disaster recovery; and more.

Identifying the physical units

Between the various departments in an organization are numerous physical units to consider. Departments may be located in separate buildings and/or in other cities. In Millennium City, for example, the Mayor's office, or City Hall, is remote from the DITT. The MCPD is spread over numerous buildings across town.

We also have intranets to deal with, as well as WANs and dedicated connections between departments that cooperate closely. The Police Department of a city of this size employs its own technical team that manages network resources and systems at both the office of the Police Commissioner and at the individual precincts. The MCPD is also hooked into the systems at the Department of Transportation, the District Attorney's Office, the Department of Corrections, and so on.

Documentation

After you have thoroughly surveyed the enterprise and are familiar with its layout and organization, you need to document your findings. Be aware that at this point in the LDS design process, the documentation is far from complete, but it nevertheless forms the basis or departure point from which the conversion or management team can begin planning and creating a blueprint. Remember, too, that the initial conversion project should be open-ended enough to permit you to slide into continuous domain administration and that the documentation should continue to evolve. It becomes the "bible" for the present and future administrative teams. The following short list is a suggestion of steps to take to complete documentation and move forward with your LDS and conversion plan:

1. Update the organizational chart and then circulate it to department heads for additions, accuracy, and comment.

2. List the KMEs throughout the enterprise and describe the extent of the administrative function in each KME. You are noting the size of the KME and its complexity. Make a

note of where the KME extends beyond departmental or divisional boundaries of the enterprise. The documentation of KMEs may take many formats. We suggest that you create a matrix on a spreadsheet, listing departments and divisions in the column headers, and the KMEs that you have discovered as rows, similar to the one started in Figure 19-2.

3. Forward the KME matrix to department heads and invite feedback. The KME list is likely to grow, and you're probably going to be informed of more KMEs that you did not uncover.

4. Divide the organizational chart into sections or make a listing of the divisions or departments you believe are the best prospects with which to begin conversion. Note the reasons and mark them for debate at the next conversion team meeting.

The next phase of the LDS plan is the investigation of the administrative models in place over IT throughout the enterprise. What we present here isn't going to get you through Harvard, but it should be enough to give you something to think about.

Administrative modeling

Administrative modeling deals with management and administrative styles and practices. The following list illustrates several core management styles that may be in place in a company for one reason or another:

- The box-oriented company
- The human-assets-oriented company
- The change-oriented company
- The expertise-oriented company
- The culture-oriented company

Understanding the definition of the term *box* is worthwhile because it influences the ultimate layout of your LDS. *Box* refers to the way that management controls a company. Enterprise analysts and corporate executives talk about soft-box companies and hard-box companies.

The *soft-box*-driven company management team does not rule with an iron fist and trusts its managers to act in the best interests of the enterprise. It goes without saying that these companies have a lot of faith in their people and have achieved a system that is comfortable for everyone. The soft-box company is likely to have a small employee handbook and provides little direct control at certain levels, giving regional managers a wide berth.

The *hard-box*-driven company is very rigid. The employee handbook at this company is likely to be about two bricks thick and probably lists rules for everything from dress code to eating in your office.

Good and bad companies are found in both models. The best exist somewhere between both extremes. A hard-box company, however, is more likely to employ a rigid, centralized administrative approach at all levels in general and with respect to IT in particular. "Softer" companies are likely to be more decentralized.

Centralized administration and decentralized administration models apply not only to general administration, but also to IT, MIS, or network administration.

Centralized administration

The *centralized* approach dictates that all management takes place from a single or central department. In a small company, you really have no alternative. Small companies that cannot afford or have no need for dedicated IT/IS administration usually outsource all their technical and IT/IS support, and the core executive team and the owners make all decisions.

Bigger companies that operate from a single location — or a clinic or a school — may employ the services of small technical teams and still outsource. The really big companies that still operate from single locations use a centralized administration model, supported by their own teams.

Decentralized administration

The *decentralized* approach dictates that management or administration is dispersed to geographically remote locations. This is usually a practice among the largest of enterprises. Departments, locations, and divisions, some of them on opposite sides of the world, are large enough to warrant their own MIS or IT departments.

Most multinationals today employ varying degrees of both approaches, and their operations dictate to what extent administration is both centralized and decentralized. This is probably the most sensible of the management models and varies from corporation to corporation.

Companies determine how much and what makes sense to delegate to the remote locations or seemingly autonomous divisions. They may, for example, dictate that remote administrators take care of responsibilities such as backup and printer management at remote centers or depots.

Other systems, even ones located at the remote sites, may make more sense managed from a central location. If you have ten sites and need to install an e-mail server at each site, for example, hiring or training people at the remote sites does not make sense if a single e-mail administrator and possibly an assistant can manage all e-mail servers from a single location. Windows Server 2008 and a dedicated reliable network make managing a highly sophisticated IT infrastructure from a remote location, with no technical staffing on site whatsoever, entirely possible. In addition, investing in products such as Exchange or Lotus Notes, which are designed to function in clusters and are managed from a single location, regardless of where the physical equipment is actually located, would make sense and go a long way toward reducing TCO. The advent of such admin-centralized technologies is making the decentralized approach more feasible to adopt. From 1998 to the present, we have managed servers in more than 20 cities throughout the United States, and we have never physically been on site.

The good, the bad, and the unwise

Each model has its pros and cons. The centralized model is often the most used from an IT point of view, and part of the reason is that legacy systems — both mid-range and Windows NT — do not lend themselves to any meaningful decentralized administration or controlled delegated responsibility. The Windows Server 2008 Security Accounts Manager (SAM), for example, can be written to only at the primary domain controllers (PDCs). Copies of the SAM on the backup domain controllers (BDCs) can be read for service requests, but not written to. If, at any time, the PDC became unavailable to remote locations (because of a loss of link, maintenance, and so on), delegated administration at remote locations becomes impossible.

Conversely, many companies go overboard and delegate willy-nilly to all departments and divisions. Some companies have carried the decentralized model to the extreme, forcing the remote or otherwise separated units to request their own budgets and acquire and support their own systems. These companies are often impossible to deal with because they have no central buying authority and integration of systems is a nightmare.

Often, newly acquired companies in mergers and takeovers end up looking after themselves as management absorbs them at an agonizingly slow pace. What you end up with is a hodgepodge of systems that are incompatible and impossible to integrate. One side may support Compaq, for example, and the other IBM. Amicable mergers or acquisitions often turn sour because IT and MIS cannot get the two or more technology departments to speak the same language.

Windows Server 2008 enables you to delegate to various levels of granularity, all the way down to the OU, in tandem with a highly distributed and redundant directory service. As such, Windows Server 2008 provides the pluses of the centralized model (such as buying like systems and technology) with the undeniable benefits of decentralized administration, permitting a controlled delegation of administrative function and partial or substantial relief of the administrative burden at HQ.

At Millennium City, you have a strong decentralized administration in place. All budget and organization-wide IT planning, however, is done at the DITT. All technical hiring, firing, and requests from Human Resources for staff takes place at the DITT. New systems, maintenance, technical support, help desk, and more is also done here.

The MCPD, however, is autonomous and distinct from the main offices of the city. MCPD is a separate administrative authority that relies on the DITT for investment decisions, choice of technology, and more, but local administrators keep it going and keep it secure.

DITT thus remains as the command center, ensuring that systems at MCPD can talk to systems at the DA's office or that crime units have familiar access to the Department of Transportation without needing to physically sit at the department's computers. DITT also ensures that an administrator at the DA's office can apply for an opening at MCPD without needing to be retrained on systems at MCPD that are different from systems at the DA's office. In short, one of the chief functions of the DITT is to strive for homogenous systems as far as possible throughout the city, and that the heterogeneous systems are interoperable and can be integrated.

Logical Domain Structure: The Blueprint

The logical container for domains in Windows Server 2008 is a forest. Forests contain trees, which have roots, and domain trees make up a Windows Server 2008 network. Understanding forests is not necessary to design a namespace, and forests are discussed in various contexts in Chapters 17 and 18.

As mentioned earlier, Windows Server 2008 lets you rename domains. Objects can be moved around domains and between domain trees if you later get stuck. You don't, however, want to be tearing down domains that are already heavily populated, so use the information culled in the enterprise analysis wisely and plan appropriately. As we emphasize in Chapter 18, test everything.

The top-level domain

You cannot start or create a Windows Server 2008 network without first creating a root, or top-level, domain. What the root should be named and what role it should play perplexes a lot of people. If you are confused, you are not alone, because no clear-cut rules work for every company.

In referring to the role played by the root, we mean whether the domain should be populated with objects or should just serve as a directory entry point, in a similar fashion to the root domains on the Internet.

Naming the root

One of the first things that you must decide is what to name the top-level, or root, of your Windows Server 2008 domain. This name involves more than just identity. It is the foundation for your corporate Active Directory namespace. Your enterprise most likely already has a domain name registered with an Internet authority, in which case you already have a namespace in existence, even if you never thought much about it as a *namespace* ... probably more as a parking space. You're probably thinking, "What the heck does the domain that we registered have to do with our corporate network?"

In our example, Millennium City is registered with the registrar as `mcity.us`. How *your* two namespaces coexist on your intranet and the Internet is not the issue. How you *integrate* the two namespaces is.

You have two options: You can leave your public domain name applicable only in the external environment, resolved by an ISP's DNS server, or you can use your public domain name as the root domain in the directory and on your intranet.

If your domain name is listed in the .com or .org levels of the DNS, it becomes published on the public Internet and is available as a point from which to resolve your public Internet resources, such as Web servers and mail servers. A query to the root (.us) for mcity.us, for example, refers the client to the DNS server addresses that can resolve MCITY host names authoritatively to servers on the public Internet. DNS servers around the world that regularly service "hits" for the mcity.us can draw on cached records to resolve IP addresses for their clients.

In your case, would you then want to use the public domain name as the domain root in your LDS? In the MCITY example, we saw no reason not to. The results of your enterprise analysis may indicate otherwise, for a number of reasons. We discuss some of them here, as pros and cons.

Reasons to have identical external and internal DNS namespaces are as follows:

- The domain suffix is identical in both environments and is less confusing for users.
- You have only one namespace to protect on the Internet.
- You have only one namespace to administer.

Reasons not to have identical external and internal DNS namespaces are as follows:

- Domains remain separate, and a clear distinction exists between resources on the outside and resources on the inside. The corporate intranet is more protected, therefore, but you still need a good firewall.
- The company may change direction and may change the name.
- Proxy configurations for separate namespaces are easier to manage. Exception lists can be created to filter the internal names from the external names.
- TCP/IP-based applications such as Web browsers and FTP clients are easier to configure. You would not need to make sure that clients that are connected to both the intranet and the Internet at the same time resolve the correct resources.

Several items in the preceding lists demand more discussion.

First, we have a way around the domain suffix problem — a late-feature addition. Windows Server 2008 clients can store more than one UPN (user principal name) to an account, as shown in Figure 19-3. This is achieved by allocating additional domain suffixes to the domain, which must be carefully managed so as not to create conflicts with users in other domains. Down-level clients are stuck with the NetBIOS name assigned to the domain. To add more domain suffixes, you can open the Active Directory and select Users and Computers, open the account of the user, and select the Account tab. The drop-down list to the right of the User logon name is where you find the additional suffixes. By the way, any suffix suffices to log the user on.

We do not believe that the intranet is any more exposed if you have a single namespace, because regardless of the name you choose as an Active Directory root domain, the domain controller is hidden behind a firewall. It is assigned an IP address that belongs to your private network and is not locatable from the public Internet — hidden by the magic of network address translation and such. Nor are any of your other resources locatable.

FIGURE 19-3

Changing the default domain suffix.

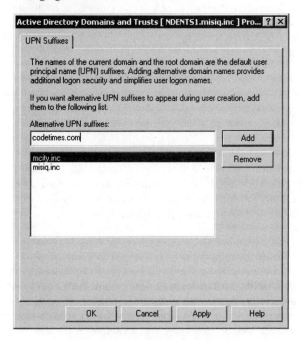

You're probably going to implement firewalls and network address translation to protect your resources, and you're likely to come under attack and face various threats regardless of whether your external DNS domain name is identical to your internal DNS domain name. Most companies already deploy mirrored sites on both sides of a firewall.

The second reason not to use your public domain name is that the identity of the company may change. You could be acquired or broken up, and changing the existing root domain to reflect the name of the new company would be almost impossible. This may, in fact, be a problem if you anticipate a merger or a name change soon (not usually something that server admins are privy to). This is why we devote such a lot of time and space to enterprise analysis.

You should be aware that the UPN suffix is not locked into the root domain name by any means — or any other domain name, for that matter. You can change the UPN suffix at any time for your users if the name of the company changes or the public domain name changes. The underlying GUIDs never change, even if you relocate the objects to other regions of the domain tree or try to clone them with various resource kit tools.

If you need to plan for a merger or acquisition down the road, or if you must deal with the outright sale of a certain division, you may be better off not naming your root domain after your public domain name at all.

Another discovery that you make in the external environment is that the public domain name and the enterprise name are different. Registering a domain name that is identical to the enterprise name is hard these days. Such a corresponding name would be nice, but obtaining it is not always possible. Take the company name Rainbow, for example. An infinite number of companies in the world must be called Rainbow something or another, but only one can be lucky enough to score the name `rainbow.com`. In such a case, you have no choice but to name the root domain the next best name.

For the sake of example and because the name was available on the Internet, we went with `mcity.us` (a week later, someone wanted to buy it from us). A city, however, is unlikely to change its name or be acquired, so if you are setting up a public institution, name changes are not a major concern.

Getting back to the subject of the supplementary UPN, however, this should definitely reflect your public domain name so that e-mail addresses are the same internally and externally. If the public domain name changes and thus e-mail address suffixes change, you can apply the new domain suffix to the UPNs of all user accounts, as shown in Figure 19-4.

The function of the root

The root domain of the first domain tree is the entry point to a forest. Forests are not part of any namespace and are located by attaching or connecting to the root domain in each forest. You can leave the domain root practically empty, with built-in accounts, or you can choose to populate it with OUs, security principals, and other objects. Most small companies never need a deep domain hierarchy, and even the root domain suffices in a company of several hundred employees. You should, however, seriously consider the following issues about the root domain:

- If the root domain is sparse, it replicates faster and provides an additional measure of fault tolerance. By ensuring that you always replicate the root, you serve to protect your domain "brainstem" in the event that a disaster takes out the lower levels. You can always create a domain and attach it to the root.

- The administrator in the root domain can reign supreme over the fiefdom like a shogun. A small group of forestwide "Samurai" administrators, serving the shogun, can be located in the root domain, which gives you tighter control over domain administrators in the lower-level domains.

The only drawback to this approach is the additional hardware for domain controllers that you need, but the root (being more ceremonial than functional) need not sit on an expensive server.

FIGURE 19-4

Adding multiple UPN suffixes to the domain.

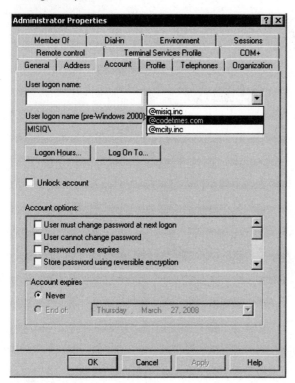

Again, enterprise analysis points the way to justifying the reasons to add additional levels to the domain hierarchy, additional domain trees, and separate forests. Figure 19-5, however, shows the hierarchy that works for the mcity namespace. This is called an *extended* namespace, because it goes beyond what was envisioned by the DNS pioneers.

Here, we have chosen to stick to one namespace on the Internet, mcity.us. This enables the name servers, Web sites, FTP servers, mail servers, and more to be correctly resolved by the Internet DNS. The first domain controller in the city (MCDC01), however, becomes the second-level domain that serves as the domain root in the Active Directory forest. As Figure 19-5 shows, this server is located behind the firewall and is further protected by network address translation.

FIGURE 19-5

The MCITY DNS-Active Directory hierarchy in an extended namespace.

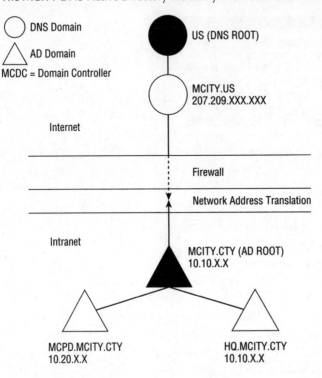

We can thus expose the directory to the Internet as LDAP.mcity.us, and it can serve as an LDAP directory global-catalog server in the so-called extranet, enabling users to look up e-mail addresses, phone numbers, locations, and more.

Under this root domain, we created second-level domains, such as cityhall.mcdc10 .mcity.us, mcpd.mcdc10.mcity.us, and ditt.mcdc15.mcity.us. These second-level domains (third level from the Internet roots) are as safe as houses on the intranet, because they cannot be resolved, and they exist on private subnets behind a firewall. Intruders would need to break into the network through other back doors, such as an unguarded modem, the PBX, the RAS servers, or stolen passwords.

This root structure also enables subsidiaries operating under the same Internet root to similarly extend the hierarchy. For example, mcnippon.mcity.us is a perfectly legitimate scenario for a domain controller in Japan, so an enterprisewide namespace/domain controller policy may be to make all first-layer domains under the root represent geographical, geopolitical, or departmental divisions. The second and third layers would then extend down into the division, as shown in Figure 19-6.

FIGURE 19-6

_____

Enterprisewide domain structure.

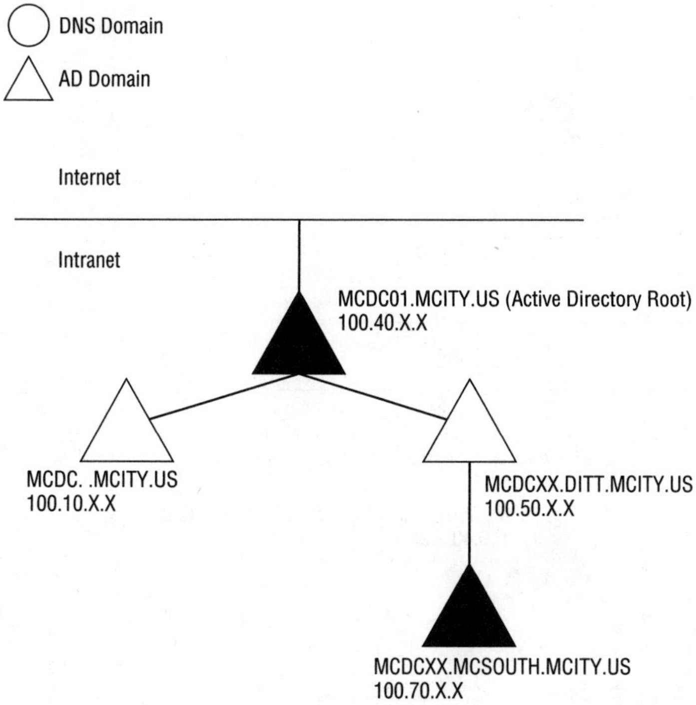

◯ DNS Domain

△ AD Domain

Internet

Intranet

▲ MCDC01.MCITY.US (Active Directory Root)
100.40.X.X

△ MCDC. .MCITY.US
100.10.X.X

△ MCDCXX.DITT.MCITY.US
100.50.X.X

▲ MCDCXX.MCSOUTH.MCITY.US
100.70.X.X

This approach involves only one caveat: Our shogun in the root domain may come under attack. However, if anyone can take him out behind our secure server room, firewalls, NAT, Kerberos security, a highly sophisticated encrypted password scheme on a smart card, and myriad other protection schemes that we don't need to mention, we can all pack our bags and go home.

Your solution, however, may be different. Following are the alternatives:

■ **Split namespace.** This namespace, shown in Figure 19-7, is not connected. The root Active Directory domain cannot be resolved from the Internet by any means, yet it _is_ a logical extension of the public DNS namespace. In other words, the Active Directory root appears to be an extension of the DNS root, yet it is in its own right an implicit namespace. The Active Directory side of the split namespace can become an extension of the DNS root at any time. Internet servers (such as DNS, mail, and FTP) can be installed on the Internet, on the intranet (protected behind firewalls and NAT), or in both places.

FIGURE 19-7

Split namespace.

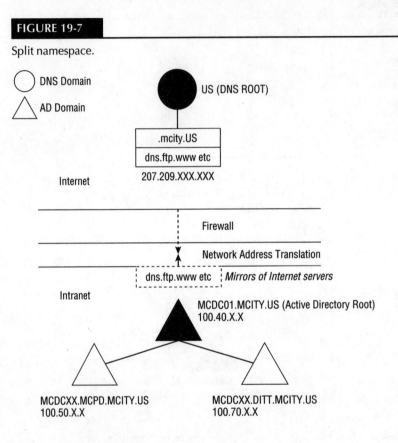

- **Separate namespaces.** Both namespaces, as shown in Figure 19-8, are registered. They cannot be joined and both represent DNS roots. In addition, one is an Active Directory root as well.

- **Illegal namespace.** The illegal namespace does not get you brought up on charges of Internet conspiracy. (*Illegal network* is a network term for an IP address range that cannot be used on the public Internet because it is already used by a registered owner.) If the name conforms to DNS standards and you have not registered it, it is *illegal* in a sense, especially if someone else owns the name. If the name cannot be registered on the Internet, as the example in Figure 19-9 indicates (possibly because of nonstandard characters or DNS root domains), it is also considered illegal. Illegal addresses are used all the time, however, on private networks.

FIGURE 19-8

Separate namespaces.

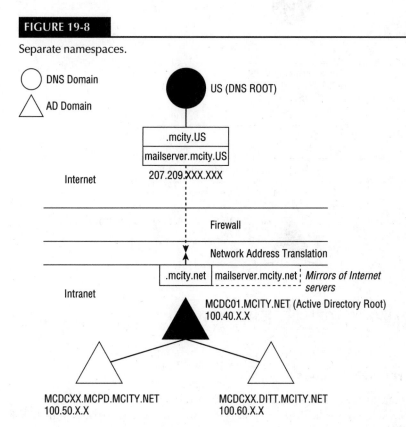

DNS naming practices

As mentioned in the section "Naming the Root" earlier in this chapter, assigning names wisely and protecting them as you would a trademark or a copyright is good practice. You should also ensure that they are registered with the Internet authorities. Start getting used to using good DNS language in the blueprint and LDS plan.

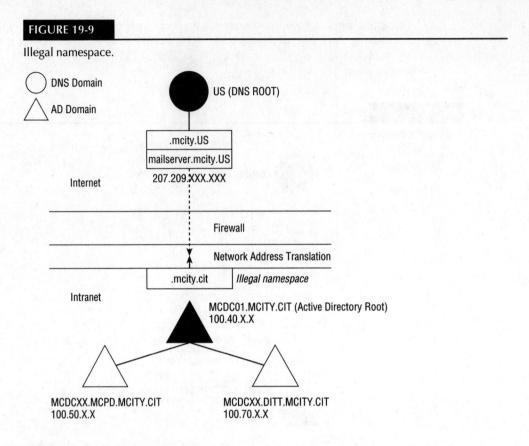

FIGURE 19-9

Illegal namespace.

○ DNS Domain

△ AD Domain

US (DNS ROOT)

.mcity.US

mailserver.mcity.US

207.209.XXX.XXX

Internet

Firewall

Network Address Translation

.mcity.cit   *Illegal namespace*

Intranet

MCDC01.MCITY.CIT (Active Directory Root)
100.40.X.X

MCDCXX.MCPD.MCITY.CIT
100.50.X.X

MCDCXX.DITT.MCITY.CIT
100.70.X.X

Use Internet DNS names

Use internationally recognized standard-approved DNS names for your Active Directory domains. See RFC 1123, which specifies that you can use A–Z, a–z, 0–9, and the hyphen (-). Notice that Windows Server 2008 supports nonstandard naming, and you can put almost any Unicode character in the name. Resist the temptation, however, even if you do not yet have a persistent connection to the Internet.

Make sure that namespaces are unique

You cannot throw an exception on a whiteboard or a legal pad, so duplicate names go unnoticed and "cloned" namespaces may make their way to networks in the enterprise that are not yet connected. If your Active Directory conversion or rollout team is divided between offices and regions, for example, you may unwittingly create two or more domain trees in your forest that are identical, but serve different divisions. After you connect them and go live, the whole kaboodle explodes like an egg in a microwave.

Keep legacy clients in mind

The deepest level in the DNS name for a newly created domain becomes the NetBIOS name for NetBIOS clients. This name need not bear any resemblance to the DNS name and can be changed. You get the opportunity to change this name only once — as you install the domain.

Pay particular attention to this name and keep in mind the following suggestions:

- **Make the NetBIOS name "palatable" to legacy clients.** Remember that they can see the NetBIOS name of the domain in the domain list when looking for a resource or trying to log on. Although Windows Server 2008 clients can log on as `someone@mcity.us`, NetBIOS clients, using the previous example, can log on only to the default NetBIOS name — such as `genesis` or `cityhall`. This isn't too bad, but what if their domain were `eggonyourface.landofoz.mcity.us`? The example seems extreme, but you never know.

  Using an alias, the NetBIOS name can easily be changed to `OZ`. However, you must remember to do it as the domain is created, because you cannot change it later short of trashing the domain controller after the installation. Check your plan and make sure that the assigned NetBIOS name is marked in red for the conversion team.

  This next suggestion may not be possible, but making the NetBIOS name the same as the last partition name in the DNS (from the top down, or reading from right to left in English) provides a consistency that your users are sure to appreciate. If `genesis.mcity.us` is your DNS name, for example, `genesis` is your NetBIOS name.

- **Make sure that NetBIOS names are not duplicated.** If you are raising a second domain in another region, make sure that the plan indicates unique NetBIOS names. The two DNS domains are different, but identical NetBIOS names do not work.

Second-level domains

To add second- and third-level domains under the root, you need good reasons. Each new domain adds administrative burden, additional expenses, and increased total cost of ownership (TCO). The following list, however, provides some valid reasons for creating additional domain levels:

- Managing separated departments
- Managing replication overhead and network latency
- Managing the decentralized administration models
- Managing autonomous divisions
- Managing a diversity of domain policies
- Managing international partitions
- Managing NT domains
- Managing security requirements

- Managing information hiding and resource publishing (a divergent view of the directory)
- Constructive partitioning of the directory

Managing separated departments

If you examine the organizational chart of Millennium City, you can easily see that some divisions or departments are remote from the Mayor's office, or City Hall, and from the other departments. In fact, MCITY is so large that few departments share buildings and physical locations. The chasm between the departments is so vast that extending the root domain out to each site may prove impractical for many reasons.

This may also be the case in your enterprise. Perhaps you have several departments spread around the city. Often, a company grows out of its present building and leases additional space across the road. In that case, you must span the network backbone or collapse it between the two locations.

Key to your decision to create second-level domains is that users and network resources need to locate a domain controller nearest to them to authenticate. If you decide to extend the domain across several city blocks or between the suburbs and downtown, users in the remote department are likely to require a partner domain controller on their segment or suffer bottlenecks in trying to locate the domain controller and other network resources in the main building. Be aware that replication and authentication traffic is also hitting the pipe, along with the general network traffic. The domain controller for a new domain does not need to deal with the replication traffic generated between partner controllers in the same domain. You have two factors to consider: the size of the separate location and its distance from the existing domain.

The number of people in the separate location should be your guide, and this information should be in your enterprise analysis documentation. If the separate location is staffed by only a handful of people, the small amount of network traffic that they generate and the additional administrative burden that they cause cancel out any perceived benefits of creating a separate domain and locating a domain controller in their offices. (Think equipment costs, installation, and administration.)

The distance from the parent domain is also an important consideration. If the site is across the road, extending the backbone is easily handled with the appropriate permissions from the city planning department. If the parent domain is in the suburbs and the department is located uptown, however, extending the backbone even several blocks is likely to prove difficult — if not very expensive and impractical. You likely need to span a full or fractional T1 circuit or frame relay circuit to connect the two locations. Still, if the department is small and does not generate a lot of network traffic, you could get away without creating a child domain.

As the population of the separate location increases, you can first locate a collateral domain controller from the parent domain on its network segment, which enables the users and resources to authenticate faster without needing to touch the link. Just remember that you must watch replication bandwidth and the size of your pipe.

Later, other reasons besides being across the road or downtown determine the creation of a new domain. Following are a few alternatives to creating a child domain for a separately located department that does not have valid reasons to act as its own domain:

- **Consider Terminal Services.** Location of domain controllers and issues such as replication do not apply in a Terminal Services implementation. Even a dedicated Internet connection may be enough, depending on the type of work that your users are doing. Plus, a myriad of other factors make Terminal Services feasible.

- **Upgrade the link (your intranet connection).** In addition, increase bandwidth between the locations to relieve bottlenecks.

- **Install a partner domain controller.** First, however, compare the costs and TCO of installing additional bandwidth with the costs of installing a partner domain controller. This subject is also tackled in the Physical Domain Structure section of the whitepaper "Planning for Windows Server 2008" which you can download from `www.misiq.com/whitepapers`.

- **A replication partner** gives you the added benefit of fault tolerance, and if you don't have one in the main location, installing one in the separate location provides this payoff.

Managing replication overhead and network latency

Replication overhead and bandwidth are causes for concern in extending the domain to remote locations that are farther away than the uptown-downtown example described in the preceding section. Again, you have many factors to consider before you create separate domains, including the following four:

- Size and nature of the remote location
- Distance from the existing domain
- Number of remote locations
- Resources required by the remote locations

Bandwidth is your primary area of focus. The larger the pipe, the less latency it has in connecting to a remote domain controller. However, dedicated networks are expensive to maintain; costs recur. A domain controller is a one-time purchase — virtually management-free if it is a partner. Conversely, creating a separate domain substantially reduces replication traffic because only a small percentage of domain data is exchanged at the global catalog (GC) level (that is, in comparison to full-blown domain objects). If you must outfit many remote locations and they are large, the cost of a dozen or more T1 or bigger circuits outweighs the cost of creating new domains, one for each remote location.

Another factor (related to the next section) is the resources required by the remote locations. They may need local DHCP services, local WINS services, and local e-mail services. If the remote location is small enough and not too critical an operation, you may get away with installing all these services on one powerful server, so the cost of the domain controller is spread over the needs of the location.

Managing the decentralized administration models

These models dictate that you must transfer administrative authority (some call it power) to local or remote facilities. Such administration need not be in IT areas; it may be pervasive throughout the child entity. In this situation, you are not dealing with technological limitations as a reason to create child domains. Rather, management has given you a valid reason to create child domains — *autonomy*.

The decision to create the child domain depends on the extent of the transference and the autonomy of the division. If delegation of administrative authority is minimal, you can achieve the decentralization or delegation initiative without needing to create a separate domain. Just delegate administrative power wisely, at the OU level or along well-defined KME-OU lines. (You find more information about KMEs and OUs in the section "Organizational Units," later in this chapter.)

Managing autonomous divisions

A good example of an autonomous division is the Millennium City Police Department (MCPD). This type of situation is also a good reason to create a separate domain. Although MCPD functions under the administration and control of the city and reports directly to the mayor — its CEO, the Commissioner, is a publicly elected official — its internal affairs and operations are very different from those of other departments. In fact, the city pays the bills and salaries of MCPD, but just about all other management decisions and administrative functions are handled by the department.

From the point of view of IT administration, MCPD has its own administrators — people who not only know IT but criminal science as well. They know how to leverage technology from the crime-fighting perspective, and their ideas of fault-tolerance, availability, and technological advantage are very different from those of the administrators in, for example, the Taxi and Limousine Commission.

A separate domain gives the MCPD the security and independence of its own domain, while still providing the benefit of being attached to the extensive systems at the DITT and City Hall. You may argue (and, in your case, you may be right) that an autonomous body such as a police department requires its own domain, in its own forest, and appropriate trust relationships between the forests. In our example, however, we believe that one forest suffices.

Managing a diversity of domain policy

As you create a domain, you need to apply domain policy to the domain. Domain policy governs many domain-wide properties, such as password expiration, account lockout, UPN style, and so on. Policy and the attributes of domain objects are generally restricted to domains. (Domains and their contents can also inherit policy from higher-level domains and from the site in which they are placed.)

So, if your situation calls for such diversity, it can be achieved by creating separate domains. You need to be really sure that the reasons are valid and that the diversity cannot be simply achieved with OUs and groups. Creating a domain with an unusually stringent security policy just to house the accounts of the network administrators seems insane. Yet, we have seen this happening — incurring the cost of a new domain controller, Windows Server 2008 server license and all, just to hold the accounts of ten people. The bottom line is to analyze, evaluate, plan, and test before you come up with weak reasons to partition your directory into numerous domains.

Managing international partitions

International offices and locations provide many good reasons to partition to second- and third-level domains. The following list shows a few of these reasons, and you can probably come up with dozens of others:

- **Language barriers.**
- **Network limitations.** We may get away with extending the domain across the inter-coastal waterway but not across the Atlantic.
- **Cultural barriers.**
- **Geographical and national remoteness.** We once needed to install an IBM OS/2 telephony system into one of Microsoft's foreign offices because the NT-based equivalent was not approved in that country (a true story). Redmond was a little upset about the "infiltration."
- **Political and security regulations.** In some countries, you may distrust the subsidiary enough to put it into a separate forest.
- **U.S. export regulations.**

Managing security requirements

Windows Server 2008 is far and away the most secure network operating system in existence. You can lock down Windows Server 2008 so tight that not even helium can get in. Lockdown, however, is a relative thing; no system is flawless, and what matters is that it knows how to heal itself and that you pay attention to the necessary security details.

If your plan calls for more severe security restrictions in a segment of the namespace, restrictions that are likely to be intolerable for the majority of your users, you are left with no alternative but to create a new domain and possibly a new forest.

A domain is a security boundary for a collection of objects, and this security boundary cannot extend past the domain boundary to other domains without a predefined trust protocol. Domain objects require the authentication of users and computers to access them. These so-called users requiring authentication are known as *security principals*. In other words, you can force all the users of one domain to log on with smart cards (say, in the MCPD domain) that have long, encrypted passwords, while requiring short, simple passwords in other domains. Domains provide this benefit, and varying levels of security can be established throughout the enterprise — specifically, as follows:

- Domain password policy, your ultimate security resource, dictates the password usage rules in each domain.

- Account lockout policy dictates the circumstances for intrusion detection and account closure.

- Kerberos ticket policy, per domain, dictates the life and renewal of a Kerberos ticket.

See Chapter 16 for more information on Kerberos tickets. Policy is discussed extensively in Chapter 24.

Managing information hiding and resource publishing

Separate domains partition the directory and can assist you in selectively publishing and hiding resources. You derive a lot of benefit from enabling users to see and know about only what they are permitted to see and know about. Active Directory enables you to publish resources and provide users with divergent views of the directory service. This publishing and hiding of information is more critically achieved by using separate domains than by publishing in the domain itself. How objects are exposed is determined first at the domain level and then at the OU level.

Constructive partitioning of the directory

The beauty of Active Directory is that it lends itself to partitioning and it is distributed. It can thus be scaled to support billions of objects (accounts, OUs, and custom objects). We don't suggest that you try to stuff a billion objects into a single domain. If you are analyzing an enterprise that supports tens of thousands of users, not partitioning into a deeper domain structure is counterproductive. The more objects you need to create, the deeper or wider the structure is likely to be.

Partitioning the Domain

Several advantages and disadvantages result from partitioning the domain. The following list identifies several advantages in creating one or more domains:

- Defined security boundaries.

- Group policies, security, and delegation need to be defined only once.

- Reduced File Replication System traffic.

- Reduced domain network traffic because of fewer changes that need to be replicated.

You also face several disadvantages in creating one or more domain partitions. You determine your needs as an organization and weigh the disadvantages against the advantages to determine the correct partitioning. Following are several of the disadvantages of creating one or more domain partitions:

- Group policies, security, and delegation need to be defined in each domain.
- Administrative overhead of managing a number of domains.
- Increased GC replication because of increased numbers of domains.
- Moving users from one domain to another is more administrative effort than moving them from one organizational unit (OU) to another.
- Increased GC size.

As discussed in Chapter 17, Windows Server 2008 domains are organized at two levels: the *organizational unit* (OU) and the *group*. Both are containers, but groups are *security principals* and OUs are not. Groups contain user and computer accounts and must be authenticated to enable their contents to access secured resources in a domain. OUs are not authenticated by the security subsystem and serve to structure and partition the domain and to apply Group Policy.

Many people have commented that OUs should have been endowed with security attributes and that Microsoft should have made them security principals. After all, Novell Directory Services (NDS) OUs are security principals, and NDS does not offer groups. However, Active Directory OUs are not NDS OUs or even X.500 OUs.

Groups are also inherited from NT 4.0 and are not derived from any austere and otherwise bloated specification, such as the X.500 directory services. Moreover, some hardened NT administrators have ridiculed Microsoft for "porting" groups to Active Directory, but groups, for whatever is deemed good or bad about them, are built into the operating system and were around before the emergence of the directory service. If Microsoft had removed groups from the NT security system, it would have been the operating system's undoing.

In this chapter, we have dispensed advice concerning the strategic analysis of the enterprise to build a directory service and a domain structure. Our style and suggestions are derived from years of enterprise analysis of many companies, from the Thai fast-food place down the road to the likes of KLM Airlines and even Microsoft's own foreign subsidiaries. We find that our own Key Management Entities (KMEs), discussed in the section "Identifying the Key Management Entities" earlier in this chapter, fit in well with the OU-group relationship and help clearly define the difference between groups and OUs.

Organizational units

OUs are, on Windows Server 2008 anyway, the *administrative principals* of the domain. They serve as an organization tool and as a keeper of Group Policy Objects (GPO), for administrative control, and as an object filing system. (See Chapter 17 for a more general discussion of OUs.)

 The term *administrative principal* is not a Microsoft term (yet). The authors coined it, and you won't find it in the Windows Server 2008 documentation.

You learn from your enterprise analysis that how a company is run and how it is organized are not the same thing. At first glance, you would think that the OU would be used to reflect the departmental organization of the company. Companies, small and large, are split into divisions, and divisions are split into departments or business units. Thus, structuring your domain by using the OU to reflect, or mirror, the organizational structure of the company may seem appropriate.

This approach may work in many situations, but enterprise organization (departments) should not be your exclusive guide. You usually find that you need to be flexible and creative in your approach and not create any shallow rules for creating OUs. Creating an OU to contain all the resources of a sales department in a small company, for example, may make sense. If the company employs ten people, you could easily create one OU for the Sales department and then add groups to the OU that controls access to the resources in Sales. Delegate an administrator to the OU (if you have one), install policy to manage the workspace of the occupants of the OU, and be done.

What if Sales employs several hundred people? One huge department would easily call for several OUs, many groups, and various levels of policy and administration. We thought about this and came up with the following suggestions for the creation of OUs (as shown in Figure 19-10):

- Create OUs not along departmental lines, but, for the most part, along KME lines.
- Nest OUs only when the KMEs are large and contain child or already physically nested KMEs.
- Group KMEs that overlap into a single OU.
- Populate OUs with groups, as opposed to individual accounts.

You then decide, with the OU leaders, the level of hardness desired in the Group Policy, access to applications, workspace control, security, and so on. From the OU level looking outward to the domain and inward to the groups, you begin to see a "social order" developing. This is not unlike the domain system that ruled Japan from the 1600s to the 1800s, where domains were also organized into units, trusted each other at the domain level, and all reported to the shogun. Management was decidedly decentralized.

Now you also see a structure taking shape — a box — and it may even influence business planners outside IT, where the shogun is the CEO sitting in HQ, and inside the forest, where the shogun is the administrator sitting in the root domain.

Look at your KME matrix and create OUs along the lines of the most significant entities. Creating an OU along the boundaries of the sales department would be a bad idea if the sales department were huge, divided up along product lines or regions. The matrix identifies several KMEs that make up the sales department, and creating OUs along those lines would make more sense, because you always find a gray area for which you need to create an OU along something other than KME or administration lines or department lines — for example, a line of business.

FIGURE 19-10

OU creation according to KMEs of the organization.

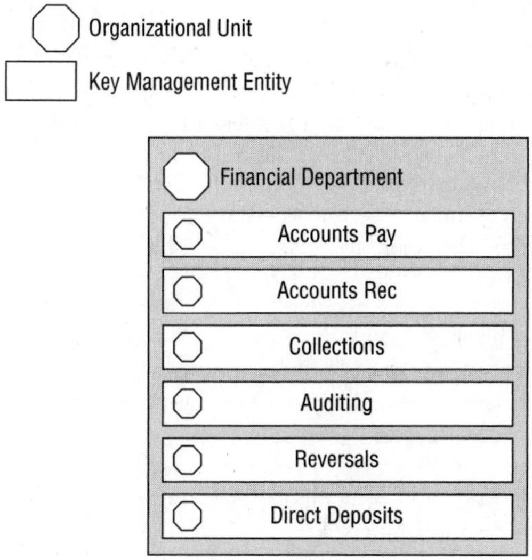

⬡ Organizational Unit

▭ Key Management Entity

We advise you to nest OUs only if the parent OU (which may turn out to be created along department lines) is large and contains child OUs. Within the financial department OU, for example, you can create OUs for accounts payable, accounts receivable, collections, and so on. If these KMEs are big or contain specialized KMEs within them, you can then create additional OUs and further nest the structure.

TIP Avoid excessively deep OU nests, which are not only harder to manage, but also require more computer resources. LDAP clients that do not understand the global catalog search long and deep and stretch the patience of your clients.

We advise you to collect all KMEs that overlap into a single OU. You could group niche KMEs in one parent OU, as long as you do not nest them just to create a hierarchy for "perspective." In some cases, you have a KME that has a wide embrace, such as accounts payable, and within that KME of, say, ten people, is one person who has a very different function or management mandate (such as a comptroller). In such a case, the smaller KME should not be defined by a nested OU but rather included in the parent OU along with its sibling.

Working with groups

After the OU is created along the KME lines, the administrators of the OU can decide, with the leaders or all members of the OU, what the OU requires in terms of resources (or, in other words, which objects the groups need to see or not see). We suggest populating your hierarchy of OUs with groups and not individual accounts.

Create groups and make the users who work in the KMEs members of the groups as needed. This practice, or policy, also serves to instill a discipline into the practice of assigning groups. NT 4.0 groups tend to show up everywhere at some lazy MIS departments. This way, unless a group is implicitly part of an OU, it should not be there.

What about users who work in KME *X*, are in OU *X*, but need access to the group in OU *Y*? Just "second" the user to the group in the other OU. You don't need to move the user account around; and, for all intents and purposes, the user may be a resident in another domain.

User and computer accounts cannot be in more than one place in the directory, but users often have more than one responsibility and, needing access to many things, appear in many groups. We may be working on applications during the week, for example, and be on call for the computer room over the weekend.

This approach — call it a philosophy — implies that all users be grouped into a single OU, possibly called HR. That concerned us, so we investigated the idea further. If you look at the attributes of user accounts, they are not variables that are managed often. Many are set once and never changed. You can then locate your user accounts in your root OU, in one OU (such as HR), or in several root OUs, at least at the top level of your enterprise, reflecting organizational policy. In fact, as long as you ensure that your user or computer accounts are linked to required GPOs (see Chapter 24), you can put the accounts in any folder.

Figure 19-11 now provides a more complete logical domain structure framework from which to expand. It shows user accounts in root OUs along department lines and OUs within the root along KME lines. The child OUs contain groups needed to serve the KMEs. After you achieve an LDS, you are in a position to decide how and where and when to delegate administration of the OUs and apply policy.

Securing the partitions

Windows Server 2008 enables administrators to efficiently manage domain partitions in very large enterprises. The new Credential Manager helps by providing a secure store of user credentials and certificates. By selecting authentication services in the catalog, you are automatically adding the Credential Manager to the system. When a user's computer requests authentication through NTLM or Kerberos, the Update Default Credentials or Save Password checkbox appears in the UI dialog box, enabling the Credential Manager to keep track of the user's name, password, and related information. The next visit causes the Credential Manager to automatically supply the stored credentials. Trusts also simplify cross-domain security issues.

If you have two Windows Server 2008 partitions or forests that are connected by a trust, authentication requests can be routed between partitions, thereby providing a seamless coexistence of resources. Authentication protocols can follow trust paths, so the service principal name of the resource computer must be resolved to a location in the partner partition. Server Principal

Names (SPNs) can be used to support authentication between a service and a client application. The SPN can be one of the following names:

- DNS domain name
- DNS host name

FIGURE 19-11

Logical domain structure.

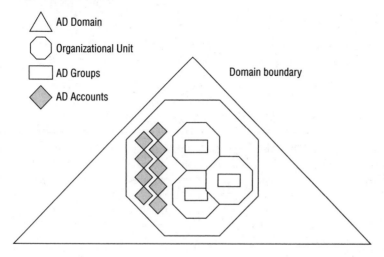

For users who access a resource from a computer located in another partition, Kerberos contacts the key distribution center on the domain controller within its domain for a session ticket to the SPN of the resource computer. Then the domain controller is responsible for finding the SPN.

Windows Server 2008 also introduced a new Group Policy management solution to unify all management of Group Policy. The Group Policy Management console integrates existing policy functionality into one simplified console. The following tools are all integrated into the Group Policy Management console:

- Active Directory Users and Computers snap-in
- Active Directory Sites and Services snap-in
- Resultant Set of Policy snap-in
- Access Control List (ACL) editor
- Delegation Wizard

These tools enable administrators to perform all necessary core Group Policy tasks from within the console. The following list shows a few benefits of the Group Policy Management console:

- Backup/restore of Group Policy Objects.

- Import/export and copy/paste of GPOs and Windows Management Instrumentation (WMI) filters.

- HTML reports for GPO settings and Resultant Set of Policy (RSoP) data. (These reports enable printing, saving, and read-only access to GPOs.)

- Scripting of Group Policy operations provided by this tool. (Note: This does include scripting of settings within a GPO.)

The Group Policy Management console also enables management across domain partitions, all within a simple user interface, by using drag-and-drop features.

Summary

Creating a Windows Server 2008 domain, especially for large and complex entities, is a daunting task. You are strongly advised not to begin an upgrade or conversion from an NT domain until you have first performed a mission-critical enterprise analysis of your organization and completed a blueprint of the logical domain structure (LDS) that is approved by the entire team and management. Additionally, you cannot start your rollout until you have done your homework in the labs and have fully signed off on the physical domain structure (PDS) — a topic we tackle in the next chapter.

Chapter 20

Active Directory Physical Architecture

This chapter reviews the physical structures of Active Directory. It also introduces you to the relationships between domain controllers (DCs) and the various roles of domain controllers, global catalogs (GCs), and sites.

Past, Present, and Future

Past operating systems had no awareness of the underlying physical network structure on which they were deployed. For small companies, or even reasonably large ones, the network layout, interconnection points and subnets, remote offices, and so on were either laid out long before Windows NT became pervasive or were installed independently of the network operating systems that depended on them.

We typically build networks for which the servers reside on 1000-Mbps media, the backbone. There are 1000-Mbps media between floors, and then this network is extended into a 20–100Mbps network down to the users. Windows NT did not care if the networks were 10 Mbps or 10,000 Mbps ... it had no built-in means of catering to the available resources.

This is no longer sufficient because Windows Server 2008's physical structure and its multimaster replication technology, GC services, public key infrastructure, directory synchronization, Kerberos authentication, and more *do* need to be sensibly and carefully built according to the physical network resources. Fortunately, the OS also enables you to build a logical network and map it to a present or future physical network. With Active Directory services, you can tailor your Windows Server 2008 deployment

697

to the available network and merge the two structures into a unified cooperative. The reason for this is Active Directory and its host domain controller server.

Legacy Windows NT and Windows Server 2008 network requirements are very different. Windows NT depended on a single primary domain controller (PDC), which held the master database of the domain configuration, accounts, security, and so on. This PDC was a single master domain controller, meaning that only the database on the PDC machine could be written to. If this machine began to shake or freak out, the network was frozen, in terms of its ability to make changes to the domain. Clearly, this was not a pleasant idea.

The old 1990s domains used backup domain controllers (BDCs) to back up the PDC. The BDCs would service the domain, in terms of logon authentication, security, and the like, but their databases could not be edited. To do that, you would have had to promote a BDC to the role of PDC. Thus, the PDC and BDC existed in a single-master or master-slave arrangement. No matter where you were on a Windows NT network, changes you made to the domain were saved to the PDC, and the PDC replicated this information out to the BDCs wherever they were. There was little else you could do to manage or customize this synchronization.

In the old days of Windows domains using NT, there was typically one BDC for every remote location and one or two resided on the local segment. The PDC functioned independently of the BDC. If the BDC went down, then the local users would have a hard time getting authenticated or using network resources, and if their segment lost connectivity to the office holding the PDC, then they would be in trouble. This legacy single-master physical domain structure is illustrated in Figure 20-1.

FIGURE 20-1

The network single-master domain structure of the Windows NT domain.

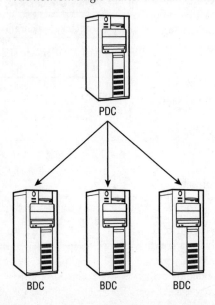

Windows Server 2000 through 2008 is very different. Although the concept of DCs and BDCs remains the same, these services operate as masters, or in a multimaster peer arrangement. There is no PDC; all domain controllers can be edited and updated. Active Directory ensures that any changes or additions made to one DC directory are distributed to the other DCs. This is known as multimaster replication technology (and you could call it a philosophy as well). The multimaster arrangement is illustrated in Figure 20-2.

FIGURE 20-2

The network multimaster domain structure of the Windows Server 2008 domain.

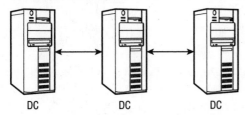

To deploy an ongoing administrative approach in Windows Server 2008, you must first design the logical structures based on the enterprise's present and future needs, as discussed in Chapter 19. Then map that model to the physical network and ensure that you have the necessary structures to support it, in terms of bandwidth, subnet design, network routes, and so on. It is also possible, as you can see, to cater to areas of your network that do not ideally fit into any logical structures you have.

Windows Server 2008 and Active Directory enable you to map your logical network model to the physical network with DCs, GCs, and sites. Moreover, Windows Server 2008 ties everything together between the DCs, the GCs, and the sites with links, bridges, and connection objects to comprise a highly sophisticated directory, directory replication, and directory synchronization service. Before we get down to the railroad work, we should talk about DCs, GCs, and sites in less abstract terms than we have in previous chapters.

Forests and Trusts

Forests consist of one or more DCs that share common schemas and GCs. If multiple domains in a forest share the same DNS naming schema, they are referred to as a domain tree, as displayed in Figure 20-3.

A forest can also be made up of one or more domain trees. The forest root domain is the first domain in the forest.

Windows Server 2008 computers use the Kerberos v5 security protocol over two-way transitive trusts to authenticate users between domains. Trust relationships are automatically created between adjacent domains when a domain is created in a domain tree. In a forest, a trust relationship is automatically created between the forest root domain and the root domain of each domain tree added to the forest. Because these trust relationships are transitive, users and computers can be authenticated between any domains in the domain tree or forest.

FIGURE 20-3

The Windows Server 2008 domain tree.

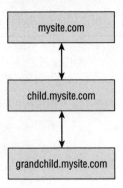

If you insist on upgrading a previous server product to the Windows Server 2008 domain, the existing trust relationships are maintained between that domain and other domains. Domain trusts enable users in one domain to access resources in another domain. Transitive trusts are two-way, meaning that both domains in the relationship trust each other. A transitive trust, therefore, is not bounded by the two domains in the relationship. Nontransitive trusts are bounded by the two domains in the relationship and don't flow to any other domains in the forest.

Table 20-1 describes the types of trusts available.

TABLE 20-1

Trust Types

Trust Type	Direction	Transitivity
External	Both	Nontransitive
Realm	Both	Nontransitive and transitive
Forest	Both	Transitive
Shortcut	Both	Transitive
Parent	Two-way	Transitive
Tree-root	Two-way	Transitive

NOTE The Active Directory Wizard automatically creates tree-root, parent, and child trusts; therefore, external, realm, forest, and shortcut trusts must be created by the New Trust Wizard.

Windows Server 2008 forests are *transitive*, meaning that their trust relationships are not bound to any two domains. Each newly created child domain automatically creates a two-way transitive trust between the child and parent domain, causing transitive relationships to flow upward through the domain tree, causing relationships among all domains in the tree. Each newly created domain tree in a forest automatically creates a relationship between the forest root domain and the new domain. If no child domains are added, the trust path is between this new root domain and the forest root domain. If child domains are added, trust flows upward through the domain tree to the domain tree's root domain, extending the path created between the domain root and the forest root domain. If new domains are added, the forest is a single root domain or domain tree, causing the transitive trust to flow through all domains in the forest. Figure 20-4 displays how transitive trusts flow through a forest.

FIGURE 20-4

Transitive trusts for Windows Server 2008.

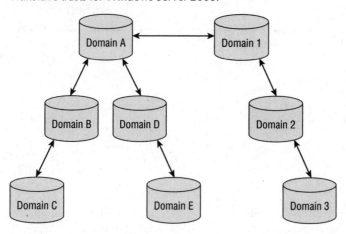

In Figure 20-4, domain 1 has a transitive trust relationship with domain 2; therefore, domain 2 has a transitive trust relationship with domain 3. Resources in domain 1 can be accessed by domain 3 users if they have the proper permissions. Domain A has a transitive trust relationship with domain 1, giving users in domain 3 access to resources in domain B, assuming they have the correct permissions.

You also have ways to explicitly create transitive trusts between Windows Server 2008 domains in the same forest or domain tree. These shortcut trust relations can be used to shorten the trust path in large and complex forests.

Nontransitive trusts are bound by two domains in a trust relationship and do not flow to any other domains in the forest.

> **NOTE**   Windows Server 2008 domains are nontransitive relationships between Windows NT domains. If you upgrade from a Windows NT domain to a Windows Server 2008 domain, all trusts are preserved.

All nontransitive trusts are, by default, one-way trusts. It is possible to create a two-way relationship by creating two one-way trusts. The following scenarios describe a nontransitive trust relationship:

- A Windows NT domain and a Windows Server 2008 domain.
- A Windows Server 2008 domain in one forest and a domain in another forest that are not joined by a forest trust.

Understanding that trusts refer to domains that are trusted to have access to resources is important. Figure 20-5 illustrates the flow of a one-way trust. *Trusting resources* means all resources, whereas *trusted accounts* refer to users that gain access to the trusted resources.

FIGURE 20-5

The one-way trust for Windows Server 2008.

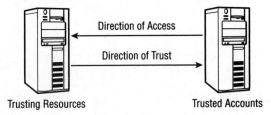

A one-way single trust relationship, as displayed in Figure 20-5, consists of nontransitive trusts. A Windows Server 2008 domain can establish a one-way trust with the following:

- Windows Server 2008 and Windows 2000 domains in a different forest
- MIT Kerberos v5 realms
- Windows NT 4.0 domains

Because Windows Server 2008 domains in a forest are linked by transitive trust, it is not possible to create one-way trusts between Windows Server 2008 domains in the same forest.

Figure 20-6 displays a two-way trust. Both of the domains shown trust each other, granting the accounts access to the resources and the resources access to the accounts. This enables both domains to pass authentication requests between themselves in both directions.

FIGURE 20-6

The two-way trust for Windows Server 2008.

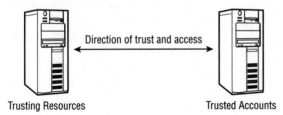

Trusting Resources   Trusted Accounts

Domain trusts in Windows Server 2008 forests are two-way transitive trusts. If you create a new child domain, a two-way transitive trust is created between the new child and the parent domains.

Forest choice design implications

Active Directory (AD) and the Security Accounts Manager (SAM) represent the cradle of security in any Windows Server 2008 (or earlier) domain. An AD network (whether a single forest containing a single domain, or multiple domains, or an AD network of multiple forests) is only as secure as the administrative practices of the enterprise or organization.

The notion that highly sensitive resources can only be secured in their own domains or forests because of the administrative and security boundaries provided by them is at best misguided and at worst a misnomer. Any value factored in from the utility of the administrative or security boundary is quickly eroded by the administrative burden in operating and managing multiple domains and forests.

Technically, a domain affords multiple entities of an enterprise (such as the subsidiaries of a company) the capability to organize and administer their own security policy, their own group policy, their own distributed file system, and so on. However, the domain boundary does not necessarily make it more secure. The reason is simple: The domains in a single forest trust each other through bi-directional, implicit, transitive trusts, and thus, the domains are not separated by impenetrable security.

Only a separate forest fully secures two domains from each other because the trusts are not transitive, are not bi-directional, and must be explicitly created (such as the trusts between NT 4.0 domains and the trusts between Windows Server 2008 and other NOSs, such as a Unix realm). However, when forests are managed by the same team of people, or resources need to be shared between them, the administrative boundaries tend to erode and are thus penetrated far easier and far quicker, and often without the knowledge of the organization, than the boundaries of a single resource domain. Doors will be inevitably opened to ease the administrative burden.

All that is needed to bring down the domain or forest boundaries is the compromising of the key administrator accounts. It is clear that if a single organization such as MCITY entertains multiple domains and multiple forests, it will result in a far more expensive and awkward architecture for its Active Directory implementation than a single forest and one operations (resource) domain for all companies.

The design and architecture described in this chapter is geared in every way, shape, and form around one operations domain — that is, a forest root domain responsible for forest-maintenance operations. This enables all administrative burdens, resources, and tools to be exploited by a single domain's security and administrative team. The security of the domain is also ensured by installing a granular and hierarchical administrative design, described in this chapter, which is backed by the most sophisticated security mechanisms available to Active Directory and Windows Server 2008.

In this regard, it is critical to be aware that, should it be determined that the single resource domain will be forgone in favor of a multiple-domain model, or possibly a multiple-forest model, this architecture must be significantly reworked to accommodate the new model, at a significantly greater cost in both the short and long terms. The architecture for hardware, software, tools, human resources, and WAN traffic will be significantly affected as a result.

Domain Controllers and Global Catalogs

The three components of Windows Server 2008 and Active Directory networks are domain controllers (the directory hosts), global catalogs, and sites. They are all interrelated, so a discussion of each individually and then collectively is warranted. We kick off with the DCs that you have been reading so much about.

Domain controllers

A *domain controller* (DC) houses Active Directory (AD); it is Active Directory's host. As you learned in the previous chapters, Active Directory is the brain, or control center, of the central nervous system that authenticates users and manages security and access control, communications, printing, information access, and so on.

Active Directory is also a lot more than just domain information. It is also a storehouse of enterprise information, a place where you can place "signposts" that point or redirect users to information and objects of functionality anywhere on the local or wide area network. It is also a place where you can go to find people, places, and things. In the future, Active Directory becomes the local "hangout" for all applications.

Active Directory also stores information about the physical structure of your network. To use the brain analogy again, Active Directory knows how your network is structured and what is required to keep it in good health and service it correctly.

The one thing we cannot do with our brains is replicate the information in them. If we could, life would be very different. Also imagine blowing out your brains and then just replacing them with a "hot" standby, *a la* plug and play. Fortunately for us, our brains, left alone, look after themselves pretty well for a period of 70 to 100 years. Active Directory brains are not as fortunate; they can be carried off, fused, trashed, and corrupted.

Imagine that the only DC running a Windows Server 2008 domain gets fried. Knowing what you do now, the network is frozen until the DC can be restored. This is not a fortunate position to be in. For starters, your backups (usually taken the night before) are only able to restore you to the state you were in 8 to 12 hours ago. Second, what now authenticates the restore service writing to the new machine? Losing the DC is not a pleasant event, akin to a human going into a coma and not returning for a few weeks or years, if ever.

Having another "equal partner" DC is essential, even for a small office. It need not cost an arm and a leg, but you should have one all the same. The number-one rule about Active Directory availability on a Windows Server 2008 network is to place the DC as close as possible to users. In larger companies, it makes sense to place DCs on remote sites, on segments, in separated offices, or in large offices, because the nearer your clients are to the DCs, the quicker they can authenticate and gain access to resources, printers, and communications. Having more than one DC also spreads the load around, a practice called *load balancing*. An office of more than 1,000 people all hitting one lonely DC does not make sense.

All the DCs in an enterprise coexist as a "cluster" of sorts, each one backing up the others. They are all responsible for maintaining the identical information about a certain domain, as well as any information that that directory has concerning the other elements and domains in the forest. The DCs keep each other abreast of changes and additions through an extensive, complex, and complicated replication topology. It is certainly far too complicated to grasp at its DNA level, and it is both with tongue in cheek and in reference to a design style that we soon discuss that we refer to a Windows Server 2008 network as a *matrix*.

The matrix, however, becomes a growing consumer of network bandwidth the larger and more complex the enterprise becomes, or the more it begins to depend on directory services. Therefore, one of the first tasks that you or your administrators have in the management of the domains and directories is the replication provisioning that must take place. The GC service also uses bandwidth and Active Directory and DC resources, as we soon discuss.

As mentioned earlier, this cooperation among all DCs on the matrix is what we call a multimaster arrangement. If the packets are routed over limited bandwidth, the router or gateway is a lot more vulnerable to bottlenecks than in the Windows NT domain arrangement of single-master operations.

Consider some core facts about DCs that cannot be ignored (and we summarize as we go):

- Each domain must have a DC (or one copy of Active Directory). As with the brain, if the last DC goes into a coma, the network comes to a dead stop.

- DCs provide users with the means to function in a workplace, to communicate, and to keep the enterprise alive. Take that away and you have a lot of unhappy people.

- You need more than one DC in a domain (or a very good backup/restore plan or even a RAID in a small office).

- The various parts of the DC that must be replicated to the other DCs in the same domain are *schema* changes, *configuration* changes, and *naming contexts*. The naming contexts are essentially the tree namespaces, the names of the actual objects on the tree, and so on.

NOTE By now, you probably realize that your DC can service only one domain. How much more sensible and easier would it be if a good machine with a ton of resources could be used to host multiple domains? We hope to see this emerge in future generations of Active Directory.

Although Active Directory replicates everything to the other DCs, it has some built-in features that facilitate replication. Before we discuss them, look at the illustration in Figure 20-7. Imagine if you poured water in either side of the tube. Your knowledge of science tells you that gravity and other forces in the cosmos act to balance the two sides. It does not matter which side you pour the water into, nature still acts to create equilibrium. This is how Active Directory works; it has automatic built-in mechanisms that ensure that when more than one DC is on the matrix, it receives the share of information it needs or deserves.

FIGURE 20-7

Active Directory replication is automatic and, for the most part, transparent.

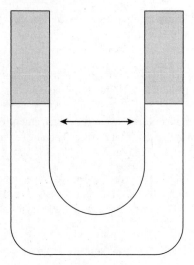

If you limit the width of the U-piece, or tunnel, however, creating the balance takes longer; and naturally, if you block the U-piece, the balance cannot occur.

Specifically, Active Directory acts in the following manner to ensure that the replication occurs and that it occurs as painlessly as possible: Only the changes to objects or new objects are replicated to the other DCs, and you can specify how the replication is handled. For example, you can schedule how often and when replication occurs.

By using these features, you can control the bandwidth usage between DCs. In addition, if you have remote sites, sensible use of replication services and bandwidth may obviate the need for a separate domain, especially if you are catering to a small office and you do not have a lot of network traffic hitting that U-piece on your network.

Global catalogs

The main purposes of the *global catalog* (GC) are as follows:

- ■ It provides the point of contact and interface for authentication of users into Active Directory domains, which means it holds a full replica of all user accounts in its custodian domain.

- ■ It provides fast intradomain and interdomain searches of Active Directory without actually iterating the trees, or performing what is known in directory service language as *deep searches*.

The GC is essentially a subset of the domain that, for search purposes, holds only the attributes or property information necessary to find an object belonging in a domain other than the one it directly serves. That may sound confusing because philosophically, the GC sits above the domain hierarchy. In fact, the GC is not in a hierarchy at all and is not part of the Active Directory domain namespace.

When you search Active Directory, you know what you are looking for, or you have at least a vague idea. (By *you*, we also mean any application that needs to look up an object for some reason.) As discussed in Chapter 17, a user object is a leaf or end node on the Active Directory domain tree that is read from right to left (or bottom to top). The user object `jshapiro.genesis.mcity.us` tells you that when you start at the top of the namespace and from `org` you work your way down three domain levels, you find `scottleathers`. Of course, you also find other objects at the end of this namespace, but at least you have limited your search to a contiguous namespace.

What if you don't have any information about the root domains? What if you or the application has no entry point (an LDAP shallow search needs at least a root from which to start a search) from which to begin? You would have to commit to a deep search of the forest to find the object. By *deep search*, we mean that you or your application would have to traverse every tree in the forest to find the object you are looking for, and this is done through a system of referrals.

A directory service with the potential of `MCITY` and all its departments would be very long and tiresome to search. That's where the GC comes in. We know this seems like a deep explanation, but many people find it confusing at first why there is a catalog when you can, theoretically, search the domain trees. The illustration in Figure 20-8 demonstrates how easy it is to search the GC.

FIGURE 20-8

Searching for a user in Active Directory.

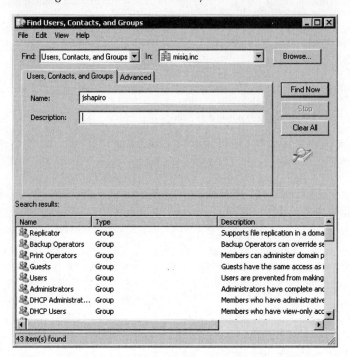

The GC contains a partial replica of every domain in the forest and a copy of the schema and configuration-naming contexts used in each forest. In other words, the GC holds a copy of every object in the forest. However, it holds only the key attributes of each object that are useful for searching. You can thus easily find an object or a collection of objects just by specifying an attribute. Figure 20-8 shows the result after we provided a letter and the search returned several objects. In this manner, a user or application can locate an object without having to know in which domain the object resides.

The GC is optimized for queries. The query mechanism is based on the LDAP system but uses basic queries that do not return referrals (LDAP referrals pass the search flow from tree to tree, but the GC is not hierarchical; it is a flat database). The following factors are important considerations:

- A GC is located by using DNS.
- A GC is created in a domain tree; it is housed on a DC.
- You should install at least one GC per DC site.

■ The members of Universal groups are stored in the GC; although local and global groups are stored in the GC, their members are not. Universal groups are available only to native-mode domains. Mixed-mode domains do not need a GC for authentication.

By the way, the GC also holds the access control information of the objects so that security is not compromised in any way.

The GC network carries an overhead separate from the DC network. Remember that they are not integrated; they are separate resources. The GC, in fact, has no understanding of how a domain works, nor does it care. Here are some specifics to keep in mind:

■ The GC generates replication and query traffic within a site and between sites, so keep in mind that your network is now going to be hit with both DC and GC traffic. In addition, a GC is required for logging on to a native-mode domain. If there is no GC on the local segment, a GC on a remote segment is used for authentication.

■ Users may need to be shown how to query the GC, which adds administrative overhead. Alternately, you must make sure that your objects are populated with relevant information. If you store only the e-mail address of a person in his or her respective object, for example, and someone looking up this person's e-mail address submits only limited information, such as a last name or first name, the chance, albeit remote, exists that the search will return NULL.

■ You need at least one GC in a domain, but if that domain is spread far and wide (which is possible), then you can add the GC to other DCs (we discuss doing exactly that in Chapter 19). Get used to the idea of managing or working with more than one GC because down the road, many applications begin taking advantage of a permanent catalog service on the network, and we are not talking about only BackOffice stuff such as Exchange and SQL Server.

GCs are built by the Active Directory replication service, which we describe shortly.

The DC and GC locator services

You may have been wondering, with all this superficial discussion of DCs and GCs, how a user locates the correct DC to log on, and how the user locates a GC to search. After all, you might imagine that you at least need an IP address or some means of locating the domain, because NetBEUI or other NetBIOS services are no longer a requirement on a Windows Server 2008 network. The answer is simple, but the architecture is a little arcane and thus may be difficult to understand initially. On a very small network, you might be forgiven if you opt out, for now, of trying to understand the locator services; but on a reasonably large network that extends beyond more than a handful of offices and network segments, understanding this is very important.

Network clients deploy a special set of algorithms called a *locator service* that locates DCs and GCs. The latest version of the Windows locator service serves both Windows Server 2008 clients and legacy Windows clients. Thus, both clients are able to use DNS and NetBIOS APIs to locate the DC and GC servers. How do they do this?

If the client can resolve DCs in DNS, which is what all Windows Server 2008 clients are empowered to do, then the client's locator service searches for the DC that is positioned closest to it. In other words, if the client is located on network segment 100.50.*xxx.xxx*, it checks a DNS server provided to it for a DC on the same network segment, regardless of whether the DC it gets is in its "home" domain.

If the domain the client is searching for is a Windows NT 4.0 domain, then the client logs on to the first DC it finds, which is either a PDC or any of the BDCs. The upshot of all this locating is that the client first logs on to a site-specific DC and not a domain-specific DC. The next steps that the client takes are worth paying attention to.

If the DC closest to the client (on the same subnet) is the home DC of the client, then well and good, and no further referral or buck-passing is required. What if the client is located in another network segment, far away from the home DC? A good example is a busy executive who spends every week in a different location, and therefore attaches to a different network each time. The notebook computer the executive is carrying around receives an IP address of a new network segment that could be many "hops" away from the last segment containing the executive's original domain.

As illustrated in Figure 20-9, the client contacts the nearest DC (A). The DC looks up the client's home site and then compares the client's current IP address with the IP address of the closest site containing a domain controller that hosts the client's domain. With that information, the client is then referred (B) to the DC in that nearest domain and obtains service.

FIGURE 20-9

The locator service used by clients to look up their domain controllers.

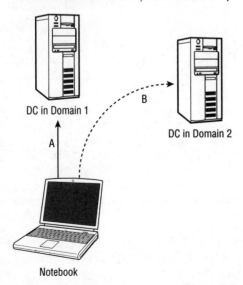

DC in Domain 1

B

DC in Domain 2

A

Notebook

Design decisions

DCs are placed according to the following rules:

- **User population.** DCs should be located where there is a high concentration of users logging on (this is a viable rule even when the link to a remote DC offers high bandwidth).

- **Bandwidth.** Where bandwidth is low, a DC is used to speed up logon and authentication times.

- **Redundancy.** Consideration must be given to how functionality will be maintained in the event that a DC fails. Consequently, multiple DCs should be available at key locations.

- **Applications.** Application reliance on DCs (such as Exchange).

Architecture

Fifty users are considered the break-even point for authentication traffic versus AD replication traffic. At a site with fewer than 50 users, Active Directory replication traffic generated by a local DC server actually creates more traffic on the WAN than authentication traffic generated by users being authenticated by a remote DC. The placement of DC servers has been modeled according to the best practices rules.

A local DC server is not required in a site when the following is true:

- There are fewer than 50 users at the site and the WAN circuit to the hub/parent site (that is, the site containing the closest DC) server has at least 64KB/sec of average available bandwidth. However, if this condition is true, then this circuit should be able to handle the authentication traffic. If this is not true, then we would consider increasing the bandwidth of the circuit by at least another 64KB/sec; and if that is not possible, we would consider implementing measures that will greatly reduce the authentication traffic needed to the site and the frequency of Group Policy updates.

- The site can tolerate the expected duration and frequency of WAN circuit failures to the hub/parent site (that is, the site containing the closest DC) server. This could be ensured or provided by a backup/alternate WAN circuit. Generally speaking, if a WAN link to a site is not 100 percent available, then WAN logon and WAN access to resources are not viable for the site.

- A local DC server is required in a site when the following is true:

  - More than 50 users work at the site, or a local Exchange server exists (likely if the site has more than 50 mailbox users and the link between the sites and a remote Exchange server is weak). Exchange servers require fast and reliable access to GC servers.

  - An application is heavily dependent on fast access to Active Directory (such as a database application that performs GC lookups and so on).

This entire matrix of DCs and GCs, replication, and referral services for logon is accomplished by a sophisticated mechanism built into Windows Server 2008 known as a *site*, a topic covered next.

Sites

A *site* is a representation of a network location or a group of network locations abstracted as an Active Directory object above one or more TCP/IP network segments. It is managed as a logical unit within the Windows Server 2008 domain controller matrix.

The concept of a site was introduced in Windows 2000. It did not exist in Windows NT. Sites provide AD with knowledge of the physical network upon which it is functioning. Sites and domains are independent concepts. A site can belong to multiple domains, and a domain can span many sites. Sites are retained as objects in AD — stored in the Configuration Naming Context (CNC). The architecture and implementation of site topology is discussed in this section.

A site is identified or addressed in Active Directory according to the TCP/IP subnet on which it resides, and it is resolved to that segment via DNS. A site is directly related to a domain as far as intrasite and intersite replication is concerned, but a site is also indirectly related to the other elements in the forest with respect to the other naming contexts, such as the GC, the schema, and so on. A site is also a logical container that is totally independent of the domain namespace.

Active Directory requires that a site be *well connected*. That term may be relative and somewhat obscure in that a well-connected site, for example, in Swaziland, may be a disaster in the United States. Nevertheless, the definition, according to Microsoft, is that the site should also be accessible via a reliable connection, which would thus preclude the term *site* being used to refer to a machine hanging off the end of a 28.8 Kbps modem. You find that, in the real world, you may need to deal with sites of 56 Kbps and 64 Kbps, which is not a lot of bandwidth.

Windows Server 2008 also requires that the site be fast enough to obtain domain replication in a timely and reliable manner. By defining a site according to a TCP/IP subnet, you can quickly structure an Active Directory network and map it to the physical structure of the underlying network.

Most important, however, is that a site is used for determining replication requirements between networks that contain DCs, and for that matter, all other replication services, such as WINS, DNS, Exchange, NDS, and more. All computers and networks that are connected and addressed to the same IP subnet are, in fact, part of this site.

A site is used to control several functions:

- **Authentication.** A site is used to assist clients in locating the DC and GC that are situated closest to them. As discussed earlier, the DC maintains a list of sites and determines which one is closest to the client, based on the IP address information it has on hand.

- **Replication.** Whenever changes occur in directories, the site configuration determines when the change is made to other DCs and GCs.

- **Collateral Active Directory services and applications.** Services such as DFS can be made site-aware and can be configured according to the site information they obtain from Active Directory. In the future, applications may also look up specific site information.

CROSS-REF   A site is also a conveyor of Group Policy, as discussed in Chapter 24.

Replication within sites

Windows Server 2008 supports a process known as the *Knowledge Consistency Checker* (KCC). This technology has been adapted from Exchange Server, which uses it to replicate between Exchange Servers. In this case, KCC is used for the replication services between DCs within a site.

The KCC essentially sets up replication paths between the DCs in a site in such a way that at least two replication paths exist from one DC to another, and a DC is never more than three hops away from the origination of the replication. This topology ensures that even if one DC is down, the replication continues to flow to the other DCs.

The KCC also sets up additional paths to DCs, but in such a way that there are no more than three connections to any DC. The additional connections swing into action only when the number of DCs in a site reaches seven, thus ensuring that the replication three-hop rule is enforced. This is illustrated in Figure 20-10. The site on the left contains six domain controllers, and each DC supports two replication or KCC connections. The site on the right contains more than six DCs, so the KCC makes additional direct connections to the DCs to ensure the three-hop rule.

FIGURE 20-10

KCC connections enforcing the three-hop rule.

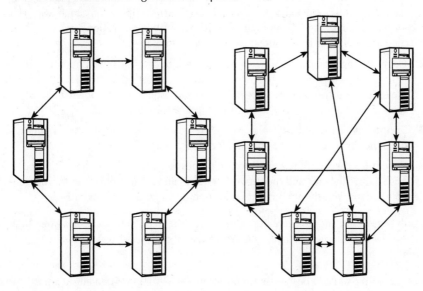

Active Directory also enables you to define *connection objects*. These are essentially manually configured points of replication between domain controllers. The KCC sets up connection objects automatically, but these objects have been made available for administrator access so that you can create a specialized replication topology of your own if needed. For the most part, you can leave the KCC to its own devices and have it set up the connection and replication environment for you.

Site links

Site links connect two or more sites together. Site links are similar to Exchange connectors and are configured similarly. The links are unidirectional and, like Exchange and WINS, are used to set up the replication network topology.

You need to do very little work to create site links because Active Directory automatically creates them when you create sites and add DCs to them. You can, however, manually configure sites, and it may become necessary as you set up links to deal with special circumstances, redundancy, and the like.

Because site links are unidirectional, you need to establish them in two directions. There are a number of options you can set, because site links are managed according to the existing infrastructure of a wide area network. The configuration options are as follows:

- **Transport provisioning.** This option governs which technology you use to transfer the actual data between the DCs. Active Directory offers you the choice of RPC or SMTP. SMTP is a mail protocol and not a reliable logon authentication data transfer protocol, but it does not require very much CPU bandwidth. RPC, on the other hand, compresses data and is thus more efficient, especially over narrow pipes. You can, however, use SMTP for replication of the GC information, schema, and file replication services (FRS), because there is no support for compression in these technologies.

- **Cost routing.** You can set a cost value for a site to determine which route to the site is the cheapest. You do not want to route over links that cost per transmission as opposed to the total monthly or annual service. You should configure cost for site links wherever you can so that Active Directory can use the route of least cost.

- **Frequency.** The frequency value of the site link is used to determine, in minutes, how often the site link should be checked for replication.

- **Schedule.** The schedule governs when replication can occur on the link. If the site is very busy during the day, and the network requires all available resources for mission-critical applications, you should prevent replication during these busy periods.

The default settings for site links are 100 minutes for the frequency and every three hours (180 minutes) for the replication schedule. You learn more about links later, when we get into the actual configuration.

Site links are simple tools to ensure that replication flows from one domain to another and vice versa. However, for complex structures, they can get a bit tedious. Site links are not transitive.

In other words, in a situation where Site A replicates to Site B, and Site B replicates to Site C, no replication between A and C takes place if B goes down.

The way around this is another feature in sites known as *site link bridges*.

Site link bridges

Breaking Active Directory into sites can reduce replication-related network traffic, but simply dividing Active Directory into sites is not enough. In order for sites to exchange Active Directory information, you must implement site links. These links provide information to Windows Server 2008, telling it which sites should be replicated and how often. When you link more than two sites using the same link transport, you are essentially causing them to be bridged. Figure 20-11 shows three sites linked by IP site links; by forming a linked bridge, these sites can communicate directly with each other.

FIGURE 20-11

Sites can communicate directly with each other through a linked bridge.

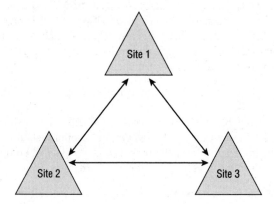

When a site is bridged it is known as transitive, meaning that when you create a site link, any sites in the link are bridged automatically. You never even need to create a site as long as all your sites are on a routed IP network.

The site link bridge costs are the sum of all the links included in the bridge. Your service provider can reconcile link costs with you.

Connection objects between sites

As discussed earlier, connection objects can be manually created and managed for replication topology design. We discussed the connection objects in terms of tools used to manage replication topology between DCs on the same site, but you can also use them to manually configure replication between DCs in different sites.

In other words, the replication topology of Active Directory is flexible (which is why we recommend you explore other uses for it, such as DNS replication). You can manage your replication manually, which means you can create all the connection objects yourself. You can also let Active Directory fully automate replication and join all sites to the site link bridges. Alternatively, you can configure some links automatically and others manually.

If you have special needs or you have a special link that can only be configured manually, use the manual options. Otherwise, leave KCC and automatic configuration to its own devices.

Active Directory Replication

If you manage a wide area network or intranet of any size, from a connection between two small sites to a worldwide service, replication in the Active Directory infrastructure is something you would do well to understand.

To recap, as soon as you have more than one DC controller on a network, you have network replication because of the multimaster replication activity that takes place between DCs of one domain and DCs and GCs of many domains. Replication takes place between DCs servicing the same domain or between DCs in the same forest. Replication is a service that enables changes made at any remote corner of the enterprise to be automatically propagated to other DCs servicing the enterprise. Replication occurs within a site and between sites.

A good example of this replication is changing policy related to certain accounts or organizational units in the Los Angeles domain (say, a lockout) and having those changes reflected in the London domain. A locked-out user may be able to gain access to the network if his or her account is disabled by logging on very far away from the DC where the account lockout was made. The locked-out user is unlikely, however, to beat the replication, and even when the remote DC does not receive the change in time, access to resources is barred.

All DCs can be updated, and their databases can be written to, which is why we call this a *multimaster* situation. However, in some special situations you do not want any DC to be able to make changes to Active Directory.

The first DC in the forest is also, by default, appointed certain exclusive forest management responsibilities. These responsibilities are related to changes that affect the forest on the whole. In this role, the DC is known as the *single-master DC*. The roles of the "root" DC are as follows:

- **The Schema Master (SM).** This DC is the only one in the forest that is allowed to make changes to the schema. Any DC can actually be the Schema Master, but you need to promote a DC to the position of Schema Master before it can play this role. This promotion leads the new SM to ask the old SM to transfer over the role of the SM.

- **Domain Naming Master.** This DC is the only one that can make changes to the domain namespace. This DC can, for example, add or delete domains or reference external directory services.

- **PDC Emulator.** Only one DC can be the PDC Emulator. This role enables a DC to provide so-called *down-level* services to the Windows NT 4.0 clients and servers. It also fools the down-level Windows NT 4.0 BDCs. In addition, as long as a PDC Emulator or advertiser exists on a mixed-mode domain, it receives preferential replication of password changes.

- **RID Master.** This DC role manages the relative identifier (RID) pool. RIDs are used to create the security principals, groups, and accounts for users and computers (which are identified according to security identifiers or SIDs). RIDs form part of the SID and are allocated to each DC in blocks of 512 RIDs. Every time a DC uses up the 512 RIDs, it contacts the RID Master for an additional allocation. The RID Master is also used to move an object from one domain to another.

- **Infrastructure Master.** This DC role maintains references to objects in other domains.

If you deploy a small network, all of the preceding roles are likely to be the responsibility of one DC. In larger, multi-domain environments, you may allocate these roles to several DCs in the domain. Be aware of these roles in case, for example, a server in charge of RIDs falls over and leaves you RID-free. Each forest must contain the RID, PDC, and Infrastructure Master roles, and these roles must be unique to each domain. The forest can contain only one instance of SM and Domain Naming Master roles. For the most part, these DC roles are self-healing between the different DCs, and you are unlikely to encounter any errors relating to the operations.

How replication works

Replication has been well designed because it is so important to Active Directory infrastructure, and Microsoft has gone to great lengths to ensure that the most up-to-date changes are distributed as efficiently and effectively as possible, without placing undue stress on already overloaded networks. In this regard, the following three crucial duties are performed by the replication algorithms:

- Identifying which changes must be replicated.
- Preventing unnecessary replication.
- Resolving conflicts.

The DC replication algorithms are self-learning and self-healing. DCs are able to keep track of the changes that have been made to their data and can discover the changes that have been made to other DCs. If the DC deduces that it is missing crucial changes made at another DC, it can request that those changes be transferred so that it can update its databases accordingly.

How does this extensive replication network remain in sync? Remember the fairy tale of Snow White and the Seven Dwarfs? The wicked witch constantly strives to stay one step ahead of Snow White by looking in the mirror and requesting updates on who is better-looking. The Active Directory replication algorithms behave in a similar fashion, but they have fortunately not been endowed with ego or one-upmanship, lest a DC decide to send a poison apple to another DC.

Romantic tales aside, every DC uses a *numerical sequence algorithm*, or *USN*, to track the changes made to its databases. Active Directory does not use timestamps to compare changes, as similar replication services do. Active Directory, in fact, only uses timestamps to settle replication collision disputes and in the timestamp field of Kerberos tickets, which checks for replay attacks.

The USN is a 64-bit number held by each DC and is important only to that DC. Each object or attribute in Active Directory has two USNs assigned to it. Each object has a *USNcreated* value and a *USNchanged* value assigned to it.

Whenever an object or property is successfully changed, the changeUSNs are advanced and the new value is stored with the object. Each DC maintains a table known as the *high-watermark vector* that states the highest changeUSN received from a DC's replication partners. Whenever a DC changes an object or a property, it sends the new USNs to the other DCs. In turn, the other DCs check their USN tables, and if the value of the changeUSN they have just received is higher than earlier ones received, or new, then the DC requests a copy of the new information, which is saved to its databases. Each DC is constantly trying to stay current with the other DCs.

This replication strategy is also extremely fault-resistant. If replication fails for some reason (for example, when the DC receiving the update is restarted), the replication attempt starts again exactly from where it left off because the receiving DC has not incremented its USNs in its high-watermark vector table. If the change does not complete, the DC that was interrupted simply requests the information again.

Obviously, because we live in a world of friction and gravity, the DCs cannot always be totally in sync. In fact, the replication model used is termed *loose consistency* because at any given time that a change may be updated or propagated, another change may already be on its way.

The only time when a DC network is 100 percent current is when there is only one DC or no changes are made to any of the DCs for a certain period of time. During quiet times or designated periods when changes are forbidden, DC states converge and become current. This is known in distributed systems lingo as *convergence*. On large networks, it is thus recommended that a change "blackout" be enforced at certain times to facilitate convergence.

Active Directory also employs some nifty algorithms that prevent both an endless cycle of updates from roaming around the network and DCs from endlessly firing off update requests and USNs. This technology is known as *propagation dampening*. Without it, a DC network simply grinds to a halt because DCs trying to update each other use up all the available bandwidth. The exact processes that are taking place in propagation dampening are fascinating, but beyond the scope of this book. If you need the torture, you can check the replication white papers at Microsoft for the excruciating details.

The same goes for collision detection. Using version numbers and the timestamp and other binary operations, Active Directory is able to resist the highly remote (but possible) chance that two administrators make a change to the same object in the Active Directory infrastructure at exactly the same time. In fact, only an application designed to do that can succeed, which is what Microsoft did to test collision resistance and assure us all that two DCs do not bump heads and blow up.

Directory Synchronization

No replication topology would be complete without synchronization traffic in the picture. At first glance, you may think that synchronization and replication are one and the same thing. They are not. Replication is information exchange between heterogeneous directories, whereas synchronization is information exchange between the same or homogeneous directories for the purpose of keeping each replica current.

For example: If you want to exchange information between Novell Directory Services and Active Directory, the technology to enable this is a *directory synchronization tool*. The following three strategies facilitate the interoperation of different directories:

- **Convert existing directories to Active Directory.** In case you decide to convert your existing directories to Active Directory, you need to obtain a directory conversion tool. One such tool for NetWare is the Microsoft Directory Migration snap-in. As a result of this course of action, the Novell directory meets the end of its life after the conversion. In this case, you replicate or transfer the information from one directory to the other. Other examples are in Microsoft's own backyard: All current network directories, such as MS Exchange and SQL Server, are converted to Active Directory.

- **Integrate directories.** If you choose instead to integrate directories, you need to deploy directory synchronization tools. These tools enable you to deploy two directories, each for its own good. Information is shared between them through the synchronization tool. A good example of such integration is an enterprise that is running both Exchange and Lotus Notes.

  Directories can be integrated with third-party tools, or you can make your own using the likes of ADSI or LDIFDE tools. (*LDIF* stands for *LDAP Data Interchange Format*, and *LDIFDE* stands for *LDAP Directory Exchange*.) Note that you can write code similar to SQL against the LDAP directory and move information between LDAP directories.

- **Deploy more than one directory.** This option is worth considering if you are a while away from deploying Active Directory, you have a huge investment in your current directory services, or your existing systems depend far too much on your current directory infrastructure. You may consider just deploying more than one directory, each one serving a special need, until you are ready to convert or synchronize.

NOTE Directory synchronization is no small matter. We recommend that you tread carefully here, letting the tools and techniques mature before you burn up time synchronizing or converting.

Whatever your decision, if you already deploy a directory service other than Active Directory or a BackOffice tool, you need to take into account the synchronization and replication traffic that is also added to your new Active Directory traffic.

Active Directory Site Design and Configuration

The first thing that you find out after you start Active Directory intersite and intrasite design is how well or how poorly your TCP/IP network has been designed, but before you start configuring anything in Active Directory, first make sure the physical network is optimized in terms of addressing, subnetting, and topology.

Confirm that the computers on the network that are attaching to Active Directory are obtaining the correct IP addresses. They should not be sitting on a different subnet from the one you are installing or getting the wrong dynamic IP addresses from a DHCP server. If the IP design is not sensible, location services are not going to resolve DCs as quickly as they should, and the logon experience becomes disappointingly slow for the user.

Topology

A good place to start when designing the physical structure is network topology. Begin by drawing a topology diagram of each site and then diagrams showing the links between each site.

After you have the site topology sketched out, you can create a network diagram showing the links between the different sites and how everything feeds back to corporate or enterprise HQ. Show the speed between the links and the different IP subnets that are in place. Also list the names of the routers on the links, the quality and transports being used, and so on. For example, in the WAN network in Figure 20-12, we indicate the IP addresses of the routers, the DHCP scope being used on that segment, the brand and model of the router, whether the site is Token Ring or Ethernet, and so on.

Also specify on the diagram or in supporting documentation the following:

- Indicate the speed of the link and the traffic. Your service provider can give you a breakdown of the bandwidth you are using, spikes in traffic, and your busiest times.

- Describe the cost of each link in as much detail as possible. Especially important to note is whether a link is pay-by-usage. This enables you to determine replication strategy to such a site.

- Describe the quality and reliability of the link.

- Define your site links by using the actual network topology that is already in place as a starting point. After all, if you have a network that is already down, no matter how bad it is, you have to start somewhere. If the links between the sites are reliable, you should map your Active Directory structure to this network as a foundation. Changes can be made later.

FIGURE 20-12

The network diagram of a portion of the Millennium City wide area network.

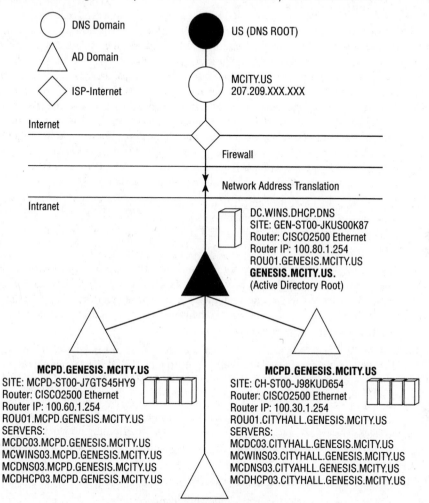

○ DNS Domain

△ AD Domain

◇ ISP-Internet

● US (DNS ROOT)

○ MCITY.US
207.209.XXX.XXX

Internet

◇

Firewall

Network Address Translation

Intranet

DC.WINS.DHCP.DNS
SITE: GEN-ST00-JKUS00K87
Router: CISCO2500 Ethernet
Router IP: 100.80.1.254
ROU01.GENESIS.MCITY.US
GENESIS.MCITY.US.
(Active Directory Root)

MCPD.GENESIS.MCITY.US
SITE: MCPD-ST00-J7GTS45HY9
Router: CISCO2500 Ethernet
Router IP: 100.60.1.254
ROU01.MCPD.GENESIS.MCITY.US
SERVERS:
MCDC03.MCPD.GENESIS.MCITY.US
MCWINS03.MCPD.GENESIS.MCITY.US
MCDNS03.MCPD.GENESIS.MCITY.US
MCDHCP03.MCPD.GENESIS.MCITY.US

MCPD.GENESIS.MCITY.US
SITE: CH-ST00-J98KUD654
Router: CISCO2500 Ethernet
Router IP: 100.30.1.254
ROU01.CITYHALL.GENESIS.MCITY.US
SERVERS:
MCDC03.CITYHALL.GENESIS.MCITY.US
MCWINS03.CITYHALL.GENESIS.MCITY.US
MCDNS03.CITYAHLL.GENESIS.MCITY.US
MCDHCP03.CITYHALL.GENESIS.MCITY.US

DITT.GENESIS.MCITY.US
SITE: DITT-ST00-JL097D76564
Router: CISCO2500 Ethernet
Router IP: 100.50.1.254
ROU01.DITT.GENESIS.MCITY.US
SERVERS:
MCDC03.DITT.GENESIS.MCITY.US
MCWINS03.DITT.GENESIS.MCITY.US
MCDNS03.DITT.GENESIS.MCITY.US
MCDHCP03.DITT.GENESIS.MCITY.US

Creating DC sites

To begin creating DC sites, take your list of segments and locations and the topological plan and follow these steps:

1. Create a DC site for each network segment, location, or collections of locations that are part of your so-called reliable WAN or intranet, and assign each location a DC site name. In our case, our first DC site name is zero-based and called GEN00-R. Formulate a naming convention for your sites and for your servers and resources (see Chapter 17). The *R* in our name means reliable. You may notice that we have used only letters, numbers, and the hyphen. This is because the DC sites are going to be used in the DNS. It is a good idea to stick to the standard RFC DNS names and resist underscores and letters that make your DNS names not only incompatible with RFC DNS but also looking like alphabet soup. Another reason for keeping the names simple is that most seasoned administrators go directly to the command line when debugging DNS. If you ask an admin to type **nslookup somethingcrazy**, you are likely to get some nasty remarks sent your way.

2. Create a DC site for each segment that is accessible only via SMTP mail. An SMTP site name on our plan would be named something like GEN05-S, the *S* standing for SMTP. You can also add information that tells a network engineer more about the site than just protocols.

3. Take network segments that are not self-contained DC sites and merge them with other sites, as long as the bandwidth between the sites is fast and reliable enough for the two segments to operate as a single combined DC site. Remember that site configuration in Active Directory has to do with replicating, so although the site may actually be a physical site, it is not a DC site, so to speak.

4. Make a list or a database of the sites that are added to your topology chart and record all the subnet address schemes. It is worthwhile to record all the sites, not only the ones that have a DC in them. You can make the site in the database a DC site. This helps you identify the site as an Active Directory site.

5. Mark on your topology diagrams where you are going to place DCs. In other words, mark the sites as being DC sites. Chapter 7 assists you in determining how to partition your forest and plan domains. Now is the time to put that planning and logical design into place.

Deploying domain controllers

Place your DCs in the sites selected in the following manner:

1. Place the root Active Directory DC in the so-called home site. In the example in this book, this site is GENESIS, and if you choose such a domain hierarchy, this site need only consist of a privately addressed subnet that uses network address translation to maintain the segment in such a way that it does not conflict with live networks. A root domain protected in this way is a worthwhile investment. Ignore the replication issue right now.

2. Place a DC in the "home" or head-office site. Your typical first-home DC is HQ. If you have followed a pilot project or you have performed lab work on Active Directory, you might also consider positioning the next site in the MIS Department. Depending on your

network and topology, MIS might be on the same subnet as HQ. In the case of Millennium City, we placed the CITYHALL domain above DITT in the namespace hierarchy, but in fact, it was the second DC that was raised.

3. Using the logical plan and the site or network topology link information, place your next DCs according to the following criteria:

   ■ Enough users are in the site to warrant a DC on their network segment.

   ■ The link is unreliable. If the link goes down a lot, users have a problem authenticating. If a DC is placed into that site, users can continue working. In the same spirit, if the link is an on-demand service, you want to drop a DC in there so that users have authentication round the clock.

   ■ The site can only receive e-mail or is open only to SMTP mail. In such a case, users must have a local DC because they cannot request logon authentication over SMTP.

While you are placing your DCs, keep in mind the need for GCs. Remember that GCs add to replication traffic, but they are also essential to log on. To refresh, GCs contain a complete copy of their parent domains and a partial replica of all other domains in the forest.

TIP Try not to get confused between sites and domains. Site links, although configured in Active Directory, are not related to domains or domain hierarchy. A site can contain any number of domains (by virtue of the presence of DCs).

Securing domain controllers

As you have discovered in the preceding chapters, DCs are packed with highly sensitive information. In fact, if a DC in a large enterprise is stolen or accessed while online, then anyone with malicious intent or thoughts of enrichment can do a lot of damage.

DCs need to be locked in secure rooms or cabinets with limited and controlled access. You may consider using a smart token (see Chapter 16). You can also install a *read-only domain controller* (RODC) in an insecure location. A RODC at least prevents an intruder from writing to the directory, which prevents a number of attack scenarios, such as denial of service (see Chapter 16).

Let's now consider the following points with respect to your architecture.

Schema Master

The Schema Master is the DC that performs updates to the directory schema. The *directory schema* is a definition of the classes and attributes within a directory. Once the directory schema is updated, it is replicated from the Schema Master to all other DCs in the directory. The Schema Master is the only role that can update the directory schema.

Products that update the directory schema include Exchange 2008, NetIQ, Microsoft Directory Synchronization Services (MSDSS), and the GroupWise Connector. These must have access to the Schema Master when they are installed. You obtain this access by logging on to the network as a member of the Schema Admins domain local security group. There is only one Schema Master per directory. You can take the Schema Master offline, and promote another DC to this role.

Domain Naming Master

A single DC needs to have the access to AD for making changes to the forestwide domain name space of the directory. This DC is the Domain Naming Master. It is the only DC that can add or remove a domain from the directory. It can also add or remove cross-references to domains in external directories. You cannot promote more than one Domain Naming Master per directory.

RID (Relative Identifier) Master

The DC that is responsible for processing RID (Relative Identifier) pool requests from all DCs within a given domain is the RID Master. This DC is also responsible for removing objects from the domain and putting them into another domain during an object move.

When a DC creates a security principal object (such as a user or user group), it attaches a unique SID (Security Identifier) to the object. This SID consists of a domain SID (the same for all SIDs created in a domain) and a RID that is unique for each security principal SID created in a domain.

A pool of RIDs for each Windows Server 2008 DC in a domain is allocated by the RID Master. When a DC's allocated RID-pool falls below a certain level, the DC issues a request to the RID Master to get additional RIDs. The RID Master responds and retrieves new RIDs from the domain's unallocated RID-pool. It then assigns them to the pool for the requesting DC.

PDC (Primary Domain Controller) Emulator

There is one PDC Emulator role holder in a Windows Server 2008 domain. This DC retains the following functions:

- It receives the password changes that are directed to other DCs in the domain. You can thus submit password changes directly to the PDC Emulator.

- If authentication failures occur at a certain DC in a domain because of an incorrect password, they are forwarded to the PDC Emulator. This takes place before a bad password failure message is reported to the user.

- All account lockouts are processed at the PDC Emulator.

  The PDC Emulator role is only necessary on a down-level domain, before member servers and DCs are upgraded to Windows Server 2008. Once a native domain is achieved, the following information applies:

- Windows Server 200X, Windows XP, and Vista clients (workstations and member servers) and down-level clients that have installed the distributed services client package no longer need to perform directory writes (such as password changes) to the PDC. They can now use any DC for the domain.

- Once BDCs (backup domain controllers) in down-level domains are upgraded to Windows Server 2008, the PDC Emulator no longer receives down-level replica requests.

In a native domain, clients and servers no longer require the Windows NT Browser service because Windows Server 2008 clients (including legacy clients that have installed the distributed services client package) will use AD to locate network resources.

Infrastructure Master

When an object in one domain is referenced by another object in another domain, it represents the reference in a variety of ways. It can use the GUID, the SID, or the DN of the object being referenced. The Infrastructure Master (IF) updates an object's SID and DN across domain boundaries.

Like the other FSMO roles, there is only one IF in a domain. In addition, only a DC that is not a GC (global catalog) server must hold the Infrastructure Master role. If the IF role is hosted on a GC server, cross-domain object references for the domain it is in will not be updated.

Miscellaneous roles for domain controllers

In addition to the aforementioned roles, two miscellaneous roles are indirectly related to Active Directory services that need to be defined for domain controllers. These are the Preferred Group Policy Administration Domain Controller and the Time Service Server. While these are not AD FSMO roles, they are also very important to be aware of.

- **Preferred Group Policy Administration Domain Controller (GPDC).** Group Policy should always be updated on the same DC, no matter how many DCs exist in the domain. This DC should always be in the first hub site of the domain. This policy serves to avoid replication collisions when administering GP and forces centralization of GPO development and assignment. The DC should also be the only DC on which GPTs (Group Policy Templates) are administered. (See Chapter 24 for more information.)
- **Time Service Server.** This is the server responsible for accessing an Internet time source and providing the domain with the time for all computer clocks to be synchronized with.

Deploying GC servers

As advised earlier, you place GC servers in your DC sites. Remember that GCs handle the logon authority for their "custody" domains and are essential for native-mode domains — and the application of Universal groups.

You should also place a backup GC in a sensitive or mission-critical domain, or have an online backup that can scream to the rescue. Losing the DC means losing the GC as well, and if that happens, your users must log on with their imaginations.

Understand that the GC holds the membership of the Universal groups, so when a logon request is made of a native-mode DC, the DC requests the GC to calculate the complete group membership access level of a particular user. With that level of security, if the GC has taken leave, your user is denied logon.

The only time that you can be lax on the GC availability scene is when you are dealing with a single domain. If this is the case, the GC is used mainly for search and seek.

Deploying DNS servers

Without DNS, you are in the dark. You can deploy a million DCs and GCs, but they run deep and silent without the locator service provided by DNS. Not only do the clients need to use DNS to locate network services and DCs, but DCs also need to use DNS to locate other DCs and other servers. We have dedicated a good part of Chapter 5 to DNS.

You should place at least one DNS on a DC site and designate secondary DNS servers on other segments and DC sites. The local DNS servers should be authoritative for the locator records of the domains in the DC site. This obviates the need for clients to query offsite servers for local resources.

You can also install a DNS server on the actual DC and have it integrated with Active Directory. The advantages are that the DNS and the DC are co-located, which saves the cost of additional equipment; Active Directory automatically keeps DNS well fed, and the DC's replication service is ideal for DNS replication. DNS-Active Directory–specific configuration information is included in Chapter 5.

Before deploying your DNS server, make sure you have done the necessary planning. The following list helps you make sure that you are ready for deployment:

- Is your domain name standard for your organization?
- Do you have a plan for dividing up your DNS domain name and network address space into forward and reverse lookup zones as needed?
- Do you have a plan to determine how many servers you need to use and where to put them on your network?
- Use DNS performance tools for optimizing and monitoring to make sure that server performance is up to par.
- If you are upgrading from a prior server product, be sure to review migration issues.
- Did you register your organization's domain name with the Internet domain name registrar?
- Do you need to consider the use of forwards for your network so that clients can resolve external DNS names?
- Create a plan for how to manage DNS client resolver configurations.
- Have you completed configuration for zones on your DNS server?
- Have you completed installation and configuration for additional DNS servers if they are to be used as secondary servers for your initial zones?
- Have you completed your DNS resource records, such as A, PTR, CNAME, and MX records?
- Consider enabling or disabling dynamic updates for zones as needed.
- Consider using the monitoring features of the DNS console to verify that DNS servers are operating correctly.

NOTE If you are planning on using a second-level, or parent, DNS domain name, it needs to be registered only if you plan to use this name on the Internet.

DNS server performance can also be very important. DNS server benchmarking helps you predict, estimate, and optimize your server's performance. Windows Server 2008 provides performance counters that you could use with System Monitor to measure DNS server activity. Performance counters help you measure and monitor server activity with the following metrics:

- Calculated statistics providing the number of queries and responses from your DNS server.

- Measurement of transport protocols such as Transmission Control, as well as Datagram protocols.

- Measurement of registration, as well as update activity by clients.

- Measurement of system memory usage and memory allocation patterns.

- Measurement of WINS lookups when WINS is integrated with DNS.

- Measurement of zone transfers.

A DDNS architecture

The DDNS architecture is characterized by the following:

- A DDNS service will be installed on all domain controllers for all sites in the forest (Active Directory integrated zones can only be hosted on a DC server for that domain).

- All clients and servers have both a primary and alternate DDNS server configured, except in the case of the root domain controllers.

- The primary and alternate DDNS servers are always located within the same regional hub as the client or server and never across the major WAN links to a remote hub site or region. (Even with high bandwidth availability across links between hub sites and regions, it is prudent to keep DNS lookup traffic local to a region and its hub site.)

Hub sites

In your hub sites, primary and alternate DDNS servers are local. Servers forward to the DMZ DNS for external (Internet) resolution. Regional sites and remote locations provide the following DNS service:

- **Regional sites.** The primary DDNS server is local and the alternate server is at the hub site.

- **Centers.** The primary DDNS server is at the regional site higher up on the spoke or at the hub site and the alternate DDNS server is at the hub site.

- **DDNS is integrated with Active Directory so no zone transfers need be carried out.** There is no notion of a primary and secondary zone with AD integrated DDNS.

- **The DNS for the domain MCITY.US will be delegated to a domain controller in the root domain.** The root DNS will therefore delegate the hosting of the DNS to the first bridgehead domain controller.

- **Resolution of external names (names on the public Internet) will be forwarded to a name server that is not part of the AD integrated namespace**.

Deploying WINS servers

As we discuss in Chapter 5, WINS is used to translate a computer name (that is, NetBIOS name) to an IP address. WINS is an infrastructure service used extensively by Windows 9.x and NT v4.0 to locate servers and resources. It is also useful as a resolution service for technology and applications that make use of NetBIOS names (such as the names of virtual servers on Microsoft Cluster Services implementations, and for DFS). However, even virtual server names can and should be resolved on DDNS. Your architecture will provide a WINS implementation at the hub sites. A replication partner can be installed on the regional site's domain controller if WINS is needed at a regional site.

Your organization may have a WINS infrastructure in place, or it may still rely on other methods of NetBIOS name resolution, such as LMHOSTS. If your organization does not currently use WINS, you need to consider deploying it based on your needs.

The strategy we use for meeting our deployment objectives considers functionality, availability, security, and total cost of ownership. If you currently have a WINS server, make sure the server meets the hardware requirements described in Chapter 1. A dual-processor machine can increase performance 25 percent, and a dedicated disk drive can help increase replication response time.

In determining the number of WINS servers needed, use the following guidelines:

- The number of WINS clients per server and the network topology help determine the number of WINS servers and their locations.

- Each server's usage patterns and storage capabilities determine the number of users it can support.

- You must be conservative when setting client counts for a WINS server to minimize client query response times.

Replication design of your WINS servers is essential to availability and performance; multiple servers distribute NetBIOS name resolution across WANs and LANs, confining traffic to local areas. WINS servers then replicate local entries to other servers. You now must determine whether you want your WINS server configured as a push or pull partner. Replication is usually set up using the Hub-and-Spoke or T Network Configuration strategies. You may want to look at Chapter 5 for more details.

Best practices

The following best practices for WINS servers are recommended:

- Do not place WINS servers on any DC that is serving a large site of down-level clients (such as Windows 95 and Windows 98). This is especially important on a DC in a hub site. If a WINS server must be placed onto a DC (for example, to consolidate servers) or into a regional site, then the service can be installed on a domain controller that services a small regional site (fewer than 50 down-level users) or a small number of Windows 95/98 clients. The reason for this advice is that WINS is a process- and disk-intensive service. It can easily impact NTDS performance when servicing environments that are heavily dependent on WINS.

- The primary WINS server value that you give to a primary WINS server must be the address of the primary WINS server itself.

- Do not provide values to secondary WINS servers.

- To minimize WAN link usage, inter-region pull replication should be less frequent (that is, 240 minutes) than intrasite pull replication (that is, 30 minutes or 120 minutes).

- You can also disable inter-region push replication (replication initiated after an arbitrary number of updates) by setting a 9,999 count.

- Inter-region replication occurs at specified intervals only (pull replication).

- To minimize intra-region convergence time, intra-region replication between well-connected sites should be more frequent (that is, pull replication 30 minutes and push replication 20 count) than intra-region replication between not-so-well-connected sites (that is, pull replication 120 minutes and push replication 40 count).

- To minimize both intra-region convergence time and intra-region WAN link usage, intra-region replication between not-so-well-connected sites should be less frequent (that is, pull replication 120 minutes and push replication 40 count) than intra-region replication between well-connected sites (that is, pull replication 30 minutes and push replication 20 count).

Deploying DHCP servers

DHCP (Dynamic Host Configuration Protocol) is used to provide DHCP clients with IP configuration details. IP configuration details include IP address, subnet mask, default gateway, primary and secondary DNS (Domain Naming Service) servers, primary and secondary WINS servers, domain name and NetBIOS node type, and so forth. DHCP configuration provides the primary and alternate DNS server configuration for all dynamically addressed computers. If a dynamically addressed client cannot access DNS information, it cannot participate on an Active Directory network.

The example shown here is a routed network characterized by more than two subnets serving the company and datacenter spread out over a large physical space. DHCP is extended to clients across the networks via the services of BOOTP relay agents and router-based IP helper services. Depending on the configuration of the IP helper devices, this service can detract from an Active Directory migration or installation if Windows Server 2008 DHCP Server configuration and router-based IP helper configuration is not coordinated.

The DHCP architecture for MCITY is thus characterized by the following best practices:

■ DHCP servers should be placed in the primary subnet of a site containing a domain controller. This will provide redundancy (using superscope/split-scope configurations) and load balancing and keep DHCP local to the subnets requiring the services.

■ As far as possible, BOOTP should be kept to a minimum on an AD/DHCP/DDNS integrated network.

■ A distribute network of DHCP servers on a large routed WAN is much preferred over one or more large DHCP servers sitting on the backbone of the WAN in a few locations.

■ The DHCP server service can be easily accommodated on the site's DC. It will be accommodated on all DC servers in all hubs sites when the need may arise.

■ All Windows Server 2008 DHCP servers on the network must be Active Directory authenticated. Non-AD authenticated servers must be either retired or authenticated to AD.

■ Only DC servers in the root domain will be DHCP servers. (DHCP services are not required for a root domain that does not have resources.)

■ The DHCP scopes will be split across DHCP servers depending upon whether the DHCP server is local or remote to the site. This is a future requirement not currently implemented.

■ Should the company grow or acquire, the DHCP scopes for the main hub sites and large regional sites will be split across two servers for redundancy. The split will be 50/50 between two domain controllers in each site.

■ Each hub's DHCP server will also contain scopes to service regional sites in the event that the regional DHCP servers cannot (failure or overflow). These scopes will be split 50/50, with the regional (local) site leasing 100 percent of the addresses needed and the hub site (remote) leasing out of the remaining 50 percent of the scope when needed (see Table 20-2).

DHCP is, of course, critical to all clients: down-level, up-level, and penthouse. The only places on a DC site that take static IP addresses are the servers.

In deploying DHCP, you should have already given the following issues some thought:

■ Determine how many DHCP servers to use.

■ Determine how to support DHCP clients on additional subnets.

■ Determine how to handle routing for DHCP networks.

TABLE 20-2

DHCP (Dynamic Host Configuration Protocol) Server Scope Splits

Server 1			Server 2		
Percent of Address Range	Address Range	# of Addresses	Percent of Address Range	Address Range	# of Addresses
Local Range			**Local Range**		
50	.21*–.137	117	50	.138–.255	117
Remote Range			**Remote Range**		
50	.138–.255	117	50	.21–.137	64

*First 20 in subnet excluded from DHCP

When determining how many DHCP servers you need, consider location and whether you want a DHCP server in each subnet. If you are planning on using a DHCP server across several networks, you may need to configure relay agents or superscopes.

DHCP segment speed is another key factor. You want to consider a DHCP server on both sides of a slower WAN or dial-up link. This helps serve clients in a more efficient manner. There is no maximum number of clients that a DHCP server can serve, although your network has practical constraints due to the IP address class you have selected to use.

When addressing performance factors of your DHCP server, consider the following:

- One of the primary factors in improving performance is the disk drives and the amount of RAM installed. Be sure to evaluate disk-access time and read/write operations.

- Limit the DHCP server to a maximum of 1,000 scopes. Adding additional scopes uses more space because of the server registry and server paging file.

- The recommended limit of clients per DHCP server is 10,000. This helps protect you from unusual traffic conditions.

DHCP servers are critical, and their performance must be monitored. When troubleshooting DHCP performance, Windows Server 2008 provides a set of tools. The tools can monitor all types of DHCP services, such as messages sent and received, processing time of message packages sent and received, and the number of packets dropped.

You may also want to consider the configuration of a standby server. You need at least one primary DHCP server, but you may want to keep a second DHCP server on standby or for backup purposes. If you plan to implement two DHCP servers for balancing scopes, you may want to consider a backup or hot standby as an alternative.

Chapter 21 takes you through actual deployment and installation of several different domains, their interconnection and replication matrix, and so on. Before you embark on this, consider the following:

- **Do a sanity check on the site concept.** It is one thing to hit a graph pad or Visio and knock out the Windows Server 2008 network of the millennium; mapping it to the physical reality is something else. If there is already an installed network, you typically need to work with what you already have, which may mean making the location a separate domain or taking care of replication as if you had the last network in the world.

- **Make network logon and access to resources your primary focus.** This should be your first consideration in the actual deployment plan. Get an idea of what slow logon or access to network resources entails and what your network feels like over low-bandwidth connections, and make that your point of departure. If it is impractical to have a new domain at the location, you must either open the pipe for better replication or be very creative with your replication scheduling.

- **Make network replication traffic your secondary focus.** As soon as you have laid the necessary foundations to ensure that your users have fast logon authentication and access to all the resources to which they are entitled, work in your replication plans. Make sure that you can pick up propagation from the other domains and that you can get all your necessary updates from the root domain controllers and other domains in the forest, as well as the updates intended for the global catalog, the other naming contexts, and so on.

DHCP parameters can be configured according to server options or scope options. In other words, where configuration is identical across all scopes hosted on the server, the configuration should be a server option. Server options automatically apply to all scopes unless they are overridden by scope options. Scope options only apply to the scope in which they are defined. See Chapter 5 for more information.

A Site Architecture

Sites in AD define locality (for service requests of domain controllers) and replication topology. Sites are thus defined to AD as locations containing domain controllers that are well connected in terms of speed and cost. A site will therefore be created and named after the location that contains a large number of users all connected to the backbone on a high-speed LAN. The site provides the key route through which remote locations and centers connect to a core data center or hub site.

Multiple domain controllers in a site (such as a hub site or a regional site with hundreds of users) replicate with each other through the built-in configurable notification system. Domain controllers in remote sites replicate using a user-configurable replication scheme. The latter scheme can be scheduled to meet the needs of the WAN topology and the available bandwidth at your disposal.

For the purposes of this architecture example, the following convention for referring to sites and locations will be followed:

- **Hub site.** This is one of three main data centers that contain the root domain controllers, FSMO role servers, bridgehead servers, and disaster-recovery architecture. The hub sites comprise the city's three redundant data centers.

- **Regional site.** This will be an autonomous location that contains at least one domain controller holding the role of Global Catalog server for LAN speed logon (typically for more than 50 users). A regional site is connected to the hub site through a WAN link.

- **Center.** This will be a remote location that does not contain a domain controller and is logically part of a larger regional or hub site. The subnets of centers that log on over the WAN to the hub site are thus included in the collection of subnets that make up a hub or a regional site.

Sites with domain controllers will be defined to AD. This means that site objects will be created in AD to provide a means for clients to authenticate to domain controllers that are locally positioned in their sites. Domain controllers in the hub sites will be load-balanced so that any domain controller can pick up the load should another domain controller fail or be taken offline for maintenance. Regional hubs should have at least one domain controller. A hub site domain controller must also be in a position to service the regional site should a DC fail.

Replication between domain controllers within sites is known as intersite replication and takes place as needed. Replication between domain controllers in different sites is known as intrasite replication and takes place on a schedule. The intrasite schedule defined in this architecture will not burden the network and cannot expose AD to potential information update latency problems.

Replication to regional sites can occur once a day, every six hours, or every two hours, depending on the requirements determined during rollout. Replication between the domain controllers in the hubs will be allowed to occur more frequently, say, every 15 minutes. This will keep the hubs as concurrent as possible. This is achieved by the availability of high-bandwidth links that exist between the hub sites. A bandwidth of at least 512 Kbits between the hubs is sufficient and recommended as a reservation of bandwidth for inter-hub replication. Replication between the hubs should be allowed to occur as frequently as possible.

As mentioned earlier, a site is defined around a collection of networks that are connected by fast, reliable backbones. A LAN (which runs at 10/100 Mbits) is considered a fast network and thus accommodating of a site. A WAN link between LANs should have a net 512 Kbits available to consolidate them into the same site. Available bandwidth even higher than 512 Kbits is preferred to consolidate the locations into sites. LAN speeds alone do not necessarily require the location to have a local DC. Most centers will have local 10/100 Mbit LANs and 1.5 Mbit connections to their nearest regional or hub sites.

You can qualify a regional site as a site that needs a domain controller. This means that the logon and authentication traffic generated by the site over the WAN must be more than the traffic generated by AD replication on the same WAN link. The general rule is that logon and authentication traffic begins to surpass replication traffic at about 50 users.

Intersite replication is very fast and very efficient as a result of the powerful data compression that takes place; and, depending on the application and user requirements, analysis may show the intersection or break-even to be at less than or more than 50 users. Server consolidation objectives may suggest upgrading the links to the regional site, rather than place a DC in the site. You can usually tell (by Windows XP or Vista logon times when Group Policy is applied and lingering hour glasses), when a GC should be located at the site.

AD uses all available site information to determine how best to use the network resources made available to it. This makes the following types of operations more efficient:

- **Service requests (that is, authentication).** The local net logon is built into Windows clients. The client makes a call to the logon API that queries AD (via DNS) for the GC situated closest to the client (determined by IP subnet information). The client is then directed to log on to a GC in the same site as the client, or the closest site that contains a DC. This process makes handling the requests more efficient. DC location is cached at the client so that repeated calls to the API are avoided. Conversely, mobile computers that connect at multiple sites request a DC when the cached information is no longer valid.

- **Replication.** Sites allow AD to streamline replication of the directory information. The directory schema and configuration information is distributed throughout the forest while domain data is distributed among all DCs in the domain. This reduces the strain on the network because Active Directory replicates directory information within a site more frequently than among sites. In other words, the best-connected DCs, those most likely to need particular directory information, receive their replications as the first priority. The DCs in other sites receive their changes to the directory less frequently. The result is a net reduction of bandwidth consumption.

Architecture

The following site architecture will be implemented:

- A site must be defined for each physical site that contains a domain controller. Hub sites and regional sites will initially represent candidates for sites.

- A site must be defined according to its subnet and the IP subnets of other regional sites or centers.

- When it is determined that there is no need to replicate DC data to and from a site, it is considered to be a "center."

- A user in a center will be authenticated by the DC in his or her site across the WAN.

- You can create site names by typically combining a site's acronym of its canonical name with other data. Site links, for example, usually include the acronym of the notification site and the partner site with which it replicates.

- Users in regional sites should only be able to log on to domain controllers in their hub sites if their local domain controllers are unavailable. They cannot log on to domain controllers in other hub sites or in other regional sites because this is prevented in DNS through the configuration of Net Logon server affinity. Users in centers that are directly connected to regional sites can use the domain controllers in the regional sites instead of one of the central hub sites. The regional site that services a center can be thought of as a mini-hub. The main sites for the MCITY architecture are listed in Table 20-3.

TABLE 20-3

Sites

Name	Description
HQ Site (phase 1)	
HQ (hub site)	Headquarters
DR Sites	
DR (hub site)	Disaster Recovery (MCI)
Other Sites	

The hub-and-spoke model to be designed for MCITY consists of three rings, with Ring 1 being the highest bandwidth ring where all sites positioned on Ring 1 connect to same backbone. We shall call this the MCITY Ring, where information is routed around the ring simultaneously to reduce replication latency.

Ring 2 sites are our so-called spoke sites and will be connected to their hub sites on lower bandwidth connections. Because Ring 2 sites attach directly to the backbone, they will become Ring 1 sites. The subnets of centers without domain controllers will use the domain controllers in Ring 2 sites as their logon servers, and the domain controllers in the hub sites will be available as backup domain controllers.

This hub-and-spoke topology and ring design is illustrated in Figure 20-13.

FIGURE 20-13

Hub-and-spoke ring topology model.

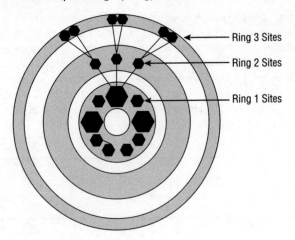

- Ring 3 Sites
- Ring 2 Sites
- Ring 1 Sites

Site link cost

The *cost value* of a site link is an arbitrary number that helps the replication system in AD determine when to use one link over others. Cost values determine the paths that replication will take through the network. To obtain cost factors, the following formula is typically used:

Cost = 1024 / Log (available bandwidth in Kb)

Following are some examples:

Available Bandwidth	Cost[1]
9.6	1042
19.2	798
38.8	644
56	586
64	567
128	486
256	425
512	378
1024	340
2048	309

Available Bandwidth	Cost[1]
4096	283
8192	261
16384	242
32768	227
65536	212
131072	200

[1]You can use a simple descending or ascending cost table (such as 100, 200, 300). However, scientifically calculated costs derived from a cost formula lessen the chance of assigning incorrect cost factors to various links.

Table 20-4 is a site link chart that can be used in the site/replication topology architected here. As you can see, Ring 1 links have the lowest cost values.

TABLE 20-4

Link Schedule/Notification Data

Ring	Schedule	Notification
Intersite		
Ring 1	Every 15 minutes	Yes
Ring 2	60 minutes	No
Ring 3	Once a day at midnight	No
Intrasite		
N/A	Automatic	Every five minutes

Site links cost factor charts

Site links assist the Knowledge Consistency Checker (KCC) in identifying the appropriate Active Directory replication topology. It is important that manually created connections be relevant to the underlying network topology.

The KCC is the application that automatically creates replication connections between AD servers within sites and between sites. For example, if Site A is network connected to Site B, which in turn is network connected to Site C, then the logical site link topology should be the same. It does not make sense to create a site link topology of "SiteA-SiteLink" connected to Site C and "SiteC-SiteLink" connected to Site B.

Site links are critical to the KCC, and without them there is no way to identify the appropriate AD replication topology. You need to thus ensure they are configured correctly.

The AD replication schedule and notification

Active Directory intrasite replication topology is automatically configured by the KCC. This is how it works: When changes are made at a DC, a timer begins a countdown from five minutes before peer domain controllers in the site are notified of the changes. As soon as notification goes out, the notified domain controllers immediately begin to pull changes from the source DC. This is the default topology created by the KCC. It will be accepted for intrasite replication and should not be changed. You only change KCC topology when the entire infrastructure is so large that automatic configuration by the KCC becomes impossible.

Intersite replication is configurable, so you can fine-tune the replication topology between sites. You can also take into consideration factors such as available bandwidth, peak times on the WAN, routes, and maintenance windows.

Site links have associated schedules that indicate at what times of the day the link is available to carry replication traffic. This is known as the replication window. Hubs sites at Ring 1 typically have all the bandwidth they need for immediate replication. The interval at Ring 1 will thus be every 15 minutes. Replication to Ring 2 sites will be every hour (refer to Table 20-4).

You cannot, under most circumstances, configure notification on intrasite links and there is no means to set notification on any dialog box on the server. However, on the links connecting the hubs (on Ring 1), notification can be enabled if you are willing to tinker with the registry settings to make the intersite replication sitting on a very high bandwidth backbone work more like intrasite replication. This will keep the hub sites in your network continuously up to date and enable them to work like a single site over the WAN.

Table 20-4 provides the schedule and notification data to be used for the implementation of the replication topology.

Transports

Intrasite replication is achieved through standard Windows Server 2008 remote procedure calls (RPCs), but different transports are used to achieve replication between DCs in different sites. This intersite replication is achieved using the following two transport types:

- DS-RPC, or Directory Services RPC (over IP)
- ISM-SMTP, or Intersite Messaging-Simple Mail Transport Protocol

Intrasite replication is always RPC-based, synchronous, and cannot be scheduled. Intersite replication uses either RPC- or SMTP-based transports. The replication data is always compressed (regardless of the transport) if the data is larger than 50KB. AD always expects intersite replication between sites to be over low-bandwidth links.

Compression algorithms run on bridgehead servers, which is why good disks and good processors are important on these "border" servers. Data is compressed to between 10 and 15 percent of the original size of the packet. Table 20-5 shows intrasite replication features versus intersite replication features.

TABLE 20-5

Intrasite vs. Intersite Replication

Feature	Intrasite	Intersite
Transport	RPC	RPC or SMTP
Topology	Ring	Spanning Tree
Replication schedule	N/A	Replication Window
Replication model	Notify and Pull	Optional Notify, Pull
Compression	None	On all packets>= 50KB
Secure channel	No	Yes (requires a CA)

In most cases, available bandwidth on an entire WAN is such that SMTP replication would not be recommended. RPC over IP is thus the preferred transport protocol to be used in all cases for high-speed WANs.

It is also worth noting that RPC links between the DCs cannot be configured to implicitly use certificates as secure SMTP can. SMTP requires that an enterprise certificate authority (CA) be made available to secure the replication traffic. This is not possible with RPC channels, so IPSec should be installed to the domain controller. Do not forget that NICs to secure the intersite replication traffic using IPSec requires a CA to be contactable (see Chapter 16).

Connection objects

The communication channels used by site links to affect the replication are called connection objects. These objects are also stored in AD and they contain attributes that provide information about replication partners, the sites to which they belong, and the transport used (RPC/IP vs. SMTP) to transfer the data.

When you first create a forest topology, the KCC creates two connection objects between two root DCs. One object is used to replicate the configuration naming context (CNC) and the schema naming contexts (SNC) and the other is used to replicate the domain naming context (DNC). When a third DC is promoted into the domain and becomes a child domain controller, no domain naming context needs to be replicated between the root and the child DCs. The reason is simple: The domain naming context is only replicated within a domain.

Connection objects are created by the KCC using a built-in process that automatically creates and then optimizes the replication topology, by automatic generation of the connection objects.

Connection objects can also be created manually, and replication can be manually forced over them. However, as mentioned earlier, this is usually only required in very large domains where the KCC needs to be manually overridden by the network engineer. Manually overriding the KCC occurs because of the built-in limitation it has on very large implementations (the KCC does not scale well when the number of sites exceeds 100).

You should not have reason to force manual creation of connection objects. Remember that if you do so, the KCC will not own or know about them and your administrative burden will climb. They will have to be manually managed and they will not be affected by any automatic replication schedule set up by the KCC.

Site link bridge

A *site link bridge* creates transitivity between a set of site links. If a site link over a slow WAN connects City Hall to DITT (CH-DITT) and a slow link connects One-Police-Plaza to Parks and Recreation (OPP-PRKS), then a site link bridge called CH-PRKS connects City Hall to Parks and Recreation. The bridge thus allows the domain controllers in the City Hall hub to create replication connections with the domain controllers in the One Police Plaza hub. In other words, the site link bridge creates a link between two sites that do not explicitly have a site link between them.

It is not necessary to explicitly create site link bridges between the hub sites because the network is powerful enough to enable the KCC to automatically develop replication topology between the DCs in hubs. This phenomenon is known as *site link transitiveness*.

Site layout and topology

Replication between sites is affected by domain controllers that are configured as bridgeheads. When bridgeheads accumulate changes for replication, they wait on remote sites to begin pulling the data through the replication window provided. The bridgehead servers in the hub sites will be configured to notify replication partners in the replication window, which is opened every 15 minutes.

Time

Time synchronization is a critical service on Windows Server 2008 networks, and all clients and servers must synchronize their time with a reliable and secure time source. This section covers the architecture for maintaining Time Services.

The objective of the forest Time Service is to ensure that all computers running Windows Server 2008 or later use a common time. Many critical services use time. For example, the Kerberos v5 protocol ensures the validity of issued keys to guard against replay attacks from hackers by checking timestamps embedded in the key data. If domain controllers are not time-synchronized, authentication services will be stopped and users will not be able to work. A Windows Server 200X or XP or Vista workstation will also fail to connect to network resources if it is not time-synchronized. For this reason (and many others), time must not be changed manually on any domain controller (or any computer for that matter) under any circumstance.

The Time Services use a hierarchical topology to ensure that all computers derive their time synchronization from a root Time Server. This topology ensures that loops are not permitted and ensures appropriate common time usage.

The following hierarchy is used on a Windows Server 2008 or later network:

- Client operating systems automatically nominate their preferred or authenticating domain controller as their in-bound time partner.

- Member server operating systems also automatically nominate their preferred or authenticating domain controller as their in-bound time partner.

- Domain controllers by default nominate the PDC Emulator domain controller in their domain as their in-bound time partner. They may also automatically use the PDC Emulator of a parent domain as their in-bound time partner based on a stratum numbering scheme (see the next section, "Time Service Architecture," for an explanation of the stratum numbering scheme).

All PDC Emulator domain controllers automatically trace the domain hierarchy in the selection of their in-bound time partner.

This design ensures that the PDC Emulator operations master at the root of the domain always becomes the authoritative time source for the forest.

Time service architecture

While the PDC Emulator domain controller at the root of the forest maintains the Time Server role, it is not the most accurate time source for a large network with multiple domains, a complex routed network, numerous remote sites, and critical dependency on Kerberos v5. The root PDC Emulator must always obtain its time from a so-called *stratum 1 source*.

Time Source accuracy levels are measured in terms of strata. A stratum 1 device is either a specialized internal clock that is always 100 percent accurate or a dedicated, highly reliable time server on the Internet (preferred). Such time servers are maintained by companies such as Cisco and Microsoft, and thousands of organizations depend on them.

The root PDC Emulator operations master in the parent domain is thus a *stratum 2 time source*. This, in essence, means it is not sufficiently accurate to be the authoritative time source for the forest (a source of last resort, so to speak). However, because it gets its time directly from a stratum 1 device, it keeps the most accurate time in the forest. By sourcing time from an external stratum 1 device, the organization is assured that its private network time is "in sync" with the rest of the world.

All other DCs in the parent domain are deemed to be *stratum 3 time sources*, which means that wherever these servers are located on the network, across routers, and other factors affecting convergence, they are deemed to have a lesser degree of accuracy than the PDC Emulator DC. In other words, as the strata level increases from stratum 1, the achievable accuracy of the clock degrades, the rate of which depends on network latencies and server clock stability.

DCs in child domains, as well as member servers and workstations in the root domain, are located at *stratum 4*. The stratum hierarchy of computers in the forest is listed in Table 20-6.

TABLE 20-6

Strata Levels for Computers in a Forest

Strata	Description
Stratum1	External Network Time Protocol Time Source
Stratum2	PDC Emulator DC in the forest root
Stratum3	DCs in root domain and PDC Emulator DCs in child domains
Stratum4	Workstations and member servers in the forest root domain; DCs in child domains
Stratum5	Workstations and member servers in child domains

Using this architecture, the PDC Emulator located in the root domain connects to an external time source. The domain controllers in the root or parent domain access time directly from the PDC Emulator. Member servers or workstations in the domain, regardless of position in the forest, source their time, by default, from their logon domain controller — one of the GCs in the site, as mentioned in the overview at the beginning of this chapter.

In subordinate or child domains, the PDC Emulator operations master can synchronize directly with the root PDC Emulator, and should. This can be checked and manually set using the NET TIME /QUERYSNTP and NET TIME /SETSNTP:<server name or IO> commands, respectively. All DCs in the child domain can then be configured to synchronize directly with the local (domain) PDC Emulator, although, by default, they may take their time from a DC at the next domain higher up on the tree. Workstations and member servers synchronize with the Global Catalog domain controller in their own domain.

Best practice

The hierarchy and configuration presented in Figure 20-13 will be adopted for MCITY. However, connecting to an external time source from the root PDC Emulator opens a security hole because a direct connection is being made to an external IP address on the Internet. For this reason, the connection must be secured with IPSec on the interface used to make the connection, or the PDC must synchronize with a secure internal time device that connects to the external device.

Summary

This chapter introduced you to the physical structure of Active Directory. We looked at the three concepts in this physical world that make up Active Directory's physical structures: domain controller (DC) servers, global catalog (GC) servers, and sites. We also discussed how essential it is, even for a small company, to either back up Active Directory regularly or maintain a redundant (hot) DC.

By maintaining a redundant DC, you ensure that the domain has a hot failover should one of the DCs stop working; however, you learned that DCs and catalogs replicate information to one another to keep the network of controllers current. The degree of currency depends on the situation. For example, DCs supporting the same domain eventually become 100 percent replicas of each other, whereas DCs belonging to different domains only partially replicate to each other.

You saw how replication is achieved by a complex collection of heuristic algorithms and how replication consumes bandwidth. On fast Ethernet networks, where there is a thick backbone, the replication traffic is tolerable. Between locations connected with slow links, however, replication traffic may be too slow to maintain a single domain. An additional domain may be needed to lessen the replication load.

You learned how you can calculate replication traffic by using information derived from the Active Directory technical specifications, such as the size of attributes. You also discovered that the attribute size remains fairly constant and that replication traffic is predictable and can easily be catered to.

Another management item on your checklist is directory synchronization. Directory synchronization differs from replication because it is an information exchange mechanism that takes place between unlike directories.

The next chapter takes the theory of the past several chapters and puts what you have learned into practice, starting with the installation of domain controllers and the deployment of Active Directory.

Chapter 21

Active Directory Installation and Deployment

This chapter deploys an Active Directory infrastructure. Working from the deployment plan blueprint described in this chapter, you will be able to identify and modify the elements of the deployment plan that will suit your configuration, be it a solution for a small network or a WAN connecting multiple domain controllers and an extensive Active Directory tree. This chapter is divided into two parts, theory and overview in the first part, and actual implementation in the second part.

IN THIS CHAPTER

Presenting the deployment plan

Rolling out the domain controllers

Planning for replication traffic

Creating organizational units

Installing and setup

Getting Ready to Deploy

This chapter takes you through the actual installation of the domain controllers for an Active Directory domain. We will be using our fictitious city, Millennium City (MCITY), as the demo. So far, we have put several structures into place according to the blueprint we discuss next. You may take this blueprint and deployment plan and use it as a template for your own project, expanding or cutting and pasting to and from it as you need, or just use the examples to establish your own strategy. If the plan appears to be a real-life example, that's because it is. This Windows Server 2008 network and namespace have actually been deployed.

What we espouse here is not the gospel on Active Directory deployment by any means. It works for our environment, situation, and the diversity of our demo organization. Smaller companies may find it too expensive to implement some of our suggestions; others may garner some deep insight. Our purpose is to show a rich implementation.

> **NOTE**   Though Millennium City is a fictitious city (modeled on the organizational chart of a real U.S. city), the following deployment plan was executed and actual domain controllers were set up across a simulated WAN in a test environment. We also upgraded a large Windows NT Primary Domain Controller (PDC) containing several hundred accounts from a live domain, and joined it to the MCITY namespace and the GENESIS forest as part of a live pilot project involving actual users.

Millennium City Active Directory Deployment Plan

The MCITY deployment plan consists of several phases. These phases are described in the plan according to the following contents:

- **A.** Executive Summary
- **B.** Deployment Phases

    Phase I: Install and Test Root Active Directory Domain

    Phase II: Install and Test Child Active Directory Domains

    Phase III: Create Organizational Units

    Phase IV: Create Groups and Users (Chapter 23)

    Phase V: Establish and Implement Security Policy (Chapter 24)

Executive Summary

The following summary describes the deployment specifics for the GENESIS forest on the `MCITY.ORG` and `GENESIS.MCITY.ORG` namespaces.

MCITY network

The MCITY network (MCITYNET) is managed in the Department of Information Technology and Telecommunications (DITT). The backbone at DITT connects to a bank of Cisco 4000 series routers that connect MCITYNET to an ATM backbone. The routers and physical network are provided and managed by a major long-distance provider that offers managed network services (MNS). MCITYNET comprises both the Internet services required by the city and the private wide area network (WAN) and intranet, known as the GENESIS network.

DITT connects to the CITYHALL and MCPD over a dedicated IP network, and to smaller departments over an MNS T1 network. Several locations are connected on smaller pipes from 64 Kbps to 250 Kbps, and so on. The configuration of the GENESIS segment of MCITYNET is outlined in Table 21-1.

TABLE 21-1

Genesis Network Configuration

LOCATION	GENESIS	CITYHALL	DITT	MCPD
Subnets	100.10.0.0	100.45.0.0	100.50.0.0	100.70.0.0
DHCP scope	100.10.2.1 to 100.10.2.254	100.45.2.1 to 100.45.5.254	100.50.2.1 to 100.50.5.254	100.70.2.1 to 100.70.254.254
Domain Controllers Reserved Names	MCDC00 to MCDC09	MCDC10 to MCDC49	MCDC50 to MCDC69	MCDC70 to MCDC129
Sites	GEN-ST00 – ST09 JKIJS09K87	CH-ST00 – ST09 J98KIJD654	DITT-ST00 – ST09 JKP09KLJ	MCPD-ST00 – ST40 JKDOP843D

The GENESIS domain

The root Active Directory (AD) domain and the forest for Millennium City will be called GENESIS. The forest is also called GENESIS because Active Directory forces the forest to take its name from the root domain. After several months of extensive research and testing of Microsoft's Active Directory services on Windows Server 2008, the Millennium City Windows Server 2008 testing team has decided how to best deploy Active Directory services.

It has been decided that for an organization the size of Millennium City, the root domain of the organization's Active Directory namespace needs to be a secure domain accessible only by a small group of senior administrators. These administrators will have the organization's highest security clearance. There will be no user accounts in the domain outside of the core administrators, and no active workplace management — other than what is needed for security, domain controller (DC) lockdown, and to protect and administer in this domain — will be put into place. There are several reasons to establish such a domain.

First, the root domain in any large organization is a target for e-terrorists. If the root domain contains many user and computer accounts and a lot of information, the organization could suffer extensive damage if this domain is destroyed either physically (removal or destruction of the DC servers) or by a concerted network attack, or if its data is accessed by unauthorized personnel. Naturally, a small concern might not need such a "bastion" root domain, but any large enterprise should seriously consider it.

Second, all MCITY first-, second-, and third-level domains are extensively populated by user and computer accounts (security principals) and many groups. There are also numerous organizational units (OUs) in these domains and thus many administrators at various levels of the domain's OU hierarchy. We thus deemed it necessary to establish a root domain with no more than a handful (preferably no more than five) of administrators who by virtue of having accounts in the root domain would have the widest authority over the city's namespace, starting from GENESIS down.

Third, the root domain is critical to the city. It might be feasible — if Microsoft makes it possible — in the future to disconnect the root domain from the rest of the domain tree and graft the tree to another root. However, at present it is not, and losing the domain root would result in the loss of the entire domain tree, taking with it all levels subordinate to the root — in fact, everything on the tree. To thus protect the root domain, we will establish partner DCs of the root domain at several remote locations, primarily for redundancy and to locate the root domain over a wide area. These locations will initially be as follows:

- Location 1: DITT's Network Operations Center (NOC)
- Location 2: City Hall's Network Operations Center
- Location 3: MCPD (Police Department) Network Operations Center

The lightweight (user accounts) nature of the root domain, which in addition to the built-in accounts only contains a handful of users, makes it easy to replicate its databases around the enterprise.

Finally, the root domain controller is also our *Schema Operations Master* and *Domain Naming Operations Master* for the forest, and holds the master schema and other naming contexts that affect the enterprise as a whole, such as the Global Catalog (GC), that can only be changed on the operations master.

The Schema Operations Master is where all schema updates will be performed, and the Domain Naming Operations Master is where we can make changes to the domain namespace on an enterprisewide basis.

Physical location of GENESIS

The GENESIS domain's first and second DCs will be secured in the main server room of DITT's network operations center (NOC). These DCs will not be attended to by DITT's operators, but instead will be administered to by the GENESIS administrators. As stated earlier, GENESIS DCs will also be placed in MCPD and CITYHALL, supported by reliable, high-bandwidth pipes.

Although it is important to locate the GENESIS root DC in a secure location, it is also important to make the services of the GENESIS DCs and GC easily available in as many GENESIS locations as possible. This will enable users to obtain the following benefits without having to contact the DC over many hops on the WAN:

- **Ease of use.** Users should not have to look up the network address of any GENESIS DC, or any DC for that matter.
- **High availability.** The GENESIS DCs need to be in as many places as possible in the city so that the most up-to-date replicas of the GC and other information are nearby.

■ **Reliable query results.** Strong and closely located GCs should facilitate rich queries, and users must be able to rely on the data's currency. They must be able to obtain information on users, groups, and other network services without any interruption in services or lack of data.

Network specifics of GENESIS

The GENESIS domain will be established on a segment of the physical network on which the Department of Technology and Telecommunications (DITT) currently runs. This network currently is supported on a 1000 Mbps backbone on which the DITT supports its AS/400, Unix, and Windows Server systems. GENESIS will be established on the same network, but on its own IP subnet. This IP address space is a network supported by Windows Server 2008 routing services. It can also be supported behind network address translation services (NAT) running on a Windows Server 2008 role server.

GENESIS site object specifics

In order to support replication to and from other MCITY domains (intersite) and between domain controllers belonging to the same domain (intrasite), an Active Directory site will support GENESIS. This site will be named GEN-ST00-JKIJS09K87, as illustrated in Table 21-1. The following DC names have been reserved for this site: MCDC00.GENESIS.MCITY.US to MCDC09.GENESIS.MCITY.US MCDC50. The NetBIOS name range of these DCs is MCDC00 to MCDC09.

GENESIS subnet object specifics

The subnet address 100.10.0.0 will be assigned to a subnet object. This subnet object will be associated with the GENESIS site object described previously.

Domain health and security

Two partner DCs will support the domain in the main DC site. The main DC site will also house a copy of the GC for the entire MCITY Active Directory namespace.

The administrators in the GENESIS domain will have administrative authority over the resources in the GENESIS domain. The GENESIS domain also has administrative and security authority over the subordinate domains.

The CITYHALL domain

The CITYHALL domain is the first of the Windows Server 2008 populated domains, and it will contain several hundred user and computer accounts. This domain will support the accounts and network resources for the Mayor's office and the various departments that fall directly under the Mayor.

Physical location of CITYHALL

The CITYHALL domain controllers will be located at City Hall and will fall under the authority of the City Hall network administrators who work directly for the Mayor. We will supply at least two DCs to support the initial deployment of Windows Server 2008 into City Hall.

Network specifics of CITYHALL

The CITYHALL domain is to be established on the actual network segment assigned to CITY-HALL by DITT. This segment is the 100.45.0.0 network. CITYHALL currently is supported on a 1000 Mbps backbone between ten floors, and the network is collapsed into a 100-Mbps network that services the workstations, printers, and other network devices.

City Hall's IT department also supports AS/400 systems, CICS on IBM S390, and several technologies supported on Unix systems, such as Oracle and Informix database management systems.

CITYHALL site object specifics

In order to support replication to and from other MCITY domains and several remote locations that will belong to the CITYHALL domain, an Active Directory site will support CITYHALL. The main site will be named CH-ST00-J98KIJD654. The following DC names have been reserved for this site: MCDC10.CITYHALL.GENESIS.MCITY.ORG to MCDC50.CITYHALL.GENESIS.MCITY.ORG. The NetBIOS name range of these DCs is MCDC10 to MCDC50.

CITYHALL subnet object specifics

The subnet address 100.45.0.0 will be assigned to a subnet object. This subnet object will be associated with the CITYHALL site (CH-ST00- J98KIJD654) object described previously.

Domain health and security

At least three partner, or peer, DCs will support the CITYHALL domain in the main DC site. We decided to locate one DC in the secure server room of the floor on which the Mayor's office is located. The remaining two DCs will be located in the main server room in City Hall's network operations center (NOC). The DCs will also house copies of the GCs for the entire MCITY Active Directory namespace.

The administrators in the CITYHALL domain will have administrative authority over the resources only in the CITYHALL domain. Some administrators in CITYHALL are also administrators of the GENESIS domain.

The DITT domain

The DITT domain contains the resources for the Department of Information Technology and Telecommunications. Several hundred user and computer accounts are in this domain, which will support the accounts and network resources for the IT staff and consultants and the various departments that fall directly under DITT.

Network specifics of DITT

The DITT domain is to be established on the network segment 100.50.0.0. See Table 21-1 for the configuration specifics of DITT.

The MCPD domain

The MCPD domain contains the resources for the Millennium City Police Department. According to the configuration, a large number of IP addresses are required for this network. The IP address range in the DHCP scope will support hundreds of workstations, terminals, and other network devices. This domain is the most complex of the four domains, because numerous domain controllers and sites will have to be configured to cover an extensive network connecting the precincts to the commissioner's offices, the DA's office, and various law enforcement agencies.

Network specifics of DITT

The MCPD domain is to be established on the network segment 100.70.0.0. Refer to Table 21-1 for the configuration specifics of the MCPD.

Installing and Testing the Active Directory Domain Controllers

Several deployment phases are outlined in this plan. Phase I covers the installation and deployment of the GENESIS, CITYHALL, MCPD, and DITT domains.

> **NOTE** Instead of repeating the full installation and deployment of each domain, we will first briefly install the root domain. We will then fully demonstrate the promotion of the CITYHALL domain controller and how it joins the GENESIS domain tree and forest. The other domains will join GENESIS in the same fashion. Each domain will then be administered as a separate entity, while still being covered by any policy that might derive from the root. The root administrators have the highest power of administration over all the domains in the forest.

The following sequence of events describes the creation of all the domain controllers. These activities will take you through machine preparation to final deployment:

1. Install the DC machine and add the Active Directory Domain Services role.
2. Promote the server to domain controller.
3. Make the server the root DC or join forest and trees.
4. Establish the DC in DNS/WINS.
5. Establish the DC in the Active Directory site.
6. Build the initial OUs.

7. Delegate OU administration.

8. Secure the DC further and follow disaster-recovery protocol.

Installing the DC machine

Follow the procedures described in Chapter 1 for installing Windows Server 2008. Ensure that the machine is stable. The best way to do this is to keep it running for about two weeks. You can use backup/restore as discussed in Chapter 7 to "burn in" the machine. After several DCs are built or acquired on the same hardware configuration, you might consider reducing the burn-in period to several days instead of two weeks. If your machine is still running under load after several weeks, consecutive machines configured on identical hardware will likely run without problems. However, a few days of tests are required to be certain.

> **NOTE**   You do not need to go to the additional expense of using Advanced Server for a domain controller. All Windows Server 2008s can be promoted to a domain controller. Providing a fail-over service or a cluster for Active Directory is also a waste of resources and money. A fully redundant server will not only be cheaper, it will make for a more secure Active Directory deployment.

Server name

Pick a name for your machine from the list provided in the deployment plan. This is the NetBIOS name you will use to construct your DNS name. This name is going to be used again when you promote your server to a domain controller. We used the name MCDC00 for the standalone machine that became the root DC for GENESIS. When we promoted this machine, we reassigned this name and DNS resolved this machine as MCDC00.GENESIS.MCITY.ORG. In the case of CITYHALL, the server name reserved for the first DC in this domain is MCDC10. Its DNS name will thus be MCDC10.CITYHALL.GENESIS.MCITY.ORG. Remember that in the case of CITYHALL, it is the first level down from the root GENESIS domain and also two levels down from MCITY and ORG, which are both Internet domain names. To check this information, open the Active Directory Domains and Trusts and select the domain in the tree, on the left-hand pane. Then, right-click the domain name and select Properties.

Server IP address

Give your machine a static IP address. You do not need to concern yourself about the subnet address you use now because you will change it later in the next phase of the deployment. However, make sure the IP address you choose is not used on any other machine on the network or as part of any DHCP scope listed in Table 21-1. Create a pool of static IP addresses, or reserve a segment of your scope, that you can use in the lab specifically for the purpose of installation and testing.

Choosing a workgroup

During the installation of the server, you will be asked to join it to a domain or a workgroup. You are also given the option of skipping the name and returning to it later. We recommend that you put it in a workgroup and that you name the workgroup after the server's name. This name cannot be the same name as the server — the installation will not allow that — so just add "wg" after the server name to keep it simple. For example, MCDC00 is the name we gave the server that was destined to become the first DC for GENESIS. The workgroup name is thus MCDCWG00. Joining a domain is not a good idea because that will force you to create a computer account for the server in the domain, which you have to remove later anyway when you install the server into its new domain. Not only is this inconvenient, you also have to then ensure that you can "see" the network and that the server will be able to find the DC of the domain it wants to join.

Services

Leave as many services out of the installation as possible. It is worth repeating here that it is better to first get a bare-bones machine running before adding additional services. However, there is one exception, as described next.

Choosing a Terminal Services mode

The one service that we deem to be the most important is Terminal Services (TS). You will have to select TS from the Windows Components dialog box. You do not have to select licensing as well; that is only for application server servers. While choosing services, you will also be asked to choose the mode for TS, so select Remote Administration mode. This will enable you to attach to the machine remotely when it is installed in the new location. The machine can be promoted from the remote location or in the lab, but you should also provide a means to administer it remotely. This is demonstrated shortly. Remote Administration mode allows up to two concurrent sessions to be used for remote administration without licensing.

Promoting to domain controller

The steps we take you through in this section demonstrate installing a root domain and a child domain into an existing domain tree. You would perform these same steps to install Active Directory for any new domain controller. The only difference is that you need to create a domain controller according to the options outlined in Table 21-2. If you are not sure what you need to install, do some more preparation and planning. Read the fine print on the dialog boxes until you are sure about your actions, but do not overly concern yourself until the last step because you can always go backward and forward in these dialog boxes until you are sure.

TABLE 21-2

Domain Controller Promotion Options

Action	GENESIS	CITYHALL	DITT	MCPD
DC for a new domain	Yes	Yes	Yes	Yes
Additional DC for an existing domain	Yes, at any time you need more DCs	Yes, at any time you need more DCs	Yes, at any time you need more DCs	Yes, at any time you need more DCs
Create a new tree	Yes	No	No	No
Create a new domain in an existing tree	No	Yes	Yes	Yes
Create a new forest	Yes	No	No	No
Place domain tree in an existing forest	No	N/A	N/A	N/A

Creating the root DC is the easiest. Follow the instructions to create a new domain and a new domain tree in a new forest. This will essentially be the first Active Directory domain you will create for your enterprise, and it is known as the root domain. We recommend a root domain structure similar to the one created here. Your own "Genesis" domain need not be on an expensive server. In fact, our first GENESIS server was a Pentium 4 233 MHz with 256MB of RAM. This does not mean you should surf eBay looking for a $50 server. Buy a server that will give you at least four years of good service. We plan to add a super-server DC for GENESIS capable of holding a huge database and taking many thousands of concurrent queries and logon requests.

Before you begin promotion, make sure your server can talk to the network. The server does not necessarily have to send packets out to other machines. Unlike Windows NT 4.0 Backup Domain Controllers, there is no need to immediately begin synchronization with a primary domain controller (PDC). However, Windows Server 2008 will not let you promote the server and install Active Directory if it cannot detect that it is attached to a network. Connecting the server to a hub is good enough, even if it is the only server in the hub.

If the server cannot be contacted from the network, you will obviously not be able to promote it remotely, nor will it be able to join the domain tree. Install the Active Directory Domain Services bits on the server as described in Chapter 1. This serves to provide the domain controller role to the server, but you still have to make the server a domain controller. This is done through the process of promoting a server. We will now begin the promotion of the DCs and the creation of domains. The following section provides a overview of the process and the screens you will encounter. Later in this chapter we will more closely follow a typical DC promotion plan for a root domain.

You need to take the following steps to complete the promotion:

1. Promote the server using the command DCPROMO at the command prompt or using the Active Directory Domain Services Installation Wizard. Upon running the command the first screen shown in Figure 21-1 loads. (You can use the DCPROMO command from the command prompt, which is quicker and easier if you plan to promote many servers or use installation scripts.) Choose the advanced mode installation as shown for more options. Click Next to arrive at the Operating System Compatibility screen. Click Next to begin the deployment.

FIGURE 21-1

The Welcome Screen of the Active Directory Domain Services Installation Wizard.

2. The next screen in the wizard prompts you to choose an existing forest or to create a new forest. This is illustrated in Figure 21-2. Choose your option and click Next.

FIGURE 21-2

Choosing the deployment configuration.

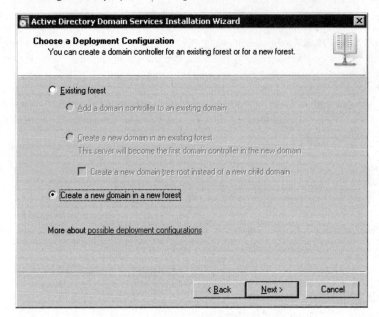

If this is a new domain you will check the option Create a New Domain in a New Forest. This is the first DC for the domain GENESIS or CITYHALL or any other new forest and domain. Creating the root domain from here is a no-brainer. Without an existing forest or domain tree, you cannot install anything else. We will now proceed to install a new domain. Click Next.

3. The Name the Forest Root Domain loads. Your screen should resemble the one shown in Figure 21-3. After you have entered the fully qualified domain name (FQDN), click Next.

4. You are now prompted to enter a NetBIOS name for the domain. This is illustrated in Figure 21-4. You would typically choose the same name as the first level of the FQDN. Refer to previous chapters for information about the choice of names. Domain names should be simple. They need to be accessible to humans, not computers. Be sure you choose the right name because you cannot change it after you promote the server.

FIGURE 21-3

Entering a name for the new forest.

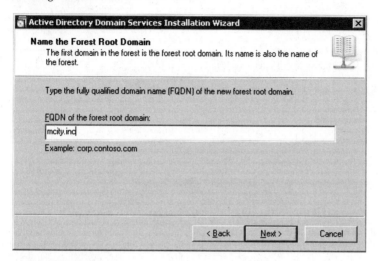

FIGURE 21-4

Entering a NetBIOS name for the new forest.

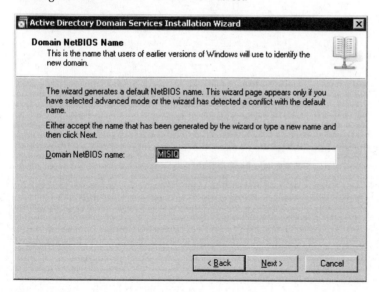

5. Click Next to choose the Forest Functional Level. Here you are given the option to provide Windows 2000, Windows Server 2003, or Windows Server 2008 compatibility. This is shown in Figure 21-5.

FIGURE 21-5

Choose the forest functional level.

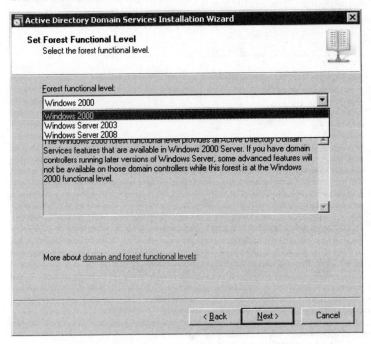

6. The next screen lets you choose additional domain controller options. These include DNS, making the sever a global catalog or a read-only domain controller. This is illustrated in Figure 21-6. Click Next after making your choices.

7. The Database, Log Folders and SYSVOL dialog box, shown in Figure 21-7, now loads. If you have separate disks, then choose a separate drive letter for the logs. This technique is inherited from Microsoft Exchange, which is the foundation for the Active Directory database and replication engines. You will get better performance if you choose two disks. If you are using RAID and only have one drive letter, then configure both locations to point to the same drive letter.

The Shared System Volume is also required. You can usually leave this to the default chosen by the server. To continue click Next.

FIGURE 21-6

Specifying DNS enables the Wizard to dynamically generate DNS entries for you.

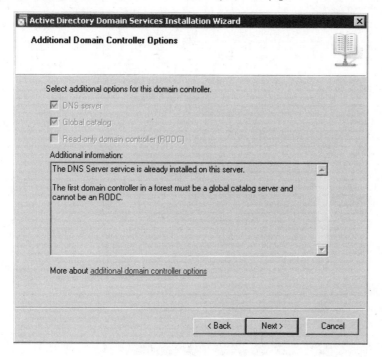

8. The Directory Services Restore Mode Administrator Password dialog box loads, as shown in Figure 21-8. This parameter is the password of the user account that is authorized to start a domain controller in Restore mode for the purpose of restoring system state. Enter the password twice and click Next.

9. The Summary dialog box loads, which means you are almost done. Check the details carefully to ensure that you have made the right choices. At this point, you can always go back and change a value or parameter. Once you click Next, however, there is no undoing any mistakes. You can only demote the server and start the whole process all over again. Click Next to begin the promotion, the installation of Active Directory, and the joining of the domain to the tree. If you see the dialog box illustrated in Figure 21-9, you are doing fine.

FIGURE 21-7

The SYSVOL folder contains a copy of information that is replicated to other servers.

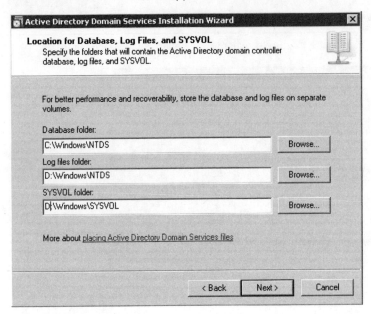

FIGURE 21-8

The Restore Mode Password is used to log in as administrator should you need to perform maintenance on Active Directory.

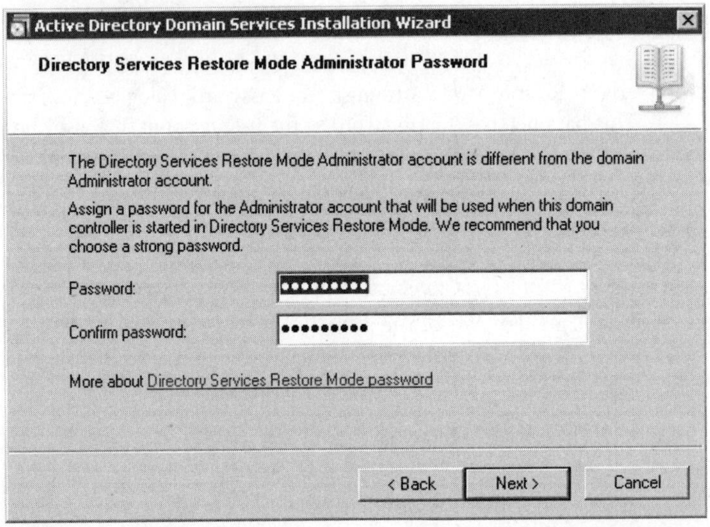

FIGURE 21-9

The Summary process of installing Active Directory is under way.

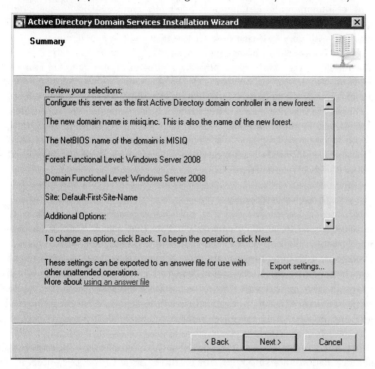

The wizard then starts the installation of Active Directory on the local server. This process can take several minutes. At this point, you can leave the DC to finish; no further human intervention is necessary.

Creating a sub-domain in the forest is a similar process. Once the new DC has been able to contact the parent DC on the network, replication is then started between the two domains. You will notice processor activity related to the replication on the parent domain; thus creating the new child domain takes a little longer.

Next, the wizard sets up a trust relationship between the new domain, CITYHALL, and its parent, GENESIS. Because the domains are part of the same domain tree in the same forest, they can exchange security credentials, which enables trusts between the domains to be transitive and bi-directional.

If all went well, and if the installation took place on the same network segment as the parent, you will notice that the new child domain was placed into the same site as the parent domain. We can leave this as is for now and move it to another site later. Also notice that the Back button has been disabled. There is no going back; the server has now been promoted to a domain controller running Active Directory services. You will now have to restart the server.

> **TIP** The entire promotion and installation process of a multi-domain forest should take no longer than an hour on a well burned-in machine and on the local area network. On a very powerful machine with very fast hard disks, it can take as little as five minutes. If the process takes longer, or if Windows Server 2008 seems to be taking hours or even the whole day to write information to the disks, then you have a problem and need to terminate the effort (just be sure the bottleneck is not due to replication that is taking place over a slow link to a remote site). Powering down the machine is the only way to terminate the effort. This, by the way, happened to us only once in more than 30 promotions. After restarting the machine, we started the effort again, and it ran all the way in about an hour.

Toward the end of the promotion period and before restarting, there is usually no way of accessing any former shares or resources on the new DC.

Establishing in DNS/WINS

Several important items needed to be taken care of when we first created the root domain GENESIS, or more correctly, GENESIS.MCITY.US. You will encounter the same issues when you install your root domain controller, the first domain in your forest. During the installation, you will be asked for the address of a Domain Name System server, or DNS, or you can choose to install DNS on the server if this was not done before you began the DNS promotion. The Active Directory installation procedure will look for a DNS server into which it must install a new zone and new domain information.

It is a good idea to choose to install and integrate DNS and WINS on the root domain controller. It will make installation a lot smoother. For example, if the new Active Directory cannot locate a DNS server, it will be unable to register any domain, host, or site-specific information into the DNS databases.

During the installation of child domains, however, you will not be prompted for DNS information, even if you installed DNS on the server when you originally set it up as a standalone server. Unless you manually install the new domain into DNS, there will be no way of authenticating to the child domain or managing it from another domain controller. You will get an error message indicating that Active Directory Domains and Trusts is unable to find the domain, or that the server was not started. If your new DC is, in fact, started, then the problem is DNS.

Let's manually install the new domain into DNS:

1. Open the primary DNS snap-in by clicking Start ➪ All Programs ➪ Administrative Tools ➪ DNS, or run the snap-in from the command line as described in Chapter 5. The DNS snap-in will load. In this example, the DNS server is hosted on our root DC, MCDC00.

2. Drill down to your root Active Directory domain. Notice that we have the higher-level Internet domains of MCITY and ORG on this DNS as well. Select the root Active Directory domain and right-click. The menu options load.

3. Go down to the menu option New Domain and select it. The New Domain dialog box will load. In this example, we are going to add the new domain MCPD to the GENESIS namespace, so we type **MCPD** in the dialog box.

4. If the domain exists, DNS will immediately pull all the records it needs into its databases. For example, CITYHALL expands down to the point where we can resolve both the Kerberos and LDAP services on the CITYHALL domain.

5. Close the DNS snap-in.

Testing DNS and WINS

If your domain controllers have been established in DNS and WINS correctly, you will be able to resolve them. The following tests provide the proof:

1. Check your DNS records: Open the command console and type **NSLOOKUP** and the domain name. If the domains have been correctly installed in DNS, you will be able to resolve them. In our example, we can correctly resolve CITYHALL and GENESIS to their respective domain controllers. Notice that you cannot yet resolve MCPD to its domain controller. There is a very good reason for this: The domain does not yet exist. Consult Chapter 5 for a more in-depth discussion of DNS.

2. Check your WINS records: Open the command console and ping the host of the domains from any workstation. If you just ping the NetBIOS name, you will be able to resolve it to an IP address. You should also be able to ping the entire DNS name, which is resolved in DNS, not WINS. Remember that clients will need DHCP-assigned IP addresses, which automatically give them DNS and WINS IP addresses. DHCP thus needs to be up and running before clients will be able to resolve anything on the network.

If DNS and WINS check out, you are on your way to happy administration. Confirm that you can open the child domain from its parent DC. This is demonstrated in the next section.

Testing Active Directory domains and trusts

If your domain controllers have been established in DNS and WINS correctly, you should be able to log on to the remote domain and administer it. Open Active Directory Domains and Trusts by clicking Start ➪ All Programs ➪ Administrative Tools ➪ Active Directory Domains and Trusts. The snap-in will load. Notice that a domain tree is now apparent. Right-click the child domain and select Manage. If trusts and authentication are all working, you will be able to enter the domain for management.

One last exercise before we look at sites and subnets again: Check the trust relationships between the newly created domains. To do this, go to the Domains and Trusts snap-in as illustrated earlier. Select a domain and right-click. Choose Properties and click the Trusts tab. You will see the child domain information in this dialog box. The Trusts tab also tells you that the trust is transitive and working. This is where you will also see that nontransitive trusts between Windows Server 2008 domains and NT networks. If your trusts are working right, you will be able to drill down to the directory and access a domain.

Creating sites

When you promote the first domain controller, Active Directory creates a default site named *Default-First-Site-Name* and places the domain controller server into that site. You can change the name of the default site to reflect the conventions in your deployment plan, or you can create a new site after the promotion and move the server into that domain. We chose the latter for demonstration purposes. This is further demonstrated when we create the CITYHALL domain.

NOTE It is not necessary to create subnet objects for replication between servers. In the GENESIS setup, Active Directory would be able to replicate to each server in the site.

Active Directory sees the root DC server in the site we created and puts the root DC of the child domain in that site. Remember that an Active Directory site is associated with an IP subnet. The Active Directory replication topology is built via the site and subnet topology, between the domain controllers, or both. This technology is derived from the Exchange replication mechanisms, and it works on the principle of joining an Exchange server to a site.

When you have two domain controllers on the same site, which is what we have done in the earlier example for expediency, the replication that takes place between the controllers happens very quickly, or at the speed of your local area network to be more precise. This could be anything from 100 to 1000 Mbps.

With subnets, Active Directory gets the information it needs to build the replication topology. In the previous example, it automatically added the second domain controller to the site we created for GENESIS because they shared an IP subnet, but we are going to take the CITYHALL DC and ship it to its new location, which is the 100.45.0.0 subnet, which means that we have to manually move the DC object from the site in which it was initially installed to the correct site. Before we do that, we need to make a new site for the DC, as follows:

1. Load the MMC snap-in Active Directory Site and Services. To find the snap-in, go to Start ➪ Administrative Tools ➪ Active Directory Sites and Services, or load it from the command line. The snap-in loads.

2. Select the Sites folder in the tree and right-click it. Choose New Site from the context menu. The New Site dialog box appears and allows you to create the new site. Enter the appropriate site information. The site transport used is now defaulted to IP. Click OK to add the site.

Let's now look at the site object more closely.

The site object

You will notice that each site has a *servers* container. This container holds the DCs that have been placed into this site. There is also an attribute named *Licensing Site Settings* and an attribute named *NTDS Settings*.

The Licensing Site Settings property is used to specify the computer and domain that licenses the site. In the NTDS Settings object, you can disable the Knowledge Consistency Checker (KCC) settings that determine the automatic generation of the replication topology within the site or between this site and other sites. These settings enable you to create additional settings to augment the replication topology of the KCC, but this depends on your situation.

Creating server objects

There is no difference between the server objects you create manually and the server objects created automatically by the AD, save that you have to remove manually what you create manually. The KCC does not know about these objects, nor does it care about what happens to them. To create such objects, perform the following steps:

1. Select the server's NTDS Settings property in the console tree and right-click it. Choose the menu option New Active Directory Connection from the context menu. The Find Domain Controllers dialog box loads.

2. Select the DC to create a connection and click OK. This will then open the New Object - Connection dialog box.

3. Supply a name for the new connection object and click OK.

You can easily change the configuration of your connection object after creating it by simply opening the connection object's Properties dialog box. You can also set the security levels and access control on the object, but most interesting is the Change Schedule button on the first tab. This enables you to change the replication schedule to suit your environment.

You can, for example, schedule replication to run at night when there is no traffic on the network. Remember, however, that the schedule for a connection object is only one way. To schedule the full replication load, you have to configure the connection object on the other domain controllers as well.

Creating the subnet objects

The Subnets folder holds the IP subnets associated with specific site objects. To create a subnet object, perform the following steps:

1. Drill down to the Subnets container in the console tree in the Sites and Services MMC snap-in. Right-click the container and choose New Subnet from the shortcut menu. The New Object - Subnet dialog box loads.

2. Type the new subnet's network address and mask. This is automatically translated into a properly bit-masked subnet.

3. Select the site in the list to which the subnet is to be associated and click OK.

Now, all servers that reside on this subnet that become DCs will automatically be added to the site associated with this subnet.

Creating the site link objects

Create the site link objects according to the criteria mentioned previously. To create an object, perform the following steps:

1. Drill down to the IP or SMTP transport listed in the console tree of the Site and Services snap-in and right-click the transport. Select New Site Link from the context menu. The New Object - Site Link dialog box loads.

2. Specify a name for the new object and then choose the sites that the link connects.

3. Click OK, and the site link object is created.

> **NOTE** When you choose site links, you need to know what you are choosing, and this should be in your deployment plan. For example, if you are going to connect sites to a T1 network, there will typically be only two sites to be linked, one at each end. Adding a third site to the link would be worthless. If you are working with a network cloud, you can also configure a site link bridge, which ensures that all sites get replication due to the transitive link structure created with site link bridges.

To configure the site link, right-click the new object and choose Properties from the context menu. The site links properties for the specific site load. Add a description for the site link and add the sites to the link by moving them from the pane on the left (Sites Not in This Site Link) to the pane on the right (Sites in This Site Link).

You can then configure the cost of the site links and any special replication schedule.

Creating the site link bridge object

The process involved in creating the site link bridge object is the same as the process for creating site link objects. The only difference is that you select two or more site links instead of sites.

Now we'll create some facilities for our administrators in GENESIS.

Creating organizational units (OUs)

To recap, OU stands for organizational unit. In the Active Directory, the OU represents a partitioning of the domain, yes, but it is more than that. An OU holds security policy, and it is the location for delegating administrative authority (also known as delegation of control).

Now and in the future, the Active Directory OU is going to be compared to the OUs of other directories, such as Novell Directory Services (NDS). Since the publishing of the Active Directory Services Interface (ADSI), the OU has already been slammed for not being a security principal. Of course, what is a spade in the hands of one gardener may be something else in the hands of another. Seasoned NT administrators may find it difficult to think in terms of another security principal to replace groups.

NOTE Had OUs replaced groups completely, it might have made upgrading very difficult.

OUs are different from groups; groups are security principals and can be given access or denied access to any network, computer, or domain resource — in fact, any object defined in the local registry or in the Active Directory. We like OUs because it is possible to model the OU to Key Management Entities (or KMEs); therefore, they play a role in enterprise administration as opposed to being gatekeepers.

To extend security policy over groups and users, you place them into OUs. OUs are themselves "locked down" with security policy and access control. The policy governs how the users and the groups are allowed to conduct themselves domainwide and forestwide. Most important for security, however, is that the OU is also your computer lockup. This is essentially how you should understand and plan the enterprise Group Policy. For now, we will take you through the steps of creating an OU.

To create an OU, open the Active Directory Users and Computers MMC snap-in and follow these steps:

1. Drill down to the domain in the console tree and right-click it. From the menu that appears, select New ➪ Organization Unit.

2. Enter the name of the OU according to the naming conventions you are using and click OK.

TIP Do not try to create an OU hierarchy for the benefit of your users. It's a waste of your resources. In fact, you should do your best as an administrator to hide the OU structure from your users and the network. The user base has a network folder hierarchy to navigate and folders that you may publish in the directory. The OU structure is there for the benefit of change control and management, security policy, and workplace administration.

You can nest an OU inside another OU hierarchy, but avoid deep OU nests because they are harder to manage.

Delegating OU administration

At this point in the creation of your Active Directory DC, you may decide to create additional OUs, or you may come back to the task of OU creation later. One of your most important chores will be to delegate administrative control and management over the OU to an administrator or responsible party. You might find it useful to assign the task of creating OUs to another individual, preferably a person trained in domain security.

There are two reasons to begin delegation at this point:

■ Delegation can help you manage a complex directory structure by delegating the work as early in the directory-building process as possible.

■ Delegation is an important security consideration. By delegating, you essentially block others from interfering with the workings of a particular OU. Delegation also obviates the need to create special OU security groups or OU administrators, which, if given power by group membership to administer an OU, essentially have the power to administer all OUs.

Start the Delegate Control Wizard to perform the delegation. This is done by first selecting the OU to which you wish to delegate control and then by right-clicking the selection. The OU context menu loads. Select Delegate Control, which is the first option in the menu. The Delegation of Control Wizard launches. Select Next and then click Add to load the list of domain security principals. Choose a user or group account from the list and then click the list of Active Directory users and groups. Click Add to add the user or group and then click Next.

The next screen enables you to select the task to delegate to the user or group. You can select from a predetermined list of tasks, or choose to build a custom list of tasks. If you choose the latter, you will be able to apply a finer level of control over the task to delegate. The customer list gives you two options: an extensive list of individual objects that can be manipulated by the intended administrator or group, or a shortcut that specifies the OU, all objects in the OU, and any new objects that are created.

If you do not want the delegated party to be able to create new objects, choose the list of objects and uncheck the specific objects that grant control.

When you are done, click Next and the summary page will appear. Check the delegation summary and then click Finish.

Securing the DC and following disaster recovery protocol

To properly secure a DC, you should ensure that all objects are properly protected by Access Control Lists (ACLs). ACLs on Active Directory objects contain Access Control Entries that apply to the object as a whole and to the individual properties of the object. This means that you can control not only the administrators or users that you want to see the object in its entirety, but also which properties should be exposed to certain groups or individuals.

Securing the directory is a complex and time-consuming task, but it is essential. Each object, just like all other operating system objects, can display a Properties page. You launch the Properties page by right-clicking the object and selecting Properties. The object's Properties page loads.

Click the Security tab. You can now add or remove security accounts from any trusted domain and select the property pages (tabs) that can be read.

In addition to protecting the directory and its contents, it is also important to lock down the server ...the domain controller. You should first ensure that the Administrator account or any other omnipotent security principal is not logged on to the console, and you should strive to ensure that such omnipotent accounts are not allowed to be disseminated. Meanwhile, lock down the server and only allow accounts to access regions of the directory to which they have been delegated.

By locking down the server, you are not only protecting the directory service, but also other critical components of a vital server, such as the registry, storage facilities, and so on.

Be sure to schedule a backup of the directory as soon as the current tasks have been completed.

Implementation

This section outlines the process of building a forest and forest root domain. It also covers the process of providing a resource and update server that will be used for OS installations, tools, utilities, and patches.

First, let's perform the setup and installation of the support server. This server is placed on the future production subnet, initially as a workgroup server, and exposes a number of shares to be used for accessing operating systems, tools, software, utilities, and patches. This server will eventually be joined to the network as a temporary software update server using Windows Software Update Services (WSUS). The server will also function as a temporary DHCP server.

This server should be installed initially as a standalone server using its old name. The base operating system is Windows Server 2008. To configure the support server, follow these steps:

1. Log on to CHBAK01 as Administrator while this server is still in the lab.
2. Create a share named `C:\ADBITS` and share as `ADBITS`.
3. Create a subfolder in the share named `C:\ADBITS\Adminpak`.
4. Create a folder named `C:\ADBITS\Support`.
5. Create a folder named `C:\ADBITS\Exchange Tools`.
6. Create a folder named `C:\ADBITS\QA documents`.
7. Crate a folder named `C:\ADBITS\Scripts`.
8. Create a folder named `C:\ADBITS\RKTools`.
9. Copy the tools you will need, including all MSI files, scripts, data, packages, and so on, to these folders.
10. Make sure this server has the latest anti-virus DAT files and that it scans the file system.
11. Install Windows Software Update Services (WSUS). This can be downloaded from Microsoft.
12. Create distribution folders, such as `C:\STDINST` (share as `STDINST`), for the Windows Server 2008 Standard Edition operating system. Repeat for each edition of the operating system, including XP and Vista.
13. Next create distribution shares (for example, `C:\..\I386`) and copy all your installation subfolders and files to these distribution shares. You can automate the process using the setup manager utility (`setupmgr.exe`) on the operating system CD's Support\Tools folder. The `setupmgr` utility is also found in the `deploy.cab` file.

14. Configure Software Update Services on MRBAK01 (see Microsoft's white paper on Windows Software Update Services Design on the Windows Update Web site at www.microsoft.com).

15. Validate this server, which should include a final scan for anti-virus.

16. Remove the server from your Lab domain and join it to a new workgroup called WORK. This will be the first instance of this workgroup. Your support server is now complete.

Install

Upon installation of the support server to the isolated network, proceed with the following installation procedures:

1. Rack and stack the server in a production rack or on the data center floor with access to an isolated network. Boot the server.

2. Log on to CHBAK01 as the local Administrator on the isolated subnet.

3. Reset the Administrator password.

4. Change your IP configuration to statically assigned addressing.

5. Assign an IP address (our example is 10.10.20.23).

6. Assign the same IP address as your gateway and DNS.

7. Install the DHCP roles and configure a new scope for the subnet.

You have now completed installation and provisioning of the support server.

IP address reservations

You can reserve IP addresses for the root domain controllers to ensure that the root DCs obtain the correct IP addresses as soon as their IP configuration is changed from static addressing to DHCP-assigned addresses.

Installation of the root domain, MCITY.US

This section covers the promotion of a root domain controller. See the section "Installing and Testing the Active Directory Domain Controllers" earlier in this chapter. By promoting root domain controllers, you are, in fact, creating the forest in which all future systems will be installed. The servers should be configured for second and third RAID-5 arrays as required.

It is critical that this process completes and proceeds as described in this chapter. If you deviate from the process or take shortcuts, you may render the root domain useless, and it will have to be rebuilt. You can also update domain controller servers with the required software updates, service packs, and security patches after promotion and after QA and validation.

Follow these steps:

1. Name the root domain DCs. Once the server installation's complete, the root domain controllers will be given miscellaneous names, and they will be members of the WORK workgroup. Change the names of the root domain controllers to the names reserved for them. For the City Hall hub, the server names would be CHRDC01 and CHRDC02. Remember to rename the servers to their DC names prior to running DC promotion because these names cannot be changed after promotion of the servers to domain controllers. If you need to change the names after promotion, you will need to reinstall the server. Do not change the workgroup when changing the names.

2. Configure TCP/IP on CHRDC01. Log on to the server designated to become the root DC (CHRDC01) as Administrator. Open the TCP/IP properties of the network interface card (NIC) and enter the parameters listed in Table 21-3.

TABLE 21-3

TCP/IP Configuration on CHRDC01

Resources	Configuration
IP Address	10.10.20.21
Subnet Mask	255.255.252.0
Default Gateway	10.10.20.1
Preferred DNS Server	10.10.20.21
Alternate DNS Server	<null>

3. Configure TCP/IP on CHRDC02. Now log on to the server designated to become the root DC (CHRDC01) as Administrator. Open the TCP/IP properties of the network interface card (NIC) and enter the parameters listed in Table 21-4.

4. Install DNS. Log on to the server designated to become the root DC (CHRDC01) as Administrator and install DNS on this server. To do so, open the Control Panel and select Add or Remove Programs ➪ Add/Remove Windows Components, which launches the Windows Components Wizard. Select Networking Services in the Wizard and click the Details button. In the Networking Services dialog box, check the option to install Domain Name System (DNS). Complete the procedures and, when prompted by the installation procedure for the Windows Server operating system CD, either provide a CD or browse to the I386 folder under the install shares on the support Server. Complete the process to install DNS on the server. You can now repeat the process for all hub root domain controllers.

TABLE 21-4

Configuration on CHRDC02

Resources	Configuration
IP Address	10.10.20.24
Subnet Mask	255.255.252.0
Default Gateway	10.10.20.1
Preferred DNS Server	10.10.20.21
Alternate DNS Server	<null>

 This process cannot be repeated on CHRDC02 or any other root server destined to become a DC.

5. Create the Forest Root Zone on CHRDC01 by using the following steps:

   a. Start up DNS and right-click the CHRDC01 icon.

   b. Select New Zone. The New Zone Wizard will now launch. Click Next.

   c. Select the option to create a Primary zone and click Next.

   d. Select Forward Lookup Zone and click Next.

   e. Enter MCITY.INC as the name of the zone and click Next.

   f. Keep the default DNS filename (it should be MCITY.INC.DNS) for the zone filename and click Next.

   g. If prompted for Dynamic Update configuration, choose the option to allow Dynamic Updates. Click Next.

   h. Complete the process by selecting Finish.

6. Create the reverse lookup zone on CHRDC01 by using the following steps:

   a. Open to the DNS console and expand the CHRDC01 server icon.

   b. Select Reverse Lookup Zones and click New Zone. The New Zone Wizard will launch.

   c. Select options for a Primary non-integrated zone and click Next.

   d. Enter the IP address range for the zone (this is the 10.10.20.X network).

   e. Click Next and select the options to allow a dynamic update.

   f. Complete the process by selecting Finish.

7. Create the forest root domain controller on CHRDC01 by using the following steps:

   a. Click Start ➪ Run and type DCPROMO on CHRDC01.

   b. Choose the options for creating a root domain controller in a new forest.

c. Choose the root domain name as the full DNS Name for the new domain (MCITY.cty).

d. Accept the default NETBIOS name of MCITY.

e. Choose the default path for the SYSVOL folder on the RAID-5 array. However, the drive letter should point to the RAID-5 array on D:\, E:\, or F:\, and not C:\ (for example, E:\Windows\...). Choose the path options provided for the NTDS Active Directory database and its log files, changing only the drive letters to point to the RAID-5 volume as mentioned.

f. Accept permissions compatible with Windows 2000 and Windows Server 2008.

g. Enter the Directory Services Restore Mode Administrator password. This should be a complex password. Choose "4NTDS@MCITY" (without the quotation marks). Remember that the server's local Administrator password will become the password required to log on to the DC after promotion.

h. Review the settings and then click Finish to begin the process. Restart the server when prompted.

8. Enable Active Directory integration of the forest root zone and the reverse lookup zone. To enable AD integration for the root zone, follow these steps:

   a. Open the DNS console and expand the root server CHRDC01 icon.

   b. Expand the Forward Lookup Zones folder and select the MCITY.CTY zone. Right-click on this zone and the select Properties.

   c. The Properties dialog box for MCITY will open. On the General tab, select the Change button on the Type option. The Change Zone Type dialog box will launch.

   d. Select the option to change the zone to Active Directory Integrated and click OK.

   e. Perform the same procedure on the Reverse Lookup Zone folder.

9. Verify CHRDC01 name registration by performing the following actions:

   a. Open the DNS console and expand the root server CHRDC01 icon.

   b. Expand the Forward Lookup Zones folder and then expand the MCITY.CTY zone.

   c. Verify that the _msdcs, _sites, _tcp, and _udp subdomains are registered under MCITY.CTY.

   d. If the preceding subdomains are not registered, then start a command prompt and type NET STOP NETLOGON. Wait for the service to stop and then type NET START NETLOGON.

   e. Repeat Steps a through c to verify the registration.

   f. Verify that the Reverse Lookup Zone has replicated.

10. Verify DNS name resolution on CHRRDC02. Before CHRDC02 can be promoted as a root DC, you must first verify DNS:

    a. Log on to the CHRRDC02 as the domain Administrator.

b. Open the command prompt, type `NSLOOKUP MCITY.CTY`, and press Enter. You should now see the following result in the console:

```
C:\>nslookup MCITY.cty
Server: CHRDC01.MCITY.CTY
Address: 10.10.20.21
Name: MCITY.CTY
Address: 10.10.20.21
```

c. If you do not see this result, confirm that the IP settings on CHRDC02 are correct. It should have CHRDC01 (10.10.20.21) as its preferred DNS server.

d. If you not have DNS working properly, you cannot proceed with DCPROMO of any other server.

11. DCPROMO CHRDC02 as follows:

a. Click Start ➪ Run and type `DCPROMO` on CHRDC02.

b. Choose the option Additional Domain Controller for an Existing Domain and then click Next.

c. You will now be prompted for access to the root domain. Choose the Administrator account because this account has Enterprise Administrator credentials. (See Step 7 g for account and password information.)

d. Choose the default path for the `SYSVOL` folder on the RAID-5 array. However, the drive letter should point to the RAID-5 array on D:\, E:\, or F:\, and not C:\. Choose the path options provided for the NTDS Active Directory database and its log files, changing only the drive letters to point to the RAID-5 volume as mentioned previously.

e. You must now enter the Directory Services Restore Mode Administrator password for this server. This should be a complex password. Choose something like 4NTDS@MCITY. DCs can and should have the same Directory Services Restore Mode Administrator password to simplify administration.

f. Review the settings and then click Finish to begin the process. Restart the server when prompted.

12. Verify CHRDC02 name registration as follows:

a. Open the DNS console and expand the root server CHRDC02 icon.

b. Expand the Forward Lookup Zones folder and select expand the MCITY.cty zone.

c. Verify that the `msdcs,_sites`, `tcp`, and `udp` subdomains are registered under MCITY.cty.

d. If these subdomains are not registered, then start a command prompt and type `NET STOP NETLOGON`. Wait for the service to stop and then type `NET START NETLOGON`.

e. Repeat Steps a through c to verify the registration

f. Verify that the Reverse Lookup Zone has replicated.

13. Update the preferred DNS parameters on CHRDC01. Log on to CHRDC01 and open the TCP/IP properties for the NIC. Change the preferred DNS server from 10.10.20.21 to 10.10.20.24.

14. Backup the domain controllers.

Quality assurance

Quality Assurance (QA) and validation should be performed before continuing with your domain building. QA can be achieved by following these steps:

1. Join a clean Windows XP SP1 or later or Vista SP1 workstation to the root domain.

2. Install the support tools on the workstation. The tools can be accessed from the ADBITS\SUPPORT\TOOLS share you created on the support server. Install the tools to the default path on the C: drive of the desktop machine.

3. Install the ADMINPAK on the workstation. This will install management tools (such as DSA.MSC) on the workstation. The tools can be accessed from the ADBITS\ADMINPAK share on the support server. Install the tools to the default path on the C: drive.

4. Install the Resource Kit tools on the workstation. This will install tools such as DNSDIAG and DSQUERY on the workstation. The tools can be accessed from the ADBITS\RESKIT share on the support server. Install the tools to the default path on the C: drive.

5. Open a command console and run DCDIAG. (You can run DCDIAG /? for the valid options like supplying a log file name for output and so on.) Perform the DCDIAG against all domain controllers. The data generated by DCDIAG will be streamed to the default log file location on the workstation.

6. DCDIAG should be carried out several times a day.

7. You can also open Replication Monitor and verify that replication is occurring without errors between the domain controllers.

8. Run DSQUERY against the domain controllers to ensure that all FSMO roles are intact. FSMO roles will most likely be moved after installation.

At this point, your root domain is ready to roll and you can proceed with a child domain or prepare for the addition of Exchange to your environment.

Summary

This chapter successfully demonstrated the promotion of several servers to domain controllers, which hold the Active Directory namespace and all the functionality that goes with it from (A)ctive to (Z)one.

You also went through the paces of creating and configuring your replication topology. We also reviewed the creation of OUs, although we did not dwell too much on them because they are discussed in detail in the remaining chapters.

Now that we have the Active Directory domain structure in place, it is time to learn a bit about managing it. Management tools, here we come...

Chapter 22

Active Directory Management

This chapter deploys an Active Directory infrastructure. Working from the deployment plan blueprint described in this chapter, you can identify and modify the elements of the deployment plan that suit your configuration. You can make changes as desired, whether you need a solution for a small network or a WAN connecting multiple domain controllers and an extensive Active Directory tree.

CROSS-REF See Chapters 1 and 2 and Chapter 17 for specifics on Active Directory Federation Services, Active Directory Lightweight Directory Services, and Active Directory Rights Management Services. For information on using Active Directory Certificate Services and read-only domain controllers, see Chapter 16.

IN THIS CHAPTER

Learn to manage replication

Familiarize yourself with catalog server installation

Learn to perform online and offline Active Directory backups

Learn how to move Active Directory among servers

Active Directory administration

Installing New Directory Services into an Existing Infrastructure

You should take several things into consideration when installing directory services into an existing infrastructure, the first of which is uptime. If you are dealing with a network that can be down for several hours at a time, perhaps after normal business hours, your job is made easier. However, if your company maintains 24/7 services, you can't very well down servers to upgrade them.

One of the most important things to remember when upgrading a Windows NT network (yes, they still exist) is to remove an existing Backup Domain Controller (BDC) to maintain network integrity. If something should go wrong during the upgrade process, you can fall back on the BDC.

If you are in a 24/7 environment, follow these steps to begin the upgrade of your domain controllers:

1. Choose a BDC on the network and ensure that it has a current copy of the User Account database. Back up this server and then unplug it from the network. If a power failure or other catastrophic event happens during the upgrade of the Primary Domain Controller (PDC), you can always promote the BDC to a Primary to resume normal network operations.

2. Begin the operating system (OS) upgrade phase on the PDCs. During this phase of the upgrade, network requests are handled by the BDCs.

3. After the operating system has been upgraded on the PDC, upgrade the OS on all the BDCs except for the BDC that was unplugged from the network.

4. When all operating systems have been upgraded, run the Active Directory Installation Wizard on the PDC, followed by all the BDCs.

If server uptime isn't much of a concern, you can upgrade concurrently, but this isn't recommended.

Replication Management

Replication management is handled with the Active Directory Sites and Services Manager, which is implemented as a Microsoft Management Console (MMC) snap-in. This is where you see how replication happens between servers; however, you lack the capability to monitor replication or to force replication to happen.

The repadmin.exe utility enables you to check replication for consistency between partners, monitor the status of replication, view the metadata contained within the replication, and force replication events.

Installing New Domain Controllers

Before you install a domain controller, verify DNS; we touch on this topic again shortly.

After you install the OS on the server, ensure that it has an active network connection and that it can properly communicate with the DNS server. During the Active Directory installation phase, the OS needs to query DNS for domain names in order for the installation to complete successfully. If you will be installing Active Directory on a server that exists within an existing forest, the network connection of this server can be configured to use more than one DNS server. This is necessary because an existing forest may have many DNS servers for each "branch" of the forest, and the Active Directory Installation Wizard on this new server must be able to locate all servers in the forest.

Don't worry if you are installing Active Directory into a network without an existing forest. The Active Directory Installation Wizard actually installs and configures a DNS server on the local machine. Keep in mind that the DNS settings of this server are automatically changed to point to the local server. You are free to change this after the Installation Wizard has completed its task. If you do change this setting, you need to point it to a DNS server that is still capable of seeing all the servers on your network. Without this, Active Directory will fail to operate correctly.

If, by chance, you already have DNS installed, you need to verify all records before you attempt the Active Directory installation. Specifically, you must verify that the appropriate service (SRV) resource records and corresponding address (A) resource records exist in the DNS server.

NOTE A DNS SRV record enables administrators to use several servers for one domain. These records designate where services are located. For example, ftp can be located on one server while another server can host a Web server or Active Directory. A DNS A record simply maps a server name to the IP address.

If these DNS records are missing or invalid, the installation will die a miserable death, so it's critical that you add or correct these records.

After you have verified that all DNS records are present and accounted for, ensure that your DNS server allows for dynamic updates. You do this in the authoritative DNS zone. To locate the authoritative DNS zone within your network, simply find the primary DNS server hosting the zone. This zone will have the DNS name of the Active Directory domain or the name of a parent zone. For example, if the name of the Active Directory domain is authors.wiley.com, the authoritative DNS could be one of the following:

- Authors.wiley.com
- wiley.com
- com

If you'd prefer not to configure your DNS for dynamic updates, you need to add all records manually. A list of all resource records that should be registered by a domain controller is stored in the following location:

```
%systemroot%\system32\Config\netlogon.dns
```

Installing New Catalog Servers

Configuring a domain controller to serve as a global catalog server is a fairly straightforward process. To begin, open the Active Directory Sites and Services management console. When it opens, expand Sites within the tree view. Below the Sites node, expand your site's name; then expand the Servers node in which your server's name is listed. Find the NTDS node, right-click it, and choose Properties. On the General page of the Properties dialog box, select the Global Catalog checkbox.

> **NOTE**   To open Active Directory Sites and Services, from the Start menu select All Programs ⇨ Administrative Tools ⇨ Active Directory Sites and Services.

Each Windows Server 2008 site or Windows 2000 site containing Microsoft Message Queue 1.0 clients running on Windows NT 4.0, Windows 98, or Windows 95 computers must contain at least one Windows Server 2008 domain controller running the Message Queuing directory service (Downlevel Client Support) configured as a global catalog server. Alternatively, you can have at least one Windows 2000 domain controller running a Message Queuing server and configured as a global catalog server from the domain of each such client. This is required to enable such clients to send queries programmatically to Message Queuing servers.

If you currently use a Windows NT 4.0 PDC, this box is automatically promoted to a domain controller configured as a global catalog server when it is migrated.

The first domain controller in a Windows Server 2008 forest is automatically configured as a global catalog server.

Protecting Active Directory from Corruption

To ensure that Active Directory operates in a smooth and consistent manner, it may be necessary to perform integrity checks, repair, move, recovery, and defragmentation of the Active Directory database.

Online and offline database defragmentation

By default, Active Directory automatically performs an online defragmentation every 12 hours as part of its garbage collection process. Online defragmentation is very effective, but it doesn't reduce the size of the database file (Ntds.dit). It does, however, optimize data storage in the database and reclaim space in the database file to create new objects. The defragmentation process prevents data storage problems, but if your database file is getting large, you won't get much help here; you will ultimately need to perform an offline defragmentation. The process of offline defragmentation creates a brand-new compacted version of the database file. If you have a large network in which objects are added and removed quite often, it is quite likely that the resulting defragmented file will be considerably smaller.

To perform an offline defragmentation of the Active Directory database, follow these steps:

1. Back up Active Directory! Regardless of the software you are using to back up your server, if you are choosing to back up everything on the server, the registry will be backed up by

default. If you choose not to back up everything on the server, ensure that you are backing up the System State, which will include all Active Directory information.

2. Open Computer Management, drill down to Services, and stop the Active Directory Domain Services Service. You can also restart the domain controller and then press and hold down the F8 key before the operating system starts. You are greeted with the Windows Server 2008 Advanced Options menu at this point.

3. With the latter option in Step 2, and if you are at the Advanced Options menu, choose Directory Services Restore Mode and press Enter. To start the boot process again, press Enter.

4. Log on to the server using the Administrator account with the local admin password defined in the offline SAM.

5. After Windows Server 2008 starts, click the Start menu and choose Programs ⇨ Accessories ⇨ Command Prompt.

NOTE The ability to simply stop AD DS is a new feature of Windows Server 2008. You can get to a console window quickly by clicking the Start menu, selecting Run, and typing **cmd** followed by Enter.

6. With either the DC in restore mode or with the services stopped, get to the command prompt and type `ntdsutil` and press Enter. First you need to set the active instance, so before going further type `ac i ntds` and press Enter.

7. After the utility opens, type `files` and press Enter.

8. Type `info` and press Enter. Current information about the path and size of the Active Directory database and its log files is displayed. Be sure to pay special attention to the path. You might want to write down this path information, shown in Figure 22-1.

FIGURE 22-1

The info command displays the location of all relevant database files.

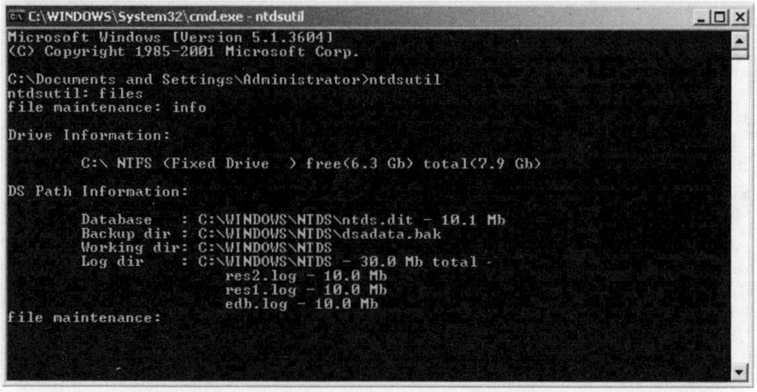

9. Locate a spot on your drive that has enough free space for the compacted version of the database to reside. Type `compact to <drive>:\<directory>` where `<drive>` and `<directory>` represent the path that you recorded in the previous step. The database file is then compacted, and a progress bar displays the compaction rate, as shown in Figure 22-2.

FIGURE 22-2

The compact process can be monitored with the progress bar.

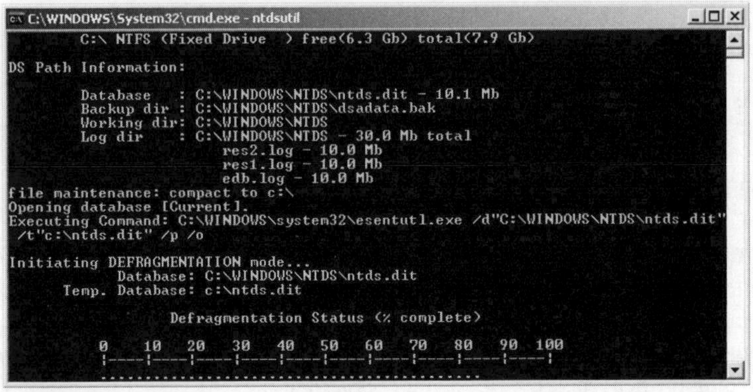

NOTE   As with any directory path, if the path contains spaces, you must surround the path with quotation marks.

When the `compact` function is finished, `ntdsutil` displays the location of the compacted database file as well as the location of the log file (see Figure 22-3).

FIGURE 22-3

Upon completion, the compact process displays the location of the resulting file.

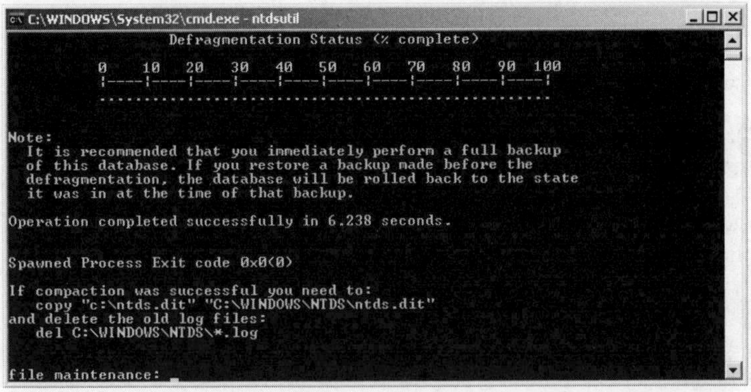

10. A new database named `Ntds.dit` is created in the path that you specified.

11. To exit, type `quit` and press Enter. To return to the command prompt, type `quit` again.

You can now copy the new `Ntds.dit` file over the old `Ntds.dit` file in the current Active Directory database path that was recorded earlier. If the services were stopped you can't do things like open Windows Explorer and mess with folder and files because AD is not online to check permissions. You are limited to simple DOS type commands such as `COPY`. Restart the services — or the computer if you were in restore mode — normally.

Ensuring database integrity

Active Directory is implemented on a transactional database system. Log files enable rollback segments, which ensure that transactions are committed to the database. In the event of a power failure, there's no chance of a partial commit of data.

NOTE The Active Directory database system is commonly referred to as the Jet database. The Jet database is the native database used by Microsoft Access. The Jet database engine has been around for quite a while and is very well established.

To check the integrity of the contents of the Active Directory database, you can use the `ntdutil.exe` tool. This tool contains a semantics checker that can be invoked by selecting the Semantic database analysis option. This tool is automatically invoked during Active Directory's Restore mode. During this time, any errors are written into `dsdit.dmp.xx` log files. A progress indicator indicates the status of the check.

The following list describes the functions that can be performed with the `ntdutil.exe` tool:

- **Reference count check.** Counts all the references from the data table and the link table to ensure that they match the listed counts for the record.

- **Deleted object check.** Deleted objects are checked to ensure that the date and timestamp have been removed.

- **Ancestor check.** Determines whether the current Distinguished Name Tag (DNT) is equal to the ancestor list of the parent and the current DNT.

- **Security descriptor check.** Looks for a valid descriptor.

- **Replication check.** Ensures that every object has property metadata.

Moving Active Directory

To move an Active Directory database, you use the `ntdsutil.exe` command-line tool in Directory Services Restore mode. In the event that you experience a corruption of a drive or a drive failure, you would need to move `Ntds.dit` or the logs files to another drive.

To move the Active Directory database to a different file system, follow these steps:

1. First and foremost, back up the Active Directory database. Windows Server 2008 Backup will handle this for you if you choose to back up the entire system. If you don't want to back up the entire machine, at least back up the System State, which includes all the Active Directory database information.

2. Stop the AD DS as described earlier either by

   ■ Restarting the domain controller and then pressing and holding F8 until the Windows Server 2008 Advanced Options menu appears.

   Or

   ■ Stopping the service from the Computer Management console or from the command prompt.

3. Choose Directory Services Restore Mode as you did earlier when you defragmented the Active Directory database.

4. Log on via the Administrator account by using the password defined for the Local Administrator account in the offline SAM (this option applies to restarted DCs).

5. From the Start menu, choose Programs ➪ Accessories ➪ Command Prompt.

6. At the command prompt, type `ntdsutil.exe` and press Enter.

7. Set the active instance; then type the word `files` and press Enter.

8. Type `info` to display the path and size information of Active Directory and the log files. Write down this path information because you will need it later.

9. Find a location that has enough drive space to hold the Active Directory database and the log files.

10. Type `move DB to <drive>:\<directory>` and press Enter. (`<drive>` and `<directory>` represent the location of the database and log files you wrote down earlier.) The `Ntds.dit` database file is moved to the location you specified.

11. Type `quit` and press Enter. To return to the command prompt, type `quit` again and press Enter.

After you have completed these steps, you can restart the computer or services as you normally would.

NOTE You can also move log files from one location to another by using the `move logs to` command, which moves the files and updates the registry entries to point to the new location of the log files.

Integrating Active Directory with Other Services

Many Microsoft products integrate very tightly with Active Directory. Installing and configuring these products is quite a long process and would merit an entire book of its own. In the following sections, however, we describe a few of the products and what you stand to gain by using them within an Active Directory domain.

Active Directory and SQL Server

Active Directory is quite capable of using SQL Server as its mechanism for data storage. The missing ingredient in this scenario, however, is access control. In the event that you need to provide both access control and the performance that only SQL Server can provide, it is recommended that you use both Active Directory and SQL Server. It is well beyond the scope of this book to describe the installation procedures involved in using both SQL Server and the Active Directory datastore.

CROSS-REF For more information on using Active Directory and SQL Server, grab a copy of the *Microsoft SQL Server 2005 Bible* by Paul Nielsen (Indianapolis: Wiley Publishing, Inc., 2002).

Active Directory and Microsoft Exchange

Like SQL Server, Microsoft Exchange is highly integrated with Active Directory. When Microsoft Exchange is installed on a server running Active Directory, it defaults to storing all user and account information in the Active Directory datastore. By doing this, the software is ensuring that there is no duplication of data and that information could not be out of sync.

Logon without the Global Catalog

If you have a WAN with many remote sites, it may be best for your network if you place the global catalog remotely to improve the performance of login times, searches, and other actions requiring the global catalog. This placement can dramatically reduce the traffic on your network. It not only provides better server response times, but also provides better response times with other applications that rely on the network to move data. For these reasons, and to reduce administrative tasks, you may choose to place a copy of the global catalog remotely. By doing so, you are essentially duplicating the functionality of the backup domain controller.

As you probably realize, there is still a problem. Even though a copy of the global catalog is placed remotely, the domain controller is still needed to authenticate users as they log in to the network. Therefore, if the remote site doesn't have a global catalog, and a global catalog server is unavailable, no one can log in. That means 100 percent down time for any remote offices that rely on a WAN connection to contact the PDC in the event that the link goes down.

CAUTION Before modifying the registry, which is discussed in the following paragraph, we strongly suggest that you back up your system and registry settings.

To remove the need for a global catalog server at a site and avoid the potential denial of user logon requests, follow these steps to enable logons when the global catalog is unavailable:

1. Start the Registry Editor (`regedit.exe`) and locate the following key in it: `HKEY_LOCAL_MACHINE\System\CurrentControlSet\Control\Lsa`.

2. Choose Edit ⇨ Add Key and add a key name of `IgnoreGCFailures`. No value is required for this key.

You can now quit the Registry Editor and restart the domain controller in order for the changes to take effect.

This key needs to be set on the domain controller that performs the initial authentication of the user.

 By bypassing the global catalog for authentication purposes, you could be introducing a major security hole. Examine all your options before making these changes to your server.

Active Directory and DNS

DNS is the means by which a Windows Server 2008 domain locates Active Directory services and servers. The clients and tools of Active Directory use DNS to locate domain controllers for administration and logon. You must have a DNS server installed within each forest of your domain to have Active Directory function correctly.

In earlier versions of Windows, NetBIOS name resolution is still required to resolve network resources on an Active Directory network. To achieve this, a WINS server, LMHOSTS file, or NetBIOS broadcast file is required. It's no secret that the WINS server is known for causing undue traffic on a network.

Installing the DNS Server supplied with Windows Server 2008 is really just a matter of pointing and clicking for simple configurations. If you are an experienced administrator, you can also install BIND on a Unix or Windows machine should you care to do so. Installing the DNS Server on Windows will quite possibly require Windows Server 2008 to complete the installation.

We recommend that you stick with the Microsoft DNS server when installing DNS on an Active Directory network. If you choose not to install the Microsoft DNS server, ensure that the server you do install supports the dynamic update protocol.

Version 8.1.2 and later of BIND (a popular DNS server implementation) support both the SRV RR and dynamic updates. (Version 8.1.1 does support dynamic updates, but it has flaws that were fixed in 8.1.2.) If you are using a version of BIND or any other DNS server that does not support dynamic updates, you need to manually add records to the DNS server.

NOTE Microsoft DNS, as included with Microsoft Windows NT 4.0 Server, does not support the SRV record. You can, however, use the DNS server supplied with Windows Server 2008 or earlier, which both support dynamic updates.

When you add a DNS server to a network that will eventually become an Active Directory network, you should install DNS on a standalone server. This server can then be promoted to a domain controller at a later time. Also ensure that this server has a static IP address. No servers on a network should use DHCP because it can cause undue network traffic when clients attempt to connect to the server.

Active Directory Administration Architecture

This section provides the architecture for the administration of Active Directory and thus the administration of the forest — the root domain and any future child domains.

A Windows Server 2008 domain is comprised of objects, the work they do, and the utility they provide to the domain. These objects are stored and administered to in Active Directory. Thus, access to and control over Active Directory objects — secured with permissions specifying authorized security principals (users and group accounts) — is what the network administrators are provided with to administer the domain.

Servers, workstations, and the file system are comprised of objects that are stored in local repositories. These are secured with security principals on the servers or workstations, which are stored in the local Security Accounts Manager (SAM). Local administrative accounts and groups have access to and rights over the local objects so that they can administer to these resources at both the local level and the domain level. To administer the local objects with domain accounts, local groups are able to admit domain membership. The local Administrators group admits membership to the Domain Admins group, which is convenient, but also represents a security risk. The Windows Server 2008 built-in groups are listed in Table 22-1.

TABLE 22-1

Built-in (Default) Security Groups

Security Groups/Built-in Domain Local (Ineligible for User or Groups as Members)	
Group	**Description**
Account Operators	Members can administer domain user and group accounts.
Administrators	Members have complete and unrestricted access to the computer/domain.
Backup Operators	Members can override security restrictions for the sole purpose of backing up or restoring files.
Cert Publishers	Members of this group are permitted to publish certificates to the Active Directory.
Cryptographic Operators	Members of this group are authorized to perform cryptographic operations.
DnsAdmins	DNS Administrators Group
Guests	Members have the same access as members of the Users group by default, except for the Guest account, which is further restricted (Guest will be disabled).

continued

TABLE 22-1   *(continued)*

Security Groups/Built-in Domain Local (Ineligible for Users or Groups as Members)	
Incoming Forest Trust Builder	Members of this group can create incoming, one-way trusts to this forest.
Network Configuration Operators	Members in this group can have some administrative privileges to manage configuration of networking features. They can also make changes to TCP/IP settings and renew and release TCP/IP addresses. This group has no default members.
Performance Log Users	Members of this group have remote access to schedule logging of performance counters on this computer.
Performance Monitor Users	Members of this group have remote access to monitor this computer.
Pre-Windows 2000 Compatible Access	A backward-compatibility group that allows read access to all users and groups in the domain.
Print Operators	Members can administer to printers.
Remote Desktop Users	Members in this group are granted the right to log on remotely.
Server Operators	Members can administer to domain servers, including DCs, without compromising security.
TelnetClients	Members of this group have access to Telnet Server on this system.
Users	Members are prevented from making accidental or intentional systemwide changes. Thus, Users can run certified applications, but not most legacy applications.
Windows Authorization Access Group	Members of this group have access to the computed `tokenGroupsGlobalAndUniversal` attribute on User objects.

Security Groups/Built-in Domain Global (Can Be Added to Domain Local)	
Domain Admins	Designated administrators of the domain (members of this group are de facto all Administrators).
Domain Guests	All domain guests.
Domain Users	All domain users.
Group Policy Creator Owners	Members in this group can modify Group Policy for the domain.

Security Groups/Built-in Domain Universal	
Enterprise Admins	Designated administrators of the enterprise.
Schema Admins	Designated administrators of the schema.

Both local and domain accounts have varying default permissions to perform a specific function. They are also afforded a range of permissions that allow varying levels of object access and a collection of rights that provide the capability to perform specific functions. These rights and permissions are listed in Table 22-2.

TABLE 22-2

Built-in Local Security Groups and Their Respective Permissions

Security Groups/Built-in Local Permissions and Rights (Default) for User, Computer, and Printer Objects	
Group	**Permissions**
Account Operators	Create/Delete Computer objects
	Create/Delete Group objects
	Create/Delete User objects
Print Operators	Create/Delete Printer objects

In Chapter 17, we discussed the advantages of a single forest in which one domain contains all the resource objects of the organization. A highly secured root domain is responsible for forest operations, such as schema changes and adding domains. A highly secured resource domain contains all of the network objects for the organization and its users. A highly secured staging or development domain is used for testing things such as Group Policy. In fact, MCITY has elected to set up a separate forest for proof of concept, testing, training, and staging.

To achieve the best security for the forest, we will set up a highly granular and hierarchical architecture to enable administrative access on a controlled and secure basis. To do this, we take advantage of Active Directory's delegation of administration capability to control access to higher levels of the administration tree, and to tightly control membership of administrative groups at various OU levels. Access to Active Directory objects is provided on an as-needed basis to certain groups. This obviates the practice of haphazardly providing users with membership in Domains Admins for narrow roles or for limited administrative responsibility.

In cases where a user spends all of his or her day performing administrative duties that require membership in the Domain Admins group, the user is given an administrative account that is a permanent member of Domain Admins. However, Domain Admins has been heavily restricted in this architecture to Active Directory work only. It enjoys very limited access to servers, and no access to workstations or mobile computers, and every member of Domain Admins is heavily audited. The Domain Admins group is also restricted, which means that membership is controlled by policy and provided through change control.

In a domain (and on local machines, for that matter), the most powerful accounts are the administrators (the Administrator and members of the Administrators group, such as Enterprise Admins and Domain Admins). These accounts, by default, have domainwide or domain-level access to all objects. To properly secure their use, membership in these domain-level accounts is kept to the absolute minimum, and given only to the most trusted and trained individuals. In some cases (such as the Domain Administrator account), use of the accounts is controlled through smart card technology (certificates), auditing, and assigned rights.

This hierarchy demonstrates how the domain-level groups have domain-level access, and, thus, control over all objects in the domain. The lower-level (Tier-1 OU) Admins have control in their parent OU and all subordinate OUs. There can be multiple Tier-1 OUs, and each Tier-1 OU can have multiple nested or child OUs (Tier-2, Tier-3, and so on). Thus, all objects inside a Tier-1 OU and its children can be administered to by these OU-level administrative groups.

Administrative control can thus be delegated in the domain without compromising the most important domain objects, and administration can be restricted to only administrators who need to administer to objects in their "home" OU and its children.

At the Tier-1 level, the Tier-1 Admins groups cannot administer to other Tier-1 OUs unless the administrator of the other OU or a domain-level administrator specifically allows this. This design provides a highly secure and controlled method of delegating administrative rights with the least administrative burden. As mentioned in Chapter 1, such practice is indeed more secure than provisioning multiple resource domains for a single organization whereby domain and enterprise administrators have accounts in all the resource domains and routinely "commute" from one domain to another.

As mentioned previously, there is a huge increase in the administrative burden of multiple resource or organization domains with no significant increase in security. The additional engineers needed to administer to the additional domains also results in a less secure forest in general. If a separate administrative boundary is indeed needed for maximum security, then a separate forest should be considered.

Groups with delegated administration at the Tier-1 level are listed in Table 22-3 and expounded upon in the following "Architecture" section.

TABLE 22-3

Tier-1 Organizational Unit (OU) Delegation of Administration

OU	Global Group	Apply to	Permissions
OU level or domain	Domain admins or <OU> admins	This object and all child objects	Full control
OU level (Tier 1 OU)	<OU> HelpDesks	<Object Type> objects (as needed)	Full control
		This object only	Create <Object Type> objects
Delete <Object Type> objects			
	<Other OU> HelpDesks	User objects	Reset password

TABLE 22-3	*(continued)*		
OU	**Global Group**	**Apply to**	**Permissions**
Enable/disable account			
Example			
HQ\Computers	\Groups\HQ HelpDesks	Computer objects	Full control
		This object only	Create Computer objects
Delete Computer objects			
	<Other OU> HelpDesks	User objects	Reset password
Enable/disable account			

Architecture

A single security and administrative boundary exists around the MCITY.INC (or NetBIOS name BC) Windows Server 2008 domain. DCs, member servers, and workstations in this domain exist in all sites, and the architecture caters to the needs of local technicians administering to the computers installed at various locations.

Without the granular security model described earlier, OU-level administrators would have full control permissions to all DCs, member servers, and workstations in the domain.

It is beneficial for OU-level administrators in root OUs such as URA, IT, and MGA (Tier-1) and subordinate OUs (Tier-2) to have full control permissions over certain resources in their OUs for future growth. It is also important that service center or help desk personnel from all upper OU tiers have full control permissions over a subset of resources (that is, Users, Groups, Printers, Servers, and/or Workstations) in their OU. Help desk personnel require minimal permissions (that is, the capability to reset user passwords and disable/enable user accounts) in their OUs.

Tier-level OU-level administrators cannot be made members of the Administrators built-in local group in the domain, or any global group, such as a Domain Admin that is a member of the Administrators built-in local group, because this grants them full and unlimited privileges throughout the domain. Individual administrative accounts, when needed, also should not be added to the Administrators security groups, but rather to the Domain Admins group, which is a member of Administrators. The custom administrative security groups are listed in Table 22-4.

The <OU Level> Admins, <OU Level> HelpDesks, and <OU Level> Other HelpDesks global groups should contain users from other corresponding <OU Level>\Users OU. Because these global groups are OU-level specific, not site-specific, they can be created in the <OU Level>\Groups OU. For example, Organization\IT\Users\<Username> could be a member of Organization\IT\Groups\IT Admins global group.

TABLE 22-4

Implementation-Specific Administrative Security Groups

Global Group	Description
<Tier level OU | Domain> Server Admins (for local access)	Members (such as service accounts and cluster service accounts) have local administrative access to a server via this group. In other words, members can install software, create folders and shares, restrict access to local objects, start and stop services, perform machine-specific activity, and so on. This group lifts dependency on the Domain Admins group, which is restricted from having interactive logon access to servers.
<Tier level OU | Domain> Workstation Admins (for local access)	Members have local administrative access to a workstation via this group. In other words, members can install software, create folders and shares, restrict access to local objects, start and stop services, perform machine-specific activity, and so on. This group lifts dependency on the Domain Admins group, which is restricted from having interactive logon access to servers.
<OU Level> Admins (AD)	Members can only create/modify/delete selected objects in their OU and child OUs. A domain can have multiple OUs and, thus, multiple <OU Level> Admin groups. For example, MGA Admins can create/modify/delete objects in the BCC OU and its child OUs.
<OU Level> HelpDesks (AD)	Members can only create/modify/delete *specific* objects in *specific* OUs. For example, MGA HelpDesk can create/modify/delete users in an OU only.
<OU Level> Other HelpDesks (AD)	Members (other <OU Level> HelpDesks) can reset passwords and enable/disable user objects in other tier-level OUs if needed.

The <OU Level> Admins global groups will not be made a member of either the Account Operators or the Print Operators built-in local groups. These built-in local groups have permissions throughout the entire domain (because members of the Account Operators built-in local group can administer user and group objects in any OU), which also exposes the domain to risk.

Members of the <OU Level> HelpDesks global group will not be able to log on locally to servers and must administer to Active Directory from a Windows Server 2008/XP/Vista Professional workstation (using Active Directory Users and Computers and any other required applications). See Table 22-2 for default permissions in the domain for the built-in local groups.

Windows Server 2008 group membership

The custom groups and accounts are not given explicit rights and permissions directly. They are given via membership in the local, domain global, and universal groups. The group memberships are listed in Tables 22-5 and 22-6.

TABLE 22-5

Security Group Membership in MCITY.INC

Group	Members
Local Groups	
Account Operators	N/A
Administrators	Domain Admins
	Enterprise Admins
	Administrator
Backup Operators	Forest Backup Operators
DnsAdmins	N/A
Guests	Domain Guests
	Guest (Disabled)
	IUSR*
	IWAM
	TSInternetUser
Pre-Windows Server 2003 Compatible Access	Authentication Users
Print Operators	N/A
Users	Authenticated Users
	Domain Users
	INTERACTIVE
Global Groups	
Domain Admins	Administrator, service administration accounts (<username>.adm.bro)
Domain Guests	Guest (Disabled)
Exchange Domain Servers	N/A
Exchange Services	N/A
Universal Groups	
Schema Admins	Administrator
Enterprise Admins	Administrator

TABLE 22-6

Security Groups (MCITY.INC)

Group	Members
Local Groups	
Account Operators	N/A
Administrators	Domain Admins
	MCITY.INC\Enterprise Admins
	Administrator
Backup Operators	Forest Backup Operators
Guests	Domain Guests
	Guest (Disabled)
	IUSR
	IWAM
	TSInternetUser
Pre-Windows Server 2003 Compatible Access	Authentication Users
Print Operators	Specific service administrator accounts
Server Operators	Specific service administrator accounts
Users	Authenticated Users
	Domain Users
	INTERACTIVE
Domain Local Groups	
DnsAdmins	Specific service administrator accounts
DHCP Administrators	Specific service administrator accounts
DHCP Users	<OU Level> HelpDesks, selected accounts or groups
Global Groups	
Domain Admins	Administrator, service administrator accounts, specified service accounts
Domain Guests	Guest (Disabled)
Exchange Services	Enterprise
Universal Groups	
NA	NA

Table 22-7 lists the membership of the built-in local groups in the MCITY.INC domain.

TABLE 22-7

Administrative Groups for Network Services

Service	Administrative Rights	Read-only Rights
DDNS	DnsAdmins, Administrators	None
WINS	WinsAdmins, Administrators	WINS Users
DHCP	DHCP Administrators, Administrators	DHCP Users

Network services administration

Only users belonging to the DnsAdmins groups (or groups in the Administrators domain local groups) can modify the DDNS (Dynamic Domain Naming Service) server configuration. Only users belonging to the WINSAdmins or Administrators domain local groups can connect to a WINS server. Only users in the Administrators domain local group can modify the WINS server configuration. Users in the WINS Users domain local group have read-only access to WINS server configuration.

Only users belonging to the DHCP Users, DHCP Administrators, or Administrators domain local groups can connect to a DHCP server. Only users in the DHCP Administrators or Administrators domain local groups can modify the DHCP server configuration. Users in the DHCP Users domain local group have read-only access to DHCP server configuration.

The <OU Level> Admins global group will not be made a member of the DHCP Administrators domain local group or the DnsAdmins domain local group (refer to Table 22-7).

The <OU Level> HelpDesks global group will be made a member of the DHCP Users domain local group and the WINS Users domain local group (see Table 22-8).

Administration of Enterprise Service Servers

Enterprise Servers — identified according to the major role the server plays (such as Exchange, SQL Server, ISA Server, IIS, Certificate Services, and so on) — will have administrative groups assigned to them that do not have membership in the domain global administrative groups, such as Domain Admins. Naturally, a member of a <Server Role> Admin might also have membership in another administrative group, which would give the engineer more privileges (or further restrict the engineer). This is because of the natural accumulation of rights assigned to lead engineers.

TABLE 22-8

Network Services Domain Local Group Members

Global Groups	Member of
\<OU Level\> Admins	DHCP Users
	WINS Users
\<OU Level\> HelpDesks	DHCP Users
	WINS Users

The restrictions placed on the logon ability of members of Domain Admins will limit their ability to log on to a server. The ability to log on interactively will be allowed for enterprise service accounts. However, it will be strongly discouraged in favor using the correct tools.

Table 22-9 identifies the groups that will be created for Enterprise Server roles. These groups will be added to the respective server's local Administrators groups, and the Domain Admins groups will be removed from the local Administrators group.

TABLE 22-9

Enterprise Network Services Domain Local Group Members

Global Groups	Role Server Administered
\<OU Level | Domain\>[1] Exch Admins	Exchange 2003
\<OU Level | Domain\> SQLS Admins	SQL Server
\<OU Level | Domain\> IIS Admins	Internet Information Services
\<OU Level | Domain\> DFS Admins	Distributed File System
\<OU Level | Domain\> SMS Admins	Systems Management Server
\<OU Level | Domain\>WSUS Admins	WSUS Server
\<OU Level | Domain\> FileServer Admins	File Server Shares and Permissions
\<OU Level | Domain\> CA Admins	Certificate Authority Services
\<OU Level | Domain\> HIS Admins	Host Integration Server
\<OU Level | Domain\> IAS Admins	Internet Authentication Service (RADIUS server)

[1]In the case of a domain-level Enterprise Services group, do not use the domain name as the group suffix.

Enterprise Services administrative groups will not have membership in any domain, forest, or network administrative groups (including the <Tier level OU> Server Admins group). This practice enables Enterprise Services administrators to fully administer the server on which the server application is running, and to remotely administer the application. For example, Exchange administrators and SQL Server DBAs will be able to administer the actual servers, as well as use tools such as Exchange Administrator (Exchange 2008) and Enterprise Manager (SQL Server 2000/2005) from their workstations. Logon to enterprise servers over Terminal Services sessions and via Telnet is envisaged.

Remote workstation administration architecture

Remote workstation administration is beyond the scope of this architecture, save to say that remote connection to XP workstations is (generally) supported. However, Active Directory administrators (at all levels) will be able to remotely connect to their Windows XP or Vista workstations to access tools needed to administer to domain controllers. In addition, whereas any person may be able to remotely connect to a workstation, administering to DCs and servers will require operation under an administrative shell.

Terminal Services policy

Terminal Services on Windows Server 2008 Servers enables remote administration of domain controllers and servers via a virtual console that can be opened from another workstation on the network. Terminal Services can operate in two modes: Application Server mode allows multiple users to run applications in virtual consoles (thin client/server architecture) and Administration mode allows two concurrent server console sessions. Terminal Services is a useful component in the administration of domain controller servers. However, if not configured properly, it becomes a security risk and it can severely hamper server administration and the ability to remotely respond to urgent alerts and service requests.

For these reasons, only members of the <Tier level OU> Computer Admins domain global group on Enterprise Services servers (which excludes domain controllers) and an Enterprise Services domain global group can use Terminal Services. Anyone who is not a member of these groups will receive the message "You do not have access to log on to this Session" when trying to use Terminal Services to log on interactively to the server. The <Tier level OU> Computer Admins group obtains permission to operate a terminal session by having membership in the local Administrators group.

The appropriate <OU Level>Admins global group will be granted Terminal Services Guest Access to each server to facilitate a "look, but don't touch policy." That is, the MGA Admins global group will be granted Terminal Services Guest Access on all MGA servers, the IT Admins global group will be granted Terminal Services Guest Access on all IT servers, and so on. However, if engineers or support personnel in any tier-level OU require full terminal server access to a server (for example, to a SQL Server machine in the MGA OU), it can be provided via the <Tier level OU> Server Admins group or the <OU Level | Domain> SQLS Admins group. Access to the sessions is provided through nested membership in the local Administrators group. Thus, only the appropriate global groups will be able to use Terminal Services on member servers.

Tier-level OU administrators can directly control how Terminal Services sessions are used through OU-level Group Policy. Terminal server policy is not configured in the EDC level (Tier 1) or in any of the domain-level policies.

As an example, the Exch Admins global group must be a member of the Administrators built-in local group on all appropriate Exchange servers. All Exchange Server Terminal Services will be configured to allow only <Domain> ExchAdmins and local Administrators terminal access to Exchange servers. The same configuration will apply to other role, line-of-business, or enterprise server servers. In other words, members of the Administrators built-in local groups on non-DCs are not subject to any interactive logon or Terminal Services restrictions.

Secure administration

As mentioned previously, a domain or forest can be easily attacked unless a commonsense security model is adopted to protect the forest and its domains. Attackers will attempt to compromise security by obtaining access to administer accounts. Damage can easily be done even without access to the Administrator account. An attacker only needs to crack membership of DnsAdmins to gain access to DDNS and wreak enough havoc to effect a complete denial of service to the organization. Several security measures are thus required to secure the forest and its domains. This security architecture comprises the following measures:

- Administrator account abuse
- Using multiple administrative accounts
- Secure administrative workstations
- Console-based administration
- Lockdown of DDNS, WINS, and DHCP
- Restricting Domain Admins
- Role-based administration

Administrator account abuse

Domain Administrator accounts are the first accounts a forest founder uses to establish both the root domain and child domains. Usage of the Administrator account in all domains should be discontinued as soon as the domains are created and administrative accounts are set up (see the following section, "Using Admin Accounts").

In earlier implementations of Active Directory and the Windows operating system, the Administrator account was often hidden and renamed, and provided a very long and complex password. There were several reasons for this practice to be adopted, and they stem from both security concerns and administrative practices.

First, the Administrator account is the highest authority in the domain. Thus, if it is compromised in the root domain, the entire forest and its domains can be destroyed. It is also possible for child or peer domain Administrator accounts to infiltrate the root domains and other child domains in a forest.

Second, overuse of the Administrator account leads to an administrative nightmare. Poor administrative practice will find this account used in a variety of places (for example, it is used for service accounts, at consoles, and for installing and running applications). This not only puts the domain at risk, but it is very difficult to hold administrators to account, to audit activities, to enforce nonrepudiation, and to troubleshoot.

Misuse of the Administrator account quickly leads to a situation in which the account cannot be protected or its password even changed without causing services to crash. This was a big problem on Windows NT 4.0 and earlier domains for which the Administrator account was used often and remained logged on at consoles. Windows Server 2008 provides more means of protecting the account.

Windows Server 2008 enables you to rename the Administrator account (and, for that matter, the Guest account as well) either directly or via Group Policy (the latter is used for domainwide renaming so that local Administrator accounts are also renamed). The policy to rename the Administrator account is found in the Default Domain Policy GPO's \ ... \Local Policies\Security Options\ folder.

Though renaming the Administrator account helps to conceal it, the main reason to do so is to thwart attempts to crack its password. Password policy protects accounts from malicious algorithms that repeatedly try user IDs with various dictionary-generated password suggestions. Given enough time and a large dictionary, an attacker will eventually find the password that accompanies the account. The domain Administrators account can also be renamed manually using the Active Directory Users and Computers console.

In Group Policy (see Chapter 24), we set up auditing to detect such activity. We also added Group Policy that locks the account after several attempts at various passwords. The Administrator account, however, cannot be locked out, so knowing the name of the account gives a potential hacker an infinite number of opportunities to try different passwords. If the attempts were not audited, the attack would go unnoticed until it was too late.

Thus, the Administrator account was often renamed and hidden. This can be done by making the account name appear to be a standard user with user-style attributes (hidden in plain sight). The security logs should also be monitored to detect any attempt to use the account without it being sanctioned by security administrators.

The steps listed in Table 22-10 are recommended best practice for preventing the abuse of the Administrator account.

TABLE 22-10

Securing the Administrator Account

Action	Purpose
Rename Administrator	Helps thwart attempts to compromise the account password.
Hide Administrator	Reduces the chance of the account being discovered.
Place in a domain-level OU	OU-level administrators do not have access to the domain-level OUs.
Provide a highly complex password	Following policy, the password should be at least nine characters and be highly complex. This will make it much harder to crack the password; and because a long password takes time to crack, the chance of being alerted to the attempt before it is cracked is more likely.
Conceal the data	The user ID and password should be known to a few of the most trusted people (if possible, no more than two people).[1] The name and password should be locked away as hard copy; securing this account with a smart card is even better.
Create a Decoy Administrator account	This practice adds another layer of protection. The account should be given no special privileges and its password should be set to complex and audited. It must never expire. This account also acts as a honey pot for exposing possible hacking.

[1]This helps to keep the account out of the hands of rogue or malicious administrators.

While any effort that helps limit the attack surface is worthwhile exploring, hacking tools are now so advanced that the renamed or hidden Administrator account can easily be discovered. In fact, all Administrative accounts can be easily identified on a domain because the security identifier of the account (SID) is well known. It thus makes more sense to protect the account with certificates (technology) and usage rules (policy) than to try hiding the account.

An administrator is often tempted to use the Administrator account on a server or workstation because it is convenient. One way to discourage this is to make the password so complex that no administrator would want to use it on the domain, or require the checking out of a token or smart card from the security administration. Setting the password to a combination of 15 complex characters would discourage any casual use of the password. It is also common to split the name and password combination between two or more people, possibly even splitting the password between two or more people.

It makes more sense to secure the Administrator account with a highly complex password, and then store the data on a smart card and enforce the logon with the smart card and not the password. The card can then be locked away in a vault and made available when needed. A simple PIN, even four digits, is sufficient. The Administrator account is thus always secure by virtue of it being relegated to a chip stored on a piece of plastic that can be locked away in a vault. Smart card PINs lock after three attempts to crack them, and this does not impact operations in any way. The same treatment should apply to any permanent account made a member of the Enterprise Admins group; or, as recommended in this architecture, we limit group membership to only the Administrator account.

These steps to secure the Administrator account are described in Chapter 24 in the section "Locking Down Domain Admins."

Using admin accounts

With the Administrator account off limits to only the most trusted and experienced engineers (and only if the work these engineers do specifically needs the access abilities of this powerful group), administrative access can be given via membership in Domain Admins. If an administrator does not need membership in Domain Admins to do his or her work, there is no need to provide the administrator with such membership. This is a domain global group that provides its members with far-reaching powers in the domain. A member of this group can even change the password of the Administrator. Members of Domain Admins have full control of every object in the domain.

Rather than make an engineer (or at least his or her user account) a member of any administrative group using a standard user ID, a second admin account should be used by the person when he or she needs to make some administrative change on the domain, configure something, or monitor services. This is a best practice recommended by Microsoft and has been found to work very well. It serves to give the engineer two "hats" to wear: One "hat" is worn for everyday work (documents, e-mail, and so on), and the other "hat" is worn when there is a need to access Active Directory or a network resource or to perform some work in an administrative shell.

The admin account can be used on a standard Windows XP machine loaded with administrative tools. When the engineer needs to access Active Directory (for example, open the Active Directory, Users, and Computers MMC snap-in), it can be opened from the engineer's own workstation under the context of her admin account, using the Run As command or an administrative shell. Alternately, the workstation itself must be restricted to a special OU that is restricted to service admin workstations.

The special admin account also makes it easier to manage engineers and their privileges. For starters, an admin account can be disabled or removed without affecting the actual user. In one action, the engineer would lose all access to administrative privileges, or be updated with new privileges without any risk to the person's ability to work, send and receive e-mail, and so on. The account is also easy to track and audit on the domain.

The most convenient style for naming the admin account is to append the suffix `.adm` onto the engineer's standard account name, and then append the entire name with the name of the domain or OU in which the account has rights. Thus, the account for Mickey Mouse at Disney World (`mmouse@disney.com`) would have the administrative counterpart `mmouse.adm.dis`.

Table 22-11 lists the pattern template for administrative accounts.

TABLE 22-11

Administrative Account Patterns

Type of Account	Template	Example
Account for AD service administrators and domain network service administrators	\<firstname initial\>	mmouse.adm.dis
	\<lastname\>.adm.	
	\<not more than first three letters of NETBIOS domain name\>	
Account for server admins (members of \<Tier level OU | Domain\> Server Admins)	\<firstname initial\>	mmouse.svr.dis
	\<lastname\>.svr.	
	\<not more than first three letters of NETBIOS domain name\>	
Account for workstation admins (members of \<Tier level OU | Domain\> Workstation Admins)	\<firstname initial\>	mmouse.wks.dis
	\<lastname\>.wks.	
	\<not more than first three letters of NETBIOS domain name\>	
Account for services	\<servicename\>\<series 01 – 99\>.sa.\<not more than first three letters of NETBIOS domain name\>. (Note that this must be the same as the actual Windows service name. See Example.)	sqlagent01.sa.dis
Account for cluster services	\<clustername\>.cl.\<netbiosdomainname\>	sqlvs01.cl.dis

The suffix mmouse.adm.dis is easier to search for in various event logs or audit trails and for reporting. When the user needs to perform extensive domain-level work on the domain, using an account that is the member of Domain Admins, the user must log in to an administrative shell using the .adm account, or run tools with the Run As command.

Secure administrative workstations

Logging on to the domain controller consoles to administer DDNS, DHCP, Active Directory, and its critical services will be prevented (in fact, only members of Server Operators can log on to a DC and restart it). As mentioned earlier, this practice of logging on directly to servers is also discouraged on MS Exchange, SQL Server, SMS Server, and other leading Microsoft server technologies. These servers should be managed from secure administrative workstations, or using an enterprise service account (see Table 22-10).

There are many different types of administrative activities taking place on a daily basis that require access to AD. These activities include GP management, user and group account management, AD publishing, site management, event log monitoring, replication monitoring, and so on. These activities are typically shared among several engineers in a large IT environment, and thus logging on to DC consoles is neither practical nor safe.

Apart from the default administrative tools that are installed on a DC during promotion and bootup into Active Directory, many more client applications may be required to administer to AD. The netIQ tools and the new Microsoft GP Management Console are good examples. A number of tools are also needed by help desk personnel, who, in any event, are not members of any group that permits local logon to a DC.

Installing all manner of administrative utilities on DCs also creates the potential for viruses to infiltrate the DCs, hostile code that can cause denial of service attacks on AD, and application incompatibility that can cause problems on the server.

Active Directory employs client-server database architecture (the same architecture that underpins MS Exchange and a number of other Microsoft technologies), so the MMC applications used to administer to both AD and Exchange should be opened from a client desktop.

Because administering AD from the console is also prevented, AD tools, Exchange tools, GP tools, security tools, the SMS Administrator consoles, SQL Enterprise Administrator, and Query Manager tools, and so on, will be installed on all engineer workstations.

Tools will be restricted to certain engineers through Group Policy, but most administrative tools will be installed on workstations (including help-desk workstations). This practice enables an engineer to be elevated to a certain level and immediately gain access to the required tool. It also enables another administrator to open a tool using Run As from a machine whose original owner cannot.

This practice of administering from workstations also enables us to actually restrict DC logon and direct DC server administration (such as restarting the server, applying service packs, and upgrading hardware) to trusted administrators who do not necessarily need to have AD administrative privileges. It also enables us to prevent direct logon to DCs by denying the right to log on to DCs (by enabling this policy setting in GP and specifying the groups to which this applies).

In addition, the data-streams between the workstations and the DCs, and servers such as SQL Server, can be compromised by sniffing the network and tapping into the text-based LDAP or tabulated data-streams (TDS). As a result, a number of AD domains have been victims of replay and denial of service attacks resulting from attacking the TDS and RPC traffic.

The best solution and practice is to create IPSec tunnels to the servers and secure them with Certificate Services (or using local certificates as a temporary solution before a CA is put in place). Though this implies additional overhead on the workstation, the amount is negligible. LDAP signing can (and should) be included in the architecture. See "Locking Down Domain Admins" in Chapter 24 for more information.

Console access

In line with the administrative model proposed earlier, console-based administration on DCs will be restricted to the members of the Server Operators group for exceptional circumstances only, such as viewing logs (except security), network and disk configuration (without the capability to change any of these), and to restart a server. All other admin accounts will be prevented from logging on to domain controllers and any workstation that is not a member of the computers OU (Service Administrators, Computers) that holds admin workstations. No other group, including Domain Admins, will be able to log on to the DC.

Policy prevents built-in administrative groups from console login everywhere in the domain except in the Service Administrators OU.

 DDNS, WINS, and DHCP will be administered, routinely, from secure administrative workstations.

Member server/workstation management

This section deals with the architecture to delegate member server and workstation management to OU administrators.

By default, the Domain Admins global group from the domain (in this case, MCITY.INC) is automatically added to the Administrators local group on the workstation or member server when a workstation or member server joins the domain. This is one of the key reasons why this group is prevented from logging on anywhere in the domain other than in the Service Administrators OU.

This prevents OU-level administrators from gaining administrative access to the machine because membership in Domain Admins is absent to prevent exposure to domain-level privileges from OU-level administrators, which is not an ideal situation. This behavior also forces workstation and member server administrators to work on computers using the local Administrator account — also not an ideal situation. While administrators might need local access to the machine, they typically also need concurrent access to the domain.

The <Tier level OU | Domain> Server Admins or the <OU Level | Domain > Enterprise Service Admins or the <Tier level OU | Domain> Workstations Admins global group from the MCITY.INC Windows Server 2008 domain must be added to the Administrators local group on the workstation or member server when a workstation or member server joins the domain. This gives members of these domain global groups full administrative privileges on workstations and servers in their region without having to expose domain administrative privileges.

OU-level administrators should not be given membership to Domain Admins in any domain because this puts critical domain services at risk. A single security boundary exists around the MCITY.INC domain. DCs in this domain exist in two of the hub sites (HQ and DR). Without a granular security model, OU-level administrators have the potential to gain full control permissions to all DCs in this domain.

Best practice dictates that tier-level administrators do not have the capability (that is, permissions, user rights, and privileges) to access DCs in the root domain. Only members of the Domain Admins in the root domain will be allowed to manage or administer the root DC servers (through RPC or command-line channels).

Tier-level administrators cannot be made members of the Administrators built-in local group in this domain, or any global (that is, Domain Admins) or universal (that is, Enterprise Admins) groups that are members of the Administrators built-in local group, because this would grant them full and unlimited privileges throughout the forest.

The best practice to protect a domain is not to create any type of administrative OU and not to delegate any administrative rights to this domain to anyone other than the founding members of the forest (the Administrator and members of the Enterprise Admins group). In addition, membership of the administrative groups in the root domain must be limited to a small contingent of the most trusted and experienced administrators because an account holder who is a member of one of the domain-level administrative groups has the potential to damage the entire forest and its resources, the child domains. However, because MCITY currently maintains a single root domain, the tighter security model for a root domain is recommended.

Summary

Management of Active Directory involves many tools and can only be effective with practice. This chapter covered the process needed to back up as well as move the Active Directory database. Using this technique, you can ensure that the database continues to provide peak performance and doesn't consume excessive disk space. You also learned how to correctly modify the registry so that a login without the global catalog is possible. When editing the registry, it is very important that you maintain an up-to-date backup of the registry. Registry changes can render your server useless, and a backup of the registry enables you to get things going again. Employ these measures and practice, practice, practice.

Part IV

Change Control and Workplace Management

Chapter 23

Managing Users and Groups

I f you are passionate about being a network or domain administrator, managing users and groups can give you a lot of satisfaction ... it can be a very powerful position in a company. On the other hand, unless you understand the fundamentals, manage the processes sensibly, and learn the tools and resources, the task can become an extremely frustrating responsibility. Our administration mantra is to use your common sense and learn to do it right before you take up the task. This chapter helps you get the best out of the Windows Server 2008 user and group-management philosophy and tools.

User and group management has become a lot more complex in Windows Server 2008. The complexity has a lot to do with the User and Group objects and their support in Active Directory. Combined with the burden of integrating Windows NT 4.0 and earlier networks, the administrative task is not easy.

However, with open interfaces and access to programmatic objects in Active Directory, administrators are developing tools for Active Directory that automate the repetitive stuff and enhance the experience of working with Active Directory (and we touch on that in this chapter). In that the directory is open and supports a widely available API (ADSI) and access protocol (LDAP), you can, for example, extend the User and Group objects to suit your enterprise requirements or custom applications. What you learn in this chapter puts you on the road to such advanced administration.

In this chapter, you examine User and Group objects and their function. You'll also look at user-management practice and policy with respect to users, groups, and computers. Finally, you will learn about the process

IN THIS CHAPTER

Understanding groups

Creating user accounts

Creating groups

Managing users and groups

of integrating legacy Windows NT Active Directory domains and how to sensibly manage users and groups on Windows Server 2008 mixed and native-mode networks.

CROSS-REF This chapter does not discuss management of the user workspace. Advanced items such as Group Policy, user profiles and logon scripts, workspace management, and so on are discussed in Chapter 24.

The Windows Server 2008 Account: A User's Resource

No one can work in a company, use any computer, or attach to any network without access to a user account. A user account is like the key to your car. Without the key, you cannot drive anywhere.

What is a user?

This question may seem patronizing at first, but in a Windows network domain (and also the local computer), the definition of *user* relates to autonomous processes, network objects (devices and computers), and humans. Human users exploit the networks or machines to get work done, meet deadlines, and get paid, but any process, machine, or technology that needs to exploit another object on the network or machine is treated as a user by the Windows operating systems. In a nutshell, the Windows Server 2008 security subsystem does not differentiate between a human and a device using its resources. All users are viewed as *security principals*, which at first are trusted.

NOTE After you install Windows Server 2008 (not do an upgrade) or create a new Active Directory domain, the operating system and many elements are exposed by default. This makes sense: Keep the doors open until the jewels have been delivered. As soon as you begin adding users to the system, and they begin adding resources that need protection, you should begin using the tools described in this chapter to lock down the elements and secure the network.

User objects are derived from a single user class in Active Directory, which in turn derives from several parents. Machine accounts are thus derived from the User object. To obtain access to the User object, you need to reference its *distinguished name* (DN) in program or script code. This is handled automatically by the various GUI objects, but if you plan to write scripts that access the object, you should be referencing the object's GUID.

What are contacts?

Contacts are objects that were introduced with Windows 2000 networks. They are derived from the same class hierarchy as the User object; the Contact object, however, does not inherit security attributes from its parent. A contact is thus used only for communication purposes: for e-mail, faxing, phoning, and so on. Windows Server 2008 distribution lists are made up of contacts.

You can access Active Directory contacts from the likes of Outlook and Outlook Express and any other LDAP-compliant client software. The Contact object is almost identical to the object in the Windows Address Book (WAB).

Local users and "local users"

The term *local user* is often used to describe two types of users: users local to machines that log on locally to the workstation service and users who are local to a network or domain. Using the term interchangeably can cause confusion among your technical staff ... and you have enough confusing things to deal with.

We believe that referring to local users as users who log on locally to a workstation or PC or a server makes sense. In other words, the local user can log on to the machine that the user is actually sitting at, where accounts have been created, or into a remote machine that has granted the user the "right" to log on locally, such as an application server that is accessed by a terminal session on a remote client.

In referring to generic users on the domain or users collectively, referring to these users as *domain users* or *domain members* makes more sense. A user can also be a member of a local domain, and such an account is also often referred to as a *local user*. On legacy NT domains, this was further confused by the capability to create a "local account," which was meant for users from nontrusted domains. This is no longer the case with Windows Server 2008 domains. Whether or not you agree, we suggest that you decide what the term *local user* means to your environment and then stick to that definition.

What is a group?

Groups are collections of users, contacts, computers, and other groups (a process known as *nesting*). Groups are supported in Active Directory (much to the horror of directory purists) and in the local computer's security subsystem. How Windows Server 2008 works with groups is discussed in the section "Groups versus Organizational Units," later in this chapter. Figure 23-1 shows the group-container philosophy.

You would be right to wonder why Microsoft provides us with both groups and organizational units (OUs) to manage. Groups, however, are a throwback to the Windows NT era. Remember that Windows Server 2008 is built on Windows 2000, and groups were thus inherited from the earlier technology and enhanced for Windows Server 2008. Although groups may appear to be a redundant object next to OUs, they are a fact of Windows Server 2008 and are here to stay. They are also extremely powerful management objects.

Specifically, you create and use groups to contain the access rights of User objects and other groups within a security boundary. You also use groups to contain User objects that share the same access rights to network objects, such as shares, folders, files, printers, and so on. Groups thus provide a security filter against which users and other groups are given access to resources. This critical role of groups is shown in Figure 23-2.

FIGURE 23-1

Groups are collections or concentrations of users, computers, and other groups.

FIGURE 23-2

Groups provide a security "filter" against which users and other groups are given access to resources.

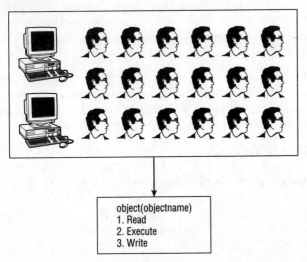

NOTE Sticking user accounts into every nook and cranny of a Windows domain is not good practice, because you'll soon have a domain that resembles a bowl of rice noodles. It is a wonder that Microsoft engineers still enable us to stick a user account anywhere, because that practice is very rare on a well-run network. We believe that the only place that you should put a user is into a group . . . even when the group never sees more than one member. Make this your number-one user-management rule: "Users live in groups. Period."

You can also use groups to create distribution lists (a new type of group). You can, for example, create a group for whom every user receives any e-mail sent to it. This is a boon for e-mail administrators.

Groups versus organizational units

Many people now believe that the Group object has been rendered redundant by the OU. That might be the case if OUs were recognized by the security subsystem and the access-control mechanisms — that is, if they were security principals — but the Group object is a sophisticated management container that can bestow all manner of control over the user accounts and other groups that it contains.

What we believe is good about the group is that it can be used to contain a membership across organizational and multiple-domain boundaries. An organizational unit, on the other hand, belongs to a domain. Complex mergers and acquisitions, along with companies that are so dispersed that their only "geographical" boundary is between the earth and the moon, are excellent candidates for groups that contain memberships from the organizational units of their acquisitions or member companies and departments. Figure 23-3 shows a group called *Accounting* that can contain the department heads and key people from several accounting departments throughout the enterprise.

A network from the viewpoint of users and groups

A *network* has several definitions. From the perspective of users and containers of users, a network is a collection of resources (a collection of network objects as opposed to devices) that can be accessed for services. Users exploit network objects to assist them with their work. Network resources include messaging, printers, telecommunications, information retrieval, collaboration services, and more.

Administrators new to Windows Server 2008 should get familiar with the meaning of *Network object*, because it is used to reference or "obtain a handle" on any network component, both hard and soft.

Exploring the Users and Computers management tools

Windows Server 2008 ships with tools to manage local logon accounts and Active Directory accounts. These tools are *Users and Passwords* and *Local Users and Groups* on standalone machines (including workstations running Windows Server 2008 Professional) and member servers and *Active Directory Users and Computers* on domain controllers.

FIGURE 23-3

The Accounting group enables its members to access resources in the departments of several corporate domains in a forest.

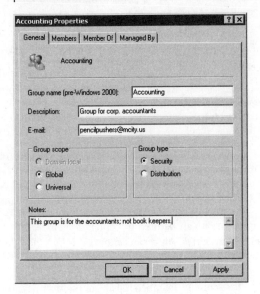

The *Active Directory Users and Computers* MMC snap-in is the primary tool used to create and manage users in network domains. It is launched by choosing Start ➤ Administrative Tools ➤ Active Directory Users and Computers. Figure 23-4 shows the Users and Computers snap-in.

FIGURE 23-4

The Active Directory Users and Computers snap-in, in advanced features mode.

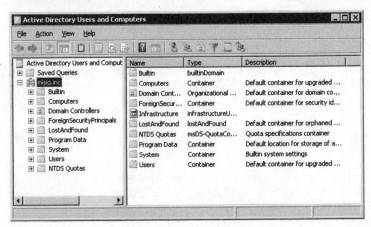

Run the snap-in. First, put the snap-in into advanced features mode so that you can see all the menu options in the Users and Computers MMC library. Select the domain node (such as mcity.us) and right-click it. Choose View ➤ Advanced Features from the pop-up menu that appears. A check mark appears on this right-click context menu, meaning that the entire snap-in is in advanced mode, and you can access all menu options.

Note that you can also select the Users, Groups, and Computers as Containers menu command from the View menu. However, this may give you too much information to deal with in the learning phase. Select this feature after you know your way around this snap-in.

In the left pane, the snap-in loads the tree that represents the domain that you are managing. You can select a number of built-in folders, as the following list describes:

- The **Builtin** folder contains the built-in or default groups created as you installed Active Directory and promoted the server to a domain controller.

- The **Computers** folder contains any computers that are added to the domain you are managing. It is empty if you have not added any computers to the domain at this stage.

- The **Domain Controllers** folder always contains at least one computer . . . the domain controller on which you are currently working.

- The **ForeignSecurityPrincipals** folder is the default container for *security identifiers* (SIDs) associated with objects from other trusted domains.

- The **Users** folder contains built-in user and group accounts. After you upgrade Windows 2000 Server to Windows Server 2008, all the user accounts from the old domain are placed into this folder. This folder is not an OU, and no OU Group Policy can be linked to it. Typically, this folder should be blank or at least should not contain any accounts as you first do a clean install of Windows Server 2008 and promote it to Active Directory. Instead, the built-in accounts should have been placed in the Builtin folder, period. We guess that it is one of those things that the folks at Microsoft did without very much forethought, but they did provide the capability to move items from folder to folder, and moving all the built-in objects to the Builtin folder may make more sense to you, especially because you cannot delete them.

- The **LostAndFound** folder contains objects that have been orphaned.

- The **System** folder contains built-in system settings.

- The **Data** folder is the default location for application data.

- The **NTDS Quotas** folder is the default location for quota specification.

Before you proceed, know that understanding how user accounts work involves two levels. You can cover the basics of user accounts by poking around in the Active Directory User and Computers snap-in MMC panels, or you can make an effort to learn about the most important attributes of user accounts at a lower level. If you are a serious network and Windows administrator, with great attention to detail, you will choose the latter for the reasons that follow.

First, as an administrator, knowing the stuff of which user accounts are made takes your management knowledge and skills to a higher level. You can contribute much more to the overall management of your enterprise network if you know how to perform advanced searches for users, scientifically manage passwords, better protect resources, troubleshoot, and so on. If you think administrators do not need to know how to program, think again; it could make a $20K difference in your salary package.

Second, senior administrators and corporate developers may need to circumvent the basic MMC panels and code directly to the Active Directory Service Interfaces (ADSI). On Windows 2000, senior administrators often created scripts that would block manipulate the accounts in the security accounts database. User Manager for Domains was often too dumb to be of use in major domain operations, such as changing the security privileges for a large number of users. Top Windows Server 2008 administrators need to know how to code to Active Directory and write scripts (which requires basic programming knowledge) that make life easier and lessen the administrative burden. Knowing everything about User objects makes your services that much more in demand.

Windows Server 2008 user accounts

A Windows Server 2008 user account can be a *domain account* or a *local account*. As you first install any version of Windows Server 2008 or promote a server to a domain controller, a number of domain and local accounts are automatically created. If you install Active Directory on a server — that is, if you promote it to a domain controller — the local accounts are disabled.

Domain accounts

Domain accounts or network accounts are User account objects that are stored in Active Directory and that are exposed to the distributed Windows networking and security environment. Domain accounts are enterprisewide. Humans, machines, and processes use domain accounts to log on to a network and gain access to its resources. Each logon attempt goes through a "security clearance," whereby the system compares the password provided by the user against the password stored in the Password Attribute field in Active Directory. If the password matches the record, the user is cleared to proceed and use network resources, perform activities on computers, and communicate.

> **NOTE** Remember that Active Directory is a "multimaster" directory service. This means that changes to users and groups are replicated to other member DCs (but not to a local account database). You can manage users on any DC on the network and not worry about locating a primary DC, as was the case in Windows NT 4.0 and earlier. User objects also contain certain attributes that are not replicated to other DCs. These attributes can be considered of interest only to the local domain controller. The attribute LastLogon, for example, is of interest only to the local network's domain controller; it is of no importance to the other domain controllers in the domain or the forest.

You can also create a user account in any part of the AD ... as long as you have rights to create or manage that User object. Although container objects such as OUs and groups serve to assist in the management of collections of users, you have no mechanism other than admin rights to prevent a user account from being created anywhere in a forest.

Local accounts

Local accounts (users) are identical to network accounts in every way, but they are not stored in Active Directory. Local accounts are machine-specific objects. In other words, a local user account can be validated only against a local security database — the *SAM*, or *Security Account Manager*. Second, local accounts provide access only to resources within the boundaries of the machine domain and no further. An analogy may be the key to your house, which enables you to enter only your house. All other houses in your neighborhood are off limits.

If you are new to Windows networking, you may be wondering why machines on a Windows Server 2008 network would have local accounts. As you know, you can create a network of machines and not manage it by using Active Directory at all, which would certainly send your cost of ownership soaring, but good reasons why these accounts are better off on the local machine rather than sitting in Active Directory also exist. Active Directory users can connect to local machines from remote services (such as to the local FTP account), which is achieved by virtue of having the right to log on locally at the target machine. Local user accounts can also exist on machines that are part of Active Directory domains and that are not the domain controllers. You can also make a domain controller an application server for a small business and enable a number of users to log on locally to the DC by way of terminal sessions.

Local user accounts are restricted to the Access Control List of the local computer. The local domain itself does not replicate this information off the local machine because it matters only to the local account system, which is not distributed.

> **NOTE** The tools to manage a local machine's local accounts and groups (although not on a domain controller) can be accessed through the Users and Passwords and Administrative Tools applications in the Control Panel.

Predefined accounts

After you install Windows Server 2008, as either a standalone or member server or as a domain controller supporting Active Directory, the operating system establishes default accounts. On a standalone machine (server or workstation), the default accounts are local to the machine native domain and established in the SAM. On a domain controller — in Active Directory — the default accounts are network accounts. Built-in accounts cannot be deleted, but they can be renamed or moved from one container to another.

The default accounts include administration accounts that enable you to log on and manage the network or the local machine. Windows Server 2008 also installs built-in machine or Guest accounts and anonymous Internet user accounts. You may notice that these so-called accounts are disabled by default and must be implicitly enabled.

A good idea, as soon as it's feasible, is to rename the Administrator account to hide its purpose and thus its access and security level. (Hiding was not possible on Windows NT but was added to Windows 2000.) If you have security fears, you can audit the activity of the Administrator to determine who or what is using the account and when.

If you demote a domain controller (DC) to a standalone server, and especially if it is the last DC on the network, the OS prompts you for the password to use for the local Administrator account. In the process of stripping away AD and its administrator accounts, the OS ensures that you can log on locally and gain access to the machine after the conversion. As AD departs from the server, it hands control of the machine back to the machine-specific domain and Security Account Manager (SAM).

Administrator account

The Administrator account is the first user account created after you install Windows Server 2008, regardless of which version of Windows Server 2008 you are installing. The Administrator account is created initially in the local SAM and then in Active Directory when the AD is added if the machine is promoted to a domain controller.

The Administrator is the CEO on Windows Server 2008 and all earlier versions. By logging on as the Administrator, you get total access to the entire system and network. Without the power of this built-in user, setting up the first objects would be impossible.

The Administrator account is dangerous, however. Over time, the password to this account gets handed around, and your network goes to hell. We have even seen situations where the Administrator's account password finds its way around the world in large corporations, even enabling users in foreign domains to mess things up without the key MIS people at HQ finding out. In one situation, it ended up in the hands of a subcontractor who managed to bring an office to a standstill for a week.

How do you protect this account from abuse? For starters, you cannot delete or disable the account because getting locked out of the system or falling victim to a denial-of-service (DoS) attack would be all too easy.

You can rename this account, however, which presents an opportunity to conceal the Administrator's true identity and lock down access to it. Recording the Administrator password in a document and then locking it away in a secure place before new (flesh and blood) administrators are added to the domain makes sense. To do so, follow these steps:

1. Rename the Administrator account. Remember to provide a UPN and rename the down-level or NetBIOS name as well, because renaming merely changes the hidden attribute and label.

2. Create a new user as a decoy Administrator and endow it with administrator power by assigning the account to the Administrators group. Alternatively, leave the account with no powers of administration.

3. Appoint the Administrator (which can be under the new name) account as the manager of this account. You do this on the Organization tab of the User Manager dialog box, in the Manager field.

4. Cease using the real Administrator and lock away the password.

You would now be correct in saying, "But that still does not stop someone from getting hold of one of the other administrator accounts and abusing it." True, but now you have accounts that can be monitored, audited, disabled, and deleted if they become a security risk, and deleting and re-creating administrators at certain intervals may pay off in some circumstances.

> **TIP** To rename the Administrator account, you need to first give an Administrator account the "right to rename the Administrator account." This right is granted by Group Policy, which is discussed in Chapter 24. After you have renamed the real Administrator, you can create a decoy Administrator account.

Another wise move is to move the Administrator and administrator type accounts out of the Users folder. This advice is backed by several reasons:

- Anyone looking for the Administrator is sure to go there first, and denying access to this folder may be impractical.

- The security policy governing the Users folder is inherited from the root domain. This means that if for any reason the default or root domain policy changes, it may affect the account without you being aware of it.

- The Administrator accounts are better grouped in the main IS OU, where access is controlled by specific OU policy, focused management, and delegated responsibility.

To move the Administrator account, follow these steps:

1. Open Active Directory Users and Computers. Double-click the Users folder.

2. Select the Administrator account in the right-hand pane and right-click it. Now choose Move from the pop-up menu. The list of folders and OUs appears.

3. Drill down to a different OU of your choice. Select that OU and click OK. The Administrator account is now moved to the new OU.

> **NOTE** Another means of protecting the network and the Administrator account and a sophisticated means of management and troubleshooting is to use the *RunAs* service. Also known as the *secondary login*, it enables a user who is logged on with his or her regular user account to perform functions with the privileges of another account — typically, an administrator's. RunAs is demonstrated in the section "Getting Familiar with RunAs" later in this chapter, where we discuss the configuration of user accounts.

> **CROSS-REF** See Chapter 24 for information on how to secure users and groups for help securing the Domain Admins group on your network.

Guest account

The Guest account is the second of the default accounts that are prebuilt as you install Windows Server 2008 the first time and after you create a domain controller and install Active Directory. The account is useful for guests and visitors who do not have accounts on any domain in the forest or whose accounts may be disabled.

The Guest account does not require a password, and you can grant it certain access and rights to resources on the computer. (See the section "Rights and Permissions," later in this chapter, for details.) We believe that the Guest account on any domain should be relocated to an OU with a security and account policy that is appropriate for managing security risks. You can leave the Guest account in the Users folder (which is a domain folder and not an OU), but the security policy governing that account in the Users folder is inherited from the root domain. Therefore, if for any reason the default or root domain policy changes, it affects the Guest account without you being aware of it. The Guest account is also automatically placed into the Guest group, which you may want to also place in the Visitors OU. You can move the Guest account by using Active Directory Users and Computers. In our Millennium City network, we've moved the Guest account to the City Hall-Visitors OU.

In the User folder, the Guest account is granted the right to log on locally to a local computer or member server. In the City Hall-Visitors OU, you can grant specific access to the domain resources, such as e-mail, access to printers and devices, and so on. You can also create several Visitor accounts for accounting and auditing purposes and to keep track of the objects that each visitor accesses.

By using logon scripts and profiles, you can track activity between each logon and logoff period and use that to generate reports. From these reports, you can run invoices, statements, bills, and so on. If you run a service bureau, this is the direction that you should be considering.

Some organizations do not believe in Guest or Visitor accounts and keep these disabled from the start. If you disable the Guest account, you are denying anyone who does not have an account from logging on. In highly secure environments, this policy may be valid; and this was, and still is, the case in many Windows NT domains that do not provide for the additional protection of the OU security policy. However, these accounts can be handy even in sensitive environments. Consider the following before taking the easy way out and disabling the account:

■ By using a Guest account, a new user awaiting a user account can get some work done on a computer. Such users can, for example, begin reading company policy or the employee handbook, and they can fill in employee forms and so on. Many companies, however, place this information on a Web server in the form of a Web application that requires more than just a guest account to access.

■ By using a Guest account, a user who has been locked out for whatever reason can at least log on to the domain and gain access to the company intranet and local resources. Suppose that you have an intranet Web site that enables users to access the help desk and open a ticket; a user who cannot log on to the domain can still generate a ticket for an account lockout problem. Lockouts can and do happen often.

If you choose not to disable the Guest account, however, make sure you take the time to severely restrict the account in the network.

The Internet user account

Windows Server 2008 also provides default or built-in accounts for anonymous access to IIS. Such accounts can be manipulated, but doing so is strongly discouraged because the default settings are generally sufficient for IIS.

Account policy

Before you create users, you must first take the time to fully understand how account policy on Windows Server 2008 affects account creation and management on an account-by-account basis.

The Windows Group Policy technology (which also includes account and security policy) governs how all accounts can be configured on both standalone servers and in the Active Directory. If you create users from the get-go, the accounts are set up with the default account policy attributes. They remain this way until Active Directory site, domain, or OU policies override this (which occurs whenever a domain controller and Active Directory is installed and sites, domains, and OUs are created).

What you should be aware of here, especially if you have been given the responsibility to create an account and set up a computer, is the order of precedence for security and account policies. The order of precedence, from the highest to the lowest, is as follows:

- Site policy
- Domain policy
- OU policy
- Local policy

The local policy governs the local accounts that you set up on the computer itself, in its native or machine-specific domain, but the local policy is overridden by the policies of higher precedence, unless you take the steps to avert that behavior.

Security principals and the logon authentication process

The onus of "good behavior" rests on the shoulders of User and Group objects in Windows Server 2008. As mentioned earlier in this chapter, these objects have the total trust of the OS on first being installed. They are often referred to as *security principals* and *trustees*. Every other object that is not a security principal or that does not exist in AD within a security context is rejected by the security subsystem and thus cannot present for rights and access. The Contact object is a good example of an object that is not a security principal. You may create other nonsecurity objects and register them in Active Directory.

Several security principals are defined to the security subsystem by default. These include groups such as Domain Users, Domain Admins, and so on.

If a user attempts to log on to Windows Server 2008 by way of the AD or the Local Security Authority (LSA), the security system determines whether the user exists and whether the password provided matches the password stored in the relevant database. If the user is authenticated, Windows Server 2008 creates an *access token* for the user.

If the domain controller does not receive the correct password or the user account is unknown, the user is gracefully returned to the logon dialog box. After a user is authenticated, Windows activates whatever rights and permissions the user has on the network.

The process that Windows Server 2008 uses to "follow" the user through the domain is known as *access token assignment*. In other words, the access token is assigned to the user for the duration of the logon and acts as a security tag that a user wears in "roaming" from computer to computer and from resource to resource. User account information is replicated to all domain controllers in the enterprise, even across slow WAN links.

Security identifiers

The *security identifier* (SID) is a unique value of variable length that is used to identify an account (known as a *trustee* to the kernel) to the security subsystem. Windows refers to the SID, rather than to the user or group name, in referencing these objects for security purposes. The SID is not the same thing as the *object identifier*, or *OID*. SIDs guarantee that the account and all its associated rights and permissions are unique. If you delete an account and then re-create it under the same name, all rights and permissions of the deceased account are gone. This is because the old SID was deleted with the original account.

As you create an account, the system also creates the SID and stores it in the security structures of AD or the SAM. The first part of the SID identifies the domain in which the SID was created. The second part is called the *relative ID* (RID), which refers to the actual object created (and is thus relative to the domain).

Whenever a user logs on to the computer or domain, the SID is retrieved from the database and placed in the user's access token. From the moment of logon, the SID is used in the access token to identify the user in all security-related actions and interactions.

Windows NT, Windows 2000, and Windows Server 2008 use the SID for the following purposes:

- To identify the object's owner
- To identify the object owner's group
- To identify the account user in access-related activity

Special well-known SIDs are also created by the system during installation to identify the built-in users and groups. If a user logs on to the system as Guest, the access token for that user includes the well-known SID for the Guest group, which restricts the user from doing damage or accessing objects to which they are not entitled.

SAM and LSA authentication

The Windows Server 2008 SAM is inherited from the Windows 2000 SAM and works the same. It no longer, however, plays a part in network domain management. Standalone and member servers use the Windows Server 2008 SAM to authenticate or validate users that have local accounts, including autonomous processes. The SAM is still buried in the registry and plays an important role in Windows Server 2008, and it is an integral part of the Local Security Authority (LSA). LSA authentication exists for several reasons:

- To process local logon requests.

- To enable ISVs and customers with special requirements to use the LSA to gain local authentication services. An access control application may use the LSA to validate holders of magnetic access control cards and so on.

- To provide special local access to devices. For a device to be installed and gain access to system resources, it may need to be authenticated by the LSA. An example is a tape-backup device driver, which may need to gain access to a local database management system or to machine-protected processes that require it to be logged on locally.

- To provide heterogeneous local authentication. Not everyone can take advantage of the Active Directory authentication and logon process, and not everyone wants to. The LSA thus provides these "users" (processes) with a local logon facility that they were accustomed to, or built for, on Windows NT 4.0 and earlier.

As you set up a standalone server, Windows creates default or *built-in* accounts. These are actually created in a local Windows 4.0-type domain stored in the local SAM. The two local domains created are `Account` and `Builtin`.

As you first install Windows Server 2008, these local domain systems are named after the NetBIOS-type name of the machine. If you change the machine's name, the domain name is changed to the new machine name the next time that you restart the server. In other words, if you set up a standalone server named LONELY1, a local domain named `LONELY1` is created in the local SAM. The OS then creates the built-in accounts for this domain. Later, you can create any local user in the local legacy domain. Services also use the local domain for system accounts.

NOTE Active Directory includes a SAM service provider that enables Windows Server 2008 domain controllers to interoperate with NT 4.0 domain controllers. Such service providers also exist for other directory services, such as Novell NDS.

User Accounts in Action

A user account is like a bank account. Without a bank account, you have no way to access the services of a bank, store money, pay bills, take out loans, and manage your financial affairs. If a user comes to work and cannot log on, the scene that ensues is like that for a bank account that has been closed unexpectedly.

Getting familiar with RunAs

Before you proceed with account creation and management, you should take some time to understand the *RunAs* application and service. It is invaluable to you in your administration endeavors, especially for troubleshooting account problems.

> **NOTE** RunAs is also known as *secondary* or *alternate logon.*

RunAs enables you to execute applications, access resources, or load an environment, profile, and so on by using the credentials of another user account, without needing to log off from the account that you initially logged on to your computer with. RunAs is a nongraphical executable that resides in the %System%\System32 folder of your server or workstation. It is a service that can be accessed from various locations in the operating system. You can link to it from the desktop or create scripts and applications that make use of its services. You can also create a shortcut to an application and enable it to be executed by using the credentials of another user account (provided that you have the password to the other account).

RunAs essentially enables you to operate an environment or application in the security context of another user account, while remaining in your current security context or in your current logged-on state. The simplest, and very useful, feature of RunAs enables you to test a logon name and account password without needing to log off from your workstation. Perhaps the best way to describe RunAs usage is to provide a simple example.

Create a shortcut to the Command Console on the desktop and enable it to be used to test a User ID and password, as follows:

1. Create a shortcut to the command prompt on your desktop.
2. Right-click the shortcut and choose Properties from the pop-up menu. On the Shortcut tab of the Properties dialog box that appears, click Advanced, select the Run with Different Credentials checkbox, and click OK.
3. Click OK again.

Now, whenever you right-click the shortcut, the Run As line is added to the context menu in bold type. You can also just double-click the shortcut icon and the Run As Other User dialog box appears. You can then enter your user's account, domain, and password.

If you investigate RunAs further, you discover that you can test alternative logons and troubleshoot problems such as access to shares, printers, and so on. You can log on and switch to the environment provided by the alternative account, and you can enable users to run an application in the context of another account.

Naming user accounts

You can make your life as a user administrator more enjoyable if you follow the recommended convention for naming user accounts. You can and should plan your user namespace carefully, publish the rules and policy surrounding the chosen convention, and stick to it. Nothing is worse than inheriting a directory of accounts in which no naming convention exists.

To set up your naming convention checklist, consider the following:

■ User account names must be unique in the domain in which the accounts are created. You cannot, for example, have two names set up as mcity\john samuels or johns@mcity.us. One must become johns1@mcity.us. You can, however, create an account with the same UPN prefix in another domain — for example, johns@mcity.mcpd.us or mcpd\johns.

■ The user account prefix can contain a maximum of 20 characters in any case. The logon process is not sensitive to case. The field, however, preserves the case, enabling you to assist in a naming convention, such as JohnS as opposed to johns.

■ The following characters are not permissible in the account name: ' < > * / \ | ; : = , + [ ].

■ You can use letters and dashes or underscores in the name to assist with convention, but remember that account names may be used as e-mail addresses. Follow the suggestions in the UPN naming conventions, described in the section "The User Principal Name" later in this chapter.

Passwords

Many administrators use a method of combining initials and numbers for passwords and keep them consistent throughout the enterprise.

To set up your password convention checklist, consider the following:

■ The passwords can be up to 128 characters in length. That does not mean that Microsoft expects you to saddle your users with a password that takes all day to input, but smart cards and noninteractive logon devices can use a field of that length.

■ Do not create passwords that contain fewer than five characters; a minimum of eight is recommended.

■ The following characters are not permissible in the password: ' / \ | ; : = , + [ ].

Password management is a nightmare for everyone. Most administrators we know keep lists of passwords in various database files and help desks because users often find themselves locked out of domains and resources for "no apparent reason." To troubleshoot and assist users, we often need to log on to a user s account and "experience" what may be going wrong. Many administrators troubleshoot this way; being in the user's context helps in troubleshooting. The new RunAs service that we describe in the section "Getting Familiar with RunAs," earlier in this chapter, is a useful tool for managing user accounts and troubleshooting passwords.

The password issuance and management-style challenges are similar from platform to platform, especially from NetWare to Windows NT and Windows Server 2008. Regarding the use of user passwords, the following three options are available:

■ Assign the passwords.

■ Enable the user to choose the password.

■ Assign passwords to certain users; enable others to set their own.

All three options have their pros and cons, and every company has a reason for going with one option or the other. If you go with the first option, you must either adopt a password-naming scheme that lends itself to easy recollection by administrators (as secure as an open field) or enter the users' passwords in a secure database.

The former is not really secure because figuring out the scheme that the administrators are using would not take much effort. A popular password-forming approach is to join a user's initials and part of his or her Social Security number, driver's license number, or some other form of number that society issues — for example, *jrs0934*. This scheme has been in place at several companies where we worked. In that several thousand accounts were set up under the scheme, changing it has been a nightmare.

The second approach, enabling users to select their own passwords, is fraught with danger. First, users who have a lot of sensitive information on their machines and in their folders often assign weak passwords that can easily be cracked. We have found users choosing *12345678* and giving us the excuse that they were going to change it later ... three months later.

Second, enabling users to choose their own passwords can be nightmarish on corporate networks. In troubleshooting problems, administrators often need to ask for the passwords over the telephone (for all to hear) and in e-mail. Then there are the occasions where you must reset the password anyway because the owner is either not present or Windows Server 2008 rejects the password.

We believe that the best policy is to let users choose their own passwords and then govern them with a sound password management policy. You can assign a password for most corporate users if you have a specific reason, and enable selected users (who demand the security and who can justify it) to set their own passwords. The latter users fall into groups that have access to company financial information, bank account numbers, credit card numbers, personnel records, and so on. Paranoid executives fall into the latter group as well. For the most part, this practice is archaic.

For service accounts, generate secure passwords (as opposed to obvious acronyms). Record the password in a secure place: either a database management system that is hard to crack, such as an encrypted Microsoft Access database file, or in an SQL Server table.

Protecting passwords is more important under Windows Server 2008 than under Windows NT — or any other OS, for that matter. The reason is the Single Sign-On (SSO) initiative and the Kerberos ticket-granting service discussed in Chapter 16. On older OSs, you need new user IDs and passwords for just about any service, such as voice mail, fax mail, SQL Server, Internet access, and so on. As more applications support the SSO, one password eventually suffices for all. This is a double-edged sword, however. If the password or access falls into mischievous hands, the culprit has access to everything authenticated in the SSO process.

Understanding logon

We have discussed the concept of local logon in various places, but this is a right and not an automatic privilege. For a user to connect to the machine standing next to him or to a remote machine across the network, he needs authority in the following two places:

- The domain that the user is a member of must enable the user to request logon permission from a machine. The default is to enable the user to request logon from any machine, which means the target machine's SAM gets to say yes or no and not the domain.

- The target machine must give the account the right to log on locally.

Unless the target machine has special software on it that requires local logon and authentication, providing access to resources on remote machines via domain groups makes more sense.

Granting remote access

Remote-access privileges are the most sought-after rights in any organization. By being given access to Remote Access Services (RAS), users may be permitted to telecommute, work from home, or access the network and servers from the road. Road warriors also give you the most headaches because remote policy is by its very nature governed by more stringent security requirements.

In setting up groups, creating remote user groups in specific OUs may also pay. You are certain to run into problems putting every remote user into an enterprisewide remote user group. Users who are restricted at certain levels as they work on the premises often find life more open and accessible in connecting from home, and users who have a wide berth in the office may find life claustrophobic on the outside.

Creating a user account

In the example in this section, we're creating user accounts for the Driver Compensation Program (DCP) in Millennium City. They exist in the DCP OU, which resides in the CITYHALL domain. Let's assume you have created the DCP OU.

Select the domain, right-click the DCP OU, and choose New ➤ User from the pop-up menu. The New Object – User dialog box opens, as shown in Figure 23-5. The most important information that you need here is either the old SAM account name of the user who is connecting or a new NetBIOS name. This is the name that the user used or still uses to log on to the legacy NT domain. It is not the name of the machine that is connecting. Remember that this is a NetBIOS name; it must contain fewer than 15 characters, and you need to avoid the illegal characters discussed earlier in this chapter.

FIGURE 23-5

The New Object – User dialog box.

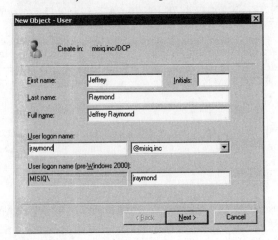

 **NOTE** You can create a new user account anywhere in the domain and later move it as needed.

The User Principal Name

In the beginning, on legacy NT, you had little flexibility with logon names. You would usually use contractions of first and last names, such as *jshapiro* or *jeffreys*, or names typically assigned to people serving 25 years to life, such as *psjrs08676*.

Now everything is different. The user's logon name and e-mail addresses are the same. Good reasons exist to do this. First, this change supports the SSO initiative, better known as Single Sign-On. As long as the resources that the user needs access to support TCP/IP, RFC 822 naming, and Kerberos authentication, the user ID or the resulting authentication certificates can be relayed to these technologies. Second, the UPN enables you to use an e-mail address to log on to the domain from anywhere on the Internet. As long as the domain controller is exposed to the Internet or the packets find the DC through a firewall, logging on and accessing resources is possible.

If you can resolve CITYHALL.GENESIS.MCITY.US on the Internet, you can log in. The prefix part of the UPN provides the so-called user ID, and the suffix identifies the domain.

Given that life would be easier if your users' logon IDs and e-mail addresses were the same, you have some serious restructuring to do. Perhaps the best place to start is at your e-mail server. Here, all the accounts are set up with UPNs already, and if you have been running an Exchange server, all the better. Simply dump all the names into a comma-separated file (.csv) and use these as the basis for your UPNs.

Using first and last names as a UPN is a good idea. RFC 822 requires that you separate the elements of the UPN with acceptable characters. Obviously, the @ sign is not acceptable, nor is the & (ampersand). Simple dot notation works the best: user.name@adomain.com or jeffrey.shapiro@mcity.us.

Figure 23-5 shows you the logon type that can be used, the UPN (jshapiro@misiq.com) but the down-level NetBIOS name (jshapiro) also works. In the first one, the user enters the prefix part of the UPN as the user ID, and the suffix as the domain name. This may be less comfortable for people accustomed to logging on to Windows NT domains or NetWare.

If you are not yet ready to move users to Windows Server 2008 but plan to in the near future, now is the time to start preparing for UPNs. If your e-mail server accounts do not make attractive UPNs (such as zp-badboy5.shapiroj@wierdestofcorps.com, for example), now is the time to change them. You seldom if ever need to type your e-mail address every time that you send a message, but you do need to type at least the prefix every time you log on to Windows Server 2008. Try keeping the UPNs as short as possible without turning everyone's name into an acronym. Using jshapiro, for example, works better than jeffrey.shapiro, which is better than js. Anyone who ends up with a UPN of more than, say, eight letters may never want to log in again.

Before you add the name, ensure that the UPN you entered as you created the account conforms to the standards that you have set for your network. This double-checking exercise is worthwhile here because the UPN often must be entered after the account is created. If you copy an account, the UPN field must be updated. Remember that the UPN conforms to the Internet standard e-mail address governed by RFC 822, such as jeffrey.shapiro@mcity.us or jeffreys@mcity.us.

Click Next to fill in the password in the next dialog box, shown in Figure 23-6. Click Finish after you're done. That's all that creating a user involves. Next, you need to set the properties for the user.

Setting properties

After the account is created, you need to set the properties that define the user's rights and privileges, access to resources, contact information, and so on. To access the property sheets of the user account object, simply double-click the account in Active Directory or right-click it and choose Properties from the context menu. In this example, you double-click Jeffrey Raymond, and Jeffrey's Properties dialog box loads, as shown in Figure 23-7.

The Properties dialog box for the user contains several tabs, which you can use to configure the User object and populate it with information. Many of the tabs are self-explanatory, so the following sections describe only the ones that you need to set when creating a new user account.

FIGURE 23-6

Adding the password to the New Object – User dialog box.

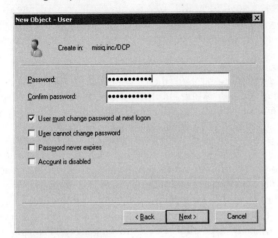

FIGURE 23-7

The user's Properties dialog box.

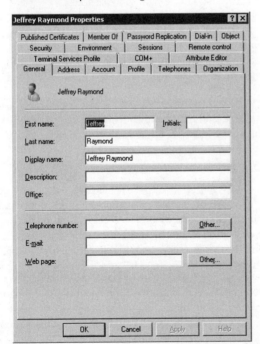

General tab properties

The options on the General tab identify the user's name and other information:

- **First Name, Last Name, and Initials.** After you enter information in these fields, the display name is formed automatically. You can also change the display name to suit a company standard or policy. You want to leave the display name as is for the current example — that way, wherever users of CITYHALL are logged on, you can spot them immediately in open file lists, connection lists, owners, and so on.

- **Description.** This information can describe the purpose of the account or it can be information that better identifies it. The bigger the network, the more important it is to fill in this field. In this case, you insert DCP Entry Team Leader to describe the purpose of the account.

- **Office.** Enter the user's physical office address.

- **Telephone Number.** Enter the user's telephone number and extension, if any.

- **E-mail.** Enter the user's e-mail address. Default to the UPN may seem intuitive, but it doesn't. This field is not e-mail format-sensitive, however, so if an SMTP format is out, you can enter a cc:Mail address, an X:400 address, or something else. Keeping the entries here consistent is important because access to this field is open via the ADSI, and the field is no doubt a key repository of information for many people-tracking tools, ERP apps, communications applications, and more. At the time of this writing, we don't know what e-mail applications may be using this field, but it is available to access.

- **Web Page.** Enter the user's home page, if applicable. The purpose of this field may be vague at first, because why would you have all your users worry about home pages? These fields can be used for other applications, however, such as an ISP with user accounts that "rent" home pages. If you are an ISP, you can set up user accounts in the directory to manage access and accounting from the directory. The field is a string data type, so an IP address is feasible here, too.

Account tab properties

The options on the Account tab are security options, and they need to be managed carefully. If you've managed user accounts before, you probably recognize many of the following options:

- **User Logon Name.** This field shows the user's UPN logon name.

- **User Logon Name (pre-Windows 2000).** This field shows the user's down-level NetBIOS logon name.

- **Account Expires.** Set this option to Never to indicate that the account never expires. Set the End Of option if you want the account to exist for only a certain period of time and expire at the end of the specified day. Locking a person out at some future date is valuable for applications services and for temps and subcontractors, who are classified a security risk at some future date.

- **Logon Hours.** See the section "Logon Hours" that follows to learn how to configure allowed logon hours.

- **Log On To.** This is the path of the workstation or server to which the users can log in. For an administrator, leave this at the default. If the employee is new or questionable, we would restrict him to the department's machine and lock the person out of the other MIS machines. For the sake of demonstration, Figure 23-8 shows this restriction in force. This restriction applies to all member machines and not just to workstations, as it may suggest. By not setting any values in this dialog box, you give the user access to all machines on the network.

FIGURE 23-8

Logon restrictions.

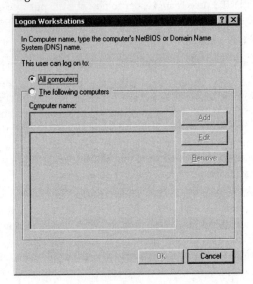

- By forcing users to log on to their own workstations, you are by omission barring them from logging on locally to any other machines. Of course, you can restrict the local logon at the target machine.

- **Unlock Account.** This option is selected if the account has been locked (such as because of repeated entry of an incorrect password). Clear the checkbox to enable the user to log on.

- **Account Options.** This is where you set password policies. To comply with the Millennium City password policy, you can select the User Cannot Change Password and Password Never Expires checkboxes. Choose a secure password for the user. Then, configure additional options as described in the following list (note that these properties are better set through Group Policy):

  - **User Must Change Password at Next Logon.** The user is prompted to change his password at the next logon.

  - **User Cannot Change Password.** This option prevents the user from changing her password.

- **Password Never Expires.** The account is not subject to password aging, and the password does not expire.

- **Store Password Using Reversible Encryption.** This option is essentially the same as storing the password in plain text. This policy is required when using Challenge-Handshake Authentication Protocol (CHAP) authentication through remote access or Internet Authentication Services (IAS). It is also required when using Digest Authentication in Internet Information Services (IIS).

- **Account Is Disabled.** Select this option to prevent the user from authenticating.

- **Smart Card Is Required for Interactive Logon.** This option requires that the user have a card reader attached to her machine before she can log on.

- **Account Is Trusted for Delegation.** This option enables the user of this account to delegate administrative function in the domain tree to others.

- **Account Is Sensitive and Cannot Be Delegated.** This option negates the option of enabling the user to delegate.

- **Use Kerberos DES Encryption Types for This Account.** DES supports multiple levels of encryption, including MPPE Standard (40-bit), MPPE Standard (56-bit), MPPE Strong (128-bit), IPSec DES (40-bit), IPSec 56-bit DES, and IPSec Triple DES (3DES). See Chapter 16 for further information on DES and security.

- **This Account Supports Kerberos AES 128 Bit Encryption.** Refer to Chapter 16 for more information on Kerberos.

- **This Account Supports Kerberos AES 256 Bit Encryption.** Refer to Chapter 16 for more information on Kerberos.

- **Account Is Sensitive and Cannot Be Delegated.** This option negates the option of enabling the user to delegate.

- **Do Not Require Kerberos Pre-Authentication.** Refer to Chapter 16 for more information on Kerberos.

Logon hours

The Logon Hours controls, shown in Figure 23-9, are available from the Account tab. By default, logon time is set to Always, meaning that users can log in whenever they want, but you may want to restrict this for several reasons. MCITY is set up to deny access to the domain controllers every Saturday night for about 12 hours. This is the time, once a week, when we power down the servers and perform maintenance. You may have a tighter security arrangement, for example, that only permits logon during working hours.

To set logon hours, follow these steps:

1. On the Properties dialog box, select the Account tab and click the Logon Hours button. The Logon Hours dialog box opens.

2. To enable a user to log on at certain hours, click the rectangle on the days and hours for which you want to deny or permit a user logon time. The blue boxes denote logon times that are permitted, and the white boxes denote logon times that are denied. By default, the entire box is blue, indicating that logon is permitted all the time.

3. After you click OK and close the dialog box, the logon hours are saved.

FIGURE 23-9

The Logon Hours controls.

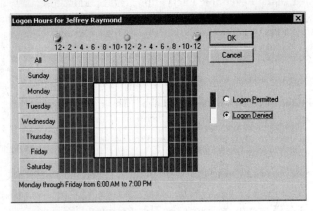

Profile tab properties

The Profile tab contains a User Profile group box and a Home Folder group box. The User Profile fields enable you to enter information specifying the resources that a user connects to as soon as that user authenticates to the domain. You can also enter logon script information, if applicable. The Home Folder fields enable you to enter the path to the user's personal folder, which can be a folder used by a group as well. This folder can also be redirected according to Group Policy. The following list describes the available options:

- **Profile Path.** Enter the user's profile path here, such as \\mcdc01\profiles \amartinez.

- **Logon Script.** If you're using logon scripts for your users, enter the appropriate filename here, such as \\mcdc01\profiles\eredmond\eredmond.scr.

- **Local Path.** Enter the path to the folder on a network server or workstation. It can be to a local folder as well, and you can just leave this field blank to default to the default local folder on the user's local hard disk. (Get used to entering information here, especially if you are going to set up resources for terminal users. Remember that terminal users' local paths are the servers that they sign on to by default, and if you redirect users to any of a number of servers, you need to define Home Folders.)

- **Connect.** This information enables you to map a drive letter to the Home Folder path.

Organization tab properties

The Organization tab enables you to provide information about the user's organization, title, and superiors. Remember that this account information is entered into a directory, which is used by people researching information related to users. The options available on this tab are as follows:

- **Title.** This is the user's title — for example, VP or CEO.

- **Department.** This is where the user works.

- **Company.** This is the name of the company.
- **Manager.** This is the user account of the individual who manages this user or account.
- **Direct Reports.** This is a list of users who directly report to this user account (information supplied in the Manager field in other accounts appear in this list).

Member Of tab properties

This tab enables you to add the user to a group on this domain or in groups in other domains in the forest. Enter the names of groups that the user is required to be a member of. You can do this by clicking the Add button and selecting the groups from a domain that appears in the Select Groups list.

Dial-in tab properties

This tab enables you to give the user dial-in (RAS) privileges, authentication options, and IP addressing options.

Renaming user accounts

Windows Server 2008 enables you to rename user accounts because the SID remains the same. All you are doing is changing the values of certain attributes in the object. To rename a user account, you can either right-click the account in Active Directory Users and Computers and choose Rename from the pop-up menu or click the entry once. After you single-click it, the entry can be renamed in the same manner as you rename any other object name in Windows Server 2008, such as a file or a folder name.

NOTE Whenever you rename an account, you are changing only the name property as you see it in the AD list. This is very different behavior from legacy NT account management, whereby the username and account name were the same thing. Changing the account name does not change the logon name (UPN) or the legacy NetBIOS name.

Deleting and disabling user accounts

Common sense tells you not to delete accounts at will. After an account is deleted, you can never get it back. The SID can be tracked, but it can never be resurrected. You have no undelete feature, and the account and SID are lost forever as active objects. If you want to render an account unusable, disable it. If you are an experienced administrator of Windows NT, this practice is not new to you, and disabling an account in Active Directory is easy. Just select the account in Active Directory Users and Computers and right-click. Choose Disable Account from the pop-up menu.

You can consider adopting a policy to delete any disabled account within a certain time frame — say, six months. Unless you have a very good reason to delete the account, however, leave it disabled indefinitely. Deleted accounts are like zombies. They return from their graves to haunt you. For example, temps often leave the company only to return six months later to perform similar duties, so re-creating the same account all over again, with the same access rights and permissions, group memberships, and so on, is a huge waste of time.

Copying accounts

Copying accounts is a no-brainer. Simply right-click the account that you want to copy and choose Copy from the pop-up menu. Copying accounts may not save you a lot of time if you have a lot of accounts to create. You may be better off using a script or special program, especially if many of the account attributes for each user are different.

Consider having new employees fill in a form in a database or on the intranet. Then parse the form and use the values to create the user account in a script.

Computer Accounts

A computer account is also a security principal, a direct descendant of the User object. For a computer to participate in a Windows network, whether Windows Server 2008, Windows 2000, or NT 4.0, it must be capable of logging on securely to a domain in some manner. Windows 2008 adds additional security and control over the computer by requiring it to have an account — just as a user does.

Whenever you join a computer to a domain, you create an account for the computer, and Windows generates a SID. The procedure is identical to that of creating human user accounts.

The first computers that you add to a Windows Server 2008 domain are the domain controllers. These servers are the domain security outposts. You cannot create a Windows Server 2008 domain without first "raising" a domain controller. The act of promoting a machine to domain-controller service demotes any authority the local SAM had. Directory services are created, and full domain security is located in Active Directory.

After you add the first member server, standalone server, or Windows 2008 Professional workstation to the domain, Windows establishes two new groups to assist with machine management: the Domain Admins Group and the Domain Users Group.

Creating a computer account is simpler than creating the user account. You select the OU in which you want to place the computer and choose New ➤ Computer from the snap-in's menu bar. Obviously, you need authority to create the account. By placing the computer into an OU, you place it under the influence of Group Policy.

Group Accounts

Group management in Windows Server 2008 is a vast improvement over legacy NT group management. The group's role as an administrator-appointed mustering or container tool has been replaced by the OU, which means that administrators can create and use groups more scientifically, now that its only purpose as a security principal is to provide and control access to computer and network resources.

A group is nothing more than a container for managing user accounts. The most important aspect of a group, however, is that you can assign permissions to it, rather than grant permissions to individual users. You rarely need to create a user who is so peculiar to an organization that she has rights and access to resources that no one else has. Even the Administrator account, of which you have only one, is placed into several groups to gain access to sensitive resources and information.

Windows 2008 groups come in two flavors: *security group* and *distribution group*:

- **Security group.** This is the standard Windows Server 2008 security principal, stored as an entry in the ACL. Security groups, however, can now be mailed to. In other words, all the members in the security group who have an e-mail address stored in their User account objects can receive e-mail.

- **Distribution group.** This group is not a security principal and is used only as a distribution list. You can store contacts and user accounts in the distribution group. Because contacts do not contain the overhead of user accounts, including contacts only in large groups makes more sense. This group is also compatible with Microsoft Exchange and can play a large part in your telephony and messaging applications as well. After you upgrade Exchange to support Active Directory, you can eliminate the Exchange distribution lists and reduce the administrative burden on the e-mail administrators. Note that this applies to pre-2000 versions of Exchange Server because latter versions integrate AD support.

The scope of groups

Both group types have three scope types. Scopes determine the capability to contain members and nest groups from other domains and forests across the enterprise and even on an intra-enterprise relationship basis. The three scope types are *Universal*, *Global*, and *Domain Local*. Windows NT supported only Global and Domain Local group types. The following list describes all three group types:

- **Universal groups.** These groups can include members from any Windows NT, Windows 2000, or Windows Server 2008 domain in a forest. The members can be groups of any of the three scope types, and they can come from any domain in the forest. This scope was created for users who need access to resources in other domains. A good example of a Universal group is a user who works mainly in USA-Domain but who frequently travels to London where the user logs onto UK-Domain. This user could log on to UK-Domain and still gain access to his USA-Domain resources. Members of Universal groups can be given access and permissions for any resource in any domain in the forest.

- **Global groups.** These groups can include members only from the originating domain. These members can be other Global groups and Contact groups. Global groups can be given access to resources in any domain in the forest, and the members can be members of any of the groups in the forest. You can nest Global, Local, and Universal groups in a global group.

- **Domain Local groups.** These groups can include members from any domain in the forest. Members of such a group can be any user or group from anywhere in the forest. However, you can nest only other Domain Local groups from the same domain. The members of this group scope cannot be members of groups set with the Global and Universal group scope types.

> **NOTE** Group scopes can be elevated only if they do not belong to other groups in the lower level and only on native-mode networks. In other words, you can move a Global group to a Universal group only if the Global group does not belong to another Global group. You may also notice that you cannot change the scope of a Universal group, because Universal scope objects are the weakest security principals of all the groups.

The following recaps common group use and management on Windows NT, which helps you understand Windows Server 2008 groups: On legacy NT domains, you create and work with two types of groups, *Domain Local* and *Global* groups. Domain Local, or just Local, groups are restricted to the domains in which they are created; they cannot be given entry into other legacy NT domains. Global groups, conversely, can be given entry into other legacy domains — and even Windows Server 2008 domains, for that matter.

Local groups can contain Global groups from the local domain and any trusted domain, but a Local group cannot contain, or nest, any other Local group.

Good management practice on legacy NT domains is to create Local groups as resource groups that access the domains as the primary security principals — almost as bastions, to borrow a Unix term. In other words, Local groups are the front-line containers holding the access and permissions control that users require to get to their resources. (This practice continues in Windows Server 2008 domains.)

If a collective of local users — or even one user — requires access to the resources in their "home" domain, you give them access or membership to the Local group. If a foreign group of users — that is, users from another domain — requires access, you give that Global group membership to the Local group. This enables you to restrict user access permissions to the local resource groups while retaining Global groups for intradomain access and organizational grouping.

The Global group is also a security principal, however, and is used to control access in the same way as the Local group. This capability has led many companies, especially those that have only one local LAN, to abolish the use of the Local group (except in the case of built-in groups) and make every group *Global*. Why worry about Local groups if Global groups serve both as security principals and as organizational "departments" into which members who do similar work and need the same resources can be assembled? Table 23-1 provides a list of scopes and their limitations.

Finding Global groups such as *Accounts Payable*, *Shipping*, and *Logistics* is not uncommon in many NT domains. Although you cannot do much harm in such management practice, Microsoft did not intend groups to function as tools of business administration. Enter the organizational unit (OU). We have touched on OUs but we need to discuss them here briefly in the context of managing groups and users. Organizational units are created to provide hierarchical administrative delegation, organizational structuring, and for setting Group Policy. Groups are used for granting and denying users access to computer and network resources. Global groups also traverse domain boundaries. A group can contain users and Global groups from other domains, both on a single domain tree and across a forest of domains. OUs are valid only on a contiguous domain space in the domain in which they were created.

TABLE 23-1

Group Scopes and Their Limitations

Group Scope	Members	Permissions	Nesting
Universal group	Can come from any domain in the forest. The members can be other Universal groups, Global groups, and users and contacts from any domain in the forest. Cannot host Local groups.	Can be granted on any domain in the forest.	Can be a member of any Local and Universal group in the forest.
Global group	Can come only from the owner domain. Can host other Global groups and users from the owner domain. Cannot host Universal groups.	Can be granted on any domain in the forest.	Can be a member of any group in the forest.
Local group	Can come from any domain in the forest. Can host Global groups and users and contacts from any domain in the forest. Can also host other Local groups from the owner domain.	Can be granted only by the domain owning the group.	Can be a member only of other Local groups in the owner domain.

Now that you have abolished the group role as an organizational tool, you need to be sure of its purpose in life. Instead of granting individuals access rights in every corner of the domain, you should instead grant them membership to certain access groups.

First creating a group with a predetermined purpose, such as "access to the very large label printer," is far easier. You would then assign security and management definitions to this group and assign any necessary permissions to the group. After the group is set up, you merely add a user to the group, and the group's restrictions and access permissions are added to the permissions that the user may have already applied elsewhere in other groups or individually and would override any weaker values assigned elsewhere. The first trait of a group is the permissions that are assigned to it. Permissions enable the users of a group to gain access to resources and information to which the group as a unit has been given access. In other words, the group permissions define the mode or level of access that members of the group gain.

Think of this in terms of classes on a plane. Businesspeople may join the First or Business Class to gain access to better meals, more room, and seating arrangements that can accommodate in-flight board meetings, room to work with files and documents, and so on. If a flyer does not have a First or Business Class ticket, she does not have access or privileges to any services paid for by the First and Business Class flyers.

The following list summarizes what you've learned in this section:

- Groups are mostly collections of user accounts.
- Users or members of groups inherit the blanket permissions assigned to a group.
- Users can be members of more than one group.
- Groups can be members of organizational units (OUs), which can be members of other OUs. Groups can also be members of other groups.

This flexibility offered by OUs and groups is somewhat dangerous, however, because it can result in an overnested organizational mess if taken to the extreme. You should plan this carefully, before you find that you can't see the forest for the trees.

The elements of groups

As do User objects, Group objects exist in two places in Windows Server 2008: in Active Directory and in the local registry. Groups are used for the following purposes:

- To manage user and computer access to network objects, local objects, shares, printer queues, devices, and so on
- To create distribution lists
- To filter Group Policy

In Windows Server 2008, you specify the purpose of the group as you create it. If the group is meant to contain security principals, you set it up as a security group. Otherwise, you specify the group as a distribution list containing contacts.

Windows Server 2008 groups operate identically to Windows NT groups but with more functionality. In fact, the underlying group technology has merely been elevated to the Active Directory level. Instead of adding individual users to resources (such as shares and device access), the best management policy is to add them to a group that needs the necessary access. Even if you have only one user who needs access to a sharepoint, create a group for that user. Do not fall into the habit of adding individuals to shares, because before long, you have these lonesome access cases spread all over the place, which is a security risk.

Installing predefined groups

Like legacy NT, Windows Server 2008 installs predefined groups as you install certain components or features of the operating system. You do not automatically get all the groups installed at the same time just by installing every service that ships with the OS. You do not see *Domain Admins*, for example, listed in the Users and Computers Snap-in until you create the first computer account. The following list defines the base built-in groups installed when you install the first domain controller and create a computer account.

Take some time to study this list and understand what each group bestows on its members. The groups are created for your convenience and serve broad purposes, but they represent a quick start to setting up a domain. Later, after your planning is underway (it is never complete), you can create new groups that serve security needs as tight as clams. These lists are not exhaustive, and you find many more groups listed in the Users and Computers snap-in. Many third-party applications also create additional groups that are specific to their applications. A good example is groupware applications such as helpdesk, CRM, and ERP applications. The following are a selection of the predefined groups, which are shown in Figure 23-10:

- **Administrators.** The only user account placed into this group at installation is the Administrator. You can add any user account to this group to immediately bestow wide access and power to the user.

  Administrators do not get access to everyone's files and folders by virtue of the wide power that they are given in this group. If a file or folder's permissions do not permit access, Administrator is also locked out. This ensures protection and enables owners or managers of sensitive shares, files, and folders to lock down their resources securely.

- **Users.** The local Users group is the default group for any user account created in Windows Server 2008. Do not confuse this group with the Users folder into which the Anonymous and Guest accounts are placed.

- **Account Operators.** This group gives wide administrative power to its members. Operators can create users and groups and can edit and delete most users and groups from the domain (permissions permitting). Account operators can also log on to servers, shut down servers, and add computers to the domain.

  Account operators cannot delete Administrators, Domain Admins, Backup Operators, Print Operators, Server Operators, or any Global or Universal groups that belong to these Local groups. They cannot modify the accounts of any members of the superior groups.

- **Backup Operators.** Members can back up and restore systems, but they can use a backup program only to back up files and folders. They can also log on to domain controllers and backup servers and shut them down.

- **Print Operators.** Members can create, delete, and manage the print sharepoints on print servers. They can also shut down print servers.

- **Server Operators.** Members can manage member servers.

- **Replicators.** This is not a group that contains human users. It contains only the user account used to log on to the Replicator service to perform replication functions.

- **Guests.** This is the built-in group that contains accounts for casual users or users who do not have accounts on the domain. Users in this group can usually log on without passwords, and they have very limited or controlled use of the system. It is an ideal group for service-based systems. Earlier in this chapter, we recommended moving the accounts from this group into a visitor's OU, which can be further secured with Group Policy.

FIGURE 23-10

Windows Server 2008's default built-in groups are created automatically on installation.

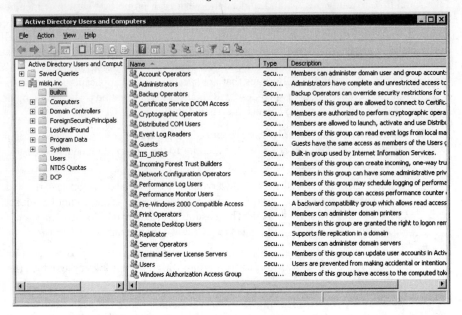

The following list presents the important Global groups. These automatically have membership in Local groups.

- **Domain Admins.** Use this group to provide administrative powers to administer the domain, domain controllers, and member servers and workstations. You can prevent anyone from accessing a member server simply by removing this group from the member's Administrators group. This group, by virtue of being a Global group, can be added to the Local groups in other domains and can be added to Universal groups.

- **Domain Users.** The Domain Users group is a Global group, so including every user in your domain in this group makes sense, regardless of the other groups they are in. You can then add this group to the Users Local group, and whenever you need to grant access to "all," simply admit the group to the object granting permission. We put "all" in quotes and did not use the term *everyone* for a good reason: The *Everyone* group that Windows admits to shares and folders by default means exactly that — everyone. If you create a user account from the command line by using the `net user` command and do not specify group destination or domain, the user is automatically sent to the Domain User group. The account is also physically located in the root of the domain, however, and not in any folder or OU. You can move it to a folder or OU after you create it.

The following list includes several "special" groups that are also created. These groups cannot be edited, disabled, or deleted, and do not offer the capability to add members. They can be removed from shares, folders, and permission lists but are not apparent in the Active Directory Users and Computers snap-in. Windows Server 2008 stores objects into these groups that need to be presented to the security subsystem:

- **Everyone.** This "group" means everyone that uses the computer and the network. By admitting this object to a share, you implicitly open all doors to the object, even if the user is an account on an alien OS on a far-away planet. If they exist, they can access your object. We believe that removing the *Everyone* group from your resource and using the Users group (containing Domain Users) is a better course. Anytime that you get a call to get someone out of an open share, you can simply knock the person out of the Domain Users or Users group.

- **Interactive.** All local users using the computer.

- **Network.** All users connected to the computer over the network. The Network group and the Interactive group are combined to form the Everyone group.

- **System.** This group contains specialized groups, accounts, and resources dependent on the operating system.

- **Creator Owner.** This group contains the owner and/or creator of folders, files, and print jobs.

Groups on member servers

There is another good reason why the Domain Admins group is a Global group: It can be admitted to the Local group on a member server (and even a workstation for that matter). As discussed, the domains created in the local machine environment are, for all intents and purposes, full-blown "domains" used to manage these computers.

The users and groups in the local domains work the same way they do in the network domains. After you attach a nondomain-controller machine to Windows Server 2008 domains, the Domain Admins group is automatically added to the member computer's Users group.

Another group worth mentioning on the local machine is the Power Users group. This group has a similar role to the domain's Domain Admins group, except that members of this group do not have total control. This setup enables the managers of these computers to keep tight control over the local users.

Nesting groups

Nesting groups is an efficient way of delegating the management of group membership. In native mode, you can create a Universal group and delegate the control over membership to an enterprise or senior administrator whose job it is to manage the membership of the Global groups. Global group administrators are the ones responsible for managing the membership of the Global groups ... granting membership to users or Local groups.

Nesting is useful in enterprises that are dispersed across geographical boundaries or that have built multiple domains. At MCITY, we have created a Universal group called GENESIS

DCP that contains the senior users from `GENESIS.MCITY.US\DCP`. In the example shown in Figure 23-11, the universal group `DCP.GENESIS.MCITY.US` has been nested into the `CITYHALL` Local DCP group.

FIGURE 23-11

Nesting in action: The local group DCP contains the universal group GENESIS DCP from the domain.

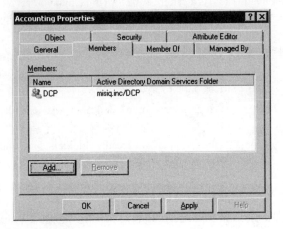

> **NOTE** Domains must be in native mode to nest security groups. The Universal group is not available in mixed mode. See the section "Mixed Mode versus Native Modes," later in this chapter.

Group creation

This section provides an example that demonstrates how to create a new group.

Run the MMC Users and Groups snap-in and double-click an organizational unit that you created earlier in this chapter. Navigate to the OU where you want to create the group. Choose Action ➤ New ➤ Group from the menu bar. This action opens the New Object – Group dialog box, as shown in Figure 23-12. The options in this dialog box are as follows:

- **Group Name.** This is the unique name that you give the new group.

- **Group Name (Pre-Windows 2000).** This is added for you automatically and is based on the name that you provided the new group. (You may need to provide a down-level name that differs from the Windows Server 2008 name.)

- **Group Scope.** The options here are Domain Local, Global, and Universal.

- **Group Type.** The options here are Security and Distribution. If you choose a group of type Security, the weak Universal group is not an option in a mixed-mode domain.

FIGURE 23-12

Creating a new group.

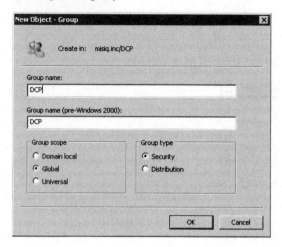

Enter the appropriate information into the fields shown in Figure 23-12 and click OK.

Setting up the group

After the group is created, navigate to the newly created group; right-click it and choose Properties from the pop-up menu. You can also just double-click its name in the list. By using the Properties dialog box for the group, as shown in Figure 23-13, you can specify the settings that you need to set.

General tab

This tab of the Properties dialog box for the group contains fields for the general information that you need to add to the Group object. You can also change some of the information that you added as you created the group, as described in the following list:

- **Group Name (Pre-Windows 2000).** Enter the legacy Windows group name here. If the name that you provided as you set up the group later causes problems, you can edit it at any time.

- **Description.** Enter a brief description of the group. What you enter here appears in the Users and Computers snap-in Description column.

- **E-mail.** Enter an e-mail address for the group. Any e-mail sent to the group is distributed to its members.

- **Group Scope.** These radio buttons enable you to change the group scope. If the group is in a mixed-mode domain, the Universal scope option remains disabled. You cannot change a group's scope from Global to Domain Local and vice versa.

- **Group Type.** These radio buttons enable you to change the group type.
- **Notes.** Enter text in this field to assist in the documentation of your domain objects.

FIGURE 23-13

Use the General tab of the group's Properties dialog box to enter or edit the base properties of the group.

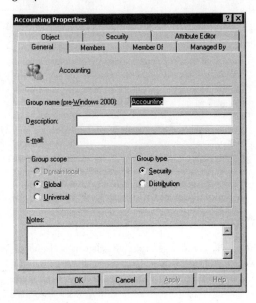

Members tab

The Members tab enables you to add members to the group. You can add computers, users, groups, and contacts to the Members list, as follows:

- **Add.** Click Add. The complete list of all objects that can be given membership to this group appears. Double-click a user, and the user's name is added to the list. Click OK.

Member Of tab

The Member Of tab provides a view of membership from the membership lists of other groups. It also enables you to join other groups, as follows:

- **Add.** Click Add. The complete list of all container objects to which this object can be given membership appears. Double-click the Users group and click OK.

Managed By tab

The Managed By tab provides a host of fields that identify the name, address, and contact information of the person who manages the group, but you change only one, as follows:

- **Change.** This is the only option that you can add or change on this tab. The other properties are inherited from the manager's User object. You can protect the object at the permissions level later.

More about adding users to groups

You can add many objects to a group. These objects, all called *group members*, can be users, other groups, contacts, or computers. Adding computers to groups has some interesting consequences for management. For now, however, we want to add only a single user account to a group of choice. To add members requires only a few steps. Simply select the group in Active Directory Management and right-click the selection. Then click Properties. The Properties dialog box appears and is labeled *YOUR DOMAIN'S GROUP* Properties. Select the Members tab and click the Add button at the bottom-left corner of the dialog box.

A second-level dialog box appears, named Select Users, Contacts, or Computers. Select the user. (Notice that you can "look in" several places or domains for the user account, and you can search the entire directory.) After you have located and selected the user account, click Add. Your user is now added into the currently selected group, as indicated in the Members list. You can select more than one user in the top list by pressing and holding the Ctrl key as you select usernames. You can also press and hold the Shift key and drag the cursor over the list to select multiple users. In this case, however, you are interested in only one user. Notice, too, that after you click Add, the accounts are listed serially in the Name field for confirmation. (This option really should have been a drop-down list.) Clicking OK puts them into the Object list at the bottom of the dialog box.

Managing groups

In Windows Server 2008, an individual or group can be delegated the task of managing users, or members, of specific organizational units. In our case, we are likely to assign the management of the GENESIS DCP group to the DCP manager, who also maintains the GENESIS DCP organizational unit. In addition, Group Policy is used to control the work environments of the users in these groups and OUs. The DCP group that we created may be refused access to the RAS, while another group that works remotely is granted access to RAS via the Group Policy.

You need to fully understand how Group Policy works, and what you learn here is insufficient to perform the task without making mistakes and needing to redo things. Only practice and a lot of experience, working with many, many users over a few years, can prepare you for the job.

Rights and permissions

The Windows Server 2008 security system controls access to network objects and protects network and machine-specific resources in two ways: through rights and through permissions. *Rights* are granted to users and groups (and don't forget that includes processes, threads of execution, and so on that operate in the context of a security principal). Many rights would not normally be exploited by a human user, such as the right to lock a file in memory, which prevents it from being paged out to disk. A thread of execution, however, requiring the capability to do so, would.

Permissions belong to the objects that are the essence of the operating system. With that bit of information in hand, you may be pleased to know that objects are given rights to perform certain things, but as objects in Active Directory, you need permission to manage them. The difference between rights and permissions has confused administrators for years. Whenever Windows Server 2008 enables you to do something on a machine or on the network, that is a right, making rights something granted to users. Rights, for example, include the right to *log on locally*, the right to *log on as a service*, and the right to *act as part of the operating system*. However, if you need to access an object in a defined way, you need to obtain permission. Permissions include being allowed to change objects, read them, execute them, delete them, and so on. A printer is a good example of an object that you need permission to use. Another way of looking at the difference is that rights involve the capability to function, while permissions control access.

Permissions are granted by both the file system (over its objects) and by the Active Directory (over its respective objects).

Rights come in two flavors: privileges and logon rights. They can be bestowed on individuals by enabling rights in a Group Policy object (User Rights Assignment and Logon Rights Assignment) and linking the object to the user account. Association does this, and it takes place whenever you place a user account into an OU. The user account can also inherit any privilege defined in the GPO of a domain or site.

Bestowing privileges and rights through group membership, rather than on an individual basis, is the best course. Whenever you need to remove a privilege or logon right, you need only remove the user account from the group.

Privileges

The rights bestowed to users and groups to provide them with the capability to perform certain functions in the computing environment are known as *privileges*. Privileges often override permissions, where necessary. A good example is the right to back up files and directories, which overrides any permission that denies access to a user. The Backup Operators group needs the capability to read and change (reset the archive bit or overwrite during a restore) the files that it is backing up, no matter what permissions the owner of the objects has. Table 23-2 explains the privileges, their purpose, and to whom they are assigned by default.

TABLE 23-2

Privileges and Predefined Groups

Right	What It Enables	Default Groups Assigned To
Act as part of the operating system.	Enables a process to operate as in the context of a secure or trusted part of the OS.	Everyone, Authenticated Users, Power Users, Administrators.
Add workstations to domain.	Enables a user to add workstations (computer accounts) to a domain.	Not assigned to a default group.
Back up files and directories.	Enables users to back up files and folders.	Administrators, Backup Operators.
Bypass traverse checking.	Moves between folders to access files.	Everyone.
Change the system time.	Sets the internal clock of the computer.	Administrators, Power Users.
Create a pagefile.	Enables the user to create a pagefile.	Not assigned to a default group.
Create a token object.	Enables a process to create an access token via the LSA.	Not assigned to a default group.
Create permanent shared objects.	Enables a user to create permanent objects.	Not assigned to a default group.
Debug programs.	Debugs low-level processes and threads.	Administrators.
Enable computer and user accounts to be trusted for delegation.	Delegates responsibility.	Administrators.
Force shutdown from a remote system.	Shuts down a remote computer.	Administrators.
Generate security audits.	Generates security audit entries.	Administrators.
Increase quotas.	Enables a user to increase the disk quotas.	Administrators.
Increase scheduling priority.	Increases the execution priority of a process.	Administrators.
Load and unload device drivers.	Installs and removes device drivers.	Administrators.
Lock pages in memory.	Enables a user to prevent pages from being paged out to `pagefile.sys`.	Not assigned to a default group.

continued

TABLE 23-2	(continued)	
Right	**What It Enables**	**Default Groups Assigned To**
Manage auditing and security log.	Specifies which objects can be audited.	Administrators
Modify firmware environment values.	Modifies system environment variables.	Administrators.
Profile single process.	Performs profiling on a process.	Administrators.
Profile system performance.	Performs profiling on a computer.	Administrators.
Remove computer from docking station.	Unlocks a computer from the docking station.	Administrators.
Replace a process level token.	Enables a user to modify a security access token.	Not assigned to a default group.
Restore files and directories.	Enables users to restore files and folders.	Administrators, Backup Operators.
Shut down the system.	Shuts down Windows Server 2008.	Administrators, Backup Operators, Everyone, Power Users, and Users.
Synchronize directory service data.	Enables a user to synchronize directory service data.	Not assigned to a default group.
Take ownership of files or other objects.	Enables the user to take ownership of all objects attached to the computer. This right overrides permissions.	Administrators.

Logon rights

Logon rights dictate how a user can log on to a computer or a domain. Logon rights are also bestowed in Group Policy. They are defined in the GPO and specifically linked to groups and users (preferably via group membership) through association with a site, domain, or OU. Table 23-3 explains the logon rights.

Mixed mode versus native mode

Your domains must be in *native mode* to use the advanced group features in Windows Server 2008. Specifically, you cannot create a Universal security group in mixed mode. (You can create only a universal distribution list, which is not a security principal.) You also cannot nest security groups in mixed mode, nor convert groups from one scope to another. This is a severe limitation, and you may want to consider promoting the scope as soon as doing so is feasible. Mixed-mode domains support Windows NT 4.0/Windows 2000 domain controllers (the legacy Backup Domain Controllers, or BDCs).

TABLE 23-3

Logon Rights and Predefined Groups

Right	What It Enables	Groups Assigned To
Access this computer from the network.	Enables a user to connect to the computer over the network.	Everyone, Authenticated Users, Power Users, Administrators.
Allow log on locally.	Enables a user to log on to a local machine at the keyboard.	Print Operators, Authenticated Users, Server Operators, Backup Operators, Administrators, Power Users, Account Operators.
Deny access to this computer from the network.	Revokes this right.	Not assigned to a default group.
Deny logon as a batch job.	Revokes this right.	Not assigned to a default group.
Deny logon as a service.	Revokes this right.	Not assigned to a default group.
Deny logon locally.	Revokes this right.	Not assigned to a default group.
Log on as a batch job.	Enables a user to log on by using a batch-queue facility.	Administrators.
Log on as a service.	Enables a security principal to log on as a service, which enables the process to operate in a security context.	Not assigned to a default group.

NOTE Before committing to new Windows Server 2008 applications, check with the ISV to determine what groups are required by the application and the features that it needs to use. Some applications may require you to promote the domain to native mode even if doing so is not practical for you.

The Zen of Managing Users and Groups

Managing users is demanding and requires an assertive personality in an administrator. Managing a small group of, say, 25 people may not be such a big deal (you think), but as the number of users grows, the task becomes more and more complex. Users depend on the network to get their jobs done, and the life of the administrator or user manager is a never-ending exercise in tolerance, assertiveness, concentration, and understanding. The less savvy are your administrative skills, the more you have your work cut out for you.

A good idea for any serious administrator is to take a course in *enterprise resource planning* (ERP), *human resources, customer relationship management* (CRM), *business management*, and *administration* in general. Understanding how the various departments function autonomously and in concert with the rest of the company goes a long way toward effective user management.

User management is not simply the task of enabling users to log on to a network. You need to provide access, protect resources, track utilization, audit activity, and much more. Setting up users and groups is often easier than managing them in the long term. Just moving a group from one domain to another can be a complex process, and if your company happens to absorb or acquire the IT department of another company, you could be saying goodbye to 40-hour weeks for a long time, especially if nobody knows who owns what shares, folders, files, and so on.

So where do you start? The preceding material in this chapter gives you a thorough understanding of Windows Server 2008 user and group architecture and how user and group accounts are created and deployed. With that information, you now need to plan the best way to use this information to manage your network. Every company is different, so you are the one who can best determine your own needs. You do, however, need to plan ahead and use common sense. We may suggest task lists as the best way to begin user and group management projects. Before you begin, establish the following protocols:

- Create an IT-HR/Windows Server 2008 physical workgroup to oversee new policy or changes in policy and change control with respect to user management and access to resources. The capability to create objects and delegate their management and control (down to the finest grain) to individuals, groups, teams, and project leaders can prove very beneficial but also very dangerous.

- Your team needs to consider new policy and the ramifications of delegated responsibility with respect to managing user accounts and the collateral services such as security, access to shares, devices, information, and other information-based resources.

- You need to set up new policy with respect to the delegation of control and management of objects. You need to decide at what level IT and MIS is prepared to give control to the department heads and group leaders and the people that they delegate.

- This team may be called the Directory Administrator's Team, with a leading figure such as the CIO or MIS in charge.

- Appoint a person (employee or consultant) to work with HR and analysts to establish or improve corporate structure. Many organizations are not remodeled or restructured for some time because few really care, but now you can involve IT directly in the corporate structure, especially as the Active Directory enables several teammates to collaborate on setting the corporate structure and model in the directory, as opposed to doing it on paper or in flowcharts and diagrams. The task ahead is to create organizational units based on the layout and scope of the entire organization.

- A term often used in business or corporate analysis is *Key Management Entity* (KME). Key Management Entities are all the key aspects of a business that need to be managed. Accounts Receivable, Accounts Payable, Materials Management, Shipping, QC, and QA are examples of KMEs. These KMEs can now be modeled in AD, inheriting directly from the models and structures typically associated with corporate analysis software and ERP technology (such as the likes of products from SAP and Baan).

- Appoint teammates who are responsible for migrating users to the new OUs and groups on a per-OU basis. If you are relocating users from Windows NT, these members need to be members of the old Domain Admins group. The problem many companies face is that shares and permissions are just dished out with no record of what groups, shares, user policies, profiles, file permissions, and so on are in place. This would need to be thoroughly documented. Adequately extracting information that documents the NT domain is almost impossible.

- Invite the people responsible for customer relationship management (CRM) to join the directory administrator's forum with a view to incorporating the help desk and the external environment into the directory. What if the group decided, for example, that setting up OUs for user groups (customers) may prove worthwhile?

Delegating responsibility

The best means of putting policy and change control under management is to involve the department heads and team leaders across the board. Several items in this regard need to be considered if you delegate:

- Do the respective department heads want the new responsibility? Do they carry sufficient weight to shirk the idea of managing their own groups? Do they carry sufficient weight to manage their peers?

- If policy dictates that they must participate, are managers behind the new initiative to enforce the policy?

- After the department heads have agreed to participate in the management of their own groups, do they need to delegate the function to a member who requires some training in managing?

Change management for users and groups is even more important under Windows Server 2008, because with the devolution of administrative power comes decentralization, even in a central location. Setting up a permissions request or user access request committee, consisting of members of HR, MIS-Security, and the network administrators, is thus worthwhile.

The teams or individuals responsible for new users (employees) should receive user and group account requests from HR after new employees are cleared. An e-mail or form is sent to the MIS-Security person responsible for setting in motion the steps to set up the user (that is, meet his basic needs) inside the organizational unit to which the user is assigned. Such a person is equipped with sensitive information about all various resources in operation at the company. This person is aware, for example, of what shares represent what on the Payroll server or how access is provided to the AS/400, the Remote Access Server, and so on.

Employees and team leaders can also motivate or request changes to the profiles and rights of the workers under them — for example, when a user is promoted or assigned new administrative functions. The user may now need certain Read-only rights changed to Full Control or rights to delete, copy, and move files. The requestors do not need to know what groups they are in. The HR manager's job is to help the department requesting a new employee clear the employee to work for the company and set the new employee up with all the resources that the person needs to do his or her job as efficiently as possible.

The MIS-Security checklist or account request and setup form may contain the following information:

- **User ID (logon).** An ID such as `jeffrey.shapiro@mcity.us`.
- **Password.** Made up according to a system or policy.
- **Devices.** Printers, drives, scanner, modems, and so on.
- **Share-points.** Folder or directory shares.
- **Applications.** For a discussion of policies and profiles, see Chapter 24.
- **Facility.** Help, training, setting up workstations, and so on.
- **Logon hours.** Regular hours and overtime.
- **Messaging.** E-mail, voice mail, fax mail.
- **Organizational Unit.** Assigned by HR.
- **Description.** Details the user's needs and any special circumstances.

After this list (which may be longer or shorter) is complete, it can be given to the network administrator or engineer responsible for user account creation in the respective organizational unit. This person does not question how or why the account is set up or what is assigned; he or she just creates the account.

Under the Windows Server 2008 domain, the preceding practice now takes place on a department or OU basis, as opposed to being enterprisewide or centralized under the control of a handful of techies. Requests from users and organizational units or departments should be directed to the help desk. A good idea is to use e-mail forms or an HTML form on the company's intranet Web site.

Of course, you can still appoint a single administrator to manage user accounts, but on Windows Server 2008, encouraging decentralized management makes sense (to a point, of course).

User and Group Management Strategies

The objective behind this section is to describe strategies that lessen the burden on the administrator. Starting with the management of groups and users, so much power is now in the hands of the Windows Server 2008 and domain administrators that, without care and forethought, becoming bogged down in a quagmire of administrative spaghetti is all too possible. As with many other management systems and technologies, you can abuse the power (such as that involving Group Policy, coming up in Chapter 24) and end up with a situation that is counter to the intention of order and sanity.

Keep your eye on TCO

TCO stands for *Total Cost of Ownership*. In a nutshell, it means that the total cost of a computer, a network, an application, or an entire IT department, for that matter, greatly exceeds the cost of its acquisition. After the asset is acquired, it must be managed and kept up, and all the functions that keep the system going contribute toward TCO.

Many habits of administrators can send TCO to the doghouse. A seemingly simple oversight can cause hours of downtime and cost the company thousands of dollars in consulting fees and technical support from Microsoft. Spending an excessive amount of money on support to resolve these issues is a good way to ensure that you are not around by the next service pack release.

Almost all the items that we discuss in the following sections affect TCO. The two basic considerations? Don't manage users, manage groups; and refuse new group requests.

Don't manage users, manage groups

Illogical user management contributes to the TCO bottom line, so where at all possible, do not manage the access and security needs and privileges of users on an individual basis. We already discussed this aspect of user management, but sometimes you may have no choice but to provide a user with "direct" access to a resource, without first putting that person into a group. If you do so, make sure that you keep that situation as temporary as possible. Then, as soon as you can, add the user to a group and get rid of the solitary assignment.

Refuse new group requests

You need to be as stubborn and assertive as possible regarding new group requests. Every time that you create a new group, you add to TCO in the following several ways:

- You add traffic to your network and systems. New groups require permission to access resources, they need storage space in the Active Directory, and they need to be replicated to domain controllers, global catalogs, and so on.

- Creating groups for every little need is a waste of time. If two groups need access to the same resource, such as a printer, why admit two groups to the resource? Keep one group and either add all users that need the same level of access to the group or nest the groups.

- You give yourself more work in documenting and maintaining the groups.

To lessen your load, first do the following before creating new groups:

1. Determine whether a built-in group can satisfy the need. Creating a group for every little device makes no sense. If a printer object admits everyone, for example, you don't need to create another group for it (unless you have specialized auditing or security needs).

2. Determine whether a group that you or someone else earlier created can suffice to meet the user's needs. Nine times out of ten, you can easily find several dozens of groups that have become redundant, because people create new ones without checking whether others exist that serve their purpose.

Determine the access and privileges needed

From the request form, you can generally determine the needs of the users or the group when deciding what group-creation or management action you need to take. If you find that you need to keep going back to people for more information, the forms are not working correctly or people are not complying with the protocols. In determining these needs, you need information concerning the following:

- **Access to applications and libraries.** If the applications are on the servers or users are Terminal Services clients, they need access to the shares and folders containing the applications. They also need access to policy and script folders, the home directory, specialized paths, connections (such as to SQL Server), and so on.

- **Access to data.** Applications and users need access to data: database tables, freestanding data files, spreadsheets, FTP sites, storage, and so on. Determine what data is needed and how best to access it.

- **Access to devices.** Users and applications need access to printers; communications devices, such as fax servers and modem pools; scanners; CD changers; and so on. All network devices are considered objects, and their access is also governed by permissions.

- **Communications.** Users need accounts on mail servers, voice messages boxes, and in groupware applications.

- **Privileges and logon rights.** Users need certain rights and power to perform their duties efficiently and in the shortest possible time.

Most of the time, requests are easily fulfilled: User X requires an account and needs to be placed in the B group for access to the C share. X needs e-mail and must have the capability to dial in to the RAS at any time of day or night and so on. This is not a difficult request, but if you get complicated requests, you need as much information as possible.

Determine the security level

The request form should be clear on the security needed over the user and the resources that the user is accessing. If the data is extremely valuable or very sensitive, you may need to consider auditing objects, tracking file and folder access, and so on. The extent to which you protect the resources depends on the needs of each organization. You may, for example, consider short-term passwords, restricting logon hours, restricting logon location, and so on.

Protect resources and lessen the load by using Local groups

The best practice in group management has been inherited from experience with Windows NT: First create *gatekeeper* groups, which are Local groups that control the access to resources and expose what needs to be exposed for broad and even tightly controlled purposes. Then nest Global and Universal (if in native mode) groups in the Local groups, providing a second level of access control and permissions.

The practice of creating gatekeeper groups also encourages a delegation of responsibility and a form of decentralized management that is still safe and not out of touch. Assign people who need to admit Global or Universal groups only as requested the responsibility of managing Local groups. Then assign the membership of the Global groups to the department or organizational unit administrators.

Delegate with care

Delegating with care is important. Over time, we expect that administrative power will become decentralized, but you still need to maintain a watchful eye over the "higher level" administrators. You may need to create admin groups for each OU where you have delegated responsibility, or create one OU admin group and manage the individuals via OU Group Policy.

Keep changes to a minimum

If you do a good job managing users and groups, you don't need to keep changing things around. The fewer changes that you need to make, the better. Remember, too, that every time you change something in the domain, the change needs to be propagated around the network to all the domain controllers. If you have a wide area network and your domain traverses geographical divides, constant changes can cause latency and costly delays while remote domain controllers lag behind in updates and replication.

Summary

In this chapter, you learned how the new User and Group objects in the Active Directory enable you to more cohesively manage users and groups on Windows Server 2008–based networks. You also learned how to create users and groups and best administer them.

We stressed using common sense in creating and managing users and groups and delegating responsibility. We move on to a more complex subject in the following chapter: managing the workspace.

Chapter 24

Change Control, Group Policy, and Workspace Management

This chapter discusses Group Policy, a collection of technologies that enable administrators to enjoy centralized workplace management and change control over workstations, servers, and services. Group Policy governs many aspects of the computing environment on a Windows network, such as security, communications, application delivery, and more.

Group Policy has been greatly enhanced in Windows Server 2008 (changes that were incorporated into Vista even before the server OS had been released). These include the following:

- New categories of Policy Management (some of which are discussed in this chapter). Internet Explorer can now be totally managed through GP and you no longer need to shell out to extensions kits or hard edit the registry.

- New format and functionality of the administrative templates. The format changed to XML in 2007 and the templates are now known as ADMX files as opposed to the old ADM format. The ADMX format has been further enhanced in Windows Server 2008 and Vista.

- Policy application is no longer reliant on the PING protocol (ICMP) and GP instead uses a new technology called Network Location Awareness. This means start-up and processing times are more efficient and GP can be applied through firewalls that filter out ICMP.

- GP has been decoupled from WinLogon and is now applied via a service. The service is responsible for applying the settings you configure, so extra care is needed to ensure the service is always operational. The service approach is long overdue, however. Like all services, it can be secured, monitored, and managed far better than previously under Windows XP and Windows Server 2003 and earlier.

What Is Change Control?

Change control is simply the capability to control change. As you are aware, nothing remains in stasis; even stasis itself "constantly" changes. For network administrators, the capability to control change at the desktop and at all layers of the network is critical. Without the capability to control change, serious network and work interruptions are inevitable.

During the writing of this chapter, one of our clients almost lost a small fortune in business because of a lack of change control. Our client is a small insurance broker (only five people). One of the brokers, Dave, writes marine insurance, and on a fine, cool January day in Florida, he got the break that the company was waiting for — an order for a policy to insure a $10 million yacht . . . the premium would be a killer.

He returned from the marina shaking and shivering, realizing that he was about to write the policy of his career. The commission would be staggering, and from this, many more deals would flow. You get a name for writing big policies such as this. Nothing would stand in his way . . . nothing but his faithful workstation.

Dave likes to fiddle with his computer. Whenever he is not looking for insurance business, he likes playing around with his desktop settings, fonts, resolution, and more. Dave lives in the Control Panel more than in his apartment. We had maintained a "loose" change-management policy in this company. In other words, we maintained minimal desktop control because Dave was the only wild card and was considered an advanced user. The company had been our client for several years, and we had never had an issue with users changing anything that could cause a problem.

On the day that Dave needed to write up his policy, his desktop went berserk. He logged in to his workstation as usual, but after he opened the insurance application, the application began to tremble and then the session froze. If you know insurance, you know that if you cannot write the policy, the client makes another call. Dave was getting ready to jump off the jetty with an anchor around his neck.

We jumped in and disabled Dave's account, and because we were deploying the Windows Desktop and Agency software applications through Terminal Services, we could get Dave back to his policy writing in record time. He admitted that he had changed his font again, along with "some other things" that he could not remember.

The client learned a lesson and decided that no employee (all four of them) could tamper with the applications or desktop sessions, but we learned a bigger lesson. Change control is as important for our small clients as it is for the big ones. It cannot be ignored anywhere.

Change control on Windows NT and other server environments has been lacking since the invention of client-server. Policy and profile maintenance is possible on Windows NT and Windows 9x desktops, but it is not secure, and users can override settings with little effort. A Windows NT workstation/server environment is more secure, but change-control empowerment is still lacking.

Windows 2000 and Active Directory changed all this in late 1999 with the introduction of *Group Policy*. Group Policy governs change-control policy for many facets of the operating system, including the following:

- Hardware configuration and administration, including power configuration and management

- Client administration and configuration (desktop settings, logons, connection, and more)

- Operating-system options and policy, such as IntelliMirror, remote OS installation, and network location

- Application options and policy (such as regional settings, language and accessibility, deployment, and more)

- Security options and policy

- Network access

This chapter doesn't cover every detail of creating and managing Group Policy objects, because the Windows Server 2008 Help system adequately handles that, but we do show you how to take control of the change-control issue, apply security policy, and more. Before we get to that, we describe the science and philosophy of change control and management.

Understanding Change Management

In the highly complex worlds of information technology and information systems, the only constant is change. The more complex and integrated that IT systems become, the more important having change control becomes. Managing change has thus become one of the most important MIS functions in many organizations. If you do not manage change, the unexpected results of an unmanaged change could render you extinct.

Processes, routines, functions, algorithms, and the like do not exist in vacuums or some form of digital isolation from the rest of the universe. Just as in life, all processes depend on or are depended on by other routines or processes. If you change the way that a process behaves, you alter its event course. In other words, you alter its destiny. Altering the event course of a process is in itself not the problem. Problems arise if processes dependent on a particular course of events are no longer afforded what they were expecting.

Think about how you feel and are inconvenienced when a person that you were going to meet does not turn up or cancels the engagement unexpectedly. In software and computer systems, such events can have catastrophic results. They in turn fail, and their event courses are also altered. Whenever processes begin to crash, an unstoppable domino effect takes place, leading to systems failure and disaster from one end of the system to the other. This is why troubleshooting is such a difficult exercise: The best troubleshooters are those who look beyond the evidence of failure and seek to discover what caused the problem or what event led up to system failure.

In addition to the example in the preceding section, when Dave's job was almost toasted, following are other examples of change control shortcomings:

- The FTP service on a server is turned off. AS/400 connections expecting to find the connection up cannot transfer route information to a network share. A process that was expecting the information to be in the FTP folder cannot calculate the daily routes for orders that need to go out. The trucks do not arrive, and the orders are not established or shipped. Clients place more than $10 million in business elsewhere.

- Norton AntiVirus causes a domain controller to hang because its update feature results in a memory leak that gradually starves the DC to death. The result is that authentication on the network comes to a halt and servers begin to drop like flies.

- A software engineer makes a change in source code that introduces a bug into the process pool. Programs begin to collapse because the receiving data function does not know how to deal with data.

- A user downloads new software from the Internet onto his company's notebook computer. The new software contains a backdoor virus that silently attacks the notebook's anti-virus suite. It inserts a replacement file into the anti-virus software and causes the software to reload the old inoculation data file, which is akin to taking an antibiotic that has expired. After the user connects back to the corporate network, the hostile code moves to the network servers and does the same thing. After it's on the servers, the virus shuts down the company systems, and the company almost goes insolvent as a result.

These examples sound far-fetched, but they are not. We have seen three of them on our own networks. Such is the need for change control. In fact, the unit of time in which no change takes place is too small to be studied by humans.

In short, you must control change; moreover, you must manage it in such a way that the effects of change are planned for and that all dependencies are informed and enabled to compensate whenever change occurs. No change can take place unless the proposed change is put to a board of change management for consideration, the consequences of the change are fully investigated, and the change is deemed necessary. Because change is always inevitable, another factor affects change control — contingency planning, of which disaster recovery is a part.

In the past, problems caused by unmanaged change affected standalone systems. Because computers were previously islands and isolated, the effects of the change were local and confined. After people started to network, change-control problems began to affect the global corporate or organizational environment, but the effect was — and still is to a large extent — confined to the corporate or enterprise information network.

In the world of e-commerce, however, change control has become critical, because any change that causes an unplanned-for, new course of events affects the external environment, where systems crashes can have catastrophic results and cause untold damages and liability. In the world of Internet banking, for example, a change-control disaster can affect many people who have no relationship with the bank, in addition to its innocent account holders.

In Chapter 25, we discuss service level and quality of support. As you know, more and more people are signing service-level agreements that guarantee availability of systems at all times. These agreements must be covered by effective change-control management.

The change-control or change-management board reviews all changes and, based on the board's research, consultation, and findings, a change request is either approved or denied. (In the companies that we consult for, all change-management approvals must be signed off by the officer in charge.)

However, problems arise if you have a fully functional board and compliant team leaders but no means of enforcing change-control policy at all levels of the enterprise. To figure out how this all comes together, you need to take a look at change-control conceptually. The respective parts of change-control or change-management systems resemble the justice system, or at least the enforcement parts of it. They include the items listed in Table 24-1.

To better understand where in the information-systems environment change control needs to be enforced, consider the change-control stack shown in Figure 24-1.

TABLE 24-1

Change Control

Description	Purpose
Change control board	A group of people in an organization responsible for reviewing change requests, determining validity, deciding change of course or procedure, and so on. This board also determines regulation and enforcement protocol and deploys change-management resources.
Change management	Functions to manage signed-off or approved change or contingency. Change management may include lab tests, pilot projects, phased implementation, incremental change, performance monitoring, disaster recovery, backup/restore, and so on.
Change control policy	Rules and the formulation thereof governing change control and management.
Change control rules and enforcement	The enforcement of policy and the methods or techniques of such enforcement.
Change control tools	On Windows 2000 to Windows Server 2008 networks, these include local security policy to protect machines, Group Policy to enforce change policy throughout the forest, security policy throughout, auditing, change request applications, and so on.
Change control stack	The change-control "stack" comprises the various layers that are covered by change control.

FIGURE 24-1

The change-control stack.

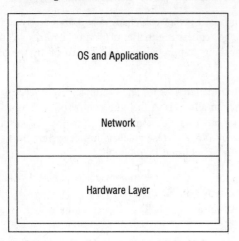

OS and Applications
Network
Hardware Layer

At the bottom of the change-control stack (CCS) shown in Figure 24-1 is the *hardware (physical) area*. The objects in this layer that you place under change-control enforcement are hardware, computer components, and hardware requirements. The following list provides an idea of what is covered by change control at the hardware or physical layer:

■ Hardware compliance with the existing infrastructure

■ Hardware acquisition and determination of hardware needs

■ Technology deemed necessary or not

■ Protection and security of storage and access to media (such as FDDs and CD-ROMs)

■ Protection of network-interface cards

■ Access to memory and system components

■ Availability and stability of hardware device drivers

■ Hardware problem abandonment point. (When do you give up trying to fix a part or computer and buy a new one?)

■ Parts replacement (such as procedure for replacing media, and so on)

■ Hardware availability (such as RAID, clustering, load balancing, and so on)

Next up is the *network layer*, which encompasses change control on the data link, network, transport, and session layers of the Open Systems Interconnect (OSI) model.

NOTE According to Newton's Telecom Dictionary, the Open Systems Interconnect (OSI) model of the International Standards Organization (at www.iso.ch) is the only accepted framework of standards for interconnection for communication between different systems made by different vendors. The OSI model organizes the communications process into a system of layers. OSI has become the foundation model for many frameworks in both software and computer hardware engineering. The OSI model is also referred to as the *OSI stack*.

The following list includes areas that are targets of change control at the network layer of the CCS:

- Security needs (encryption, IPSec, access to routers, circuits, hubs, and so on)
- Quality of service
- Network bandwidth
- Topology
- Transport technology (for example, Ethernet, SNA, Token Ring)
- Routing, bridging, switching

As you get higher up in the CCS, the number of variables begins to increase. (You have more opportunities for change and thus change control, because you are getting into the area where the user lives.) The following list includes areas that are targets of change control at the operating systems and applications layer of the CCS:

- Logon/user authentication
- Network services
- File systems and storage
- Network protocols
- Device driver installation and version control
- Device operation
- Application services
- Disaster recovery services
- Internet/intranet services
- Media services and telephony
- File transfer
- Sharing and access control
- Virus protection
- Directory services
- User levels/access to resources
- Communications
- Desktop configuration (menus, shortcuts, icons, access to folders, and so on)
- Access to information (such as access to the Internet)
- Cultural and regional options

- Accessibility (the ease of access to computing resources, specifically to people with handicaps)
- Access to software/applications
- Access to data

Not only are more factors or "opportunities" for change control in this top layer, but it also is the most vulnerable of the layers. Although certain parts of the operating system and the lower layers provide a barrier to entry because of their complexity, change control should not be any more lax or less important. The more obscure the service is, regardless of the layer on which it resides, the higher the risk of a skilled attacker doing undetectable and lasting damage. The biggest threat to the stability or health of IT/IS systems, however, comes from users. Most of the time, the problem is just a case of "curiosity killed his computer" (remember Dave?), but users also generate security threats, introduce viruses, download hostile applications (most of the time unwittingly), and so on.

The user

The term *user* rarely refers to a single biological unit. This is why you have security groups, as discussed in Chapter 23. As soon as you define or categorize the levels of user groups that you need to support in your organization, you can enforce change-management procedures on those groups.

If you are involved in client management, you should make an effort to become a member of the change-control team. You should also get to know your users, the type of software and applications that they need, and how they work with their computers, treat their computers, and interact with their computers.

You have two main types of user or worker, as described in the following list:

- **Knowledge workers**. Your knowledge workers are usually the workers who are applying a particular skill set or knowledge base in their job. These people are your engineers, technical-support people, accountants, lawyers, designers, and so on. Knowledge workers usually have a permanent office, and they use their computers for most of the day. Because their machines are constantly in use, losing them would be costly for the company. They can be considered advanced users.
- **Task-oriented workers**. These workers are data-entry personnel, receptionists, office assistants (to varying degrees), order takers, and so on. Most of these users would not need more than a terminal and a terminal service account to perform their duties. These users can be considered your basic users.

The computer

The two main types of users are further broken down into the following categories (by computer resource used):

- **Stationary (office) workstation user**. These users (usually knowledge workers) do not need a notebook computer because they need the machine only at work. The machine is usually a small-footprint workstation running Windows Vista or Windows XP Professional.

- **Remote workstation user**. This worker connects to the network from home or a remote office across a WAN connection or modem. These users still use a fixed desktop computer because they do not move around.

- **Notebook/docking station user**. These users use their computer at work *and* at home. The user is usually accommodated with a docking station at home and at the office, which makes connecting and disconnecting from the network easier.

- **Multi-user workstation**. This computer does not belong to any specific user. Users making use of this resource are usually guests, users who move around from location to location, temporary staff, shift staff (such as call-center or customer-service representatives), and so on. This computer is also known as a *kiosk*.

- **Mobile computer**. This computer is usually a notebook or laptop computer, sans docking station, that spends most of its life in a carrying case stuffed inside the cubby of a jetliner. Mobile users can either connect to the office from the road (such as a hotel or conference center) or from branch locations where they can connect to the corporate network.

In each of these cases, you need to establish workstation and user-management policy for each type of user and computer. Further tagging your users as advanced or basic in the literacy level of computer usage often makes more sense than dumping them in one group. We have had knowledge workers who caused endless problems for the administrators and basic workers who should be writing software instead of using it. We return to the subject of how much power to give users in the section "Workstation Lockdown" later in this chapter. First we need to deal with the issue of applications.

Create a list or database of these categories. In each category, list a computer name and a user-name. Take, for example, the following list of mobile computers:

- Mobile Computer Accounts
  - MCPD98
  - MCPD99
  - MCPD100
  - MCPD101
- Mobile Computer Users
  - Henry R. James
  - Catherine H. Anderson
  - Jill J. Smith
  - Michael F. Wolf

Taking Control

You, the network administrator, have control over a number of critical areas. The three main areas are easily identified according to the following high-level network administration areas:

- **Applications**. This area is one of the most important to put under strict change control. Users must in no way, shape, or form install and manage their own software.

- **Security**. To maintain a secure network, you need the authority to set security policy or to enforce the policy required by the business owners at both the servers and the workstations.

- **Operating-system environment**. Our modern operating systems, such as Windows 2000 and Windows XP, are extremely complex. Management and control of these systems and their myriad configuration needs to be firmly in the hands of experienced network technicians, support personnel, and administrators.

These three areas merely encapsulate what amounts to thousands of possible management scenarios. We discuss each one in more detail in the following sections.

Applications

What's the big deal about enabling users to obtain and install their own applications? First, users really do not understand (for the most part) software piracy laws and how easily they can run afoul of them. Many people borrow software from friends and family, often unaware that they are committing a felony that carries a penalty of as much as 20 years in jail.

Falling victim to software piracy laws is very easy. All that's necessary is for one disgruntled employee to report that your company steals software, and the ensuing raid by the software piracy police makes an IRS raid seem like Sunday at the church fund-raiser.

If application usage is managed by the IT department and only technical-support people can install software, the risk is greatly reduced. Software metering and strict adherence to licensing requirements can keep the CEO or CIO out of jail.

Enabling users to install their own software can cause administrative burdens to go through the roof. Most users do not understand the changes that an operating system undergoes whenever software is installed on the operating system.

Software should also be distributed from a central location or server. This practice saves technicians from needing to make the trip to the users' desktops for the installation. Remote software deployment or electronic software distribution goes a long way toward keeping administrative burden to a minimum.

To protect your company from extensive application support and administrative burden, users need to use only the applications that are approved or sanctioned by the company. The best way to manage this approach is to create groups or collections of users and assign to them various applications. These groups and collections can be named after the applications that the members use, such as Office07Users and AcrobatUsers.

For each user, you need to create another list that specifies what software and hardware that user requires to perform his or her functions. You create two lists. The first is for basic users who need no more than the standard applications adopted by the enterprise. If your company has adopted Microsoft Exchange 2007, for example, Outlook 2007 and later is on that list, as is MS Word, Excel, and other applications (if, of course, the company has standardized on Microsoft Office components, which is very common).

A second list next to the first one is an advanced-user choice list. These users (if policy permits) can choose a specialized list of software for which they must justify deployment. This justification, by the way, is presented to change control or management for review. A good example is a software engineer who is hired to create a certain application. She then requests that a development tool or component be installed or made available to complete the task.

Managing software is a daunting task for anyone. In a small organization, one person can typically be saddled with the job of managing anywhere in the region of 10 to 20 applications. In large companies, the number of software components can run into the thousands. Defining and enforcing policy regarding installation and configuration of applications is thus critical. Consider the following problems that may occur if you permit users to install their own applications:

■ The application may be unstable and could damage existing systems. During the early beta testing of Windows Vista, for example, a technical-support engineer at one of our clients installed the Release Candidate code for SP1 on his workstation to check it out. The code corrupted his workstation and shut him down for several days.

■ Applications may not be legally obtained. If you do not enforce change-control policy, your enterprise may be risking lawsuits and criminal charges. You cannot claim ignorance of users using illegal or pirated software. Your boss goes away for 20 years or more if your users steal software.

■ The act of installing the software can introduce viruses and security risks to the network. If the user installs from a source on the Internet, the download may bring with it hostile applications. We have seen backdoor viruses pop out of downloaded zip files and kill a machine in less than a minute.

■ Users are likely to run into problems and come to you for help with an application that you know nothing about. (Isn't it amazing how the network or server administrator is expected to know everything about every application that has ever been invented?)

Another category in addition to applications is *application management and configuration*. This involves determining and managing the deployment process, local and remote installation, configuring the software, user education, user support, and so on. Windows Server 2008 provides some services to manage automatic deployment and configuration.

Security

Like application management, security must be managed centrally. In fact, whenever you join a workstation to a domain, any security settings that you apply or enforce at the local workstation level are overridden by domain security settings.

Security policy needs to govern and enforce issues such as password usage, lockouts, and attempts to crack passwords by using elimination processes. If users maintain short passwords that never change or that can be easily figured out (such as the names of their dogs), before long, an intruder can learn the password and do some damage.

Other security policies that you need to manage centrally include public keys, certificates, digital signatures, and so on. What a user can and cannot do on the workstation or at a server is also important. The capability to log on to a domain controller, for example, is a privilege that only a handful of administrators should have.

Operating-system environment

The operating system is a complex piece of machinery, and it is becoming more complex to manage as software and hardware become more sophisticated and powerful. Consider the Windows Vista operating system: Tens of thousands of settings and preferences can be set on it.

For your own sanity, all workstations in the enterprise must be managed as a single unit — or at least in only a handful of variations.

You should strive, for example, to make sure that all workstations have the same screen-saver settings — usually the corporate logo — and that users do not have the capability to change the corporate screen saver. If you don't, before long (a few days at the most), you can count on having as many as 20 different screen savers in use. Not only can the custom screen savers be doing damage (especially if they are freebies found on the Internet), but some may also be downright offensive. A few years ago, some male users in a company were downloading screen savers that portrayed a female in an offensive manner. A sexual-harassment lawsuit ensued after the requests to remove the screen saver were ignored.

You don't want users constantly changing display settings, fiddling with network devices, and installing hardware that can damage the computer systems.

Workstation lockdown

Of course, the capability to centrally control and manage your user's computing experience can also be too powerful for some situations. Certain classes of users may need more administrative control over their work environment.

Remote users on notebook computers that connect to the network for no more than 30 minutes a day may need more privileges to manage their own computers than do users who work from the office.

Although roving notebook users should possibly be permitted to set their own printer drivers and configurations, because they typically move from one printer to another during their sojourns, this does not mean that they should have the capability to change their network-device settings. Remote notebook users rarely need to set static IP addresses, and the DHCP stuff that they receive at each site is sufficient for them.

You find many settings in the Control Panel, however, that users rarely need to modify. Leaving these locked down until the user comes into the office and the notebook is handed to the technical people for a tune-up is usually sufficient.

Getting ready for change-control policy

You now have a lot of information with which to determine how best to lock down workstations. The following list recaps what you know, or should know, before you enter the world of the Group Policy creators:

■ You should know what type of user you support (basic to advanced or technically inclined).

■ You should know the category of workstation that the user needs (mobile, workstation, handheld, and so on).

■ You should know what applications are required and how they are used (usage level). For example, is the user advanced or basic? If the user is given Access 2008, can he wreck Access 97 databases?

■ You should know the list of applications that your classes of users need.

In addition to the preceding list, understand the following information before you begin to determine how best to enforce policy:

■ Have users logged on to their computers as the local administrator or as a member of the local Administrators group? (This is common practice on workstations where logging on to the domain is not always possible or desirable.) If users can access the local account and registry, they may circumvent change-management policy. Decide which users fall into this category and which may be candidates to obtain a Windows XP or Vista desktop or session. Then ensure that these workstations have a local policy that as far as possible shadows Group Policy.

■ Do your users install their own unauthorized software on their computers? If you do not have a policy to control this scenario in an enterprise, you need to formulate one as soon as possible.

■ Do your users store data on their own workstations? If they do, you need to devise a strategy to have them move the data to network sharepoints or folder resources published in Active Directory folders. Understand that the data is at risk in such a practice, because workstations are not typically backed up, which means that data can be lost if a computer crashes or is stolen. A feature of Windows 2000 and Windows Server 2008 called *folder redirection* is a way of ensuring that a user's documents or data folders reside on the server where the data is backed up. You find more information about this in the section "Types of Group Policy," later in this chapter.

■ How often do users call with "broken" workstations or desktop configurations? A broken configuration is usually the outcome of a user trying to install his software or hardware on the machine. Another form of broken configuration results from users tampering with the operating systems, fiddling with registry settings, modifying Control Panel applets, and so on. The problem often stems from users who have a false sense of confidence because they have mastered a home computer. They then eschew policy that strips them of that power at work. Only your administrators — and only a few, at that — or power users who are testing software as part of change-management board activity, however, should have such rights over the enterprise or corporate computer property. The risk of a change causing damage to the workstation or network services is too high to entrust that level of control to users who consider themselves "kings of computers."

Users also need to use the Internet wisely and in a way that does not compromise the enterprise. Although you can trust some users to do just that, you also need power and tools to ensure that users use the Internet only according to the organization's business rules. You can and should control Internet Explorer use and enforce proxy-access rules, browsing preferences, and so on.

Windows 2000 and Windows Server 2008 security is extremely powerful, but unless you can extend the security to workstations and ensure that users follow corporate requirements and business rules with respect, your life as a network or workstation administrator can prove very frustrating (and short).

Understanding Group Policy

The change-control tool on Windows Server 2008 is the Group Policy Management console (GPM console or just GPMC.MSC from the command line). Shown in Figure 24-2, this application is an MMC snap-in from which policy can be applied to the security principals — computer, users, and groups — of a Windows Server 2003 and Windows Server 2008 network.

FIGURE 24-2

The Group Policy Management console snap-in.

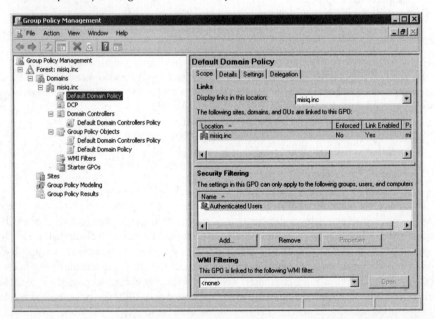

Group Policy, which gets its name from the idea of grouping policy, can be applied to items such as security management and hardware configuration.

Group Policy is applied by creating an object that contains the properties that extend control of the computer and the user's access to network and machine resources. This object is known as the *Group Policy Object*, or *GPO*. The policy is created from various templates stored on the workstation or server.

If an object is a member of a container that is associated (linked) to the GPO, that object falls under the influence of that GPO. If a container is linked to multiple GPOs, the effects of all GPOs on the linked container are merged, as illustrated in Figure 24-3.

FIGURE 24-3

Multiple Group Policy Object policies merge to affect the container.

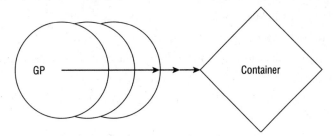

NOTE   Sophisticated object-oriented engineering is at work in the GPO application process. The Group Policy architecture is complex, spans hundreds of pages, and is beyond the scope of this book. It is, however, well worth studying if you are an engineer at heart, because such advanced knowledge can only make you a better server or network administrator. You can search for the GPO architecture papers on the Microsoft Web site by searching Microsoft's white papers.

Group Policy is not applied directly to an individual security principal (although you can attain such granular control by creating specific OUs). Instead, it is applied to collections of security principals. Security principals gather under one roof on a Windows Server 2008 network in three places: the *site*, the *domain*, and the *organizational unit*. Because GP applies to all three types of containers, you can refer to this as a *GP hierarchy*.

Group Policy is vast and extremely powerful. It takes some getting used to and you need to spend a lot of time trying different things. In large companies, the role of managing GP should be assigned to individuals, possibly members of the change-management board. Managing GP can easily become a full-time occupation for an administrator. GP becomes your main technology with which to manage change, user configuration and desktop settings, workstation lockdown security, software installation, and so on.

GPOs have more than 100 security-related settings and more than 700 registry-based settings, and the GP technology can also be extended or enhanced with certain APIs and custom templates. Specifically, GP technology provides you with the following functionality:

- The GPO is configured and stored in Active Directory. GP can also be defined at the local level — that is, at the workstation. Standalone computers are secured or locked down with local policy, and we provide more information about that in the section "How Group Policy Works" later in this chapter. GP, however, depends on Active Directory.

- You apply GPOs to users and computers in AD containers (sites, domains, and OUs).

- The GPO is secure. You can lock down a GPO just as you can any other object in the operating system.

- The GPO can be filtered or controlled by membership in security groups. This, in fact, speeds up application of policy for the membership of the security group.

- The GPO is where the concentration of security power is located on Windows networks.

- The GPO is used to maintain Microsoft Internet Explorer.

- The GPO is used to apply logon, logoff, and startup scripts.

- The GPO is used to maintain software, restrict software, and enable software installation.

- The GPO is used to redirect folders (such as My Documents).

- The GPO does not expose the user profile to tampering if policy is changed, as was the case with Windows NT 4.0.

- GP settings on the computer are not permanent. Unlike older technologies for management or locking down workstations, the registry is not permanently tattooed. The settings and configuration can be lifted at any time and easily changed.

Types of Group Policy

Group Policy has influence over just about every process, application, or service on a Windows network. Both servers and workstations are influenced by GP, so unless you deploy Windows Vista or Windows XP, or Windows Server 200X, GP is *not* pervasive throughout the enterprise. Windows 9x and NT 4.0 workstations are not influenced to the same extent as Windows 2000/XP/Vista clients, because client-side extensions that pull down and read policy are not present in these legacy desktop operating systems.

A network consisting of many different versions of Windows (in some cases, as many as five), therefore, is also going to be less secure or at least not as manageable. Obviously, a hard-to-manage or hard-to-control network is going to be a lot more expensive to maintain in the long run. The initial cost of upgrading to Windows Server 2008 throughout the enterprise pays off in the long run. In terms of security, such as the capability to stave off a hacker thanks to encryption or the capability to save critical data thanks to folder redirection — and we could give you many more examples — not only can you save a bundle by going "native," but you may even save the company as well. The more versions that you eliminate, the more secure and more manageable life is going to be for you.

You can have many different types of Group Policy "collections." (The term *policy collection* is not a Microsoft term as far as we know, but it is useful for describing the policy types.) The following list describes the "intent" of these collections:

- **Application deployment**. These policies are used to govern user access to applications. Application deployment or installation is controlled or managed in the following ways:

  - **Assignment**. GP installs or upgrades applications and software on the client computers. The assignment can also be used to publish an icon or shortcut to an application and to ensure that the user cannot delete the icon.

  - **Application publication**. Applications can be published in Active Directory. These applications are then advertised in the list of components that appears whenever a user clicks the Add/Remove icon in the Control Panel.

- **File deployment**. These policies enable you to place files in certain folders on your user's computer. You can, for example, take aim at the user's My Documents folder and provide her with files that she needs to complete a project.

- **Scripting**. These policies enable you to select scripts to run at predetermined times. They are especially useful for ensuring that scripts are processed during startup and shutdown or whenever a user logs off a machine and a new user logs on to the same machine. Windows Server 2008 can process VB scripts, JScripts, and scripts written to the Windows scripting host.

- **Software**. These policies enable you to configure software on user workstations on a global or targeted scale. This is achieved by configuring settings in user profiles, such as the desktop settings, Start menu structure, and the other application menus.

- **Security**. Perhaps no other collection in Windows Server 2008 is as important as the security policies, given that the next hacker who wipes out the assets could be the kid next door.

In addition to *eventually* reducing the total cost of ownership (through lowering the cost of administration), you should consider that Group Policy has other roles. It exists not to create problems for users and administrators, but to secure the environment and enhance the work and user environment. You thus need to make sure that you have the wherewithal to balance the two needs; if you don't, you could end up with cold pizza instead of glazed sirloin for dinner.

In your endeavors to secure the environment, you no doubt come across conflicts that violate the tenet to maintain a "user-friendly" environment. Going wild on password length is a good example. If you set password length too long to increase security, users not only get peeved, but they also start sticking the passwords on their monitors because they are so hard to remember. That is not security. If you must have tight security, your best option may be to take the security need to management and suggest smart cards or biometrics. Remember that locking down an environment should not lock out the user at the same time.

The environment can be enhanced in many different ways. If users need access to new software, you need to determine which of the following three methods of delivery is more pleasing or enhancing to the user from the user's perspective:

- Waiting hours or days for the administrator to show up at your desk with the new software

- Being asked to log on to a network distribution point and install the software yourself

- Taking a break while the software mysteriously installs itself onto your machine with seemingly no human intervention

Enhancing the users' environment also means helping them easily locate applications, intelligently redirecting folders or mapping their folders to resources, and automating processes during the twilight times of the workstation — namely, at logoff and logon.

Before you study how Group Policy works, take some time to familiarize yourself with the technology.

The elements of Group Policy

A programmatic discussion of the Group Policy elements is beyond the scope of this book, but understanding the various elements with which you interact is a good start. Several components make up GP from the administrator's perspective, including the following:

- The Group Policy Object
- Active Directory containers
- Group Policy links
- The policy of Group Policy (such as the Group Policy refresh intervals)
- Explain text, which elaborates on the objective of the policy
- The Group Policy Editor
- Computer Configuration and User Configuration nodes
- GP Containers and GP Templates
- The gpt.ini file

The Group Policy Object

The *Group Policy Object*, or *GPO*, is the object that contains Group Policy properties. The GPO is really a container, at the highest level, into which properties or attributes are stored. Policy is conveyed by association with a GPO — that is, its properties "rub off" on a user or computer object contained inside a GP recipient. GPOs must be created and named before their policies can be used.

Active Directory containers

Active Directory containers are the default targets of the GPO. In other words, the contents of a container to which a GPO is linked receive the Group Policy settings by default. By establishing a link with a GPO, a container falls under the influence of the GPO and its policies. This happens automatically if you create a GPO. The containers that can be linked to GPOs are *sites*, *domains*, and *organizational units*. However, GP can also be associated with a standalone computer; and all computers can be linked to their local GPO.

Group Policy links

GP links are the means by which containers are associated with GPOs. You can research links for a particular domain, as discussed in the section "How Group Policy Works," later in this chapter. By "discovering" the links, you can establish which GPO is influencing a particular container and therefore, its members.

The policy

The *policy* is the *property* of the GPO. The policy is the actual setting that is applied through the association as discussed in the section "Active Directory Containers" earlier in this chapter. All GPOs have the same policies. You do not add or remove a policy from a GPO, but policy is activated in several ways. The policy first must be *defined* and then possibly *enabled* or *disabled* or otherwise activated in the particular GPO or applied to a security group. After it is enabled or defined, you can then manipulate the settings that comprise the policy.

Figure 24-4 shows a policy that needs to be defined before it can be made useful. We have chosen to define a policy for the DNS server. After the policy is defined, you can set its startup criteria. In this case, we have defined the DNS server and set its startup parameter to *Automatic*. Other policies require you to simply enable or disable the policy, whereas others require definition, enabling, and then further configuration or setup.

FIGURE 24-4

Defining a policy.

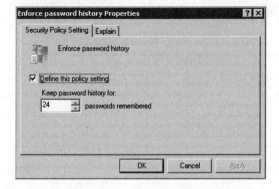

Explain text

The *explain text* is accessed on the Explain tab of a policy, also shown in Figure 24-4. Not all policies have an Explain tab. Explain text essentially describes what the policy achieves, any instructions related to applying the policy, and even circumstances in which you *shouldn't* apply the policy.

The Group Policy Editor

The *Group Policy Object Editor* (GPOE) is the Microsoft Management Console (MMC) snap-in that provides access to the configuration of a GPO. To edit or create a GPO for a container, you first must load a used or new GPO into the GPOE. The GPOE is shown in Figure 24-5.

FIGURE 24-5

The Group Policy Management Editor, showing User Rights Assignment expanded.

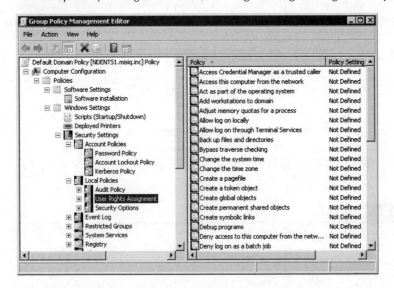

Computer Configuration and User Configuration

A GPO is divided into two nodes, known as the *Computer Configuration* and the *User Configuration*. Each node contains the policies for the respective security principal. You can apply policy to either of the nodes for any GPO.

Where GPOs live

All GPOs store their information in two locations: the *GP Container* (GPC) and a *GP Template* (GPT). These objects are identified by a globally unique identifier (GUID), which keeps the objects in the two locations synchronized. After a GPO is born, information associated with it is transferred to the two locations.

For the GPT, the OS creates a folder for its use in the `Sysvol` structure in the `systemroot`. The actual folder name of the GPT is its GUID. A typical GPT folder looks as follows:

```
%systemroot%\SYSVOL\sysvol\genesis.mcity.us\Policies\{31B2F340-016D-
11D2-945F-00C04FB984F9}
```

The GPC lives in the Active Directory. It builds itself a hierarchy of containers in the space that it is given in the directory in which to store computer and user configuration information.

The GPC deals with the version (used for synchronization), status (enabled/disabled), and settings (of extensions), and any policy settings defined by extensions. The SYSVOL side of the GPO holds a list of client-side extensions, user configuration settings, computer configuration settings (`registry.pol`), and registry settings that derive from administrative templates.

As a general rule, policy data that is small and seldom changes is stored in the GPC, and data that is large and changes often is stored in the GPT.

Group Policy Template structure

The default contents of the Group Policy Template structure are security related, but as you configure the user and machine environment, the GPT structure begins to fill up with folders and information related to a broad range of GP and change-management information.

Table 24-2 lists some of the folders and information that find their way into the GPT structure.

TABLE 24-2

The Group Policy Template Structure

Folder	Purpose
\ADM or ADMX	This holds the ADM or ADMX files that are associated with a GPT.
\MACHINE	This holds the `registry.pol` file that relates to machine registry settings.
\MACHINE\APPLICATIONS	This holds the AAS files used by the Microsoft Windows Installer.
\MACHINE\DOCUMENTS & SETTINGS	This holds files that are used to configure a user's desktop whenever the user logs on to this computer.
\MACHINE\MICROSOFT\WINDOWSNT\SECEDIT	This holds the `gpttmpl.ini` Security Editor file.

continued

TABLE 24-2 *(continued)*	
Folder	**Purpose**
\MACHINE\SCRIPTS	This contains the startup and shutdown folders.
\MACHINE\SCRIPTS\STARTUP	This holds scripts and other files related to startup scripting.
\MACHINE\SCRIPTS\SHUTDOWN	This holds scripts and other files related to shutdown scripting.
\USER	This holds the registry.pol file that relates to user registry settings.
\USER\APPLICATIONS	This holds the AAS files used by the Microsoft Windows Installer.
\USER\DOCUMENTS & SETTINGS	This holds files that are used to configure a user's desktop.
\USER\SCRIPTS	This holds logon and logoff scripts.
\USER\SCRIPTS\LOGON	This holds scripts and other files related to logon scripting.
\USER\SCRIPTS\LOGOFF	This holds scripts and other files related to logoff scripting.

The gpt.ini file

In the root folder of each GPT, you also find a file called gpt.ini. Two important entries in this file are related to local GPOs:

- Version = x. This entry is the version number of the GPO, where x is the placeholder for a number specified by a version-counter function. Typically, the version number is zero-based, and each time you modify the GPO, this counter is incremented by 1. However, this number is a decimal representation of an eight-digit hexadecimal number (a DWORD), which is the data type the group policy processes understand. The four least significant digits represent the Computer Settings version number, and the four most significant digits represent the User Settings version number. In other words, if you see Version = 65539, the computer understands this as hexadecimal 0X00010003, which tells it that the Computer Settings version is 3, and the User Settings version is 1.

- Disabled = y. This entry refers to the local GPO and tells the dependent functions whether the local GPO is disabled or not. If you disable the GPO, the value placed here is 0; and if you enable it, the value is changed to 1.

How Group Policy Works

The Windows Server 2008 Group Policy (GP) application hierarchy is typically site first, domain next, and then OU. In other words, if GP is set for a site, all objects in that site feel the effects of the GP, including the domain and all its members. If you then apply GP to a domain, the merged GP for all objects in the domain is inherited from the site and the domain. If you further apply GP to an OU, if GP is set for the domain and the site, the GP on any object in the OU is a combination of all three.

In other words, the combined control in the OU may be derived from the domain policy and the site policy as well, unless the inherited policy is expressly blocked by a built-in override mechanism that can be enabled or disabled (discussed in the section "The Policy" later in this chapter) and the access-control mechanisms on groups and users.

You can also force policy directly on an object by linking the GPO to the object and then setting the link to forbid overriding.

Local or nonlocal Group Policy Objects

Group Policy Objects also come in two flavors — *local GPOs* and *domain-bound GPOs* — and because the local GPO is applied to a computer before the domain GPO, the actual inheritance hierarchy for a computer is local GPO, nonlocal site, domain, and finally OU. Local GPO is first applied to the computer, and then any policy that is to be applied from the DC takes place after the user logs in.

What happens to the policy that is applied to the computer? Group Policy application is successively applied. In other words, the last policy that is enabled for a setting is applied, so if a local policy is defined and a site policy undefines it, then the site policy setting wins. If the domain setting then defines the setting again but the OU policy undefines it, then the setting is undefined and does not affect the objects that are affected by the GPO. In this example, the OU policy wins over all others.

For a local GP, if the setting is undefined from on high, then the local policy wins. To keep your network secure while ensuring that users can continue to work, to some extent, with their computers, you should set up local policy as though no domain policy were forthcoming.

One part of GP, however, always wins over local policy, and that is the security policy from the domain. Security policy always overrides local security policy, even if the local security policy is stronger. If no security policy is defined at the domain level, the security policy at the local level remains undefined. You can test this by running a report for a Resultant Set of Policy. Each Windows computer has only one local GPO that governs it. You can open the local GPO by running `gpedit.msc` from the command line on any Windows Server 2008, Windows 200X Server, and Professional or Windows XP/Vista computer, or you can pull up the MMC snap-in from installed menu items. (To customize the MMC, refer to Chapter 2.) Remember that a nonlocal GPO can override the local GPO. More about this is coming up in the following section.

Group Policy application

The architecture of Active Directory dictates that policy applied later to an object overrides policy that is applied earlier. In other words, if you remove the rights that enable a person to log on to a computer locally in the local GPO and then later restore that right in a site or domain GPO, the restored setting becomes the effective control because it was applied later — possibly even last. The exception is that anything not defined does not change the existing control, and any control specifically enabled or disabled earlier persists.

> **TIP** Any GPO control state that is disabled or enabled in an earlier container persists, but if something higher up is undefined, and then, at the local level, it is defined, the defined setting survives. This is useful for controlling access and certain security mechanisms on individual computers, where specifically disabling an option prevents an administrator from enabling it unintentionally or on purpose at the nonlocal (domain) level.

You also can create multiple GPOs for a container. The order of control application specifies that policy applied later overwrites policy applied earlier. In other words, if you have two GPOs to an OU, any settings that say "yea"; in the first GPO in the list are then overwritten by GPOs that say "nay" later in the list. This is called *administrative order*, and the order can be rearranged by using the Up and Down arrows in the Group Policy Management console, as shown in Figure 24-6.

FIGURE 24-6

Applying the GPO link.

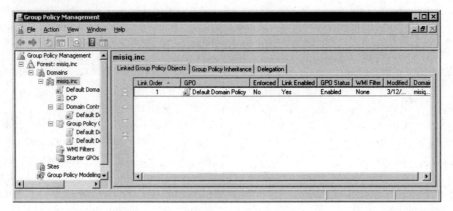

If you set Enforced on a GPO by right-clicking the policy, GPOs that are linked at the lower levels cannot override the higher GPO's effective settings. The use of Enforced also prevents GPOs that are linked at the same level from overriding. If several links at the same level in the AD are set to Enforced, you need to arrange them according to a priority that you determine. Links that are higher in the list have priority.

Understanding priority in applying GP to a domain or even to a site is important. You want numerous settings to remain in force, and a local administrator may attempt to override you. As long as you set the Enforced on the higher GPO, the setting that you enable is enforced at the lower levels of the directory.

The Enforced setting is applied to a link, rather than to the actual GPO. The Block Policy inheritance setting is applied to the domain or OU, and it thus applies to all GPOs linked at that level or higher. Sites do not have a higher authority.

Conversely, you can also block inheritance of GP from higher GPOs. You do this by checking Block Inheritance on the domain or one of its OUs. This option does not apply to sites, because in terms of GP, they are the highest in the hierarchy. There is a catch (just when you thought you found a security flaw): the Enforced option — if enabled — takes precedence.

Whenever you edit a GPO, any settings that you change are not immediately applied to the container's possessions, but the change in policy is immediate. The GPO settings are then applied to the object by default every 90 minutes. The refresh time can be changed, however, as described in the section "Group Policy Refresh Rate" later in this chapter.

Conflicts can possibly arise from the application of GP. An account lockout, for example, can occur if you set the number of attempts at a logon password too low. If a user gets the password wrong several times in succession, which can easily happen if the user has the Caps Lock key on, you need to reset the lockout post haste.

An account lockout could be the result of several security policies doing what they were supposed to do but with unintentional results. To unlock an account in such a case, open the Active Directory Users and Computers snap-in and right-click the user account. Select Properties from the menu. On the Properties page that appears, select the Account tab. You see that the Account Lock Out checkbox is selected. The OS did this in compliance with GP. Deselect the box, and the user can now log in (as long as the Caps Lock key is off).

TIP Although the GP of a parent container can override a child's GP, if the child's GP contradicts the parent, then the child prevails. Rather than create a tug of war between the override, inheritance, and access control associations, strive to keep things simple, and fully document all GP, group memberships, and any peculiar associations.

Filtering policy

GP can also be filtered out of the range of security principals residing in security groups. In other words, you can narrowly define which security group of users or computers is influenced by GP, irrespective of the relationships the group has with an OU. This is achieved by setting the discretionary access control list (DACL) permissions on the group. Not only does the GPO take effect on the security principals much faster, but you can also restrict a specific security policy from creating AD links to GPOs.

The DACL is a list of permissions on an object (in this case, a GPO). You use the DACL to permit or deny access to the GPO according to membership in the group. You can apply the filter in either of the following two ways:

- Right-click the root node of a Group Policy Object in the GPOE it is open in; then choose Properties from the pop-up menu. The Properties dialog box loads. Select the Security tab, which shows groups and users and their associated permissions.

- You can also open to the container in Active Directory (site, domain, or OU), right-click it, and choose Properties from the pop-up menu. Then click the Group Policy tab on the Properties page that appears and select the GPO in the GPO list. Right-click the GPO, choose Properties from the pop-up menu, and then select the Security tab on the dialog box that appears. (You can also simply click the Properties button to get to the same destination.)

Now you can specify which groups are influenced by the container by checking or unchecking the Apply Group Policy access control entry (ACE). You should also know that, by default, authenticated users have both the Apply Group Policy and Read permissions checked but not Write or Full Control. What this means is that users cannot modify the GPO, enabling you to apply more stringent access to it.

These techniques also enable you to use the Security tab on the GPO to determine which administration group can modify GP. We use such techniques to tighten the security of our domain, as demonstrated in the section "Security at the Local Group Policy Objects" later in this chapter.

Delegating control of GP

GP can be delegated as follows:

- Delegate GP link assignment for a site, domain, or OU (link GPOs).
- Perform group policy modeling analysis.
- Read group policy results data.

Delegation is further performed through the delegation of rights to use MMC consoles and particular management snap-ins related to GP. These are themselves controlled through GPOs. To delegate access to GPO duties, you essentially control who has access to the Group Policy MMC snap-ins. The path to this is as follows: Expand the container in the GPMC. Select a GPO or, if one is not yet created, make one. Click Edit to load the Group Policy Management Editor. Expand the User Configuration node of the Group Policy Object to Administrative Templates ➤ Windows Components ➤ Microsoft Management Console ➤ Group Policy. Under the Group Policy node, you'll find several folders and policies related to Group Policy snap-ins.

Administrators can administer Group Policy by being a member of a domain administrator group or the built-in administrators group. Non-administrators must be given *log on locally permission* before they can administer GP, which is done by expanding Computer Configuration to Windows Settings ➤ Security Settings ➤ Local Policies ➤ User Rights Assignment ➤ Allow Log On Locally. Enabling many people to log on to the DC is not very secure or wise; your best bet is to assign Active Directory tools, such as the Active Directory Users and Computers tool, which invokes the Group Policy Editor console, to network administrators or the help-desk consultant's workstations. Given the appropriate rights, these administrators need never enter the server room and camp out at the DC.

Security at the local Group Policy Objects

The local GPOs that exist on every Windows Server 2008 machine have only security settings configured (and most of them are disabled). The local GPO is stored in the %SYSTEMROOT%\SYSTEM32\GROUPPOLICY directory. The following permissions are set through the DACLs:

- Administrators (Full)
- System (Full)
- Authenticated Users (Read and Execute)

How Group Policy is processed

Group Policy is almost entirely processed from the client side. The only service using GP that processes entirely from the server is the Remote Installation Service, and that's because a client-side OS does not yet exist to process policy.

A group of DLLs called *client-side GP extensions* performs client-side processing after first making a call to a DC for a GPO list. The processing order is obtained from the GPO list. The rule of precedence in processing is that computer configuration gets preference over user configuration. What if a user is placed in one OU and his computer is placed in another OU? Which GPO becomes the effective GP conveyor? I suggest putting all your users into a small collection of OUs and then placing their computers into other OUs that can be associated with key management entities (KMEs).

The following GP behavior attempts to keep a sanity check on things. A feature known as the *Group Policy loopback* enables you to bestow GP based or dependent on the computer used. The loopback feature enables you to choose two modes by which you can govern the choice of user or computer configuration.

Merge mode

Whenever a user logs on to a computer and the loopback feature is in *merge mode*, the GP objects are read according to the user configuration and then again according to the computer configuration. By reading in the computer configuration last, the computer configuration is given priority, so the computer-related GP has a higher precedence than the user's GP. If the user's specific GP is not affected by the computer's configuration, the user-configuration policy is applied.

Replace mode

The *replace mode* forces GP to ignore the user's GP configuration. In other words, only the GP in the computer configuration applies.

The merge mode and replace mode setting, as well as all GP processing options, can be toggled in a GPO by selecting Computer Configuration ➢ Administrative Templates ➢ System ➢ Group Policy.

GP processing streams

GP processing can be performed asynchronously or synchronously. Asynchronous processing can occur on other threads, and thus the processing happens much quicker. Synchronous processing threads wait for one process to complete before they start. You can customize the behavior of GP processing, but you would consider this only for specialized applications in which you need to apply the GP as quickly as possible. The rule is that, for speed, use asynchronous processing; for reliability, use synchronous processing.

Although the latter rule worked well for Windows 2000, the Windows XP and Vista operating system muddies the GP pool a bit. Windows XP and later are designed to start up fast when GP is applied asynchronously, and thus it can start up too fast. Users may therefore be on their desktops and working before all policy is applied. Have no fear, because that does not mean that while your user is working, some policy, such as folder redirection, comes along ten minutes into a document edit and whips the word-processing file away from the user's fingertips. Some policies — and folder redirection is one of them — are not processed synchronously.

One annoying issue with asynchronous processing is how software distribution is affected. If you assign applications to workstations, you may need to force the user to log on and off numerous times before the software policy takes root and the software is installed. This is not a cool scenario if your idea of software distribution is that the software is installed now and not after the user logs off for the whole morning just to pick up another new application.

Group Policy refresh rate

The default refresh rate is every 90 minutes. Thus, any changes made to the GP that apply to a particular user or computer become effective only during this default period. You can change the default by using the GP setting in Administrative Templates. A setting of zero forces the refresh to kick off every seven seconds. You would configure a narrower refresh interval for tighter security application or for a specialized processing situation. The default refresh rate seems long and can be shortened to at least 60 minutes.

> **NOTE** Setting shorter refresh intervals causes increased network traffic, and very tight intervals on user computers can interfere with the work environment. Very long refresh intervals are easier on the network but result in a less secure environment. The longest time is 45 days, and if you need to make a security policy change, such a time would be useless.

To change the setting, you need to edit the Default Domain Controller's GPO. This is linked to the DC's OU. Open the GPO and select the Computer Configuration node of the GPO. Then select Administrative Templates and expand it through System and Group Policy until you arrive at the Group Policy Refresh Interval for the Computers node.

> **TIP** On several domain controllers that we installed, the refresh policy was disabled. You may want to verify that this is not the case on your DCs. The documented DC refresh rate is five minutes.

Administrative GP settings, such as Folder Redirection and Software Installation, take place only during or after the computer starts up or after the user logs on, and not during the periodic refresh period described earlier in this section. Obviously, you would not want software to start removing itself while a user was still using it.

Optional Group Policy processing

Every client-side extension has a policy parameter for controlling the processing of GP. By default, the client-side extension updates the GP only if it determines at the refresh interval that the GP has changed. This is done for performance optimization, but for security purposes, you can make sure that at every refresh interval, GP is refreshed even if the policy has not changed.

Be very selective when using this setting, because you see increased network bandwidth and slower GP refresh as a result.

Group Policy processing over low bandwidth

Group Policy sets a flag on the client-side extension if low bandwidth networks are detected. If the flag is raised, the following GP processing takes place:

- Security policy is always processed.
- Policy in Administrative Templates is always processed.
- Software installation is skipped.
- Scripts are turned off.
- Folder redirection is skipped.
- Internet Explorer maintenance is turned off.

How does GP detect low bandwidth? The client-side extensions simply ping the DC and analyze the response data. However, low bandwidth is relative. What's low to you and me in Miami could be as fast as blazes in the Land of Oz.

Using a built-in algorithm, GP works out the response rate based on data and time parameters and the connections being used. If the result of the calculation is equal to the 500-Kbps default, GP considers that a slow link and makes the necessary adjustments in GP processing. You can change the default as you deem fit in the Group Policy options of the GPO. The exact policy is *Group Policy slow link detection*. Remember to set this for users as well in the User Configuration node. The target policy in User Configuration is identical.

User Profiles also have a timeout policy over slow links. This is located in the Computer Configuration node, and the target policy is the Logon node of the GPE. If the extension cannot ping the server, it defaults to measuring file-system performance, which is how NT measures performance. The policy can be configured for a connection speed threshold in Kbps and a threshold transit time in milliseconds.

We are currently administering a domain in which hundreds of Windows XP workstations have been scattered around the U.S. They have been configured to receive policy over a 32-Kbps connection once a day. So far, they are not complaining.

Specifying domain controllers for GP

In setting up your Active Directory infrastructure, you need to make sure that GP settings are correctly propagated and disseminated throughout the enterprise and that replication is not a course for corrupted GP information.

You have several considerations. If you support a small enterprise that usually contains one DC on the same network as everyone else, you should not need to concern yourself about where GP is edited. In a large enterprise, you may want to studiously control the target DCs for GP changes and who has the capability to make such changes.

We have discussed how you can delegate (or restrict) power to edit GP; you can also determine which DC is the target to receive the changes. Problems can occur if you have more than one DC receiving GP edits and more than one administrator applying changes. Your GP edit may become overwritten during replication, and you could suffer GP editing collisions. In addition, depending on the location of the DC, it may not always be accessible for GPO editing and creation.

You have two options for setting domain controller behavior for GP. One way is via the GPO Editor snap-in. The other way is via GP settings that enable you to set DC options by editing policy in the Administrative Templates node.

To access the setting in the former option, you need to open the Default Domain Policy in the GPOE and then select the root. Choose View ➤ DC Options from the menu bar. The dialog box shown in Figure 24-7 appears.

FIGURE 24-7

Choosing the domain controller to receive changes.

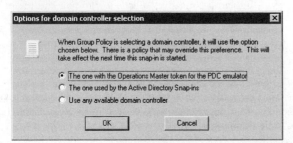

The dialog box contains three options. Choose the option that best applies to your network environment, as follows:

- **The One with the Operations Master Token for the PDC Emulator**. This is the default option according to Microsoft documentation, but we have found that isn't always the case, especially if you have more than one DC on the same network segment. This option ensures that only one DC is the target for GPO creation and editing, however, and that the other DCs receive GP updates from one source. This option forces the console to use the same DC every time that you or someone else uses it, which is why the option is part of the console and not the snap-in in the first place. You should limit the number of people that can apply GP in a certain domain, or you should schedule the GP tasks as part of change management. (The DC with the Operations Master token is usually the first DC created for a forest, but it can abdicate this honor when forced to.)

- **The One Used by the Active Directory Snap-ins**. Snap-ins include an option that enables you to change the DC that is the focus of the snap-in. (All MMC consoles enable you to choose a computer.) As long as you are sure that you are "aimed" at the right DC, this option works, but if you don't pay attention to detail, this could become a problem down the road.

- **Use Any Available Domain Controller**. This option is the least desirable but would suffice in a situation where you're working with a close-knit group or cluster of DCs on a fast network.

The option that we prefer overrides all the preceding ones . . . by setting the option in GP. The GPO makes sure that all snap-ins select the primary domain controller emulator for a domain in editing a GPO.

You can also use the policy to specify how GP chooses the domain controller. In other words, you can specify exactly which DC should be used by setting the option as policy.

To configure the correct settings, open the default domain GPO as just described and in User Configuration, select Administrative Templates ➤ System ➤ Group Policy. The options in the policy are the same as the ones demonstrated in the DC Options dialog box shown in Figure 24-7 and discussed earlier (although the various help texts describing these option vary). The exact policy is called *Group Policy domain controller selection*.

Putting Group Policy to Work

As discussed in the section "How Group Policy Works" earlier in this chapter, two key areas of GP and change management are *software change control* and *security*. These represent two main areas in change control and change management, which are serviced by the GP technology of Windows Server 2008.

The software policies

The software policies include policy to manage applications and Windows Server 2008 and its respective components. In the following examples, we demonstrate the modification and manipulation of the settings and environment by using the GPE snap-in.

889

To edit software GPOs, follow these steps:

1. Open the GPM console snap-in and go to the site, domain, or OU in which you want to locate your GPO. (These are often referred to as the *SDOU containers*, which stands for *S*ite, *D*omain, or *O*rganizational *U*nit container.)

2. Right-click the container and choose Edit.

3. Expand the User Configuration node from its root through Administrative Templates and Control Panel to Display. In this example, you are going to set a policy by disabling the Background tab so that the user cannot change the pattern and wallpaper on the desktop. The policy that does this is called "Prevent changing wallpaper."

4. Right-click the policy to modify it and then choose Properties from the pop-up menu.

5. Check to determine whether the policy is implemented, defined, or enabled. If it is not enabled, define or enable the item by checking it. Then choose the setting for the policy. Click Apply and OK to get back to the console.

That's all that making a simple policy change involves. You may notice as you browse the software-related policies that some of them require you to add more details, such as the path name and similar information.

Security policies

These policies govern the extent of the security configuration of Windows Server 2008 networks and are exposed under the Security Settings node in the GPM console. Security GP is available for deployment at every port that poses a security risk to the system as a whole, such as logon/logoff, communications, file systems, hardware and media, and so on. (For the complete list of policies open the GPM console).

Table 24-3 describes the GP related to security areas.

TABLE 24-3

Security Group Policy

GP	Purpose
Account Policies	These policies configure passwords, account lockout, authentication, Kerberos, and so on.
Local Policies	These policies configure auditing, user-rights definitions, and so on.
Event Log	These polices configure the Event Log.
Restricted Groups	These policies govern group membership for security-sensitive groups. The built-in Administrator group is an example of a restricted group.
System Services	These policies configure security and the default startup behavior for services running on the computer. (Refer to Figure 24-4, which provides an example of applying policy on a service.)

TABLE 24-3 *(continued)*	
GP	**Purpose**
Registry	These policies configure security on the registry keys.
File System	These polices configure security on the file system.
Active Directory	These polices configure security on directory objects in each domain.
Public Key	These policies configure the encrypted data-recovery agents, trusted certificate authorities, and other parameters related to your public-key infrastructure or PKI.
Wired Network (IEEE 802.3)	These policies govern wired network administration.
Network List Manager	These policies govern network location.
Wireless Network (IEEE 802.11)	These policies govern wireless network administration.
Software Restriction	These polices govern how software is used, trusted, and managed on the network.
Network Access Protection	These policies configure policies related to network access protection (NAP).
Windows Firewall with Advanced Security	These policies are used for configuring the Windows firewall.
IP Security	These policies configure policies related to IPSec.

Group Policy and Change Management: Putting It All Together

The number-one rule of change-control policy engagement is this: *Change control policy is enforced over the user by way of the computer.* In other words, the target of change control is the user's computer.

If you can enforce change policy over the computer, you are effectively enforcing the policy over the user. If a user has no control over her computer, she is no longer in a position to circumvent policy. Although the GPO is divided into two configuration nodes, user and computer, the computer configuration takes precedence.

CAUTION With the power that GP yields, all the elements of Windows — access control, GP inheritance, GP override blocking, GP refreshing, GPO links, OU nesting, domain nesting, and more — you can potentially cook up a GP soup that no one can fathom, so take care in the planning stage.

Restricting a user to any particular computer becomes impractical. Terminal Services sessions are impossible to manage, and you have a hard time managing computers for roaming users and task-oriented staff. Therefore, the user's identification to the network, or logon ID, *and* the workstation's identification on the network are merged to provide the change-control "blanket" that filters rights and privileges, thus controlling the user on the computer that he uses.

This power is not only a boon with security and change control, but it is also the main player in the functionality of IntelliMirror — having the user's desktop follow him to any PC, local or remote. After you have determined that you need change management and control, you also need enforcement. In other words, you create the change-control body, provide policy to carry out the whims of the change-control board, and enforce change control at all levels of the enterprise through GP (and other mechanisms that you find and customize to suit your environment).

Don't accept the default policy

In dealing with GP, it's unsafe to assume that whatever Microsoft has installed as default Group Policy is adequate. Believing that the default settings are adequate is foolish for several reasons. First, every enterprise is different, so what you set in GP may work for you but not for the company around the corner. Second, the criteria that Microsoft has used to set the default GP is not widely known and is not appropriate for the majority of users (and we don't think that Microsoft intended that either). Third, in many cases, what Microsoft documented as the default was found not to be the actual default after we installed and tested the services and components.

Where then do you start with GP? You can follow the cowboys who have stated that planning is for politicians and that the best way to tackle a Windows network is to just install it and to heck with all this ramp-up, pilot-project, testing, lab tripe. Or you can take the more conservative approach and perform testing and validation. You may find a place for yahoo-type antics. If you need to get a server up and running just to use a particular service as soon as possible, you can get away with the install-and-run approach.

What we recommend is that you go back to the lab and browse GP. This is probably the best method of getting to know it; and at the same time, you find out how the server is configured from the time that you reboot it, after Active Directory promotion.

Without worrying about desirable change-management policy for now, open the GPE of your new domain controller and start at the top of the directory. Starting with the site, work your way down through each container in the SDOU hierarchy and investigate the GPO links that are in place (refer to the section "How Group Policy Is Processed," earlier in this chapter) by opening the Properties page of the container and selecting the Group Policy tab. Edit each link that you see in the container and then investigate the settings defined or enabled in each object, in both User and Computer Configurations.

At the birth of a new domain, any settings are unlikely to be blocked or overridden in any way, so you can safely assume that the policy that has been set up for the site into which you have placed your root DC filters, down to the "bottom" of the directory. In other words, any OU that you now create inherits from higher up. The domain, of course, is in the middle of this hierarchy, so you need to investigate the GP that is applied at the domain level to determine what effects that may have on your desired control at the OU level. Each domain created gets a default domain GPO. Study the information and document it on your help desk or change-management system. If you do not have a change-management system, even a database or word-processing document works — it may get unwieldy eventually, but for now it serves the purpose.

Establishing a GP attack plan

We discussed OU strategy and groups and users extensively in the previous chapter, but before you start, first sit down with the policy required by change management and security and separate policy required from one end of the forest to another from policy that is required from one end of a domain to another. If only one domain is in the tree, this process should not take long. This research does not need to be exhaustive because the list is going to change and get very much longer.

With that Global Policy wish list, you edit the GPO first for the site in which you have located your root DC — the one that sits at the very top of the namespace in the twilight world between the Active Directory domain and the Internet domain or namespace. In that site, establish the policies that you want to see defaulted throughout the enterprise. A good example is password length. If no GPO is linked to the site, create one and open it for editing.

Whatever policies that you set at this level then filter down to the various domains and OUs that you create. Notice that as you first went into the policy, the setting for password length was not even set. Then, if you open the domain GPO, you find that the default length is 0 characters. That level of security is about as secure as an unlocked door. That's like asking the burglar to mind the store while you go out for five minutes.

Go through all the policies in the site and define what satisfies your change-management and security plans for now. Your first objective is to lock down the network and install some form of security. Later, and before you deploy, you can batten down the hatches further as your needs dictate.

Dealing with computer accounts

Look at the logical plan discussed in Chapter 18. Concentrating your computer accounts into the OUs that represent your KMEs is feasible most of the time (and we say "most of the time" because every company has its own requirements). With that in mind, you can create OUs along key management entity (KME) lines or functions and collect your computers for the KME into the respective OU. You can also group all your computer accounts into a Computers or Workstations OU, which is done often, and all of your users into one large Users OU.

You can also — and doing so makes more sense — add a bunch of computers to a security group and then locate that security group in the respective OU. Wherever that computer group is added — and the group may be linked to other OUs through association — the computers are influenced in the order that they receive policy. For a group of computers, that order is first the OU in which they reside alone or in a group, and then, later, any other structure affected by GP to which that group is admitted. Remember that the last GP applied overrides the previous GP unless you expressly forbid it or block inheritance.

Getting Started

Discussing all the possible ways and means of enabling change control and management would exceed the scope of this book. The best place to start, however, is to ensure that you fully understand the concepts. First, understand that the change control and management or configuration technologies deployed in Windows Server 2008 fall under an umbrella philosophy called *IntelliMirror*, which started with the *Zero Administration Windows* (ZAW) initiative almost a decade ago.

You could literally start implementing the IntelliMirror technologies anywhere in your enterprise. You may start with installation and rollout of the operating system, with software installation and configuration, or with user settings and so on. Every segment of the change-management matrix is extremely complex.

The following suggestions provide a starting point for change configuration using GP- and IntelliMirror-related technologies. We prefer to start by configuring the logon/logoff scenario, locking down desktops, customizing and locking down the Start menu, redirecting folders, and configuring various settings in the Administrative Templates. For us, these areas represent the most urgent needs for clients already in business for some years and who are well entrenched in their business processes and resources. We can't cover everything here because Group Policy alone has more than 700 settings to consider, so after you digest this introduction, review all related technologies and stack them up against the change management that you have begun to implement or are planning.

Customizing logon/logoff

A void time (when the user stares at the screen) exists between the computer starting up and the presentation of the login screen (when the user is asked to press Ctrl+Alt+Del). A void time is also present just after the user logs off.

In this void time, you can use policy to run various options. You can run an anti-virus checker, for example, or pull or push something to the network, synchronize offline files and folders, run diagnostics, or gather intelligence into a data file that represents the user's activities while logged on at the machine. Depending on the applications, you can have a million reasons to run something (via scripts, of course) in void time during logon/logoff.

Locking down the desktop

Locking down the desktop is an important component in change control, and takes you back to the first anecdote at the beginning of this chapter.

You can also create custom configurations for Internet Explorer to enforce download and browsing policy and so on. Other policies that are extremely useful can achieve the following:

- Prevent users from changing the path to their My Documents folders. This policy is often used if you need to ensure that users' documents and other work-related files are redirected to a server folder where they are certain to be backed up.

- Disable the Control Panel, which prevents users from fiddling with the settings that govern their displays, network connections, communications, and so on. You can also hide specific Control Panel programs if your users need access only to certain items.

- Hide access to the CD-ROM and the floppy disk drive. By taking away these ports, you prevent users from introducing viruses or rogue software into the network, and you ensure that the enterprise can control software piracy. (Remember that you need to lock down access to the Internet and e-mail as well to be 100 percent sure that no viruses are being introduced to the systems.) You can also hide the hard disk drives from the users.

- Disable the Command Console so that users cannot execute commands from the command line. For hackers, accessing the command line on a computer is like making it to the first floor.

- Disable access to the registry editing tools such as Regedt32 or Regedit.

Controlling the Start menu

GP enables you to disable portions of the Start menu so that they are not visible to the user. You can also customize the Start menu to reflect the needs of change management. You can, for example, do any of the following:

- Remove the Run menu item from the Start menu. This option also locks down the keyboard shortcut that opens the Run menu.

- Add the Logoff item to the Start menu, which you want to do for terminal session users.

- Disable the drag-and-drop shortcut menus on the Start menu. This serves to prevent users from removing items or reordering the sequence of items from the Start menu.

Folder redirection

Each user is given access to a number of personal folders on a domain and on a workstation. These include My Documents, My Pictures, and Application Data. To protect a user's files, the intellectual property of the enterprise, and application data, a valuable feature of Group Policy enables you to redirect every user's collection of personal folders and application data to a network server.

This practice bestows three important benefits on the enterprise. First, by forcing data to be stored on the network server, both personal and application data can be regularly backed up.

Second, the data and files can be regularly frisked for viruses. Data that is stored on local machines in an enterprise is usually never backed up, and forcing antiviral technology onto every workstation is not a 100-percent surefire solution to the virus malady. Despite installing virus checkers onto every workstation, you can never ensure that everyone has the latest data file on the thousands of new viruses that are being launched every month. Protecting one server is easier than setting up processes to ensure that every computer is adequately protected.

Third, you can ensure that no matter where users log on, even as terminals on an application server, they always have access to their same folders, and their application data is always saved and remains accessible from the same place.

Redirecting folders is easy and can be done from any special folders that you place into service. You can also redirect everyone to a sharepoint, and folder redirection can be enabled by group membership as well.

To enable folder redirection, expand the User Configuration node through Windows Settings to the Folder Redirection node in the SDOU of choice, as explained in the section "Putting Group Policy to Work," earlier in this chapter.

To redirect a folder, follow these steps:

1. Right-click the folder — for example, My Documents — and choose Properties from the pop-up menu. The dialog box for that folder loads. (In this example, it would be the My Documents Properties dialog box.)

2. Select the Basic – Redirect Everyone's Folder to the Same Location option from the Setting drop-down list. Alternatively, to redirect according to group membership, you can choose the Advanced – Specify Locations for Various User Groups option.

3. Enter a target folder in the Target Folder Location field. Enter a UNC name here and use the `%username%` variable if necessary. You can also select the path via the Browse option. If you selected Advanced in Step 2, select the group that this policy applies to by clicking the Add button in the dialog box.

4. Click the Settings tab on the dialog box to further configure the redirection criteria, such as rights, removal policy (which kicks in after policy is removed), and so on. Click Apply and then OK after you are done configuring the redirection criteria.

After all that work, ensure that your backup and virus checkers "sweep" the new redirected resources.

Older versions of Windows

As mentioned in the section "Types of Group Policy" earlier in this chapter, a mixed environment is problematic. No user or computer logging in to versions of Windows earlier than

Windows 2000 can be influenced by Windows Server 2008 GP. To protect your environment, you need to continue to work with the older technologies, such as the System Policy Editor on Windows NT 4.0 (`poledit.exe`). Consider moving the older environments to Windows Server 2008 as soon as possible. Of course, this means upgrading to Windows Vista.

Change Control Management for Group Policy

It's ironic that the premier technology for managing change control in Windows Server 2008 could use some change management itself. One of the biggest problems with the development, deployment, and management of GP is that the technology is extremely difficult and complex to manage. Microsoft has been promising better tools to make management of GP easier, but they have been slow in coming.

Before we discuss this difficulty, consider how technology is usually deployed under strict quality-management and validation procedures. First, systems are designed on paper and in Visio or Rational Rose before discovery and proof of concept in the lab. Then, on approval of the design and testing in the lab environment, the systems are migrated from the lab or torn down and built anew according to design specifications. After this process is complete — and following essential change control — a formal validation is carried out. This formal validation involves checks to ensure that systems are installed correctly, that they operate correctly, and that they meet performance metrics.

After the systems are deployed, they are maintained according to maintenance procedures, disaster recovery practices, and change control.

Group Policy implementation should follow the same practices in design and build-out, as described in Chapter 23. The technology has profound and far-reaching influence on the technical operations of an enterprise, yet it is neither practical nor possible to follow good design and management philosophy because of several shortcomings in the GP creation and application architecture itself.

For starters, you can design and test Group Policy in the lab and get it approved, but copying and pasting it into production is not possible because GP must be created from scratch in a production environment. You have no way to migrate GP into production by using Windows Server 2008 tools, so you must document, usually in spreadsheets or databases, exactly what was tested in the lab, and then you must re-create everything in production.

Not only must the Group Policy be created from the ground up, but after the object is saved — which occurs as soon as you exit the editor — it is immediately in production and starts to work. Therefore, any validation or testing is meaningless. The GP is immediately linked to the container in which it was created. If the GPO is created in the main OU and turns out to have hostile tendencies toward all computers, you cannot always undo the damage easily or quickly.

From development to production with Group Policy

To ease the burden of deploying GP, you should thus create a staging OU in your domain where all GP is created. This OU must be at the lowest level in any OU tree — preferably, one that is not nested too deeply. This enables you to create the GPO without it linking to any production OU that is populated with unsuspecting computers and users, or that affects any users or computers beneath it. After the GPO is created, it can be unlinked from the staging OU (deleting the link) and linked to any OU of your choosing, or it can be applied to a group somewhere in the domain.

This form of GP quarantine thus enables a measure of phased implementation. After the GPO is created, you can gather a collection of test computers and users in a test OU and move the GP out of the staging area. If the GPO is doing what it is designed to do, you can then take it through change control and roll it out into production As you saw in the section "How Group Policy Works" earlier in this chapter, this is achieved by simply linking the GPO to another container or by applying it against a group of users or computers.

Change control for Group Policy

The next biggest headache that you face is maintenance and change control of Group Policy. You cannot extend or test or return the GPO to the lab for a tune-up without affecting your live users, so you typically must create a new GPO for the new features, extend the old one, or partition it.

Wrecking and corrupting a GPO is certainly possible. Applying a setting that has less or more than the desired effect is also possible. Sure, you want to implement strict change control for GP, but for the most part, managing change in your GP architecture is extremely difficult.

Extending an existing GP is difficult. The new definitions and settings of the GPO add to the complexity of the object. The more stuff that you implement in a GPO, the harder maintaining it or moving it around your domain becomes. Think about this concept for a second. A GPO with fancy login script settings is difficult to extend. If you add administrative settings for Access 2008 in the GPO, users who are affected by the login script settings also feel the effect of the Access 2008 restrictions. You cannot, therefore, scale the GPO to all users of Access without interfering with login script settings.

Planning and troubleshooting GP by using the Group Policy Results Wizard

If you have experience in GP management, you know that you have no easy way to troubleshoot problem GPOs or to easily predict or test how a GPO will work in production. *Resultant Set of Policy* (RSoP), which was introduced in Windows XP, goes a long way toward providing the means to both plan GP and troubleshoot problems that arise at workstations that have applied GP. It now comes built into Windows Server 2008 and is called Group Policy Results or GP results. A handy wizard will enable you to determine the resultant set of policy applying to an object.

GP results enables you to obtain a report of all the GP settings that apply to a user and machine. It thus enables you to troubleshoot GP and determine how the GP results change the desktop and work environment of a user's computer.

The native Windows Vista and Windows Server 2008 GP results functionality enables you to extract GP results from both the machine that you are sitting at or any machine on the domain. You can also use the command-line utility, GPRESULT, to discover the sum of GP settings affecting a user and her computer. GP results and GPRESULT are discussed extensively under the topic of troubleshooting GP in Windows Server 2008's Help files.

To use GP results to plan GP application, open the GPM console, right-click the Group Policy Results node, and select Group Policy Results Wizard (shown in Figure 24-8).

FIGURE 24-8

The Resultant Set of Policy Wizard.

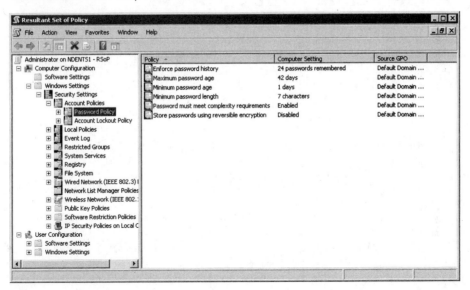

Use this wizard to simulate GP application on a target OU, or users, computers, and groups, with various settings such as loopback mode, slow network connection, and Windows Management Instrumentation (WMI) filters.

You can also bypass the wizard and either run GPRESULT (which runs in the command window) or the RSOP.MSC tool. To build a report of GP results on a target user and computer, open the Resultant Set of Policy console (rsop.mmc) on the target computer. Before loading the console, the RSoP gathers GP information targeting the current machine and logged-on user. The RSoP console then launches with this information. You can use the same console to target other machines (mainly workstations) and computers.

The RSoP console is available on Windows XP and Vista and you can target other workstations and users from a Vista support computer . . . provided you have permission, as the target machine's local administrator (which, by default, includes members of the Domain Admins group), to generate an RSoP report.

That said, generating reports for troubleshooting and simulating the resultant GP is about all that RSoP is good for. Making a mistake in the GPO — and even trashing it — is still very possible. It is not unheard of for a perfectly functional GPO to be ruined because some administrative templates overcooked the GP. Can you undo the changes, get a backup of the GP from the lab, or restore a backup? Unfortunately, that's not possible with the standard first-party tools that ship with the operating system. With these shortcomings in mind, you need to turn to a third-party software vendor for help.

Architecting Group Policy

An architecture for GP creation and application is outlined in the following sections. First, you must consider the base policies to be implemented, and these are listed in Table 24-4. Notice the naming convention that we have chosen to use here. Later we will focus on one policy in particular as an example of application.

The essential and minimal configuration defined in the domain-level GPOs are controlled in the following sections:

- Password Policy
- Account Lockout Policy
- Kerberos Policy (see Chapter 16; these policies are set in the Default Domain Policy)
- Audit Policy
- Event Logs
- User Rights Assignments
- Security Options
- System Services
- IP Security Policies
- Group Policy
- Display
- Start Menu and Task Bar

Every domain has a Default Domain Policy, and this GPO will be modified in the root domain (MCITY.US). A Default Domain Policy is always linked (active), although it initially contains default settings that provide the default implementation of security policy. Microsoft revises the default for each version of the operating system.

TABLE 24-4	

Base Policies

Tier 1	
Policy Name	**Purpose**
Default Domain Policy	Defines the base and required security, account, and audit policy for the domain
FirstDomainSecurityPolicy	This policy is created for additional security policies designed to eliminate as far as possible the potential attack surfaces.
SecondDomainSecurityPolicy	This policy cannot be overridden and is created for additional security policies designed to eliminate (as far as possible) the potential server and domain attack surfaces.
ThirdDomainSecurityPolicy	Defines base services (functionality) in the domain. On approval, services enabled or disabled in this policy can be overridden as needed by policy that follows this policy.
DomainEnterpriseServerPolicy	Defines base settings for the enterprise data center and function-specific servers throughout the domain. A baseline policy for servers will be defined in this GPO that will apply to all servers in the domain. Each server will then obtain an additional policy that is customized or tailored to the role the server plays in the data center or in an OU. For example, the enterprise Certificate Authority servers are more locked down than the standard print servers.
Default Domain Controllers Policy	The Default Domain Controllers Policy will be modified in the root domain (MCITY.US) and any future child domain. The purpose of this policy is to impose a Group Policy definition on all domain controllers in the forest (that is, it defines the base and required policies that affect domain controllers).
FirstDomainControllersPolicy	Defines an extended policy for domain controllers. This policy cannot be overridden.
SecondDomainControllersPolicy	Defines an extended policy for domain controllers that can be overridden.

The Default Domain Policy is the broadest security policy that needs to be defined for a domain. This GPO is the one intended to extend certain mandatory security settings to all users and computers in the domain, no matter where they reside in the directory. Policies in the Default Domain Policy are not overridden by GPOs that are applied after its application.

Account policies affect local and domain-connected computers. When applied to a local computer, the account policies apply to the local account database that is stored on the computer. When applied at the domain controller, the account policy affects all domain accounts; that is, for users logging on to the domain from Windows Server 2008 or XP computers.

Domainwide account policies are defined in the Default Domain Policy. DCs pull the domainwide account policy from the Default Domain Policy, so it is imperative that a paper copy of the GPO (listing the settings) be maintained in the event that the GPO becomes corrupted. The use of a third-party GPO management tool such as NetIQ's Group Policy Administrator or the Group Policy Management Console (GPMC) obviates this need. These tools store the settings of GPOs offline and they can be easily moved to various storage locations, and restored or rolled back if the GP becomes corrupted. The default policies are also easy to re-create. There can be only one account policy for a domain. In other words, the Default Domain GPO is the single enforcer for all domain accounts.

Member servers that are not DCs also receive the Default Domain Policy, but this can be blocked. To do so, enable the No Override option on the GPO. However, as long as a member server is joined or authenticated to the domain, its local policy is overridden by mandatory domain policy. Thus, you cannot specify a local security account policy and succeed at applying it unless the server or workstation is removed from the domain or no longer pulls down AD Group Policy.

Under Local Policies in the Default Domain Policy, you should define the minimal audit policy for the domain. User Rights Assignment and Security Options are also defined under Local Policies, but these will be configured on the Default Domain Controllers Policy and GPOs at the root OU levels for the various server groups (such as file servers and print servers). A Default Domain Controller Policy is always linked for a domain, although it initially contains default settings that are insufficient for secure implementation of security policy. Let's now review these so-called "default" GPOs.

Password policy

The password policy proposed for MCITY has been designed according to Microsoft's recommendation for password complexity and management. Password complexity is enforced using a custom-built password filter or the default filter provided with the Windows NT 4.0 SP2 password filter (`passfilt.dll`). The password filter is a dynamically linked library (DLL) accessed when password complexity is defined at the Group Policy level.

The password policies include the following options:

- **Maximum Password Age**. This option specifies the number of days a password can be used before the user is given notice to change it. Changing passwords regularly is one way to prevent passwords from being compromised. Your default should vary from 30 to 42 days.

- **Enforce Password History**. This option specifies the number of unique, new passwords that must be associated with a user account before an old password can be reused. When you use this option in conjunction with Minimum Password Age, it prevents repeated use of the same password. This setting should be a value greater than 10 to prevent reuse of the same password, which is a security risk.

- **Minimum Password Age**. This setting specifies the number of days a password must be used before the user can change it. The default value is zero, but you should reset it to a few days. When used in conjunction with Enforce Password History, this option prevents repeated reuse of the same password.

- **Minimum Password Length**. This is the minimum number of characters to be used in the password. The default value is zero. A minimum of seven characters is recommended.

- **Passwords Must Meet Complexity Requirements**. A built-in algorithm now ensures that passwords meet the following complexity requirements:

  - The password does not contain your name or user name.

  - The password contains at least six characters.

  - The password contains characters from each of the following three groups: uppercase and lowercase letters (A, a, B, b, C, c, and so on); numerals; and symbols (characters that are not defined as letters or numerals, such as !, @, #, and so on).

Table 24-5 lists the password policy for MCITY and the GPO in which it is configured.

TABLE 24-5

Password Policy

Setting	Policy	Default Value	Required Policy	Unit	GPO
Windows Settings\ Security settings\ Account Policies					
	Enforce password history	1	15	Passwords remembered	Default Domain
	Maximum password age	42	45	Days	Default Domain
	Minimum password age	0	4	Days	Default Domain

continued

TABLE 24-5 *(continued)*

Setting	Policy	Default Value	Required Policy	Unit	GPO
	Minimum password length	0	8	Characters	Default Domain
	Passwords must meet complexity requirements	Disabled	Enabled		Default Domain
	Store the password using reversible encryption for all users in the domain	Disabled	Disabled		Default Domain

Account lockout policy

This facility enables the administrator to block continuous attempts to break passwords, and to detect attempts to hack into the network using random password generators, known to hackers as "war dialers." The facility provides the following three criteria that will cause an account lock-out. A locked out account cannot be reused until the administrator or another authorized user resets it.

- **Account Lockout Threshold**. This option specifies the number of failed logon attempts the security system will allow to go unnoticed until the lockout is activated. The threshold can be set from 1 to 999 failed attempts. If set to 0, an account is never locked out. Failed attempts at Ctrl+Alt+Del or failed attempts to cancel a password-protected screen saver do not count toward the threshold. Remote logon failures, however, do count toward the lockout threshold. To apply this setting, drill down to the following GP configuration path:

```
Computer Configuration\Windows Settings\Security Settings\
Account Policies\Account Lockout Policy
```

- **Account Lockout Duration**. This option specifies the number of minutes (1 to 99999) that must elapse before an account is unlocked automatically. To require an administrator to be the only means to unlock the account, you can set the duration to zero. By default, this policy is not defined because it only has meaning when an "account lockout threshold" is specified.

- **Reset Account Lockout Counter After**. This option enables you to determine how many minutes (1 to 99999) must elapse before the failed logon counter for an account is reset to 0.

By default, account lockout settings are disabled in the Default Domain Group Policy Object (GPO), and in the local security policy of workstations and servers. Table 24-6 outlines the policy chosen by MCITY.

TABLE 24-6

Account Lockout Policy

Setting	Policy	Default Value	Required Policy	Unit	GPO
Windows Settings\ Security Settings\ Account Policies					
	Account lockout duration	Not Defined	0	Minutes	Default Domain
	Account lockout threshold	0	51	Invalid logon attempts	Default Domain
	Reset account lockout counter after	Not Defined	43202 (72 hrs)	Minutes	Default Domain
Windows Settings\ Local Policies\ Security Options	Interactive Logon: Prompt user to change the password before expiration	Not Defined	Enabled	10 days	Default Domain

Audit policy

Audit policy for the root (MCITY.US) is defined as follows:

Audit account logon events: Logon events are processed at a DC. If auditing of account logon events is defined for the domain, then the logon activity associated with the logon event will be recorded in the event log of the DC that processes the logon attempt. The event is processed when the security subsystem processes and validates the user's credentials. Account logon events are only processed at DCs and are only recorded in the DC event logs.

Audit policy for security settings can be viewed under the Security tab of the server's event viewer. If credentials are presented to the local Security Accounts Manager (SAM), which means the user is not authenticating to the domain but rather to the local machine, the event is recorded in the local server's security event log.

By consolidating the event logs for the domain, security administrators are able to track and analyze all account logon events, regardless of which DC receives the logon request. A report should be created for the account logon events, which would filter out all other event logs and provide security administrators with a clean audit trail for all logon authentication for the domain. A well-designed report can quickly highlight disconcerting logon patterns in the domain.

Following are some key audit policies:

- **Audit account management**. This policy is used when users and groups (security principals) are created, changed, or deleted in the domain. This audit tells the security administrator when a security principal was created, and who created the object.

- **Audit directory service access**. All Active Directory objects have a *System Access Control List* (SACL) associated with them, so object access can be extensively audited by the security administrators. AD user and group accounts are audited using Account Management facilities. However, you can also audit the modification of other objects in the directory naming contexts, such as the Configuration and Naming contexts. This is achieved by auditing for object access, which is accomplished by defining the SACL for the specific objects to be audited. Audit information is generated when user and group lists on the SACL of the AD object attempt to access the object.

- **Audit logon events**. Logon events record when a user logs on or off a computer, which is not the same thing as account logon events. Logons can be generated at any time after a user logs on with an account. In other words, the logon events are generated after a user authenticates to the domain, whereas account logon events usually only occur once.

  When a user logs on to a remote server — say, using the Terminal Services client — the logon event is generated in the remote server's security log. These logon events are created when the user's logon session and access tokens are created and destroyed.

  Logon events are useful to security administrators to track attempts to log on interactively to servers. They can be used to investigate potential security violations launched against servers from specific locations. *Success audits* generate an audit entry when a logon attempt succeeds, and *failure audits* generate an audit entry when a logon attempt fails.

- **Audit object access**. Auditing for all objects throughout a Windows Server 2008 domain can be achieved using the SACL of the objects. Each object's SACL contains a list of security principals (usually groups) that specify actions to audit. Just about every object created in a Windows Server 2008 domain has its own SACL; therefore, it can be audited for access control. Important objects to audit include files, folders, drives, printers, and even registry keys.

The SACL contains *Access Control Entries* (ACEs). Each ACE contains three items of information critical to the object auditing process:

- The security principal to be audited (a user or group object).
- The specific access type to be audited. This is known as the *access mask*.
- A flag that indicates whether to audit for failed access, successful access, or both.

For events to appear in the security log, Auditing for Object Access must first be enabled in Active Directory. Then the SACL for each object must be defined.

- **Audit policy change**. By auditing for policy changes, the security administrator can monitor attempts to change policy. Not only can you audit to track and monitor attempts to change policy that governs user rights and other policies, but also attempts to alter audit policy itself.

- **Audit privilege use**. Administrators at various levels in a Windows Server 2008 domain exercise certain rights they are given in order to administer a domain. Such privileges include backup of files and folders, restoring files and folders, changing the system time, shutting down the system, and so on. Auditing the use of privileges for success and failure generates an event each time a user attempts to exercise a user right.

    Enabling the Privilege Use audit does not automatically audit use of every user right. By default, the following rights are excluded:

    - Bypass traverse checking
    - Create a token object
    - Replace process level token
    - Generate security audits
    - Backup files and directories
    - Restore files and directories

- **Audit process tracking**. Processes running on Windows Server 2008 computers can be audited to provide detailed information showing attempts to create processes and end processes. Security administrators can use this facility to audit the attempt of a process to generate a handle to an object, or even to obtain indirect access to an object. It is very useful in the hacker prevention arsenal.

- **Audit system events**. System events are generated every time a user or process alters an aspect of the computer environment. The security administrator can thus audit for events such as attempting to fiddle with system time (often a target in a hacking scenario) or shutting down a computer.

This facility also enables you to audit attempts to clear the security log. This is important because users or hackers planning to infiltrate the network almost always attempt to cover their tracks by purging the security logs, thereby hiding changes they make (or attempt to make) to the environment. Thus, it is important to constantly pipe event log information to SQL Server or a similar repository (the archiving process) so that in the event that a hacker succeeds in purging the event log, the event leading up to the purge, or events close to the actual purge event, are logged.

The minimum audit policy defined for MCITY's domains is described in Table 24-7.

TABLE 24-7

Audit Policy

Setting	Policy	Default Value	Required Policy	Unit	GPO
Windows Settings\ Local Policies\ Audit Policy	Audit account logon events	Not Defined	Success and Failure		Default Domain
	Audit account management	"	Success and Failure		Default Domain
	Audit directory service access	"	Success and Failure		Default Domain
	Audit logon events	"	Success and Failure		Default Domain
	Audit object access	"	Failure		Default Domain
	Audit policy change	"	Success and Failure		Default Domain
	Audit privilege use	"	Failure		Default Domain
	Audit process tracking	"	Failure		Default Domain
	Audit system events	"	Success and Failure		Default Domain

It should be noted that audit policy for Application, Security, and System applies on all computers in the domain, including workstations.

Base policy for auditing on desktops should be enabled with custom settings defined for desktop events. These will then take precedence for the desktop over the domain-level settings. Only events that apply to the local workstation are recorded, which provides a useful record of activity on a workstation and the necessary data required for troubleshooting. Remote access tools such as the SMS client can read these logs to determine the cause of application or system failure or security breaches.

Event log

Table 24-8 lists the required event log settings. These are typically set in the Default Domain Policy.

TABLE 24-8

Event Log Settings

Setting	Policy	Default Value	Required Policy	Unit	GPO
Windows Settings\ Event Log	Maximum application log size	Not Defined	65,536	KB	Default Domain
	Maximum security log size	"	184,320	KB	Default Domain
	Maximum system log size	"	65,536	KB	Default Domain
	Restrict guest access to application log	"	Enabled		Default Domain
	Restrict guest access to security log	"	Enabled		Default Domain
	Restrict guest access to system log	"	Enabled		Default Domain
	Retain application log	"			Default Domain
	Retain security log	"			Default Domain
	Retain system log	"			Default Domain

continued

		Default	Required		
Setting	**Policy**	**Value**	**Policy**	**Unit**	**GPO**
	Retention method for application log	"	Override events as needed		Default Domain
	Retention method for security log	"	Override events as needed		Default Domain
	Retention method for system log	"	Override events as needed		Default Domain
	Shut down the computer when the security audit log is full	"	Disabled		Default Domain

TABLE 24-8 *(continued)*

Let's now extend the base for a specific purpose to illustrate the points made earlier in this chapter.

Locking down Domain Admins

You should always ensure that your administrator accounts do not end up in the wrong hands, because once an intruder manages to obtain the administrator login somewhere, he or she can use it — interactively via a user interface or at some command line — to trash your domain.

The most dangerous object in Active Directory is an account that has administrator privileges. This account gets its administrator privileges from the domain groups (such as Schema Admins, Domain Admins, Administrators, and Enterprise Admins). To reduce the "attack surface" on your existing network as much as possible, start with the Domain Admins group.

The Domain Admins group is a dangerous group because an account that has membership in it can do just about anything on the network. Domain Admins accounts are often handed out to engineers who don't really need them to do their work. Prevent the casual use of Domain Admins accounts completely from the network, limiting the capability of an account in this group to log on only to a few secure workstations. To enforce this, you can perform the following steps:

1. Create an OU at the highest level in AD, where a folder for secure workstations will act as a barrier against a policy that restricts logon by Domain Admins. Add the secure workstation into this OU and ensure that members of Domain Admins can log on to these machines.

2. Create administrative groups (domain local) for each of your line-of-business servers and administrative groups for your workstations. These groups can be named according to the role of the server on which they are being used (such as SQLServerAdmins, Exchange Admins, and so on).

3. Create a WorkstationAdmins (or DesktopAdmins) group and add this group to your workstation's local Administrators group. All members of the local Administrators group will be able to work on these servers and workstations, just as a member of Domain Admins would be able to do, without having to be a member of Domain Admins.

4. With administrative access to your servers and workstations, and when you can log on with an account that is not a member of Domain Admins, configure a GPO to prevent local logon to Domain Admins on the domain on all but a few of the most secure machines (that is, the workstations you set up and installed to the OU described in Step 1).

On your secure and reliable workstations positioned in the Service Administration, Computers OU, you can install the necessary administration tools to manage the domain. Ensure that they are working properly. They include the Active Directory tools, such as Active Directory Users and Computers (DSA.MSC), and the Group Policy Management Console (GPMC.MSC).

Now create the GPO (for example, ServiceAdminPolicy) and link it to the Service Administration OU. The objective is for this GPO to affect only computers contained in the Computers OU, encapsulated in the Service Administration OU. In this GPO, ensure that you have the following settings enabled. Under Local Policies ➢ User Rights Assignment, enable the following rights:

- **Allow Logon Locally**. This provides access to BUILTIN\Account Operators, BUILTIN\Administrators, BUILTIN\Backup Operators, and Domain Admins.

- **Allow Logon Through Terminal Services**. This provides access to Domain Admins (enabling you to log on to the workstation remotely). The other groups do not need this.

- **Deny Logon Locally**. This setting enables you to enter groups (such as BUILTIN\Server Operators, and your custom ServerOperators) that you do not want to be able to log on to your secure administration workstations.

- **Shutdown the System**. This setting gives this right to your Domain Admins, which it implicitly already has, so that only Domain Admins can shut down the admin workstation. This policy overtly excludes all other groups from shutting down your Service Administration machine.

Enable the policy and update GP using GPUPDATE/FORCE or leave it to propagate automatically. As soon as you have confirmed that the GP has updated on your machine, without GP errors, and your account (as a member of Domain Admins, and the Administrator) can log on to the Service Administration machines, you can proceed to the last, and most sensitive, step.

Edit your Default Domain Policy and enable the policy "Deny logon" locally for Domain Admins. You can call this GPO DenyLogonPolicy. It is recommended that you create a new GPO for this setting, rather than risk it in the Default Domain Policy. Administrators who now have a Domain Admins account will no longer be able to use them everywhere.

If you have accounts that are being used for standard network login that are members of Domain Admins, you should remove them before you activate this policy. If you don't, your users will find that they cannot log on to their workstations. Give technicians who have legitimate reasons for using Domain Admin accounts their own administrative machines. In addition, create two user accounts for network engineers who need Domain Admins membership for their jobs. They can use one account for working with the privileges (such as `jshapiro.adm`) and the other account for day-to-day network access just like any other employee (`jshapiro`). A third account for server operators (such as `jshapiro.svr`) is also an option and recommended on a large network.

Summary

This chapter discussed the importance of change control and change management, and how you can use Windows Server 2008 Group Policy to satisfy, as far as possible, the needs of the enterprise for change and security.

You examined how unmanaged change can lead to disaster, and you looked at the importance of assessing your user and security environment to better understand the elements that need to fall under change management in the enterprise.

Chapter 25

Service Level

Preliminary benchmarks of Windows Server 2008 declare it a very capable operating system for running server-based applications. The speed increase in the operating system will appeal to many, and is noticeable from the moment the machine is booted and the OS starts. This will place tremendous burden and responsibility on Windows Server 2008 administrators to ensure the maximum availability of systems, and that too much software clutter doesn't slow down the system. This chapter discusses service level and provides an introduction to Windows Server 2008 performance monitoring.

Understanding Service Level

If there is anything to be learned by this book, it is this: Windows Server 2008 is a major-league operating system. In our opinion, it is the most powerful operating system in existence ... for the majority of needs of all enterprises. Only time and service packs will tell if Windows Server 2008 can go up against the big irons such as AS/400, Solaris, S/390, and the like.

Microsoft has aimed Windows Server 2008 squarely at all levels of business and industry and at all business sizes. You will no doubt encounter the rush of diatribe in the industry: 99.9 percent this, 10,000 concurrent hits that, clustering and load balancing, and more. However, every system, server, or OS has its meltdown point, weak links, single point of failure (SPOF), "tensile strength," and so on. Knowing, or at least predicting, the meltdown "event horizon" is more important than availability claims. Trust us, poor management will turn any system or service into a service level nightmare.

> **NOTE**   One of the first things you need to ignore in the press from the get-go are the crazy comparisons of Windows Server 2008 to $75 operating systems and the like. If your business is worth your life to you and your staff, you need to invest in performance and monitoring tools, disaster recovery, quality of service tools, service level tools, and more. Take a survey of what these tools can cost you. Windows Server 2008 out of the box has more built into it than anything else, as this chapter will illustrate. By our calculations, Windows Server 2008 is the cheapest system out there on performance-monitoring tools alone.

With application service providing (ASP), thin-client, quality of service (QoS), e-commerce, distributed networking architecture (DNA), Web Services, and the like becoming implementations everywhere, as opposed to being new buzzwords, you, the server, or network administrator are going to find yourself dealing with a new animal in your server room. This animal is known as the *service level agreement* (SLA).

Before we discuss the SLA further, we should define service level and how Windows Server 2008 addresses it.

Service level (SL) is simply the ability of IT management to maintain a consistent, maximum level of system uptime and availability. Many companies may understand SL as quality assurance and quality control (QA/QC). Examples will better explain it, as follows.

Service level: example 1

Management comes to MIS with a business plan for application service providing (ASP). If certain customers can lease applications online, over reliable Internet connections, for *x* rate per month, they will forgo expensive in-house IT budgets and outsource instead. An ASP can, therefore, make its highly advanced network-operations center, plus a farm of servers, available to these businesses. If enough customers lease applications, the ASP will make a profit.

The business plan flies if ASP servers and applications are available to customers all the time from at least 7 A.M. to 9 P.M. The business plan will only tolerate a .09 percent downtime during the day. Any more and customers will lose trust in the business and bring resources back in house. This means that IT or MIS must support the business plan by ensuring that systems are never offline for more than .09 percent of the business day. Response, as opposed to availability, is also a critical factor. Quality of service addresses this in SL (discussed shortly in this chapter).

Service level: example 2

Management asks MIS to take its order-placing system, typically fax-based and processed by representatives in the field, to the extranet. Current practice involves a representative going to a customer, taking an order for stock, and then faxing the order to the company's fax system, where the orders are manually entered into the system. The new system proposes that customers be equipped with an inexpensive terminal or terminal software and place the orders directly against their accounts on a Web server.

MIS has to ensure that the Web servers and the backend systems, SQL Server 2005, Windows Server 2008, BizTalk 2006 Server, the WAN, and so on, are available all the time. If customers find the systems offline, they will swamp the phones and fax machines, or simply place their orders with the competition. The system must also be reliable, informative, and responsive to the customers' needs by fully automating the process with auto-response confirmation e-mails and all the frills that go along with online ordering.

The service level agreement

The first example may require a formal service level agreement. In other words, the SLA will be a written contract signed between the client and the provider. The customer demands that the ASP provide written — signed — guarantees that the systems will be available 99.9 percent of the time. The customer demands such an SLA, because it cannot afford to be in the middle of an order-processing application, or sales letter, and then have the ASP suddenly disappear.

The customer may be able to tolerate a certain level of unavailability, but if SL drops beyond what's tolerable, the customer needs a way to obtain redress from the ASP. This redress could be the right to cancel the contract, or the right to hold the ASP accountable with penalties, such as fines, discount on service costs, waiver of monthly fees, and so on. Whatever the terms of the SLA, if the ASP cannot meet it, then MIS gets the blame.

In the second example, it is highly unlikely there will be a formal SLA between a customer and the supplier. Service level agreements will be in the form of memos between MIS and other areas of management. MIS will agree to provide a certain level of availability to the business model or plan. These SLAs are put in writing and usually favored by the MIS, who will take the SLA to budgeting and request money for systems and software to meet the SLA.

However, the SLA can work to the disadvantage of MIS, too. If the SL is not met, the MIS staff or CTO (Chief Technology Officer) may be fired, demoted, or reassigned. The CEO may also decide to outsource or force MIS to bring in expensive consultants (which may help or hurt MIS).

In IT shops that now support SL for mission-critical applications, there are no margins for tolerating error. Engineers who cannot help MIS meet service levels will not survive long. Education and experience are likely to be high on the list of employment requirements.

Service Level Management

Understanding service level management (SLM) is an essential requirement for MIS in almost all companies today. This section examines critical SLM factors that have to be addressed.

Problem detection

This factor requires IT to be constantly monitoring systems for advanced warnings of system failure. You use whatever tools you can obtain to monitor systems and focus on all the possible points of failure. For example, you will need to monitor storage, networks, memory, processors, power, and so on.

Problem detection is a lot like earthquake detection. You spend all of your time listening to the earth, and the quake comes when and where you least expect it. Then, 100 percent of your effort is spent on disaster recovery (DR). Your DR systems need to kick in to recover from preceding events. According to research from the likes of Forrester Research, close to 40 percent of IT management resources are spent on problem detection.

Performance management

Performance management accounts for about 20 percent of MIS resources. This factor is closely related to problem detection. You can hope that poor performance in areas such as networking, access times, transfer rates, restore or recover performance, and so on, will point to problems that can be fixed before they turn into disasters. However, most of the time a failure is usually caused by failures in another part of the system. For example, if you get a flood of continuous writes to a hard disk that does not let up until the hard disk crashes, is the hard disk at fault, the controller card, or should you be looking for better firewall software?

The right answer is a combination of all three. The fault is caused by the poor quality of firewall software that allows passage to a denial-of-service attack. In the event that this happens again, you need hard disks and SCSI controllers that can withstand the attack a lot longer.

Availability

Availability, for the most part, is a post-operative factor. In other words, availability management covers redundancy, mirrored or duplexed systems, *failovers*, and so on. (Note that failover is emphasized because the term itself denotes taking over from a system that has failed.)

The clustering of systems, or load balancing, conversely, is also as much disaster prevention as it is a performance-level maintenance practice. Using performance management, you would take systems to a performance point that is nearing threshold or maximum level; then you switch additional requests for service to other resources. A failover is a machine or process that picks up the users and processes that were on a system that has just failed, and it is supposed to enable the workload to continue uninterrupted on the failover systems. A good example of failover is a mirrored disk, or a RAID-5 storage set: The failure of one disk does not interrupt the processing, which carries on oblivious to the failure on the remaining disks, giving management time to replace the defective components.

NOTE   There are several other SL-related areas that IT spends time on and which impact SLM. These include change management and control, software distribution, and systems management.

SLM by design

SLM combines tools and metrics or analysis to meet the objectives of SL and service level agreements. The SLM model is a three-legged stool, as illustrated in Figure 25-1.

FIGURE 25-1

The SLM model is a three-legged stool.

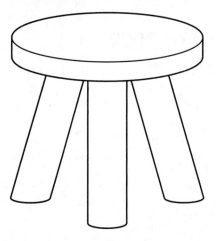

The *availability* leg supports the model by guaranteeing the availability of critical systems. The *administration* leg ensures 24-7 operations and administrative housekeeping. The *performance* leg supports the model by ensuring that systems are able to service the business and keep the systems operating at threshold points considered safely below bottleneck and failure levels. If one of the legs fails or becomes weak, the stool may falter or collapse, which puts the business at risk.

When managing for availability, the enterprise will ensure that it has the resources to recover from disasters as soon as possible. This usually means hiring gurus, or experts, to be available onsite to fix problems as quickly as possible. Often, management pays a guru who doesn't do anything for 95 percent of his or her time, which seems to be a waste, but when that expert can fix a problem in record time, they will have earned their keep several times over.

Often, a guru will restore a system that, had it stayed offline a few days longer, would have cost the company much more than the salary of the guru. However, it goes without saying that the enterprise will save a lot of money and effort if it can obtain gurus who are also qualified to monitor for performance and problems, and who do not just excel at recovery. This should be worth 50 percent more salary to the guru.

Administration is the effort of technicians to keep systems backed up, keep power supplies online, monitor servers for error messages, ensure that server rooms remain at safe temperatures and have air circulation, and so on. The administrative leg manages the SL budget, hires and fires, maintains and reports on service level achievement, and reports to management or the CEO.

The performance leg is usually carried out by analysts who know what to look for in a system. These analysts are paid the big bucks to help management decide how to support business initiatives and exploit opportunity. They need to know everything there is about the technology and its capabilities, such as which databases should be used, how RAID works and the level required, and so on. They must be able to collect data, interpret data, and forecast needs.

SLM and Windows Server 2008

Key to meeting the objective of SLM is the acquisition of SL tools and technology. This is where Windows Server 2008 comes in. Whereas clustering and load balancing are included in Advanced Server and Datacenter Server, the performance and system monitoring tools and disaster recovery tools are available to all versions of the OS.

These tools are essential to SL. Acquired independently of the operating systems, they can cost an arm and a leg, and they might not integrate at the same level. These tools on Windows NT 4.0 were seriously lacking. On the 200X versions of Windows Server and especially Windows Server 2008, however, they raise the bar for all operating systems. Many competitive products unfortunately just do not compete when it comes to SLM. The costs of third-party tools and integration for some operating systems are so prohibitive that they cannot be considered of any use to SLM whatsoever.

The Windows Server 2008 monitoring tools are complex, and continued ignorance of them will not be tolerated by management as more and more customers demand SL compliance and service level agreements. The monitoring and performance tools on Windows Server 2008 include the following:

- Reliability and Performance Monitor (includes the System Monitor component)
- Task Manager
- Event Viewer
- Quality of Service
- Windows Management Instrumentation (WMI)
- Simple Network Management Protocol (SNMP)

This chapter does not provide an exhaustive investigation into the SLM tools that ship with Windows Server 2008, programmatic models and interfaces such as WMI, or how to use each and every one. Such an advanced level of analysis would take several hundred pages, and is thus beyond the scope of this book. Performance monitoring is one of the services and support infrastructures that ships with Windows Server 2008 but it takes some effort to get to know and master. However, the information that follows will be sufficient to get you started.

Windows Server 2008 System Monitoring Architecture

Windows Server 2008 monitors or analyzes storage, memory, networks, and processing. This does not sound like a big deal, but the data analysis is not done on these areas per se.

In other words, you do not monitor memory itself, or disk usage itself, but rather how software components and functionality use these resources. In short, it is not sufficient to just report that 56 MB of RAM were used between time *x* and time *y*. Your investigations need to determine what used the RAM at a certain time and why so much was used.

If a system continues to run out of memory, there is a strong possibility, for example, that an application is stealing the RAM somewhere. In other words, the application or process has a bug and is leaking memory. When we refer to *memory leaks*, this means that software, which has used memory, has not released it after it is done. Software developers are able to watch their applications on servers to ensure they release all the memory they use.

What if you are losing memory and you do not know which application is responsible? Not too long ago, Windows NT servers used on the Internet and in high-end mail applications (no fewer than 100,000 e-mails per hour) would simply run out of RAM. After extensive system monitoring, we were able to determine that the leak was in the latest release of the Winsock libraries responsible for Internet communications on NT. Another company in Europe found the leak at about the same time. Microsoft later released a patch. It turned out that the Winsock functions responsible for releasing memory were not able to cope with the rapid demand on the sockets. They were simply being opened at a rate faster than the Winsock libraries could cope with.

The number of software components, services, and threads of functionality in Windows Server 2008 are so numerous that it is literally impossible to monitor tens of thousands of instances of storage, memory, network, or processor usage.

To achieve such detailed and varied analysis, Windows Server 2008 includes built-in software objects, associated with services and applications, which are able to collect data in these critical areas. When you collect data, the *focus* of your data collection is on the software components, in various services of the operating system, that are associated with these areas. When you perform data collection, the system collects data from the targeted object managers in each monitoring area.

Two methods of data collection are supported in Windows Server 2008. The first one involves accessing registry pointers to functions in the performance counter DLLs in the operating system. The second supports collecting data through the Windows Management Instrumentation (WMI). WMI is an object-oriented framework that enables you to instantiate (create instances of) performance objects that wrap the performance functionality in the operating system. WMI can be programmed against by C/C++ tools as well as languages in the NET Framework.

The OS installs a new technology for recovering data through the WMI. These are known as managed object files (MOFs). These MOFs correspond to or are associated with resources in a system. The number of objects that are the subject of performance monitoring are too numerous to list here, but you can look them up in the Windows Server 2008 Performance Counters Reference, which is on the Windows Server 2008 Resource Kit CD. They include the operating system's base services, such as the services that report on the RAM, paging file functionality, and physical disk usage, and the operating system's advanced services, such as Active Directory, Active Server Pages, the FTP service, DNS, WINS, and so on.

To understand the scope and usage of the objects, it helps to first understand some performance data and analysis terms. There are three essential concepts to understanding performance monitoring: *throughput*, *queues*, and *response time*. Once you fully understand these terms, you can broaden your scope of analysis and perform calculations to report transfer rate, access time, latency, tolerance, thresholds, bottlenecks, and so on.

Understanding rate and throughput

Throughput is the amount of work done in a unit of time. If your child is able to construct 100 pieces of Lego bricks per hour, you could say that his or her assemblage rate is 100 pieces per hour, assessed over a period of x hours, as long as the rate remains constant. However, if the rate of assemblage varies, through fatigue, hunger, thirst, and so on, you can calculate the throughput.

Throughput increases as the number of components increases, or the available time to complete a job is reduced. Throughput depends on resources, and time and space are examples of resources. The slowest point in the system sets the throughput for the system as a whole. Throughput is the true indicator of performance. Memory is a resource, the space in which to carry out instructions. It makes little sense to rate a system by millions of instructions per second when insufficient memory is not available to hold the instruction information.

Understanding queues

If you give your child too many Lego bricks to assemble, or reduce the available time in which he or she has to perform the calculation and assemblage, the number of pieces will begin to pile up. This also happens in software and IS terms, where the number of threads can begin to back up, one behind the other, in a queue. When a queue develops, we say that a *bottleneck* has occurred. Looking for bottlenecks in the system is key to monitoring for performance and troubleshooting or problem detection. If there are no bottlenecks, the system might be considered healthy, but a bottleneck might soon start to develop.

Queues can also form if requests for resources are not evenly spread over the unit of time. If your child assembles one piece per minute evenly every minute, he or she will get through 60 pieces in an hour, but if the child does nothing for 45 minutes and then suddenly gets inspired, a bottleneck will occur in the final 15 minutes because there are more pieces than the child can process in the remaining time. On computer systems when queues and bottlenecks develop, systems become unresponsive. Additional requests for processor or disk resources are stalled. When requesting services are not satisfied, the system begins to break down. In this respect, we reference the response time of a system.

Understanding response time

Response time is the measure of how much time elapses between the firing of a computer event, such as a read request, and the system's response to the request. Response time increases as the load increases because the system is still responding to other events and does not have enough resources to handle new requests. A system that has insufficient memory and/or processing ability will process a huge database sort a lot slower than a better-endowed system with faster hard disks and CPUs. If response time is not satisfactory, you will have to either work with less data or increase the resources.

Response time is typically measured by dividing the queue length over the resource throughput. Response time, queues, and throughput are reported and calculated by the Windows Server 2008 reporting tools.

How performance objects work

Windows Server 2008 performance monitoring objects contain functionality known as *performance counters*. These so-called counters perform the actual analysis. For example, a hard disk object is able to calculate transfer rate, while a processor-associated object is able to calculate processor time.

To gain access to the data or to start the data collection, you first have to create the object and gain access to its functionality. You do this by calling a `create` function from a user interface or other process. As soon as the object is created, and its data collection functionality invoked, it begins the data-collection process and stores the data in various properties. Data can be streamed out to disk, files, RAM, or to other components that assess the data and present it in some meaningful way.

Depending on the object, your analysis software can create at least one copy of the performance object and analyze the counter information it generates. You need to consult Microsoft documentation to "expose" the objects to determine whether the object can be created more than once concurrently. If it can be created more than once, you will have to associate your application with the data the object collects by referencing the object's instance counter. Windows Server 2008 enables you to instantiate an object for a local computer's services, or you can create an object that collects data from a remote computer.

Two methods of data collection and reporting are made possible using performance objects. The objects can *sample* data. This means that data is collected periodically, rather than when a particular event occurs. All forms of data collection place a burden on resources, which means that monitoring in itself can be a burden to systems. Sampled data has the advantage of being a period-driven load, but the disadvantage is that values may be inaccurate when a certain activity falls outside the sampling period or between events.

The other method of data collection is *event tracing*. Event tracing, introduced in Windows Server 2003, is able to collect data as certain events occur. Because there is no sampling window, you can correlate resource usage against events. For example, you can watch an application consume memory when it executes a certain function and monitor how and if it releases that memory when the function completes.

The disadvantage of event tracing is that it consumes more resources than sampling, so you would only want to perform event tracing for short periods where the objective of the trace is to troubleshoot, and not to just monitor.

Counters can report their data in one of two ways: instantaneous counting or average counting. An instantaneous counter displays the data as it happens; it is a snapshot. In other words, the counter does not compute the data it receives; it just reports it. Conversely, average counting computes the data for you. For example, it can compute bits per second or pages per second.

Other counters are able to report percentages, difference, and so on.

System monitoring tools

Before you rush out and buy a software development environment to access the performance monitoring routines, you should know that Windows Server 2008 is equipped with two primary, ready-to-go monitoring tools: the Reliability and Performance Console and Task Manager. Task Manager provides an instant view of systems activity, such as memory usage, processor activity, process activity, and resource consumption. Task Manager is very helpful for immediate detection of system problems. The Reliability and Performance Console is used to provide performance analysis and information that can be used for troubleshooting and bottleneck analysis. It can also be used to establish regular monitoring regimens such as ongoing server health analysis.

Reliability and Performance Console comes with tools built in: Performance Monitor and Reliability Monitor ... but more about them later. The first tool, due to its immediacy and as a troubleshooting and information tool, is Task Manager.

Task Manager

Task Manager provides quick information on applications and services currently running on your server. It provides information such as processor usage in percentage terms, memory usage, task priority, response, and some statistics about memory and processor performance.

Task Manager is very useful as a quick system sanity check, and it is usually evoked as a troubleshooting tool when a system indicates slow response times, lockups or errors, or messages pointing to lack of system resources, and so on.

Task Manager, illustrated in Figure 25-2, is started in several ways:

- Right-click the taskbar (the bottom-right area where the time is usually displayed) and select Task Manager from the context menu.
- Press Ctrl+Shift and press the Esc key.
- Press Ctrl+Alt and press the Del key. The Windows Security dialog box loads. Click Task Manager.

When Task Manager loads, you will notice that the dialog box has six tabs: Applications, Processes, Services, Performance, Networking, and Users. You can perform several useful tricks with Task Manager:

- The columns can be sorted in ascending or descending order by clicking the column heads. The columns can also be resized.
- When Task Manager is running, a CPU gauge icon displaying accurate information is placed into the system tray on the bottom-right of the screen. If you drag your mouse cursor over this area, you will see a pop-up menu of the current CPU usage.

■ You can keep the Task Manager button off the system tray if you use it a lot. You do this by selecting the Options menu and then checking the Hide When Minimized option. The CPU icon next to the system time remains, however.

■ You can control the rate of Refresh or Update from the View ➤ Update Speed menu. You can also pause the update to preserve resources and click Refresh Now to update the display at any time.

FIGURE 25-2

Task Manager, opened to the Performance tab.

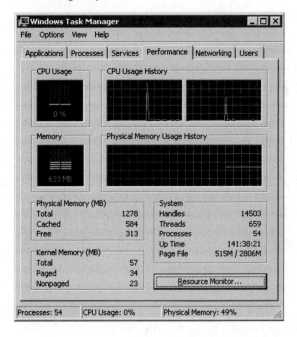

The Processes tab is the most useful, providing a list of running processes on the system. It measures their performance in simple data. These include CPU percent used, CPU time allocated to a resource, and memory usage.

Several additional performance or process measures can be added to or removed from the list on the Processes page. Select View ➤ Select Columns. This will show the Select Columns dialog box, which enables you to add or remove process counters.

A description of each process counter is available in Windows Server 2008 Help.

You can also terminate a process by selecting the process in the list and then clicking the End Process button. Some processes are protected, but you can terminate them using the kill or remote kill utilities that are included in the operating system. You will need authority to kill processes, and before you do, you should fully understand the ramifications of terminating a process.

The Performance tab (shown in Figure 25-2) enables you to graph the percentage of processor time in kernel mode. To show this, select the View menu and check the Show Kernel Times option. Kernel times is the measure of time that applications are using operating system services. The remaining time, known as user mode, is spent in threads that are spawned by applications.

If your server supports multiple processes, you can click CPU History on the View menu and graph each processor in a single graph pane or in separate graph panes.

The Application tab lists running applications. You can terminate an application that has become unresponsive or that you determine is in trouble or is the cause of trouble on the server.

Reliability and Performance Console

The Reliability and Performance Console includes the System Monitor (as Performance Monitor), which is discussed first, and Reliability Monitor (which incorporates the Performance Logs and Alerts from earlier versions of the OS), which is discussed next. These tools, albeit much simpler, were known as *perfmon* on Windows NT. It can be opened by selecting Administrative Tools ➤ Reliability and Performance Monitor. The console can be loaded like all Microsoft Management Console (MMC) snap-ins from the Run console, Task Manager, or command line as perfmon.msc.

When the Performance Console starts, it loads a blank Performance Monitor graph into the console tree.

Performance Monitor

Performance Monitor enables you to analyze system data and research performance and bottlenecks. Using this utility you can create graphs, histograms (bar charts), and textual reports of performance counter data. Performance Monitor is ideal for short-term viewing of data and for diagnostics.

Performance Monitor, illustrated in Figure 25-3, includes the following features:

- Performance Monitor is hosted in MMC, which makes it portable. The snap-in can take aim at any computer and monitor remote processing on that computer.

- It provides a toolbar that can be used to copy and paste counters, purge or clear counters, add counters, and so on.

- You have extensive control over how counter values are displayed. For example, you can vary the line style and width and change the color of the lines. You can also change the color of the chart and then manipulate the chart window.

■ Legends indicate selected counters and associated data such as the name of the computer, the objects, and object instances.

■ Performance Monitor is an ActiveX control named sysmon.ocx. You can load the OCX into any OLE-compliant application, such as Microsoft Word or Visio, and even an HTML page on a Web site. The OCX is also useful in applications that can be specifically created for performance monitoring and analysis.

 NOTE OCX is the file extension of certain ActiveX controls.

FIGURE 25-3

The Performance Console.

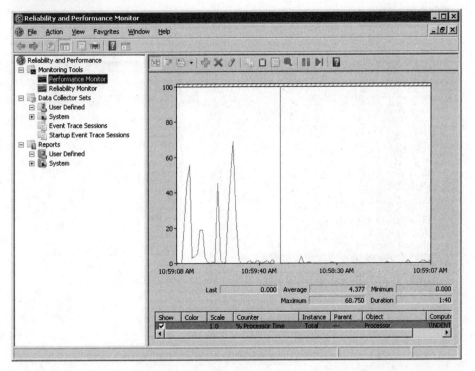

The monitor can be configured using the toolbar or the Shortcut menu. The Shortcut menu is loaded by right-clicking in the blank graph area and selecting the appropriate option. The toolbar is available by default.

Using the toolbar, you can configure the type of display to view by clicking the View Chart, View Histogram, or View Report buttons. In other words, the same information can be viewed in chart, histogram, or report format.

The differences in the view formats should be noted. The histograms and charts can be used to view multiple counters; however, each counter only displays a single value. You use these to track current activity, and view the graphs as they change. The report is more suited to multiple values.

Your data source is obtained by clicking the View Current Activity button for real-time data. You can also select the View Log File Data button, which will enable you to obtain data from completed or running logs.

Of course, you first have to select counters. The counter buttons in the middle of the toolbar include Add and Delete. When you click the Add button, the dialog box illustrated in Figure 25-4 is shown.

FIGURE 25-4

The Add Counters dialog box.

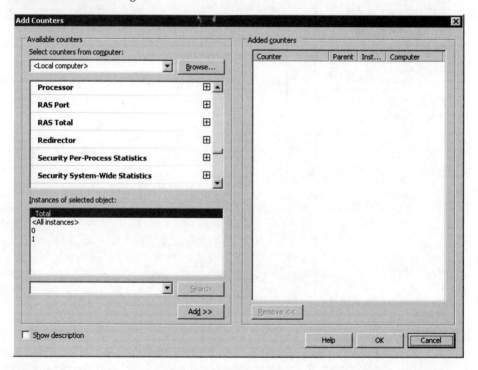

This dialog box enables you to select the computer you want to monitor, and to select performance objects and counters. You can click the Show Description checkbox to learn more about the individual counters you select.

In addition, on the monitor pane you update the display with the Update Data button. You can also freeze the display with the Freeze Display button, which suspends data collection. Click the Update Data button to resume collection.

The display can also be exported. You can, for example, save it to the Clipboard. Conversely, a saved display can be imported into the running display. Access these features by right-clicking in the display to reveal a context menu.

Finally, the Properties button enables you to access settings that control fonts, colors, and so on. When you click it, the properties dialog box loads, as shown in Figure 25-5.

FIGURE 25-5

The Performance Monitor Properties dialog box.

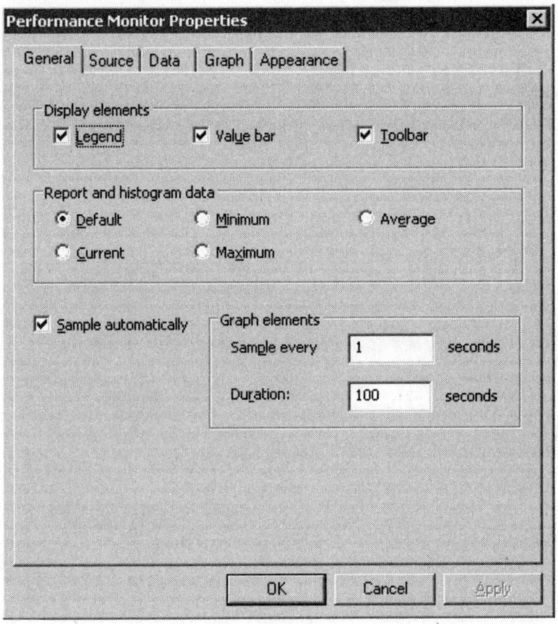

There are several ways you can save data from the monitor. Besides the Clipboard option described previously, you can add the control to a host application, as discussed earlier. By far the easiest means of preserving the look and feel of the display is to save the control as an HTML file. Right-clicking the pane and saving the display as an HTML file does this, and it is the default Save As format.

Alternatively, you can import the log file in comma-separated (CSV) or tab-separated (TSV) format and then import the data in a spreadsheet, database, or report program such as Crystal Reports.

Working with the Add Counters dialog box, you can select all counters and instances or specific counters and instances to monitor from the list. Keep in mind that the more you monitor, the more system resources you will use. If you monitor a large amount of monitors and counters, consider redirecting the data to log files and then reading the log file data in the display. It makes more sense, however, to work with fewer counters and instances.

 It is possible to run two instances of Performance Monitor (in two performance consoles). This may make it easier to compare data from different sources.

In the Instances list box, the first value, _Total, enables you to add all the instance values and report them in the display. The lines in the display can also be matched with their respective counters by selecting the line in the display.

Performance Logs and Alerts

The Windows Server 2008 Performance utilities can produce two types of performance-related logs: counter logs and trace logs. These logs are useful for advanced performance analysis and record-keeping that can be done over a period of time. There is also an alerting mechanism. The Performance Logs and Alerts are incorporated into the console for use in a provided or user-defined data collection set. This is shown in Figure 25-6.

FIGURE 25-6

The Performance Logs and Alerts tree.

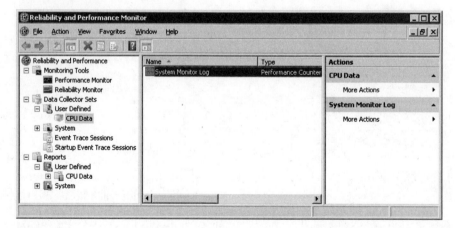

The Counter Logs record samples data about hardware resources and system services based on the performance objects described earlier. It works with counters in the same manner as System Monitor. The Performance Logs and Alerts Service obtains data from the operating system when the update interval has elapsed.

Trace logs collect event traces. With trace logs, you can measure performance associated with events related to memory, storage file I/O, and so on. As soon as the event occurs, the data is sent to the logs. The data is measured continuously from the start of the event to the end of the event, as opposed to the sampling that is performed by the System Monitor.

The Performance Logs data is obtained by the default Windows Server 2008 kernel trace provider. You can analyze the data using a data-parsing tool.

The alerting function is used to define a counter value that will trigger an alert that can send a network message, execute a program, or start a log. This is useful for maintaining a close watch on systems. You can, for example, monitor unusual activity that does not occur consistently and define an alert to let you know when the event has been triggered. Security-related events are good candidates for the alert service. When you are trying to catch a hacker, there is no better time than when he or she is in the act.

You can also configure the alert service to notify you when a particular resource drops below or exceeds certain values, thresholds, or baselines that you establish.

Counter logs can also be viewed in the console, and the counter log data can be saved to CSV and TSV files and viewed in spreadsheet or report software. You can configure the logs to be circular, which means that when the log file reaches a predetermined size, it will be overwritten. Logs can also be linear, and you can collect data for predefined lengths of time. Logs can be stopped and restarted based on parameters you set. You can save files to various formats, such as HTML, or import the entire control OCX into an OLE container.

Creating Data Collector Sets

To work with Logs and Alerts you first need to create Data Collector Sets. Expose the Data Collector Sets node and right-click the User Defined folder and select New ➢ Data Collector. The Create New Data Collector Set Wizard shown in Figure 25-7 loads.

Create a name for the Data Collector Set (such as the one shown in the figure) and then choose to either create the set from a template or manually, which will allow you to pick options. The figure shows a set created from a template; in this case the Active Directory Collector set. Click Next.

NOTE To use Logs and Alerts, you need to have Full Control access to the following registry subkey: `HKEY_CURRENT_MACHINE\SYSTEM\CurrentControlSet\Services\SysmonLog \Log_Queries`. This key is open to administrators by default, but access can also be given by way of the Security menu in Regedit32. To run or configure the service, you need the right to start or configure services on the system. Again, administrators have this right by default, but it can be conveyed through security group membership and Group Policy.

The next screen lets you choose a template. So here we need to pick the Active Directory Diagnostics template. This is shown in Figure 25-8. After choosing the template click Finish.

FIGURE 25-7

Creating a Data Collector Set.

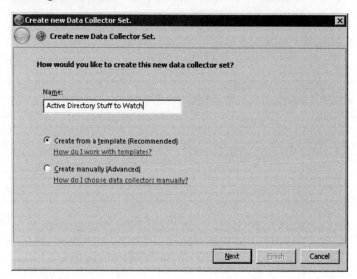

FIGURE 25-8

Choose a Data Collector Set template.

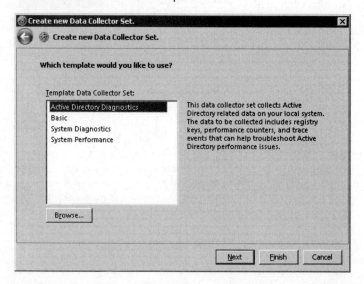

To configure alerts, you first need to configure counters for the alerts, the sample interval, and the alert threshold. You then need to configure an action to take when an event occurs. These can include running a program, sending a message, triggering a counter log, or writing to the event log.

Alert startup can also be configured by providing Start and Stop parameters.

To configure counter logs, you need to set the counter log counters and provide a sample interval. To write to log files, you need to provide a file type, size, path, and any automatic naming parameters needed. The counter logs should be defined as SCV files or TSV files, text files, or binary linear or circular files.

Counter logs can be scheduled to start automatically, but you cannot configure the service to automatically restart if a log file is configured to stop manually. The same criteria apply to trace logs.

Getting to Know Your Servers

To maintain service level and keep servers and applications available, you need to become familiar with each of your machines, the applications running on them, and the resources they use. However, it is insufficient to maintain a subjective feel for how a server is "supposed" to operate. Mission-critical applications, server attacks, and system failures can happen suddenly. System monitoring is thus a task in which you should be engaged continuously.

When you first begin to monitor a system, you basically have nothing to compare it against. After a considerable amount of data has been collected, you will have a data set to work with. You will need to collect data over several weeks, possibly even months; and then based on the assessment of that data, you need to establish baselines against which to base future observation. Normal for some machines may be aggressive CPU usage, whereas other machines may sit idle for most of their lives.

NOTE   If a system is unstable collecting data, setting alerts like crazy is only going to compound the problem. Your first option is to determine the cause of the instability and then set up monitoring and alerts to determine the cause of the instability in the first place. In the event of an unresponsive system, your first option is to run Task Manager and attempt to end the tasks, applications, and processes that are causing the problems.

With a baseline in hand, you will quickly be alerted to performance that is out of the ordinary. For example, if you notice that at night your mail server's responsiveness begins to diminish suddenly, you may find that the server is being hacked for its relay services, which can be compared to riding on a train without paying the fare. A memory counter would be the object that alerts you as to when this is taking place.

Your information should also reflect various points in system performance. You should note what constitutes normal on a server. For example, we noticed that a client's mail server was low on RAM and had begun to page out to disk excessively. When we queried this with the MIS, he advised it was "normal" for this time of the day due to replication services.

Therefore, it is important to note periods of low usage, average usage, and high or peak usage. Systems that provide real-time communications are good examples of servers that should be monitored continuously for this type of information.

TIP Make baseline performance information available within an arm's reach of your server. This can be in the form of clipboards or journals into which you can paste data. This enables other system operators to look up a server and determine what might be considered normal.

Do not expect to obtain any meaningful insight into system performance from the get-go, because the baselines you develop will establish typical values to expect when your system is not experiencing problems.

Monitoring for bottlenecks

As described earlier in this chapter, when system performance deviates from your established baselines, bottlenecks occur. It helps to have some guidelines, so Table 25-1 suggests thresholds for a minimum set of system counters.

TABLE 25-1

Suggested System Counter Thresholds

Item	Resource	Object	Counter	Threshold
1	Disk	LogicalDisk	%Free Space	15%
2	Disk	LogicalDisk	%Disk Time	80%
3	Disk	PhysicalDisk	Disk Reads/sec; Disk Writes/sec	Check the manufacturer's specifications
4	Disk	PhysicalDisk	Current Disk Queue Length	Number of spindles plus 2
5	Memory	Memory	Available Bytes	4 MB; best not to go below 16 MB
6	Memory	Memory	Pages/sec	20 per second
7	Network	Network Segment	% Net Utilization	30%
8	Paging File	Paging File	% Usage	Above 70%
9	Processor	Processor	% Processor Time	85%

Item	Resource	Object	Counter	Threshold
TABLE 25-1 *(continued)*				
10	Processor	Processor	Interrupts/sec	1,500 per second
11	Server	Server	Bytes Total/sec	N/A
12	Server	Server	Work Item Shortages	3
13	Server	Server Work Queues	Queue Length	4
14	Multiple Processors	System	Processor Queue Length	2

Some of these options may vary and still be satisfactory for your server. The following list of notes provides some additional guidance (the notes reflect the numbering in Table 25-1):

- **Item 1.** A threshold of 15 percent free space may be too low depending on the purpose of the machine. You can ensure that the threshold is never suddenly exceeded with disk quotas. Although not all processes can be blocked from using disk space, it is a good idea to configure alerts to signal you when the threshold is exceeded.

- **Item 2.** The value given for Disk Time is a usage period. We are saying that the disk should not be used more than 80 percent of the time. Check this value against the advice of the manufacturer. Disks that exceed this usage may not last long. We have seen disks easily overheat and crash when the threshold scaled to 100 percent.

- **Item 3.** The transfer rate information of your disk is usually printed on the disk. The program alerts you if the monitor reports that your rates are exceeding this rate. If the applications are hammering your disks, upgrade to faster technology, such as Ultra Wide SCSI.

- **Item 4.** The number of spindles is a snapshot; you should observe this value over several intervals. You can also use the Avg. Disk Queue Length counter.

- **Item 5.** If memory drops below 4 MB, paging activity will begin to increase and the system response will begin to wane. If the condition continues, you will get an error message advising that system resources are getting low.

- **Item 6.** If memory use increases, watch that this threshold does not exceed your baselines.

- **Item 7.** This value depends on the type of network you are running. For an Ethernet network, your typical threshold will be around 30 percent.

- **Item 8.** You should fully understand how paging works before trying to make sense of this counter, because the threshold varies according to the nature of the hardware and the number of applications you have.

- **Item 9.** Processor Time can be easily observed in Task Manager, as described earlier in this chapter. Any processor usage at the 85 percent or higher mark is cause for concern.

You can also use Task Manager to identify the process that is using up your CPU's bandwidth. If it is a critical function, such as Exchange or SQL Server, you might need to add another processor or upgrade to a faster CPU. On stable or inactive machines, you will notice that the System Idle Process uses the CPU most of the time.

- **Item 10.** This counter can be used to signal hardware problems. If the counter increases dramatically without a corresponding increase in server activity, a piece of hardware is responsible for the flood in interrupts. The hardware could be a disk controller, a network interface card, or something similar.

- **Item 11.** Using the server counter, you can sum the total Bytes Total/sec for all servers, and if the value is equal to the maximum transfer rate for the network, then you may have some segmenting to do.

- **Item 12.** If the value exceeds three, you may have to change parameters in the registry. Look up information on work items in the Microsoft knowledge base for a complete discussion of the Work Item Shortages counter.

- **Item 13.** Server work queues is another snapshot counter that may signify a processor bottleneck. You should observe this counter over several intervals.

- **Item 14.** The processor queue length is also a snapshot, and you should monitor the counter over several intervals. A value higher than two over several intervals requires investigation.

Understanding server workload

In addition to the starting points just described, you might find useful the following monitoring suggestions for workload monitoring on some standard server configurations. The following list provides a short description of objects to monitor by the server role:

- **Application servers.** These include standard application servers and Terminal Services, or application, servers. Terminal Services are more demanding and require constant performance monitoring. The heaviest resource usage on these servers is memory and CPU. Objects to monitor include Cache, Memory, Processors, and System.

- **Backup servers.** These servers can create bottlenecks on the network and suffer from extensive CPU usage. They may also place a burden on the remote computer to which they connect. Consider monitoring the System, Server, Processor, and Network Segment objects.

- **Database servers.** Disks and CPU are the most taxed resources on database servers. You would think that available memory is a taxed resource, but most advanced database server technologies, such as SQL Server 2005, only keep a small amount of "hot" data in memory (by caching records) for the majority of queries. You particularly need fast hard disks for database servers, such as SQL 2005 or Oracle. Objects you should monitor include the PhysicalDisk, LogicalDisk, Processor, and System.

- **Domain controllers.** Domain controllers can eat up a lot of different resources, including CPUs, disks, memory, and networks. You should monitor Memory, CPU, System, Network Segment, Network Interface, and protocol counter objects, such as TCP, UDP, IP,

NBT, connection, NetBEUI, NetBIOS, and so on. You can also monitor Active Directory's NTDS service objects and the Site Server LDAP service objects. WINS and DNS also have applicable objects that can be observed.

■ **File and print servers.** These servers consume a lot of hard disk space and network resources. Intensive color and graphics rendering can tax a CPU. Monitor here for CPU, Memory, Network Segment, Physical Disk, and Logical Disk. You can also monitor the PrintQueue object to troubleshoot spooling, and so on.

■ **Mail servers.** Mail servers, such as Exchange, use CPU, disks, and memory the heaviest. You can monitor the memory collection, Cache, Processor, System, PhysicalDisk, and LogicalDisk objects. Exchange also ships with specialized counters.

■ **Web/Internet Information Services.** These servers consume extensive disk, cache, and network components. Consider monitoring the Cache, Network Segment, PhysicalDisk, and LogicalDisk objects.

Performance Monitoring Overhead

Monitoring performance requires resources, which can adversely affect the data you're trying to gather. Therefore, you need to decrease the impact of your performance monitoring activities. There are several techniques you can use to ensure that performance monitoring overhead is kept to a minimum on any server you are monitoring:

■ The System Monitor application can be demanding on resources. You can use logs instead of displaying a graph, and then import the data into report programs and databases. Save the logs to storage that is not being monitored, or to a hard disk that is not the object of analysis. In addition, ensure that the logs are not growing too big. Set a quota and alert on the disk space, or be sure to keep your eye on the disks.

■ Do not use many counters at the same time. Some counters are costly and can increase overhead, which will be counterproductive. In addition, it is hard to monitor too many things at once. What each counter consumes in overhead is available on the Windows Server 2008 Resource Kit.

■ Tight collection intervals can also be costly. Microsoft recommends a ten-minute interval for data collection.

■ While taking care not to impact available resources, continue monitoring during peak usage periods to obtain the best assessment of resource usage. It makes no sense to monitor a system that is idle.

■ Consider monitoring remotely. Remote monitoring allows for centralized data collection. You can also collect data from several servers and save the data to the local machine. Be aware, though, that what you save on the swings you might lose on the roundabout. Network bandwidth increases with more data collection and the more often you collect. Consider keeping the number of servers in a monitored group to no more than about 10 or 15. To increase network bandwidth, consider saving the remote data to log files on the remote servers and then either copy the data to the local computer or view it remotely.

Service Level with Microsoft Systems Center Operations Manager

So far, this chapter has provided information about the myriad of tools available to you for managing servers, but don't you wish a system were available that could automatically do everything described in the first part of this chapter and in previous chapters? Enter Microsoft System Center Operations Manager (formerly Microsoft Operations Manager [MOM]).

Microsoft System Center Operations Manager is the flagship product that comprises Microsoft's offering of system and operations management products. To counter IBM with its Tivoli enterprise management system, HP with OpenManage, and so on, Microsoft set out to dominate the systems-management market. It did this long before Windows 2000 to create products that would specialize in the systems and operations management of its own operating systems.

Both Microsoft System Center Operations Manager and Microsoft System Center Configuration Manager (formerly Systemd Management Server or SMS) are integrated into part of Microsoft System Center. A comprehensive discussion of these powerful tools is beyond the scope of this book. We are primarily interested in Microsoft System Center Operations Manager, however, as the key tool to monitor system performance and operations management. To make sure our high-performance and highly available systems remain operating and available, we need to use a high-performance and highly available operating tool.

Microsoft System Center Operations Manager's central task in your operations arsenal is to provide comprehensive event management, monitoring and alerting, reporting, and operational trend analysis. The software has the capability to consolidate events and to analyze the data in such a way that it can be configured to report to you in real time which events are of critical importance to you. You configure Microsoft System Center Operations Manager to respond to these events by contacting you, the help desk, or IT staff by phone, e-mail, page, fax, and so on. You can also configure Microsoft System Center Operations Manager to resolve events automatically.

Further exploration of Microsoft System Center Operations Manager is beyond the scope of this chapter. In fact, Microsoft System Center Operations Manager itself is worth more than one book.

Summary

This chapter introduced service level (SL) and service level management (SLM). More and more companies and business plans are demanding that MIS maintain SL standards. To ensure that MIS or IT and IS managers adhere to the performance requirements of the business, the service level agreement, or SLA, is going to be seen a lot more often in many enterprises.

As the e-commerce phenomenon continues to explode, so too will the number of applications and business processes that demand SL adherence. The customer will be more and more directly involved in the health of your systems. These include data interchange systems, Web servers, applications servers, ISP equipment, and so on.

SL and SLM have, for the past few years, been the domain mainly of mid-range and legacy systems. SL tools have been lacking on server operating systems for years. Now Windows Server 2008 rises to the challenge by providing an extensive performance monitoring and reporting architecture that enables you to monitor systems' health in the ongoing effort to support SL, methodically troubleshoot problems, and maintain server and service health. These tools also enable you to plan for capacity and provide feedback to management to ensure that IT continues to support the business models and marketing plans being adopted.

We have discussed the Reliability and Performance Console, System Monitor, Log and Alerts, and Task Manager in very loose terms. Our definitions have also been very broad. The number of monitoring objects is so extensive that you will need to fully understand what they collect and how they impact the available resources.

Index

Symbols and Numbers

. (dot), domain name syntax and, 180
64-bit platform, .NET Framework
        supporting, 363
6bone, 115

A

A (host) records
    creating, 195
    overview of, 185
    verifying before installing AD, 779
access control
    administering/managing printers,
        403–405
    overview of, 579
    security access levels in NTFS,
        488
    security registry and, 347
    user and group management and,
        856
access control entries (ACEs), 884,
        907
access time, hard disks, 413
access token assignment, 822
access tokens, 632, 822
accessibility, Ease of Access applet, 81
account credentials, DHCP, 172
account lockout, 232, 904–905
account policies, user accounts, 821
accounting, RRAS, 268–270
    overview of, 268–269
    RADIUS accounting, 269–270,
        280
    Windows accounting, 269
accounts, auditing, 906
ACEs (access control entries), 884,
        907
ACID (atomic, consistent, isolated,
        durable), 460
ACLs (Access Control Lists)
    AD objects and, 621

DCs and, 768–769
local accounts and, 817
name servers and zones and, 209
.NET Framework supporting, 363
overview of, 579
ownership and, 526
registry keys and, 347
security management and, 632
action planning, for disaster recovery,
        325–326
Active Directory Certificate Services
        (AD CS), 22
Active Directory containers, Group
        Policy, 877
Active Directory Domain Controller
        role, 557–558
Active Directory Domain Services (AD
        DS), 22
Active Directory Domain Services
        Installation Wizard,
        755–762
Active Directory Federation Services
        (AD FS), 22
Active Directory Lightweight Directory
        Services (AD LDS), 22
Active Directory preparation tool
        (ADPrep.exe),
        651–652
Active Directory Rights Management
        Services (AD RMS), 22
Active Directory Service Interfaces
        (ADSI), 627–628, 816
Active Directory Sites and Services
        Manager, 778, 779–780
Active Directory Users and
        Computers, 814–816
Active Directory Wizard, installing
        domain controllers, 23–24
ActiveX controls, 45
AD (Active Directory)
    ACLs and access tokens, 632
    APIs, open, 607
    APIs for custom needs, 627–628
    application management, 601–602

auditing access to, 906
authorizing DHCP servers, 152
CAs integrated with, 591–592
change management, 601
database structure, 615–616
DBMS for, 612–614
defined, 602
deploying. See deploying Active
        Directory
DFS namespaces and, 467
directories, 599
distributed administration, 601
DNS integration with, 209
DNS namespace planning, 33–34
domain objects, 621–623
domains, 631
Exchange integration with, 27
features in Windows Server 2008,
        25
GC (global catalog), 626–627
Internet and, 611
intra-domain trust relationships,
        631–632
LDAP and, 605–607
LDS and, 660
legacy Windows domains and,
        628–630
managing. See managing Active
        Directory
namespaces, 610–611
naming conventions, 620–621
objects, 616–618
open standards as basis of,
        609–610
OUs, 623–624
overview of, 597–599, 633–634
path names, 618–620
physical architecture. See physical
        architecture, AD
planning. See planning Active
        Directory
printers in, 391–392
publishing shares, 495
recovering, 332–333

939

NTFS, 461
NTLM, 573–574
online security, 285
overview of, 551–552
PKI. *See* PKI (public key infrastructure)
planning, 580
proxies and bastions and, 582
RIP configuration, 247
router settings, 244–245
second-level domains for managing, 689–690
server roles and, 556–557
smart cards. *See* smart cards
SNMP configuration, 137
SSL, 581
SSL/TLS, 571
staffing domain security position, 662
summary, 595
templates, 74
threats list, 553–554
security, registry
auditing access, 347–349
overview of, 346–347
permissions applied to keys, 347
preventing access, 347
securing remote access, 350
Security Account Manager. *See* SAM (Security Account Manager)
security administration, AD, 798–805
administrative workstations, 803–804
administrator account abuse, 798–801
administrator account use, 801–802
console access, 804
member servers/workstations, 804–805
overview of, 798
security associations, IPSec, 570
Security Configuration Wizard. *See* SCW (Security Configuration Wizard)
security groups, AD
built-in, 787–789
group membership and, 792–795
implementation-specific, 792
types of groups, 837
security identifiers. *See* SIDs (security identifiers)
security levels, AD users and groups, 856

security model, LDAP, 606
security policies. *See also* Group Policy
actions, 71
names, 74
overview of, 875
Viewer page showing policy settings, 75
security principals
computer accounts, 836
in domain plan, 634
KDCs and, 581
Kerberos and, 565
locations of, 873
logon authentication and, 821
users viewed as, 810
seek time, hard disk parameters affecting capacity, 413
separator pages, printer management, 397–399
serial interface, local print monitor, 380
Server Core install
benefits of, 4–5
performing, 14
server recipes, 6
unattended install, 14–15
Server Manager
installing server roles with, 21
installing Windows Server 2008 features, 23
Server Principal Names (SPNs), 694–695
server recipes, Windows Server 2008, 6–10
hardware guide, 10
types of, 6–9
server roles
domain controllers, 23–27
member servers, 20–21
overview of, 19
role servers, 21–23
security enhancements in, 556–557
standalone servers, 19–20
servers
application. *See* application servers
backing up, 305–306
configuring server support during AD deployment, 769–770
creating server objects during AD deployment, 765
installing, 770
IP address reservations, 770

monitoring for bottlenecks, 932–934
naming DC machine, 752
overview of, 931–932
print servers, 382
root servers, 180
server extensions, 70
static addressing, 752
workload monitoring, 934–935
servers, Windows
DDNS support, 210–211
domain functional levels and, 662
server-side print problems, 406–408
service level. *See* SL (service level)
service level agreements. *See* SLAs (service level agreements)
service level management. *See* SLM (service level management)
Service Location records. *See* SRV (Service Location) records
services
AD integration with, 784–785
application services, 31–33
bare bones installation of, 753
database, 30–31
delegating administration, 648
dependencies, 61
DHCP service, 150
Exchange and communication services, 27–29
general properties, 58–59
IIS and ASP.NET integration, 31
logon options, 59–60
mirroring, 332
name resolution, 33–35
NAT configuration, 255–257
overview of, 57
print. *See* print services
recovery options, 60–61, 332–333
RS (Removable Storage), 291–293
starting/stopping, 57–58
system monitoring, 29–30
Services for Network File System. *See* SNFS (Services for Network File System)
Services for Unix. *See* SFU (Services for Unix)
session keys, Kerberos, 562, 568
session tickets, Kerberos, 567–568
Setup, registry settings and, 336
Setup Wizard, 16–17

The books you
read to succeed.

**Get the most out of the latest software and leading-edge technologies
with a Wiley Bible—your one-stop reference.**

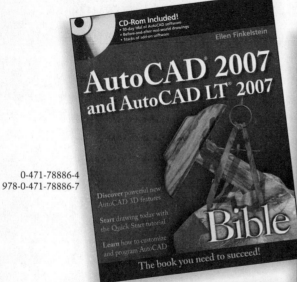